Psychology
for A Level

ERIKA COX

OXFORD
UNIVERSITY PRESS

Great Clarendon Street, Oxford OX2 6DP

Oxford University Press is a department of the University of Oxford. It furthers the University's objective of excellence in research, scholarship, and education by publishing worldwide in

Oxford New York

Athens Auckland Bangkok Bogotá Buenos Aires Cape Town Chennai Dar es Salaam Delhi Florence Hong Kong Istanbul Karachi Kolkata Kuala Lumpur Madrid Melbourne Mexico City Mumbai Nairobi Paris São Paulo Shanghai Singapore Taipei Tokyo Toronto Warsaw

with associated companies in Berlin Ibadan

Oxford is a registered trade mark of Oxford University Press in the UK and in certain other countries

© Erika Cox 2001

Database right Oxford University Press (maker)

First published 2001

British Library Cataloguing in Publication Data

Data available

ISBN 0 19 832 838 9

Typeset by Hardlines, Charlbury, Oxon
Printed in Italy by G. Canale & C.S.p.A., Borgaro, T.se, Turin

The author and publishers would like to thank the following for permission to reproduce photographs:

Cover photo Science Photo Library; p13 Professor Albert Bandura, Stanford University; p48 Tografox/Bob Battersby; p55 Harlow Primate Laboratory, University of Wisconsin; p57 Science Photo Library; p92 Science Photo Library/Martin Dohrn; p107 Mary Evans Picture Library; p129 Professor Phillip G. Zimbardo, Stanford University; p132 Moviestore Collection; p134 Popperfoto; p135 from the film 'Obedience' by Stanley Milgram; p244 Popperfoto/Reinhard Krause,

Reuters; p264 Moviestore Collection; p268 Moviestore Collection; p279 Science Photo Library/ Mark Thomas; p280 Science Photo Library/ Dr Monty Buchsbaum, Peter Arnold Inc; p291 Topham Picturepoint; p294 Topham Picturepoint; p339 (happiness) Topham Picturepoint/Peter Jordan; p339 (disgust) Press Association; p339 (surprise) Popperfoto; p339 (sadness) Topham Picturepoint/Press Association; p339 (anger) Popperfoto; p339 (fear) Press Association; p353 Science Photo Library/ Ed Young; p386 Bridgeman Art Library/ Arts Council Collection, Hayward Gallery, London; p393 © Exploratorium; p394 © Exploratorium; p396 Ascending and Descending by M. C. Escher. © Cordon Art, Baarn, Holland. All rights reserved; p399 © Exploratorium; p428 The Autistic Society; p478 Popperfoto; p491 Wellcome Trust Photo Library; p538 (top) OSF/Rudie H. Kuiter; p538 (bottom) Windrush Photos/ Michael Gore; p558 BBC Natural History Unit/Bruce Davidson; p569 BBC Natural History Unit/Jürgen Freund; p574 (top) BBC Natural History Unit/John Cancalosi; p574 (centre) FLPA/Leonard Lee Rue III; p574 (bottom) BBC Natural History Unit/John Cancalosi; p582 William Munoz; p588 GSU Language Research Center, University of Georgia State; p609 (Van Gogh) The Art Archive Musée D'Orsay Paris/Dagli Orit; p609 (Virginia Woolf) Popperfoto; p609 (Handel) Popperfoto; p609 (Coleridge) Bridgeman Art Library/ Private collection; p632 Moviestore Collection; p640 Network Photographers/Fritz Hoffmann; p652 Science Photo Library/ Tim Beddow; p662 Popperfoto; p676 Science Photo Library/Will McIntyre.

Illustrations by Bill Piggins, Robert Cox and Hardlines.
Special thanks to Bexhill Photographic for their assistance.

The author and publishers also acknowledge permission to reproduce statistical tables in Chapter 26:

Appendix 1: 'Critical values of U for (Mann-Whitney)' reprinted from R Runyon and A Haber: *Fundamentals of Behavioural Statistics* 3e (McGraw Hill, 1976), reprinted by permission of The McGraw Hill Companies. Appendix 2: 'Critical Values of T in the Wilcoxon Signed Ranks Test' adapted from R Meddis: *Statistical Handbook for Non-Statisticians* (McGraw Hill, London 1975). Appendix 3: 'Critical Value of Spearman's r' data reprinted from Table 1, Critical values of the Spearman Rank Correlation Coefficient r_{S1} for two-tailed and one-tailed probabilities, $\alpha(2)$ and $\alpha(1)$ respectively, p 579 from J H Zhar: 'Significance testing of the Spearman Rank Correlation Coefficient' in *Journal of the American Statistical Association*, Vol. 67, No 399, September 1972, pp 578-80, by permission of the American Statistical Association. Appendix 4: 'Level of significance for a one-tailed test' abridged from R A Fisher & F Yates: *Statistical Tables for Biological, Agricultural and Medical Research* 6e, (Longman, 1974), copyright © R A Fisher and F Yates 1963, reprinted by permission of Pearson Education Ltd. Appendix 5: 'Critical Values in the Binomial Sign Test' reprinted from F Clegg: *Simple Statistics* (Cambridge University Press, 1982), by permission of the publisher.

We have tried to trace and contact copyright holders before publication but this has not been possible in all cases. If notified, the publisher will be pleased to rectify any errors or omissions at the earliest opportunity.

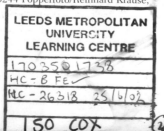

Contents

Acknowledgements   ii
Preface   vii

1   An introduction to psychology   1
1.1   What is psychology?   1
1.2   The philosophical roots of psychology   3
1.3   The beginnings of modern psychology   3
1.4   Perpectives in psychology   5
1.5   Psychology and common sense   16
1.6   What do psychologists do?   17
      Notes on activities   18

2   Human memory   20
2.1   The nature of memory   20
2.2   Early studies of memory   20
2.3   Models of memory   21
2.4   Theories of forgetting   34
2.5   Reconstructive memory   38
2.6   Critical issue: eye-witness testimony   41
      Notes on activities   50

3   Attachments in development   51
3.1   Investigating attachment   51
3.2   Attachment difficulties   60
3.3   Are early difficulties reversible?   64
3.4   Other factors in social and emotional
      development   65
3.5   Critical issue: day care   67
      Notes on activities   71

4   Stress   73
4.1   What is stress?   73
4.2   Models of stress   74
4.3   The physiological response to stress   75
4.4   Sources of stress   78
4.5   Personality differences and stress   86
4.6   Stress and illness   87
4.7   Critical issue: stress management   91
      Notes on activities   99

5   Abnormality   100
5.1   What is abnormal psychology?   100
5.2   Defining abnormality   100
5.3   Cultural and subcultural differences
      in the definition of abnormality   104
5.4   Models of abnormality   106
5.5   Critical issue: eating disorders   112
      Notes on activities   120

6   Social influence   121
6.1   Conformity   121
6.2   Obedience   132
6.3   Individual differences in response to
      social influence   140
6.4   Independent behaviour   141
6.5   Critical issue: the development of
      ethical guidelines for research   143
      Notes on activities   149

7   Research methods   152
7.1   Methods in psychological research   152
7.2   Quantitative and qualitative data   162
7.3   Variables, operationalisation, and
      hypotheses   162
7.4   Populations and samples   164
7.5   Experimental design   166
7.6   Reliability, validity, and
      standardisation   169
7.7   Levels of measurement   170
7.8   Descriptive statistics   172
7.9   Ethics in psychological research   177
      Notes on activities   178

8   Social cognition   182
8.1   What is social cognition?   182
8.2   Attribution theories   182
8.3   Errors and biases in attribution   186
8.4   Social and cultural influences on
      perception and impression formation   189
8.5   Social and cultural stereotypes   192

8.6	Prejudice and discrimination	196
8.7	The reduction of prejudice and discrimination	203
	Notes on activities	207

9	**Relationships**	**209**
9.1	Why do we form relationships?	209
9.2	Types of relationship	210
9.3	Factors in interpersonal attraction	211
9.4	Theories relating to the formation of relationships	217
9.5	The maintenance of relationships	220
9.6	The dissolution of relationships	222
9.7	Psychological explanations of love	226
9.8	Cultural and subcultural differences in relationships	228
	Notes on activities	239

10	**Pro- and anti-social behaviour**	**241**
10.1	The nature of aggression	241
10.2	Theories of aggression	242
10.3	Environmental stress and aggression	247
10.4	Altruism and bystander behaviour	249
10.5	Media influences on pro- and anti-social behaviour	264
	Notes on activities	270

11	**Brain and behaviour**	**272**
11.1	Methods of investigating the brain	272
11.2	Localisation of function in the cerebral cortex	281
11.3	Lateralisation of function in the cerebral cortex	288
11.4	The effects of cortical damage	295
11.5	Recovery from cerebral lesions	302
	Notes on activities	303

12	**Biological rhythms, sleep and dreaming**	**304**
12.1	Bodily rhythms	304
12.2	Sleep	308
12.3	Dreaming	318
	Notes on activities	323

13	**Motivation and emotion**	**325**
13.1	What is motivation?	325
13.2	Brain mechanisms of motivation: hunger and thirst	326
13.3	Theories of motivation	329
13.4	What is emotion?	338
13.5	Brain structures in emotion	339
13.6	Theories of emotion	341
	Notes on activities	349

14	**Attention and pattern recognition**	**351**
14.1	What is attention?	351
14.2	Theories of focused attention	353
14.3	Divided attention	362
14.4	Pattern recognition	373
	Notes on activities	380

15	**Perceptual processes and development**	**382**
15.1	What is perception?	382
15.2	The visual system	383
15.3	Perceptual organisation	389
15.4	Theories of visual perception	397
15.5	Perceptual development	403
	Notes on activities	411

16	**Language and thought**	**412**
16.1	What is language?	412
16.2	Language and culture	413
16.3	Language development	419
16.4	Problem-solving and decision-making	430
	Notes on activities	442

17	**Cognitive development**	**445**
17.1	Development of thinking	445
17.2	Development of measured intelligence	462
17.3	Development of moral understanding	472
	Notes on activities	481

18	**Social and personality development**	**483**
18.1	Personality development	483
18.2	Gender development	489
18.3	Adolescence	499
	Notes on activities	509

19 Adulthood   **511**
19.1 Early and middle adulthood   512
19.2 Family and relationships in adulthood   516
19.3 Late adulthood   523
19.4 Social changes in late adulthood   529
       Notes on activities   533

20 Determinants of animal behaviour 534
20.1 Darwin's theory of evolution   534
20.2 Evolutionary explanations of
       co-operation and altruism in
       non-human animals   538
20.3 Learning theory   542
20.4 Social learning in non-human animals 555
       Notes on activities   562

21 Animal cognition   **565**
21.1 Animal navigation   565
21.2 Animal communication and language   572
21.3 Memory in non-human animals   589
       Notes on activities   593

**22 Evolutionary explanations of
       human behaviour**   **596**
22.1 Evolutionary theory and
       human behaviour   596
22.2 Human reproductive behaviour   596
22.3 Explanations of mental disorders   606
22.4 Intelligence   612
       Notes on activities   618

**23 Issues in the classification and
       diagnosis of psychological
       abnormality**   **620**
23.1 Classifying abnormal behaviour   620
23.2 Multiple personality disorder
       (dissociative identity disorder)   630
23.3 Culture-bound syndromes (CBSs)   639
       Notes on activities   644

24 Psychopathology   **645**
24.1 The aetiology of mental disorders   645
24.2 Schizophrenia   646
24.3 Depression   655
24.4 Anxiety disorders   661

       Notes on activities   670

25 Treating mental disorders   **672**
25.1 Introduction   672
25.2 Biological (somatic) therapies   673
25.3 Behavioural therapies   679
25.4 Alternatives to biological and
       behavioural therapies   685
25.5 Issues in evaluating therapies   693
       Notes on activities   697

26 Research issues   **699**
26.1 Planning research   699
26.2 Inferential statistics   700
26.3 Carrying out statistical tests   701
26.4 Writing research reports   710
       Notes on activities   715

Appendix 1: Tables for Mann–Whitney
                  U test   716
Appendix 2: Tables for Wilcoxon signed
                  ranks test   720
Appendix 3: Tables for Spearman's
                  coefficient r_s 721
Appendix 4: Tables for chi square (χ^2)   722
Appendix 5: Tables for the binomial sign test 723
Appendix 6: Sample research report   724

27 Issues and debates in psychology   **730**
27.1 Gender bias   730
27.2 Cultural bias   734
27.3 Ethical issues   737
27.4 The use of non-human animals   742
27.5 Free will and determinism   746
27.6 Reductionism   749
27.7 Is psychology a science?   751
27.8 The nature–nurture debate   754
       Notes on activities   757

References   762
Index   800

Preface

This textbook is precisely targeted at AQA A Level Psychology, Specification A. It will also be of interest to those who are new to psychology, and who want to get a flavour of the kinds of topics in which psychologists are interested.

It aims to be a user-friendly text which explains the material clearly and in simple language, while at the same time giving good coverage to the sometimes complex ideas psychologists have put forward. There are frequent summaries (marked by ❺ symbols) throughout each chapter; these can be used to provide an overview of each topic and should also be useful when it comes to revision.

The text contains a range of activities (questions, short tests, mini-practicals, and so on) to encourage you to engage with the material. Many of these activities are designed to help you remember the information being put across and check your understanding of it. The mini-practicals will help you get a feel for how psychologists go about their research, and experience for yourself some of their findings.

I would like to thank Sue Cave, Julie Harris and Jackie Malone for their useful contributions to chapters 2 and 5, and Nick Oliver for his many helpful suggestions, which I am sure have made the book much better than it would otherwise have been. I would also like to thank Helen Kara, for her patience in editing the constantly changing versions of the text, and my editor Don Manley for helping to keep me on track. Last but not least, my thanks to Robert as an endless source of support and cups of tea.

Psychology is a fascinating subject. I hope you enjoy using this book as an introduction to what it can offer.

Erika Cox
Fakenham, May 2001

01

An introduction to psychology

In this chapter we will be looking at:

1.1 What is psychology?

1.2 The philosophical roots of psychology

1.3 The beginnings of modern psychology

1.4 Perspectives in psychology:
   The psychodynamic perspective
   The behaviourist perspective
   The physiological perspective
   The cognitive perspective
   The humanistic perspective

1.5 Psychology and common sense

1.6 What do psychologists do?

1.1   WHAT IS PSYCHOLOGY?

What is psychology? The general view of what psychology is all about is often rather narrow. When I tell people I am a psychologist, I often get one of two responses. One is: 'I'll have to be careful what I say to you'. The other is: 'I hope you're not going to psychoanalyse me'.

The first response seems to imply that psychologists have developed skills which allow them to read people's minds and easily unearth their deepest secrets in a casual conversation. It is true that when you start to study psychology, you are likely to notice and think about behaviour, and perhaps what people say, and relate it to what you have learned, in the same way that someone starting to learn about geology might notice different rock formations. But psychology is not a basis for reading people's minds.

The second response assumes that psychology and psychoanalysis are the same thing. This is understandable in a way, since Freud is probably the best-known name in psychology. Many of his ideas (though perhaps in a distorted form, such as 'Freud is all about sex') are widely known, and some terms associated with psychoanalytic theory have filtered down into general use. You may perhaps have heard of the **Oedipus complex**, the **ego** or **repression**. But there is a vast amount of psychology beyond Freud.

The *Concise Oxford Dictionary* defines psychology as 'the scientific study of the human mind and its functions, especially those affecting behaviour in a given context'. This definition is not without its problems. There are very many different kinds of psychologist. As we will see, each of these concepts – 'scientific', 'mind' and 'behaviour' – can be considered to be either more or less important, depending on what kind of psychologist you are. As a working definition, though, this gives us some general idea of what psychology is about. But what exactly does this study entail?

As you have chosen to study psychology, you probably have an idea of some of the kinds of questions in which psychologists are interested. We will look at this a little more closely in activity 1:

◖ Activity 1: topics in psychology

Which of these topics do you think psychologists might be interested in?

◆ why people help others (or don't)
◆ treatments for depression
◆ how children learn language
◆ the relationship between stress and illness
◆ the behaviour of animals
◆ astrological signs and personality
◆ why some people are more outgoing than others
◆ the causes of schizophrenia
◆ extra-sensory perception
◆ how people solve logical problems
◆ improving performance in sport

When you have finished, see the notes on page 18.

This activity should have given you some idea of the broad range of topics in psychology. Obviously not all psychologists are interested in all of them; just as in other disciplines, psychologists specialise.

There are six main topic areas with which most psychologists are concerned. **Cognitive** psychologists are interested in the ways in which we process information – for example, when we use our memory. **Developmental** psychologists are mainly interested in the ways in which children develop – for example, the way that they become attached to their caregivers, and how their thought processes and personality develop. More recently, the developmental approach has also looked at changes across the lifespan. **Physiological** psychologists are interested in the way in which the body functions, and how these physiological processes can be linked to psychological experience and behaviour. Emotion, stress and the effects of brain damage are examples of the kinds of topic in which they are interested.

While these three areas are interested in establishing general laws – the functioning of people in general – psychologists are also interested in **individual differences** – for example, personality, intelligence and mental disorders. **Social** psychologists focus on the idea that people are essentially social creatures, and that therefore much of a person's behaviour is influenced by others. They are interested in topics such as relationships, helping behaviour and obedience. Finally, **comparative**

psychologists study animal behaviour, both as a subject that is interesting in its own right – for example, predator–prey behaviour – and because an understanding of animals may help to establish general principles which also apply to humans. Theories of learning fall into this category, as we will see later in this chapter. Each of the following five chapters covers one topic from the first five areas.

Psychologists vary in their basic beliefs about the nature of people, the questions they think are important and the methods which they think are appropriate to the study of psychology. To get some idea of how these differences have come about, we need to turn now to the history of psychology as a discipline.

◉ Psychology covers a wide range of topic areas. It can be generally defined as 'the science of mind and behaviour'.

◉ The boundaries of the subject are not clear-cut. Some topics are seen as marginal by some psychologists.

◉ The six main areas of psychology in which psychologists are interested are cognitive, developmental, physiological, individual differences, social and comparative.

1.2 THE PHILOSOPHICAL ROOTS OF PSYCHOLOGY

Psychology has its roots in philosophy, going back at least as far as the ancient Greeks. Plato argued, for instance, that we need to make a distinction between mind and body (this belief is known as **dualism**). He also believed that we have innate ideas and knowledge, so that learning is not so much a matter of experience, but rather a process by which we reveal to ourselves knowledge we already have. The motivation to do this is also innate. This general approach is known as **rationalism** or **nativism**.

In your study of psychology, you will come across many examples of modern psychological theories which have their roots in rationalist ideas. Later in this chapter, we will be looking in some detail at one of them, Freud's psychodynamic theory.

Aristotle was a pupil of Plato, but disagreed fundamentally with Plato's belief in innate ideas. He argued that all learning must come from experience, and that we learn by associating aspects of the world which commonly occur together. This approach is known as **associationism**. These general ideas were taken up by a group of seventeenth century philosophers, in particular Locke, Hobbes and Hume. They argued that **experience** is the basis of all knowledge of the world. They are referred to as **empiricists**, from Greek words meaning 'from experience'. In other words, we find out about the world not because of innate knowledge, but through our experience of it. Again, you will come across many examples of modern psychological theories which have their roots in associationism, notably the learning theory of Skinner, which we will be discussing later.

A further tradition in psychology, bringing together rationalism and associationism, has its roots in the rather more recent ideas of the eighteenth-century philosopher, Immanuel Kant. In his *Critique of Pure Reason* (1991), written in 1781, he agreed with the associationist position that experience is important to learning. At the same time, he argued, something must already be present in the mind if we are to make any sense of reality. In brief, we have an innate rule-forming capacity which enables us to *construct* models of reality on the basis of this experience. For this reason, this point of view is known as **constructivism**. A major theorist whose work has its roots in this philosophical position was Jean Piaget (1896–1980), who was interested in the development of thinking in children.

Psychology, then, did not emerge from a vacuum; many of the beliefs that psychologists have and the ideas which they explore go back a long way. At the same time, producing philosophical arguments is far removed from modern psychology. In order to provide a framework for the kind of psychology you will find in this course, we now need to turn to the end of the nineteenth century, to the time when psychology became a discipline in its own right, separate from philosophy.

- ◔ Psychology has its roots in philosophy, starting with the ideas of Plato and Aristotle.
- ◔ The three different philosophical positions – **rationalism**, **associationism**, **constructivism** – are reflected in the different beliefs of modern psychologists about the nature of people.

1.3 THE BEGINNINGS OF MODERN PSYCHOLOGY

In 1879, Wilhelm Wundt opened the first psychology laboratory at the University of Leipzig in Germany. This is usually thought of as the beginning of psychology as we know it.

While philosophy involves speculation about the mind, Wundt was aiming to do something rather different. He and his co-workers were attempting to analyse the workings of the mind in a rather more structured way, with the emphasis being on **measurement** and **control**.

Participants were exposed to a standard stimulus (e.g. a light or the sound of a metronome) and asked to report their sensations. Asking people to report on their mental processes is known as **introspection**. The aim here was to record thoughts and sensations, and to analyse them into their constituent elements, in much the same way as a chemist analyses chemical compounds, in order to get at the underlying structure. For this reason, the school of psychology founded by Wundt is known as **structuralism**.

Around the same time, other psychologists were also investigating mental experience. The American psychologist William James published *The Principles of Psychology* in 1890. He was opposed to the structuralist approach, believing that we ought to study mental experience as a whole. Like Wundt, however, he used the introspective method. His work covered a wide range of topics in psychology, among them the perceptual experience of newborn babies, human instincts and emotion. Many of his ideas can still be related to modern-day theories.

The German psychologist Hermann Ebbinghaus published *Concerning Memory* in 1885. He carried out a considerable amount of research into human memory, using nonsense syllables in an attempt to eliminate the effect of meaning in memory, and with himself as the sole participant. His work is covered in more detail in chapter 2. While still generally within the introspectionist tradition, his work is also notable for its carefully controlled experimental approach.

◖ Activity 2: evaluating introspection

Introspection involves asking people to report on their mental processes. Can you think of any problems which might arise in relying on this kind of information to form theories and test ideas?
When you have finished, see the notes on page 18.

Because of the problems with introspection, a new kind of psychology emerged with J. B. Watson (1878–1958), whose ideas have their roots in the **associationism** mentioned above. He argued that psychology should be like any other science, and that its methods should be those of a science.

◖ Activity 3: the scientific method

What procedures do scientists go through to collect information, and form and test theories? You will need to think about the methods of investigation you are familiar with from your study of chemistry, physics or biology.
When you have finished, see the notes on page 18.

Watson argued that if psychology is to be a science, the scientific method should be adopted. The introspective data produced by psychologists like Wundt and James were inappropriate, since they were not **objective**. He asserted that psychology could find its objective data in behaviour, which is observable, public information, and therefore this should be central to the study of psychology. For this reason, the school of thought started by Watson is known as **behaviourism**, and we will be coming back to it in more detail in the next section. He believed that all human functioning can be studied in this way, even claiming (mistakenly) that thinking is expressed in tiny movements of the vocal cords.

But not all psychologists have gone along this route. Sigmund Freud (1856–1939) started to develop his **psychodynamic theory** around 1900. For him, the unconscious mind is central. Although unconscious factors can be inferred from behaviour, his methods relied very much on talking to patients with problems. Necessarily this involved quite a lot of interpretation of the information the patients supplied, and so was quite different from the methods of a behaviourist.

Freud's method of studying the individual in depth is known as a **case study**, which will be discussed in more detail in chapter 7. Up to a point it can be regarded as scientific; Freud thought of himself as a scientist, and he was trained as a neurologist. The case study method has some of the features of the scientific method: the careful collection of data, and analysis (though not necessarily statistical analysis) of those data. It can also be used to support a hypothesis or a theory.

While an experimental approach has been the dominant tradition within psychology, more recently several different approaches to psychology have emerged. They vary in what they see as the proper subject matter of psychology, the kinds of questions which they believe to be important and their 'model of the person', i.e. the assumptions they make about the nature of people. Given these differences, the methods they use also vary. In the next section we shall be looking more closely at these distinctions and how they relate to different models.

❺ Modern psychology began with researchers like Wundt, whose methods relied heavily on **introspection**.

❺ Watson criticised introspection as being **subjective**. He argued that psychology should be a science and adopt the methods of other sciences. The study of behaviour would supply **objective** data. The movement he started is known as **behaviourism**.

❺ Not all psychologists have accepted Watson's model. Different approaches to psychology have emerged, each with its own **model of the person**. They vary in their assumptions, aims and methods.

1.4 PERSPECTIVES IN PSYCHOLOGY

Different approaches in modern psychology can be summarised under five major headings: psychodynamic; behaviourist; physiological; cognitive; and humanistic.

The psychodynamic perspective

The **psychodynamic** or **psychoanalytic** model is based on the work of **Freud**. Freud was a major theorist, and probably the most widely known in psychology. Although they are controversial, his ideas have been applied to many areas of psychological investigation – for example, aggression, gender development, moral development, mental disorders and personality – so we will look at his theory in some detail.

There are a number of fundamental ideas which formed the basis of Freud's theory: the principle of **psychological determinism**, the role of the **unconscious**, and the importance of **childhood** in determining adult behaviour.

Psychological determinism refers to the idea that all behaviour is motivated, and the reasons we behave as we do are often unconscious. Unconscious motivation can be illustrated by Freudian slips or **parapraxes**, where a person says or does something which they had not consciously intended to say or do. Here is a parapraxis reported by Freud:

▶ Activity 4: a parapraxis

Read through this description of the behaviour of one of Freud's patients:

A young man who was rather cautious about commitment finally proposed to his girlfriend and was accepted. When he had taken her home, he got on a tram to go home himself, and asked the conductress for two tickets.

Six months after his wedding, he was not entirely happy with married life. He missed his friends and did not get on with his parents-in-law. One evening he fetched his wife from her parents' house, got on a tram with her and asked for one ticket.

What unconscious reasons might the young man have had for the mistakes he made in asking for tram tickets?

When you have finished, see the notes on page 18.

The concept of the **unconscious** is one of the unique contributions Freud made to psychology. This was not in itself a new idea, but before Freud, the unconscious was seen as a dumping ground for experiences which were no longer of any importance, and so the unconscious itself had no particular status. Freud conceived of a **dynamic unconscious**, an active force, motivating much of our behaviour. He believed that a lot of material in the unconscious, far from being unimportant, is there because it is too painful for us to acknowledge consciously, and that this kind of material can only be accessed using the special techniques of the therapy he developed called **psychoanalysis**. The unconscious can be contrasted with the preconscious, ideas of which we are not at the moment conscious but which we can recall if we want to – for example, a friend's telephone number. There is also the conscious, those ideas we are currently aware of.

The idea of **unconscious conflict** is central to Freud's theory. It can show itself as parapraxes, as disturbing emotional states, and can also be revealed in dreams, where conflict expresses itself through the use of symbols.

Freud believed that adult behaviour is shaped by our experiences in **childhood**. He saw instinctual needs such as hunger, thirst and sex as being very important sources of motivation; at the same time, however, he thought that the social environment, which constrains the gratification of these instincts, was crucial to a child's development. He placed particular emphasis on the conflict between instinctual needs and the demands of society as the basis of personality development and the development of mental disorders.

The experiences of the first five years of life and the conflicts which arise during this time are seen as particularly important to the development of an individual's personality, and we will be coming back to Freud's ideas about children's development later in this section.

The structure of the mind

Freud proposed a theoretical (i.e. non-anatomical) account of the structure of the mind. He believed it consisted of three parts: the **id**, the **ego** and the **superego**.

Figure 1: the structure of the mind

id The id is present at birth. It is the seat of our instincts, and is unconscious. It operates on the **pleasure principle**, in that it tries to get immediate gratification and to avoid pain. It is the source of psychic energy, the **libido**.

ego This develops in childhood out of the id, as children learn that immediate gratification is not always possible and that pain cannot always be avoided. The ego works on the **reality principle**. It decides what actions are appropriate, and which id impulses will be satisfied, and how. The ego tries to balance the demands of the id, the realities of life, and the demands of the **superego**. Many ego processes are conscious, but some are preconscious and

others, especially the **ego defences** we shall come to later, are unconscious.

superego This consists of the values and morals of the child, and develops around the age of five. It is the child's **conscience** and **ego-ideal**, a model of what the child would like to be.

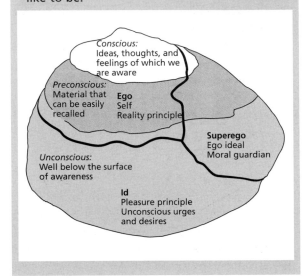

The forces of the superego and the id are often in opposition, with the superego curbing the primitive impulses of the id when they don't fit in with socially acceptable behaviour. For example, your superego would find it socially unacceptable if you decided to have sex on a crowded bus, no matter how frustrated your id was. So your ego would then decide that the action was inappropriate and must wait until later, or be expressed in some other more socially acceptable way. The dynamics of personality, according to Freud, are rooted in this conflict, originating in the id and fuelled by the libido. The way conflict is resolved is a crucial part of the way people develop.

- One major principle of Freud's theory is **psychological determinism**; all behaviour is seen to be motivated. This idea can explain **parapraxes**. Another central idea is the **dynamic unconscious**. **Childhood experience** is seen as being crucial to later development.
- The mind consists of the **conscious**, the **preconscious** and the **unconscious**.

❺ Freud suggested that personality is made up of the theoretical constructs of the **id**, the **ego** and the **superego**. **Unconscious conflict** between them is important to personality development.

Defence mechanisms

States of conflict may lead to the unpleasant sensation of anxiety developing, and people deal with this in different ways. One way is by the use of ego **defence mechanisms**, coping mechanisms which allow id impulses to be expressed, and so reduce anxiety. They are quite effective, particularly in the short term.

Displacement is one defence mechanism: where feelings cannot be expressed towards their real targets, substitute objects on which feelings can be taken out are chosen. For example, if a child is angry with its mother, these unacceptable feelings may be expressed by being unkind to a younger sibling.

Sublimation is a type of displacement where a socially acceptable activity is found to express an unacceptable impulse. For example, you might play squash to re-channel either your aggressive impulses, or sexual energy which lacks a sexual outlet. This is the only defence mechanism which can be effective long-term.

There are several other defence mechanisms. In **denial**, a fact which is too painful to cope with – such as the knowledge that you have a life-threatening illness – is denied. **Repression** is motivated forgetting (discussed in the section on **forgetting** in chapter 2). A person may unconsciously 'forget' something that is too distressing to remember, such as memories of being abused as a child, or the death of a relative. **Rationalisation** involves finding superficially acceptable reasons for a behaviour. You might, for example, blame your awful exam results on the fact that you had a cold on the day you sat the exam, to protect yourself from feelings of inadequacy. In **reaction formation**, a person consciously feels or thinks the exact opposite of their unconscious feelings or thoughts. For example, a person who is deeply prejudiced against a minority group could protect themselves from these unacceptable feelings by becoming actively involved in the Campaign for Racial Equality. **Regression** involves a symbolic return to an earlier stage of development, for example, sucking your thumb to comfort yourself.

Psychosexual development

As we saw earlier, the importance of childhood is central to Freud's theory, and he describes how children progress through a sequence of **psychosexual stages**. Everyone goes through these stages in the same order, and their experience of them is crucial not only to the child, but also to the adult. At each stage, interest is focused on the pleasurable sensations associated with different **erotogenic** (pleasure-giving) zones.

The **oral stage** lasts from birth to around one year. During this time, the source of pleasurable sensations is the mouth. You may have noticed that babies and very young children automatically put anything new into their mouths, and seem to derive pleasure from doing so. This stage is divided into two sub-stages. In the first few months, in the **incorporative** sub-stage, the baby is relatively passive; activity is largely focused on sucking and swallowing. This is followed by the **aggressive** sub-stage, when biting and chewing become important.

The **anal stage** lasts from around one to around three. Once weaned, the libido focuses on the anus and the muscles of the urinary system. Again, there are two sub-stages. In the **expulsion** sub-stage, the child gets great pleasure from defecating, while in the **retention** sub-stage, there is pleasure from holding in faeces. During this stage, the child comes up against external restrictions in terms of where and when defecation is acceptable, and will find that this aspect of behaviour has social implications in terms of pleasing parents, or not.

The **phallic stage** lasts from around three to around five. In this stage, pleasure centres on the genitals, and the stage is experienced differently by boys and by girls.

The young boy goes through a crisis which Freud called the **Oedipus complex**, during which he develops unconscious sexual feelings towards his mother. He is envious of his father, and jealous of the love and attention he gets from his mother. The way in which the boy's feelings for his mother and rivalry with his father is resolved is crucial for development. Similarly, a girl will experience the **Electra complex**.

In the **latency period**, from five to puberty, children turn aside from their sexuality, concentrating instead on developing socially and intellectually. This continues until the onset of adolescence. At adolescence, the child moves into the **genital stage**. In this stage, recognisably adult sexual feelings develop, and mature love becomes possible.

Freud suggested that the developmental stages which a child goes through help to form the personality of that child as an adult. The adult personality is determined not only by the interaction of id, ego and superego, together with the use of particular defence mechanisms, but also by **fixation**, an unconscious preoccupation with a particular psychosexual stage. This causes problems with adult personality if the child experiences frustration or overgratification while passing through a stage. If this happens, these early fixations are expressed symbolically in adult behaviour.

- Unconscious conflict causes **anxiety**, which can be dealt with using ego **defence mechanisms**. Only the mechanism of **sublimation** is effective in the long term. People differ in the kinds of mechanisms they use, and the extent to which they use them.
- Children develop through **psychosexual stages: oral, anal, phallic, latency** and **genital**. **Fixation** in one of these stages has implications for adult personality characteristics.

Overview of the psychodynamic model

The basic model here is of behaviour being shaped by **unconscious** forces. The idea of **conflict** is also central, with problems being created as the result of conflict between different parts of the personality. These in turn are determined by the **psychosexual development** which takes place in childhood, considered to be an extremely important time within this tradition, since our experiences at this time can affect us throughout our lives. Freud's is a **nativist** theory, since psychosexual development is determined by the sex into which we are born. On the basis of our sex, we are shaped by early childhood experiences.

The aims of this approach are twofold. Firstly, Freud seeks to explain development and behaviour within this general framework. However, this is not only a theory, but also a therapy: **psychoanalysis**. The aims here are to uncover unconscious conflict and help the patient understand its causes. They

can then come to terms with their problems.

In developing his theory, Freud used a clinical method known as the **case study**. Talking to patients and exploring their problems allowed him to understand the course of development which he claimed we all go through. Psychoanalysis is often referred to as the 'talking cure'. The methods here involve asking patients to talk about their concerns (**free association**) and to describe their dreams. This material allows the analyst to uncover unconscious conflict and start the process of curing the patient.

The behaviourist perspective

As we have seen, behaviourism had its roots in the ideas of **Watson**. Watson argued that if psychology was to be carried on in a scientific way, and to gain wide acceptance as a science, it needed to be objective. It must use the same methods and collect the same kinds of data as other sciences. The contents of a person's consciousness were not objectively measurable and were therefore not valid data; studying behaviour would provide observable, measurable events. He therefore saw behaviour as the only acceptable data.

Darwin's evolutionary theories had already suggested that there was a continuity between humans and other animals. This meant that animal behaviour could be studied in psychology experiments, and would provide valid, objective, measurable data which could also throw light on human behaviour.

Activity 5: using animals in experiments

Many psychologists have used animals in experiments, instead of humans.
What advantages does this have?
When you have finished, see the notes on page 18.

In proposing what a science of psychology should be, Watson was concerned with the connection between an event in the environment (e.g. touching something hot, or a voice saying your name) and the behaviour which follows (e.g. taking your hand away quickly, or turning your head towards the sound of the voice). The environmental event is called a stimulus, and what a person does as a result of the stimulus is called a **response**. For this reason, the behaviourist approach to psychology is sometimes called stimulus–response (or S–R) psychology. Watson saw learning as the process of associating stimulus and response, and believed this would prove a fertile area for psychological research. These ideas were developed by others interested in the nature of learning, and their theories are grouped together as **learning theory**.

Classical conditioning

Watson's ideas tied in with research being carried out by Pavlov (1849–1936), a Russian physiologist interested in the digestive processes of dogs, in particular the salivation reflex. A **reflex** is a fixed and automatic response to a particular stimulus; the response cannot be controlled. Pavlov was interested in accurate measurement of the relationship between the **stimulus** of food in the mouth and the **response** of salivation. In the course of his research (which won him a Nobel prize), Pavlov developed a technique for collecting the saliva secreted by the dog as part of the digestive process, and this made accurate measurement of the strength of the salivary reflex possible.

Pavlov noticed that the dog would salivate not only when it could taste the food, but also when it could only see it. The experiments he carried out demonstrate a phenomenon known as **classical conditioning**, one of the two kinds of learning processes in the behaviourist tradition. The other is **operant conditioning**, which we shall come to later.

Box A: Pavlov (1927)

Procedure: A dog was held in a harness so that little movement was possible. A bell, which the dog had not heard before, was rung to check that the dog didn't have an automatic salivary response to this sound. Pavlov called the bell a **neutral stimulus (NS)**, because there was no automatic response to it. The experimenter then rang the bell and

immediately afterwards presented food to the dog. The pairing of bell and food was repeated several times. Finally, the bell was rung on its own.

Results: The paired presentation of bell and food automatically produced the response of salivation on each presentation. Finally the bell alone also produced salivation.
Conclusion: The bell which had previously not produced salivation eventually did so because of its repeated pairings with food. This response came about as the result of an **association** being formed between bell and salivation.

We need now to look at a few technical terms. Pavlov referred to the food in this experiment as the **unconditional stimulus** (**UCS** or **US**) because it automatically or unconditionally causes salivation. Salivation in response to the food is referred to as the **unconditional response** (**UCR** or **UR**), for the same reason. The bell is originally referred to as a **neutral stimulus** (see box A). After its pairing with food, it becomes a **conditional stimulus** (**CS**), because it can only cause salivation *on condition* that it has been paired with food. The salivation caused by the bell on its own is the **conditional response** (**CR**), because it only occurs on condition that the bell–food pairings have taken place.

With the dog salivating to the sound of the bell, we have an objectively measurable change in behaviour, so the dog can be said to have *learned* to salivate to the sound of a bell.

It is possible to condition any reflex. Humans as well as animals have reflex responses – for example, the knee-jerk or patellar response. We also show the reflex response of blinking when air is blown into our eyes.

Watson was enthusiastic about Pavlov's work, since it was an example of the scientific study of behaviour he wanted to see in psychology. He used Pavlov's procedure for experiments into human learning. A classic study is shown in box B:

Box B: Watson and Rayner (1920)

Procedure: An eleven-month-old child known as Little Albert was the participant in this study. Two months earlier, his reactions to various stimuli had been tested: a white rat, a rabbit, various other animals, cotton wool and burning newspapers. He showed no fear of any of these, and seems to have been a rather unemotional child. However, hardly surprisingly, he did show a fear reaction to a loud noise behind him, a hammer hitting a steel bar. The experimenters made this noise several times, at the same time presenting him with a white rat.

Results: Albert developed a fear of the white rat. The fear response to the rat became less extreme over time, but was still evident a month later.

Conclusion: Classical conditioning is one way of explaining fear responses. This is an example of a **conditioned emotional response** (CER). It is possible that people develop phobias through forming this kind of association.

Activity 6: questions on 'Little Albert'

Read through the Little Albert experiment in box B and answer these questions:

a Identify the NS, UCS, UCR, CS and CR.

b What are the ethical problems here, and how might they be overcome?

When you have finished, see the notes on page 19.

The case of Little Albert shows that Pavlov's findings do have some relevance to human learning. Psychologists have made use of this in various ways, most notably in **behaviour therapy**. If behaviour is learned, it can also be unlearned, and more appropriate behaviours learned instead. These ideas have been used to help people who suffer from disorders such as phobias, and are discussed in a little more detail in chapter 5.

- Watson wanted a scientific psychology, using objective methods. He saw behaviour as the only legitimate data for psychology.
- Studies of **animals** have often been carried out within the behaviourist tradition. Their use has several advantages.
- Watson was interested in the relationship between a **stimulus** to which an animal is exposed and its **response**. His ideas have been incorporated into **learning theory**.
- Pavlov's work on the salivary reflex in dogs led him to demonstrate what has come to be known as **classical conditioning**. His ideas can also be used to condition humans. The principles of classical conditioning are used in **therapy**.

Operant conditioning

The most famous name in operant conditioning is Skinner (1904–1990). The term 'operant' means an action: the animal operates on its environment. While sharing some general principles of classical conditioning – the emphasis on observable behaviour and explaining behaviour in terms of learning theory – operant conditioning is a move away from looking at associations between stimulus and response. In operant conditioning, what is important is the association between **behaviour** and the **consequences** of that behaviour. The basic principle behind Skinner's theory is that behaviour is shaped and maintained by its consequences.

While Pavlov's work related to reflex behaviour, Skinner's theory applies to any behaviour. He believed that all behaviour is learned, apart from the few reflexes we have at birth, and that any organism, human or animal, could be taught to produce any behaviour of which it was physically capable by the use of appropriate techniques.

Two key terms in Skinner's theory are reinforcement and shaping. **Shaping** is a way of gradually changing behaviour. **Reinforcement** refers to a positive consequence of a behaviour, which makes the behaviour likely to be repeated. To understand the theory, we will need to look at what he meant by these terms in a little more detail.

Shaping

If you wanted to train a rat to produce a behaviour, you might have quite a long wait before the rat produced the desired behaviour spontaneously. To shorten this time, Skinner used **shaping**. For example, if you want a rat to press a lever, you would reinforce a hungry rat with food when it moved in the direction of the lever. Once this behaviour was established, the rat would have to come a bit closer to what was required before being reinforced – for example, it might have to touch the lever. You would then require the rat to get even closer to lever-pressing – perhaps a slight lever press – to receive food, and then finally only reinforce when the rat produced a full lever press. In this way, you would be reinforcing **successive approximations** to the behaviour you were aiming at. Skinner himself managed to train pigeons to play table tennis using these methods!

Reinforcement and punishment

Although most of his original work was carried out on rats and pigeons, Skinner also applied his ideas to humans, and his research into the effect on learning of both reinforcement and punishment is of considerable relevance to human behaviour. He distinguished between positive and negative reinforcement. **Positive reinforcement** is when something with pleasurable consequences, which is likely to encourage a particular behaviour, is introduced into a situation. An example could be food for a hungry animal. It could also be praise or attention; it doesn't have to be anything tangible, just something which is pleasurable for the animal (or human) who is being reinforced. **Negative reinforcement** is when something aversive is removed from a situation. An example could be taking your hand away when you have accidentally touched a hot iron.

Both positive and negative reinforcement *strengthen* a particular behaviour. **Punishment**, on the other hand, weakens behaviour. It also differs from both positive and negative reinforcement, because it involves introducing something aversive into a situation, or taking something pleasurable away from it. These distinctions are summarised in figure 2.

In discussing ways of changing behaviour, Skinner himself was strongly in favour of the use of positive reinforcement, and to a lesser extent negative reinforcement. Punishment may be necessary to put an immediate stop to dangerous behaviour, like stopping a child playing with a knife, but otherwise Skinner was very much against it.

One of the reasons for this was practical: if you try to use punishment to change behaviour, initially it seems to work. What typically happens, however, is that this change is only temporary, and the undesired behaviour comes back, perhaps even more strongly than before. Although punishment may not be a good way of stopping a behaviour once and for all, it is very effective in temporarily suppressing unwanted behaviour. It could perhaps be useful, then, in stopping unwanted behaviour for long enough to allow desired behaviour to occur; this desired behaviour could then be shaped and reinforced, using positive reinforcement.

Figure 2: reinforcement and punishment			
term	**what happens**	**effect**	**examples**
positive reinforcement	something pleasurable is added to a situation	behaviour is strengthened	praise, food if hungry
negative reinforcement	something aversive is removed from a situation	behaviour is strengthened	pain stops
punishment	something aversive is added to a situation	behaviour is weakened	physical punishment
	something pleasurable is removed from a situation	behaviour is weakened	pocket money taken away

The implications of operant conditioning

Skinner and his followers believed that all behaviour is learned, apart from the few reflexes we have at birth. This is true both for animals and for humans. Our behaviour is shaped and maintained by its consequences. It therefore follows that, in theory, anyone can be taught to do anything which is physically possible.

Skinner considered that the principles of behaviour change which he had established could be very widely used well beyond the laboratory. His principles have been applied in many areas; for example, helping children with learning difficulties to acquire skills, and behaviour management in the classroom.

⊖ **Operant conditioning** is the term used to refer to the work of Skinner and his followers. Skinner explained learning as the association between a behaviour and its consequences. He believed all behaviour except reflexes is learned through **shaping** and **reinforcement**.

⊖ Behaviour is **reinforced** when the consequences are positive. **Shaping** allows behaviour to be developed which would not occur spontaneously.

⊖ Skinner distinguished between **positive reinforcement**, **negative reinforcement** and **punishment**. He strongly advocated the use of positive reinforcement as a way of changing behaviour. Punishment is an ineffective long-term measure, but it may have a place in behaviour change if it is used alongside positive reinforcement.

⊖ The principles of operant conditioning have been applied in a variety of contexts.

Social learning theory

Social learning theory is based on the principles of operant conditioning, in that it suggests that all behaviour (including social behaviour) is learned, and is likely to be repeated if it is positively reinforced.

Bandura, one of the foremost proponents of this theory, claimed that all social behaviour is learned through **modelling**. He suggested that there were three main sources of models: the family, the subculture (the people we mix with outside the immediate family) and the mass media.

Social learning theory: sources of models

We learn through observing the behaviour of others, and seeing the results of their behaviour. This is called **observational learning**. Modelling is rather more than just imitation, since Bandura sees the psychological effects of modelling as being much broader than just copying what we see; it is general rules and principles which are learned. This theory therefore also introduces cognitive factors to behavioural theory, such as attending to relevant features of the modelled behaviour, and remembering its critical features so that they can be accurately reproduced. He and his co-workers have shown this effect in a series of studies. One is described in box C:

Box C: Bandura *et al.* (1963)

Procedure: Children observed an adult behaving aggressively towards a large, inflatable Bobo doll. The adult attacked the doll in unusual ways (e.g. hitting it with a hammer, and saying things like 'Pow ... boom ... boom'). The children were then left in the playroom and their behaviour was observed. A control group of children also played in the playroom with the same toys, but did not observe the adult model attacking the doll.

Results: The behaviour of the experimental group was very similar to that of the adult model. The control group did not display similar behaviour.

Conclusion: Children imitated the behaviour of the adult model they had observed.

In a later study (Bandura, 1965), one group of children went straight into the playroom after they had observed the adult model. A second group saw the adult being rewarded for aggressive behaviour before they were let into the playroom, while a third group saw the adult punished. There was little difference in the number of imitated aggressive behaviours shown by the first two groups, but the third group showed significantly fewer imitated behaviours.

This seems to suggest that seeing a model punished leads to less learning. However, Bandura then offered rewards to the children who had seen the adult punished if they could reproduce the behaviour they had observed. The number of imitated aggressive behaviours shown by this group then rose to the level of the other two groups. Bandura concluded from this that **modelling** is sufficient for behaviour to be *learned*, but **reinforcement** is necessary for behaviour to be *performed*.

⊖ **Social learning theory** is a development of operant conditioning which introduces a cognitive element. It proposes that all behaviour is learned through **modelling**.

⊖ **Observation** of models is sufficient for learning to take place, but **reinforcement** is necessary if it is to be reproduced.

Overview of the behaviourist model

The behaviourist model claims that behaviour can be accounted for within the framework of **learning theory**, with S–R associations being learned within a classical conditioning framework, and behaviour which is reinforced being strengthened and therefore likely to recur within an operant conditioning framework.

Behaviourism emphasises the continuity between humans and other animals, since the same principles of learning are believed to apply in both cases. It assumes that very little is innate, and that therefore most of our behaviour needs to be learned. It is fundamentally an **associationist** approach.

Its aims are to establish by experimentation the rules which establish and change behaviour. This is often done by studying **animal behaviour** to establish basic principles. This has the advantage of control, in that animal behaviour is very much less complex than human behaviour, so it is easier to isolate particular variables. These principles may then be helpful in understanding human behaviour.

Human behaviour has also been studied directly using behavioural methods. These methods are also relevant to therapies; since all behaviour is learned, it can be unlearned and more appropriate behaviour learned in its place. This principle forms the basis of behavioural attempts to help people with problems, for example those suffering from phobias.

The physiological perspective

All the wide range of behaviour and experience which adds up to being human must have a physiological basis. Some psychologists therefore believe that to understand human functioning, we need to focus on the basic physiological processes which underlie it. We will look briefly at some of the topics with which biopsychologists are concerned.

One area of interest is **localisation of function**, i.e. how the functioning of different areas of the brain relates to behaviour and experience. In chapter 2, for example, some of the areas of the cerebral cortex which are known to be involved in different kinds of memory are discussed.

Biopsychologists are also interested in biochemical processes. **Neurotransmitters**, for example, are chemical messengers which allow neurons (nerve cells) to communicate with each other. In chapter 4, the role of neurotransmitters in the stress response is discussed. These substances are also implicated in mental disorders; for example, an excess of the neurotransmitter dopamine has been offered as one explanation for the development of schizophrenia. **Hormones** are another kind of biochemical; it has been suggested that the hormone CCK-8 may be related to the development of eating disorders. This is discussed in chapter 5.

Genetics is another area of interest. Physical characteristics (such as eye colour) and some physical disorders (such as cystic fibrosis) are passed on through the genes from parent to child. Biopsychologists have investigated the possibility that psychological characteristics (such as intelligence) and mental illnesses (such as schizophrenia) can be inherited in the same way.

Can psychological characteristics be inherited?

These are just a few of the topics in which biopsychologists are interested, but this should have given you a flavour of the kinds of areas with which they are concerned. The aims of this approach are to provide a detailed picture of aspects of physiology related to psychology, and to see how they relate to behaviour and experience. Given the nature of this approach, the scientific method is used. As in the behaviourist approach, animal research can often be a starting point.

The cognitive perspective

While behaviourism was a very popular approach in the 1940s and 1950s, some psychologists have pointed out that internal mental processes play a large part in many human functions, and therefore study of these processes should have a place in psychology. While behaviourists acknowledge the existence of processes such as thinking and emotion, they do not consider them an appropriate focus of study since they are not directly observable. Many psychologists believe, however, that to focus entirely on observable behaviour and ignore the mental processes which lead to the behaviour being produced provides an unnecessarily limited account of psychological functioning.

Cognitive psychologists are particularly interested in the mental processes involved in perception, attention, memory, language and thinking. They propose that the human mind can be compared to a computer, where information is taken in, processed in some way, and in turn affects behaviour and experience. The underlying model here is of people as **information processors**, and the aims are to establish the rules which govern our cognitions.

While it is not possible to observe cognitive processes directly, they can be observed indirectly by looking at the *results* of processing information. As you will see in chapter 2, much research into memory asks people to carry out memory tasks in controlled conditions; the results of these studies have helped psychologists to understand the nature of the cognitive processes involved in memory. Most research into memory is carried out using scientific research into other areas of cognition.

A recent development has been **artificial intelligence**, combining cognitive psychology with computer science. This has focused on the development of computer programs which can carry out the kinds of complex cognitive tasks typical of human functioning. The most recent theoretical framework taking this approach is **connectionism**, which has been influential in such areas as explaining how children develop language and why they make particular kinds of linguistic errors.

The cognitive approach is a move away from the use of animals, since some of our cognitive functions, such as the spontaneous development of language, are not shared by animals, and in any case human cognitions are vastly more complex than those of animals.

This approach has also been influential in the development of **therapies**, which try to help people with problems by encouraging them to reappraise the ways they think about themselves and others. This is discussed in chapter 6.

The humanistic perspective

The humanistic approach grew out of dissatisfaction with the rather piecemeal approach of the other perspectives we have described. In particular, some psychologists were unhappy with the behaviourist approach, with its disregard for conscious experience, as well as the rather pessimistic view of the psychodynamic approach, which saw people as being at the mercy of unconscious forces. In response to the huge influence of behaviourism and psychodynamic psychology, humanistic psychology therefore emerged as a third force, concerned with people's conscious experience and their ability to direct their lives.

Humanistic psychologists also question the use of the scientific method as the most useful one for psychologists to follow. This method has been dominant in much of psychology, and aims at objectivity. It is interested in the measurement of behaviour and exploring cause and effect relationships through rigorously controlled experiments. In contrast, humanistic psychologists argue that what is important is the experience of being a person, and that the methods used in the more traditional sciences are inappropriate for this kind of study. A rigorously scientific approach constrains our understanding of the individual. Like Freud, humanistic psychologists prefer to use a **case-study** method, and to make use of **introspective** data, which allows the psychologist to understand the individual in depth.

There are three basic principles of humanistic psychology. Firstly, what is important is the **experience** of being human. Instead of analysing people in an objective way, the humanistic psychologist is interested in people's experience. This is known as a **phenomenological approach**. An important aspect of this is that we are aware of our own existence as distinct individuals, moving through life towards old age and death.

The second principle is that we should take a **holistic approach** – in other words, look at the **person as a whole**. You will remember from earlier in the chapter that a similar viewpoint was put forward at the end of the nineteenth century by William James. Instead of studying specific psychological processes in isolation, the focus should be on the whole person, the physical person with thoughts and feelings, within a particular social context.

The final principle is that we all have **personal agency**. In most situations, we are aware of having choices. There may well be social constraints on our choices, and we may not be fully aware of the alternatives open to us. We may even be afraid of the consequences of making particular choices. Nonetheless, we do have the potential to choose. An extension of this principle is that we can play a part in the kind of person we become. Humanistic psychologists believe that people can be helped to change and develop by becoming as aware as possible of their feelings and motivations and the influences upon them. This process of change is referred to as **personal growth**.

The aims of humanistic psychology are to explore the experience of the individual, and to facilitate personal growth. Perhaps the major figure in humanistic psychology is Carl Rogers (1902–1987), whose work is particularly relevant to **therapies**. The aim of humanistic therapy is to help a person explore the changes they wish to make in their lives, and thus help them to grow as individuals.

Activity 7: identifying perspectives

Try to match each of the following statements to one (or more) of the perspectives described above **psychodynamic behaviourist physiological cognitive humanistic**

1 It is important to study what makes an individual unique.
2 Like any other science, psychology needs to use scientific methods.
3 Animal research can be useful in helping us to understand how people function.
4 The principles of psychology can be used in therapies.
5 It is important to focus on people's unconscious processes.
6 We need to understand how the body works if we are to understand behaviour and experience.
7 We have no direct access to internal psychological processes; we should therefore concentrate on what is observable.

When you have finished, see the notes on page 19.

This section should have given you some insight into the different ways in which psychology can be carried out. As you study different topics, you can consider each perspective: what its assumptions are, what its aims are, and what methods are used. You may also find it useful to come back to this section later, when you have more knowledge to which these distinctions can be related.

- There are five major approaches to psychology: **psychodynamic, behaviourist, physiological, cognitive** and **humanistic**.
- They vary in their assumptions, aims and methods.

1.5 PSYCHOLOGY AND COMMON SENSE

It may seem questionable whether psychology has much to tell us which is not just a matter of common sense. After all, we all observe what is going on around us and how people behave, and we draw conclusions about what people are like from what we observe. We seem to understand people quite well without the help of psychologists. So what does psychology have to offer?

One way of looking at this is to think of psychology as *organised* common sense. Psychology can give us a more detailed understanding of people, supported by evidence. This evidence has been reached in a systematic way, compared with the rather sporadic observations we may make of a very limited number of cases.

Common sense also has its problems. We may assume, for example, that what is true for us is also true for everybody else. Given the nature of Western society, for example, we could assume that people are 'naturally' competitive. Research in other cultures, which are based more on co-operation, suggests that this may not be the case. These assumptions, then, may have come about because we are particular individuals, who live in a particular community, in a particular culture, at a particular time. In a different setting, common sense could let us down. Psychology can take a wider view.

Some of the subject matter of psychology may not be within the experience of all of us. The physiological basis of behaviour is an obvious example, if we are not trained physiologists. For example, common sense can tell us little about the relationship between brain damage and behaviour.

Finally, common sense is sometimes wrong. For example, common sense tells many of us that if you punish someone for doing something, they will not do it again. (We know this in spite of prisons being full of people who have reoffended!) The findings of behaviourists, such as Skinner, however, show that punishment is not the best way of stopping behaviour, and can also suggest more effective ways of changing behaviour.

Common sense can of course be useful. It may give us useful insights, which start us off on a more precise psychological investigation. At the same time, psychology can extend and organise our understanding.

- Psychology can be thought of as organised common sense. It can provide evidence for common sense theories, and can take a wider perspective than the individual.
- Sometimes the findings of psychologists may contradict common sense.

1.6 What do psychologists do?

Psychology is one of the most popular subjects at A-level, and also at university, with large numbers of students graduating each year. What can a psychology graduate do with their degree once they have it? Of course many psychology graduates, like graduates in other disciplines, work in areas where a degree may be required, but the subject of the degree is not really important. But what about jobs in psychology?

Psychology **teaching** is one possibility. Psychology graduates can train to teach GCSE or A-level psychology in schools or colleges of further education. They can also combine teaching with research in a university department. Most people working in a university psychology department will have taken a PhD after their first degree.

Educational psychology is another option. Educational psychologists have teaching experience, and a masters degree in educational psychology. Most are employed by the local educational authority, and work with 5–16 year olds. Their work includes testing and assessing children with learning difficulties, and planning remedial programmes.

Postgraduate training is also necessary to become a **clinical psychologist**. Clinical psychologists work in general and psychiatric hospitals, often as part of a team of healthcare professionals, which includes a psychiatrist and a psychiatric social worker. Psychiatrists are *not* psychologists; they have medical training first, and then further training in psychological medicine. They assess patients with psychological problems, and plan and carry out therapy. **Forensic psychology** is a branch of clinical psychology. Forensic psychologists are employed by the prison or probation service. They may work with young offenders, run courses on anger management, or carry out risk assessment when certain prisoners are being considered for release. Another area related to clinical psychology is **counselling**. Many diploma courses in counselling are now available.

Another major area is **industrial** or **occupational psychology**. Occupational psychologists are often employed by large firms, though some work on a consultancy basis. They work in the personnel field, assessing people for job suitability, training people for jobs and retraining people for a new career after accident or redundancy. They are also involved in **ergonomics**, which involves designing machinery and equipment to optimise the working environment and maximise productivity. Specialised areas within this field include **advertising** and **sports psychology**.

The **British Psychological Society (BPS)** is the professional body for psychologists. Suitably qualified psychologists can apply for **Chartered Psychologist** status under its charter.

- Psychology graduates work in a range of fields, not always directly related to psychology.
- Some psychologists teach psychology. In a university department, teaching is combined with research.
- Professional psychologists work in three other main areas: educational, clinical and industrial or occupational psychology.
- Suitably qualified psychologists can apply for Chartered Psychologist status.

Notes on activities are on page 18.

Notes on activities

1 You would be right in thinking that psychologists are interested in nearly all these topics. There are some areas, though, which are controversial. An interest in animal behaviour is one example. Many psychologists believe that since animals and people are all living creatures, insight into the behaviour of rats and dogs may give us a head-start in understanding human behaviour. Others argue that people are unique, and we therefore need to concentrate directly on the behaviour and experience of people.

The relationship between astrological signs and personality is *not* a topic in psychology, though perhaps psychologists could be interested in the relationship between personal characteristics and a *belief* in astrology. There are also some areas (e.g. extra-sensory perception) which many psychologists would not regard as psychology, and others would regard as being, at best, on the fringes of psychology.

2 One obvious drawback is that you are relying on the skill (and honesty) of the person you are testing. The participants Wundt tested were carefully trained to try to overcome this problem, but they would still be dependent on their own level of awareness, and their ability to turn this awareness into words. It is also possible that describing a sensation may actually interfere with that sensation. In addition, reporting is always retrospective – you are describing something which has happened, not something which is happening, and this may present further difficulties.

It may well be possible to get useful information when the sensations which are to be reported are relatively straightforward and relate to simple events. All the problems outlined, though, are likely to become more serious as the stimulus to which a person is exposed becomes more complex.

A key point here is that introspection is essentially **subjective** – only the individual concerned can observe these internal processes. The accuracy of a subjective account cannot be checked, and it does not lend itself easily to measurement and precise analysis.

3 First of all, a precise area to be studied needs to be identified. This is followed by **observation** of a phenomenon, and from this observation, a general explanation or **theory** can be produced (though in practice, much new research is triggered off by an existing theory or research). This in turn will lead to a specific and testable **hypothesis**: a precise prediction of what the results of an experiment will be.

An **experiment** or test must then be set up, which isolates the factor in which you are interested, and controls other factors which are not relevant to your research. Information or **data** must be collected. This needs to be **objective**, so that someone else running a similar experiment could check their results against the results you have found. This is in contrast to the **subjective** data produced by introspection. **Conclusions** can then be drawn on the basis of the findings.

4 Freud believed that on the first occasion, the young man asked for two tickets because he wished his fiancée was with him. Asking for only one ticket on the second occasion expressed the unconscious wish for her *not* to be there, as he was dissatisfied with his marriage.

5 There are various ideas here which you could have come up with:

a Animals can be bred for laboratory experiments. This means that animals who are genetically identical can be bred, and their environment from birth onwards can be closely controlled. It is therefore possible to eliminate confounding variables from the study.

b It is also possible to treat animals in ways that would not be allowed if humans were to be tested – for example, keeping them hungry, or rearing them in isolation. There are ethical problems here, but national bodies like the British Psychological Society (BPS) have laid down guidelines which must be strictly followed.

c   Animals are less likely to be affected by demand characteristics, i.e. to change their behaviour in line with what they think the purpose of the study might be.

d   The kinds of animals which are used in laboratories, such as rats and pigeons, have much shorter lives than humans. This makes it easier to study learning at different stages of the lifespan.

e   There are no problems in finding enough participants for a study, they don't drop out and they don't need paying!

6   You should have identified the NS (and later the CS) as the rat. The initial UCS–UCR bond here is between noise–fear. The final CS–CR bond is between rat–fear.

There are serious **ethical problems** here. Researchers have a duty of care to protect participants from short-term stress and long-term harm, and this research fails on both counts. Albert obviously could not give his informed consent to what was to happen in this experiment, and it is not clear whether Watson had explained the experiment fully to his mother. Albert and his mother moved away soon after this study, before Watson had done anything to remove the fear response. Extinguishing Albert's learned fear would have gone at least some way to addressing the ethical concerns this study raises.

7   The first statement very much describes the humanistic approach. Scientific methods are a major feature of behaviourist, physiological and cognitive psychology. Remember, though, that Freud thought of his methods as scientific. Animal research has been important in behaviourist and physiological psychology. All five perspectives can have therapeutic applications. You should have identified the emphasis on unconscious processes as being associated with psychodynamic psychology, and how the body functions with a physiological perspective. The final statement typifies the behaviourist view, though it could also relate to physiological and to some extent cognitive psychology.

Human Memory

In this chapter we will be looking at:

2.1 The nature of memory

2.2 Early studies of memory

2.3 Models of memory
    The multi-store (structural)
     model of memory
    Working memory
    Levels of processing

2.4 Theories of forgetting
    Inaccessibility
    Unavailability

2.5 Reconstructive memory

2.6 Critical issue: eye-witness testimony
    (EWT)
    Registration
    Storage
    Retrieval
    Face recognition

2.1 THE NATURE OF MEMORY

Imagine life without memory! You wouldn't be able to talk, to read this chapter, to use a knife and fork... Nor would you be able to learn anything from experience – you would in effect spend your whole life as a new-born baby. You use memory to get dressed in the morning, carry on a conversation, pass exams, know people's telephone numbers, recognise faces – the list is endless. So studying memory is an area of psychology that seems relevant to all our lives. The ultimate goal of memory research is to apply its findings to practical problems such as helping people to use their memory more effectively and improving eye-witness accounts of crimes.

The three main processes involved in memory are **registration**, **storage** and **retrieval**. Registration is the process by which your sense organs detect information and enter that information in the memory system; storage is the process by which information is kept or stored in the memory; and retrieval is the process by which information in memory can be recovered or recalled. All these aspects are considered in the theories and research we will be looking at in this chapter.

2.2 EARLY STUDIES OF MEMORY

Psychologists have studied memory experimentally for more than 100 years. In 1885, Ebbinghaus's research was published, research in which he was the only participant. The study in box A is only one of many that he carried out to look at such things as how the position of a word in a list affects its recall:

Box A: Ebbinghaus (1885)

Procedure: Ebbinghaus used **nonsense syllables** of three letters such as KED and MOZ. He read a long list of these syllables at a steady pace, then covered up the list and tried to recite it from memory. He counted the syllables he remembered correctly, then read the list again, and repeated the procedure until he could recall the whole list. He tested his memory of the lists at various times after he had learned them.

Results: Ebbinghaus discovered that forgetting the syllables occurred quite quickly at first, but gradually slowed down.
Conclusion: The first, quick forgetting is the loss of material from a short-term memory system. The more gradual forgetting is their loss from a more long-term system.

Activity 1: evaluating Ebbinghaus

Having read Ebbinghaus' study, now evaluate its design. Try to think about the advantages and disadvantages of the way in which he carried out his research.

When you have finished, see the notes on page 50.

Although criticisms can be made of Ebbinghaus' work, he carried out a series of pioneering pieces of research, and was the first to suggest that memory consists of more than one system or store. His distinction between a short-term memory system and a longer-term memory system is similar to that made by William James (1890) between **primary memory** and **secondary memory**. The modern terms for such a distinction are **short-term memory (STM)** and **long-term memory (LTM)**.

Ebbinghaus believed that memory depends on the association of ideas, so that the process of learning a list of words or numbers consists of forming associations between the items. Another early theorist called Bartlett, whose work we will be looking at later in the chapter, published a book called *Remembering* (1932) in which he argued against the associationist standpoint. He took a **constructivist** approach to memory, seeing memory as a reconstructive process, and what we recall as a reconstruction rather than an exact copy of the original information. He believed that to get a clearer picture of how memory works, we should investigate memory using meaningful material.

- Memory involves **registration**, **storage** and **retrieval**.
- Ebbinghaus took an **associationist** approach to memory. He was the first to distinguish between a **short-term memory** store and a **long-term memory** store. William James described these as **primary** and **secondary** memory.
- Bartlett took a **constructivist** approach to memory. He saw remembering as **reconstruction** rather than reproduction.

2.3 MODELS OF MEMORY

Sometimes in psychology, a **model** of a particular process is used. A model is a sort of metaphor – a way of representing a process that makes it easier to understand, and for this reason models are often drawn up to try to produce a framework that explains complicated processes such as memory, and which enables us to investigate the processes involved.

The multi-store (structural) model of memory
This model is also often called the two-process model because of the importance attached to the two stores of **short-term memory (STM)** and **long-term memory (LTM)**. You may also find it referred to as the modal model; 'modal' here means 'most frequently occurring', and this model shares a number of common features with other, similar, models.

Figure 1: Atkinson and Shiffrin's model of memory (1968 and 1971)

This model describes memory in terms of information flowing through a system. In figure 1, you can see that information is detected by the sense organs, and enters the **sensory memory (SM)**. If we attend to this information, it enters the **STM**. Information from the STM is transferred to the **LTM** only if that information is rehearsed. If **rehearsal** does not occur, then the information is forgotten.

There are different types of rehearsal. Craik and Watkins (1973) distinguished between **maintenance rehearsal**, where, for example, you repeat a word out loud a number of times to keep it in STM, and **elaborative rehearsal**, in which information is processed in terms of its meaning. They suggested that maintenance rehearsal may be enough to keep information in STM, while elaborative rehearsal is the type necessary to transfer information from STM to LTM.

Psychologists often contrast memory stores in terms of how much information they can hold (their **capacity**), how long they can hold that information (the **duration** of the storage), and how information is coded (**encoding**). The characteristics of the different stores in the Atkinson and Shiffrin model are shown in figure 2:

Figure 2: comparing SM, STM and LTM

	SM	STM	LTM
Capacity	small	7±2 items	unlimited
Duration	0.25–2 seconds	up to 30 seconds	indefinite period of time
Encoding	modality specific	mainly acoustic	semantic/ visual/acoustic

Sensory memory

SM is what happens after information has reached the sense organs, and it travels to the brain for interpretation. This lingering of information in the nervous system (very briefly) gives the brain time to interpret it. There are two types of sensory storage: **iconic storage**, the store associated with visual information, and **echoic storage**, associated with heard, or auditory information. You can probably imagine iconic storage if you remember what happens when someone takes your photograph with

a flash – you often see an after-image of the flash for a brief moment, and this is iconic storage. Box B explores the nature of SM:

Box B: Sperling (1960)

Procedure 1: Replicating many previous studies, Sperling asked participants to look at an array of letters. He used a device called a tachistoscope, a machine which can display letters or numbers on a screen for very short and accurately controlled periods of time. In one trial, the participants were shown three rows of four letters (such as that shown below) for 50 milliseconds. They were then asked to recall as many letters as they could from the whole display.

sample display:

G	B	T	F
S	R	D	W
E	N	Z	X

Results: Participants could recall on average about 4.5 of the 12 items.

Procedure 2: Sperling then introduced his own idea, a partial report condition in which the participant was asked to recall only part of the display. A tone was played just after the display – if the tone was a high-pitched tone they should recall the top row of the display, a low-pitched tone indicated the bottom row, and a medium-pitched tone indicated the middle row.

Results: When the participants were cued to recall one row of the display immediately after the display was switched off, their average recall was 3.3 letters. As the tone was increasingly delayed, the average number of letters recalled decreased as the after-image faded.

Conclusion: Since the proportion of items remembered was greater in the partial report condition than for the total display, participants must have been reading the letters from an after-image – their iconic stores. Iconic storage lasts approximately half a second.

A study by Averbach and Coriell (1961) has provided a more sensitive measure of the capacity of SM, with information about how material is lost from this store:

Box C: Averbach and Coriell (1961)

Procedure 1: Participants were shown two rows, each of 8 letters chosen at random, for 50 milliseconds. A small mark then appeared just above one of the letter positions. Participants were asked to state which letter had been in the position of the marker.
Results: Letter identification was 75% accurate.
Conclusion: 12 letters can be held in SM, i.e. 75% of the 16 letters shown.

Procedure 2: Using a tachistoscope, participants were shown a letter, followed after a short time interval by another letter. They were asked to identify the first letter.
Results: If the time interval between the presentation of the two letters was less than 100 milliseconds, **superimposition** occurred (e.g. F followed by L was reported as E). If the time interval was longer than 100 milliseconds, backward visual masking (**displacement**) occurred (e.g. F followed by L was reported as L).
Conclusion: The iconic store forgets by displacement; the second letter displaces the first. For this to occur, there must be at least 100 milliseconds between the original stimulus and the displacing stimulus.

Treisman (1964) found that echoic memory has similar characteristics.

Short-term memory (STM)

If you look back to figure 2, you will see that the capacity of STM is said to be 7±2 items. This idea was put forward by Miller (1956). '7±2' means 'seven plus-or-minus two', so Miller was suggesting that STM can store between 5 and 9 pieces of information. STM can store only a limited number of items because it has only a certain number of 'slots' in which items can be stored. But Miller didn't specify the amount of information that could be held in each slot – indeed, his idea was that we can increase that amount by **chunking** the material; for example, by grouping letters together into words or into abbreviations that have meaning for us.

Activity 2: chunking

Write the letters listed below on a large piece of paper, and test some volunteers to see how many of the letters they can recall in a free recall task (they should try to remember as many as they can, in any order):

M S C G N V Q G C S E P H D B S C A S

Now group the letters so that they form the chunks below, and write them on a second large piece of paper. Test a different set of volunteers to see how many of the letters they can recall.

MSC GNVQ GCSE PHD BSC AS

Which task led to greater recall?

You probably found that the second condition allowed people to recall significantly more letters than the first. In terms of Miller's idea, the first set of letters (19 items) would be too many for the 7±2 slots of STM to hold. But if we group the letters so that they form the chunks MSC, GNVQ, GCSE, PHD, BSC and AS, they give six 'chunks' of information (at least to English-speaking people who know something about the English education system) which is within the range of STM.

A further task to investigate STM which you could try on your participants is what is known as the **Brown–Peterson technique**. Peterson and Peterson (1959) asked their participants to remember **trigrams** – groups of three consonants like KMG or PNS. But to prevent the participants from rehearsing the trigrams, they were asked to count backwards aloud in threes, from a number such as 176. This is a very effective way of preventing rehearsal (try it!) and they found that information was rapidly forgotten; they concluded that without rehearsal, material in STM is forgotten within 6–12 seconds. Although Atkinson and Shiffrin believe it lasts rather longer (see figure 2), these findings give a general indication of the **duration** of STM, and show that **rehearsal** is necessary to enable information to be transferred to LTM.

Activity 3 investigates how material is encoded in STM:

▶ Activity 3: coding in STM

You will need to find some participants to help you carry out this activity.

Draw each of the letters listed below on to a separate piece of white card, in large clear lettering. Put the letters into two piles – list 1 and list 2.

> **List 1:** B V T C D G E P
>
> **List 2:** M R W L Z Y Q A

Now show each letter of list 1 to your participants and ask them to look at each letter carefully and try to memorise it. When all the letters have been shown, ask them to write down as many of the list of letters as they can.

Next, repeat the procedure with list two. To make it a better test, you should really present half your participants with list 1 first and list 2 second; the other half of the participants should be presented with list 2 first and list 1 second. This technique is known as **counterbalancing**. It eliminates **order effects**, such as practice, fatigue or boredom, and is discussed in more detail in chapter 7.

Work out which list was remembered most accurately. What is the difference between the two lists?

You may have noticed that the letters in list 1 all sound like each other – they are acoustically similar. You may have found that your participants were far more likely to make errors when recalling the letters that were acoustically similar than when recalling different sounding letters, so made more mistakes when they tried to recall list 1 than with list 2. Bear in mind that this happened even though the letters were presented visually – you didn't read the letters out loud and in doing so show that list 1 letters all sounded similar. The results of this study imply that information stored in STM is stored in an **acoustic code**. Other studies have given similar results:

Box D: Conrad (1964)

Procedure: Participants were shown sequences of 6 letters, chosen from B C F M N P S T V X. They were asked to write them down as they appeared, but presentation was too fast for participants to keep up, so the information had to be held in STM. The errors made were analysed.

Results: The errors were generally acoustic confusion errors, where the original letters were replaced by ones with a similar sound, e.g. S for X or M for N.

Conclusion: Coding in STM is acoustic, even when material is presented visually.

Long-term memory (LTM)

Figure 2 shows that according to the multi-store model, LTM can hold unlimited amounts of information for an indefinite period of time, and that this store uses mainly **semantic coding** (i.e. based on the meaning of information) together with **visual** and **acoustic** coding.

Box E: Baddeley (1966)

Procedure: Participants were presented with a short list of words which were semantically similar (e.g. neat/clean/tidy/smart). He also gave them a list of words that were acoustically similar (e.g. heat/sweet/greet/sheet). Recall was tested immediately, and again after a period of time had elapsed.

Results: When testing immediate recall, there was acoustic confusion between acoustically similar words, while those with similar meanings were easily remembered. When participants were tested again later, however, the words with similar meanings caused problems.

Conclusion: The confusion on semantically similar lists after a period of time is evidence that LTM mainly uses a semantic code. The confusion on lists that sounded similar is evidence that encoding in STM is acoustic.

⊝ Atkinson and Shiffrin's **multi-store model** described information flowing through a memory system composed of **sensory memory (SM)**, **short-term memory (STM)** and **long-term memory (LTM)**.

⊝ **SM** is **modality-based** and lasts up to 2 seconds.

⊝ **STM** uses an **acoustic code** and has a capacity of 7±2 items. It lasts between 6 and 12 seconds, but can be extended by **rehearsal**.

⊝ **LTM** has unlimited **capacity** and can potentially last indefinitely. It mainly uses a **semantic code**.

Evidence for the multi-store model of memory

Evidence for this model comes from a number of sources, one of which you can test for yourself in activity 4.

▶ **Activity 4: a free recall task**

You can try this activity on a few friends or on members of your family. The more people you try it on, the better the test will be.

Read out the following instructions to your participants: 'I am going to read you a list of words. I would like you to listen carefully to the words. When I have finished, I would like you to write down as many of the words as you can remember, in any order.'.

Now read out the following list of words in order (first 'scissors' then 'file' etc) to your participants – slowly and clearly, with a gap of a second or two in between each word. (Don't read out the numbers!)

1. scissors	2. file	3. grass	4. lion
5. computer	6. carpet	7. room	8. knife
9. book	10. dish	11. idea	12. sand
13. card	14. cushion	15. parrot	16. fire
17. milk	18. house	19. pencil	20. wall

Then say to your participants: 'Now please write down as many of the words as you can remember, in any order.'.

To analyse your results, write down a list of the 20 words in the order in which you read them out. Now go through your participants' recall lists, and count up how many people recalled each word. Your results table should look something like this:

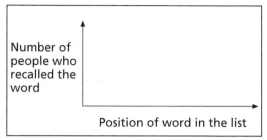

word	position of word in list	number of people who recalled that word
scissors	1	3
file	2	2
grass	3	3
lion	4	0

When you have finished the table, plot a graph like the one below:

Was the position of the word in the list related to the number of people who recalled it?

You may have found no particular pattern in your graph, especially if you were limited to only a couple of participants. On the other hand, you may have a curve that looks like the one in figure 3:

Figure 3: serial position curve

Position of word in the list

Your participants performed what is called a **free recall task** – that means that they recalled the words in any order. Similar experiments were carried out by Ebbinghaus whose work on nonsense syllables was mentioned earlier. He had similar results to those shown in figure 3. Displaying results in this way is known as a **serial position curve**. Typically, words near the beginning and end of the list are better recalled than those in the middle. The effect whereby the first few words are well recalled is known as the

primacy effect (**P** on the graph) and the effect whereby the last few words are well recalled is known as the **recency effect** (**R** on the graph).

◖ Activity 5: interpreting the serial position curve

Look carefully at the serial position curve above. What does it show? Try to explain what the shape of the curve means. How does it support the two-process model?

When you have finished, see the notes on page 50.

Evidence that the recency effect is due to retrieval from STM is given by Glanzer and Cunitz (1966) who found that the recency effect occurs only if the last items on the list are recalled immediately; if recall is delayed, then the recency effect disappears. You could try this as a further experiment, if you still have willing participants!

Clinical evidence also supports the two-process model:

Box F: Milner (1996)

Scoville and Milner described the now classic case study of HM, a man who had drastic brain surgery to cure his epilepsy. One consequence of this procedure was that he suffered from **anterograde amnesia** – he could recall events that happened before the operation, such as details of friends he knew before the surgery, but very little of what occurred afterwards. He re-read newspapers unaware that he had just read them, and only knew what time it was for about 15 seconds after he looked at the clock. All the people he met after the surgery had to be 're-met' each time they visited him, as he couldn't remember who they were.

The case of HM supports the two-process model, because it supports the idea that the brain uses different mechanisms for holding information for a short time, and for holding it relatively permanently. HM could remember a lot from before the surgery, so presumably his LTM was unaffected by the operation, but he did not seem able to transfer new information from his STM into his LTM.

Further clinical evidence for the idea of separate STM and LTM processing systems comes from cases of amnesia resulting from the type of brain damage caused by chronic alcoholism. This is called the **Korsakov syndrome** and patients suffering from it have a fairly intact LTM but a severely faulty STM.

One other piece of evidence for the two-process model is that different types of coding are used in STM and LTM, as previously discussed (see box E). The fact that short-term coding is so different from long-term coding supports the idea that there are two distinct stores.

Criticisms of the multi-store model of memory

Atkinson and Shiffrin's model affected psychological research into memory for many years. It has made a valuable contribution to memory research as it clearly distinguishes between the *structures* and the *processes* of memory. However, the model is no longer accepted as entirely plausible, and has been criticised on many counts.

One problem is that it implies that to reach LTM, information needs to flow through STM. Shallice and Warrington (1970) carried out a case study of KF, who suffered brain damage as the result of a motorcycle accident. His STM was seriously impaired, but his LTM was relatively intact, including memory for information *after* his accident. This suggests that information does not have to flow through the STM in order to reach LTM.

The multi-store model can also be criticised for its lack of detail about the nature of LTM; it does not go beyond defining capacity, the coding involved and duration of storage.

Another major problem with the model is that there is evidence that neither STM nor LTM is a unitary store. Each may more usefully be seen as being made up of different subsystems. This approach has been taken in the theory of **working memory** which we shall be looking at in the next section.

Similarly, Tulving (1972) suggested that there are two systems within LTM: **semantic memory**, consisting of facts, such as that Lima is the capital of Peru, and **episodic memory**, personal memories such as where you went on holiday last year, and public events which have happened in your lifetime, such as earthquakes or assassinations. He also described **procedural memory**, memory for complex skills such as how to type, and how to combine words appropriately when speaking your native language. Evidence for these distinctions comes from clinical evidence, such as the study reported by Blakemore (1988) of Clive Wearing. After suffering brain damage as the result of a brain infection, Clive Wearing's semantic and episodic memory were severely affected, while his procedural memory was relatively intact.

A further problem is that the multi-store model takes no account of the *nature* of information to be recalled, concentrating only on *quantity* of information. It treats all information as the same, whereas we know intuitively that *what* we are trying to remember is very important in whether or not it is remembered. Some people find it very easy to remember golf scores or astronomy facts, for example, but cannot for the life of them recall capital cities or relatives' birthdays.

The importance of the nature of the information to be recalled is shown by the phenomenon of **flashbulb memories**. This is where people have a particularly strong and often detailed memory of where they were and exactly what they were doing when a specific major event occurred. For example, you may know people who remember in great detail where they were on VE day at the end of the second world war when the Germans surrendered unconditionally (1945) or when the American president John F Kennedy was shot (1963) or when Mrs Thatcher resigned as Prime Minister (1990) or when they heard that Diana, Princess of Wales had died (1997), depending on their age.

Brown and Kulik (1977) found that people were likely to remember six kinds of information in memories of this kind: where they were when they heard the news; what they were doing at the time; the person who gave them the news; how they felt about it; how others felt about it; and the aftermath of the event. The most important factors in triggering a flashbulb memory were that the event was surprising, was seen to be important and was associated with a high level of emotional arousal. These ideas were demonstrated in their findings that of the 80 people asked about their memories of the Kennedy assassination – an unexpected event of national importance in the USA, and about which most people had very strong feelings – 79 remembered where they were and what they had been doing at the time. Similarly, very high levels of flashbulb memory for the resignation of Mrs Thatcher were found by Conway *et al.* (1994).

A further study has produced similar findings:

Box G: Pillemer (1984)

Procedure: In this American research, people were asked about their memory for the attempted assassination of the American president Ronald Reagan in 1981. They were asked about this event a month after it happened, and again six months later.

Results: People had vivid memories of where they were when they heard the news, and who told them about it. They reported strong visual images. The amount of emotional arousal people experienced was related to the vividness, elaboration and consistency over time of the memory.

Conclusion: Flashbulb memories are associated with an event being unexpected, seen as important, and creating strong emotional arousal.

As well as public events, we can also have flashbulb memories of personal events. Rubin and Kozin (1984) asked people to describe their three clearest memories. Many of these memories related to accidents or injuries to themselves or those close to them, while others related to love affairs, sports, animals and their experiences when starting college. National events, such as those described above, made up only three per cent of the sample. As with the other research in this area, surprise was an important factor; the number of times people had rehearsed the memory, i.e. gone over it in their minds, was also important.

Activity 6: investigating flashbulb memories

Carry out a small-scale replication of the Rubin and Kozin study. Use your own three clearest memories as a starting point.

a Do they include the kinds of events Rubin and Kozin describe?

b Was there a strong element of surprise associated with these memories?

c Have you often thought about these events since they happened?

Ask other people the same questions, and compare what they say with your own answers and the findings of the Rubin and Kozin study.

One of the factors associated with flashbulb memories is **distinctiveness**: the fact that an event is so unusual means that it stands out from our everyday memories. Distinctiveness is a factor in memory which applies more widely than just to flashbulb memories, a phenomenon which is known as the **von Restorff effect**.

More everyday personal factors are also important:

Box H: Morris *et al.* (1985)

Procedure: Participants were asked to fill in a soccer knowledge questionnaire. They were then asked to memorise that day's football results and a set of simulated scores.

Results: There was a high positive correlation (0.82) between soccer knowledge and memory for the real scores. For simulated scores, the correlation was only 0.36.

Conclusion: Interest and knowledge are factors in whether or not information is retained.

● The **primacy** and **recency effects**, the case of **HM**, the **Korsakov syndrome** and the fact that different **codes** are used in **STM** and **LTM** are all evidence for the multi-store model.

● This model has been criticised for being too simplistic in its assumption that memory flows in one direction through the different stores.

● This model gives little detail of **LTM**.

● There is evidence that neither the **STM** nor the **LTM** is a unitary store.

● This model does not take into account the nature of the material to be remembered.

In the light of the criticisms made of the multi-store model, several other models of memory have been suggested. The **working memory** model of Baddeley and Hitch (1974) offers an alternative explanation of STM. **The levels of processing** model of Craik and Lockhart (1972) moves away from an emphasis on separate stores, while providing insight into the importance of how material is processed for retention.

Working memory

In contrast to the multi-store model, the working memory model of Baddeley and Hitch (1974) deals only with STM and recently activated parts of LTM. The working memory model concentrates on systems by which information is processed in STM, and emphasises the idea of an **active processor**. If you look back to the work by Atkinson and Shiffrin, you will see that the stages of their model are passive stores through which information flows, in strong contrast to this idea of memory as an active process.

Baddeley and Hitch suggested that working memory consists of a **central executive** which controls three **slave systems**. The central executive is used when you are dealing with difficult mental tasks such as problem solving. Information can be briefly held within a slave system while new information is being processed. In doing a complicated addition sum, for example, the number to be carried forward from one column of figures can be held while the next column is added up. The central executive also acts as a sort of attention system, deciding which information entering from the sense organs should have attention allocated to it, and directing the work of the slave systems.

The central executive is the most important part of the system as it controls all the other systems. It is very flexible: it can process information from any of the senses, and can even store information for a short period of time. The three slave systems are the **visuo-spatial scratch pad**, the **articulatory loop** and the **primary acoustic store**.

Figure 4: working memory (Baddeley Hitch, 1974)

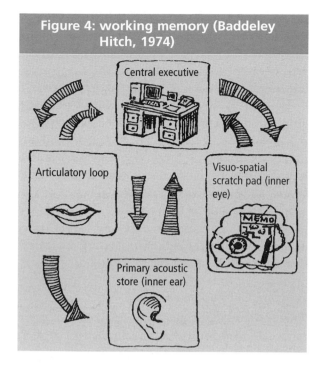

The **visuo-spatial scratch pad**, also known as the **inner eye**, uses a visual code and deals with visual and spatial information, such as the layout of the inside of your house or where the plants are situated in your garden. Activity 7 looks at the ways information is coded using the visuo-spatial scratch pad and the articulatory loop:

▶ Activity 7: coding in working memory

You will need to draw carefully the display grid below on a large piece of paper. You also need to draw a number of blank grids, exactly the same as the first one but without the letters in. Then you will need to draw two patterned grids similar to the one shown below, each with a slightly different pattern of squares coloured in.

Display grid

M			K		
		Z			
			A		G
F		R			

Patterned grid

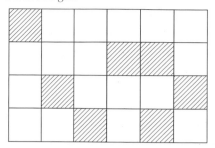

Half your participants will be performing a verbal task in between seeing the display and recalling it; the other half will perform a visual task.

Show half your participants the display for 10 seconds. Then ask them to count backwards aloud from 100 and time this counting for 10 seconds. (This is the **verbal task**). Finally, ask them to fill in one of the blank grids you prepared earlier, to see how much of the display they can recall.

If they remember a letter but not where it went, they should put it anywhere. If they remember there was a letter in a particular square, but can't remember what it was, they should put any letter in the square.

Repeat this procedure with the rest of your participants, but instead of the verbal task, ask them to look at two of the patterned grids you prepared earlier, and tick which parts of the two grids match (time them doing this for 10 seconds) – this is the **visual task**.

You should score your participants' answers separately in two ways. For each condition each participant should have a score out of 7 for number of letters recalled correctly, and a score out of 7 for the number of positions recalled correctly.

Activity 7 is similar to an experiment carried out by Den Heyer and Barrett (1971). You probably found that your participants' recall of the letters was more disrupted by the verbal task, and their recall of the letters' positions in the grid was more disrupted by the visual task. Den Heyer and Barrett suggested that the experiment gives evidence that the letters themselves were encoded acoustically (because the verbal task prevented their recall) and that the position of the letters was encoded visually.

The **articulatory loop** is known as the **inner voice**. It is a **verbal rehearsal loop** which holds words in an articulatory code. It is like an inner voice because you 'hear' in your head the telephone number you are attempting to remember; for example, while you search for a pen and notepad. The capacity of the articulatory loop was discovered when Baddeley *et al.* (1975) showed that people involved in a recall task could immediately recall as many words as they could read out in two seconds, but no more. The articulatory loop therefore works rather like a continuous cassette loop: the amount of information it can hold is determined only by how long it takes that information to be spoken out loud, and not by the number of items.

You may have unwittingly come across evidence for the articulatory loop. Perhaps you have had the experience of asking somebody 'What did you say?' when you thought you hadn't heard them correctly, but in the time it took you to ask the question, you realised that you did know what it was they said. This is your articulatory loop in action; like a cassette loop, the information was played back to you, and you heard what was said.

You can also try out for yourself how the articulatory loop works. If you repeatedly say a phrase out loud, you are occupying your articulatory loop so that it can't be used to hold other information in working memory at the same time. The idea of repeating a phrase at the same time as learning a list of words, or reading a book, is called concurrent verbalisation. If the task being carried out is hampered by the **concurrent verbalisation** task, then you can assume that the task normally utilises the articulatory loop.

▷ **Activity 8: a concurrent verbalisation task**

Pick a textbook that you sometimes use in your studies, but that you have previously found fairly difficult. Read a page of the text silently, simultaneously saying the phrase 'cognitive psychology' out loud. When you finish reading the page, see how much of the text you can remember.

You may well have found that you could not remember much of the text you had read, because your articulatory loop was being used to repeat the phrase 'cognitive psychology'. This is called **articulatory suppression**. The reason it was suggested that you pick a fairly difficult textbook was because concurrent verbalisation has more effect if the material is quite difficult to understand.

Very little is known about the **primary acoustic store**, or **inner ear**, which was added to the original model in 1982; it is thought to receive auditory information directly from the ears or via the articulatory loop, and to store it in an acoustic code. It was added to the original model when it was found that information which is presented acoustically is not affected by articulatory suppression. This can be contrasted with the silent reading you used in activity 8.

Evaluation of working memory

Although working memory is one of the most recent models of memory, it is limited in that it considers only STM, and also because comparatively little is known about the central executive, the most important part of the whole system.

However, it seems to make more sense to see STM as a group of processing mechanisms rather than as a single store in which information is passively held. In terms of coding, the working memory model gives more emphasis to the use of visual coding in STM, compared to the multi-store model which sees coding as primarily acoustic.

Its main advantage is the way it portrays memory as an **active process**, and not merely a series of passive stores. Cognitive psychologists also find it useful to see attention and memory as part of the same system, since we tend to use the two processes together. Further research may well provide more information about the nature of the central executive part of the model.

Another strength of the working memory model is that it ties in neatly with PET scan studies of brain activity during different memory tasks, carried out by the Wellcome Foundation. PET stands for positron emission tomography, and this type of scan displays a three-dimensional representation of the brain's structures and provides images which show brain activity in different areas while carrying out different tasks. Activity in different areas corresponds with the four systems the model proposes:

Figure 5: brain localisation and working memory (from Carter, 1998)

Articulatory loop

Primary acoustic store

Central executive

(a) Articulatory loop and primary acoustic store (left side of brain)

Visuo-spatial scratch pad

Central executive

(b) Visuo-spatial scratch pad (right side of brain)

Working memory has potential practical applications – for example, in teaching children to read. If children with normal intelligence are having difficulties learning to read, and they also have trouble in recognising rhyme, it suggests a problem with their articulatory loop. When we understand the systems better, we will be in a better position to help such children and put our theoretical knowledge to good use.

- The working memory model of Baddeley and Hitch is a model of short-term memory.
- This memory system is seen as an active processor, consisting of a **central executive** in control of three slave systems – **the visuo-spatial scratchpad**, the **articulatory loop** and the **primary acoustic store**.

- Concurrent verbalisation tasks give evidence that the articulatory loop is involved in processing information.
- The model places more emphasis on visual aspects of STM.
- The idea of different subsystems is supported by evidence from **PET scans**.
- The working memory model has been criticised on the grounds that the central executive is not fully understood.
- Applications of the working memory model include helping children learn to read.

Levels of processing

The levels of processing model was put forward by Craik and Lockhart (1972), partly as a result of the criticisms levelled at Atkinson and Shiffrin's model. Instead of concentrating on the stores involved, i.e. STM and LTM, this model concentrates on the *processes* involved in memory. The basic idea is that memory is really just what happens as a result of processing information. What is important is what you do with the information to be remembered.

Craik and Lockhart suggested that storage of information varies along a continuous dimension depending on the depth to which it has been encoded. They defined 'depth' in terms of the meaningfulness extracted from material. They proposed that information which has been processed deeply, i.e. more extensively, will be better stored, and is therefore more likely to be recalled; whereas information which has been processed in a more shallow way, i.e. more superficially, is more likely to be forgotten.

Although depth is a continuous dimension, this idea has generally been tested using three levels:

Figure 6: possible levels in Craik and Lockhart's levels of processing model (1972)

structural level	What does the word *look* like? e.g. capitals or lower case letters?	shallow
phonological level	What does the word *sound* like? e.g. does it rhyme with 'cat'?	↓
semantic level	What does the word *mean* ? e.g. is it a type of food?	deep

An example of a study to test the levels of processing model is shown in box I:

Box I: Craik and Tulving (1975)

Procedure: Participants were shown a series of words, on each of which they were asked a question. The questions required either **a** structural, **b** phonological or **c** semantic processing, e.g:

a is the word written in capital letters? (e.g. CAT or cat)

b does the word rhyme with 'stable'? (e.g. table or chair)

c does it fit into the sentence 'she climbed up the...' (e.g. stairs or goat)

They were then given an unexpected recall task in which they were asked to pick out the words they had been shown from others they had not seen.

Results: Participants were significantly better at recognising words they had processed semantically.

Conclusion: The effectiveness of recall is related to the level at which material has been processed, with deeper processing producing better recall.

Elias and Perfetti (1973) also tested the levels of processing model. They asked participants to work through a list of words, performing different types of processing on each word (such as thinking of a word that rhymes with each word on the list, or finding a word with a similar meaning). Their participants were not told that they would later have to recall the words, but when they were tested, they recalled significantly more words which had been semantically processed, giving evidence for the levels of processing model.

You can test the levels of processing model for yourself:

▶ Activity 9: testing the levels of processing model

Make up two sets of 18 cards. For each set, each of these words should be written on a separate card:

celery   carrot   plumber   lawyer   ferret
bear   spinach   broccoli   secretary   painter
hamster   hyena   potato   parsnip   doctor
printer   tiger   rabbit

For the first set, write each word in the same kind of writing so that they are as uniform as possible. For the second set, write two vegetables, two professions and two animals in fairly small lower case letters (but so they can still be read easily), two of each group in fairly large lower case letters and the remaining six words in capital letters:

celery	plumber	FERRET

For the first set (condition 1), prepare instructions asking participants to sort the cards into three groups of words which are related in meaning. For the second set (condition 2), ask them to sort the cards into three groups by the style of writing in which they are written.

Participants should not be told that this is a memory test; tell them you will explain what the study is about after they have carried out the task. When each participant has carried out the sorting task, remove the cards and ask them to write down as many words as they can remember in any order. You will need to test different participants in each condition. Test as many as you can; if you are working in a group, pool your data.

In which condition did people tend to recall more words correctly?

According to levels of processing theory, you are likely to have found that the people you tested recalled more words if they were asked to sort them by meaning than by writing style.

The distinction Craik and Watkins (1973) made between maintenance rehearsal and elaborative rehearsal, which we mentioned earlier, is relevant here. You will remember that in **maintenance rehearsal**, a word or number is repeated again and again, and this is enough to keep it in STM. For example, if a friend reads out their telephone number to you, you might well repeat that number out loud again and again while you search frantically for a pen and notepad. This is **phonological** processing, and in the levels of processing model it is relatively shallow.

Elaborative rehearsal, on the other hand, is where you elaborate the material to be remembered in terms of its meaning. For example, you might remember the phone number 2954, by thinking: 'Uncle Jim is 29 and he lives at number 54'. This elaborative rehearsal which is necessary to retain information in the LTM involves deeper **semantic** processing.

Evaluation of the levels of processing model

Craik and Lockhart's model of memory has contributed to research in this area of psychology because it concentrates on the *processes* of memory. It emphasises that how likely you are to retrieve a particular item from your memory successfully depends on how you process that piece of information, and not on how hard you try to rehearse it. However, the model is criticised for being descriptive rather than explanatory, and for its failure to explain *why* deeper processing leads to better recall – an opinion which Craik and Lockhart themselves counter by claiming that their idea was not intended to be a theory of memory, but rather a 'conceptual framework for memory research'.

One of the main problems of their approach is that it is very difficult to measure how deeply a piece of information has been processed. It is a circular argument to say that something you remember well is something that you have processed deeply; but the only way to tell whether it has been processed at a deep level is by seeing if you can recall it!

There is also a problem because the levels of processing model makes no distinction between STM and LTM, and you have already read about the evidence which suggests that there are two quite distinct memory processes.

One further problem is that the improved recall of some words could be due to **processing effort** rather than depth of processing:

Box J: Tyler *et al.* (1979)

Procedure: Participants were given two sets of anagrams to solve. Some of the anagrams were easy (e.g. FAMIYL); others were difficult (e.g. YMALFI). Participants were later given an unexpected recall test.

Results: Significantly more of the difficult anagram words were remembered than the easy ones.

Conclusion: As all words were processed at the same depth (i.e. semantically), recall of the words depended on the effort that was put into processing them, and not the depth of processing.

You can probably see that the participants would also have spent more *time* processing the more difficult anagrams, and this is another potential **confounding variable**. It is impossible for a researcher to work out which variable is having an effect (processing effort, *or* length of time spent processing, *or* depth of processing) if the variables cannot be separated.

There may also be factors other than depth of processing which influence how well something is remembered:

Box K: Craik and Tulving (1975)

Procedure: Participants were shown a word and a sentence containing a blank. They were asked whether the word would fit into the sentence. On some trials, the sentence was complex (e.g. 'the great bird swooped down and carried off the struggling ...') and in some trials less so (e.g. 'she cooked the ...).

Results: Using cued recall, participants recalled twice as many words accompanying complex sentences.

Conclusion: As both kinds of trial required semantic processing, increased recall for the words accompanying more complex sentences can be explained by greater *elaboration* of processing, i.e. the amount of processing of a particular kind.

The **von Restorff effect**, mentioned earlier, suggests that distinctiveness, too, is a factor in whether or not information is recalled.

There is also evidence that semantic processing does not always lead to improved recall:

> ### Box L: Morris *et al.* (1977)
>
> **Procedure:** Participants were presented with words and asked to answer questions involving either meaning or rhyme. Recall was tested either by a standard recognition test (see box H) or by a rhyming recognition test, in which they were asked to pick out words which rhymed with the stimulus words.
>
> **Results:** On the standard recognition test, recall was better for words which had been processed semantically than for those where questions about rhyme had been asked. On the rhyming recognition test, however, the opposite was true.
>
> **Conclusion:** Semantic processing does not always lead to superior recall compared with phonological processing. Recall may depend on the relevance of the kind of processing to the memory test.

- Craik and Lockhart's levels of processing model suggested that information is processed at one of three levels – at the **structural** level, the **phonological** level, or the **semantic** level.
- The deeper the information is processed, the better it is recalled.
- The levels of processing model has been criticised on the grounds that it is difficult to measure how deeply information has been processed.
- It has also been suggested that **processing effort** and the time taken to process information, rather than depth of processing, are responsible for improved recall with semantically processed information.
- **Elaboration** and **distinctiveness** are also factors in recall. On some tasks, semantic processing may not be the most effective technique.

2.4 THEORIES OF FORGETTING

To understand the nature of forgetting, it is important to make a distinction between availability and accessibility. **Availability** is whether the information you are trying to recall is still actually stored; **accessibility** is whether or not it can be retrieved at will. Obviously information that is not available (because it wasn't stored in the first place or is no longer stored) will not be accessible.

Inaccessibility

Many years ago, psychologists such as Freud believed that memories were permanent, and forgetting was merely a failure to retrieve information successfully. Evidence for this idea came from Penfield (1969). He stimulated the surface of the brain of epileptic patients on whom he was operating, to try to identify which area of the brain was involved in producing the epileptic attacks:

Figure 7: Penfield (1969)

Places where stimulation elicited snatches of memory during Penfield's investigations

He found that this procedure led to some people recalling long-forgotten memories with great clarity. Given this idea, it follows that failure to retrieve information should be because memories are inaccessible.

Theories of forgetting based on the idea that memories are inaccessible include **interference**, **cue-dependent forgetting** and **repression**.

Interference

The idea behind this theory is that memories may be interfered with either by what we have learned before, or by what we may learn in the future. Similarity is the main factor in forgetting. Forgetting increases with time because of interference from competing memories that have been acquired over time.

If you have ever sunburnt your left arm and put your watch on your right wrist for a few days, you are likely to glance at the wrong wrist on the first few occasions you try to tell the time. This is **proactive interference (PI)** — wearing your watch on the left wrist (old knowledge) has interfered with the new knowledge that your watch is actually on your right arm.

When the sunburn heals, you return your watch to the original left wrist. Now you have learned to look at your right wrist, and this new learning will interfere with the old knowledge of where to look for the time. This is **retroactive interference (RI)**.

Figure 8: proactive and retroactive interference

PI: learn A: learn B: interference from A
affects recall of B
RI: learn A: learn B: interference from B
affects recall of A

This theory is basically associationist. In the example of the watch, the stimulus of wondering 'What time is it?' is associated with the response of looking at your wrist. Interference comes from the very similar responses of looking at your right or left wrist.

McGeoch and Macdonald (1931) found that for participants learning a word list, forgetting was greatest when a subsequent interference task was similar to what had been learned originally. There was little effect on recall from interference when the subsequent task involved unrelated material, but more when it involved antonyms of the original list. Most forgetting occurred when the interference task involved synonyms of the original list.

One problem with this theory, though, is that it doesn't apply very widely to everyday forgetting. As Baddeley has pointed out, PI in particular has been very hard to establish outside the laboratory.

There is some disagreement as to whether interference should be thought of as lack of accessibility or lack of availability. There is some evidence, however, that interference is due to lack of accessibility:

Box M: Tulving (1962)

Procedure: Participants were given a list of words to remember. Recall was tested on three different trials.
Results: Participants recalled similar numbers of words on all three trials. What the specific words were, however, varied from trial to trial. Only about half the words were remembered on all three trials.
Conclusion: Recalling words on later trials which had not been recalled on the first trial suggests that the initial lack of recall could not have been due to lack of availability. It is likely that different retrieval cues were used on each trial.

Cue-dependent forgetting

The term cue-dependent forgetting has been used by Tulving (1974). It refers to two related phenomena: **context-dependent forgetting** and **state-dependent forgetting**.

Research such as that by Abernathy (1940) has shown that it is much easier to remember something if you are in the same context in which you originally learnt it. For example, if you learn a set of A-level facts in a particular room over a long period of time, you would remember those facts significantly better if you were asked to recall the facts in that same room. This has obvious implications for examination technique – unfortunately, it is unlikely that you will be able to sit the exam in the room in which you learnt the material; nor is it practical for you to learn the material in the exam hall! What may help, however, is *imagining* the environment in which you learnt the information. Zechmeister and Nyberg (1982) showed that this can help recreate the conditions in which you learned the information.

An interesting study showing the effect of context is described in box N:

Box N: Godden and Baddeley (1975)

Procedure: Diver participants learned a list of words either on land or underwater. Later, both groups were tested for their recall either on land or underwater.
Results: The divers who learned the words underwater recalled more accurately when tested underwater. The divers who learned the words on land recalled them more accurately when tested on land.
Conclusion: Recall is affected by external context.

You may have experienced how memory is related to context if you have ever visited a place where you once lived, or somewhere you regularly went on holiday as a child. Often such a visit helps people recall lots of facts and experiences about the times they spent there – facts that they did not realise were stored in their memory.

To explain why this effect occurs, it has been suggested that information about the environmental context is stored while you are learning. Using that context later on, when you are remembering the information, makes recall easier by providing you with **retrieval cues** which trigger memory for relevant information. Being able to remember something depends on having the information stored (i.e. it being available) *and* having an appropriate cue that brings it back into consciousness. This type of remembering is known as **cued recall**.

While external context has been shown to affect recall, it has also been found that you are much more likely to remember something if you are in the same **internal state** (physical or emotional) in which you learnt it. A good example of this is if you lose something while under the influence of alcohol. You may find it impossible to find the item when sober the following morning, but retrieve it quite easily the next time you drink. Similar results have been shown to be true for mood.

Goodwin *et al.* (1969) found that memory loss was greater for those participants who acquired information while under the influence of alcohol, and were then asked to recall when sober, than vice versa. This shows that physical state does indeed affect recall.

Memory can also be dependent on emotional state:

Box O: Bower *et al.* (1978)

Procedure: Participants were hypnotised, and imagined a happy or unhappy mood while learning information.

Results: Those participants who recalled in the same mood as that created during learning recalled better than those who recalled in a different mood.

Conclusion: The participants were affected by the internal context in which they learned the information.

Repression

Repression also emphasises the role of emotion in forgetting. Freud suggested that we forget because there is great anxiety associated with certain memories, and the psychological pain of recall would be too great to cope with. When this is the case we may use the unconscious defence mechanism of repression to push such memories out of consciousness. The memories continue to exist, but in the unconscious mind. For example, memories of being abused as a child may be too disturbing for a person to cope with, and may be outside conscious recall.

Part of psychoanalytic therapy involves bringing such repressed memories into consciousness. Memories retrieved during therapy are known as **recovered memories**. However, such memories are reconstructed, often long after the event, and so are not always reliable. This has given rise to the concept of **false memory syndrome**. People sometimes 'recall' traumatic childhood abuse, usually with the help of their therapist, which their families claim could not have happened. Loftus (1994) described the case of a woman who 'remembered' during therapy having been involved in a Satanic cult, having sex with animals and watching an eight-year-old friend being murdered. When she left therapy, she realised that these memories were fantasies brought about during therapy.

However, memories accessed during therapy *may* indeed be recovered memories despite the obvious problems in deciding what is true about events many years in the past.

In addition, you will remember that research on **flashbulb memory** found that people have clear memories of events which they found traumatic, and remember in some detail the circumstances in which they became aware of these events. This suggests that high emotional distinctiveness of an event leads to a better ability to recall it, in contrast to Freud's suggestion that if an experience is traumatic, it will be repressed.

Unavailability

Not everybody agrees with Penfield's idea that memories are available but not accessible. In particular, only a small percentage of Penfield's stimulation triggered vivid memories, and it has been suggested that many of the 'memories' were merely fantasies (a bit like dreams) resulting from the stimulation. If this is the case, then forgetting must be due to **unavailability** – because the memory is no longer stored. Theories of forgetting based on the idea that memories are unavailable include **displacement**, **trace decay** and **brain damage**.

Displacement

It has been suggested that forgetting in STM is due to **displacement**. Displacement refers to the limited number of slots in STM – 7±2. When more items are introduced into STM than there are slots, some of the old information must be knocked out of its slot, or 'displaced'. It also follows that this would lead to forgetting: as you put a new piece of information into your STM, the displaced piece of information is lost. This suggests that information in STM must be processed if it is to be retained in LTM.

Evidence for displacement comes from the **Brown–Petersen technique** discussed earlier, where participants were asked to recall trigrams, but

after presentation were asked to count backwards in threes to prevent rehearsal. If this technique is used when participants are asked to learn a list of words, such as that in activity 4, the recency effect (see figure 3) is lost. The last few items on the list are displaced from STM by the counting task.

Trace decay

Peterson and Peterson (1959) suggested that forgetting in STM is due to **trace decay**. Learning something creates a memory trace or **engram**, which gradually fades. Rehearsal prevents forgetting because it replenishes the trace before it decays completely. A similar explanation may also explain why some information in LTM is lost.

In a study by Shallice (1967), participants were presented with numbers at different speeds. Forgetting was less when the numbers were presented more rapidly, which suggests that time is a factor, and so supports the idea of **trace decay**. However, what was even more important than speed of presentation was how many numbers followed the ones to be recalled, suggesting that **displacement** is also important.

Brain damage

Sometimes memories may become unavailable because of **brain damage**. Brain damage can cause either **retrograde amnesia** (i.e. loss of memory from the period before the brain damage) or **anterograde amnesia** (i.e. loss of memory for new information after brain damage). Retrograde amnesia can result from electro-convulsive therapy or **ECT**, where a brief electric shock is passed through the brain, which is sometimes used as a therapy for severe depression. Patients often cannot recall what happened immediately before treatment. The **Korsakov syndrome**, which is the result of advanced alcoholism, mentioned earlier in relation to the STM/LTM distinction, is an example of anterograde amnesia, as is the case of HM (see box F). Changes which occur in the brain as the result of ageing can also lead to amnesia.

Post-traumatic amnesia often follows a blow to the head; for example, as the result of a fall. The person may have retrograde amnesia and often cannot remember what happened immediately before the blow. Yarnell and Lynch (1970) investigated this phenomenon by asking footballers who had been concussed during play what strategy their team had been using immediately before the incident. The footballers could answer this question if asked straight away, but had forgotten if asked twenty minutes later. This suggests that a period of **consolidation** is necessary for something to be remembered.

In contrast, a study by Sacks (1985) showed that brain damage can also lead to remembering rather than forgetting. He described an elderly woman who suffered a mild thrombosis in one of the temporal lobes of her brain, after which she remembered Irish songs which her mother had sung to her when she was a child in Ireland. Unfortunately, as she recovered, these memories also disappeared.

- Information is forgotten because it is not **available** or not **accessible**.
- Theories relating to lack of **accessibility** include **interference**, **cue-dependent forgetting** and **repression**.
- **Interference** theory suggests that similarity between competing memories can result in forgetting.
- **Cue-dependent forgetting** can be divided into state-dependent and context-dependent forgetting. This theory suggests that we cannot recall information without the use of **retrieval cues**.
- Freud believed that forgetting of painful memories may be due to the defence mechanism of **repression**.
- Theories relating to lack of availability include **displacement**, **trace decay** and **brain damage**.

2.5 RECONSTRUCTIVE MEMORY

Bartlett (1932), argued that memory is affected by the store of relevant prior knowledge we have, and not just by what information is presented. He regarded memories not just as reproductions of information but as reconstructions influenced by prior knowledge.

Activity 10: Bartlett's War of the Ghosts (1932)

Read this story, which is the native American story Bartlett used in his research:

One night two young men from Egulac went down to the river to hunt seals, and while they were there it became foggy and calm. Then they heard war-cries and they thought: 'Maybe this is a war-party'. They escaped to the shore and hid behind a log. Now canoes came up, and they heard the noise of paddles, and saw one canoe coming up to them. There were five men in the canoe, and they said: 'What do you think? We wish to take you along. We are going up the river to make war on the people.' One of the young men said: 'I have no arrows'. 'Arrows are in the canoe,' they said. 'I will not go along. I might be killed. My relatives do not know where I have gone. But you,' he said, turning to the other, 'may go with them.' So one of the young men went, but the other returned home. And the warriors went on up the river to a town on the other side of Kalama. The people came down to the water, and they began to fight, and many were killed. But presently the young man heard one of the warriors say: 'Quick, let us go home: that Indian has been hit.' Now he thought: 'Oh, they are ghosts.' He did not feel sick, but they said he had been shot. So the canoes went back to Egulac, and the young man went ashore to his house, and made a fire. And he told everybody and said: 'Behold I accompanied the ghosts, and we went to fight. Many of our fellows were killed, and many of those who attacked us were killed. They said I was hit, and I did not feel sick.' He told it all, and then he became quiet. When the sun rose he fell down. Something black came out of his mouth. His face became contorted. The people jumped up and cried. He was dead.

Now cover up the story and write down as much of it as you can remember.

Bartlett's studies showed that a number of changes occurred to the story as it was recalled by his participants. He found that typically people gave shorter, more simplified versions of the story. You may also have found as you recalled the story that some of your errors made the story sound more like a standard English one, and less like a native American story. For example, you might have written down 'boat' instead of 'canoe'; or said that the man went 'home' rather than 'ashore to his house'. Sometimes new information is introduced to make the story more logical by our standards. For example, some of Bartlett's participants introduced a reason for the fighting, or reproduced 'something black came out of his mouth' as 'blood came out of his mouth'.

This type of reconstruction Bartlett termed **rationalisation**. Such distortions are used to make sense of unfamiliar things. But the most important thing was that the central ideas of the story were not really changed at all. Bartlett suggested that what happens is that people store a few main facts about the story and then **reconstruct** it from those facts. This act of reconstruction Bartlett referred to as **effort after meaning**.

Mr Benson tripped in the refreshment tent and broke his ankle

Old Benson went over in the beer tent and his leg's in plaster

shame

Young Benson was falling about plastered in the bar and now his leg will be in plaster for weeks

Can't hold their beer those lads

Even memories which seem very clear can sometimes be inaccurate. You will remember that earlier in this chapter we discussed **flashbulb memories**, very vivid memories of surprising and emotionally-charged events. Brown and Kulik (1977) believed flashbulb memories to be both long-lasting and very accurate, but there is some evidence that even these memories may become distorted over time. One person interviewed by Linton (1979) gave a vivid account of studying in her college library when told about the Kennedy assassination by a friend. The friend, however, was actually at a different college in a different state at the time. Similar inaccuracies were reported by McCloskey *et al.* (1988) in their study of people's memories of the explosion of the space shuttle Challenger. They also found changes in what people remembered of the event over time, suggesting that their memories were in part a reconstruction.

Bartlett's notion of reconstruction in memory can be linked to **schemas**. A schema is a way of summarising events which enables us to predict what is likely to happen in various situations. Bartlett defined a schema as 'an active organisation of past reactions, or past experiences'. A schema provides the background knowledge that enables us to understand a situation, since we can predict what is likely to happen. For example, if you were asked to say what your schema of 'getting on the bus' involved you would probably include:

> getting on the bus; stating your destination; paying the fare; thanking the driver; finding an empty seat and sitting down.

Schema theory, then, gives us a way of looking at how information is organised in memory: new information is related to what we already know. But while schemas are useful in helping us to organise information, at the same time our reliance on them may lead to distortion of what we remember.

Most memories are at least in part reconstructions. If asked to remember what you were doing three Tuesdays ago at 2 pm, you could probably make an educated guess and might even be correct – but what you remember will in all likelihood be more of a reconstruction of what sort of thing you usually do on Tuesdays rather than an accurate memory of the day in question. This has been shown experimentally:

Box P: Brewer and Treyins (1981)

Procedure: Thirty participants were asked individually to wait in an office while the experimenter supposedly checked the laboratory to see if the previous participant had finished. After 35 seconds, he returned and asked them to go into another room where they were asked to recall everything in the waiting room.

Results: People tended to recall items consistent with an 'office schema'. Nearly everyone recalled the desk and chair, but only eight people recalled the skull, while just one recalled the picnic basket. However, nine people 'recalled' books, which had not been there.

Conclusion: Schemas can produce distorted recall, with items consistent with the schema being incorrectly recalled, and inconsistent items forgotten.

Reconstructive memory can also be affected by stereotypes, leading to distorted memories:

Box Q: Buckhout (1974)

Procedure: Participants were shown a series of counter-stereotypical pictures, each for a very short time. One picture, for example, set in a subway, showed a scruffily dressed white man, holding a razor, threatening a well-dressed black man. It was assumed in this instance that many white people would have a stereotype of black people as having criminal tendencies.

Results: Approximately half the participants remembered the black man as holding the razor.

Conclusion: Memory can be distorted by the stereotypes we hold.

Another study tested this idea more naturalistically:

Box R: Duncan (1976)

Procedure: Participants were shown a video of two men having a discussion. They were told it was a live event shown over closed circuit TV. At one point, the discussion became heated, and one man gave the other a shove. At this point the video stopped. Participants were asked to classify the shove, choosing from 'playing around', 'dramatising', 'aggressive behaviour' and 'violent behaviour'. There were several versions of the video, varying the race of the actors.

Results: When the shove was given by a black man, participants were more likely to classify it as 'violent behaviour' than when it was given by a white man. This was particularly true when a black man shoved a white man.

Conclusion: Classification was affected by racial stereotypes. Behaviour is interpreted in line with the stereotypes we hold.

The distortion of recall shown by Duncan's participants could have far-reaching consequences in some contexts. If you forget to buy spaghetti from the supermarket, it is unlikely to be too tragic an event. But in the area of **eye-witness testimony**, where people give evidence in court cases, the accurate recall of events can mean someone's imprisonment or freedom. In the next section we will look at factors which affect the reliability of eye-witness testimony.

- ⑤ A **schema** is a summary of what happens in a certain situation. Schemas simplify the processing of new information.
- ⑤ Bartlett used schema theory to suggest that memory is reconstruction. He saw the major determinant of human memory as **effort after meaning**.
- ⑤ Schemas allow us to predict what is likely to happen in particular situations, but may make us inflexible when we come across something unexpected.
- ⑤ Reconstructive memory can also be influenced by **stereotypes**.

2.6 CRITICAL ISSUE: EYE-WITNESS TESTIMONY (EWT)

Jurors seem to find eye-witness testimony amongst the most convincing evidence of all. The Devlin Report (1976), which was concerned with eye-witness testimony, found that in more than 300 cases, eye-witness identification was the *sole* evidence of guilt, yet the conviction rate was 74%.

Building on the idea of memory as reconstruction, a lot of research has been carried out, notably by Loftus and her associates, which demonstrates that memory can be affected by the wording of questions testing the memory of an experience. Her studies have shown that people's accounts of events that they have witnessed can be extremely unreliable. One part of a study is shown in box S:

Box S: Loftus and Palmer (1974)

Procedure: One hundred and fifty participants were shown a film of an accident between two cars, and then asked to fill in a questionnaire about the accident. The important question involved the speed of the cars at the point of impact. The question was phrased differently for different groups of participants – some were asked 'How fast were the two cars going when they *hit* each other'; others were asked the same question but with *smashed, collided, bumped,* or *contacted* replacing the word 'hit'.
Results: The average speeds the participants gave in answer to the question are listed below.

verb used	speed given
hit	34mph
smashed	41mph
collided	39mph
bumped	38mph
contacted	32mph

Conclusion: The speed at which the participants thought the cars were going was affected by the verb used in the question. Recall can be distorted by the wording of a question.

As well as the choice of words, asking **leading questions** which imply that a certain answer is expected can significantly affect a person's testimony. Loftus and Zanni (1975) showed participants a film of a car accident. They found that more participants recalled (incorrectly) seeing a broken headlight if they were asked 'Did you see *the* broken headlight?' than 'Did you see *a* broken headlight?'.

Another part of Loftus and Palmer's study is relevant here:

Box T: Loftus and Palmer (1974)

Procedure: One hundred and fifty participants were shown a film of a car accident. The subsequent questionnaire asked a third of those participants 'How fast were the cars going when they *smashed* into each other?' A third was asked 'How fast were the cars going when they *hit* each other?' The final third (the control group) was not asked about the speed of the cars. One week later, the same people were all asked whether they had seen any broken glass in the film of the accident. (There had been no broken glass shown in the film.)
Results: Twelve per cent of the control group claimed to have seen broken glass in the film and 14% of those who had heard the word *hit* said they had seen broken glass. But 32% of the participants who had heard the word *smashed* remembered seeing broken glass.
Conclusion: The leading question asked a week previously affected the participants' recall. The people who heard the word *smashed* recoded the accident as being more serious than those who heard the word *hit*. This information was added to their earlier memory of the film, and changed it.

So it is clear that leading questions not only affect recall of material, but can actually change information that has previously been stored in memory – they can, in effect, make us **reconstruct** memories. It is argued that this may be what happens in **false memory syndrome**, discussed earlier in the section on **repression**.

At the same time, however, it is less easy to mislead witnesses about something which is central to what they have witnessed than something which is more peripheral. Loftus (1979) found that 98% of people who had watched colour slides of a man stealing a red purse from a woman's bag correctly remembered it as red, even when it was implied that it was brown.

We will look now at research into factors affecting the accuracy of eye-witness testimony in terms of the three processes involved in memory: registration, storage and retrieval.

Registration

Factors which influence people's initial perception of an incident can be categorised as **witness factors** – characteristics of the witness – and **event factors** – factors to do with the situation.

Witness factors

Age can play a part in the accuracy of recall. Several studies (e.g. Dent, 1988) have shown that children typically give fewer details about an event they have witnessed than adults. Similarly, List (1986) found that older people may also recall less than younger people. In terms of responding to misleading information, as in the Loftus studies described in the previous section, Ceci *et al.* (1987) found that children were more likely to be misled than adults, and Loftus *et al.* (1991) found the same to be true of older people, particularly males.

The levels of **stress** experienced when witnessing a crime can also affect accuracy of recall. This relationship can be shown by the Yerkes–Dodson law (see chapter 4, figure 1).

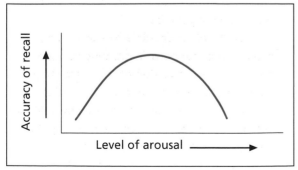

The Yerkes–Dodson law applied to recall

This law suggests that at very low levels of arousal (i.e. low levels of stress), performance is poor. It improves with moderate levels of arousal, and then falls off again when stress is further increased. The law has been supported by research:

Box U: Peters (1988)

Procedure: People going to a clinic to receive inoculations met a nurse who gave them the injection and another person (the researcher). They were exposed to each person for equal periods of time. They were later asked to identify the nurse and the researcher from a set of photographs.

Results: Participants were significantly better at identifying the researcher than the nurse.

Conclusion: The stress of having an injection, associated with the nurse who gave it, led to comparatively poor memory when asked to pick out her photograph.

However, stress does not always have this effect:

Box V: Yuille and Cutshall (1986)

Procedure: Thirteen people who witnessed an armed robbery in Canada gave evidence to the police. They then agreed to take part in interviews with psychologists between four and five months after witnessing the robbery. During that later interview, participants were asked two misleading questions.

Results: Being asked two misleading questions did not affect the participants' recall four months after the event. There were few, if any, facts recalled by the participants that had been made up or reconstructed. There was no relationship between the levels of stress reported at the time of the crime and accuracy of recall.

Conclusion: In real-life situations, recall is not necessarily inaccurate, or susceptible to misleading questions. The level of stress experienced is not related to accuracy of recall.

This study shows that EWT of events occurring in a real-life situation is not necessarily as inaccurate as laboratory studies might lead us to expect. This is a good example of a study with high **ecological**

validity: it was carried out on people who had witnessed a genuine armed robbery, and not merely watched a video of such an event, and therefore is more convincing as a piece of research.

However, one problem with this study is that those witnesses who experienced more stress were closer to what was going on. It is possible that the higher level of stress they experienced was counteracted by having better access to information, thus improving their recall of the event.

Expectations can also influence the registration of information. In the previous section, the influence of people's beliefs and expectations was shown by the studies in box Q and box R.

Event factors

One important factor here is **exposure time**, i.e. the length of time for which a witness is exposed to an event. It was shown as long ago as 1885, in a study by Ebbinghaus, that the longer we are exposed to something, the better our perception of it is. However, people are often very poor at estimating exposure time:

Box W: Loftus *et al.* (1987)

Procedure: Participants were shown a 30-second video of a simulated bank robbery and asked to estimate how long it had lasted.

Results: On average, the robbery was estimated to have lasted two and a half minutes. Very few participants correctly estimated the time, or underestimated it.

Conclusion: People tend to overestimate the length of time of an event which they have witnessed.

▶ Activity 11: overestimation of time

Why might this tendency to overestimate time be important in a legal context?
When you have finished, see the notes on page 50.

A further event factor is what is known as **detail salience**. In an armed robbery, for instance, the presence of a gun may be a salient feature for witnesses. They may focus on the gun and so have

their attention distracted from other important features of the situation, such as the characteristics of the robbers. This is known as **weapon focus**, and has been shown experimentally:

Box X: Loftus *et al.* (1987)

Procedure: Participants were shown one of two versions of a restaurant scene on video. In one version, a man pointed a gun at the cashier and she gave him money. In the other version, he gave her a cheque, and she gave him money. The eye movements of participants were monitored, and their recall for the event tested.

Results: Participants in the 'weapon' version fixated more on the gun than those seeing the 'non-weapon' version. Their recall for other details was also poorer, and they were less able to identify the man from a set of photographs.

Conclusion: A salient detail can focus attention, and so lead to poorer recall for other details of the event.

The violence of the event witnessed can also affect recall:

Box Y: Loftus and Burns (1982)

Procedure: Participants were shown one of two versions of a simulated armed robbery on video. One version included a scene of a boy being shot in the face while the robbers were making their getaway.

Results: Recall of details of the event was much higher for participants who had seen the 'non-violent' version of the event. Those who had seen the 'violent' version had less accurate and less complete recall, not only for events immediately before the shooting, but also for events up to 2 minutes earlier.

Conclusion: The shock associated with the 'violent' event disrupted the processing of information into memory, and its consolidation.

---

๑ Eye-witness memory for details of an event can be affected at the **registration** stage by **witness factors** and **event factors**.

๑ **Witness factors** include age, stress and expectations.

๑ **Event factors** include detail salience, in particular weapon focus, and the violence of the event.

Storage

Information is lost with the passage of time, which can be explained by the **trace decay** theory of forgetting, covered in an earlier section. As with the influence of exposure time on memory, this too was demonstrated by Ebbinghaus (1885). It has also been shown in a naturalistic study of long-term forgetting:

Box Z: Wagenaar and Groeneweg (1990)

Procedure: Seventy-eight survivors of Camp Erika (a second world war Dutch concentration camp) were interviewed between 1984 and 1987 about their camp experiences. The information they gave was compared with earlier evidence they had given just after the end of the war.

Results: There was general agreement in the later interviews on basic information. All but three of 38 people who had been tortured by the camp commandant, for example, remembered his name. However, much of the detail had been lost. The names of guards, for instance, given at the earlier interviews, were largely forgotten.

Conclusion: While basic information may be well remembered over time, details tend to be lost.

The studies by Loftus and Palmer, described in box S and box T, have shown that memory can also be distorted once it has been stored; memories of an event can be reconstructed as a result of the way in which questions are asked, i.e. depending on the choice of words and the use of leading questions.

Studies (e.g. Bekerian and Bowers, 1983) have also shown that mentioning details of an event to a witness after they have witnessed it can lead to

these details being 'recalled' later; new information has been incorporated into what is remembered. Sometimes this effect is only partial:

Box AA: Loftus (1975)

Procedure: Participants were shown a 3-minute video of a lecture being disrupted by eight demonstrators. They were later given a 20-item questionnaire. For some participants, this included the question: 'Was the leader of the 12 demonstrators a male?' For the others the question was: ' Was the leader of the 4 demonstrators a male?' A week later, they were asked how many demonstrators there had been.

Results: Those who had earlier been given the '12 demonstrators' question reported on average that there had been 8.9 demonstrators; those who had been given the '4 demonstrators' question reported on average that there had been 6.4 demonstrators.

Conclusion: Participants' memory had been distorted by the misleading information they had been given. Most participants compromised between the actual number of demonstrators they had seen and the misleading number.

However, as shown in the study carried out by Loftus (1979), described after box T, this is less likely to happen when people are asked about something which is central to the event they have witnessed.

It has also been argued by McCloskey and Zaragoza (1985) that the influence of misleading information – the **misinformation effect** – has little to do with memory impairment, but more to do with two sources of bias in the testing procedure. The first of these they call **misinformation acceptance**. They suggest that one reason that participants can be misled is that they have failed to register relevant information when witnessing an event, and this is why they accept misleading information as being accurate. The second source of bias is **demand characteristics**, i.e. features of the testing situation which may lead participants to (mis)interpret the task. In this case, participants might accept the misinformation as accurate because it was provided by the researcher, or because they wanted to 'do well' on the test.

- ❺ Storage factors can affect recall. Basic information is often retained, but detailed information is lost over time.
- ❺ Memory can be **supplemented** by later information. It can be **distorted** by misleading information, known as the **misinformation effect**. This can also lead to completely **inaccurate information** being given.
- ❺ The misinformation effect has been challenged in terms of whether it is the result of **memory impairment** or the effects of **bias** in the testing situation.

Retrieval

As we have seen, techniques to collect information may affect the detail and accuracy of EWT. This is of particular importance in the light of the work of Loftus and others, which suggests that the way in which questions are asked can distort memory. This has important implications for people like the police and solicitors, who have to consider the phrasing of their questions very carefully.

Recently, psychologists have begun to evaluate police interview techniques, and have found that British police officers have little formal training in the interviewing of witnesses, and that they are often unaware of the shortcomings in their interview technique.

Officers typically aim to elicit descriptions of gender, height, age, dress, and so on. They ask for information which seems immediately useful, rather than accessing information which may be useful later on. Standard police interviewing techniques may not be the best way to get the maximum amount of useful information from the witness.

It is widely believed that **hypnosis** may be a way of improving recall, but this is somewhat controversial. A comprehensive review of hypnosis research led Orne *et al.* (1984) to claim that testimony produced under hypnosis was not reliable, and that it should not be accepted unless it was confirmed by independent evidence. People who have been hypnotised are very susceptible to suggestions made by the interviewer, and for this reason alone, testimony produced under hypnosis needs to be treated with caution.

However, a technique called the **cognitive interview** has been developed as a way of trying to ensure that police interviews are carried out in such a way as to get maximum accurate recall from witnesses. This technique is now widely used by police forces in the UK and the USA.

The cognitive interview

Geiselman *et al* (1984) developed a procedure called the **basic cognitive interview**, based on two principles of memory research: firstly, that there may be a number of retrieval paths to a memory, and that a memory may be accessible if a different retrieval cue is used; secondly, that a memory trace is made up of several features and the effectiveness of a retrieval cue depends on how much of it overlaps with the memory trace.

From these principles, a **memory retrieval procedure** was derived. Incorporating all these ideas reflects the common view of memory as a complex group of features. It may remind you of research you read earlier in the chapter on what affects the accuracy of remembering:

Figure 9: the basic cognitive interview

This technique involves:
- an eye-witness mentally reinstating the environmental and personal context of the crime. This includes reporting what was going on at the time, both in terms of the event witnessed and the witness's own thoughts and feelings
- the eye-witness being asked to report everything they can recall about the event, regardless of how unimportant it might seem
- encouraging an eye-witness to recount what happened in a variety of orders
- asking them to report from a variety of perspectives and points of view

Witness being encouraged to recall every detail

> ◗ **Activity 12: linking the cognitive interview to memory research**
>
> Look back at the previous sections in this chapter. Can you make links between some of this material and the principles of the cognitive interview? When you have finished, see the notes on page 50.

The cognitive interview can also be linked with the **spreading activation model** of organisation in memory, proposed by Collins and Loftus (1975). This suggests that concepts in LTM are interlinked. Closely related concepts have short links between them, and links that are often used become stronger (shown as thicker lines in figure 10) than links that are rarely used. When one concept is activated, this activation spreads out to related concepts, so activating the word 'robin' would also activate the related concepts of 'red', 'bird' and 'Christmas'. In turn, these could lead on to apparently unrelated concepts.

This model suggests that there is a complex interrelationship of links in memory, so asking a witness to recall information in different orders and from different perspectives increases the probability of a seemingly irrelevant piece of information triggering off something which may be useful.

When the basic cognitive interview was used, Fisher *et al.* (1987a) found it to be significantly superior to the standard police interview, in terms of the amount of information accurately recalled. Geiselman *et al.* (1986) found that this technique also seemed to strengthen resistance of witnesses to misleading information.

The technique has now been refined further through an analysis of real, taped police interviews, which has the advantage of high **ecological validity**. On the basis of this research Fisher *et al.* (1987b) recommended additional techniques for interviewing eye-witnesses. This is known as the **enhanced cognitive interview** technique.

Figure 10: spreading activation model (Collins and Loftus, 1975)

Figure 11: enhanced cognitive interview

This technique includes:
- minimising distractions
- getting the eye-witness to speak slowly
- tailoring language to suit the individual eye-witness
- reducing anxiety
- avoiding judgmental and personal comments

Tailoring language to suit the individual

All these techniques are designed to help the witness to focus on the task and to reduce anxiety. Fisher *et al.* (1990) found that these techniques elicited 45% more correct statements than even the basic cognitive interview. A field test with detectives of the Police Department in Miami showed that detectives trained in this enhanced cognitive interview technique collected 63% more information than a control group of untrained detectives. Wilkinson (1988) found that such techniques could raise the EWT of children to adult level.

The cognitive interview seems to be a way that really can make a difference both to the amount of potentially useful information obtained from witnesses, and to the accuracy of that information.

- **Hypnosis** as a way of improving recall is controversial.
- The **cognitive interview** has shown itself to be an effective way of increasing the completeness and accuracy of EWT.
- The **enhanced cognitive interview** can produce even more relevant information.

Face recognition

An important aspect of EWT can be identifying people suspected of carrying out a crime, so we will turn now to the topic of face recognition.

Having a memory for faces, which enables us to recognise other people, is of great significance in our lives. You can imagine how difficult life would be if you didn't recognise your mother, brother, best friend or partner. Human beings seem to have an amazing ability to recognise faces. Standing (1973) showed participants 10,000 faces over 5 days. When they were shown pairs of faces, one of which they had previously been shown, together with a new one, they were able to identify the face they had seen 98% of the time. This ability is also impressive when people are asked to identify faces which they have not seen for some time:

Box BB: Bahrick *et al.* (1975)

Procedure: Fifteen years after their graduation, participants were shown five pictures from year books. One picture of the five was a person with whom they had graduated from high school.
Results: The participants were accurate in identifying 90% of their classmates. It was found that even those participants who had graduated more than 40 years previously could identify 75% of their classmates correctly.
Conclusion: People have a well-developed ability to recognise faces.

Just as psychologists have learned a lot about memory from clinical cases of patients with disorders such as amnesia or the Korsakov syndrome, so they have learned about the processes of face recognition from people suffering from **prosopagnosia**. People with this disorder can't recognise the faces of people they know well – sometimes they cannot even recognise their own face in a mirror. They can, however, recognise friends and family from their voices, so the problem is not due to people having been forgotten.

There are two types of theory that try to explain this disorder. One suggests that it takes more precise discrimination to tell the difference between two faces than it does to tell the difference between a book and a pencil, for example, so failure to discriminate faces may lie in the lack of the ability to make this kind of fine distinction. The other type of theory suggests that there are specific processes that are needed if we are to recognise a face, and that these are lacking in prosopagnosics.

The idea that an inability to recognise faces is due to a lack of fine discrimination is not widely accepted. De Renzi (1986) worked with a prosopagnosic man who could make very good fine discrimination between different people's handwriting, for example, and between Italian coins, but could not recognise relatives' and friends' faces. Similarly, McNeil and Warrington (1991) reported the case of a farmer with prosopagnosia, who was nonetheless able to identify each of his 36 sheep without hesitation. It therefore does not seem likely that prosopagnosia is due to an inability to make fine discriminations.

The alternative theory, relating to processes specific to face recognition, is more likely. It is supported by the finding that there are areas of the brain which deal specifically with face recognition. Hay and Young (1982) suggested that familiar faces are stored in the brain in neural circuits known as **face recognition units (FRUs)**. When we see a face, we scan our FRUs for a match, to decide whether or not the face is familiar. If a match is found, we can then access information about the person, such as their job and biographical information, which in turn may generate their name.

Ellis *et al.* (1979) investigated what information is most important when recognising familiar and unfamiliar faces. They found that recognition of unfamiliar faces depends more on external features,

such as the shape of the face and the hairline. For familiar faces, internal features are more important. According to Roberts and Bruce (1988), the area round the eyes is the most important, while the area round the nose is of least importance.

While people are usually extremely good at recognising faces, especially familiar faces, Shapiro and Penrod (1986) found that in eye-witness identification, people show inferior recall compared with traditional studies of face recognition. One reason for this may be that, unlike laboratory studies, the circumstances in which a face is first seen and when identification needs to be made may be quite different.

Quite often an identification may need to be made from footage supplied by security cameras:

▶ Activity 13: identification of faces from video

video picture

The man in the CCTV picture?

Are these pictures of the same man or of different people? How sure are you? Why is it difficult to make a judgment using this kind of material? Why might it be easier if the images were of someone you knew?

When you have finished, see the notes on page 50.

Other characteristics of face recognition also make identification problematic. Shepherd *et al* (1974), for instance, found that people have more difficulty in recognising faces of people from another race. Older people also have more difficulty than younger people in recognising faces they have only seen once (Farramond, 1968).

In many cases, people need to describe to the police the faces of people whom they have seen carrying out a crime. For many years, police forces have been using aids to help witnesses, one of the earliest of which was the **PhotoFIT** system, developed by Penry (1971). This consisted of sets of photographed features – hair, eyes, nose, mouth and chin – from which the witness could select elements to build a representation of the face they had seen. This system could produce a general likeness, but was found to be poor in terms of creating a close likeness.

More recently, **E-FIT** (electronic facial identification technique) has been developed, using computer graphics. Again, faces are built from a library of features, selected on the basis of a verbal description by the witness. As well as giving a picture which is of similar quality to a photograph, this system has the advantage of being much more flexible in terms of the modifications which are possible.

Sergent (1984) has shown that configural information, i.e. the way in which different facial features relate to each other, is important in the representation of faces in memory. The E-FIT system takes this into account, in that it allows very subtle adjustments to be made to the configuration of features making up the face.

A system called **FRAME** (facial retrieval and matching equipment), described by Shepherd (1986), uses verbal descriptions of faces given by witnesses to retrieve possible matches from mugshots. The advantage of this system is that it uses the information which witnesses can give, while making use of our well-developed capacity to recognise faces. It also saves witnesses the time-consuming task of searching through albums of mugshots. Its effectiveness has been tested experimentally:

Box CC: Ellis *et al*. (1989)

Procedure: Each participant saw a target face for 10 seconds, which they were later asked to identify. Using a database of 1000 male faces, a comparison was made between the effectiveness of the FRAME system and a mugshot album search.

Results: The FRAME system produced 69% correct matches, compared to only 44% for the album search. There was also a much higher percentage of false alarms when mugshot albums were used.

Conclusion: The use of verbal descriptions together with mugshot albums is more effective in leading to face recognition than the use of mugshot albums alone.

- EWT can require witnesses to identify people whom they have seen committing a crime. While people are in general very good at face recognition, particularly of familiar faces, they tend to be less good at eye-witness identification.
- Several systems have been developed to aid this process. FRAME, which combines verbal descriptions with possible matches from a database of mugshots, has a high success rate.

Notes on activities are on page 50.

Notes on activities

1 Testing only one person is not really the best way to establish the general rules of psychological functioning. It is impossible to generalise to the rest of the population, as you can't guarantee that one person is representative of everyone.

It is also possible that experimenters carrying out research on themselves might be tempted to influence the results to fit their expectations, or do so unconsciously.

The research also has **low ecological validity** – it is arguable whether nonsense syllables adequately represent the richness of information we hold in our memories. It is not something we generally spend time doing! Using nonsense syllables does, however, ensure that the material is not distinctive, and hence avoids the problem that some information may be more memorable to some participants than others.

5 The shape of the curve implies that the first few words on the list are recalled well because they have been stored in LTM, whereas the last few words are recalled from STM. The first few words go into LTM because time has elapsed and they have been processed semantically, whereas the last few words have not had time to be transferred into LTM so are still in STM. The shape of the graph therefore gives evidence for the fact that we have two distinct stores in memory, as Atkinson and Shiffrin suggested. This should also remind you of Ebbinghaus' explanation of forgetting which you read about earlier in this chapter (box A).

11 How long events lasted can be crucial in a criminal trial. When people overestimate the length of time they were exposed to an event, they create the impression that they had longer to look at something than they actually did, and this may falsely increase their credibility as witnesses.

12 Many of the ideas of the cognitive interview are based on **cue-dependent forgetting**. Talking about how the witness and other people present at the time might have felt is linked to state-dependent forgetting, so that reinstating the emotional state will provide cues which may trigger off additional information. Mentally reinstating the context may have a similar effect.

13 Burton *et al.* (1999) found that people had great difficulty in making the kind of identification required in activity 18. The video images are of poor quality, and there are differences in the lighting of the pictures and the angle at which the faces are seen. However, people do not find the task is so difficult if the person is known to them, presumably because they are familiar with what a known person looks like from different angles, and there may be additional information from the way in which the body moves.

Attachments in development

In this chapter we will be looking at:

3.1 Investigating attachment
    Patterns of attachment
    Why is an infant–mother attachment
      formed?
    The maternal deprivation hypothesis
    Critique of the maternal deprivation
      hypothesis

3.2 Attachment difficulties
    Privation, disruption, and distortion
    Long-term effects of insecure
      attachment

3.3 Are early difficulties reversible?

3.4 Other factors in social and emotional
    development

3.5 Critical issue: day care

3.1 INVESTIGATING ATTACHMENT

Attachment can be defined as a strong emotional bond with another person; in babies attachment to their mother or major carer is particularly evident. They become distressed when their mother leaves the room and are often unwilling to be comforted by someone else. They seek her out when they are stressed, and are generally oriented towards her: looking at her, moving to stay close to her and making sounds directed at her.

Schaffer and Emerson (1964) described the stages of attachment which take place during the first 18 months of a child's life. They used two measures of attachment. The first was **fear of strangers**, the response of an infant to the arrival of a stranger, whether or not the mother is there. The second was **separation anxiety**, the amount of distress shown by a child when separated from the mother, and the degree of comfort and happiness shown when they are reunited. They found that attachment could be described in terms of three stages (figure 1).

There is, however, a lot of individual variation in the development of attachment. For example, Schaffer and Emerson found that the second stage of specific attachment could start at any time between six months and a year, and was not necessarily formed with the mother. There was also variation in the number of multiple attachments formed, and when they were formed (see box A).

Figure 1: stages of attachment (Schaffer and Emerson, 1964)		
stage	**approximate age range**	**characteristics**
indiscriminate attachment	up to about 6 months	It does not matter who is holding the baby. The baby smiles at anyone, and protests when put down, whoever is holding them.
specific attachment	from about 7 months to a year	One specific attachment, usually to the mother. Fear of strangers and separation anxiety are intense for 3–4 months.
multiple attachments	from about one year onwards	Shows attachment to one other person, then to a number of other people important in their life.

Box A: Schaffer and Emerson (1964)

Procedure: Sixty babies were observed during monthly visits to the family home during the child's first year, and a follow-up visit was made at 18 months. Patterns of attachment were noted. Mothers were interviewed about how the babies behaved with people they were brought into contact with.

Results: In the first six weeks, babies showed no preference for a particular person. During the first six months, they became more sociable towards anyone who wanted to interact with them. By seven months, nearly a third had formed several attachments; 10% had 5 attachments by this time. Most, however, showed a preference for their major carer at seven months, and were wary of strangers. By ten months, however, nearly 60% had more than one attachment, rising to 87% at 18 months. Only a half were mainly attached to their mothers, with a third showing a preference for their fathers. Others had formed a major attachment to a grandparent, or to a brother or sister.

Conclusion: While there was a general pattern of attachment development, there was wide individual variation.

The **indiscriminate attachment** phase is a period of preparation for the intense carer–child relationship which follows. During this time, the infant's experience of responding to others establishes a pattern which later will be directed away from numerous people to focus on just one person. As we shall see, the **specific attachment** phase may set a pattern for future relationships. It also provides the child with emotional security, a secure base from which to explore and to which they can return for emotional support. Attachments formed when the child enters the **multiple attachment** phase are usually less intense than the one formed during the specific attachment phase.

This pattern of the development of attachment behaviours has also been found in cross-cultural studies. For example, figure 2 shows a similarity in the development of separation anxiety in four very different cultures:

Figure 2: culture and the development of attachment behaviour

Development of separation anxiety

Bowlby (1969) suggested that as a result of their experience of the stages of attachment, children develop an inner representation of the mother–child bond, which serves as an **internal working model** of the relationship they have with their primary carer. By this he meant a cognitive representation, or schema, based on day-to-day interactions with the carer. (See chapter 2 for a fuller account of schemas.) He believed that this internal working model persists, relatively unchanged, throughout life, and becomes a model or guide for all future close relationships.

The effects of attachment can be seen when infant and attachment figure are separated. In the 1950s and 1960s, mother and child were separated when either needed to spend time in hospital. Visiting was not encouraged, as it was thought likely to be too upsetting. Robertson and Robertson (1967–73) made a series of films to demonstrate the effect of this practice, which they believed caused unnecessary distress to young children. One example is given in box B:

Box B: Robertson and Robertson (1967–73)

Procedure: John (17 months) spent time in a residential nursery while his mother was in hospital. His behaviour during this time was observed.

Results: For the first few days, John's response was one of protest. He tried to gain attention and form attachments with the nurses, but they had other demands on their time. He showed considerable distress. After a few days, John showed despair. He cried a lot, refused food and had difficulty sleeping. Finally he seemed to give up altogether. His behaviour showed detachment. He stopped trying to attract attention and showed little interest in other people. When his mother came to pick him up, he ignored her and wouldn't allow her to comfort him.

Conclusion: Children who have formed an attachment to a carer go through three stages when they experience separation: protest, despair and detachment.

This attachment of young babies, and what happens when there is a separation between a child and the main carer has been a major focus of interest to developmental psychologists.

Patterns of attachment

One major method of carrying out research investigating mother–infant attachment has been the use of the **Strange Situation** technique, developed by Ainsworth *et al.* (1978). This is described in figure 3.

Using this technique, Ainsworth *et al.* identified three contrasting patterns of attachment (Types A, B and C). Further studies using this technique, e.g. Main and Solomon (1990), have added a fourth pattern (Type D). These are shown in figure 4.

Figure 3: Strange Situation

(a) A mother and child in a playroom. The child is exploring a new environment

(b) A second female adult who is a stranger to the child comes in and talks, first to the mother and then to the child

(c) The mother leaves the room at some point while the stranger is talking to the child

(d) The stranger interacts with the child

(e) The mother returns and the stranger leaves

(f) The mother leaves the room, so the child is alone

(g) The stranger returns to be with the child

(h) The mother returns to the room again

Each episode (a) – (h) lasts three minutes (or less if the child becomes distressed). A video measures the child's behaviour in terms of seeking, maintaining, avoiding, and resisting contact.

Figure 4: types of attachment

Type A: anxious–avoidant – the child ignores the mother when she returns, or mixes welcome with avoidance behaviour, such as turning away. The child treats the mother and the stranger in very similar ways.

Type B: secure – the child cries during separation from the mother, but is easily comforted when she returns. The child tries to stay close to the mother, and prefers her to the stranger.

Type C: anxious–ambivalent – the child is very upset when the mother leaves the room, but is not easily comforted when she returns. The child is angry and tries to avoid contact when she comes back, but this is combined with attempts to be close to her.

Type D: disorganised – the child seems dazed and confused, without any coherent way of dealing with separation and reunion.

Figure 5: cultural variation in the Strange Situation

How infants react in the Strange Situation

Ainsworth found most children showed Type B behaviour. Types A, C and D all show insecure attachment. Typically, research using this classification method has found that approximately 20% of children show a Type A response, 70% Type B and 10% Type C. Type D behaviour is extremely rare and is associated with children who have been abused, or where there is parental pathology. However, cross-cultural research suggests that culture may be important in patterns of attachment and how they are shown. Van Ijzendoorn and Kroonenberg (1988) collected data from 32 studies using this technique, and in all the samples, secure attachment (Type B) was the most common response. However, they also found quite wide cultural variations. For example, in a Chinese sample only 50% showed secure attachment (Type B), and in a German sample, 35% showed anxious–avoidant behaviour (Type A). Takahashi (1990) found high proportion of anxious–ambivalent behaviour (Type C) in Japanese babies.

It seems improbable that babies in China, Germany and Japan are less likely to form secure attachments than the British babies studied by Ainsworth and others. A more convincing conclusion is that different patterns of mother–child relationships in different cultures can lead to a different pattern of responses to the Strange Situation. Takahashi (1990), for example, reports that Japanese infants are normally never left alone at this age, which could account for their extreme distress in the Strange Situation. When observed outside the Strange Situation, they did not appear to be insecurely attached. Similarly, according to Grossmann *et al.* (1985), German parents encourage their infants to be non-clingy and independent. The pattern of response of German children to the Strange Situation may therefore be the intended result of cultural beliefs and practices.

We therefore need to be aware that there may be a cultural bias in methods of assessing attachment such as the Strange Situation, and be careful of the conclusions we draw from this kind of research. There are common factors in the mother–child relationship across cultures which contribute to a secure attachment. At the same time, different cultures place different values on particular behaviours and characteristics, so there are likely to be wide cultural differences in the way these patterns are expressed.

Why is an infant–mother attachment formed?

Several theories have been put forward to provide an explanation of why the infant becomes attached to the mother.

An influential early theory was the **secondary drive hypothesis**, proposed by Dollard and Miller (1950). This theory, taking a behaviourist approach, suggested that attachment is a learned response. Feeding plays a central role in the infant–carer relationship. The baby's hunger is a **primary drive**, a motivational state arising from a basic physiological need. Since this need is repeatedly satisfied by the mother, her presence is associated with the satisfaction of this need, and so becomes a **secondary (or learned) drive**. The child is therefore motivated to seek the mother's presence and is distressed when she is not there.

More generally, **operant conditioning** suggests that if there is a positive outcome to a behaviour, it is likely to be repeated. Since the child is close to the mother during feeding, feeding positively reinforces attachment.

Feeding is also central to a **psychodynamic** explanation of attachment. You will remember from chapter 1 that for Freud, sucking provides oral gratification, so attachment behaviours are related to feeding.

There are some problems with theories which explain attachment in terms of feeding. You will remember from the Schaffer and Emerson study (box A) that human infants can form a main attachment to family members who seldom if ever feed them. Feeding alone may therefore not be an adequate explanation. This has been demonstrated further in animal research:

Box C: Harlow and Zimmerman (1959)

Procedure: Rhesus monkeys were separated from their mothers shortly after birth. They were raised individually with two surrogate mothers. These were models bearing some resemblance to adult monkeys, one consisting of a wire frame, and the other covered in soft cloth. Milk could be obtained through a teat on the wire mother. The monkeys were deliberately frightened by introducing into the cage a clockwork teddy bear, beating a drum.

Results: The infant monkeys showed their extreme distress in behaviours such as screaming, crouching, rocking and thumb-sucking. They spent most of their time clinging to the cloth 'mother', even though it did not give milk. They also clung to her when frightened by the teddy bear. They made no attempt, however, to cling to the wire mother.

Conclusion: Mothering is not only about the basic routine care involved in feeding. Primates also need a source of psychological warmth. What Harlow called the **contact comfort** provided by the cloth mother was important.

A rather more convincing theory has been put forward by Bowlby (1969). He proposed that the attachment of infants to their carers is the result of evolution, in that it is a behaviour which has developed because it is adaptive. The human infant is extremely helpless at birth, and could not survive without adult care. Behaviours which lead to the infant staying close to the mother mean that the baby is protected, and thus more likely to survive. Social behaviours such as smiling attract the mother to the baby, creating a relationship between mother and baby which will motivate the mother to care for the infant. We will look at Bowlby's work in more detail in the next section.

- An infant who is securely attached shows distress at separation from the mother, and seeks her out when stressed. Gazing, following and vocalising are examples of attachment behaviour.
- Attachment has been investigated using the **Strange Situation** technique developed by Ainsworth *et al*. They identified different kinds of attachment. Different patterns of attachment behaviour may be expressed in different cultures.
- Attachment has been explained as a learned behaviour related to **feeding**. More convincingly, it may have developed as an **adaptive behaviour** contributing to survival.

The maternal deprivation hypothesis

The British psychiatrist, John Bowlby, was the first major theorist to become interested in attachment. He was asked by the World Health Organisation to study the effects of being without their mother on children made homeless in the second world war. Bowlby's report for WHO was later published as a book: *Child Care and the Growth of Love* (1953). In it he proposed the **maternal deprivation hypothesis:**

> What is believed to be essential for mental health is that an infant and young child should experience a warm, intimate and continuous relationship with his mother (or permanent mother-substitute – one person who steadily 'mothers' him) in which both find satisfaction and enjoyment. (Bowlby, 1953, p.13)

▷ ## Activity 1: the maternal deprivation hypothesis

Read carefully through the quotation. What do you think Bowlby means by the terms 'warm', 'intimate' and 'continuous'? What do you think he means by 'mental health'? What kinds of problems does this term imply? How is the idea of unsatisfactory parenting used now to explain the emotional and behavioural problems of older children? Are Bowlby's beliefs about what makes satisfactory parenting still current today?

When you have finished, see the notes on page 71.

The origins of Bowlby's theory

According to Bowlby, if children do not form a close bond with one main carer, which is unbroken in the early years, emotional, social and cognitive problems will be the result. What led Bowlby to propose the maternal deprivation hypothesis?

His ideas drew on a number of sources. In his work with children, Bowlby had noticed that at around the age of 9 months, children start to protest and show distress when separated from their mother. As we saw earlier in Schaffer's stage description of attachment, this kind of behaviour is rare before 5 or 6 months, reaches a peak at around the age of 12–16 months and then decreases. Bowlby suggested this distress showed that a bond had been formed with the mother. The fear of strangers served the purpose of preventing other attachments being formed. Bowlby used the term **monotropism** to describe a child's need to become attached to only one particular person if the child is to be mentally healthy. It is perhaps worth noting that Bowlby was a trained psychoanalyst, so Freud's emphasis on the importance of childhood experience was also an influence. Bowlby, too, believed that the first five years were crucial.

Two research studies were also influential in shaping Bowlby's ideas. One of them Bowlby carried out himself:

Box D: Bowlby (1944)

Procedure: Forty-four juvenile thieves in a child guidance unit were compared to 44 juveniles who had emotional problems, but had not committed a criminal offence.

Results: Seventeen of the thieves but only two of the other group of juveniles had been separated from their mothers for a period of at least a week in the first five years of their lives. The group of thieves showed what Bowlby called **'affectionless psychopathy'**, an inability to feel affection or care about other people.

Conclusion: Maternal deprivation was the cause of the thieves' delinquency and their serious emotional problems.

▷ ## Activity 2: criticisms of the 'juvenile thieves' study

Can you think of any flaws in this study? You will need to think about the methodology and the conclusions Bowlby drew from his findings.

When you have finished, see the notes on page 71.

Another study which influenced the maternal deprivation hypothesis looked at the effects on children of being raised in an institution:

Box E: Goldfarb (1943)

Procedure: Two groups, each of 15 children, were compared. The 'institution' group were raised in a children's home until they were about 3½. They were then placed in foster homes. The 'fostered' group went straight from their birth mothers to foster homes.

Results: At 3, the institution group were behind in language development, they showed an inability to form relationships, a lack of guilt and a craving for affection. When tested later between the ages of 10 and 14, the institution group compared very poorly to the fostered group. Their average IQ was 72 (95 for the fostered group). They were restless, had problems concentrating and were unpopular with other children.

Conclusions: The inability of the 'institution' group to form an attachment with one person during the first three years led to social and intellectual retardation.

Activity 3: criticisms of Goldfarb's study

Are there any other factors, which Goldfarb did not take into account in drawing his conclusions, which could have brought about the differences between the institutional and fostered groups?

When you have finished, see the notes on page 71.

In his later book *Attachment and Loss* (1969), Bowlby reinterpreted many of his original ideas on the basis of animal studies. We will look at these in the next section.

- Bowlby proposed the **maternal deprivation hypothesis**. This states that a warm, continuous relationship in the early years between an infant and one, permanent carer is necessary for mental health.
- In his work as a psychiatrist, Bowlby noticed a pattern of distress shown by young babies when separated from their main care-giver. On the basis of his observations, he proposed that infants show **monotropism**, i.e. an exclusive attachment, which Bowlby believed necessary for mental health.

- His own research on **juvenile thieves** found that they were more likely than a comparison group to have experienced separation from their mothers in their early years. There are, however, flaws in this research.
- Additional evidence came from research into children living in **institutions**. These children showed long-term social, emotional and intellectual damage, though again the research can be criticised.

Attachment in animals

Bowlby's belief in the importance of a close and permanent bond with a mother or other carer also received support from animal research. An important theoretical area was the work of Lorenz on imprinting. In the period immediately following birth or hatching, young birds and mammals show a following response to a moving object. Usually the moving object will be the mother. The process of learning which object to follow is known as **imprinting**.

This behaviour has obvious survival value. The mother will protect her young from predators, feed them and generally cater for their needs. It was initially thought that imprinting had a **critical period**, i.e. a restricted period of time in which it had to take place. If it did not happen then, it could not happen, and once the bond was formed, it was irreversible. Although the principles of imprinting have since been modified, and it has been found to be rather more flexible than initial research suggested, the notion of a critical period was still current as Bowlby was developing his ideas.

Goslings imprinted on Lorenz

Lorenz demonstrated that goslings would imprint on him. He found in the course of his studies that these goslings, and other animals which had failed to imprint on an appropriate carer, had serious social and sexual problems as adults. His researches led him to believe that this abnormal behaviour was irreversible.

Bowlby extended these ideas to attachment in infants. In evolutionary terms, those infants genetically predisposed to form strong attachments would be more likely to survive to sexual maturity in a sometimes harsh environment, and so pass their genes on to their own offspring, demonstrating the Darwinian notion of **fitness**. Bowlby suggested that the critical period for children to form this bond is from around 6 months to 3 years. He believed that the social and emotional wellbeing of children would be seriously affected if they were unable to form a strong, stable attachment during this period, or were separated from their primary carer for any length of time.

It is of course necessary to be cautious when extrapolating from goslings to people. Imprinting is a reflex leading to following behaviour, whereas attachment involves the development of emotions. While imprinting is superficially similar to attachment, therefore, it may not be an adequate model for human attachment. However, other evidence from research on maternal deprivation in monkeys, carried out in a series of studies by Harlow and his associates, is perhaps more convincing. One of these studies has already been described in box C.

Harlow and Harlow (1962) showed the long-term effects on monkeys of the early experience of being reared without a mother. When monkeys reared in this way were later put together with normally reared monkeys, they were unable to interact normally. Some were withdrawn, clasping their heads in their hands and rocking back and forth repetitively. Some were self-harming, chewing and biting their own bodies until they bled, or were aggressive to others. Males could not mate successfully. Females, if they did mate, were cruel and unsatisfactory mothers, rejecting their infants and refusing to let them nurse.

It seems, then, that infant monkeys do not develop normal behaviour without a live mother; social and sexual behaviour is much impaired. This suggests that the importance of attachment behaviours goes far beyond obtaining nourishment. Attachment may have far-reaching consequences for the later social development of infants.

You probably found reading about these studies rather upsetting. It is unlikely that they would meet the ethical standards required today when carrying out research on animals, although this is partly because we already have the information they provided; if this research had not already been done, it is possible that a case could be made for carrying it out. The studies do serve to show that not having an attachment figure has devastating consequences for infant monkeys. Given that monkeys and humans are closely related, these findings lent support to Bowlby's belief in the importance of attachment in human infants.

- ⑤ Bowlby's ideas were partly influenced by animal research.
- ⑤ Lorenz' work on **imprinting** suggested that young animals form an exclusive and permanent bond with a moving object soon after birth. This must happen within a **critical period**. Failure to imprint appropriately leads to later problems with mating. Imprinting may not, however, provide a close parallel to attachment.
- ⑤ Harlow's work on monkeys lends more convincing support to Bowlby's ideas.

Critique of the maternal deprivation hypothesis

There would now be little agreement with Bowlby's maternal deprivation hypothesis in its original form, and Bowlby himself modified his ideas in his later writings. When his hypothesis was first proposed, however, what he had to say was extremely influential. To understand why this was so, we need to look briefly at the social and political climate of the time.

During the war while the men were away fighting, a lot of women had needed to join the workforce, and they were still working when the war had ended. Since one of the circumstances likely to damage children, listed in *Child Care and the Growth of*

Love, was 'mother working full time', Bowlby's ideas were a powerful argument for women not working. Large numbers of servicemen were now returning to Great Britain after the war and needed jobs.

It was thus in the interests of those in power to give Bowlby's ideas publicity, both to provide jobs and to save the expense of providing care for children who could be looked after at home. Since Bowlby's ideas meshed with public concerns, people were generally receptive to what he had to say.

A lot of research has since been carried out to evaluate the maternal deprivation hypothesis, and it has been questioned on several counts.

▶ Activity 4: assessing the maternal deprivation hypothesis

Look back to the quotation from *Child Care and the Growth of Love* on page 56 to remind yourself of Bowlby's original formulation of the maternal deprivation hypothesis. You should also look at your notes on activity 1. What reservations do you have about Bowlby's claim? What aspects of it do you think need further investigation?

If you know any very young children, you might find it helpful to think of the patterns of care they experience. Are they different from what Bowlby is describing as essential? How? What do you think might be the effects of different kinds of care?

When you have finished, see the notes on page 72.

As the discussion of activity 4 suggests, several aspects of Bowlby's views have been questioned by later researchers. We will look at what this later research has to tell us in the next sections.

- ⊖ Bowlby's **maternal deprivation hypothesis** has been very influential. The political climate of the time ensured that it received wide publicity.
- ⊖ Many aspects of Bowlby's theory have been questioned. Bowlby himself modified his ideas in his later writings.

Can fathers be 'mothers'?

Up to now, we have been discussing maternal deprivation; fathers haven't been mentioned. Clearly children also form attachments to fathers, and the Schaffer and Emerson study (box A) suggests that

this can be an important influence in a child's life. Many children could indeed be said to suffer *paternal* deprivation. For example, their fathers may work long hours, or be in prison, or children may live in single-parent families, which usually means with their mother. This emphasis on the mother reflects the traditional attitudes of our culture, where men and women are seen as having different roles in society and the family. The anthropologist Margaret Mead went so far as to claim that a father is a 'biological necessity, but a social accident'.

Although Bowlby recognised that children form more than one attachment, he claimed that the attachment to the mother or permanent mother substitute is the strongest and the most crucial. The question here is what Bowlby means by a 'permanent mother substitute'. Could this be the father? The evidence of the Schaffer and Emerson (box A) study supports the idea that fathers can indeed be 'mothers'.

The Schaffer and Emerson study also suggests that the vast majority of young children form multiple attachments, and we shall now look at this in a little more detail.

One attachment or many?

Stacey *et al.* (1970) studied four-year-old children in Wales who went into hospital to have their tonsils removed. They stayed four days, and their parents were not able to stay overnight. Some coped very well, and it was found that they had experienced this kind of separation before, mostly staying overnight with their grandparents or a friend. Like the Schaffer and Emerson study, these findings suggest that children are indeed capable of forming more than one attachment, and that other attachments mean that they do not find temporary separation from the major carer as distressing as Bowlby was suggesting.

Attachments to grandparents can be very important to young children. For many of the children in Dunn and Kendrick's (1982) study of family relationships, a grandmother was a major presence in their lives. This is particularly likely to be the case when the mother is a single parent, and the grandmother can share childcare. We need also to look at patterns of attachment in cross-cultural research:

Box F: Werner (1991); Tyszkowa (1991)

Werner (1991): In black extended families in the USA, the maternal grandmother is seen both by her daughter and herself as actively involved in childcare. In cases where the mother works, the grandmother is often the primary carer. In Native American families, the role of grandparents in child-rearing is seen as crucial. When there is no biological grandparent, an unrelated older person is often adopted into the family to fulfil this role.

Tyszkowa (1991): Grandparents also have a central role in Poland. They are additional attachment figures, but are also valued for the ability their experience gives them to pass on family and social history to the child.

There is, however, a limit to the number of attachments which can be formed:

Box G: Tizard and Rees (1975); Tizard and Hodges (1978)

Procedure: Sixty-five babies in institutional care were studied. They had all entered an institution before 4 months, and remained until at least two. By the age of $4\frac{1}{2}$, 15 had returned to their mothers, 24 had been adopted and 26 had stayed in the institution. The institutions offered a far more stimulating environment than that described in the Goldfarb study (box E). By the age of 2, the children who were to stay in the institution had had on average 24 carers. This had risen to 50 at $4\frac{1}{2}$.

Results: At $4\frac{1}{2}$ and 8, there were differences between those who stayed in the institution and the other two groups. More than two-thirds of the children staying in the institution were described at $4\frac{1}{2}$ as 'not to care deeply about anyone'. Many were said to be very attention-seeking. When followed up at 8, they were seen by teachers to have severe problems. They were attention-seeking, restless, unpopular and antisocial.

Conclusion: For normal social and emotional development, there are limits to the amount of shared care a child can tolerate.

- For many young children, their main attachment is to the **father**. For many children, the **grandmother** is an important attachment figure.
- Most also form multiple attachments in their first year. At the same time, there are limits to the number of attachments a child can make if that child is to develop normally.

3.2   ATTACHMENT DIFFICULTIES

We need to look now at whether the circumstances which lead to some young children failing to form or maintain secure attachments affect the outcome for the child.

Privation, disruption, and distortion

The three key terms here are:

privation: the child has never had the opportunity to form a close attachment

disruption: a bond has been formed which has later been broken

distortion: a bond exists between child and carer but there is conflict and unhappiness

Rutter (1972) pointed out that *de*privation implies the loss of maternal care, whereas the child may never have had the opportunity to form close bonds in the first place. He suggested that instead of deprivation, we need to make this distinction by using two new terms: **privation** and **disruption**.

Activity 5: privation and disruption

What kinds of circumstances could lead to the disruption of early attachments? Do you think the circumstances you have described might lead to different long-term outcomes? Do you think privation and disruption might have different effects? Refer to your notes on this activity as you read this section.

Box H: Pringle and Bossio (1960)

Procedure: Children in long-term institutional care were studied. The aim was to find out why some of these children were much less maladjusted than others.

Results: Children who had stayed with their mother during the first year were generally better adjusted than those who had entered the institution soon after birth, and who had not formed a stable attachment. These children had difficulty in forming relationships.

Conclusion: There is a better outcome when a relationship has been disrupted than when a child has not had the opportunity to form an attachment.

Disruption of attachment can come about through the death of a parent, or a child being taken into care by the local authority, or when the parents separate or divorce. Bowlby emphasised the relationship between a broken home and later delinquency, and believed that it was lack of maternal care which led to later problems. There are other problems, however, associated with family break-up. There is likely to be tension and discord in the home in the time leading to the break-up, and this may well continue afterwards. This led Rutter to make a further distinction between disruption brought about by bereavement, and the **distortion** of relationships associated with divorce.

There has been a lot of research comparing the effects of disruption and distortion of attachments. Going back to Bowlby's notion of delinquency, Rutter (1972) reported that the delinquency rates for boys who had lost a parent (**disruption**) was very similar to that for boys in intact families. However, the rate for boys whose parents had divorced (**distortion**) was significantly higher. There was also a higher delinquency rate for boys who lived in intact but unhappy families (**distortion**), compared with those whose parents were divorced, but where relationships remained good (**disruption**). It seems that disruption is less of a problem than distortion.

The effects of divorce were confirmed in a study by Hetherington *et al.*, which also identified an additional factor:

Box I: Hetherington *et al.* (1979; 1982)

Procedure: This longitudinal study studied 4-year-old children of divorced parents living with the mother.

Results: Initially, when compared with a control group from intact families, these children showed less mature play, and tended to be negative, attention-seeking, dependent and aggressive. Two years after the divorce, there was no difference between the girls with divorced parents and controls. For boys, however, problems continued, though they had become less extreme. Four years later, the differences between boys and girls persisted. Boys were more aggressive and lacked social skills compared with controls.

Conclusion: There are gender differences in adjustment to disruption and distortion.

Long-term effects of insecure attachment

From research described in earlier sections, it is clear that the lack of a secure attachment can have short-term effects. You will remember that Bowlby's **maternal deprivation hypothesis** proposed that there would also be long-term effects.

His study of 44 juvenile thieves, described in box D, and Goldfarb's longitudinal study, described in box E, lend some support to this idea. In addition, we have looked briefly at other research findings, e.g. the Rutter study (mentioned in the previous section), the Tizard and Rees and Tizard and Hodges studies in box G, the Pringle and Bossio study in box H, and the Hetherington *et al.* study in box I, which have all supported the idea that the effects may also be relatively long-term.

This links in with the suggestion made by Bowlby, mentioned earlier, that children develop an **internal working model** of the relationship they have with their primary carer which has long-term implications. We will look briefly at some further research in this area.

Box J: Main and Cassidy (1988)

Procedure: A variant of Ainsworth *et al.*'s Strange Situation technique was used with children aged 3–6.

Results: There were considerable differences between children in terms of their behaviour and their self-image:

1. some children see themselves as lovable, and value close relationships with others.
2. some see themselves as unlovable, and act in ways which are likely to make others reject them; they are more interested in activities than people.
3. some children interact inappropriately, responding to parents with unnatural enthusiasm or hostility.
4. some are still upset by separation from the parent at this age, showing whiny, clinging behaviour.

Main and Cassidy related these different patterns to the four types identified in Strange Situation studies of infants.

Conclusion: There are pronounced individual differences in relationship types at age 3–6 which can be related to attachment patterns seen in younger children.

▶ Activity 6: the Strange Situation revisited

Main and Cassidy found patterns of attachment in older children which they related to the distinctions made by Ainsworth *et al*. Can you match each of the kinds of relationship they describe in box J with one of the four types of attachment found in infants? You will need to look back to the descriptions in figure 3.

When you have finished, see the notes on page 72.

Moving on from this work, Main and her colleagues developed the **Adult Attachment Interview (AAI)**, to find out whether these patterns of attachment could influence adult relationships, as Bowlby suggested, and whether in particular they could be related to the quality of the adult's attachment to their own child. Four main patterns emerged from the AAI:

Figure 6: patterns of adult attachment based on the AAI (Main and Goldwyn, 1984)

1. autonomous–secure: even if their early attachment experiences were not entirely positive, these adults could recall them objectively, and valued relationships. They were likely to have securely attached children.
2. dismissing–detached: these adults had few childhood memories, or produced idealised recollections. They placed little value on relationships. Their children tended to be anxious–avoidant.
3. preoccupied–entangled: these adults were still preoccupied with their relationships with their parents, and still tried to please them. Conflicts with them were often unresolved. Their children were likely to be anxious–ambivalent.
4. unresolved–disorganised: these adults had suffered traumatic separation from the attachment figure, with which they had not come to terms. They had often been abused. Their children tended to show insecure disorganised behaviour patterns.

The findings of Main and Goldwyn suggest a link between early attachment experience and the quality of mothering that the adult provides. Hazan and Shaver have extended this idea by investigating a possible link, using Ainsworth *et al.*'s categories, between the kind of mothering experienced and experience of adult romantic love:

Box K: Hazan and Shaver (1987)

Procedure: Using Ainsworth *et al.*'s three basic attachment types (see figure 3), the experimenters wrote descriptions of three types of corresponding adult attachment. They produced a 'Love Quiz' for a newspaper, and readers were invited to pick which description of adult relationships best applied to them, and were also asked to complete an adjective checklist to describe the kind of parenting they had received as children. ✍

🖎 Ainsworth *et al.*'s categories and the linked descriptions of adult attachment and type of parenting received are shown in figure 7.

Results: There was a significant relationship between the kind of parenting received as a child and the choice of description of participants' adult attachments.

Conclusion: There is a link between early attachment experience and the nature of relationships formed as an adult.

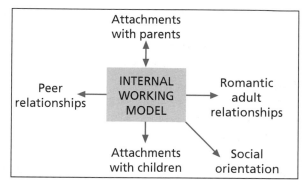

The internal working model through the life span

Figure 7: Hazan and Shaver (1987)

attachment style	type of parenting	adult relationships: self-description
securely attached	readily available attentive, responsive	I find it relatively easy to get close to others and am comfortable depending on them and having them depend on me. I don't often worry about being abandoned or about someone getting too close to me.
anxious–avoidant	unresponsive, rejecting, inattentive	I am somewhat uncomfortable being close to others; I find it difficult to trust them completely, difficult to allow myself to depend on them. I am nervous when anyone gets too close, and often, love partners want me to be more intimate than I feel comfortable being.
anxious–ambivalent	anxious, fussy, out of step with child's needs. Only available/responsive some of the time.	I find that others are reluctant to get as close as I would like. I often worry that my partner doesn't really love me or won't want to stay with me. I want to merge completely with another person, and this desire sometimes scares people away.

Both the Main and Goldwyn study and that of Hazan and Shaver give some support to Bowlby's idea of an internal working model which persists into adulthood. This relates both to the kind of parenting they themselves provide, and their experience of adult relationships.

There is also some evidence that the quality of early attachments is not only relevant to later relationships, but also to wider social orientation, for example the response to crises within society.

Box L: Mikulincer *et al.* (1993)

Procedure: The response of young Israeli adults to the Iraqi Scud missile attacks during the Gulf War was investigated, to find out whether there was a relationship between attachment style and responses to this threat to their society.

Results: Securely-attached individuals (Type B) coped with the trauma by seeking emotional support from others. Ambivalent types (Type C) showed a more extreme emotional response, while avoidant types (Type A) tried to distance themselves psychologically from these events. For people with patterns of insecure attachment, the psychological distress experienced was greater than for securely-attached people.

Conclusion: Early patterns of attachment are related to how people respond to crises.

- Rutter distinguished between **privation, disruption** and **distortion** of relationships. Privation and distortion seem to have more serious effects than disruption.
- **Distortion** may come about through divorce, and may also happen in intact but unhappy families.
- Bowlby believed that children develop an **internal working model** of relationships, which persists relatively unchanged into adult life.
- The **Adult Attachment Interview (AAI)** technique shows that early attachment experience can affect a carer's relationship with their own child, adult relationships, and their response to social crises.

3.3 ARE EARLY DIFFICULTIES REVERSIBLE?

The discussion in the previous section suggests that there may indeed be long-term effects from insecure early attachment. But are such effects inevitable? We will start by looking at some animal research in this area.

Look back now to box C to remind yourself of Harlow's research on infant monkeys. This was followed up by a study to see if the extreme effects of maternal deprivation Harlow noted could be overcome:

Box M: Suomi and Harlow (1972)

Procedure: Monkeys were raised in isolation for 6 months. They were then placed with normally-reared 3-month-old monkeys.
Results: The isolated monkeys were withdrawn, and showed the stereotyped rocking behaviour observed in earlier studies. When placed with adults or peers, they were attacked, and could not respond appropriately to others. After a few weeks with the normally-reared younger monkeys, however, they started to explore their environment and take part in social play. Stereotyped behaviour decreased. After 6 months, their social behaviour was virtually normal.
Conclusion: Interaction with monkeys who were younger helped to reverse the effects of early deprivation.

There is of course the problem that this research was carried out on monkeys, and we need to be careful when extrapolating these findings to human infants. At the same time, it does present a fairly optimistic picture of the reversibility of early deprivation, which has been supported by research into the role of peers in human attachment:

Box N: Freud and Dann (1951)

Procedure: A case study was carried out of 6 Jewish war orphans whose parents had been killed in the genocide of the second world war. They had been brought up in a concentration camp by a succession of short-term carers. Though little is known about their early lives, it is likely that they had had traumatic experiences during this time. The study was carried out at the Bulldogs Bank children's home. The children were between 3 and 3 years 10 months at the start of the study. To begin with, they were aggressive and destructive, had very limited language, and poorly developed social skills. They were not potty trained, for example, and could not use a knife and fork. However, they were extremely attached to each other, did everything together and refused to be separated.
Results: They gradually started to make progress and were adopted. They went on to lead reasonably successful lives.
Conclusion: A close attachment to a primary carer early in life is not as crucial as Bowlby suggested. The outlook is positive if the child is able to form attachments with someone, not necessarily an adult carer.

In addition, adoption studies have indicated that the time during which secure attachments can be formed is not as limited as Bowlby's maternal deprivation hypothesis suggested. Kadushin (1970) studied 91 families who had adopted children over the age of 5. In over 4 out of 5 families, strong attachments had been formed between child and carer, and in only two cases had the child left the adoptive home.

Finally in this section we will look at some cases of severely deprived children:

Box O: Davis (1947)

Procedure: Davis described a case study of a child who had been kept in virtual isolation for the early part of her life. Isabelle was illegitimate, which at that time was considered extremely shameful, so she had been hidden away. She could not speak, since her mother was a deaf mute. She had been kept in a dark room with almost no social contact. After she was found at 6½, she was given a lot of loving care, as well as considerable attention, to help her development.
Results: Eighteen months later, the change in Isabelle was dramatic. She did well at school and made friends with other children. She was a happy and cheerful little girl.
Conclusion: The effects of early deprivation can be overcome later than Bowlby suggested.

The case of Genie is another example of an isolated child:

Box P: Curtiss (1977)

Genie spent the first years of her life alone, tied to a potty chair and fed on baby food. She had lived her life in virtual silence, not being spoken to and being punished for making any sound herself.
She was found at the age of 13½. She developed attachments to her foster carers, but after a settled period in their care, she was moved to a succession of short-term carers, some of whom mistreated her.
Her mother eventually refused to allow anyone access to her, and it is not known what happened to her later in life. During the years when her whereabouts were known, Genie only acquired limited language skills.

Even in this extreme case, it seems that it is still possible for children to form attachments later in life. Genie's inability to develop language suggests that she suffered cognitive deficits as a result of deprivation. It is not possible to know, though, whether these deficits were the result of the lack of an early attachment figure or other aspects of the deprivation she experienced. It is also possible, of course, that Genie was hidden away because she was in some way not a normal infant.

In general, it seems that the outlook for children who suffer early deprivation, even if this is very severe, is not as bleak as Bowlby originally suggested.

- Animal research has suggested that the effects of early deprivation can be reversed by the company of **peers**. There is evidence that this is also true for humans.
- Studies of **late adoption** suggest that attachments can be formed and the effects of early deprivation reversed much later than Bowlby suggested.
- Even in cases of **severe deprivation**, normal intellectual and social development is possible.

3.4 OTHER FACTORS IN SOCIAL AND EMOTIONAL DEVELOPMENT

Activity 7: other factors in social and emotional development

Up to now we have concentrated on the effects of carer behaviour on the child. Can you think of any other factors which might affect how infants and children develop?
When you have finished, see the notes on page 72.

Buss and Plomin (1984) noted that very early on, infants show wide individual differences in **temperament**. This can be defined as the consistent ways in which children respond to their world, which is relatively stable across different situations. Buss and Plomin's **EAS** model believes distinctions can be made on three dimensions:

65

emotionality: some infants become upset very much more easily than others.

activity: infants have different preferred levels of activity.

sociability: they differ in their preferred amount of interaction with others.

It could be that temperamental differences affect early infant–carer interactions, which may in turn affect attachment and later development. For example, Waters (1978) found that infants who do not readily attend to people and objects are more likely to develop insecure attachments.

We need also to consider here what is known as **goodness-of-fit**. What this means is the extent to which the characteristics of child and carer are compatible. For example, it may be difficult for a mother who wants to spend a lot of time interacting with her child if the child is low on sociability.

This can be related to the **transactional model** of infant–carer interaction described by Sameroff (1991). This model emphasises the active role of a child in its own development. Both carer and child influence each other's behaviour. An example is shown in figure 8:

> **Figure 8: an example of the transactional model of mother–child interaction (from Sameroff, 1991)**
>
> 1. After a difficult childbirth, a mother is anxious and behaves inconsistently to her child.
> 2. In response to this inconsistency, the child develops irregular patterns of feeding and sleeping.
> 3. As a result of this irregularity, the mother perceives the child as having a difficult temperament. She spends less time interacting with the child.
> 4. Due to the relative lack of interaction, the child is slow in developing language.

It is difficult here to pick out one particular cause for the mother–child problems. It would certainly be simplistic to see the outcome purely as the result of poor parenting. Both mother and child are involved in a complex developmental sequence.

We also need to look beyond children's relationship with their primary carer to explain later development. Rutter (1972) suggested that there are four factors associated with later behavioural problems: family discord, parents having psychiatric problems or a criminal record, social disadvantage (e.g. poor housing and poverty) and a poor school environment. He found that these factors were good predictors of problem behaviour in children.

It is necessary to look at wider family characteristics, then, and factors outside the family, in order to explain why children develop problems. It would be interesting to know how many of the factors Rutter identified applied to the 44 juvenile thieves studied by Bowlby (box D).

⊖ We need to look beyond maternal behaviour in order to explain developmental problems.

⊖ Children's **temperament** may contribute to developmental difficulties. This can also be related to **goodness-of-fit** between the characteristics of child and mother, and Sameroff's **transactional model** of mother–child interaction.

❺ Wider social and economic factors may also influence development.

3.5 CRITICAL ISSUE: DAY CARE

You will remember that Bowlby believed that young children need continuous care from their mother or permanent mother-substitute. For children to enjoy good mental health, they should not be cared for by someone other than the major carer, so any form of day care would be damaging. In his 1951 report to the World Health Organisation, Bowlby claimed that the use of day care would lead to 'permanent damage to the emotional health of a future generation' (WHO, 1951, quoted in Tizard, 1991).

Bowlby's ideas continued to be extremely influential for many years. Penelope Leach, a popularly accepted authority for new mothers, was writing in 1979:

I believe that for children under three there should be no form of socially approved *group-care*. My ideal society has no day nurseries ....Babies and very small children each need a 'special' and continuous person or people and they need to have their daily lives based on somewhere they know as 'home'.

However, a child being continuously cared for by a mother is no longer the norm. Many young children spend at least part of their time at a nursery, with a childminder or being cared for by people other than their mothers in some more informal arrangement. In a survey carried out by the US Bureau of the Census (1994), for example, it was found that 60% of mothers with a child under two were employed, and their children were therefore experiencing day care.

There has been a good deal of research into the effects of the separation from the main carer which this entails, to find out whether it is harmful to children, as Bowlby and others have suggested, and in particular whether it weakens the bond with the mother.

As we will see, most studies have concluded that day care need not have an adverse effect on young children. Clarke-Stewart and Fein (1983), for example, found that children of mothers who work

still form attachments to their mother, and prefer them to other carers. There is one exception to these general findings, however:

Box Q: Belsky (1988)

Procedure: The quality of attachment shown by young children who spent time in day care was compared with the quality of attachment shown by children remaining at home with their mothers. Attachment was assessed using the Strange Situation technique.

Results: There was a greater risk of children forming insecure attachments if they had been in day care for at least 4 months before their first birthday, and if they spent more than 20 hours per week in care. While a large number of children in day care developed secure attachments, a larger proportion of children showing insecure attachments was found among those experiencing day care than those who did not.

Conclusion: In certain cases, children who spend time in day care are more likely to show insecure attachments than those kept at home with the mother.

Figure 9: security of attachment and extent of non-maternal care (Belsky, 1988)

	Extent of non-maternal care	
	More than 20 hours/week	Less than 20 hours/week
Secure attachment	59%	74%
Insecure attachment	41%	26%
N = 464		

Taken at face value, this conclusion seems rather worrying. It implies that day care may prevent a secure attachment being formed and that the child's future development may therefore be at risk. However, are there other ways of interpreting these findings?

▶ Activity 8: day care and insecure attachments

The Belsky study used the Strange Situation as a measure of attachment. Look back to the earlier section discussing this technique. In the light of this discussion, is there another way in which the findings of this study could be interpreted? In coming to a conclusion, you will need to consider the child's experience of separation and reunion. When you have finished, see the notes on page 72.

Given the problems of interpreting the results of the Strange Situation, it seems possible that day care may not be as harmful as Belsky's research suggests. There is also evidence that it may have some very positive outcomes, and we will look now at research investigating this possibility.

The effects of day care on children has been investigated in the Thomas Coram Research Institute Study, described in box R:

Box R: Melhuish *et al.* (1990a and 1990b)

Procedure: Eighteen-month-old children were observed in a day care environment and at home. About a third in day care were cared for by a relative, half by a childminder and the remainder attended a nursery. Further measures were taken when the children were three years old.

Results: Some behaviour was very similar in all the settings observed, e.g. the amount of individual play and crying. There were differences in attention and verbal interaction (highest in the home and least in nurseries). Affection shown to and by the child was highest in the home and lowest in nurseries. Aggression was highest in the nursery setting. The behaviour of children in the Strange Situation when reunited with the mother was comparable across all the settings.
At the age of 3, affectionate interactions were more frequent where mothers and relatives were caring for the child. Sharing

and empathy were more likely to be shown by the nursery children.
Conclusion: Different kinds of day care are associated with different patterns of behaviour. Day care may have some negative effects, but may also have some positive effects on social behaviour.

Melhuish *et al.* pointed out that we need to look not only at the nature of the care provided, but also at the quality of care. The nurseries they observed had a relatively high child to carer ratio, compared with the other settings, which meant that staff needed to become more involved in controlling the children, and had less time to interact with them. Many of the staff were young, without experience of children of their own, and staff turnover was high. All these factors might contribute to lower-quality care.

In poor daycare...

The nurseries had a high child-care ratio

The staff were young

The staff had no experience of children of their own.

The staff turnover was high

The question of quality of care was also investigated by Kagan *et al.* (1980):

Box S: Kagan *et al.* (1980)

Procedure: This was a longitudinal study into the effects of day care. It looked at children who were in day care for seven hours a day, five days a week, over 5 years. Children were tested at intervals for cognitive development (e.g. language skills), social development (e.g. relationships with other children), and attachment to the mother.

Results: The day care group was compared with a control group of children being cared for at home. There were no differences, provided the day care facility was staffed by experienced carers, there was a good child-to-carer ratio, and there was appropriate equipment.

Conclusion: Good-quality day care has no serious negative effect on children's development.

There is also evidence that good-quality day care may have a very positive effect on children's development:

Box T: McCartney *et al.* (1985)

Procedure: The development of young children in Bermuda was investigated, where 85% of children enter day care before the age of two.

Results: Verbal stimulation by carers and overall rating of the quality of day care predicted enhanced cognitive, language and social skills in the pre-school years.

Conclusion: Good-quality day care can make a broad contribution to children's development.

There were similar findings in a Swedish study (Andersson, 1992) of children entering good-quality day care before the age of 12 months.

The key issue here is the quality of care provided. In America, guidelines have been produced which define the characteristics of good-quality care in a day care setting, many of which relate to aspects of good quality care noted by Kagan *et al.* (box S).

Figure 10: appropriate infant and toddler day care (National Association for the Education of Young Children, 1991)

characteristic	signs of quality
physical setting	clean, well-lit, well-ventilated and uncrowded environment; fenced outdoor play space available
carer-to-child ratio	ratio of no more than 1:3 for infants and 1:6 for toddlers; consistent staffing so that relationships with particular carers can be formed
daily activities	schedule includes active play, quiet play, naps and meals; flexibility to meet children's individual needs
adult–child interaction	prompt carer response to distress; carers hold, talk to and read to children, and are responsive to the needs of the individual child
carer qualifications	training in child development, first aid, and safety
relationships with parents	parents are welcome at any time; carers discuss children's behaviour and development with them
toys and equipment	appropriate play materials, both for indoor and outdoor play, are available, and within reach of the children

Activity 9: the quality of day care

If you can arrange to do so, visit a local day care centre. Make an assessment of the facilities it offers, using the signs of quality in figure 9 to guide you. Talk to the children to find out what they enjoy about the centre. You could also talk to the staff (if they are not too busy with the children!)

In most of Europe, the provision of day care is regulated. In the USA, however, standards are set at state level and are very variable. Zigler and Gilman (1993) found that many young children attend unlicensed day care homes where there is no check on health and safety standards, and where one carer may be responsible for as many as 12 babies. Phillips *et al.* (1994) found that many children who attended poor-quality day care came from poor homes, suggesting that these children may be doubly disadvantaged, both at home and in the day care environment. So what are the effects of poor-quality day care?

Box U: Howes (1990)

Procedure: Children entering poor-quality day care before the age of 12 months, and who stayed there throughout the pre-school period, were assessed during their first year at school.

Results: Teachers rated these children as being very easily distracted, with difficulty focusing on an activity and becoming involved in it. They were also less considerate of others than children who had not experienced day care.

Conclusion: Poor-quality day care is associated with a lack of the skills necessary for cognitive development, and poor social relationships with other children.

Poor-quality day care can have serious effects on children's social, emotional and cognitive development, and it is children from already disadvantaged backgrounds who are more likely to experience such care. At the same time, however, good-quality day care can help to reduce the negative impact of a disadvantaged background for such children:

Box V: Campbell and Ramey (1991)

Procedure: In the Carolina Abecedarian project, over 100 children from disadvantaged homes, aged from 3 months to 3 years, were enrolled in a full-time year-round day care programme. They received stimulation aimed at developing motor, cognitive, language and social skills. Their development was compared with a group from a similar background who were not on the programme.

Results: On intelligence tests, scores for the group which had experienced day care were significantly higher than for the controls. This advantage was still apparent at 12 years old. The effects were greater for those who had entered the programme at a younger age.

Conclusion: For disadvantaged children, appropriate day care can help to develop cognitive skills.

It is encouraging, given that many mothers need to make day care arrangements for their children, that the effects of day care (provided it is of good quality) do not seem to be as negative as Bowlby suggested. However, just as Bowlby's ideas need to be seen in the social and political context in which they were put forward, it could be argued that findings that day care is not necessarily harmful to young children, and might even have positive effects, could have found ready acceptance in an industrial climate which welcomes women into the workplace as cheap and tractable labour.

Day care: the mother's perspective

In the quotation from *Child Care and the Growth of Love* given earlier, Bowlby pointed out that the relationship between mother and child should be one in which 'both find satisfaction and enjoyment'. But is this always possible?

When a parent (usually the mother) gives up work outside the home, her life will change drastically. She may feel cut off from the adult company and conversation which she is used to in her work environment, and she may miss the challenges work has provided. If she has had a stimulating job, she may feel bored at the prospect of life at home, where one day is very much like the next. A study by Boulton (1983) found that women in this situation can experience depression and loss of identity. Over half the mothers interviewed found fulfilment in parenting, but a large minority did not.

Schaffer (1990) has also pointed out that the mother's perspective needs to be taken into account when considering what is best for the child. It is likely that a child will develop better with a mother who is happy and enjoys work than with one who is bored and frustrated as a full-time carer. In a review of 122 studies of working mothers, Hoffman (1974) found that dissatisfied

mothers were more likely to be inadequate mothers. This was true whether or not the mother was working, and was also true across social class boundaries. In these circumstances, day care may be beneficial for both child and mother, and for the relationship between them.

- Research into **day care** suggests that it may have negative effects on a child. It may also have a positive effect.
- The **quality** of day care is important.
- Good quality day care can help to **reduce negative aspects of development** associated with children coming from a disadvantaged background.
- The **mother's perspective** also needs to be taken into account when considering day care.

Notes on activities

1 The terms 'warm' and 'intimate' indicate that in Bowlby's view, adequate routine care is not enough. He is concerned with the *quality* of the relationship between baby and carer. 'Continuous' implies that mothering in the early years should be full-time. 'Mental health' relates to how well a child is adjusted, both in early infancy and later as an older child and an adult. A child with good mental health is happy and emotionally secure. Poor mental health can be shown in a range of behaviours, such as clinging, aggression, social withdrawal and so on.

There is still a widespread belief that problems in childhood are associated with the child's early experience. Parents are often blamed when children show poor social skills, are aggressive or show other problem behaviours. The precise connection made, though, can vary: perhaps parents are thought not to have given their children enough attention, perhaps children may be seen as lacking discipline and so on.

2 In considering the methodology, you may have thought that this study would have been stronger if there had been a more adequate control group. Both groups had emotional

problems; it would have been interesting to compare these samples with children who showed no such problems, since Bowlby was proposing that emotional problems would be the outcome of maternal deprivation.

In addition, this is a correlational study, looking for a relationship between two factors. This method has the drawback that it can't establish whether any relationship which is found is causal, i.e. that one factor (in this case, maternal deprivation) causes the other (affectionless psychopathy). It could be that a further factor, e.g. family problems, was responsible both for the lack of continuity of care and the serious emotional problems experienced.

In addition, since the study is retrospective, it is difficult to identify what other factors – physical, social, emotional and so on – might have been involved in bringing about these children's problems.

3 The children who were studied were matched to an extent on such factors as mothers' occupation and level of education, but there may well have been other important factors – for example, temperamental differences or general health –

on which the groups were not matched. Characteristics such as how alert or intelligent or outgoing they seemed to be may have been factors in deciding whether they found foster homes straight away, or spent their early years in the institution.

It is also possible that it is not the lack of a permanent carer so much as the general lack of stimulation which was at least in part responsible for the differences between the two groups. In the institution Goldfarb studied, babies under 9 months were kept isolated from each other, in order to prevent the spread of infections, and had little contact with adults except for routine changing and feeding. There was a high turnover of carers, and for this reason, carers were discouraged from forming bonds with the children in their care. Throughout the time before they were fostered, then, they experienced considerable social isolation.

4 You have probably come up with similar questions to those investigated by later researchers. You may know children who regularly spend time away from their major carer – for example, who go to a nursery. So how continuous does care need to be? Bowlby focused very much on infant and mother in the development of attachment, but what about the role of the father? Should we accept the concept of monotropism or can the child form attachments with more than one person? What about the reasons why the close bond Bowlby saw as vital cannot be established or maintained? Do the circumstances make a difference? Does what Bowlby sees as an inadequate start in life mean there will necessarily be later problems, as the idea of a critical period implies, or can the effects of early experience be reversed? Are there individual differences between children in terms of the effects of their early experience? Does continuous care such as Bowlby describes guarantee the development of mother–child attachment?

6 The first description relates to Type B, a secure attachment. The second relates to Type A, the third to Type D and the last one to Type C.

7 Two possible factors here are the characteristics the child brings to early relationships and the impact of wider social and economic conditions.

8 It could be argued that children in day care have learned that separation is only temporary and is always followed by reunion with the mother. For these children, separation would not be such a threatening experience as for those who have seldom or never experienced it. This might be reflected in their response to the Strange Situation; the patterns of behaviour they showed could reflect the pattern of care they had experienced, but would not necessarily mean that they had not formed a secure attachment. You might like to relate this to the response of Chinese, German and Japanese children to the Strange Situation discussed earlier.

It is possible also that there are reasons other than being in day care which lead to these children showing insecure attachment. For example, it could be that there are differences between those mothers who choose or need to work, and so put their children in day care, and those who do not.

04

Stress

In this chapter we will be looking at:

4.1 What is stress?

4.2 Models of stress

4.3 The physiological response to stress

4.4 Sources of stress
    Environmental factors
    Physiological factors
    Psychological and social factors

4.5 Personality differences and stress

4.6 Stress and illness
    The immune system
    Animal research
    Stress and illness in humans

4.7 Critical issue: stress management
    Biological approaches
    Behavioural approaches
    Cognitive approaches
    The psychodynamic approach
    Social support
    Reducing stressors

4.1 WHAT IS STRESS?

Most people at one time or another have claimed to be suffering from stress. As with many other concepts, however, the use of the term 'stress' is rather more complex in the context of psychology than in everyday situations.

We tend to think of stress as unpleasant, and as something to be avoided. However, stress can broadly speaking be seen as a response to any kind of stimulation, so a complete lack of stress would relate to a complete lack of stimulation; in this sense, a certain amount of stress is beneficial. This can be related to the **Yerkes–Dodson law**, which links arousal and performance:

Figure 1: Yerkes–Dodson law

How arousal affects performance

According to the Yerkes–Dodson law, we need a certain amount of arousal in order to perform well. There is an optimal level of arousal, however, and if we move beyond that point (see the shaded part of the diagram in figure 1), performance drops off, and we experience what we would generally refer to

Figure 2: optimal arousal and task complexity

The Yerkes–Dodson Law

as stress. The more complex the task we are asked to perform, the lower the optimum level of arousal.

Selye (1974) distinguishes between **distress** and **eustress**. Distress refers to the kind of stress which is experienced as unpleasant, when we feel that we can't cope with what is being asked of us. Eustress, however, refers to pleasant stress, such as we experience when we take part in moderate exercise. Even though stress has its positive side, though, we will be concentrating here on its more negative aspects.

4.2 MODELS OF STRESS

Cox (1975) has proposed that there are three different models of stress. These different approaches vary in the emphasis they give to external and internal factors.

The first is the **engineering model**, and focuses on characteristics of the environment related to stress. In the same way that the metal from which a heavily-used bridge is constructed will become weakened and eventually suffer from metal fatigue, so people become stressed as the result of their experiences. This model looks at the kinds of factors which lead people to experience stress, and thus focuses on the *causes* of stress.

The **physiological model** is concerned with how our bodies respond to stress. Selye (1956) defines stress as 'the non-specific response of the body to any demands made upon it', and we will be looking at his work in more detail in the next section. This model is concerned with our *reactions* to a **stressor**, i.e. anything which causes stress.

The third model is the **transactional model**. As the name implies, this model sees stress in terms of the interaction between people and their environment. Stress can therefore be defined as an imbalance between a person's perception of the demands a situation makes of them and their estimation of their ability to meet those demands. Note that this model is concerned not with an objective appraisal of the demands a person is faced with, but an individual's *perception* of these demands in relation to their ability to cope with them. This model is therefore concerned with the relationship between external stressors, the physiological stress response and ways of coping with it.

Cox (1975) shows how these elements can be linked:

Figure 3: the transactional model of stress (Cox, 1975)

How arousal affects performance

There are individual differences in what is felt to be stressful, the precise physiological response to stressful situations, and in coping strategies:

▶ Activity 1: stress and individual differences

a What kinds of events do you find particularly stressful?
b How does your body react to this kind of event?
c What coping strategies do you use?
Ask a few other people the same questions and compare their answers with your own. Did everyone give similar answers, or were there differences?

In the next sections, we will look in more detail at the different elements of stress which have been outlined.

❺ Stress can be defined as the physiological state which prepares an organism for action. A **stressor** is something which causes stress.

- A certain amount of stress is beneficial, but most research has focused on the **negative effects** of stress.
- Researchers are interested in the **physiological response** to stress, the **causes** of stress, and **coping strategies** for dealing with stress.

4.3 THE PHYSIOLOGICAL RESPONSE TO STRESS

Selye (1956) proposed that there is a similar pattern of physiological response to stressors, irrespective of the nature of the particular stressor. He came to this conclusion on the basis of studies of rats. They were exposed to extreme cold, fatigue, electric shocks and surgical trauma, and in each case the physiological response was the same, which led him to believe that there was a non-specific reaction of the body to any kind of damage. He called this the **general adaptation syndrome (GAS)**. It is also known as the **pituitary–adrenal stress syndrome**, since the pituitary and adrenal glands are involved in the stress response. Selye described three stages of the stress response: the **alarm reaction**, the **resistance** stage and **exhaustion**.

The **alarm reaction** is concerned with the physiological changes associated with arousal. The first part of this reaction is the **shock phase**, an immediate reaction to a stressor. The person experiences tachycardia (an abnormally rapid heartbeat), and both temperature and blood pressure are lowered. This is followed by the **countershock phase**, as the body marshals defensive forces against the stressor. The mechanisms of the alarm reaction centre on the **autonomic nervous system (ANS)** and the **pituitary gland**.

The ANS regulates many aspects of our functioning over which we do not need to have conscious control, such as breathing and digestion. It controls a number of internal organs – for example, the heart muscle and the gut, and a number of glands, such as the salivary and adrenal glands. It has two branches, the **sympathetic nervous system (SNS)** and the **parasympathetic nervous system (PNS)**, which are generally in balance. When the SNS is dominant, there is a pattern of arousal, associated with situations which demand activity. When the PNS is dominant, there is a pattern of relaxation. It is the SNS which is involved in the alarm reaction. In a situation of possible threat, your body needs to prepare itself for action, so high levels of SNS activity help to cope with the demands of the situation by increasing your heart rate and the blood supply to your muscles.

The main system involved in the stress response is called the **hypothalamic–pituitary–adrenal axis**, and it is highly sensitive to environmental change. We will look briefly at the elements which go to make up this system.

The **hypothalamus** plays a central role in the stress reaction. It is a small structure in the forebrain, just above the pituitary gland, to which it is connected by a structure called the **infundibulum**. Through this connection, it controls the secretion of all the hormones released by the pituitary gland. It controls ANS centres in the brainstem, which in turn control the ANS. It is particularly involved in states of arousal, and for this reason is important in the stress response.

We have two **adrenal glands**, two small glands above the kidneys, each of which is made up of the **adrenal medulla** and the **adrenal cortex**. The **pituitary gland**, a gland at the base of the brain, controls the adrenal cortex. When the adrenal cortex is stimulated by the pituitary hormone **ACTH (adrenocorticotrophic hormone)**, it secretes **corticosteroids** into the bloodstream. Even very mild stimuli, if they are unexpected, can trigger the release of ACTH, and set this process in motion. There are many different corticosteroids, but those relevant to stress are the **glucocorticoids**, e.g. cortisone and hydrocortisone. These substances facilitate the conversion of stored fat and protein into energy. They also suppress the body's **immune system**.

The ANS controls the **adrenal medulla**. When it is stimulated, the adrenal medulla releases two hormones into the bloodstream, **adrenaline** and **noradrenaline**. They increase heart rate, blood pressure and sweat gland activity. They also mobilise fat reserves, in preparation for energy expenditure, so they prolong the effects of SNS arousal.

Activity 2: the stress reaction

Use the words from this list:
ACTH, adrenaline, blood pressure, cortex, corticosteroids, energy, heart rate, hypothalamus, immune, medulla, noradrenaline, pituitary, stressor, sweat gland activity, sympathetic to complete this diagram and show the processes involved in the stress response:

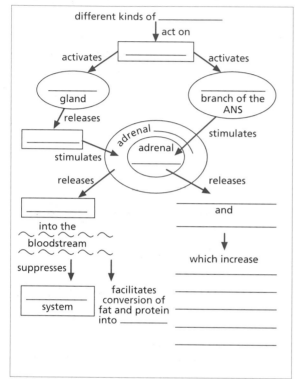

different kinds of _____

act on

_____

activates _____ activates

_____ gland

branch of the ANS

releases

adrenal _____

adrenal

stimulates

stimulates

releases

releases

_____

and _____

into the bloodstream

which increase

suppresses

facilitates conversion of fat and protein into _____

_____ system

The alarm reaction makes the body more alert and active, and prepares it for what Cannon (1929) has termed **fight-or-flight**, i.e. a behavioural response to a stressful situation. This response can be understood in evolutionary terms. At the beginning of our evolutionary history, when a person was under extreme stress – such as being faced by a predator, or having a stranger encroaching on his territory – only two choices were available: to fight off the attack or to run away. The physiological boost provided by SNS activity would facilitate either of these responses. Although we have the same autonomic responses as our distant ancestors, most of the stressful events and situations which we encounter cannot easily be resolved by the physical response of fight or flight, but need to be responded to in a more rational way. The response of the ANS is therefore now maladaptive; there is no outlet for the physical responses caused by stressors, with the result that they can be detrimental to health.

The effects of the alarm reaction include **pupil dilation**, **deeper breathing**, a **faster heartbeat**, and **digestive changes** (where sugar metabolism is speeded up, but not the processing of foods like proteins and fats which take longer to work their way through the digestive system). The spleen releases stored red blood cells.

Activity 3: the alarm reaction and fight-or-flight

If you were exposed to physical threat, how would these elements of the alarm reaction help you to produce a fight-or-flight response?
a pupil dilation
b deeper breathing
c faster heartbeat
d conversion of stored fat and protein
e release of red blood cells
When you have finished, see the notes on page 99.

As well as these changes, additional **blood platelets** are produced. These help clotting, and so prepare the body to repair physical damage. The brain produces neurotransmitters called **endorphins**, which block out the immediate feelings of pain. **Sweating** helps to cool down the body. All these contribute to an effective fight-or-flight response. The physiological response to stress in the alarm reaction can be assessed by measuring the levels of corticosteroids and adrenaline in the urine.

The pattern of physiological activity in the fight-or-flight response cannot be maintained for long, and the body moves into the **resistance stage**. In this stage of the stress response, the body starts to recover from the alarm reaction. There is full adaptation to the stressor, during which symptoms improve or disappear altogether. There is a decrease in the activity of the SNS branch of the ANS, with a lower output of adrenaline and noradrenaline. However, there is an increase in output from the adrenal cortex. Blood sugar levels, which have been raised during the alarm reaction, return to normal. If the stressor is removed, the body reverts to normal functioning, though increased hormone levels persist for some time. However, there is little likelihood of there being any permanent physiological damage.

If the stressor is not removed, the PNS branch of the ANS acts to return the functioning of internal organs, such as the heart, to normal. However, while the body is attempting to defend itself against stressors, it is only partially successful. Cell repair is inhibited, and the immune system may be damaged, increasing the likelihood of infection and a lowered ability to cope with physical damage. If there is a second stressor, resistance is lower, and the final (exhaustion) stage is reached sooner (see figure 4).

Figure 4: the effects of a second stressor

Resistance to stress in the general adaptation syndrome

If the stressor is severe, and experienced over a prolonged period of time, the final stage of **exhaustion** follows. Heart rate and blood pressure return to apparently normal levels, but the excessive levels of adrenaline and noradrenaline in the bloodstream cause the adrenal glands to stop functioning properly. Body tissue and internal organs are damaged. Even mild sources of

additional stress cause an immediate and strong reaction. Symptoms reappear, and if stress continues, death may be the result.

Solomon (1969) found that at this stage resistance to illness is lowered. People have a tendency to fatigue, and feel generally weak and unwell. These effects are linked to the suppression of the immune system, discussed earlier. It is in this stage that what Selye called **diseases of adaptation** occur, such as ulcers and coronary heart disease (CHD). In the long term, the individual will suffer from **burnout**, where they are no longer capable of functioning adequately.

Figure 5: the stages of Selye's GAS

General adaptation syndrome

Selye's model is a useful guide to the physiological response to stressors. However, it was developed as the result of work with non-human animals, so it does not take into account psychological factors in the stress response. For example, people are likely to make a cognitive appraisal of a stressful situation – to what extent is this situation threatening? how able am I to cope? – which will affect their response.

⊖ Selye proposed the **GAS** as a non-specific physiological response to stress of any kind. There are three stages: the **alarm reaction**, the **resistance stage** and the **exhaustion stage**.

⊖ The **alarm reaction** involves the **hypothalamus**, the **pituitary gland** and the **adrenal glands**. It prepares the body for **fight-or-flight**.

⊖ Long term exposure to a stressor leads to **physiological damage**, including a damaged **immune system**. This stage is associated with the development of diseases of **adaptation**. It can lead to **burnout**.

4.4 SOURCES OF STRESS

Three main factors influence whether or not something is experienced as stressful. The first is **predictability**. Stimuli which are either totally unpredictable (such as crashing your car) or totally predictable (such as the noise of a television from next door in the evening) have both been found to be stressful, though most of the time it is unpredictability which is more of a problem.

Something predictable or something unpredictable – both can be stressful.

The second factor is **controllability**. When things are out of our control, we feel more stressed by them. The neighbour's television may upset us, for example, but our own will not. Seligman (1975) showed the effects of lack of control in his work on **learned helplessness**. Rats were given shocks to their feet; there was nothing they could do to avoid being shocked. When they were later put in the same situation, they failed to take action to avoid being shocked, even though escape was possible: they had learned to be helpless. Hiroto and Seligman (1975) carried out a similar experiment with human participants. They were exposed to inescapable loud noise, and were later asked to carry out a task, again accompanied by loud noise. Although the noise was now controllable, the participants failed to control it.

We will be returning to the issues of predictability and control later in the chapter. These factors may be related to the development of stress-related illness, and are also important in stress management.

The final factor is **threat and loss**. These seem to be common to a wide range of stressful events; even pleasant events, such as holidays, can be threatening because we are in a new environment, and life events such as divorce clearly involve loss in many cases.

In all of these areas, it is important to note that it is not important that stimuli are objectively unpredictable, uncontrollable, or threatening, or that loss is likely; what matters is that we perceive them in this way – it is our cognitive appraisal of the situation that is important. We may be totally wrong!

A number of sources of stress have been identified and researched. These include environmental, physiological and psychological factors, and we will look at each of these in turn.

Environmental factors

One major source of environmental stress is **noise**, which can be defined as unwanted sound. Very loud noise will cause physical discomfort, but even fairly quiet noises will cause annoyance if they are not wanted in that situation. The classic example here is the dripping tap, or the buzzing fly which emerges just when you are trying to revise for an examination! Rosen (1970) has shown that noise leads to physiological responses associated with stress. In line with the Yerkes–Dodson law described earlier, it also affects task performance:

Box A: Glass *et al.* (1969)

Procedure: Participants were asked to carry out a simple clerical task in noisy conditions. The GSR (galvanic skin response, which measures the change in electrical resistance of the skin, and is an objective way of measuring arousal) was used as a measure of stress, together with the number of errors made. The researchers also looked at the effects of predictability and controllability.

Results: The GSR showed a stress reaction when work was carried out in noisy conditions. Fewer errors were made when the noise was predictable, and even fewer when it was controllable.

Conclusion: Noise is a source of stress, but predictability and controllability are factors which influence the extent to which it is experienced as stressful.

Stress resulting from noise can also have physical effects. Cohen (1980) found that there was a relationship between prolonged exposure to noise and the incidence of physical illness.

Another environmental factor is **temperature**. Baron and Ransberger (1978), for example, found that the occurrence of riots and civil disturbance in America was related to hot weather. The relationship peaked when temperatures were in the mid-80s, and then dropped off – presumably because it was too hot to make the necessary effort! It should be noted, however, that it is something of an assumption that rioting is necessarily a symptom of stress.

Pollution is also related to stress. Rotton *et al.* (1978) found that there was a correlation between the level of air pollution and mood. People reported feeling less happy when there were high levels of pollution. Again, though, this study rests on the assumption that negative mood can be seen as a straightforward symptom of stress.

Overcrowding can be another source of stress:

Box B: Calhoun (1962)

Procedure: Rats were provided with an environment with abundant food, water and nesting materials, and no predators. The behaviour of the rats was observed as the population of rats grew in size.

Results: Under crowded conditions, the rats were extremely aggressive. Male rats attacked pregnant females and often ate the new-born. Females often abandoned their young. The rats were more likely to become physically ill. Some animals became hyperactive, while some were withdrawn and appeared depressed. The population levelled off at about 150 animals, though the environment could theoretically have supported many more.

Conclusion: Stress induced by overcrowded conditions can lead to pathological behaviour in rats.

Activity 4: a critique of Calhoun's study

What criticisms could be made of this study? Can you think of any positive outcomes it might have had? When you have finished, see the notes on page 99.

Finally, living in an **urban environment** may be stressful. It is likely to contain all the elements we have discussed so far, and there will also be other factors which may lead to stress, such as the **invasion of personal space**.

Physiological factors

Selye (1956) listed several physiological sources of stress. These include infections, trauma, nervous strain, heat, cold, muscular strain and being X-rayed.

One important physiological source of stress is the disruption of circadian rhythms. Many of our physiological functions, such as heart rate, metabolic rate and body temperature, vary across a 24-hour period. They all have maximum values in the late afternoon and minimum values in the early hours of the morning. These patterns of variation are known as **circadian rhythms**. These rhythms persist even when our activity pattern is reversed, for example when we work at night and sleep during the day, and reversal can take some time.

What happens when a circadian rhythm is disrupted can be seen by looking at the effects of jetlag and shift work; in both cases, people have problems in adjusting to changes because they occur so rapidly.

In the case of **jetlag**, modern transport systems are capable of taking us across time zones so quickly that when we arrive at our destination, the local time (the **Zeitgeber**, or external cues which help to regulate circadian rhythms) tells us that the situation is different from that based on the information given by our own biological clock. The result is that we feel tired and disoriented; we are awake when others are asleep and vice-versa, hungry at the wrong times, and so on. It may take up to ten days for our system to adjust; some rhythms (e.g. body temperature) adjust more quickly than others (e.g. ACTH production). There are also individual differences, however, in how easy people find it to adapt; some may never do so completely.

What happens when circadian rhythms are disrupted has also been shown in the effects of **shift work:**

Box C: Blakemore (1988)

Procedure: Workers in a chemical company in Utah were studied. They worked a three-shift system, whereby they would work a day shift for a week, a night shift for the second week and an evening shift for the third week. The cycle would then start again. The effects of lengthening the period between shift changes and rotating the shifts in the opposite direction, in line with the body's preference for a longer rather than a shorter period of wakefulness, were investigated.
Results: As a result of the changes, productivity rose and workers were healthier.
Concusion: The constant shifts in circadian rhythms to which the workers had been forced to adapt had stressful effects in terms of productivity and health.

Similarly, Gold *et al.* (1992) found that nurses on rotating shifts made twice as many errors at work than those on permanent day or night shifts, again suggesting that the disruption of circadian rhythms causes stress, leading – as the Yerkes–Dodson law predicts – to poorer task performance.

⊖ Environmental factors which can lead to stress include **noise**, **temperature**, **pollution**, **overcrowding** and the **urban environment**.
⊖ It is also stressful when **bodily rhythms** have to be adjusted. These effects can be seen in **jetlag** and **shift working**.

Psychological and social factors

One basic psychological source of stress, mentioned earlier, is the **perception of threat**. We may assess a situation to which we are exposed as posing a threat to our physical well being, for example being asked to do something which we think is physically dangerous, or to make more physical effort than we feel capable of making. Similarly, we may feel that our psychological well being is threatened when we are asked to work very long hours, for example, or asked to provide more psychological support for someone with problems than we feel capable of giving.

Another psychological source of stress is **frustration**, which can be defined as: 'a negative emotional state which occurs when we are prevented from reaching a goal'. Frustration can come about through our own inadequacies – for example, wanting to be a ballet dancer but being too tall, or not being able to get to grips with a difficult concept in psychology – or from external factors beyond our control – for example, being late for an appointment because the bus was late, or the weather being stormy when we had planned a walk in the country. Many frustrations are relatively minor everyday events, and we shall return to this idea later in this section.

A further source of stress is **response conflict**. This can take three forms:

Figure 6: conflict and stress

type of conflict	examples
approach–approach conflict: choosing between two attractive options.	deciding between two university courses which both sound interesting.
	choosing which of two invitations for the same evening to accept.
avoidance–avoidance conflict: choosing between two unattractive options.	choosing to go to the dentist or put up with toothache.
approach–avoidance conflict: choices which have both pleasant and unpleasant characteristics.	wanting to go to a party that all your friends are going to, but knowing that someone you want to avoid is also likely to turn up.

Approach–approach

Avoidance–avoidance

Approach–avoidance

In general, approach–approach conflict is the easiest to resolve, and therefore the least likely to cause stress, because there will be some positive outcome whatever choice is made. In contrast, avoidance–avoidance conflict is the most stressful, since the choice made inevitably leads to unpleasant results.

Activity 5: resolving conflict

Identify a current example of a conflict you are facing. This can be an approach–approach, an avoidance–avoidance or an approach–avoidance conflict. Complete the chart below to help you to decide how to resolve it.

Firstly, identify the logical outcome or outcomes of each choice. Then on a scale of 1–5 rate the probability of each outcome occurring (from 0 = won't occur to 5 = certain to occur). Now rate the importance to you of each consequence, from 0 = not at all important to 5 = extremely important.

You may find it helpful to multiply the probability and significance ratings for each outcome, and compare the results for each alternative.

Another psychological approach to stress has been to look at the effect of **life changes**. Holmes and Rahe (1967) developed the **social readjustment rating scale (SRRS)** which linked life events to stress and illness. This scale ranked 43 events in terms of their stressfulness, using a numerical scale up to 100. The scale was developed using patients' records to identify events in patients' lives in the months before they became ill. One hundred independent people were then asked to think about each event and to rate it in terms of how much change it would bring about in a person's life. Figure 7 shows some of the events identified, together with the **LCUs (life change units)** of each.

type of conflict			
alternatives	logical outcome	probability	significance

Figure 7: sample items from the SRRS (from Holmes and Rahe, 1967)

life event	LCU
death of a spouse	100
divorce	73
marital separation	65
death of a close family member	63
gaol sentence	63
marriage	50
fired from work	47
marital reconciliation	45
gain of new family member	39
sex difficulties	39
change in financial state	38
change in number of arguments with spouse	35
son or daughter leaves home	29
outstanding personal achievement	28
trouble with the boss	23
change in residence	20
change in social activities	18
holiday	13
Christmas	12

Holmes and Rahe claimed that a score of 300+ LCUs in the preceding year were associated with a range of serious health problems, e.g. diabetes, heart disease, stroke and leukaemia, as well as less serious everyday problems such as headaches and stomach upsets. Rahe and Arthur (1977) found that people with high LCU scores were more likely to develop physical and psychological illnesses, more susceptible to sports injuries and more likely to have traffic accidents.

▷ Activity 6: evaluating the SRRS

1 Bearing in mind that some of the life events here are pleasant, e.g. 'holiday' and 'marital reconciliation', what is it about a life event which leads to stress and increases vulnerability to illness?

2 Holmes and Rahe were suggesting that life experiences may lead to illness. Since the relationship they found was correlational, what alternative causal relationship would be possible? Use items from the list to illustrate this explanation.

3 How might individual differences between people having these life experiences make the relationship Holmes and Rahe were suggesting a complex one?

4 The SRRS looks at stressors in terms of single events. Why might this be a limited way of identifying sources of stress?

Compare your ideas with the discussion which follows.

You will have noticed that the crucial factor is not that the events are necessarily unpleasant (getting married or going on holiday are likely to be seen in quite a positive light), but the extent to which they bring change into our lives, to which we have to adapt.

Since the relationship Holmes and Rahe found was correlational, a cause-and-effect relationship such as they propose cannot be assumed. In some instances quite a good case could be made out for illness causing life events, rather than vice versa. For example, it might well be that stress and the early stages of illness could themselves cause such events as 'sex difficulties', or 'change in number of arguments with spouse'. Similarly, it is possible that illness could lead to inattention to work, which in turn would lead to mistakes being made and so 'trouble with the boss'.

Individual differences also mean that the pattern may be rather more complex than Holmes and Rahe suggest. Christmas, for example, can be very stressful for some people; if you are very short of money and have several children expecting expensive presents, for example, or if you have in-laws coming to stay who you don't get on with. But for others it could just be a few days away from work and not really anything very special. Even the most stressful event – 'death of spouse' – could vary in terms of the stress involved, depending on one's religious beliefs, whether the person died suddenly or at the end of a long and painful illness, and so on. In many cases, then, it is something of a generalisation to give overall numerical values to life events.

The detailed nature of these events, then, and how they are perceived by the individual are important. Lazarus and Folkman (1984) carried out many studies to look at these effects, and found that the central factor in the effects of life events was cognitive appraisal, or how we perceive and manage such events. This idea has also been linked to ways of coping with stressful events, and we will be looking at this later in the chapter.

A further problem is that the SRRS focuses very much on crisis events, which by definition don't happen very often. It does not take into account the gradual effects on the individual of, say, being in a job you don't like month after month, or the long-term care of a family member. Under these circumstances, people could become stressed who have not recently experienced any of the stressors on the SRRS.

Kanner *et al.* (1981) suggested that it may be not so much the impact of major events which leads to stress but the more minor everyday stressors which we all experience. To test this idea, they designed a **hassles and uplifts** scale, consisting of relatively minor experiences which have a negative or positive effect. The scale consisted of 117 hassle items, such as 'misplacing or losing things' and 'worries about weight' and 135 uplift items, such as 'feeling healthy' and 'relating well with spouse/lover':

Box D: Kanner *et al.* (1981)

Procedure: One hundred men and women aged 45–64 were studied over 12 months. The relationship between hassles and uplifts and psychological symptoms, both positive and negative, was investigated.
Results: Hassles were positively correlated with psychological symptoms associated with stress. There was a negative correlation between stress symptoms and uplifts. Hassles were a better predictor of stress symptoms than the SRRS.
Conclusion: Everyday stressors are a better predictor of stress (and therefore vulnerability to illness) than life events.

Activity 7: testing hassles and uplifts

Create your own hassles and uplifts scale. If you are working with other people, brainstorm possible items which could be included.
Set the scale out so that participants have a choice of responses, e.g:

I worry about my weight
often   sometimes   rarely   never

Work out a scoring system so that hassles score high (e.g. 3 for 'often', 2 for 'sometimes', 1 for 'rarely' and 0 for 'never'), with the scores reversed for uplift items.
Find participants who are willing to complete your scale (they should not know what the scoring system is). You will need to work out standardised instructions. Ask them also to rate how stressed in general they feel themselves to be on a scale of 0 – 10, where 0 = completely stress free and 10 = extremely stressed. Don't forget to thank them for taking part in your study and to debrief them when it is complete.
Draw a scattergram (see chapter 7) to show the relationship between the scores for the hassles and uplifts scale and the stress ratings. Do your findings support the idea of Kanner *et al*?

Work is also an important source of stress. Cox *et al.* (1981) asked a sample of people what they perceived to be the major source of stress in their lives. Fifty-four per cent identified work, while for a further 12% it was trying to balance the demands of work and home. Work seems to be an important source of stress, then, but what are the factors which may make it so?

One common source of stress at work is quantitative; people feel that they are overloaded and have too much to do, or are required to work too fast. Overload can also be qualitative, when people find their work too difficult or to require too much concentration. For example, Spector (1987) found that people who reported heavy workloads also experienced high levels of anxiety and frustration.

However, French *et al.* (1982) found that work underload can also be stressful. When people feel they do not have enough to do, or that their skills and abilities are not being fully used, they can become bored and frustrated.

A further source of stress in the workplace relates to **roles**. While the idea of roles is usually associated with the acting profession, we also adopt roles every day, including in the workplace, in the sense that at work we are expected to act in particular ways.

▷ Activity 8: work roles

What does the role of a teacher involve? Make a list of the kinds of behaviours which are associated with being a teacher.

When you have finished, see the notes on page 99.

The ways in which others expect a role occupant to behave are known as **role expectations**. However, there may be an element of **role ambiguity**, when an employee is not clear as to his or her precise role within the organisation. A person may be unclear as to their aims and objectives, and the expectations others have of them. They may also be unsure about the scope and responsibility of their job. Spector *et al*.

(1988) found an association between role ambiguity and frustration and anxiety.

A further source of stress in the context of work is **role strain**, also known as role stress, which refers in general to any situation in which a person has difficulty in meeting a role expectation. In many cases, role strain results from **role conflict**, where there is difficulty as a result of conflicting role expectations.

Nine possible sources of role strain are shown in figure 8 below.

▷ Activity 9: identifying role strain

Listed below are nine examples of possible role strain at work. Can you match each of them with one of the nine sources of role strain in figure 8 which they might be likely to experience?

a a working mother, with sick children at home

b a general labourer

c a sales person in a shop selling fur coats

d a shy office clerk asked to take over a receptionist's duties

e a vet asked to put down a healthy animal

f a poorly-paid worker in a nuclear power plant

Figure 8: sources of role strain

source	example
1. role ambiguity	the job description may be unclear
2. intra-role conflict (conflict within a role)	librarians are expected both to lend books out and to keep them safe
3. inter-role conflict (conflict between different roles)	a doctor treats members of his own family
4. costs of fulfilling the role outweigh the rewards	a worker is poorly paid for a job which involves exposure to radiation
5. personality, self-concept or attitudes are incompatible with the role	a vegetarian is working in a meat packing factory
6. cultural ideology conflicts with role expectations	a man works as a lumberjack in a society where environmentalists are concerned with preventing the logging of forests
7. role overload (the job is demanding more than the individual can possibly do)	a doctor works in a war zone
8. role underload (the job is felt not to be demanding enough)	an overqualified new member of staff
9. the perceived role differs from the expected role	an office cleaner who thinks that she has to tidy everyone's desk as well

g a college graduate who takes a job stacking supermarket shelves

h a bricklayer who is proud of how quickly he can work, but is told that he must concentrate on making neater joints

i a salesman whose territory has been doubled in size in the last year

When you have finished, see notes on page 99.

Role strain can lead to severe problems at work, as a result of the stress it causes. In a study of the American restaurant industry, Whyte (1948) found that waitresses were under a lot of strain (and were frequently reduced to tears) because they were caught between the customers on the one hand, who wanted their food quickly, and the chefs on the other, who felt they needed time to produce the food properly.

▶ Activity 10: dealing with role strain

Make a list of ways which could help to deal with the role strain Whyte's waitresses were experiencing. When you have completed your list, see the notes on page 99 and compare your ideas with the suggestions put forward by Hall and Savery in figure 9.

Hall and Savery (1986) have put forward some suggestions for ways of reducing the effects of role strain. These are shown in figure 9.

The extent to which work may be stressful depends in part on the nature of the work, since some occupations seem to be more stressful than others. A study by Wolfgang (1988), using self-report questionnaires, found the highest levels of stress to be among nurses. People in positions of middle management are also particularly liable to suffer from stress, which Ivancevich *et al.* (1982) related to work overload and role conflict.

- Psychological causes of stress include the **perception of threat**, **frustration** and **conflict**.
- Holmes and Rahe used the **SRRS** to show that major **life events** are associated with vulnerability to illness. This idea has been criticised since the research is **correlational**. In some cases, any causal connection could be in the opposite direction to that suggested. Individuals' **perceptions** of these events are likely to be a factor. The theory cannot account for stress symptoms in people who have not experienced any of these events.
- The hassles of daily life may be a better predictor of stress than major life events. This idea has been supported by research using the **hassles and uplifts** scale.
- **Work** can be a major source of stress. Both **overload** and **underload** can be stressful. **Role ambiguity** and **role strain**, particularly where there is **role conflict**, are associated with stress. The extent to which workers are vulnerable to stress is related to the nature of their occupation.

Figure 9: reducing role strain (Hall and Savery, 1986)

1. restructure the organisation to clarify roles, and priorities within roles, and to improve communications
2. select staff who are carefully matched to roles in terms of their abilities, personality, motivation and interests
3. make role expectations clearer, e.g. by providing a detailed job description
4. devise carefully planned, progressive programmes for staff induction, training and development
5. change to a more participative management style, so that workers have more say in what goes on
6. improve relationships between and within groups
7. screen staff for signs of stress
8. give staff advance warning of any changes, especially if these changes mean that there will be extra demands on them

4.5 PERSONALITY DIFFERENCES AND STRESS

It has been suggested that personality differences affect stress levels. Friedman and Rosenman (1974) believed that people could be divided into Type A and Type B, each type showing different behaviour patterns. Before reading on, try this test to find out which type you are:

◑ Activity 11: Type A or Type B personality?

Work through the following statements, each time circling the box which you feel most applies to you. Do not think too long about the statements – it is usually best to give your immediate response. If possible, try to avoid the 'cannot say' option.

1 I never seem to have enough time to finish everything I need to do.

   disagree   cannot say   agree

2 It doesn't really bother me if I have to wait in a queue.

   disagree   cannot say   agree

3 When I play games, I play to win. I get angry with myself when I lose.

   disagree   cannot say   agree

4 My life would be much easier if other people did their job properly.

   disagree   cannot say   agree

5 I find it helps to confide in someone when I have problems.

   disagree   cannot say   agree

6 It is important to me to be best at everything I do.

   disagree   cannot say   agree

7 I enjoy just sitting and watching the world go by.

   disagree   cannot say   agree

8 At the end of a meal, I like to sit and chat for a while.

   disagree   cannot say   agree

9 I usually try to do only one thing at a time.

   disagree   cannot say   agree

10 I tend to fidget when I am just sitting and listening to somebody.

   disagree   cannot say   agree

11 I don't really mind if I don't finish what I had planned for the day.

   disagree   cannot say   agree

12 I function best under pressure.

   disagree   cannot say   agree

When you have finished, see the notes on page 99.

People with a **Type A** personality are extremely competitive, and are highly motivated to achieve. They are restless, more than usually alert, and continually feel that they do not have enough time to fit in everything they need to do. They can't bear to wait their turn, have to do several things at once, and need to be admired by peers to sustain their self-esteem. They are hostile, cynical, angry and speak vigorously.

People with a **Type B** personality, on the other hand, may be equally ambitious, but this does not dominate their whole lives. They make time in their lives for family and friends, and their leisure pursuits tend to be less competitive than those chosen by Type A personalities.

It has been suggested that people with Type A personality are more likely to suffer from high blood pressure and CHD than people who do not have these characteristics, and we will be looking at this link more closely in the next section.

A further link between stress and personality has been suggested by Kobasa's concept of the **hardy personality**. Some people appear to cope very well with stressful situations, while others break down under very little pressure. Kobasa (1979) carried out a study to investigate the role of personality in these differences (box E).

Since this was a correlational study, it has been criticised on the grounds that the personality characteristics Kobasa identified could be the result rather than the cause of illness. For example, it would be difficult for a person to become involved in work and social life if they were ill. However, this criticism was countered by the findings of a longitudinal study (Kobasa *et al.*, 1982), which monitored executives over a two-year period. This study found that those who had a more positive attitude were less likely to become ill.

Box E: Kobasa (1979)

Procedure: Six hundred executives and managers were asked to complete two questionnaires, a personality questionnaire and one listing the illnesses and stressful events which they had experienced in the previous three years.

Results: The responses could be put into two groups, those who had scored above average and below average on illnesses. For both groups, the scores for stressful events were high. However, in contrast to the high stress/high illness group, the high stress/low illness group were likely to:

- feel more in control of their lives.
- have a sense of commitment and purpose in their work and social lives.
- welcome change as a challenge.

Conclusion: A person with these personality characteristics can be described as a 'hardy' personality, i.e. one who is better able to cope with stress.

Kobasa's concept of the hardy personality raises the question: to what extent is it possible to develop the kinds of characteristics which she identified as important in combating stress? Her participants had the kinds of work which would provide challenge and change, and which was stimulating enough to encourage commitment. Her conclusions might not apply so easily to someone in a monotonous and routine job, or one leaving them too tired to make a commitment to outside interests.

- ⊖ A link between **Type A** personality and stress-related illness has been suggested.
- ⊖ People with a **hardy personality** are better able to cope with stressful experiences.

4.6 STRESS AND ILLNESS

Selye's GAS, discussed earlier, predicts that the experience of stress, particularly if it is prolonged, has long-term effects on physiological functioning. This includes damage to the immune system, leading to an increased probability of illness. Before looking at evidence for the link between stress and illness, we need to look briefly at how the immune system works.

The immune system

When **antigens** (dangerous foreign bodies such as bacteria or viruses) are detected, the immune system stimulates **leucocytes** (white blood cells) to destroy them. It also produces **antibodies** which bind to antigens, and identify them as targets to be destroyed. Antibodies remain in the bloodstream and continue to be effective if the same antigens are later present again.

The immune system also plays a role in **inflammation**. If you cut yourself, the blood vessels first of all contract to stop the bleeding. They then dilate, so more blood can flow to the damaged area. The blood carries leucocytes to combat any foreign bodies which might gain access through the wound. It follows that if the immune system is damaged, we become more vulnerable to the effects of foreign bodies, such as infection.

The persistent secretion of steroids (described in the GAS) interferes with the production of antibodies. Inflammation is therefore decreased, reducing the activity of leucocytes. As well as affecting the response to infection, it also seems to be the case that stress impairs the healing process. Sweeney (1995) found that for people who were highly stressed as the result of looking after relatives with dementia, a small cut took significantly longer to heal than for a non-stressed control group.

Animal research

The link between stress and illness has been investigated in animal studies, one of the most famous of which is called 'Ulcers in executive monkeys' (see box F over the page).

Box F: Brady (1958)

Procedure: Pairs of monkeys were linked up to an apparatus which gave electric shocks. Shocks were delivered over a period of 6 hours at 20-second intervals, continuing over several weeks. One monkey of the pair (the **executive**) could prevent shock to both monkeys by pressing a lever; the other (**yoked**) monkey also had a lever, but pressing it did not stop the shock.

Results: The executive monkeys developed ulcers, while the yoked monkeys did not.

Conclusion: The executive monkeys had to remain constantly vigilant to avoid being shocked, while their partners could do nothing to influence the situation. Constant vigilance is highly stressful, and this stress led to physical ill-effects.

While this study seems to support the link between stress and physical illness predicted by the GAS model, there have been some criticisms of it. Seligman *et al.* (1971) pointed out that the monkeys had not been randomly allocated to the executive and yoked conditions. The animals had to learn that pressing the lever was the required response to avoid shock; those who were able to learn this became executives, while the others were in the yoked condition. There were therefore individual differences between the monkeys in the two conditions, which may have had a part to play in the outcome.

Brady's study was later repeated in rather better controlled studies using rats:

Box G: Weiss (1972)

Experiment 1:
Procedure: A yoked design similar to that of Brady was used, with rats as participants. Shocks were delivered through tail electrodes so that the rats could not avoid shocks by adopting particular postures. Rats took part as triplets:

rat 1 – had control; could avoid shock by pressing a lever.

rat 2 – yoked to rat 1, no control; received shock when rat 1 failed to avoid shock.

rat 3 – control rats; put into apparatus but received no shock.

Results: The amount of ulceration was most for rat 1, less for rat 2 and least for rat 3.

Conclusion: The psychological factor of lack of **control** can affect ulceration.

Experiment 2:
Procedure: A similar method was used:

rat 1 – received a shock preceded by a warning signal, but avoiding the shock was not possible.

rat 2 – received the same shocks but with no warning.

rat 3 – a control who received no shocks.

Results: The amount of ulceration was most for rat 1, less for rat 2 and least for rat 3.

Conclusion: The effect of the shocks was related to **predictability**.

A link can be made between this study by Weiss and the relationship between stress, predictability and control at the start of the section on sources of stress; stress is more likely to be experienced where the stressor is either predictable, or highly unpredictable, and there is no control.

Using data from these studies, Weiss found that **response rate** affected ulceration. Those rats who produced a lot of responses suffered worse ulceration than those who made few responses. By pairing data from high-responding rats with control and yoked rats making few responses, he found the same effect as Brady had shown.

- The effect of stress on the **immune system** suggests that there should be a link between stress and **vulnerability to illness**.
- Stress leads to ulceration in monkeys, supporting a link between stress and **physical illness**.
- Similar studies using rats have demonstrated a link between **control**, **predictability** and stress.

Stress and illness in humans

A link between stress and illness in humans has also been investigated. Since stress affects the functioning of the immune system, people are more likely to catch colds after a stressful experience, because the body has a lowered resistance to cold viruses:

Box H: Cohen *et al.* (1991)

Procedure: Healthy volunteers were injected either with a common cold virus or a harmless salt solution. They were also given a stress index, based on the number of stressful events they had experienced in the past year, the extent to which they felt able to cope, and the incidence of negative feelings such as anger and depression.

Results: Almost all of those injected with the cold virus showed signs of infection, but only about a third developed colds. Even when other factors were taken into account (i.e. age, exercise, diet, use of nicotine and alcohol), there was a positive relationship between the stress index and cold symptoms (see figure 10).

Conclusion: There is a positive relationship between stress and vulnerability to infection.

Figure 10: Cohen *et al.* (1991)

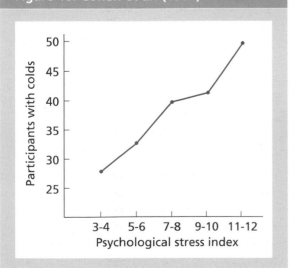

It has been suggested that stress is linked with headaches and asthma. It has also been related to more serious illnesses – cancer, CHD and hypertension – and we will look now at research in these areas.

Cancer

Since stress depresses the immune system, it reduces the body's ability to fight off attacks in the form of infections and viruses. A weakened immune system may also lower resistance to cancer cells.

Cancer occurs when a body cell begins to replicate out of control, so that there are many more of this type of cell than there should be. These cells then begin to invade areas of healthy cells, and unless they are destroyed or removed, they eventually cause damage to tissues and organs, and ultimately death. Cancers appear to be caused by an interaction between a hereditary predisposition, environmental factors such as cigarette smoke or asbestos fibres, and changes in the body's immune system.

Whenever cancer cells start to multiply, the immune system acts to check their uncontrolled growth. In a normal healthy person, the immune system manages to keep cancer cells in check. However, if the immune system has been weakened by exposure to stress, cancer is more likely to develop.

This has been demonstrated in animal research. Visintainer *et al.* (1983) injected animals with cancer cells and then exposed them to an uncontrollable stressor. The cancer cells developed more rapidly in animals who had been stressed than in controls.

The link between stress and cancer in people has also been investigated:

Box I: Jacobs and Charles (1980)

Procedure: Cancer patients were asked about stress in their lives before cancer was diagnosed.

Results: Patients often reported higher than normal levels of stress at this time.

Conclusion: The experience of stress may be linked to the development of cancer.

Activity 12: stress and cancer

Read through the study in box I. Why might it be unwise to draw the conclusion from these findings that stress leads to cancer?

You will need to think about the possible ways in which the link established by Jacobs and Charles could be interpreted, and the method used in collecting the data.

When you have finished, see the notes on page 99.

Coronary heart disease

CHD results from **atherosclerosis**, a thickening of the walls of the coronary arteries which reduces or blocks the blood supply to the heart. There are several risk factors which affect the probability of a person developing CHD, including smoking, heavy drinking, obesity, poor diet and lack of exercise.

In the late 1950s, two cardiologists, Friedman and Rosenman, found that men were far more likely than women to develop CHD, although there were no real gender differences in such factors as diet. It was therefore clear that some other factor was also implicated. Since at this time most men worked, while most women did not, they suggested that work-related stress could also be a contributory factor. They investigated this possibility in a classic study, where stress was defined in terms of the behaviour shown by those with **Type A** personality traits:

Box J: Rosenman *et al.* (1975)

Procedure: A longitudinal study in the USA, starting in 1960, followed 3000 men, aged 39–59, for a period of $8\frac{1}{2}$ years. All were healthy at the start of the study. Participants fell into two approximately equal groups classified as Type A or Type B.

Results: Of the 257 men who died in the course of the study, 70% were Type A. Men who were Type A were almost two and a half times as likely to develop CHD than those who were Type B. Even when risk factors for CHD (like smoking and heart disease in the family) were taken into account, they were still twice as likely to develop the illness.

Conclusion: Type A individuals are significantly more likely to develop stress-related illness than Type B.

These findings have been replicated in a number of countries, including England, Canada, Belgium, Sweden and New Zealand. Some studies, however, have not found such a strong relationship (e.g. Mathews, 1984). Ragland and Brand (1988) found that there was no difference between Type A and Type B men in the likelihood of developing CHD, and their findings gave some indication that Type A men might actually be at less risk.

So how can we make sense of these contradictory findings? It is possible that not all the personality characteristics associated with Type A contribute to the link with heart disease. Dembroski and Costa (1988) suggest that the key factors are hostility, anger and vigorous speech. Williams (1984) found that Type A people with a cynical, hostile outlook on life have an increased risk of heart disease, while Type A people with a positive outlook actually have a lowered risk.

So how does stress contribute to heart disease? You will remember that the fight-or-flight response releases noradrenaline and cortisol into the bloodstream, with the result that heart rate is increased and stores of fat are released to give muscles a quickly available source of energy. If some physical action is taken, this fat is used as energy, but if not, the fat may be deposited on the walls of blood vessels. These fatty deposits then create the blockages which restrict the blood supply to the heart, leading to CHD.

Hypertension

Hypertension is a state of chronically high blood pressure. In a small percentage of cases, there is a physical cause, such as kidney disease, but in the vast majority of cases, there is no medical cause. Hypertension, which carries an increased risk of stroke and can lead to CHD, has also been linked to stress:

Box K: Harburg *et al.* (1973)

Procedure: Participants living in Detroit were divided into 'high stress' and 'low stress' groups on the basis of the area of the city in which they lived. 'High stress' areas were defined as those with a high crime rate, high population density and high poverty.

Results: Those in the 'high stress' group were more likely to suffer from hypertension than those in the 'low stress' group.

Conclusion: There is some evidence of a link between environmental stress and hypertension.

Care must be taken in interpreting this kind of evidence, of course, since many factors in this kind of study cannot be controlled. At the same time, these findings do offer some indication that stress may be a factor in the development of hypertension.

There is also a lot of evidence (e.g. Goldstein, 1981) that people with high blood pressure tend to react to stressful situations with a more exaggerated and prolonged increase in blood pressure.

- A link has been established between stress and a vulnerability to **viral infection**. There is also a link with **headaches** and **asthma**.
- Damage to the immune system caused by stress reduces the ability of the body to destroy cancerous cells. Being highly stressed is one factor which may therefore make a person more likely to develop **cancer**.
- There is also a relationship between stress and **CHD**. This has sometimes been shown using **Type A** personality characteristics as an indicator of stress. However, it may be that only certain aspects of the Type A personality are linked with heart disease.
- **Hypertension** may also be caused by stress.

4.7 CRITICAL ISSUE: STRESS MANAGEMENT

As we have seen, stress is not only psychologically damaging but is also associated with a risk of developing illnesses such as cancer and CHD. It is therefore important to think about ways in which stress can be handled and reduced. We will look in this section at some of the ideas which have been put forward: biological and behavioural treatments, cognitive and psychodynamic approaches, together with the importance of social support and reducing stressors.

Biological approaches

Stress is often experienced as **anxiety**. **Anxiolytic drugs**, also known as **minor tranquillisers**, are frequently used to help people with anxiety disorders. Until recently, barbiturates were used, but their use has now been largely discontinued. This is because they are extremely dangerous in overdose, are highly addictive, and there are often unwanted interactions with other medicines a patient may be taking.

The most common drugs in current use are the **benzodiazepines**, for example **diazepam**, e.g. Librium or Valium. These drugs regulate the neurotransmitter **GABA** (see chapter 1 for more information on neurotransmitters). Diazepam is prescribed for short-term use (no longer than 2–4 weeks is recommended) where anxiety is severe and disabling, and the patient is suffering extreme distress.

One of the problems with these (or any) drugs is possible side effects. Possible side effects of diazepam include drowsiness, confusion, amnesia, headache, low blood pressure and occasionally apnoea (i.e. the patient stops breathing). Diazepam is also addictive, leading to psychological and physical dependence, so withdrawal has to be gradual.

An alternative anxiolytic drug is **buspirone**, which acts on **serotonin** receptors. While buspirone also has possible side effects, it does not lead to dependency, so withdrawal is not a problem. **Beta blockers** may also be used. They treat the physical symptoms of stress, reducing ANS symptoms such as palpitations and tremor. The reduction of physical symptoms may in turn lead to an improvement in the psychological symptoms of anxiety.

A major criticism of the use of drugs to reduce anxiety is that they do not deal with possible environmental factors contributing to the problem – such as having several young children or an elderly relative to look after, or having serious money worries – but only the physical symptoms. They may best be seen as short-term ways of dealing with stress, and may need to be used in combination with other therapies, such as counselling, if the problem is to be dealt with more radically.

Sometimes **alcohol** is used to reduce stress. It has a sedative effect, slows down neural function and loosens inhibitions. The same criticisms which can be made of other drugs, however, also apply to alcohol. Additionally, there is a positive relationship between alcohol consumption and stroke, so the use of alcohol to reduce stress can be counter-productive.

Behavioural approaches

Biofeedback is a behavioural approach to dealing with stress symptoms, using the principles of **operant conditioning**, outlined in chapter 1. The principle of biofeedback is simple: people's physiological functions, such as heart rate and blood pressure, are monitored and then this information is made known to them. They are trained in methods – usually involving relaxation – to bring these biological processes under voluntary control. Feedback can be visual (e.g. by a changing line on a TV screen) or auditory (e.g. a tone which changes in pitch). It requires specialist equipment, but this is relatively cheap and readily available. Erbeck *et al.* (1983) found that people could lower their blood pressure using biofeedback.

One problem with this method, however, is that some people find the necessary control quite difficult to acquire. Very often it may take many months for appropriate techniques to be acquired and beneficial effects to be seen. For these reasons, alternative ways of changing these functions could

A biofeedback machine

be preferable, for example meditation, in which relaxation plays an important part.

The principle behind **meditation** is the focusing of consciousness, using rituals and exercises designed to empty the mind. The process includes physical exercises – such as regulating breathing and practising yoga positions – and mental exercises – such as focusing on a symbol or chant which is repeated over and over again. The result is a mild change in consciousness, in which the individual feels in a pleasant state of physical and mental relaxation. With practice, this may lead to mystical experiences in which there is a loss of awareness of individual identity, and a feeling of being at one with a wider consciousness.

▶ Activity 13: meditation

Try this exercise, using meditation techniques:
a Sit quietly in a comfortable position with your eyes closed.
b Deeply relax all your muscles. Start with your feet, and work your way up to your face. Keep your muscles relaxed.
c Breathe through your nose and concentrate on your breathing. As you breathe out, silently say the word 'one' to yourself.
d Continue this exercise for 20 minutes. (You can open your eyes to check the time but do not use an alarm).
e When the 20 minutes are up, sit quietly for a few minutes, first with your eyes closed and then with them open.
Did you feel relaxed, both physically and mentally, after this exercise?

As well as psychological effects, you may also have noticed physiological changes. The feeling of relaxation leads to a decrease in arousal. The parasympathetic branch of the ANS comes into action, leading to a reduced breathing rate, reduced oxygen consumption, a slower heart rate and lower blood pressure. There may also be release of endorphins, the body's natural pain-killers, leading to reduced sensitivity to pain.

Cases have been reported of people who have been able to control their metabolic processes to an incredible extent through meditation. In 1970, for example, Ramanand Yogi survived for over 5 hours in a sealed box, using only half the amount of oxygen which would normally be necessary to stay alive.

Meditation has been found to help in reducing anxiety, and has been used in sport psychology to help with relaxation and stress reduction (e.g. Syer and Connolly, 1988).

A broader approach involves encouraging the person to use appropriate behaviours to combat the effects of stress. One example is **exercise**. For example, Blumenthal *et al.* (1987) found that people who exercised were less likely to experience anxiety, depression and tension than those who did not.

Physiological changes during stress prepare the person for action, so exercise is an appropriate response to these changes; it uses up the blood sugars released by the hormones secreted into the bloodstream during stress. It also helps to work out tension that has built up in the muscles, and increases strength, flexibility and stamina, so making the person more able to combat future stressors. Aerobic exercise, such as brisk walking or swimming, also improves the efficiency of the cardiovascular system. Exercise also has the advantage of removing the person, albeit temporarily, from the situation which is causing stress.

Behavioural methods have also been used effectively to modify **Type A** behaviour. There have been two basic approaches here.

The aim of the **shotgun approach** is to change all the behaviours associated with the Type A personality. Friedman *et al.* (1986) in their Recurrent Coronary Prevention Program used a combination of behavioural methods, including advice on changing behaviour in terms of diet and exercise, and encouraging people to carry out behaviours which are incompatible with their personalities. They were asked, for example, to listen to people without interrupting, or deliberately to stand in the longest queue at the supermarket.

The **target behaviour approach** focuses only on those Type A behaviours which are likely to lead to heart disease. You will remember from the section on heart disease that Williams (1984) suggested that cynicism and hostility were the crucial factors.

It is argued that if behaviours associated with these characteristics can be modified, the risk of heart disease will be lowered.

While these are good ways of coping with stress, they still largely only deal with symptoms rather than causes. Behavioural programmes can also help to combat the underlying problem, however, e.g. help with time-management planning if a person feels overwhelmed by the demands made on them.

Social situations, e.g. meeting new people, taking part in meetings, and so on, can be experienced as very stressful. Cohen and Williamson (1991) found that people lacking the necessary social skills to deal with these kinds of situation were more likely to become ill. Stress can therefore be reduced if people learn to develop the necessary social skills through observation and role-play practice, before using them in real-life social situations.

- Stress can be treated in the short term with **drugs**. There may be problems with **side effects**, and they do not deal with environmental factors contributing to stress.
- **Biofeedback** can be used to control physiological stress responses. **Meditation** and **exercise** can also be effective.
- Behavioural methods have been used to modify the behaviour of those with a **Type A personality**, and to help people acquire relevant **social skills**.

Cognitive approaches

It has been suggested that people adapt best to stressful events by changing the way they think about them, and consciously taking control of their situation.

Activity 14: the perception of stressful events

Do a small survey among your friends to find out what they think are the five or six most stressful things that have happened to them in the last few months.

Where there are events in common, ask your friends how they coped with these events. Did people who found them less stressful perceive them differently, or use different coping strategies? Think of a current stressor in your life. Can you think about it differently, in ways which may make it less stressful?

As we saw earlier, one factor which affects the extent to which stress is experienced is **control**. The **locus of control** theory put forward by Rotter (1966) is relevant here. 'Locus' means 'place', and the theory makes a distinction between people who have an **internal** locus of control, believing that they have some control over life events, and those who have an **external** locus of control, who feel that they are controlled by external forces and have little control themselves.

People with either an internal or an external locus of control can suffer from stress; people with an internal locus of control are likely to blame themselves when things go wrong, while people with an external locus of control may feel helpless in the face of what life throws at them. However, Johnson and Sarason (1978) found that people with an external locus of control were more likely to experience stress. Similarly, experiences over which we feel we have some control are usually less stressful than those over which we feel we have none. This idea has been used to help people cope with anxiety.

When I visit my dentist, he always tells me to raise my hand at any time if I want him to stop what he is doing. Visiting the dentist is now much less of a problem for me than it used to be. Brown (1986) discusses several studies using this system in a simulated dental surgery. The effect of the control this gives patients is usually less anxiety, and sometimes an increased tolerance for pain. It is perhaps worth noting that these findings contradict those of Brady (box F); this contradiction is best explained by the constant vigilance over long periods required of Brady's monkeys if they were to avoid shocks.

One form of control is **information control**. Explaining to people undergoing a medical procedure what is going to happen and why is a good example of an effective way of reducing anxiety and stress.

The role of this kind of control has been shown in research:

> ### Box L: Bourne (1971)
>
> **Procedure:** Levels of stress hormones in US soldiers in Vietnam were tested before, during and after a Viet Cong attack.
>
> **Results:** On the day when ordinary soldiers were preparing for the attack, their levels of stress hormones dropped; levels rose in the officers and radio operators.
>
> **Conclusion:** The training the soldiers had received provided them with mechanisms which they could use in dangerous situations. Many of them believed that what they had been taught would protect them from harm. The preparations they made before an attack – e.g. checking weapons and filling sandbags – gave them a sense of control over the situation. The officers and radio operators did not have this protective routine.

Another study looked at this kind of control in a medical context:

> ### Box M: Janis (1971)
>
> **Procedure:** The relationship between pre-operative characteristics of patients waiting for abdominal surgery and their post-operative adjustment was investigated.
>
> **Results:** Compared with patients with high or low levels of pre-operative fear, those with a moderate level of fear were more likely to ask for realistic information before the operation took place, and were the least likely to show emotional disturbance after the operation.
>
> **Conclusion:** Information control can be beneficial to adjustment after an operation.

This study is interesting in finding that people with low levels of pre-operative fear were likely to experience more emotional disturbance than those with moderate levels. It is possible that very low-fear people were using ego defence strategies, such as denial, in the pre-operative situation, and did not ask for information about the operation for this reason. They were therefore not well equipped to cope with the effects of the operation.

Another kind of control is **cognitive control**. This involves encouraging people to think in different ways about an experience which they find stressful. These two kinds of control have been compared:

Box N: Langer *et al.* (1975)

Procedure: Participants were patients waiting for elective surgery, i.e. non-emergency surgery such as hysterectomies and hernia repairs. The 'cognitive control' group were asked to focus their attention on the positive aspects of their surgery, such as avoiding daily hassles, and the positive changes it would bring to their lives, and to avoid thinking about the negative aspects. The 'information control' group were told what was going to be done and how they would feel afterwards. Both groups were compared with a control group who were not prepared in this way.

'...asked to focus on the positive aspects of their surgery'

Results: Both information control and cognitive control helped patients to cope, compared with the control group. Cognitive control was more effective than information control in reducing anxiety.

Conclusion: Information control and cognitive control are both effective in stress reduction. Cognitive control, used together with information control, may be the most effective way of reducing stress.

A further cognitive approach to the control of stress has been developed by Meichenbaum (1985). This is a method of **cognitive restructuring** called **stress inoculation**. It is a three-stage procedure carried out with the help of a therapist, and aims to control the **catastrophising thoughts** which people often have in stressful situations. A person attending a job interview, for example, might think: 'I just know I'm not going to get this job'.

Figure 11: stress inoculation (Meichenbaum)

1. **conceptualisation:** the therapist helps the person to identify and talk about their feelings and fears, and how they have tried to cope with them.

2. **skill acquisition and rehearsal:** general techniques for coping with stress are taught and practised, such as relaxation and making a realistic appraisal of stressful situations. Specific skills, such as effective interpersonal communication, may also be taught.

3. **application and follow-through:** the therapist guides the person through a series of stressful situations. This helps the person to develop and practise the cognitive strategies necessary for coping with stressful situations.

Kobasa, whose concept of the 'hardy personality' was discussed earlier (see box E) also takes a cognitive–behavioural approach to coping with stress in her suggestion as to how hardiness may be developed. Again, there are three elements:

Figure 12: coping with stress (Kobasa)

1. **focusing:** the person is trained to recognise the physiological signs of stress, such as increased heart rate or sweating. This helps them to recognise sources of stress.

2. **reconstructing stressful situations:** the person is helped to think about a recent stressful situation and consider ways in which it could have turned out better or worse. This aims to help the person make a realistic appraisal of the stresses they experience.

3. **compensation through self-improvement:** the person is encouraged to take on challenges they can cope with. Through this they learn that they are capable of coping with stressful situations.

The methods of reducing stress suggested by Meichenbaum and Kobasa can be linked with the **transactional model** of stress described at the start of this chapter. You will remember that this model suggests that stress can be defined in terms of a mismatch between the perceived demands a situation makes of us and our perceived ability to meet these demands. Both these methods aim to help us make a realistic assessment of the demands made of us, while at the same time improving our ability to cope with them. They also both involve the experience of coping successfully with stressful situations, so that we develop a feeling of control; as we have seen, control is an important element in successfully handling stress.

⊖ Increasing a person's feeling of **control** in stressful situations can be useful in coping with stress. People with an **external locus of control** tend to experience higher levels of stress than those with an **internal locus of control**.

⊖ Both **information control** and **cognitive control** can be effective.

⊖ Meichenbaum and Kobasa have both suggested methods of reducing stress which aim to help people make **realistic assessments** of stressful situations, and develop **coping strategies.**

The psychodynamic approach

Freud has suggested that we deal with anxiety, which is the psychological manifestation of stress, by the use of unconscious **ego defence mechanisms** such as denial (mentioned in relation to Janis's study, box M). You will remember from chapter 1 that Freud's theory proposes that anxiety arises as the result of unconscious conflict.

▷ Activity 15: ego defence mechanisms

Some of the mechanisms described by Freud which we use to deal with anxiety are:

repression	denial
reaction formation	sublimation
rationalisation	regression

What do each of these involve? Which is the only one which is effective in the long term? Check your answers with the information in chapter 1.

Because these mechanisms are unconscious, they involve self-deception: the whole point of them is that they prevent us becoming aware of unpleasant or threatening material. They rest on a distorted view of reality, both the reality of our own inner feelings and the reality of our social and physical world. They help us to cope effectively in the short term, but because they rely on self-deception and distortion, they are fundamentally unhealthy as long-term coping mechanisms. The only exception to this is sublimation, since it provides an acceptable outlet for unacceptable impulses.

Grasha (1983) has used Freud's suggestions about the nature of ego defence mechanisms to describe a range of **coping mechanisms**. In contrast to Freud's account, these are *conscious* ways of trying to cope with anxiety in a positive and constructive way. The coping mechanisms he describes involve looking for support from other people, thinking of ways to solve our problems, acknowledging our true feelings, and making decisions about what our aims are and how to achieve them. He redefines Freudian terms from this point of view:

Figure 13: coping mechanisms (Grasha, 1983)

coping mechanism	definition
suppression	consciously putting something out of your mind until an appropriate time to deal with it
substitution of thoughts	consciously substituting other thoughts and feelings for how we really think and feel to cope with the situation we are in
playfulness	using past feelings and ideas to help solve problems in an enjoyable way
concentration	deliberately putting aside thoughts and feelings unrelated to what we need to do
logical analysis	analysing problems to help us make realistic plans to solve them

Sublimation is both an ego defence mechanism and a coping mechanism, since it is a positive and constructive way of dealing with anxiety.

▷ Activity 16: defence mechanisms and coping mechanisms

Match each of Grasha's coping mechanisms in figure 13 with the equivalent ego defence mechanism from activity 15. Then match each with one of these scenarios:

a On Thursday, Martin is asked to work late by his boss, but this is also the day when he usually visits his mother in a nursing home. She will be disappointed if he doesn't go. There is no time to do both. He starts to think of various options: asking his boss if he can take work home, speaking to his mother on the phone and arranging to go the next day, and so on.

b Wendy has been asked to plan a Halloween party for the badminton club she belongs to. She is worried it will turn out to be a disaster. She remembers a similar party she went to a few years previously. She thoroughly enjoyed this party, and everyone else seemed to have a good time too. She starts to think about how some of the ideas from the previous party could be adapted for the Halloween party.

c It is Saturday evening. Viri is waiting to hear whether he has got a job he applied for. He is very keen to get the job, as his current job will be finishing in a few weeks. He decides to go to the pub with his friends, and ring up about the job on Monday morning.

d Helen is working hard on a report which needs to be handed to her boss the next day. She has a hospital appointment next week which she is worried about. She puts her worries to the back of her mind and focuses on getting the report finished.

e Anne is a head of department at a comprehensive school and has to work with other members of her department on the development plan for the coming year. She does not get on very well with David, and doesn't think he is very competent. When David arrives at the meeting, she greets him with a smile, and asks him what ideas he would like to include.

When you have finished, see the notes on page 99.

The effectiveness of both ego defence mechanisms and more cognitive coping mechanisms has been shown in a study by Greer *et al.* (1979). This study found that for women with breast cancer, who had had a mastectomy, the prognosis in terms of being free of cancer five years after treatment was much better for those who reacted with denial or who were determined to beat the disease. However, strategies such as denial can also be dangerous. For example, if a person with a heart problem does not follow his doctor's recommendations for lifestyle changes because to do so would mean acknowledging that he is ill, there could well be life-threatening consequences.

🆂 Freud believed we use unconscious **ego defence mechanisms** to cope with anxiety. These are only effective in the short term.

❺ We may also use similar but conscious **coping mechanisms**.

Social support

Another way of dealing with stress is to draw on **social support**. Winnurst *et al.* (1988) found that the support of others – friends, family or social organisations – can be very helpful in reducing the stress experienced when undergoing a divorce or coping with a bereavement or the loss of a job. Similarly, Tache *et al.* (1979) found that adults who were widowed, divorced or separated were more likely to develop cancer than controls, a finding which could be interpreted in terms of the lack of social support.

The support of other people can help reduce stress

House *et al.* (1988) found that support groups can be a very useful resource for people faced with long-term stressful situations, such as illness or poverty. Support groups can help people to cope, not only because they provide other people to lean on, but also because people belonging to these groups can learn ways of coping from each other.

Reducing stressors

A final way of coping with stress is to look at the problem from a different angle. Instead of accepting that stress is inevitable, in some cases it may be possible to change the circumstances which lead to stress being experienced.

▶ Activity 17: reducing stressors

Amanda is 35 and has a daughter aged 6, a son aged 5 and a six-month-old baby. Every morning she is up at 5.30 to make packed lunches for the older children, hoover the house, prepare food to be cooked for the evening meal and get the baby ready to go to the childminder's.

She drops the children off and drives through the rush hour to get to work. She is in charge of a department at work, and it is her responsibility to make sure that the other people in her department are working efficiently. Every week she has a meeting with them to discuss any problems which have arisen, and she often stays until well after six to check that work has been completed satisfactorily. She is very ambitious and intends to rise high in her profession, so she often volunteers for extra responsibility.

On her way home she picks up all three children from the childminder's, takes them home and cooks an evening meal. She puts the children to bed, washes up and makes sure that the kitchen is clean. She feels she is not doing her job properly unless the house is immaculate. She then usually has papers from the office to look through for the next day or reports to write. She is the chairperson of the local PTA, and complains that she often seems to be doing all the work as well as chairing meetings. She finally stops work at around 11, and goes to bed, though she often has difficulty in getting to sleep.

Her husband also has a high-powered job. She has asked him to give her more help, but he also brings work home, and is often away at weekends for his job. At weekends she has work to prepare for the week, but leaves this till after the children are in bed. She regularly takes them swimming on Saturdays. On Sundays, her in-laws always come for lunch, and she prides herself on cooking them a wonderful meal.

She says she always feels very stressed, but can't see what she could do to make things any easier.

How could Amanda reduce the stressors in her life? Based on the sections in this chapter on coping with stress, what other advice would you give her? When you have finished, see the notes on page 99.

❺ **Social support** increases our ability to cope with stress.

❺ **Reducing stressors** is also a useful strategy.

Notes on activities

3 **Pupil dilation** would allow you to become more aware of external stimuli, and thus better able to respond to them. **Deeper breathing** takes more oxygen into the lungs; your muscles require oxygen if they are to work effectively. A **faster heartbeat** speeds up blood circulation, and so carries oxygen to the muscles more quickly. Speeding up **sugar metabolism** creates an instant supply of energy; the danger could well be past by the time proteins and fats were metabolised. Stored red blood cells from the **spleen** mean that the blood can carry more oxygen.

4 There are clear ethical problems here, in terms of the suffering of the rats. The ecological value of the study has also been questioned, in that the environment provided for the rats was not a natural one, so we need to be cautious in the conclusions we draw from the findings. As with all animal studies, we need to be cautious about extrapolating the behaviour of rats to people. This study nonetheless suggests that overcrowding can have far-reaching physical and psychological consequences, and it inspired a lot of research into the effects of overcrowding on people.

8 You have probably listed such things as presenting classes with structured information relevant to the curriculum in the subject being taught; maintaining classroom discipline; setting and marking homework; attending meetings with management; involving parents and management when there are problems; attending training days, and so on.

9 **a** 3; **b** 1; **c** 6; **d** 5; **e** 2; **f** 4; **g** 8; **h** 9; **i** 7.

10 You might have suggested that the waitresses and the chefs should communicate with each other more, to clarify how they feel. The waitresses and the chef could discuss what is a reasonable length of time for customers to wait, and make customers aware of what they have agreed. They could make sure that management are aware of the situation and can intervene when there are problems. Staff training to help them deal with stress might also be a good idea.

11 For questions 1, 3, 4, 6, 10 and 12, 'agree' scores 2, and 'disagree' scores 0. For questions 2, 5, 7, 8, 9 and 11, 'disagree' scores 2 and 'agree' scores 0. For all questions, 'cannot say' scores 1. If you are close to the maximum score of 24, you show signs of being a Type A personality, while if your score is close to 0, you are a Type B personality.

12 One major problem is that this study is retrospective, i.e. it asks people to talk about events which happened before the illness developed, and so relies on their memory being accurate. Another weakness is that there was no control group of people who had *not* developed cancer.

16 suppression = repression (**c**), substitution of thoughts and feelings = reaction formation (**e**), playfulness = regression (**b**), concentration = denial (**d**), logical analysis = rationalisation (**a**).

17 Amanda has taken a lot on, and it is not surprising that she feels stressed. There are several aspects of her life where stressors could be reduced: she could let the children have school meals instead of packed lunches, lower her standards about housework, prioritise what needs to be done at work and delegate more to the people in her department, perhaps mark time in her career for a few years and not take on extra responsibilities, drop her PTA commitment, suggest that her family should visit the in-laws sometimes on a Sunday or eat out, and so on. You have probably come up with several other ideas.

One problem is that she sounds very much like a Type A personality, so she would find making these changes difficult. She might need help in changing the way she thinks about her life and her behaviours. She would also be well advised to take exercise and perhaps put time aside for meditation.

Abnormality

In this chapter we will be looking at:

5.1 What is abnormal psychology?

5.2 Defining abnormality
   Deviation from statistical norms
   Violation of social norms
   Maladaptive behaviour
   Defining normality

5.3 Cultural and subcultural differences in the definition of abnormality

5.4 Models of abnormality
   Historical models
   The biological (medical) model
   The behavioural model
   The cognitive model
   The psychodynamic model

5.5 Critical issue: eating disorders
   Anorexia nervosa
   Bulimia nervosa
   Biological explanation of
      eating disorders
   Social and psychological expla-
      nations of eating disorders
   Explanations of eating
      disorders: an overview

5.1 WHAT IS ABNORMAL PSYCHOLOGY?

Abnormal psychology, or **psychopathology**, is the area of psychology which relates to mental disorders. There is considerable controversy about how 'abnormality' should be defined. Psychologists also differ in what they see to be the causes of mental disorder, or indeed whether we actually need to concern ourselves with causes at all. This is important, because what is seen as the cause (or **aetiology**) of a disorder may determine the treatment (or **therapy**) given.

This is an important area, since mental disorders cause a lot of unhappiness to millions of people, and research in this area aims to alleviate suffering. We will be looking in this chapter at some of the problems associated with this topic.

5.2 DEFINING ABNORMALITY

Problems in this area start with definition:

Activity 1: defining abnormal behaviour

Make a list of the characteristics or features of a person whose behaviour you consider to be 'abnormal'. You could picture someone you know and would describe as abnormal, or you may find it easier to think back to a film you have seen that portrayed someone as abnormal.

What criteria would you use to define someone as showing abnormal behaviour?

Keep your notes to compare with the discussion which follows.

Deviation from statistical norms

One way in which abnormality may be defined is as a characteristic or behaviour which is **statistically infrequent**, or which deviates substantially from the average or typical behaviour of the group to which an individual belongs. For example, someone may have an abnormally well-developed memory for word lists: their memory for this kind of information is much better than it is for the majority of others in the population. However, there are problems in defining abnormal behaviour as being behaviour which is significantly different from that of most other people.

One problem here is that using the statistical criterion of abnormality does not include any assessment of whether the behaviour is desirable or not. We would probably be satisfied to define people like Hitler as abnormal, but it doesn't seem sensible or useful to define the statistically rare talents of someone as intelligent as the scientist Steven Hawking or as creative as Picasso in this way.

Another difficulty is that some conditions which clearly constitute a problem are relatively frequent. Depression, for example, is quite common in Western cultures, and is regarded as a mental disorder, but it would not be described as abnormal using this criterion.

A further difficulty arises when deciding where the cut-off point between normal and abnormal should lie. How good a memory would a person need to have, for example, before being described as having an abnormally good memory? At the extremes, there would be little difficulty in deciding that someone had or didn't have an abnormally good memory, but the grey area between these two extremes is problematic.

In one area, however, the statistical criterion is used. **Mental retardation** is defined in the classification system ICD-10, which we will be looking at later, as having a measured IQ which is two or more standard deviations below the mean. In general, though, while this criterion may go some way towards a definition of abnormality, it is clearly not enough to provide a definition on its own.

The distribution of IQ scores in the population. Each division represents 1 standard deviation from the mean

Violation of social norms

An alternative definition of abnormal behaviour sees it as behaviour which violates **social norms**. Scheff (1966) introduced the idea of **residual rules**, unwritten rules in a society of which people are somehow aware and to which they generally conform. For example, you do not stand staring vacantly into space in the middle of a busy pavement, or spit on the piano. People who break these rules, and go against social norms, could be defined as behaving abnormally.

Residual rules

One problem with this definition, however, is that we can only judge normality according to the situation. For example, singing loudly and tunelessly is not a problem if someone is in the shower, but would be seen as abnormal in a library or on a bus. Killing people during wars may be regarded as heroic, but can be seen as murder at other times.

Defining behaviour as abnormal according to social norms is also difficult, since social norms change from one period of history to another as social trends change. You can perhaps think of behaviours, like dyeing one's hair pink, or sunbathing topless, which would have been considered abnormal 40 years ago, but which are now accepted as issues of personal choice. Homosexuality is one behaviour which until 1973 was listed as a mental disorder in DSM-II, a classificatory system widely used by psychiatrists, and to which we will be returning later in the chapter. Homosexuality is now legal between consenting adults over 18, and most people in the UK now accept homosexuality as falling within social norms.

Some norms, it could be said, also need to be broken. In the 1950s, it was quite common to find rooms to let with notices saying 'No coloured. No Irish', a practice which, thankfully, has become both socially unacceptable and illegal.

However, this definition of abnormality has been applied: repressive political regimes, such as that in the former USSR, have frequently classified those who disagreed with them as having a mental disorder, and confined them to psychiatric hospitals for publicly condemning the actions of the government.

Maladaptive behaviour

If behaviour is adaptive, it contributes to a person's sense of individual worth and allows them to function adequately as a member of a larger social group. If a person's behaviour fails to meet these criteria, and disrupts their ability to work or to have relationships with other people, it can be said to be maladaptive, and the behaviour can be defined as abnormal.

Within this framework, one criterion for defining abnormality is **personal distress**. As we have noted, disorders such as depression are common, and therefore can't be defined statistically as abnormal. They do, however, make the person thoroughly miserable, and as such are abnormal. Symptoms such as loss of appetite, insomnia and general aches and pains can be indicative of a mental disorder, even if friends or relatives of the person concerned have noticed no real differences in that person's behaviour.

There are, however, problems with this criterion. Distress is a perfectly natural reaction in some circumstances – for example, when someone close to you has died. In contrast, there are some disorders where no personal distress is felt. For example, someone with an antisocial personality behaves violently and with no concern for the feelings of others, but does not themselves feel distressed.

This leads to another criterion related to maladaptive behaviour, that of **causing distress to others**; this criterion would certainly apply to antisocial personality disorder. A person cannot be said to be functioning adequately if their behaviour frightens or upsets other people. However, many disorders would not meet this criterion.

Another aspect of failure to function adequately is that the person with a mental disorder shows **unexpected behaviour**, a term used by Davison and Neale (1994). Although behaviour is affected by the nature of the situation in which we find ourselves, to some extent our behaviour is predictable, and this is one of the things which allow us to interact appropriately with other people. If a person is extremely unpredictable, interacting with them is likely to be very difficult, and their behaviour would therefore be maladaptive. Again, though, it is a matter of where the line is to be drawn between expected variations in behaviour and unexpected behaviour.

Finally, behaviour which is **bizarre** is another example of a failure to function adequately. Some people with schizophrenia, for example, hear voices in their head with which they may carry on a conversation. This leads to the bizarre behaviour of someone walking along apparently talking or arguing with themselves. People with obsessive–compulsive disorder may need to carry out a behaviour such as washing their hands as often as 500 times a day, developing painful sores in the process, and leaving little time for anything else. At the same time, though, a lot of mental disorders are not associated with bizarre behaviour.

All the criteria for defining abnormality which we have looked at so far apply to some aspects of some mental disorders, but none on its own provides an adequate definition. In most cases, psychologists have found that it is best to consider a person's behaviour against all of the criteria we have looked at.

In line with this way of thinking, Rosenhan and Seligman (1989) listed six criteria, shown in figure 1, for judging behaviour as abnormal:

Figure 1: six criteria for judging behaviour as abnormal (Rosenhan and Seligman, 1989)

1. personal distress
2. maladaptiveness
3. irrationality
4. unpredictability
5. unconventionality and statistical rarity
6. observer discomfort

They put forward the idea that any combination of these criteria could indicate mental illness. This seems to be a useful way forward. The problem remains, though, that the criteria require a subjective judgement to be made; different people could assess a person differently on each point.

Psychologists have also, on the whole, seen that there can be no precise distinction between normal and abnormal behaviour, so abnormality now tends to be seen as a **continuum** with 'normal' at one end, 'abnormal' at the other and various degrees of normality in between. This is a more realistic model, as it takes account of the fact that we have all probably experienced irrational thoughts and feelings or felt distress at one time or another, but do not all need to be defined as abnormal or suffering from a mental disorder.

- ⊝ Abnormal behaviour has been defined as behaviour which is **statistically infrequent**, **violates social norms**, and is **maladaptive**.
- ⊝ There are many difficulties associated with defining behaviour as abnormal, notably the fact that assessment may be **subjective**.
- ⊝ There is no single straightforward criterion for defining abnormality. Taken together, however, different definitions may help to define abnormality.
- ⊝ Abnormality is now seen to be a **continuum** from normal to abnormal, with varying degrees of mental health in between.

Defining normality

Many of the problems associated with defining abnormality have led to a different approach, that of attempting to define normality. This approach started with Freud, who said that the goal of therapy was a well-balanced individual 'able to love and to work'. Defining abnormality in terms of maladaptive behaviour rests on the assumption that certain aspects of our behaviour are necessary for mental health. Jahoda (1958) suggested a range of characteristics, shown in figure 2, which describe a mentally well-adjusted person:

Figure 2: characteristics of a well-adjusted person (Jahoda, 1958)

1. self-acceptance
2. potential for growth and development
3. autonomy
4. accurate perception of reality
5. environmental competence
6. having positive interpersonal relations

More recently, Atkinson *et al.* (1983) listed six personality traits which they suggest a normal person exhibits to a greater degree than an individual who is classified as abnormal. In other words, they are stressing the idea that mental health and mental illness exist as a continuum:

Activity 2: what is mental health?

Compare the ideas of Atkinson *et al.* in box A with the characteristics Jahoda suggests. In what ways are they similar? How do they differ?
When you have finished, see the notes on page 120.

Box A: Atkinson *et al.* (1983)

Efficient perception of reality
Normal people have a realistic idea of their own capabilities and can fairly accurately understand what is going on around them. Those people with mental disorders may consistently overvalue or underestimate their own abilities, and misunderstand what other people say and do.

Self-knowledge
Normal people have some awareness of their own motives and feelings – they are more self-aware than those people with a mental disorder.

An ability to exercise voluntary control over behaviour
Although all normal people sometimes act impulsively, they can control their urges if

they decide to do so. Even if they do exhibit bizarre behaviour which does not conform to what society expects, they have voluntarily decided to act in that way.

Self-esteem and acceptance

Well-adjusted people don't always bow to peer pressure. They have an idea of their own self-worth and feel comfortable that they are accepted by others. Mentally ill people frequently feel worthless and unaccepted by other people.

An ability to form affectionate relationships

Normal people can form satisfying, intimate relationships with others. People with mental disorders can be extremely self-centred and concerned with their own feelings, leading to a lack of success in relationships.

Productivity

Normal people have an enthusiasm for life and are productive – whether that be at work or in leisure time. People with mental disorders often suffer from a lack of energy and tiredness.

This approach has intuitive appeal, and could provide some indication of whether a person's characteristics and behaviour would be classed as abnormal. It is not without its problems, however. Like some of the definitions we considered earlier, subjective judgements are necessary, and there may well be differences between the assessment on these criteria – for example, as made by a mental health professional or by the person who is being considered.

In essence, these lists outline ideal mental health. The question arises as to how many of us could be said to enjoy good mental health using these criteria. There is no very clear dividing line between normal and abnormal, and many people who would not be defined as abnormal may still not fully meet all the criteria Atkinson *et al.* and Jahoda have proposed.

- An alternative approach to defining abnormality and mental disorder is in terms of **mental health**.
- The criteria proposed present an **ideal** which many people may not meet. Assessment is **subjective**.

5.3 CULTURAL AND SUBCULTURAL DIFFERENCES IN THE DEFINITION OF ABNORMALITY

Cultures vary in their beliefs, attitudes, values and customs, and may therefore differ in their concept of abnormality. This makes it difficult to define psychological abnormality in terms which can be universally applied. While there are no problems with identifying physical illnesses, such as measles, in a Welsh person and a Chinese person, with mental disorders it is not quite so straightforward.

Some disorders such as schizophrenia are present in most cultures, and are universally considered to be a disorder. Children with attention deficit hyperactivity disorder (ADHD), on the other hand, a condition seen as a disorder in our culture, would be considered naughty or badly behaved but not abnormal in some cultures. Similarly, in some cultures it is considered normal to see and hear a person who has died during the bereavement period. Within Western culture, this would be considered abnormal.

There are also disorders which are recognised and even common in some cultures but are unknown in others. For example, it would be very unusual in Britain to come across someone suffering from **koro**, an anxiety disorder found among the Chinese, where the sufferer is afraid that his penis will withdraw into his abdomen. Sufferers may even tie a string to the penis to stop this from happening. **Amok** – where males have periods of aggression and try to kill or injure others – is not recognised as a specific mental disorder in the West, but is recognised as such in Malaysia. Another example is **dhat**, a disorder found among Indian men, who complain of loss of semen through the urine. They suffer from multiple aches and pains, and believe that the loss of semen is causing them weakness.

Disorders such as these, which are strongly related to particular cultures, are known as **culture-bound syndromes.** Helman (1994) has suggested that anorexia nervosa, which we will be discussing towards the end of this chapter, is a Western culture-bound syndrome. Pre-menstrual syndrome and agoraphobia may be other examples.

As an aid to the diagnosis of mental disorders, mental health professionals use systems which classify disorders into diagnostic categories. The two most well-known current systems of classification are **ICD (International Classification of Diseases)** and **DSM (Diagnostic and Statistical Manual of Mental Disorders)**. ICD-10, the most recent version of this system, is currently used in Britain and in most other parts of the world, whereas DSM-IV, the most recent version of this alternative system, is used in North America. Until recently, it was assumed that Western diagnostic categories of mental disorders used in these systems could be applied universally, and that disorders in non-Western cultures were just variations of Western disorders. However, the most recent version of DSM now takes cultural variation into account and includes a list of culture-bound syndromes in an appendix; ICD-10 has a similar section.

There may also be subcultural factors in defining abnormality. At a subcultural level, there are significant differences in the prevalence of diagnosis of certain mental illnesses, and therefore what is defined as abnormal, between ethnic groups in Britain. Cochrane (1977), for example, found that Afro-Caribbeans are calculated to be between 2 and 7 times more likely than whites to be diagnosed as schizophrenic. They are also far more likely to be compulsorily admitted to secure hospitals.

It is possible that the disproportionate number of Afro-Caribbeans diagnosed as schizophrenic may be related to **stereotypes**, e.g. the stereotype that violent behaviour is more likely to be associated with black people. Behaviours of the majority white population may be seen as **social norms**, with deviations being considered abnormal and indeed pathological. It has been suggested that there is a **Eurocentric bias** in defining people as abnormal.

This seems to suggest that culture should be taken into account when diagnosing someone as having a mental disorder. On the other hand, it has also been suggested that taking account of cultural variation may not necessarily be helpful:

Box B: Lopez and Hernandez (1986)

Procedure: A large number of mental health professionals in California were surveyed about the relationship of ethnicity to their diagnostic work.

Results: There was sometimes a tendency to explain the problems experienced by patients in terms of subcultural norms. One clinician, for example, believed that blacks were more likely than whites to suffer from hallucinations, so did not consider a diagnosis of schizophrenia for a black patient.

Conclusion: Being aware of cultural differences can lead to problems being minimised, an appropriate diagnosis not being made, and therefore less chance of appropriate intervention.

Another example of subcultural variation is gender. There are gender differences in the incidence of diagnosis of particular disorders which are related to sex-role **stereotypes** in our society. This can be illustrated by differences in diagnosis for the disorders shown in figure 3:

Figure 3: four personality disorders from DSM-IV

disorder	characteristics
histrionic personality disorder	extravagant displays of emotion, attention-seeking, manipulative and demanding
dependent personality disorder	lack of self-confidence, passivity, oversensitiveness to criticism
narcissistic personality disorder	grandiose view of their own abilities, lack of empathy in relationships, craving the admiration of others
obsessive–compulsive personality disorder	perfectionist, work-oriented, lack of warmth, requirement that everything be done their way

▶ Activity 3: diagnosis and sex-role stereotypes

For each of the disorders in figure 3, decide whether the characteristics best fit the sex-role stereotypes of males or females.

When you have finished, see the notes on page 120.

For all the disorders shown in figure 3, there is a higher incidence of diagnosis for the gender who fits the stereotypes than for the other gender. This has also been tested experimentally:

Box C: Broverman *et al.* (1981)

Procedure: Mental health professionals were asked to rate the characteristics of the 'healthy man', the 'healthy woman' and the 'healthy adult'.

Results: The ratings for 'healthy adult' and 'healthy man' were similar. The characteristics included 'assertive', 'decisive' and 'independent'. The 'healthy woman' was regarded as 'submissive', 'dependent' and 'emotional'.

Conclusion: Diagnosis of a person as suffering from a mental disorder may be related to the different gender stereotypes of what ideal mental health (and therefore abnormality) is for a man and for a woman.

- ⊖ There are cultural variations in what is considered to be abnormal. Behaviour considered normal in one culture may be seen as abnormal in another.
- ⊖ Disorders specific to a culture are called **culture-bound syndromes**. They are included in the most recent versions of the classificatory systems DSM and ICD.
- ⊖ There may also be **subcultural variations,** e.g. related to **ethnicity** or **gender**, in defining abnormality.

5.4 MODELS OF ABNORMALITY

There are several models of abnormal behaviour which vary in terms of what are seen to be the causes of abnormal behaviour. This in turn has implications for what is seen as the appropriate therapy for someone with a mental disorder.

Historical models

Historically, abnormal behaviour has often been explained in terms of possession by evil spirits. **Demonology** is the idea that some sort of evil being is responsible for a person's behaviour. Treatments therefore centred on ridding the body of such evil spirits, and included starvation (to ensure the body was unsuitable for the devils to reside in), trepanation (drilling holes in the skull to let the spirit out) and various forms of exorcism.

It is now widely thought that people who in the Middle Ages were called witches were often merely people with a mental disorder. Religious fervour was strong at the time, and the poorly-educated masses believed abnormal behaviour to be a sign of moral wickedness. Women accused of witchcraft were tortured if they did not confess; and it was said that people who had lost their sense of reason could have the demon exorcised by burning. You may also have read of witches being ducked under water; those who did not drown were thought to be in league with the devil. Those unfortunates who did drown were thought not to be witches, although it was then too late for their innocence to be of much use to them!

Poor "witch"!

Another historical model, dating back to the second century, took a more medical approach. Galen suggested that normal brain functioning depended on the balance of four fluids, or **humours** – blood, black bile, yellow bile and phlegm. Since mental disorders were considered to be the result of an imbalance of these humours, various treatments intended to restore that balance were employed. These included blood-letting to rid the body of an excess of blood, the effect of which was (hardly surprisingly) to calm the most violent of patients!

The development of **asylums** began in the sixteenth century. Originally the asylums admitted mentally disordered people, beggars, and some people with leprosy. The first hospital specifically designed to contain people with mental problems is said to be the Priory of St Mary of Bethlehem in London, founded for the containment of the mentally disordered in 1547. This is the origin of the modern term 'bedlam'. However, the inmates of such asylums were chained to cell walls by iron collars, treated like criminals, and fed an appalling diet.

Treatments included the idea that so-called lunatics could be cured merely by frightening them; this is related to the idea of demonic possession, since evil spirits would be frightened and therefore leave the body. It is perhaps worth mentioning that 'lunatic' means 'controlled by the moon', and is therefore another example of an early aetiology. The fact that the patients were seen as sub-human is well illustrated by the fact that the middle-classes were encouraged to pay to view the antics of the lunatics, and asylums became a huge tourist attraction.

Conditions in the asylums did not improve until in 1793 a Frenchman called Pinel took over La Bicêtre, a large asylum in Paris, and was shocked at the way in which the patients were treated. He advocated a humanitarian approach, removing the chains from the inmates, feeding them healthily and treating them with compassion.

These examples of how historically abnormality has been explained and treated are, thankfully, in the past. However, it is perhaps worth noting that some other cultures had a more positive approach to people with a mental disorder. For example, among many nomadic Asian peoples abnormal behaviour was seen as a sign of special sensitivity to, and the ability to communicate with, the spirit world. The mentally-disordered person would hold a particularly privileged position as a shaman (or priest) within the society. In *The Politics of Experience and the Bird of Paradise* (1967), R. D. Laing put forward a similar suggestion about schizophrenics, but this remains an extremely unusual point of view in Western medicine.

We will turn now to more modern models in abnormal psychology.

The biological (medical) model

The medical approach is the most traditional and widely accepted model of mental disorder. As its name suggests, this kind of disorder is seen as a medical problem, so the term 'mental illness' is widely used in this context. There are clear parallels between the medical model of physical illness and the medical model of mental illness.

The **medical model of illness** proposes that **symptoms** are caused by an **organic lesion**, i.e. a change in the structure of body tissue caused by disease or injury. **Diagnosis** involves the identification of the lesion from the symptoms. **Prognosis** gives a likely outcome to the illness. **Treatment** involves treating the lesion by **physical means**. Patients are not considered to be in control of their symptoms.

The **medical model of mental illness** considers abnormal behaviour to be a **symptom** caused either by a **hypothetical lesion**, or by a **physical lesion** which has not yet been identified. Since **diagnosis** is not possible in the absence of a lesion, **classification** (making use of classification systems such as DSM-IV and ICD-10, mentioned above) provides a guide for **prognosis** and **treatment**.

(a)

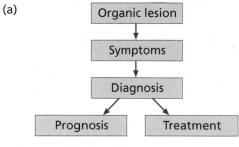

Medical model of physical illness

(b)

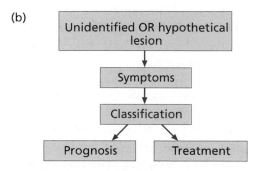

Medical model of mental illness

The medical model uses terms associated with physical illness when it talks about mental disorders. Patients are treated by specialist *physicians* (doctors) called psychiatrists, or by general practitioners. The –*pathology* part of the term psychopathology (the study of mental disorders) is taken from medicine. The abnormal behaviour of the patient is seen as a *symptom* of a physical problem. The doctor will aim to observe the patient carefully and then *diagnose* the illness, using one of the classificatory systems, together with further examination and tests to assist diagnosis. They will then decide on a suitable treatment. Some treatments can be given against the will of the patient, by detaining them forcibly and providing treatment under the relevant section of the 1983 Mental Health Act (a process sometimes known as '**sectioning**').

Abnormal behaviour may be seen as caused by **genetic factors**. Some physical disorders, such as cystic fibrosis and haemophilia, can be passed on from parents to children, and the medical model of mental illness suggests that mental disorders can be inherited in the same way. There is strong evidence for a genetic basis to some mental disorders, in particular schizophrenia and bipolar disorder (manic depression). The evidence is far less strong, however, for other disorders such as depression. Genetic factors do not fully explain the development of mental disorders. It seems to be more likely that genetic factors predispose someone to develop a mental disorder; whether it in fact develops seems to depend on environmental factors.

Mental illness can also be seen as having a biochemical cause. Some abnormal behaviours have been linked to the endocrine system, which produces the body's **hormones** and regulates their activity. For example, certain disorders of the thyroid gland have been linked with depression.

Imbalances in particular **neurotransmitters**, chemical messengers which carry information between neurons, have also been linked to mental illness. Schizophrenia, for example, is associated with an excess of the neurotransmitter dopamine. However, there is insufficient evidence to claim that this kind of chemical imbalance causes a particular disorder. Both the disorder and the chemical imbalance could be caused by a further factor; for example, they could both be genetic.

Neurological damage is seen as another possible cause of mental illness. As an example, we will look at **Fregoli's delusion**. People who suffer from this delusion believe strangers to be people whom they know, even though they do not look like them. The sufferer may try to make sense of their experiences by believing that people they know are going about in disguise. A case study of a patient with this disorder is described in box D:

Box D: Ellis and Szulecka (1996)

Miss C believed that she was being stalked by an ex-lover and his girlfriend, who followed her everywhere. She believed they disguised themselves by wearing wigs or dark glasses, or by changing their clothes and driving different cars. She reported their activities to the police.

She would go up to strangers and demand that they took off their disguises, and believed that the gas man who had come to read her gas meter was one of them, who had adopted a disguise to get into her house.

The false recognition of strangers as people she knew was eliminated by drugs, but the delusion remained. Miss C believed that the police had made the stalkers go away.

A CAT scan of Miss C's brain showed that, as the result of a stroke, there was quite severe damage to the cerebral cortex. (CAT stands for computerised axial tomography, and this type of scan displays a three-dimensional representation of the brain's structures and can therefore be used for such tasks as locating tumours.)

Since mental disorder is seen to have an **organic** (i.e. physical) basis, it is treated with physical or **somatic** therapies. These include drugs, ECT (electroconvulsive therapy, described in chapter 2), and psychosurgery. Psychosurgery involves making lesions in the brain, and cannot be carried out without the patient's consent.

There are several positive aspects of the medical model. Firstly, for many disorders the treatments offered can be very effective. The idea that there is an organic or physical cause for some types of mental illness is supported by the fact that some somatic therapies do relieve the symptoms of many mental illnesses. ECT, for example, is often very successful in treating severe depression, and the symptoms of schizophrenia can be controlled by anti-psychotic drugs such as chlorpromazine.

Additionally, considering abnormal behaviour to be a symptom of 'illness' means that the person cannot be blamed for their disorder; they are not 'bad' but 'ill'. The hope, therefore, is that people will be sympathetic towards those with a mental illness. However, there are stereotypes about people with a mental disorder which mean that this doesn't necessarily happen in practice. For example, research by Jones and Cochrane (1981) showed that British people's stereotype of mental disorder fitted the symptoms of schizophrenia. It is possible that this formed part of your answer to activity 1. Sufferers from this disorder can be violent and their behaviour is often bizarre. For this reason, many people may be afraid of such individuals, and tend to avoid them rather than showing sympathy.

Some theorists, sometimes known as **anti-psychiatrists**, take a very different view of mental disorders from that advocated by mental health professionals. In his book *The Myth of Mental Illness* (1972), Szasz suggested that most mental disorders are not organic (i.e. having a physical basis) but **functional** (i.e. with no known physical cause). These disorders are attributed by Szasz to what he termed 'problems in living'.

Szasz argued that the word 'depression' simply describes an unhappy person, and that if we consider the term to be a medical diagnosis, this allows us to put into place various practices that we consider will 'cure' the patient, whether or not that person wishes to be treated. To Szasz, mental illnesses are termed 'illnesses' because they go against our idea of normality, and not because they are true, physical illnesses. This makes psychiatry a form of **social control**, made acceptable by the existence of psychiatrists, but really a way of taking away a person's rights and responsibilities.

In his book *The Divided Self* (1965), another anti-psychiatrist, R. D. Laing, suggested that 'sanity or psychosis is tested by the degree of conjunction or disjunction between two persons where one is sane by common consent'. He was here stressing the idea that judging someone to be psychotic is very subjective, and that there are important implications regarding who decides which people are mentally ill. Many researchers find it of great concern that the lack of power of some people's social position seems to attract the label 'mentally ill' more readily than others. As we saw earlier, this applies particularly to members of ethnic minorities and women.

This argument raises an ethical issue. If psychiatrists are justified in believing that a person's abnormal behaviour is caused by an organic problem that is preventing them from functioning adequately, then they are right to treat those people, even if treatment is resisted. The psychiatrist must act for the patient's own good, and take responsibility for their well-being, while attempting to free the patient of the misery of mental illness.

Alternatively, if the anti-psychiatrists are correct, then hospitalisation can be seen as imprisonment which violates people's human rights. People who may never have broken the law have their freedom taken away from them, and if this is true, society is persecuting unconventional people for behaviour that society itself cannot cope with. On the other hand, Szasz's ideas could mean that those with mental disorders are not helped during what is often a very distressing time in their lives.

- **Historically**, mentally ill people have been thought to be possessed by **evil spirits**, suffering from an imbalance of the **humours**, or morally **wicked**.
- The **medical model** sees mental illness as having a physical basis. In particular, **genetic factors**, an imbalance in **neurotransmitters** or other **neurological problems** are seen as important. There is some evidence that these factors play a major part in some disorders.
- Since the causes are presumed to be physical, **physical treatments** such as drugs are offered. They are helpful in treating the symptoms of some disorders.

❺ **Anti-psychiatrists** take issue with the medical model of mental illness. Szasz believed that there is no such thing as mental illness, and that the concept is used to **control** people. Laing objected to the processes and procedures used as **dehumanising** to the patient.

The behavioural model

As with other areas of psychology, behaviourists relate abnormal behaviour to learning. Behaviourists believe that all behaviours, apart from the few simple reflexes we are born with, are learned. They therefore see mental disorders as learned, inappropriate behaviours which they call **maladaptive behaviours**.

You will remember from chapter 1 that the two main theories relating to this model are classical and operant conditioning. According to **classical conditioning**, behaviours are learned by forming an association between an environmental event (a stimulus) and a physiological reaction (a response). This idea has been particularly influential in explaining the development of phobias. In the same way that Pavlov's dogs learned to respond by salivation to the sound of a bell, a person may learn to produce a fear response when they see a snake or find themselves in an enclosed space.

In **operant conditioning**, an association is formed between a behaviour and its consequences. If a behaviour has favourable consequences (**positive reinforcement**), it is likely to be repeated. For example, these principles have been used to explain conduct disorders in children where inappropriate behaviour may have been reinforced by attention.

The behavioural model of mental disorders, however, is not concerned with causes. It claims that we do not need to know what has brought about a maladaptive behaviour. The problem is the behaviour, so the focus of therapy is on helping people to unlearn these behaviours, and to learn new, more adaptive ones.

For example, in the case of someone who is phobic, one way in which the principles of classical conditioning can be applied in therapy is through the use of **systematic desensitisation**. The phobic person is gradually exposed to the situation or object of their phobia and learns to relax. Exposure is gradually increased until the phobia has disappeared. This works on the principle that it is not possible to have competing responses (fear and relaxation) to the same stimulus. Another possibility is **flooding**, where the person is exposed to the phobic object or situation in an extreme form, on the principle that extreme fear cannot be maintained.

Behavioural therapy has the advantage of being relatively quick and straightforward, and is very successful with some disorders, such as phobias. The behavioural approach, however, has been criticised as being unduly reductionist, since it focuses only on behaviour, and does not take higher mental processes such as thoughts, feelings and memories into account. Many therapists also believe that we need to uncover the root causes of the behaviour in order to find out what underlying emotional problems a person is experiencing. If this is not done, and these problems are not dealt with, there may be **symptom substitution**, where the problem behaviour which has been unlearned is replaced by another, equally maladaptive behaviour.

The cognitive model

You will remember from chapter 1 that cognitive psychologists focus on internal mental processes. In the area of psychopathology, cognitive theorists have suggested that the root of disorders lies in the way people think about events and experiences. In Personal Construct Theory, for example, George Kelly (1955) suggested that every individual made sense of the world using **bipolar constructs**, such as happy–sad or honest–dishonest. These constructs are useful because they provide each of us with a **personal reality**, built on constructs which relate to our individual experience of the world, which can help us to understand the events and people we encounter. This creates a sense of predictability and therefore control over our lives.

According to Kelly, psychological disorders are due to faulty thinking processes, such as the failure of a person's construct system. For example, he explained anxiety in terms of the realisation that our construct system is inadequate for making sense of the events we experience and the people we meet. A person with a mental disorder may be using inappropriate constructs to make sense of the world, or constructs which are too limited or too vague to be helpful. People with psychological disorders continue to use inappropriate constructs rather than altering them, despite the fact that their predictions about events and other people are repeatedly shown to be wrong. This leads to mentally ill people anticipating events with very little accuracy. The implications of this for therapy are that the therapist needs to help the person with problems to change the way they understand the world by adapting their construct systems.

Other cognitive theorists are Aaron Beck and Albert Ellis. They explain mental disorders in similarly cognitive terms to Kelly, but focus on irrational beliefs and negative thoughts rather than explaining inappropriate thinking in terms of bipolar constructs. Beck (1967), for example, related depression to negative thoughts in three areas, which he called the triad of negative assumptions – the self, circumstances and the future:

Figure 4: Beck's triad of negative assumptions

- **Negative view of self**
  (e.g. I am a worthless person)
- **Negative view of circumstances**
  (e.g. everything is bleak and I cannot cope with what people expect of me)
- **Negative view of the future**
  (e.g. things can only get worse, and there is nothing I can do to change them)

Problems occur when these kinds of faulty thinking prevent the person from behaving adaptively.

The therapies cognitive theorists think are appropriate are cognitive (Kelly) or cognitive–behavioural (Beck and Ellis). For Kelly, the person with a mental disorder needs to be helped to develop a more adaptive construct system. For Beck and Ellis, faulty thinking needs to be challenged, and more positive ways of thinking need to be translated into behaviour during the therapeutic process in order to be effective.

Inappropriate ways of making sense of the world and faulty cognitions have been found to be associated with a range of mental disorders. For some disorders, in particular depression but also phobias and anxiety disorders, cognitive therapy can be very effective.

At the same time, however, it has been suggested – by Beck (1991) himself among others – that irrational and maladaptive thinking may be the *result* of a mental disorder rather than its cause. A further criticism of this approach is that it focuses very much on the individual who is experiencing problems; it may therefore not give enough weight to the contribution made by environmental factors (such as poor housing or the characteristics of other family members) to the development of a disorder.

The psychodynamic model

The psychodynamic model centres round the ideas of Freud. According to this model, mental disorder is due to **psychic conflict**, and has its roots in **childhood experience**. The causes of mental disorders lie in the **unconscious**. You may find it useful at this point to look back to the outline of Freud's theory in chapter 1 to remind yourself of its basic principles.

According to Freud, the three parts of the mind are the id, the ego and the superego. In the mentally healthy person, the ego is in control. Mental disorder will result from conflict between the different parts of the mind with which we are unable to cope.

Freud believed that early experiences are crucial to our development. Unresolved and unconscious conflicts relating to our experience of psychosexual development will lead to a mental disorder.

One of Freud's main ideas is that the unconscious mind is all-important. According to Freud, our lives are controlled by internal, unconscious forces of which we are mainly unaware. Ego defence mechanisms are used to prevent the anxiety resulting from psychic conflict from reaching consciousness. However, using defence mechanisms distorts our perception of reality. The conflict which has become unconscious has not been dealt with, so still continues to affect how we experience the world and our behaviour.

Since the causes of mental disorder lie in the unconscious, the aim of therapy is to bring our unconscious conflicts into consciousness so that they can be resolved. Psychodynamic therapy is called **psychoanalysis**. It is a talking therapy, and the main method used is **free association**, where the patient talks freely about anything which comes into their head. With the help of a psychoanalyst, unconscious material is brought into consciousness and interpreted by the analyst, who helps the patient to 'work through' the underlying problems.

There are problems with this model of mental disorder, since it relies very much on interpretation, and many people find the underlying ideas about psychosexual development unconvincing. It has also been accused of being overly reductionist, since it sees people as basically driven by animal instincts over which they have no control. Many people claim to have been helped by psychoanalysis, but it is difficult to evaluate its effectiveness objectively.

▷ Activity 4: which approach?

Match each of the following statements with one or more of these approaches:

medical   **behavioural**
cognitive   **psychodynamic**

a We do not need to know what has caused a person to have a particular problem in order to treat them.
b Therapy consists mainly of talking.
c People need to be helped to make sense of how they experience the world.
d The root causes of problems are to be found in childhood experiences.
e Drugs are a useful way of helping people with problems.
f Mental illnesses have an organic cause.
g This approach can be criticised as being reductionist.

When you have finished, see the notes on page 120.

❺ The **behavioural** model explains mental disorders in terms of faulty **learning**. Treatment therefore involves learning more appropriate behaviour.

❺ In the **cognitive** model, mental disorders are linked to faulty ways of **making sense** of our world, implying that treatment should focus on developing more appropriate cognitions.
❺ The **psychodynamic** model sees the roots of abnormal behaviour in **psychic conflict**. Treatment involves dealing with unconscious conflict through psychoanalysis.

5.5 CRITICAL ISSUE: EATING DISORDERS

The classification system DSM-IV characterises eating disorders as physically and/or psychologically harmful eating patterns. The two disorders we shall be looking at in this section are **anorexia nervosa** and **bulimia nervosa**. There is some discussion about whether anorexia and bulimia should be thought of as separate disorders or variants of the same disorder. As we will see, some of the evidence relating to the causes of these disorders relates to one or the other, and some to both.

Anorexia nervosa

Anorexia has a high profile in the media, so it is likely that you already know something about it:

▷ Activity 5: anorexia – true or false?

Read through these statements and decide whether you think they are true or false:
a Anorexia is most likely to affect teenage girls.
b People with anorexia do not feel hungry.
c Most people with anorexia recover.
d Anorectics see themselves as fatter than they actually are.
e Anorexia usually starts as an attempt to lose weight.
f There is a similar incidence of anorexia across cultures.

Check your answers by reading through the rest of this section.

Anorexia nervosa means 'nervous loss of appetite', though sufferers do experience hunger. The problem is that they do not respond to it by eating appropriately. Anorectics refuse to maintain the minimum expected body weight and are at least 15% below what is regarded as normal. Typical characteristics are shown in figure 5:

Figure 5: typical characteristics of anorectics

a a fear of gaining weight or becoming fat

b a distorted body image: although they are thin, they believe that they are fat

c denial that they have a problem

d perfectionism

e obsession with food and its preparation, with a tendency to hide food to conceal the fact that they are not eating it

f avoidance of high-calorie food

g excessive exercising

h amenorrhoea in females: one diagnostic criterion is three missed periods

Although they are thin they believe they are fat

Of course some of these characteristics are also true of non-anorectics, but figure 5 gives some idea of the general overall pattern typically found in anorectics. DSM-IV divides anorectics into two types, **bingeing** and **non-bingeing**. Between 30 and 50% of anorectics also binge and vomit.

Ninety per cent of anorectics are females, with the onset of the disorder usually between the ages of 13 and 18. Some cases are as young as 8, and sufferers may be older than 18. Anorexia also seems to be on the increase among males, of whom around half are homosexual. DSM-IV claims that the incidence is 0.5–1% among young females. The top two social classes (professional and managerial) are over-represented, as are certain professions; according to Garfinkel and Garner (1982), dancers and models account for 7% of cases.

Twenty per cent of anorectics have one episode but make a full recovery. Sixty per cent have a pattern of weight gain and relapse over several years. The remaining 20% are severely affected and usually need

to be hospitalised. The mortality rate in this group is more than 10%; anorectics die from starvation, suicide or electrolyte imbalance. Hsu (1990) reports that anorexia is fatal in 5% to 15% of cases.

Figure 5 described the psychological and behavioural characteristics typically associated with anorexia. Someone with this disorder may also show changes in their physical appearance apart from extreme thinness. Typically the skin of anorectics is dry, rough and dirty-looking. They may grow hair on cheeks, neck, forearms or thighs, known as **lanugo hair**, and may lose scalp hair. They have an abnormal intolerance of cold, so have bluish fingers and toes, a condition known as **cyanosis**.

There are several physical and psychological effects of the disorder. Sufferers have a low metabolic rate. They sleep less than normal, and have a low or non-existent sex drive. They suffer from constipation, and sometimes swollen ankles (**peripheral oedema**). They are likely to develop a mood disorder, e.g. depression, or an anxiety disorder. They also show a high rate of alcoholism. They often suffer from anaemia and dehydration, and are liable to die from heart failure.

Bulimia nervosa

'Bulimia' comes from the Greek, meaning 'ox hunger'. It is typified by binge eating followed by behaviour to prevent weight gain, i.e. vomiting, misuse of laxatives and diuretics, excessive exercise or fasting. Non-bulimics may also binge and purge occasionally; it is the frequency of this behaviour which defines the bulimic – it takes place on average 2–3 times a week, and sometimes as often as 30 times.

Bulimics usually have normal weight but a distorted body image, so they see themselves as fatter than they are. They indulge in secretive overeating – up to 10,000 calories at a time – of fattening foods, eaten rapidly with little chewing. Eating stops when the food runs out or when the bulimic experiences severe abdominal pain. They may use coloured marker foods to ensure that all food is eliminated by vomiting. Depression and guilt are common. Bulimics recognise their behaviour is abnormal; the sufferer is aware of loss of control. They often have swollen features with puffy parotid glands, caused by vomiting. Parry-Jones and Parry-Jones (1993) found that four bulimics of the 25 they studied were self-mutilators, i.e. they cut themselves, which they suggest may be a way of reducing anxiety. Parkin and Eagles (1993) described three bulimics who showed similar behaviour, using blood-letting to reduce tension and anxiety.

Nearly all sufferers – 95% – are female. The average age of onset is slightly later than for anorexia; many bulimics have previously suffered from anorexia. It is difficult to establish how prevalent bulimia is, because bulimics usually have normal body weight and they are also secretive about their eating habits. It may be more common than anorexia; it has been suggested that it affects up to 5% of females in their late teens or early twenties.

Bulimia is associated with cardiac problems, sometimes epileptic seizures, kidney damage, hair loss and metabolic disturbances. There is often also throat damage and dental erosion from the corrosive effects of stomach acids as a result of repeated vomiting.

❺ The main characteristic of people suffering from **anorexia** is a refusal to maintain normal body weight, together with a belief that they are fat, and a refusal to acknowledge that they have a problem. The disorder is associated with a range of psychological and behavioural characteristics, and can result in severe medical problems and even death. Sufferers are typically females in their teens.

❺ **Bulimia** usually has a slightly later onset. It involves bouts of bingeing and purging. Incidence is difficult to establish because sufferers have normal body weight. As with anorexia, there are serious medical implications.

As with other disorders, the suggested aetiology of eating disorders is a much disputed area. Some theorists focus on possible **biological** factors while others stress the importance of **social** and **psychological factors**.

It is also possible that biological and social/psychological factors interact. The **diathesis–stress model** suggests that some people may be predisposed to develop a particular disorder (**diathesis** refers to this vulnerability), either for genetic reasons or as the result of early experience. Whether they in fact develop the disorder will depend on the amount of **stress** in their lives.

It is important to know as much as possible about the causes of a mental disorder, so that an appropriate therapy can be offered to the patient. For example, if the disorder has a biochemical cause, then it would seem most sensible to use a drug therapy; if the disorder is related to faulty cognitive processes, then cognitive therapy, which aims to change the way someone views the world, would seem to be a good place to start treatment. As we will see, however, a range of explanations has

Anorexia	Higher prevalence in middle and upper socio-economic group	Bulimia
Underweight Bingeing (for some)	Mainly female	Normal weight
Denial of problem	Distorted body image	Frequent bingeing
Depression (for some)	Fear of gaining weight	Awareness of problem
Peak onset: mid-teens	Secretive about eating behaviour	Guilt and depression
Life threatening	Likelihood of heart problems	Peak onset: early 20s
Damage to kidneys and gastrointestinal system	Metabolic disturbances	Rarely life threatening

been offered for eating disorders, and in no case does any one theory provide a definitive explanation.

Biological explanations of eating disorders

One possibility is that eating disorders may have a **genetic** basis. One way of exploring this has been through the use of **family studies**. Family studies look at the incidence of a particular disorder within families. If the cause is genetic, it would be expected that if one member of a family has the disorder, other members are also more likely than unrelated people to have it, particularly if they are close relatives. This approach usually relies on interviewing family members about the family, both current and past generations.

Activity 6: family studies

Can you think of any problems with the technique described above? Why might we need to be wary of drawing conclusions, using this method, about the contribution of genes to a disorder?
When you have finished, see the notes on page 120.

DSM-IV states that there is an increased risk of an eating disorder in first-degree relatives of sufferers, i.e. parents, brothers and sisters or children. However, because of the problems associated with family studies, this does not necessarily mean that the cause of eating disorders is genetic.

Twin studies are another way in which a possible genetic influence can be investigated. Twins can be **fraternal** (**dizygotic** or **DZ**: they develop from different fertilised eggs within the mother) or **identical** (**monozygotic** or **MZ**: developing from only one fertilised egg). Fraternal twins share on average 50% of their genes, the same proportion as any brother or sister. Identical twins, as the name suggests, have 100% of their genes in common.

The reasoning behind twin studies is that if one identical twin suffers from a disorder, and the disorder is genetically caused, then the other twin must also suffer from the same disorder, since they have all their genes in common. In other words there should be 100% **concordance** between

identical twins. For fraternal twins, however, there should be a much lower concordance rate, approximately 50%, similar to that between brothers and sisters who are not twins. If the environment is important, a low concordance between MZ twins reared apart would be expected.

Twin studies have been more informative than family studies in investigating a possible genetic basis for eating disorders:

Box E: concordance for eating disorders in twin studies

Holland *et al*. (1984) – anorexia:
MZ twins: 55%   DZ twins: 7%

Kendler *et al*. (1991) – bulimia:
MZ twins: 23%   DZ twins: 8.7%

These studies support the idea that there may be a genetic link in eating disorders, but at the same time concordance is a long way off 100%, particularly for bulimia, so other factors are clearly involved.

It is possible that eating disorders are caused by a **neurotransmitter** imbalance in a structure in the brain called the **hypothalamus**, which is known to be one of the structures controlling eating behaviour:

Figure 6: the hypothalamus and eating behaviour

lateral hypothalamus (LH) →	stimulates eating (neurotransmitters: noradrenaline and dopamine)
ventromedial hypothalamus (VMH) →	inhibits eating (neurotransmitter: serotonin)

Activity 7: neurotransmitters and eating disorders

How could each of the following help to account for either anorexia or bulimia?
a low levels of noradrenaline
b low levels of serotonin
When you have finished, see the notes on page 120.

Further evidence of neurotransmitter involvement comes from the use of antidepressant drugs which influence neurotransmitter levels, and have sometimes helped to reduce binge–purge behaviour in bulimics. However, the results of research in this area have been inconsistent.

A further idea links eating disorders with **hormones**. One piece of evidence comes from Lydiard *et al.* (1993), who found low levels of the hormone **CCK-8** in bulimics. Park *et al.* (1995) suggested the possibility of a viral or immune system disorder, since four anorectics he studied had had glandular fever. This could affect the production of **corticotrophin releasing hormone (CRH)**, which would in turn affect the functioning of the **hypothalamus**, which as shown in figure 6 controls eating behaviour.

One problem with looking to hormones for the cause of eating disorders, however, is that hormone function can be influenced by emotional factors, so it is difficult to establish the direction of any causal connection between hormonal function and eating disorders.

A recent suggestion, put forward by Kennedy (1997), is that anorexia may be due to abnormality in the **temporal lobes** of the cortex. Scanning techniques have shown reduced blood flow to these areas in anorectics. This could explain their distorted body image, since these lobes are involved in the interpretation of what we see.

- **Twin studies** suggest a **genetic** link in eating disorders, particularly **anorexia**.
- **Neurotransmitters** may also be involved, with low levels of **noradrenaline** being associated with **anorexia**, and low levels of **serotonin** with **bulimia**.
- **Hormones** and **temporal lobe abnormality** could also be implicated.

Social and psychological explanations of eating disorders

A range of social and psychological explanations for eating disorders has been proposed: behavioural explanations, cultural factors, cognitive explanations, psychodynamic explanations, and the nature of family relationships.

Behavioural explanations

Attempts have been made to account for eating disorders as learned behaviour, using the principles of conditioning theory. If we use the **classical conditioning** model, the UCS of admiration produces the UCR of feeling good about yourself. When slimming is paired with admiration, slimming itself becomes a CS producing the CR of feeling good about yourself. Using the **operant conditioning** model, admiration for slimness reinforces dieting behaviour. It may also be reinforced by attention; for example, from parents. In this way, slimming may become a habit.

Anorexia has also been explained as a **weight phobia**, brought about by social norms. Advertising puts across the message that 'slim is beautiful', and dieting in Western cultures is often seen as 'normal'. Garner *et al.* (1980) found that Playboy centrefolds and contestants in the Miss America Pageant had become thinner over the previous twenty years, while over the same period the average weight for women had increased. Similarly, Wade and Tavris (1993) reported that Miss Sweden of 1951 was 5'7" tall and weighed 151 pounds, while Miss Sweden of 1983 was 5'9" tall and weighed only 109 pounds.

While these ideas are perhaps not entirely successful in explaining such features of anorexia as distorted perception of body size, and the willingness to pursue the goal of thinness even if it leads to death, they do have some intuitive appeal, and link in well with explanations which focus on culture.

Cultural factors

It has been found that anorexia and bulimia are more common in industrialised societies, where there is an abundance of food, while at the same time slimness is seen as attractive. Immigrants from non-industrialised societies, once they are assimilated, are as likely to develop these disorders as the indigenous population. All this suggests that eating disorders may be linked to cultural factors.

Support for this comes from Sui-Wah (1989), who pointed out that eating disorders are rare in China, and suggested that this may be linked to the respect the Chinese have for food. There is a cultural norm in China of meals being seen as social occasions, so there is pressure to conform to family eating patterns.

The idea of cultural influences is taken further in a feminist perspective on eating disorders. This points out that the images of ideal women presented by our society are constructed by men, since they have the power within society. Images of males concentrate on action, while those of females focus on appearance. Therefore it is only through their appearance that women can exert power, by conforming to the 'ideal' body shape. Orbach (1978) has suggested that bingeing is an expression of anger at social pressure to be thin, while purging is a way of regaining control.

The idea of control is also raised by Lewis and Blair (1991). They argued that women in our society receive conflicting messages about their role: they need to achieve academically and in a career, while at the same time raising a family and putting partner and children first. Anorexia may be a way of regaining control over at least one aspect of their lives.

Cognitive explanations

The underlying principle of cognitive explanations for eating disorders is that attitudes and beliefs influence eating behaviour – for example, the belief that 'thin = successful, happy and attractive'. In bulimics, a broken diet may lead to uninhibited eating (the **disinhibition hypothesis**). A cognitive explanation for this could be the reasoning: 'I broke my diet. What's the use? I failed so I may as well go all the way.' There is some research evidence supporting a cognitive explanation of bulimia:

Box F: Cutts and Barrios (1986)

Procedure: A group of bulimics and a control group were asked to imagine gaining weight. Their heart rate and muscle tension were monitored as indicators of emotional arousal.
Results: The bulimics, but not the controls, showed an increased heart rate and muscle tension.
Conclusion: There are cognitive differences between bulimics and non-bulimics in relation to weight gain.

Cognitive ideas also link well with the distorted body image of anorectics, and we will look at this aspect of the disorder in a little more detail here. Three techniques are used to assess body image:

Figure 7: investigating body image

moving caliper technique
The person is asked to imagine their body silhouetted on a screen, and to mark the width of the face, shoulders, waist and hips using sliding calipers. This is then compared with the actual body measurements.

image-marking technique
The person is asked to face a large sheet of paper and imagine it is a mirror. They are then asked to mark the width of the body at various points.

distorting image technique
An image of the person is projected on a screen through a lens. The image can be adjusted horizontally to make it more or less fat. The person is asked to adjust the image until it seems right to them. This technique is the most realistic and reliable, but requires more elaborate equipment.

There is some evidence of a link between overestimation of body width and anorexia:

Box G: Slade and Russell (1973)

Procedure: Anorectics and controls were asked to estimate their body width. They were also asked to estimate their height, and the width of other objects.
Results: Anorectics overestimated the width of their bodies by 25–55%, while controls estimated body width accurately. There was no difference between anorectics and controls in the accuracy of their estimations of their height and the width of other objects.
Conclusion: There is a strong link between anorexia and distorted body image.

Other research in this area, however, has produced conflicting results. Crisp and Kalucy (1974) found that controls also overestimated body width, but this may be because the group they tested was younger, and estimation of body size becomes more accurate with age. Thompson (1986), however, showed that 95% of women in fact overestimate their weight; it is possible, though, that anorectics overestimate by a greater margin. Even if distorted body image is related to anorexia, it could be that the distortion is a result of the disorder, rather than its cause. A further problem, as Yager *et al.* (1986) have pointed out, is that there are blind anorectics; though of course they will still have a body image based on senses other than sight.

Psychodynamic explanations

Several ideas have been put forward from a psychodynamic perspective. For Freud, eating can be a substitute for sexual expression, so eating disorders could be a symbolic way of repressing sexual impulses. You will remember that one of the characteristics of anorexia is amenorrhoea, which returns the body to a prepubescent state, so the disorder could be a way of avoiding the issue of sexuality. This idea has been given a rather broader focus in the suggestion that anorexia may be a way of avoiding the demands of adulthood by regressing to childhood.

Many patients with eating disorders report in therapy being sexually abused as children, so an eating disorder may be a response to early traumatic experiences. Sexual abuse may lead people to reject their own bodies in adolescence, so anorexia and bulimia may express an unconscious desire to destroy their own bodies.

> ## ◗ Activity 8: evaluating psychodynamic explanations
>
> Look back through the psychodynamic explanations outlined above. Can you identify any problems with what they suggest?
>
> When you have finished, see the notes on page 120.

Research findings have questioned psychodynamic explanations. The idea that amenorrhoea could be the aim of anorexia has been challenged by Halmi *et al.* (1977). They found that in almost 40% of

anorectics, menstruation ceased *before* significant weight loss occurred, suggesting that an underlying endocrine problem is the cause of amenorrhoea.

Similarly, of the 18 patients with eating disorders studied by Piran *et al.* (1985), eight had shown symptoms of depression at least a year before the eating disorder had developed, suggesting that any link between childhood trauma and developing an eating disorder is likely only to be indirect.

Family relationships

Eating disorders have also been related to problems in family relationships, especially the struggle of young people to establish their own identity. Bemis (1978), for example, argued that anorectics are often well-behaved and co-operative girls, who may feel that they are overly controlled by others. Overcontrolling parents may lead young people to feel that they lack a separate identity, which in turn leads to low self-esteem. Anorexia may be one way of taking control.

The fact that anorexia is more common in middle-class families, where there is likely to be considerable pressure on young people to succeed, lends some support to this idea. Similarly, Pike and Rodin (1991) found a link between eating disorders and mothers who thought their daughters were unattractive and should lose weight.

Coming from a psychodynamic background, Bruch (1973) made a link between anorexia and early relationships between infant and mother. She suggested that distorted body image and faulty hunger awareness both come about as a result of the mother failing to respond to the infant's signals. This leaves the infant with the feeling of being an ineffective individual.

Family systems theories suggest that we need to look at the dynamics within the family in order to understand why one member has an eating disorder. Bruch (1973) believed that anorexia may be mutually rewarding for mother and child: the mother retains the child and the child remains dependent. According to Minuchin *et al.* (1978), anorexia may be a way of diverting the attention of parents who are having marital problems away from each other and on to the child, as a way of preventing family break-up.

All these ideas imply that family therapy is the most useful way to treat eating problems, and it is widely used, with some success.

▷ Activity 9: explanations of eating disorders

Read through the following suggestions which have been put forward to explain eating disorders, and sort them under these headings:
biological, cultural, psychodynamic, family relationships, cognitive, learning

a Women are under pressure from the media to be thin.

b Women are encouraged to be thin by praise and attention from others.

c Tensions within the family may trigger eating disorders.

d Low levels of noradrenaline are related to anorexia.

e Anorexia may be the expression of a weight phobia.

f Eating disorders express the relative powerlessness of females in our society.

g Anorexia may be a way of retreating from sexuality and adult responsibilities.

h Distorted thoughts and beliefs about food and eating lead to eating disorders.

When you have finished, see the notes on page 120.

Explanations of eating disorders: an overview

We have looked at a range of suggestions as to why people might develop eating disorders. There are several levels of explanation. Biological explanations focus on genetic and neurochemical factors in the individual. Learning theory, psychodynamic and cognitive explanations also have their focus very much on the individual, while psychologists interested in family relationships look more at the individual within a social context. The focus can be even broader, taking in aspects of the cultural context.

As we have seen, all these approaches have something to offer, while none seems to provide a complete explanation of eating disorders. However, these different kinds of explanations are not necessarily mutually exclusive. Biological factors may interact with cognitions, influenced by social norms and expectations, and further influenced by particular patterns of family interactions, to lead to the development of anorexia and/or bulimia.

- ❺ **Learning theorists** explain eating disorders in terms of classical and operant **conditioning**. They suggest that such disorders may be a **weight phobia**.
- ❺ **Cultural factors** may be implicated in eating disorders; they are more common in Western cultures, where slimness is presented as the 'ideal'. They have been related to the relative powerlessness of women in society, and may be used as a way of exerting control over their lives.
- ❺ According to **cognitive** theorists, eating disorders are the result of **inappropriate beliefs** and attitudes.
- ❺ **Psychodynamic** explanations make a link with **regression** to childhood, and avoidance of adult sexuality and responsibilities. These ideas are, however, difficult to test.
- ❺ It has been suggested that the cause of eating disorders may lie in **family relationships**. They may be a way in which young people seek to establish their own identity, separate from an over-controlling parent; the result of inappropriate maternal feedback to an infant; or an attempted solution to distorted family relationships.
- ❺ These different explanations are not necessarily mutually exclusive. The **interaction** of different factors may lead to eating disorders.

Notes on activities are on page 120.

Notes on activities

2 There are some parallels between these two systems. The term 'affectionate relationships' used by Atkinson *et al.* seems to be expressing a similar idea to Jahoda's 'positive interpersonal relationships'. Also, 'voluntary control' is similar to 'autonomy', and 'efficient perception of reality' is similar to 'accurate perception of reality'.

Jahoda's term 'self-acceptance' brings in aspects of 'self-knowledge' and 'self-esteem' from the Atkinson *et al.* list, though 'self-esteem' is rather more positive than 'self-acceptance'. 'Productivity' from the Atkinson *et al.* list has something in common with 'potential for growth and development', though the latter focuses more on the individual and the former relates also to interaction with others. 'Productivity' therefore shares some aspects of Jahoda's term 'environmental competence', though it goes further in its emphasis on interaction with the external environment.

3 The first two correspond to female stereotypes, and the last two to male stereotypes.

4 **a** behavioural; **b** psychodynamic; **c** cognitive; **d** psychodynamic; **e** medical; **f** medical; **g** behavioural and psychodynamic.

6 The technique asks ordinary people, untrained in diagnosing mental disorders, to draw conclusions about the mental health of members of their family. Information about past generations relies on the accuracy of the memory of the interviewee. These kinds of problem have been overcome to some extent by looking at the medical records of family members, but of course this can only be done when people have presented for treatment. Even if it is clear that family members do have similar disorders, we cannot assume that the disorder is inherited; close family members are likely to share the same physical and psychological environment, and this could account for the similarity.

7 Low levels of **noradrenaline** acting on the lateral hypothalamus could be insufficient to stimulate eating and so could be a partial explanation for **anorexia**. Similarly, low levels of **serotonin** may not be enough to inhibit eating and so could partially explain bingeing in **bulimics**.

8 As with all psychodynamic ideas, these suggestions are not easy to test in a rigorous way. The link with amenorrhoea can only relate to females; while most people with eating disorders are female, males are also affected. Similarly, while the onset is most frequently in the early teens, the idea of avoiding sexuality or adult responsibilities cannot explain why the onset is often later, particularly for bulimics. It could also be that any connection between childhood trauma and eating disorders is rather indirect; for example, sexual abuse could lead to depression, which might then be expressed in an eating disorder.

9 **a** learning; cultural   **b** learning   **c** family relationships **d** biological   **e** learning   **f** cultural **g** psychodynamic   **h** cognitive

Social influence

In this chapter we will be looking at:

6.1 Conformity
   Ambiguous and unambiguous
      situations
   Cultural differences in conformity
   Why do people conform?
   Conformity and social roles
   Minority influence
   Evaluation of conformity research

6.2 Obedience
   Milgram's research
   Ethical factors in Milgram's research
   Gender, culture and victim
      characteristics
   Milgram and after

6.3 Individual differences in response
      to social influence

6.4 Independent behaviour

6.5 Critical issue: The development of
      ethical guidelines for research
   Consent
   Deception
   Debriefing
   Right to withdraw
   Confidentiality
   Protection from harm
   Observational studies
   Giving advice
   The morality of carrying out
      research: psychology and
      the ethical imperative

One area in which social psychologists have been particularly interested is the effect that other people can have on our behaviour. This general area can conveniently be described by the term **social influence.** This is relevant to very many areas in social psychology, and we will be focusing in this chapter on only two forms of influence: conformity and obedience.

6.1 CONFORMITY

Conformity refers to behaviour change as a result of group pressure. This pressure doesn't necessarily need to be expressed, and may even just be in the mind of the person who experiences it; for example, Mary may feel that she should study languages at university because this is what her two older sisters have done. Sometimes, though, there is explicit pressure; for example, if the rest of the family suggest that this is what Mary should do.

Ambiguous and unambiguous situations

Research into conformity goes back a long way. Allport (1924) asked participants to judge the pleasantness of smells, and found that if people made this judgement in groups, individual judgements tended to be in general agreement with the average judgement for the group as a whole. Similarly, when Jenness (1932) asked participants to judge the number of beans in a bottle, and then revise their estimates after discussion in a group, the second estimate tended to move towards the average group judgement. Another study, shown in box A, demonstrated conformity using a visual illusion called the **autokinetic effect**: when there is a point of light in an otherwise darkened room, it seems to move about:

Box A: Sherif (1935)

Procedure: Participants were asked individually to estimate how far and in what direction the point of light moved. Average scores were worked out for each participant over a series of trials. They were then divided into groups, each group containing participants with very different averages calculated from the individual trials. Participants were then asked to make individual judgements while in their groups.

Results: After a few trials, individual judgements tended to move towards agreement within the group. The effect was still evident when the tests were repeated later, with participants tested individually.

Conclusion: When making judgements in a group, there is a tendency for individual judgements to drift towards group consensus, i.e. to conform to the average for the group.

Box B: Asch (1951)

Procedure: All participants were given the simple task of matching a standard line with one of three comparison lines (see figure 1). They were tested in groups of seven, of whom six were confederates of Asch. They were asked for their decisions in order, going round a table, with the genuine participant sitting last but one. On some trials, the confederates were asked to give the (same) wrong answer.

Results: Participants conformed to the group's incorrect judgements in about 32% of trials on average. This can be compared to a control group, with no confederate participants, where judgements were virtually 100% correct.

Conclusion: In a group situation, there is a tendency to conform to the judgements of others, even where this judgement is clearly incorrect.

It is worth noting that Sherif's study did not *ask* participants to arrive at a group estimate. It is a nice example of conformity where there is no direct and explicit pressure to change behaviour; influence comes about through the individual's perception of the situation.

This study has not been without its critics, however. Asch, who went on to carry out his own series of studies on conformity (see box B), pointed out that Sherif's study had put participants into a situation of uncertainty, i.e. where a correct answer was not apparent: since the light does not actually move at all, but only seems to move, there is no right or wrong answer.

He argued that for a real understanding of conformity, we need to look at what happens in an *un*ambiguous situation. In other words, there should be one clearly correct solution to the task, and we should look at whether participants move from a position held with certainty to conform to obviously wrong answers given by others.

Figure 1: the Asch task

a Standard line   **b** Comparison lines

Asch found that about a quarter of his participants *never* conformed to the group's wrong judgement, leaving three-quarters who *did* conform at least once. Some participants conformed on only a few trials where incorrect judgements were made, and only about 1 in 20 conformed each time. We will be returning to the question of individual differences in susceptibility to social influence later in the chapter.

Participants who conformed to the majority gave a variety of reasons for conforming.

▷ Activity 1: explaining Asch's findings

Imagine you had taken part in this study, and conformed at least occasionally to the incorrect judgements of the group. How might you explain what you did?

When you have finished, see the notes on page 149.

Asch followed up his original study with some variations, to look in more detail at some of the possible variables which could affect conformity.

▷ Activity 2: other conformity research by Asch

Here are some of the questions Asch investigated in later studies. What do you think his findings were? Try to give reasons for your answers:

a How would more/fewer confederates affect conformity?

b What would be the effect of having one of the six confederates giving the *right* answer?

c What would happen if someone agreed with the genuine participant (as in question 2) to start with, but then gave the majority answer in later trials?

d What would happen if the task were more difficult, i.e. the lines closer in length?

e How would a majority of naive participants react to only *one* confederate in the group giving a wrong answer?

f Would the effect be the same if the genuine participant could give his answer in private?

When you have finished, see the notes on page 149.

Another question is whether other people need to be physically present for conformity to occur, or if the belief that others are carrying out the same task is all that is necessary. To investigate this question, Crutchfield set up an experimental situation where participants worked in booths on their own, so were not directly exposed to other participants. They were asked to indicate agreement or disagreement by means of switches which would turn on lights. They were aware of the judgments of other people from a display of lights, and believed that their own responses were similarly available to other participants (see box C).

Box C: Crutchfield (1954)

Procedure: More than 600 participants were tested, including American college students and military personnel. They were tested for conformity on a range of tasks, including clearly incorrect factual statements and personal opinions, e.g:

a agreement with statements such as: 60–70% of Americans are over 65 years old; Americans sleep 4–5 hours a night, on average

b an Asch-type task

c agreement that a star had a larger surface area than a circle (in fact it was a third smaller)

d agreement with the statement 'I doubt that I would make an effective leader.'

e agreement with the statement 'Free speech being a privilege rather than a right, it is proper for a society to suspend free speech when it feels itself threatened'. Participants might have been expected not to agree with this opinion, given that free speech is enshrined as a right in the American constitution.

Results: The degree of conformity varied with the nature of the task. There was 46% conformity to **c**, for example, and only 30% conformity to **b**. Thirty-seven per cent agreed with **d**, none of whom did so when asked on their own. Substantial numbers of participants agreed with the 'facts' given in **a**, and the opinion given in **e**.

Conclusion: There was conformity both to incorrect facts and to opinions. The extent to which conformity was shown depended on the nature of the task.

The information they were given about other judgements was, of course, actually manipulated by the experimenter.

Crutchfield's results were in broad agreement with those of Asch, and extended Asch's work by demonstrating conformity not only in factual judgements, but also opinions. Like Asch, Crutchfield found that some participants never conformed to an incorrect judgement made by the majority, some always conformed and most conformed some of the time.

⊝ Early studies into conformity used situations in which the answer was uncertain. The classic study by Asch, using a task where there was a clearly correct answer, found a high rate of conformity. Variations on this study isolated particular factors such as group size which affect conformity.

⊝ Some conforming participants in Asch's study showed **public conformity**, but no **private change**. Others changed their judgement as a result of social influence.

⊝ Crutchfield's study extended conformity research to opinions.

Cultural differences in conformity

You will have noticed that many of the studies referred to were carried out some time ago, and mostly used American students as research participants, i.e. they provided a snapshot of a particular culture at a particular time. But can these findings be generalised to other populations, and more recent times?

Larsen (1974) replicated Asch's original experiment with American college students, to investigate whether cultural changes in the preceding twenty years would affect conformity rates. Participants still conformed, but at a lower rate than the 32% of the Asch study. Perhaps at that time the US had become a less conformist culture? A further replication in 1979, however, found a rise in conformity.

There may be some variation as culture is modified with the passing of time, but what about **cross-cultural** differences? Using Asch's technique, there have been findings similar to those of Asch in Brazil, Hong Kong and the Lebanon. A higher conformity rate, however, was found among the Bantu in Zimbabwe (Whittaker and Meade, 1967). Every culture needs a degree of conformity, to simplify social life by giving it order and predictability. How this need is translated into practice, though, would be expected to vary across cultures, since what are regarded as important **social norms** – i.e. what is considered to be appropriate behaviour within a particular social group – will vary from culture to culture.

⊝ The conformity rate has been found to alter across time within a **culture**, though overall trends are far from clear. There is also variation between cultures. These differences are related to **social norms**.

Why do people conform?

Let us start by looking again at the Asch study. Those of Asch's participants who conformed to judgements which were clearly incorrect fell into two groups. A distinction was made between those who changed their behaviour, but not their opinion (**public conformity**), and those who changed both their behaviour and their opinion (**private change**).

Kelman (1958) picked up on this distinction, referring to **compliance** (i.e. public conformity) and **internalisation** (i.e. private change). These two different kinds of conformity have been related to two different kinds of influence: what Deutsch and Gerard (1955) have called **normative influence**

Figure 2: public conformity and private change			
Asch's terms	Kelman's terms	what happens	influence
public conformity	compliance	behaviour changes opinion doesn't	normative
private change	internalisation	behaviour changes opinion changes	informational

and **informational influence** (see figure 2).

Normative influence refers to the social influence of others which may lead a person to conform to social norms. Informational influence may bring about change as the result of information gained from other people. Asch's study highlights the effect of normative influence, but it may also be that some participants asked themselves: 'Can it be possible that what I think is the right answer is not actually correct here?' This is suggested by the increased conformity found with variation (d) in activity 2.

Let us look first at **normative influence**. As you will remember from the last section, **social norms** relate to behaviour which is considered appropriate within a particular social group. There are norms, for example, about queuing at supermarket checkouts and apologising when you accidentally step on someone's toes.

▷ Activity 3: identifying and understanding norms

What are the social norms when you are:
a at a psychology lecture?
b in a restaurant?
What kinds of behaviour would go against these norms?
Why are there unwritten social conventions and how do we know what they are?
What are the consequences when we do not observe these conventions?
When you have finished, see the notes on page 150.

The observation of social norms helps to explain the conformity people show in some of the studies we have looked at. People very readily identify themselves as part of a group; Tajfel *et al.* (1971) found that people quickly identified themselves as members of a group artificially created by the experimenter even when group membership was decided by something as arbitrary as the toss of a coin. Asch's participants said they felt it was important to maintain group harmony, and that disagreement would damage this. The importance of acceptance and approval emerge clearly in the phrases which they used when Asch asked them after the study why they had conformed to the majority answer; many said they didn't want to 'create a bad impression', 'be different' or 'look stupid'.

This kind of concern has also been verified by physiological measures. Bogdonoff *et al.* (1961) looked at autonomic arousal in participants in a study similar to Asch's. (Autonomic arousal is related to anxiety and stress and is covered in more detail in chapter 4. Blood pressure and heart rate are examples of some of the ways in which it can be measured.) A high level of arousal was found when the participant was faced with an incorrect majority judgement. This dropped if the participant conformed, but remained high if they disagreed with the judgement.

Informational social influence is another factor, which stems from the desire to be right:

▷ Activity 4: decision making and social influence

Imagine you are taking up a new sport, e.g. skiing or tennis, and are planning to buy some equipment. You have heard of a few brand names, but don't know much about the different makes available. How would you go about choosing what to buy? When you have finished, see the notes on page 150.

▶ Activity 5: summarising conformity theory

To link these studies and ideas, complete the blanks in these sentences, picking a word or phrase from those given underneath.

One form of conformity is ...., where there is public acceptance of a group decision, but private disagreement. It depends heavily on .... influence, and is motivated by .... It is more likely in .... situations, such as the study by ....

The other form of conformity is ...., where there is both public and private acceptance. It depends more heavily on .... influence, and is motivated by .... It is more likely in .... situations, such as the study by ....

> **internalisation   normative   compliance**
> **the need for approval/acceptance   Asch**
> **informational   the need to be right**
> **unambiguous   Sherif   ambiguous**

When you have finished, see the notes on page 150.

But is the distinction between the two processes as clear-cut as activity 5 suggests? It has been suggested that both normative influence and informational influence may be factors at the same time:

Box D: Insko et al. (1983)

Procedure: Participants worked in groups of six. They were shown a colour slide, and had to decide which of two other slides had the more similar colour. A control condition tested participants alone, to establish the most frequent answers. Four confederates answered before the genuine participant, disagreeing with these answers. There were two independent variables:

  a public vs. private answers
  b determined vs. undetermined

'Determined' referred to trials where the experimenter claimed to have apparatus which could check the accuracy of the judgements made. In the 'undetermined' trials, it was claimed that there was no possibility of making this check, and that the degree of similarity between the colours was simply a matter of opinion.

Results: Conformity was more frequent in the 'public' than the 'private' condition. It was also greater in the 'determined' than the 'undetermined' condition. There was greater conformity, both 'public' and 'private', in the 'determined' condition.

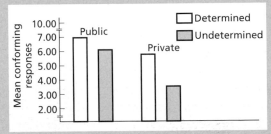

Mean conformity data from Insko *et al.* (1983)

Conclusion: The 'public' vs. 'private' comparison showed normative influence. The 'determined' vs. 'undetermined' comparison showed informational influence. The final finding suggests that informational influence can add to normative influence, so the two can work together to increase conformity.

Conformity and social roles

Another important reason why people conform is to do with **social roles**. A role is a set of behaviours which are thought to be appropriate to a person in a particular kind of situation. The role of 'student', for example, implies dressing casually and having a wild social life, as well as studying and writing essays. We all play roles in social situations and our in-role behaviour is shaped by our beliefs about the demands of the situation and the expectations of other people.

A major study in this area, carried out by Zimbardo *et al.* (1973), was interested in how people adapted their behaviour to fit the roles which they had been asked to take on:

Box E: Zimbardo *et al.* (1973)

Procedure: Student volunteers were asked to role-play prisoners and guards in a simulated prison situation. They were chosen to participate on the basis of tests for emotional stability and physical health, as well as having clean legal records. They were then randomly assigned to be prisoners or guards. For the prison, the basement of Stanford University was converted to be as authentic as possible. 'Prisoners' were arrested, charged, finger-printed, strip-searched and deloused. They were then issued a uniform. 'Guards' were also issued uniforms, together with whistles, handcuffs and dark glasses, to make eye-contact with 'prisoners' impossible.

Results: Both prisoners and guards acted in character to an extreme degree. Guards became increasingly more aggressive, and seemed to

Zimbardo's volunteers

enjoy the control they had over the prisoners. They went far beyond the minimum requirements for fulfilling their role, e.g. making prisoners clean out toilets with their bare hands. Prisoners became passive, and showed extreme stress reactions, such as uncontrolled crying and depression. Some prisoners, wanting to withdraw from the study, asked to 'be paroled'. One developed a serious rash when his 'parole' was rejected. It had been intended to run the study for two weeks; it had to be stopped after six days because of the extreme reactions of the prisoners.

Conclusion: People easily respond to roles assigned to them, particularly where the environment supports these roles. The behaviour people demonstrate 'in role' may be very different from their normal behaviour.

▷ Activity 6: Zimbardo's prison simulation experiment

Read through the prison simulation experiment in box E, and answer these questions:

1 Why do you think potential participants were screened before being accepted?
2 Why were they not allowed to choose which role to take?
3 Both prisoners and guards assumed their roles very rapidly, and showed extreme behaviour. How could you explain this?
4 Participants were paid for taking part in this study. How might this have affected their behaviour?
5 What are the implications of Zimbardo's findings for the prison system?

Compare your ideas with the discussion which follows.

The first two questions relate to Zimbardo's attempts to make his study as unbiased as possible, and so avoid methodological criticisms. Screening the participants ensured that the participants were 'ordinary' people. They had had no direct experience of the law which might have distorted their role-play. They were not unstable, and so were not likely to behave in pathological ways, but could be taken to be representative of people in general. They were also not likely to be badly affected in what was expected to be something of a stressful experience (though not as stressful as it in fact turned out to be).

The behaviour shown cannot be accounted for in terms of existing personality differences, or differences in relevant experiences, then, but can be taken to show how ordinary people are affected by roles allocated to them, and the environment in which they find themselves. If participants had been allowed to choose their roles, it is possible that this might have biased the results; for example, with aggressive people choosing to be guards. (In fact, all the participants had stated a preference for being a prisoner.)

The relative ease and thoroughness with which roles were adopted perhaps has something to do with the media. The prisoners–guards scenario is, after all, a standard one on TV, and the behaviour of both prisoners and guards in Zimbardo's study reflects rather stereotypical pictures of how in general prisoners and guards might be expected to behave. Other role models involving power and subordination are also very widespread in people's lives, e.g. parent–child; teacher–pupil; boss–employee. We can call on our experience of this kind of relationship when it is required in a particular situation.

The fact that participants were paid quite well for taking part may have encouraged them to throw themselves wholeheartedly into their roles. It may also have made it harder for them to withdraw from the study. It is possible, then, that payment may have biased the study in some way.

Zimbardo's study was heavily criticised on ethical grounds, particularly since the participants were clearly distressed by their experience. However, Zimbardo claimed that the study had provided a lot of information which could not have been established any other way. The feedback from the students themselves is interesting; for example, many of the guards mentioned the pleasure they had experienced from their control over others. It is not just 'monsters' or disturbed individuals who have these feelings, but ordinary well-balanced people, if the environment is right.

Perhaps even more importantly, though, Zimbardo's study was instrumental in bringing about changes to the prison system in America, in particular providing support for the notion that an institution itself can have a substantial effect on behaviour.

A final factor in conformity is the power of **reference groups** – people we like or admire, who we conform to because we want to be like them. Relating to role models in this way is known as **identification**.

⑤ In explaining conformity, a distinction can be drawn between **compliance** (public conformity, but no private change) and **internalisation** (public and private change).

⑤ Compliance can be linked to **normative influence**, where people are motivated to observe social norms in order to have the acceptance and approval of others. This kind of conformity is more likely in **unambiguous** situations.

⑤ Internalisation is linked to **informational influence**, where people are motivated by the desire to be correct. It is most likely in **ambiguous** situations.

⑤ The distinction is not necessarily very sharp: both kinds of influence may simultaneously underlie conforming behaviour.

⑤ **Social norms**, the often unwritten rules which allow social groups to function, help to explain social influence.

⑤ Zimbardo's prison simulation study showed how roles and the environment can affect behaviour in situations involving power and subordination.

⑤ **Reference groups** – people we adopt as role models – may also be associated with conformity. This is known as **identification**.

Minority influence

A limitation of most conformity research is that its design only allows a one-way influence; individual participants can either conform to the majority or not. Other research has looked at the possibility of influence in the other direction. To what extent can a minority affect the judgement of a majority? There are many examples in history where a single person has changed majority opinion. For example, Galileo's belief that the earth moved round the sun contradicted opinion at the time, but is now accepted.

An early research study in the area of minority influence is described in box F:

That's a fine cheese tonight

Fact or majority opinion?

Box F: Moscovici *et al.* (1969)

Procedure: Participants were tested in groups of six. Two were confederates of the experimenter. Each participant was asked to judge the colour of 36 slides, all of which were blue. The confederates consistently judged them to be green. Participants were also asked to name the colour of the after-image. (This is the colour which is perceived when you have been staring at a colour, and then look at a white surface; the complementary colour is seen.)

Results: A third of all genuine participants judged a slide to be green at least once. They also tended to label the after-image red/purple. Controls who had not taken part in the judgement task used yellow/orange labels.

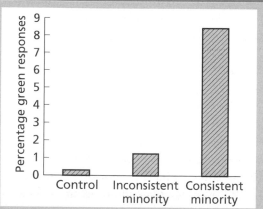

Conclusion: A minority can influence a majority if they are consistent in their judgements. The label given to after-image colours suggests that change was genuine and lasting.

Moscovici proposed that different factors are at work in majority influence and minority influence. He distinguished between compliance (when a majority influences a minority) and conversion (when a minority influences a majority).

In **compliance**, change is to do with the power of greater numbers and factors connected with social norms; people respond to normative influence. There is public agreement with the majority, but private agreement may not last long when a person is no longer in the presence of people holding the majority opinion.

In **conversion**, however, Moscovici believed that an undecided person may pay attention to the viewpoint of a minority because they are interested in the reasons for this different viewpoint. Minorities may therefore respond to informational influence, and there is likely to be lasting change in the opinion held, i.e. **internalisation** in Kelman's terms.

This suggests that minority influence should be linked to **behavioural style**; Moscovici has suggested that a minority is more likely to bring about conformity by a majority if the minority point of view is put across confidently and consistently.

Research has demonstrated the role of confidence in minority influence. Lee and Ofshe (1981), for example, confirmed the effectiveness of a confident non-verbal behavioural style, while Nemeth and Wachtler (1973) found that minorities who appear certain about their position achieve more conformity than those who seem less confident. However, while confidence is important, this should not be allowed to tip over into dogmatism if minority influence is to be effective. Mugny (1984) found that opinion statements putting forward minority viewpoints were far less effective in bringing about change when they were written in slogan-like terms than when they were expressed in more moderate language. It seems that flexibility on the part of the minority, defined as a willingness to make concessions to others to reduce conflict, while at the same time remaining consistent, is more effective than dogmatism.

The study by Moscovici *et al.* in box F demonstrates the importance of consistency. In a variation of the basic study, Moscovici *et al.* (1969) found that an inconsistent minority had little effect on the judgements of the majority.

Other factors may also be important:

Box G: Moscovici and Nemeth (1974)

Procedure: Groups of five people (four participants and one confederate of the experimenter) were asked to take jury-type decisions. The confederate took a minority view. In one condition, he chose to sit in either position A, B or C at the table (see figure 3), while in the other he was assigned to one of these seats.

Results: There was little minority influence when the confederate was assigned to a seat. When he chose where to sit, he was highly influential when he sat in position C, but not when he chose seats A or B.

Conclusion: Minority influence is more likely when a person holding a minority opinion is seen to act autonomously and when he is the focus of attention.

Figure 3: seating in the Moscovici and Nemeth (1974) study

The status and power of the individual is also relevant. If someone putting forward a minority viewpoint is perceived by others as having high status or as being able to exert power over others, these characteristics can help to bring about change in a majority viewpoint. However, Wiggins *et al.* (1967) found that these characteristics are of little use if the person hinders the group from reaching its goal.

Other factors also work against minority influence. If the minority is seen as having something to gain from the opinion they are putting forward, their perceived self-interest is likely to make them less effective in bringing about change in the majority. The same is true if two or more people are in the minority and cannot agree among themselves.

Group size may also be a relevant factor in whether a minority can influence a majority:

Activity 7: conformity and group size

Imagine yourself as one of a group of 12 people, who need to come to a unanimous decision. You are in a minority of one. Then imagine the same situation with a smaller group, say six. In which group would you be more likely to conform to the majority? Why?

When you have finished, see the notes on page 150.

This question is relevant to jury size. The Supreme Court in the USA has shown some interest in reducing the size of juries. This would cut costs, and could well lead to greater efficiency in terms of the time taken to reach a verdict. At the same time, a jury decision will affect people's lives, so every effort must be made to find the size of group which will make the best quality decisions.

In the film *Twelve Angry Men*, made in 1957, a murder case jury, about to vote 'guilty', was persuaded to change its verdict by one doubting member. The behaviour shown by the one man wanting to bring in a 'not guilty' verdict was very much in line with Moscovici's suggestions for conversion: he was consistent, he argued his case and discussed the objections of the other jury members, rather than just dogmatically repeating his view. This is of course fiction, but nonetheless provides a nice example of how a minority can influence majority opinion.

Henry Fonda acts persuasively in 'Twelve Angry Men'

In a jury of 12, one member who does not agree with the others is under considerable social pressure to conform, whereas fewer people will mean less pressure. The Supreme Court was influenced by Asch's work. They came to the conclusion that a jury of six would be efficient in terms of cost and time, and would also have the advantage of being less likely to be under pressure to conform (though it is worth noting that Asch's studies did not find that a group of six was under less pressure to conform than a group of twelve!). This could well ensure a more just verdict.

- A distinction can be made between **compliance**, where a majority can affect the judgement of a minority, and **conversion**, where a minority can affect the judgement of the majority.
- **Conversion** is best achieved if a minority view is put consistently and not dogmatically.
- This research could be relevant to considerations of effective **jury size**.

Evaluation of conformity research

Much of the research into conformity has been criticised on methodological grounds. As you read through the previous section, you may have had doubts about the **ecological validity** of studies such as those of Asch and Sherif. Can we really find out much about a social phenomenon like conformity within the confines of a laboratory situation? While this approach does have the advantage of controlled conditions, in which exact measurements can be made and compared (e.g. the estimates of the distance the light appeared to move in Sherif's study in box A), it also has a number of disadvantages.

If we take the Asch study as an example, we are often put into situations where we can conform or not, but we are seldom faced with a task as artificial as line-matching. There would seem to be room to test the basic ideas suggested by this kind of research in a more naturalistic way. Crutchfield's technique could arguably be seen as being even less realistic than the Asch studies.

There is also the question of **demand characteristics**. Even when participants are not aware of the true nature of an experiment, they are aware of taking part in a psychological experiment of some sort. This knowledge may lead them to think about what the study may be investigating and so to behave in ways which do not necessarily correspond to the way they would act naturally.

Another problem is the sharp distinction made between 'fact' and 'opinion' in accounting for different findings. There are of course judgements which fall neatly into one or other category. The Asch study (box B), for example, is concerned with a fact: one line of the three comparison lines was the same length as the standard line. Some of the judgements in the Crutchfield study (box C), on the other hand, looked at what were clearly matters of opinion.

However, there seems also to be a grey area between fact and opinion, which could be explored in more depth. There is quite a lot of knowledge which we might define as 'fact', but which is in truth culturally determined. Opinions which are widely held within a particular culture are often considered to be 'fact', but are majority opinions and facts the same thing? Before Galileo, for instance, it was an accepted 'fact' that the sun moved round the earth. Similarly, the distinction between normative and informational influence is not clear-cut, as the Insko study (box D) suggests.

You may also have had ethical concerns. As we saw earlier, Bogdonoff et al. (1961) showed that participants experienced the situations they were put in as stressful.

You may have come away from these studies with the impression that conformity is somehow wrong or ridiculous; this emerges quite clearly in Asch's work, and is a judgement he himself explicitly made. It is not the job of psychological research to provide answers about social desirability, and it is in any case open to question whether conformity is necessarily undesirable.

As pointed out earlier, conformity serves a very positive and necessary function in helping social interaction to run smoothly. Normative influence helps us to make the compromises necessary in social life to fit into social situations. If a friend were to take you to an event at the local Conservative Club, for example, you might wear a suit and keep your radical green views to yourself. Informational influence helps us to learn appropriate behaviour in times of uncertainty; for example, learning how to taste wine involves a lot of acceptance of others' definitions of what makes a wine 'good', when to the beginner it may not taste very pleasant at all. However, most conformity research has tended to focus on demonstrating conformity, rather than broadening its scope to consider in detail the functions it might serve in different situations.

At the same time, these studies do give us a good basis for understanding conformity. This research has implications for group situations: we can't expect disagreement and therefore discussion to arise naturally in groups, and at the same time, we can't assume that agreement shows consent.

- ❺ Conformity research has attracted a certain amount of criticism. Its **ecological validity** is often poor, and there are also **ethical concerns**.
- ❺ It may also rest on questionable **assumptions**, e.g. drawing a sharp distinction between fact and opinion, and normative and informational influence. It tends to be **descriptive** rather than providing functional explanations.
- ❺ Research has given us some understanding of conformity, which may be applicable in practical situations.

6.2 OBEDIENCE

Milgram's research

After the second world war, German war criminals who had been involved in the Holocaust – the wholesale killing of Jews, together with other 'undesirables' such as gypsies, homosexuals and the mentally ill – were put on trial for war crimes. These trials continued for a number of years and roused considerable public interest.

Those on trial did not appear to be monsters. On the contrary: Hannah Arendt, writing about the trial of Adolf Eichmann, was struck by just how ordinary he seemed, using the phrase 'the banality of evil'. Yet at the same time, he had been very directly involved in the concentration camp programme. His defence against the charges brought against him, like that of many other war criminals, was that he was 'only obeying orders'.

Adolf Eichmann in the dock

Milgram was intrigued by the apparent contradiction between the ordinariness of the men involved and the terrible deeds they had carried out. He was interested in how the idea of obeying orders fitted into the picture, and in the extent to which ordinary people would obey orders to harm an innocent fellow human being. He brought these factors together in a series of studies. The basic study is described in box H opposite.

Milgram later ran a number of variations of the basic study, to find out more about the particular factors which might influence obedience. Some of these, together with the results, are listed in box I.

Box H: Milgram (1963)

Procedure: Male volunteers, aged 20–50, were recruited through a newspaper advertisement to take part in a 'scientific study of memory and learning'. Each worked in pairs with Mr Wallace, apparently another participant, who was in fact a confederate of Milgram and an accountant in his late fifties. His part in the study had been planned in advance and was scripted.

The study was run at Yale University Psychology Department by a young man in a white lab coat. He told the participant and Mr Wallace that the study was investigating the effects of punishment on learning. The two men drew lots to decide who was to be the teacher and who the learner in the experiment, though this was rigged so that Mr Wallace was always the learner. In view of the teacher, Mr Wallace was strapped into a chair and attached to electrodes, linked to a shock generator. At this point, Mr Wallace said he had a heart condition, but was assured that though the shocks were painful, there would be no permanent damage. The teacher's job was to administer a shock every time the learner made a mistake in learning a list of paired associates.

Milgram's (1963) apparatus and Mr Wallace being connected up to it

The teacher was then taken to another room containing the shock generator. This had a 30-point scale showing an increasing level of shocks from '15 volts–mild shock' up to '450 volts–XXX'. The size of shock was to be increased every time an error was made. The teacher was given a 45 volt shock in case he had any doubts that the shock apparatus was real. No further shocks were given, though the teacher was unaware of this.

Results: All the participants gave increasing shocks in the early part of the experiment. No one stopped below '300 volts–intense shock'. Some participants were unwilling to continue, but did so when told by the experimenter: 'Please continue' or 'The experiment requires that you continue'. These instructions (which Milgram called 'prods') were followed despite Mr Wallace banging on the wall, refusing to continue to take part in the experiment, and asking for the shocks to stop. Many teachers continued to give increased shocks even when, at 315 volts, Mr Wallace let out a violent scream, and when at 330 volts there was complete silence from the next room – the teacher had been told that no response counted as a wrong response. In all, two-thirds of the men (65%) continued to increase the shocks up to the maximum level of 450 volts.

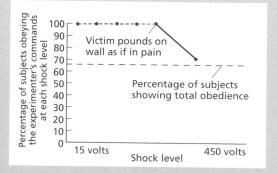

Conclusion: Ordinary people are likely to follow orders given by an authority figure, even to the extent of killing an innocent human being.

Box I: variations on Milgram's experiment

disobedient models: When the 'teacher' was in the presence of two other participants (actually confederates of the experimenter) who refused to administer shocks, the level of obedience fell from 65% to 10%.

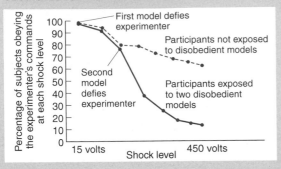

Just under 50% of participants continued to increase the shocks to the maximum 450 volts.

proximity of the learner: When the learner was in the same room as the teacher, the obedience level dropped to 40%. It dropped still further to 30% when the teacher had to force the learner's hand on to the shock plate.

proximity of the experimenter: When the experimenter left the room and gave instructions over the phone, the obedience level dropped to around 20%.

two teachers: A teacher was paired with another (confederate) teacher who administered the shocks. The genuine participant had only to read out the words. The obedience level was 92.5%.

encouragement: The participant was not instructed to increase the shock each time an error was made. The average shock given remained around 50 volts across the series of trials. When two confederates urged the participant to increase the shock level, the average strength of the shock given after 20 trials was more than 150 volts.

location: The study was carried out in a run-down office, rather than at Yale University.

◗ Activity 8: explaining Milgram

Use the information in box H and box I to identify:

a the factors which influenced obedience in this series of experiments

b the relative strength of each.

Can you explain exactly how each factor might have influenced behaviour?

Compare your ideas with the discussion which follows.

The degree of personal **responsibility** which participants experienced is obviously of major importance here. In the original study, it was easy for participants to hand over responsibility to the experimenter, since he was giving them instructions and reminding them of their role when they protested (i.e. 'prods'). Participants were also assured by the experimenter that he was responsible for the welfare of the learners. There was therefore plenty of reason for the participants not to accept personal responsibility.

In the 'two teachers' variation, the high level of obedience can perhaps be explained in terms of the situation allowing the participant to shift responsibility from themselves to the person actually administering the shocks. In the 'disobedient models' variation, the refusal of the models to follow instructions is likely to have demonstrated to the participant that it was possible to take responsibility and act accordingly. This may be one reason why there was such a dramatic drop in obedience in this situation. Taking personal responsibility would also have been an important factor in holding down the hand of the 'victim', though the effect here was much smaller. We will be coming back to the question of responsibility later in this chapter, when we discuss reasons why some participants did *not* obey the experimenter.

The marked drop in obedience when the experimenter was in the next room (from 65% to 20%) also underlines the importance of the physical **presence of the experimenter**. Together with the effect of a disobedient model, this is one of the most important factors.

A related factor is the **authority of the experimenter**. Given the mention of a 'scientific study' in the advertisement, the experimenter's white coat and the prestigious setting of Yale University, the experimenter would be seen as a legitimate authority figure. When in one variation the experimenter was 'called away' and a stand-in (introduced as a research participant) suggested the stepwise increase in shocks as his own idea, obedience was greatly reduced, again suggesting the importance of authority.

The **location** does not seem to have played a major part here, though, since obedience only dropped by 15% when the location was changed.

Another factor is the **gradual** change in the behaviour required from the participant. A 15-volt shock is extremely mild, and willingness to deliver it paves the way for the next shock, also pretty mild, and so on.

Social influence clearly played a major role, since the encouragement of others was enough to produce a major increase in disobedience. The fact that 35% of participants ceased to be obedient before the end of the experiment suggests that some of the remaining 65% who did obey may well have had qualms about their behaviour; in fact, many participants showed clear signs of conflict and distress, stuttering, twitching and verbally abusing the experimenter. In a few cases, participants had seizures. In this case, a disobedient model would be enough to tip the balance towards disobedience. It is possible that the behaviour of disobedient models reminded participants of a possible alternative response: some participants made remarks at the end of the basic study, where they were not exposed to disobedient models, such as 'I didn't realise I could'. At the same time, participants tended to increase shocks when encouraged by others to do so; social influence can work both ways.

The effect of the presence of the learner in the same room as the teacher, and in particular of the teacher having to hold the learner's hand on the shock plate, is perhaps surprising. Obedience dropped in both these conditions, but was still at quite a startling level. Being brought face to face with the consequences of your actions does not seem to have as much influence as you might suppose.

Activity 9: the ethics of Milgram's study

Milgram's work has been widely criticised on ethical grounds. What are the ethical objections to this study? You may find it helpful to look at figure 5 towards the end of this chapter, which shows the British Psychological Society guidelines for carrying out research with human participants. How justified are these objections? How, if at all, could they be overcome?

Compare your ideas with the discussion which follows.

Ethical factors in Milgram's research

There are two main considerations here: **deception** and the **stress** or loss of self-esteem which may have been experienced by participants as a result of taking part.

The participants were deceived about the nature of the experiment, so they were unable to give their informed consent to participate in it. They were also not informed that they could withdraw from the experiment at any time. On the contrary, they were explicitly instructed to continue, and clearly felt under some pressure to do so. One way of avoiding this kind of criticism would be to give participants full information about the experiment, and to ask them to role-play their usual behaviour, but in this case role-play would be unlikely to be a true representation of normal behaviour. Alternatively, naturally occurring behaviour could be observed, but such an approach does not lend itself easily to this particular topic.

One way of mitigating this kind of ethical problem, where participants cannot be given full information about the nature of the study, is the use of **debriefing**. This involves giving participants as much information as possible about the study after it has taken place. They are told about the aims of the investigation, and any deception that was necessary. They are also encouraged to ask questions, and the use to be made of the findings is discussed. They are reassured that the way they behaved was perfectly natural in the circumstances, and not in any way unusual or shameful. Given the nature of Milgram's study, though, this last aspect of debriefing might be both inappropriate and ineffective.

A further study looked at the value of debriefing:

Box J: Ring et al. (1970)

Procedure: Milgram's experiment was replicated, using female students as participants. One group was thanked after the experiment, but not debriefed. A second group was thanked and debriefed, and reassured that their behaviour was quite normal. A third group was debriefed, but not reassured about their behaviour. They were told they should have defied the experimenter.

Results: Both group 1 (who thought they had really hurt the learner) and group 3 (who were not reassured about their behaviour) were very upset about the experiment, compared to group 2. However, only group 1 regretted having taken part in the experiment.

Conclusion: Careful debriefing, which includes both information and reassurance, can go a long way towards overcoming ethical problems.

NB: *All* participants received a complete debriefing at the end of the study.

Perhaps even more serious is the stress caused by participation in Milgram's experiment – at least one participant suffered convulsions – and the loss of self-esteem which many participants experienced as a result of taking part in this study. Baumrind (1964) argued that adequate measures had not been taken to protect participants from psychological harm.

In replying to this kind of criticism, Milgram argued that the study was not intended to cause stress for the participants, and that Baumrind was confusing

the outcome (i.e. stress experienced by participants) with what was expected to happen. He pointed out that before carrying out the study, he had asked many people, including psychiatrists, what they expected the outcome to be. There was general agreement that perhaps only one person in a hundred would obey throughout the experiment, and that most would stop at 150 volts. Milgram also carried out a follow-up study (Milgram, 1964) when he surveyed those who had taken part. He reported that 84% were glad to have taken part in the experiment, 75% said they had learned something useful and only 1.3% were sorry or very sorry to have taken part. Milgram argued that the ethics of a study are best judged by those who have taken part, rather than in absolute terms.

However, many if not all of the participants must have experienced some loss of self-esteem, knowing that they had been prepared to hurt another human being, and had been unable to resist obeying an authority figure. This must have been all the more hurtful, since the experimenter had no real authority; although the participants were paid for taking part in Milgram's study, they were paid before the study started, so there was no real incentive to continue.

In answer to those who point to the loss of self-esteem suffered by those who took part in the experiment, it has been argued that it is not the duty of psychologists to hide from people truths about their own nature, however much they may not wish to know those truths.

This leads on to the question of the extent to which stress was *caused* to the participants by taking part in this study. It could be argued that it was the way the participants *responded* to the situation which led them to experience stress. As Milgram points out, the whole point of the study is that participants had a choice, and that most chose obedience.

A further justification of this study is that the ends had justified the means: his study had gathered valuable information about human behaviour which could not really have been established in any other way. Perhaps more than any other experiment, Milgram's study highlights the capacity of ordinary people for homicidal – even genocidal – behaviour. This carries clear implications for international courts, but it also changes our perceptions of ourselves. By knowing about this study, we are ourselves less likely to obey in similar situations.

With these kinds of considerations in mind, Elms (1972) considered Milgram's experiment to be one of the most significant ever carried out in modern psychology, and one of the most moral, both in its attempts to understand important phenomena and its concern for the welfare of its participants.

☉ Milgram was interested in the defence offered by war criminals that they were 'only obeying orders'. He carried out a series of studies to investigate obedience.

☉ In his original study, 65% of his participants were prepared to give what they thought were lethal electric shocks to someone they believed to be a fellow-participant in a learning experiment.

☉ Variations of the study looked at various factors in more detail. There was, for example, a drop in obedience when the participant was exposed to disobedient models. The authority of the experimenter, cues to reduce the sense of personal responsibility and the gradual increase in the strength of shocks given all seem to be important factors.

☉ Milgram's study has been criticised on **ethical** grounds: participants were deceived and subjected to stress and loss of self-esteem. However, Milgram found that very few participants regretted taking part in the study. The stress experienced can be seen in terms of the participants' choice of behaviour. Valuable information has been gained with important implications.

Gender, culture and victim characteristics

▷ Activity 10: gender, culture and obedience

Would you expect gender and/or culture to be a factor in obedience in this kind of study? Give reasons for your answer.
When you have finished, see the notes on page 150.

The participants in Milgram's original study were all men, but the effect of gender has been explored in similar studies. The Ring *et al.* study (box J) found no difference between levels of obedience in men and women, and a later study by Milgram (1965), using a relatively small sample of 40 females, had similar findings. Another study focusing on gender produced even more startling results:

Box K: Sheridan and King (1972)

Procedure: Male and female participants were asked to give a puppy genuine electric shocks of increasing strength. Participants could see the puppy yelping, howling and struggling to free itself in response to the shocks.
Results: High levels of obedience were found in both men and women. Every female participant gave the puppy the maximum shock.
Conclusion: Women are just as likely as men to obey orders involving the infliction of pain.

You probably feel that this is a very distasteful study, but it does address the issue of gender very directly. It is perhaps also worth noting here that many women were among the concentration camp personnel involved in the Nazi programme of killing Jews and members of other 'undesirable' groups.

To investigate possible cultural differences, several researchers have replicated Milgram's study at different times and in different countries. For example, Mantell (1971), using a German sample, found an obedience level of 85%, while Kilham and Mann (1974), using an Australian sample, found somewhat lower rates of obedience than the 65% recorded by Milgram.

It is difficult to draw any very definite conclusions from these findings, though, since the behaviour of some participants in these later studies may well have been affected by knowledge of Milgram's original work. Another problem in making comparisons is that the studies were not exact replications of Milgram's work. In any case, even relatively small differences in the make-up of the sample – age, educational level, and so on – make direct comparisons unreliable. At the same time, the possibility that there are cultural differences in obedience cannot be excluded.

Let us look finally in this section at a study investigating the characteristics of the *victim*:

Box L: Farina *et al.* (1966)

Procedure: Milgram's basic procedure was followed. The teacher was introduced to the learner before the experiment began, on the pretext that getting to know someone helps communication. The learner then talked about himself and his past in either a negative way (unhappy childhood, history of illness, parents divorced and so on) or positively.

Results: More intense shocks were given to the learners who had talked about themselves negatively. Teachers also showed through questionnaire answers that they were less interested in getting to know the 'negative' learners than the 'positive' ones.

Conclusion: The results support what has been called the 'just world hypothesis': people who suffer do so because in some way they deserve to suffer. The 'negative' learner identifies himself as a loser in a world where people get what they deserve. He is therefore a legitimate target.

You may have found the results of this study a little surprising. There is quite a widespread belief that people are sympathetic to the underdog, but in practice this doesn't seem to be the case. It is perhaps worth noting that the Nazis went to a great deal of trouble to put across the idea of Jews as underdogs, and this may perhaps have had a part to play in the readiness of the camp guards to kill them.

- Most studies have found no **gender** difference in obedience levels.
- There are **cultural differences** in obedience levels, but precise comparison is difficult.
- Characteristics of the **victim** may also be relevant. The widespread belief that we show sympathy for the underdog seems to be false.

Milgram and after

We have already looked at criticisms made of Milgram's studies on ethical grounds. There has also been considerable criticism of their methodology. One suggestion (Orne and Holland, 1968) was that participants did not actually believe that they were giving genuine electric shocks to the learners. Far from the participants being deceived, they suggest, it was Milgram himself who was deceived into thinking that his participants accepted the experimental situation at face value!

▶ Activity 11: Milgram's methodology

Imagine you were a participant in Milgram's study. What aspects of the experimental situation might have struck you as rather odd and would perhaps have made you suspect you were being deceived? When you have finished, see the notes on page 150.

One way to clear up the question of whether Milgram's participants behaved as they did because they did not believe that the 'victim' was genuine was to set up a study in which participants also serve as their own victims:

Box M: Kudirka (1965)

Procedure: Participants were instructed to eat 36 quinine-soaked biscuits.

Results: Grimaces, moans and occasional gagging showed that this was clearly unpleasant. Nonetheless, virtually all the participants ate the biscuits.

Conclusion: Suggestions that participants are obedient because they don't accept the experimental situation as real are not supported. There are still high levels of obedience when the reality of the situation is quite unambiguous.

A second question mark hangs over the **ecological validity** of the study: can the findings of an artificial laboratory study be related to real-world situations?

It has been argued that there were some crucial differences between Milgram's studies and obedience in Nazi Germany. Firstly, the experiments were presented to participants in a positive way, i.e. as aiming to increase knowledge about human learning, while many Germans recognised the aims of the Nazis as immoral. Secondly, there were no penalties for disobeying Milgram's orders, whereas it would have been very dangerous to have disobeyed orders in Nazi Germany. Finally, Milgram's participants were told explicitly that the shocks they would give would cause no permanent damage, while people like Eichmann knew they were sending other people to their deaths.

These differences may not be so very clear-cut, however. The Nazi programme was presented to the German people in a very positive way, in terms of racial purification and the creation of a Nazi homeland. Most of Milgram's participants, on the other hand, recognised what they were doing to be wrong – as we have seen, many became very upset in the course of the experiment and protested at what they were being asked to do – but they nonetheless continued to give the shocks. Similarly, although participants were told that the shocks would do no permanent damage, it is hard to see what other interpretation could be put on the pleas from the victim for the experiment to stop, followed by a scream and then silence. Indeed, when they were reunited with Mr Wallace after the experiment, many 'teachers' stated that they thought they had killed him.

In one very important way, Milgram's study mirrored the experience of the Nazis who were 'only obeying orders'. In both cases, people were put into a situation unlike any they had ever experienced and instructed to carry out an extremely distasteful task. In real life, people being given orders to harm or kill others is not an everyday situation. For example, during the Kosovo conflict newspapers carried reports of groups of Kosovan men being machine-gunned to death and then set on fire, and of refugees being herded on to a bridge to be bombed, so that they would appear to be victims of NATO aggression. Presumably the people who obeyed these orders were not in a normal, everyday situation. It could be that it is the strangeness of the situation which makes obedience more likely. It could therefore be argued that as Milgram's participants were in an unusual situation, his studies had *higher* ecological validity.

This leads to the question of whether people show the same level of obedience in a more everyday situation. This can only really be tested by carrying out a naturalistic study, in such a way that the participants are not aware of being studied:

> **Box N: Hofling *et al.* (1966)**
>
> **Procedure:** A man claiming to be a doctor rang a hospital on 22 separate occasions. Each time, he asked a nurse to give medicine to a patient. This would require the nurse to break three hospital rules:
> a they were not allowed to accept instructions over the phone.
> b the dose was double the maximum limit stated on the box.
> c the medicine itself was unauthorised, i.e. not on the ward stocklist.
> On each occasion, the nurse's behaviour was monitored.
> **Results:** In reply to questionnaires, most nurses said they would not obey such an order. In reality, 21 of the 22 nurses followed the orders they were given.
> **Conclusion:** There is some support for obedience to authority in less extreme situations than that tested by Milgram: a very high proportion of people follow unjustified orders if told to do so by an authority figure.

When they were debriefed, some of the nurses said that this kind of situation often arose. They followed instructions because otherwise the doctors would be annoyed. This doesn't really explain away what they did, however, but rather says something about the relationships between authority figures and their subordinates which may lead to orders being obeyed.

Stimulated by Milgram's original experiments, a more recent set of 19 studies, the Utrecht Studies of Obedience, was carried out by Meeus and Raaijmakers in the 1980s. In these studies, participants were asked to inflict what Meeus and Raaijmakers termed 'administrative violence' on people who they thought were their fellow-participants. This involved making negative remarks about their performance on tests, and denigrating remarks about their personality. Two sample studies are described in box O:

Box O: Meeus and Raaijmakers (1986)

Procedure: In a bogus personnel selection procedure, 39 participants aged 18–55 were instructed to make job applicants nervous, and to disturb them while taking a test as part of the application procedure. In consequence, applicants failed the test and remained unemployed. Forty-one participants aged 18–55 took part in variations of this basic study, when the experimenter was out of the room and when another participant was present who refused to obey the orders given by the experimenter.

Results: In the basic experiment, more than 90% of participants – a much higher percentage than in Milgram's experiment – complied with the orders they had been given, even though they considered them unfair and did not enjoy carrying out the task. In the variations of the study, obedience was much lower than in the equivalent variations of the basic Milgram study.

Conclusion: Participants show willingness to obey orders to inflict mental harm on others when instructed to do so. As in Milgram's studies, however, obedience is reduced in the absence of an authority figure, or in the presence of a disobedient peer.

On the basis of observing participants' behaviour, analysis of questionnaire responses and debriefing, Meeus and Raaijmakers concluded that participants had found the task stressful but had attempted to hide the stress they were experiencing and act as though nothing were wrong, behaving as an official. They therefore explained their findings in terms of attitudes to social institutions, and distant relationships with fellow citizens.

- Milgram's studies have been criticised on methodological as well as ethical grounds.
- The studies may have given rise to **demand characteristics**, and their **ecological validity** has been questioned. Later studies have gone some way towards refuting these criticisms. It may be unwise to assume, however, that the findings of laboratory studies can be directly extrapolated to behaviour in Nazi concentration camps.

6.3 INDIVIDUAL DIFFERENCES IN RESPONSE TO SOCIAL INFLUENCE

Up till now we have been considering social influence in general terms. Another approach has been to look at individual differences between people in terms of the extent to which they are affected by such influence.

In all the conformity studies discussed earlier in the chapter, you will remember that there were individual differences in conformity, with some people being much more likely to conform than others. This kind of pattern has been found in other research, looking at conformity both on judgements of facts, as in the Asch studies (box B), and on opinions, included in the Crutchfield study (box C).

Several researchers have looked at individual differences in conformity and obedience, including Crutchfield (1955) and Elms and Milgram (1966), and links with various characteristics have been found. For example, higher levels of obedience have been found among prejudiced and intolerant people, those achieving lower educational levels, and scientists and engineers (compared to doctors and teachers). Sub-cultural differences have also been found, with the military and Catholics (compared to Jews and Protestants) being more likely to conform. But the correlations are often weak, so any one factor of this kind is unlikely to play a large part in determining susceptibility to social influence.

One important theory, however, which links conformity and obedience to personality is Adorno's work on the **authoritarian personality**. Adorno *et al.* (1950) were interested in prejudice, and whether it was related to a particular kind of personality. Adorno himself was a Jewish American at a time when anti-Semitism was rife in the USA. He produced scales to measure personality, the most famous of which is called the **F-scale** (F standing for 'fascist'). Some sample items are shown in figure 4:

Figure 4: sample statements from the F-scale

The most important thing to teach children is obedience to their parents.

Homosexuals are hardly better than criminals, and ought to be severely punished.

Any good leader should be strict with people under him in order to gain respect.

When a person has a problem or worry, it is best for him not to think about it, but to keep busy with more cheerful things.

People can be divided into two distinct classes, the strong and the weak.

Some day it will probably be shown that astrology can explain a lot of things.

The F-scale measures characteristics such as conventionality, submission to those in authority, aggression to those over whom you are in authority, toughness, destructiveness and superstition. The scale was successful in identifying people who were likely to be prejudiced, since prejudiced people would be likely to have these characteristics and so to agree with all these statements. Adorno referred to a high scorer on these scales as an **authoritarian personality**.

One characteristic typical of the authoritarian personality was a tendency to conform. A relationship has been shown between high scores on the F-scale and obedience in studies like that of Milgram (box H). There is some evidence that a tendency to conform is related to upbringing.

Frenkel-Brunswik (1942) found that as a child, someone with an authoritarian personality was likely to have been strictly disciplined, and punished for disobedience.

From Adorno's work, it emerges that the authoritarian personality has a greater need than most for approval and acceptance. You will remember that **normative influence** is related to these needs, and is one factor in conformity; conformity is a way of satisfying these needs. Support for this comes from Stang (1973), who found that people with high self-esteem (and therefore less in need of the approval and acceptance of others) were less likely to conform than those with low self-esteem.

- There is some support for the idea that personality plays a part in conformity.
- One of the characteristics of the **authoritarian personality** identified by Adorno is conformity.
- This kind of personality has a high need for the approval and acceptance of others. It is related to a harsh, disciplinarian upbringing.

6.4 INDEPENDENT BEHAVIOUR

Why people conform to the behaviour of others or obey orders are interesting questions, but equally interesting is why others do not. After all, 13 of the 50 participants in Asch's experiments (box B) did not conform with the majority, and 35% of the participants in Milgram's experiment resisted the order to continue giving shocks, at least to the extent of refusing to give the most extreme shocks.

Asch interviewed his participants after his experiment, and found that those who had not conformed fell into one of three groups. For one group, the essential factor was that they were **confident** that their judgement was correct. This can be related to the findings of Perrin and Spencer (1981), who replicated Asch's study. Very few of their participants conformed. In order to avoid using participants who knew about the Asch series of studies, they used medical and engineering students. Both these groups deal with physical phenomena, where accurate observation and measurement are crucial. Given the nature of the task, their knowledge and skills could have made them more sure of the judgement they were asked to make. This study also confirms the findings of Wiesenthal *et al.* (1976), that people who see themselves as competent at a particular task are much less likely to conform to a majority.

A second group maintained their independence by **withdrawal**, mentally withdrawing from the group, avoiding eye contact with the others, and so on. A third group experienced tension in the situation, but chose to *focus* on the requirements of the task.

Another factor in independent behaviour is past experience. Convincing evidence for this idea comes from one of Milgram's studies, and in particular from two participants who would not follow the experimenter's instructions.

One of them, Gretchen Brandt, refused to obey when the voltage was raised to 210V. It emerged that she had grown up in Nazi Germany. When she was asked to explain why she had not obeyed the order to give shocks, she replied: 'Perhaps we have seen too much pain'. The other, Jan Rensaleer, had lived in Holland during the second world war. He also had direct experience of the potentially terrible consequences of unquestioning obedience. To return to a previous point made in the discussion of Milgram's studies, unlike some of the other participants, both accepted responsibility for their own behaviour, rather than giving control to the experimenter.

Here we are looking at people affected by unusual and extreme experiences. What about people without this kind of experience? A study set up to investigate independent behaviour is described in box P:

Box P: Gamson *et al.* (1982)

Procedure: Participants were told the study was to investigate community standards, and was being carried out by a human relations company. In groups of nine, they were asked to fill in questionnaires on a wide range of topics. This was to establish the extent of anti-authority attitudes for each participant.

They were also asked to sign an agreement to be videotaped, which stated that the tape would remain the property of the company. They were then asked to discuss the case of a petrol station manager, who was living with someone he wasn't married to. They were told that the company had fired him on moral grounds, and he was suing for breach of contract. The co-ordinator asked three of the participants to argue as if they were offended at the manager's conduct. Their discussion was videotaped. This was repeated for three more members of the group. They were then asked to repeat these views individually in front of the camera, and sign an agreement that the videos could be used as evidence in a court case.

Results: Out of 33 groups, only one followed the procedure all the way through. There was a high correlation between anti-authority attitudes and disobedience, but there was also disobedience in groups where anti-authority attitudes were low. In some groups, some of the participants signed the affidavit, but in many groups, disobedience became the group norm.

Conclusion: There is considerable readiness to disobey when people feel they are being manipulated. Although disobedience is linked to anti-authority attitudes, this is not enough to explain disobedience.

Activity 12: comparing Milgram and Gamson *et al.*

Look back to Milgram's study (box H). Compare this with the Gamson *et al.* study in box P. What factors could have influenced people to be more ready to disobey in the Gamson *et al.* study? When you have finished, see the notes on page 151.

⊖ **Personality**, **competence** and **experience** may all influence non-conformity and disobedience.
⊖ Disobedience is more likely when people are aware that they are being manipulated.

6.5 CRITICAL ISSUE: THE DEVELOPMENT OF ETHICAL GUIDELINES FOR RESEARCH

Because of the subject matter of psychology, research is carried out on people (or in some cases animals), and this raises special concerns in terms of the way those who take part in psychological research are treated. Ethical issues arise for psychologists more than for other scientists mainly because they study living organisms – human beings and animals. They are sentient beings; they can feel pain and fear. The humans involved are also thinking beings, and may experience an experimental situation as threatening, embarrassing, stressful or belittling. It is generally considered unacceptable for a person to induce feelings of self-doubt or inadequacy in another person, so researchers need to think carefully whether what they are planning to do could affect participants in this way.

It is unacceptable to induce feelings of self-doubt and inadequacy

Until fairly recently, people taking part in psychological research were known as 'subjects', and you may find this term used in older textbooks. However, the term 'participants' is now widely used, and recommended by the British Psychological Society. This change in terminology emphasises the fact that people freely give their time and effort when they offer to take part in a psychological study, and so deserve respect and concern for their well-being.

'Unethical' refers to procedures which are not only morally wrong but which are also professionally unacceptable. As we saw earlier, Milgram's work has been widely criticised on ethical grounds, and is perhaps the study most psychologists think of first when the topic of ethics in research involving human participants is raised. As we have seen, there are still differences of opinion about the ethical justifications of his research, with some psychologists seeing it as highly unethical and some seeing it as work of the highest moral quality. It is perhaps worth noting that the American Psychological Society investigated the ethics of Milgram's research shortly after it appeared, and concluded that it was morally acceptable, while in 1965 the American Association for the Advancement of Science awarded him a prize for his outstanding contribution to psychological research.

One undoubted result of Milgram's study, and the debate on ethics which arose from it, was an increased focus on ethical issues in psychological research. To help researchers consider these issues, professional bodies such as the British Psychological Society (BPS) in Great Britain and the American Psychological Association (APA) in the USA produce regularly updated guidelines. Both these sets of guidelines stress that the aims of psychological research should be a better understanding of people and the promotion of human welfare, which require an atmosphere of free enquiry. At the same time, research needs to be carried out responsibly, and with concern for the welfare of people who take part in it.

We will be looking in this section at the Ethical Principles for Conducting Research with Human Participants (1993), produced by the BPS. The BPS has a register of chartered psychologists who work professionally in research or applied fields. People can be struck off the register if they fail to maintain professional standards, and it is hoped that this system will create an accredited body of professional psychologists in whom the general public can have confidence.

Figure 5: summary of BPS Ethical Principles for Conducting Research with Human Participants (1993)

1. **introduction:** in good psychological research, there should be mutual confidence and respect between participants and researchers. Guidelines are necessary to help to establish whether research is acceptable.

2. **general:** researchers have a duty to consider the ethical implications of their research before it is carried out. They should eliminate possible threats to the physical and psychological well-being of participants. When researchers do not have sufficient knowledge of possible implications of their research for people varying in age, gender or social background, they should consult people with relevant characteristics.

3. **consent:** whenever possible, participants should be given full information about an investigation so that they can make an informed decision about whether or not to take part. Especial care should be taken with research involving children or others who may be unable to give full informed consent. Participants should not be pressurised into taking part in research when the researcher is in a position of influence or authority over them, or by financial reward.

4. **deception:** deception should be avoided wherever possible, and particularly if participants are likely to feel troubled when debriefed.

5. **debriefing:** when participants are aware of having taken part in a study, at the end of their participation the researcher should offer full information. They should discuss any aspects of the research which may have had negative consequences for the participant.

6. **withdrawal from the investigation:** participants should be told at the outset that they have the right to withdraw from the study and have their data destroyed, even when the study has been completed, and whether or not they have been paid to take part.

7. **confidentiality:** information gathered about participants during research should be kept confidential, and if published should not be identifiable.

8. **protection of participants:** participants should be protected from any physical or psychological harm greater than that experienced in everyday life. Where personal information is collected, participants should be protected from stress and assured that personal questions need not be answered.

9. **observational research:** unless consent is given for behaviour to be observed, observation only of behaviour which could normally be observed by strangers is acceptable. Researchers should be sensitive to cultural values, and to intruding on the privacy of people being observed, even if they are in a public place.

10. **giving advice:** if the researcher becomes aware of physical or psychological problems of which the participant is apparently unaware, these problems should be raised with the participant. An appropriate source of professional advice should be recommended.

11. **colleagues:** a researcher who is aware of a colleague carrying out research not following these principles should encourage the colleague to consider the ethical issues arising from their research.

We will look in a little more detail at some of the issues considered by these guidelines.

Consent

In order to give consent to take part in a study, participants need to be given full information beforehand on which to base their decision. There is some evidence that sufficient information is not always routinely provided. Epstein and Lasagna (1969), for instance, found that only a third of people volunteering to take part in a study had any real understanding of what was involved. However, this study was carried out some time ago, and with ethics emerging in recent years as a very real issue in psychological research, it may be that researchers are now more aware of the importance of giving full information.

In some circumstances, it can be difficult to obtain consent based on a full understanding of the implications of taking part in a study. The study of children poses problems here, since they may not be able to understand the situation. It is generally agreed that if children are too young to understand the research aims, or below the legal age of consent, their parents must be asked for consent in their place. Informed consent can also be a problem for some adults; for example, people with a mental disorder or people with learning difficulties.

There may be further problems when there is an existing relationship between potential participants and the researcher, particularly when the researcher is in a position of authority over participants. For example, many studies are carried out by university lecturers in psychology, using their students as participants. In this case, steps must be taken to ensure that consent is freely given, with no inducements offered for taking part, such as participation being counted towards course grades, nor any suggestion that there might be negative consequences in deciding not to take part.

Within the university system of the United States, psychology undergraduates have to take part as participants in research, and participation counts towards their final grades. The choice is not whether to take part or not, but only which research to participate in. They are paid for participation. However, students are aware that this is a course requirement, and it could be argued that participation may provide the students both with insights into psychological procedures and a sensitivity towards their participants when they carry out research themselves.

Deception

Menges (1973) found that 80% of a sample of 1000 experiments involved giving participants incomplete information about the study. They were given full information about the dependent variable in only 25% of the studies, and complete information about the independent variable in only 3%. (The terms 'dependent variable' and 'independent variable' are explained in chapter 7.) In other words, deception appeared to be widespread in psychological research. Again, however, it is worth noting the date when this research was carried out; it is possible that deception is now no longer as widespread as Menges suggested.

Deception is linked to informed consent: if participants have been deceived about the nature of the study, it is not possible for them to make an informed decision as to whether or not they are willing to take part. Deception is also likely to have wider repercussions, in that participants who have been deceived are likely to be angry, and disillusioned about the way psychology studies are carried out, and so psychology may be brought into disrepute. For these reasons, the use of deception should be considered very carefully, and only used when it is essential to the study.

It has been argued that some forms of deception are worse than others. For example, if you turned up to take part in a psychology study which you thought was investigating memory, and were then told that the study was actually researching the type of person who replied to advertisements requesting volunteers, it is unlikely that you would be unduly distressed. On the other hand, deception such as that suffered by Milgram's participants, where there may be damage to people's self-image and self-esteem, is clearly potentially more serious.

One way of approaching the question of whether deception is acceptable is to consult people, similar to those to be tested, before carrying out the study. They should be given full information about the aims and procedures of the proposed study, together with the nature of the deception involved and why it is considered necessary. If they say they would have agreed to take part given this information, then there is some support for the use of deception.

Kelman (1967) has suggested that one way to overcome the problem of deception is to ask people to role-play. In some experiments, this may be a valuable strategy. At the same time, there are clearly limitations to the kind of research where this might be useful, and there will in any case inevitably be some doubt about the extent to which role-play accurately represents participants' normal behaviour.

Debriefing

Debriefing can be linked to the idea of protecting participants from harm (guideline 8). Participants are given full information about the study in which they have taken part (if this has not taken place beforehand) and are reassured about their own performance. In many cases, this is not problematical.

However, many people who have had no previous experience of taking part in psychology experiments – and these are ideal participants, since they are less likely than, for example, psychology students to be influenced by previous knowledge of psychology – are concerned that in some way judgements will be made either about their ability or their mental health. Careful and thorough debriefing does therefore need to be given serious consideration.

It is perhaps worth noting that debriefing can provide additional benefits for both researcher and participant. During debriefing, participants can often provide additional information about their performance which may be useful to the researcher in understanding the phenomenon being investigated. For the participant, the understanding gained during debriefing can be an educational experience shared with the researcher.

Right to withdraw

This guideline has links with the need for informed consent. Informed consent may be given at the outset of the study, but participants have the right to withdraw their consent and decide at any point that they no longer wish to take part. This right should be made clear to them, and that it applies even if (as in the case of Milgram's participants) they have accepted payment for participation. They should also know that they have the right to withdraw any data they have provided, and to have it destroyed, even when the study is completed.

In some circumstances, the right to withdraw needs to be given particular consideration. For example, in the earlier example of psychology lecturers using their students as participants, it is particularly important that the right to withdraw at any time without negative consequences is emphasised.

Confidentiality

The importance of confidentiality is highlighted in the BPS guidelines, unless participants have agreed in advance to waive this right. Confidentiality is a legal right under the Data Protection Act, but a further argument for its importance comes from Coolican

(1990), who points out that potential participants in psychology studies would soon become very hard to find if they were not assured of confidentiality!

It is standard practice in most psychology studies to assign participants a number. If their results are to be singled out for discussion in a research report, they can then be referred to by this number, and so not be identified. In some areas of research, the case study method is used, where one person or a small group of people with some unusual psychological characteristic are studied in some detail. In this case, participants are usually identified only by their initials, for example the case of HM reported by Milner (chapter 2, box F).

However, there may be exceptions to the practice of maintaining confidentiality, when psychologists feel they have a wider ethical duty. If we take as a hypothetical example research involving participant observation of gang behaviour, during which a researcher became aware that a crime was being planned, the researcher might consider that his ethical responsibility should be to society as a whole, and that he should therefore report the planned crime. Similarly, on a more personal level, if a researcher became aware that a participant was planning to commit suicide, he might not feel bound to respect the participant's confidentiality, if he considered this not to be in the person's best interests.

Protection from harm

There is seldom any risk of physical harm to participants in psychology experiments. Some experiments have used electric shocks or loud noise, or have deprived participants of food or sleep, or have induced nausea. However, if this is the case, participants are warned beforehand so that they can decide whether or not they wish to take part.

When it comes to psychological harm, Aronson (1988) proposed that researchers should ensure that participants leave the experimental situation in a frame of mind that is at least as sound as when they entered it. In most studies, this is not problematic if participants are given as much information as possible beforehand and fully debriefed at the conclusion of the study, and reassured that their performance is in no way out of the ordinary.

A well accepted principle of psychological research is that if a researcher is unsure about a study and its effects on participants, they should seek advice from a colleague. This should preferably be someone who has carried out similar research before, and who is not likely to be affected by the outcome of the research, and will therefore be unbiased in the advice they give. Milgram, whose studies were outlined in the previous section, kept to this principle, and consulted 14 psychology students and 40 psychiatrists before he carried out his first experiment. These people suggested that participants were very unlikely to obey the orders they were given. As we now know, however, their predictions were very inaccurate. However, following this basic principle can help to ensure that any possibility of harm to participants is minimised.

In some studies – again, notably those of Milgram – protection from harm is a contentious issue. It is clear that participants did not leave Milgram's studies in the same frame of mind as when they entered it, since the vast majority of them had gained an awareness of their willingness to inflict harm on an innocent human being when ordered to do so. But does the psychologist have a responsibility to protect people against self-knowledge, however unwelcome?

A cost–benefit analysis might be useful here, weighing up the costs of the immediate distress of the participants in Milgram's study against the benefits both to them personally (suggested by the proportion who felt that they had learned something useful) and more generally, in increasing our understanding of human psychological functioning in this area.

Observational studies

In many observational studies, people are unaware that their behaviour is being observed. This usually means that they have not consented to take part in the study and are not debriefed afterwards. In some cases a situation may be set up by the researcher, such as someone pretending they need help because their car has broken down, so deception may also be involved. This kind of study involves what is called **involuntary participation**, and may involve **invasion of privacy**.

It could be argued that if normally occurring behaviour in a public place is observed, consent is implicitly given. If the study you are carrying out involves observing whether men or women are more likely to hold a door open for someone passing through the door after them, the ethical considerations are fairly minimal. But if you are observing rather more sensitive behaviour – perhaps the way mothers interact with their children, or public courtship behaviour – you need to be aware of possible ethical objections. A study illustrating this problem was carried out by Humphreys (1970) who investigated the behaviour of consenting homosexuals, himself acting as a 'lookout' at a public convenience. Those being studied were completely unaware that they were being studied and that their car registration numbers were recorded in order to obtain more background information later on.

Giving advice

There is one problem that is encountered by psychologists far more frequently than by other scientists. People sometimes take the opportunity of talking to a psychology researcher about educational or mental health problems, mistaking the researcher for a clinical psychologist or a counsellor. In this case, the researcher is advised to recommend an appropriate source of professional help, and explain the misunderstanding to the person involved.

The BPS guidelines go even further than this, suggesting that advice should be offered if the researcher becomes aware that the participant may have a problem, even when the participant apparently does not realise it and has not asked for advice.

The morality of carrying out research: psychology and the ethical imperative

One further aspect of ethics in psychological research needs to be mentioned. As Brehm (1956) has pointed out: 'We must not overlook the other side of the ethical issue: the ethical imperative to gain more understanding of important areas of human behaviour'. This idea is echoed by Aronson (1988), who pointed out that psychologists have an 'ethical responsibility to society as a whole'. The BPS guidelines suggest that increasing our understanding of people's behaviour improves people's lives, and 'enhances human dignity'. In other words, if we are to understand people's behaviour and improve the quality of their lives, we must carry out research. But it must be carried out with an awareness of the rights of the participants involved.

All the ethical considerations discussed here are relevant to many pieces of research. One overall question, however, applies to every piece of psychology research: 'Do the ends justify the means?'. In other words, will the knowledge gained from the research outweigh any possible costs to the participants?

Aronson (1988) has suggested that psychologists may face an ethical dilemma when there is a conflict between their responsibility towards research participants and to society as a whole. For example, it could be argued that Milgram's research into obedience has highlighted aspects of important social issues with potential benefit to society, and this benefit may be considered to outweigh the cost to participants.

◯ Psychology research can raise serious ethical issues. Various professional bodies have produced **ethical guidelines**.

Psychology research should avoid causing physical or psychological **harm** to participants.

Participants should give **informed consent** to taking part in a study, and should be made aware that they can **withdraw** at any time. Special care must be taken with participants who cannot give informed consent. Researchers need to be aware of possible problems in invading the **privacy** of others.

Deception is sometimes unavoidable, but **debriefing** can help to minimise its effects.

A **cost–benefit analysis** should be made before embarking on research.

Psychologists also have an ethical responsibility to carry out research to increase knowledge about human behaviour and so potentially improve the quality of our lives.

We have looked in some detail at the ethical concerns raised by Milgram's experiments, but his is not the only study to have raised such concerns. To end this chapter, we will look briefly at another study which has attracted criticism on ethical grounds, which was carried out by Zimbardo (1973 – box E).

Since his study was carried out some time after Milgram's studies, Zimbardo went to considerable lengths to make the study as ethical as possible. Participants were given reasonably full information before the study was carried out, so that they knew that the study would involve invasion of privacy, the loss of some civil rights, and harassment. They were not informed, however, that they would be 'arrested' by the police, in part because approval for this aspect of the study was only received just before the study started, and partly to make the study more realistic.

Not only were participants aware that they were free to withdraw at any time – indeed, some asked to do so – but Zimbardo himself stopped the study as soon as it became clear that the effects on the participants were far more severe than had been anticipated.

Participants were debriefed individually and in groups immediately after the experiment, and everyone who had taken part was asked to return questionnaires several weeks later, several months later, and at yearly intervals. On the basis of this information, Zimbardo claimed that the suffering experienced by people who had taken part did not extend beyond the experimental situation.

Activity 13: the ethics of Zimbardo's study

Look back to the account of Zimbardo's study (box E). In the light of this information and the additional information given above, to what extent do you consider Zimbardo's study to have been unethical? To reach your assessment, you will need to consider the ethical guidelines described above.

Notes on activities

1 A variety of reasons were given. Some participants claimed that they thought a mistake had been made; they did not want to upset the experiment, which might create a bad impression; they did not want to seem different from everyone else; they did not want to look stupid. All these reasons show **public conformity**, i.e. changing the answer they would have given if asked on their own, but no **private change** – their actual judgement of the lines was not affected.

Some participants, however, seemed to believe that the incorrect decision of the majority was actually correct; they showed private change as well as public conformity. They suggested reasons why their own judgements might have been wrong; perhaps they were suffering from eye strain, or the position of their chair did not allow them to see properly.

2 a Asch found that the conformity effect emerges with only three confederates; increasing the size of the group beyond this does not increase the size of the effect. There was a less marked effect when there were only two confederates. What seems to be crucial here is not the size of the group, but the fact that there is complete agreement among group members.

b The reverse is also true: if the judgements made are no longer unanimous, and there is one confederate who gives the correct answer, the rate of conformity drops to about 5%. Allen and Levine (1971) found this to be true even when the non-conforming confederate wore glasses with pebble lenses; his judgements might not be very reliable! Curiously, this also seems to happen if one confederate gives a different *wrong* answer from the other confederates. However, this only seems to apply to physical judgements, like Asch's lines task; if a social or political judgement is involved, another answer diverging from both the majority and the participant results in the participant conforming to the majority decision (Allen and Levine, 1968). This may be because we expect there to be a variety of opinions on social questions, but we expect consensus on physical judgements.

c When the dissenter from the group changes to agreement with the majority, the conformity effect reappears, with the same strength as in the original situation.

d Making the task more difficult tends to increase conformity; presumably participants then have less confidence in the correctness of their judgments.

e If only one person in the group gives a wrong answer, the rest of the group tend to be sarcastic and make fun of him. It seems that the participants in the original study who were afraid of being ridiculed were justified!

f This perhaps helps to explain why, when Asch allowed the genuine participant to write down his answer, while still being aware of the answers of the confederates, conformity dropped to just over 12% – he would no longer be vulnerable to this kind of reaction.

3 In a lecture, you listen to the information you are given and make notes. You are quiet; any talking is done in a whisper. It would be inappropriate to stand up and start singing a rugby song, or to take all your clothes off. Similarly in a restaurant, you

order food, eat it with the cutlery provided and pay before you leave. You wouldn't take your own food and ask the waiter to cook it for you, or sit with your elbows in the soup.

Social conventions help to ensure that social interaction with others runs smoothly. Because these conventions are unwritten, many of them are acquired as part of the socialisation process. What is (and is not) appropriate behaviour is picked up by observing the behaviour of others. The consequence of not observing social conventions is loss of the acceptance and approval of others.

4 You would probably ask the advice of people you know who are already involved in the sport, and could well end up buying the same make of equipment as they did. This kind of conformity doesn't have anything to do with needing their approval. The fact they have more *information* than you is what is crucial in your decision to conform, so this is known as **informational influence**. It has a role in particular in situations where there is some degree of uncertainty, i.e. lack of information.

5 In the first paragraph, you should have linked **compliance**, **normative**, the **need for approval/acceptance**, **unambiguous** and **Asch**, leaving the other terms for the second paragraph.

7 You probably decided that you would be more likely to conform in a group of twelve. Convincing eleven people that you are right is much more of an uphill struggle than convincing five!

10 Gender might be expected to make a difference. In our society and many others, a woman's role has traditionally been that of carer, protecting others from harm rather than inflicting it. Social behaviour reflects the varying cultural norms and values of different societies. It therefore seems probable that obedience, like other social behaviours, will vary from culture to culture.

11 Firstly, this was presented as a study on the effects of punishment on learning, but participants were not doing anything which the experimenter could not have done just as well for himself. It must also have seemed very odd when the experimenter showed no reaction when the learner pounded on the wall and demanded that the experiment should be stopped. There were possibly other subtle clues which could have been picked up. It is very difficult, for example, to treat a confederate in exactly the same way as a complete stranger. These factors could well have led to participants trying to guess the *real* purpose of the study, i.e. **demand characteristics**. They may have come to realise that they themselves were actually the ones being studied.

In reply to this, Milgram claimed that a follow-up survey showed that 80% of participants had no such doubts. Additionally, many participants showed clear and unambiguous stress responses, such as trembling, stuttering and sweating.

12 The Gamson *et al*. study was carried out nearly 20 years after Milgram. During this time, there were many social changes, one of which could have been that it had become more acceptable to question authority, a change to which knowledge of Milgram's studies could itself have contributed. Milgram's study received widespread publicity. One of the participants in the Gamson *et al*. study even referred to Milgram's work as a reason for not conforming!

Perhaps also the participants were less intimidated by a company representative than by a researcher from a prestigious university.

In addition, people were working in groups. You will remember from our discussion of Milgram's study that obedience was reduced to 10% when the participant was exposed to disobedient models.

Finally, the participants in this later study can have been in no doubt that they were being cynically manipulated, whereas in the Milgram study they might have believed that what they were doing was of some academic value.

Research methods

In this chapter we will be looking at:

7.1 Methods in psychological research
    The experimental method
    Non-experimental methods

7.2 Quantitative and qualitative data

7.3 Variables, operationalisation, and hypotheses

7.4 Populations and samples
    Sampling methods

7.5 Experimental design
    Evaluation of independent
        measures design
    Evaluation of repeated
        measures design
    Matched pairs design
    Pilot studies

7.6 Reliability, validity, and standardisation

7.7 Levels of measurement

7.8 Descriptive statistics
    Measures of central tendency
    Measures of dispersion
    Graphical representation

7.9 Ethics in psychological research

7.1 METHODS IN PSYCHOLOGICAL RESEARCH

You will remember from chapter 1 that psychology goes beyond common sense in that it attempts to set about the task of understanding behaviour and experience in an organised and systematic way. It does not rely on casual observation to support its ideas because this approach is very limited and can be misleading. For these reasons, psychologists carry out studies to investigate their ideas in a structured way which will enable them to collect information or data which can provide objective evidence to support or challenge psychological ideas.

Not all psychologists give priority to research, however. As we saw in chapter 1, for humanistic psychologists, with their focus on the experience of the individual, research is of much less importance than for, say, cognitive psychologists, although Rogers did carry out research into clients' experience of client-centred therapy. The work of most psychologists, however, is focused on research, and a wide range of methods has been used to try to understand how people function.

The experimental method, which is the traditional method of scientific enquiry, has been the main method used by psychologists. However, alternative ways of carrying out research also have their place, and may be more suitable for some research areas. We will look first at what the different methods used in psychological research involve.

The experimental method

There are two criteria which define a piece of research as an experiment. Firstly, an **independent variable (IV)** is manipulated by the experimenter, with all other variables being kept constant. Secondly, there is an element of **random selection** and/or **allocation** of participants to conditions. There are other methods which do not fully meet these criteria yet which may loosely be called experiments, but we will start by looking at each of these two criteria in turn.

A variable is anything which can vary, i.e. can have different values. The **IV** is the variable in which the experimenter is interested, in terms of its effect on the **dependent variable (DV)**, i.e. the performance of participants in an experiment.

In terms of manipulation of the independent variable, in an experiment the researcher creates two or more different conditions. The differences between the conditions constitute the **independent variable**, with all other variables being kept constant. The effect of these different conditions on the **dependent variable** is measured and compared.

To give a simple example, a researcher may be interested in how different instructions for carrying out the memory task of learning a word list affect the number of words remembered. One group of participants could be instructed to learn the words by reading through the list over and over again, repeating them in their heads, i.e. rehearsal. A different group of participants could be asked to use story linkage, making up a story in which all the words appear. Both groups would then be asked to write down as many of the words as they could remember. The independent variable here is the instructions given to the participants, since it is the difference between the groups. The dependent variable is the number of words remembered, since that is what is being measured.

Activity 1: identifying the IV and DV

For each of these studies, identify the IV and the DV:

a A researcher is interested in whether older or younger people are more helpful. Drivers are observed at a junction. The number of older people (apparently over 45) and younger people (apparently under 25) who give way to another vehicle (and who do not give way to another vehicle) are counted.

b Do people work more efficiently first thing in the morning or later in the day? The productivity of workers making soft toys in a factory is compared between 9–10am on the morning shift and 7–8pm on the evening shift on a given day.

c Participants are asked to remember word pairs, either by rehearsing the pairs of words to themselves or by forming a mental image linking the two items. They are tested by being given the first word of each pair and then asked to supply the word with which it was paired. When you have finished, see the notes on page 178.

The experimenter would also need to control **confounding variables**. These are any variables which could affect the outcome of the study but are not the IV in which the researcher is interested. It is important to control or eliminate confounding variables in an experiment in order to be sure that any differences between conditions in the dependent variable can only be the result of the manipulation of the independent variable.

A confounding variable can take the form of a random error or a constant error. A **random error** is any uncontrolled or inadequately-controlled variable which could affect the results in an unpredictable way. For example, performance on a task could be affected for some participants by a disturbance outside the room in which they are being tested, or by not being able to get to sleep the night before, or by not being motivated to perform the task they are asked to carry out. A **constant error** is something other than the IV which consistently affects the DV – for example, participants in one condition being given unclear instructions.

Confounding variables can also be classified as **subject variables**, i.e. differences in the participants in the two conditions, or **situation variables**, i.e. differences in the testing situation. For an example of a subject variable, let us go back to the memory experiment described above. If all the participants in one condition were male and all the participants in the other were female, gender could be a confounding variable: it is not the variable in which the researcher is interested but could be the reason for any differences in the test scores of the two groups.

Similarly, in the same experiment, time of day could be a situation variable. For example, if one group were tested early in the morning and the other group late at night, any differences found between the scores of the two groups could be explained in terms of the time they were tested (e.g. people may be more alert in the morning) rather than in terms of the instructions they were given.

Condition 1   Condition 2

A possible subject variable

◗ Activity 2: identifying confounding variables

Look back to the studies in activity 1. In each study, identify possible confounding variables. Say whether each is a subject or a situation variable. When you have finished, see the notes on page 178.

Laboratory experiments are carried out in many areas of psychology, because they give the researcher more control over the procedure. Laboratory conditions make it easier to control confounding variables and isolate the one variable in which the researcher is interested, i.e. the IV. If this is done successfully, the researcher can claim that there is a cause and effect relationship between the IV and the DV. The control the laboratory experiment offers makes it easy for other researchers to repeat or **replicate** the experiment to check the findings. It also means that researchers can set up the conditions they need, and do not have to wait for a suitable opportunity to present itself naturally. Another advantage of this kind of experiment is that it can easily be structured to provide **quantitative data**, i.e. results in a numerical form. These can be analysed using statistical tests which indicate how likely the results are to have come about by chance. A laboratory experiment also means that sophisticated technical equipment can be used, e.g. presenting a visual stimulus for a precisely measured fraction of a second.

Laboratory experiments also have their drawbacks, however. A major problem is **ecological validity**, i.e. the extent to which a laboratory study shares the characteristics of a real-life situation. For example, in the Strange Situation, described in chapter 3, the conditions in which the children experienced separation and reunion with caregivers were somewhat artificial, and so it might be unwise to generalise from the results of this technique to the effects of temporary separation in familiar surroundings. Similarly, Ebbinghaus' use of nonsense syllables to investigate the nature of memory (see chapter 2) allowed the role of meaning in memory to be controlled. However, this kind of material is very different from the kinds of things which we would normally try to learn.

A related problem is what Orne (1962) called **demand characteristics**. In a laboratory situation, participants are usually well aware that they are taking part in an experiment, and so may try to make sense of what they are being asked to do. They may pick up cues from what the researcher says and does, or from the layout of the laboratory. They could then change their behaviour in a way that they see as being helpful to the researcher, or possibly set out deliberately to go against what they perceive to be the experimenter's aims, which Masling (1966) has termed the **'screw you' effect**. If participants are responding to demand characteristics, clearly the ecological validity of the study is compromised.

A study carried out by Berkowitz and LePage (1967) provides a good example of the possible role of demand characteristics. This study investigated Berkowitz' **aggressive cue theory**, and was interested in the effect of contextual cues – in this case, the presence of weapons – on aggression. Participants were made angry by being given a series of seven mild electric shocks by a confederate of the experimenter, supposedly as a way of assessing the effects of stress on problem-solving behaviour. Participants were more aggressive (in terms of giving more small electric shocks to the confederate, as a way of evaluating his performance on a problem-solving task) when there was a shotgun and a revolver in the room than when no weapons were present.

However, it is possible that the participants guessed the nature of the study. The presence of weapons in a psychology laboratory must have seemed very odd, and the cover story – that the weapons were needed for an experiment later on – seems rather unconvincing.

Page and Scheidt (1971) replicated the 'weapons effect' study, and interviewed the participants afterwards. Eighty-one per cent claimed to have suspected that the investigation was about revenge against the confederate, and many of these had guessed that the weapons were there to increase their aggressive response. The results of the Berkowitz and LePage study could therefore be explained by the participants co-operating with what they (correctly) saw to be the aim of the study.

In answer to this criticism, Berkowitz pointed out that it was just as likely that participants could have decided to behave in such a way as to go against the hypothesis being tested. Either way, though, demand characteristics could have reduced the ecological validity of the study and distorted the research findings.

Related problems are **evaluation apprehension**, where participants' performance may be affected by concern that their behaviour will be judged by the experimenter, and **social desirability** effects, where behaviour may be distorted in an attempt to give what the participant believes to be a good impression.

Experimenter effects are a further problem. These occur when the characteristics or behaviour of the experimenter may influence the behaviour of the participants. For example, experimenter characteristics could include gender, race, age or physical attractiveness, while experimenter behaviour which might affect participants' behaviour could include being very friendly or patronising.

A related problem is **experimenter bias**, when the experimenter shows unintentional bias when recording the data from an experiment. One way to overcome this kind of problem is to use a **double blind** technique. In most research, participants are unaware of what the experimenter is expecting the study to show (though of course demand characteristics may make this less true). Keeping participants unaware of the nature of the study is known as the **single blind** technique. In a double blind study, the collection of data is carried out by someone other than the experimenter, so that neither the participant nor the person running the study is aware of what the results are expected to be.

Not all studies carried out in a laboratory, however, are experiments. Observational studies which look at naturally occurring behaviour can also be carried out in laboratory conditions. For example, Smith and Lloyd (1978) made many video recordings of the interaction between mothers and babies, in such a way that the activity and verbalisation of both mother and baby could be viewed simultaneously. They found that a turn-taking pattern emerged, in which both baby and mother took an active part, and concluded that this kind of early interaction formed the basis in very young babies for their later acquisition of language.

Conversely, not all experiments are carried out in a laboratory. Some experiments are **field experiments**. These are studies which take place in natural conditions, but where the criteria for an experiment are met. Field studies are carried out when it is thought to be important that what is being studied happens in the natural environment. A good example here would be the study by Hofling *et al.* into nurse compliance, described in the section on obedience in chapter 6.

The main advantages of field experiments are that they have high ecological validity and reduce the possibility of people responding to demand characteristics. However, control is more of a problem, with an increased likelihood of the study being influenced by confounding variables. This also makes replication more difficult. While high ecological validity may mean that the results of field experiments can be more readily generalised, i.e. the conclusions drawn from the experiment can be assumed to apply to similar situations, it may also be more difficult to apply general conclusions from a field study to other situations which differ from the situation in which the study was carried out. There are also ethical problems, which we shall come to later in this chapter; in particular, participants will not have given consent to having their behaviour observed if they are unaware that they are taking part in a study. Field experiments can also take longer to carry out than laboratory experiments, since the researcher may have to wait for behaviour to occur, and they do not allow complicated technical equipment to be used.

A final kind of experiment is the **natural experiment**. This is a procedure which takes advantage of a naturally occurring event. For example, **adoption studies** have been carried out to establish the extent to which schizophrenia has a genetic cause. To do this, the incidence of schizophrenia in adopted children with birth mothers with the disorder, and those with birth mothers with no history of mental disorder, is compared. This kind of study has similar advantages and disadvantages to the field experiment. Such studies are not strictly speaking experiments, since random allocation is not possible; experimenters cannot randomly allocate children to birth mothers.

There are also **quasi-experiments**, which take a broadly experimental approach but where the criteria for an experiment are not completely met. Studies (a) and (b) in activity 1 are examples of quasi-experiments. Random allocation of participants to age groups in study (a) would not be possible – participants would come to the study already allocated as over 45 or under 25! Similarly, in study (b) it would be unlikely that the researcher would be able to allocate workers randomly to shifts.

⑤ In the **experimental method**, researchers manipulate an **independent variable** to find its effect on the **dependent variable**, while controlling **confounding variables**.
⑥ **Laboratory experiments** take place in controlled conditions, while **field experiments** take place in the natural environment. **Natural experiments** take advantage of a naturally occurring situation, while **quasi-experiments** do not completely meet the criteria for an experiment.
⑤ All these kinds of experiment have both advantages and drawbacks.

Non-experimental methods

As well as experiments, psychologists have a range of other methods open to them. Because none of these methods involves manipulating the independent variable, they do not offer the control of an experiment, and so it is more difficult to establish cause and effect relationships. They do, however, enable researchers to carry out research in more natural conditions than those of a laboratory, and they can be more suitable than the experimental method for some kinds of investigations.

Correlational analysis

Correlational analysis is a statistical technique which measures the relationship between two variables. An example of research using correlational analysis is Kanner *et al.*'s study, described in chapter 4, of the relationship between the experience of everyday hassles and the psychological symptoms of stress. A positive correlation occurs when as values for one variable increase, values for the other also tend to do so; in Kanner *et al.*'s example, people who experienced more hassles tended to suffer more from stress, while those who scored low on the hassles scale tended also to score low for stress. A negative correlation occurs when as values for one variable increase, values for the other tend to decrease. There would probably be a negative correlation, for example, between the amount of alcohol people had drunk and how well they performed on a test of hand-eye co-ordination.

Statistical tests measuring correlation produce a value or **coefficient** between +1 (a perfect positive correlation) and −1 (a perfect negative correlation). A coefficient of 0 shows that an increase in one variable does not predict a consistent increase or decrease in the other variable. A correlation coefficient must always have a value between +1 and −1. In practice, coefficients are rarely as high as +1, and negative correlations are rarely as low as −1, but usually fall somewhere in between these extreme values. A correlation of 0.7, for example, would show a fairly strong positive relationship between two variables, while a correlation of -0.3 would show a fairly weak negative relationship.

Activity 3: correlation

For each of these pairs of variables, say whether you would expect to find a positive correlation, a negative correlation or no correlation. Estimate what value between +1 and −1 you would expect the coefficient to have:

a height and shoe size
b scores on a French test and scores on an English test
c how stressed a person feels and their state of health
d bodyweight and scores on a video game

When you have finished, see the notes on page 179.

This technique allows us to measure the strength and direction of relationships between two variables. It can also be used at the start of research to establish whether there is a phenomenon which could be investigated more thoroughly using the experimental method. As we shall see later, it is also used to establish the **reliability** and **validity** of tests.

Its main drawback is that it cannot establish cause and effect. There is likely to be a strong positive relationship between the number of puddles that you see and the number of umbrellas, but there isn't a causal relationship between puddles and umbrellas, since both are caused by a further variable, i.e. rain.

Correlation also cannot show non-linear relationships. As discussed in chapter 4, the relationship between arousal and performance is initially a positive one, but when arousal becomes too great, and can be described as stress, performance drops off and the relationship becomes a negative one. These two trends would cancel each other out to give a correlation coefficient close to 0, masking the real relationship between these two variables. This kind of relationship is called a **curvilinear relationship**.

● **Correlational analysis** shows the direction and strength of the relationship between two variables. A major drawback is that it cannot establish **cause and effect**, nor can it show **curvilinear relationships**.

Observational studies

This method makes no attempt to manipulate variables, but simply records aspects of behaviour in a particular situation as they occur. As we saw earlier, this technique can be used in a laboratory setting, but more often takes place in a more natural setting. It therefore has high ecological validity and avoids demand characteristics. It allows researchers to collect a wide range of interesting data.

In **participant observation**, the researcher joins in with the group of people being studied. Hargreaves (1967), for example, investigated social relationships at a school by becoming a teacher at the school for a year. Similarly, Marsh (1978) investigated the extent to which the behaviour of football fans comes about as the result of them conforming to the rules developed by the groups of fans themselves. To do this, he went to football matches, travelling with groups of fans, and observed their behaviour. In **non-participant observation**, such as observations of children's play, the researcher remains apart from those being studied, who may or may not be aware that their behaviour is being watched.

It is often possible to record on video the behaviour which is being observed. This has the advantage of allowing the behaviour to be viewed as many times as is necessary for a full analysis to be carried out. Where this is not possible, the methods of time sampling and event sampling may be used to make the observation more manageable.

In **time sampling**, observations are made for only short periods of time during the observational period. For example, if a researcher was interested in the kinds of play shown by children in a playground, it would be impractical to observe the children's behaviour and at the same time make detailed notes. Time sampling could be used by watching the children for a two minute period in every quarter of an hour, using the rest of the time before the next observation to make notes on what had been observed. If the observer was interested in the frequency of particular kinds of play, this method would be a manageable way of making comparisons across the period of the observation.

In **event sampling**, observations are made of a specific event each time it occurs. If the researcher observing children's play, for instance, was interested in whether boys show more aggression in their play than girls, each example of behaviour from both boys and girls which could be classified in this way would be noted.

Naturalistic observation is a useful technique when the researcher is interested in something which would be very hard to recreate in a laboratory – for example, the behaviour of drivers or the interaction of children at school. It can also be used in exploratory studies, to establish which phenomena could be explored in more detail in a laboratory setting.

One practical problem of observational techniques is the **observer effect**, where observing a phenomenon may in itself affect what is being observed. A good example is the **Hawthorne Effect**, which takes its name from the Hawthorne works of the Bell Telephone Company where it was first observed. It refers to the fact that in an industrial setting, productivity may improve simply as the result of changes being introduced, even if this was not the intention behind introducing the change. In psychological research, the Hawthorne effect is often referred to when a research participant's behaviour may have been affected by their awareness of being observed.

Observer bias is also possible. As rigorous measurement is not taking place, observers may interpret what they see in line with the expectations and beliefs they bring to the study. One way of trying to overcome this problem is to have two people making observations of the same event(s), and to check that their observations are similar. This is known as **inter-observer reliability**, and we will be returning to it later in the section on reliability.

A further problem of observational techniques is the difficulty of **replication**; it is very unlikely that all aspects of an observational study would remain the same if the study were to be repeated. For this reason, too, there are difficulties with **generalisation**, i.e. applying the conclusions drawn from a study of this kind more widely. For example, it might be unwise to draw general conclusions about the nature of children's play from observation of a particular playgroup, since there are likely to be a number of uncontrollable variables which could have affected the observations. For instance, the skills of the playgroup staff, the kinds of toys and materials available and the number of children attending the group could all have an effect on children's behaviour.

It is also more likely in this kind of study than in an experiment that relevant aspects of the behaviour being observed could be missed. For example, in an observation of children's play in a group situation there could be so much movement that it would be difficult to keep track of everything which took place. As noted already, this kind of difficulty can be minimised by making a filmed record, which can be replayed as often as is necessary for a complete record.

- **Naturalistic observation** focuses on naturally occurring behaviour. In **participant observation**, observers themselves take part.
- **Time sampling** and **event sampling** may be used.
- It is a useful technique when studying behaviour which could not easily be translated to a laboratory setting.
- There may be **observer effects**, and **replication** may be difficult. Carrying out this kind of study can present **practical problems**.

Case studies

Unlike the methods we have talked about so far, a case study is a detailed study of one individual or a small group of individuals. A range of methods can be used, including interviews, detailed observation, records such as a medical history, information from others about the person being studied, and so on. Quite often at least some of the data is **qualitative**, being largely descriptive, rather than **quantitative**, i.e. providing precise measures. A case study is an **idiographic** approach, since it is an in-depth study, focusing in detail on particular characteristics of the individual(s).

This method is widely used in clinical psychology; Freud's research, for example, consisted entirely of case studies of patients. It can be a very useful approach for increasing understanding of all relevant aspects of a person's experience and behaviour. It is also useful for investigating the characteristics of people who are unusual in some way, for example Curtiss' study of Genie, described in box P of chapter 3.

One of the advantages of this method is that it can increase our knowledge within a certain topic area, such as mental disorders, when a more experimental technique would be unethical. For example, if people with a mental disorder were randomly allocated to conditions, in one of which they were offered a specific treatment which they were likely to find beneficial, and in the other condition were not offered treatment, there would be serious ethical problems in withholding treatment from people who might benefit from it.

The case study method can be useful in the initial stages of researching a topic, to identify particular areas which might usefully be followed up using other methods. The detail it provides means that it can also be used as the basis for challenging an existing theory, if the results of the case study call the theory into question. It also gives detailed information about a real person or people, where techniques such as the experimental method are more interested in general trends, i.e. take a **nomothetic** approach, and so may lose valuable information about individual differences. Finally, since the numbers of participants are so small, it

lends itself to a **longitudinal** approach, where people are studied over time, e.g. the Freud and Dann Bulldog Bank study of concentration camp survivors, described in box N of chapter 3.

However, there are also some drawbacks to this method. A major problem is **generalisability**; we cannot conclude that what is true of one person or a small group of people is also true of people more generally. **Researcher bias** is also a problem; for example, Freud's case studies have been criticised on the grounds of the high level of interpretation they involved. Finally, if a case study involves in-depth interviews, this relies heavily on the person being interviewed giving accurate answers. For instance, an adult asked about their childhood may not be able to remember relevant information or may inaccurately reconstruct their memories. The problem of **recovered memory** and **false memory syndrome** is discussed in chapter 2.

- ❺ **Case studies** are in-depth studies of one or a small number of people. They provide detailed, often **qualitative**, data.
- ❺ They are a useful way of studying unusual characteristics, particularly where a more experimental approach would raise ethical difficulties.
- ❺ The results are not necessarily **generalisable**. **Researcher bias** may also be a problem.

Interviews and surveys

Interviews and surveys cover a wide range of related techniques – **interviews**, **questionnaires**, **attitude surveys**, and the **clinical method** used in diagnosing psychological problems – but they all involve asking people for information about themselves. Interviews can be **structured**, where every respondent (the person being interviewed) is asked the same questions, or more **unstructured**, where there is room for flexibility in terms of what is asked.

Questionnaires and surveys may use open-ended or closed-ended questions. **Closed-ended questions** provide the respondent with answers from which they must choose, while **open-ended questions** allow them to answer in any way they feel is appropriate:

Activity 4: closed- and open-ended questions

A closed-ended question:

Why did you choose to take A-level psychology? Was it because:

a it sounded more interesting than the other options?

b it was recommended by a friend?

c you like the teacher?

d you thought it might be easier than the other options?

An open-ended question:

Why did you choose to take A-level psychology?

What are the advantages and disadvantages of each of these types of question?

When you have finished, see the notes on page 179.

One example of the use of surveys is to measure people's attitudes to various issues. Likert (1932) developed the principle of measuring attitudes by asking people to respond in a structured way to a series of statements relevant to the attitude being measured. A series of statements – perhaps 30 – is prepared, relevant to the particular attitude to be measured, with half the statements being favourable and half unfavourable. This balance is necessary in order to eliminate **response set**; if all the statements were favourable to the attitude being measured, participants might respond without reading each statement carefully, and so reduce the accuracy of the information being gathered. Statements are presented in random order and participants rate each statement on a five-point scale, to which numerical values are attached.

Examples of the sorts of items which might be used to measure attitudes to the royal family, together with the scoring system, are shown in figure 1. You will see that a high score shows a favourable attitude to the royal family, and a low score an unfavourable attitude. A person's attitude is the sum of their scores from all the items. The numbers would not appear on the questionnaire completed by participants; they are only there to show you how the system works.

In a different area, **Eysenck's Personality Inventory (EPI)** is a personality **questionnaire** using a similar approach. It is an example of a **psychometric test**, i.e. a test which aims to measure particular psychological characteristics. In this case the characteristics being measured are extroversion and neuroticism, the two dimensions which Eysenck believed are sufficient to describe an individual's personality. A typical extrovert is sociable, gregarious, impulsive and enjoys taking risks, while a typical neurotic is guilt-ridden and anxious. Sample questions relating to extroversion are shown in activity 5:

Activity 5: measuring extroversion

Here are some sample questions on extroversion. For each one, answer 'yes' or 'no'.

You can answer '?' if you really cannot decide, but try to avoid this if possible.

Don't spend too long thinking about how to respond – it is usually best to stay with your first reaction.

Figure 1: sample of a Likert scale to measure attitudes

1. The royal family are good ambassadors for this country

strongly agree	agree somewhat	undecided	disagree somewhat	strongly disagree
5	4	3	2	1

2. It would be a good idea to have a president instead of the royal family

strongly agree	agree somewhat	undecided	disagree somewhat	strongly disagree
1	2	3	4	5

1 Are you inclined to be slow and
   deliberate in your actions?   Y ? N
2 Do you often buy things on impulse?   Y ? N
3 Do you often change your interests?   Y ? N
4 Are you rather cautious in novel
   situations?   Y ? N

Did any problems occur to you as you were answering these questions? Are there any ways you think this method of measuring personality could be criticised?

When you have finished, see the notes on page 179.

Given the kinds of problem often found with these kinds of questionnaires, Eysenck included a lie scale in the EPI. This uses questions such as: 'Have you ever been late for an appointment?', working on the principle that we have all at some time been late for something, even if only slightly late for something not very important. This is perhaps a little limited, but it is one way of alerting the tester to the possibility of a **social desirability** effect.

A structured approach has the advantage of focusing on specific questions which are of interest to the researcher, and is likely to produce quantitative data, i.e. in the form of scores, which are more easily analysed using statistical methods. This is particularly the case where the range of possible answers to questions is limited. In their written form, techniques such as attitude surveys and personality questionnaires allow a lot of information to be gathered relatively easily from large numbers of respondents. Given the constraints on what is asked using this kind of structured technique, interviewer bias is less likely than with a more unstructured approach.

An unstructured interview, on the other hand, while being more open to bias, allows the interviewer to follow up responses which are of particular interest, and thus to collect potentially richer data. It has the advantage of being very flexible and giving access to information which might not easily be gained using other methods.

In practice, a **semi-structured interview** technique is often used to tap into the advantages of both the structured and unstructured approaches. An example of a semi-structured

technique is the **clinical interview**, used to assess a person with a mental disorder. Specific questions are asked, but there is also the possibility of following up responses in more detail if this is thought to be useful. This technique may be used not only to diagnose the particular disorder from which the person is suffering, and so form a basis for deciding which kinds of therapeutic intervention might be appropriate, but also to provide material for research purposes. Mental health professionals use this technique to collect information about the psychiatric, medical, personal and family history of the patient; their social circumstances; and their personality. In addition, they use a more structured approach to make a cognitive assessment, e.g. of memory and IQ, test the functioning of the central nervous system and make a physical examination.

One of the drawbacks to unstructured or semi-structured techniques, where the range of possible answers is open, is that they may be limited by how easily respondents can express themselves. This in turn may be affected in face-to-face interviews by the sensitivity and skill of the interviewer. The interviewer must also be aware of ethical considerations. Respondents should not feel coerced into giving replies, nor feel that judgements are being made about them on the basis of the information they give.

Sometimes postal interviews are carried out, usually anonymously, which go some way to addressing these concerns. With this method, though, flexibility is lost and the return rate is usually very low. More importantly, the kinds of people who choose to return completed postal interviews or questionnaires are a **self-selected sample**, and so may not be typical of the group of people in whom the researcher is interested. We shall be returning to sampling later in the chapter.

❺ **Interviews**, **questionnaires**, **attitude surveys** and **clinical interviews** are techniques which ask people directly for information. They can be **structured** or **unstructured**. A structured approach offers precision and ease of analysis, while an unstructured approach offers richness of data.

7.2 QUANTITATIVE AND QUALITATIVE DATA

Many of the research methods used by psychologists are concerned with collecting **quantitative data**, i.e. numerical data which can be put in categories, or in rank order, or measured in units of measurement. This emphasis on quantitative data is the result of psychologists adopting a similar approach to research to that used in traditional sciences such as physics and chemistry. This approach is **positivist**, which means that it sees only measurable events as worthy of scientific study.

However, we have also looked at methods which do not have this focus, and are more interested in collecting much more loosely-structured **qualitative data**, which do not easily yield this kind of numerical information.

▶ Activity 6: qualitative data in research

Look back through the different methods used in psychology outlined at the start of this chapter. Which of the methods described could provide qualitative data?
When you have finished, see the notes on page 179.

An interest in qualitative data came about as the result of the dissatisfaction of some psychologists with positivism. Since psychologists study people, the traditional approach to science is not seen as an appropriate way of carrying out research, since it fails to capture the totality of human experience and the essence of what it is to be human. Exploring the experience of participants is known as a **phenomenological** approach.

It is argued that to focus on isolated pieces of behaviour, as is most often the case in studies interested in collecting quantitative data, is rather superficial, and ignores the social context within which behaviour takes place. Given that psychological research is something which happens in a social context, the objectivity of the researcher, central to traditional methods, is seen as essentially false within psychology. As people studying people, researchers necessarily have attitudes and values

which they bring to their research. It is therefore more honest that researchers' attitudes and values should be acknowledged, and form part of the context of research.

Experimental methods limit the possible ways in which a research participant can react to and express appropriate social behaviour. Findings are therefore likely to be context-bound and simply a reflection of the assumptions which the researcher brings to the investigation.

The traditional method of using research to confirm or falsify a particular theory, model or hypothesis is also seen as inappropriate. Rather, theories, models and hypotheses should emerge from the data, as a co-operative effort of researcher and participant. These ideas also link to the **deconstructionist** approach and the **feminist perspective**. According to many who work within this perspective, the traditional positivist approach is seen to be very male-oriented, with its emphasis on control, manipulation and objectivity, and as such is dehumanising.

Qualitative methods necessarily involve interpretation of data, which from a traditional viewpoint could be seen as a criticism. However, psychologists interested in a qualitative approach believe that objectivity is unattainable in psychological research, and given the nature of the subject matter, they consider that even to attempt to be objective is undesirable.

❺ Some psychologists have challenged the traditional emphasis on **quantitative data** using a scientific model in psychological research.
❺ They have argued that **qualitative methods** may be more appropriate, given the subject matter of psychology.

7.3 VARIABLES, OPERATIONALISATION, AND HYPOTHESES

In the section on the experimental method in psychology, we discussed how the aim of a piece of research is to find out whether an IV affects the DV. This is done by manipulating the IV between conditions, and controlling possible confounding variables. Correlational research, on the other hand, looks for a relationship between two variables.

The variables in a particular piece of research need to be **operationalised**, i.e. defined in terms of how they are to be used in a particular study. For example, the Loftus and Palmer study in box T of chapter 2 was interested in whether the wording used in a question about an event (IV) affected memory of that event (DV). The IV here was operationalised as the inclusion of the word 'hit' or 'smashed' in a question about the speed of a car in a video showing a car crash, and the DV was the answer a week later to the question: 'Did you see any broken glass?'

Activity 7: operationalisation

Here are some research ideas. For each one, identify the IV and the DV and suggest ways in which each could be operationalised:

a Do people remember more about a topic they are interested in than about one in which they have little interest?

b Are there gender differences in the amount of aggression shown by children in play?

c Are neurotic people more likely to suffer from phobias?

When you have finished, see the notes on page 179.

Much psychological research aims to test a specific **hypothesis**. This is a precise prediction about the expected findings of a study, and includes the IV and DV in their operationalised form, or the two co-variables in the case of correlational analysis. A study uses two hypotheses, the **null hypothesis** and the **alternative hypothesis** which is also known as the **research** or (in an experiment) the **experimental hypothesis**.

The **null hypothesis** predicts that there will be no difference between the conditions, or no relationship between the co-variables, in the case of a correlational study. For example, in the Loftus and Palmer study the null hypothesis would predict that there would be no difference between the conditions they tested in the percentage of people claiming to have seen broken glass. Statistical tests tell us what the probability is that the results of a study have come about by chance. If this probability is relatively high, then the null hypothesis has to be retained. If it is relatively low, then the null hypothesis can be rejected, and the alternative hypothesis accepted.

In a study, the null hypothesis is what is being tested when data are analysed using statistical tests. The **alternative hypothesis** (i.e. the alternative to the null hypothesis) predicts that there will be a difference between conditions, e.g. in the Loftus and Palmer study that a higher percentage of participants in one group would report having seen broken glass. In a correlational study, the alternative hypothesis will be that there is a relationship, not necessarily causal, between the two variables.

Alternative hypotheses can be **one-tailed** (**directional**) or **two-tailed** (**non-directional**). In an experiment, a two-tailed hypothesis predicts that there will be a difference in the DV between the conditions of the study, e.g. that there will be a difference in the number of words remembered by participants using rehearsal and those using story linkage in a memory task. In the case of a correlational design, it predicts a relationship between the variables, e.g. that there will be a relationship between extroversion scores and preference for bright colours on a colour preference questionnaire. It does not, however, specify what the difference or relationship will be.

If the hypothesis is one-tailed, the direction of the difference or relationship is also predicted. In the above examples, one-tailed hypotheses would be: 'participants using story linkage will remember *more* words than those using rehearsal' and 'there will be a *positive* relationship between extroversion scores and preference for bright colours on a colour preference questionnaire'.

Activity 8: hypotheses

Read through these examples of alternative hypotheses, and identify whether each is one- or two-tailed:

a There will be a difference in scores on an intelligence test between people who eat fish and those who do not eat fish.

b There will be a relationship between extroversion and a preference for loud music.

c People will remember more words in a foreign language if the information is presented in picture form, rather than as words alone.

Now rewrite these hypotheses. For each one, if it is one-tailed, rewrite it as a two-tailed hypothesis. If it is two-tailed, rewrite it as a one-tailed hypothesis. When you have finished, see the notes on page 180.

⑤ Variables need to be **operationalised** in terms of how they are to be used in the context of a particular piece of research.

⑤ The **alternative (researcher/experimental) hypothesis** proposes that there will be a difference or a relationship between two or more sets of data. The **null hypothesis** proposes that there will be no such difference or relationship.

⑤ Experimental hypotheses can be **directional** (one-tailed) or **non-directional** (two-tailed).

7·4   POPULATIONS AND SAMPLES

A target population is a group of people who share specific characteristics, and who the researcher is interested in testing. Populations can be small (e.g. female A-level physics students in a particular sixth-form college) or large (e.g. people living in Britain). Populations are usually too large, however, for every individual to be tested, so only a subset of the population – a sample – is tested instead. Ideally this should be a **representative sample**, i.e. one in which all the characteristics of the parent population are represented. If the sample is representative, any conclusions drawn from the results of the study can be generalised to the population as a whole, since the sample will be accurate in terms of representing important aspects of the population.

▷ Activity 9: representative samples

Imagine you are planning to use A-level students at your college as participants in an investigation into the relationship between study habits and exam success, and you intend to select a sample to test. Which characteristics would need to be included in your sample to make it representative of A-level students as a whole?

When you have finished, see the notes on page 180.

The larger the sample, the more likely it is to be representative of the population from which it is drawn. If the sample in activity 9, for example, consisted of only five students, it would be very unlikely that all the different characteristics which might be important to the research would be represented. If the sample is not representative of the population, it is said to be **biased**, i.e. some characteristics of the population are either over- or under-represented, so the sample does not reflect accurately the characteristics of the population.

The problem in deciding on an appropriate size for a sample is essentially a practical one. A very small sample is likely to be biased, but on the other hand a very large sample will take a long time to test, and could be expensive in terms of additional materials which may be necessary. Whatever the sample size, there is likely to be **sampling error**, i.e. inaccuracies in the sample in terms of its representativeness of the parent population. This is reduced (though not necessarily eliminated) by testing a larger sample.

A small population: left-handed trainspotters living in Norwich with their birthdays in May

Sampling methods

There are several ways of selecting a sample. In a **random sample**, every member of the parent population has an equal chance of being included in the sample. To select a random sample, a list of all the members of the population is necessary, e.g. in the study in activity 9, a list of all the students taking A-levels at your college.

There should be no bias in who is selected as part of the sample. This could be achieved by putting all the names into a hat, stirring them round, and then picking out names to make up the sample until the planned sample size is reached.

Alternatively, if the population is too large for this to be practicable, every member of the population could be given a number. A computer program which generates random numbers could then be used to select the sample, matching up the numbers given by the computer with the numbers given to the members of the population.

The strength of this method is that it avoids possible experimenter bias in selecting a sample. The drawback is that a random sample may well not be representative of the population. For example, a random sample of A-level students could by chance consist entirely of males. However, this kind of bias becomes less likely as the size of the sample increases.

Another possibility is a **systematic sample**, where members of the population are picked on the basis of some system. A sample of voters, for example, could include every tenth person on the electoral roll. This is not strictly speaking a random sample, since only those who are in the relevant position on the roll can be selected, but it is likely to be relatively unbiased, and a faster process than random sampling. It is sometimes called a **quasi-random** sample.

An **opportunity sample** is frequently used. This means that the sample is selected on the basis of who is available at the time of testing and willing to take part. Since it is so straightforward, it is frequently used by students carrying out A-level psychology coursework.

> ### Activity 10: problems with opportunity sampling
>
> Imagine you are planning to carry out the research into study habits and exam success described in activity 9, and you decide to test an opportunity sample. What kinds of factors might lead to this not being a representative sample?
>
> When you have finished, see the notes on page 180.

In practice, the problems associated with opportunity sampling may often not be too serious. For example, in a study measuring physiological responses to stress, people forming this kind of sample would be unlikely to produce results which would differ radically from those of samples selected in other ways.

In a **self-selecting sample**, people volunteer either directly or indirectly to take part in a study. This kind of sampling technique was used in Milgram's study on obedience (see chapter 6) when he advertised in the newspaper for volunteers. The problem here is that those who volunteer directly may not be typical of the target population, so the sample would be biased. This problem has already been mentioned in the discussion of postal interviews.

People may also volunteer indirectly. For example, if you were interested in possible gender differences in superstition you could set up a ladder and note how many males and how many females avoided walking underneath it. The people you were observing would be unaware that they were taking part in a study, but would indirectly be volunteering to take part by walking where the ladder was set up.

In **quota sampling**, the sample is selected so that particular characteristics of the population are represented in the same proportion in which they occur in the target population. Let us take as an example a research study into the study habits of psychology students at a college. Thirty females and 10 males are in their second year of studying psychology, and 40 females and 20 males are in their first year. A quota sample would need to draw a sample of males and females in the ratio of 3:1 from the second year, and 2:1 from the first year.

A self-selecting sample

This is the only sampling method which tries to ensure representativeness, rather than simply making it likely.

Activity 11: identifying sampling techniques

In each of these studies, identify the sampling technique used, choosing from:

random	**systematic**
opportunity	**self-selecting**

a A student research group is interested in a possible relationship between age and attitudes to the use of drugs. People are stopped in the street and asked to complete a questionnaire.

b A psychologist is investigating attitudes of English schoolchildren to learning French. At a local high school, he gives a questionnaire to the third boy and the third girl listed in each of the class registers.

c A psychology student carrying out a study on the effects of stress on problem-solving puts up a notice on the college notice board asking people willing to take part in her study to sign up.

d Students in a psychology class have been asked to carry out a memory test on one participant each. Some ask people in the library and the study area, some ask those in the canteen, while others go to find participants in the common room.

In each case, why might the sample not be representative of the parent population?

When you have finished, see the notes on page 180.

- ○ A study tests a sample of the population in which the researcher is interested. If this is a **representative sample**, results can then be **generalised** to the population as a whole.
- ○ In a **random sample**, every member of the population has an equal chance of being part of the sample. A **systematic sample** selects on the basis of some kind of system. An **opportunity sample** consists of members of the population who are available at the time of testing, and willing to take part. In a **self-selecting sample**, participants offer themselves, either directly or indirectly, as part of the sample. In **quota sampling**, characteristics of the population are represented in the sample in the same proportion in which they occur in the population.
- ○ Sampling methods can introduce **sampling error** which can lead to a **biased sample**.

7.5 EXPERIMENTAL DESIGN

Some of the factors which need to be taken into account when planning experimental research have already been discussed. The IV and the DV need to be operationalised, and possible confounding variables need to be eliminated as far as possible. The size of the sample to be tested and the sampling method need to be considered. Another decision which needs to be made is the design of the study, and we will be looking in this section at three possible designs.

One possibility is an **independent measures** design. You may also find this referred to as an **unrelated design** or a **between-groups** design. In this design, different participants are tested in each condition of the experiment, and participants are randomly allocated to conditions. To go back to the earlier example of a study comparing the effectiveness of rehearsal and story linkage on recall, one set of participants would take a memory test using rehearsal, while a different set of participants would be asked to use story linkage.

The experiment could consist of two or more conditions, where each condition receives a different experimental treatment (as in the memory test example), or one or more experimental conditions and a control condition. In a **control condition**, participants are given no particular treatment; in this example they would be asked to memorise a list of words with no strategy being suggested. The principle here is that the data from this group provides a baseline with which the experimental condition(s) can be compared.

Manipulation of the IV is one criterion for defining a study as an experiment. The second is random allocation of participants to conditions. Randomly allocating participants to conditions means that all participants should have an equal chance of taking part in either condition, or in any condition if there are more than two; in the memory experiment example, a third condition could be introduced where participants were asked to use a third method to help them remember the words, e.g. putting pairs of words into a meaningful sentence. The principle of random allocation is to prevent any kind of bias in selecting which participants will take part in which condition, and so avoid bias in the way in which the experiment is carried out.

To achieve random allocation the person conducting an experiment may 'take names out of a hat' or use random number tables. In natural or quasi-experiments, however, discussed in the section on methods in psychology, this is not possible.

In a **repeated measures design** (sometimes known as a **related design** or **within-groups design**), participants take part in both (or all) the conditions. Their performance in the different conditions is compared. Since participants take part in both (or all) conditions, random allocation does not apply in quite the same way. The order in which they carry out the conditions, however, should be randomised.

Evaluation of independent measures design

The main advantage of the independent measures design is that it eliminates the possible problem of **order effects**. If all participants take part in both

or all conditions in the same order, there may be a **practice** effect. They may do better in the second condition in which they take part, not because of the nature of the condition itself, but because they may be helped through practice. Alternatively, **boredom** or **fatigue** as they work through the conditions could account for differences in performance. Taking part in only one condition eliminates this possibility.

Using this design also helps to reduce the effect of **demand characteristics**. If people take part in more than one condition, they are more likely to guess the aim of the experiment and perhaps adjust their performance than if they take part in only one condition. In some cases, fewer materials are needed, since the same materials (e.g. the list of words to be remembered) can be the same in both or all conditions, as each participant will be exposed to them only once.

The major drawback to an independent measures design is the possibility of the results being affected by **individual differences** between the participants in each condition. In the memory test example, any difference between the two conditions could come about as the result of participants in one group having in general better memories than those in the other, rather than the manipulation of the IV, i.e. the strategy they have been asked to use. Random allocation of participants helps to minimise this source of bias. This design also requires more participants (i.e. twice as many in a two-condition experiment) than a repeated measures design, in which each participant provides data in both or all conditions.

Evaluation of repeated measures design

The main advantage of a repeated measures design is that it eliminates the influence of **individual differences**, since each participant's performance in one condition is compared with that same person's performance on the other(s). As noted above, it also requires fewer participants.

The main drawback, however, is the possible influence of **order effects**, i.e. practice, boredom and fatigue. Sometimes it is possible to minimise these effects by **counterbalancing**, i.e. varying the order in which participants carry out conditions. In the memory test example, half the participants could start with the rehearsal condition, and then go on to use story linkage, while for the other participants, this order would be reversed.

Counterbalancing is not always a solution, however. For example, in the memory experiment, participants who started with the story linkage condition could find it so effective that they used it in the rehearsal condition as well in spite of the instructions they were given. Counterbalancing may not even be possible. If the effectiveness of two methods of teaching French were to be compared, it would only be possible for participants to take part in one condition. In these cases, an independent measures design would need to be chosen.

With a repeated measures design, **demand characteristics** are likely to be more of a problem. It is also possible that additional materials would need to be prepared. For instance, in the memory test example, different word lists would need to be constructed for each condition; otherwise participants might remember more words on the second condition simply because they had already seen them once. The word lists would also need to be matched in terms of word length and how common the words are, which could be a time-consuming process. A word list in one condition with words like 'cat', 'tree' and 'chair' matched with a word list in the other condition with words like 'bagatelle', 'chandelier' and 'antigropeloes' would clearly introduce an unwanted bias!

Matched pairs design

A final design possibility is a **matched pairs design**. This aims to pick up on the advantages of both independent measures and repeated measures designs, while avoiding some of the drawbacks of both. In this design, each participant is matched with another participant on characteristics which are considered relevant to the experiment. These characteristics could include age, sex, personality or intelligence. One participant from each pair is then allocated at random to each condition, and each participant takes part in only one condition. This method assumes that the matching process creates pairs which are so similar that for the purposes of the study they can be treated as if they were the same person.

To return to the memory experiment example, potential participants could be matched on the basis of their memory ability. They would be given an initial memory test requiring them to learn a list of nonsense syllables, for example, and would be put into pairs on the basis of having similar recall scores. One member of each pair would then be randomly allocated to each condition.

Activity 12: matched pairs design

Look back through the discussion of the advantages and drawbacks of the independent measures and repeated measures designs. Identify the strengths of each which are incorporated in a matched pairs design.
What are the drawbacks of this design?
When you have finished, see the notes on page 180.

Pilot studies

Whichever design is selected, a **pilot study** is normally carried out before starting the process of gathering data. A pilot study is a small-scale study carried out with a few participants to highlight any possible problems in the planned study. For example, the instructions given to participants may not be clear, or the statements used in an attitude questionnaire may be ambiguous. A pilot study also clarifies aspects of the research such as whether the method used to collect data in an observational study is workable, or how long the optimal time would be for a participant to be exposed to materials in a study on memory. If the time allowed is too long, there is likely to be a **ceiling effect**, where most of the participants remember virtually everything, and so the procedure fails to discriminate between the performance of different participants. Similarly, if it is too short, there may be a **floor effect**, where very little is remembered by anyone.

❺ An experiment has one or more **experimental conditions**, where participants receive particular treatments. For the purposes of comparison, it may also have a **control condition**, where there is no experimental intervention.

- In an **independent measures** design, different participants take part in each condition of a study. In a **repeated measures design**, each participant provides data in both or all the conditions.

- Each design has both strengths and weaknesses in terms of **order effects**, **demand characteristics** and the influence of **individual differences**.

- A **matched pairs** design attempts to combine the strengths of independent measures and repeated measures designs. It is, however, an unwieldy and time-consuming method.

- A **pilot study** is usually carried out before starting full-scale research in order to identify any possible problems with the design of the study.

7.6 RELIABILITY, VALIDITY, AND STANDARDISATION

The term **reliability** in psychological research relates to consistency. For example, Eysenck's EPI is a reliable test, since it provides relatively consistent results if the same person takes it more than once. Researchers need to be sure that the measures they are using are reliable, and so provide a consistent measure. A tape measure which measured out a metre differently every time it was used would be of little use. The same idea is important in psychological measures.

Test–retest reliability assesses external reliability, i.e. the reliability of a test over time. It involves giving participants the same test on two different occasions. If the test is reliable, the results should be very similar. The timing here is important; if participants take the test for the second time too soon after the first test, it is possible that they may remember their previous answers. On the other hand, if there is too long a time gap, participants may have changed in some important way.

Split-half reliability assesses the internal consistency of a test, i.e. the extent to which all parts of the test contribute equally to what is being measured. This is done by comparing the results from half the test with the results from the other half. A test can be split in half in several ways,

e.g. the first half and the second half, odd number and even number questions, or at random.

Inter-rater (or **inter-observer**) **reliability** refers to the extent to which two people rating the same event agree on the ratings they give. If more than one person is to be involved in using a rating scale (for example in a study rating passers-by on helpfulness when asked for change for the phone) it is necessary that they are able to use the scale consistently. A scale would need to be worked out in advance and then tested for reliability before the main study begins.

In all these cases, reliability can be checked by using **correlational analysis**; if a measure is reliable, the two measures should show a very high positive correlation.

Validity refers to the extent to which a test is actually testing what it sets out to test. A test can be reliable but not valid. This is a criticism often made of intelligence tests; they are reliable, in that they give consistent results, but it has been argued that they are not valid tests of intelligence because they only measure a very narrow range of abilities. In order to be useful, a test needs to be both reliable and valid.

There are two overall types of validity. The first is **content-related validity**, i.e. is the content of the test appropriate for what the test aims to measure? The second is **criterion-related validity**, i.e. does the test tally with other measures to which it is considered to be related?

A very straightforward way of assessing whether the content of a test is valid is to see whether it *seems* to be testing what it aims to test. This is called **face validity**. For example, items which tap into individual differences in the ways in which people respond to situations and other people seem on the face of it to be testing personality. People who are expert in the field which a test covers may also decide whether material which is appropriate – both in terms of the nature of the content and the range the content covers – is included. **Construct validity** relates to the extent to which test items are in line with the hypothetical constructs underlying them, e.g. the questions on extroversion in Eysenck's EPI relate to the theoretical constructs of his theory of personality on which the test is based.

One way of testing the validity of a test in terms of its relationship with known criteria is to assess its **concurrent validity**. A new personality test, for example, might well be evaluated in terms of the extent to which it produces similar results to an existing test. Tests of **predictive validity** are another way of establishing the criterion-related validity of a test. The old 11+ test is a good example of a test whose use was based on the assumption that it had predictive validity. All children used to take this test, which determined whether they went on to either a grammar school offering an academic education or a less academically-orientated secondary modern school. The use of this test rested on the assumption that results at 11+ could predict how well someone was likely to do later on in their academic life (see figure 2).

Concurrent validity and predictive validity can be tested using correlational analysis. If a test has concurrent validity, there should be a strong positive correlation between the results it provides and results using the existing measures with which it is being compared. If it has high predictive validity, there should be a strong positive correlation with later performance on the related criterion.

A final kind of validity is **ecological validity**. This has already been mentioned. You will remember that this refers to the extent to which the results of an investigation can be generalised to other places and other conditions.

Measures of reliability and validity are used in the **standardisation** of tests. When new tests or new versions of existing tests are being developed, items to be included need to be adjusted in order to make the test a reliable and valid measure of the population with whom it is intended to be used. It would not be enough, for example, to translate an American test into Danish and assume that it would then be suitable for use with Danes. The translated version would need to be tested on a large sample of Danes, and appropriate adjustments made.

Standardisation also refers to the procedures used when studies are carried out. For example, the instructions given to participants should be identical, so that there is no possibility that slight variations in wording could affect the results of the study. The timing and presentation of stimulus material, together with the techniques used in scoring, also need to be standardised for the same reason.

- **Reliability** refers to the consistency of a test. Measures of reliability include **test–retest**, **split-half** and **inter-rater** reliability.
- **Validity** refers to the extent that a test measures what it claims to measure. Validity can be **content-related** (**face** validity and **construct** validity), and **criterion-related** (**concurrent** and **predictive** validity).
- Measures of reliability and validity are used to **standardise** tests for use with a particular population.
- Standardisation also refers to carrying out the procedures of a research study consistently.

7.7 LEVELS OF MEASUREMENT

When carrying out research, psychologists collect data. While sometimes the data are qualitative, many of the techniques described produce quantitative data, and it is this kind of data which will be discussed here. The information collected varies in how precise it is, and the term 'levels of measurement' refers to these differences in precision. It is important to assess the level of

Figure 2: types of validity	
CONTENT-RELATED VALIDITY (appropriate content)	**CRITERION-RELATED VALIDITY** (relationship to other measures)
face validity: does the test appear to test what it aims to test?	**concurrent validity:** does the test relate to existing similar measures?
construct validity: does the test relate to underlying theoretical concepts?	**predictive validity:** does the test predict later performance on a related criterion?

measurement of a particular set of data because this will determine how it can be analysed statistically. The different levels can be illustrated by the example shown in figure 3:

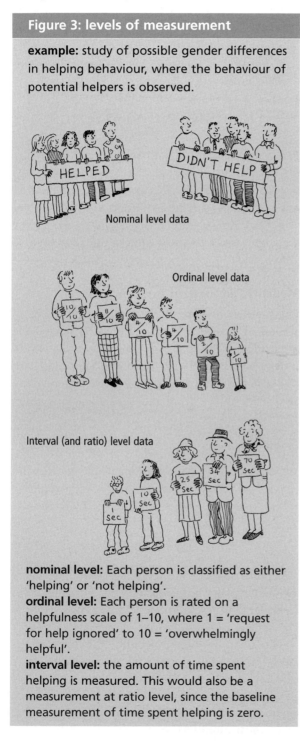

Figure 3: levels of measurement

example: study of possible gender differences in helping behaviour, where the behaviour of potential helpers is observed.

Nominal level data

Ordinal level data

Interval (and ratio) level data

nominal level: Each person is classified as either 'helping' or 'not helping'.
ordinal level: Each person is rated on a helpfulness scale of 1–10, where 1 = 'request for help ignored' to 10 = 'overwhelmingly helpful'.
interval level: the amount of time spent helping is measured. This would also be a measurement at ratio level, since the baseline measurement of time spent helping is zero.

At its simplest, measurement is at **nominal level**. This is sometimes also referred to as category data, because it means that each piece of data is put into a category. Measurement at this level is basically a head count. It gives us very little information. For example, in figure 3, someone classified as 'helping' could be someone who barely helped at all or someone who was so overwhelmingly helpful that you wished they would stop.

The next level of measurement is **ordinal level**. This goes beyond the simple categorisation of nominal data in that each piece of data is in the form of a score, and so the data can be put in order. However, the measurement is still not very precise. In figure 3, for example, we cannot assume that someone rated 8 for helpfulness is exactly twice as helpful as someone rated 4; all that can safely be said is that someone rated 8 is more helpful than someone rated 4. Since the measuring scale is so imprecise, the data are reduced to rank-ordered scores, i.e. the researcher will focus on the order of the scores rather than the scores themselves.

Interval level measurement is more precise, since it refers to measures which, in contrast to ordinal level measurement, have equal intervals between the points on the scale being used; there is exactly the same distance between 2 cm and 3 cm, for example, as between 14 cm and 15 cm. The most common examples of interval level measurement are measures of temperature, length and time.

Length and time are also examples of **ratio level** data. This is the same as interval data, but additionally the scale has a genuine zero or starting point; it is not possible, for example, to measure something as being −3 cm. Measures of temperature provide interval level data, but not ratio level. 0°C or 0°F are not a baseline measure since temperatures such as −13° are possible.

It needs to be noted that data do not come ready labelled with a particular level of measurement, but the level to be used must be decided by the researcher. If we go back to the example from figure 3, the amount of time spent helping is interval (and indeed ratio) level data. We could, however, choose to ignore the actual number of seconds spent helping, and focus instead on the order of the scores, i.e. reduce the data to ordinal level. It would also be possible to assign participants to categories, e.g. 'helped for less than 10 seconds', 'helped for 10–30 seconds' and 'helped for more than 30 seconds', thereby treating the data as nominal.

Activity 13: levels of data

For each of the following examples, decide the level at which data is being analysed:

a A psychologist believes that tiredness affects co-ordination. Two groups of people, woken after different amounts of sleep, are tested on a task which requires them to move a small metal ring along a curved loop of wire without touching the wire. The number of times each participant makes contact with the loop of wire is noted.

b Researchers are interested in possible gender differences in choice of play activity. Eight-year-old participants are given a list of 12 play activities, four of which can be described as make-believe, four as construction and four as physical activity. From the 12, they are asked to choose their favourite activity. The number of choices of girls and boys which fall into each category are compared.

c A psychology teacher is interested in whether there is a relationship between the amount of time students spend on writing an essay and essay grades. Students are asked to note down the time spent on an essay. The normal essay grades of A – E are translated into a numerical scale, i.e. A = 10, B = 8, etc. The teacher investigates a possible correlation between these two measures.

d A researcher is interested in how instructions on how to learn a list of words affects the number of words recalled. One group of participants uses rehearsal. The other group uses story linkage. The number of words remembered by participants in each group is noted.

When you have finished, see the notes on page 180.

❺ Data can be described in terms of different **levels of measurement**. The level of measurement determines appropriate statistical analysis.

❺ **Nominal level**, where data are put into categories, is the least precise level. Ordinal level gives more information since it uses scores. It focuses on the order of the scores rather than the scores themselves. More precise still, **interval level** refers to data where there are equal intervals between the points on the measuring scale. Where there is a genuine zero, this is also **ratio level** data.

7.8 DESCRIPTIVE STATISTICS

The term 'descriptive statistics' refers to ways in which sets of data can be summarised. Two important ways in which this can be done are by using measures of central tendency and measures of dispersion. A range of charts and graphs can also be used to present a clear overview of the data obtained from a study.

Measures of central tendency

These measures are ways of reducing a set of numerical data to one value which represents the whole set. Look back to sample study (d) in activity 13. If you had carried out this study with 40 participants in each condition, it would be quite hard work to see from the sets of scores which method was more effective in leading to recall. A good way of summarising these data to provide an easy comparison of how many words were remembered in each condition would be to work out the average, or **mean**; all the scores would be added together and the total divided by the number of scores.

The **median** is another measure of central tendency. If a set of scores is put in numerical order, the middle score of the sequence is the median. If there are two middle scores (i.e. an even number of scores in the set), the mean of these two scores is the median.

The final measure of central tendency is the **mode**. This is the most frequently occurring score in a set of scores. Sometimes there may be two equally frequent scores (in which case there are two modes, known as **bimodal** values), or even more, giving **multimodal** values.

⊳ Activity 14: mean, median and mode

a These are the scores on a psychology test for a class of students. Work out the mean, the median and the mode:

7 7 8 10 11 11 11 13 13 15 15

b The mean number of children in the average British family is 2.4. Why might this not be the best way of expressing this kind of information? Which measure of central tendency do you think might be better, and why?

c These are people's scores on a general knowledge test. Which measure of central tendency do you think would be the best way of summarising the data? Give your reasons:

5 6 12 17 18 18 25 29 31 31 36 37 64

When you have finished, see the notes on page 181.

The three measures of central tendency all have their uses and are appropriate in different circumstances. If you are collecting very precise data, i.e. interval data, like reaction time in seconds, it makes sense to use the mean to summarise the data, as it is the most precise of the three measures.

It would make less sense to use the mean where the data itself is ordinal and so is less precise, as in the use of rating scales. In general, the median is used to summarise this kind of data.

The mode is in practice rarely used except with nominal data. It would, however, make sense to use it to summarise data which fall into a limited number of categories. For example, if people were being rated on a three-point helpfulness scale (1 = didn't help; 2 = quite helpful; 3 = very helpful), identifying the category which was used most would seem to be the most effective way of summarising the data.

To highlight the usefulness and limitations of each of the measures of central tendency, work through activity 15:

⊳ Activity 15: mean, median and mode: advantages and drawbacks

For each measure of central tendency, answer the following questions:
a is this measure always an actual score?
b does it use all the scores?
c does it use the values of all the scores?
d is it distorted by an extreme value?

Decide whether your answer to each question is an advantage or a drawback of this measure, and enter each answer in this table:

measure of central tendency	advantage	disadvantage
mean	1_____ 2_____	1_____ 2_____
median	1_____ 2_____	1_____ 2_____
mode	1_____ 2_____	1_____ 2_____

When you have finished, see the notes on page 181.

Measures of dispersion

A measure of dispersion is another way of summarising data. This measure gives an indication of the spread of scores, i.e. the extent to which scores deviate from the measure of central tendency. In these sets of scores:

13 14 15 16 17   and   5 10 15 20 25

the mean for each sample is 15, but the second set of scores shows a much greater spread than the first. A measure of dispersion is therefore a further way of summarising data and gives more useful information than a measure of central tendency alone.

A simple way of expressing this spread of scores is to use the **range**. This is simply the smallest score subtracted from the largest score. In the above example, the range for the first set of scores is therefore 4, and for the second set 20. For technical reasons, if there is an even number of scores, 1 is usually added to this figure. If values are calculated to one decimal place, e.g. 7.6 and 5.8, the range is the difference between the extreme scores plus .1, while .01 is added if values are calculated to two decimal places, e.g. 7.64 and 5.83.

The range is very simple to work out, but where there is an extreme score (as in activity 14, c), the range can give a distorted picture of the data. To overcome this drawback, the **interquartile range** may be calculated. This is the range calculated using the 25% of the scores immediately below the median, and the 25% of the scores immediately above it, to give an indication of the range of the central 50% of the scores.

The **standard deviation** is a more sophisticated measure of dispersion, since it calculates the average distance from the mean of all the scores. It is a more powerful measure of dispersion than the range, since the values of all the scores contribute towards the calculation. Because it is a more precise measure, it is usually used when the data are precise, such as the time taken to react to a visual stimulus. Where the data are less precise, e.g. in the form of ratings on a rating scale, the range is more likely to be used as a measure of dispersion.

Another measure of dispersion is the **variance**, which is simply the standard deviation squared. This statistic is sometimes required in order to carry out statistical tests on the data.

Finally, the **variation ratio** is a simple measure of dispersion, and is used where the mode is used as a measure of central tendency. It is the percentage of non-modal scores in the sample. In this set of scores:

2   3   5   5   5   7   8   8   9   9

the mode is 5, since it is the score which appears most frequently, as three of the ten scores. The number of non-modal scores is therefore 7 out of ten, so the variation ratio is 70%.

⊖ **Descriptive statistics** are ways of summarising data.

⊖ The **mean**, the **median** and the **mode** are three **measures of central tendency**, i.e. a way of representing a set of scores with one statistic.

⊖ The **range** (including the **interquartile range**), the **standard deviation**, the **variance** and the **variation ratio** are **measures of dispersion**, which give information about the spread of scores.

Graphical representation

Psychologists carrying out research often present their data graphically. This way of summarising results has the advantage of presenting the data very clearly, in such a way that the overall findings are immediately accessible to the reader of a research report. Four of the most frequently used types of graphical representation are histograms, frequency polygons, bar charts and scattergraphs. We will look at each of these in turn, and consider when they are an appropriate way of presenting data, the underlying principles of their use and how they are interpreted.

Histograms

A histogram is used when representing interval- or ratio-level data. It divides data into categories, each represented as a bar. The bars are of equal width, and are drawn touching each other. Since histograms can only be used with continuous data, i.e. where there are no gaps between scores for the categories, categories which do not contain scores must also be shown, as in the first category in activity 16 (see opposite). The categories are shown on the x-axis, with the mid-point of each category being identified, and the frequency with which each category occurs is shown on the y-axis.

Let us take as an example the results of a memory test, where participants have been asked to learn a set of 30 words and then write down as many as they can remember.

◗ Activity 16: interpreting a histogram

Look at this histogram and answer the questions below:

Histogram showing the number of words recalled on a memory test

1 How wide is the range of scores within each category?
2 What is the range of scores making up the category on the extreme right?
3 How many participants had scores in the largest category?

When you have finished, see the notes on page 181.

Frequency polygons

A frequency polygon is an alternative to a histogram. Instead of using bars, the mid-points at the top of each bar are joined. It is a useful technique to show the results of two or more conditions at once. To take the data from activity 16 as an example, these scores could be data from a condition in an experiment in which participants were asked to use rehearsal as an aid to recall. Data from another condition, where participants were asked to use story linkage, could be shown on the same frequency polygon, so that comparison of the results of the two conditions could be made (figure 4).

Bar charts

Bar charts look similar to histograms, in that they consist of bars of equal width, but there are important differences. They are used with ordinal or nominal data, and so can be used with non-continuous frequencies on the x-axis. They are often used to show the means for different conditions in an experiment. They are usually

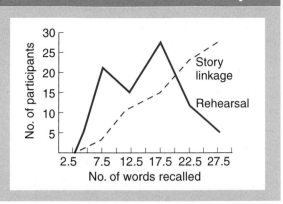

Figure 4: frequency polygon showing the number of words recalled on a memory test

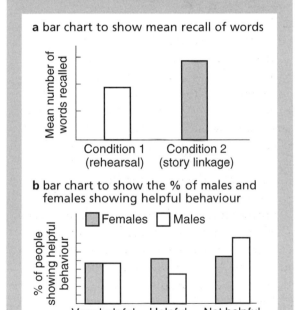

Figure 5: examples of bar charts

a bar chart to show mean recall of words

b bar chart to show the % of males and females showing helpful behaviour

drawn so that one bar does not touch the next, so that they do not seem to suggest that the data are continuous. Two examples of bar charts are shown in figure 5. The first shows means for the two conditions of a memory experiment, comparing the effectiveness of rehearsal and story linkage on recall of words. The second compares the helpfulness of males and females in terms of opening doors for someone carrying heavy shopping.

Activity 17: interpreting a bar chart

Look at this bar chart and answer the questions below:

Bar chart to show the number of aggressive acts observed in children at play

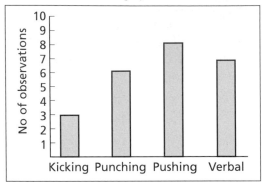

1 Which behaviour was observed most frequently?
2 Which behaviour was observed least frequently?
3 How many acts of verbal aggression were observed?

When you have finished, see the notes on page 181.

Scattergraphs

Scattergraphs (or scattergrams) are used to show sets of data where a correlational technique has been used. Each of the two variables being correlated is represented on one axis. The crossing point of the two scores for each individual being tested is marked on the scattergraph.

Figure 6: scattergraphs

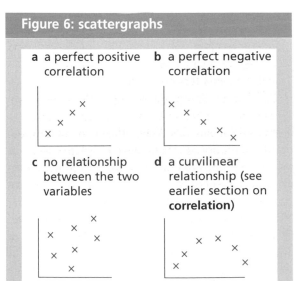

a a perfect positive correlation
b a perfect negative correlation
c no relationship between the two variables
d a curvilinear relationship (see earlier section on **correlation**)

In practice, a perfect positive or a perfect negative relationship is extremely rare, particularly as the number of observations increases, so a scattergraph can be used to assess the direction and strength of any relationship between the two variables being correlated. It can be helpful to draw a line of best fit on a scattergraph to help show whether the relationship between the two variables is generally a positive or a negative one, and to show the strength of that relationship.

To work out where a line of best fit should go, the average value of each variable is worked out, and the resulting point – the **pivot point** – is marked on the scattergraph. A straight line is then drawn through this point in such a way that each point is as close to the line as possible, and with the same number of points above and below the line:

Figure 7: scattergraph with line of best fit

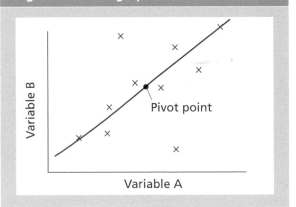

In figure 7, since the line of best fit is in the same direction as in figure 6a, the relationship between the variables being correlated is a positive one. As most of the points are reasonably close to the line, the correlation is fairly strong. There are two points which are quite a distance from the line of best fit; these are called **outliers**, and mean that the strength of the correlation is reduced.

Activity 18: drawing and interpreting a scattergraph

Here are data from a correlational study to investigate a possible relationship between IQ (scores on an intelligence test) and points scores at A-level (where A=10, B=8, C=6, D=4, E=2):

participant	IQ scores	A-level scores
1	125	20
2	110	14
3	127	24
4	135	18
5	118	22
6	142	20
7	122	16
8	112	10
9	128	18
10	108	10

Use these data to draw a scattergraph, and draw on a line of best fit.

a Does your scattergraph show a positive or a negative relationship?

b Are there any outliers?

c How strong is the relationship between IQ and performance at A-level?

When you have finished, see the notes on page 181.

- **Graphical representation** provides a clear way of displaying data.
- **Histograms** take the form of bars, and are used with continuous data, of at least interval level.
- **Frequency polygons** are an alternative to histograms, and are useful for showing two or more sets of data at once.
- **Bar charts** can be used with non-continuous data at ordinal or nominal level. They can also be used to show the **means** for different conditions in an experiment.
- **Scattergraphs** are used to display correlational data. They give an indication of the direction and strength of the relationship between two variables.

7.9 ETHICS IN PSYCHOLOGICAL RESEARCH

Carrying out psychological research is not just a matter of operationalising the variables in which you are interested, choosing an appropriate design, controlling possible confounding variables and handling the data which have been collected. It is also extremely important that researchers make sure that they take full account of the ethical guidelines laid down by professional bodies such as the British Psychological Society. These point out the kinds of issues which researchers need to bear in mind when planning and carrying out research. The Association for Teachers of Psychology (ATP) has produced similar guidelines specifically aimed at students studying psychology at pre-degree level. The Experimental Psychology Society has laid down similar guidelines for work with animals.

You have already read about the development and role of ethical guidelines in the critical issue section of chapter 6, where the ethical aspects of research are discussed in detail. The following activity, however, should serve to remind you of some of the issues raised there:

Activity 19: identifying ethical issues

Read this account of a (fictional) psychology study. List what you consider to be the ethical problems which it raises. Compare your notes with the discussion which follows it on the next page.

Dr Smith is carrying out a research project. She tells her group of 20 students that they will take part in her experiment, but does not say what the research involves. The students turn up at the required time, and are told by a man in a white lab coat that they should sit down and wait for Dr Smith to arrive. They are kept waiting for nearly two hours in the laboratory.

After about an hour, two students get up to leave. They say they have waited long enough, and won't wait any longer. They are told to sit down, and the laboratory door is locked.

When Dr Smith finally arrives, the students are told to fill in the questionnaire they are given as honestly as possible. When they have all finished, the laboratory door is unlocked, and they leave.

They think their ordeal is over, but the following week, Dr Smith starts one of her lectures with an amusing anecdote, in which she divulges one of the answers given to an item in the questionnaire by a student, whom she identifies. Everyone in the lecture theatre roars with laughter. The student whose answer has been quoted runs out of the room in embarrassment, vowing never to take part in another psychology experiment ever again.

Dr Smith did not ask for volunteers for her study. The students were *told* they had to be involved in her research. This violates one of the most basic ethical guidelines, that participation should be voluntary. In addition, the students were told nothing about the nature of the research, so they did not have enough information to decide whether or not they wished to participate in the study. In other words, they could not give informed consent.

The students could also have been intimidated because they were put in a position where refusing to take part in the study would be very difficult. The power relationship between Dr Smith and her students is a very unequal one, as she is in a position to influence their academic progress. The students could also have found the man in the lab coat intimidating. This is sometimes known as the power of the investigator. You may remember that in the studies carried out by Milgram, discussed in chapter 6, this kind of intimidation was a factor in many of the participants being prepared to give powerful electric shocks to another person when they were instructed to do so. Researchers have to be aware that their participants may see them as threatening or in a position of influence, merely because they are carrying out research.

Dr Smith also breached confidentiality when she let other people know of a student's answers in her study. All participants should be guaranteed anonymity when they volunteer to take part in research. In case studies, participants are usually referred to by initials for this reason. Participants should also be able to withdraw from the study at any stage (and withdraw their data), should they wish to do so. They should not be subjected to stress or discomfort. Waiting in a laboratory for two hours is not acceptable research practice!

It is also good practice to debrief participants at the end of a study. This involves explaining to them the aims and purpose of the experiment, if they wish to know, and answering any questions they may have. It can also include reassurance about the way they have responded in the experimental situation; participants in psychology experiments are often concerned that their performance has been inadequate, or that their behaviour has been in some way unacceptable. The aim of debriefing is that participants should leave the research situation, as far as possible, in the same psychological state in which they entered it. There is no indication that Dr Smith debriefed the students who had taken part in the study.

You may not have spotted all the ethical dilemmas in activity 19, but you were probably able to work out most of them. It is really a question of treating people sensitively and with respect, and appreciating them giving up their time to take part in research.

Ethical issues have been touched on only briefly here, but this topic is raised in connection with a number of studies in this book. Even where ethics are not specifically mentioned, you will need to bear these issues in mind when you read about psychological research.

⊖ There is a range of **ethical issues** which need to be considered when planning and carrying out research.

Notes on activities

1 a IV = age. DV = whether or not they give way at the junction.

   b IV = time of day. DV = number of soft toys produced.

   c IV = instructions. DV = number of words correctly remembered.

2 There are any number of possibilities. Here are a few suggestions:

   a **possible subject variables:** the gender of drivers; how pressed for time they were.

   possible situation variables: how far away from the junction each driver was; the speed at which they were travelling.

   b **possible subject variables:** different kinds of workers could be employed on each shift, e.g. younger workers on the early shift and older workers on the evening shift.

   possible situation variables: only one shift might cover a loo break; different toys, one more complicated than the other, could be produced by the different shifts.

c possible subject variables: some participants might find it easier to form mental images than others; those with better memories might by chance be allocated to one group.

possible situation variables: if the groups were tested in different places, there might be more distractions in one place than the other.

3 a a fairly strong positive correlation, say 0.8. The correlation would not be perfect because there are some tall people with relatively small feet and some short people with big feet.

b since both tests are to do with words, some positive correlation would be expected; this would probably not be particularly strong – say 0.4 – since some people who are good at English might well have little interest in French.

c a fairly strong negative correlation, say –0.8, might be expected, since there is good evidence for a relationship between stress and poor health (see chapter 4); again, there would be exceptions, since some people seem to thrive on moderate amounts of stress.

d there doesn't seem any reason why there should be a relationship between these variables; perhaps people who spend a lot of time developing skills on video games might lead a more sedentary lifestyle and so be more likely to be overweight, so there might be a very small positive correlation, say 0.1.

4 Closed-ended questions provide data which are easier to analyse. For example, the percentage of participants choosing each response would be very easy to work out. However, it is possible that none of the answers corresponds with how the person answering the question would ideally like to respond. In the example here, the person could be taking A-level psychology because it was the only option available which would fit in with their timetable for other subjects, and for which there were still places available. Open-ended questions may lead to more detailed information being given, but it is likely to be more difficult to analyse.

5 You may have thought it was pretty obvious what the questions were testing; you probably realised here that 'no' answers to questions 1 and 4, and 'yes' answers to questions 2 and 3, would contribute to a high score for extroversion. This awareness could possibly affect the way you answered the questions, i.e. you could respond to the **demand characteristics** of the procedure. Your answers could also be influenced by **social desirability**; people could answer so as to put themselves in a good light (this is known as 'faking good'). It is of course rather unfair to form a judgement on the basis of a few questions; in reality, these items would be embedded in a much longer questionnaire, and one covering neuroticism as well as extroversion.

The range of possible answers could be seen as constraining; sometimes people find it hard to limit themselves to Y/N answers (even with ?). Another problem here is that the questions are a little vague and don't relate to a defined context, e.g. what kind of novel situation is meant in Q4? This could perhaps affect how you would want to answer the question. Eysenck has shown, however, that people do respond consistently over time to this kind of question, in other words the questionnaires have been shown to have good **test–retest reliability**, a concept which we will be looking at later in this chapter.

More generally, you may have thought that answering this kind of question requires you not only to be prepared to answer the questions honestly (which may be problematic, particularly if something important – like being offered a job – depends on the outcome) but also to have enough insight to be able to do so.

6 Open-ended questionnaires, unstructured interviews, case studies, participant observation and to some extent clinical interviews are all likely to produce qualitative data.

7 a IV = interest. People could be asked to use a scale of 1 (very boring) to 10 (extremely interesting) to rate for interest potential topics on which they might be tested. The operational definition of interest would be the interest ratings.

DV = memory. People could be given questionnaires on passages they were asked to memorise. The operational definition of memory would be the questionnaire scores.

b **IV = gender,** i.e. whether children were boys or girls.

DV = aggression. Both boys and girls could be observed at play. A list of aggressive behaviours could be drawn up (e.g. pushing, name-calling etc). The number of times these behaviours were shown during the observation period would be the operational definition of aggression.

c **IV = neuroticism.** This could be operationalised as the N scores on Eysenck's EPI. People scoring above a certain point on the scale would be classed as 'neurotic' and those below a certain point as 'non-neurotic'.

DV = the extent to which participants suffer from phobias. A questionnaire could be used to establish which phobias people suffer from and the extent to which they fear phobic objects and situations. The operational definition would be the scores on the phobia questionnaire.

8 **a** two-tailed. One-tailed = people who eat fish will score higher on an intelligence test than those who do not eat fish.

b two-tailed. One-tailed = there will be a positive relationship between extroversion and a preference for loud music.

c one-tailed. Two-tailed = there will be a difference in the number of words remembered in a foreign language when the information is presented in picture form and as words alone.

9 Some suggestions here are that the sample should include: both sexes; mature students as well as students studying for A-levels immediately after finishing their GCSEs at school; students in both their first year and second year of study; those taking different combinations of A-levels, e.g. science, languages and so on.

10 This kind of sample is very easily biased. You might, for example, tend to approach people you are friendly with, and they might differ in important respects from the parent population, i.e. the population from which they are drawn. For example, in activity 9 these could be students following similar A-level courses, leaving out those studying other courses.

11 **a** This is an **opportunity sample**. It may not be representative because members of the group may only ask passers-by who seem approachable. There could also be something about the location – it could, for example, be near a school or a leisure centre – which might bias the kinds of people in the street at the time.

b This is a **systematic sample**. It may not be representative because it could be, with this relatively small sample, that the children chosen happen to be those who are keen on learning French.

c This is a **self-selecting sample**. It may not be representative because people who volunteer to take part in studies may be a particular type of person.

d This is an **opportunity sample**. It may not be representative for the same reasons as those given for (a).

12 **Independent measures:** order effects are eliminated; demand characteristics are reduced; fewer materials are required.

Repeated measures: individual differences are reduced, though not eliminated.

Drawbacks: the main drawback of the matched pairs design is the time involved in matching up participants, or indeed in finding participants who can be matched in this way. Complete matching is not really possible, and it may be that participants have not been matched on a characteristic which turns out to be important. If one participant drops out of the study, the nature of the design means that two participants are lost.

13 **a interval (and ratio) level** – for example, there is the same difference between people who make one contact and two contacts as there is between people who make five contacts and six contacts.

b nominal level – the first choice of each participant is assigned to a category by gender and by type of play.

c the amount of time spent is **interval (and ratio) level**. The grades are better reduced to ordinal level – it cannot be assumed that an essay given a B grade (8 marks) is exactly twice as good as one given a D grade (4 marks).

d possibly **interval level**, on the grounds that ten words, say, is twice as many as five. This could also be regarded as ordinal level data, since all the words might not be equally easy to remember, so there are not equal intervals between the points on the scale (i.e. one word, two words, three words, and so on.)

14 a the mean, median and mode are all 11.

b nobody actually has 2.4 children. The mode, i.e. the number of children a family is most likely to have, might be a more realistic way of putting this information across.

c the mode could be used. This would be a bimodal distribution, with modes at 18 and 31. On the other hand, there are a lot of scores which have different values from these. The mean could be used, but would give a rather distorted picture, since the score of 64 is extreme, well out of line with the other scores. The median would probably give the most accurate picture.

15 mean: advantages **b** (yes) and **c** (yes); disadvantages **a** (no) and **d** (yes).

median: advantages **d** (no) and **b** (yes); disadvantages **a** (only with an odd number of scores) and **c** (no).

mode: advantages **a** (yes) and **d** (no); disadvantages **b** (no) and **c** (no).

16 1 five words; **2** 26–30; **3** four participants.

17 1 kicking; **2** pushing; **3** seven times.

18 The scattergraph should look like this:

1 The line of best fit indicates a positive correlation.

2 Most of the points lie fairly close to the line of best fit, though there are some outliers.

3 This indicates a reasonable but not particularly strong positive correlation between IQ and A-level points scores.

Social cognition

In this chapter we will be looking at:

8.1 What is social cognition?

8.2 Attribution theories
   Correspondent inference theory
   Kelley's covariation model
   Causal schemata

8.3 Errors and biases in attribution
   The fundamental attribution error
   The actor-observer effect
   Self-serving bias

8.4 Social and cultural influences on perception and impression formation
   Social identity theory
   Social representations

8.5 Social and cultural stereotypes
   The development and maintenance of stereotypes
   Are stereotypes a bad thing?

8.6 Prejudice and discrimination
   Individual explanations of prejudice
   The interpersonal approach to prejudice
   The intergroup approach to prejudice

8.7 The reduction of prejudice and discrimination
   Equal status contact
   Superordinate goals
   Other influences in the reduction of prejudice

8.1 WHAT IS SOCIAL COGNITION?

Just as we try to make sense of the physical world around us, we also try to make sense of our social world. We do not passively observe other people, but actively use the information available to us to seek to understand, and draw conclusions about, what people are like and why they behave as they do. This allows us to make predictions about what is likely to happen in social situations, and thus gives us some feeling of control over what is going on around us. Social cognition looks at the ways we process information about other people and draw conclusions about them based on this information.

8.2 ATTRIBUTION THEORIES

An attribution is the process of giving reasons for why things happen. Heider (1944) laid the foundations of attribution theory. He proposed that people have a strong need to make sense of their social world, and that we do this by developing ideas and theories about what is going on around us. Some of these ideas relate to the *causes* underlying events and behaviour, and it is with this aspect of social cognition that attribution theory is concerned. The strength of this tendency to identify the causes behind what we observe was shown in an early study:

Box A: Heider and Simmel (1944)

Procedure: Participants were shown an animated cartoon of three geometric shapes (a large triangle, a small triangle and a circle) moving around, and in and out of, a square. They were asked to describe what they saw.

Results: There was a tendency to talk about the shapes as if they had human intentions. Many people saw the two triangles as men fighting over a woman (the circle). The large triangle was seen as an aggressive bully, the small triangle as a defiant hero, and the circle as shy.

Conclusion: There is a strong tendency to link behaviour with personality and intentions, even when the behaviour being observed is that of inanimate objects.

According to Heider, one major way in which we explain a person's behaviour is by seeing the causes either as lying within the person (a **dispositional attribution**), or within the situation they find themselves in (a **situational attribution**). For example, if Mary gets a good pass in her Business Studies exam, a dispositional attribution could be that she has done so well because she is very clever. A situational attribution could be that the exam was very easy.

Various theorists have contributed ideas in the general area of attribution theory, and we will be looking at some of them in the following sections. As you read through this section, it may help to bear in mind that these ideas are not really in conflict with one another, but rather offer us different insights into the attribution process.

Correspondent inference theory

According to Jones and Davis (1965), the first thing we do in establishing causes is to decide whether an action is deliberate or not. If we believe an action to be deliberate, we then look for a personal characteristic which could have been responsible for the action. This matching of a behaviour with a personal characteristic to which it corresponds is what Jones and Davis referred to as a **correspondent inference**. For example, if Jane assists an elderly lady with her heavy shopping, the behaviour can be labelled 'helpful' and Jane's disposition can be labelled 'kind'.

In this theory, developed originally by Heider, there are three important concepts. The first is that we prefer to find **stable causes** for behaviour. It is only stable causes which can fulfil the need to be able to predict what is likely to happen in a given situation. Secondly, we need to be able to judge whether or not an action is **intentional** in order to be able to interpret it. The final distinction is between dispositional and situational attributions, mentioned above.

Let us take as an example Jack throwing a ball which hits Robert. If we decide that Jack did this on purpose, we would try to explain his action in dispositional terms, e.g. that Jack is an aggressive person. This would be a stable cause because aggression is seen as an enduring aspect of Jack's character. If we interpreted his action as accidental, on the other hand, we would be more likely to make a situational attribution, e.g. that the ball flew out of his hand when he stumbled.

Jones and Davis suggested that we have a tendency to assume that actions are deliberate, and to make dispositional rather than situational attributions. Once we have decided that an action is deliberate, we can then attempt to make the correspondent inference about the aspect of the person's disposition underlying that action. Correspondent inference theory can only be applied where the actor is seen as having a choice of action, since the correspondent inference process rests on the judgement that the action is deliberate.

However, there is some evidence that the tendency to make dispositional rather than situational attributions does not always hold true and may be related to experience:

Box B: Guimond and Palmer (1990)

Procedure: Students taking social science, commerce and engineering courses were asked to give explanations of poverty and unemployment at the beginning and again at the end of their first year of study.

Results: There were no differences between student groups in the explanations offered at the beginning of the year. At the end of the year, social science students were more likely than the other groups to give explanations related to the sociopolitical system.

Conclusion: Background information can affect whether a dispositional or a situational attribution is made.

Jones and Davis identified three major factors which influence whether or not a dispositional attribution is made. One is the **principle of non-common effects**. For example, let us say that Anne has to choose between three resorts for her skiing holiday. All three resorts offer similarly priced holidays and all have a good snow record. Only one, however, is known for its lively après ski, i.e. a factor which the three resorts do not have in common. If this is the resort Anne chooses, we are likely to make a dispositional attribution about her choice of holiday, and conclude that she has decided to go to that particular resort because for her après ski is an important part of the holiday.

Personalism refers to the extent to which an action affects us personally. We are more likely to see behaviour as intentional, and to make a dispositional attribution, if the effects of an action have personal consequences for ourselves. For example, if a driver knocks down a close friend or relative of ours, we are more likely to condemn them as 'negligent' than if they had knocked down a stranger.

Finally, **hedonic relevance** relates to the extent to which we experience the effects of an action as pleasant or unpleasant. Actions are more likely to be judged as intentional, and dispositional attributions made, if the effects of the outcome are either pleasant or unpleasant rather than neutral. For example, a driver whose failure to apply his handbrake has no serious consequences is less likely to have a personal attribution made about his behaviour than a driver whose car runs into a school playground, causing the death or injury of children.

Kelley's covariation model

Kelley's model (1967; 1973) again focuses on whether we see the causes of someone's behaviour as internal (dispositional) or external (situational). He has suggested that we look for three kinds of information: consensus, distinctiveness and consistency.

To illustrate what Kelley meant by these terms, let us take the hypothetical situation of Jane getting a low mark for a psychology assignment. **Consensus** refers to the extent to which other people behave in a similar way. If most of the other students in the class also get low marks, then consensus will be high. If Jane is the only one, then consensus is low.

Distinctiveness relates to whether Jane behaves in a similar way in comparable situations. If she gets low marks for assignments for her other subjects, then distinctiveness is low; there is nothing distinctive about psychology. Distinctiveness is high if she gets high marks in her other subjects.

Consistency relates to how stable Jane's behaviour is over time. If she usually gets low marks for psychology assignments, then consistency is high, but if this is unusual, then consistency is low.

Kelley suggested that it is the pattern produced by these three kinds of causal information which determines what kind of attribution we make.

Kelley's covariation model

Activity 1: making attributions

Read through these scenarios and decide for each what reasons you might use to explain the behaviour described. Make a note in each case of whether your attributions are dispositional or situational, and whether each shows high or low consensus, distinctiveness and consistency:

Heather always buys organic potatoes. Her friends don't buy organic fruit and vegetables. Heather usually buys organic fruit and vegetables.

Marie goes to a local meeting to discuss the possibility of a bypass round her village. Many of her friends have gone to the meeting. Marie does not usually become involved in local issues.

When you have finished, see the notes on page 207.

Kelley believed that the combination of low consensus, low distinctiveness and high consistency will lead to a dispositional attribution, and that any other combination will lead to a situational attribution. There has been some support from research into Kelley's ideas. One example is shown in box C:

Box C: McArthur (1972)

Procedure: Participants were given a series of one-sentence descriptions of actions, opinions and feelings, e.g. Sue is afraid of the dog; George translates the sentence incorrectly; John laughs at the comedian. With each sentence, information was supplied showing high or low consensus, distinctiveness and consistency, similar to the information given in activity 1. Participants were asked to make causal attributions.

Results: Participants were likely to make dispositional attributions when there was low consensus, low distinctiveness and high consistency. Other combinations were likely to produce situational attributions.

Conclusion: Information on consensus, distinctiveness and consistency is important in determining causal attribution. The patterns that Kelley suggested allow us to predict whether a dispositional or a situational attribution will be made.

Activity 2: investigating Kelley's covariation theory

Try a replication of the McArthur study described in box C. You can use his descriptions and/or make up some of your own. You will need to look back to the definitions of consensus, distinctiveness and consistency in order to provide the additional information to go with each description. Make sure that you use a range of different combinations of high and low for each kind of information.

Your findings were probably similar to what Kelley suggested. However, there are a few problems with his theory. One problem is that people do not seem to use all three sources of information equally. Major (1980) found that participants tend to focus mostly on consistency, and much less so on distinctiveness and consensus, with consensus in particular having a very weak effect. Other studies have shown similar findings. This could be another aspect to explore in activity 2.

People may also use other kinds of information when making attributions. Garland *et al.* (1975) found that people prefer to use information about personality and the context in which a behaviour is taking place, if such information is available.

A further problem is that the theory implies that a lot of mental effort is involved in using all the relevant information in making causal attributions. As we will see, people tend to make as little effort as possible in making sense of their social world – they act as 'cognitive misers' – and so use relatively little information to reach conclusions. It is also possible that in real situations, people do not act as logically as the theory suggests.

Causal schemata

In response to some of these criticisms, and to try to explain attributions in situations where we do not have information about consensus, distinctiveness and consistency, Kelley (1972) developed another model.

In situations where we have little information he suggested that we use **causal schemata**, which he defined as 'general conceptions a person has about how certain kinds of causes interact to produce a specific kind of effect'.

One kind of schema is that of **multiple sufficient causes**. For example, there could be a whole range of reasons why someone might choose to go to an evening class in German. They could be planning to go to Germany on holiday, or some knowledge of German might be useful to them for their job, or they might go to the class to keep a friend company, or they may have just moved into the area and are hoping to make new friends. Any one of these causes would be sufficient to account for their behaviour.

A further schema, showing our tendency to situational rather than dispositional attribution, is the **discounting principle**. Sometimes we have reason to believe that one explanation is more likely than the others. We are then likely to accept this reason and discount the other possibilities. For example, an actress advertising a brand of shampoo could be doing so because she believes it is a really good product, or as a favour for a friend in the company which makes the shampoo, or because she is very well paid to do so. Any one of these causes is sufficient to account for what she is doing. If it seems to us that the last is the most likely, we assume that money explains her behaviour and discount the other possible reasons.

Similarly, when behaviour is 'in role', we are likely to make a situational rather than a personal attribution, and vice versa. For example, a doorman who holds a door open does so because it is his job; a passing stranger does so because he is considerate.

A principle which may apply within a schema is that of **multiple necessary causes**. Some behaviour can only be explained by a combination of causes. For example, to explain why someone won a marathon we would need to consider them to have been very fit, to have undergone a period of training, to have worn appropriate shoes, to have been highly motivated, and so on. One of these reasons alone would not be enough to explain their success.

- ❺ **Attribution theory** is about how we explain the causes of behaviour. Attributions can be **dispositional** or **situational**.
- ❺ **Correspondent inference theory** claims that we prefer to make dispositional attributions. We need to decide whether a behaviour is intentional before we can make sense of it, and we prefer to make stable attributions. 'Correspondent inference' refers to the process of matching a behaviour to a stable personal characteristic.
- ❺ **Kelley's covariation theory** focuses on **consensus**, **distinctiveness** and **consistency**. The pattern of this information determines whether we make a dispositional or situational attribution.
- ❺ Sometimes people do not use all this information or choose to use other kinds of information.
- ❺ Kelley suggested we use **causal schemata** when we have insufficient information on consensus, distinctiveness and consistency.
- ❺ One type of causal schema is that of **multiple sufficient causes**, where several ways of explaining behaviour are possible. If one way seems much more likely than the rest, the **discounting principle** comes into play.
- ❺ A principle which may apply within a schema is **multiple necessary causes**, where several reasons are required to explain behaviour.

8.3 ERRORS AND BIASES IN ATTRIBUTION

It has already been suggested that people do not necessarily draw conclusions as logically and rationally as Kelley proposed. Because we take short cuts, such as focusing on some sources of information and ignoring others, perceptions and judgements of our own and other people's behaviour get distorted; errors and biases are liable to creep in.

The fundamental attribution error

Ross (1977) defined the fundamental attribution error (FAE) as 'the tendency to underestimate the importance of situational determinants and overestimate the degree to which actions and outcomes reflect the actors' dispositions'. In other words, we are more likely to make a dispositional attribution, even though a situational explanation may be equally possible. For example, we are more likely to believe that someone drops a cup because they are clumsy than because the cup was wet.

The fundamental attribution error (FAE)

This again fits in with the idea that we behave as 'cognitive misers'. Individual behaviour is conspicuous, and so is simpler to focus on than the context of a situation. We don't feel the need to take possible situational influences into account unless there is no adequate personal explanation. The FAE has been demonstrated experimentally:

Box D: Ross *et al.* (1977)

Procedure: Participants were randomly allocated to be questioners or contestants in a general knowledge quiz. The questioners made up their own questions, and additional participants watched the quiz. Afterwards questioners, contestants and observers were asked to rate the general knowledge of questioners and contestants.

Results: Both observers and contestants (but not questioners) assessed the questioners as being more knowledgeable.

Conclusion: The observers and contestants overestimated dispositional factors in making their ratings. They ignored the situational factor of questioners being able to draw on their particular areas of expertise in setting the questions.

Similarly, Bierbrauer (1979) found that participants watching a film of Milgram's experiments on obedience (these are described in chapter 6 in the section on obedience) were more likely to use dispositional attributions to explain the behaviour of the 'teachers' (e.g. 'they were cruel') than situational attributions (e.g. 'they were intimidated by the experimenter'). There is some evidence, then, to support the idea of the FAE.

It has also been found that once a dispositional attribution has been made, it is quite difficult to change:

Box E: Ross *et al.* (1974)

Procedure: Female students were told they had done either well or badly on a problem-solving task. They were then told that the scores they had been given were false, and the feedback they had been given on their performance was not necessarily true. They were then asked to rate their ability at the task, to estimate how well they had done, and to say how well they thought they might do if they were to carry out the task again.

Results: Those who were initially told they had done well gave themselves higher ratings and made more positive estimates than those who had been told they had done badly.

Conclusion: Participants made dispositional attributions (i.e. in terms of their ability) on the basis of the initial feedback they received. Even though they knew the feedback had been false, the attributions they had made affected their self-ratings.

Activity 3: does the FAE always occur?

Look back through the last section on causal schemata. Can you find an example when the FAE was less likely to occur?

When you have finished, see the notes on page 207.

Fiske and Taylor (1991) have suggested that the idea of the FAE is something of an over-simplification. They also suggested that the FAE should not be thought of as an error, but rather as a bias. That term may be more appropriate, since this kind of judgement represents a distortion rather than something which is necessarily wrong.

It is also possible that the FAE may be related to culture. Miller (1984) found that Indian children were more likely to make situational attributions than North American children, though this study has been criticised on methodological grounds.

The actor–observer effect

Activity 4: explaining choices

Write down brief reasons why you have chosen to study psychology.

Write down also brief reasons why someone you know well has chosen to take one of the subjects they are studying.

When you have finished, see the notes on page 207.

There is a tendency to see our own behaviour as a response to a particular situation, and so quite variable in different situations. At the same time, we tend to explain the behaviour of others in terms of personal characteristics and intentions. This pattern is known as the actor–observer effect (AOE).

How might this be explained? The actor has more direct information about the event and his own previous behaviour than the observer. An observer may be at some distance from the event, so might not be aware of a situational cause. In addition, the focus of attention is different for actor and observer. The actor focuses outwards on the situation, while the observer focuses on the actor. A study by Storms (1973) illustrates the relevance of this point:

The actor–observer effect

Box F: Storms (1973)

Procedure: Two participants took part in a short conversation. Questionnaires were used to assess participants' attributions about their behaviour in the conversation. In one condition, participants saw a video of the conversation they had taken part in before completing the questionnaire.

Results: Participants who had seen themselves on video made more dispositional attributions than those who had not.

Conclusion: When actors become observers, they are more likely to make dispositional attributions. This confirms the attentional explanation of the AOE.

Self-serving bias

Activity 5: reasons for success and failure

Think back to an exam or test in which you did well, and one in which you did badly. Why did you do well in one and not so well in the other?

When you have finished, see the notes on page 207.

According to the **self-serving bias**, we tend to make dispositional attributions to account for our success. This tendency has been called the **self-enhancing bias**. We tend to make situational attributions to explain our failure. This is known as the **self-protecting bias**. This kind of effect is perhaps best explained in terms of **self-esteem**. Self-esteem is increased if we take credit for good performance, and is protected if we do not take responsibility when things go wrong.

These kinds of effect were shown by Johnson *et al.* (1964). They found that teachers accounted for poor performance by their pupils as being the fault of the pupils, while they saw themselves as responsible when pupils' performance improved.

This kind of bias can also work at the group level. For example, if you are a member of a successful football team you are likely to see success as the result of skill, hard training and so on, while failure could be seen to be due to unexpected injury or a biased referee.

Abramson *et al.* (1978) found that depressed people are an exception to this bias. They tend to explain success in terms of external factors such as luck and chance, and failure in terms of their own shortcomings. There is also some evidence that women are more likely to show this reversed pattern than men.

An offshoot of the self-serving bias is what Berglas and Jones (1978) have called **self-handicapping**.

◖ Activity 6: self-handicapping

Imagine that you are waiting with your friends to go into an exam room. You are rather worried about the exam, and think it quite likely that you will not do very well. What kinds of things are you likely to say to your friends?

When you have finished, see the notes on page 207.

In this kind of situation, people often provide reasons to account for possible failure before it happens. If they then do badly, creditable reasons which do not damage their self-esteem are already in place.

As an example of self-handicapping, Berglas and Jones (1978) have suggested that alcoholics may drink too much in order to provide themselves with an external attribution for failure; poor performance can be put down to alcohol, rather than to any lack of ability.

⑤ The attribution process shows errors and biases. The FAE refers to our tendency to prefer dispositional attributions to situational ones. Once made, this error is difficult to reverse.
The FAE is not always made. It may be culture-specific.

⑤ The AOE refers to the tendency of people to explain their own behaviour using situational attributions, and the behaviour of others using dispositional attributions.

⑤ Explanations for our own success or failure often show the **self-serving bias**. We are likely to make dispositional attributions for success and situational attributions for failure. This bias helps to maintain **self-esteem**.

⑤ We are engaged in **self-handicapping** when we provide acceptable reasons in advance of possible failure.

8.4 SOCIAL AND CULTURAL INFLUENCES ON PERCEPTION AND IMPRESSION FORMATION

When we try to make sense of social information, our judgements are affected by those around us. In this section we will be looking at two frameworks within which this can be explored: **social identity theory** and **social representations**.

Social identity theory

Social identity theory (SIT) was put forward by Tajfel (1978) and Tajfel and Turner (1986). This theory proposes that our self-image has two components: personal identity and social identity. Personal identity relates to our perception of our personal traits, our relationships with those around us and so on. Social identity is formed as the result of our group membership. We tend to put people into categories, and this applies also to ourselves.

For example, you may define yourself as a mother, a teenager, a Labour voter or a choir member.

Since we all strive for a positive self-image, we emphasise the positive aspects of the different groups to which we belong; if the group is good, then our association with it makes us good also. One way of enhancing the positive aspects of groups to which we belong (**ingroups**) is to think less positively of groups to which we do *not* belong (**outgroups**), and to overemphasise differences between the two. This tends to lead to biases in the ways in which we see and behave towards other people, in particular the **ingroup favouritism effect** and **negative outgroup bias**. These effects have been shown experimentally:

The ingroup favouritism effect and negative outgroup bias

Box G: Tajfel (1970)

Procedure: Schoolboys were divided into groups using arbitrary criteria such as the toss of a coin. There was no contact between group members; all that each knew about the others was whether they were members of the same group or not. Their task was individually to allocate points (later to be exchanged for money) either to members of their own group (the ingroup) or the other group (the outgroup).

Results: There was a strong tendency for the boys to allocate more points to their own group. They were also likely to maintain the differentials between the two groups, even where this meant allocating fewer points in total to members of their own group.

Conclusion: Group membership is in itself sufficient to lead to ingroup favouritism and a negative bias against an outgroup.

Tajfel carried out a series of these **minimal group** experiments, i.e. with groups which were formed using arbitrary criteria, and whose members may have had little in common and little or no contact with their group members. The findings were similar across these studies. The same kinds of bias were shown even when participants were *told* that they were being randomly allocated. Other research has supported these findings, using participants of different ages in several different countries.

Tajfel's study in box G can perhaps be criticised on the grounds of demand characteristics. It is possible that the boys guessed the purpose of the experiment, or felt in some way constrained to act as they did by the way in which it was run.

The minimal groups paradigm has also been criticised for its artificiality. Can we generalise from these studies to normally occurring social interaction? However, the use of such groups shows that even membership of a group which has little validity can give rise to ingroup favouritism and intergroup rivalry, which suggests that these effects are likely to be even stronger in more natural groups.

We also need to be aware of possible limitations to cross-cultural validity. Wetherall (1982), in a study of white and Polynesian children in New Zealand, found that Polynesian children were much more generous to the outgroup. These findings can possibly be explained in terms of cultural norms, with the kinds of bias Tajfel found being less likely to occur in cultures which emphasise co-operation rather than competition.

At the same time, the wealth of research supporting Tajfel's findings lends weight to the conclusion that our social judgements are not just an individual matter, but depend also on the powerful effect of group membership.

Social representations

A further angle on social perception is supplied by social representation theory, put forward by Moscovici (1984). Social representations are defined as beliefs and explanations, shared by a social group, which are used to account for their social experience. For example, the concept of *the unemployed* is for many people not just a term referring to people who are not currently in work, but relates to a complex of beliefs about individual differences in industriousness, initiative, moral strength, and so on.

This theory suggests that we do not always aim to achieve a full understanding of our social world, but rather to achieve a social representation of it, drawing again on the idea that people act as 'cognitive misers'. Shared social representations allow people to communicate effectively with one another, and to share a model of social reality. They are also an important influence on behaviour.

Different groups of people are likely to have different social representations, which can lead to misunderstandings and a breakdown in communication. An example is shown in box H:

Box H: Di Giacomo (1980)

Procedure: The social representations of student protesters in Belgium were investigated using interviews and a content analysis of the students' associations to key words.

Results: There were differences in the social representations of the student leaders and ordinary students. For example, the concept of *student–worker solidarity* was an important concept for the student leaders but not for the ordinary students.

Conclusion: The discrepancy between the social representations of these different groups could be one explanation for why ordinary students failed to support the demands made by their leaders.

Differing social representations can also occur on a cultural level. A good example is cultural beliefs about education. In Britain, there is a tradition of believing that intelligence is largely inherited and fixed, and that therefore only the few can benefit fully from education. In the USA, on the other hand, the role of training and the effect of environmental influences is seen as much more important. These differing social representations express themselves in differences in the teaching profession in the two countries.

This is not to suggest, however, that social representations are fixed. What is generally considered to be the body shape of the ideal woman is one example of changing representations. In the 1960s a boyish figure was seen as the ideal; one of the major models of the time was known as Twiggy. Currently models like Naomi Campbell and Cindy Crawford have a more defined body shape, and the idea of a strong and fit body, achieved through exercise, has become part of the ideal. Beliefs about what constitutes a healthy diet have also changed considerably over the past few decades.

Social representations are on the one hand enduring, but at the same time open to change. This apparent contradiction can perhaps be explained by Moscovici's suggestion that social representations have a central **figurative nucleus**, as well as peripheral (i.e. less important) elements. Flament (1988) has suggested that it is the peripheral elements which are most likely to adapt and change, while the central element only changes with major changes to most of the peripheral elements. To take the example of ideal body shape, the central element here might be the ideal of slimness, while peripheral elements might be the degree of slimness which is seen as desirable and the importance of muscle tone.

This model could account for fundamental change in a society's social representations, and for the formation of completely new social representations. Moscovici and Hewstone (1983) used split-brain research, described in chapter 11 on brain and behaviour, as an example. They described how the basic ideas of brain specialisation demonstrated by this research have been transformed into a widely-shared and much more general social representation among non-scientists about the relationship of the brain to such topics as personality and gender.

These kinds of shared 'common sense' ideas can be related to the theory of **lay epistemology**, proposed by Kruglanski (1980). This theory is concerned with how ordinary (lay) people develop and make use of knowledge in their everyday lives. As Moscovici and Hewstone pointed out, non-specialists often find scientific ideas difficult to understand. But they can become easier to grasp using short cuts, two of which are personification and figuration.

As an example of **personification**, Moscovici (1961) pointed out that many people know the names of Freud and Einstein, and these names are linked with simple (and sometimes mistaken) ideas about psychoanalysis and relativity. Attaching ideas to a name is one way of simplifying difficult concepts. **Figuration** refers to the use of visual images to express complex ideas. An often used example is the relationship in Freudian theory between id, ego and superego, described in chapter 1. A way of using figuration to make sense of these concepts and the relationship between them is shown in figure 1.

The kinds of social representations which these methods produce help us to make sense of our world. They simplify information processing, and at

Figure 1: figuration as a way of expressing the Freudian concepts of id, ego and superego

SUPER EGO

ID

EGO

the same time make communication easier. On the other hand, it is easy for such representations to become distorted.

- **SIT** suggests that social identity is one part of our **self-concept**. We can increase self-esteem by thinking positively about groups to which we belong (**ingroups**), and negatively about groups to which we do not belong (**outgroups**).
- Tajfel's studies of **minimal groups** have shown that membership of a group is sufficient in itself to create **ingroup favouritism** and **negative outgroup bias**.
- **Social representation theory** suggests that we have shared beliefs which form the basis for drawing conclusions about our experience.
- These shared beliefs simplify information processing and facilitate communication. They may also be inaccurate.

8.5 SOCIAL AND CULTURAL STEREOTYPES

A major way in which we simplify our social world is through stereotyping. Stereotypes have been defined as 'widely shared assumptions about the personalities, attitudes and behaviour of people based on group membership, for example ethnicity, nationality, sex, race and class' (Hogg and Vaughan, 1995). All members of that category or social group are perceived as sharing the same characteristics, and any individual belonging to that category is assumed to have these characteristics.

Stereotypes can be formed on the basis of something as simple as first names:

Box I: Harari and McDavid (1973)

Procedure: Teachers were asked to pick attractive and unattractive names. Other teachers were then asked to grade essays, identified only by attractive (e.g. David/Lisa) or unattractive (e.g. Elmer/Bertha) first names. The names were randomly allocated to essays.

Results: Essays supposedly written by those with attractive names were graded on average a letter grade higher than those with unattractive names.

Conclusion: Stereotypes can be formed on the basis of names. These stereotypes may affect how we behave towards a person with that name.

We also have stereotypes about physically attractive people: we assume that if someone is physically attractive, they are also likely to have a range of other positive characteristics. This assumption that one positive characteristic is associated with others is known as the **halo effect**. Dion *et al.* (1972) found that photographs of attractive people, unlike those of unattractive people, were consistently associated with positive characteristics, e.g. they were judged to be kind, sensitive, interesting, to be professionally more successful and to lead fulfilling lives.

Much research into stereotyping has focused on **ethnicity** and **gender**. An early method of investigating ethnic stereotypes is shown in box J:

Box J: Katz and Braly (1933)

Procedure: American university students were given a list of nationalities and ethnic groups (white Americans, African Americans, Germans, Irish and so on), and a list of 84 personality traits. They were asked to pick out 5 or 6 traits which they thought were typical of each group.

Results: There was considerable agreement in the traits selected. White Americans, for example, were seen as industrious, progressive, ambitious, materialistic and intelligent, while African Americans were seen as superstitious, lazy, happy-go-lucky, ignorant and musical. There was a greater tendency to agree about derogatory traits. Participants were quite ready to rate ethnic groups with whom they had had no personal contact.

Conclusion: Ethnic stereotypes are widespread, and shared by members of a particular social group.

This research was replicated, using students from the same institution, by Gilbert (1951), who found that participants were less ready to make this kind of generalisation. In a similar study by Karlins *et al.* (1969), participants again showed ethnic stereotyping, but were more likely to use positive terms. This variation over time indicates that stereotyping is a social and cultural phenomenon, affected by social change and the ethos of the time. However, it should be noted that this kind of study, which relies entirely on verbal reports, is extremely

Ethnic stereotypes

low in ecological validity. The limited information that participants are given is also likely to create demand characteristics.

Activity 7: ethnic stereotypes

You might like to replicate these studies in a modified form. Focus on just a few ethnic groups, e.g. French, Germans, Japanese and Irish, and ask participants to write down 5 or 6 words which they think best describe a typical member of each group.

How willing were your participants to carry out this task? Was there any similarity in the descriptions they used? Were they more likely to use positive or derogatory terms? This information should help you to compare your findings with the three studies described above.

We will turn now to stereotyping related to gender.

Activity 8: gender stereotyping

Run a small-scale study to investigate gender stereotyping. Give your participants the following list of characteristics, and ask them to indicate for each one whether they think it is more typical of a man or a woman:

1 emotional	2 resourceful	3 witty
4 forgiving	5 rational	6 cautious
7 affectionate	8 cruel	9 hard-headed
10 fussy	11 warm	12 confident

Gender stereotypes

These are sample items from the 300 descriptions used in a study by Williams and Best (1990). In a series of studies carried out in 30 countries all over the world, they found considerable agreement in gender-stereotyping using this kind of material. This is rather at odds with the findings on ethnic stereotyping, discussed above. One way of explaining this could be that gender stereotypes reflect real differences between males and females, which could be innate and genetically-determined. However, it could also be that women's status and the roles they are expected to fill are similar across many of the cultures studied.

In activity 8, numbers 1, 4, 6, 7, 10 and 11 are commonly associated with females, and the others with males. It is worth noting here that some of these stereotypical associations are positive, e.g. warm and confident. While stereotypes are usually negative, it is also possible to have positive stereotypes – for example, of nurses and children – as in the Dion *et al.* (1972) study.

We create stereotypes based on gender very early on. Condry and Condry (1976) showed participants film of a baby. Some were told the baby was a boy, and others that it was a girl. They found that beliefs about the gender of the baby affected how his/her behaviour was interpreted.

The development and maintenance of stereotypes

Like other aspects of social cognition which we have discussed in this chapter, stereotyping makes it easier for us to make sense of our social world. But why do specific stereotypes develop?

The **illusory correlation** explanation was put forward by Chapman and Chapman (1967). They suggested that if two distinctive events occur at the same time, we tend to see them as connected. At the time they put this idea forward, seeing someone who was of a minority ethnic group and seeing someone being mugged, for example, were both relatively rare. They suggested that in these circumstances the two events are likely to be seen as being correlated, and so lead to the stereotype of the black criminal.

The problem with this explanation, of course, is that many people hold this kind of stereotype who have never witnessed this kind of event, so at best it can only provide a partial explanation.

LeVine and Campbell (1972) suggested that many stereotypes are rooted in social and cultural facts. For example, the stereotype of Jews as being mercenary and grasping could be explained by their history of persecution. With many ways of earning a living closed to them, trading was one of the few remaining options. Similarly, before slavery was abolished, it was illegal to educate slaves, so the stereotype of black people as being less intelligent should not really be surprising.

You might like to relate this to activity 8. There may be some truth in the gender stereotypes which people hold, because society expects and values different kinds of behaviour in men and women, to which men and women within that society are likely to conform.

It is worth noting that we tend to create stereotypes of groups of which we are not personally members. This can be related to SIT, discussed earlier. You will remember that group membership affects how ingroup and outgroup members are perceived, and how we behave towards them. One aspect of the way we perceive members of an outgroup is the **outgroup homogeneity effect**. Stereotypes are produced in terms of perceived similarities between outgroup members, and specifically ways in which they differ from the ingroup.

By definition, we are likely to interact more with our ingroups, and lack of contact with members of other groups is likely to lead to an oversimplified view of their characteristics.

Once stereotypes are formed, they are very resistant to change. Two processes which help to maintain them are **selective remembering** (we remember information which supports the stereotypes we hold) and **negative memory bias** (we tend to remember information which is critical of groups against whom we are prejudiced).

Stereotypes can also be maintained by a **self-fulfilling prophecy**. The classic example to illustrate what this means is the fall of the Last National Bank in the USA. The bank was sound, but it was rumoured to be about to collapse. As a result of the rumours, people rushed to draw out their money, causing the bank to collapse. In other words, an initially false definition of a situation brought about a behaviour which made the originally false idea come true.

> ## Activity 9: stereotypes and the self-fulfilling prophecy
> A teacher believes that black children are unintelligent. How might the self-fulfilling prophecy support her stereotype?
> When you have finished, see the notes on page 207.

Are stereotypes a bad thing?

The oversimplification stereotyping involves is likely to lead to overgeneralisation about group characteristics, and so cause us to make faulty judgements. But is this always the case?

Asch (1952) pointed out that in a lot of situations, our behaviour is indeed determined by group membership. For example, active Christians tend to go to church. Stereotyping can therefore be seen as a useful way of understanding the social world.

It is also worth noting that much of the research in this area was carried out in the USA, where political ideology demands that everyone who lives in the USA is 'American' first, whatever their cultural or ethnic origins. Stereotypes, with their focus on difference, present a challenge to this political ideal, and are therefore seen negatively.

Tajfel (1969) has argued that within a European tradition, cultural diversity is seen in a more positive way, so stereotyping can be seen as straightforward cognitive processing. It is purely an example of categorisation, which involves picking up on similarities within groups, and exaggerating differences between groups, in order to help us understand our social world.

However, one problem with stereotypes is that they can influence our other cognitive processes, and cause us to draw incorrect conclusions. This is shown by the studies by Buckhout (chapter 2, box Q) and Duncan (chapter 2, box R). The kind of bias in reporting behaviour shown in these studies might have far-reaching consequences, e.g. for a defendant in a court case.

Campbell (1967) pointed to the serious problems stereotypes can cause. They overestimate the differences between groups and underestimate the differences within groups. They distort reality, and are usually negative. They are seldom questioned and can therefore be used to justify hostility and discrimination, and we shall be looking at this in the next section.

- **Stereotypes** are judgements made about people on the basis of their **group membership**. They may have a social or cultural basis.
- **Ethnic stereotyping** is widespread, but the readiness with which people are prepared to stereotype others has been shown to vary across the decades of the mid-20th century. This suggests a socio-cultural basis for stereotyping. Stereotyping on the basis of **gender** is also very common.
- The **illusory correlation** can partially explain the development of stereotypes. There may also be historical and cultural reasons which explain particular stereotypes. Stereotypes may contain some truth, which serves to maintain them.
- SIT links stereotyping with the **outgroup homogeneity effect**.
- Stereotyping helps us to simplify our social world. It may be seen negatively because of the

cultural traditions in the USA where much research in this area has taken place.
- Stereotypes can influence the interpretation of behaviour. These aspects of stereotyping have implications for the reliability of **eye-witness testimony**.
- Stereotyping is related to **prejudice**.

8.6 PREJUDICE AND DISCRIMINATION

Baron and Byrne (1991) defined prejudice as 'an attitude (usually negative) toward the members of some group, based solely on their membership in that group'.

Just as stereotypes can be positive, so too can prejudice. This is known as **ingroup favouritism**. Hastorf and Cantril (1954) showed students film of a football match played between teams from the two universities they attended. Students from each university thought that their own team had committed fewer fouls than the other team, and that the other team's fouls were more serious.

In practice, however, psychologists have been interested in investigating prejudice in its negative sense. A study of history suggests that prejudice, together with the violent mistreatment of some people by others which arises from it, has always been widespread, and is likely to remain so. Examples come only too readily to mind – the apartheid regime in South Africa, Nazi genocide in the second world war, killings of Catholics by Protestants and Protestants by Catholics in Northern Ireland, and the 'ethnic cleansing' by Serbian forces of Albanians in Kosovo.

Racism has been a particular focus of research. Again, recent examples are not hard to find. In England in 1993, Stephen Lawrence was apparently killed by a group of white youths just because he was black. In America in 1997, three white men dragged James Byrd to his death behind a pick-up truck for the same reason.

Psychologists try to explain what causes prejudice and what function it serves for the individual. They are also interested in using theory and research to suggest ways in which prejudice can be reduced.

Since prejudice is an attitude, in common with other attitudes it has three components: **cognitive** (our beliefs about a particular group: our stereotypes), **affective** (how we feel about them: hostility) and **behavioural** (how we act towards them). The behavioural part of prejudice is **discrimination**, which Secord and Backman (1964) defined as 'the inequitable treatment of individuals considered to belong to a particular social group'.

▷ Activity 10: expressing prejudice

Think of examples of how extreme hostile attitudes have been expressed in the past. Think also about how prejudice is expressed in society today; looking through current newspapers may help you with this. Make a list of as many different examples as you can. If you are working in a group, pool your ideas.

Keep your notes to compare with Allport's stages described in figure 2.

Allport (1954) distinguished five different levels of the behavioural component of prejudice:

Figure 2: Allport's five stages of the expression of prejudice

1. *antilocution:* expressing hostility verbally, e.g. making derogatory and insulting remarks about the target group, and telling jokes about them.

2. *avoidance:* making efforts to avoid any kind of contact, physical or social.

3. *discrimination:* excluding the target group from housing, civil rights and employment opportunities.

4. *physical attack:* violence against members of the target group, or their property.

5. *extermination:* extreme violence against an entire group, up to and including genocide.

You should be able to match the items on the list you made in activity 10 against Allport's five stages. Examples of all five stages are (unfortunately) not hard to think of.

While cognitive, affective and behavioural elements of prejudice usually occur together, this is not always the case:

Box K: LaPiere (1934)

Procedure: LaPiere travelled round America with a Chinese couple, expecting to meet discrimination as a result of anti-Chinese feeling. They visited 67 hotels and 184 restaurants. Six months after their return, all the establishments they had visited were sent a letter, asking whether they would accept Chinese guests.

Results: They were only refused at one of the establishments they visited, and were generally treated very politely. Of the 128 establishments which responded to the letter, however, 91% said they were not willing to accept Chinese guests.

Conclusion: Cognitive and affective components of prejudice are not necessarily expressed in discrimination.

▷ Activity 11: inconsistency in LaPiere's findings

Can you think of any possible reasons to explain the discrepancy between the way in which LaPiere and the Chinese couple were treated on their journey and the negative responses to the letter?

When you have finished, see the notes on page 207.

Prejudiced beliefs and feelings are not inevitably expressed in behaviour, then. It makes more sense to think of these aspects as *predisposing* someone to act in a prejudiced way; whether they do so or not is affected by situational factors.

It is also possible to act in a discriminatory way without being prejudiced. For example, women are not allowed to play in the men's singles at Wimbledon, but this does not imply prejudice against women.

There are three broad approaches to explaining prejudice which we will be considering. The

individual approach looks for causes within the individual, e.g. personality characteristics. This approach is also interested in differences between people. The **interpersonal** approach focuses on processes occurring within social groups; for example, shared beliefs, stereotypes within a culture and conformity to cultural norms. The **intergroup** approach looks at relationships between different groups of people, e.g. inter-group competition.

Splitting up the various theories in this way provides a manageable framework within which we can look at prejudice. At the same time, it is likely that the three different approaches complement rather than contradict each other; they all have something to contribute to our understanding of prejudice.

- **Prejudice** is an attitude towards people based on their group membership.
- It has **cognitive**, **affective** and **behavioural** components. The behavioural component is **discrimination**.
- Allport distinguished five **stages** of the expression of prejudice, ranging from antilocution to extermination.
- The three components usually occur together, but it is possible to have prejudiced beliefs and feelings without behaving in a prejudiced way. It is also possible to show discrimination without the cognitive and affective components of prejudice.
- Theories of prejudice focus on the **individual**, **interpersonal** or **intergroup** levels.

Individual explanations of prejudice

There are two possible ways of explaining prejudice based on the individual. One way focuses on individual differences, and investigates whether prejudice is associated with a particular personality type. The second assumes that individuals are basically the same, and looks at the processes which can lead to prejudice in any of us. However, both kinds of explanation are examples of **externalisation**: the individual deals with personal problems and conflicts by projecting them on to others.

The authoritarian personality

Personality differences are at the heart of the theory of the **authoritarian personality**, proposed by Adorno *et al.* (1950). An outline of this theory has been given in chapter 6, in the section on individual differences in response to social influence. The characteristics of the authoritarian personality, and behavioural measures associated with this personality type, are shown in figure 3:

Figure 3: the authoritarian personality (Adorno *et al.* 1950)	
characteristics	**associated behaviours**
hostile to inferiors	pro-police
servile to superiors	anti-pornography
inflexible	susceptible to social influence
intolerant of ambiguity	likely to bring in 'guilty' verdicts
doesn't introspect about his/her feelings	in favour of longer sentences
conventional	sexist
superstitious	politically right wing
fatalistic	
puritanical about sex	likely to go to the extreme in a Milgram-type study (see chapter 6)
	strict with their children

Adorno *et al.* were initially interested in devising a questionnaire to measure anti-semitism, but then became interested in measuring wider prejudice against ethnic groups. This is known as **ethnocentrism**, i.e. the belief that one's own ethnic group is superior and the standard by which other groups should be judged.

Initial research involved interviewing a wide sample of white, native-born, non-Jewish, middle-class Americans about their political beliefs and childhood experiences. **Projective tests** were also used, drawing on the Freudian defence mechanism of projection discussed in chapter 1. In a projective test, people are asked to respond to ambiguous material, on the principle that the ambiguity will lead people to project their own unconscious ideas, beliefs and feelings on to the material. In this case, the **Thematic Apperception Test** (**TAT**) was used. This test involves showing people ambiguous pictures and asking them to make up a story to describe what is happening, what the people in the picture are thinking, what they want to happen and what the outcome will be.

▷ Activity 12: a picture similar to those used in the Thematic Apperception Test

Have a look at this TAT-type picture and write a brief story about it. Who are the people? What is happening, and what led up to this situation? What are the people thinking and feeling? What do they want to happen? What will the outcome be?

If you are working with a group, compare your story with those written by other students. It is likely that the stories will vary a great deal. Does your story relate to your own private concerns?

The principle behind this test is that this kind of indirect method would be more likely to uncover unconscious attitudes – in this case towards minority ethnic groups – than asking people directly. As a result of this research, Adorno *et al.* became interested in a possible link between political ideology and personality.

In parallel with this research, several scales were developed. All took the form of statements, assessed by a **Likert scale** (see chapter 7), where the respondent indicates the extent to which they agree or disagree with the statement. One scale measures **anti-semitism** (**AS**), one **ethnocentrism** (**E**), one **political and economic conservatism** (**PEC**) and one **potentiality for fascism** (**F**).

The **F-scale**, sometimes called the **authoritarianism scale**, has been most closely identified with investigations into prejudice. In its final form, it contained 38 items, looking at nine different issues. Some sample statements are listed in chapter 6, figure 4. You may like to link these items back to the characteristics listed in figure 3. As you will have seen, none of the items relates directly to attitudes towards minority ethnic groups, but they aim to tap into the general personality characteristics which Adorno *et al.* believed were linked to prejudiced attitudes.

Adorno *et al.* explained the development of the authoritarian personality within the framework of Freud's theories (see chapter 1). They believed that the causes lay in childhood experience. On the basis of the interview and TAT data they had collected, they claimed that people who scored high on the F-scale had often experienced a harsh upbringing, where they were punished for any misdemeanour and were seldom shown affection.

Freudian **defence mechanisms**, in particular **displacement** and **projection,** also formed part of the picture. Consciously, people with an authoritarian personality thought highly of their parents, but often showed unconscious hostility towards them. Adorno *et al.* believed that this unconscious hostility was displaced on to minority groups. The authoritarian personality also projects his or her own unacceptable sexual and aggressive impulses on to these groups, and so sees them as threatening.

Evaluation of the authoritarian personality theory

There is supporting evidence that some people are more likely to be prejudiced than others. One example is shown in box L:

Even when a group does not exist people can still be prejudiced against them

---

Box L: Hartley (1946)

Procedure: Participants were asked their opinions about mythical but plausible-sounding ethnic groups (Wallonians, Danerians and Pirenians); for example, how they would feel if a member of this group came to live next door to them, or wished to marry their daughter.

Results: While some participants refused to answer, many expressed extreme prejudice against these groups. These people were also very prejudiced against Jews and black people.

Conclusion: This prejudice could not have developed through experience, since the groups did not exist. The roots of prejudice must therefore lie within the person.

However, the theory has been criticised both on methodological and conceptual grounds.

▷ Activity 13: methodology and the F-scale

Look back at the sample statements from the F-scale shown in chapter 6, figure 4. Can you identify a possible source of bias?

When you have finished, see the notes on page 207.

A further methodological problem is that the people carrying out the interviews knew the F scores of the people they were interviewing, so there is a possibility of **experimenter bias** when they came to analyse the results. Adorno *et al.* have also been criticised for their limited sample.

A conceptual problem has been raised by Hyman and Sheatsley (1954). They suggested that we do not need to use personality to explain ethnocentrism; levels of education, linked to socioeconomic status, are a more plausible explanation. They found that the percentage of people agreeing with questions from the F-scale decreases as educational levels increase. However, correlation does not necessarily imply causation. It may be, for example, that a low level of intellectual ability underpins both high scores on the F-scale and low socioeconomic status.

A further problem is that a theory which focuses on the individual cannot account for prejudice which is widespread in a particular community at a particular time; for example, anti-semitism in Nazi Germany. It also cannot explain rapid changes in levels of prejudice. Again taking Nazi Germany as an example, anti-semitism rose rapidly over a period of about ten years. It does not seem credible that a whole generation of Germans changed their child-rearing patterns over so short a time.

A final criticism is that this theory associates prejudice with extreme right-wing ideology. In his book *The Open and Closed Mind*, Rokeach (1960) suggested that authoritarianism is associated with the extreme left as well as the extreme right. People at both extremes are likely to have 'closed minds', i.e. to be rigid thinkers, intolerant of those different from themselves. He referred to this as **dogmatism**, and developed a questionnaire to measure it.

As he had predicted, dogmatism was found among people at both extremes of the political spectrum. Rokeach's dogmatism questionnaire is structured in a similar way to Adorno *et al.*'s F-scale, and so can also be criticised on the grounds of possible **response set**. At the same time his theory makes an important distinction, between the nature of political beliefs and their strength, in investigating the association with authoritarianism.

Eysenck (1954) put forward a similar idea to that of Rokeach, again suggesting that authoritarianism applies to the extreme left as well as the extreme right. He used a dimension of tough- vs. tender-mindedness, with the authoritarian personality showing extreme **tough-mindedness**. Tough-mindedness is related to **extroversion** in Eysenck's personality theory (see chapter 7, activity 5). A tough-minded person would be likely to support the death penalty and long prison sentences to punish criminals, while in contrast the tender-minded person would support the abolition of the death penalty and the re-education of criminals. In practice, there has been little support for Eysenck's idea that both Communists and Fascists will show extreme tough-mindedness, and Rokeach's link with dogmatism is generally considered to be more useful.

Frustration and aggression

The **frustration–aggression hypothesis** of Dollard *et al.* (1939) provides another explanation of prejudice which focuses on the individual. It is not interested in individual differences, though, but rather in the processes which can lead to prejudice in people in general.

This hypothesis states that frustration always leads to aggression, and aggression is always caused by frustration. Frustration is used here to refer to

goal-directed activity being prevented from achieving the goal at which it is directed. The connection with prejudice is based on Freud's ego defence mechanism of **displacement** (see chapter 1), where aggressive impulses which cannot be expressed directly are displaced on to someone or something else. For example, if someone is frustrated by being unemployed they might blame the government. There is no direct way of expressing their aggression against the government, so a **scapegoat** is found on whom the aggressive feelings can be displaced. When an individual is frustrated, they will express their aggression as prejudice against an outgroup which is used as a scapegoat.

This idea has been tested experimentally:

Box M: Weatherley (1961)

Procedure: Participants were two groups of students, high- and low-scorers on an anti-semitism questionnaire. Half of each group were insulted, in order to create frustration, while filling in another questionnaire. All participants were later asked to write stories about some pictures of men, two of whom were given Jewish names.

Results: Those who scored high for anti-semitism responded more aggressively to the 'Jewish name' pictures than those who scored low. There was no difference between high and low scorers who had been insulted in the amount of aggression directed at the other pictures

Conclusion: When frustrated, highly anti-semitic people target their aggression specifically at Jews.

However, the choice of scapegoat is not random. In England in the 1930s and 1940s, Jews were the main scapegoat, followed by West Indians during the next two decades, and later by Asians, in particular Pakistanis. The fact that these particular groups were picked out at these periods, rather than prejudice being more widely targeted at other minority groups, suggests that groups chosen as scapegoats are in some way socially approved. This in turn suggests that in order to explain prejudice, we need to look beyond the individual and focus on their social group, and this approach is explored in the next section.

❺ Adorno *et al.* suggested that prejudice is linked with the characteristics of the **authoritarian personality**. This personality type is associated with extreme right-wing ideology. It has its roots in childhood experience.

❺ While there is some support for the theory, methodological and conceptual criticisms can be made.

❺ Both Rokeach and Eysenck linked this type of personality with extreme political ideology of both left and right. Rokeach describes it as **dogmatism**, and Eysenck as **tough-mindedness**.

❺ The **frustration–aggression hypothesis** suggests that we displace aggression on to minority groups when we are frustrated. They become **scapegoats**.

The interpersonal approach to prejudice

Ideas about prejudice which look at processes within groups of people focus on stereotyping, discussed earlier, and conformity to **social** and **cultural norms**.

Social norms shared by members of a social group are one possible influence on prejudice and discrimination. People may have prejudiced beliefs and feelings and act in a prejudiced way because they are conforming to what is regarded as normal in the social groups to which they belong:

Box N: Minard (1952)

Procedure: The behaviour of black and white miners in a town in the southern United States was observed.
Results: Below ground, 80% of the white miners were friendly towards the black miners. Above ground, this dropped to 20%.
Conclusion: The white miners were conforming to different norms above and below ground. Whether or not prejudice is shown depends on the social context within which behaviour takes place.

Pettigrew (1959) also investigated the role of conformity in prejudice. He investigated the idea that people who tended to be more conformist would also be more prejudiced, and found this to be true of white South African students. Similarly, he accounted for the higher levels of prejudice against black people in the southern United States than in the north in terms of the greater social acceptability of this kind of prejudice in the south.

A study by Rogers and Frantz (1962) found that immigrants to Rhodesia (now Zimbabwe) became more prejudiced the longer they had been in the country. They gradually conformed more to the prevailing cultural norm of prejudice against the black population.

Conformity to social norms, then, may offer an explanation for prejudice in some cases. At the same time, norms change over time, so this can only go some way towards explaining prejudice.

❺ People may be prejudiced because they are conforming to **social** and **cultural norms**.

The intergroup approach to prejudice

At the intergroup level, prejudice has been explained in terms of **intergroup conflict**. One theory using this idea is **relative deprivation theory**: when people feel that they are deprived in relation to other groups, they become prejudiced against the groups with whom they are comparing themselves.

In support of this idea, Vanneman and Pettigrew (1972) found that white people who were most prejudiced against black people also believed that white people were badly off compared to black people. They were actually better off, but the idea of relative deprivation depends on a subjective evaluation of a situation, rather than a realistic assessment.

Another approach is **realistic conflict theory**, proposed by Sherif (1966). He carried out a series of experiments investigating aggression in boys at a summer camp. A sample study is described in box O:

Box O: Sherif (1966)

Procedure: The participants in this study were 11- and 12-year-old boys at an American summer camp. In the first stage of the study, the boys mixed with each other and took part in sports and outdoor activities. During this period, friendships were formed.

The boys were then divided into two groups, with friends being split up. Each group again took part in the normal range of camp activities, but only within their own group. There was no contact with the other group. Each group shared a dormitory and took their meals together. Very soon, friendships were formed, and a strong sense of group identity had developed. A leadership structure emerged, and each group gave themselves names, the Eagles and the Red Devils.

In the next stage, competitions in various activities were arranged between the two groups.

Results: A lot of intergroup hostility was shown, e.g. name calling, raids on each other's dormitories and graffiti.

Conclusion: Competition between groups can result in aggressive behaviour.

On the basis of this research, Sherif suggested that intergroup conflict comes about as the result of a conflict of interest. He claimed that this is enough to create hostility and discrimination. There is a lot of evidence that when people compete for scarce resources, there is a rise in intergroup hostility. For example, many studies have shown that in times of high unemployment there are high levels of racism among white people who believe that black people have taken away their jobs.

However, Tyerman and Spencer (1983) have challenged Sherif's conclusions. In a similar study of a summer camp, they found that competition did not lead to the hostility Sherif described. This could have been because the boys all knew each other well, and the cohesiveness of the whole group was encouraged by the leader.

If competition is not in itself enough to create hostility, is it necessary at all? You will remember from the discussion of Tajfel's minimal groups studies (box G) that being in groups is enough in itself to cause hostility and discriminatory behaviour.

We need finally to look at historical explanations of prejudice, based on relationships between groups. Racial prejudice against some minority ethnic groups in Britain may have its roots in colonialism. For example, when India was a British colony, white men ran its tea plantations while the labour was supplied by the native Indians. The two groups thus had very different roles, and the prevailing British view of the inhabitants of the colonies was that they were inferior to white Britons. Prejudice in Britain today against people from former British colonies may be, in part at least, a hangover from this attitude. A similar argument applies to prejudice against black people in America, in the historical context of slavery.

Finally, the role of the mass media in encouraging prejudice against particular groups of people should not be forgotten. For example, Nazi propaganda films depicted Jews as vermin, thus laying the foundation for the genocide which was to follow. Similarly, the Serbian assault on Kosovo followed years of intensive anti-Albanian propaganda.

- Prejudice has been explained in terms of **intergroup conflict**. Two theories taking this approach are **relative deprivation theory** and **realistic conflict theory**.
- There may be historical reasons for hostile intergroup relationships.
- Media propaganda can play a role in encouraging prejudice.

8.7 THE REDUCTION OF PREJUDICE AND DISCRIMINATION

Activity 14: reducing prejudice

Look back through the theories of prejudice and their related ideas discussed above. Focus in particular on:

a authoritarian personality

b frustration-aggression hypothesis

c social and cultural norms

d stereotypes

e relative deprivation theory

f realistic conflict theory

How might these theories suggest we go about reducing prejudice?

When you have finished, see the notes on page 207.

In *The Nature of Prejudice*, Allport (1954) proposed that 'prejudice ... may be reduced by equal status contact between majority and minority groups in the pursuit of common goals'. Cook (1978) suggested that five factors were necessary for prejudice to be reduced: equal status contact; exposure to non-stereotypical individuals; personal acquaintance; environmental support for intergroup contact; and co-operation between groups. Since prejudice and discrimination are such major social problems, there has been a lot of psychological research exploring the effectiveness of these (and other) ideas.

Equal status contact

Increased contact between groups should help to break down stereotypes. Our negative stereotypes are often maintained by avoiding contact with members of groups about which we have the negative stereotypes, which means that our stereotypes are not challenged. Avoidance helps to maintain the emphasis on differences between groups, while contact will lead to recognition of similarities. Wide contact also challenges the outgroup homogeneity effect; if contact is limited to one or two individuals, they may be seen as untypical. Positive attitudes to individuals may not generalise to a group as a whole.

However, increased contact on its own does little to reduce prejudice and may even reinforce stereotypes. Aronson (1980) pointed out that for many white Americans, the only black people they had contact with worked as dishwashers, toilet attendants and domestic servants, and this kind of contact would be likely to reinforce the stereotype of black people as inferior. It is only contact with people of equal status which challenges stereotypes and emphasises similarities.

One early study of equal status contact is described in box P:

> ### Box P: Deutsch and Collins (1951)
>
> **Procedure:** Residents of two housing projects were interviewed. One project was integrated, with black people and white people living together, and one segregated.
> **Results:** White people in the integrated housing project showed less prejudice against black people.
> **Conclusion:** Contact between people of similar status helps to break down prejudice.

However, research has not always been so positive. In a review of studies looking at the effect of desegregating American schools, Stephan (1978) concluded that integration had had little effect on inter-racial prejudice, and there was even some evidence that black people's prejudice against white people had increased as a result. However, desegregation was still relatively recent when this review was undertaken, and it would be helpful to look at possible long-term effects.

The Sherif (1966) summer camp study, described above, also investigated whether equal status contact would reduce aggression. They found that just bringing the boys together; for example, to watch a film or to share a meal, was not in itself effective. The groups needed to work together at achieving **superordinate goals** in order for hostility to be reduced, and we shall consider this next.

Superordinate goals

Superordinate goals are goals which can only be achieved through co-operation. Sherif (1966) found that aggression between the groups of boys at summer camp was reduced when both groups needed to work together to achieve something which neither group could achieve alone. For example, when they had to co-operate to mend a damaged water supply, or club together in order to hire a film, divisions between the groups disappeared.

Superordinate goals can only be achieved through co-operation

This effect has also been shown in a study using the **jigsaw classroom technique**:

Box Q: Aronson *et al.* (1978)

Procedure: The jigsaw classroom technique was used in small learning groups of children of different races. Each child was given material relating to one part of the lesson, to be communicated to other members of the group. All were later to be tested on the lesson as a whole. Each child was therefore dependent on all the others to achieve the goal of learning the lesson.

Results: Academic performance, self-esteem and to some extent inter-racial perceptions were improved, and there was increased liking for classmates. The children who had worked together liked each other as individuals, but this did not necessarily generalise to ethnic groups as a whole.

Conclusion: Contact and co-operation may go some way to helping to reduce prejudice.

Activity 15: limitations of the jigsaw classroom technique

As you have seen, while there were several positive outcomes to the jigsaw classroom technique, it was not very effective in reducing prejudice. What factors might account for this relative lack of success?

When you have finished, see the notes on page 208.

The effectiveness of working towards superordinate goals in a more long-term situation has been shown in a study by Stouffer *et al.* (1949). They found that there was less prejudice among racially mixed units in the American army than among segregated ones. Here there was equal status contact, and the men needed to co-operate to fight a common enemy (a superordinate goal). In effect they were re-categorising themselves as one single group.

However, the picture may be a little more complex than these studies imply. Worchel *et al.* (1977) found that we need to look at the history of the two groups, and whether they experience success or failure at a superordinate task, before we can predict whether co-operation is likely to lead to more positive attitudes between groups.

They found that if groups had been co-operative in the past, then success or failure at the superordinate task was irrelevant; in either case, little prejudice was shown. If, on the other hand, groups had been in competition with each other in the past, then failure at a superordinate task was likely to lead to an *increase* in prejudice.

The groups involved also needed to have distinctive roles to play in achieving the task, and to feel that both groups were making a defined contribution. Otherwise negative feelings between the groups were likely to increase.

Other influences in the reduction of prejudice

A classic study, known as the **brown eyes, blue eyes** study, demonstrates that **education** can have a role in combating prejudice:

Box R: Elliott (1977)

Procedure: Jane Elliott, a schoolteacher, decided to give her class of 9-year-olds direct experience of what it is like to be discriminated against. She told them that people with blue eyes were inferior to those with brown eyes. The brown-eyed children were given extra privileges, while the blue-eyed children had to wear special collars to

---

show their low status. The following day, she said she had made a mistake, and that it was in fact brown-eyed people who were inferior. The next day the children were debriefed.
Results: On the first day, the brown-eyed children were cruel and unkind to the blue-eyed children. The blue-eyed children did badly at their work, and described themselves as 'sad', 'bad' and 'stupid'. The following day these behaviours were reversed. Ten years later, Elliott found that the children were actively opposed to prejudice, and tolerant of group differences.
Conclusion: Education, particularly through direct experience, can help to combat prejudice.

Blue eyes, brown eyes

While Elliott's findings are encouraging, there are nonetheless problems in relying on education to eliminate prejudice. School is only one part of a child's experience, and targeting the home is only likely to work if parents accept that they are prejudiced. They are likely to think that the opinions they have are reasonable, particularly if these opinions are widespread within their social group.

McGuire (1964) has suggested that we need to take an **inoculation** approach to the education of our children against prejudice. They need to be given counter-arguments which will protect them from the prejudiced attitudes and behaviour they are likely to come across in life, and be encouraged to act on those counter-arguments.

Education can also help by encouraging children to see people as unique individuals rather than to focus on their group attributes, and by limiting the competitive atmosphere of the classroom in favour of one where co-operation is valued.

Counter-stereotyping can also be effective, and the media can play a role in this. Many television programmes present members of minority ethnic groups in ways which challenge our stereotypes. The sitcom *The Cosby Show* is one example where a black family is shown whose members are high academic and social achievers, in contrast to the common stereotype of black people as less intelligent than white people. This kind of example may help to change our perceptions and our behaviour. By bringing about a change in social norms, the reality of the situation may also be changed, which in turn will further change our perceptions of minority groups.

Legislation may also have a part to play in changing both people's behaviour and their attitudes. For example, the Race Relations Act made it illegal to advertise a job indicating that black people should not apply, and few people would now consider that kind of advertisement acceptable. Legislation may, however, cause resentment, which could be counter-productive.

๑ Research into prejudice can suggest ways of reducing it. **Equal status contact** and working towards **superordinate goals** can be effective.

๑ **Education, counter-stereotyping** and **legislation** can also have a part to play.

Counter-stereotyping can be effective

Notes on activities

1 You probably concluded that Heather buys organic potatoes because she believes that organic produce is a healthy option, or because she is worried about possible chemical contamination in non-organic produce. This is a dispositional attribution, and Heather's behaviour shows low consensus, low distinctiveness and high consistency. Marie is likely to have gone to the meeting because the issue of the bypass is a particular concern for her. This is a situational attribution, and Marie's behaviour shows high consensus, high distinctiveness and low consistency.

3 The example of the celebrity advertising shampoo is one case where a situational attribution (getting paid) is likely to be preferred over an equally plausible dispositional attribution (the celebrity thinks the shampoo is an excellent product). The example of a doorman holding open the door is another.

4 When Nisbett *et al.* (1973) asked students to carry out this task, they found that the students tended to make dispositional attributions when asked to give reasons for a friend's choices (e.g. in terms of personality), while using situational attributions to account for their own (e.g. in terms of what the course had to offer). A similar pattern of attributions was made in giving reasons for their own and a friend's choice of girlfriend or boyfriend.

5 You are likely to have made dispositional attributions for your success; for example, you worked hard or were good at that particular subject. You are also likely to have made situational attributions to explain your failure; perhaps the subject wasn't interesting, or the teaching was poor.

6 Quite often in this situation, people talk about their lack of revision, or say they are not feeling very well, or couldn't sleep the night before.

9 She might spend less time with the black children in her class, preferring to concentrate on children she thinks are more likely to benefit from her help. She might also set the black children less challenging tasks, which do not stretch them. The black children might then fail to make good progress, and so confirm her initial belief.

11 It is possible that the presence of LaPiere himself could have made the Chinese couple more acceptable, and more difficult to refuse, when looking for accommodation or getting served in a restaurant. However, he did try to avoid his presence becoming a factor by letting his friends enter hotels and restaurants ahead of him, while he concerned himself with the car or luggage. It would also not be in the financial interests of hotel keepers to turn away custom. It should also be noted that LaPiere's Chinese friends were well dressed, with good quality luggage, and very polite; these factors may have affected how they were treated in a face-to-face situation.

13 You may have noticed that all the statements are structured in such a way that they score positively for authoritarianism; there are no statements with which an authoritarian personality would disagree. This is true for all the items on the scale. The trouble with this is that a person filling in the questionnaire might develop a **response set**, i.e. once they had agreed with the first few statements, they would mechanically agree with the others without reading the items carefully. In this case, the questionnaire might not be measuring authoritarianism, but acquiescence.

14 The concept of the **authoritarian personality** suggests that prejudice is an inevitable consequence of a particular personality type. The child-rearing patterns which lead to this personality type would also be difficult to change. However, the relationship to education suggests that widening educational access might be one way of tackling the problem.

The **frustration–aggression hypothesis** suggests that reducing frustration might be helpful, though it cannot of course be eliminated. Ways of displacing aggression which do not involve scapegoating minorities could also be encouraged.

If people's behaviour is affected by **social and cultural norms**, these norms could perhaps be modified by information and education. Similarly, contact with members of outgroups could help to break down stereotypes, and in particular challenge the outgroup homogeneity effect.

Relative deprivation theory suggests that information could help to create realistic expectations, while according to **realistic conflict theory**, replacing competition with co-operation would seem to be a good way forward.

15 The finding that positive feelings about individuals fail to generalise to ethnic groups as a whole may perhaps be explained by the small-scale and short-term nature of the study. You may also have pointed out that children spend a relatively small proportion of their time at school, and their home environment is likely to play an important role in their developing beliefs and attitudes. Nonetheless, this study has been widely replicated, with very similar results, and does suggest a way in which we might start to combat prejudice.

Relationships

In this chapter we will be looking at:

9.1 Why do we form relationships?

9.2 Types of relationship

9.3 Factors in interpersonal attraction
    Situational factors
    Personal characteristics

9.4 Theories relating to the formation of
    relationships
    Reinforcement/affect theory
    Sociobiological theory
    Stage and filter theories

9.5 The maintenance of relationships
    Economic theories
    Communal and exchange
      relationships
    Strategies in maintaining a
      relationship

9.6 The dissolution of relationships

9.7 Psychological explanations of love

9.8 Cultural and subcultural differences
    in relationships
    Individualist and collectivist cultures
    Gay and lesbian relationships
    Relationships formed on the
      Internet

9.1 WHY DO WE FORM RELATIONSHIPS?

There are rare examples of people who go to great lengths to avoid being with other people, but in general we have a need for the company of others, known as **affiliation**.

McClelland (1961) proposed that affiliation is one of the basic human needs which motivate our behaviour. This idea has been supported by studies where participants are deprived of the company of others:

Box A: Schachter (1959)

Procedure: Five male volunteers were each kept in a room on their own in conditions of social deprivation. They were given plenty to do, but were always alone.

Results: At one extreme, one participant felt an uncontrollable need to leave after 20 minutes, while at the other extreme, one participant managed to remain in isolation for 8 days. All of them admitted to feeling nervous and uneasy, and were apathetic and withdrawn. They reported that they thought and dreamed about other people.

Conclusion: There are individual differences in our need to be with others, but even a relatively short period of isolation from others has marked psychological consequences.

Even short periods of social deprivation have marked psychological consequences

There is evidence, then, of a need for affiliation, to seek out and be with other people. However, a dyadic (two-person) relationship goes beyond simple affiliation. We form a special bond when we form a relationship with another person; it is not the case that anyone could just as easily be considered a friend or partner as anyone else. The rest of this chapter will be looking at the factors which lead to us forming such relationships, how we keep them going, and why and how they sometimes break down.

It is perhaps worth noting that there are similarities between forming adult relationships and the attachments infants make to caregivers. Hazan and Shaver (1987) (see chapter 3, box K and figure 7) demonstrated a link between the attachment styles of infants and the kinds of romantic relationship people form as adults.

9.2 Types of relationship

We have many different kinds of relationships in our lives. For example, your relationship with a fellow student at college, whom you know only casually, is very different from your relationship with a close friend, which in turn is different from your relationship with someone you would choose as a partner to live with. Berscheid and Walster (1978) distinguished between three different kinds of personal relationships, which can be described in terms of the kinds of emotional states associated with them:

Figure 1: relationship types (Berscheid and Walster, 1978)

liking: the positive feelings we may have for casual acquaintances

companionate love: the affection we have for those with whom our lives are deeply entwined, such as family or close friends

passionate love: relationships associated with intense physiological arousal and absorption in the other person

Gottman (1994) has also distinguished between different types of relationships within marriage, in terms of how couples interact and communicate in both stable and unstable marriages:

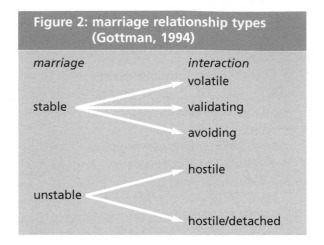

Figure 2: marriage relationship types (Gottman, 1994)

marriage → *interaction*

stable → volatile / validating / avoiding

unstable → hostile / hostile/detached

Within a stable relationship, **volatile** refers to a marriage where there are intense emotions, with big fights and great times making up. When there are disagreements, each partner is very intent on bringing the other round to their point of view. However, this kind of relationship runs the risk of deteriorating into endless quarrels, and even violence.

Validating describes stable marriages where the relationship is calm, and attempts to convince your partner of your point of view are moderate and good-natured. The risk here is that romance can be replaced by boredom.

In **avoiding** marriages, areas of disagreement are skirted round. These marriages have very low emotional intensity. However, this style of relationship means that unresolved problems have to be lived with, there is a fear of negative emotions, and the couple may lose the skills required to settle conflicts.

Both types of unstable marriage are characterised by hostility. In marriages in the **hostile** category, there is direct conflict, with each partner watching the other to detect any criticism. People in this kind of marriage complain about and attack each other, and react defensively when attacked themselves.

In the **hostile/detached** style of marriage, the partners seem detached and uninvolved, but now and again one of them will launch a hit-and-run attack.

Activity 1: relationship typology

In what way(s) are these attempts to classify relationships useful? How might they be criticised? When you have finished, see the notes on page 239.

⊖ **Affiliation** is the basic need to seek out and be with other people.

⊖ Forming a relationship can be seen as an **attachment** process.

⊖ Some theorists have produced relationship **typologies**.

9.3 FACTORS IN INTERPERSONAL ATTRACTION

We can't choose our family, but we can choose our friends. A lot of researchers have been interested in what determines the choices we make.

Activity 2: choice of relationship

Look back to the three kinds of relationship outlined in figure 1. Think of someone from each category with whom you have a relationship. What factors were important in forming relationships with those particular people and not with others? Compare your ideas with the discussion which follows.

There are several factors which may influence the choices we make. The relative importance of each depends to some extent on the kind of relationship; for example, choosing someone to spend your life with is rather different from choosing someone to sit next to in a lecture.

Many studies have found that two main groups of factors are involved: **situational factors** and **personal characteristics**.

Situational factors

Situational factors include exposure and familiarity. Proximity, i.e. physical closeness, is often cited as a further factor, though as we shall see, its influence can in general be explained in terms of exposure and familiarity.

Exposure and familiarity

When we are often exposed to a person, that person becomes familiar to us. There is quite a lot of evidence that exposure and familiarity can be important influences on our choice of people with whom we wish to form a relationship.

Provided that we don't actually dislike a person, liking tends to increase with additional contact. We tend to like things or people to whom we have been frequently exposed and which have therefore become familiar. Zajonc (1968) called this the **mere exposure effect**, and it has been shown in various studies:

Box B: Saegert *et al.* (1973)

Procedure: Female participants were asked to rate the taste of various drinks. During the course of the experiment, they were brought into contact with other women either once, twice, five times or ten times. This contact was limited to seeing each other; at no time did participants talk to each other or have any other kind of interaction.

Results: Participants preferred the women they had been exposed to more often to those they had seen only once.

Conclusion: Exposure to others can on its own lead to positive feelings towards them.

In a similar study by Moreland and Beach (1992), experimenters posing as students attended varying numbers of classes. Those who attended most classes were rated by other students as more likeable than those who had attended fewer.

This does not only hold true for face-to-face exposure. Zajonc *et al.* (1971) asked participants to rate photographs of strangers. They gave more positive ratings for the ones they were shown more often. Nor is it restricted to our liking for other people. We have a preference for the mirror-image of our own face, which we see more frequently than the view other people have of us (Mita *et al.* 1977) and for more frequently-heard nonsense words (Zajonc, 1968). Gross (1992) reported that similar effects have been found over a range of stimuli, including paintings, Pakistani music and political candidates.

Cross *et al.* (1967) played Mozart to young rats, and found that as adults they preferred Mozart to Schoenberg. However, young rats reared on Schoenberg showed no preference for this music when adult. This could be an example of the polarising effect of similarity: while liking tends to increase with familiarity, if we dislike something to start with, familiarity may increase this dislike. However, most studies in this area have found positive effects of exposure and familiarity.

Exposure and familiarity are important factors in forming a relationship

Proximity

Bossard (1932) found that couples in Chicago who lived one block away from each other were more likely to marry than those who lived two blocks away, while Clarke (1952) found that 50% of people in Columbus, Ohio had married people who lived within walking distance. The effect of proximity was shown in a classic study:

Box C: Festinger *et al.* (1950)

Procedure: The friendship patterns of students living on campus in university housing were studied.

Results: Students were most friendly with those living next door to them, less friendly with those living two doors away, and least friendly with those living at the end of the corridor. When the accommodation was on different floors, students tended to form friendships with those living on the same floor as themselves. Those who lived near stairs, and so were in frequent contact with others, tended to have more friends.

Conclusion: Physical proximity can be an important factor in establishing friendships.

Other studies looking at the effects of proximity in different situations have had similar findings. For example, Whyte (1955) found that people are more likely to become friendly with people living next door to them, particularly if there is a shared driveway. In a study of police cadets, who were seated in alphabetical order by surname, Segal (1974) found that surname was a better indication of whether friendships would be formed than similarity in terms of religion, age, education or hobbies.

In all these cases, the findings can be explained by exposure and familiarity; if we are in close physical proximity with someone, we are likely to see them often, and so they become familiar. Hogg and Vaughan (1995) suggested that a second factor is availability. You may have experienced a friend moving away to a different part of the country; it takes more effort to keep this friendship alive than to maintain friendships with people who still live near you. They also suggested that if we know that we are going to be in regular contact with someone, it pays to make an effort to get on with them. Living next door to someone with whom you don't have a friendly relationship can be very uncomfortable.

- **⊗ Situational factors** in the formation of relationships include **exposure**, **familiarity** and **proximity**.
- **⊗** While exposure and familiarity usually lead to increased liking, increased exposure and familiarity with something or someone which we dislike can increase dislike. These factors may **polarise** existing feelings.
- **⊗ Proximity** is usually associated with **familiarity** and **exposure**.

Personal characteristics

Personal factors include physical attractiveness, similarity and complementarity, and competence. We will look at what research has to offer in each of these areas.

Physical attractiveness

Feingold (1992) found that physical attractiveness was particularly important in the early stages of a relationship. Aronson *et al.* (1994) claimed that it is the secret of popularity from preschool to adulthood for both sexes. There is a lot of evidence that our judgements of people are affected by physical attractiveness:

Box D: Dion *et al.* (1972)

Procedure: Participants were shown photographs of people, and asked to make judgements about their personal qualities.

Results: There was a **halo effect**, i.e. people who were more attractive were considered also to have positive psychological characteristics. They were judged to be more moral, more intelligent, warmer, happier and more successful.

Conclusion: Physical attractiveness can influence the broader psychological impression we form of others.

Many studies into the role of physical attractiveness in the formation of relationships have used the computer dance technique. Participants – usually college students at the start of the academic year – independently buy tickets for a dance and are asked to fill in a form giving information which a computer can use to match each of them with an ideal partner; in fact they are randomly allocated a partner. This technique allows each person buying a ticket to be rated for physical attractiveness:

Box E: Walster *et al.* (1966)

Procedure: The computer dance technique was used to find out how many of the men paired up in this way would ask their partner for a second date, and what would influence whether they asked or not.

Results: The most influential factor was the physical attractiveness of the woman.

Conclusion: Physical attractiveness can be important in establishing a dating relationship.

However, the role of physical attractiveness in the formation of relationships can be a complex one. In particular, the **matching hypothesis** proposed by Murstein (1972) suggested that we may seek to form a relationship not with the most physically attractive person around, but with someone who is roughly as attractive as we are ourselves. We compromise in terms of picking the best person available who is likely to accept us on the same basis, and so try to avoid rejection by someone more attractive than ourselves.

We may seek to form a relationship with someone who is roughly as attractive as we are ourselves

▶ Activity 3: the matching hypothesis

You can test the matching hypothesis for yourself. You will need to collect pictures of couples; a dozen couples would probably be enough. The pictures need to be more or less the same size, and either all coloured or all black and white. You could use magazine pictures (avoiding pictures of recognisable people such as film actors), or the wedding photos carried in some local newspapers. Separate the pictures of each couple so that you have one group of females and one group of males. Code each individual with a letter, and use these codes to keep a note of which female was the partner of which male.

You will need to find some participants, ideally at least 9 or 10. Ask each participant to rate each of the pictures separately for physical attractiveness using a 5-point scale, where 1 = very unattractive, 2 = quite unattractive, 3 = averagely attractive, 4 = quite attractive and 5 = very attractive. You could use a more detailed 10-point scale if you prefer.

When all your participants have completed their ratings, work out an average rating for each picture, using either the median or the mode. Draw up a list of the females and match each to their partner. Are the average ratings of each pair similar? A scattergram could help to show you this.

In a further study of the matching hypothesis, Price and Vandenberg (1979) studied married couples aged 28–60. They found that couples through the different generations tended to be matched in terms of physical attractiveness.

However, there is some ambiguity in the matching hypothesis. It is not entirely clear whether it is meant to be an explanation of the cognitive processes we go through in deciding who we are attracted to, or an explanation of the process by which we tend to end up with someone who is roughly as attractive as we are ourselves.

While there is some evidence that physical attractiveness can be important in the formation of relationships, there are also some limitations to this idea. To start with, it refers only to the type of relationships which have the potential to develop into what Berscheid and Walster (1978) classified

as passionate love (see figure 1). Interestingly, Krebs and Adinolfi (1975) found that those who were most physically attractive were more likely than physically unattractive people to be rejected by members of their own sex.

The methods typically used to investigate the influence of physical attractiveness can also be criticised. Much of the research in this area involves asking people to respond to photographs – usually just of faces – which have previously been rated for attractiveness. Some studies, e.g. Franzoi and Herzog (1987), have included body shape as part of the presentation. However, this approach in general can be criticised as being very far removed from the way we develop relationships with real people, in particular because of the lack of face-to-face interaction and the emphasis on immediate judgement.

There are also gender differences in the importance of physical attractiveness. Buss (1989), in a study of 37 cultures, found that when establishing a relationship, physical attractiveness was a more important criterion for males than for females. Similarly, Reis et al. (1980) found that in long-term real-life relationships, physical attractiveness had a greater effect for men than for women. Sigall and Landy (1973) found that physical attractiveness in a female partner raised a male's status and increased the respect he was given by others. Bar-Tal and Saxe (1976) found that the reverse was not true; a good-looking male partner did not have the same effect on a female's status and the respect she was given.

Similarity and complementarity

A further personal factor in the formation of relationships is similarity, i.e. the extent to which others share our beliefs, attitudes and values. It has also been suggested that complementarity may be important. This is the extent to which someone has characteristics which we feel that we personally lack, but which we value, and which complement the characteristics we do possess.

Most of the research evidence has suggested that **similarity** is the more important factor. People tend to like others who are similar to themselves on a wide variety of factors: age, religion, being a morning or an evening person, attitudes, and so on. Duck and Barnes (1992) found this to be true for all ages, from children to the elderly.

Activity 4: similarity

Think of two or three close friends. To what extent are they similar to you? Do you think that similarity is an important basis for your relationship with them? How and why might similarity be important in a relationship?

When you have finished, see the notes on page 239.

The influence of similarity has been shown in several studies, for instance:

see the notes on page 239.

Box F: Griffitt and Veitch (1974)

Procedure: A sample of 13 males was paid to spend 10 days in a fallout shelter to find out what factors influenced the relationships they developed.

Results: Participants most liked the others who shared their attitudes and opinions, particularly about things which they considered important.

Conclusion: Similarity is a strong determinant of whether or not a relationship will develop.

The tendency for like to select like also plays a role in the stability of relationships. For example, Caspi and Herbener (1990) found that married couples tend to be similar on all personality dimensions. However, this may partly be a function of the length of the relationship, as other studies (e.g. Zajonc *et al.* 1987) have shown that as a result of their interactions, people become more alike in verbal skills, open-mindedness and even physical appearance.

However, similarity is not necessarily a major factor in the formation of relationships:

Box G: Newcomb (1961)

Procedure: Male students were offered free board and lodging to take part in this study. In the first year, students were randomly assigned a room-mate. In the second year, different participants were assigned a room-mate whose attitudes, beliefs and values were either very similar or very dissimilar to their own.

Results: In the first year, similarity was the major predictor of whether friendships would be formed. In the second year, room-mates became friends much more often than would have been predicted on the basis of similarity.

Conclusion: Familiarity may be more important than similarity in determining whether a friendship is formed.

Kerckhoff and Davis (1962) suggested that similarity may be more important in the early stages of a developing relationship, with complementarity becoming more important as relationships become better established; we will be returning to their theory later in the chapter. However, Winch (1958) suggested that perceived **complementarity** is also a factor in initial attraction; we may be attracted to someone because they seem to have qualities which we feel we lack. Rodin (1978) pointed out that this will only be the case if we value these perceived qualities.

It has also been suggested that what seems on the surface to be a partnership of opposites can at a deeper level indicate a similarity in the ways in which the couple view the world. Let us take for example a marriage in which both husband and wife take very sex-typed roles, e.g. dominant/submissive; decision-maker/decision-accepter. On the surface, the partners in the relationship are very dissimilar; however, at a deeper level, they share a common belief that there are 'appropriate' masculine and feminine roles.

Competence

Another factor which influences how we respond to others is their perceived competence:

Box H: Aronson *et al.* (1966)

Procedure: Participants were played a tape recording of a Quizbowl, a televised competition similar to University Challenge. Some contestants were 'superior', answering 92% of difficult questions correctly. Participants were also told that the contestant was the editor of the college yearbook, a member of the athletics team and so on. Others were 'average', answering 30% of the questions correctly. The other information given indicated a lower degree of competence in other areas, e.g. they were a proofreader on the college yearbook. Half the contestants in each condition were heard to spill coffee during the recording.

Participants were asked to rate how much they liked each contestant.

Results: 'Superior' contestants were preferred to 'average' contestants. 'Superior' contestants who spilled coffee were preferred to those who did not. 'Average' contestants who spilled coffee were liked least.

Conclusion: People who are competent are liked more, and liking is increased if they are also fallible and capable of making mistakes. If people seem to be too perfect, liking for them is decreased.

The influence of fallibility could relate to similarity. If we consider ourselves to be generally competent, a competent person who also makes mistakes may be seen as being more similar to ourselves than one who does not. Someone who is not competent and also clumsy may be seen as less like us, and this could be why we feel less positively towards them.

Aronson also made a link with **self-esteem**. Another study (Helmreich *et al.* 1970) found that a preference for coffee-spilling 'superior' contestants was true only for those of average self-esteem; this kind of contestant was liked less by those with very high or very low self-esteem. This suggests that it is relative competence, compared with our perception of our own competence, which is related to attraction.

❺ **Personal characteristics** in the formation of relationships include physical attractiveness, similarity and complementarity, and competence.

❺ **Physical attractiveness** can be important in the formation of relationships; its importance is related to gender. The **matching hypothesis** suggests that we tend to like people who are of similar attractiveness to ourselves. The **interpretation** and **methodology** of research in this area has been criticised.

❺ A lot of research has established that **similarity** is important in establishing a relationship. However, it is possible that familiarity is more important. **Complementarity** may also be important if another person has qualities we do not have ourselves, but which we value.

❺ We tend to like people who are **competent**, especially when they show they can also be **fallible**.

9.4 THEORIES RELATING TO THE FORMATION OF RELATIONSHIPS

We do not necessarily form a relationship with everybody to whom we are attracted. This section looks at theories which seek to explain the processes of proceeding from initial attraction to forming a relationship.

There are several theories which provide a framework to explain the underlying factors which influence the formation of relationships. We will look here at the role of reinforcement, sociobiological ideas, and stage and filter theories.

Reinforcement/affect theory

Reinforcement is a central concept in operant conditioning. We associate behaviour with its consequences; if the consequences are positive, the behaviour is likely to be repeated. Byrne and Clore (1970) applied this general principle in explaining the formation of relationships. We tend to like people whose behaviour is rewarding to us:

▶ **Activity 5: rewards in the formation of relationships**

What kinds of behaviours might be thought of as rewards in the context of relationship formation? You may find it useful to think back to the start of a current relationship and identify aspects of the other person's behaviour which could be seen in this way.

When you have finished, see the notes on page 239.

One major limitation of this theory is that it cannot really be used to predict who will form relationships with whom; it is very difficult to assess what will be rewarding to different people in different situations.

It also rests on a basically circular argument: Why do people form relationships? Because relationships bring rewards. How do we know these things constitute rewards? Because people engage in relationships to get them.

This kind of theory also neglects gender and cultural differences. Lott (1994) suggested that in many cultures, women are socialised into being more concerned with the needs of their partner than their own needs. This may also be relevant at a subcultural level: Hays (1985) found that in student friendships, as much value was attached to giving as to receiving rewards.

Sociobiological theory

Sociobiological or evolutionary explanations of relationship formation suggest that the basis of evolution, producing viable offspring, leads to differences in mate choice for men and for women.

The reproductive possibilities are fewer for women than for men; a woman is limited in the number of children she can produce. It therefore makes sense for her to be selective in her choice of sexual partner, in terms of finding a mate who has sufficient resources to maximise the chances of the few offspring she is capable of producing reaching maturity, and being able to mate themselves. The limits on a woman's reproductive potential mean that there is no advantage to her in having more than one sexual partner.

A man, on the other hand, can theoretically produce many more offspring. His chances of reproductive success will be increased if he chooses to mate with young and healthy women. In addition, promiscuity might serve him well, since the more sexual partners he has, the more likely he is to produce viable offspring.

Evolutionary theory is discussed in chapters 20 and 22; this aspect of it is considered in rather more detail at the start of chapter 22. Its implications in relation to jealousy have been investigated by Buss:

Box 1: Buss (1992)

Procedure: Both men and women were asked if they would be more jealous if their partner had sex with someone else, or if they formed a deep emotional attachment to another person.

Results: Of the men, 60% said they would be more jealous of their partner's sexual infidelity. Of the women, 85% said that they would be more jealous if their partner formed a deep emotional attachment to someone else. These subjective responses were supported by physiological measures, such as heart rate and GSR.

Conclusion: If a man invests resources in a woman, he would need to be sure that any children were his, and is therefore more likely to be jealous of sexual infidelity, which would make this uncertain. A woman would want commitment from her partner to help to ensure that any children produced would survive to maturity. A deep emotional attachment to another person would be more of a threat to this than sexual infidelity.

One problem with sociobiological theory is that it is not falsifiable. It is very good at explaining observations after the event, but less good at prediction. For example, male promiscuity can be explained by the evolutionary imperative of maximising reproductive chances. At the same time, male monogamy can be explained by two-parent care being adaptive in improving the viability of children.

A further criticism is the reliance on animal studies; there is no place for historical and cultural factors in its account of relationships.

Kitzinger and Coyle (1995) also pointed out that it fails to account for homosexual relationships, which we will be looking at towards the end of this chapter. While this is not in itself a criticism of the theory, it does limit its usefulness in explaining relationships.

Sociobiological theory remains highly contentious, not least because it could be seen as serving patriarchal ideas of male sexual freedom and the control of women.

Stage and filter theories

These theories see the development of relationships as passing through a series of stages. As such, their area of interest extends beyond the formation of relationships, but they nonetheless have something to contribute in this area.

Kerckhoff and Davis (1962) saw the formation and development of relationships in terms of stages which progressively filter people out, and so narrow down our choices. The first and second filters are relevant to the formation of relationships:

Figure 3: the filter theory of Kerckhoff and Davis (1962)

first filter: demographic similarity (e.g. similarity of race, religion, and social class)
second filter: similarity of psychological characteristics (e.g. similarity of values)
third filter: complementarity of emotional needs

Kerckhoff and Davis based their theory on a comparison of couples who had been in a relationship less than 18 months and those whose relationship was of longer standing. The first filter determines the potential friends and partners we are likely to meet. Social factors such as similarity of religion narrow what Kerckhoff (1974) has called the 'field of availables'. Kerckhoff and Davis found that the second filter was the factor most closely associated with the relationship becoming stronger, while the third filter was most closely associated with it developing into a long-term commitment; this was found to be more important for couples who had been together for more than 18 months.

Murstein (1976) also put forward a stage theory of relationships:

Figure 4: the stimulus–value–role (SVR) theory (Murstein, 1976)

stimulus stage: couples are firstly influenced by physical attributes, e.g. looks
value stage: the match between their values and attitudes becomes important
role stage: couples are concerned whether their performances of the roles they have in their partnership complement each other, and so make for a satisfactory relationship

The factors which come to the fore at each stage have some influence throughout the relationship; they will be more or less significant depending on the stage which the relationship has reached.

As with the filter theory of Kerckhoff and Davis, the 'value' stage of relationship formation focuses on similarity. This is again reflected in the last stage theory we will look at, the processes in the development of relationships outlined by Lewis (1972). The first stage combines the first two filters of the Kerckhoff and Davis model:

Figure 5: processes in the development of relationships (Lewis, 1972)

1. *perceiving similarities:* sociocultural, values and interests
2. *achieving pair rapport:* deep liking develops; there is greater ease of communication and satisfaction with the relationship.
3. *inducing self-disclosure:* the process of 'falling in love', which leads to a degree of intimacy beyond 'liking'. Increasingly more personal and private matters are shared and discussed.
4. *role-taking (empathy):* those who show greatest role accuracy, based on self-disclosure and observation of the other person, make greater progress towards a dyadic relationship.
5. *achieving interpersonal role-fit:* observed personal similarity; complementarity of roles and needs (compare Murstein's role stage and the third filter of Kerckhoff and Davis)
6. *achieving dyadic crystallisation:* the life of the individual becomes more and more entwined with that of their partner; the relationship becomes more committed. At the same time, boundaries are established, i.e. areas which are 'me', not 'us'.

This theory breaks down the stages of the development of a relationship in rather more detail than the other stage theories we have looked at. It also has the advantage of linking both feelings and thoughts with the development of a relationship.

As with the other stage theories we have looked at, it is only the early stages which offer ideas which are relevant to the formation of relationships. However, the later stages in all these theories suggest factors – in particular, the linking of disclosure, intimacy and empathy in Lewis's model – which may be important in the maintenance of relationships, which we will be looking at in the next section.

- ☻ **Reinforcement/affect** theory explains the formation of relationships in terms of the rewards offered by a potential friend or partner. However, this theory is limited in its ability to predict who will form relationships with whom, and its reasoning is somewhat circular.
- ☻ **Sociobiological theory** uses evolutionary principles to explain the differences between men and women in selecting a partner. However, it has been widely criticised.
- ☻ In **stage** and **filter theories**, the early stages in the development of a relationship suggest factors which lead to relationship formation. The later stages are more relevant to the maintenance of relationships.

9.5 THE MAINTENANCE OF RELATIONSHIPS

Theories of attraction and the formation of relationships can be seen as distinct from maintenance theories, which are concerned with reasons why people who have established a relationship choose whether to remain in that relationship or not. Economic theories, which are all a refinement of reinforcement/affect theory (discussed in the previous section), have been influential in this area. This group of theories has looked at four different factors related to rewards and costs: outcome, alternatives, investment and fairness.

Economic theories

The **social exchange theory** proposed by Thibaut and Kelley (1959) suggests that whether or not a

relationship is maintained depends on the benefits that a relationship offers, and the costs it involves. The benefits include such things as stimulation, love and emotional support, money and so on. In terms of costs, it takes time and effort to establish and maintain relationships and they may involve providing financial support. If for both partners in a relationship the benefits outweigh the costs, the relationship is likely to be maintained.

An important aspect of this theory is comparison of a relationship both with what you expect from a relationship (**comparison level or CL**) and with what alternative relationships might have to offer (**comparison level for alternatives or CL alt**). Relationships are seen as dynamic, in that making comparisons is a continuous process. It is possible that what you or your partner expect from a relationship, i.e. the CL, might change, perhaps because other people seem to be getting more from their relationships than you. Your CL alt may change if you meet someone who seems to have a lot to offer.

Equity theory is a modification of exchange theory, in that it focuses on what people see as fair (i.e. equitable) in a relationship. Walster *et al.* (1978) suggested that we try to establish equity between the outcomes for both people in a relationship in terms of the effort each puts in. If both people receive the same outcome, but one has put in more effort, the relationship is seen as inequitable. On the other hand, if one person has put in less effort, but also receives a lower outcome, the relationship may be seen as equitable.

Economic theories such as these see relationships as being based on self-interest. However, while some relationships may be maintained on the basis of balancing costs and benefits, not all relationships are like this, as we shall see in the next section.

Communal and exchange relationships

Economic theories apply to exchange relationships which weigh up the costs and benefits involved. Mills and Clark (1982) have distinguished between these kinds of relationships and communal relationships, which are more altruistic and are more concerned with the needs of the other person than is the case in exchange relationships.

The differences between these two kinds of relationships can be seen early on. Kerckhoff and Davis (1962) found that disclosure in an exchange relationship was on a reciprocal basis; disclosure from one person was likely to be 'repaid' by disclosure from the other. On the other hand, in communal relationships, a partner will disclose freely without expecting anything in return.

Once a communal relationship is established, it can be characterised by the giving of gifts, in its broadest sense, without expecting gifts to be given in return. Indeed, Mills and Clark (1979) found that in communal relationships, 'exchange' acts could be seen as negative; for example, if a person felt they had to repay a close friend for a favour.

At the same time, costs and benefits can still be relevant. Imagine you have a friend who always turns to you for help, never gets in touch unless they need something from you, and is not available to help you when you need it. The benefits of the relationship are all on their side, and the costs on yours. It is unlikely in these circumstances that your relationship will be maintained.

The broad distinction between exchange and communal relationships has been shown experimentally:

Box J: Clark (1984)

Procedure: Participants were pairs of friends or strangers. They were given a matrix of numbers (rather like a wordsearch) and asked to take it in turns to look for specific sequences. A reward was offered for completing this task, which they could divide up as they wished. Two pens, a red and a black, were provided.
Results: Pairs of friends were more likely to use the same pen, while strangers were more likely to use different pens.
Conclusion: The relationship between strangers was an exchange one. Different pens were used so that the contribution each person had made to the task could be assessed and the reward divided fairly. Friends had a communal relationship, where fairness in dividing up the reward was not an issue, so different pens were not necessary.

Strategies in maintaining a relationship

In any relationship, problems are likely to arise. Research has tried to identify the strategies people use to overcome these problems and so maintain the relationship.

Research has identified some of the maintenance and repair strategies couples use:

Box K: Dindia and Baxter (1987)

Procedure: A sample of 50 married couples was interviewed about the maintenance strategies they used to keep a relationship going and to deal with problems.
Results: A total of 49 different strategies were identified. Maintenance strategies focused on doing things together and interacting, such as spending time together with friends and talking about their day. Repair strategies tended to focus on the relationship itself, such as by talking about the problem, or one partner giving the other an ultimatum.
Conclusion: Couples develop a range of strategies to maintain and repair a relationship.

Activity 6: long- and short-term relationships

Dindia and Baxter also found that long-term relationships did not use as many maintenance strategies as more short-term ones.

Can you think of any reasons for this?

When you have finished, see the notes on page 239.

Ayres (1983) has pointed out that people are not necessarily concerned just with maintaining their relationship. While some may wish to maintain a relationship at its current level, some may want it to develop further, and some to reduce it. These different aims are associated with different strategies:

Figure 6: aims and strategies within relationships

avoidance strategies: strategies such as avoiding talking about the relationship are used by a person who wishes it to remain at its current level when faced with a partner who wishes it to develop further.
balance strategies: increasing effort is put into the relationship by a partner who wishes it to develop further; less effort is put into it by a partner who wishes to reduce its intensity.
directness strategies: strategies such as talking about the relationship are usually used by people who wish a relationship to be maintained at its current level.

- **Social exchange theory** sees relationships as being assessed in terms of **costs** and **benefits**. A relationship is maintained if the benefits outweigh the costs for both partners. We **compare** a relationship with our **expectations** of it, and with possible **alternative relationships**.
- **Equity theory** extends this to focus on what is seen as **fair** in terms of effort and outcome.
- These theories are less useful in explaining **communal** relationships.

- Couples use a range of **maintenance** and **repair strategies**, particularly in the early stages of a relationship.
- Different strategies are used depending on whether a person wishes the relationship to **develop**, to be **maintained** at its current level, or **reduce** its intensity.

9.6 THE DISSOLUTION OF RELATIONSHIPS

A close and intimate relationship brings both partners many benefits. For example, Cochrane (1996) found that people were considerably more likely to die when single than when married, with an even higher death rate for divorced people. Similarly, Cramer (1994) found that married people have lower rates of mental disorder than single people. Since marriage contributes to physical and mental health, it seems surprising that so many relationships come to an end. We will look here at some of the reasons for the dissolution of a relationship.

Duck (1992) has identified several demographic factors which are linked to the likelihood of a relationship breaking down:

Figure 7: factors associated with the dissolution of a relationship (Duck, 1992)

a. marriages in which the partners are very young
b. early parenthood
c. being in a lower socioeconomic group
d. poor education
e. partners are of different race or religion
f. one or both partners have parents who themselves divorced
g. a greater number of sexual partners before marriage

Activity 7: making sense of Duck's factors

Think about the factors listed in figure 7. Why do you think each may make it more likely that a relationship will end?

When you have finished, see the notes on page 239.

These factors cannot be seen as direct causes of relationship breakdown, but rather as associated factors. However, several interpersonal factors which may lead to the dissolution of a relationship have been identified:

Figure 8: some interpersonal reasons for relationship breakdown (from Baron and Byrne, 1997)

a. People may think they agree more than they do. There may be conflict if this emerges when problems arise.
b. Differences in the way people interact, e.g. the extent to which they are able to express their feelings may cause tensions in a relationship.
c. Jealousy (see box I).
d. People may change their attitudes or values. This is a particular problem when this change involves something which is very important to the other person, e.g. politics or religion.
e. The relationship may become routine and boring. Even if only one person becomes bored, the couple will then develop differing goals, leading to possible relationship breakdown.
f. Lack of sexual satisfaction.

Rusbult and Zembrodt (1983) have described four possible reactions to problems in a relationship which are linked to the likelihood of the relationship breaking down. These vary along two dimensions: destructive–constructive and active–passive. Different combinations lead to different strategies:

Figure 9: reactions to problems in a relationship (Rusbult and Zembrodt, 1983)

	destructive	
active	EXIT	NEGLECT
	VOICE	LOYALTY	passive
	constructive	

According to Rusbult (1987), deciding which strategy to use depends on the degree of satisfaction experienced in the relationship. Satisfied people tend to use the constructive strategies of **voice**, i.e. talking about their concerns, and discussing how problems might be overcome, or **loyalty**, i.e. waiting for an improvement. Those who are dissatisfied use the destructive strategies of **exit**, i.e. ending the relationship, or **neglect**, i.e. waiting for the inevitable break-up. 'Exit' and 'neglect' are strategies associated with the breakdown of the relationship.

There are gender differences in which strategies are used. Rusbult *et al.* (1986) found that women are more likely than men to choose 'voice' and 'loyalty', perhaps because they have more at stake in maintaining the relationship. Other factors may also influence the choice of options:

Box L: Yovetich and Rusbult (1994)

Procedure: Students were asked to role-play likely responses to problems, e.g. 'I'd be better off without you!'. The amount of time they were given to consider their responses varied from less than 10 seconds up to 30 seconds.
Results: Those who had more time to think about their response were more likely to use constructive options.
Conclusion: Spontaneous reactions can be destructive to a relationship. Giving yourself time to consider how to respond is more likely to lead to a constructive response to problems.

Strategies in conflict resolution have also been linked to attribution theory. **Attribution theory** looks at the way we assess the causes of behaviour. For example, we may make an **internal** attribution (the person behaves that way because of personal characteristics) or an **external** attribution (the person behaves that way because of the situation). We may also make a **global** attribution (this is the way the person behaves across different situations) or a **specific** attribution (this is the way the person behaves in this kind of situation). Finally, we may make a **stable** attribution (the person always behaves in this way) or an **unstable** attribution (this is unlike the person's usual behaviour).

Bradbury and Fincham (1990) suggested that couples have different attributional patterns. Satisfied couples use what Bradbury and Fincham call a **relationship-enhancing** pattern, while dissatisfied couples use a **distress-maintaining** pattern:

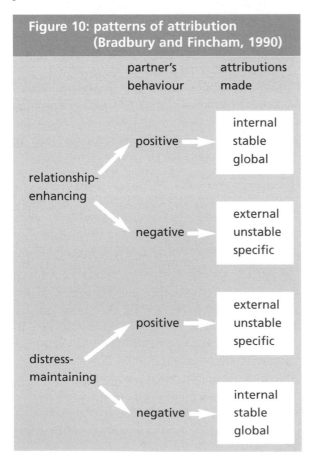

Figure 10: patterns of attribution (Bradbury and Fincham, 1990)

partner's behaviour	attributions made
relationship-enhancing → positive	internal stable global
relationship-enhancing → negative	external unstable specific
distress-maintaining → positive	external unstable specific
distress-maintaining → negative	internal stable global

Activity 8: applying attributions

1 Elaine's partner brings her flowers. What attributions might she make using **a** a relationship-enhancing and **b** a distress-maintaining pattern of attribution?

2 Kate's partner starts shouting at her. What attributions might she make using **a** a relationship-enhancing and **b** a distress-maintaining pattern of attribution?

In each case you will need to use all three dimensions, i.e. internal vs. external, stable vs. unstable and global vs. specific.

When you have finished, see the notes on page 239.

It is worth noting that relationship-enhancing and distress-maintaining attributional styles correspond to the attributional styles used respectively by non-depressed and depressed people when explaining their successes and failures. You can read more about attribution theory in chapter 8.

Stages of breakdown of a relationship

Relationships do not break down overnight; breakdown is a process which happens in stages. Duck (1982) suggested that there are four phases:

Figure 11: stages of relationship breakdown (Duck, 1982)

a. *intra-psychic phase:* one of the partners decides that they can not stand the relationship any more. They start thinking about negative aspects of the relationship, the costs of withdrawal and the possible positive aspects of an alternative relationship. It is called 'intra-psychic' because these thoughts are in the individual's head and not yet shared with their partner.

b. *dyadic phase:* the individual considers they would be justified in withdrawing from the relationship, and involves the other partner. Negotiations and attempts to repair the relationship take place, and the costs of ending the relationship are assessed.

c. *social phase:* the dissatisfied partner decides that they want the relationship to end. The social implications of ending the relationship are considered, and the state of the relationship is made known and discussed among the couple's social circle. Family and friends may be asked to try to help repair the relationship.

d. *grave-dressing phase:* The end of the relationship is inevitable. Others are made aware of each person's version of events, as part of getting over the relationship breakdown.

Lee (1984) suggested that there are five stages:

Figure 12: stages of relationship breakdown (Lee, 1984)

a. *Dissatisfaction* is experienced.
b. There is *exposure* of this dissatisfaction.
c. *Negotiation* about the dissatisfaction takes place.
d. Attempts at *resolution* are made.
e. Finally there is *termination* when the relationship breaks down.

Lee has also investigated the experiences of people passing through these stages of relationship breakdown:

Box M: Lee (1984)

Procedure: A survey was carried out of the experiences of 112 couples experiencing premarital breakdown.

Results: Exposure and negotiation were the most intense and emotionally exhausting stages. Couples who moved straight from dissatisfaction to termination experienced reduced post-relationship intimacy with their partner. Where the passage through the stages was long and drawn-out, couples reported feeling more attracted to their partner, but also increased fear and

loneliness during the stages of negotiation and resolution.

Conclusion: There is considerable variation in how relationship breakdown is experienced depending on how the different stages are negotiated.

The first two stages of relationship breakdown are identical in the models proposed by Duck and by Lee. Duck's third and fourth stages then go on to consider the wider social context within which the breakdown takes place, while Lee's remaining stages focus only on the couple whose relationship is breaking down. This difference reflects the focus of Lee's model exclusively on *premarital* relationships. Both these models could be useful to relationship counsellors in assessing which stage in a relationship crisis clients have reached, and so how best to help them.

More recently, Femlee (1995) has put forward what she calls the **fatal attraction model of relationship breakdown**. She suggested that the characteristics which attract us to a particular partner in the first place may be the very characteristics which lead to a breakdown in the relationship. Someone who is initially seen as 'exciting', for example, may later be seen as 'unpredictable', while someone who is seen as 'caring' may later be seen as 'clinging'.

- Some **demographic characteristics** of couples whose relationship is likely to end in breakdown have been identified, together with a range of possible **causes**.
- The choice of **strategies** used to respond to the situation when a person is dissatisfied with a relationship can be linked to the likelihood of the relationship breaking down.
- There is a link between the **patterns of attribution** used to explain a partner's behaviour and the probability of relationship breakdown.
- Theorists have described the **stages** through which a couple passes as a relationship breaks down.

9.7 PSYCHOLOGICAL EXPLANATIONS OF LOVE

What is love? Reber suggested that psychologists would have been 'wise to have abdicated responsibility for this term and left it to the poets.' (1985, p409). However, psychologists have had some interesting ideas to put forward in this area.

Rubin (1973) made a distinction between liking and loving. When we like someone, we feel positively about them, with affection and respect. He saw loving as completely different, and made up of attachment, caring and intimacy. **Attachment** refers to the need to be with the person we love, and the feelings of loss when this is not possible. **Caring** refers to the concern and responsibility we feel for the other person's welfare. **Intimacy** refers to the emotional closeness we feel for someone with whom we are able to share our innermost thoughts and feelings.

Rubin has developed a scale to measure these components of love:

Figure 13: sample items from Rubin's Love Scale

a. I am very concerned about ....
b. I feel very close to ....
c. If I could never be with .... I would be miserable.
d. I would do anything .... asked me to do.
e. If .... were feeling bad, my first duty would be to cheer him/her up.
f. I need to be with ....
g. I feel that I can confide in .... about virtually everything.

▶ Activity 9: identifying Rubin's components of love

Match each of the sample items in figure 13 with either:
    attachment   caring   intimacy
When you have finished, see the notes on page 240.

Rubin found that lovers tended to give very similar (although not identical) responses to items on this scale. In addition, people who score high on this scale are more likely to expect the relationship to become permanent.

There are differences in love between men and women. Rubin and McNeil (1983) found that men channel attachment, caring and intimacy into a single relationship with one person, whereas women may experience these feelings across a wider range of relationships.

Sternberg (1986) has suggested that there are different kinds of love, typified by the presence or absence of three basic components: **intimacy**, **passion** and **commitment**, which can be represented graphically as sides of a triangle, the area of which represents the amount of love:

Figure 14: Sternberg's triangular theory of love

Different combinations of the three components lead to different kinds of love. For example, romantic love has high passion and intimacy, but is low in commitment, while companionate love has high commitment and intimacy, but low passion. He suggested a third kind of love which is high in all three components, consummate love, which is the most satisfying as it fulfils more needs.

He goes on to suggest that intimacy alone leads to liking, passion alone leads to infatuation, and commitment alone leads to what he describes as 'empty' love. Where there is passion and commitment but little intimacy, he suggests we have 'fatuous' love, the kind of love associated with a whirlwind romance.

This kind of geometric representation allows different kinds of love to be represented visually, e.g.:

Figure 15: representations of variations in the components of love

high commitment/intimacy low passion – a representation of the kind of love experienced by a couple who have been together for several years

high passion/commitment low intimacy – a representation of 'fatuous' love

It also allows us to make comparisons of the shape and size of the triangles for two partners in a relationship. They might match fairly closely, so that the two show roughly equal amounts of the same components. They might also be the same general shape, but differ in size because one partner has less passion, commitment and intimacy than the other, and so brings less love to the relationship.

Sternberg suggested that the satisfaction that two partners find in the relationship ought to be based on the amount of overlap between the triangles, and a study by Sternberg and Barnes (1985) has supported this idea.

Schneider (1988) believed Sternberg's theory to be more a way of representing aspects of love than a theory. However, at the same time he pointed out that it is valuable in orienting us to asking all kinds of questions about relationships. For example, is there a particular shape that is 'best', in terms of leading to more satisfying relationships? How do the shapes of love triangles alter during the course of a relationship? Do homosexual and heterosexual relationships differ in the relative importance of the components? Can we predict the success of a relationship by knowing the shapes of the partners' triangles early in the relationship?

Hendrick *et al.* (1988) have suggested that there are different kinds of romantic love. They use terms taken from ancient Greek ideas about types of love and love-related emotions:

Figure 16: six styles of love (Hendrick *et al.*, 1988)

1. game-playing love *(ludus)*: playful love, without strong commitment or jealousy
2. possessive love *(mania):* love with a strong physical component but little commitment
3. logical love *(pragma):* a rational choice of love partner, with an emphasis on what they can offer
4. altruistic love *(agape):* selfless caring
5. companionate love *(storge):* friendship type of love, with little passion
6. erotic love *(eros):* a strong element of physical passion

However, it is open to question whether the six styles of love proposed by Hendrick *et al.* offer any more than Sternberg's theory:

▶ Activity 10: comparing Sternberg and Hendrick *et al.*

Can Sternberg's three components of love – commitment, intimacy and passion – be used to describe the six styles of love suggested by Hendrick *et al.*?

When you have finished, see the notes on page 240.

However, Levy and Davis (1988) found a link between the love styles identified by Hendrick *et al.* and attachment styles, mentioned at the start of this chapter: ludus-style lovers tend to be anxious-avoidant, mania-style lovers tend to be anxious-ambivalent, and both agape- and eros-style lovers tend to be securely attached. This suggests that both attachment styles and love styles are based on deep underlying psychological differences.

⊜ Rubin conceptualised love as **attachment**, **intimacy** and **caring**. He devised a **scale** to measure love.

⊜ The **triangular theory of love** proposed by Sternberg describes love in terms of different combinations of **commitment**, **intimacy** and **passion**. This theory allows comparisons to be made between partners in a relationship, and offers a potential tool for future research.

⊜ Hendrick *et al.* suggested that there are **six kinds of love**. Links can be made with **attachment theory**.

9.8 CULTURAL AND SUBCULTURAL DIFFERENCES IN RELATIONSHIPS

At the start of this chapter, we noted that much of the research into the nature of relationships, how they are formed and maintained, and how they break down, has tended to focus on heterosexual relationships in Western cultures. In this last section we will broaden this focus to look at relationships which do not fall within this category.

Individualist and collectivist cultures

In recent years, cross-cultural psychologists have tried to establish broad distinctions between different kinds of culture which can help to explain the differences in behaviour of people living within different societies. Hsu (1971) has drawn a major distinction between individualist and collectivist cultures.

In **individualist** cultures, the emphasis is on the goals and needs of the individual, and the importance of personal choice. Priority is given to personal achievement and self-reliance. This is the typical pattern of Western cultures, of which the USA is a good example.

In contrast, in **collectivist** cultures, the emphasis is on the goals and needs of the social group, and the duties of the individual towards the group to which they belong. Priority is given to the welfare and the unity of the group. This is more typical of non-Western cultures, of which mainland China is a good example.

Moghaddam *et al.* (1993) have built on this distinction to suggest that Western relationships are dominated by different concerns from non-Western relationships:

Figure 17: Moghaddam et al. (1993)

Western relationships are characterised by being:

voluntary: individuals select their own partners

individualistic: the partnership is the concern of the two people involved

temporary: the partnership lasts until either partner wishes to finish it

Eastern relationships are characterised by being:

involuntary: individuals do not select their own partners

communal: the partnership is the concern of the wider community

permanent: the partnership is seen as being 'for ever'

SHE SAYS SHE WANTS AN ARRANGED MARRIAGE....

The distinction between individualist and collectivist cultures has been found useful in providing a general point of comparison in investigating cross-cultural variation in personal relationships. Cross-cultural research of this kind also allows us to examine theories of relationships to establish whether what they have to say applies universally, or whether they are the result of particular cultural or historical conditions. For example, it has been suggested by Berman *et al.* (1985) that the principles of exchange which operate in the early part of a relationship, in which the couple offer each other similar-sized rewards, appear to apply less well in collectivist cultures, where the emphasis is more on meeting the needs of the other person.

There are both benefits and costs for the individual within each kind of culture. In an individualist culture, people have more personal freedom, but they are more likely to suffer from loneliness and are at greater risk of divorce. In a collectivist culture, social support is provided by the extended family, and loneliness and divorce are less likely. At the same time, however, personal freedom is more limited, and there is a greater risk of more powerful members of the group controlling those who are less powerful.

This distinction between types of culture is reflected in the criteria which are seen to be important in selecting a partner. Dion and Dion (1988) found that people from individualist societies tended to stress the importance of personality compatibility in choosing a mate. Those from collectivist cultures were more likely to mention socially valued characteristics, such as financial resources and social status. Hofstede (1980) has pointed out that these priorities expressed by members of collectivist cultures are logical, given that young people in these cultures may have very limited economic freedom. Economic interdependency with their family or small social group makes these factors important, particularly when – as in many collectivist cultures – material resources are scarce.

In Western individualist cultures, romantic love is seen as the basis for marriage, with each individual making their own choice of life partner. However, the passionate love popularly shown in Hollywood movies is very much a Western, individualistic concept. While India – a collectivist culture – also has a thriving film industry portraying

this kind of love, it does not correspond to what happens in real life. Marriage within collectivist cultures is often arranged. The term 'arranged marriage' may be associated in Western cultures with unwilling teenage girls being forced into marriage with someone they have never met. There are extreme cases where this does happen, but generally the stereotype presents a far from accurate picture. In practice, families often select possible partners for their children, from among those with a similar social background, with the individual making a choice from among these possibilities. Romantic love, however, is not seen as a prerequisite for marriage.

▶ Activity 11: Sternberg's components of love revisited

Look back to figure 14 showing Sternberg's three components of love. Which component is the basis for **a** marriage in a Western individualist culture and **b** an arranged marriage in a collectivist culture?

When you have finished, see the notes on page 240.

The basis for marriage is in general different for these two kinds of culture, but in a good relationship, the other components will also develop within marriage. In an arranged marriage, it is assumed that love will develop after a couple has married, and there is some evidence that this is what happens:

Box N: Gupta and Singh (1992)

Procedure: A sample of 50 couples in Jaipur in India, some in arranged marriages and some in love marriages, completed Rubin's love scale at various points of time after their marriage.

Results: Those in arranged marriages felt less love at the start of their marriage than those who had married for love. However, this love increased over the first five years of marriage, and was maintained at this new high level ✍

over the following five years. For those in love marriages, the degree of love started at a higher level and was maintained over the first five years, but by ten years had fallen well below the level experienced by those in arranged marriages.

Conclusion: Love is likely to develop and be maintained in arranged marriages, but is likely to decrease after an initial period in love marriages.

▷ Activity 12: explaining contentment in arranged marriages

What reasons might there be for people in arranged marriages finding such satisfaction in their relationship with their partner? The earlier section of this chapter which discusses factors leading to the maintenance of relationships may help to give you some ideas. You will also need to think about the nature of collectivist cultures, discussed at the start of this section.

When you have finished, see the notes on page 240.

At the same time, there are some limitations to the study carried out by Gupta and Singh. Since this was a natural experiment, it is likely that the two sets of couples differed systematically in ways other than the type of marriage they had made. In addition, it is more than likely that those marrying for love were in relationships which were, at the time of marriage, substantially more developed than those of couples whose marriages were arranged. It is possible that the lack of an increase in love after marriage in the love marriages simply reflects the greater maturity of these relationships compared to the love marriages.

The individualist/collectivist distinction is not without its problems, and is not really as clear-cut as might be supposed. Let us take the issue of the choice of partner as an example. As we have seen, in the arranged marriage system common in collectivist cultures, there is often quite a large element of choice, even though the choice is

restricted. At the same time, it is questionable whether people within an individualistic Western culture have a completely free choice, with no influence from outside pressures.

Another issue is what happens when people change cultures, for example Asians coming to live in Britain. According to Goodwin (1995), it is not unusual for immigrants to fall into two groups: those who wish to maintain traditional values, which stress the role of the family and community in the selection of a partner, and those who adopt the values of their new society, where there is more freedom of choice. However, Hanassab and Tidwell (1989) claimed that whichever stance is taken, there are likely to be problems, with individuals feeling torn between the two competing cultural traditions.

It should also be remembered that societies change, sometimes slowly but often dramatically, affecting the values and traditions of people living in those societies, and often giving rise to tensions:

Box O: Goodwin (1995)

Procedure: Research into relationships was carried out in Russia, after the fall of the Communist regime. People of different ages and backgrounds were interviewed.

Results: Individualistic relationship values were found among the young and affluent. More collectivist values were found among older people and among manual workers. The speed with which new individualistic values were being adopted was seen as causing problems between different sections of society.

Conclusion: Times of change may bring about a shift in values, including attitudes towards relationships. Rapid change in particular can lead to tensions within a society.

While there appears to be a general trend towards individualism and Western values, there are also cultures where religious values have brought about changes which have reversed this trend and promoted a move towards collectivist values – for example, Iran (Tashakkori and Thompson, 1991). With the growth of fundamentalist Islam in many countries, this trend looks set to continue.

While the individualist/collectivist distinction is a useful way of illustrating ways in which personal relationships vary across different cultures, research in this area is still very much in its infancy. There are several areas which would repay further research and provide a much more detailed picture of the link between culture and patterns of relationships. The effect of societal change on relationship patterns, how culture affects different subgroups, and how individuals and subgroups within a culture may express views which go against broader cultural norms are all topics for future research to investigate.

● **Individualist** and **collectivist** cultures differ in their values and priorities. These differences are reflected in their patterns of relationships. Both kinds of culture have advantages and limitations for the individual.

● While individualist cultures tend to see love as a prerequisite for marriage, collectivist cultures expect love to develop within marriage. There is some evidence that this is the case.

● While the distinction between individualist and collectivist cultures is useful, it is not clear-cut. Interesting questions arise as to what happens when people change cultures, or when the culture itself changes.

Gay and lesbian relationships

While there has been quite a lot of research into gay and lesbian relationships over the past twenty-five years, early work in this area did little more than provide descriptive accounts of the lives and sexual preferences of gays and lesbians. Indeed, according to Kitzinger and Coyle (1995), until the mid-1970s, most research into homosexual relationships saw homosexuality as pathological and these relationships as being of no value. Since it was only in 1973 that homosexuality was removed from DSM (the Diagnostic and Statistical Manual of Mental Disorders) as a category of disorder, this is hardly surprising. This attitude has

by no means disappeared; in a speech at the Conservative Party Conference on 8 October 2000, Shadow Home Secretary Ann Widdecombe asserted that homosexual relationships do not have equal validity with heterosexual relationships, a view which she presumably believed would find resonance both with party members and the wider public.

Although there is still a long way to go before we understand gay and lesbian relationships in the same depth as heterosexual relationships, recent years have seen a growth in gay and lesbian studies within what Kitzinger (1987) calls a 'liberal humanistic' framework. This has four over-lapping themes:

> **Figure 18: the liberal humanistic framework of research into gay and lesbian relationships (from Kitzinger, 1987)**
>
> a. There is a basic underlying similarity between homosexual and heterosexual people.
> b. Homosexuality is not seen as the central organising principle of personality; rather, the diversity of individual lesbians and gay men is recognised.
> c. Homosexuality is as natural, normal and healthy as heterosexuality.
> d. Lesbians and gay men do not pose a threat to children, the nuclear family or society.

While this approach is clearly an improvement on the earlier pathologising of homosexuality, at the same time it has also led to attempts to force homosexual relationships into patterns considered to be typical of heterosexuals, with the implication that deviation from these patterns is pathological.

There are of course similarities between gay and lesbian relationships and heterosexual relationships. For example, Peplau noted that homosexuals and heterosexuals experience 'a similar range of joys and problems' (1991, p182), and as with heterosexual relationships, gay and lesbian couples' relationships tend to last longer if the partners are from similar backgrounds. Similarly, Anthony said of the lesbian clients who came to her for counselling that they needed to 'struggle with the same issues as other people; that is, how to live self-actualising lives through gaining a strong sense of self-esteem, establishing and maintaining meaningful relationships, and pursuing satisfying work' (1982, p53).

However, there are also important differences:

▷ Activity 13: what are the differences?

Think about the differences between a gay or lesbian couple and a heterosexual couple. Make a list of your ideas.

When you have finished, see the notes on page 240.

As we will see, the many differences between homosexual and heterosexual couples highlighted in activity 13 all have implications for the nature of relationships between gay and lesbian couples. The implications for gay men and for lesbians also vary.

Because of these differences, traditional models of relationships which relate to heterosexuality may not be appropriate for gay and lesbian relationships. As Peplau (1991) pointed out, to try to apply them to these relationships may lead to questionable conclusions, and conceal useful information about how lesbian and gay couples organise their relationships.

As an example, think about how you might define a successful heterosexual relationship. One of your criteria is likely to be that the relationship is long-lasting. Huston and Schwartz (1995) noted that the 'lifetime marriage' model is not one accepted by homosexuals. They do not place the length of the relationship above other factors, but give rather more emphasis to satisfaction and happiness in measuring success.

Most of the research in this area takes the form of interviews. Before we look at what such research has to tell us, it should be noted that there are problems in trying to interview a representative sample of gays and lesbians. Interviews will exclude people who are not 'out',

they may under-represent people living in rural and isolated communities, and may also under-represent older couples who are less willing to talk about their private lives. Nonetheless, research has gone some way towards providing insight into the nature of gay and lesbian relationships.

Relationship formation

Since homosexual relationships are still not acceptable to a large proportion of the mainstream heterosexual population, a problem faced by gays and lesbians looking to start a relationship is identifying possible partners. There is, of course, a smaller pool of eligible partners than for heterosexuals.

There is a growing number of bars and other meeting places, mainly in cities, especially for gay men. According to Huston and Schwartz (1995), lesbians are more likely than gay men to be 'closeted', so these meeting places may be less useful for them. However, for both gays and lesbians living in rural or isolated areas, meeting potential partners may not be so easy.

Warren (1974) found that both lesbians and gays were more likely to meet potential partners through being introduced by mutual friends, though given the spread of organisations and meeting places for gays and lesbians over recent years, this may no longer be the case.

There are differences in the criteria used by gays and lesbians when choosing a partner. Right across the animal kingdom, males tend to be the aggressive sexual hunters and females the choosy customers. In evolutionary terms, these are adaptive differences, and are reflected in the typical early stages of gay and lesbian relationships. Wolf (1979) reported that lesbians are likely to seek emotional involvement before having sex with a partner; in contrast, Warren (1974) found that for gay men, sex tends to come first, with emotional involvement developing later. However, not all gay men are comfortable with the idea of casual sex. The appearance of AIDS has meant that casual sex is extremely problematical, and more recent research (e.g. Davidson, 1991) has found a growing number of partnership-oriented gay males.

Socialisation processes have also caused problems for lesbians in seeking to start a relationship. While in Western culture it is generally accepted that males will be sexually aggressive, females are encouraged rather to respond to the sexual advances of others. This may lead to neither woman interested in a potential relationship approaching the other. However, there is some suggestion in the research literature that some women adopt more assertive roles.

The characteristics gay men and lesbians look for in a partner also tend to differ:

Activity 14: looking for a partner

Find a 'lonely hearts' column which caters for gay men and lesbians as well as heterosexuals, for example the 'Guide' in *The Guardian* on Saturdays.

Carry out a brief content analysis of advertisements for gay and lesbian partners. Compare the frequency with which gay men and lesbians refer to

a physical characteristics

b financial resources and

c socioemotional characteristics.

Does a different pattern emerge for gay men and lesbians?

Davidson (1991) found that gay men tend to focus on the physical characteristics of potential partners: an attractive face, a good physique, and a well-groomed appearance. They also value the status symbols associated with manliness in our culture: a well-paid career and the material possessions associated with the good life.

In contrast, Huston and Schwartz (1995) suggested that lesbians are less likely to focus on physical characteristics and more likely to value socioemotional ones. Since many lesbians are involved in the women's movement, many lesbians also value emotional strength and self-sufficiency in a partner. Job status, however, is not as important to them as it is to gay men.

What many gay and lesbian young people cannot do, of course, is to court a potential partner openly.

To 'come out' as gay or lesbian is to expose oneself to the widespread homophobia of the mainly heterosexual peer group. It is even less likely that they will feel that they can confide in their parents. For these reasons, for many homosexual young people serious courtship is likely to start rather later than for heterosexuals; they may therefore have fewer relevant social skills, and less practice at judging who is right for them.

Relationship maintenance

Once a relationship is formed, there are several factors which contribute to its stability and the satisfaction the couple find within it:

Box P: factors in maintaining gay and lesbian relationships

Eldridge and Gilbert (1990): for lesbians, an equitable balance of power, a high level of emotional intimacy and high self-esteem all contribute to maintaining a relationship.

Jones and Bates (1978): for gay men, avoiding conflict, high appreciation of one's partner, stability and co-operation are all important.

Kurdek (1993): for both lesbians and gay men, frequently becoming involved in destructive arguments is negatively correlated with satisfaction.

A further study has examined the extent to which maintenance behaviours are similar to those used by heterosexual couples, and whether gays and lesbians use maintenance behaviours which apply more particularly to homosexual relationships:

Box Q: Haas and Stafford (1998)

Procedure: An open-ended survey approach was used to explore the maintenance behaviours of gay and lesbian couples.

Results: Although many of the maintenance behaviours were the same as those used by heterosexual couples, other behaviours emerged which were unique to gay and lesbian couples. These included: being 'out' ✎

as a couple to their social circle, and seeking 'out' gay/lesbian supportive environments to strengthen the relationship.

Conclusion: As well as the maintenance behaviours used by heterosexual couples, gay and lesbian couples use additional behaviours relating to their being a stigmatised group within mainstream heterosexual society.

However, although the support of the gay community can be a way of helping to maintain a relationship, this community may at the same time threaten relationships. For example, Blumstein and Schwartz (1983) found that lesbians who were heavily involved in their community were more likely to break up. They suggested this was the result of falling in love with other women also active in the community.

Communication is also a necessary part of maintaining a relationship. There is a lot of research suggesting that men and women tend to have different styles of communication. In general, women use conversation as a way of becoming intimate with another person, and are willing to play a supportive role to facilitate this. In contrast, men tend to play a dominant role. They often see conversation as a point-scoring competition which can help them assert their status.

It has been suggested that these differences arise as the result of men and women being socialised into different patterns of communication. An alternative suggestion is that the differences reflect the relative power of men and women. The communication style of men is the style of the privileged and dominant, so the differences between the communication styles of men and women are really differences between 'powerful' and 'less powerful' styles. Within heterosexual couples, the 'dominant–supportive' model of communication is to some extent preprogrammed, which is not the case in gay and lesbian couples.

The different communication styles of men and women underpin the way in which problems are solved and decisions made in gay and lesbian couples. For example, Tannen (1990) found that lesbian partners tend to avoid dominant conversational techniques, and to seek consensus. Gay men, on the other hand, tend to use dominant communication techniques – for example, interrupting and not seeking the other's opinion – to assert their own authority. Decision-making may be achieved by the more powerful partner being allowed to get his way.

Lesbian partners seek consensus

Relationship breakdown

Although there are exceptions, gay and lesbian relationships in general tend not to last as long as heterosexual relationships:

Box R: Blumstein and Schwartz (1983)

Procedure: As part of a wider study, a survey was carried out to compare the percentage of gay, lesbian and heterosexual couples who ended their relationship within two years of the start of the study.

Results: In the different categories, the percentages were:

- Lesbian couples 48%
- Gay couples 36%
- Hetrosexual couples 29%
- Married couples 14%

Conclusion: Homosexual relationships tend to be less durable than heterosexual relationships.

Activity 15: differences in relationship breakdown

Why do you think homosexual relationships tend not to last as long as heterosexual ones? You will need to consider reasons why some married couples may stay together, even if the relationship is not a happy one, which do not apply (or not so commonly) to gay and lesbian couples. You might also find it useful to look back to your notes on activity 13.

Compare your ideas with the discussion which follows.

For married couples, there are quite serious barriers to leaving the relationship. Since marriage is a legal agreement, couples usually want a judicial separation or divorce, which can be both painful and costly. They are more likely than homosexual couples to have children, with both partners being the biological parents of those children; this again has implications in terms of custody and maintenance, and the distress divorce is likely to cause the children. There may also be quite strong financial incentives for a married couple to stay together. Since wives usually have lower earning power, it may be difficult for them to leave a bad marriage.

Gay and lesbian couples, on the other hand, have fewer barriers to leaving a relationship. For one thing, they are less likely than heterosexual couples to live together: Harry (1983) found that only about 75% of lesbian couples lived together, and only 50% of gay couples.

Both gay and lesbian couples are, moreover, less likely to have the support of parents and other family members, thus depriving them of a source of help and support when their relationship is in difficulties. There is also the question of the likelihood of finding an alternative partner. Most gay men have few barriers to leaving a relationship, and a wide choice of alternative partners. For lesbians, there are usually fewer barriers to leaving a relationship than for a heterosexual couple. However, Kurdek and Schmitt (1986) found that for lesbians the chances of finding an alternative partner are relatively poor, since most lesbians are already in a relationship. Older lesbians tend to be 'closeted', making them harder to find.

There are also some differences between gay men and lesbians in the reasons for the breakdown of relationships. Blumstein and Schwartz (1983) reported that among lesbians, arguments about sex tend to lead to dissatisfaction with a relationship. Arguments about money, family, friends or unequal power within the relationship are also factors (Peplau *et al.*, 1982). As with heterosexual relationships, affairs and the jealousy they cause can lead to relationship breakdown. For gay men, the most frequently mentioned cause for relationship breakdown is a large power difference between the partners which cannot be resolved.

- In recent years, gay and lesbian relationships have been studied within a **'liberal humanistic'** context. While they are in some ways **similar to heterosexual relationships**, there are also important **differences**. There are difficulties in studying a **representative sample** of lesbians and gay men.
- **Meeting potential partners** is likely to be more difficult than for heterosexuals. **Gay men** tend to focus on **physical characteristics** in selecting a partner, while **lesbians** are more interested in **socioemotional characteristics**. Open courtship can be problematical, especially for young people.
- Gay and lesbian couples use similar strategies to heterosexual couples to maintain their relationship. Additionally, they seek **social support** from gay friends and the wider gay community.
- Differences between men and women in **communication patterns** have implications for the maintenance of gay and lesbian relationships.
- Gay and lesbian relationships tend to be **less durable** than heterosexual relationships. There are **fewer barriers** to leaving a relationship, and **less support** when a relationship is in difficulties. While some reasons for relationship breakdown apply to both gay and lesbian relationships, other reasons apply more to gay or to lesbian relationships.

Relationships formed on the Internet

The Internet is a huge global medium linking many millions of people who are able to communicate through email and discussion groups. Given its size and the wide variety of people who use discussion groups, there has been considerable interest in the nature of relationships formed in this way.

Two opposing views have been proposed. On the one hand, it has been suggested that on-line relationships are shallow and impersonal, the 'relationships lost' perspective. On the other hand, cyberspace can be seen as liberating relationships from the limitations of physical locality, the 'relationships found' perspective.

Support for the first point of view came from studies which compared groups communicating by means of a computer (CMC) and those communicating face-to-face (FtF). For example, Kiesler and Sproull (1992) found that CMC groups had greater difficulty in recognising and moving towards a shared point of view, while Dubrovsky *et al.* (1991) found that CMC groups showed more verbal aggression.

▷ Activity 16: CMC and FtF groups

Which aspects of the communicative situation vary between CMC and FtF groups? How might these variations help to explain the differences shown by this research?

When you have finished, see the notes on page 240.

However, Parks and Floyd (1996) suggested that the key factor is time. While social cues speed up FtF communication, CMC can nonetheless convey relational and personal information; it just takes longer to do so. They therefore suggested that many of the negative aspects of CMC identified by research come about because much of this research, carried out under laboratory conditions, imposed strict time limits on interaction. In contrast, field studies (e.g. McCormick and McCormick, 1992) have found that email users report that they use email for social purposes, to maintain relationships, to play games and to receive emotional support. In

other words, these on-line relationships are considered to be genuine personal relationships.

Some of the ideas about personal relationships covered earlier in this chapter certainly seem to pose problems for on-line relationships:

▷ Activity 17: factors in the development of relationships

Look back through the earlier part of this chapter. Make a list of factors which have been identified as being important in the development and maintenance of relationships. Which of these factors present difficulties for on-line relationships? How might these difficulties be overcome?

When you have finished, see the notes on page 240.

However, it is questionable whether the kinds of factors identified as important by traditional theories are a prerequisite for the development of relationships. It may be that these factors are helpful, but it is far from clear that any of them are necessary. The 'relationships lost' position may therefore not acknowledge the possibilities of on-line relationships, or recognise the conditions under which such relationships develop and are maintained.

How often are personal relationships formed on-line?

A major study to investigate how often people form relationships on the Internet was carried out by Parks and Floyd:

Box S: Parks and Floyd (1996)

Procedure: A sample of 528 people (22 randomly selected from each of 24 discussion groups covering a range of topics) were sent surveys by email. Replies were received from 176 people, ranging in age from 15 to 57. The typical respondent was male, single, and in his early thirties. They were asked if they had formed a relationship with someone 'met' on-line, and if so to provide further details about the nature of the relationship.

Results: Nearly two-thirds had formed a personal relationship. Opposite-sex relationships were slightly more common than same-sex relationships, but not significantly so. Only a few (7.9%) were romantic. Over two-thirds of the relationships were less than a year old, though some had been in existence for up to six years. Nearly a third of the participants communicated with their partners at last three or four times a week; just over half communicated with them on a weekly basis.

Conclusion: On-line relationships are not uncommon among Internet discussion group users, across a wide age range, and with different interests.

participating in their particular newsgroup for longer, and had contributed to it significantly more often than those who had not.

Conclusion: The typical profile of someone who has formed an on-line relationship is a female who has been involved with a newsgroup over a period of time and is a frequent contributor.

Activity 18: gender and on-line relationships

Parks and Floyd made several suggestions as to why women should be more likely to form on-line relationships than men. Can you think of any possible reasons?

When you have finished, see the notes on page 240.

Who has on-line personal relationships?

The stereotype of the kind of person who would form a personal relationship on the Internet is of someone who is lonely and possibly dysfunctional; to quote Jack Dee: You're not surfing. You're sitting in your bedroom typing. The question of who is likely to form an on-line relationship was also investigated in the Parks and Floyd study:

How developed do on-line personal relationships become?

Relationships of all kinds develop from the impersonal to the more personal. For example, they show an increase in interpersonal dependence, in self-disclosure, and in commitment. To what extent is this also true of relationships formed on-line? The Parks and Floyd study also addressed this question:

Box T: Parks and Floyd (1996)

Procedure: The characteristics of the sample of participants described in box S was analysed, with a comparison being made between those who had formed an on-line relationship and those who had not.

Results: Significantly more women (over two-thirds) had formed such a relationship than men (just over half). Age and marital status did not differ between those who had formed relationships and those who had not. The most important factors correlated with the likelihood of a relationship being formed were the duration and frequency of participation in newsgroups. Those who had formed on-line relationships had been

---

Box U: Parks and Floyd (1996)

Procedure: The quality of on-line relationships was investigated using questionnaires with items to be rated on a seven-point scale, covering: interdependence; breadth of communication; depth; code change; predictability; commitment; and network convergence. Examples of positively- and negatively-scoring items are shown in figure 19. The mean score on each scale was compared with the midpoint, and the overall mean score was compared with the overall midpoint.

Results: There was a spread of scores for interdependence, with the mean close to the midpoint. Moderate to high levels of breadth and depth were reported. There were low average scores for code change, predictability and network convergence. Moderate levels of commitment were found. The overall mean was well below the midpoint. However, there were wide individual differences, with about 30% of respondents having highly developed personal relationships.

Conclusion: While many on-line relationships are relatively shallow, there is evidence that some people have highly-developed relationships of this kind.

Do on-line relationships spread to other settings?

There is some evidence that relationships which start on-line often use additional forms of communication. Parks and Floyd (1996) found that around a third of their sample made additional contact by telephone, a third FtF, and rather fewer by post. Nearly two-thirds of those who had formed on-line personal relationships made contact other than by computer.

Overall, the picture seems to support the 'relationships found' perspective. However, research in this area is still very much in its infancy. Traditional theories of relationships cannot easily accommodate some aspects of on-line relationships, which raise unique questions.

- ☉ **Early studies** suggested that there were **difficulties** in forming genuine on-line relationships. However, more **recent research** has suggested that such relationships are **not uncommon**.
- ☉ The **typical profile** of someone who has formed an on-line relationship is a female who has regularly contributed to newsgroups over a period of time.
- ☉ While some on-line relationships are relatively shallow, many are well-developed. People often supplement their on-line relationship with **additional forms of communication**.

Figure 19: sample items from Parks and Floyd (1996)

interdependence:	The two of us depend on each other.
	The two of us have little influence on each other's thoughts.
breadth of communication:	Our communication ranges over a wide variety of topics.
	Our communication is limited to just a few specific topics.
depth:	I feel quite close to this person.
	I would never tell this person anything intimate or personal about myself.
code change:	The two of us communicate in ways outsiders would not understand.
	There is not much difference between the way I communicate with this person and the way I generally communicate on the Net.
predictability:	I can usually tell what this person is feeling inside.
	I do not know this person very well.
commitment:	This relationship is a big part of who I am.
	I do not expect this relationship to last very long.
network convergence:	This person and I do not know any of the same people.
	We contact a lot of the same people on the Net.

Notes on activities

1 These kinds of classifications are helpful in reminding us that psychological ideas about relationships need to focus on the different nature of different relationships. For example, reasons for becoming friends with someone may be rather different from the reasons underlying the choice of a sexual partner.

Even where relationships can in some ways be classified together, as Gottman has done for types of marriage, the subgrouping reminds us of variations which may be differently affected by different factors.

Both these kinds of typology provide a framework within which research can take place. They can help us to identify links between the nature of a particular relationship and the factors which influence its formation, maintenance and possible breakdown.

At the same time, this kind of typology can be something of an oversimplification. If we take the Gottman example, you are likely to know many couples who do not fit tidily into one of the five categories. There is also the issue of cultural bias. The kinds of patterns these typologies describe refer to a large extent to heterosexual relationships in Western cultures. Very different patterns are found cross-culturally and within subcultures, and we will return to this issue later in the chapter.

Finally, the nature of the types arrived at in any typology does not necessarily reflect objective differences in the phenomenon being typed; the types are at least as likely to be a reflection of the preconceptions of the researcher.

4 Rubin (1973) suggested several reasons why similarity is important. Firstly, similarity can provide a basis for doing things together. If both partners in a relationship enjoy sailing or train-spotting, doing these things brings shared enjoyment. People who agree with us increase our confidence in our opinions and attitudes, and therefore also our self-esteem. Shared views also make it easier to communicate; it is very hard to communicate with someone with whom you have no common ground. We also tend to have a reasonably good opinion of ourselves, so are likely to think positively about people who are like us. Finally, we may assume that people who are similar to us will like us, and so we like them. This is known as **reciprocal liking**.

5 There are lots of possibilities here. These may include: being interested in us (e.g. by wanting to get to know us), kindness (e.g. being helpful when we need help), showing concern when we are upset, being pleased to see us, enjoying our company, and so on. Foa and Foa (1975) proposed eight categories: help, goods, information, love, money, respect, sex and status.

6 It is possible that long-term relationships do not need as many maintenance strategies because the partners have come to understand each other better as time has passed. It is also possible that for some people, long-term relationships continue through force of habit.

7 Some of these factors relate to similarity, e.g. **e**, but also perhaps **a**, where people may not yet have clearly established their identity. It is possible that after marriage, they will continue to develop in ways which make them less compatible. Factors **c** and **d** suggest that there could be financial problems. These couples are also those who are likely to have children early in their marriage **b**, again possibly linked with financial problems, but also not allowing the parents to develop their relationship as a couple before the arrival of a third person. For **f**, we discussed in chapter 3 the idea that children develop an internal working model of relationships which can affect their own adult relationships (e.g. the Hazan and Shaver study in chapter 3, box K). Factor **g** could be linked to CL alt, discussed under social exchange theory.

8 **1a** He is a kind and thoughtful person, he often brings her flowers, and shows his thoughtfulness in many ways.

1b He just happened to pass a flower shop, he doesn't usually bother with bringing her gifts, so he must be feeling guilty about something.

2a Something must have upset him at work, he does not usually shout at her so he must be having a really bad day.

2b   He is an unpleasant person, he is always shouting, and all his behaviour shows what an inconsiderate pig he is.

9   **a** caring **b** intimacy **c** attachment **d** caring **e** caring **f** attachment **g** intimacy

10   eros: high passion; ludus: low commitment, low intimacy; storge: high commitment, high intimacy; pragma: low passion; mania: high passion, low commitment; agape: high commitment.

11   **a** passion **b** commitment

12   Possible reasons include:

a Couples are likely to be more similar, since possible partners are chosen on the basis of similarity of education and social status. As we have seen, similarity can be an important factor in relationships.

b They may be less focused on their own needs than couples who have married for love, and more concerned with the practicalities of the marriage.

c It is the expectation within collectivist cultures that marriage is a lifetime commitment. Without the option of ending the relationship, couples may be more motivated to try to make it work.

d The social group can be relied on to offer support when the relationship is in difficulties.

13   **a** The partners in the relationship are the same sex.

b Their homosexuality is not assumed by others in the way that heterosexuality is.

c Either or both of them may not be 'out' as individuals.

d Even if both individuals are 'out', they may not be 'out' as a couple, so the relationship may be ambiguous to others.

e They are unlikely to receive social support or encouragement in forming their relationship or continuing it.

f They may experience hostility from others because of their sexual orientation.

g Their relationship cannot be formalised legally in marriage.

h They will not both be the biological parents of any children in the relationship.

16   In CMC groups, there is more anonymity, which is a major factor in deindividuation, discussed in chapter 10. Research into deindividuation has suggested that it can cause aggression. Secondly, FtF relationships include a lot of social cues missing in CMC relationships. For example, factors such as tone of voice and facial expression form part of a FtF communication and can help to overcome communicative difficulties. CMC communication is therefore likely to be more impersonal than FtF communication.

17   Proximity is one obvious factor, as is the importance of physical appearance. However, these can to an extent be overcome by arranging meetings, sending photographs, and so on. It is also worth noting that other factors which have been found to be important, such as similarity, can work well on-line. For example, being part of a particular discussion group guarantees that participants at least have something in common on which to base a relationship.

18   Parks and Floyd suggested that it is possible that a greater proportion of women than men are using the Internet to find friends. It may also be that they are more willing to label as 'a relationship' the communication they have with someone they have met on-line. Bearing in mind that there are more male users of the Internet than women, women may simply be more sought after. However, this is a question which would repay further research.

10

Pro- and anti-social behaviour

In this chapter we will be looking at:

10.1 The nature of aggression

10.2 Theories of aggression
   Social learning theory
   Deindividuation
   Aggression between groups

10.3 Environmental stress and aggression

10.4 Altruism and bystander behaviour
   Latané's information-processing
      approach
   Piliavin's arousal:cost-reward model
   Batson's empathy–altruism
      hypothesis
   Cultural variation in prosocial
      behaviour

10.5 Media influences on pro- and
   anti-social behaviour
   Anti-social behaviour
   Prosocial behaviour

10.1 THE NATURE OF AGGRESSION

There are many different types of anti-social behaviour – for example, dropping litter, or playing loud music in the middle of the night – but we will be focusing here solely on aggression.

To start this topic, we need to look at how 'aggression' may be defined. We all have a general understanding of what we mean when we say that someone is aggressive, or is behaving aggressively, but 'aggression' is a term whose precise definition can cause some problems.

Activity 1: defining aggression

Write a definition of what you understand by 'aggression'. Then read through the following scenarios. Decide whether or not you think each one is an example of aggression. Give reasons for your decision:

1 A soldier fires at an enemy soldier.
2 Darren tries to punch his older brother. His brother holds his wrists, and laughs at him.
3 A cat pounces on a mouse.
4 Sophie throws a stone at a girl she doesn't like, but misses.
5 Karl has drunk several pints of lager, but drives himself home from the pub. On the way, his car hits and kills an old lady crossing the road.
6 Shihan is talking to her boyfriend. She says some very unpleasant things about one of her classmates.
7 Luisa has had a row with her friend Lucy. She tears up Lucy's psychology essay.
8 James has been made a fool of in public by a workmate. He plans various hurtful ways he can get his own back.
9 Priscilla steps back suddenly from the kerb. She collides with a passer-by, who falls and hurts her arm.
10 Anna hits a boy who has been bullying her little sister.
11 Two young men are fighting outside a pub. One says: 'Got you that time!' and they both laugh and go off together.

If you are working in a group, compare your answers with those of other students. How much agreement was there? Having read through these examples, would you need to change your original definition of aggression?

This activity should have helped you to identify some of the problems in defining aggression. Does actual harm need to be involved, or is the intention to harm enough (2, 4 and 8)? What about unintentional harm (5 and 9)? Does the object of aggression need to be a living thing, capable of feeling pain (7)? What about verbal aggression (6)? Is it aggression when you are obeying orders (1) or when there is some justification (10)? Can only humans be aggressive (3)? And who decides whether or not behaviour is aggressive (11)?

In many if not all cases, you probably felt that you would have liked rather more information before coming to a decision. At the same time, it is likely that you found it fairly easy to decide whether or not aggression was involved in each of these examples, and to justify your decision. It is also likely, though, that there was some disagreement with others in the group, and that your initial definition needed adjusting to take the various factors identified above into account.

Baron (1977) has proposed a possible definition of aggression:

a. The aggressor must have an intention to harm the victim.

b. The victim must be another living thing.

c. The victim must be motivated to avoid such treatment.

▷ Activity 2: applying Baron's definition of aggression

How does this definition relate to the scenarios in activity 1? Does this classification agree with the decisions you made?

When you have finished, see the notes on page 270.

How useful Baron's definition is in relation to activity 1 is for you to decide. It is likely that you will not be entirely happy with it, but it does have the advantage of giving us something to work with

in an area where definition seems highly problematic.

❺ There are problems in producing a precise **definition** of aggression.

10.2 THEORIES OF AGGRESSION

A great many theorists have put forward ideas to help us understand human aggression. They have tried to explain it on a number of different levels. Some theories explain aggression in terms of causes which lie within the individual. For example, Lorenz (1965) suggested that we have an aggressive instinct, and this instinct generates energy which needs to be discharged through aggressive behaviour. Other theories explain aggressive behaviour in terms of brain functioning. For example, Papez (1937) considered aggressive behaviour to be caused by activation of a particular circuit in the limbic system of the brain, now known as the Papez circuit. However, we will be focusing here on some of the theories which are interested in the social context within which aggression takes place.

Social learning theory

Social learning theory (SLT) is based on **operant conditioning**, which suggests that behaviour is learned, and is likely to be repeated, if it is positively reinforced. In learning social behaviour, the reinforcement is vicarious: we are more likely to imitate the behaviour of a model if we see the model being reinforced. There is an outline of SLT in chapter 1; you may find it useful at this point to have another look at that section of the chapter.

In the 1960's Bandura claimed that much of our social behaviour, including aggression, is learned through **observational learning** and **modelling**. We learn through observing the behaviour of others, and seeing the results of their behaviour. He and his co-workers showed the effects on aggressive behaviour of observational learning and modelling in a series of studies using a Bobo doll, one of which was described in chapter 1, box C.

Another of these studies looked at the role of reinforcement in the modelling of aggressive behaviour:

Box A: Bandura (1965)

Procedure: In the first stage of the study, children who had observed an adult model attack a Bobo doll were divided into three groups. Group 1 went straight into the playroom, group 2 saw the model being rewarded for their aggression against the doll, while group 3 saw the adult model punished. In the second stage of the study, after the children had played with the doll, all the children were offered rewards to behave as the adult model had done.

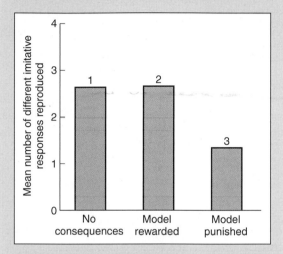

Results: In the first stage of the study, group 3 children showed significantly less aggressive behaviour towards the dolls than groups 1 and 2. In the second stage of the study, there was no difference between the groups in the mean number of imitated aggressive actions.

Conclusion: Observation of a model is sufficient for aggressive behaviour to be learned, but the consequences of the behaviour, both for the model and the observer, influence whether the behaviour is reproduced.

Further variations of the Bobo doll studies carried out by Bandura and his colleagues identified other factors which influence whether or not behaviour is modelled:

Figure 1: factors in modelling

Factors making imitation more likely:

a. *similarity:* if the child saw themselves as similar to the model (for example, if they were the same sex).

b. *presentation:* if the aggressive model was seen live rather than on film.

c. *warmth:* if the model was warm and friendly, rather than cool and distant.

d. *prestige:* if the model was of high status.

e. *appropriateness of behaviour:* if the model was male rather than female. This relates to stereotypes relating to sex-role differences; for example, many studies have found that in Western culture it is more acceptable for males to be aggressive than females.

▶ Activity 3: chapter 1, box C revisited

Why did the adult models attack the Bobo doll in unusual ways?

Are there any ways in which the methodology of this study could be criticised?

When you have finished, see the notes on page 270.

Bandura's studies may be limited in what they can tell us about real-life aggression, in that they did not involve realistic attacks on real people. Neither are we likely to find in real life an exact similarity between an observed situation and one in which the observer later acts.

Nonetheless, Bandura's ideas have been extremely influential. There has been considerable research interest in the idea that aggression can be acquired simply through observational learning. You will remember that Bandura suggested that there are three main sources of models: the family, the subculture and the mass media. The effects of the media, and in particular the effects of violence on television, have been very widely researched and we shall be looking at this in more detail towards the end of this chapter.

⊙ **SLT** proposes that aggressive behaviour is learned by **observational learning** and **modelling** the behaviour of others.

⊙ Bandura showed that seeing a model punished inhibits imitation of aggressive behaviour, but does not prevent the behaviour from being learned. Modelling is sufficient for behaviour to be learned, even where it is seen to be punished, but **reinforcement** is necessary for it to be performed.

⊙ Several factors influence the likelihood of observed behaviour being imitated.

⊙ SLT has stimulated research into the effects of the **media**.

Deindividuation

People as a group sometimes act in ways which they would not do as individuals. Everyday observation of group behaviour – for example, in riots, demonstrations and football matches – suggests that very often people behave more violently in groups than as individuals, and this observation has often been confirmed experimentally.

One suggestion put forward to explain why being part of a group may lead to aggression is deindividuation, a concept first proposed by Le Bon (1895). This concept suggests that we may lose some of our sense of being an individual and become more anonymous when we are part of a group. This may lead to our control over our own behaviour being weakened. We are less concerned with observing social norms and with how our behaviour will be evaluated by other people, and are less likely to think about the consequences of what we do. Our inhibitions are lowered, and aggressive behaviour – as well as other anti-social behaviour, such as vandalism – becomes more likely.

◗ Activity 4: factors in deindividuation

Imagine yourself as part of a group; for example, at a football match. You find yourself acting in ways in which you would not behave as an individual, such as shouting abuse at the referee. How might you explain these changes in your behaviour? Compare your ideas with the discussion which follows.

One suggestion is **diffusion of responsibility**. When we act as an individual, we must take responsibility for our own behaviour. When we are part of a group, responsibility is shared across the group. For example, if a group of 20 people is behaving violently, each individual can be thought of as carrying only one-twentieth of the responsibility for the violence.

This idea is also relevant in other areas of social psychology. Investigations of helping behaviour have found that people are less likely to offer help to someone if there are other potential helpers than if they are alone; the responsibility for helping is reduced by the presence of other potential helpers. This is discussed later in this chapter in the section on **prosocial behaviour**.

A further factor is **disinhibition**. If we behave aggressively as an individual, we know that we can be easily identified, so there are likely to be unpleasant consequences, such as punishment or social disapproval. As a member of a group we are less easily identifiable, so our behaviour is less likely to lead to unpleasant personal consequences. With the fear of punishment reduced, we lose our inhibitions, and so are less concerned with observing social norms and are more free to behave in anti-social ways.

Aggression within groups can also be linked to **anonymity**. Being a member of a group can be very positive for a person, in that belonging to a group can give them a sense of identity and belonging. In **social identity theory**, Tajfel (1981) suggested that part of our identity, our sense of who we are, comes from the groups with which we identify. At the same time, however, our personal identity can merge with the group identity: we become more anonymous.

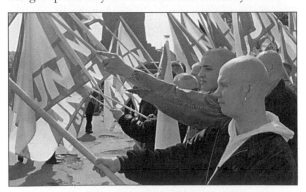

Our personal identity can merge with the group identity

The effect of anonymity on behaviour has been investigated experimentally:

Box B: Diener et al. (1976)

Procedure: In a field study, the behaviour of 1300 children at Halloween was observed. They were following the American custom of 'trick-or-treat', where children go from house to house asking for sweets or money.
Results: Those children in large groups, wearing Halloween costumes which made them impossible to identify, were the most likely to steal sweets or money.
Conclusion: There is a link between anonymity and anti-social behaviour.

However, this study is essentially correlational, and cannot therefore establish a cause-and-effect relationship between anonymity and anti-social behaviour. Possibly the children behaved in an anti-social way because they were anonymous. However, it is also possible that children with anti-social tendencies chose to make themselves anonymous by their choice of costume.

Zimbardo (1969) proposed that anonymity was the key factor leading to deindividuation. He carried out a study, focusing specifically on anonymity as a possible cause of anti-social behaviour:

Box C: Zimbardo (1969)

Procedure: In a study similar to that of Milgram (see chapter 6, box H), female participants took part in what was described as an experiment into the effect of electric shocks on learning. They were asked to give electric shocks to the learner (actually a stooge of the experimenter), although in fact no shocks were delivered. The participants could see the learner, who pretended to be in great discomfort, through a one-way mirror. Half the participants sat in a darkened room, wore bulky coats and hoods which hid their faces, were only spoken to as a group, and were not addressed by name. The other

participants wore ordinary clothes, were given large name tags, and were introduced to each other by name. All participants were given information about the 'learner', either positive (e.g. that she was warm, sincere and honest) or negative (e.g. that she was conceited or critical). The degree of the 'shocks' given by each group was compared.
Results: Participants in the 'anonymous' condition gave twice as much shock as those in the control condition. Those in the control condition decreased the level of shock given when they had been given positive information about the 'learner'. 'Anonymous' participants did not.
Conclusion: The anonymity of the hooded participants led to deindividuation, which in turn led to aggressive behaviour.

Wearing a uniform also increases anonymity. The function of uniform is to minimise individual identity by focusing on the individual as a member of a particular group, e.g. the army or the police; its aim is to bring about deindividuation. This can be linked to the prison simulation study carried out by Zimbardo et al. (1973), discussed in chapter 6, box E. Participants acting as guards wore a uniform, as well as dark glasses, which increased their anonymity. Zimbardo found that many of the 'guards' acted extremely aggressively towards the 'prisoners', in ways which were unexpected in participants who had been selected to take part in the study on the basis of being well-adjusted.

However, while wearing a uniform can be linked to aggressive behaviour, the deindividuation it brings about can also make individuals wearing it appear less human. For example, it may be that rioters are more likely to act aggressively towards the police because they see the person they are attacking not as an individual but as a member of the police force. Putting prisoners in uniforms can dehumanise them, which can lead to a disregard for their human rights.

There is some support, then, for deindividuation as an explanation of the increased aggression of groups compared to individuals. However, there are some problems with the theory. One question which arises is whether, as the theory suggests, group behaviour arising from deindividuation is always extreme and uncontrolled. Brown (1988) discussed the behaviour of people taking part in the urban riots in the USA in the 1960s. He pointed out that the looting and violence which took place at that time had some element of control, with people being selective in the targets for their anti-social behaviour. Another piece of research supports this idea, and suggests that the group itself may have norms which limit aggression:

> ### Box D: Marsh (1978)
>
> **Procedure:** Marsh researched the behaviour of football fans. He used the method of participant observation, travelling to football matches with a group of fans. He also interviewed them, and analysed video recordings made at matches.
>
> **Results:** Although the behaviour of football fans seems chaotic, it is in fact governed by rules, to which the fans conform. Aggression was part of the behaviour expected by the group, but carrying knives was frowned on. It was also expected that once a rival fan had been kicked to the floor, no further violence would be inflicted.
>
> **Conclusion:** Where aggression is one of the norms of the group, group membership is likely to lead to aggressive behaviour. However, group membership can also serve to control aggression.

Marsh was looking at aggression in a group of young males, but aggression related to being part of a group is not just a masculine phenomenon. Campbell carried out studies of girls from a young offenders institution (1981) and working-class girl gangs (1984). In both cases the vast majority of the girls had been involved in fights. However, as with Marsh's findings, group membership also imposed constraints on what was thought to be acceptable

violence; for example, the use of bottles and knives was considered unacceptable.

A further question is whether deindividuation always leads to an increase in aggression. There have been conflicting findings in research in this area, with some studies finding that deindividuation increases aggression, some finding that it has no effect, and some even finding that it reduces aggression. It has also been found that in some circumstances deindividuation can have positive consequences:

> ### Box E: Gergen *et al.* (1973)
>
> **Procedure:** A group of participants spent an hour together either in a room with normal lighting or in a completely dark room.
>
> **Results:** Those spending time in the light room chatted to each other for an hour. Those in the dark room started by chatting, then began to discuss serious subjects and finally made physical contact with each other. Ninety per cent of these participants deliberately touched others, nearly half the participants hugged each other and a large majority found that they were sexually aroused.
>
> **Conclusion:** The anonymity created by the dark room led to deindividuation, which in turn led to behaviour beneficial to the participants.

Emergent-norm theory, proposed by Turner and Killian (1973), has tried to accommodate these conflicting findings. This theory suggests that extreme forms of behaviour, such as aggression, are more likely to be shown in a group not because people lose their inhibitions and are less concerned with conforming to social norms, but because new norms develop within the group to which the individual conforms. For example, in a confrontation between police and demonstrators, the group norm could develop that people should defend themselves against the police, leading to aggressive behaviour towards the police.

▶ Activity 5: emergent-norm theory

Look back at the studies by Marsh (box D) and Gergen *et al.* (box E). How would emergent-norm theory explain their findings?

When you have finished, see the notes on page 270.

If anonymity weakens the pressure to conform to social norms, emergent-norm theory would predict that under the conditions of anonymity, aggressive behaviour should be weakened if the situation demands aggression. Conforming to the situational norm of aggression should be most likely when individuals are easily identifiable. In contrast, deindividuation theory would predict that anonymity reduces inhibitions, and so leads to aggressive behaviour; being easily identifiable should reduce aggression.

Research has been carried out to test these predictions and so evaluate the claims of deindividuation theory against those of emergent-norm theory. Mann *et al.* (1982) claimed to have found support for both theories: anonymous individuals were more aggressive in a situation where aggressive behaviour was the norm, but less so where aggression was inappropriate. In a further study, Rabbie *et al.* (1985) found that male participants acted more aggressively when anonymous, while female participants were more aggressive when easily identifiable.

This seems to suggest that both theories have something to offer, but additional factors, such as gender, are important in determining the relationship between group membership and aggression in a particular situation.

🅢 **Deindividuation** refers to the diminished sense of personal identity and responsibility experienced when a person is a member of a group. Groups are more likely to show anti-social behaviour than individuals. This has been explained in terms of **diffusion of responsibility**, **disinhibition** and **anonymity**.

🅢 While some research supports the idea that deindividuation can lead to aggression, the findings are not clear-cut. Apparently uninhibited anti-social behaviour has been found to be to some extent controlled. It has also been found that deindividuation can decrease aggression.

🅢 **Emergent-norm theory** explains behaviour in groups by the development of group norms. Where the norm is aggression, people in groups will behave more aggressively. This will not be the case where there is no such norm.

🅢 There is evidence for both deindividuation and emergent-norm theory. It is also likely that additional factors such as **gender** affect whether people in groups are likely to behave more aggressively than individuals.

Aggression between groups

The theories of aggression we have looked at up to now have focused on the individual within a social context. Other social psychological theories explain aggression in terms of relationships between groups of people. We have already looked at two such theories – **relative deprivation theory** and **realistic conflict theory** – in chapter 8, under the section headed 'the intergroup approach to prejudice', in the context of explaining prejudice. You might find it useful to re-read this material now, to provide a broader view of possible social psychological causes of aggression.

🅢 **Relative deprivation theory** and **realistic conflict theory** consider aggression in terms of relationships between groups.

10.3 ENVIRONMENTAL STRESS AND AGGRESSION

In chapter 4, in the section headed 'sources of stress', we looked at environmental factors which can lead to stress, in particular **noise**, **temperature**, **pollution**, **overcrowding** and the **urban environment**. We saw that the stress induced by these factors could lead to poor task performance, negative mood and even illness. The Baron and Ransberger (1978) study described in that section established a link between temperature and rioting, and the Calhoun (1962) study described in box B of the same section found that rats in overcrowded conditions became extremely aggressive. These studies therefore suggest that environmental stressors can also lead to aggression. Other studies have also investigated this link. We will start by looking at a study into the effects of **noise**:

Box F: Donnerstein and Wilson (1976)

Procedure: Half the male participants were angered by having work which they had written negatively evaluated by a confederate of the experimenters; the other half received positive evaluations. All participants were then able to give the confederate electric shocks of varying intensity when she made mistakes in a learning task. During this part of the experiment, all participants wore headphones through which they received either slightly or extremely unpleasant noise. Aggression was measured by the strength of shock given to the confederate.

Results: For both levels of noise, angry participants gave higher intensity shocks than those who had not been angered. The shock given was greatest for angry participants exposed to extremely unpleasant noise. Non-angry participants did not increase the shocks in the unpleasant noise condition.

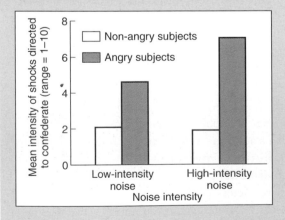

Conclusion: Noise experienced as unpleasant can increase aggression, but only in angry participants.

The Calhoun study into the effects of **overcrowding** was carried out on rats. Results from investigations into the effect of overcrowding on people have been less clear-cut. Some studies (e.g. Freedman *et al.*, 1972) have found that overcrowding is linked to increased aggression, while other studies (e.g. Hutt and McGrew, 1967) have found that there is a decrease in aggression in crowded conditions.

▶ Activity 6: explaining conflicting findings on the effect of overcrowding

Make a list of situations where you have been in crowded conditions, with very little space around you. Are there any differences between the situations which might affect the likelihood of aggression?

When you have finished, see the notes on page 270.

The relationship between **temperature** and aggression is also a complex one. Archival studies provide statistical data on the frequency of various kinds of aggressive crimes, such as murder, rape and aggravated assault, at different periods of time. These data can then be compared with climatological data, in particular temperature differences, at the same times. In a review of a large number of these kinds of study, Anderson (1989) concluded that there was indeed a positive relationship between higher temperatures and the incidence of aggressive crimes.

However, the link between temperature and aggression has also been tested experimentally, with somewhat different results:

Box G: Baron and Bell (1975)

Procedure: Using a procedure similar to that of Donnerstein and Wilson (box F), aggression was measured by the duration and intensity of electric shocks given to a confederate of the experimenters. At the start of the study, some participants were angered and some treated in a friendly manner. Aggression for

---

both groups at different temperatures was compared.

Results: Aggressive behaviour decreased as the temperature increased from 20° to 30°C. Participants who had been angered behaved less aggressively under heat conditions, while those who had been treated in a friendly way behaved more aggressively.

Conclusion: The relationship between aggression and temperature depends on mood, with the relationship between negative mood and aggression being curvilinear.

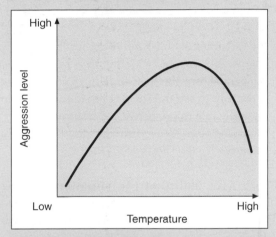

For people in a neutral mood, an unpleasantly high temperature can worsen their mood and make aggression more likely. If people are already in a negative mood, an unpleasantly high temperature can make them feel so bad that all they want to do is to escape from the situation, making aggression less likely.

The results of investigations into the relationship between temperature and aggression therefore seem to be conflicting. However, it is possible that in real-life situations people may not be able to escape from unpleasant heat, leading to a straightforward positive relationship between heat and aggression. On the other hand, in laboratory studies such as that by Baron and Bell described in box G, the possibility of escape from an intolerable situation may make this relationship rather more complex.

We should also not overlook the possible effect of other variables on the relationship between heat and aggression found in archival studies. For example, it may be that people – both criminals and victims – are able to spend more time outdoors during the hot summer months. To give us a clearer picture, future research in this area would need to focus on the influence of these kinds of factors.

- ➎ There is some evidence to link environmental stressors, such as **noise**, **overcrowding** and **heat** with increased aggression.
- ➎ **Mood** mediates the relationship between aggression and both noise and heat, while overcrowding may lead to aggression if it is experienced as unpleasant.

10.4 ALTRUISM AND BYSTANDER BEHAVIOUR

Some time ago, the newspapers carried a report of a fatal accident, involving a young girl trying to rescue her dog which had fallen through thin ice into a pond. She got into difficulties herself, and a passing off-duty policeman, together with another man out for a walk, went to her rescue. Tragically, no one survived. The kind of behaviour shown by the two men – acting to help somebody else, at considerable personal cost, not expecting anything out of it for themselves – is known as **altruism**.

It is not unusual to come across this sort of story, and you can probably think of many other examples of such selfless behaviour. However, the term **prosocial behaviour** also includes more everyday behaviour: for instance, holding a door open for someone carrying heavy bags, or giving directions. Examples such as these, where the potential costs of helping are considerably lower than rescuing a child from a pond, are usually referred to as **helping behaviour**. Because this kind of behaviour is fairly common, and lends itself both to naturalistic observation and more experimental methods, it has been of interest to many psychologists concerned with prosocial behaviour.

As well as investigating helping, there has also been considerable interest in why people *don't* help.

The case of Kitty Genovese (activity 7) played a large role in this interest, and was the source of the concepts of **bystander apathy** and the **unresponsive bystander**:

Activity 7: bystander apathy – the case of Kitty Genovese

Read this account of a crime which took place in New York in 1964:

At 3.20 am, a 28-year old woman, Kitty Genovese, was returning home from her job as manager of a bar. She parked her car, and started to walk the 30 yards to the apartment house where she lived, in a middle-class suburb of New York.

A man grabbed her from behind. She screamed: 'Oh my God! He stabbed me! Please help me!' Lights went on in the surrounding apartment houses, and someone called out: 'Let that girl alone!' The attacker walked away, and the lights were turned off.

He returned and grabbed her again. She shrieked: 'I'm dying!' Again the lights came on, and the attacker drove off in his car. When the lights were switched off again, he returned a third time, and stabbed her to death.

These events had taken over half an hour, and 38 people had witnessed the assault. No one intervened, and no one phoned the police while the attack was going on. One person phoned when the attack was over, after ringing a friend for advice.

Why do you think no one came to Kitty Genovese's aid? Many of the witnesses said they had been afraid to phone. Here are some additional comments from the witnesses to the crime, made to the police in their door-to-door enquiries, which you may also find helpful:

'We thought it was a lovers' quarrel.'

'Frankly, we were afraid.'

'I didn't want my husband to get involved.'

'We went to the window to see what was happening, but the light from our bedroom made it difficult to see the street. I put out the light and we were able to see better.'

Compare your ideas with the discussion which follows.

At first sight, **defining the situation** as one in which help was required doesn't seem to be a problem; it seems obvious that Kitty Genovese needed help. But supposing it were just a lovers' quarrel? Interfering in domestic arguments is often a bad move, with both people involved turning on the would-be helper. Remember, too, that this was a middle-class neighbourhood, with little crime; the very unlikelihood of the attack on Kitty could have affected how the onlookers interpreted what they saw. The one man who did phone felt he needed to consult a friend before phoning the police, and the final comment makes it sound as if this couple were watching television, not a real-life event.

Perhaps one of the most important factors in this case is the number of witnesses; each of them would have been aware of lights on in other windows, and so could have assumed that someone else watching would call the police, or had already done so. This phenomenon – where everyone in a group thinks someone else in the group will take or has taken action – is called **diffusion of responsibility**.

There would also be **costs** involved in helping. True, it doesn't cost much to make a phone call, but there would also probably be costs in terms of time (and hassle) spent talking to the police, possible court appearances as a witness, and so on. The onlookers might also have felt that if it came to a court case, they could be in danger from the attacker or his friends. The positive side of making a call would be the satisfaction of knowing that you had helped to save someone's life, but only if that life was in danger in the first place – we have already noted problems in defining the situation. The costs here might well seem to outweigh the rewards. This is not, of course, to suggest that people *consciously* work out the balance of costs and rewards; making a decision whether to help or not is a fairly instantaneous process.

You may of course have thought of other possible reasons for the lack of help Kitty received. We shall look now at theories of helping behaviour, including how these three general principles are incorporated into them.

- Prosocial behaviour includes extreme acts of **altruism**, as well as more everyday **helping behaviour**.
- The Kitty Genovese case sparked interest in why bystanders offer or withhold help.
- Some of the factors which influence this decision are: **defining the situation**; whether a bystander assumes responsibility for helping, since **dissolution of responsibility** may occur; and the relative **costs and rewards** of helping.

Latané's information-processing approach

A model which links together some of the possible reasons why no one helped Kitty Genovese, together with other factors which help to determine whether help is offered or not, has been proposed by Latané and Darley (1970). Their theory applies particularly to emergency situations. They take an information-processing approach to explain the decision whether or not to help, and suggest that the decision-making process goes through several stages:

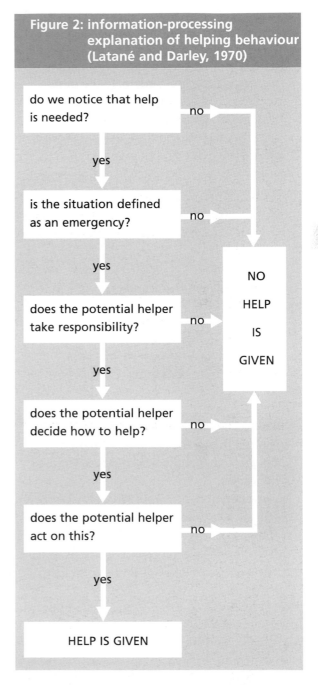

Figure 2: information-processing explanation of helping behaviour (Latané and Darley, 1970)

do we notice that help is needed?

is the situation defined as an emergency?

does the potential helper take responsibility?

does the potential helper decide how to help?

does the potential helper act on this?

NO HELP IS GIVEN

HELP IS GIVEN

Latané and Darley's account of the decision-making process includes some of the suggestions which were made to explain why witnesses failed to help Kitty Genovese. An inaccurate definition of the situation is one possibility which has been investigated experimentally:

Box H: Latané and Darley (1968)

Procedure: Participants were taken to a room to fill in a questionnaire. In one condition, they were alone in the room. In the other condition, two other people were completing the questionnaire in the room with them. Once they had started their task, steam was let into the room through a vent. The researchers were interested in the percentage of participants in each condition reporting the problem.

Results: Of participants working alone, 75% reported the escape of steam within six minutes, compared to 12% of those working with others.

Conclusion: The interpretation of the escape of steam as a problem was less likely when other people were present. Circumstances can affect the way we interpret a situation, and therefore whether or not we respond to it.

The presence of other people affecting the interpretation of a situation is sometimes known as **pluralistic ignorance**. In a group situation, each person may be looking to the others for signs of anxiety to help them decide whether or not there is a problem. In the meantime, everyone is trying to appear calm themselves, for fear of looking foolish if there is no emergency. They each accept the others' apparent interpretation of the situation as one which requires no action, and so fail to act.

Another study in this area is interesting, in that it relates to one of the comments made by witnesses in the Kitty Genovese case: 'We thought it was a lovers' quarrel':

Box I: Shotland and Straw (1976)

Procedure: The experimenters set up a fight, apparently a real event, between a man and a woman. In one condition, participants heard the female scream: 'I don't even know you!' and in the other: 'I don't even know why I married you!'

Results: Three times as many participants intervened in the first condition as in the second.

Conclusion: People are far less likely to intervene in 'domestic' acts of violence than when the attack is being carried out by a stranger.

Another suggestion made to account for the lack of help offered in the Kitty Genovese case, and which also forms part of the sequence outlined in the Latané model, is the problem of deciding who is responsible for offering help. You may remember it was suggested that when there are several people available to help, **diffusion of responsibility** may occur, with individuals accepting only a small part of the responsibility to help. This idea has been supported experimentally:

Box J: Darley and Latané (1968)

Procedure: Participants, each in a separate cubicle, were asked to discuss social problems with other participants over an intercom system (to avoid embarrassment). They supposedly heard one of the group (actually a tape recording made by a confederate of the experimenter) say that he was liable to seizures when stressed. They later heard him apparently having a seizure. Participants were told that the discussion was taking place with either 2, 3 or 5 other participants, though in fact they were the only participant, the others being recordings. The percentage of

participants who, within 4 minutes, went to help the person having a seizure was noted.
Results: When the participant thought there were 2 other participants in the group, 85% helped, compared to 62% if they thought there were 3 other participants, and only 31% if they believed there were 5 other people taking part.
Conclusion: As the number of people they believed were also in a position to help increased, people were less likely to help. This can be explained by diffusion of responsibility.

However, Piliavin *et al.* (1981) interpreted these findings rather differently. They argued that the lack of response to Kitty Genovese showed diffusion of responsibility, as witnesses accepted and shared responsibility. On the other hand, in the Darley and Latané situation, participants could not observe the behaviour of others. Their behaviour can therefore be explained in terms of reasoning that someone else must have helped and so not accepting responsibility. Piliavin *et al.* termed this **dissolution of responsibility**.

However, the availability of more potential helpers does not always lead to diffusion or dissolution of responsibility. Piliavin *et al.* (1969) studied helping behaviour in the New York subway. They found that, contrary to the idea of diffusion of responsibility, people were *more* likely to offer help to someone collapsing on the platform if there were more people about. Perhaps this was because the situation was unambiguous; perhaps also, since the subway is not a very safe place, people might have felt there was safety in numbers, and therefore have been more relaxed about helping when the risks of doing so were minimised by the presence of others.

Another of the stages in the decision-making process Latané and Darley described is deciding how to help:

Activity 8: deciding how to help

In each of these scenarios, would you offer direct help? Why might you not be able to do so? If you were unable to help directly, what other kind of help might you offer?
1 You are walking along the street, when a middle-aged man collapses on the pavement and seems to be having a heart attack.
2 You are on a river bank. Your attention is drawn to someone in the water waving and calling for help.
When you have finished, see the notes on page 270.

If we feel we are competent to help in a particular situation, we are likely to offer direct help. If not, we may offer indirect help. However, if we believe someone else is more capable of helping, diffusion of responsibility may occur:

Box K: Bickman (1971)

Procedure: This study replicated the Darley and Latané study (box J), with the additional variable of how close the participant believed themselves to be to the 'victim'. The assumption here was that someone believing themselves to be closer to the 'victim' than other potential helpers would perceive themselves as being better able to help.
Results: Participants who believed that there were other potential helpers, as close to the 'victim' as they were, showed diffusion of responsibility. However, when they thought that other potential helpers were further away, participants in groups were as likely as individuals to offer help.
Conclusion: Diffusion of responsibility does not occur when people believe that they are the best placed to offer help.

Evaluation of Latané's information-processing model

While naturally occurring events like the case of Kitty Genovese can provide useful information, ideas from this kind of source can only be speculative. The Latané and Darley model provides a framework within which intuitive ideas about why people decide to offer help or withhold it can be tested. The theory breaks down the decision-making process into discrete steps, allowing the researcher to isolate and manipulate particular variables in controlled experiments. It therefore has the potential to allow a more stringent test of the influences on helping behaviour, which can help us towards rather more precise knowledge. Although the model was developed to explain why help is given or withheld in emergency situations, it has also been successfully applied more widely to helping behaviour in general.

However, the theory is limited in that it has more to say about why people do *not* help than about why they do. It also focuses on cognitions, and does not consider emotional factors in the decision about whether or not to help. In the next section we will be looking at Piliavin's arousal:cost-reward model which attempts to redress the balance by explaining what motivates people who do help, taking into account emotions as well as cognitions.

The model successfully identifies some of the factors which influence the decision whether or not to help. However, several important kinds of factors are not covered, notably the characteristics of the person needing help, the characteristics of the potential helper, the nature of the situation, and cultural factors. All of these have been shown to affect whether or not help is given, and we shall be looking at research relating to these factors later in the chapter.

- Latané and Darley proposed an **information-processing model** of helping behaviour in an emergency situation, linking factors which are important in the decision about whether or not to help.
- There have been many empirical studies into helping behaviour which have identified important factors influencing such behaviour, and which support the Latané and Darley model.
- **Definition of the situation** has been shown to be important, with the presence of others tending to lead to **pluralistic ignorance**.
- Both **diffusion of responsibility** and **dissolution of responsibility** are also important factors.
- Perception of one's own **competence** is an additional factor.

- The theory provides a useful **theoretical framework** within which research can be carried out. However, it is largely **descriptive**, and focuses more on why people do not help than why they do. It does not cover **other influences** on the decision-making process which have been shown to be important.

Piliavin's arousal:cost-reward model

One factor discussed in relation to the Kitty Genovese case was the cost to the potential helper of offering help. Cost and reward are considered by **exchange theory**, a theory which has applications in several areas of social psychology. It states that **profit = rewards − costs**. For example, costs of helping may include time, money, effort and potential danger. Rewards can be either **extrinsic** (such as money or the gratitude of the person helped) or **intrinsic** (such as satisfaction in knowing that you have helped save a life, or avoiding guilt feelings caused by not helping). In any situation, if the costs are outweighed by the rewards, then there is a net profit in helping. If not, the potential helper is unlikely to offer help.

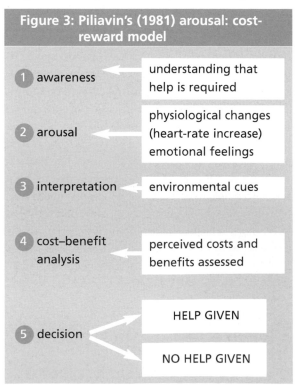

Figure 3: Piliavin's (1981) arousal: cost-reward model

1 awareness	understanding that help is required
2 arousal	physiological changes (heart-rate increase) emotional feelings
3 interpretation	environmental cues
4 cost–benefit analysis	perceived costs and benefits assessed
5 decision	HELP GIVEN / NO HELP GIVEN

Piliavin *et al.* (1981) built on this theory in their **arousal:cost-reward** model of helping behaviour, intended to apply to helping in both emergency and non-emergency situations. The cost-reward part of the model uses the principles of exchange theory, but Piliavin *et al.* argued that this only covers the cognitive elements of the decision-making process, i.e. thoughts, judgements and so on. They suggested that emotional factors also need to be taken into account. They pointed out that we have an emotional reaction to what is going on around us. Seeing someone who needs help creates negative emotional states such as anxiety, and we are motivated to act in such a way as to reduce these unpleasant emotions (**negative state relief**). We then carry out a cost–benefit analysis to reach a decision as to whether the rewards of helping, including the relief of our distress, are worth the costs involved.

The model goes on to predict whether or not help is likely to be given, taking into account both the costs of helping and the costs of *not* helping. Staying with someone who has been injured while an ambulance arrives would be a high cost if you were in a hurry, whereas spending a few moments to tell someone the time would be a low cost. Believing that someone might have died because of your failure to help would be a high cost of not helping, whereas knowing that there were plenty of potential helpers around would mean that not helping was low cost; if something went wrong, you would feel less guilty because of the presence of others. The model also predicts whether if help is given, it will be direct help:

		costs of helping	
		LOW	HIGH
costs of not helping	HIGH	direct help	indirect or no help
	LOW	help depends on social norms	no help

Figure 4: the likelihood of helping (Piliavin *et al.* 1981)

Indirect help here refers to behaviour such as phoning for an ambulance, or asking someone else to help. Where costs of helping and costs of not helping are both low, Piliavin *et al.* suggested that there is quite a high probability of help being given, but this will largely depend on the person and how responsive they are to social norms. **Social norms** are accepted ways of behaving in particular social situations. Two social norms in particular have been related to helping behaviour. The first is the **principle of reciprocity**, i.e. behaving towards others as you would expect them to behave towards you. The second is the **social responsibility** norm; people feel they have a social obligation to give help to people who need it.

▶ Activity 9: relating examples to Piliavin's predictions

In each of these scenarios, decide whether you would offer help, and if so, whether you would offer direct or indirect help.
Then decide in each situation whether:
    a the costs of helping are high or low and
    b the costs of *not* helping are high or low.
1 A small child is about to run past you to retrieve his ball which has rolled into the road. There is quite a lot of traffic about.
2 In a fairly busy street, you notice a tourist looking at a map, and then looking around, clearly unsure as to where they are.
3 You are in a hurry to keep an important appointment. An elderly woman has had a fall and is lying on the pavement, clutching her head and groaning.
4 Just ahead of you, a man – staggering slightly and carrying a bottle – approaches several passers-by, saying he feels ill and asking whether they will take him to a doctor. His speech is slurred.
Do your decisions relate to the predictions made by Piliavin's model, shown in Figure 3?
When you have finished, see the notes on page 270.

Most research in this area has investigated the effect of costs on providing help. For example:

Box L: Gross *et al.* (1975)

Procedure: Participants were asked to volunteer to take part in an experiment which would last about 20 minutes and involve filling in a questionnaire. In the high-cost condition, participants were asked to go to the university to complete the questionnaire. In the low-cost condition, they were given stamped envelopes and told they could fill in the questionnaire at home and send it in.

Results: Of participants in the low-cost condition, 81% agreed to take part, compared to only 49% in the high-cost condition.

Conclusion: High costs reduce the likelihood of help being offered.

However, Piliavin's model looks not only at the effect of costs but also at possible rewards against which the costs may be balanced:

▶ Activity 10: costs and rewards in helping behaviour

For each of the following scenarios, list the costs and rewards of helping. Use this to decide how likely it is that you would offer help. Use a rating scale from 5 (extremely likely) to 0 (extremely unlikely):

1 As you are walking along the road, you see a letter lying on the ground. It has a stamp on which hasn't been postmarked. It looks as if the letter were dropped on the way to the post box 100 metres up the road.

2 You are walking through the city centre on Saturday afternoon on your way to visit a friend. A young man comes up to you and asks if you have any spare change.

3 You are in a crowded shopping mall. A child of about 5 years of age is standing alone and crying: 'Mummy! I want my mummy!'

4 You are walking home late at night. No one is about. There is a man lying on the pavement, talking to himself and groaning occasionally. There is a bottle lying in the gutter nearby.

5 Your little sister wants you to take her to see the latest Disney film. It is half term and you have a psychology practical to write up.

If you are working with others, did your assessments roughly agree with the rest of the group?

You might have found that this is quite a good way to get a rough idea of how likely it is that help will be offered. You probably also found that there were many factors in each situation which you identified as important in assessing costs and rewards. These are likely to relate to the characteristics of the person needing help, the characteristics of the potential helper, and characteristics of the situation. All of these kinds of factors mediate our assessment of costs and rewards, and can be accommodated in Piliavin's model. We will now look at each of them in turn.

● Piliavin's **arousal:cost-reward model** includes both **cognitive** and **emotional factors** in the decision-making process.

● The model predicts the likelihood of help being offered in terms of the costs both of helping and of not helping.

Characteristics of the person needing help
There has been considerable research into this area, and a few examples will serve to show that characteristics of the person needing help may indeed be an important factor in determining whether or not help is offered. One classic piece of research is shown in box M:

Box M: Piliavin *et al.* (1969)

Procedure: A scene was staged in the New York subway, where a man appeared to collapse as the train pulled away from the station. In one condition, the man was carrying a cane; in the other condition he was carrying a bottle. The percentage of people offering help within 10 seconds was noted.

Results: In the 'cane' condition 95% of bystanders helped, compared to 50% in the 'bottle' condition.
Conclusion: Judgements about the person needing help can affect whether or not help is given.

An important concept here is that of **causal attribution**, in other words what we believe has led up to a particular situation. This idea was originally put forward by Heider (1944), and has been found useful in several areas of psychology. It is discussed in more detail in chapter 8. In the area of helping behaviour, it suggests we make assumptions about the reasons leading up to a person needing help. We may make **external** attributions (reasons outside the person's control, e.g. luck) or **internal**

attributions (reasons over which the person has some control, e.g. attitudes and beliefs).

The second example in activity 10 can help to illustrate this idea and its effect. It is possible that you thought something along the lines of: 'Poor man, there's not much work around. No wonder he can't get a job.' You might also have thought: 'Lazy man, can't be bothered to go out and look for work.' In the first instance, you would be making an external attribution (the man is a victim of the economic situation) and in the second, an internal attribution (it is his own fault he is in this situation). In the Piliavin *et al.* study (box M), the man with the cane could be seen as a victim of illness, whereas the man with the bottle could be seen as responsible for his (apparently) drunken state. An external attribution is more likely to lead to an offer of help than an internal one.

But judgements about others, and hence the likelihood of them being offered help, are not based solely on attributions. Unambiguous characteristics of the person needing help also have a part to play. Box N gives examples of some factors which have been shown to be important:

Box N: characteristics of the person needing help

1. physical attractiveness: Benson et al. (1976)
Job applications with an attached photograph were left in a busy telephone box. The form was much more likely to be returned to the applicant where the photo was of a physically attractive person.
2. race: West et al. (1975)
Black drivers in a black neighbourhood who seemed to be having problems with their car were helped faster than white drivers. The same was true of white drivers in a white neighbourhood.
3. gender: West et al. (1975)
A female driver standing at the side of the road with a car with a raised bonnet, which had apparently broken down, was helped significantly faster than a male in the same position.

4. age: Tipton and Browning (1972)

People aged 50–60 who dropped groceries were helped to retrieve them more often than 20–30-year-olds.

5. appearance: (a) Graf and Ridell (1972)

A student stood near a car which had apparently broken down, and tried to get a lift to a petrol station from passing motorists. In one condition, the student had short hair and was neatly dressed. In the second condition, he had shoulder-length hair and was casually dressed in jeans and sandals. Drivers stopped significantly more often for the student in the first condition.

(b) Piliavin *et al.* (1975)

The percentage of people offering help to a person with an ugly facial birthmark who had apparently collapsed in the subway was considerably lower than the percentage offering to help a person with no birthmark.

6. similarity between the potential helper and the person needing help: Karabenick *et al.* (1973)

In the USA, on Election Day, an experimenter posing as a campaign worker dropped a pile of political posters supporting either Nixon or McGovern. The experimenter observed whether help was offered or not, and later asked participants about their political preference. Help in picking up the posters was given more often to those supporting either the Republican or the Democratic party, i.e. with similar political views to the helper.

The study on race (see 2, above) also illustrates similarity.

▶ Activity 11: characteristics of the person needing help

How could you relate each research example outlined in box N to Piliavin's arousal:cost-reward model of helping behaviour?

When you have finished, see the notes on page 271.

Characteristics of the potential helper

If, as suggested in box N, similarity influences whether or not we offer help, there are likely to be **individual differences** between people in their willingness to help in any given situation. You will remember that Piliavin *et al.* suggested this in the prediction they made about the probability of help being offered in a situation where the costs of both helping and not helping are low. If you carried out activity 10 in a group, you could check this by comparing the ratings you made with those of others in the group, as suggested at the end of the activity.

There is also evidence to suggest that there are considerable personality differences between people, with some being ready to help in almost any situation, and some being in general much less helpful:

Box O: Oliner and Oliner (1988)

Procedure: This study investigated the personality characteristics, attitudes and beliefs of 231 non-Jews who helped save Jews during the Nazi persecution of the second world war, and compared them with 126 non-Jews who did not intervene in this way.

Results: The former group had a stronger belief in equality. As predicted by the arousal:cost-reward model, those who showed greater empathy for people who were suffering were more likely to help.

Conclusion: Personality differences are a factor in willingness to help.

This is an interesting study in that it relates to a real situation, and it looks at enduring facets of personality. Similar results were reported by Bierhoff *et al.* (1991), in a study of first aiders who helped traffic accident victims. Those who helped scored high on a social responsibility scale and an empathy scale.

However, characteristics of the potential helper also relate to more transient factors, such as mood and what their immediate preoccupations are:

Box P: Darley and Batson (1973)

Procedure: Students at Princeton Theological Seminary were told they were to make a videotaped speech. Some were to talk about jobs for seminary students and some about the parable of the Good Samaritan. After a few minutes to make notes, they were told to go to another building to make the recording. Some were told that they were running late, others that they were on time, and others that they were early. To get there, they needed to go down an alley, where they passed a man lying in a doorway, moaning.

Results: The topic on which they were to give a speech had some effect on whether or not the man was offered help. The 'hurry' variable, however, had a much stronger influence:

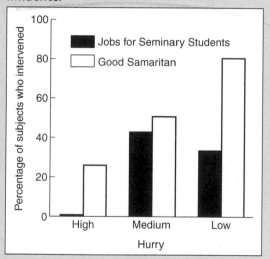

Conclusion: Immediate preoccupations can affect willingness to help.

It is perhaps worth noting that even after thinking about helping behaviour in the parable of the Good Samaritan, only four out of five of the group with time to spare stopped to help. This could perhaps be related to making an internal attribution: when asked later, some of the students said the reason why they didn't stop to help was that they thought the man might have been drunk. This helps to highlight the idea that in any decision whether to help, there are likely to be several different factors which determine whether help is offered or not.

Characteristics of the situation

We have already considered some situational factors which affect whether or not help is offered: for example, diffusion (or dissolution) of responsibility, and how competent a person feels to help in a particular situation. Latané (1970) showed that the decision whether or not to help can also be influenced by whether we are alone or in the company of others. In New York, 2091 passers-by were asked for a subway fare. Those alone were significantly more likely to give the requested money than people walking in groups of two or three.

Many studies have also found that if someone responds to a small request for help, they are more likely also to respond to a further, larger request. This is known as the **foot-in-the-door technique**. An example could be someone asking on the street for 50p for a cup of coffee; if this is successful they would then follow this up with a request for £5 to get some food. This phenomenon has been demonstrated experimentally:

Box Q: Freedman and Fraser (1966)

Procedure: Housewives were asked a few questions about some of the household products they used. They were later asked to allow a team of researchers to list and classify all the products they used.

Results: Women who agreed to answer the initial set of questions were more likely to agree to all their household products being surveyed than women who were not asked the initial questions.

Conclusion: Agreeing to a small request makes it more likely that a larger request will then be complied with: the foot-in-the-door phenomenon.

Freedman and Fraser found similar results in a second study, where suburban housewives were more likely to allow a large unattractive sign promoting safe driving to be erected in their gardens if they had previously agreed to sign a petition or place a small sign in their window.

Activity 12: the foot-in-the-door technique

How would you explain the effectiveness of the foot-in-the-door technique?

When you have finished, see the notes on page 271.

- **Characteristics of the person needing help** influence the decision whether or not help is offered. These include **physical characteristics**, such as race, gender and physical attractiveness. We also make **attributions** about the causes underlying the need for help. If we make internal attributions, we are less likely to offer help than if we make external attributions.
- **Characteristics of the potential helper** are also important. People differ considerably in their willingness to offer help. Such differences may be fundamental and rooted in their personality, or influenced by more transient factors such as mood or current preoccupations.
- Factors relating to the **situation** include the presence of others, and previous helping. The foot-in-the-door technique can be effective in getting people to offer help.

Evaluation of Piliavin's arousal:cost-reward model

The arousal:cost-reward model is useful in adding the important element of emotional response to exchange theory, and in providing a framework within which research in this area can be carried out. It is more flexible than Latané's information-processing model, in that it can accommodate a range of factors in the decision-making process which have been shown to influence whether or not help is offered.

At the same time, it is questionable whether the principles it proposes apply equally to both emergency and non-emergency situations. While these ideas are appealing in the context of non-emergency situations, do people really carry out the sort of calculation the model suggests when faced with an emergency?

The model proposes that help is least likely to be given in high-cost situations. However, selfless behaviour – such as that shown by the two men mentioned at the start of this section, who tried to rescue a girl who had fallen through thin ice into a pond – is not unusual. The level of arousal of bystanders is likely to be high in an emergency situation, and the idea that they would then calmly weigh up costs and rewards is not entirely convincing.

However, Piliavin *et al.* (1981) introduced a modification to the model which takes this into account. They suggested that when people are faced with an emergency situation, they become extremely aroused. This narrows their focus of attention, so that they consider only the plight of the victim, so weighing up the costs of offering help becomes of only secondary importance.

- Piliavin's **arousal:cost-reward model** relates to helping in both emergency and non-emergency situations, and allows the likelihood of helping to be predicted. It can accommodate the range of factors which have been found to be important in the decision whether or not to help.
- The extent to which it can be applied to helping in an emergency situation has been questioned. This is taken into account in a modification of the model.

Batson's empathy–altruism hypothesis

Piliavin's arousal:cost-reward model suggests that while helping behaviour on the surface seems to be for the benefit of someone else, the motivation for helping is ultimately selfish. The 'arousal' part of Piliavin's model suggests that we experience an unpleasant emotional response in situations where someone requires help, so we act to reduce these feelings. In the cognitive element in the decision-making process, we weigh up the relative costs and benefits to ourselves before we offer help. In other words, the motivation for helping is egotistical.

But not all theorists share this view. Batson (1990) did not deny that some altruistic behaviour rests on selfish concerns, but he also proposed the **empathy–altruism hypothesis**. This suggests that helping behaviour can arise from genuine concern for others. Seeing another person's need or suffering creates empathy, a personal understanding of their feelings and experiences. We focus on *their* needs, not our own, and are motivated to help for *their* sake.

Some theorists have even argued that this ability to empathise may be innate, part of the essence of being human. Hoffman (1981) found that newborn infants in the first few hours of life become distressed and cry if they hear another baby crying; if this is an expression of empathy, its early appearance supports the idea that it may be inborn. Most people admit to crying (or at least feeling very sad) when watching a sad film, so empathy seems at least to be an adult characteristic.

The possible link between helping and empathy has been tested experimentally:

Box R: Batson *et al.* (1981)

Procedure: Female participants observed Elaine, a confederate of the experimenters, apparently receiving painful electric shocks. Some participants were led to believe that Elaine had similar attitudes to themselves (high attitude similarity), while some believed her to have dissimilar attitudes (low attitude similarity). In addition, some participants were told that they could leave the room after the second trial, and so not continue to observe Elaine's apparent suffering (easy escape condition), while others were told that they would need to observe Elaine's behaviour till the end of the experiment (difficult escape condition). Each participant was asked whether she would be willing to take Elaine's place.

Results: In the easy-escape/low-attitude-similarity condition, participants were unwilling to help Elaine. The proportion of helpers was much greater in the other three conditions.

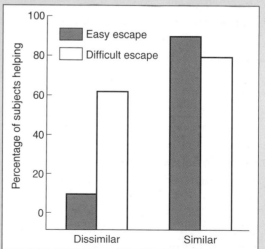

Conclusion: If people are egotistically oriented, they might prefer to escape to reduce negative arousal. However, people motivated by empathy would not be as likely to leave the situation, since their desire to help a victim would persist after they had left. Empathy was increased in high attitude similarity conditions, but helping was greater in the easy escape condition, suggesting that participants in the easy-escape/high-attitude-similarity condition were motivated by empathy.

However, other studies investigating the role of empathy in helping behaviour have not always supported these findings. For example, Cialdini *et al.* (1987) carried out a partial replication of the study in box R. They found that participants in the high-empathy/easy-escape condition showed a low rate of helping if they were offered financial incentives to take Elaine's place. This could possibly have come about because accepting financial benefits changed their self-perceptions; they would see themselves as helping for their own gain, rather than because of empathy for Elaine.

It is possible that the kind of pattern of helping behaviour Batson *et al.* observed only emerges in certain situations. Batson *et al.* (1983) have also suggested that there are individual differences between people in whether helping behaviour is motivated by altruism or egotism.

The main problem with this theory seems to be that it is in practice very difficult to discriminate between helping for egotistical and altruistic reasons. If we behave empathically, we put ourselves in the position of the victim and to this extent share their suffering. However, at the same time, reduction in the suffering of the victim reduces our negative feelings. The relief we experience then serves an egotistical purpose.

❺ **Batson's empathy–altruism hypothesis** suggests that we may help for genuinely altruistic rather than egotistical reasons.
❺ There is some evidence that this may be true in some circumstances. However, it is difficult in practice to differentiate between altruistic and egotistic motivation.

Cultural variation in prosocial behaviour

All the research on helping behaviour we have looked at so far was carried out in the USA, so is rather limited in the range of people studied. These studies have shown a range of basic factors to be important in the decision whether or not to help. However, is it safe to assume that the same factors apply equally to any human population? The tendency to make this assumption is something we need to be very aware of when drawing broad conclusions about human behaviour from a limited sample.

Each cultural group has **social norms**. Cultures also share **values**, which specify what kinds of behaviour are considered desirable. We all need to go through the processes of socialisation to acquire the norms and values relevant to our culture. If we behave differently from the prescribed cultural norms, there are likely to be negative consequences, such as the disapproval of others.

Norms and values vary considerably between cultures and subcultures because there is such wide cross-cultural variation in social structure. We need to remember, then, that what may be true of the social behaviour of Americans does not necessarily apply to people living in the Kalahari Desert or Australian sheepshearers.

Hsu (1971) proposed that cultures can be divided into two broad groupings, individualist and collectivist. In **individualist** cultures, such as the USA and other Western cultures, emphasis is placed on individual freedom and looking after our own interests, with less concern for the welfare of others. In **collectivist** cultures, such as China, Japan and some other Asian cultures, together with some Latin American countries, individual wishes are seen as less important than the well-being of the group. It might therefore be expected that prosocial behaviour would be more apparent in collectivist cultures:

Box S: Eisenberg and Mussen (1989)

Procedure: An overview of cross-cultural research into children's prosocial behaviour was carried out. The kinds of behaviour studied included kindness, consideration for others and co-operation.

Results: North American children were in general less kind, considerate and co-operative than children who had grown up in Mexican villages, Hopi children reared on Indian reservations or Israeli children reared in kibbutzim.

Conclusion: There is a relationship between the type of culture within which children grow up and the degree of prosocial behaviour they show. Children reared within a collectivist culture tend to show more prosocial behaviour than those reared in an individualist culture.

However, the distinction between individualist and collectivist cultures may be too broad to give a clear picture of cultural differences in helping behaviour, since members of cultures which can be in general classified under one heading may also vary in their willingness to help:

Box T: Feldman (1968)

Procedure: Passers-by in Paris, France; Athens, Greece; and Boston, Massachusetts were asked for help by a compatriot couple and a foreign couple. In the first situation, they were asked for directions, while in the second they were asked to post a letter which was either stamped or unstamped.

Results: In the first situation, Bostonians were the most helpful overall to both compatriots and foreigners, and helped both equally. Parisians and Athenians helped compatriots more than they did foreigners. In the second situation, Athenians treated compatriots worse than foreigners, while Bostonians treated foreigners worse than compatriots. Parisians treated compatriots and foreigners the same. There was no difference between the treatment of foreigners in Athens and Boston.

Conclusion: There are wide variations between individual cultures in prosocial behaviour. The extent to which help is offered in a particular culture is influenced by the situation in which it is required.

A further study has investigated the effect of specific cultural beliefs:

Box U: L'Armand and Pepitone (1975)

Procedure: A comparison was made between altruistic behaviour in the United States and India. The attitudes to and beliefs about helping in the two cultures were also explored.

Results: In contrast to what would be predicted from the individualist versus collectivist distinction, Americans were in general more altruistic than Indians, but only in low-cost situations. There was a cultural belief among Indians that all types of rewards are fixed and limited, so one person's gain is another's loss.

Conclusion: Cultural beliefs and attitudes can affect helping behaviour.

There has also been a certain amount of research looking at subcultural differences in helping behaviour within a particular culture and, in particular, differences between classes:

Box V: Muir and Weinstein (1962)

Procedure: In a study in the USA, middle-class and lower-class women were questioned about helping behaviour and the principles that they used in deciding whether or not to help.

Results: Middle-class women worked on exchange principles, i.e. according to what is 'fair', following the same general principles as financial help. They felt obliged to help others who had helped them in the past, but did not help again people who had not 'repaid' the help they had already been given. Lower-class women, on the other hand, were more likely to help when they were able.

Conclusion: There are class differences in helping behaviour.

This research was carried out over 30 years ago, so it is quite possible that there have been sufficiently large cultural changes in that time to make the validity of this conclusion questionable. There does not seem to have been much recent research in this particular area. However, it is perhaps worth noting that similar results have been found in other countries, e.g. Turkey (Ugurel-Semin, 1952) and Israel (Dreman and Greenbaum, 1973).

❺ It is unwise to draw general conclusions based on the behaviour of a particular culture or subculture. Cultures and subcultures have different **social norms** and **values**, acquired through socialisation, which affect social behaviour.

❺ People in **collectivist** societies are likely to be more helpful than those in **individualist** societies, though this is not always the case. This distinction may be too broad to account for the cultural differences which have been found in helping behaviour.

❺ Studies have also demonstrated **subcultural** and in particular class differences in helping behaviour.

10.5 MEDIA INFLUENCES ON PRO- AND ANTI-SOCIAL BEHAVIOUR

An important social and political issue is the extent to which the mass media can influence behaviour, in terms of encouraging both anti-social and prosocial behaviour. Certainly direct media appeals for violent behaviour can be appallingly effective; for example, in Rwanda in 1994, radio appeals to Hutus to go out and murder Tutsis resulted in hundreds of thousands of members of both communities being murdered.

This section looks at two specific media, television and film, and their influence on one type of anti-social behaviour, i.e. violence, and on prosocial thought and behaviour.

Anti-social behaviour

In social learning theory (SLT), discussed at the start of this chapter, Bandura *et al.* (1963) suggested that the media are one source of models for learning social behaviour. In one version of his Bobo doll studies, children watched a video of an adult

attacking the Bobo doll. While imitation of aggressive models was less than in the experiment using live models, children nonetheless imitated the adult models. This seems to lend support to Bandura's claim that the media are a source of models. This is an idea which has found quite wide public acceptance, and the question of censorship is frequently discussed in the press. For example, there has been a lot of discussion about the V-chip which would allow children's television viewing to be censored.

There are frequent examples in the press of murders which are said to have been inspired by films. When *Natural Born Killers* was released in 1994, a 14-year-old boy in France killed a 13-year-old girl. He claimed that he 'wanted to be famous, like the Natural Born Killers'. A further case in the USA concerned a young man called Nathan Martinez, who had seen the film ten times. He shot his mother and stepsister, and fantasised about driving off with a friend, like Mickey and Mallory had done in the film. It was also suggested that the two young boys who abducted and killed James Bulger had been influenced by watching the video *Child's Play 3*.

It is possible that murders have been inspired by films such as *Natural Born Killers*

However, this evidence is anecdotal and only correlational. For example, it cannot tell us whether the children were violent because of the films they watched, or whether they were violent individuals who chose to watch these films, and in doing so picked up ideas about how their violence might be expressed. In any case, claims made by defence lawyers that their clients had acted violently as the result of watching particular films are unlikely to be objective.

There has been considerable research into this area, focusing especially on the effects of violence on television, particularly on young children.

▷ Activity 13: violence on television

Make a list of as many kinds of TV programmes as you can which contain aggressive behaviour.

When you have finished, see the notes on page 271.

It has been estimated that 80% of programmes contain violence, rising to 93% at weekends, and that a child watching for four hours a day will have witnessed 13,000 murders by the age of 16. If verbal aggression is included, there is an average of 1.96 violent events an hour.

A survey carried out by Cullingford (1984) found that 80% of 7–12 year olds had watched television the previous night. Typically they had watched between three and six programmes. Many 9-year-olds and most of the older children had at some time watched programmes after midnight.

However, a more recent study of the incidence of violence on British TV (Frean, 1995) found that violent acts made up only 1% of the programme content on terrestrial TV and less than 2% on satellite channels. They also found that 1% of programmes contain 19% of all violent acts. It is possible, then, that children may not be exposed to as much violence on television as is generally thought.

There seems no doubt, though, that children are exposed to violence on television. But does this exposure lead to aggression in children? It is perhaps worth bearing in mind that Bandura found that while exposure to violent behaviour leads to the behaviour being learned, it does not necessarily follow that the behaviour will be imitated. You will remember from box A that Bandura (1965) found

that spontaneous imitation of the observed behaviour only occurred when there was no negative outcome for the aggressive model.

One example of a study to investigate a possible causal link between viewing violence and aggressive behaviour is described in box W:

Box W: Ellis and Sekgra (1972)

Procedure: Children were shown either an aggressive or a non-violent cartoon. The researchers then observed the levels of aggressive behaviour the children displayed.

Results: Children watching the violent cartoon behaved more aggressively than the controls shown the non-violent cartoon.

Conclusion: Watching media violence causes aggressive behaviour in children.

▷ Activity 14: laboratory studies of media violence

What criticisms could be made of accepting a link between media violence and aggression, based on research such as the study in box W?

When you have finished, see the notes on page 271.

More naturalistic field studies have also been carried out:

Box X: Friedrich and Stein (1973)

Procedure: Children in a nursery school were observed over a period of 3 weeks, in order to establish a baseline measure of aggressive behaviour. Over the next 4 weeks, they were shown either violent cartoons, non-violent cartoons or prosocial cartoons. Their behaviour during this time and for the following two weeks was observed.

Results: Children who were initially above average in terms of aggressive behaviour were affected by the violent cartoons, and showed more aggressive behaviour. Other children were not affected.

Conclusion: Watching violent cartoons can lead to a rise in aggressive behaviour, but only for children who are already aggressive.

This study has the advantage of looking at more naturally occurring behaviour, and also takes a rather more long-term approach than the typical laboratory study. It is also interesting in that it looks at individual differences; the conclusions drawn from it suggest that it may be something of an oversimplification to propose a straightforward cause-and-effect relationship between being exposed to TV violence and aggressive behaviour.

Possible long-term effects of TV violence have also been investigated:

Box Y: Williams (1985)

Procedure: In this study, Williams carried out a natural experiment, taking advantage of a naturally occurring event. Children's behaviour was monitored in a town in British Columbia, before and after it was able to receive television.

Results: Two years after the arrival of television, children were found to be more aggressive, both verbally and physically. There was no increase in aggression over this period in similar communities which already had television.

Conclusion: Television violence is associated with an increase in children's aggressive behaviour. These effects can be long-term.

Activity 15: evaluating the Williams (1985) study

What reservations do you have about the conclusion drawn by this study?

Are there other factors which the study might need to take into account?

When you have finished, see the notes on page 271.

The above studies, however, are either correlational studies (e.g. Williams, box Y) or experimental studies (e.g. Friedrich and Stein, box X), in which demand characteristics may have played a part in influencing children's behaviour. This has led some researchers to claim that although there seems to be a link between exposure to violence on television and aggressive behaviour, it is also possible that naturally aggressive people actively seek out violent programmes:

Box Z: Eron *et al.* (1972)

Procedure: The amount of TV violence to which 9-year-olds were exposed was measured by asking parents what their children's favourite TV programmes were. The children's peers were also asked to rate them for aggressiveness. Peer ratings and measures of the amount of TV violence watched were also taken 10 years later.

Results: For the 9-year-olds, there was a high measure of correlation between peer ratings for aggression and exposure to TV violence. For boys, there was a high correlation between watching violent TV at 9 and peer-rated aggression at 19. There was no correlation between watching violent TV at 19 and peer-rated aggression at 9. The findings were much less clear for girls.

Conclusion: The idea that watching TV violence leads to aggression is supported, especially for boys. The alternative possibility, that being aggressive leads people to seek out violent TV programmes, is not supported.

Activity 16: problems in studying the effects of TV violence

In reading through this section, what problems have you identified which make it difficult to establish a clear connection between watching violent programmes on television and aggressive behaviour? (Hint: ethics and methodology) Compare your ideas with the discussion which follows.

Aggression has often been studied through controlled research, where the experimenter manipulates the material to which the participants are exposed. This has the advantage of allowing the researcher to control possible confounding variables, but may present problems in terms of possible demand characteristics and low ecological validity. Although children often do watch this kind of material on their own, they may not often be in an unfamiliar situation when they do so, and instructed to watch by an unfamiliar adult.

These studies are often carried out using children as participants. Because of this, the material used has often been quite mild, in particular cartoons. There would be a serious ethical question over the use of anything more extreme, though many children are exposed to much more violent material outside the laboratory. But this does mean that this kind of research can be criticised for not giving us a realistic picture of possible links between exposure to TV violence and aggressive behaviour.

Non-experimental methods, such as correlational studies and naturalistic observation, are one way of trying to overcome these methodological and ethical problems. At the same time, findings using these methods are also more likely to be affected by confounding variables, and so it is extremely difficult to establish a clear relationship between the factors

being investigated. This has already been noted in the discussion of the Williams study (box Y).

Explaining the effects of media violence

Although the picture is far from clear, the research we looked at in the previous section has given some support to the idea that watching violent TV programmes is associated with aggressive behaviour. SLT offers one explanation for this link: children learn through observational learning and modelling. The use of violence may be reinforced by seeing it used effectively as a way of coping with difficulties.

Several other ideas have been put forward to explain why watching TV violence might lead to aggressive behaviour. One key idea is **desensitisation**. If we are continually exposed to violence, we become less sensitive to it; it has less and less effect on us. It can be compared to taking a drug, to which we gradually become tolerant – we need more and more to achieve the same effect. While desensitisation does not itself explain violent behaviour, it can explain a tendency to watch increasingly violent television.

There is some evidence that desensitisation may be a factor in aggression. Cline *et al*. (1973) looked at physiological responses to violence, e.g. increased heart rate and raised blood pressure. They found that children who watched a lot of television showed less physiological response when shown a violent film, suggesting that they were less sensitive to what they were seeing.

In a further study carried out by Drabman and Thomas (1974), children saw either a violent or a non-violent TV programme. They then witnessed a fight, which was staged, but which the children thought was real. Children who had seen the violent TV programme were less likely to report the fight to an adult, presumably because they had been desensitised to violence as a result of watching the violent TV programme.

Watching TV may also shape our beliefs and attitudes. If we watch others behaving aggressively, we can come to see this kind of behaviour as a legitimate way of dealing with problems. This can lead to **disinhibition**. Watching other people behave aggressively may remove the restraints we have put on our behaviour; we lose the inhibitions we have about behaving in this way.

Activity 17: advising parents on TV violence

Look back through this section. On the basis of this material, what advice would you give to parents who are worried about their children watching violent television programmes?

The advice you give has to be a personal response to this information, but this activity should have helped to reinforce the idea that there are no very straightforward answers here.

⊖ There is some evidence that exposure to violent television programmes is related to aggressive behaviour. It is more likely that watching violence leads to aggressive behaviour than that aggressive people seek out violent programmes.

⊖ There are **ethical** and **methodological problems** in carrying out research in this area. It is therefore hard to establish a clear-cut connection.

⊖ Bandura's **SLT** can explain the connection between media violence and aggressive behaviour. **Desensitisation** and **disinhibition** have also been suggested as reasons for the link.

Prosocial behaviour

The term 'prosocial behaviour' refers to helping behaviour, but is also applied more widely to any behaviour which has a positive outcome. If Bandura is right, children should model not only anti-social but also prosocial behaviour. There has been some research into this possibility.

One approach has been to use instructional films. For example, O'Connor (1969) looked at the usefulness of models for children who had difficulty in relating appropriately to others. They were shown a film of children their own age interacting with others, with their behaviour having a positive outcome. Watching the film had a beneficial effect on the children's behaviour.

A further study also looked at the possible **therapeutic applications** of this kind of material. For example, Bandura and Menlove (1968) showed

pre-school children who were afraid of dogs a series of films showing children playing with dogs. This experience helped them to overcome their fear.

Educational broadcasts can also have a prosocial effect, and some are designed with this in mind. For example, *Sesame Street* and *Mister Rogers' Neighbourhood* were developed to help children from a deprived background to learn basic literacy and numeracy skills, together with social skills. Coates and Pusser (1975) found that children did indeed benefit from such programmes, and particularly those from the poorest backgrounds.

Educational broadcasts, such as *Sesame Street*, can have a prosocial effect

Other programmes, not specifically developed with an educational aim, can also contribute to children's prosocial behaviour:

Box AA: Sprafkin et al. (1975)

Procedure: Children aged 5 and 6 watched one of three films. Group A saw an episode of *Lassie*, in which a boy risked his life to save a puppy. Group B watched a *Lassie* episode carrying a positive message about dogs, but with no incident of a human helping a dog. Group C watched an episode of *The Brady Bunch*, a family-based situation comedy.

All the children then took part in a button-pressing game where they could win prizes. At the same time, they wore headphones through which they could (supposedly) hear a kennel, and were asked to press a button if they heard the barking of a puppy in distress. This would mean breaking off from the prize game, so they needed to make a choice between the prize game and helping the puppy.

Results: Group A children chose to help the puppies more quickly and for longer periods than children in the other two groups.

Conclusion: Programmes showing prosocial behaviour can encourage children to behave unselfishly.

The study in box AA shows a prosocial effect when the behaviour being modelled is very similar to the behaviour shown by the children. However, the effects of watching prosocial material can also be more generalised. For example, Baran (1979) compared children who had watched an episode of *The Waltons*, where characters were generally helpful to each other, with children who had seen another programme with no prosocial content. Those who had watched *The Waltons* were more likely to help the experimenter when he dropped a pile of books.

The studies we have looked at up till now have all been laboratory studies. An example of a study which has investigated children's natural viewing habits is described in box BB:

Box BB: Sprafkin and Rubinstein (1979)

Procedure: The programmes watched by the group of children being studied were classified according to the amount of prosocial and anti-social material they contained. The amount of TV watched was also noted. Ratings for the children's prosocial behaviour were obtained from the children themselves and their teachers.

Results: There was a positive correlation between watching programmes with a high prosocial content and children's prosocial behaviour. There was a negative correlation between the amount of TV watched and prosocial behaviour.

Conclusion: Both the amount of TV watched and the kinds of programmes watched are related to prosocial behaviour.

Another way in which it has been suggested that TV can have a prosocial effect (e.g. by Rydin, 1976) is that it encourages children to think about moral problems, and therefore has the prosocial effect of encouraging the development of **moral reasoning**. There is some evidence that this may be the case. However, findings have been mixed, and seem to relate not only to the kind of TV programmes watched, but also to the amount of TV watched overall (a link already suggested in the findings of the research in box BB) and the age of the child.

For example, Gunter *et al.* (1991) found that children aged 10–16, asked to talk about TV dramas, could talk about the moral themes in these dramas, understand the difference between right and wrong, and criticise wrong behaviour even when it was carried out by their favourite characters.

However, Rosenketter *et al.* (1990) found that for 4- and 5-year-olds, watching a lot of television was associated with poorer moral reasoning. However, for 7- and 8-year-olds a preference for watching situation comedies was associated with a better understanding of the importance of helping people in need. Children aged 10 and 11 preferred shows high in action and adventure. Children who watched these programmes also more often had poorer moral reasoning skills. However, it is difficult to draw any firm conclusions here. For example, it may be that children who have poor moral reasoning skills are those who take refuge in TV. Alternatively, it could be that being passive and sedentary, rather than watching a lot of TV, underlies the poor development of these skills.

Most research has tended to focus on investigating a possible link between watching violent TV programmes and anti-social behaviour, and has tended to downplay TV's potential prosocial influence. However, many TV programmes have a high prosocial content, and overall there is some evidence that watching TV in moderation can have prosocial effects on children, both in terms of their behaviour and their moral understanding.

❺ **Instructional films** can help children develop social skills and cope with problems.

❺ **Educational programmes** can help with literacy and numeracy skills.
❺ Children's behaviour is affected by prosocial **models** in mainstream TV programmes.
❺ There is some evidence that prosocial programmes can also have a positive effect on children's **moral understanding,** though findings are not clear-cut.

Notes on activities

2 Only 5, 7, 9 and 11 would not be classed as aggressive using Baron's definition.

3 a The researchers needed to be sure that the children had imitated the behaviour they had observed. Ordinary aggressive behaviour could have been produced spontaneously.

b Since these were laboratory studies, the children were put in an unfamiliar situation which could lead to **demand characteristics**; they were likely to have looked for cues as to what they were supposed to do in this situation. In addition, the kinds of play opportunities offered by a Bobo doll are limited; it is difficult to see how else the children could have responded to it. The experimental situation also had low **ecological validity**; it is not often that children experience such a simple demonstration of behaviour and its consequences, nor one where aggression is rewarded. Demand characteristics and ecological validity are discussed in chapter 7.

5 According to emergent-norm theory, in the Marsh study, a group norm of aggression had developed, and so group members behaved aggressively. In the Gergen *et al.* study, a norm of intimacy developed, to which the group members conformed.

6 Having to travel in a crowded underground train is likely to be experienced as unpleasant, and these conditions may make aggression more likely. However, if you are in a crowded club, you have chosen to be there, and the presence of lots of other people contributes to the atmosphere. In

this case, crowding is likely to be experienced as pleasant, and in these circumstances may be less likely to lead to aggression.

8 a You could offer direct help if you were a doctor, or perhaps a nurse or medical student, or someone with first aid training. Otherwise you could help indirectly by phoning for an ambulance and/or finding out if anyone else around at the time had any kind of medical training.

b You would need to be at least a competent swimmer and preferably have life-saving training to offer direct help. Otherwise you could offer indirect help by shouting to alert other people to the emergency, or by finding a stick to hold out for the person in the water to take hold of.

9 1 The costs of helping are low (you only have to catch hold of the child). The costs of not helping are high (he could get run over). The model would predict that you would be very likely to offer direct help.

2 The costs of helping are low (it would not take long to help with directions). The costs of not helping are low (there are other people around he can ask). The model would predict that the likelihood of offering help would be quite high here. However, social norms such as the principle of reciprocity and social responsibility could be outweighed by other norms common in some cultures, such as not approaching strangers, which might reduce the likelihood of offering help.

3 The costs of helping are high (offering help is likely to take time and you are in a hurry). The costs of not helping are high (she could be seriously hurt). The model would predict that the likelihood of offering help is high, but is more likely to be indirect, e.g. phoning for an ambulance, alerting someone else to the situation.

4 The costs of helping are high (the man appears to be drunk and could turn nasty, and the help he asks for is likely to be time-consuming). The costs of not helping are low (it doesn't seem to be an immediate emergency, and there are other people around who could help). The model would predict that the likelihood of offering help is low.

11 Examples **1** and **5a** can be linked to the idea of costs and benefits; the costs are not seen to be so high when we are helping someone towards whom we have a more positive attitude. Example **3** is likely to relate to social norms and attitudes to females in Western society. It may also relate to potential costs – we are less likely to be harmed by a female than a male. Examples **2**, **4**, **5b** and **6** relate to empathy; we are able to put ourselves in the place of the person needing help. Helping in this situation could be to do with negative state relief, but we will also be looking at the empathy–altruism hypothesis, which has a rather different explanation of how empathy leads to helping. In the example in **5b**, less empathy was felt with the person with the birthmark, resulting in a lower level of negative drive, leading in turn to lowered motivation to help, and a reduced likelihood of help being offered.

12 Freedman and Fraser explained this phenomenon in terms of a change in the way people see themselves. Once someone has agreed to a minor request, they may self-define as a helpful person, as someone who co-operates with good causes, and who therefore is ready to help again. More recent studies (e.g. Uranowitz, 1975) have tested and supported this explanation. It is also possible that initial helping makes the person more aware of behaviour which is socially approved, and this increases the likelihood of further helping. It is of course perfectly possible that both these explanations could have a part to play in the foot-in-the-door phenomenon; they are not mutually exclusive.

13 It is hard to think of a type of programme that *couldn't* potentially include aggressive behaviour. Crime series like *The Bill* come immediately to mind, but news and current affairs programmes often contain scenes of war and rioting, and sports programmes like boxing also show aggression. Programmes considered unsuitable for children are meant to be shown only after the 9 o'clock watershed, but you might also have included programmes intended for children, e.g. *Power Rangers* and *Tom and Jerry*.

14 First of all, this was a laboratory study. It is possible that the children were responding to demand characteristics, and behaving as they thought the experimenter wanted them to behave. Children in particular are often very eager to co-operate in an experimental situation. In addition, the situation itself is highly artificial and so may lack ecological validity. The children are instructed to watch cartoons by an unfamiliar adult in an unfamiliar environment, and are then put into another unfamiliar situation in which they may or may not show aggressive behaviour.

Another problem is that this kind of study can only show the *immediate* effects of TV violence. Violence on television is more of a problem if the effects are lasting, and a study of this kind cannot tell us this.

15 The conclusion would be more convincing if the study had looked at the amount of exposure to TV violence (and indeed TV in general) of the children who were being investigated. Did those who watched more TV show more aggression than those who watched less? What were children doing less of because of time spent watching TV? Could the increase in violence be related to lack of exercise, perhaps, or lack of interactive play? Were there individual differences in children's responses, as suggested by the study in box W? What other societal changes were there during this two-year period which might have affected levels of aggression?

Brain and behaviour

In this chapter we will be looking at:

11.1 Methods of investigating the brain
    Classic techniques
    Brain scanning techniques

11.2 Localisation of function in the
    cerebral cortex
      Motor and sensory areas
      Association areas
      Thought and language in the
        cortex

11.3 Lateralisation of function in the
    cerebral cortex
      Studies of normal lateralisation
      'Split-brain' research

11.4 The effects of cortical damage
      Disorders of visual perception
      Disorders of action and movement
      Spoken language disorders
      Disorders of reading and writing
      Disorders of memory
      Disorders of emotional expression

11.5 Recovery from cerebral lesions

11.1 METHODS OF INVESTIGATING THE BRAIN

One of the earliest attempts at mapping cortical functions was the system of **phrenology**, introduced by Gall in the early part of the nineteenth century. This approach claimed to be able to associate bumps on the skull with the development of the underlying areas of the brain, and made links between specific abilities and specific parts of the skull. For instance, language was supposedly located in the area below the left eye socket. As more scientific techniques for investigating the structure and function of the brain have been developed, both of these claims are now known to be false.

The system of phrenology

Current methods of investigating the brain can be broadly divided into **invasive** methods, where the brain is physically interfered with by the experimenter and the results are observed, and **non-invasive** methods, where the activity of the brain is recorded without such radical interference taking place. The more invasive techniques are used in animal research rather than in research using human participants; however, the effects of accidents or surgical procedures can also give us information about the effects of brain damage in humans.

Since much of the research on the functioning of the brain is carried out on animals, it is important to think carefully about how applicable the findings might be to human behaviour. This is particularly important when considering the **cerebral cortex**, the part of the brain which is most highly developed in humans compared with other animals. In addition, of course, animals cannot report back to the experimenter about sensations they may be experiencing.

Brain research methods also differ in the extent to which they are **macro-level** methods, studying relatively large parts of the brain, or **micro-level** methods, studying a single cell or small group of cells. Macro- and micro-level methods complement one another: by using both, researchers can find out how organs within the brain function, and also how those complete organs are built up from individual neurons.

In addition, research methods can be divided into those which give **functional** information, i.e. about what different parts of the brain do, and those which give purely **structural** information, i.e. how the brain is organised anatomically.

Another useful distinction can be made between **classic techniques** used in earlier research, and the more recent **brain scanning techniques** (or computed tomographies), which rely on computer-based analysis of recordings made of the brain.

Classic techniques

Anatomical techniques

Anatomical techniques are used on the dead brain, to investigate its structure. After death, the brain must first of all be perfused, i.e. the blood must be drained away and replaced with a dilute salt solution. This makes it easier to observe the structures it contains. Then it is fixed, to prevent it decomposing and to harden it, usually by using formalin solution. Further hardening, using freezing or soaking in paraffin, may be employed to make the brain easier to slice into the very thin sections needed to look at

it under the microscope. After sectioning it and mounting it on slides, different types of tissue or even transmitter substances can be stained with dyes to make them show up more clearly.

Using animals, nerve tracts and pathways can be traced by injecting radioactive amino acids into the area of the brain being studied. The animal is then killed so that slides can be made to clarify where the nerves go.

There are two drawbacks with these anatomical techniques. Firstly, they can only tell us about structures, and can give no information about the function of different areas. Secondly, they can only be used with the dead brain.

Some research which would previously have been carried out by anatomical studies can now be carried out by scanning using computerised axial tomography (CAT) or magnetic resonance imaging (MRI), techniques which are described later in the chapter.

Investigating the effects of brain damage

Investigating how the damaged brain works can help researchers find out how the normal, undamaged brain functions. If damage to a particular area of the brain results in the loss of a particular ability, it is tempting to conclude that the damaged part of the brain controlled the ability that was lost. This may not necessarily be the case, though. It may be that the damage disrupted communication between other areas, or caused inflammation and biochemical change to adjoining areas, or that the damaged area contributed to the ability lost, but only in a very specific way.

Even so, studying the damaged brain has generated a great deal of knowledge about the workings of the normal brain. One method is that of **clinical studies**, in which the brain is damaged by accident or by necessary surgery, and the effects studied. The other method is **ablation** or **lesioning studies**, in which damage is done to animals solely for the purpose of observing the effects.

A famous example of a clinical study arising from accidental damage is the case of Phineas Gage, an American railway worker, who in 1848 had an iron bar shot into the frontal part of the brain when an explosive charge went off prematurely. The main effect of this on his behaviour was that he became much less inhibited than previously, swearing, removing his clothes in public, and generally being more impulsive and less conscientious.

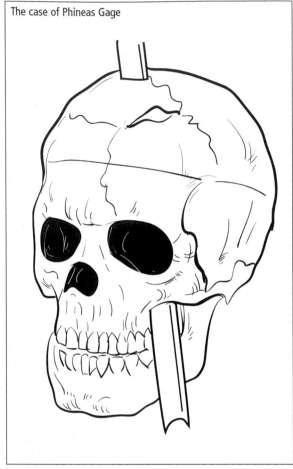

The case of Phineas Gage

A tamping iron, over 1m long, and tapering from $1\frac{1}{4}''$ in diameter, entered under the left cheekbone and came out through the top of the head.

Another useful source of information is the study of patients who have suffered strokes or cerebral haemorrhages. Although strokes are the result of blood clots, and haemorrhages the result of burst blood vessels, the results are similar. In both cases, the blood supply to the neurons of the brain is interrupted and the neurons are starved of oxygen. Because the two sides of the brain have separate blood supplies, it is often the case that only one side of the brain is affected. For example, stroke patients may be paralysed down one side

only. An example of this type of study can be seen in the case study by Broca of a stroke patient who had lost the ability to speak, which will be discussed later in this chapter.

Sometimes surgery may be carried out with the specific intention of changing a patient's behaviour; this is known as **psychosurgery**. For example, this was used by Moniz (1937), who injected alcohol into the frontal lobes of schizophrenic patients, carrying out what has come to be known as a **frontal lobotomy**, on the assumption that destruction of the frontal lobes would cure them of their problems (it didn't!).

However, these approaches have their limitations. Some of these limitations are common to all forms of brain damage, and have already been discussed. In addition, assessment of the behaviour change after brain damage is far from straightforward, since an accurate record of behaviour prior to the damage may not be available. Moreover, the damage may also extend over several areas of the brain, making it impossible to reach any definite conclusions about the functions of any one area. Finally, it has not always been possible to determine the extent of the brain damage from the outside, though this can now be done using the brain scanning techniques discussed later. An autopsy after death may provide the information, but this may require a long wait until the patient dies. It is not even certain that permission to carry out an autopsy will be obtained.

Some of the problems associated with clinical studies can be overcome by the use of studies which involve deliberate interference with or removal of particular areas of the brain, thus permitting an evaluation of the effects of precisely controlled brain damage. There are different techniques related to the amount of damage inflicted. In a **lobotomy**, such as that used by Moniz, an entire lobe of the brain (each side of the cortex contains four) is destroyed. Simply cutting the connections between a lobe and the rest of the brain is known as a **leucotomy**. Destruction of a large area of the cortex, but less than a lobe, is called an **ablation**, and destruction of a small area is a **lesion**. This technique was used by Lashley in the 1920s to study in rats the effects on memory of removing areas of the cortex.

This destruction can be carried out in several different ways. The area concerned can be burnt out electrically. Suction can be used – the brain is quite soft and easy to suck out. Specific poisons or neurotoxins can be used to affect the functioning of the brain cells, either temporarily or permanently, like the alcohol used by Moniz. Finally, radio waves can be used to destroy tissue. This last method is thought to be the best, because it is less likely to leave residues which affect the functioning of the cells which remain.

One advantage of these techniques is that the damage can be precisely located, particularly when it is produced using a **stereotaxic apparatus** in conjunction with a **stereotaxic map** of the brain:

Figure 1: a stereotaxic apparatus for performing brain surgery on rats

The stereotaxic map is a three-dimensional drawing of the brain on which the position of the various structures is marked. Measurements are given of their position relative to particular seams in the skull where bones have joined together during development.

The animal can be put into the apparatus, the skull exposed, and a needle inserted into the correct site in the brain with the use of the map, thus allowing a precise lesion to be carried out. This method has been used to identify the different areas of the brain involved in different behaviours. For example, different parts of the hypothalamus are involved in eating and drinking behaviour.

In humans, the method has been used surgically to eliminate some of the excessive trembling that occurs in Parkinson's disease. The area which is malfunctioning can be located, and then burnt out using lasers or radioactive rods. Another example, to which we will return in section 11.3 of this chapter when we come to consider **split-brain** research, is the use of surgical lesions to split the two sides of the brain by severing the connection between them. This is done to prevent the spread of severe epileptic seizures from one side of the brain to the other.

Research using these techniques is useful in pin-pointing specific areas involved in various behaviours. However, the use of animals in many studies means that findings must be regarded with caution. There is also a problem with the interpretation of findings, in that areas being investigated may simply be part of the pathway that co-ordinates behaviour, rather than being the prime organiser. In fact it seems likely that brain areas are so interconnected and behaviour so complex that no one area can be considered to be responsible for any particular behaviour.

Electrical recording and stimulation studies

Another group of methods are those which rely on electrical techniques. There are a great variety of these, and they can be used in several different ways. What they have in common is that they rely on the electrical nature of communication in the nervous system. By recording or stimulating this communication, it is possible to explore the functions of different areas of the cortex.

The electrodes used to do this may be **macroelectrodes**, which deal with the activity of a large number of neurons, or **microelectrodes**, which deal with the activity of single neurons.

Macroelectrodes are made out of wire which can be inserted into the brain. Microelectrodes are made out of very fine metal wires or glass tubes, and are inserted into the brain using a stereotaxic apparatus, with a socket glued to the skull for long-term use:

Figure 2: a permanently attached set of electrodes, with a connecting socket cemented to the skull

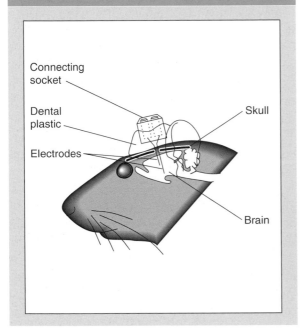

These can be used in two different ways. One possibility is to present a stimulus, and record, amplify and display visually the activity of the nerve cells which respond to it. This method was used by Hubel and Wiesel (1962) in their study of the type of stimulus which would trigger a response in cells in different parts of the visual system. By implanting microelectrodes in single cells in the visual cortex of an anaesthetised cat, they were able to show the existence of cortical cells which respond to patterns of light falling on the retina. An example of their research is given in chapter 14, box M.

Alternatively, the electrodes can be used to stimulate the nerve cells in the brain by passing an electric current through them. This is known as **electrical stimulation of the brain** or **ESB**. The effects which this has on behaviour can then be

observed. This approach was used by Olds and Milner (1954) in their study of the pleasure centres of the brain:

Box A: Olds and Milner (1954)

Procedure: Olds and Milner were investigating the effects of electrical stimulation of a region of the brain called the **reticular formation**, which is involved in arousal and sleep. They accidentally inserted the electrode into a different part of the brain, with the result that the animal kept returning to the area of the cage where it had received the stimulation, evidently looking for more. They then devised a system whereby the rats could administer the electric shocks themselves, known as **self-stimulation**.
Results: Rats would stimulate themselves in this way more than 700 times an hour. The area of the brain responsible for this behaviour is the **medial forebrain bundle**, a bundle of nerve fibres which passes through the lateral part of the **hypothalamus**.
Conclusion: ESB was a useful technique for identifying the function of this area of the brain, known as the pleasure centre.

Later studies replicating this study have shown response rates of thousands of times per hour, with no sign of satiation. Another well-known set of studies was carried out by Penfield on human patients being prepared for brain surgery. These are discussed later in this chapter in the section on motor and sensory areas.

As an extension of the electrical techniques already discussed, **electrical recordings** can be made of the electrical activity of the brain by means of electrodes attached with electrode jelly to the surface of the scalp. This technique was discovered by Caton in 1875 (Caton, 1977), who tried it out on animals. Berger applied it to humans and called it the **electroencephalogram** or **EEG**.

The electrodes can detect activity in the underlying brain cells, which is then amplified and either drawn on paper or displayed on a computer:

Figure 3: an EEG record

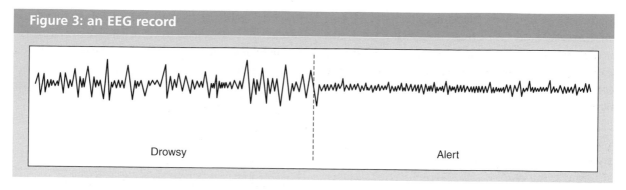

Drowsy   Alert

The resulting EEG pattern is termed **synchronised** when the individual is asleep or drowsy. In these circumstances, it is made up of waves of a particular **amplitude** (height) and **frequency** (measured in the number of waves per second). When people are awake, aroused, or asleep and dreaming, the EEG becomes **desynchronised**. It is irregular in activity and no clear wave form can be seen.

Different cortical regions produce different patterns of 'brain waves', as do different mental states. For example, when we are alert and awake we produce EEG beta waves, showing a typical frequency of 13 or more Herz, i.e. cycles per second. When we are relaxed, there are more alpha waves (8-13 Herz). When we are asleep, theta (4-7 Herz) and delta (1-3 Herz) waves appear. This technique has been used in the study of **sleep**, and is discussed in more detail in chapter 12. It can also be used to diagnose possible epilepsy, as affected individuals often show abnormal patterns of electrical activity. Another possible technique is to present stimuli and observe the pattern of EEG responses.

Further analysis of the EEG record can produce what is known as the **average evoked potential (AEP)**. This is produced using a computer to tidy up the response record and eliminate irrelevant electrical activity. The brain waves recorded over a short period of time are added and averaged; this average response can then be regarded as characteristic for the person in that situation, unlike any single response which might be produced.

Electrode stimulation can be carried out invasively (using electrodes inserted into the brain) or non-invasively (stimulating the surface of the brain before surgery). Electrodes can be used with great precision to stimulate small groups of cells, and can give an immediate demonstration of the effect of electrical stimulation on behaviour. If the brains of conscious patients are being stimulated, the researcher can obtain verbal feedback about the experience.

However, there are also some limitations to electrical techniques. For example, the use of microelectrode recording to map the responses of individual cells in the cortex is a very slow way to build up a picture of how the brain operates. Stimulation techniques are also limited in that they do not necessarily elicit the same behaviour when used on different occasions. For example, stimulation of the same point may produce different memories at different times. Moreover, electrical stimulation cannot tell us that a particular part of the brain *initiates* a particular behaviour or experience. It can also give the impression that each behaviour is only determined by one area of the cortex, which as we shall see is not in fact the case.

Chemical techniques

As well as electrical activity, the brain communicates by chemical means, so it is possible either to record this information or to interfere with it, and then look for links with behaviour.

Stimulation techniques involve the use of a **micropipette** which delivers drugs or other chemicals through a cannula, a thin glass tube inserted into the brain at the required site. Different drugs or neurotransmitters can be delivered through this, to see which chemicals the neurons in that particular area respond to, and observe the behavioural effects of the drugs.

Radioactive chemicals can also be introduced, and their uptake by different areas of the brain measured after the animal has carried out a particular behaviour. For example, if glucose were introduced this technique would show which areas of the brain have used glucose and were therefore active during the behaviour. This is the principle on which the positron emission tomography (PET) scanner works, described in the section on brain scanning techniques.

As well as stimulation by chemicals, it is possible to measure responses using chemical analyses. For example, cerebrospinal fluid can be analysed to detect the effect of drugs on neurotransmitter levels. The fluid collected is analysed by **high-precision liquid chromatography (HPLC)**, a very sensitive method of detecting the presence of transmitter substances. For example, this has shown that many addictive drugs, such as cocaine, cause the neurotransmitter dopamine to be released in certain parts of the brain known as **reward pathways**, which is why they are so pleasurable to take. Chemical techniques such as these are useful, but again can be criticised for being based on animal research.

▶ Activity 1: cortical function: the classic techniques

Complete the gaps in this passage using one of the items given below. Each should be used only once:

dead	perfused	neurotransmitters
fixed	lesioning	microelectrodes
clinical	chemical	cerebrospinal fluid
ablation	stereotaxic	macroelectrodes
micropipette		inflammation

Anatomical techniques are based on the .... brain, which has been .... and ...., so that it can be examined under the microscope.

.... studies look at the effects of brain damage which has been caused for non-experimental reasons. .... and .... studies, on the other hand, are carried out exclusively on animals, and involve deliberate destruction of parts of the brain, often using a .... apparatus.

A limitation of these methods is that brain damage causes .... which can disrupt the functioning of areas adjacent to the damaged area. Electrical techniques can use either .... or .... to record electrical activity or stimulate the brain.

.... techniques either deliver drugs via a .... into the brain, or analyse extracts such as .... for the presence of ....

When you have finished, see the notes on page 303.

Brain scanning techniques

These techniques all rely on the enormous calculating power of modern computers, which can generate pictures of slices of the brain from radiation either passing through or coming from the brain. For this reason, they are known also as **computed tomographies**. The name 'tomography' comes from the Greek 'tomos', meaning 'slice', and 'graphein' meaning 'to draw'.

As well as being ethically more sound than some of the classic techniques, and therefore able to be carried out on human beings, brain scans have the advantage of allowing us to examine the function of different areas of the cortex much more directly than was previously possible.

There are several different types of brain scanning techniques. As with the classic techniques, these techniques can be classified according to the extent that they are invasive or non-invasive, and whether they give functional or only structural information. They are also classified in terms of their **spatial resolution** (how small an area can the technique identify and describe?) and their **temporal resolution** (how quickly can it update itself?).

The earliest technique was the **X-ray**, which relies on the principle that dense material such as bone absorbs the rays, and this makes bones show up on a photographic plate. The brain is not dense enough to do this unless a dye is injected into the bloodstream to make it more visible, a technique known as an **angiogram**. This has been used to show if the blood supply has been blocked or diverted to one side (for example, as the result of the

❺ The brain can be investigated using **classic** or **brain scanning** techniques.

❺ **Classic** techniques include **anatomical**, **clinical**, **ablation**, **lesioning**, **electrical** and **chemical** approaches.

❺ Brain scanning procedures include **CAT**, **MRI**, **fMRI**, **PET**, **SPECT** and **MEG**.

❺ Major differences in procedures include: the extent to which they are **invasive**; whether they work at the **macro-** or **micro-level**; and whether they show **function** or only **structure**.

❺ Brain scanning techniques also differ in their levels of **spatial** and **temporal resolution**.

11.2 LOCALISATION OF FUNCTION IN THE CEREBRAL CORTEX

The **cortex** is the outer layer of the brain, and it is the area which is most highly developed in humans compared with animals. In appearance it is deeply wrinkled. These wrinkles serve to increase the surface area and allow more active cells to be packed into the available space. The parts of the brain which lie beneath the cortex are known as the **subcortex**.

The cortex is divided from front to back into two symmetrical halves, known as the right and left **hemispheres**. Between the two hemispheres is the longitudinal fissure, but the two remain joined by a mass of nerve fibres known as the **corpus callosum**.

Each hemisphere can also be divided into four **lobes**: the **frontal** lobe (at the front), the **temporal** lobe (at the side); the **occipital** lobe (the lower part at the back) and the **parietal** lobe (the upper part at the back). They are marked off from one another by two deep fissures, the **central** and **lateral fissures**.

One important debate about the cortex centres on the issue of localisation of function. In the days of phrenology, discussed at the start of this chapter, it was thought that specific areas of the brain, indicated externally by bumps on the skull, were associated with specific functions, such as language or emotional behaviour.

Figure 7: the hemispheres of the brain

View from above
Back

Right hemisphere
Front
Left hemisphere

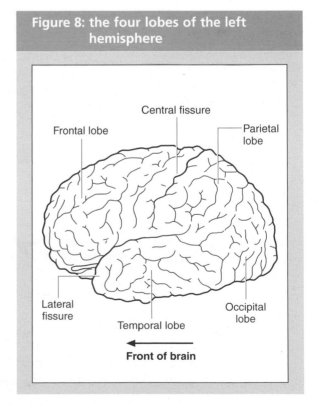

Figure 8: the four lobes of the left hemisphere

Central fissure
Frontal lobe
Parietal lobe
Lateral fissure
Temporal lobe
Occipital lobe
Front of brain

Another example of an early localisationist is Kleist, whose 'map of the brain' is shown in figure 9:

The modern version of this idea argues that distinct areas of the cortex are associated with specific behaviours, i.e. functions are localised. This is also referred to as the **modular** approach. Different parts of the brain are believed to be specialised for different mental capacities, such as memory and language. Each module has its own processes and will only deal with certain types of data. For example, it is argued by some (e.g. Marr, 1982) that the visual system consists of modules which process different aspects of visual information, such as colour or movement. This is discussed in more detail in chapter 15.

The alternative to this is the argument that there is very little localisation of function, and the cortex tends to work as a whole. The **law of mass action**, proposed by Lashley (1929), stated that the severity of the effects of cortical lesions depended on the size of the lesion and not its location. The **law of equipotentiality** suggested, in its extreme form, that all areas of the cortex were equally capable of carrying out all functions. The extreme form of this law is unlikely to be acceptable, as we shall see from studies of the effects of brain damage in section 11.4 of this chapter. Lashley himself probably had in mind a weaker form, which is that the cortex as a whole is equipotential for some processes, such as learning or problem-solving (Milner, 1970).

Another principle which is relevant here is the **principle of multiple control**, which suggests that a particular part of the brain may well be involved in many different types of behaviour. For example, the **hypothalamus** is a subcortical structure which is involved in both eating and drinking behaviour, while **Broca's area**, in the left frontal lobe, is involved in both word production and grammar. A particular behaviour may therefore be produced with the involvement of many different brain areas. This has been shown by PET scans carried out during speech.

Figure 9: Kleist's (1943) 'map of the brain'

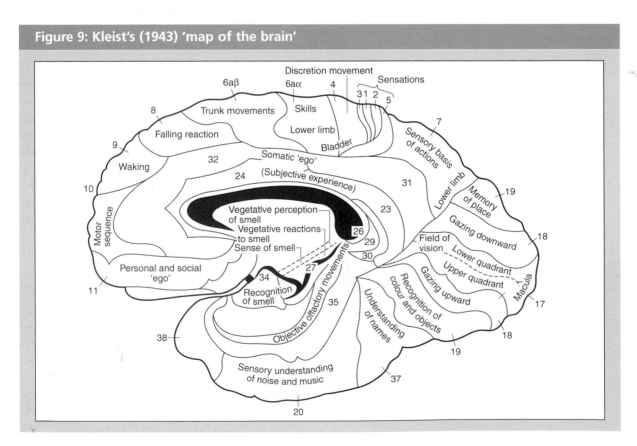

Some early research on localisation of function was carried out by Lashley in the 1920s:

Box B: Lashley (1920s)

Procedure: Rats were trained to run through a maze. An area of the brain was then destroyed and they were tested again to see if they could still remember how to get through the maze. Lashley was searching for the **engram,** a memory trace thought to be laid down in the brain during learning.

Results: There did not seem to be any one area which appeared to contain the memory in the way he had expected. The most important determinant of whether the rats could remember the way or not was the amount of cortex destroyed.

Conclusion: These experiments supported the law of mass action. All areas of the cortex were equally involved in learning.

The modern version of the antilocalisation stance is the idea of **distributed functions** (or **connectionism**), which takes the holistic view that the brain functions as a whole. All areas are interconnected, and have multiple tasks to carry out. Information is distributed in networks made up of millions of neurons. For example, based on the original Gestalt theory of stimuli producing electrical fields in the brain, modern Gestalt theories look at perception in terms of neural networks, and interactions between them to produce networks of networks (Palmer, 1992).

In the following sections, we will be looking at evidence for and against localisation of function by considering research on motor, sensory and association areas of the cortex, and looking at the organisation of memory and language skills in the brain.

Motor and sensory areas

Pioneering early work on the sensory and motor areas of the brain was carried out by Penfield in the 1950s. These areas are shown in figure 9, together with some other areas associated with specific functions:

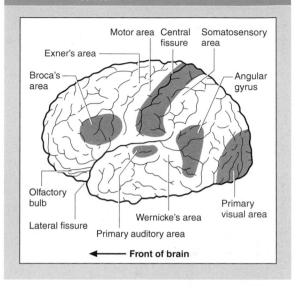

Figure 9: localisation of function in the left cortex

Figure 9 shows only the left cortex. The motor and sensory areas are found on both sides of the brain in all species (including humans) which have a well-developed cortex. They include motor, somatosensory (concerned with sensory input from the skin, i.e. temperature, touch, pain and movement), visual, auditory and olfactory areas. Other areas shown here are only found on one side of the brain. These include **Broca's area, Wernicke's area,** and **Exner's area** which are to do with producing and understanding language, and which we will be discussing later, together with the **angular gyrus,** which is involved in matching the visual form of a word with its sound. The right side of the brain, as we shall see later, also has its own specialised functions, including some aspects of music perception and the analysis of complex visual scenes.

Penfield used patients who were waiting for brain surgery to explore the effects of delivering electrical stimulation to different cortical regions. He found that stimulation just in front of the central fissure produced bodily movements. For example, stimulation on the left side of the brain would cause a movement of the right leg. This suggests that each hemisphere controls the opposite side of the body, known as **contralateral representation**:

Figure 10: contralateral system

He also found that the body is represented upside down in the brain, so that stimulation near the top of the head produced movement of the lower body, and stimulation lower in this motor area led to movement of the upper body:

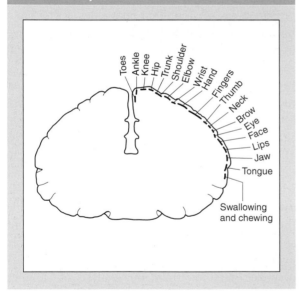

Figure 11: representation of different body parts in the motor cortex

Another important finding was that some parts of the body had large areas of the brain devoted to them, while others only had small representations. These differences did not relate, as you might expect, to differences in the size of the body parts. They were instead found to depend on the amount of control, co-ordination and sensitivity needed. For example, the fingers and mouth have large cortical representations.

Although this motor area is not responsible for making the decision to move, it is responsible for carrying out commands and for ensuring smooth movement, so fine control will be lost if it is damaged.

The **primary sensory areas** of the cortex deal with incoming messages rather than outgoing ones. Several different areas have been identified, dealing with information from different senses.

The **somatosensory area**, shown in figure 12, is to the rear of the central fissure in the parietal lobe. It deals with information from the bodily senses and from the taste receptors. As in the motor areas, the information received comes from the opposite side of the body. The body is represented upside down, so the face is lower and the legs are higher in the cortex:

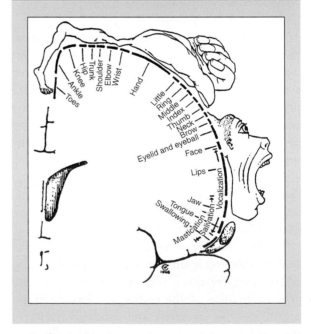

Figure 12: representation of different body parts in the sensory cortex

As figure 12 shows, the size of the area devoted to a particular bodily region again depends on sensitivity and use. For example, rats have a large area of cortex devoted to input from their whiskers, which they rely on a great deal for information about their environment. Robertson (1995) found that people who use Braille to read have larger cortical areas for some fingertips than normally sighted people. From this, it is possible to conclude that allocation of space within the somatosensory cortex is flexible; parts of the body which are used more for sensory activities will expand their cortical areas. This ability of the cortex to be flexible in its response to differing needs is known as **plasticity**.

Damage to the primary sensory areas of the cortex can lead to a variety of problems, such as the inability to tell the difference between different temperatures.

The **primary auditory area** is in the temporal lobe beside the lateral fissure. It receives input from the ear via the auditory nerve and a subcortical structure called the **thalamus**. When it is stimulated electrically, sounds will be reported, the nature of which will depend on the precise area stimulated. Damage to the left auditory cortex tends to result in problems in identifying and naming sounds, while damage to the right auditory cortex leads more to difficulties with the perception of pitch, rhythm and melody.

Hearing is a **partially-crossed system**. It is partly **contralateral**, i.e. each hemisphere receives input from the ear on the opposite side of the body, and partly **ipsilateral**, i.e. some information is dealt with by the hemisphere on the same side as the ear. Around 90% of auditory information is processed contralaterally, with the remaining 10% being processed ipsilaterally:

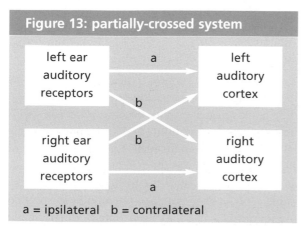

Figure 13: partially-crossed system

The **primary visual area** is at the back of the occipital lobe, and receives input from the eyes via the optic nerve. Each hemisphere deals with information from the same side of each eye, e.g. information from the right side of each eye is passed to the right hemisphere. The visual system, then, shows the same partial crossing as the auditory system. This means that damage to the primary visual area can cause loss of sight on just one side of the visual field, or a hole in vision. Equally, loss of one eye means that vision can still be quite good, as information will go to both hemispheres. You can read more about the visual system in general and the primary visual area in particular in chapter 15.

Activity 3: locating motor and sensory areas

In which lobe of the brain is:
  a the primary motor area
  b the primary somatosensory area
  c the primary auditory area
  d the primary visual area?
When you have finished, see the notes on page 303.

Association areas

Each of the sensory areas mentioned above has an association area next to it, to which it sends information. Motor association areas, by contrast, are areas adjacent to the motor area which send information to the motor area.

Motor association areas deal with planning and carrying out movements as a result of the information they receive. These orders are then dealt with by the primary motor area. For example, the left parietal lobe contains an area which helps us to follow the movements we make. Damage to this area results in severe difficulties in drawing.

The sensory association areas lie alongside the primary sensory areas. The **somatosensory association** area operates to provide awareness of the body through the skin. If it is damaged, a condition called **sensory neglect** results (Halligan, 1995), which leads the individual to ignore one side of the body. For example, when shaving only one side of the face will be shaved:

Box C: Halligan (1995)

Procedure: Patients with right hemisphere damage to the somatosensory association area were asked to produce drawings. They were also asked questions about pictures, and to imagine and report a view from a building when they were facing towards it and then facing away from it.

Results: Their drawings showed only the right side of what they were drawing, e.g. the right half of a flower with no corresponding left side. When they were shown a picture of a burning house, the flames were not reported if they were shown on only the left side of the house. However, patients reported a preference for living in a house that was identical, except that it was not on fire! When asked to imagine a building, they did not report details on the left of the building when they imagined they were facing it. However, when facing away from it, they reported details from the left side, in spite of having left them out of their previous description.

Conclusion: Information from the left side reaches the brain, but cannot always be used. This may be because it cannot enter conscious awareness.

The **auditory association area** is in the posterior part of the occipital lobes and deals with encoding and decoding sound in order to make sense of it. Damage to this part of the left hemisphere can lead to an inability to understand and to produce spoken language, while damage to the right leads to an inability to recognise rhythms.

There are **visual association areas** in the temporal, parietal and occipital lobes. These carry out higher-level visual processes, such as the ability to recognise faces and objects, and distinguish an object from its background. Damage to these areas can cause a variety of difficulties associated with visual recognition, which are known as **visual agnosias**. The famous case reported by Oliver Sacks (1985) of the man who mistook his wife's head for a hat is an example of a visual agnosia. Other patients with damage to these areas find it difficult to integrate details into a whole object, as seen in drawings by patients with this kind of damage, and produce drawings which contain all the correct elements but in a disjointed form.

Other areas on the borders between the different association areas combine information from different sensory modalities, linking sight, sound, taste, smell etc to give a complete representation of a scene.

Overall, then, the different lobes of the brain appear to have different functions. The frontal lobes deal with motor responses, the occipital lobes with vision, the temporal lobes with hearing, taste and smell, and the parietal lobes with somesthetic senses, i.e. somatosensory input, and with movement.

- ⊖ The **cortex** is divided into right and left cerebral **hemispheres**, each of which is divided into four **lobes**: **frontal**, **temporal**, **parietal** and **occipital**.
- ⊖ There has been a major debate about whether functions are **localised** in different cortical areas (**modular**) or whether they are **distributed**.
- ⊖ Primary **motor** and **sensory** areas have been located in different lobes, each of which has an **association area** linked with it.

Thought and language in the cortex

Obviously we carry out a great many other activities not yet mentioned, such as thinking and remembering. Where in the brain do these take place?

The frontal lobes appear to play an important part in planning, decision-making and creativity. When they are damaged, people become impulsive, with little thought for the future and an inability to delay rewards. You will remember that in the case of Phineas Gage, this was the area which was damaged, and his behaviour after the accident showed these kinds of changes. A phenomenon called **perseveration** has also been noted, when people will carry on with tasks or with methods of problem-solving long after they have been completed or proved useless. Inability to concentrate and lack of emotional reactivity are also seen. It was these kinds of problems which led to the rejection of the prefrontal lobotomy introduced by Moniz as a treatment for schizophrenia, discussed in chapter 25. As we shall see later, damage to the frontal lobe was found by Broca (1861) to be associated with loss of the ability to produce language.

The temporal lobes are involved in memory and learning. Penfield found that stimulation in some areas led to reliving a past experience. Although it is difficult to verify such reports, other research has looked at the effects of removal of parts of the temporal lobes. This has been carried out in animals and humans, e.g. tumour and epilepsy patients. It has been found that this produces severe impairment of the ability to form new memories. This is now known to be due to the removal of the **hippocampus**, a structure embedded in the temporal lobes which seems to serve as a 'printing press' for new memories.

Other effects of damage to the temporal lobes include the impairment of emotional responses (also possibly due to damage to another subcortical area called the **limbic system**) and the ability to understand either written or spoken language (Wernicke, 1874).

Activity 4: terms in localisation of function

What is:
  a contralateral representation
  b ipsilateral representation
  c sensory neglect
  d perseveration
  e Broca's area
  f Wernicke's area?
Look back over the previous section to check your answers.

As mentioned in the previous section, two areas of the cortex appear to play a major part in language skills. In 1861, French physician Paul Broca reported a case study of a patient called 'Tan', because that was the only word he was able to say. After he died, an autopsy revealed that as the result of a stroke, he had suffered damage to the lower part of the left frontal lobe. Observation of similar cases led Broca to propose that this area, now called Broca's area and shown in figure 9, was responsible for the *production* of spoken language; however, *understanding* of speech did not seem to be impaired. The problem suffered by Tan was termed **expressive aphasia**. Aphasia refers to disorders in the comprehension or production of speech; they may be called **dysphasia**, if they are not too severe.

The role of Broca's area in language has been demonstrated in studies of patients who suffer damage to this part of the cortex. This kind of damage may lead to the patient suffering from **Broca's aphasia**, discussed in detail in the section on language disorders later in this chapter.

In 1874, Carl Wernicke reported his research on patients who appeared to be able to speak fluently – although their speech often made little sense – but were unable to understand the speech of others. This was termed **receptive aphasia**, and seemed to be associated with damage to the top of the left temporal lobe, now called Wernicke's area (see figure 9).

The key theory of language which links the activities of Broca's area and Wernicke's area is known as the **Wernicke–Geschwind theory**:

Box D: the Wernicke–Geschwind theory

The processes involved in language: Speech is heard and passed to the **auditory cortex** via the **auditory nerve**. It then goes to Wernicke's area, where the sounds are analysed, and the words identified and analysed for meaning. When speech is being produced, the motor plans for how to say words are activated in Broca's area. These are passed to the **motor cortex**, and converted to instructions to the speech muscles so that the words can be said.

Reading and **writing** also appear to have specific mechanisms. Writing is a motor skill, and is therefore dealt with by the motor cortex acting on instructions from Exner's area, just above Broca's area. Reading involves the visual system sending information to the **visual cortex**, and these visual patterns then have to be identified as particular words. The area responsible for this is the angular gyrus (see figure 9) which assembles visual word patterns. These are then transmitted to Wernicke's area nearby for comprehension.

▷ Activity 5: identifying areas of the cortex

On this diagram, label these areas:

Broca's area   Wernicke's area   the angular gyrus
motor areas   visual areas   Exner's area

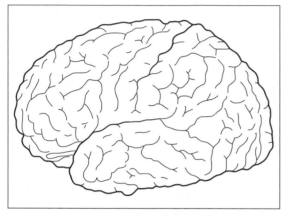

Check your work by looking back at figure 9.

In conclusion, there is some evidence that particular areas of the cortex may have key roles in the organisation of some behaviours. However, other behaviours are more difficult to pinpoint, as shown by Lashley. Even where there is localisation, it is not very precise, and may involve relatively widespread areas.

One way of resolving this is by looking at the structure of the cortex more closely. The cortex consists of layers of cells which are arranged in columns (Hubel and Wiesel, 1962). According to Milner (1970), the lateral interconnections between columns are not very important in normal functioning. What is more relevant in connecting columns are axons which leave the cortex and pass through the underlying white matter before returning to another part of the cortex, creating a distributed network which links modules. This fits well with what is believed to be the most likely arrangement for visual processing.

Humphreys *et al.* (1992) pointed out that a system which combines partial information from different processing modules may well be the best

way of dealing with the input received. Clearly, as shown by scanning studies, even the most simple activities involve a wide range of interconnected areas. A useful analogy offered by Ramachandran and Blakeslee (1999) is that of a television programme, which cannot be localised to any one part of the television.

- ❺ **Planning, decision-making** and some aspects of **language** are the responsibility of the **frontal lobes**. **Memory**, **emotionality** and other aspects of **language** are dealt with by the **temporal lobes**.
- ❺ The **Wernicke–Geschwind** model of language explains the production and comprehension of both written and spoken language with reference to four areas of the cortex: **Broca's area**, **Exner's area**, **Wernicke's area** and the **angular gyrus**.

11.3 LATERALISATION OF FUNCTION IN THE CEREBRAL CORTEX

We will look now at whether the two hemispheres of the brain have different roles, i.e. whether each hemisphere specialises in different activities. We have already seen that for some senses, each hemisphere deals with information from the opposite side of the body (contralateral representation), and issues motor commands to the opposite side of the body. It has also been suggested that they have even more differences in functioning.

One area which has been extensively researched in this respect is language. The language areas mentioned in the previous section were originally identified in the left hemisphere in right-handed patients, leading to the suggestion that they may be in the right hemisphere for left-handed patients.

▷ Activity 6: brain surgery and handedness

Penfield and Roberts (1959) carried out a study on patients who had had brain surgery on either the left or the right side of the brain. Some patients were left-handed and some right-handed. They noted the percentage who showed speech defects after surgery:

	operation on left	operation on right
right-handers	70%	0.4%
left-handers	38%	9%

What do these figures tell you about the location of the language centres in the two groups?

When you have finished, see the notes on page 303.

Subsequent research has confirmed this general pattern, using the **Wada test**. This involves injecting sodium amytal into one or other of the carotid arteries (each carotid artery supplies blood to one cerebral hemisphere) and seeing whether or not language is impaired.

Box E: Beaumont (1988)

Procedure: An overview was carried out of research over 40 years into handedness and hemisphere dominance for language.
Results:

	right-handers	left-handers
left hemisphere dominance	95%	75%
right hemisphere dominance	5%	
bilateral representation		25%

Conclusion: For most people, the left hemisphere is dominant for language. A small number have right hemisphere dominance, and a sizeable minority have bilateral representation.

The finding that the left hemisphere of the brain is mainly responsible for language has led many people to describe it as the dominant hemisphere. However, more recent thinking suggests that it may not be so much a matter of dominance, but more a case of the two hemispheres being specialised for different functions. These differences have been investigated in two ways: studies of **normal lateralisation** and studies of **split-brain patients**.

Studies of normal lateralisation

In the normal brain, the left hemisphere is almost always larger than the right, and contains shorter nerve fibres which provide richer interconnections over a smaller area. The right hemisphere contains longer fibres which cover more ground. According to Zaidel (1978), these differences only become apparent after about 5 years of age. If there is damage before this, the surviving hemisphere can take over the functions of the damaged area. This demonstrates the principle of **equipotentiality**, mentioned earlier in this chapter, and also the phenomenon of **developmental plasticity**, whereby the brain can reorganise itself during development.

We will look first at studies asking participants to respond to visual information. The visual pathway from the eye to the brain is different in items presented on the right and left sides of the visual field. Those presented on the left will reach the right hemisphere before they reach the left hemisphere. It follows that if a verbal response is required, people should do better when the information is presented on the right side, since this will reach the left (language) hemisphere first. If the response is non-verbal, e.g. picking out a picture, the side on which the item is presented should make no difference. Rasmussen and Milner (1977) carried out a study based on these principles:

Box F: Rasmussen and Milner (1977)

Procedure: Participants were asked to carry out various tasks, presented to either the right or the left side of the visual field. The tasks included analytical problems, spatial tasks and artistic tasks.
Results: The left hemisphere was better and quicker than the right at responding to analytical problems. The right hemisphere was better at spatial and artistic tasks.
Conclusion: Some activities show differential hemisphere superiority.

These findings are supported by research by Springer and Deutsch (1985). They found that an EEG showed increased activation in the left hemisphere during verbal tasks, and in the right hemisphere during spatial tasks.

Another approach is to present different auditory information simultaneously to the two ears. This is known as **dichotic listening**, and is described in more detail in the section on **focused attention** in chapter 14. Bryden and Ley (1983) found that when this information is verbal, it is more likely to be reported from the right ear, showing left hemisphere superiority for this type of material. When it is non-verbal, e.g. music, it is more likely that the left ear will be reported, showing right hemisphere superiority.

Another area of difference relates to emotions. Researchers in this area argue that information received directly by one hemisphere is richer and more detailed than that which has been presented initially to the other hemisphere, and therefore has had to be passed on by the corpus callosum, the mass of fibres which interconnect and allow communication between the two hemispheres. Based on this, Ley and Bryden have explored the responses of the two hemispheres to tasks requiring the recognition of emotional expression:

Box G: Ley and Bryden (1979)

Procedure: Using a tachistoscope, participants were shown very briefly cartoon drawings of faces showing different emotional expressions. Each drawing was presented to either the right or the left visual field, and participants were asked to identify the emotion shown. In other trials, participants were asked to identify emotions from tone of voice.

Results: The right hemisphere was superior to the left at the accurate identification of emotions in drawings. This superiority was even more marked with tone of voice. The left hemisphere was more accurate at identifying the literal meaning of the words.

Conclusion: The identification of emotions shows right hemisphere superiority.

Figure 14: stimulus material used by Ley and Bryden (1979)

This research has been supported by studies of clinical cases. Tucker *et al.* (1977) found that after right hemisphere damage, the ability to recognise whether two sentences were spoken in the same or different tones of voice, and therefore varying in the emotion expressed, was reduced. A case study by Bowers and Heilman (1981) of a patient with a tumour in the right hemisphere showed that he could distinguish between people's faces, but not their emotional expressions.

There are similar findings in studies of emotional expression rather than the identification of emotions:

Box H: Sackheim and Gur (1978)

Procedure: Photographs were taken of people showing different emotions. The photographs were cut in half, and mirror images made of each half. The two identical halves were then pasted together to make a whole face (see figure 15), and participants were asked to rate how expressive they were.

Results: Those made from left halves were rated as more expressive than those made from identical right halves.

Conclusion: There is right hemisphere superiority in the expression of emotions.

Figure 15: Sample stimulus material used by Sackheim and Gur (1978)

| Original face | Composite of right side of face | Composite of left side of face |

In a more natural situation, Moscovitch and Olds (1982) observed people in restaurants and parks. They found that the left sides of their faces had stronger emotional expressions. This could account for an observation by Goldstein (1948) that people with left hemisphere damage are more likely to show a strong emotional response to their condition, whereas those with right side damage often appear to be indifferent to their problems. If the latter group has lost the areas responsible for emotional expression, this would be perfectly understandable.

Clinical cases show similar effects. Buck and Duffy (1980) found that right hemisphere lesions impair the expression of emotion both facially and by tone of voice. Morrow *et al.* (1981) found that patients with right hemisphere lesions showed less change in galvanic skin response (or GSR – an indicator of emotional arousal) than normal, when presented with emotive stimuli.

As a result of such research, Ornstein (1986) proposed that there may be two types of thinking and two types of consciousness, one generated by the left hemisphere and one by the right. The left hemisphere is specialised in language and number, and thinks sequentially and analytically, applying logical rules. It attends to details. The right hemisphere, by contrast, thinks in a more diffuse way. It is sensitive to shape and spacing in time, processes many pieces of information at a time (parallel processing), and attends to the whole stimulus rather than detail. For example, in language comprehension the literal meaning will be deciphered by the left hemisphere, but any metaphorical meaning, or additional meaning dependent on the tone of voice or context, will be deciphered by the right hemisphere.

A nice example of the association of holistic skills with the right hemisphere and the association of attention to detail with the left hemisphere was given by Carter (1998). When shown this display:

D
D
D
D
D
D D D D D

concentration on the overall 'L' shape creates activity in the right hemisphere, while concentration on the 'Ds' creates activity in the left hemisphere.

This suggests that the two hemispheres are at least independent in their actions, if not in direct opposition, but Levy (1985) suggested that it is more likely that they act in an integrated way. For example, when reading, the left hemisphere may deal with the language content, but the right will integrate what is read into a meaningful whole, and work out what the emotional connotations are.

- In most people, the **left hemisphere** is dominant for **language**, whether they are right- or left-handed. It is also better at **analytical problems**.
- The **right hemisphere** is better at **spatial, artistic** and **musical** tasks, and at the identification and expression of **emotions**.
- For most tasks, the two hemispheres normally work together.

'Split-brain' research

In order to prevent the spread of epileptic seizures from one hemisphere to the other, patients may undergo an operation called a **commisurotomy**. In these people, the corpus callosum, which connects the two hemispheres of the brain, has been severed, so they have what is known as a 'split brain'. The two sides of the brain are still connected at the subcortical level, but the cerebral hemispheres are separated. In everyday life, there do not seem to be any side effects, despite the fact that the patient has what in many respects are two independent brains.

Sperry (1961) devised an experimental situation in which different stimuli could be presented to either of the two hemispheres independently, and the patient's responses tested. He eventually received a Nobel prize for his work. His method relies on the way in which visual information is transmitted from the eyes to the cortex. When the corpus callosum is cut, information presented to one side of the visual field cannot cross to the other hemisphere; a stimulus presented on the left side will only register in the right hemisphere and vice versa.

Normally this is not a problem, because the patient can move his eyes and pass information to the cortex through both eyes. Sperry's idea was to present the stimulus so briefly – for just 1/10 of a second – that this was not possible. He carried out a series of experiments using this method.

The person being tested was asked to look straight ahead. The stimulus was then flashed very briefly on to the screen to either the right or the left visual field, so passing to either the left or the right hemisphere respectively. The ability of the person to report or respond to what was shown could then be tested in various ways to provide an indication of what the two hemispheres are capable of separately. The apparatus Sperry used is shown in figure 16:

Figure 16: Sperry's apparatus for testing lateralisation

Box I: Sperry; three studies

study 1
Procedure: Using the apparatus shown in figure 16 and the method described above, patients were presented with words to the right or the left visual field, and asked to report what they had seen (see figure 17).
Results: Patients could read and report the words presented to the right visual field, going to the left hemisphere. They were unable to report the words presented to the left visual field, going to the right hemisphere. Using the left hand they were able to select by touch, from a group of objects on the other side of the screen, the item whose name they had been shown. However, they were unable to say why they had selected the object.
Conclusion: The left hemisphere can identify words and name them. The right hemisphere can identify words but cannot name them.

study 2
Procedure: Different words were presented on each side of the screen. Patients were asked to report what they had seen (see figure 18).
Results: Patients were able to report only those words which had been presented to the right visual field (i.e. going to the left hemisphere).
Conclusion: The left hemisphere can identify and name words. The right hemisphere can read words but not say them out loud.

study 3
Procedure: Participants were asked to write with their left hand the word which had been presented to the left visual field, and to report what they had written (see figure 19).
Results: They could write the word they had seen, but with the screen in place, they were unable to report what they had written.
Conclusion: The right hemisphere seems to have some language skills. It can identify and write words, but it cannot name them.

Figure 17

Figure 18

Figure 19

Three experiments by Sperry

◗ Activity 7: making sense of Sperry

What general conclusions would you draw about the language skills of the two hemispheres from the three experiments carried out by Sperry described in box I?

When you have finished, see the notes on page 303.

More recent work by Zaidel (1983) has used a contact lens which moves with the eye and enables stimuli to be presented to only one hemisphere for a longer period than is possible using Sperry's technique. This has the added advantage that different types of task can be given. For example, participants can be asked to choose from different pictures presented to the right and left visual fields a picture which corresponds to a word they have seen. Zaidel found that on this task, the right hemisphere could equal the linguistic skills of the average 10-year-old. It also seemed to have a better understanding than the left hemisphere of metaphors such as the phrase 'turning over a new leaf'.

The right hemisphere is better than the left at copying drawings and recognising faces. When different faces are presented to the two visual fields, the participant will select the one shown to the right hemisphere and ignore the other:

Box J: Levy *et al.* (1972)

Procedure: Participants were presented with **chimerics**, i.e. photographs which had been cut in half; the left eye was presented with half of one face and the right eye with half of a different face, together making up a face with two different halves. They were asked to select the picture they had seen, or to describe it.

Results: Participants pointed to the image received by the right hemisphere (presented to the left visual field), and described in words the one received by the left hemisphere (presented to the right visual field) (see figure 20).

Conclusion: The right hemisphere has visual superiority, and the left hemisphere has language superiority.

Figure 20: responses given by the left and right hemispheres to a chimeric

'Man, dark hair and dark eyebrows'

The right hemisphere was also shown by Sperry (1974) to be better at copying designs (with the left hand) using coloured blocks.

In general, it can be concluded that the two hemispheres may have different skills, but they normally act together in an integrated way. Most tasks – for example, language tasks – involve contributions from both hemispheres:

Box K: Hermelin and O'Connor (1970)

Procedure: Blind children, who were predominantly right-handed, were tested to see whether they could read Braille better with their left or their right hand.

Results: They could read better with the left hand.

Conclusion: The spatial information from Braille goes to the right hemisphere. It then goes to the left hemisphere to be translated into language.

Finally, it needs to be noted that research on split-brain patients needs to be treated with caution, since the fact that they suffer from epilepsy may mean that their performance is the result of side effects. More importantly, the surgery itself may exaggerate the differences between the hemispheres. Ellenberg and Sperry (1980) found that the performance of such patients is better than normal if they are given two tasks to do at once, suggesting that their hemispheres are working in a more independent way.

However, this is not always an advantage. Carter (1998) described instances of split-brain patients facing difficulties with simple tasks such as getting dressed. As fast as the right hand (under the command of the left hemisphere) buttons up their shirt, the left hand (under the control of the right hemisphere) unbuttons it again. This sort of problem, peculiar to split-brain patients, is known as **inter-manual conflict** (or **alien hand**). It demonstrates both the extent to which split-brain patients have two minds working in one head, and also the way that, in the normal brain, one hemisphere (usually the left) inhibits the commands sent out by the right.

▶ Activity 8: left or right?

For each of the following activities, decide whether the left or right hemisphere is primarily responsible. Draw up a table with two columns, one for the left hemisphere and one for the right, and put each in the appropriate column:

calculation   music
artistic skills   emotional expression
imagery   logic
language   holistic perception
spatial skills   focus on detail

left	right

When you have finished, see the notes on page 303.

❺ Research on normal and **split-brain** people has shown that the two hemispheres appear to have different roles.

❺ The **left hemisphere** is logical, analytical, mathematical and verbal. The **right hemisphere** is artistic, spatial, musical, emotional and holistic.

❺ Split-brain studies carried out by Sperry have shown that the right hemisphere can identify and write words, while the left hemisphere can also name them. The right hemisphere may be better at understanding metaphors and recognising faces than the left.

❺ The two hemispheres of split-brain patients may not operate in the same way as those of normal individuals.

❺ The two hemispheres normally work in an **integrated** way.

11.4 THE EFFECTS OF CORTICAL DAMAGE

Damage can result in disorders of visual perception, action and movement, spoken language, reading and writing, memory and emotional expression. We will consider each of these in turn.

Disorders of visual perception

Disorders of visual perception can be divided into two groups, those which result from damage to the primary visual areas (V1-V8), and those resulting from damage to the visual association areas.

Patients suffering from damage to the V1 primary visual area may suffer from **blindsight**. This makes the individual 'blind' to objects in the opposite visual field. For example, if the damage is on the right, objects on the left will be ignored. However, if patients with this kind of damage are asked to reach for an object on the blind side they will be able to carry out this task. This indicates that the visual information is present, but is not able to reach conscious awareness:

Box L: Weiskrantz (1986)

DB had had an abnormal clump of brain cells removed from the right primary visual cortex. This resulted in him being blind to the left half of the world.

DB was asked to look straight ahead at a fixation point. He was asked to indicate when he could see spots of light which were flashed up in different areas of his visual field. He responded only to the spots in his right visual field.

However, over a series of trials, a stick was held up either vertically or horizontally to his left visual field, and DB was asked to give its orientation. He claimed he could not see the stick, and was asked to guess. He made almost no errors.

Damage to V4 may result in an inability to perceive colours, while damage to V5 can result in the world being seen as a series of still snapshots:

Box M: Ramachandran and Blakeslee (1999)

Ingrid was a young woman who had damage to the V5 area. Her eyesight was in most ways normal. For example, she could recognise and name shapes and people, and read a book with no difficulty.

However, Ingrid was terrified to cross the street because she could not estimate the speed of oncoming cars. She reported that talking to someone was like talking on the phone, because she couldn't see their changing expressions. Even pouring a cup of coffee was difficult, because she didn't know when to slow down or change the angle of the coffee pot, since she couldn't estimate how fast the liquid was rising up the cup.

The second group of disorders of visual perception are visual **agnosias** ('failure to know'), which result from damage to the visual association cortex. The visual system is intact, but objects cannot be identified from drawings or by sight. However, if an object is held it can be identified, so the problem is not a language difficulty.

One special form of this disorder is **prosopagnosia**, the inability to recognise faces, described in chapter 2. This can occur even when objects can be recognised, indicating that there are special circuits for face recognition. It results from bilateral damage to the occipital and temporal cortex (Damasio *et al.* 1982).

Associative visual agnosia is a different form. Perception of objects appears to be normal, in that they can be drawn accurately, but they cannot be named or drawn from memory (Ratcliff and Newcombe 1982):

Generally the agnosias are thought to result from problems with transferring information from the visual to the verbal mechanisms of the cortex, possibly due to disruption of the neurons beneath the occipital and temporal lobes.

Disorders of action and movement

Disorders of action and movement are called **apraxias**, and they result from damage to the corpus callosum, or the frontal or parietal lobes. There are four main types.

Limb apraxia is a problem with movement of the arms, hands or fingers:

Figure 22: lesions associated with limb apraxia

Figure 21: associative visual agnosia

(a) Stimulus   (b) Patient's copy, looking a stimulus   (c) Patient's drawings, from memory

Either the wrong part is moved or the sequence of movements is incorrect. For example, when pretending to open a door with a key a patient may rotate his hand first and then insert the key.

Constructional apraxia results from lesions of the right parietal lobe, and causes problems with drawing pictures, following maps or assembling objects:

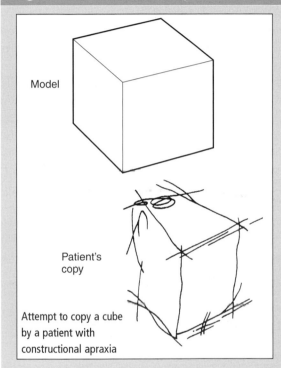

Figure 23: constructional apraxia

Model

Patient's copy

Attempt to copy a cube by a patient with constructional apraxia

Movements can be controlled, but patients are unable to imagine what the movement looks like.

Oral apraxia is a disorder of the muscles used in speech, shown in difficulties in articulating sounds. **Apraxic agraphia** is a writing problem.

Spoken language disorders

Disorders in the comprehension or production of speech are called **aphasia** (or **dysphasia**, if they are not too severe). Carlson (1991) identified seven different types.

Wernicke's aphasia results in poor comprehension of speech, together with confident, fluent and grammatical production of meaningless speech. Kertesz (1981) gave this example: 'and he roden all o these arranjen from the pedis on from iss pescid'. Because patients with Wernicke's aphasia are unable to comprehend even their own speech, they are typically unaware that there is any problem.

In **word deafness**, words can be heard, but there is no understanding of speech. The patient's own speech is unaffected, and reading and writing are normal. It results from damage to the connections between Wernicke's area and the primary auditory cortex:

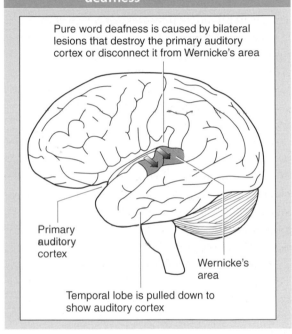

Figure 24: brain damage producing word deafness

Pure word deafness is caused by bilateral lesions that destroy the primary auditory cortex or disconnect it from Wernicke's area

Primary auditory cortex

Wernicke's area

Temporal lobe is pulled down to show auditory cortex

Unlike the previous two, **Broca's aphasia** is an expressive disorder, where speech is slow and lacks fluency. The words used are correct, but the patient has difficulty in finding them. Speech tends to be telegraphic, and important grammatical function words like 'the', 'in' or 'some' are omitted. There are three separate speech deficits: **agrammatism** (inability to use grammatical constructions), **anomia** (difficulty in finding words) and **articulation difficulties** (producing an incorrect sequence of sounds, such as 'lickstip' instead of 'lipstick'). An example of the kinds of problems associated with this disorder was given by Gardner (1975):

Box N: speech of a patient with Broca's aphasia (Gardner, 1975)

I: Were you in the Coast Guard?

P: No, er, yes, yes ... ship ... Massachu ... chusetts ... Coast Guard ... years (raises hands twice with fingers indicating '19').

I: Oh, you were in the Coast Guard for 19 years.

P: Oh ... boy ... right ... right.

I: Why are you in the hospital?

P: (points to paralysed arm) Arm no good. (points to mouth) Speech ... can't say ... talk, you see.

I: What happened to make you lose your speech?

P: Head, fall, Jesus Christ, me no good, str, str ... oh Jesus ... stroke.

I: Could you tell me what you've been doing in the hospital?

P: Yes, sure. Me go, er, uh, PT nine o'cot, speech ... two times ... read ... wr ... ripe, er, rike, er, write ... practice ... get-ting better.

Comprehension can appear to be relatively unaffected, although there are problems in understanding differences in word order. For example, Schwartz et al. (1980) found that patients were unable to say with any accuracy who is doing what to whom in sentences such as 'the horse kicked the cow' (see figure 25). Scores were only 62% correct, just above chance level. The disorder results from lesions of the frontal association cortex, which suggests that the basic problem is one of sequencing, since that is one of the functions of this area.

Conduction aphasia involves good speech and comprehension, but poor ability to repeat what is heard when nonsense words such as 'rilled' are presented, or if words are unconnected (Margolin and Walker, 1981). Meaning is therefore an important determinant of whether or not what is heard can be repeated. This disorder results from damage to the parietal lobe, which disrupts the axons connecting Broca's area and Wernicke's area (Damasio and Damasio, 1980). The axons transmitting information about sound appear to be disrupted, but those in another pathway between the two areas and which deals with meaning are not.

Anomic aphasia is the inability to find appropriate words, while speech, grammar and comprehension remain intact. Many patients have to speak about things in a roundabout way – called **circumlocution** – in order to get round the problem. It can be produced by lesions to either Broca's area or Wernicke's area. An example of the speech of a patient with this disorder is given by Margolin et al. (1985):

Figure 25: sample stimuli from Schwartz et al. (1980)

 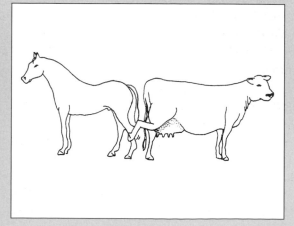

Box O: Margolin *et al.* (1985)

The patient was asked to describe this picture. What she said is given below. The pauses, when she is having difficulty in finding appropriate words, are marked with three dots. The words in brackets are the words the researcher thought she intended to use:

'It's a woman who has two children, a son and a daughter, and her son is to get into the ... cupboard in the kitchen to get out (*take*) some ... cookies out of the (*cookie jar*) ... that she possibly had made, and consequently he's slipping (*falling*) ... the wrong direction (*backward*) ... on the ... what he's standing on (*stool*), heading to the ... the cupboard (*floor*) and if he falls backwards he could have some problems (*get hurt*), because that (*the stool*) is off balance.'

The same patient was asked to name common objects from pictures. Here is her response when she was shown the picture of a saw:

'I know what it is. I can't tell you – maybe I can. If I was to carry the wood and cut it in half with that ... you know, if I had to cut the wood down and bring it in ... It's called a ... I have 'em in the garage. They are your ... You cut the wood with them ... it ... sah! ... ah ... Ss ... sahbing ... I can't say it.'

Transcortical sensory aphasia is loss of memory for the meanings of words, as a result of not being able to access the memories associated with a particular word. For example, memories associated with the word 'tree' include what various trees look like, the feel of bark, seasonal changes, knowledge about how trees grow, and so on. Normally this depends on circuits in Wernicke's area being linked with other areas in the posterior association cortex, where memories are stored. If these are disconnected, patients can repeat what they hear, and recognise words, but they have no understanding and no spontaneous speech (Kertesz, 1979). Normal speech production must therefore involve the flow of information from these association areas to Wernicke's area. Comprehension involves the reverse process:

Figure 26: the role of the speech areas and association cortex

(a) Repeating a word

(b) Spontaneous speech

(c) Answering a question

Transcortical motor aphasia is characterised by good comprehension and repetition of speech, but little spontaneous speech output (Damasio and Van Hoesen, 1983). Patients seem to have no interest in speech. This is caused by damage to the connections between Broca's area and the supplementary motor cortex in the frontal lobe (Damasio, 1981).

Disorders of reading and writing

Disorders of reading are referred to as **alexia** (or **dyslexia** if they are not too severe). Disorders of writing are referred to as **agraphia** or **dysgraphia**, again depending on the severity of the disorder. Reading disorders have been more widely investigated than writing disorders, and it is those which we will deal with first.

Alexia is also known as **word blindness**. In its pure form, the patient can write, but is unable to read back what has been written. It is caused by lesions to the angular gyrus in the parietal lobe, which disconnect it from visual input. Objects can still be recognised and named, showing that there are different mechanisms for the analysis of objects and words.

Dyslexia breaks down into five types:

Figure 27: five types of dyslexia

a. *word-form dyslexia*: a disorder acquired after the person has learned to read, which results in slow reading. Words cannot be recognised as a whole, but only by the naming of individual letters

b. *phonological dyslexia*: the inability to link letters with sounds, making it impossible to read phonetically

c. *direct dyslexia*: written words can be read but not understood. Visual word recognition is no longer linked with comprehension

d. *deep dyslexia*: the inability to read phonetically, so reading (especially of abstract words) is very poor

e. *developmental dyslexia*: the inability to learn to read fluently

There appears to be a genetic component to developmental dyslexia, as it runs in families. It also appears to be more common in males. Rutter and Yule (1975) have suggested that the male link may implicate the Y chromosome or the presence of **androgens** (male hormones) during foetal development.

Dyslexia is associated with abnormalities in a part of Wernicke's area called the **planum temporale**.

This is normally larger in the left hemisphere, but in dyslexics it is reduced in size and of abnormal appearance (Galaburda *et al.* 1988). It is more common in left-handed people; this is also true of immune disorders such as diabetes and rheumatoid arthritis. Geschwind and Behan (1984) have suggested that suppression of left hemisphere development could result in left-handedness and language abnormalities. Galaburda and Geschwind (1982) proposed that the presence of the male hormone testosterone may slow down the development of the brain and the immune system.

Disorders of writing are rare, but motor disturbances can result in apraxic agraphia, the inability to make the movements necessary for writing. Dysgraphia occurs in two forms. Phonological dysgraphia is a problem with writing words phonetically, although Shallice (1981) found that they could be written from memory using visual images instead. In **orthographic dysgraphia**, words can be sounded out but irregular words cannot be spelled.

Disorders of memory

These are known as **amnesias**, and fall into two groups. **Retrograde amnesia** is loss of memory of events before the damage occurred, while **anterograde amnesia** is the inability to form new memories after the damage. Chorover and Schiller (1965) produced retrograde amnesia in rats by inducing electroconvulsive seizures following a learning task. Provided the seizure occurred within a second or two of the learning experience, it disrupted short-term memory. This type of amnesia can also be seen in humans who have been given electroconvulsive therapy for depression (see the section on **somatic therapies** in chapter 25).

Anterograde amnesia is generally the result of damage to the hippocampus, a subcortical structure which lies beneath the temporal lobe, or to its connections with other areas. This appears to be responsible for converting short-term memories into long-term memories. One condition which is commonly linked with anterograde amnesia is **Korsakov's syndrome.** This is associated with chronic alcoholism and is thought to be the result of dietary deficiencies, leading to a shortage of vitamin B (thiamine). Patients appear to have a relatively normal short-term memory, but cannot form new long-term memories.

Disorders of emotional expression

This kind of disorder is known as **aprosodia**. There are several different forms, resulting from damage to different areas of the cortex:

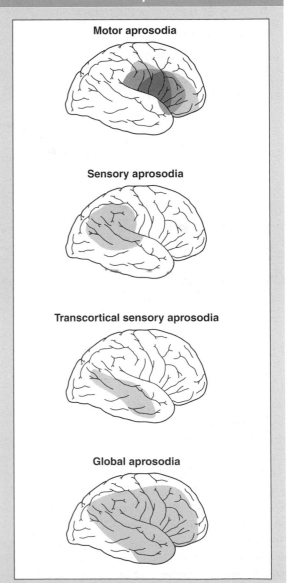

Figure 28: brain damage causing different forms of aprosodia

Motor aprosodia

Sensory aprosodia

Transcortical sensory aprosodia

Global aprosodia

According to Ross (1981), there are circuits in the right hemisphere which are responsible for the comprehension and expression of emotions. **Motor aprosodia** is the inability to express emotion, although emotions expressed by others can be recognised by their tone of voice or from facial expressions. This is the result of frontal damage. **Sensory aprosodia** results from posterior lesions, and affects the ability to comprehend emotions, but not to express them. Finally, there are also global and transcortical varieties.

▷ Activity 9: defining disorders

Link each of these names of disorders with the appropriate definition:

1 agnosia		a	disorder of memory
2 apraxia		b	disorder of emotional expression
3 aphasia		c	disorder of perception
4 dyslexia		d	disorder of writing
5 dysgraphia		e	disorder of movement
6 amnesia		f	disorder of spoken language
7 aprosodia		g	disorder of reading

When you have finished, see the notes on page 303.

❺ **Brain damage** can lead to agnosias, apraxias, aphasias, alexia and dyslexia, agraphia and dysgraphia, amnesia and aprosodia.

11.5 RECOVERY FROM CEREBRAL LESIONS

Research in this area suggests that a variety of repair processes can take place over a period of about one year. For example, when neurons are damaged as the result of the swelling that occurs after a head injury or infection the patient may recover fully when the swelling goes down. Moscovitch and Rozijn (1989) reported that draining off the excess cerebrospinal fluid assists the recovery process.

When neurons are destroyed, new connections will sometimes be formed to take over their role. Neighbouring healthy neurons grow branches called **collateral sprouts**, which may become attached to the empty synapses left by the dead neurons (Veraa and Grafstein, 1981). If they become attached to other sites, they can of course become disruptive instead.

Repair can also take place as a result of external interventions; for example, through the transplantation of brain tissue:

Box P: Bjorkland *et al.* (1983)

Procedure: Foetal rat brain tissue was transplanted into the brains of adult rats with lesions which produce the symptoms of Parkinson's disease, i.e. shaking and difficulty with motor control. Foetal tissue was used because it is still plastic and adaptable.

Results: The new tissue established itself in the host brain, leading to a reduction in symptoms. An increase in the neurotransmitter dopamine was also found; there is a lack of dopamine in the brains of Parkinson's sufferers.

Conclusion: Transplantation may offer a way of repairing some forms of brain damage.

Another example relates to **Alzheimer's disease**. This affects 5–10% of people over 65. It involves loss of memory, disorientation and a general decline in mental functioning. This is thought to result from the degeneration of neurons which produce **acetylcholine**, another neurotransmitter, in the base of the forebrain. These have links with the cortical association areas and with the hippocampus, so are involved in memory.

Coyle *et al.* (1983) found that rats with lesions to this area developed memory problems, which improved when they were given transplants of foetal tissue from the same area. This seems to be a promising technique, but one which raises ethical issues regarding its use in humans, since it depends on the use of aborted human foetuses as donors of the brain tissue for transplantation.

If brain damage, such as the loss of one hemisphere, occurs early in life, i.e. up to the age of about 8, it is possible that functions normally carried out by the damaged area can be taken over by others. Remember that Zaidel (1983) found that the two hemispheres only became different after 5 years of age. It was previously thought that this was unlikely to occur if the damage took place after puberty. However, Gooch (1980) has reported that this has happened even in adult patients who have had a left hemispherectomy, i.e. removal of the left hemisphere as the result of an accident or to remove a tumour. Motivation appears to be an important factor in how successful the technique is. In all four cases reported, the language function was regained after surgery. This suggests that the hemispheres are not in fact fundamentally different in their skills.

In general, the effects of cortical damage (for example, after a stroke) are not as drastic as might be expected, due to the plasticity or flexibility of the way that the brain is organised. Since there is no specific group of neurons which is entirely responsible for a particular function, it is possible (if the need arises) for a dominant part of the system to take over. For example, Altman and Kien (1989) found that in patients who had suffered a stroke, PET scans showed that areas which are normally only involved in complex tasks became active during simple movements.

Alternatively, regeneration of nerves may be possible.

It seems that rather than being hierarchical, as has been suggested, the cortex is organised into relatively independent loops or units which operate in parallel. Another possibility is that functions like memory may be organised in the form of a hologram, so that if part remains, the rest can be re-created.

⊖ The effects of damage may be lessened by **repair** and **plasticity**.

Notes on activities

1 dead; perfused; fixed; clinical; ablation; lesioning; stereotaxic; inflammation; macroelectrodes; microelectrodes; chemical; micropipette; cerebrospinal fluid; neurotransmitters.

2 **a**7; **b**5; **c**2; **d**3; **e**6; **f**4; **g**1

3 **a** frontal; **b** parietal; **c** temporal; **d** occipital

6 The fact that most right-handers showed defects after surgery to the left side of the brain suggests that right-handers have their language centres in the left hemisphere. However, since 29.6% showed no speech disturbances, it could be concluded that they had language centres in both hemispheres; this is known as **bilateral representation**. Alternatively, it is possible that they too had language in the left hemisphere, but that the surgery left the language areas intact. At least 0.4% of right handers must have language only in the right hemisphere.

At least 38% of left-handers also have language only in the left hemisphere, though it seems that many have bilateral representation. At least 9% have language only in the right hemisphere.

7 The left and right hemispheres have different language skills:

   left: read, identify and name

   right: read, identify and write

8 left: calculation; language; focus on detail; logic

   right: spatial/artistic skills; imagery; holistic perception; music; emotional expression

9 1c 2e 3f 4g 5d 6a 7b

Biological rhythms, sleep and dreaming

In this chapter we will be looking at:

12.1 Bodily rhythms
    Circadian rhythms
    Infradian rhythms
    Ultradian rhythms

12.2 Sleep
    The stages of sleep
    The mechanisms of sleep
    Sleep disorders
    Theories of sleep
    Sleep deprivation studies

12.3 Dreaming
    The nature of dreams
    Theories of dreaming

12.1 BODILY RHYTHMS

A bodily rhythm can be defined as a pattern in physiological or psychological processes which repeats itself over a specified period of time. What this means is that certain features of our behaviour are repeated on a regular basis. There are five different types of bodily rhythm, the difference between them being the period of time that elapses before the behaviour is repeated. These rhythms are accompanied by physiological and psychological changes:

Figure 1: bodily rhythms	
description	**length of cycle**
circadian	approximately 24 hours
diurnal	changes during the waking day
circannual	approximately one year
infradian	longer than a day, e.g. monthly
ultradian	more than once within a day

In this section, we will be looking at three kinds of bodily rhythms: circadian, infradian and ultradian.

Activity 1: examples of bodily rhythms

An example of a diurnal rhythm is variation in performance on cognitive tasks carried out at different times of the day; for example, the 'post-lunch dip', when people feel they are not thinking as clearly or working as efficiently as earlier in the day. An example of a circannual rhythm is hibernation, or Seasonal Affective Disorder (SAD), associated with depression during different seasons of the year.

Read through the definitions of circadian, infradian and ultradian rhythms in figure 1. Can you think of at least one example of each, relating to humans or animals? If you get stuck, there are many examples, most of which will be familiar to you, as you read through the next few sections.

Circadian rhythms

Circadian rhythms are repeated approximately every 24 hours – the word 'circadian' comes from the Latin 'circa' meaning 'about' and 'dies' meaning 'a day'. **Sleep** is the most researched example; in normal circumstances, we follow a regular pattern of sleeping and waking over a 24-hour period.

Circadian rhythms are influenced and kept synchronised to the 24-hour clock by exogenous factors , i.e. external cues, such as dark and light or mealtimes. These are known as **Zeitgebers** from the German for 'timegivers'. These Zeitgebers lead us to function on a 24-hour cycle, and light seems to be the most important. Perhaps the most famous study of circadian rhythms in humans was carried out by the French explorer Michel Siffre:

Box A: Siffre (1972)

Procedure: Siffre spent 7 months underground. He was adequately fed, had opportunities for exercise and was able to make contact at all times by telephone, but he totally lacked any cues about when it was day or night. Changes in his sleep pattern were noted.

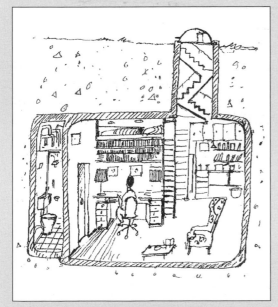

Results: He eventually settled to a 25-hour cycle of sleep and activity.
Conclusion: Patterns of sleep and waking persist, even when there are no external cues. However, the natural pattern is slightly longer than 24 hours.

Miles *et al.* (1977) found that blind people show the same pattern as sighted people. Since they cannot respond to light, this suggests that although external Zeitgebers produce a 24-hour cycle, there are also endogenous factors, i.e. internal cues – sometimes referred to as **pacemakers** – which maintain rhythms when Zeitgebers do not provide appropriate information. As Siffre found, our internal pacemaker in the sleep/waking cycle works to a 25-hour cycle, which is slightly modified by external cues. Groblewski *et al.* (1980) found that rats also operate on a 25-hour cycle when kept in conditions of constant dim illumination.

Sleep is probably the circadian rhythm we are most aware of, and we will be looking at it in more detail later in this chapter. However, there is also a whole range of other changes which share this rhythm: it is estimated that in mammals, there may be as many as 100 biological changes taking place during 24 hours. Heart rate, urine secretion, metabolic rate (i.e. chemical changes), respiration (i.e. breathing) and temperature are all highest in the late afternoon at around 4 pm, and lowest in the early morning at around 4 am. Hormone levels also vary. For example, prolactin, which stimulates milk production in females, rises in the middle of the night.

So what are the mechanisms, or **biological clocks**, that govern these rhythms? The principal one appears to be the **suprachiasmatic nuclei (SCN)** of the **hypothalamus**. Ibuka and Kawamura (1975) have shown that lesions of these nuclei disrupt circadian rhythms, and Rusak and Groos (1982) have found a correlation between the cyclical changes in behaviour which we have described above and the activity of neurons in that area.

There may well be other clocks which regulate specific rhythms, such as temperature changes, but even so the SCN seem to have some controlling function. The SCN are well situated to do this task because they receive nerve input directly from the retina of the eye, so they are kept informed about the Zeitgebers of light and darkness. This information is transmitted to the **pineal gland**, which manufactures **melatonin**, a hormone which regulates the activity of many of the body's systems, and is involved in bringing about sleep.

The SCN clearly govern some of these rhythms via nerve connections with the rest of the hypothalamus and with the pineal gland. They may also control others by the secretion of **neuromodulators**, chemicals which affect the behaviour of neuro-transmitters. Ralph *et al.* (1990) found that grafted SCN, even when they have not grown any connections with the rest of the brain, can establish circadian rhythms within a few days. Interestingly, Hurd and Ralph (1998) found that if the donor animal happens to have a slightly different cycle, this will be adopted by the recipient after the transplant.

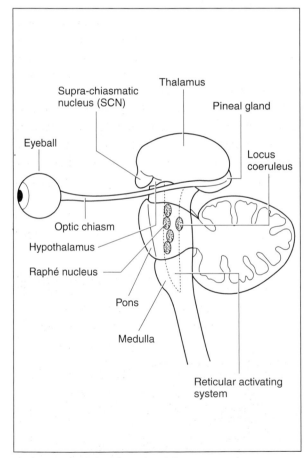

Supra-chiasmatic nucleus (SCN)
Thalamus
Pineal gland
Eyeball
Locus coeruleus
Optic chiasm
Hypothalamus
Raphé nucleus
Pons
Medulla
Reticular activating system

The brain physiology of arousal and sleep

There has been much research into what happens when circadian rhythms are disrupted. This disruption can take the form of **desyn-chronisation**, when different rhythms adapt at

different rates, and **flattening**, when the amount of circadian variation is reduced.

As we saw in chapter 4, in the section on physiological sources of stress, the effects of jetlag and shift work are examples of what happens when the circadian rhythm is disrupted. In the case of jetlag, problems are caused by desynchronisation. For example, Hauty and Adams (1966) found that physiological measures took from between four days (body temperature and heart rate) and eight days (palmar sweating) to adjust. Behaviour took less time to adjust than physiological functioning. Colquoun (1970) concluded that flattening was implicated in the problems associated with shift work, with only body temperature being affected also by desynchronisation.

In both jetlag and shift work, people have problems in adjusting to changes because they occur so rapidly. So how can these problems be overcome?

In the case of **jetlag**, the easiest way to adapt is to try to stay awake longer, shifting sleep to a later time. You will remember from box A that in the absence of external Zeitgebers, circadian rhythms establish themselves in a cycle which is slightly longer than 24 hours, so extending the waking part of the cycle is more effective than trying to shorten it.

▶ Activity 2: understanding jetlag

New York is five hours behind London: when it is noon in London, it is 7 am in New York. If you were flying out from London to New York, and then back a week later, on which journey would you be more likely to feel jetlagged?

When you have finished, see the notes on page 323.

Culebras (1992) has shown that exposure to properly timed bright light can help to reset the clock, and in hamsters the drug triazolam (a relative of valium, which works on the neurotransmitter GABA) has been found by Turek and Losee-Olson (1986) to be helpful in shifting the activity cycle.

Blakemore's study (chapter 4, box C) showed what happens when circadian rhythms are disrupted by **shift work**. Workers were unhappy, were more likely to become ill and were not as productive as they might have been.

Activity 3: the effects of shift work

In the Blakemore study, workers in a chemical company in Utah worked a three-shift system, whereby they would work a day shift for a week, a night shift for the second week and an evening shift for the third week. The cycle would then start again.

From what you know about circadian rhythms, why is this a bad system? What recommendations would you make for improving it, but keeping a shift system?

When you have finished, see the notes on page 323.

Akerstedt (1985) found that many people get 1–4 hours less sleep than normal when they have to sleep during the day. The importance of this is shown by accident rates. As we saw in chapter 4, Gold *et al.* (1992) found that nurses on rotating shifts made twice as many errors at work as those on permanent day or night shifts, since rotating shifts disrupt sleep even more than sleeping during the day. Similarly, the high risk periods for motorway accidents are midnight–2 am, 4–6 am, and 2–4 pm. Horne (1992) found that falling asleep at the wheel was responsible for most accidents, the result of having been awake for 18 hours or more, getting up very early, or having irregular sleep patterns, perhaps as a result of shift work.

Exposure to light can go some way towards helping shift workers overcome adjustment problems. Dawson and Campbell (1991) found that a 4-hour exposure to bright light on the first night of shift work could help people to adjust, as shown by recordings of body temperature.

- **Physiological** and **psychological processes** generally show a rhythm or cycle that recurs over a period of time. There are **five rhythms**, relating to different cycle lengths: circadian, infradian, circannual, ultradian, and diurnal.
- **Circadian rhythms** are repeated approximately every 24 hours. They are governed by external

Zeitgebers and internal **pacemakers** involving the **SCN** and **pineal gland**.
- **Jetlag** is the result of having to adjust circadian rhythms, especially when these cycles need to be shortened to accommodate to different time zones.
- **Shift workers** also have problems because a change of shift means that these rhythms have to be adjusted.
- Having to adjust sleeping patterns is associated with a greater risk of motor **accidents**, and **errors** at work.
- Exposure to **light** can help with adjustment.

Infradian rhythms

This refers to rhythms which last for longer than a day. They include the menstrual cycle (28 days), testosterone secretion in males (21 days) and seasonal mating. Of these, the **menstrual cycle** has been the most researched.

The menstrual cycle relates to the endocrine activity which prepares the womb for the possibility of conception after egg cells are released. The process involves the activity of a range of hormones, which are co-ordinated by the **pituitary gland**. This in turn may be influenced by light levels, and by the secretion of melatonin, mentioned previously. A study which supports this viewpoint is described in box B:

Box B: Reinberg (1967)

Procedure: A young woman spent three months in a cave. The only lighting she had was a miner's lamp. The effect on bodily rhythms was investigated.

Results: Her day lengthened (as in the Siffre example in box A) to 24.6 hours. Her menstrual cycle shortened to 25.7 days. When the three months were up, it took a year for the menstrual cycle to return to normal.
Conclusion: The menstrual cycle may be affected by levels of available light.

This idea is further supported by the fact that blind girls begin to menstruate earlier than those who can see.

As well as light, the menstrual cycle may also be influenced by smell, since females who spend a lot of time together show synchronisation of their cycles, i.e. they tend to menstruate at the same time. Russell *et al.* (1980) showed that synchronisation could be produced by simply transferring samples of underarm sweat from one woman to another.

A problem associated with the menstrual cycle is the phenomenon known as **pre-menstrual syndrome (PMS)**, which refers to negative psychological effects experienced by up to 60% of females about 4–5 days before menstruation begins: irritability, depression, headaches, lethargy, insomnia and sometimes changes in appetite – both increases and decreases have been reported. Some researchers, e.g. Dalton (1964), have claimed that during this part of the menstrual cycle, females are more likely to commit child abuse, to have accidents, to carry out crimes, to commit suicide and to have reduced scores on IQ tests. However, more recent studies have not supported these claims, with only a small proportion of women showing impairment of normal functioning.

- **Infradian rhythms** last longer than a day. The most widely researched is the **menstrual cycle**. This cycle is thought to be affected by **light** and possibly **smell**.
- During the part of the cycle just prior to menstruation, some women suffer from **PMS**. Research into its effects are somewhat contradictory.

Ultradian rhythms

These rhythms are shorter than a day. They include heart rate, sleeping and oral activity, such as smoking. The most extensively researched of these are the stages of sleep, which we will be looking at in detail in the following sections.

12.2 SLEEP

The physiological changes that occur during sleep have been well documented. A great deal of research has also been devoted to trying to discover the mechanisms which bring about these changes. A related area of interest is that of sleep disorders, where research attempts to shed light on the mechanisms of sleep by examining what happens when these mechanisms fail to function adequately. Another area of interest is the question of why we need to sleep. Several theories have been put forward to try to explain what function it serves. One way of trying to establish what these theories have to offer has involved research into the effects of sleep deprivation. We will be looking at all these aspects of sleep research in the following sections.

The stages of sleep

As well as being part of the circadian cycle of rest and activity, sleep has its own internal rhythms, based on a 90 minute ultradian cycle. Within this cycle there are a number of stages, which can be shown by looking at EEG, EOG and EMG recordings taken during sleep. Figure 2 shows how these recordings are made:

Figure 2: ways of recording the stages of sleep

EEG (electroencephalogram): measures electrical activity in different parts of the brain
EOG (electrooculogram): shows the electrical activity as a result of eye movements
EMG (electromyogram): records electrical activity from the chin muscles, and so gives information about muscle tension

One particular kind of sleep is known as **REM** (which stands for rapid eye movement) sleep. People experience several periods of REM sleep every night. During this kind of sleep, the eyes make rapid movements which produce intense EOG activity. An early study looked at the characteristics of the different stages of sleep, and in particular investigated the relationship between REM sleep and dreaming:

Box C: Dement and Kleitman (1957)

Procedure: Five participants were studied. An EEG recorded changes in brain activity during the various stages of sleep. Each was wakened on average 5–6 times a night, when their dream recall was tested. They were wakened either 5 or 15 minutes into a period of REM sleep and asked to say whether their dream had lasted 5 or 15 minutes.
Results: REM sleep was predominantly associated with dreaming. Participants were in general accurate in identifying how long they had been dreaming.
Conclusion: There are clearly differentiated stages in sleep. REM sleep shows a distinctive pattern of brain activity. It is connected to dreaming.

Following on from this early work, Rechtschaffen and Kales (1968) categorised the different kinds of sleep we experience.

Stage 0 is wakefulness, identified by the presence of **beta waves** in the EEG, which are low amplitude and high frequency. As we relax, these are replaced by **alpha waves**, which are higher in amplitude but slower in frequency (8–12 cycles per second).

Stage 1 sleep is characterised by the appearance of **theta waves** in the EEG; these are slower (4–7 cycles per second) and more irregular. Breathing and heart rate slow down, body temperature falls, and muscles relax. There may also be slow eye rolling, shown on the EOG.

Stage 2 sleep usually occurs after about a minute, and is characterised by the appearance of brief bursts of high frequency EEG activity known as **sleep spindles**, lasting about one second. There are also **K-complexes**, which represent the brain's response to stimulation; either external, e.g. a noise in the room where we are sleeping, or internal, e.g. a muscle movement. Very slow (1–3 cycles per second) high amplitude **delta waves** start to appear as well. The EOG shows little activity, and the EMG is reduced still further.

Stage 3 sleep occurs after about 20 more minutes. In this stage, there is 20–50% **delta activity** in the EEG.

Stage 4 sleep follows shortly, when delta activity has increased to over 50% of the total, and become even slower. Heart rate, blood pressure and body temperature are at their lowest, and the muscles are very relaxed. At this stage, people are very difficult to wake, and do not respond to external stimuli as readily, so this is regarded as a deeper stage of sleep. This will last for about 40 minutes.

Stages 3 and 4 are often known as **slow-wave sleep**, and stages 1 to 4 as **non-REM (NREM)** sleep.

Having descended what is known as the **sleep staircase** into deeper and deeper sleep, the sleeper then starts to climb back through stages 3 and 2. However, instead of going back into stage 1, REM sleep comes next. In this stage, the EEG pattern resembles that in the waking, relaxed state, with a high level of **alpha activity**. There are also **PGO spikes**, which are short bursts of high frequency, large amplitude activity from the pons, thalamus and visual cortex (PGO stands for pontine geniculate occipital). Heart rate, blood pressure and respiration rates increase and become more irregular. Rapid eye movements occur, where the eyes may flick from side to side rapidly. The EMG record shows that, despite all these signs of activity, the muscles are in a state of virtual paralysis, apart from occasional twitches of the toes and fingers.

This is thought to be the deepest phase of sleep, since this is when people are hardest to wake. It is also known as **paradoxical sleep** – the brain is alert, but the body is not. As we have seen (box C), this is the stage of sleep when people are most likely to report dreams if woken up. It has been argued that people may be more difficult to wake at this time not because they are more deeply asleep, but simply because they are absorbed in their dreams.

After about 10 minutes, there is a return to stage 2 sleep, and the sleep staircase is descended once again. During the night, we normally experience around five of these cycles, each of which will last for about 90 minutes. Stages 3 and 4 only occur in the first two cycles, and periods of REM sleep get longer in the course of the night.

Figure 3: EEG, EOG and EMG recordings in the various stages of sleep

The exact pattern of sleep varies from person to person, and can also vary in the same person from night to night. There are also changes with age. Newborn infants sleep for around 16 hours, half of it REM sleep, dropping to around 12 hours a day at 12 months, a third of which is REM sleep. Adults will sleep for about 8 hours, and have 2 hours REM sleep. In old age, there will be even more reduction both in the total amount of sleep and the amount of REM sleep. We also have less stage 4 sleep as we get older; by the age of 60 it has virtually disappeared, which is why elderly people are often easily wakened. There are also systematic differences, in that long sleepers (i.e. 9 hours or more) have more REM sleep than short sleepers (i.e. under 6 hours).

⑤ Ultradian rhythms are shorter than a day. The most extensively researched ultradian rhythms are the stages of sleep.

⑤ EEG, EOG and **EMG** are measures of electrical activity which show variation during the stages of sleep. Researchers are particularly interested in **REM** sleep and its link with **dreaming**. The four other stages are **non-REM** sleep. Each stage has a distinct **pattern of electrical activity**.

⑤ During **wakefulness**, the EEG shows beta waves, replaced by alpha waves as we relax.

Stage 1 sleep is characterised by theta waves. **Stage 2 sleep** shows sleep spindles and K-complexes. An increase of delta waves marks **stage 3 sleep**. When these are more than 50% of the EEG, we are in **stage 4 sleep**. This is followed by **REM sleep**, with high levels of alpha activity.

⑤ These stages of sleep follow a typical pattern, with some variation between **individuals**. The pattern also changes with **age**.

Figure 4: characteristic profile of a night's sleep

Figure 5: changes in sleep pattern with age

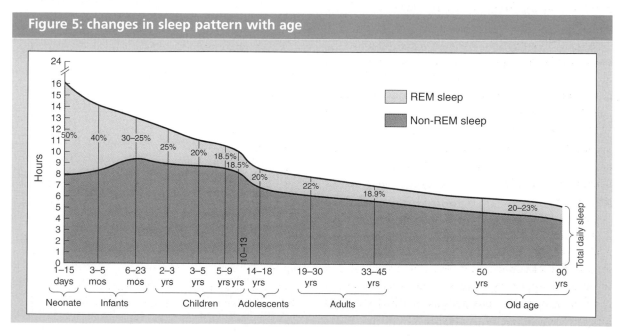

The mechanisms of sleep

Research into the mechanisms of sleep has looked at neurochemicals, circulating sleep-inducing chemicals, and at neurological mechanisms involved in sleep, i.e. sleep centres and circuits.

The link with circadian rhythms has already been mentioned; when it gets dark, the eyes send messages to the SCN of the hypothalamus, and from there to the pineal gland. The pineal gland starts to secrete melatonin, which makes us feel drowsy. Melatonin in turn influences neurons in the **raphé nuclei** in the brain stem, which produce the neurotransmitter **serotonin**. Serotonin in turn influences activity in the **reticular activating system (RAS)** which is nearby.

The RAS is concerned with arousal, and has been implicated in sleep since Moruzzi and Magoun (1949) showed that low levels of activity in the RAS were associated with the onset of sleep, and French (1957) found that a sleeping cat could be woken by stimulation of the RAS. More recent research seems to indicate that the RAS is involved in movement rather than arousal. In the context of sleep, serotonin is an inhibitory transmitter, and lesions of the raphé nuclei, which are known to produce sleeplessness, will produce an almost complete loss of brain serotonin. Drugs which reduce levels of serotonin in the brain prevent sleep, and those which increase serotonin levels reverse the effect.

Another system appears to be responsible for the production of REM sleep. Jouvet (1967) found that destruction of the **locus coeruleus**, located in the pons, eliminates REM sleep. The locus coeruleus produces the neurotransmitters **noradrenaline** and **acetylcholine**. REM sleep occurs when there are increases in activity in acetylcholine systems, and is brought to an end when there are increases in activity in noradrenaline systems. This fits in with the finding that **monoamine oxidase inhibitors** (**MAOIs**), which are drugs that have been used to treat depression, and which increase levels of noradrenaline and serotonin, also eliminate REM sleep.

Other research has focused on the idea that substances which promote sleep or wakefulness might be produced, accumulating in the blood during wakefulness and being destroyed during sleep. However, there are problems with this idea. Mukhametov (1984) has shown that the two hemispheres of the brain sleep separately in dolphins, which they would not be able to do if sleep was being produced by chemicals in a shared blood supply. Even more convincingly, conjoined twins, who also share the same blood supply, have different sleep patterns.

However, Monnier and Hosli (1964) were able to extract **DSIP** (**delta-sleep-inducing-peptide**) from rabbits, which induced sleep when injected into rats. Pappenheimer *et al.* (1975) obtained **Factor S** from the cerebrospinal fluid of sleep-deprived goats, which had the same effect; it has also been found in human urine (Garcia-Arraras and Pappenheimer, 1983). However, the role of these chemicals is still unclear, as they have other effects as well, such as raising body temperature and stimulating the immune system.

🖙 The **hypothalamus**, **pineal gland** and **RAS** are involved in NREM sleep, which is influenced by the neurotransmitter **serotonin**. The **locus coeruleus** governs REM sleep. The neurotransmitters **acetylcholine** and **noradrenaline** are involved. Other chemicals may also be important in regulating sleep.

Sleep disorders

A sleep disorder can be thought to exist whenever the inability to sleep properly produces impaired functioning or excessive sleepiness during the day. There are many different kinds of sleep disorder. We will look briefly here at three examples: **insomnia**, **sleep apnoea** and **REM sleep behavioural disorder**.

The most common sleep disorder is insomnia, which is thought to affect at least 20% of the population at some time during their lives. Patients complain about the quantity or quality of sleep they are getting. Insomnia can be caused by depression, pain, illness or even looking forward to an exciting event.

Generally insomniacs get more sleep than they think, around 6 hours (Horne, 1988). Their feelings of tiredness during the day are often due to stress or anxiety; in some cases this may be due to thinking they need more sleep than they do. There are large individual differences in sleep requirements. For example, Meddis *et al.* (1973) reported the case of a 70-year-old woman who felt fine sleeping only one hour a night.

Sleeping pills given for insomnia are hypnotics, such as the **benzodiazepines**. Unfortunately they are addictive, since they supplant the brain's natural mechanisms for bringing about sleep. When a patient stops taking them, there is a rebound effect, and even worse sleep, since the natural mechanisms no longer work properly.

In sleep apnoea, breathing stops while asleep. It can be caused by an obstruction of the windpipe, which can be corrected by surgery, or by excessive relaxation of the muscles which hold the windpipe open. According to Guilleminault and Bliwise (1994), it may also be the result of a fault in the area of the brainstem which controls breathing, in which case it can be treated by brainstem-stimulating drugs. When a sleeping person stops breathing, the reduced oxygen levels in the blood cause the secretion of emergency hormones which in turn cause the sleeper to wake up and start breathing again.

It is thought that sleep apnoea is in some cases responsible for **Sudden Infant Death Syndrome (SIDS)**, although according to Kemp and Thach (1991), up to around 50% of cases are due to accidental suffocation caused by sleeping face down. The use of monitors which give the alarm when the child stops breathing appear to deal well with this problem.

REM sleep behavioural disorder, described by Schenck *et al.* (1986), is a condition where people act out the contents of their dreams. For 44% of sufferers this involves attacking their partners! Schenck *et al.* gave the example of a man who had a very vivid dream that he was playing American football. When he woke up, he found that he had got out of bed in his sleep and run around, knocking lamps and mirrors off the furniture, and had hit his head and his knee.

You will remember that muscle paralysis normally accompanies REM sleep. Damage to the area of the brainstem which produces this paralysis leads to REM sleep behavioural disorder, but the effects can be controlled by drugs in 90% of cases.

❺ There are many kinds of **sleep disorder**. They include **insomnia**, **sleep apnoea** and **REM sleep behavioural disorder**.

Theories of sleep

In this section we will be looking at theories and research which try to establish why we sleep and what function it serves.

▶ **Activity 4: explaining sleep**

Why do we need to sleep? We will be looking at several theories, so it is likely that you will have ideas which coincide with at least one, and perhaps more. If you have ever missed a night's sleep, think about what it felt like – could this help to explain why sleep is necessary?

Compare notes with fellow students and the discussion which follows.

There have been many theories about the functions of sleep, some of which we will look at in this section. Some theories are related to sleep in general, while others deal with a specific type of sleep.

Evolutionary theories of sleep

One major theoretical explanation of sleep takes an evolutionary approach. Meddis (1975) emphasised the adaptive function of safety and energy conservation. His theory focuses on the fact that some species seem to sleep for longer than others, and at different times. For example, predators like lions who are unlikely to be attacked sleep for longer than sheep, who have little defence against predators and have to spend a long time feeding to get enough nutrition.

The evolutionary theory of sleep

This leads to the idea that sleep has evolved because it aids survival by reducing unnecessary energy expenditure. It does this by immobilising us for long periods. **Hibernation theory**, a similar approach, argues that sleep keeps us out of harm's way by immobilising us at night when we are vulnerable.

Activity 5: evaluating evolutionary theories of sleep

Can you see any problems with these theories from an evolutionary point of view? (Hint: you will need to think why sleeping less might serve an evolutionary purpose, and what the implications of this are; for hibernation theory, you will need to consider why many animals hunt at night.)

When you have finished, see the notes on page 323.

Restoration theory of sleep

An important alternative approach is **restoration theory** (Oswald, 1966). This theory argues that the purpose of sleep is to restore energy levels and repair the brain and the body. NREM sleep operates to restore bodily processes, e.g. to restore hormone levels, and REM sleep restores brain processes, e.g. by stimulating the synthesis of proteins.

There are several important lines of evidence which could support this idea. Firstly, it accounts for the fact that babies sleep for longer than older people, and in particular need more REM sleep to assist the development of the **central nervous system**. Secondly, Shapiro et al. (1981) found that people who had taken part in an ultra-marathon of 57 miles slept longer than normal (especially stage 4 sleep) on the next two nights, presumably to help their bodies recover. Similarly, people who have had **electroconvulsive therapy (ECT)**, where an electric shock is delivered to the brain as a treatment for depression, or who have taken drug overdoses, show an increase in REM sleep for a period of 6–8 weeks afterwards, which is approximately how long it would take to replace half the brain's total protein.

People who suffer from fibrositis (which causes pain and stiffness in the back muscles) have also been found to suffer lack of stage 4 sleep, which is when the pituitary gland releases growth hormone. Growth hormone is essential for the promotion of protein synthesis (and therefore for tissue growth) and the formation of red blood cells. Lack of stage 4 sleep has been found to produce similar symptoms in healthy volunteers. Further support for the theory comes from Hartmann (1973), who found that stress, which may increase the need for restoration, also increases the need for sleep.

On the other hand, inactivity does not seem to reduce the need for sleep. For example, Ryback and Lewis (1971) found no change in sleep requirements in healthy individuals who spent 6 weeks in bed.

However, Horne (1988) argued that in humans, the purpose of both REM and stage 4 sleep is to restore brain functioning. Body tissue repair takes place during periods of relaxed wakefulness, observed in humans though not in other animals, when energy expenditure is minimal. As we shall see in the next section, **sleep deprivation** studies, which indicate that the main effects of sleep loss in humans are psychological rather than physiological, support this approach.

Alternative theories

The other theories of sleep which we will be looking at all relate exclusively to REM sleep. One of the main functions of REM sleep is that it produces dreams; theories as to why we dream are discussed in section 12.3 below. It has also been suggested that REM sleep is important for **memory consolidation**. Empson and Clarke (1970) gave people a test in the morning on material presented before they went to sleep. When they had been deprived of REM sleep, their memory was poorer. This idea could also be supported by the evidence about differences in the amount of REM sleep in children and old people, given the differences in the amount of new information which they will have taken in during the day.

Sentinel (or **cognitive arousal**) **theory**, proposed by Snyder (1966), suggests that REM sleep serves the purpose of bringing the individual closer to wakefulness, which would allow the environment to be checked for danger. The problem with this argument is that it is limited as a theory, since the function of the rest of sleep still has to be explained. It also raises the issue of whether REM sleep is in fact a lighter or a deeper form of sleep, which as we have already seen is far from clear.

Oculomotor system maintenance theory (Berger, 1969) argues that the function of REM sleep is to keep the eye muscles toned up. As we have seen, sleep deprivation can affect the ability to focus the eyes, but this is not restricted to REM sleep deprivation. It does seem rather an elaborate system to have developed if that is its only function!

From what we have said about theories of sleep, it is clear that we do not yet fully understand why we need to sleep in general, and why we need particular kinds of sleep like REM sleep. At the same time, research is beginning to give us some of the answers, and has provided a useful foundation on which further research can build.

Activity 6: theories of sleep

Match each theory named on the left with the appropriate explanation on the right. State whether each theory applies to the whole of sleep (S), to REM sleep (REM), or to non-REM sleep (NREM):

1 evolutionary (a) storing new memories
2 restoration (b) immobilisation and energy conservation
3 memory consolidation (c) toning up the eye muscles
4 sentinel (d) physiological and psychological replenishment
5 oculomotor (e) bringing closer to wakefulness

When you have finished, see the notes on page 323.

- There are several theories about the function of sleep. **Evolutionary theories** focus on its **adaptive** functions in terms of safety and energy conservation.

- **Restoration theories** explain it in terms of restoring energy levels and restoring the brain and body.
- Alternative theories include **memory consolidation**, **sentinel (cognitive arousal) theory**, and **oculomotor maintenance**.

Sleep deprivation studies

To investigate the reasons for sleeping, many researchers have looked at the effects of sleep deprivation. The argument here is that if lack of sleep can be seen to have specific ill effects, it follows that the purpose of sleep is to avoid these effects. However, it is important when considering the results of these studies to take into account exactly which type of sleep is involved, since some studies use selective deprivation of only REM sleep, or only stage 4 sleep. It is also important to note how much sleep volunteers have been deprived of, since there may well be quite different outcomes over different periods of time.

There are not many studies of total sleep deprivation in humans, for obvious ethical reasons. In a case study reported by Dement (1972), a DJ called Peter Tripp carried out a 'wakeathon' for charity, staying awake for eight days. At the end of this time, he displayed hallucinations and delusions amounting to a severe paranoid psychosis.

A similar attempt to stay awake for a long time was studied in its latter stages:

Box D: Gulevich et al. (1966)

An attempt was made on the world record for going without sleep by a student, Randy Gardner, in 1965. He managed to stay awake for 11 days. As time went on, his mood became more negative, and task performance deteriorated and became more variable.

Physiologically, he showed slowing of the EEG and decline in body temperature. After his successful attempt, he spent 14 hours and 40 minutes asleep, mainly in stage 4 and REM sleep. This need for REM sleep after deprivation is known as the **REM rebound effect**, and suggests that the need for REM sleep is greater than the need for non-REM sleep.

Overall the effects were not nearly as dramatic as those displayed by Peter Tripp.

The psychological effects of sleep deprivation, taken from a number of studies which were somewhat more controlled than the ones we have looked at, have been described by Hüber-Weidman (1976). They include impairment in tasks that require sustained attention and the processing of complex information, and an increase in irritability and delusions. However, physiological changes are slight, the main problems being focusing the eyes and the development of hand tremors. Overall, this seems to suggest that generally lack of sleep is not really physically harmful, so sleep does not serve any useful physiological purpose. Webb (1975) has suggested that the main result of going without sleep is to make us want to sleep!

However, longer term studies in animals show a somewhat different picture:

Box E: Rechtschaffen *et al.* (1983)

Procedure: Rats were deprived of sleep by using an apparatus that forced them to walk whenever they showed signs of sleepiness. If they did not do so, they fell into water. Control rats were exposed to the same apparatus, but allowed to sleep normally.

Results: After 33 days, all the sleep-deprived rats had died, while the controls seemed to have suffered no ill effects. The sleep-deprived rats also showed a dramatic loss in body weight, despite having increased their food consumption. They also had other problems – stomach ulcers, respiratory infections and enlarged adrenal glands.

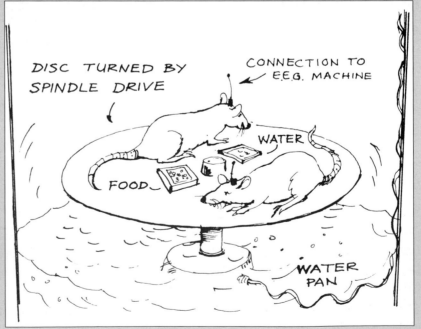

Conclusion: The rats died as the result of sleep deprivation and their temperature regulation mechanisms failing.

Many of the physical problems shown by the sleep-deprived rats are symptoms of **stress**, and death could therefore be due to the stress brought about by lack of sleep. However, it is not clear whether or not stress is the mediating mechanism which leads to death. It is also not certain that humans would react in the same way as rats if sleep deprivation went on for long enough.

While testing animals allows us to carry out procedures which would not be ethical if applied to humans, you probably nonetheless have ethical concerns about this study. It would certainly be very unethical to expose humans to anything like the same period of sleep deprivation as that experienced by the rats. Instead, studies of humans have used **partial sleep deprivation**, when people are allowed to sleep only for about 4 hours per night. The results show less effect on performance, especially if the amount of sleep is gradually reduced over a period of time. On recovery, there is an increase in stage 4 sleep. However, Bonnet and Webb (1979) found that abrupt reduction of the amount of sleep leads to impaired intellectual functioning and irritability. This is a rather worrying finding, as this is the kind of situation faced by junior hospital doctors. They are often 'on call' for extended periods, during which they may be woken several times to treat patients.

Selective deprivation studies have focused on deprivation of REM or stage 4 sleep, by waking volunteers when they seemed to be entering those stages:

Box F: Dement (1960)

Procedure: Over several nights, participants were woken whenever they entered REM sleep. A control group was woken up the same number of times, but only during NREM sleep.

Results: REM deprivation more than doubled the frequency of REM periods; on the first night, REM-deprived participants had to be woken on average 12 times. This rose to 26 times by the seventh night. There was also an REM rebound effect at the end of the study, leading to a 60% increase in REM sleep.

Behavioural changes were mild and temporary. Participants showed impaired concentration, increased eating, irritability and anxiety.

Conclusion: The immediate psychological effects of lack of REM sleep are not severe. At the same time, it must serve some purpose, since the body attempts to make up for its lack.

Agnew *et al.* (1964) found that **stage 4 deprivation** had similar effects on mood, but little effect on performance. There was some physical lethargy and increased sensitivity to pain.

The importance of REM sleep has been demonstrated in a study by Jouvet (1967):

Box G: Jouvet (1967)

Procedure: The 'flowerpot technique' was used. This involved placing an animal, in this case a cat, on a flowerpot just large enough to hold it. The flowerpot was surrounded by water. The animal could sleep during slow wave stages, but when it entered REM sleep, the loss of muscle tone caused it to fall into the water, and so woke it up.

Results: Cats deprived of REM sleep showed hypersexuality and eventually died.

Conclusion: Extreme and continuous deprivation of REM sleep has serious behavioural and physical consequences.

Apart from ethical concerns, this study is problematical in that it relates to animals rather than people. At the same time, however, it suggests that REM sleep may be important in ways which we don't yet understand.

It seems that attempts to use sleep deprivation to answer the question: 'why do we need to sleep?' have not been as successful as we might have hoped. They have shown that sleep must have some useful purpose, since the body reacts to lack of sleep and tries to make up the deficit. At the same time, there have been difficulties with carrying out sleep deprivation studies, and interpreting the results.

- Sleep deprivation research has demonstrated a need to make up sleep afterwards, particularly stage 4 and REM sleep. This is called the **REM rebound effect**.
- Deprivation in humans has been found to lead to some **detrimental changes** in behaviour, task performance, and emotional response. Longer term studies of animals have indicated more extreme effects, though these may be the effect of stress rather than specifically lack of sleep.
- Similar results have been found with **partial deprivation** studies, which focus on stage 4 and REM sleep. Problems of **irritability** and **cognitive impairment** are more apparent when sleep is *abruptly* reduced than when the process is gradual.

12.3 DREAMING

Activity 7: true or false?

Read through these statements. From your own experience, decide whether each is true or false:
a Some people do not dream.
b Sometimes dreams are in black and white, not colour.
c People who have been blind from birth have auditory dreams.
d The events in dreams do not actually last as long as they would in real life.
e We may sleepwalk while we are dreaming.
f External events can affect the content of dreams.
g There are differences in the dreams of men and women.

When you have finished, see the notes on page 323.

' You "mostly dream in black and white with just a touch of red" ... er ... what would the red be exactly?'

The nature of dreams

Dreams are psychological activities which occur during sleep. They are distinctly different from normal waking mental activity in several ways. Firstly, they involve **hallucinatory** imagery, mostly visual, although auditory, tactile and movement sensations may also be reported. Taste, smell and pain are rarely involved.

They can be considered **delusional** because at the time they seem quite real. We do not usually realise that we are having a dream. This is all the more surprising given that dreams defy physical laws – for example, you may have experienced a dream in which you could fly – and involve discontinuities in content, i.e. places and people may change suddenly within the dream.

Barely known places and people can become very important in dreams; people can become **hypermnesic**, with memory recall being better than usual, but after the dream it is unlikely that anything will be remembered. It has been estimated that at least 95% will be forgotten.

Emotional responses have different patterns in dreams: emotions are vivid and changeable; anxiety, fear and surprise are more common, sadness and guilt less common. We often have obsessional thoughts in dreams – for example, about things we

318

haven't completed – and there may be repetition.

One aspect of dreams that shows **cultural differences** is what is known as **lucid dreaming**. This refers to the person being aware of dreaming, and able to influence what goes on in the dream. It appears to be uncommon in our culture, but is well documented in others, e.g. in aboriginal Australians.

An analysis of **dream content**, carried out by Hall (1951), has shown that the setting is usually familiar, based on leisure rather than work. Characters are predominantly strangers (43%) and friends (37%), rather than family (19%). The plot tends to involve negative emotions and hostile actions (64%). Colour occurs in 29% of dreams, with females tending to experience it rather than males.

Real events occurring prior to or during sleep may also relate to content. For example, Dement and Wolpert (1958) found that a dripping tap could lead to dreams about water. Additionally, Bokert (1970) found that thirsty subjects would dream of drinking, so a dream can compensate for reality.

If we are woken out of NREM sleep, as would normally be the case, we are unlikely to recall our dreams. As we saw in the Dement and Kleitman study (box C), it is when we are woken out of REM sleep that we are more likely to recall them. However, this study also found that some participants reported dreams when they were woken from NREM sleep.

- Everybody dreams, though dreams may not always be remembered. They vary in vividness and take place in 'real time'. There are differences in the dreams of men and women.
- Dreams have distinctive psychological characteristics, such as **hallucinations**, **delusions**, **hypermnesia**, **obsessional thinking**, vivid **negative emotions** and emphasis on particular types of content.
- They mainly occur during REM sleep, and we are more likely to remember them if we wake up during this stage of sleep.

Theories of dreaming

Activity 8: the function of dreaming

Apart from occurring during sleep rather than when we are awake, how do dreams differ from normal mental waking activity? From the characteristics which you have identified, what purpose(s) do you think dreams have?

Write down a dream you have had recently, together with your own ideas about why you had that particular dream. Compare your comments with the following sections, to see if your ideas correspond with any of the theories which have been put forward.

As with sleep, several theories have been put forward to explain why we dream. We will look here at five theories: **psychoanalytic** theory, **problem-solving** theory, **reprogramming** theory, **activation synthesis** theory and **reverse learning** theory.

The psychoanalytic theory of dreams

Perhaps the best known theory of dreaming is that of Freud (1901), who wrote that dreams were the 'royal road to the unconscious'. What he meant by this was that during sleep the **unconscious** is more free to express itself. You will remember from chapter 1 that Freud believed that a lot of material is pushed into the unconscious, but because the unconscious is dynamic, these repressed wishes and impulses seek expression. Dreaming is one way in which this can happen.

In order not to create too much anxiety and wake the sleeper, it has to do this by using **symbolism** to convey its needs and anxieties. So Freud saw dreams as using imagery to keep disturbing and repressed material in the unconscious, and in this way having the function of 'protecting sleep'. Much of this repressed material has to do with sexuality. Examples of symbols commonly found in dreams are shown in figure 6:

Figure 6: sexual symbols in Freudian dream interpretation

(a) sexual intercourse

(b) male genital organs

(c) female genital organs

Freud referred to the events occurring in the dream as the **manifest content**, and what lies behind them – the true meaning which is being symbolised – as the **latent content**. Freud believed that there is always some logic to a dream, however absurd it may seem on the surface, and that **psychoanalytic techniques** can tease out this meaning, i.e. uncover the latent content.

Interpreting dreams can be important in **psychoanalysis**, the therapy associated with Freud's theories, which is described in more detail in chapter 25. **Dream analysis** is an important psychoanalytic technique in helping people with problems. At the same time, Freud accepted that it may be dangerous to interpret the meaning of symbols occurring in dreams by looking only at the dream's content. The dreamer's waking life also needs to be taken into account.

Figure 7: example of Freud's analysis of a dream

This dream was reported by one of Freud's patients:
I was at home, and I was arranging flowers in the centre of a table for a birthday celebration. The flowers were expensive – lilies of the valley, violets and pink carnations. I was decorating them with green paper to hide the untidy parts and make the display more attractive.

The interpretation given was:
The dream represents the woman's desire to be married, and the birthday mentioned is the birth of a baby. The table is the woman and the flowers are her genitals. The cost of the flowers represents the value she puts on her virginity, and white lilies are the purity it stands for. The pink carnations represent flesh, and violets are a symbol for violation. She is concerned to make herself look beautiful and hide the parts which she considers ugly.

As with other aspects of Freud's work, Freud's theory of dreams can be criticised on the basis that dream analysis relies very much on interpretation. Decoding the symbols of a dream is not an objective process, but is heavily influenced by the analyst's view. In addition, Fisher and Greenberg (1977) have argued that worries are not always concealed but may be dreamed about directly. For example, they suggested that a person who is worried about being impotent is just as likely to dream about being impotent as to express this concern symbolically, such as by dreaming about broken candles.

Problem-solving theory

An alternative theory has been proposed by Cartwright (1978). Problem-solving theory suggests that dreams help us, often through the use of symbols, to deal with real-life problems, e.g. problems with work, health or relationships. There have been reports of dreams which have led to important insights and even scientific discoveries. The most famous example of this kind of dream, quoted by Borbely (1986), is Kekulé's discovery of the benzene ring: his dream of a snake swallowing its own tail gave him the idea of a continuous ring, and so helped him to understand the structure of benzene.

Cartwright doesn't make the same distinction as Freud between the manifest and latent content of dreams. Although we sometimes use metaphors in dreams, these can be directly understood and do not need interpretation. For example, a teacher who dreams about being buried under a pile of paper could be expressing her worries about preparing documents for a forthcoming OFSTED inspection, i.e. being metaphorically 'buried' with paperwork.

A teacher who dreams about being buried under a pile of paper could be metaphorically 'buried' with paperwork.

There is some support for this idea. Hartman (1973) found that people who are experiencing problems spend longer in REM sleep, when most dreaming takes place.

Reprogramming theory

Evans (1984) uses a computer analogy to argue that the brain needs to reduce input from the outside world so that it can 'file' new information. It does this on a daily basis during sleep. Dreams are the result of our efforts to clarify, organise and sort this material. This is supported by the finding that REM sleep is increased in people who have been given complex tasks before going to sleep:

Box H: Herman and Roffwarg (1983)

Procedure: Participants wore distorting lenses which made them see things upside down. They therefore had to use a lot of mental effort to adjust to their environment.
Results: More time than usual was spent in REM sleep the following night.
Conclusion: Additional REM sleep allowed more dreaming to take place, during which this experience could be processed.

Additional evidence comes from the fact that the amount of REM sleep decreases with age, presumably because as we get older we have fewer new experiences which need to be processed.

Koukkou and Lehman (1980) suggested that dreams allow us to make sense of new experiences in terms of existing ideas and cognitive strategies. A similar theory, put forward by Foulkes (1985), considers that dreams are related to cognitive processes. They represent our attempt to integrate new information and experiences with our general knowledge and our knowledge about ourselves, and may help us to prepare for events which might happen in the future. Evidence in support of this idea comes from Winson (1992), who showed that important events are 'marked' as they occur by the theta rhythm in the EEG, for later storage; this appears to be reactivated during sleep.

Dreams are the result of our efforts to organise new material.

Activation synthesis theory

Hobson and McCarley (1977) considered dreams to be purely the result of biological activity in the brain. They have no meaning in themselves. The neurons in the brain fire randomly during sleep, starting in the pons and spreading elsewhere. This pattern of firing is then interpreted by higher centres in the cortex to produce dreams. The activation is synthesised into a meaningful story. The idea of meaningless material having meaning imposed on it could perhaps be seen as complementary to, rather than incompatible with, the psychoanalytic idea of dream content as an expression of the unconscious.

This theory fits well with evidence about dreams often relating to events of the day – it could be that the neurons which have registered these events are easier to reactivate. Lack of smell and taste sensations in dreams could be because those areas are not stimulated. Experiences of falling or floating could be the result of stimulation of the neurons in the areas of the brain that are normally responsible for this kind of sensation.

Reverse learning theory

This is a neurobiological theory put forward by Crick and Mitchison (1983). They argued that we dream in order to forget. During dreaming the brain

is trying to have a 'clear-up' and get rid of unwanted or what they call parasitic information. This process allows the nervous system to keep functioning efficiently. The lack of REM sleep in certain mammals (notably dolphins) is attributed to their very large cortex, which can store all of the information accumulated. They therefore do not need to go through this process. Another possibility is that they have developed a large cortex because they have no REM sleep.

During dreaming, the brain is trying to clear out unwanted information.

This theory sees dreams as essentially meaningless events. However, this idea has been challenged by dreams which clearly do seem to have a meaning, such as Kekulé's snake dream, described above.

One problem shared by all these theories is that they cannot explain the fact that REM sleep seems to occur in the developing foetus. It is hard to imagine what kinds of unconscious wishes a foetus could have, or what kind of parasitic information would need to be forgotten. Jouvet (1983) suggested that foetal REM sleep is the result of innate, genetic behaviour, which is practised during the foetal stage but does not have a real function until after birth.

Recent research suggests that dreaming assists us to assimilate new information, identify patterns in memory, and learn and improve new skills. Karni *et al.* (1994) trained people in a simple perceptual task, and found that performance improved overnight, with this improvement lasting for years. However, if REM sleep was blocked that night no improvement occurred, so it seems that there is a critical period for dreaming to have this effect. There is also anecdotal evidence for this idea, with people reporting the practice of new skills, such as riding a bicycle or skiing, in their dreams.

⑤ Several theories have been put forward to explain why we dream. Freud's **psychoanalytic theory** claims that dreams are the symbolic expression of **unconscious wishes** and anxieties.

⑤ Cartwright's **problem-solving theory** suggests that dreams allow us to deal with everyday problems, sometimes using symbols.

⑤ According to Evans' **reprogramming theory**, dreams allow us to organise new information.

⑤ The **activation synthesis theory** of Hobson and McCarley explains dreams as a by-product of neural activity. They are the cortical interpretation of random firing in neurons.

⑤ According to Crick and Mitchison's **reverse learning theory**, dreams allow us to get rid of unnecessary information.

⑤ While all these theories are plausible, none accounts fully for the phenomena of dreaming.

Notes on activities

2 Travelling west-to-east (i.e. from New York to London) is more likely to result in jetlag than travelling east-to-west, since it shortens the day. In a study of people flying between London and Detroit, involving a five-hour time change, Nicholson *et al.* (1986) found that people flying eastward (from Detroit to London) took significantly longer to fall asleep on the five nights after travelling than those flying westward.

3 There are two main ways in which this system can be criticised. First of all, changes which mean that the body has to adapt its rhythms need to be made every week, which is a very short period for adjustment. It would make sense to get people to change shifts less often, say every three weeks. The other problem is that each shift change has the effect of shortening the day, and as we have seen in the discussion of jetlag, this is more likely to lead to problems than when the day is lengthened. The shifts should therefore rotate forwards in time. These were in fact the recommendations Blakemore made to the company. The workers preferred the new system, their health improved and productivity rose. This outcome gives a good example of the association of psychological factors with physiological adaptation.

5 The difficulty with this approach is that sleeping for longer or shorter periods could *both* be seen as advantageous from an evolutionary viewpoint. Long periods, as has been argued, would keep us from harm and save energy. On the other hand, short periods would allow us to remain alert (a possible defence against predators) and have longer to feed. Similarly, hibernation theory does nothing to predict which animals will be diurnal and which nocturnal – if most animals are out hunting for food during the day, the night would surely be a safer time to be out and around. These theories cannot be falsified, since whatever the sleep pattern of a species, it can be explained in evolutionary terms.

6 1bS; 2dNREM and REM; 3aREM; 4eREM; 5cREM.

7 Some people claim not to have dreams, but their sleep patterns are the same as those of everyone else. If they are woken during REM sleep, they report dreams. However, it is likely that some people are better at remembering dreams than others.

Dreams vary in their vividness; while some are in full colour, they may also be in black and white. People blind from birth have auditory dreams which are just as vivid and complicated as those of sighted people.

Dreams tend to take place in 'real time'. While time may seem longer or shorter in dreams, perhaps covering events that last several days, the actual events of dreams last as long as they would in real life. Distortions in time are likely to be the result of editing out stretches of time – we may jump in a dream from an event that is happening in the morning to one which is happening in the evening.

Since dreaming takes place during REM sleep, sleepwalking cannot take place while we are dreaming. You will remember that our muscles are virtually paralysed during these periods of sleep. This was illustrated in the study by Jouvet (box G).

Dreams can be altered by external events. Dement and Wolpert (1958) sprayed water on the faces of people having dreams. Their participants were significantly more likely to report dreams involving water than controls. This effect is more likely to occur when the event is meaningful to us; for example, someone saying our name.

There is some evidence that there are differences in the dreams of men and women. For example, Cohen (1973) found that women are more likely to dream about indoor settings and men about events taking place outdoors. It has also been found that men are three times more likely than women to have clearly sexual dreams.

13

Motivation and emotion

In this chapter we will be looking at:

13.1 What is motivation?

13.2 Brain mechanisms of motivation: hunger and thirst

13.3 Theories of motivation
    Cannon's homeostatic drive theory
    Hull's drive-reduction theory
    Expectancy (incentive) theory
    Maslow's hierarchy of needs

13.4 What is emotion?

13.5 Brain structures in emotion

13.6 Theories of emotion
    The James–Lange theory
    The Cannon–Bard theory
    Schachter's cognitive labelling theory
    Lazarus' appraisal theory

13.1 WHAT IS MOTIVATION?

Psychologists interested in motivation are interested in the causes of behaviour; for example, why we eat, or help someone in the street, or remember a particular event. On another level, though, the concept of motivation has its own difficulties, since the kinds of explanations for behaviour which psychologists seek and are prepared to accept will depend on their theoretical orientation. In other words, the 'model of the person' which you hold will influence which kind of theory you find useful.

Activity 1: psychological orientation and theories of motivation

Look back to chapter 1, where the different perspectives or theoretical orientations to psychology were introduced:

psychodynamic   behaviourist
humanistic   neurobiological
cognitive

How would each of these perspectives try to explain human behaviour? What would be the differences between theories of motivation associated with each of these approaches?
You may not be able to do this for each perspective if you have not looked in detail at theories and research representing a particular approach, but try, in general terms, to cover as many as possible. When you have finished, see the notes on page 349.

This activity should have given you some idea of the range of explanations of motivation which psychologists have to offer. It may help if you think of theories of motivation as falling into three fairly broad categories, as shown in figure 1:

Figure 1: categories of motivation theories

physiological: the neurobiological approach, with motivation related to neurological structures. It focuses on basic organic needs, e.g. hunger, pain avoidance and so on.

> **behavioural:** drive reduction theories, again concerned with organic needs, but explaining behaviour in terms of reinforcement, rather than focusing on physiological processes.
> **psychosocial:** concerned with more complex psychological and social factors, sometimes still with an emphasis on the individual, but also looking at wider social influences. Cognitive, psychodynamic and humanistic theories fall within this general category.

❺ Different **theoretical orientations** provide different kinds of explanations of motivation. How useful each orientation is will depend on the kinds of questions being asked, and the kinds of phenomena which you are trying to explain.

❺ Theories of motivation can be fitted into three broad **categories: physiological, behavioural** and **psychosocial**.

13.2 BRAIN MECHANISMS OF MOTIVATION: HUNGER AND THIRST

Hunger

The main area of the brain associated with hunger is a subcortical area called the **hypothalamus**. At the beginning of the twentieth century, Frohlich (in Hess 1957) found that tumours near the hypothalamus caused **hyperphagia** (i.e. overeating). When more precise methods of investigating the brain became possible (see the section on **stereotactic procedures** at the start of chapter 11), it was possible to explore in more detail the effects of damage to this area on eating behaviour.

Different areas of the hypothalamus appear to be responsible for different aspects of eating behaviour. The **lateral hypothalamus (LH)** is a **feeding centre**, which stimulates eating behaviour. Anand and Brobeck (1951) found that rats with lesions to the LH showed **aphagia**; they would stop eating, even when palatable food was readily available, and would starve to death.

The **ventromedial hypothalamus (VMH)** is a **satiety centre**, which stops feeding behaviour.

Hetherington and Ranson (1942) found that rats with lesions to the VMH would overeat till they became hugely fat. Later research showed that VMH hyperphagia has two phases. To start with, the animal overeats for several weeks and becomes obese. It then eats in such a way as to maintain its new body weight. If it is then deprived of food, it will overeat until the weight it has lost has been regained; if it is force-fed, it will reduce its food intake until the extra weight it has gained through force-feeding has been lost.

Cross-section of rat brain

The VMH of the rat on the left was destroyed.

The influence of these two areas of the hypothalamus in hunger has also been shown in humans. For example, Quaade (1971) successfully lesioned the LH of obese patients to reduce eating. If the LH was stimulated electrically, they reported feeling hungry. Similarly, Reeves and Plum (1969) carried out a post mortem on a patient who had doubled her weight in two years, and found a tumour in the VMH.

However, it is likely that the complete picture is more complicated than physiological 'start' and 'stop' centres. Research carried out on rats by Teitelbaum and Stellar (1954) found that appetite could be recovered after LH lesions. Furthermore, this part of the hypothalamus is not only involved in feeding behaviour but also in drinking, temperature change and sexual activity. Systems other than the hypothalamus are also likely to be involved in hunger. For example, damage to nerves involved in chewing and swallowing was found by Zeigler and Karten (1974) to produce similar effects to LH lesions.

A further complication is that while a rat with damage to the VMH eats more food than normal, it will only do so if the food is readily available. If it has to work to obtain food – for example, by pressing a lever – it will actually eat *less* than a normal animal. It is therefore not simply a case of a VMH-obese rat being more motivated to eat than a normal rat. This also seems to be true of obese people:

Box A: Schachter (1971)

Procedure: Obese participants and normal-weight controls were given access to nuts, shelled in one condition and unshelled in the second condition.

Results: Controls ate roughly the same amount of nuts in both conditions. Obese participants ate more of the shelled nuts than controls, but ignored the unshelled nuts.

Conclusion: Obese humans are motivated to eat more than those of normal weight only when access to food is easy.

HE LIKES TO BURN OFF A FEW CALORIES SHELLING HIS OWN PEANUTS

It is believed that the LH and the VMH function in response to a **set point**, an optimal weight which the body seeks to maintain. They work to maintain a relatively constant level of satiety, 'switching on' and 'switching off' eating behaviour appropriately. To do this, they need to know the state of the body's energy reserves. Two possible sources of this information are changes in blood glucose levels and the amounts of fat in the body.

Weight loss

Weight loss thermostat is at the set point of 150 lbs

After inital weight loss, the weight thermostat adjusts to 'starving' message by slowing body metabolism

Weight loss thermostat makes further adjustments and it becomes even more difficult to lose weight

Weight loss thermostat is at the set point of 140 lbs

Weight gain

Weight thermostat makes further adjustments and it becomes even more difficult to gain weight

After inital weight gain, the weight thermostat adjusts to increased weight by increasing body metabolism

Set point theory

Originally **blood glucose levels** were seen to be the most important factor. **Glucostatic theory** proposes that when blood glucose levels drop below their set point, we become hungry and are motivated to eat. When they reach their set point again, we become satiated. Since glucose is the primary food of the brain, this theory seems logical.

There is evidence that detectors of blood glucose levels might be found in the liver. Russeck (1971) investigated hunger in dogs. Glucose was injected into the bloodstream or directly into the liver. The dogs stopped eating only in response to injections into the liver, which supports the idea of detectors in the liver being important in feeding behaviour. Furthermore, if neural connections between the liver and the brain are blocked, an injection of glucose into the liver no longer has this effect. It seems that the liver assesses the situation, and then sends signals to the brain, which in turn causes hunger to stop.

Lipostatic theory, related to body fat, is another set point theory. Fats are stored in **adipocytes**, which make up the fatty (or **adipose**) tissue of the body. As the level of fats in the adipocytes falls, we are motivated to eat to adjust the level. As it rises, we are motivated to stop eating. There is support for this theory in that most adults maintain a relatively constant body weight.

Glucostatic theory and lipostatic theory are complementary rather than competing theories. Glucostatic theory is seen as accounting for feeding motivation in the short term, with lipostatic theory explaining long-term regulation of body weight.

However, there are some problems with theories which assume that feeding motivation can be explained purely in physiological terms, particularly in humans. There are factors other than hunger which affect feeding behaviour, such as the variety of food which we are offered and whether we are eating alone or with others. We will return to these kinds of factors later in this chapter.

- ❺ The **hypothalamus** regulates hunger. The **LH** stimulates feeding, while the **VMH** stops it. Information about energy levels is derived from **blood glucose** levels and **fat** levels.
- ❺ The amount of **difficulty** involved in obtaining food is also important.

❺ **Psychological** and **social factors** also influence eating behaviour.

Thirst

As with hunger, the hypothalamus is central to the control of thirst. Since water is needed for the digestion and metabolism of food, feeding and drinking often occur together, so a system which in some respects is common to both is not surprising.

So how does the system detect low levels of fluids, leading to thirst? One important signal is **cellular dehydration**. A fluid deficit is detected by certain cells called **osmoreceptors** in the **lateral preoptic area** of the hypothalamus **(LPH)**. When there are high levels of salt in the blood, water leaves these cells by **osmosis**, and the cells become dehydrated, causing them to shrink. This shrinkage causes the hypothalamus to stimulate the pineal gland to produce **antidiuretic hormone (ADH)**, which in turn causes the kidneys to reabsorb water which would otherwise be excreted as urine, thus retaining fluid which would otherwise be lost. A second effect of the shrinkage of osmoreceptors is to produce thirst.

Another signal of low fluid levels is lowered **blood volume**. Low levels of water lead to a reduction in the volume of blood in the body, leading in turn to lowered blood pressure. As a result, **baroreceptors** – sensory receptors sensitive to pressure – are stimulated. These are found in the heart, kidneys and veins. As with cell dehydration, the baroreceptors trigger the secretion of ADH, causing the kidneys to reabsorb water. The kidneys release a hormone called **angiotensin**. When it reaches the hypothalamus, it produces thirst.

The mechanism which 'switches off' thirst is not so clear. The main problem is that we usually stop drinking before the effects of rehydration on blood volume and osmoreceptors are completed. However, it seems likely that thirst is 'switched off' by the combined effects of water receptors on the tongue and feedback from the weight of water in the stomach. It is possible that the small intestine communicates with the hypothalamus when enough liquid has been taken in.

As with feeding behaviour, an understanding of the physiology of thirst is not enough to explain drinking behaviour. For example, if you are in a pub on a Saturday night, it is likely that very little of the drinking you do is related to dehydration.

❺ Thirst is also regulated by the hypothalamus, triggered by **cell dehydration** and **blood volume**. Thirst too is affected by **non-physiological factors**.

⏺ Activity 2: physiological factors in hunger and thirst

Complete each of these statements with one of the words or phrases given below:

1 The .... 'switches on' hunger. Damage to this area of the hypothalamus can cause .... (i.e. excessive overeating).
2 The .... 'switches off' hunger. Damage to this area can cause .... (i.e. excessive undereating).
3 Glucostatic theory suggests that the action of the hypothalamus is triggered by information about .... This explains hunger regulation in the .... Detectors can be found in the ....
4 Lipostatic theory suggests that the action of the hypothalamus is triggered by information about .... This explains hunger regulation in the ....
5 Low levels of fluid are detected by ...., cells in the ...., which shrink when fluid levels are low, leading to ....
6 ..... (cells sensitive to pressure) also provide information about fluid levels. One organ in which they are found is the ....
7 We know less about the precise mechanism which .... thirst than about what .... thirst.

osmoreceptors	lateral hypothalamus
fat levels	hyperphagia
short term	blood glucose levels
switches on	cell dehydration
aphagia	long term
baroreceptors	liver
hypothalamus	heart
switches off	ventromedial hypothalamus

When you have finished, see the notes on page 349.

13.3 THEORIES OF MOTIVATION

Cannon's homeostatic drive theory

Homeostasis refers to regulatory mechanisms which allow the body to maintain a relatively constant internal state. The body is able to adapt so that it functions at or very close to optimal levels. The optimal level of a particular function is referred to as a set point.

A homeostatic system has three components. There must first be some mechanism which defines the set point. There must also be some way of detecting deviations from this set point. Finally there must be ways to eliminate these deviations. This kind of system is known as a **negative-feedback system**, since changes in one direction trigger compensatory effects in the other direction.

If we take drinking as an example, lack of water will lead to dehydration and ultimately to tissue damage. As we saw in the previous section, the body picks up on physiological signals, and readjusts the balance by bringing about thirst and thus the motivation to drink. If on the other hand body fluids rise above their optimal levels, then the flow of urine increases to eliminate this excess.

Homeostatic drive theory looks at the physiological basis of these adaptations. Cognitions – e.g. the knowledge that 'I am thirsty' – are not a necessary part of this explanation. The emphasis is rather on physiological responses. Tissue needs lead to a physiological imbalance, which brings about a homeostatic drive to correct it. The term 'drive' relates to an aroused, goal-directed tendency of an organism in response to physiological change, in other words a motivational state. This in turn leads to appropriate behaviour (in this case, drinking) which reduces the drive.

Feeding behaviour is another example where homeostatic principles apply. As we saw in the previous section, the LH stimulates hunger when a drop in energy levels is detected, and the VMH inhibits hunger when energy levels are restored.

◐ Activity 3: physiological responses to needs

Feeding and drinking are two examples where homeostatic mechanisms apply. Can you think of another example where the body responds automatically to less than optimal functioning? How does it make adjustments?

When you have finished, see the notes on page 349.

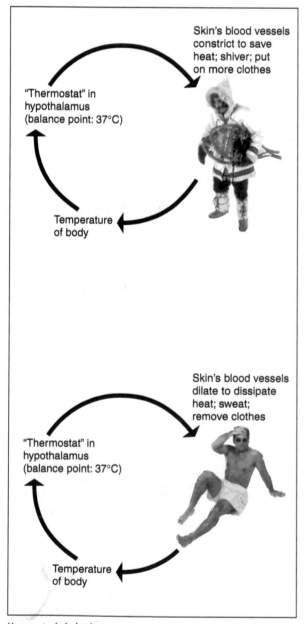

Skin's blood vessels constrict to save heat; shiver; put on more clothes

"Thermostat" in hypothalamus (balance point: 37°C)

Temperature of body

Skin's blood vessels dilate to dissipate heat; sweat; remove clothes

"Thermostat" in hypothalamus (balance point: 37°C)

Temperature of body

Homeostasis in body temperature

In the previous section, we saw the homeostatic role of the hypothalamus in hunger and thirst. Cannon himself believed that information about hunger was sent to the brain from the **stomach**, by way of the **vagus nerve**, the connection between the stomach/intestinal tract and the brain. At first sight, this seems a reasonable proposal; as the walls of the stomach contract, we experience 'hunger pangs', and we are aware of being full when we have eaten. Cannon carried out a study to demonstrate the role of the stomach in hunger:

Box B: Cannon and Washburn (1912)

Procedure: Washburn swallowed a deflated balloon attached to the end of a tube. The tube was connected to a water-filled U-shaped tube, so that Washburn's stomach contractions could be monitored by a change in the water level in the U-shaped tube.

Rotating drum

To clock timer

Stomach contractions

Time

Hunger pangs

Balloon   Stomach

Results: Washburn's reports of the experience of hunger pangs corresponded with a rise in the water level in the tube.

Conclusion: The experience of hunger, and thus the motivation to eat, is closely related to stomach contractions. The motivation for basic human functions can be explained on a physiological level.

There are, however, some problems with this study. It is open to criticism as a single-subject case study, though there is no reason to suppose that in this instance Washburn's reports were idiosyncratic, and that other people might have responded differently. At the same time, since we are looking here at a *correlation* between stomach contractions and the report of hunger pangs, we can not necessarily assume that one *causes* the other.

It would also seem to be unwise to assume that even if a causal link has been established, stomach contractions are the *only* cause of hunger. Other research evidence suggests that while the stomach is usually involved in hunger, other factors may be equally if not more important. Pinel (1993) studied patients whose stomachs had been removed because of disease. Their stomachs had been bypassed by linking the oesophagus directly to the duodenum. These patients needed to maintain their body weight by eating smaller meals more frequently. In spite of the absence of a stomach, they still reported feeling hungry (and satiated).

As we saw in the previous section, homeostatic drive theory has been supported by later research which has identified the precise mechanisms which 'switch on' and 'switch off' hunger. However, the theory is limited in that it looks only at physiological mechanisms related to motivation. Eating and drinking behaviour are not governed only by hunger and thirst.

There are psychological factors which influence these behaviours. For example, when we have eaten a meal and are no longer hungry, we may still be tempted by a pudding which looks or smells delicious, or we may eat when we are bored or stressed. Eating can also be a learned habit. For example, we may eat because it is a mealtime, or because as children we were expected to eat everything on our plate. We may eat and drink because we are in a social situation which includes eating and drinking, at a party or barbecue. Bellisle *et al.* (1999) asked people to keep a food diary for a week, recording both what they ate and whether they ate alone or with others. They found that people ate more when they were with others.

Variety is also a factor. Rolls *et al.* (1981) found that people would eat more sandwiches if there were four different types of fillings rather than just one. The effect of variety of food on eating behaviour has also been shown in rats:

Box C: LeMagnen (1967)

Procedure: Every day for 4 days, rats were given access for a 2-hour period to one of four different foods, A, B, C or D, each with a slightly different taste. After this initial period, on the first day the rats were given 30 minutes access to food A, 30 minutes to food B, 30 minutes to food C and 30 minutes to food D. On the second day, they were given 2 hours access to food C. This 2-day pattern was repeated on successive days.
Results: In the initial 4-day period, there was little difference in the amount of food eaten; the four foods seem to have been equally attractive. In the subsequent period, much more food was ingested when the rats were offered a variety of foods.

Conclusion: More food is eaten when there is a variety of foods available.

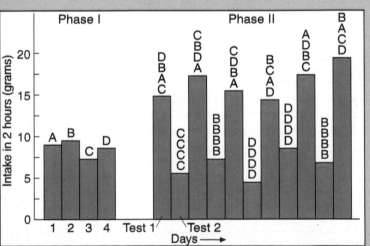

Eating disorders again indicate the limitations of this theory. While the eating behaviour of most people is to a certain extent influenced by psychological motives, anorexia nervosa and bulimia nervosa, discussed in chapter 5, can provide an extreme example of psychological influences. Many anorectics experience hunger cues, but override them by refusing to eat, while bulimics overeat in the absence of hunger cues, or long after they have disappeared.

⊖ Cannon (1929) proposed the **homeostatic drive theory** of motivation. The body responds automatically to correct physiological imbalances. Motivation is explained in terms of the **physiological processes** which achieve homeostasis. The physiological mechanisms involved in eating and drinking behaviour are more complex than Cannon proposed.

⊖ While the principle of homeostasis is sound, this approach to motivation is limited in that it does not take into account **psychological factors** in motivation.

Hull's drive-reduction theory

A behavioural account of motivation, rooted in learning theory, was put forward by Hull (1943). As in Cannon's theory, needs and drives are central. The distinction between needs and drives is important here. **Needs** are *physiological* deficit states, which can be defined objectively, e.g. in terms of blood sugar level or temperature. **Drives** on the other hand are *psychological*, referring to internal events which cannot be objectively measured. They are hypothetical constructs which allow us to explain behaviour.

The focus in Hull's theory is less on the physiological processes which are central to homeostatic drive theory, and more on the role of **reinforcement** in motivation; reinforcement in learning theory is explained in chapter 1. Hull used the concept of **drive-reduction** in his account of learning theory to explain how reinforcement brings about behaviour change.

Hull believed that all human behaviour has its roots in the satisfaction of **primary drives** – drives which are universal in a species, unlearned and which have an organic basis. Hunger, thirst and avoiding injury are examples of primary drives. The processes involved in Hull's theory are summarised in figure 2:

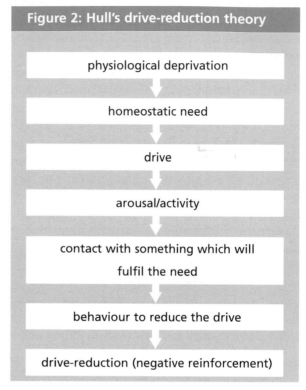

Figure 2: Hull's drive-reduction theory

physiological deprivation

↓

homeostatic need

↓

drive

↓

arousal/activity

↓

contact with something which will fulfil the need

↓

behaviour to reduce the drive

↓

drive-reduction (negative reinforcement)

▷ Activity 4: applying drive-reduction theory

Use the information in figure 2 to describe hunger and feeding behaviour.

When you have finished, see the notes on page 349.

Hull used this formulation to produce equations linking the various parts of the process, and which would allow the theory to be tested in laboratory conditions. One major example is:

$$sEr = D \times V \times K \times sHr$$

where sEr is the likelihood of a particular behaviour occurring. To calculate this, the four factors on the right of the equation need to be known. Again, we will use feeding as an example.

Here D is drive, the strength of which would need to be measured using some objective criterion, e.g. the number of hours that a rat has been deprived of food. V is the strength of the signal for feeding behaviour, K is the strength of the incentive, perhaps here the palatability of the available food, and sHr is habit strength, usually described in terms of the number of times a particular behaviour has been reinforced.

Hull's theory has the advantage of making a clear distinction between the concepts of needs and drives. In doing so, it shifts the emphasis from the purely physiological account of Cannon's theory to more psychological factors. It provides a link between physiology and behaviour, within the general context of learning theory, and the equations Hull suggests allow these links to be tested. It certainly seems to be an adequate explanation of some behaviour, e.g. the feeding example given above.

On the other hand, drives can occur where there is no obvious physiological need. To quote a previous example, little of the drinking which takes place in the pub on a Saturday night is to do with thirst. A classic example of a non-homeostatic drive is electrical stimulation of the brain:

Hull was very much concerned with primary drives – hunger, thirst and so on. A lot of human behaviour does not fit into this framework very well. For example, it would clearly not be sensible to propose that we have a video-watching drive or a football-playing drive.

However, it is possible to fit these kinds of behaviour into Hull's theory if we bring in the notion of **secondary (acquired) drives** and **secondary reinforcement**: something which is not innately reinforcing but has become so through learning, by association with primary drives. While Hull emphasised primary drives, other theorists have modified his theory to take secondary drives into account. For example, the motivation to acquire money is a learned secondary drive. It is the source of our ability to buy food, and is therefore associated with the reduction of a primary drive. This association has led us to find money reinforcing; it has become a secondary reinforcer. Mowrer (1950) saw anxiety reduction as one of the main secondary drives.

- **Hull's drive-reduction theory** links **primary drives** to behaviour through the process of **reinforcement**. Physiological needs create psychological drives. The reduction of these drives through appropriate behaviour is negatively reinforcing.

Box D: Olds and Milner (1954)

Procedure: Rats had an electrode implanted in the brain, in the medial forebrain bundle area of the hypothalamus. The electrode could be activated by the rat pressing a lever.

Results: Rats made between 3000 and 7500 lever-pressing responses in a 12-hour period. This is a much more frequent response than lever-pressing for food, typically around 25 responses per hour. They preferred to self-stimulate than eat when hungry, drink when thirsty or receive attention from a sexually receptive female.

Conclusion: This area of the brain can be thought of as a pleasure centre. This kind of electrical stimulation is a drive unrelated to a physiological deficit.

❺ Hull's ideas provide a good explanation of some kinds of behaviour. However, a lot of behaviour is not easily linked to primary drives. Other theorists have extended Hull's theory by giving more emphasis to **secondary drives**.

Expectancy (incentive) theory

Both Cannon's homeostatic drive theory and Hull's drive reduction theory focus very much on internal states which *push* an organism to carry out a particular behaviour. An alternative approach to motivation, put forward by Bolles (1972), does not look at internal physiological states, but rather proposes that external events (or **incentives**) *pull* us in particular directions. We are motivated to carry out a particular behaviour when we expect that this will lead to a desirable outcome – hence **expectancy theory** – and motivated *not* to carry out a particular behaviour when we expect that this will lead to an undesirable outcome. This theory is therefore very much a cognitive one.

If we relate this to eating behaviour, a person may initially eat because their hunger 'pushes' them. However, when they are no longer hungry they may still eat a pudding because the sight or smell of it 'pulls' them to carry on eating.

There is plenty of evidence that incentives can be strong motivators:

Box E: Sheffield and Roby (1950)

Procedure: Rats were offered unlimited access to saccharin, a sweet substance with no nutritional value.
Results: The rats ate the saccharin for hours, even though ingesting it fulfilled no nutritional need.
Conclusion: Feeding can be influenced by incentives.

Expectancy theory has been applied extensively in occupational psychology to the topic of work motivation, i.e. the tendency to spend time and put effort into the job we are doing. For example, Mitchell and Larson (1987) suggested that there are three factors which are necessary to lead to a high level of work motivation:

1. We need to believe that working hard will improve our **performance**.
2. We must believe that good performance will result in various **rewards**.
3. These rewards must be rewards which we **value**; for example, praise from a line manager for whom we have no respect will not act as a reward, whereas a salary increase, if money is important to us, will be rewarding.

This suggests that it is not only our expectations which affect motivation, but also our values.

Rewards can be either **intrinsic** (i.e. coming from within) or **extrinsic** (i.e. coming from outside us). When we have carried out a task well, an intrinsic reward might be our own satisfaction with our performance, while an extrinsic reward might be praise from someone whose opinion we value.

Administering extrinsic rewards, however, can be problematical. The extrinsic reward of recognition of our performance can add to the intrinsic reward of satisfaction with a job well done. However, in some cases, if we are given extrinsic rewards for a behaviour which we found intrinsically rewarding, our enjoyment of that behaviour is lessened:

Box F: Lepper et al. (1973)

Procedure: Children were studied in a nursery school, where they had a free choice of a range of toys and activities. For a few days before the experiment, their interest in a set of magic markers (which had not been previously available) was measured, in terms of how long each child spent using them. Each child was then tested alone in a different room, and asked to draw a picture with the markers. Group 1 were shown a 'good player award', told that they would be given it if they drew a good picture, and given it when they had finished. Group 2 were not told about the award beforehand, but were given it when they had completed their drawing. Group 3 were not told about the award, nor given it. Two weeks later, the

---

markers were again put out in the classroom, and the amount of interest shown by the groups compared.

Results: Group 1, whose drawings had been extrinsically motivated by the promise of the award, showed far less interest in the markers than the other two groups, compared with the baseline measurement taken before the experiment. Their drawings were also less detailed and original than those of the other two groups.

Conclusion: Extrinsic motivation can decrease intrinsic motivation.

● Activity 5: extrinsic and intrinsic rewards

Make a list of the possible reasons why a person might work hard at his or her job in terms of the time and effort invested in it. Which of them refer to intrinsic and which to extrinsic rewards?

Pick out one of the intrinsic rewards you listed. How might this be decreased by an extrinsic reward?

When you have finished, see the notes on page 349.

Incentives in eating behaviour

In the **positive-incentive theory** proposed by Bolles (1980), the motivation underlying eating and drinking behaviour is explained in terms of the interaction of various factors, both physiological and psychological. Hunger is affected by physiological factors such as blood glucose levels; psychological incentives could include the anticipated taste of the food on offer, and social factors such as the presence of others who will be eating. This theory therefore incorporates both physiological accounts (e.g. Cannon's homeostatic drive theory) and psychological factors (as in expectancy (incentive) theory), which must be included in a complete theory of motivation.

On the basis of this idea, Wirtshafter and Davis (1977) suggested that instead of using the concept of a set point in explaining feeding behaviour, it may be more appropriate to think of body weight fluctuating round a much less rigid settling point, affected by both the physiological and psychological factors which influence eating behaviour. Pinel (1997) described **settling point** theory using the image of a leaky barrel:

Figure 3: the leaky barrel model (Pinel, 1997)

The water pressure at the nozzle is analogous to the incentive value of the available food

The amount of water entering the barrel is analogous to the amount of consumed energy

The amount of water entering the hose is analogous to the amount of available food

The weight of the barrel on the hose is analogous to the strength of the satiety signal

The amount of water leaking from the barrel is analogous to the amount of energy being expended

The water level in the barrel is analogous to the level of body fat

This model is useful in helping us to understand and predict changes in body weight as the result of a variety of factors. In suggesting how different factors which influence energy intake and output may contribute to these changes, it may also have practical applications in helping people with obesity to bring about a change in their body weight. However, it is not as yet specific enough about the factors which contribute to these changes to be immediately useful in this way.

- ❺ **Expectancy (incentive) theory** takes a **psychological** view of motivation. Behaviour is motivated by the expectancy of **rewards**, or incentives.
- ❺ Rewards can be **extrinsic** or **intrinsic**, and must be valued if they are to act as motivators. Extrinsic rewards can reduce the effectiveness of intrinsic rewards.
- ❺ The effect of incentives has also been applied in **positive incentive theory** to explain eating motivation. This has led to the suggestion that the concept of a **set point** should be replaced by a **settling point**.

Maslow's hierarchy of needs

We will look finally at a theory of motivation proposed by Maslow (1954). His ideas fit into a humanistic perspective; you will remember that humanistic psychologists focus on human experience and people's capacity for change and development. Maslow suggested that there is a range of human needs which form a hierarchy on seven different levels.

Maslow believed that we all have a range of needs which compete for expression. At any one time, different needs will have more or less importance. For instance, if you have not eaten for some time, hunger needs will dominate needs for affection and intimacy. Maslow used the term **prepotence** to refer to the relative strengths of different needs.

This model proposes that basic needs, those at the bottom of the hierarchy, need to be satisfied before we can move to a higher level. Survival needs are more prepotent than those at the higher levels. As the needs at lower levels are satisfied, we can then move up through the levels of the hierarchy to meet the other deficiency needs of safety, belongingness and so on.

At the highest level is **self-actualisation**, a 'being' need. This differs from the other levels in that it is a need which cannot be satisfied, but whose expression is an end in itself. Since it is to do with realising our own potential, how this need is expressed varies from person to person; it depends on how we would like to develop and what we would like to work towards. For example, for a professional footballer, these needs could include training and practising skills, working towards playing an increasingly effective part in his team's performance. For a musician, they could include developing creativity in writing and performing songs.

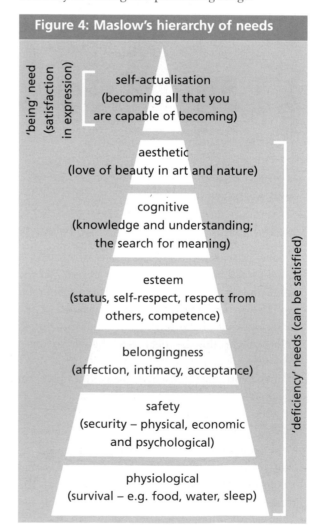

Figure 4: Maslow's hierarchy of needs

'being' need (satisfaction in expression)

- self-actualisation (becoming all that you are capable of becoming)

'deficiency' needs (can be satisfied)

- aesthetic (love of beauty in art and nature)
- cognitive (knowledge and understanding; the search for meaning)
- esteem (status, self-respect, respect from others, competence)
- belongingness (affection, intimacy, acceptance)
- safety (security – physical, economic and psychological)
- physiological (survival – e.g. food, water, sleep)

Activity 6: needs for self-actualisation

Make a list of half a dozen people in different areas of public life, and try to identify how their needs for self-actualisation might be expressed. Then try to identify your own needs in this area. To do this, you will need to think about what is important to you – creativity? understanding the world? being a good parent? academic achievement?

This activity should have helped you to realise the wide range of ways in which this kind of need can be expressed.

Maslow originally suggested that deficiency needs must be met before the process of self-actualisation can take place. At the same time, he does point out that the distinction between them is not necessarily clear-cut. For example, a chef or a gourmet could satisfy part of the need for food in a 'being' way, by finding satisfaction and pleasure in the way food is prepared and presented. It is also possible that what seems to be a process of self-actualisation could be pursued in a 'deficiency' way. For example, this would be true if a professional footballer was developing his skills purely to achieve the respect of others, rather than as part of his self-development.

Maslow accepted that for some people the self-actualisation level is more developed than for others. To identify the personal characteristics which help this process, he looked at the qualities of people he knew and people in public life (e.g. Einstein and Schweitzer) to find out what they had in common. His suggestions are shown in figure 5:

This approach is perhaps open to criticism. The sample of people Maslow analysed was rather biased, and the characteristics he described are impressionistic rather than precise. You may also feel that some of the features he lists show rather circular reasoning: people seem to have been selected for study using criteria which then appeared in the list of features shown by self-actualisers. On the other hand, his research is an interesting way of looking at human motivation, and his ideas can be related to specific examples.

Activity 7: evaluating Maslow's theory

Now that you have some idea of Maslow's hierarchy of needs, here are some aspects of it which you might like to think about. Try to think of examples to support your ideas. If you are working in a group, you could also discuss these questions with other members of the group:

1 Do we always need to satisfy needs at the bottom of the hierarchy before seeking to satisfy those higher up?
2 Does everyone reach the top of the hierarchy, and move towards self-actualisation?
3 Maslow was an American, whose major work was carried out from the 1950s to the 1970s. Is his theory a result of the times in which it was produced?
4 Can Maslow's ideas be applied to all cultures?

When you have finished, see the notes on page 349.

Figure 5: qualities of self-actualisers

positive characteristics:
involved in something outside themselves
working on/devoted to something precious to them – the work/joy distinction disappears
creative – seeing the world in unstereotyped and original ways
capable of deep relationships, but also happy alone

but sometimes also:
impersonal; emotionally cold; ruthless; stubborn; vain; anxious

❺ **Maslow's hierarchy of needs** takes a **humanistic** approach to human motivation.

❺ Physiological needs are at the bottom of the hierarchy, followed by safety, belongingness, esteem, cognitive and aesthetic needs. These are all **'deficiency' needs**, and are capable of being met.

❺ At the top of the hierarchy is the **'being' need** of **self-actualisation**. Complete self-actualisation is not possible; the expression of this need is an end in itself.

❺ Deficency needs must be satisfied before self-actualisation can be worked on. Maslow has been criticised for this claim.

❺ The theory has also been criticised for being heavily influenced by a particular **culture**.

> ## Activity 8: comparing theories of motivation

For each of these statements, say whether it applies to (a) Cannon's homeostatic drive theory, (b) Hull's drive reduction theory, (c) expectancy (incentive) theory or (d) Maslow's hierarchy of needs. Some statements apply to more than one theory:

1 Motivation is rooted in physiological needs.
2 Psychological factors are important in explaining motivation.

3 This is a behavioural approach to motivation.
4 Motivation can be explained in terms of an interaction between physiological and psychological factors.
5 Cognition is central to motivation.
6 The emphasis is on personal change and development.
7 Motivation must be explained in terms of measurable changes.
8 Reinforcement is an important concept in explaining motivation.

When you have finished, see the notes on page 350.

13.4 WHAT IS EMOTION?

Chambers dictionary defines emotion as: 'a moving of the feelings; agitation of mind.' Up to a point, this makes sense. But to an extent this is also something of a circular definition, substituting 'feelings' for 'emotion'. Considering how commonly the term is used, it is surprisingly hard to define.

There seem to be four elements involved in emotion. Firstly, emotion is something we **experience** to which we can attach a label, like 'happy'; we are aware of feeling excitement, fear or sadness. **Cognition** also comes into it; we usually make a link between a feeling and its cause. For example, we may be excited because we are setting off on a holiday we have been looking forward to for a long time, frightened at the thought of the plane trip and sad when the holiday is over and it's time to come home. It is also possible that emotions are triggered not by events but by internal factors, like thoughts; we may feel sad because we happen to think of a friend who is ill in hospital. In addition, we may be aware of **physiological changes** associated with emotional arousal. You may have experienced 'butterflies in the stomach' when you have had to give a presentation to your class, or play the piano in public. Finally, emotion is associated with **behaviour**. We may cry when we are sad or scream when we are frightened. How these four factors link together has been a focus of interest to psychologists interested in emotion.

Activity 9: the elements of emotion

How would you make the link between the four elements of: feelings, their perceived immediate cause, physiological changes and behaviour? Which comes first? How does each affect the other? Make a note of your ideas so that you can compare them with the various theories which have been put forward to explain emotion.

Several psychologists have tried to classify emotions. Wundt (1896) suggested that all emotions can be described using three dimensions: pleasantness/unpleasantness, calmness/excitement and relaxation/tension. This conclusion was reached on the basis of asking participants to introspect about their feelings, so is open to criticism as not being very scientific.

More recently, however, Ekman (1972) used pictures of models' faces expressing different emotions. He tested participants in the USA, South America and Japan, as well as tribes in New Guinea. He found that people recognise the facial expressions associated with six basic emotions: happiness, sadness, anger, fear, disgust and surprise. These emotions are recognised, and expressed facially in the same way, by people belonging to all the cultures that were tested. This suggests that emotional expression may be universal, which in turn implies that the six emotions may themselves be innate. To these six, Plutchik (1980) added a further two, acceptance and expectancy.

- ❺ Emotion is difficult to define. Four elements seem to be important: **subjective experience**, relating this to an external or internal **cause**, **physiological change** and **behavioural response**.
- ❺ Several attempts have been made to classify emotions. Basic emotions are universally recognised from facial expressions, suggesting an **innate** element.

13.5 BRAIN STRUCTURES IN EMOTION

Before we explore the more psychological aspects of emotion, we need to know something about related physiological systems. In particular, psychologists have been interested in establishing the relationship between brain structures and emotion. Much of this research has been carried out on animals. Since animals can't tell us what emotions they are experiencing, research has mainly concentrated on emotions which can be easily identified from behaviour: rage, aggression, fear and placidity.

Early work on cats by Bard (1928) involved ablating (i.e. removing) the cortex. This produced what is known as **sham rage**. The cat showed extreme but undirected aggression. Bard also found that sham rage disappeared if the hypothalamus was removed, suggesting that this structure is involved in emotional expression.

Figure 6: the six basic emotions (Ekman, 1972)

Happiness   Disgust   Surprise   Sadness   Anger   Fear

Bard concluded that aggressive behaviour is organised in the midbrain and hindbrain, and that its appropriate expression is controlled by higher brain centres, in particular the **limbic system**. The limbic system is a set of structures which are interconnected by neural pathways. They include the **hippocampus**, **septum**, **mammillary body**, **amygdala** and **cingulate cortex**, all of which have direct connections to the hypothalamus. Later research has concentrated on the limbic system, investigating the effect of lesions and electrical stimulation of its various structures on emotional response.

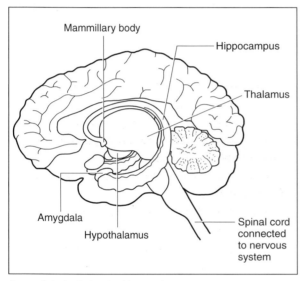

Areas of the brain involved in emotion

Papez (1937) made a connection between increased aggression in rabies and damage to the hippocampus. He proposed that the hippocampus and other limbic structures make up a circuit controlling how emotion is expressed. These ideas were expanded by MacLean (1949), giving us the **Papez–MacLean limbic model** of emotion.

Other research by King and Meyer (1958) showed that damage to the septum resulted in increased emotional reactivity in rats and mice.

However, the connection between limbic structures and emotion is far from straightforward. Flynn (1972) stimulated different parts of the cat hypothalamus, resulting in different kinds of aggressive response: a quiet, biting attack or an affective response, with raised hackles, claws out and

hissing. The first kind can also be stimulated from the **thalamus**, and the latter from the amygdala. It is not possible, then, to make a clear connection between a particular part of the brain and a particular emotion.

But can research into the limbic system be related to humans? There is some evidence of an association in humans between aggression and **limbic tumours**. In addition, the brain waves of **sociopaths** show positive spikes which indicate a dysfunctional limbic system. Amygdala lesions in monkeys were shown to result in a calm, placid animal, and this led to similar operations (**amygdalectomies**) in aggressive human psychiatric patients. This is one form of **psychosurgery**, which is covered in more detail in chapter 25.

But it is not only the limbic system which mediates emotional responses. Klüver and Bucy (1939) carried out research on monkeys. They removed the **temporal lobe**, resulting in extreme changes in affective and social behaviour. Monkeys became very placid, and showed orality (repeatedly putting objects in the mouth) and increased sexual behaviour. This pattern is known as the **Klüver–Bucy** syndrome.

Brain **lateralisation** also seems to have a part to play. One interesting piece of research is described in box G:

Box G: Gainotti (1972)

Procedure: Patients with lesions in different parts of the brain were tested on verbal and emotional understanding of statements.
Results: Patients with left hemisphere damage could not understand the words, but responded to the emotional content. This difference was reversed for those with right hemisphere damage.
Conclusion: The right hemisphere is involved with emotional response.

However, the left hemisphere is also involved in emotion. For example, Gur *et al.* (1994) found that when people were asked to think about sad events, the right hemisphere was more active, and conversely, the left hemisphere was more active when they were asked to think about happy events.

Finally, **neurotransmitters** need to be mentioned. There is some evidence that **serotonin** is related to aggression. For example, amphetamines reduce serotonin, and taking them is related to aggressive behaviour. Surges of **dopamine** are associated with happiness, while **noradrenaline** is implicated in several emotions. The role of **adrenaline** is discussed, in relation to stress, in chapter 4.

⊖ Emotions are generated by a wide range of hindbrain and midbrain structures, with their expression mediated by the **limbic system**. The two **cerebral hemispheres** play different roles in emotion.

⊖ Much of this research has been carried out on **animals**, but there is some evidence that these research findings are relevant to humans.

13.6 THEORIES OF EMOTION

The James–Lange theory

The psychologist William James and another psychologist named Lange independently produced very similar theories. Their ideas, described by James (1884), have come to be known as the **James–Lange theory**, and at first glance seem to be contrary to our common sense understanding of emotion. They suggested that when we are exposed to an emotional event, an internal physiological response and/or an overt behavioural response is made. We become aware of how we are responding, and supply an appropriate emotional label. The theory tends to give more weight to behavioural responses. If for example we see a weepy film, we may cry. We become sad because we cry, rather than the other way round.

Activity 10: explaining emotion

Pardeep is nervous about playing the piano in public. Lisa finds herself in a field with an angry bull, and feels her heart pounding. How would the James–Lange theory explain what is happening here?

When you have finished, see the notes on page 350.

Let us look at the implications of this theory. Firstly, it suggests that the more highly aroused we are, the more intense the emotion that we experience. There is some evidence, described in box H, which supports this idea:

Box H: White *et al.* (1981)

Procedure: Male college students were asked to run on the spot, one group for 120 seconds (high arousal), and another group for 15 seconds (low arousal). Both groups were then shown videos of either attractive or unattractive women, and asked to rate them for attractiveness.

Results: The high arousal group rated attractive women as more attractive, compared with the ratings made by the low arousal group. They rated the unattractive women as more unattractive, compared with the ratings made by the low arousal group.

Conclusion: The strength of emotion experienced is related to the strength of physiological arousal.

Figure 7: the James–Lange theory of emotion

emotion-producing stimulus → physiological response → emotion

emotion-producing stimulus → behavioural response → emotion

The theory also implies that we can control our emotions by changing our behaviour. If you smile you should start to feel happy, because you are using an appropriate label for smiling behaviour. Try it! While you may not be totally convinced, a study by Laird (1974), described in box I, suggests that there may be an element of truth in this idea:

Box I: Laird (1974)

Procedure: Thirty-two students were misled into thinking they were taking part in a study to measure the activity of facial muscles, using electrodes which were attached to their faces. In fact, no measures of muscle activity were made. Participants were instructed to relax and contract particular facial muscles.This had the effect of making them frown, smile and so on, without them being consciously aware of the emotional significance of what they were doing. During this procedure, they were shown cartoons, and asked to rate how funny they found them. They were also asked to rate their own emotions.

Results: Cartoons seen while they were 'smiling' were rated as funnier than those seen when 'frowning'. Participants also described themselves as happier when they were 'smiling'.

Conclusion: Participants in the 'smiling' condition were amused more by the cartoons, and felt happier, *because* they were smiling. Behaviour can *cause* subjective feelings.

◖ Activity 11: a critique of Laird (1974)

The study in box I lends some support to the James–Lange theory of emotion. Can any criticisms be made of it, which might make it unreliable as a source of evidence?

When you have finished, see the notes on page 350.

A study by Valins (1966) provides further evidence to support the James–Lange theory:

Box J: Valins (1966)

Procedure: Male participants were shown slides of semi-nude female models. They were given what they believed to be genuine feedback about the effect on their heart rate of viewing each picture. In fact they were given false feedback: they were told that their heart rate increased for half the pictures. They were asked to rate each picture they had seen for attractiveness.

Results: Participants rated the females who were supposedly associated with an increased heart rate as more attractive than the ones where they believed their heart rate was unchanged. This is known as the **Valins effect**.

Conclusion: Emotion can occur without arousal, when participants *believe* that they have been aroused.

This study supports the James–Lange theory, since it demonstrates that participants do respond emotionally to their own arousal, even when they only *believe* themselves to have been aroused. Since there was no actual arousal, though, we need to go beyond the James–Lange model to understand fully the processes involved in emotion. In particular, this study suggests that arousal may not be necessary for an emotional response. Perhaps we should look instead to cognitive factors, since Valins' participants' *beliefs* about their own arousal seem to have played a crucial part in their emotional response to the slides of models.

A further implication of the James–Lange theory is that if we are able to use a range of labels for different emotions, there must be quite distinct physiological changes corresponding to each of the different emotional labels we use. Is there any evidence that this is the case? The research in box K looked at this:

Box K: Ax (1953)

Procedure: Participants were told that they were taking part in a study of hypertension, and were wired up to an apparatus measuring GSR (galvanic skin response). While they were being wired up, fear was induced in one condition by the technician 'accidentally' giving the participant a small electric shock, and hinting that the apparatus might be faulty. In the second condition, anger was induced by the technician handling the participant roughly, being rude to him and grumbling. The pattern of physiological changes in each condition was measured.
Results: Physiological changes in the fear condition were those associated with adrenaline (raised heart rate, breathing rate and so on), while the changes in the anger condition were those associated with noradrenaline.
Conclusion: Different emotions are associated with different kinds of physiological responses.

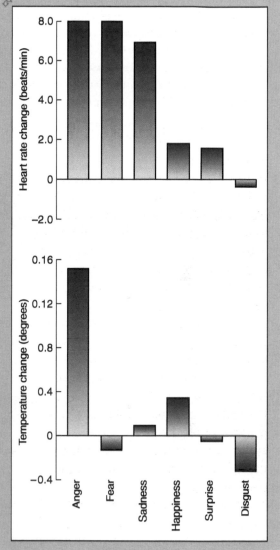

Conclusion: Physiological changes vary with the expression of different emotions.

Ax's study is useful evidence that different emotions correspond to different physiological changes. On the other hand, it doesn't indicate whether the changes cause the emotions, as the James–Lange theory suggests, or vice versa. It is also rather limited, in that it only investigates two emotions. The James–Lange theory implies that there must be a distinct pattern of physiological changes corresponding to each of the wide range of emotions we experience. There is some support for this idea:

Box L: Ekman et al. (1983)

Procedure: Participants were trained to hold for 10 seconds expressions relating to various emotions. Changes in their heart rate and temperature for each emotion were recorded.
Results: Changes in heart rate and temperature varied with the emotion being expressed.

However, a study by Marañon (1924) contradicts the James–Lange theory. Participants were injected with adrenaline, which as we have seen is associated with fear. Seventy-one per cent reported only physical sensations, with no emotional change. The others used phrases like 'It's *as if* I was afraid'. The theory suggests that the physiological changes should lead to an emotional response, which was not the case for most of the participants. It seems that physiological arousal is not enough on its own to produce emotional experiences.

● The **James–Lange** theory of emotion suggests that we have an internal physiological and/or overt behavioural response to an event or thought, and then provide an appropriate emotional label for this response.

● The implication of the theory that **increased arousal** should lead to an increased emotional response has been supported by research. Support for the idea that inducing physiological change or behaviour should create an appropriate subjective response has not been so clear-cut.

● An emotional response can be produced with no arousal. This suggests that **cognitive factors** need to be brought into a theory of emotion.

● There is some evidence that different emotions are associated with different physiological changes. However, it is not clear that these changes *cause* emotions.

The Cannon–Bard theory

Other criticisms of the James–Lange theory have been made by Cannon, within the framework of his own theory. This theory was later modified by Bard, so it has come to be known as the **Cannon–Bard theory** of emotion (Cannon and Bard, 1931).

One of the problems with the James–Lange theory, noted by Cannon, was that each emotion would need to be associated with a particular pattern of physiological change. At the time he was writing, it seemed unlikely that this was the case, but as we have seen, this criticism may be somewhat misplaced. In addition, he argued that physiological changes do not necessarily cause different emotions. He also pointed out that we often feel emotions very rapidly. Physiological change is often relatively slow, which suggests that emotions cannot easily be fitted into the James–Lange framework.

The Cannon–Bard theory tries to take all these factors into account. It suggests that the conscious experience of emotion and the physiological changes associated with it are quite independent, but happen at the same time. They both come about in response to an emotion-producing stimulus:

Figure 8: The Cannon–Bard theory of emotion

emotion-producing stimulus

stimulus is interpreted by the brain, causing feeling of emotion

stimulation of the autonomic nervous system causes physiological change

The Cannon–Bard theory suggests that all that is necessary for an emotion to be experienced is exposure to an emotion-producing stimulus; arousal of the autonomic nervous system (ANS) is not necessary. However, this idea has been challenged.

Hohmann (1966) studied patients with spinal cord injuries, with corresponding damage to the ANS. If the Cannon–Bard theory is correct, it would be expected that they would be able nonetheless to experience emotion at the same level as they had before the damage. However, they reported 'as if' experiences, similar to those described earlier by Marañon, rather than emotions. On the other hand, these 'as if' statements did relate to specific emotions. Taken together with the study by Marañon described earlier, this suggests that physiological arousal is not sufficient on its own but is nonetheless necessary to produce emotional experiences.

The Valins study in box J implies that cognition is important to emotion. The Cannon–Bard theory, with its emphasis on our interpretation of emotion-producing stimuli, also recognises the importance of cognition. We will now look at a theory of emotion which brings together elements of both the James–Lange theory and the Cannon–Bard theory, in which both arousal and cognition have a part to play in emotional experience, and where cognition is central.

❺ Cannon made several criticisms of the James–Lange theory of emotion. These criticisms formed the basis of the **Cannon–Bard** theory.

❺ **Physiological arousal** and **emotional experience** are independent but simultaneous responses to an **emotion-producing stimulus**.

❺ Research has challenged the implication of this theory that ANS arousal is not necessary for emotion to be experienced. An adequate theory of emotion needs to explain emotional arousal in terms of both **arousal** and **cognitions**.

Schachter's cognitive labelling theory

Schachter's (1964) theory brings together the two elements of physiological **arousal** and **cognition**, in terms of the attributions we make about this arousal. For this reason, it is sometimes known as the **two-factor** theory of emotion. For an emotion to be experienced, a physiological state of arousal is necessary. Situational factors will then determine how we interpret this arousal. For example, if you are being charged by an angry rhinoceros, arousal will be interpreted as fear. If on the other hand you are talking to someone you find physically attractive, arousal will be interpreted as attraction.

Figure 9: Schachter's cognitive labelling theory

The strength of physiological arousal will determine the strength of emotion experienced, while the situation will determine the *type* of emotion. These two factors are independent of each other; both are necessary for emotion to be experienced.

▷ Activity 12: comparing theories of emotion

Look back to the descriptions of the James–Lange theory and the Cannon–Bard theory. In what ways is Schachter's theory similar to each of them? In what ways does it differ from them? You will need to consider the role of physiological arousal, the role of cognition, and the sequence of events which leads to us experiencing emotion.

When you have finished, see the notes on page 350.

A classic study by Schachter and Singer (1962) supports Schachter's ideas:

Box M: Schachter and Singer (1962)

Procedure: Participants were asked to help test, through injections, what they believed to be a new vitamin compound. However, in the experimental conditions adrenaline was injected, which is produced naturally when we experience such emotions as fear. There were four conditions:

A Participants were injected with adrenaline and correctly informed about its side effects, i.e. dizziness and palpitations.

B Injection as A, but participants were misinformed about side effects: they were told to expect numbness of the feet.

C Injection as A, but participants were given no further information.

D As C, but saline injected. This was the control condition.

They were then put in a room with a confederate of the experimenter, who acted either as if he were angry (complaining about and tearing up the questionnaire which he and the participant had been asked to complete) or euphoric (laughing out loud and playing with paper aeroplanes). In condition B, only a euphoric and not an angry confederate was used. Participants were rated on the extent to which they joined in with the behaviour of the confederate, and were also asked to report on the emotions which they experienced.

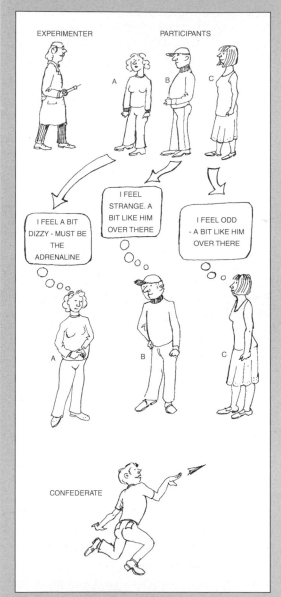

Results: Participants in conditions B and C were quite likely to behave in a similar way to the 'angry' or 'euphoric' confederate. Participants in conditions A and D were less likely to behave in a similar way to the confederate. They were also less likely to report feeling angry or euphoric.

Conclusion: In conditions B and C, participants needed to explain the arousal they were experiencing. The behaviour of the confederates acted as a cue to identify this arousal as anger or euphoria. In condition A, participants could account for their arousal in terms of the information they had been given, so no further explanation was necessary.

These findings were confirmed by a further study by Schachter and Wheeler (1962). Participants were injected either with adrenaline (causing arousal) or chlorpromazine (which inhibits arousal). Those injected with adrenaline laughed more at a slapstick comedy than controls, who had received a placebo injection. The controls in turn laughed more than those injected with chlorpromazine.

The original Schachter and Singer study has also been criticised on several counts, notably by Green (1996). Firstly, he has pointed out that the only significant differences between conditions were in terms of behaviour, not participants' reports of emotional experience; differences here would also be predicted by the theory. Secondly, there is also the problem of individual differences; there was no control of participants' emotional state at the start of the study, which could have introduced a confounding variable. Moreover, the study assumes that everyone will respond in the same way to a measured amount of adrenaline. In fact, this is not the case. Data for five of the participants in this study had to be excluded, because they were not aroused by the injection of adrenaline. Thirdly, the study was a highly artificial situation, and therefore had low ecological validity. Finally, later attempts to replicate Schachter and Singer's findings have not been successful. For example, Marshall and Zimbardo (1979) repeated the Schachter and Singer study using only the 'euphoric' condition. The participants in this study who were injected with adrenaline reported feeling less happy than controls, the opposite effect to that predicted by Schachter and Singer.

The relationship between arousal and the identification of emotion has also been investigated in a more realistic situation:

Box N: Dutton and Aron (1974)

Procedure: Naive male participants were interviewed on a high suspension bridge or on a low wooden footbridge, by an attractive female. They were asked about scenic attractions. One of the questions required them to describe a picture, and their descriptions were later analysed for sexual content. It was assumed that the sexual content would reflect the degree of sexual arousal experienced. The results for these participants were compared with those of participants interviewed by males.

Results: Participants interviewed on the high bridge by the female interviewer showed more sexual arousal than the comparison groups.

Conclusion: Arousal created by the fear of height was misinterpreted as sexual arousal, because of the situational cue provided by the female interviewer.

CASANOVA UP THERE ON THE BRIDGE, TURNED INTO BORING BILL BLOGGS DOWN HERE.

But is cognitive labelling theory correct in its claim that arousal comes first, *followed* by appropriate labelling, on the basis of situational cues?

Box O: Speisman *et al.* (1964)

Procedure: Participants were shown a film 'Subincision in Arunta'. In the film, as part of aboriginal puberty rites, a boy's penis is cut with a jagged knife. By changing the accompanying soundtrack, four conditions were created. The emphasis was on:

A the pain and jaggedness of the knife (trauma)

B the boys' keenness to achieve manhood (denial)

C the traditions of the tribe (intellectualisation)

D a control condition, with no soundtrack.

Results: Highest arousal was shown in condition A, followed by D, B and C.

Conclusion: Cognitive response to a situation can affect the degree of arousal shown. Cognition can come *before* arousal.

In the light of the problems identified with this theory, it seems sensible to draw the general conclusion that both physiological change and cognitions are involved in emotion. However, since research evidence in this area is somewhat flawed, we don't yet have a complete picture of how they relate to each other.

- Schachter's **cognitive labelling theory** proposes that an emotional situation creates **arousal**. We then give this arousal an emotional label, based on situational cues.
- There is some evidence to support Schachter's idea that arousal comes before **cognition**. Other research suggests that cognition may come before arousal.
- **Methodological** and **conceptual flaws** in the main study on which this theory is based make it difficult to draw any firm conclusions.

Lazarus' appraisal theory

While there are some problems with Schachter's theory, it has nonetheless been an important influence on theoretical accounts of emotion. Other theorists have built on his ideas, and most current theories of emotion agree that cognition must be a central factor.

The **cognitive appraisal** approach of Lazarus (1982) is a development of cognitive labelling theory. He suggested that we initially make a brief cognitive analysis of a situation, in terms of whether or not it represents a threat. Lazarus suggested that this analysis may happen at a preconscious level. Preconscious analysis has been shown in research into **subliminal perception**: participants are exposed to a stimulus, but too briefly for the material to reach conscious awareness. Changes in the GSR show an autonomic response, which shows that some preconscious analysis must have taken place.

This initial appraisal leads to an immediate behavioural or cognitive reaction. A response could take the form of fight-or-flight. The use of Freudian defence mechanisms such as denial or rationalisation would also fit in here. As we have seen, the Speisman *et al.* study in box O lends some support to the idea that cognition can come before arousal. Lazarus then proposed a third stage. This is also cognitive, and involves a reappraisal of the situation. It is at this stage that a specific emotion is identified.

⬤ Activity 13: Lazarus' appraisal theory

In activity 10, Pardeep's nervousness at playing the piano in public and Lisa's flight from an enraged bull were explained within the framework of the James–Lange theory. How would Lazarus' theory explain them?

When you have finished, see the notes on page 350.

Another formulation of this theory has been proposed by Smith and Ellsworth (1987). They suggested that how we describe emotions depends on cognitions in a particular situation.

⬤ Activity 14: identifying emotions

Imagine you have a friend who is ill in hospital. What emotions would you experience if she is there because:

a she has been knocked down by a hit-and-run driver.

b she was hurt when she fell downstairs after tripping over something you dropped.

c she is ill, with no apparent immediate cause – it's just one of those things.

When you have finished, see the notes on page 350.

Smith and Ellsworth claim that the **control** you and others have over the situation is important to emotions; it is likely that you took this into account in activity 14. Smith and Ellsworth's ideas have a lot in common with **attribution theory**, discussed at the start of chapter 8. Other cognitive factors which they see as important include judgements about the **desirability** (i.e. (un)pleasantness) of the situation, the amount of **effort** you expect to be involved and the amount of **attention** you want to give to it.

⊖ Most current theories of emotion recognise the importance of cognition.

⊖ **Lazarus' appraisal theory** suggests that the emotional response is in three stages: an initial superficial **appraisal** of the situation, a cognitive or behavioural **response**, and finally a **reappraisal** which identifies a specific emotion.

⊖ Other theorists have taken a similar approach, identifying in detail the cognitive factors involved.

⬤ Activity 15: activity 9 revisited

Now you know something about some of the theories of emotion which have been put forward, look again at your answers to activity 9. To what extent did your ideas agree with those of the various theorists we have considered? Do you need to modify your ideas in the light of what you have read?

Notes on activities

1 **Psychodynamic theories**: while recognising conscious motives, to do with current concerns, psychodynamic theories are in general more interested in unconscious motives, often rooted in childhood experience. **Behaviourist theories**: the notion of motivation is rather too mentalistic for behaviourists, since they are concerned with observable behaviour, rather than the internal states which the term 'motivation' implies. Explanations focus on finding links between stimulus and response, or schedules of reinforcement which maintain behaviour. There is no real need for a separate concept of motivation. However, some learning theorists try to explain reinforcement in terms of drives and drive reduction, and as we shall see, this can be related directly to motivation. **Humanistic**: motivation is a central concept, since humanistic psychologists are interested in personal growth and how people can change and develop. **Neurobiological**: motivation is seen in terms of physiological processes; for example, in the nervous system and the endocrine system. **Cognitive**: motivation is seen in terms of how we process information, and the relationship between thinking and behaviour.

2 1 LH; hyperphagia 2 VMH; aphagia 3 blood glucose levels; short term; liver. 4 fat levels; long term 5 osmoreceptors; hypothalamus; cell dehydration 6 baroreceptors; heart 7 switches off; switches on

3 **Body temperature** is another example. Our optimal body temperature is around 37°C. If body temperature rises above this level, the sweating response helps to cool us down. If temperature drops, we shiver. This generates heat through muscle activity, and so helps to raise the temperature. We may also show a behavioural response, e.g. opening a window if we are too hot or putting on a jersey if we are too cold.

4 If a rat has been some time without food (physiological deprivation), blood sugar levels will drop (homeostatic need). This results in hunger (drive). Because this state is unpleasant, it leads to arousal and activity, i.e. searching for food. When the rat finds food, it will eat. This reduces the hunger drive. Eating is negatively reinforcing, because it reduces the unpleasant sensations associated with hunger. Because of this reinforcement, food-seeking behaviour and eating are likely to recur as a response to the stimulus of hunger.

5 Extrinsic rewards could include being paid or given a bonus, praise from others, and opportunities for promotion, while intrinsic rewards could be satisfaction at having completed a job effectively and feeling that your work has contributed to something worthwhile. Being paid a bonus for doing something which was done because it was enjoyable could decrease the pleasure taken in the work. It might lead a person to make a different self-attribution as to why they carried out the task – away from 'I did it because I enjoyed it' to 'I did it to earn a bonus'.

7 You have probably thought of various examples where needs at the bottom of the hierarchy are not met, in order to fulfil higher needs. One case might be a mother going short of food herself in order to feed her children. It may be that Maslow overstated the importance of satisfying basic needs. It is probably fair to say that basic needs are met when possible, but that in some circumstances, complete satisfaction of lower level needs doesn't happen.

Maslow has also been criticised for being **ethnocentric**, i.e. reflecting the beliefs and values of a particular culture. The emphasis in his theory is very much on the individual, in line with the Western capitalist society from which it emerged. It also reflects the general belief in the USA at that time that anyone was capable of becoming anything they wanted to become. It may be a useful framework for understanding motivation within that particular culture. In cultures where the emphasis is more on the social group and less on the individual, though, it may have less to offer. It would also seem to be of rather less value in countries where survival itself is a constant priority, leaving little room for focusing on higher needs.

8 **1** a; b. **2** c; d. **3** b **4** b; c. **5** c. **6** d. **7** a; b. **8** b.

10 The thought of playing the piano creates the physical sensation of 'butterflies in the stomach', dryness in the mouth and perhaps trembling. Pardeep becomes aware of these sensations and labels them 'nervousness'. He is nervous because he has butterflies in his stomach and is trembling. Lisa is aware that she is breathing faster than normal. She interprets this as fear.

11 Participants may have responded to **demand characteristics**. They were supposedly unaware of the true purpose of the study, but being asked about their emotions and to judge how funny they found cartoons may have given them some idea of what was actually going on, and so influenced their responses.

12 Schachter's theory is similar to the James–Lange theory since it suggests that there must be a physiological response before an emotion is experienced. The Cannon–Bard theory does not believe that physiological arousal is necessary for emotion to be experienced. Like the Cannon–Bard theory, Schachter believed that cognitions are important in emotion. This theory is different from the Cannon–Bard theory, though, because it suggests that physiological responses and the cognitive element of emotion are related, rather than independent.

13 Pardeep and Lisa have both made an initial appraisal of the situation they are in and identified it as threatening. Pardeep responds to this initial appraisal with stress symptoms, which he then relates to the situation and identifies as fear. Lisa's initial appraisal leads to her running away. Her reappraisal leads to her identifying her emotion as fear.

14 It is likely that you included anger in **a**, guilt in **b** and sadness in **c**.

Attention and pattern recognition

In this chapter we will be looking at:

14.1 What is attention?

14.2 Theories of focused attention
    Broadbent's filter theory
    Treisman's attenuation theory
    Late selection models of attention

14.3 Divided attention
    Factors in divided attention
    Kahneman's capacity model
    Action slips

14.4 Pattern recognition
    Bottom-up theories
    The top-down approach
    Face recognition

14.1 WHAT IS ATTENTION?

While you are looking at the words on this page, you are still probably aware at some level of other people around you, the colour of the walls in the room, the view outside the window, and so on. At the same time you are probably aware of sounds – perhaps someone near you talking or the sound of pages being turned over. You could be aware of the chair you are sitting on and the feel of the pen you are holding. In other words, there are lots of elements in your environment of which you are partially aware, and on which you could choose to concentrate.

Selective attention refers to our ability to select one element to attend to among all the things going on around us, and ignore everything else. It is also called **focused attention**, because it is concerned with our ability to focus on a particular sensory input. In this case, you are focusing your attention on what you are reading (I hope!) and largely shutting out a lot of the other things that are going on around you.

Attention theorists are also interested in our ability to attend to more than one thing at a time, or **divided attention**. It is possible that while you are reading this, you are also listening to music on a Walkman, and so paying attention to two things at once. Another example would be a skilled car driver, who would have no trouble in carrying on a conversation with a passenger, or eating a sandwich, at the same time as driving.

At first glance, neither selective nor divided attention seems problematical, but nonetheless they both raise questions which are of interest to psychologists.

Theorists concerned with focused attention ask such questions as:

◆ how do we select what we attend to?
◆ how much awareness do we have of the other sensory information we have chosen to ignore?
◆ to what extent do we consciously *choose* what we attend to?

Researchers investigating divided attention look at such questions as:

◆ how many different things can we attend to at once?
◆ what are the constraints on this ability?

An information-processing model of attention

In order to answer the kinds of questions posed by attention theorists, we need a theoretical framework which allows us to develop and link ideas about attention. One way of considering these questions has been to see the brain as an information-processing system, using the analogy of a computer. In the same way as information is fed into a computer, information reaches our senses from the environment: these are **input processes**. Just as a computer works on the information it has been given, the brain will then select, manipulate and store information (**storage processes**). Finally, appropriate responses are produced (**output processes**). This can be shown in a diagram:

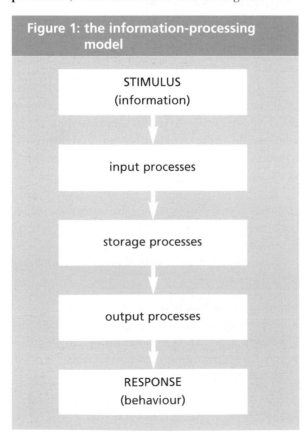

Figure 1: the information-processing model

STIMULUS
(information)

↓

input processes

↓

storage processes

↓

output processes

↓

RESPONSE
(behaviour)

We can relate this model to the driving analogy. We receive a wide range of information from the environment as we are driving, and from this we select the information we need in order to drive safely. This information is compared with what we have in our memory, e.g. what a red light means, thinking about where we are going and how our driving needs to be adapted for the conditions. This information is then fed along the system so that it can be processed and translated into appropriate behaviour, e.g. changing gear and steering. So this model talks about information being processed by the brain through a series of stages.

Different sensory inputs can be thought of as different **communication channels**, and we have to choose which will have our attention. It may help to compare this with deciding which television channel to watch; when you switch to a particular channel, you are setting up a flow of information through the transmission system. In the same way, we have to select from our immediate environment what to attend to and process, and what to ignore. The idea of **stages** of processing allows us to look at each part of the process individually and in detail, to see how each contributes to the overall picture.

Another important idea here is that of **attentional capacity**. In the same way that only one television programme can be watched at a time, so the information that can be processed by our systems is limited: we can only deal with a certain amount of information at once, and this fact has been central to the information-processing model of attention.

❺ Attention theorists are concerned with two aspects of attention: selective or **focused** attention (the ability to focus on one particular stimulus), and **divided** attention (the ability to divide attention across two or more activities).
❺ An **information-processing model**, using the analogy of the brain as a computer, provides a framework within which questions of attention can be explored.
❺ This model emphasises the idea of a **one-way flow** of information along a communication channel, through various stages of processing. The capacity to handle information is limited.

14.2 Theories of focused attention

There are several theories of focused attention, based on the information-processing model. The theories vary in two main ways. Firstly, where in the system does the selection of items for attention to take place? Secondly, to what extent does non-attended information continue to flow through the system?

Broadbent's filter theory

One of the earliest theories of selective attention was developed by Broadbent (1958). His interest arose out of his work with air traffic controllers. In their job, they are faced with a vast amount of information from pilots, and selecting what is important is obviously vital if air disasters are to be avoided. Broadbent wanted to find out precisely what processes were involved in their ability to do this.

The work of air traffic controllers is very complex.

Given the complex nature of their job, it would not have been practical to have carried out research by looking at their performance in real-life situations. For example, it wouldn't have been very ethical to manipulate the conditions under which they were working – the result might have been fatal! Broadbent therefore carried out experiments in a laboratory, where he could isolate and manipulate various aspects of selective attention. Obviously this approach may not have high **ecological validity**, but at the same time it does permit very precise data to be collected. Broadbent reasoned that by

overloading the attentional system, and analysing the errors people made on the tasks he devised, it would be possible to find out about the precise processes involved.

He developed a procedure called **dichotic listening** ('dichotic' means 'two ears') in which the two ears receive different messages simultaneously. A typical experiment uses the **split-span procedure**, and an example is described in box A:

Box A: Broadbent (1958)

Procedure: Participants were required to listen through headphones to a set of three numbers coming to the right ear, while at the same time, a different set of three numbers reached the left ear. They were then required to report all six numbers either (a) ear-by-ear or (b) pair-by-pair:

(a) reporting ear-by-ear

(b) reporting pair-by-pair

Results: Participants found it very much harder to report pair-by-pair than ear-by-ear, and made more errors in this condition.
Conclusion: Switching physical channels decreases efficiency in tasks requiring focused attention.

Before we discuss Broadbent's results, you may like to try dichotic listening yourself. Broadbent used fairly sophisticated apparatus, but the simplified version in activity 1 will help to give you some idea of what it is like:

▷ Activity 1: dichotic listening

You will need to work in a group of three, two of you saying the numbers and the third being a 'dichotic listener' and reporting back, either ear-by-ear or pair-by-pair. Take it in turns to be the listener.

Prepare sets of six numbers. Each set should contain six different single-figure numbers in no particular order. Ten sets is about right, so that the listener can have five trials reporting ear-by-ear and five reporting pair-by-pair.

The two speakers will need to speak their sets of numbers simultaneously, so a bit of practice will be necessary before you start. You might find that nodding your head as you speak helps you to keep time with each other.

When you are ready, each of the speakers should position themselves reasonably close to one ear of the listener. Before each trial, remind the listener whether they are to report ear-by-ear or pair-by-pair, and write down what is reported.

You will find it easier to draw up a table before you start, which can be filled in as you go along, e.g:

Numbers	Ears/Pairs	Response
259 176	ears	259176
462 983	pairs	

and so on ...

When all the trials have been completed, make a rough analysis of which condition, ear-by-ear or pair-by-pair, was more difficult. How many numbers were not reported, or were wrong, or in the wrong order? Ask your participant for an introspective report too.

Though there are usually quite wide differences in people's ability to carry out this task (a point we shall be coming back to later), it is likely that you found it quite difficult. Probably, though, you had similar results to Broadbent and found the ear-by-ear condition relatively easier than pair-by-pair.

How can we explain Broadbent's results? When recalling pair-by-pair, it is necessary to switch from one ear to the other and back again, making at least three switches to group the numbers in pairs. In the ear-by-ear condition, only one switch is necessary, so an explanation of the differences between the conditions is likely to have something to do with the frequency of switching that is necessary to carry out the task. To see why this should make a difference, we need to look at Broadbent's theory. He suggested the model in figure 2, where the arrows represent information passing through the system:

Figure 2: Broadbent's model of selective attention

senses

sensory buffer store

selective filter

limited capacity processor

output processes

In the dichotic listening experiment, Broadbent assumed that the ears were acting as separate communication channels, and so gave two sources of auditory input. This sensory information is passed to the **sensory buffer store**. This is a memory store which only lasts a very short time, where incoming information is held until it can be processed. He suggested that the processing system could only deal with one channel at a time, which is why his is a **single-channel theory** of attention. There is a **selective filter** operating which selects the channel we will attend to. He also suggested that the channel was chosen only on the basis of **physical characteristics**: for example, acoustic features, such as whether the sound was loud or soft, high-pitched or low; or the actual physical channel through which it was received, depending on the direction it was coming from. In the dichotic listening experiment, the key factor is the ear to which each input is coming. The incoming information is only analysed for meaning *after* selection.

In the dichotic listening experiment, switching between channels takes up time, and more time is taken up with the extra switches needed for the pair-by-pair condition. This time lapse means that the material in the sensory buffer store has decayed, and so is no longer available, which explains why people tend to do less well on the pair-by-pair condition.

Further support for Broadbent's theory came from research using a technique called **shadowing**, originally developed by Cherry. One study he carried out using shadowing is described in box B:

Box B: Cherry (1953)

Procedure: Through headphones, participants were played two different passages of prose simultaneously, one to each ear. Their task was to repeat aloud one of the passages (called the **attended message**) as they heard it, while at the same time ignoring the material being played into the other ear (the **unattended message**). They were then asked what they had noticed about the *unattended* message.

Results: Participants could give information about the physical characteristics of the unattended message (e.g. whether the voice was high or low, or whether the message changed from speech to a tone), but were unable to say anything about what the passage had been about.

Conclusion: These findings support Broadbent's ideas. Input channels are distinguished by physical characteristics. Meaning plays no part in selection.

Problems with Broadbent's model

One problem is how we define a channel. On the face of it, the idea of the ears acting as two separate channels seems plausible. In real life, though, we seldom have two entirely separate sets of information coming to each ear individually. For example, if you are listening to a piece of music played by a band or orchestra you can pick out different voices or instruments, even though this information is going to both ears, but it doesn't seem sensible to think of all the different instruments and voices as separate channels.

Secondly, how does the selective filter operate? Broadbent claims that selection is on the basis of physical characteristics, and that meaning is not a factor. His dichotic listening experiments used information whose channels couldn't be selected on the basis of meaning (since both channels carried numbers) so there doesn't seem a very sound basis for this claim. Gray and Wedderburn (1960) decided to test whether meaning could be used as a basis for message selection:

Box C: Gray and Wedderburn (1960)

Procedure: The procedure was basically the same as that followed by Broadbent (1958). The only difference was that instead of two sets of numbers, each ear received a mixture of words and numbers, e.g.:

Participants were asked to report ear-by-ear or category-by-category, i.e. grouping the numbers together and the words together.

Results: Participants found it as easy to report category-by-category as ear-by-ear. Dividing the stimulus material into meaningful categories made switching less of a problem than in Broadbent's experiment.

Conclusion: Meaning must be analysed *before* selection.

- Broadbent used a technique called **dichotic listening**.
- His **filter model** suggests that there is a filter which lets only one channel of information through to the limited capacity processor. This filter operates on the basis of physical characteristics. Meaning is only analysed *after* selection.
- Broadbent's definition of a channel is problematic. His technique eliminates any possible effect of meaning.
- Evidence from Gray and Wedderburn suggests that meaning must be analysed *before* selection.

Treisman's attenuation theory

Treisman followed Cherry's shadowing technique for further studies into the basis of selection, using a variety of materials. In a series of experiments (examples are given in box D) she found considerable support for the conclusion drawn by the Gray and Wedderburn study (box B), i.e. that meaning is a factor in the selection process. It seems that the studies of Broadbent and of Cherry do not give us the complete picture.

Box D: Treisman (1960; 1964)

(a) Bilingual participants were asked to carry out a shadowing task. The attended message was in English, and the unattended message was a French version of the English. If the French version followed the English version after a slight lapse in time, most participants were aware that the messages had the same meaning.

(b) Participants were asked to shadow a string of words similar to English sentences (e.g. I saw the girl song was wishing …) which was presented to one ear. A similar word string to the other ear was to be ignored. There were intrusions from the unattended channel when the words from that channel would make sense in the context of the attended channel.

Conclusion: Even though participants were focusing attention on one input, the meaning of the other input was unconsciously monitored. The meanings of messages are recognised before selection takes place.

Activity 2: cocktail party effect

Imagine you are at a party and are having a very interesting conversation with someone you have just met. Suddenly your attention switches to something that is said on the other side of the room. What might have been said to make your attention switch in this way?

When you have finished, see the notes on page 380.

The cocktail party effect

The **cocktail party effect** was first described by Cherry (1953). It has also been shown experimentally; Moray (1959) found that participants recognised their own name on the unattended channel of a shadowing task. The phenomenon can only really be explained if we accept that we are monitoring much more of the information around us than we are consciously aware of, and that we have some knowledge of the meaning of this information. It is the nature of the information which causes us to switch attention when there is something of particular relevance to us.

These findings led Treisman to suggest a modified version of Broadbent's theory of selective attention:

Treisman's model partly follows Broadbent's. She agrees with him that there is a selective filter where one channel is selected on the basis of its physical features. However, she suggests that other channels are not blocked off entirely, but instead are **attenuated**. This means that the information those channels carry is only passed on in a weakened form. Imagine the various input channels as radios, broadcasting different programmes. In the attenuation process, one of them is turned right up and all the rest are turned down so they are just a low background murmur. In figure 3, the selected channel is represented by the heavier arrow going from the selective filter to the next stage in the system, while the attenuated

Figure 3: Treisman's attenuation model of selective attention

input sensory processes	selective filter (attenuation)	dictionary (semantic analysis)	output processes

channels are shown by the arrows with thinner lines.

There is then a further selection process, where material is selected through **semantic analysis**, i.e. on the basis of its meaning. This stage of selection consists of a mental **dictionary**, listing words and their meanings. Each item is known as a **dictionary unit**, each of which has a specific **threshold**. The threshold is the intensity a word needs to have to trigger that particular dictionary unit. For some words, such as our own name, this threshold is very low. This means that even if this information is carried on an attenuated channel, the words will be very easily triggered. We can relate this to the party example, where you catch the sound of your own name across the room (on an attenuated channel), not in the conversation you are actually having (the selected channel).

Our own name is always important to us, and so will have a permanently low threshold. Thresholds can also change according to the situation. For example, if you are hungry then words associated with food will temporarily have a low threshold until you have had something to eat. They will then have a higher threshold (unless, of course, food is something which is always of major interest to you!)

Activity 3: thresholds and dictionary units

a Which of these words have a permanently low threshold for most people?
For which particular kinds of people might the other words have a permanently low threshold?

kennel   help   Olympics   fire   mummy

b For each of these situations, give examples of words whose threshold may be temporarily lowered:

taking your driving test   going on holiday

When you have finished, see the notes on page 380.

It is at the dictionary stage, then, that the final selection is made. If there is nothing on attenuated channels with a particularly low threshold, then the already selected channel will be attended to and

information on the other channels lost. But the originally selected channel can be overridden if an attenuated channel contains something with a permanently or temporarily lowered threshold. In this case, attention will switch (as in the party example) to this attenuated channel.

Activity 4: Broadbent and Treisman

For each of these statements, indicate whether they refer to Broadbent's theory, Treisman's theory, or both:

a all input channels are initially processed simultaneously
b one channel is selected on the basis of physical characteristics
c information from the other channels is blocked
d information from the other channels is passed on in a weakened form
e a response can include items from an unattended channel

When you have finished, see the notes on page 380.

On the face of it, Treisman's model can account for phenomena, like the cocktail party effect, which Broadbent's theory doesn't really cover, but how satisfactory is it? There are two ways in which it has been criticised:

Firstly, the concept of attenuation is tricky. It seems clear what the *function* of attenuation is, i.e. to reduce the amount of information being processed through the system and facilitate the selection process. But how does it actually operate? In what sense is the information content of the attenuated channels reduced?

There is also a problem in the notion of a selection process based on the *meaning* of the various inputs. The findings of Gray and Wedderburn (box C) and the cocktail party effect as well as Treisman (box D), suggest that unattended channels are processed for meaning. But processing for meaning must be a complex process, and Treisman's model does not really explain very clearly what the semantic mechanisms are which allow switching between an attended and an unattended channel.

⑤ Treisman used the technique of **shadowing**. Her **attenuation theory** of selective attention suggests that the selective filter does not block unattended information; it attenuates it.

⑤ We can (and do) switch to another channel when material on that channel has a low **threshold** for us.

⑤ Like Broadbent's filter theory, attenuation theory claims that we are only able to attend to one channel at a time.

⑤ The theory has been criticised for failing to explain how attenuation works. It also fails to explain clearly the semantic mechanisms involved in switching.

Late selection models of attention

The theories of Broadbent and Treisman are both **bottleneck theories**. This means that only some of the information available to us can pass all the way through the attentional system, with the rest blocked along the way. They agree that the bottleneck occurs at the recognition stage, and so some selection must take place before this is reached. Other theorists have suggested that *all* incoming stimuli are processed for meaning. This processing is virtually automatic, and so makes few demands on the system. Only after this initial analysis is one input selected for further processing. The bottleneck in the system comes nearer to the response stage.

This framework was first proposed by Deutsch and Deutsch (1963) and later revised by Norman (1968). It is illustrated in figure 4 below.

Deutsch and Deutsch suggested that all incoming stimuli are recognised and processed by

being matched against information in long term memory. The recognition process is not a bottleneck, as Broadbent and Treisman proposed, but nonetheless acts as a filter. The filter weighs up the relative importance of the stimuli, and only what is most pertinent, i.e. relevant, in a particular context is selected for further processing and is consciously attended to. For this reason, this model of attention is sometimes known as the **pertinence model**. Other stimuli will only be attended to if they become more relevant.

▷ Activity 5: pertinence

In each of these scenarios, what event might cause unattended stimuli to become pertinent, and so reach conscious awareness?

1 Sarah is watching her favourite soap opera, and is engrossed in a particularly interesting twist in the story. There is the steady sound of cars passing

Figure 4: late selection models of attention

sensory processes → semantic analysis (recognition processes) → response processes the house. She is looking forward to going out that evening with a friend, who is coming to pick her up in his car. He is already a little late.

2 Malik is playing football with his brother in the garden. He is concentrating on not letting his brother shoot goals past him. Their father is cooking lunch on the barbecue. It is already well past Malik's normal lunchtime.

When you have finished, see the notes on page 380.

The pertinence theory suggests that in a dichotic listening experiment, the fact that participants are unaware of unattended material doesn't mean that this material has not been recognised. Rather, it means that it has not reached consciousness.

However, if we want to test this distinction between recognition and consciousness, relating it to an observable response, we come up against a problem. Participants would respond in exactly the same way to material that had been recognised, and then forgotten before they became conscious of it, as they would to material which had not been recognised at all. This is illustrated by the Treisman study described in box D (a). Participants realised that the two stories were the same, but only if they were very close together in time. This suggests that the information in the unattended message was recognised, but quickly forgotten. An ingenious way of overcoming this problem is described in the experiment in box E:

The fact that Corteen and Wood found that a GSR was produced by city names not included in the original list strongly suggests that the unattended material was processed quite deeply, to a level in which the semantic category of an item was recognised.

Von Wright *et al.* (1975) carried out a similar study. They found a GSR on only a few of the trials. It seems that thorough processing of unattended information only happens some of the time, challenging the Deutsch and Deutsch view that all input must be analysed before selection. A further challenge comes from a study by Treisman and Riley:

There is some evidence, then, that Treisman's ideas about attenuation may be more accurate than the full semantic analysis required by late selection theories.

The Deutsch and Deutsch theory has also been criticised for proposing a rather rigid processing system. A more flexible model has been suggested by Johnston and Heinz (1978). They suggested that selection may be possible at various stages of processing. They made two assumptions. Firstly, the more stages of processing that take place before selection, the greater the demands on processing capacity. Secondly, in order to minimise these demands, selection takes place as early as possible, depending on the specific demands of the situation. There is some support for the flexibility they suggested:

The original debate about selective attention assumed that information passes through the attentional system, and that at some point there is a bottleneck, where selection takes place. The issue was at what point in the system this bottleneck occurs. Early selection theories placed the bottleneck at the recognition stage, whereas late selection theories suggested that the bottleneck occurs nearer to the response stage.

The argument now seems to have shifted somewhat, to the nature of recognition. Broadbent's original theory suggested that recognition was an all-or-nothing process, but Treisman's theory and more particularly late selection theories suggest that recognition is not that simple; there may be degrees of recognition.

Box G: Johnston and Wilson (1980)

Procedure: Using a dichotic listening technique, participants were asked to identify target words belonging to a particular semantic category, e.g. clothing. 'Socks' would be a sample target word. Each target word was ambiguous, having at least two meanings. The presentation of each target word was accompanied by a non-target word. This would either bias appropriately (e.g. 'smelly'), bias towards the inappropriate meaning (e.g. 'punches') or was a neutral word (e.g. 'Tuesday'). On some trials, participants were told the ear in which they would hear the target words. On some trials they were not given this information.

Results: When participants did not know which ear targets would arrive at, appropriate non-target words improved target detection, and inappropriate ones impaired it. These effects were lost when participants knew in which ear they would hear the target words.

Conclusion: Non-target words were processed for meaning only when participants did not know in which ear they would hear the target words. Whether or not semantic processing of unattended material takes place depends on whether it is necessary to the task.

The Johnston and Heinz model goes further, to suggest that the degree of recognition will depend on the demands of the task.

❺ The Deutsch and Deutsch/Norman **pertinence model** suggests that all incoming information is processed for meaning, and that the bottleneck is at the response stage. As with the Broadbent and Treisman models, only one channel can be attended to at a time.
❺ Attention switches when unattended information becomes more pertinent.
❺ Research evidence does not entirely support this model. It has also been criticised for being too rigid. Johnston and Heinz have proposed a more flexible model, in which processing depends on the requirements of the task.
❺ The nature of recognition is problematical. There may be different degrees of recognition.

14.3 DIVIDED ATTENTION

The models of attention we have covered so far all assume that there is some kind of selection mechanism which chooses between the various channels of information available to us at any one time, and that there is a single, general-purpose mechanism which deals with attention. They also all assume that only one channel can be attended to at a time. This is known as **serial processing**.

However, some theorists have questioned these assumptions, since it is possible to some extent to process information in parallel. For example, if you are a skilled driver, you can carry on a conversation with your passenger at the same time as responding appropriately to the task of driving. This is **parallel processing**, i.e. making sense of two inputs (driving information and the conversation) at the same time. Many attention theorists have looked at what is involved when we divide our attention between two tasks. The most common method used in this approach is the **dual task** (or concurrent task) method. It is demonstrated in activity 6:

▶ Activity 6: dual task method

Work with a partner and see how easy (or difficult.) it is to attend to two things at once. Try carrying out these pairs of tasks at the same time, and afterwards rate how difficult you found each combination on a scale of 1 (no problem) to 10 (impossible):

1 Ask your partner to tell you the story of a television programme or film they have seen recently. Shadow the story as they tell it to you ('shadowing' is repeating the story as it is told to you – discussed in the section about Treisman's work on selective attention). At the same time, draw a row of cats on a piece of scrap paper.

2 Sit with your partner on your left. Shadow what your partner is telling you, as in the previous task. At the same time, try to listen to a pair of students working near you to your right, so that you could repeat the main points of the story they are using.

3 You won't need a partner this time. Copy out a short section of your psychology notes. At the same time, with your other hand, draw the outline of a square with your finger on the table next to you.

NB: The first two combinations can be carried out on your own if you like, by using the radio and/or television.

You probably found that the first pair of tasks were fairly easy to do, and rated this about 2 or 3. But you may well have had more of a problem with the second and third combinations, and rated them around 7 or 8. We will now turn to research investigating why some pairs of tasks may be more easily carried out than others.

Factors in divided attention

Two of Allport's studies into factors which influence the extent to which we are able to divide our attention between two (or more) tasks are described in box H. Compare his findings with your own experience of activity 6.

Box H: Allport *et al.* (1972)

First study:

Procedure: Participants were asked to shadow a continuous passage of prose which they heard in both ears through headphones. At the same time, they were shown a set of fairly complicated pictures, and asked to study and memorise them for a later test.

Results: There was little difference in the participants' scores for recognising the pictures, whether they had shadowed the prose at the same time or just seen the pictures on their own. Their ability to shadow the prose was also unaffected by memorising the pictures at the same time.

Second study:

Procedure: Participants were all skilled piano players. They were asked to play by sight a musical score which they had not seen before, and at the same time shadow a continuous piece of prose.

Results: These two tasks were performed as well together as either one of them separately. There was very little interference experienced.

Conclusions: In both these studies, the lack of interference suggests that different processing mechanisms were involved in the concurrent tasks.

In both cases, Allport argued that it was fairly easy for participants to carry out these two tasks simultaneously, because the **input modalities** (the way the information was received, e.g. as a visual or auditory input) and the **output modalities** (the nature of the task, e.g. articulatory or motor) were different for the two tasks. This is true of the first task you carried out in activity 6. On the other hand, there are problems if the two tasks share input or output modalities. The second pair of tasks in activity 6 shared their input modality (both inputs were auditory) and the third pair shared their output modality (both outputs were motor). According to Allport, then, modality is one factor which can affect the ease with which we do two things simultaneously. But is it the only factor?

Box I: Shaffer (1975)

Procedure: A skilled copy typist was asked to copy type a passage of prose in German (a language she did not understand) while at the same time shadowing a passage over headphones. She was then asked to type a passage in English presented through headphones, while reading aloud a passage presented visually.

Results: The typist had little difficulty in carrying out the first pair of tasks. There was considerable interference between the second pair of tasks.

Conclusion: There was no problem with shared input or output modalities in the second pair of tasks: the input modalities were auditory and visual, and the output modalities motor and articulatory. There must therefore be another factor causing the problems the typist experienced. In the second condition, both tasks involved processing meaningful English prose. The *nature of the material* being processed must be another factor in determining whether we are able to carry out two tasks at once.

To sum up, then, we have shown that we can attend to two tasks at once, provided they have different input and output modalities, and the nature of the material to be processed is not too similar. But even this does not explain everything. For example, a skilled cook can carry out a routine task such as stirring a sauce as it thickens, and chat to a friend at the same time. There is no conflict of modalities here (for stirring, the input is kinaesthetic, the output motor; for chatting, the input is auditory, the output articulatory). The tasks are not at all alike, so no problems are experienced. But if the sauce starts to go lumpy, the conversation is likely to stop while attention is focused on a rescue operation on the sauce. So how do we explain the shift from easily doing two things at once to focusing attention on just one? Box J suggests that a distinction between automatic and attentional processing may be useful:

Box J: Shiffrin and Schneider (1977)

Shiffrin and Schneider carried out a series of studies which led them to suggest that there are two different modes of processing information, **attentional** and **automatic**, with quite different characteristics.

Attentional processes:
◆ have limited capacity and mean that we have to concentrate on the task.
◆ mean that we can only concentrate on one thing at a time, i.e. serial processing.
◆ enable us to learn a new skill fairly quickly, and mean that how we do it can easily be modified.
◆ mean that we are often consciously attending to what we are doing.

In contrast, **automatic processes**:
◆ have much greater capacity.
◆ allow more than one task to be attended to at a time, i.e. parallel processing.
◆ involve learning skills which require a lot of practice, and which are hard to change once learned.
◆ are usually relatively unconscious.

If we apply this distinction to the sauce example, we switch from automatic processing to attentional processing when it starts to go lumpy. Since this involves serial processing, we can't attend to the conversation we are having at the same time. We will look at some examples of the distinction between automatic and attentional processing in activity 7:

Activity 7: automatic and attentional processing

Using Shiffrin and Schneider's criteria, identify each of these activities as involving mainly (a) automatic or (b) attentional processing:
1 washing your hands
2 solving a crossword puzzle clue
3 driving a car the first time you've tried
4 driving a car ten years after getting your licence
5 tying a shoelace
6 balancing your cheque book stubs
When you have finished, see the notes on page 380.

The distinction between automatic and attentional processing can also be related to Allport's studies (box H) and Shaffer's work (box I). For example, in the second Allport study the participants were all experienced musicians. Sight-reading would be a well-practised task for them, so would use automatic rather than attentional processing. Attention could therefore be given to the shadowing task. In Shaffer's experiment, the participant was a skilled copy typist. For her, typing had become a skill requiring virtually no conscious attention, allowing her to focus on the concurrent shadowing task.

Norman and Shallice (1986) have pointed out that it is a little simplistic to draw a sharp distinction between automatic and attentional processing. They suggested that it would be more realistic to talk about three different levels of functioning: fully automatic, partially automatic and deliberate control. The distinction, though, is still relevant.

To sum up: as well as the nature of the input and output modalities, and the kind of material to be processed, our ability to do more than one thing at a time is also affected by the extent to which at least one of those things has become a relatively

automatic activity, needing little if any focused attention. If this is the case, our attentional capacity can be much increased. But when there is a problem with an automatic task (e.g. the sauce becoming lumpy), processing becomes attentional. This means that it is more difficult to carry out another activity at the same time (e.g. chatting).

While automaticity makes it possible to extend this capacity, it may at the same time have its drawbacks.

Activity 8: automatic processing

Read quickly through this sentence, counting the number of times the letter 'h' occurs:

The hungry horse ate the whole sackful of fresh hay

If you can find some willing participants, ask them to carry out this activity as well. Do their answers support the idea described in the next paragraph?

In our culture, one of the activities which has become most automatic is reading. It fits perfectly the criteria for automatic processes that Shiffrin and Schneider put forward: we need a lot of practice to acquire this skill, but once we have become fluent readers, it is almost impossible not to read clearly printed material in our direct line of vision. The process has become so automatic that short and frequently occurring words such as 'and', 'on', 'if' and so on are processed not as a set of individual letters but as units in themselves. In activity 8, the letter 'h' occurs seven times, but is often only counted five times. Two of the occurrences are in the word 'the', a very frequently occurring word, which can therefore be thought of as being processed as a single unit, rather than a set of three individual letters.

This is a simple example of automatic processing (reading short, common words as single units rather than as a set of different letters) interfering with an attended task (counting the number of times 'h' occurs). An even more dramatic example of this kind of interference, demonstrating possible drawbacks to automatic processing, is shown in box K. It is known as the **Stroop effect**:

Box K: Stroop (1935)

Procedure: Participants were shown two sets of words written in a variety of coloured inks. One set of words was made up of colour names, but each word was never written in the colour the word spelt; e.g. the word BLUE could be written in red, green or yellow, but never in blue. The other set of words used were neutral words, similar to the first set, but with no colour associations. These too were written in a variety of ink colours. Participants were asked to identify for each word the ink colour it was written in.

Results: Participants took longer to identify the ink colour of the colour words than the ink colour of the neutral words.

Conclusion: Since reading is an automatic process, the words themselves are processed automatically. The meaning of the colour words conflicts with the ink colour in which they are written, so the participant has to try to overcome the automatic processing of reading in order to perform the attended task of naming the ink colour.

▶ Activity 9: the Stroop effect

If you have willing participants, try for yourself a modified form of the Stroop task, based on a study carried out by Flowers *et al.* (1979).

Show a participant each of the displays below in turn:

condition A	condition B
4 4	• •
3 3 3 3 3	• • • • •
2 2 2	• • •
5	•
1 1 1 1	• • • •
2 2 2 2 2	• • • • •
5 5 5	• • •
4	•
3 3	• •
4 4 4 4 4	• • • • •
1 1 1	• • •
5 5 5 5	• • • •
3	•
2 2 2 2	• • • •
1 1	• •

The task is to work down each column, saying out loud how many items there are in each row. This should be done as fast as possible, but without making any mistakes. For each condition, you should time how long the participant takes to carry out the task, and how many errors are made.

If you are testing more than one participant, some should carry out condition A followed by condition B; for some the order should be reversed. Counterbalancing in this way will help to avoid order effects (e.g. practice or fatigue).

Since number recognition is much more automatic than counting, you should find – like Flowers *et al.* – that people have a tendency to say the written numbers in condition A, and that this condition takes longer to complete.

If you have a minimum of five participants, you could use the Wilcoxon signed ranks test to analyse your data (see chapter 26).

- ❺ Theories of **selective attention** rest on the assumption that we can only attend to one channel of information at any one time.
- ❺ Studies of **divided attention** using **dual task** methods have challenged this idea. They have altered the focus of attention research by looking at what constraints there are on our ability to process various inputs in parallel.
- ❺ We can attend to more than one thing at a time if:
  – the input and output modalities of the tasks are different.
  – the material to be processed is also different.
  – at least one of the tasks is automatic and does not require focused attention.
- ❺ Automatic processing enlarges our attentional capacity, but may also have drawbacks if it produces a conflict with an attended task.

Kahneman's capacity model

Kahneman's capacity model of attention (Kahneman, 1973) brings together ideas from research on both selective and divided attention.

It seems clear that some tasks require more attention – more **mental effort** – than others. If a task does not require our complete attention, it is possible to attend to something else at the same time. There are also limits to the number of things which we can attend to at once, however little of our attention each takes up. You would probably find it extremely difficult, if not impossible, to read a book, hum a tune, tap your foot and sew on a button, all at the same time, even if all these tasks are routine and well-practised.

There are limits to the number of things we can attend to at once.

This seems to suggest that there is a pool of attentional resources which, although limited, can be flexibly allocated to tasks. Kahneman's model includes a **central processor** which governs **resource allocation**. The model assumes that we have considerable control over how resources are allocated.

Another important factor is **arousal**. Arousal determines how much processing capacity we have, which in turn influences allocation. For example, if you are half asleep you might find that a simple task like getting out of a car takes all your concentration;

you have less attentional capacity than if you are fully alert, so there is no spare capacity to be given to another task.

Finally, the central processor allocates resources in response to external factors. Kahneman differentiates between **enduring dispositions**, i.e. aspects of the environment which are always of interest to a person, and **momentary intentions**, i.e. those aspects which are only of current interest.

▶ Activity 10: momentary intentions and enduring dispositions

In each of these scenarios, imagine that the person is in a TV shop where the sets are tuned to different channels. Pick out from the list at the bottom which programme s/he is likely to attend to, relating to (a) momentary intentions and (b) enduring dispositions:

◆ Peter is a keen runner, running several miles a day. This evening he and his girlfriend are on their way to see a film.

◆ Tonya has got her driving test this afternoon, and is really worried she won't pass. She needs to have her licence so that she can get to the drama course she is about to start.

a report on the London Marathon
a drama workshop   the Grand Prix
a report from the Cannes film festival
a trailer for a new crime series
the weather forecast   a cookery programme
an athletics meeting in Gateshead

When you have finished, see the notes on page 380.

How relevant a stimulus is to a person is one factor in whether it is attended to. Generally, current goals are most important in deciding resource allocation. However, there are also other factors. Enduring dispositions include factors to do with survival, which would explain why attention switches very rapidly when someone shouts 'Fire!' The intensity of a stimulus, and its novelty, can also be important in overriding attention to the current goal.

All these elements come together in Kahneman's model shown in figure 5:

Figure 5: Kahneman's capacity model of attention

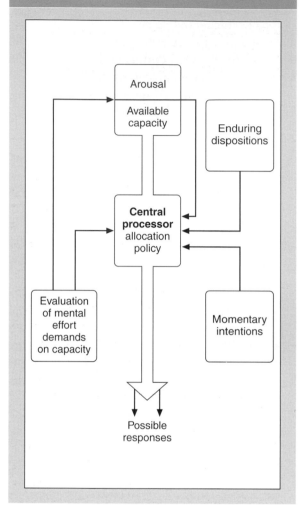

This model is much more flexible than those proposed by earlier theorists such as Broadbent, and takes account of the wide range of factors which research has shown to be important. What it still has in common with earlier models, though, is the idea of attention as a process.

▶ Activity 11: automatic and attentional processing

Look back to box J. How can the idea of attention as a skill be related to Shiffrin and Schneider's distinction between automatic and attentional processing?

When you have finished, see the notes on page 380.

Neisser has suggested that we may need to think of attention as a skill.

▶ Activity 12: attention as a skill

You will remember that Broadbent's early work was concerned with air traffic controllers. Their work demands that they focus on one particular piece of information, while at the same time being aware of other messages to which they are not currently attending.

It is possible that when they start training, some air traffic controllers find this easier than others but, experience is likely to have helped all those working in this field to become more expert at it.

Can you think of other examples of jobs or occupations where people would develop the skill of attending selectively to a particular stimulus, while at the same time monitoring unattended information?

When you have finished, see the notes on page 380.

Neiser illustrated his idea with the example of two participants in a study he carried out with colleagues (Spelke *et al*. 1976). After considerable training over a period of weeks, they could write and understand dictated words, while being able *at the same time* to read a different text, and understand that as well. It is also worth noting, though, that even with practice there is *some* disruption when two complex tasks are performed together. However automatic a task, it does use some attentional resources. Broadbent (1982) found this was also true of the Allport (box H) and Shaffer (box I) studies.

The idea of attention as a skill is relevant to simultaneous translating. This involves hearing a message in one language and, as it is heard, producing a spoken translation in another language. Training for this work involves first of all shadowing a heard message in the translator's native language. This gets the translator used to dealing with combining 'language-in' with 'language-out'. They can then move on to the more difficult task of translating the 'language-in', and speaking the translated version as 'language-out'.

The idea of attention as a skill would also help us to understand individual differences in attention:

Alternatives to Kahneman's model

Kahneman's model assumes that attention is a unitary system. However, not all theorists accept this idea. For example, Allport (1989) preferred a **modular model**. Instead of one system dealing with any of the tasks presented to it, he suggested that there are several specialised subsystems (**modules**), each dealing with particular kinds of task. When two tasks are very similar, they are competing for the same modules, and this explains some of the difficulties we may experience in a dual-task situation. An example would be the second pair of tasks in the Shaffer study (box I), where both tasks involved processing meaningful English prose.

There is some evidence for this idea, particularly from studies of brain-damaged patients, which have shown that skills such as reading are complex skills which involve several separate processing mechanisms. This kind of model is not very detailed, though, in terms of the number and nature of these modules, and how they would co-ordinate when operating together.

Other theorists (e.g. Eysenck, 1982) have produced **synthesis theories**, bringing together features of capacity and modular models. They suggest that attention has a hierarchical structure, with a central executive at the top, and specific processing mechanisms at a lower level. The central executive is modality-free, and controls and co-ordinates the processing mechanisms, which function relatively independently. The idea of a central executive is similar to the central processor of Kahneman's capacity model, while the specific processing mechanisms are similar to modules. An example of this kind of model is the **working memory** model of short term memory, put forward by Baddeley and Hitch, discussed in chapter 2.

The main problem with the compromise suggested by synthesis theories – and with theories of selective attention, and Kahneman's capacity model – is the assumption that there is a unitary attentional system, dealing with all aspects of attentional processing. This seems not to be the case. For example, Posner and Petersen (1990) identified three separate processes involved in visual attention:

Figure 6: abilities involved in visual attention (Posner and Petersen, 1990)

- *disengaging* attention from a particular stimulus
- *shifting* attention from one stimulus to another
- *engaging* attention on a new stimulus

This idea of distinct processes within attention is supported by studies of visual disorders in patients suffering brain damage, where different kinds of visual problems can be related to these different abilities. This is discussed further in chapter 11. A modular model of attention therefore seems to offer the best framework within which attention can be understood.

- ◓ Kahneman's **capacity model** brings together much of the information we have about attention.
- ◓ Attention is flexibly allocated by a **central processor** between one or more tasks. Overall capacity is related to **arousal**. Allocation decisions are influenced by **enduring dispositions** and **momentary intentions**.
- ◓ Neisser has suggested that attention should be regarded as a **skill** rather than a process.
- ◓ Other theorists prefer to think of attention as a **modular system**. **Synthesis models** propose a hierarchy, with a central executive co-ordinating different modules. Evidence from studies of brain-damaged patients challenges the idea of a unitary attentional system.

Action slips

Action slips can be defined as the performance of actions which were not intended. We often relate this kind of slip to absent-mindedness, suggesting that we make these slips because of lack of attention to what we are doing. Psychologists are interested in these slips because of what they can tell us about the processes involved in planning and carrying out sequences of behaviour. As we will see, the distinction between automatic and attentional processing, discussed earlier, is also relevant to action slips.

Diary studies are one way of studying action slips. An example of a diary study is described in box L:

Box L: Reason (1979)

Procedure: A sample of 35 participants kept diaries of their action slips over a period of two weeks. Over 400 action slips were reported, which were sorted according to five categories.

Results: The five categories were:

1. **storage failures** (40%). Intentions and actions are forgotten or misremembered, e.g. going into the kitchen to make a cup of tea and then not remembering why you went there.

2. **test failures** (20%). A planned sequence of behaviour is not sufficiently monitored at crucial points, e.g. going to get the car out, but putting on gardening clothes on the way to the garage.

3. **subroutine failures** (18%). Failure to carry out an action sequence, by leaving out, repeating or reordering the sequence, e.g. trying to take off your glasses when they have already been taken off.

4. **discrimination failures** (11%). Mistaking one object for another, e.g. trying to shave with toothpaste.

5. **programme assembly failures** (5%). Combining actions inappropriately, e.g. unwrapping a sweet, putting the paper in your mouth and throwing the sweet in the bin.

(The percentages of the whole sample in each category are given in brackets – the other six per cent were unclassifiable.)

Conclusion: There are different kinds of behaviour which demonstrate absent-mindedness. These can occur at any stage in a planned sequence of behaviour. Storage failures are the most frequent.

Activity 13: action slips

Think back over the last couple of weeks. Can you think of any examples of your own behaviour, or your observations of the behaviour of other people, which show absent-mindedness? If you are working in a group, pool your examples with those from the rest of the group. See if you can fit them into the behaviour categories used in the study in box L.

This activity is a variant of a diary study. How might diary studies be criticised as a way of finding out how often action slips are made? Why might they be an unreliable way of finding out the frequency of the different kinds of slips, relative to each other? What are their limitations?

When you have finished, see the notes on page 380.

Because of problems with diary studies, some theorists have carried out laboratory research in this area. One technique is to observe action slips which come about because a misleading context has been produced. Try this yourself in activity 14:

Activity 14: action slips in a misleading context

For this activity, you will need a participant. Tell them that you are going to ask them a series of questions, which they are to answer as quickly as possible (but don't read the answers):

What do we call the tree that grows from acorns?
(oak)
What do we call a funny story?   (joke)
What sound does a frog make?   (croak)
What is Pepsi's main competitor?   (Coke)
What is another word for 'cape'?   (cloak)
What do you call the white of an egg? (albumen)
You can probably think of other examples yourself!

In his discussion of this study, Reason (1992) reported that 85% of participants answered 'yolk' to the final question, compared to only 5% who were asked this one question alone.

Activity 15: laboratory research into action slips

What criticisms could be made of studying action slips under laboratory conditions? Why is this kind of study of absent-mindedness particularly open to criticism?

When you have finished, see the notes on page 381.

- **The term action slips** refers to absent-minded behaviour. There are several different kinds of slips.
- The method of **diary studies** has been used, but its limitations have led to laboratory-based research.
- **Laboratory studies** can be criticised for their low ecological validity. This is a particular problem given the nature of action slips.

Theories of action slips

Most theorists, e.g. Reason (1992), relate action slips to the automatic/attentional distinction which was discussed in the section on divided attention. You might find it useful to look back to box J at this point to remind yourself of the difference, as well as the advantages and drawbacks of each kind of processing.

There are assumed to be two possible modes of control in carrying out a task. The **automatic** mode is controlled by **schemas**, or organised action plans (schemas were discussed in more detail in chapter 2 on **memory**). The **conscious control** mode uses attentional processing.

When we use the automatic mode, conscious control is only necessary when we switch from one practised routine to another. Failure to switch into attentional mode means that an inappropriate schema can be activated or allowed to run on.

Let us take as an example a very common kind of action slip, where an action is repeated unnecessarily, e.g. going to switch on a light that you have just switched on, or looking for your glasses when you have just put them on. These well-practised actions take place in automatic mode, but failure to switch out of the appropriate schema once the action is completed means that the action is repeated.

These basic principles have been elaborated by Norman (1981) and Sellen and Norman (1992) in **schema theory**. They suggest that we have hierarchically organised schemas which bring about our actions. At the highest level is the schema related to **intention**, e.g. going to work, and at lower levels schemas of the **actions** necessary to carry out the intention (making sure that you have with you what you need, getting in the car, driving to work, and so on). A schema is translated into action when its level of activation is high (you are motivated to go to work) and when the situation triggers off action (e.g. you get to the car).

This model suggests several reasons for action slips. Firstly, there could possibly be an **error in forming the original intention**, e.g. intending to go to work on a Sunday. Secondly, there could be **errors in the activation of appropriate schemas**; the wrong schema could be activated (e.g. going through the kitchen on the way to the garage could trigger off coffee-making behaviour), or an appropriate schema could lose its activation (e.g. not driving off to work once you are in the car). Finally, there could be **errors in the triggering of active schemas**, so that an action is triggered by the wrong schema (e.g. putting on gardening clothes instead of work clothes).

One of the positive points of this theory is that it seeks to explain action slips within the general framework of attention theory, rather than seeing them as special events which need to be explained in their own terms. However, there is something of a problem in its reliance on the distinction between automatic and conscious modes of control to explain such slips. As we have seen, a clear-cut distinction is rather an oversimplification. In addition, it assumes that there is a unitary attentional system, and as we have seen, this too has been challenged by modular and synthesis models.

The theory predicts that action slips are most likely to occur with highly practised tasks, carried out automatically, and this is usually the case. On the other hand, take as an example a forestry worker who routinely uses a chainsaw. For him this will be a highly practised activity, but because it is potentially lethal, the automatic mode of control is not likely to be used. Theories of action slips are not yet in a position to accommodate this kind of phenomenon.

❺ The distinction between **automatic and attentional processing** is helpful in explaining action slips.

▷ Activity 16: a schema hierarchy

Think of an activity you intend to carry out today, e.g. washing your hair. Construct a schema hierarchy, with the intention at the top, and the series of actions required to carry it out on the lower level.

What kinds of action slips would be possible here? How would they be explained by schema theory? Try to relate your explanations to the kinds of errors described above, and Reason's five categories (box L).

A hierarchically-organised schema

❺ **Schema theory** builds on this distinction. Intentions and actions are related hierarchically. Action slips are related to problems in the activation of schemas.

❺ Schema theory looks at action slips within the general framework of attention theory. Some of the assumptions it makes about the nature of attention are questionable. There are still phenomena which it can not easily explain.

14.4 PATTERN RECOGNITION

One of the most important features of visual perception is our ability to identify objects despite variations in the image they produce. A simple example is letter recognition:

Figure 7: letter recognition

While there are differences in the way these letters are presented, each one is easily identified as a capital E.

There are several theories which explain how this kind of identification is possible. One major distinction in these theories is the relative importance given to bottom-up and top-down processing. Some psychologists emphasise the importance in explaining perception of starting with the analysis of sensory inputs, i.e. sensory data. This information is then transmitted to higher levels of analysis, so that sensory information builds up to a mental representation. This is known as **bottom-up** processing, or **data-driven** processing, since perception is driven by sensory data.

Other theorists, in contrast, claim that sensory information is not enough to explain perception, since it is fragmentary and may be ambiguous. They emphasise the importance of stored knowledge in processing sensory information. This is called **top-down** (or **context-driven**) processing, since knowledge and expectations work downwards to influence how we interpret sensory inputs.

Bottom-up theories

Several theories have taken a bottom-up approach in explaining object recognition. In this section, we will look at some of them, together with the evidence on which they are based.

Template matching hypothesis

The **template matching hypothesis (TMH)** suggests that stored in long-term memory we have tiny copies (or **templates**) of patterns we have seen in the past. We compare visual input with these templates in order to identify them. This theory sees processing as being essentially bottom-up.

▷ **Activity 17: evaluating the TMH**

Can you think of any problems with this idea? When you have finished, see the notes on page 381.

To try to overcome the problem of the huge number of templates required by the TMH, Biederman (1987) has proposed the **geon theory of pattern recognition** ('geon' is short for *geo*metrical ic*on*). He suggested that all shapes could be made up of combinations of as few as 36 geons. Figure 8 shows some of the geons and possible combinations to represent objects:

Figure 8: geons in combination

Prototype theories

Prototype theories are an alternative to the TMH. It is possible that instead of storing a huge number of templates, we store prototypes instead. Prototypes are defined by Eysenck (1993) as 'abstract forms representing the basic elements of a set of stimuli'. One problem here is that, like the TMH, a very large number of prototypes would be necessary. Identifying what would be the prototype or 'best' representation of a particular stimulus is also problematic. In addition, this kind of theory does not take into account the effect of context on perception, as we shall see.

Feature detection theories

Feature detection theories are a major approach in this area. The suggestion here is that the perception of objects is built up from the detection of their elementary features, so it is a bottom-up approach. Perhaps the best known model is Selfridge's (1959) **pandemonium model.** This proposes that we have detector cells (called **demons** in Selfridge's theory) which are sensitive to particular elements of visual input. The detection of an element contributes to the final identification of the object. Lindsey and Norman (1972) have applied this model to letter recognition:

The response of the demons to elements of the retinal image is shown here by the lines leading from one column of demons to the next. This can be thought of as a shriek (hence 'pandemonium'). The strength of the shriek relates to the weighting given to each figure. If the feature is definitely present, the demon will shout loudly (indicated by a heavy black arrow), while if the evidence is not so strong, it will shout less loudly (shown by a thin arrow), and if the feature is not present it will not shout at all.

There is some evidence to support this general idea. It relates well to what we know about neural processes in the visual system which is organised as a hierarchy. Each layer of cells responds to the firing of lower levels of cells. This is described in more detail at the start of chapter 15.

Supporting evidence comes from a classic study described in box M:

Box M: Hubel and Wiesel (1959)

Procedure: A microelectrode was implanted in a single cell of the visual cortex of an anaesthetised cat. The background electrical activity of the cell was recorded to form a baseline against which any change could be

Figure 9: Selfridge's (1959) pandemonium model

image demon

line demons

angle demons

pattern demons

decision demon

measured. A screen was placed in front of the cat on to which a pinpoint of light could be projected. The cat's head was fixed so that there was a one-to-one correspondence between the screen and the cat's retina. Changes in the firing rate of the cell when the light was moved around the screen were measured using an oscilloscope.

Results: Each cell in the visual cortex fired in response to light stimulation on some areas of the retina, while firing was inhibited in other areas. Complex patterns of light stimulation were necessary to increase or decrease firing activity. The receptive fields were often a slit-like shape.

Conclusion: Cortical cells respond to bars of light falling on specific parts of the retina. The patterns of light which excite or inhibit these **feature detection cells** provide information corresponding to edges between slit-shaped areas of light and dark. This would help to indicate boundaries of objects in the environment and so facilitate object recognition.

Feature detection theory is also supported by **visual search** studies, originally carried out in a series of experiments by Neisser (1963). In a visual search task, participants are asked to scan a display and pick out target items from among background items. Try the method for yourself in activity 18:

Activity 18: visual search

You will need to find a participant to carry out this activity. Ask your participant to scan through each of these sets of letters in turn, starting from the top and working down. In each set, they should tap the table when they have found the letter G. Use a stopwatch to time how long it takes for each set. It is a good idea to cover the sets of letters. Expose the one to be scanned as you instruct your participant to start, and at the same time start your stopwatch.

CUPOJR	VATILM	BROPPD	XVTELZ
OCQSQJ	YZMXYT	QDOCSQ	XHZKYL
CDOQRC	XKHNXY	DUPQOB	FEAYXZ
BUOPRS	FELKNH	DROBRP	VNEAWX
CUPOJR	VATILM	BROPPD	XVTELZ
OCQSQJ	YZMXYT	QDOCSQ	XHZKYL
BRUGUP	VXNMTA	PORDOC	VTGYXN
BUPOCP	NIYXML	BSROPU	XILKET
CDOQRC	XKHNXY	DUPQOB	FEAYXZ
BOUSRQ	VEAGIK	RSGUPR	FTELIH
CUPOJR	VATILM	BROPPD	XVTELZ
BUOPRS	FELKNH	DROBRP	VNEAWX

Add together the search times for the first and third sets, and for the second and fourth sets. Which were faster, and why?

When you have finished, see the notes on page 381.

The G was in the seventh row of the first and fourth sets of letters, and in the tenth row of the second and third sets, to make a fair comparison between sets 1 and 3 and sets 2 and 4 possible.

Neisser (1963) found that when participants were asked to find target letters from a display of letters, this was easier when the distractor items were different in shape from the target letters than when they were similar. It is likely that your participants identified the G faster in sets 2 and 4. The difference here is in the shape of the background letters. G is a curved letter, and the background letters (known as **distractor items**) for sets 1 and 3 are other curved letters, whereas the background letters of sets 2 and 4 are all angular.

In this task, presumably every non-target letter must be compared with a representation of the target stored in the memory, before it can be rejected. If non-target items are fully recognised, there is no reason why the nature of the distractor items should make a difference to search time. The relative speed of picking out the G from the angular background letters suggests that analysis is only partial. Features of each non-target item are analysed, but analysis only needs to be sufficient to establish that the item is not a target.

The top-down approach

There are some problems with feature detection theories, and with a strictly bottom-up approach in general. Some aspects of object recognition are best explained in top-down terms. For example, we do not need every bit of information in order to perceive an object; often there is quite a lot of redundancy in the retinal image, and we can predict what the object is from fairly sketchy information.

This is supported by point light studies:

Box N: Johansen (1975)

Procedure: Participants were shown films of actors wearing black clothes against a black background, so that they were completely invisible except for lights attached to their joints.

Results: Participants could identify the actors' movements, posture and gender, and could even recognise friends filmed under these conditions.

Conclusion: By focusing on the whole display, very limited sensory input was organised in such a way as to provide a lot of perceptual information.

A further problem with bottom-up theories is that they fail to take into account the effect of context. A lot of research has shown that object recognition can be strongly affected by the context in which the object is seen:

Box O: Palmer (1975)

Procedure: Participants were asked to identify objects from briefly presented line drawings. On some trials, they were shown a picture of a scene (e.g. a garden). The drawing which followed was either relevant to the scene (e.g. a wheelbarrow) or inappropriate (e.g. a skull). This technique is called semantic priming. A control group was not shown a scene.

Results: Accuracy of identification of objects was highest when the drawing followed an appropriate scene and lowest when it followed an inappropriate scene. The 'no scene' condition fell in between.

Conclusion: The context provided by the scene facilitated or inhibited object recognition.

Although many psychologists favour either top-down or bottom-up processing, neither approach alone, if taken to extremes, can provide a full explanation. Bottom-up processing cannot account for rapidly and accurately perceiving objects where little or ambiguous sensory information is available. Top-down processing alone cannot account for our ability to handle totally new objects or situations. Neisser's **cyclic theory** (1976), described in more detail in chapter 15, integrates these two approaches, and so may give a clearer picture of how object recognition takes place.

- Theories of pattern recognition differ in their emphasis on processing as **bottom-up** or **top-down**.
- The **template matching hypothesis (TMH)** and **prototype theories** are two bottom-up explanations of how pattern recognition takes place. There are problems with both these accounts.
- **Feature detection theories** also take a bottom-up approach. They suggest that perception of objects is built up by detection of their individual features. There is some empirical support for this idea, but there are also some aspects of perception which it does not account for.
- A top-down approach recognises that pattern recognition can take place when there is very little information, and is affected by the **context** within which perception takes place.
- Neisser's **cyclic theory** brings together bottom-up and top-down elements in pattern recognition.

Face recognition

We will turn now to a specific kind of object recognition, the ability to recognise faces that we have seen before. You will remember from the section on face recognition at the end of chapter 2 that people are highly skilled at recognising a familiar face, even when they haven't seen the face for a number of years. When we fully recognise a face, we also recall other information about the person, including their name. For example, when we see a friend, we may remember that his name is Andy, that he works for an insurance company and that he enjoys wind-surfing. Any theory of face recognition must therefore also include our ability to put a name to a face and to remember personal details.

Different areas of the brain are involved in the different aspects of face recognition. Regions of the temporal lobes of the cortex specialise in face recognition. In extreme cases, damage to this area leads to **prosopagnosia**, the loss of ability to recognise familiar faces, discussed in the last section of chapter 2.

Information is also relayed to a subcortical area of the brain called the **limbic system**. It is here that emotional responses to familiar faces are generated. Where this pathway is damaged or underactive, the result may be **Capgras syndrome**. For Capgras patients, people they know look the same as usual, but something does not feel right emotionally when they see them. They may deal with this mismatch between appearance and feelings with the belief that those close to them have been replaced by imposters or even taken over by aliens. Blount (1986) refers to the case of a man who was so sure that his father had been abducted and replaced by a humanoid robot that he slit his father's throat to look for the wires which made him work.

Prosopagnosia and Capgras syndrome are extreme examples of what happens when the face recognition systems malfunction. What happens when part of this process fails in less extreme cases is also interesting, in that it can help us to understand the normal processes which take place when we recognise a familiar face:

Box P: Young *et al.* (1985)

Procedure: A sample of volunteers was asked to keep a diary of any errors they made in person recognition.
Results: 1008 incidents were recorded, four-fifths of which fell into four main categories. The number in each category is shown in brackets:

a *failure to recognise a familiar person* (114). This typically happened when the appearance of the person had changed, for example if they had grown a beard or lost weight.

b *misidentifying one person as another* (314). People thought they recognised a stranger; this was likely to happen in poor viewing conditions.

c *recognising a person but not being able to place them or remember their name* (233). This was most likely to happen if the person was an acquaintance seen in an unfamiliar context, for example a familiar shop assistant seen in a restaurant.

d *inability to remember someone's name* (190). Even though the name could not be recalled, some personal details were recalled, such as the person's job or where they were usually seen.

Conclusion: There are at least three separate systems involved in successful face recognition. Stored representations of familiar faces are held in a **face recognition** system. A **semantic** system includes general knowledge about people you know. The third system stores **names**.

▶ Activity 19: systems in face recognition

For each type of error described in box P, identify which of the three systems contains a failure. What do these errors suggest about the order in which the different aspects of face recognition take place?
When you have finished, see the notes on page 381.

On the basis of this and other research into face recognition, Bruce and Young (1986) proposed the model of face recognition shown in figure 10:

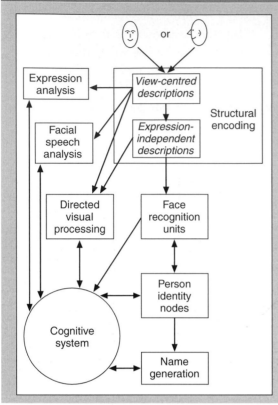

Figure 10: Bruce and Young's model of face recognition (1986)

In figure 10, each box represents a separate processing mechanism or store, with arrows indicating the flow of information between them. Working down the right-hand side of the model, information is first encoded. This information is **expression-independent**, firstly because we recognise faces irrespective of their expression, and also because there is clinical evidence that faces and emotional expression are processed separately. Some patients with neurological damage can recognise faces but not emotions, while others can recognise emotions but not faces.

This structural encoding stimulates the **face recognition units (FRUs)**. The closer the correspondence between the face which is seen and information stored in a FRU, the stronger the activation will be. The FRUs are linked to both the cognitive system and to **person identity nodes (PINs)**. Face recognition makes available other information about the person from which

identification can be made, such as their job or their hobbies. Information from the cognitive system to the PIN is included because we may often recognise someone using information other than their face, e.g. the sound of their voice or the way they walk. The PIN is the point at which recognising a person can be said to have taken place. After this, **name generation** can occur.

The directed visual processing unit is included because we can choose to focus on certain aspects of a face. For example, if we are meeting a friend in a crowded bar we may scan for someone with their style and colour of hair. The facial speech analysis unit is included because there is clinical evidence that lip reading is a separate ability from face recognition, as some patients with brain damage can read lips but not recognise faces, while others can recognise faces but not lipread.

▶ Activity 20: errors in face recognition

Look back to the kinds of errors described in box P. How would the Bruce and Young model explain these kinds of errors?

When you have finished, see the notes on page 381.

Burton *et al.* (1990) have used the Bruce and Young model to develop a model (see figure 11) which can be simulated by a computer program:

Like the Bruce and Young model, this model has three separate groups of interlinked units: one for FRUs, one for PINs, and one for semantic information. However, unlike the Bruce and Young model, semantic information is linked to PINs but not to FRUs. In this model, recognition occurs when activation in the relevant PIN reaches a given threshold. This excitation is then transmitted to other linked parts of the system.

The Burton *et al.* model has been very successful in simulating findings in face recognition research, such as the effects of **semantic priming**, discussed earlier. Bruce and Valentine (1988) asked people to identify whether a face was familiar. They found that people recognised a familiar face more quickly if they had been primed by being previously shown another familiar associated face, rather than a

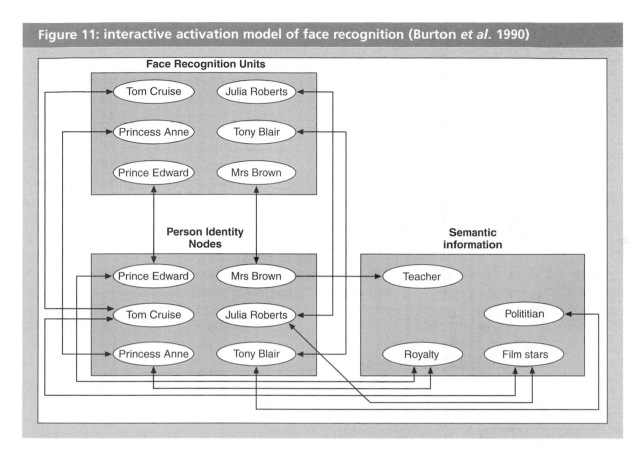

Figure 11: interactive activation model of face recognition (Burton *et al*. 1990)

familiar but unassociated face. For example, Bill Clinton's face would be recognised more quickly as familiar after seeing Hillary Clinton's face, compared with seeing Julia Roberts' face. The Burton *et al*. model can simulate this priming effect by producing easier recognition when an associated face follows seeing a particular face than when the second face is unconnected with the first.

It can also simulate the **distinctiveness effect**, the finding that distinctive faces are more quickly recognised than more typical faces (e.g. Valentine and Ferrara, 1991). The model assumes that distinctive faces share fewer features than more typical faces, and this difference in the number of shared features was included in the computer model. When the model was run, the PINs for distinctive FRUs were more quickly and more strongly activated than those for more typical faces.

Unlike the Bruce and Young model, Burton *et al*. suggested that it is not necessary to assume that there is a separate name store. Burton and Bruce

(1992) pointed out that unlike most semantic information about a person, their name is connected to only one PIN. For example, knowing that a particular person has a daughter is information which is likely also to apply to other known people, whereas someone's name is likely to be a unique link between the name and the PIN. When the computer model was run, it was found that names received the least activation of all the semantic information units, which could account for the difficulty people have in recalling them.

- The Bruce and Young model of face recognition proposes different modules in face recognition: **FRUs**, **PINs** and **name generation**.
- Burton *et al*. have developed this model using **computer simulation**. Their model can account for a range of findings in face recognition research. It also suggests that a separate name generation module is not necessary.

379

Notes on activities

2 Something that almost always catches our attention is someone saying our own name: we seem to be very keen to know if anyone is talking about us. Attention switching can also happen with other topics which we find interesting. For example, if you're a Spurs fan, the words 'Tottenham' or 'White Hart Lane', or the name of one of the players, are all likely to catch your attention.

3 Because they relate to possibly dangerous situations, 'fire' and 'help' are likely to have a permanently low threshold for everyone. 'Kennel' would be likely to be picked up by someone interested in dogs, perhaps a dog breeder, and 'Olympics' by a sports enthusiast. Mothers often automatically respond to 'mummy' from other people's children long after their own have left home. And of course Egyptologists might too!

If you are taking your driving test, words like 'driving instructor', 'Highway Code' and 'pass' have a temporarily lowered threshold. Once the test is over and done with, they will soon lose their significance and be no more likely to be picked up on an attenuated channel than thousands of other words. Similarly, if you are going on holiday, the threshold for words like 'airport', 'passport' or the name of the place you are visiting is likely to be lowered temporarily.

4 Statements **a** and **b** refer to both theories, while **c** refers only to Broadbent's model, and **d** and **e** only to Treisman's model.

5 Sarah is unconsciously aware of the traffic outside. She might find her attention switching if she hears a car pulling up in front of the house. Malik is hungry, and is aware at an unconscious level that his father is cooking. It is likely that his attention will switch from saving goals when the smell of cooked food drifts towards him. What Sarah and Malik are unconsciously aware of – the sound of a car stopping and the smell of food – have become pertinent, i.e. more relevant than what they are consciously attending to.

7 **1**, **4** and **5** need relatively automatic processing; **2**, **3** and **6** require much more focused attention.

10 Based on enduring dispositions, Peter is likely to attend to the London Marathon report, or the athletics meeting, while for Tonya the drama workshop is likely to be more relevant. Momentary intentions could make Peter switch his attention to the report from the Cannes film festival, particularly if the film he is planning to see is mentioned. The words 'drive', 'car' and so on could be enough to make Tonya's attention switch to the Grand Prix.

11 One of the features of automatic processing is that it relates to tasks which are well-practised. Reading, knitting and so on only become automatic after considerable practice, i.e. when we have developed appropriate skills.

12 There are several possibilities here. For example, you may have suggested that this would be a useful skill for primary school teachers, or mothers with several very young children. It could be that because their attentional skills have developed through practice, these people would be quite competent at dichotic listening tasks.

13 You may have found it hard to fit some of your examples neatly into one of the categories Reason uses. In addition, it is possible that two action slips may on the surface seem very similar, but have rather different causes. An example is given by Grudin (1983), who looked at typing errors which involved hitting the key next to the correct one. Sometimes this came about through using the correct finger on the wrong key, and sometimes by hitting the wrong key with the finger which normally uses it. Though the *outcome* is the same in both cases, the *causes* are different. Diary studies can only describe action slips; they tell us nothing about the underlying processes which cause them.

Just counting the number of times different kinds of action slips occur gives very limited information. Firstly, this method only tells us how often people *detect* action slips. This may not be a good reflection of how often they actually occur. Counting is also only meaningful if we know how often each kind of slip *might* have occurred, but didn't. For example, it is possible that storage failures form such a large proportion of recorded slips because there are more opportunities for this kind of slip to happen.

15   As with many studies carried out in this way, there is the problem of ecological validity. We cannot assume that conclusions drawn from the results of laboratory research necessarily apply to naturally occurring behaviour. This is a particular problem in this case because these kinds of slips normally occur in familiar surroundings, and when both the intended action and the wrong action are well practised and automatic. In a laboratory study, these conditions are extremely unlikely to apply. Participants are often asked to carry out unfamiliar activities, in unfamiliar surroundings. They are likely to be motivated to carry out the task well, and so will be consciously attending to what they are asked to do.

17   The first problem is storage. It would need an unfeasibly large amount of space to store all the possible variations of all the objects we have seen. Even if this were possible, it would need an extremely long search time to find one matching template among so many, whereas recognition is instantaneous. Finally, we are able to identify variations which we have never seen before. For example, you were able to identify all the items in figure 7 as Es, even if one of the fonts was unfamiliar to you.

18   You are likely to have found that the G was found more quickly in the second and fourth sets, where the background letters (distractor items) were angular, than in the first and third sets where the background letters were curved. The kind of analysis which seems to be taking place here would fit well with Broadbent's ideas. You will remember that he suggested that we select inputs on the basis of their physical characteristics, and here the angularity or curved shape of the letters is the criterion. As in Broadbent's theory, meaning does not seem to be important. Neisser found that many of his participants were unaware of the nature of the distractor items, which again suggests that meaning has no part in the selection process.

19   **a** and **b** show a failure in the face recognition system. **c** shows a failure in the semantic system, while **d** shows a failure in the name system. The errors in groups **a** and **d** suggest that face recognition comes first, while the errors in **c** and **d** suggest that the semantic system is activated before the name system.

20   **a** The change in someone's appearance would mean that there was not sufficient stimulation of a FRU for the face to be recognised.

b The similarity of the face which is seen and a familiar face is sufficient to activate wrongly a FRU.

c The relevant FRU has been activated, but the stimulation has not been strong enough to activate the cognitive system or the PIN and so retrieve more information about the person.

d There is a problem at the final stage between the PIN and the name generation system.

15

Perceptual processes and development

In this chapter we will be looking at:

15.1 What is perception?

15.2 The visual system
　　Structure of the visual system
　　Visual processing in the cortex
　　Colour vision and colour constancy

15.3 Perceptual organisation
　　Depth perception
　　Perception of movement
　　Constancies
　　Visual illusions

15.4 Theories of visual perception
　　Gregory's constructivist theory
　　Gibson's theory of direct perception
　　Neisser's cyclic theory

15.5 Perceptual development
　　The perceptual abilities of neonates
　　Cross-cultural research

15.1 WHAT IS PERCEPTION?

At first sight, perception does not seem problematical; we become aware of information which reaches the sense organs – eyes, ears, tongue and so on. It seems to be such a simple and automatic process that we take it for granted. However, we need to make a distinction between sensation and perception. Detecting sensory information through the sense organs is called **sensation**, while **perception** involves making sense of that information by interpreting and organising it. Roth (1986) defined perception as: 'the means by which information acquired from the environment via the sense organs is transformed into experiences of objects, events, sounds, tastes, etc.'.

To illustrate this distinction, try activity 1:

◗ Activity 1: what do you see?

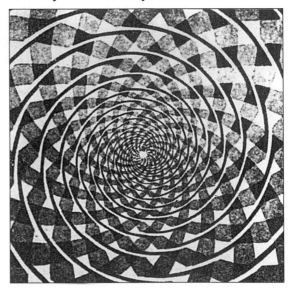

When you have finished, see the notes on page 411.

While perception relates to all the senses, we will be focusing in this chapter on visual perception. This is the dominant sense in human beings, and far more is known about it than about the other senses.

> ❺ **Sensation** refers to information reaching the sense organs. **Perception** refers to interpreting and organising this information, and thus making sense of the external world.

15.2 THE VISUAL SYSTEM

Structure of the visual system

The eye

The eye is the sense organ responsible for receiving visual information and translating it into electrical impulses so that the brain can process, interpret and respond to it. This information comes to the eye in the form of light energy or waves. The wavelength of the light energy to which the human eye responds is between 380 and 760 nanometers (a nanometer is one billionth of a metre). Infrared, ultraviolet and X-rays are all outside this range, but some animals are sensitive to them. This is discussed in the section on animal navigation in chapter 21.

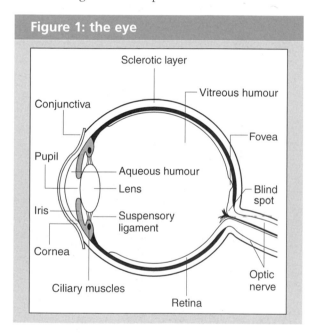

Figure 1: the eye

Sclerotic layer
Vitreous humour
Conjunctiva
Fovea
Pupil
Aqueous humour
Lens
Blind spot
Iris
Suspensory ligament
Cornea
Optic nerve
Ciliary muscles
Retina

The outer layer of the eye is a thin transparent membrane called the **conjunctiva**, which the light waves pass through first of all. They then reach the **cornea**, a slightly curved transparent membrane, which protects the lens, and which bends the light rays towards the centre of the eye. This bending process is assisted by the **aqueous humour**, the fluid in the **anterior chamber** between the cornea and the lens.

The light then passes through the **pupil**, an adjustable opening in a band of muscle called the **iris**, the coloured part of the eye. The iris is held in place by the **suspensory ligaments**. The size of the pupil can be adjusted to let more or less light through. This is an automatic process, and not under our conscious control. When light is dim, the pupil dilates to let more light in; when it is bright, the pupil contracts to shut out some of the light. The iris has tiny sets of muscles which dilate and contract the pupil; the **ciliary muscles** also regulate pupil size.

The light then reaches the **lens**, just behind the iris. The lens is a transparent oval structure which focuses the light on the **retina** at the back of the eye, producing an upside-down image. The shape of the lens can be altered by muscles pulling on it at each end – a process known as **accommodation** – so that it can focus light rays from both close and distant objects on to the retina. When we focus on objects which are close to us, the ciliary muscles contract, and the lens thickens and becomes more curved. When we focus on things which are further away, the ciliary muscles relax and the lens becomes flatter.

Behind the lens is the **posterior chamber**, filled with **vitreous humour**. Both aqueous humour and vitreous humour give the eyeball its shape, and help to keep it firm.

It is at the retina that coding takes place, i.e. the light waves are translated into electrical messages.

The retina is the innermost layer of the eyeball, and consists of five layers of cells. Receptors called rods and cones are located in the **sclerotic** layer, at the very back of the retina. The **rods** are sensitive to changes in light intensity (light and dark), and allow us to see when the light is dim. They are located mainly towards the edges of the retina, and contain a chemical called **rhodopsin**, which is bleached by light and triggers a nerve impulse. If we go from a brightly-lit place into a dark room, we cannot see very well at first, but our eyes soon adapt to the dark. This is the result of rhodopsin in the rods having been bleached by the light, making the rods insensitive. The rhodopsin is regenerated by the rods after a little while, and they become sensitive again.

The **cones**, on the other hand, are responsible for colour vision, vision in bright light, and vision of fine detail. They are less sensitive than rods, and there are fewer of them. They are mainly located in the centre of the retina around an area called the

fovea, which is where we can focus most clearly. There are no rods in the fovea.

To reach these receptors, light must pass through the other four layers, which include **horizontal cells**, **bipolar cells** (in the **choroid** layer), **amacrine cells** and **retinal ganglion cells**. The electrical charge generated by the receptors then passes back through the layers to the front of the retina, where nerve fibres join to form the **optic nerve**. This leaves the eye, creating a **blind spot** where it does so, and carries impulses to the brain. However, the brain copes with this gap in the visual image by a process loosely referred to as 'filling in'.

Figure 2: the retina

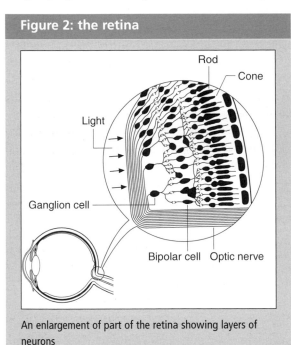

An enlargement of part of the retina showing layers of neurons

▷ Activity 2: the blind spot

Shut your right eye and look at the black dot on the right of the diagram below with your left eye. Hold the page about 18 inches away from you, and gradually move it towards you. At some point, the hatched disc on the left will fall entirely on your blind spot and disappear.

Notice that when the disc disappears, you are not aware of a hole in its place. This area is seen as being covered with the same colour as the background. This phenomenon is 'filling in'.

Now repeat the procedure with this diagram:

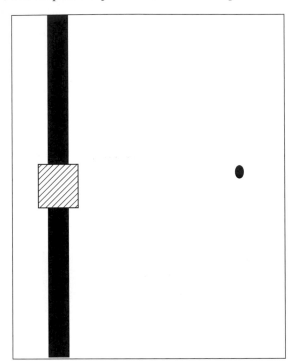

Most people find that when the hatched square on the left falls on the blind spot, the black line on the left is 'filled in' and seen as a continuous black line.

There are three types of retinal ganglion cells. They vary in terms of their **receptive field**, i.e. the region of the retina in which stimulation affects their firing rate. **On-centre** cells are more active when the centre of their receptive field is stimulated. **Off-centre** cells are more active when the edges of their receptive field are stimulated. **Transient** cells have larger receptive fields than the other two kinds of cell; they respond to movement.

▷ Activity 3: features of the eye

Match each of the terms on the left with a definition on the right:

a retina   1 A thin transparent membrane which forms the outer layer of the eye.

b fovea | **2** Receptors sensitive to light and dark.

c iris | **3** An oval disc which focuses light on the retina.

d conjunctiva | **4** A layer of nerve cells at the back of the eye which convert light waves into electrical impulses.

e sclerotic | **5** Colour-sensitive receptors.

f cornea | **6** The opening in the iris which controls the amount of light entering the eye.

g pupil | **7** A layer in the retina where the rods and cones are situated.

h lens | **8** A curved transparent disc, which bends light rays towards the centre of the eye.

i rods | **9** The area in the centre of the retina where we can focus most clearly.

j cones | **10** The coloured part of the eye perforated by the pupil.

When you have finished, see the notes on page 411.

Visual pathways

Each eye has its own optic nerve, and these meet at a point called the **optic chiasma**, where the information is divided.

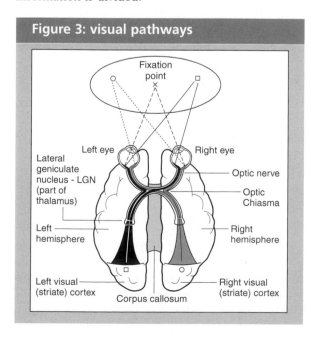

Figure 3: visual pathways

The axons within each nerve that come from the *outer* halves of each retina carry on to the cerebral hemisphere on the same side, i.e. the left side of the left eye to the left hemisphere and the right side of the right eye to the right hemisphere. Those from the *inner* half of each eye cross over, so the right side of the left eye goes to the right hemisphere, and the left side of the right eye goes to the left hemisphere. The net effect is that information from the left side of each eye, which picks up what is called the **right visual field** (i.e. information presented on the right of the point of visual fixation or what the person is looking at directly) goes to the left cerebral hemisphere, and vice versa.

These two **optic tracts** then go to the **lateral geniculate nuclei (LGN)** of a subcortical structure called the **thalamus**, and from there pass on to the primary visual (striate) cortex in the occipital lobe. This is known as the **retina–geniculate–striate system**. It contains two channels. The first, known as the **parvocellular (P) pathway**, transmits input from the cones, and is therefore sensitive to colour and fine detail. The second is the **magnocellular (M) pathway**, which transmits information from the rods, and is most sensitive to movement.

- Information reaches the eye in the form of **light energy**. When it reaches the **retina**, it is recoded as **electrical impulses**. **Rods** respond to light and dark. **Cones** respond to colour.
- The electrical charge leaves the eye via the **optic nerve**, creating a **blind spot** where it does so. Information from each eye passes via the **thalamus** to both sides of the **visual cortex**.

Visual processing in the cortex
Contrast

In order to detect objects, and features of objects, it is essential first of all for the visual system to perceive edges. Edges are perceived where there is a contrast between two adjacent areas.

Mach (1886) noted an effect called **contrast enhancement**; the difference between a light area and a dark area next to it is most noticeable where they meet. At that point, the dark area looks darker, and the light area looks lighter. These patterns of stripes are sometimes called **Mach bands**. This is the result of a process called **lateral inhibition**, in which the firing of one receptor inhibits those close to it. This will affect the firing of receptors in the middle of the bright area. However, those on the periphery, next to the receptors in the dark area, will be less inhibited, and so will fire more compared with those in the bright area. The lateral inhibition process is carried out by the retina, which can therefore be said to be a processor of information, rather than simply a copier.

Features

Hubel and Wiesel (1977) found that the primary visual area of the brain, the striate cortex, consists of three types of neurons – simple, complex and hypercomplex – which respond to different visual features.

Simple cells respond to a line of a particular orientation in a specific part of the visual field. They are inhibited from responding if the line is moved. They respond most strongly to areas where there is contrast, and therefore help to locate the edges of objects.

Complex cells are also responsive only to a particular orientation, but will continue to respond if the line is moved. They encode texture or pattern.

Hypercomplex cells respond to lines of a particular orientation anywhere in their receptive field, but if the line (or a part of it) moves outside that field, they will stop responding. These cells are probably a hybrid between simple and complex cells.

An alternative approach to feature detection is that of De Valois and De Valois (1988). They argued that cells in the visual cortex are more responsive to the spatial frequency of changes in light intensity than they are to straight lines and edges. Using fuzzy parallel bars of alternating dark and light (known as **sine-wave gratings**), they were able to obtain stronger responses from most cells in the primary visual cortex than by using lines and edges. This approach has been made use of in art, notably in op-art paintings by Bridget Riley.

Cells are organised in the visual cortex into 2500 rectangular modules, each containing approximately 150,000 neurons (Livingstone and Hubel, 1987).

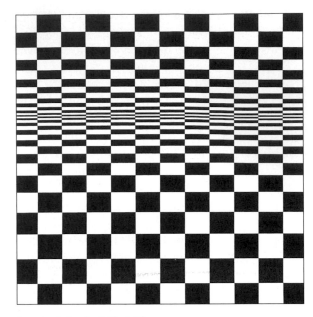

Op-art painting by Bridget Riley

Each module analyses just one part of the visual field. Half of each module receives input from the left eye and the other half receives input from the right eye. In the centre of each module is a column of neurons called a **blob**. Neurons in the blob are sensitive to colour, and those outside are sensitive to orientation or movement if they are complex cells. Yet other neurons respond to retinal disparity, i.e. the differences in input between the two eyes. Registration of these differences is important in distance perception, which we will be returning to later.

This form of organisation in the cortex may well be genetically programmed, but visual experience is necessary to develop and maintain the system. This was shown by the research of Blakemore and Cooper (1970), who restricted the visual experience of kittens and found this limited their ability to respond to visual stimuli.

Visual association area

As we have seen, the primary visual area (also known as the **striate cortex** or **V1**), consists of modules which each respond to just a part of the visual field. For object recognition to occur, this information has to be integrated, and this is the job of the visual association area (or **prestriate cortex**).

Figure 4: areas in the visual association area

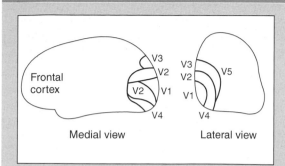

Area V1 has separate neuronal connections with areas V2, V3, V4 and V5 in the visual association area, and these areas seem to respond to different visual features (Zeki, 1978). V2 neurons respond to orientation and colour, V3 to shape, V4 to colour and V5 to movement. At this level, then, there is an intermediate analysis of these aspects of visual input separately. Using PET scans, Zeki (1992) confirmed that activity levels in these areas differ according to the task being performed.

Identification of objects, the highest level of analysis, takes place in the lower part of the temporal lobe, the inferior temporal cortex. Cells here respond better to three-dimensional objects than to two-dimensional drawings. Areas V3, V4 and V5 also send information to the parietal lobe, which is involved in spatial perception. Damage to these areas can result in **visual agnosia**.

Apperceptive visual agnosia is shown by a failure to perceive shapes, suggesting a V3 deficit, although visual acuity and perception of size and colour may be intact. **Associative visual agnosia** occurs when object perception is intact but objects cannot be named.

Damage to V4 results in **achromatopsia**, the loss of colour perception, while damage to V5 is associated with **akinetopsia**, when moving objects cannot be seen. **Chromatopsia** is a condition in which colour vision remains intact while all other aspects of visual perception are impaired.

What is known about visual information processing in the cortex fits in well with **bottom-up models** of perception such as the pandemonium model, described in chapter 14 in the section on pattern recognition where the distinction between bottom-up and top-down processing is also discussed. However, there are reasons to believe that the system is more complex, and **top-down processes** such as expectation and attention have an important part to play:

Box A: Moran and Desimone (1985)

Procedure: In an experiment on monkeys, recordings were taken from single cells in area V4 (colour). The monkeys were trained to watch a computer screen for coloured bars and make a response if the bar shown in a particular spot matched a target for colour. In a second condition, another set of bars flashed alongside the target bar as a distractor.

Results: In the first condition, the V4 cells fired as expected when the monkeys were exposed to a bar of the particular colour they were tuned in to. However, in the second condition, the cells failed to respond or responded only weakly if the distractor bar was presented. This was the case even when the distractor bar was in their receptive field and was the colour they were tuned to. For example, a cell tuned to green responded to a green target but not a green distractor bar.

Conclusion: Attentional demands of the task had changed the response of the cells. The system is fluid rather than fixed.

Activity 4: the visual association area

a Match each of these areas with its function:
  V1 colour
  V2 movement
  V3 orientation/colour
  V4 shape
  V5 primary visual area

b What are these disorders? With which area is each associated?
  akinetopsia
  apperceptive visual agnosia
  achromatopsia

When you have finished, see the notes on page 411.

- ❺ **Edges** are perceived where two adjacent areas meet. The contrast is heightened by **lateral inhibition**.
- ❺ Different types of neurons respond to different visual features. It may be that cells in the visual cortex are more sensitive to changes in **light intensity** than to **edges**.
- ❺ Different **modules** of cells in the visual cortex respond to different parts of the visual field. Within each module, some cells respond to **colour**, some to **orientation**, some to **movement** and some to **retinal disparity**. This organisation may be genetically programmed, but **visual experience** is necessary to maintain it.
- ❺ The **visual association area (prestriate cortex)** integrates information. Different areas deal with different kinds of information. Visual **deficits** resulting from **damage** provide information about the function of each area.
- ❺ Both **bottom-up** and **top-down** processing are important in visual information processing.

Colour vision and colour constancy

There are three major theories of how we perceive colour.

According to the Young–Helmholtz theory (Helmholtz, 1962), also known as the **trichromatic theory**, we have three different types of cone cell. Each responds to different wavelengths of light – blue, green or red. Because other colours can be made up from these, colour vision can be explained by looking at their different rates of firing. For example, yellow would be perceived when the green and red cones fire together. It is the pattern of firing rates, i.e. the ratio of blue-, green- and red-sensitive cells, which determines the colour we see.

Support for this theory comes from the finding that there are indeed different types of cone receptor which vary in sensitivity to different wavelengths of light (Dartnell *et al.*, 1983), although these are actually blue–violet, green and yellow–green. Land (1964) found that a full range of colour sensations could be produced by mixing red, green and blue light, also lending support to this theory.

However, one limitation of the theory is that it does not explain the most frequent forms of colour blindness (red/green and blue/yellow). It also fails to deal with **negative after-images**. For example, if you look at a red light and then look at a white wall, you will see a green after-image of the light.

An alternative to this is the **opponent-process theory**, put forward by Hering (1878), who suggested that there are three types of cell in the visual system, each with two modes of response. One type encodes brightness, and produces white or black. The other types encode colour, and respond either to red/green or blue/yellow. The colour produced by each cell depends on the way in which it responds, i.e. the nature of the opponent process.

There is some evidence to support this theory. Firstly, it can account for after-images. In addition, an inability to distinguish red from green is the most common form of colour blindness; people with this kind of colour blindness are sensitive only to red or to green, not both.

A two-stage theory, drawing on elements of both the trichromatic theory and opponent-process theory, seems to represent the best explanation of what actually occurs. The cones do appear to be of three types, and there are also opponent-process cells in the ganglion layer of the retina. The red/green ganglion cells signal red when they are excited, and green when inhibited. The blue/yellow ganglion cells signal yellow when excited, and blue when inhibited. Thus a red light will stimulate the red cones and excite the red/green opponent-process cells.

This theory explains the different types of colour blindness and after-images. It can also account for us not being able to see reddish greens or bluish yellows, although we can perceive reddish yellows and bluish greens. For example, in the red/green process, the neurons involved can only signal one colour at a time by being either excited or inhibited; they cannot do both.

Colour constancy

Perception of colour, like perception of other aspects of the visual stimulus, is not a simple mechanical process. This has already been demonstrated in the study by Moran and Desimone (box A). The phenomenon of colour constancy is another example.

Colour constancy is the tendency for an object to be perceived to be the same colour when viewed in different light conditions. We seem to be able to compensate for darkness, or even for coloured light shining on an object, and still make fairly accurate judgements about its colour. For example, colours still appear to be much the same when you are wearing green-tinted sunglasses.

The colour we perceive is not only determined by the wavelength composition of the light reflected from the object we are looking at. It is also influenced by **prior stimulation** of the retina (as shown by the phenomenon of negative after-images), the colour of the **surroundings**, and our **knowledge** of an object's colour; we often know what colour particular objects are likely to be. Land (1964) carried out a study which provides a good demonstration of colour constancy:

Box B: Land (1964)

Procedure: This study used a large display of around 100 pieces of matt coloured paper, which Land called a 'colour Mondrian', from the painter whose work consisted of large blocks of colour. Participants were asked to identify the colours of squares of different coloured papers, e.g. white and red. The amounts of red, green and blue light coming from each were measured. Using red, green and blue filters, the illumination of the red square was then adjusted so that the same amount of red, green and blue light came from the red paper as from the previously-tested white paper. Participants were again asked to identify the colour of the paper.

Results: Participants continued to report the red paper as 'red'.

Conclusion: The participants showed colour constancy.

Land's research showed that the colour of the surroundings is an important cue. If coloured light is shining on to an area, the colour of an object in that area will be perceived fairly accurately, i.e. colour constancy will be shown.

If, however, the coloured light is restricted to just that object, colour constancy breaks down. Zeki (1993) supports Land's findings by reporting the presence of dual-opponent colour cells. These are neurons which respond to any differences in the wavelength (i.e. colour) of light reflected by nearby surfaces.

Land (1977) went on to propose the **retinex theory** of colour constancy. The word 'retinex' is a combination of 'retina' and 'cortex', and Land used it to designate the mechanism that generates independent long-, middle- and short-wave lightness images, suggesting that the retinal–cortical structure acts as a whole. He suggested that each of these sets of receptor mechanisms generates a separate lightness image. A comparison of the three determines how colour is perceived. The formation of lightness images and the comparison between them can happen in either the retina or the cortex.

- ❺ **Trichromatic theory** explains colour vision in terms of different types of cones responsive to blue, green or red. **Opponent-process theory** suggests that each of these three types of cells has two modes of response. Colour vision is best explained by a **combination** of these two theories.
- ❺ **Colour constancy** is the tendency to see an object as being the same colour under different lighting conditions. The **retinex theory** proposed by Land explains colour constancy in terms of a comparison of different lightness images in the retinal–cortical structure.

15.3 PERCEPTUAL ORGANISATION

We will be looking in this section at a range of visual phenomena which need to be accounted for in any theory of perception: **depth perception**, the **perception of movement**, **constancy** and **visual illusions**.

Depth perception

Human beings are able to perceive the world as three-dimensional although the image received on the retina is two-dimensional. The retina of each eye receives different light energy as each eye is in a different position on the face. The brain, however, builds up the information from both eyes into a single three-dimensional perception. For this to occur, both eyes must **converge**, i.e. move to focus on an object. If this does not happen, double vision will occur:

Activity 5: double vision

Gaze steadily at an object some distance away. Press lightly on the side of one eye. You should see two objects instead of one. Why do you think this is?

Now hold your arms out, parallel and straight in front of you. Point your two middle fingers towards each other. Close one eye and try to bring your two fingers together. Now try this again with both eyes open. You probably found it much easier to do this when both eyes were open. Why do you think this is?

Compare your answers with the discussion that follows.

The 'double vision' phenomenon occurs because shifting one eye by pressing on it causes the light energy from the object you were looking at to fall on a different part of that eye's retina than of the other eye's retina. In the other exercise, the eyes cannot converge to focus on your fingers so it is difficult to line them up.

The ability to see objects in three dimensions is called **depth perception**. The cues which are used to transform two-dimensional retinal images into three-dimensional perceptions can be **binocular cues**, which require information from both retinal images together, or **monocular cues**, which are available from the information from just one retinal image.

Binocular cues

One binocular cue is **convergence**; the eyes turn inward to a greater extent for nearer objects. You become cross-eyed when your eyes converge on a really close object, such as the end of your nose. The degree of convergence provides the brain with information about distance. **Stereopsis**, the process the brain uses to put together the two retinal images into one three-dimensional perception, provides further information. This is possible because of **retinal disparity**, the difference between the images received by each eye:

Activity 6: retinal disparity

Hold your finger directly in front of your nose. Look at it with each eye in turn, keeping the other eye closed. Now hold your finger at arm's length and repeat the procedure. Note each time how much your finger appears to move, relative to what is behind it.

It will appear to move much more when it is held close to, because the difference in the retinal images is much greater than when it is held at arm's length.

Monocular cues

One monocular cue is **linear perspective**. Lines appear to converge as they get further away, e.g. railway lines stretching into the distance, which influences the perceived distance of an object. **Relative size** provides a further cue. For example, if I can see a tennis ball and a house, and they both create the same size retinal image, I can infer that the house is further away since I know that it is larger than the tennis ball. There is also **interposition**; an object which blocks the full view of another object is perceived to be in front of it.

If you look out of the window of a moving car or train, you will be aware of **motion parallax**: objects which are closer appear to move across the field of vision more quickly than distant objects. The apparent **texture** of objects becomes smoother as they become more distant; for example, the textured nature of cobblestones in a cobbled street is more apparent close to you and less so further away.

Two-dimensional objects do not usually cast **shadows**, so a shadow can be a cue that an object is three-dimensional. Finally, relative **brightness** and **colour** cues give us information about distance. Objects closer to us reflect more light to the eyes, and the colour of objects close to us is perceived as more intense. There is also a 'blue shift' when light rays travel a long distance from an object; for example, distant hills appear blue.

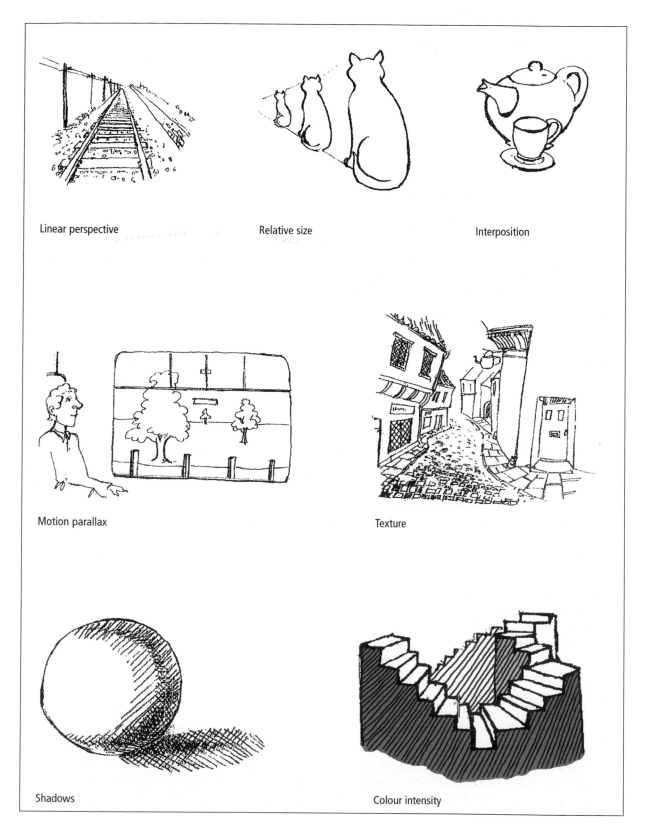

Linear perspective

Relative size

Interposition

Motion parallax

Texture

Shadows

Colour intensity

A final cue is **accommodation**. This refers to the lenses of the eyes changing shape when we focus on an object. As we saw in the previous section, they become thicker when the object is close to us and flatten when the object is further away, thus providing a muscular cue to distance.

◉ From a two-dimensional retinal image, we build up a three-dimensional perception. This ability is **depth perception**.

◉ There are a number of **binocular** and **monocular cues** which influence depth perception.

Perception of movement

The perception of movement also raises interesting questions. Sometimes rapidly changing retinal images do not register as movement. For example, when we look round a room, the succession of retinal images we receive are not perceived as movement of the furniture we are looking at. In contrast, as we watch a tennis match, we may track the movement of the ball so that its image falls on the same part of the retina, but we still perceive the ball as moving.

Similarly, we sometimes perceive movement when it is *not* there; for example, when the succession of still images we receive while watching a film are interpreted as the characters moving. This is known as **stroboscopic motion**, and is one example of **apparent movement**, i.e. the illusion of movement which is not actually happening.

Another example of apparent movement is the **phi phenomenon**: when two lights are close together, and are switched on and off alternately, they may be seen not as two separate lights but as one light moving from one location to the other and back again. You may have noticed a similar phenomenon in road signs which remind drivers of the speed limit (see figure 5); the top and bottom pairs of lights flash on and off in turn, giving the impression that the lights are moving up and down.

Figure 5: a road sign showing apparent movement

A further example is the **autokinetic effect**. In a totally dark room, a single stationary spot of light will appear to move. Gregory (1972) suggested that this is the result of tiny involuntary eye movements. It could also be something to do with the lack of any frame of reference against which the spot of light is seen.

Induced movement occurs when we perceive an object to be moving when it is actually stationary and the background is moving. Films sometimes make use of back projection to achieve this effect: people may appear to be in a moving car when in fact it is the background projected behind them which is moving.

Finally there are **motion after-effects.** For example, workers at a conveyor belt in a factory sometimes see the belt as moving backwards when it stops. While most of the other movement illusions are the result of normal perceptual strategies used inappropriately, movement after-effects are likely to have a physiological explanation. This probably works in much the same way as negative after-images, discussed earlier. The phi phenomenon has also been explained in terms of the stimulation of normal physiological mechanisms; different still images closely related in time are integrated to create the perception of movement.

⊖ There are different kinds of **apparent movement**: **stroboscopic motion**, **induced movement** and **motion after-effects**. The **phi phenomenon** and the **autokinetic effect** are also examples of apparent movement.

⊖ Some effects are the results of inappropriately applying normal perceptual strategies, while some are likely to have a physiological basis.

Constancies

We recognise objects despite variation in retinal information. For instance, we may perceive a cup from the side or from the top, close to us or further away, in bright or dim light. All these factors lead to variation in the image which reaches the retina, but the cup is still recognised as the same object. The ability to do this is known as **constancy**. We have already considered colour constancy – the tendency to perceive an object as remaining the same colour in spite of changes in lighting – in an earlier section.

Constancy is necessary if we are to cope effectively with the environment. If our perception of objects did not have this kind of stability, our perception of the environment would be extremely confused. Constancy shows how the brain uses memory, knowledge and expectation in interpreting environmental stimuli.

We see objects as having more or less constant brightness even though this changes with the level of illumination. This is **brightness constancy**. If illumination is constant, white things reflect more light than black things. However, snow in deep shadow still looks white, and coal in bright sunlight still looks black, even though the intensity of light reaching the retina is stronger in the case of the coal than the snow.

Shape constancy refers to the ability to perceive an object as remaining the same shape, as in the cup example above, in spite of changes in the angle at which we see it.

When we watch a person moving away from us, the image they form on the retina gets smaller. We don't perceive the person as actually getting smaller, though, but as someone of constant size getting further away. This is **size constancy**, and comes about as a result of taking into account distance cues, discussed in the previous section:

▶ Activity 7: size constancy

Look at the picture of these two men and note their relative size:

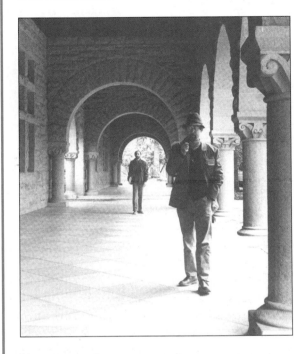

Now turn to the picture on the next page.

In the first picture, the bareheaded man is perceived as being the same size as the man in the hat although his image on the retina is smaller. The smaller picture of the man from the next page is probably much smaller than you would have expected. To maintain size constancy, the brain adjusts the image of objects which are further away; this is called **constancy scaling.** The picture of the two men on the next page shows the degree of adjustment the perceptual system is able to make.

⊖ We recognise objects in spite of changes in the angle from which they are seen. The adjustment which makes this possible is **shape constancy**. We also have **size constancy**,

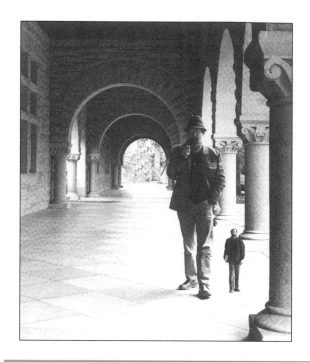

compensating for changes in the size of the retinal image. **Brightness constancy** compensates for the degree of illumination with which objects are seen.

Visual illusions

We experience an illusion when what we perceive does not correspond to the physical characteristics of what we are looking at. We started this chapter with a visual illusion to demonstrate the difference between sensation and perception. In this section, we will look at some other illusions to see what they can tell us about the nature of perception.

Gregory (1983) divided visual illusions into four categories: distortions, ambiguous figures, paradoxical figures and fictions.

Distortions are geometrical illusions. Some examples are shown in figure 6:

Figure 6: distortions (geometrical illusions)

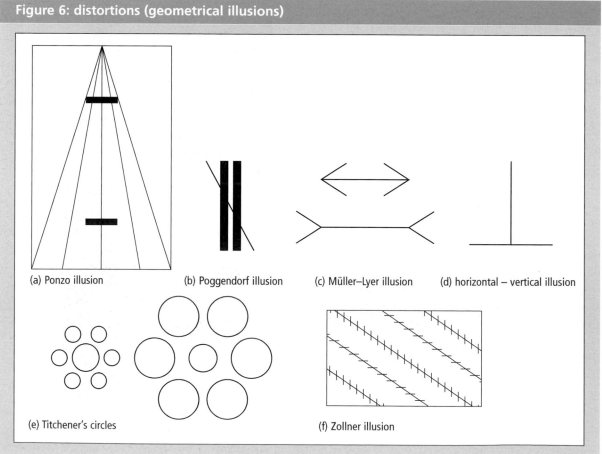

(a) Ponzo illusion   (b) Poggendorf illusion   (c) Müller–Lyer illusion   (d) horizontal – vertical illusion

(e) Titchener's circles   (f) Zollner illusion

Activity 8: exploring distortions

Look at the illusions in figure 6, then answer these questions:

a Which of the two horizontal lines appears longer?

b Does the diagonal line seem continuous or discontinuous?

c Which of the two horizontal lines appears longer?

d Which of the two lines appears longer?

e Which of the central circles seems larger?

f Do the long diagonal lines appear to be parallel? What can these illusions tell us about the nature of perception?

Figure 7 shows some examples of **ambiguous** (or **reversible**) figures:

In all these examples, the information can be interpreted in two ways. In the Necker cube, the face marked with crosses can be seen as either the front face or the back face. Boring's old woman–young woman can be seen as an old woman with a hooked nose and a pointed chin, or as a young woman with her head turned away. The third example can be seen as either a duck or a rabbit, and the final one as either a Native American or an Eskimo.

Both ways of perceiving these figures are equally valid in terms of the visual information provided. The visual system therefore has no way of deciding which is the 'correct' view, and so what is perceived tends to switch spontaneously from one possibility to the other.

Figure 7: ambiguous (reversible) figures

(a) Necker's cube

(b) Old woman or young woman

(c) Duck or rabbit

(d) Native American or Eskimo

Paradoxical figures are figures which could not actually exist:

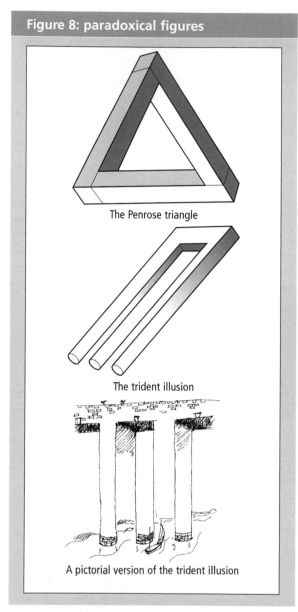

Figure 8: paradoxical figures

The Penrose triangle

The trident illusion

A pictorial version of the trident illusion

This idea has been used in the work of Escher (see figure 9), whose elaborate pictures depict scenes which are three-dimensionally impossible:

Figure 9: impossible picture by M. Escher

Fictions are illusions in which we see something that isn't actually there:

Figure 10: fictions – Kanizska's triangles and square

b.

If you focus on the crosshatching of the Penrose triangle, there is no third front face to fit with it, and this is also true if you focus on the white or the grey faces. The trident illusion has two prongs at one end but three at the other. In each case, we find it impossible to focus on the whole figure because we are automatically translating a two-dimensional picture into three dimensions, which in these cases is impossible.

In (a), you should see a white triangle, in (b) a white triangle with curved sides, and in (c) a white square. These kinds of illusion relate to our use of contours to identify shapes. In these figures, the perceptual system uses **subjective contours** rather than physical ones, which Kanizsa (1976) defined as the boundaries of a shape perceived in the absence of physical contours.

In the Kanizsa triangles, there are some physical contours where the white triangle and the discs overlap. However, these would probably not be enough to trigger closure, i.e. to lead us to perceive a complete figure, and they certainly don't account for the curves we see in (b). The white square we see in (c) can perhaps be related to interposition, discussed earlier under depth perception.

All these illusions are, of course, extremely artificial compared to real-life perceptions. However, they do relate to real-life illusions. For example, two-dimensional pictures make use of perspective cues so that they are seen in three dimensions. Illusions may still therefore help us to understand how perception works, and we shall be returning to them in the next section.

❺ **Visual illusions** fall into four categories: **distortions**, **ambiguous figures**, **paradoxical figures** and **fictions**. They give some insight into the way the perceptual system works.

15.4 THEORIES OF VISUAL PERCEPTION

There are several theories of visual perception, which vary in the relative importance given to bottom-up and top-down processing. We will look now at some of these theories, and discuss how their ideas relate to the perceptual organisation described in the previous section.

Gregory's constructivist theory

Gregory (1972) claimed that we construct our perceptions 'from floating, fragmentary scraps of data signalled to the senses and drawn from the brain memory banks, themselves constructions from the snippets of the past'.

Gregory's theory of visual perception is a **constructivist** model because it claims that we actively construct our perception of reality, drawing on our past knowledge and experience. This idea is similar to the constructivist view of memory discussed in chapter 2. What we perceive goes beyond the often incomplete sensory information received through the sense organs. We may also need to select which aspects of the visual input we attend to. Gregory suggested that we form a **perceptual hypothesis**, i.e. make a 'best bet' about what we see, and then check this hypothesis against the available data. This account of perception makes Gregory's theory a top-down model.

Some visual illusions are one source of support for these ideas. We attempt to make sense of visual illusions in the same way that we normally make sense of our visual environment, but in the case of illusions these attempts are misleading. Illusions are examples of inappropriate perceptual hypotheses which are not confirmed by the data.

Look back now to the distortions shown in figure 6. The Ponzo illusion can be explained in terms of our past experience of using depth cues provided by perspective. A similar explanation can be offered for the Müller–Lyer illusion, where the arrow heads pointing inwards suggest that the horizontal line is close to us, while the arrow heads pointing outwards suggest that the horizontal line is further away; we use size constancy scaling to make automatic adjustments to the perceived length of the horizontals.

The Zollner illusion and Titchener's circles both show the effect of context on what we perceive. Our perceptions of the diagonals in the Zollner illusion and the central circles in Titchener's circles are influenced by the context provided by the other parts of the presentation.

The figures in figure 7 provide ambiguous information. Our interpretation therefore switches between the alternatives, probably influenced by where our attention is focused.

We have problems interpreting the paradoxical figures shown in figure 8. There should be no difficulty in taking in the sensory data these figures provide, but we have trouble seeing the whole stimulus in each case because we automatically try to interpret the two-dimensional stimulus as a three-dimensional representation, which in these cases is not possible.

Finally, in the fictions shown in figure 10, the subjective contours of the white triangles and square go beyond the available information. The triangles and the square are perceived because there is enough evidence for us to assume that they exist. We do not simply take in information; we go beyond it to draw conclusions.

A further source of support for Gregory's ideas comes from constancy phenomena, already noted above in the discussion of the Müller–Lyer illusion. What we perceive does not necessarily correspond to the retinal image, since the brain makes automatic adjustments to our perception of colour, size, shape and brightness in line with our knowledge of the physical world and our past experience of it.

There is also support from cross-cultural studies, which show that depth perception needs to be learned and is therefore the result of experience. We shall be returning to this in the final section of this chapter.

The idea of **perceptual set** also supports Gregory's ideas. Set can be defined as a bias or readiness to interpret visual stimuli in a particular way. For example, a study by Bruner and Minturn (1955) found that participants were more likely to perceive the fourth item in this sequence:

$$E \ C \ D \ B \ A$$

as a B and in this sequence:

$$16 \ 15 \ 14 \ 13 \ 12$$

as 13, although they are identical. What was perceived was affected by expectation and context.

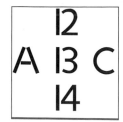

Perceptual set

While there are good sources of evidence for Gregory's ideas, there are also possible problems. To return to the Müller–Lyer illusion, Gregory's explanation in terms of misplaced size constancy has been challenged by other research. Delboeuf (Delboeuf, 1892) used variants of the illusion:

Figure 11: variants of Müller–Lyer

In spite of changing the arrows to the dumb-bells, brackets and curves shown in figure 11, the illusion was still effective. It would be hard to explain this effect in terms of misapplying depth cues. Another variant was used by Morgan (1969):

Figure 12: Morgan's variant of the Müller–Lyer

The dot here is in the middle of the horizontal line, but appears to be closer to the right-hand end. This implies that the arrow is seen as sloping away from us, which seems no more likely than that it is sloping towards us.

A more general problem is that knowledge may not lead us to modify our perceptions. For example, even when we know that the two horizontal lines of the Müller–Lyer are the same length the illusion still remains – we are not able to change our perceptual hypothesis in the light of additional information, as Gregory suggested. Simply knowing that a perception is inaccurate cannot remove the illusion. Clearly 'visual knowledge' needs to be incorporated at an unconscious level.

This inflexibility is shown even more startlingly in the Ames room illusion:

In this illusion, the figure on the left is seen as very much larger than the figure on the right. This effect is achieved by using a distorted room, shown schematically in figure 13. We come to this illusion knowing that the perceived difference in size of the people is a virtual impossibility, but the illusion is none the less effective.

Figure 13: Ames room

The Ames room

The Ames room explained

A further criticism is that visual illusions are static and two-dimensional, and are therefore very far removed from the richness of detailed information which usually reaches the visual system in real-life situations. It may therefore be unwise to generalise too freely from this source of information.

❺ Gregory's **constructivist** theory of perception takes a **top-down** approach. We form **perceptual hypotheses** which are then checked against the sensory data.

❺ Visual **illusions** can be seen as inappropriate perceptual hypotheses. They lend support to Gregory's ideas. His theory is also supported by **cross-cultural** findings that depth perception needs to be learned, and by the phenomenon of **perceptual set**.

❺ Some variants of illusions have questioned Gregory's interpretations. His theory cannot provide satisfactory answers to some perceptual phenomena.

Gibson's theory of direct perception

In contrast to Gregory's emphasis on the importance of top-down processes in perception, Gibson (1986) believed that we receive enough sensory information to allow us to perceive the environment in a direct way. There is no need for any kind of processing, since the information we receive – about size, shape, distance, movement and so on – is sufficiently detailed to enable us to interact directly with the environment.

For Gibson, sensation *is* perception. There are no intermediate stages between light falling on the retina and the response of the perceiver. No interpretation needs to take place, no hypotheses need to be formed. With its emphasis on the richness of sensory data, this theory is in tune with bottom-up theories of perception, though it is not strictly speaking a bottom-up theory, since it claims that no processing is necessary for perception to take place.

Gibson pointed out that vision is not static, but the result of people moving around in a visual environment. Because of this movement, there are continuous changes in what Gibson calls the **ambient optic array** – all the transmitted and reflected light rays from the environment – and these changes give us new information.

Gibson called his theory an **ecological approach**, since it emphasises the direct contact between the perceiver and meaningful aspects of the environment. Gibson sees perception as a necessarily adaptive process: if animals are to survive, they need to be able to respond both to relatively unchanging aspects of their environment, such as sources of water, and aspects which change, such as the presence and location of other animals.

Gibson developed his theory as a result of his experience in training pilots. During the second world war, he was asked to provide training films for pilots, and in particular to focus on the problems experienced by pilots during take-off and landing. These two manoeuvres require skill and concentration, and Gibson became interested in researching just what information pilots had available to them at these times; he called this information **optic flow patterns**:

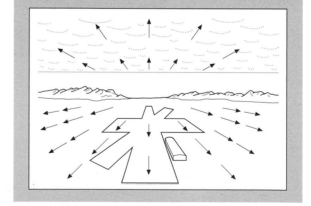

Figure 14: the optic flow patterns as a pilot approaches the landing strip

Gibson pointed out just how much information was available. The point to which the pilot is moving is invariant, i.e. static within the display, but all around that point is a moving display giving a great deal of unambiguous information about speed, direction and altitude. Gibson also pointed to the importance of texture gradients, discussed earlier in the section on depth perception, which are a rich source of information about depth and distance, without any need for analysis.

He extends the idea, that all this information is received and responded to directly, to the concept of **affordances**. Affordances refers to the function of perceived aspects of the environment, i.e. the possible uses an object affords, such as for shelter or for use as a tool. For example, a chair is perceived as something to sit on.

The main strength of Gibson's model is that it stresses an **ecological approach**; it relates to the perceptual experience of people and animals in real-life situations. He is right to point out that we spend a lot of our time in motion, producing moment-by-moment changes in the optic array which increase the richness of sensory data available to us. This approach is in stark contrast to the impoverished visual information available in the artificial setting of many traditional laboratory experiments.

There are, however, some problems with these ideas. Firstly, there are serious problems with Gibson's assertion that no processing is needed to analyse the visual world. We discussed at the start of this chapter some of the processing of visual information which takes place. To quote Hampson and Morris (1996): 'Data from a large number of sources, including neurophysiology, indicate that a large number of internal transformations, both analytic and constructive, are performed on the visual input before people are able to say that they perceive and recognise anything at all.'

In addition, the theory cannot explain illusions, which we also discussed earlier. Gibson's argument is that illusions come about as the result of deliberately ambiguous information in artificial situations, and therefore cannot tell us anything very useful about real-life perception. He has a point here, but some illusions do hold true in real life:

Activity 9: the vertical–horizontal illusion

Look back to figure 6 for this illusion. To reproduce this illusion in a real-life setting, you will need a cup, a saucer and two similar teaspoons. Put one spoon in the saucer next to the cup, and the other upright in the cup.
Which spoon looks longer? You should find that the spoon in the cup (vertical) looks longer than the one on the saucer (horizontal).

The theory also has difficulties in explaining the influence of perceptual set, mentioned earlier, and cannot explain cultural differences in perception, which we shall be looking at later in this chapter.

The links made between humans and other animals may also not be entirely appropriate in this instance. As we will see in chapter 21 in the section on animal navigation, animals appear to be preprogrammed to attend and respond to particular aspects of their environment which are relevant to this activity. A lot of human behaviour, on the other hand, is governed by higher-order processes, such as remembering and planning, between stimulus and response.

When we come to the idea of affordances, the parallel between humans and other animals seems particularly weak. Clearly we need to draw on culturally-relevant knowledge to understand that a pencil affords drawing or a washing machine affords cleaning clothes.

Gibson's theory seems to be better at explaining some aspects of perception than others. This can be related to the distinction referred to by Fodor and Pylyshyn (1981) between 'seeing' and 'seeing as'. They illustrate this with the example of a man lost at sea who sees the Pole Star. If he sees it as just another star ('seeing'), then he will be just as lost as ever, whereas if he sees it as the Pole Star ('seeing as'), it is a potential navigational aid which could help him to find his way. Gibson's theory is better at explaining 'seeing', while having little to say about 'seeing as'.

Activity 10: Gregory and Gibson

Read through these statements. For each one, decide whether it applies to Gregory's constructivist theory, Gibson's theory of direct perception or both:
a The environment provides us with a vast amount of unambiguous information.
b Illusions are a good way of helping us to understand perceptual processes.
c Perception is an active process.
d Top-down processes are important in perception.
e The environment provides the necessary information for making sense of visual stimuli.

f Visual perception is mediated by light reflected by surfaces and objects.

g Basing conclusions on illusions lacks ecological validity.

h Memory and experience are important in making sense of visual stimuli.

i A physiological system is necessary for perception.

When you have finished, see the notes on page 411.

❺ Gibson claimed that there is a vast amount of information in the **ambient optic array** as a person or animal moves round their environment. This means that perception does not need to depend on processing but is direct.

❺ **Affordances**, i.e. the function of objects in the environment, are also perceived directly, though this may be more true for animals than humans.

❺ The main strength of the theory is Gibson's **ecological approach**, but the theory is better at explaining 'seeing' than 'seeing as'. It has difficulty in explaining **visual illusions**, **perceptual set** and **cross-cultural differences** in perception.

Neisser's cyclic theory

While Gibson's theory of direct perception suggests that processing is unnecessary to perception, its emphasis on the richness of sensory data available to the perceiver is very much in line with a bottom-up approach. Gregory's constructivist model takes a much more top-down approach. One theory which attempts to combine the best of both approaches is Neisser's cyclic theory:

In Neisser's theory, top-down and bottom-up processes are used in a continuing cycle during perception. He assumes that perception starts with **schemas**, i.e. ideas and expectations of what we expect to see in a particular context. Schemas influence the way we explore our perceptual environment as we seek to confirm our expectations. We sample the information available in the environment in a preliminary analysis of the sensory cues, and on this basis we form a **perceptual model**, i.e. a mental representation of a likely object or event.

The perceptual model is then used to initiate an active search of the sensory cues in the environment. If sensory cues are found to confirm the perceptual model, there is an **elaborative effect**, i.e. details are added to the model. If not, the perceptual model will need to be revised, i.e. there is a **corrective effect**. Perception therefore involves a continuous process of checking and rechecking sensory data in line with modifications to the perceptual model we have formed.

Neisser calls his model an **analysis-by-synthesis** theory, since perception involves extracting information about aspects of the environment (analysis) and generating a perceptual model (synthesis), as a cyclical process.

A major strength of Neisser's theory is that it attempts to show that the interaction of bottom-up and top-down processing is important in perceiving the environment; we have already seen that both have a part to play. It has a lot in common with Gregory's idea of perceptual hypotheses, though in Neisser's model, the hypotheses we form are much

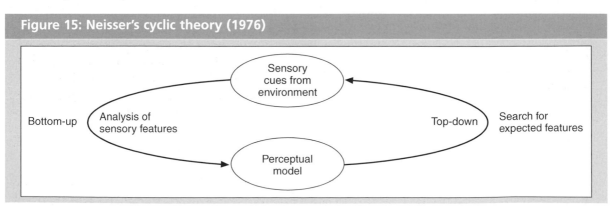

Figure 15: Neisser's cyclic theory (1976)

more general than those suggested by Gregory. Both models also see perception as an active process. Another positive point about Neisser's model is that it makes a link with attention, in that the process of checking sensory data is directed towards aspects of the environment which are relevant to the perceptual model we have formed.

However, there are some limitations to this theory. For one thing – as with the theories of Gregory and Gibson – it does not actually specify the neural mechanisms involved. The processes described by Neisser – directing, sampling and modifying – constitute a 'broad framework' (Hampson and Morris, 1996) rather than an explanation of how a perception is built up. The amount of processing which may be involved also raises the question of where exactly in the cycle perception can be said to have taken place. Does this happen when an initial hypothesis is formed, or not until the perception is fully confirmed? Finally, there are problems when it comes to trying to test this theory in a natural environment; given the cyclical nature of perception, it is difficult to see how this could be done.

Neisser's model is perhaps best seen not as an alternative theory to those of Gregory and Gibson, but as an attempt to integrate Gregory's constructivist approach and Gibson's theory of direct perception into an overall explanation of how visual perception occurs.

- In Neisser's **cyclic model**, we generate a **perceptual model** based on expectations. The model is then checked against **sensory data** and revised if necessary, in a continuing process.
- One strength of the model is that it combines **top-down** and **bottom-up** processing in an interactive model. It has been criticised, however, for being **vague**, and **descriptive** rather than explanatory.

15.5 PERCEPTUAL DEVELOPMENT

An important area of debate within perception is the extent to which the ability to perceive is innate and the extent to which it depends on learning. This is an example of the **nature–nurture debate**. In perception, this question has been explored using a range of methods.

One major area of research has looked at the abilities of very young babies to make sense of the world around them. This has been a fruitful area of research, using some very ingenious ways to test the abilities of **neonates**, i.e. newborn babies. Another way of investigating this question has been to carry out **cross-cultural research**. We will turn now to what these approaches can tell us about the nature of perception.

The perceptual abilities of neonates

Activity 11: visual perception in neonates

Do you think these statements are true or false?
- **a** For newborn babies, the visual environment is very blurred.
- **b** All aspects of adult vision are fully developed within the first year.
- **c** Babies respond to bright light from birth.
- **d** Within about the first two months of life, colour vision is at an adult level.
- **e** A lot of the development of the visual system must take place after birth.
- **f** It is many months before babies can track a moving object.

Check your answers with the information in the rest of this section.

In a famous quotation, William James (1890) described the world of the newborn infant as being one of 'blooming, buzzing confusion'. He is suggesting here that there is sensation, but no organisation of this sensation into meaningful perception. An infant's visual system is not fully developed at birth, but James may have underestimated the visual abilities of infants.

The difficulty of finding out what those abilities are, of course, is that small babies cannot tell us directly what they are able to see, but several possible behaviours which give us this information have been explored.

One method is **habituation**. A baby is given a dummy to suck, and the baseline sucking rate is noted. If the child is then presented with a visual stimulus, the sucking rate may increase or decrease. After a time, habituation occurs, i.e. the sucking rate returns to the baseline level. If the sucking rate changes when a new stimulus is shown, it is inferred that the child recognises that there is a difference between the two stimuli. Bornstein (1976) used this technique to investigate **colour vision** in babies. He found that three-month-old babies could discriminate blue from white, and yellow from green. The retina and the rods and cones, necessary for colour vision, are fairly well developed at birth.

Newborns respond to **brightness** in a similar way to adults. In response to bright light, they show the **pupillary reflex**, i.e. pupil contraction, and the blink reflex. A response to brightness can even happen in the womb; if a bright light is shone on a pregnant woman's belly, the baby often moves towards it.

Very young babies also respond to **movement**, and can track a slowly moving object within two days of birth. Horizontal movement is tracked rather better than vertical movement, and the ability to adjust focus to the distance of objects is fully developed by about four months.

Point light studies are also informative. An example of the technique is given in chapter 14, box N. At three months, babies are sensitive to this kind of display, indicating that they can discriminate and that they prefer biodynamic motion patterns.

Visual acuity takes time to develop fully, and is about 30 times poorer in a newborn than in an adult. This has been tested using the **preferential looking technique**, where infants are presented with two visual stimuli. The logic here is that if babies spend significantly more time focusing on one stimulus rather than the other, then (a) they can see that they are different and (b) they prefer looking at one rather than the other. To test visual acuity, babies are shown sets of stripes like those in figure 16, each pattern matched with a grey square of equal overall brightness. Up to the age of one month, babies show a preference over the grey square only for the thickest set of stripes. By the age of six months, they are able to distinguish the finest set of stripes from the grey square.

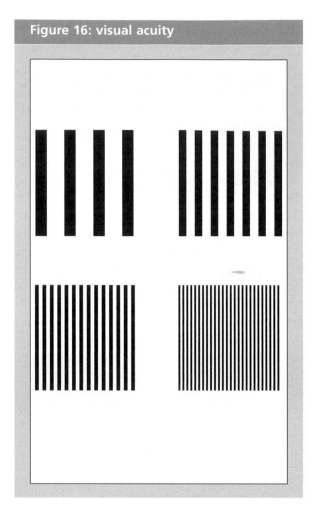

Figure 16: visual acuity

A classic study into **pattern perception** in infants, also using the preferential looking technique, was carried out by Fantz:

Box C: Fantz (1961)

Procedure: Babies from two months old were shown a series of visual stimuli (called targets) in random order. The total fixation time for each target was measured.

Results: The babies focused significantly longer on more complex targets, and in particular a face-like target (see figure 17).

Conclusion: Babies can perceive patterns in the first few weeks of life. They show a preference for complexity and representations of a face.

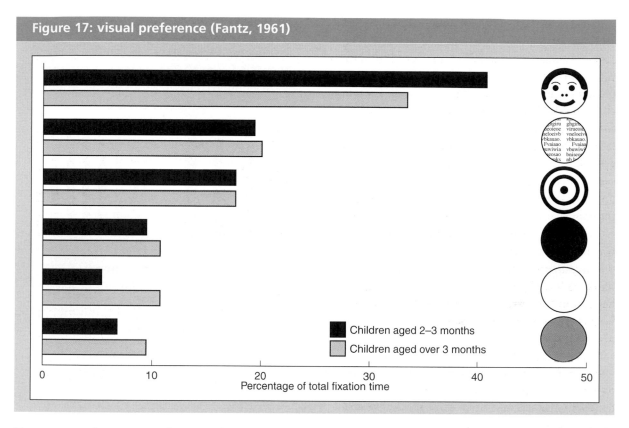

Figure 17: visual preference (Fantz, 1961)

Children aged 2–3 months
Children aged over 3 months

Percentage of total fixation time

Fantz carried out another study comparing preferences for the three targets shown in figure 18:

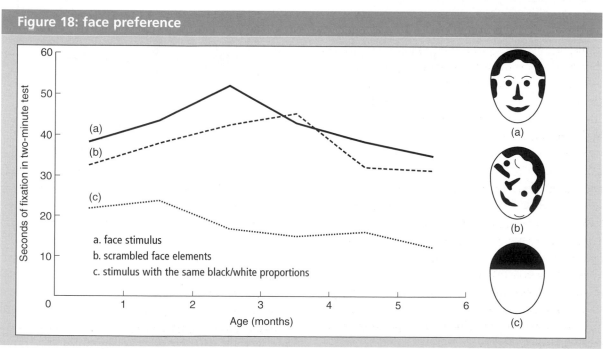

Figure 18: face preference

(a)
(b)
(c)

a. face stimulus
b. scrambled face elements
c. stimulus with the same black/white proportions

Seconds of fixation in two-minute test

Age (months)

(a)
(b)
(c)

There was still a small preference for (a) over (b); both were preferred to (c). In a later study (Fantz, 1963), Fantz replicated his research with infants as young as two days old, with similar findings, so there is quite strong evidence here for an innate ability (a) to perceive patterns and (b) to focus on the human face.

It is possible that face preference could be to do with the symmetry or complexity of this target, rather than its face-like qualities. There is also the problem of ecological validity here, in that Fantz' studies used schematic rather than real faces. Hershenson *et al.* (1965) used realistic targets and controlled for complexity; all the targets, including a face, were equally complex. Their results failed to show a preference for the face stimulus. However, Dziurawiec and Ellis (1986) found that with a moving display, infants less than an hour old were more likely to track non-scrambled than scrambled faces.

A further study developed the idea of face preference to investigate a possible preference for the mother's face over the face of another woman:

Box D: Walton *et al.* (1992)

Procedure: Infants from 12–36 hours old were tested. They were shown videos of their mother's face, and the face of a stranger with similar eye and hair colour, complexion and hairstyle. Using operant conditioning (see chapter 1), the baby could control which of the two faces was shown on the screen by changing their sucking rate on a dummy.
Results: The babies brought their mother's face to the screen for a significantly longer period than the face of the stranger.
Conclusion: The preference for the mother's face is learned within the first few hours of life. We may be preprogrammed to focus on our mother's face as part of the bonding process.

Another classic experiment explored infants' **perception of depth**:

Box E: Gibson and Walk (1960)

Procedure: The 'visual cliff' apparatus used is shown in figure 19. Twenty-seven babies from 6–12 months old were placed on the central board. Their mothers were asked to encourage them to crawl across both the visually solid part of the apparatus and the visual cliff.
Results: All the babies crawled to their mothers across the visually solid side. Only three infants crawled over the visual cliff, even though some of them patted the glass over the drop.
Conclusion: By the age of 6 months, babies have developed depth perception.

Figure 19: the visual cliff

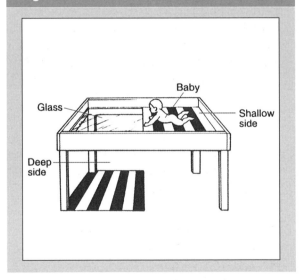

One of the problems with the visual cliff method used by Gibson and Walk was that response to depth was shown by a refusal to crawl over the apparent drop. It is possible, as Gibson and Walk suggested, that this response to depth is innate. It is also possible that depth perception is not innate, but learned in the period before babies are able to crawl.

Campos *et al.* (1970) used the visual cliff method to test depth perception in babies younger than those in the Gibson and Walk study. They found that the heart rate of babies as young as 55 days changed on the two sides of the apparatus. From

2–5 months, the heart rate decreased. Babies were attentive and less likely to cry, suggesting that they were interested in what they could see. Above 6 months, the heart rate increased and the babies showed signs of distress and fear. These findings led them to suggest that understanding of the implications of depth develops with experience.

Depth perception is related to object perception, in that if a baby can distinguish between a three-dimensional object and a two-dimensional representation of the same object, they must be sensitive to depth cues. Fantz (1961) found that infants prefer a three-dimensional sphere to a two-dimensional circle, and a more ecologically valid study by Slater *et al.* (1984) found that babies under nine days of age showed a visual preference for real objects over photographs of the same objects. This suggests that at a very early age, babies are sensitive to the three-dimensional qualities of objects.

You will remember from earlier in this chapter that constancy refers to the way that we recognise objects in spite of variations in retinal information. To what extent is this innate, and to what extent must it be learned? Babies have been tested for **size constancy**:

Box F: Bower (1966)

Procedure: Two-month-old babies were conditioned to turn their heads in response to a 30cm cube at a distance of 1 metre. The reinforcement used was an adult popping up in front of the baby in a game of peek-a-boo. The apparatus used is shown in figure 20. Babies were then tested on the original presentation and three different ones:

    a. 30cm cube at 3 metres
    b. 90cm cube at 1 metre
    c. 90cm cube at 3 metres

The number of conditioned responses in each condition was noted.

Results: The original presentation produced a total of 98 conditioned responsess, condition (a) produced 58 responses, (b) produced 54 and (c) 22.

Conclusion: The babies showed some degree of size constancy.

Figure 20: Bower's apparatus

Activity 12: evaluating Bower's study

1 Which condition – (a), (b) or (c) – produced the same retinal image as the original presentation?
2 In which condition would a conditioned response show size constancy?
3 Which comparison is the critical one for testing size constancy?
4 On the basis of these comparisons, do you think that size constancy is innate or learned?

When you have finished, see the notes on page 411.

There is some evidence, then, that size constancy is innate. This may also be true of shape constancy. Bower (1966) conditioned two-month-old infants to respond to a rectangle, and found that they still showed a conditioned response when the rectangle was turned slightly to produce a trapezoidal retinal image.

● A range of techniques has been used to determine the extent to which perception is **innate** or needs to be **learned**.
● Very young babies have well-developed vision for **colour**, **brightness** and **movement**. **Acuity** develops in the early months.
● Very young infants prefer **complex patterns**; this preference develops with age. They prefer **curved shapes** to shapes with straight lines.
● The evidence for a preference for **faces** is unclear. In the first day of life, infants show a preference for their **mother's face** over the face of a stranger.
● **Depth perception** is present very early in an infant's life. The implications of depth are learned through experience.

❺ Babies show a sensitivity to **three-dimensional** presentations in the first few days of life.

❺ At two months, they show **size** and **shape constancy**.

Cross-cultural research

Research into the perceptual abilities of infants has given us a good deal of information about perceptual development, but there are some problems with this kind of research. The findings are seldom clear-cut. A degree of interpretation is always necessary, and this may be biased. Ethical restrictions on what babies can be exposed to mean that research is limited. You may also have thought that many of the studies you have read about in the previous section have poor ecological validity.

For these reasons, other research methods have been used to provide a clearer picture of perceptual development, one of which is **cross-cultural** research. Cross-cultural studies, which make comparisons between different cultures, have identified a variety of cultural differences in perception. As well as being interesting in their own right, studies of this kind can also provide useful psychological information. If there are consistent differences between cultural groups, then these differences must be due to environmental factors – for example, social practices or the nature of the physical environment – rather than innate factors. In the area of perception, such studies can help to shed light on the nature–nurture debate.

There is a lot of evidence that the ways in which we perceive the world are influenced by cultural factors. We will start this discussion with a simple exercise:

▶ Activity 13: what do you see?

How would you describe what you see in this picture? Show it to other people to see what answers they give. When you have finished, see the notes on page 411.

Several studies have used visual illusions to examine cultural differences in perception. Probably the earliest study in this area was carried out by Rivers (1901), who compared English adults and children with adult and child Murray Islanders. The Murray Islanders were less susceptible to the Müller–Lyer illusion and more susceptible to the horizontal–vertical illusion (see figure 6).

Allport and Pettigrew (1957) used a rotating trapezoid:

Figure 21: the rotating trapezoid

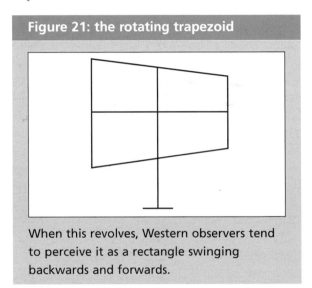

When this revolves, Western observers tend to perceive it as a rectangle swinging backwards and forwards.

They believed that this illusion depends on our perceiving the display as a window, and that therefore people from cultures which do not have this kind of window would be less likely to experience the illusion. Tests on rural Zulus supported this idea.

Segall *et al.* (1963) carried out a similar study testing people from a range of cultures:

Box G: Segall *et al.* (1963)

Procedure: The Müller–Lyer and horizontal–vertical illusions (see figure 6) were tested on members of three African cultures: the Batoro and Bayankole who live in open country, and the Bete who live in dense jungle. Filipinos, South Africans of European descent and Americans from the mid-western state of Illinois were also tested.

Results: The Africans and Filipinos were less susceptible to the Müller–Lyer than the other groups. However, on the horizontal–vertical illusion, the Batoro and Bayankole were the most susceptible, and the Bete the least susceptible.

Conclusion: The open country where the Batoro and Bayankole live makes it possible to see for long distances. Vertical objects are therefore important indicators of distance and an important part of visual experience, so people from these cultures are more susceptible to the horizontal–vertical illusion. The opposite is true of the Bete who live in dense jungle.

Based on these findings, Segall *et al.* (1963) put forward the **carpentered world hypothesis**. People in Western societies live in a world of straight lines in which most retinal images of lines meeting at an angle can be realistically interpreted, using shape constancy, as right angles. For example, in the Müller–Lyer illusion, it would make sense to interpret the figure with fins extending out from the vertical as the corner of a room, with the fins defining the walls coming towards us.

Segall claimed that we interpret two-dimensional drawings in three-dimensioinal terms; we add the extra dimension of depth which is not actually there. You might find it useful to look back at this point to Gregory's constructivist theory of perception, which says something similar.

Some studies have supported Segall's hypothesis. Annis and Frost (1973) found that Cree Indians living in a non-carpentered environment were good at making judgements about whether two lines were parallel, irrespective of the angle at which the lines were shown. Crees living in a carpentered environment were good at judging horizontal and vertical lines, but less good when the lines were at other angles. However, the results of a study by Jahoda (1966) which tested Ghanaians and one by Gregor and McPherson (1965) with Australian aborigines were not in line with what this hypothesis would predict.

Illusions have not been the only method of investigating cross-cultural differences in perception. An interesting insight relating to real-world experience was given by Turnbull (1961). He took a pygmy, whose home was in dense rainforest, to a plain where a huge herd of buffalo was grazing. The pygmy said he had never seen such insects before. As they rode towards the buffalo, the pygmy believed their increasing size was due to magic. His lack of depth perception and size constancy, at least over large distances, supports the idea that these aspects of visual perception are influenced by experience. However, this kind of evidence is only anecdotal.

Studies have also used pictorial material:

▷ Activity 14: interpreting drawings
                 (pictures adapted from
                 Hudson, 1960)

In each of these pictures, at which animal is the man aiming his spear: the antelope or the elephant? Which animal is nearer to the man? Which cues in the pictures give you this information?

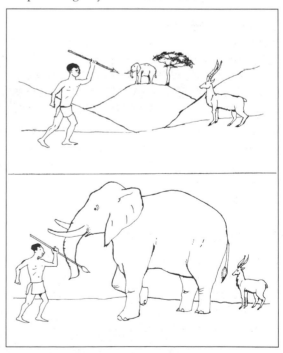

When you have finished, see the notes on page 411.

People from several African cultures were shown these pictures, and believed that in (a) the man was aiming his spear at the elephant. They did not perceive depth in this picture, in other words see the picture as a two-dimensional representation of a three-dimensional scene, as Westerners do.

However, the methodology of this kind of study is open to criticism. Deregowski (1972) found that the Me'en of Ethiopia were better at recognising pictorial representations when they were made on cloth (with which they were familiar) rather than unfamiliar paper, and when there were no distractions such as borders.

A further problem is the relative lack of depth cues in Hudson's material. If you look back to the section on depth perception, you will find that there are quite a number of potential sources of information about depth other than those used by Hudson. Serpell (1976) described a study by Kingsley *et al.* in which texture gradients were added to Hudson's pictures. This made it more likely that the Zambian children who were tested would give three-dimensional answers about pictorial material.

Serpell went on to suggest it could be that cultural differences in perception may instead be stylistic preferences. Deregowski (1972) found that several African cultures preferred the 'split elephant' to the top view perspective (see figure 22), though one person was not keen on the split elephant, which seemed to him to be jumping around dangerously.

Figure 22: Deregowski (1972)

'split elephant'

top view perspective elephant

There are other conventions in the pictorial representation we are familiar with which we take for granted, but which could be very confusing to someone who does not share our understanding of these conventions.

Activity 15: interpreting pictures

Have a look at picture (a). What information is the artist giving us about the character in the way he has been drawn? How would you interpret picture (b)?

(a)

(b)

Compare your ideas with the discussion which follows.

Duncan *et al.* (1973) tested rural African children on items like (a). Conventions such as the stars in this picture showing that the person has been stunned, and the curved lines indicating a staggering movement, were not understood by African children. In the same way, a Western observer would not understand that in ancient Egyptian art, a figure with feet apart depicts a live person, while one with feet together signifies that the person is dead.

This idea of conventions which may confuse research into perception should be even more clear from (b). This is an example of American Indian art, showing a beaver. The significant parts of what is being drawn have been picked out to describe them graphically for the observer. Without some background knowledge it is impossible for the Western observer to understand clearly what is represented.

- There are differences between cultures in their susceptibility to **visual illusions.** One explanation is the **carpentered world hypothesis,** though research evidence is ambiguous.
- There is anecdotal evidence of the influence of culture on perception.
- Other studies using **pictures** have found cultural differences in **depth perception.** The use of pictures can be criticised since **interpretation** of the findings is necessary, which may be influenced by **cultural bias.**

Notes on activities

1 Most people see a spiral, radiating from a central point. However, if you try to trace the spiral with your finger, you will find that it is not a spiral at all but a series of circles. Your sense organs – in this case your eyes – have provided accurate information about the figure, but what you see is rather different. When you perceive the spiral, you are interpreting the information which reaches your eyes. There is a discrepancy here between sensation and perception.

3 a4; **b**9; **c**10; **d**1; **e**7; **f**8; **g**6; **h**3; **i**2; **j**5.

4 V1 – primary visual area; V2 – orientation/colour; V3 – shape; V4 – colour; V5 – movement. Akinetopsia – failure to perceive movement (V5); achromatopsia – failure to perceive colour (V4); apperceptive visual agnosia – failure to perceive shapes (V3).

10 *Gregory:* **b d h** *Gibson:* **a e g** *both:* **c f i**

12 The retinal image was the same in conditions (a) and (c). The much larger number of conditioned responses to condition (a) suggests that babies were responding to the actual size of the cube, not the size of the retinal image. Since the babies were so young, the results give some support to the view that size constancy is innate.

13 Many people describe this as a staircase going up and a staircase going down. But of course there is no reason why you shouldn't go down the 'up' staircase and up the 'down' one. The reason people choose to describe what they see in this way is probably related to the Western convention, not shared by all cultures, of reading from left to right.

14 The hunter in (a) is aiming at the antelope, even though the tip of the spear is pointing at the elephant. We know this using the depth cues of relative size and interposition.

16 Language and thought

In this chapter we will be looking at:

16.1 What is language?

16.2 Language and culture
    Language and thought
    Social and cultural aspects of
    language use

16.3 Language development
    The process of language acquisition
    Skinner's theory
    Chomsky's theory
    Social interactionist theories
    Recent developments

16.4 Problem-solving and decision-making
    Problem-solving
    Decision-making

16.1 WHAT IS LANGUAGE?

Language is used every day in rather general terms to mean social interaction which communicates a message. Used in this way, we can say that animals have language. For example, bees communicate the distance and direction of pollen when they return to the hive, and chimpanzees and gorillas have a range of calls and gestures which carry meaning to others in the group. We also talk about 'body language'; for example, we interpret dilated pupils in someone we are talking to as signifying interest in us and what we are saying, or arms crossed tightly over the chest as a defensive gesture. However, it is clear that human language goes beyond this rather general definition.

One important feature of human language is that it uses words as **symbols**. The symbols a language uses are arbitrary. There is no reason, for instance, why the sound 'curtain' rather than 'splot' should mean a piece of cloth in front of a window, or why 'Vorhang' should carry the same meaning in German. We are capable of combining these symbols in an infinite variety of patterns which make sense to others who share our language. We can refer to past events and plan for future ones. We can use language to think about abstract ideas, like beauty or the nature of love, and to consider hypothetical circumstances ('What would happen if ...?'). Human language has two main functions: **external** (to communicate with others) and **internal** (to represent our thoughts). The everyday use of the word 'language' concentrates only on its external function.

Linguists study the structure of language. They look at four main aspects: syntax, the lexicon, semantics and phonology.

Syntax refers to the grammar of the language; how words can be put together to make structurally acceptable sentences. 'The dog barked at the postman' is a grammatical utterance, so is syntactically acceptable. 'The dog barking at the postman' is not a grammatical sentence in standard English. Word order is another aspect of syntax, which explains why 'The postman the barked dog at' is not a grammatical sentence.

The **lexicon** is the vocabulary of a language, so 'curtain' is part of the English lexicon, whereas 'splot' (as far as I know) is not. **Semantics** brings together syntax and the lexicon, since it refers to putting words together to make sentences that are both grammatical and meaningful. So 'The dog barked at the postman' is semantically acceptable, while 'The dog slept at the postman' is not, although there is nothing wrong with it as a sentence as far as syntax and the lexicon are concerned.

▶ Activity 1: syntax, the lexicon and semantics

Say whether each of these sentences is correct in terms of:

a English syntax
b the English lexicon and
c English semantics:

The cat sat quietly on the mat.
The cat laughed at the mat helpfully.
The plink sat feltfully on the flong.
When you have finished, see the notes on page 442.

Phonology is the study of the sounds of a language. When children develop language, phonics are learned first, followed by lexical items. Finally, syntax is acquired.

A final aspect of language with which social psychologists are particularly concerned is **pragmatics**. This relates language to the social context in which it is used. For example, when we communicate with others we take into account what the person we are communicating with already knows. If we say 'The postman came today', the person we are communicating with can assume that he delivered a letter or a package, although this has not been stated explicitly. In addition, we adjust what we say, and how we say it, depending on the situation and who we are communicating with.

▶ Activity 2: pragmatic rules

Imagine that you are explaining why you want a particular job. What differences might there be in the way you explain this to:

a the person interviewing you for the job
b your best friend

When you have finished, see the notes on page 442.

⊖ Language is used loosely to refer to meaningful communication. Human language, with its use of **symbols**, stands alone in its ability to be detached from the immediate environment and to let us think abstractly and hypothetically.

⊖ Linguists are concerned with three aspects of language: **syntax** (grammar), the **lexicon** (word meanings) and **semantics** (the production of meaningful utterances).

⊖ Social psychologists are particularly interested in **pragmatics**. This relates utterances to the particular social context in which they occur.

16.2 LANGUAGE AND CULTURE

Language and thought

How are language and thought related? This may seem to have a fairly straightforward answer: we have thoughts which we can then express in language. But this is an area where there is considerable disagreement.

Some theorists (e.g. Watson, 1913) have proposed that thinking and language are identical. For Watson, thought processes were 'motor habits in the larynx', an idea put to the test in a study described in box A:

Box A: Smith *et al* (1947)

Procedure: Smith injected himself with curare, a drug which brings about total paralysis. Because of its effects, his breathing had to be carried out artificially.

Results: When the effects of the drug had worn off, Smith reported that he was still able to think, in spite of any movement being impossible.

Conclusion: Thinking does not depend on movements of the larynx.

Watson's theory, then, was mistaken. But are language and thought related? If so, to what extent, and what kind of relationship is it?

There are numerous examples of thought without language. Koehler (1925) showed how apes given sticks of different lengths could construct a tool to retrieve a banana out of reach of a single stick. To do this, the ape must be reasoning, and without language being involved. If this is true of apes, it may also be true of humans.

If we look directly at human activity, babies attempt to solve problems, and so show reasoning, before they have developed language. You have probably also experienced the 'tip of the tongue' phenomenon, where you are aware of an idea, but have temporarily forgotten the word you need to express it.

The creative process may also take place without language being involved. Einstein (in Ghiselin, 1955) described his creative processes: 'The words of language ... do not seem to play a role in my mechanism of thought. The ... elements in thought ... are more or less clear images ... in my case of visual and some of muscular type. Conventional words ... have to be sought for laboriously only in a secondary stage'. While we need to be cautious in accepting this kind of introspection at face value, nonetheless it does seem to indicate that at least some kinds of thinking can take place without words.

So thought and language need to be seen as separate. But does thought shape language? This idea has been turned on its head by two theorists, Sapir and Whorf. They independently suggested that people around the world do not think about the world in the same way. Rather, the language that people speak determines the way they see the world and think about it. This theory has come to be known as the Sapir–Whorf hypothesis, or **linguistic relativity hypothesis**. In other words, thought is *relative*, and depends on the way concepts are expressed in a particular language.

Whorf gave many examples to support this idea. Perhaps the most famous is that the Eskimo people have very many more words for snow than, say, English speakers – falling snow, snow on the ground, snow packed hard like ice, slushy snow and so on. He argued that Eskimo people therefore perceive and think about snow very differently from English people. What evidence is there that the way people see and think about different categories of objects is affected by the way they are labelled?

Box B: Carmichael *et al.* (1932)

Procedure: Participants were shown simple line drawings which could be interpreted in various ways. They were later asked to reproduce them. One group was shown the drawings with one set of labels. Another group was shown them with a different set of labels. A control group saw the drawings with no labels.

Results: Participants produced very different drawings depending on which set of labels they had seen. Here are some examples:

Conclusion: Verbal labelling can affect memorising and recall.

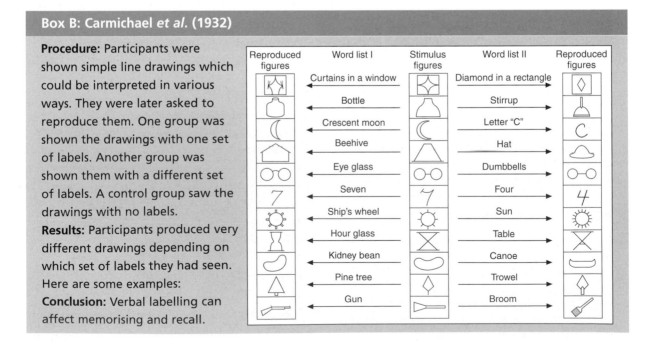

But is this the same as Whorf's claim that our whole world view is determined by the language we speak? There are several points which argue against this. First of all, it is relatively easy to translate into English the kinds of snow which the Eskimo language distinguishes. We may not have a one-word label for 'snow which is good for building', but we can express the idea in a phrase. This suggests that there must be some universal, shared knowledge of the physical world. Wherever you live and whatever language you speak, the sky is blue, rain falls more or less frequently, some things are heavy and difficult to move, and so on. It may also be that Whorf's argument is based on thinking too literally. This is illustrated in activity 3:

Activity 3: things that fly

How many different things can you think of that fly? Make a list of as many as possible in 30 seconds, but don't include birds.

You have probably come up with quite a long list. In the Hopi language, though, there is one word (masa'ytaka) for everything that flies, except birds. This would include insects, aeroplanes and pilots. But although the same word is used, it would seem very odd to suggest that the Hopi cannot see any difference between a bee and a plane.

In addition, perhaps differences in culture shape language in the first place. For the Eskimo people, snow is an important part of the environment. They need to draw attention to differences, and the words they have invented reflect this need. It could be, then, that the nature of the environment determines the *labels* used in a particular language, rather than language constraining the way in which the environment is perceived. It is perhaps also worth noting that expert skiers have a wide variety of terms for different types of snow such as 'powder', which lends support to this idea.

Some of the most important studies in this area have been concerned with colour labels. There is a wide range of colour labels in different languages. Berlin and Kay (1969) studied 98 languages and found that they all use terms from among the 11 basic (or focal) categories shown in figure 1:

Figure 1: focal colour categories

white black | red | green yellow | blue | brown | purple pink orange grey

There is a reason why the 11 focal colours have been set out in this way. Many languages use fewer than 11 colours. For example, the Jale language has only two colour terms, and Ibibio only four. But these terms are not chosen randomly from the 11 possibilities. If a language has one of these colour terms, then it must also have terms for all the colours to the *left* of it in the diagram.

Activity 4: colour terms

Which two colours does the Jale language name? Which are the four colours in Ibibio?
When you have finished, see the notes on page 442.

The universal order in which colours are encoded in different languages suggests that there are universal (natural) categories in colour naming, which in itself challenges the linguistic relativity hypothesis. However, Whorf's belief would also suggest that speakers of languages with few colour terms, like Jale or Ibibio, should be unable to make colour discriminations in the same way that speakers of, say, English can. This has been explored in the research in box C:

Box C: Rosch (1973)

Procedure: A colour memory test was given to American participants, and to Dani speakers, whose language distinguishes only between bright and dark. They were presented with a range of colour samples, including both focal colours (i.e. 'good' examples of the 11 colours shown in figure 1) and non-focal colours. After a 30-second delay, they were asked to pick out the colours they had been shown from a large array of colours.

Results: Both groups recognised the focal colours better than the non-focal colours.
Conclusion: The lack of colour names in a language does not affect the ability to recognise colours. The better performance of both groups in recognising focal colours suggests that there is a universal response to basic colour categories, even when relevant terms are not used in the language.

What we have been discussing so far is the 'strong' form of the linguistic relativity hypothesis: language *determines* thought. As we have seen, this idea has very little support. However, the 'weak' form – that language *influences* thought – is more persuasive:

Box D: Carroll and Casagrande (1958)

Procedure: Native American children, all living on the same reservation in Arizona, were tested. Children who were predominantly Navaho speakers and children who were predominantly English-speaking were presented with groups of three objects, e.g:

(a) yellow stick   blue rope   yellow rope
(b) blue cube   white cube   blue pyramid

They were asked to decide which two objects of the three presented 'went best' together.
Results: The Navaho speakers tended to group by form, e.g. in (a) putting the ropes together, and in (b) putting the cubes together, while the English speakers tended to group by colour, e.g. in (a) putting the two yellow items together and in (b) putting the two blue items together.
Conclusion: The Navaho language has different words for 'give', depending on the nature of the object; for example, whether the object to be given is flat and flexible like cloth, or long and rigid like a stick. This led them to favour form or shape over colour when carrying out the task.

However, Carroll and Casagrande carried out the same task with white middle-class children living in a suburb of Boston. Their responses were more similar to the Navaho-dominant children, with a tendency to group by form and shape rather than by colour. Carroll and Casagrande suggested that this finding could be explained by the influence of toys which focus attention on form, such as where shapes have to be fitted into holes. They therefore suggested that while language may influence thought, other characteristics of the environment will modify this influence.

The relationship between language and thought has also interested other psychologists. Piaget took the opposite view to Whorf. He did not believe that language *determines* thought, but rather that language *reflects* thought. For Piaget, thinking develops as the result of our actions on the environment. Language then allows these concepts to be expressed. However, the Russian psychologist Vygotsky believed that thought and language had quite separate and independent roots. At about the age of two, there is a fusion of internal thinking and external social language, which then determines social and intellectual development. The theories of Piaget and Vygotsky are discussed in more detail in chapter 17.

- Whorf proposed the **linguistic relativity hypothesis**. In its strong form, this states that language determines thought. The weak form is that language influences thought.
- Research into different languages, particularly on colour naming, does not support the strong version of the hypothesis, though there is more general acceptance of the idea that language influences thought.
- **Piaget** believed that thinking determined linguistic development. **Vygotsky** believed thinking and language to be initially separate. They later come together to determine intellectual and social development.

Social and cultural aspects of language use

▶ Activity 5: conversations at a bus stop

Read through these two imaginary conversations:

conversation A:

Mother:	Come back here.
Child:	Why?
Mother:	Come back.
Child:	Why?
Mother:	You'll get knocked down.
Child:	Why?
Mother:	I told you to come back here, didn't I?

conversation B:

Mother:	Come back here, darling.
Child:	Why?
Mother:	If you don't, you could fall into the road and get knocked down.
Child:	Why?
Mother:	The pavement's very slippery, and there's lots of cars whizzing past.
Child:	Why?
Mother:	Now come back here, darling, and stand by me.

What differences can you see between these two conversations? Think about vocabulary, grammar and the kinds of ideas which are being expressed. Compare your notes with the discussion which follows.

Bernstein (1961) was interested in the relationship between language, social class and school achievement. He claimed that working-class and middle-class people speak two different kinds of language, or codes. Working-class people use what he referred to as a **restricted code**, while middle-class people use an **elaborated code**. A summary of the differences between these two codes is shown in figure 2:

Figure 2: restricted and elaborated code	
restricted code	**elaborated code**
short, simple sentences; much meaning conveyed non-verbally	complex sentences, with greater use of subordinate clauses; precise descriptions
few adjectives and adverbs	greater use of adjectives and adverbs
much of the meaning is implicit, making sense only within a context, e.g. 'put it in there'.	much of the meaning is explicit, making specific stand-alone sense, e.g. 'put the teddy in the basket'.
stress on the present	stress on the past and future
frequent use of commands/questions	frequent use of prepositions to show logical, temporal and spatial relationships
does not allow abstract/hypothetical ideas to be expressed	allows abstract/hypothetical ideas to be expressed

Many of these differences can be identified in the two conversations in activity 5. The mother in conversation B, for example, talks hypothetically about what might happen, using longer and more complex sentences, while three of the utterances of the mother in conversation A are commands, the final one in the form of a question.

Bernstein argued that while middle-class children learn to use both restricted and elaborated code, working-class children have access only to restricted code. These language differences will affect how children relate to their world. The deprived language of working-class children will limit the extent to which they can benefit from education.

Box E: Bernstein (1961)

Procedure: A working-class group of 61 messenger boys and a middle-class group of 45 public school boys were compared. All the participants were tested using a non-verbal intelligence test (Raven's Progressive Matrices) and a verbal intelligence test (Mill Hill Vocabulary Test).

Results: The middle-class boys performed similarly on both tests. The working-class boys scored higher on the non-verbal than the verbal test.

Conclusion: The restricted code of the working class limits the ways in which their intelligence can be expressed.

The differences in language use which Bernstein identified have been interpreted in two ways. The **language deficit** interpretation is that restricted code is not as 'good' as elaborated code, and its use means that working-class people are restricted in their thinking and so lack the ability to reason logically. The deficit model was very influential, particularly in the United States in the 1960s and 1970s. An important political issue at that time was that poor and black children were failing in the education system. Money was put into various projects, most famously **Project Head Start**, which was started in 1965. Its aim was to try to promote equality of opportunity by compensating for some of the deficiencies in the environment of disadvantaged children. Language was one aspect of the environment which was singled out as important.

On the other hand, the **language difference** interpretation is that variations of language reflect the ways that speakers use language in different social contexts. This interpretation does not accept that some varieties of language are somehow 'better' than others, and variations in language use do not reflect differences in intellectual functioning.

The main name associated with the language difference viewpoint is Labov. He based his ideas on

his work with black New York children, speakers of **Black English Vernacular (BEV)**. Labov claimed that the BEV dialect is just as complex, organised and rule-governed as standard English. Linguistically, you cannot say that one is better than the other. If they are seen as unequal, this is because the social status of their users is unequal. Users of BEV are just as able to reason logically as users of standard English. He gives a nice example:

Box F: Labov (1970)

A black 15-year-old was asked why he thought God would be white:

'Why? I'll tell you why! Cause the average whitey out here got everything, you dig? And the nigger ain't got shit, y'know? Y'understan'? So – um – in order for that to happen, you know it ain't no black God that's doin' that bullshit.'

Conclusion: The language here is non-standard and uses restricted code, but the speaker is clearly using abstract reasoning.

Labov also claimed that much research in this area was biased, since researchers (usually middle-class) did not know enough about working-class children to allow them to make judgements. Leading on from this, he pointed out that interviews of black working-class children by white middle-class interviewers would have an inhibiting effect on the children. They would therefore not be in a situation which allowed them to demonstrate their linguistic skills. The importance of the situation is shown in another example:

Box G: Labov (1970)

Procedure: A young black boy, Leon, was invited to chat:

(a) by a white interviewer
(b) by a black interviewer
(c) by a black interviewer using BEV

Results: In condition (a), he was mostly silent, in condition (b) he tended to give very brief answers to questions, while in condition (c) he was very much more chatty.

Conclusion: In investigating children's language skills, the situation needs to be taken into account. Performance may not reflect capability.

The importance of situation can be related to educational achievement. Teachers are users of elaborated code, and most teaching needs children to be able to operate within it. If children are not used to being spoken to in elaborated code, and using it themselves, there is going to be a mismatch between the children and the situation. These children are going to be limited in what they can gain from their educational experience.

It may also be that the use of restricted code may cause the teacher to expect less of those children. This raises the worrying possibility of a **self-fulfilling prophecy**, where children will underachieve because they are expected to do so.

- Bernstein distinguished between working-class language, using **restricted code**, and middle-class language, using **elaborated code**.
- A **language deficit** interpretation associates the use of restricted code with constraints on the ability to think logically. This interpretation has influenced compensatory programmes.
- Labov takes a **language difference** approach. Different varieties of language are of *linguistically* equal status. The difference lies in their *social* status.
- Restricted code use may disadvantage children within the education system.

16.3 LANGUAGE DEVELOPMENT

The process of language acquisition

There has been considerable research into the acquisition of language, focusing in particular on how grammar develops. It has been found that children go through a series of stages, which are very similar, whether they learn English, Urdu or Swedish.

The prelinguistic stage
Condon and Sander (1974) found that newborns show a preference for human speech over other sounds. It therefore seems reasonable to assume that the ability to focus on and discriminate in favour of this aspect of the environment is innate. In the first month, crying dominates. Babies use several types of crying, to communicate pain, hunger and so on, which caregivers learn to discriminate between. In the second month, cooing develops.

At about 6 months, babies start to babble, producing a range of sounds which combine consonants and vowels, e.g. 'ma' and 'goo'. Babies spend a lot of time making these noises, and they seem to enjoy it. Until around 9–10 months, babbling sounds are similar in babies from different linguistic backgrounds, suggesting that babbling develops as the result of maturation. It is only from around 10 months that sounds which do not occur in the mother tongue are dropped, showing that the learning of phonics is taking place. The sounds produced, although not yet meaningful, have the rhythms and the variations in pitch which characterise speech.

Following on from this, Crystal *et al.* (1976) identified seven different stages:

Stage 1 (9 months–$1\frac{1}{2}$ years)
At this stage, single words appear, such as 'milk' and 'sock'. Each of these words can be used to carry different meanings. For example, 'milk' could mean 'I want some milk' or 'That's the milk' or 'The milkman has brought the milk'. It is hard to argue that these utterances have any grammatical structure, though, since the exact meaning depends a lot on interpretation.

Stage 2 ($1\frac{1}{2}$–2 years)
Two words now appear in combination.

Activity 6: two-word utterances

A baby says 'Sock foot'. How many different things could that mean?
When you have finished, see the notes on page 442.

The context is still important in understanding what the child wants to communicate.

Braine (1963) found that when combining two words, children were following rules. He found that there was one group of words (which he called the **pivot class**) which always occurred in one position in an utterance. One example is 'all gone' which he found always came first, another is 'pretty' which always came second. A second class of words (**open class**) could come either first or second. Two open words could occur together, or one pivot and one open, but no utterance could contain two pivot words. By this stage, then, children are using grammar, since a regular word order is used.

Stage 3 (2–2½ years)
Three or four words are now used in combination. Different patterns emerge for statements ('mummy gone work'), questions ('where my teddy?') and commands ('let me go'). Inflections begin to appear, e.g. the addition of '-ing' to a verb, as well as pronouns, e.g. 'me' and 'you'.

Stage 4 (2½–3 years)
Sentences now become longer and more complex. Most sentence patterns and inflectional endings are now used. Question forms and negatives are now incorporated into the sentence, e.g. 'where daddy go?' becomes 'where's daddy going?' and 'more milk no' becomes 'I don't want more milk'.

Stage 5 (3–3½ years)
More complex sentences are used, with co-ordinated clauses ('the dog *who is sitting in the garden* belongs to Julie') and subordinated clauses ('he's crying *because he hurt his foot*'). Very long sentences, linked by 'and' and 'then' are also common: 'Karim sat on the table and he falled off and he cried and then …'

Stage 6 (3½–4½ years)
Children are by now handling adult grammar competently, but there are still some structures to learn. At this age, they start to use passives, e.g. 'it *was eaten* by a monster', as well as complex noun phrases ('some of the little children') and verb phrases ('I should have been able to'). However, the development of this kind of complex structure will continue for some time.

Stage 7 (4½ years onwards)
In this final stage, there are three main areas of development. Firstly, children learn to connect sentences, using words like 'afterwards' and 'however'. Children also use word order and intonation for emphasis, e.g. 'It was the juice I wanted'. Secondly, as children start school, they learn to use language differently in different contexts, and for different purposes. Finally, although linguistic structures are used appropriately, their use is not always fully understood yet. An example is given in box H:

> ### Box H: Sinclair *et al.* (1978)
>
> **Procedure:** Children were asked to act out a set of sentences using dolls, e.g.:
> (a) the girl pushed the boy
> (b) the boy was pushed by the girl
> (c) the truck hit the car
> (d) the car was hit by the truck
> (e) the wand was waved by the fairy godmother
>
> **Results:** Young children had no difficulty in understanding the passive form where it could not easily be reversed and still make sense, e.g. in (e). Before the age of about 5, however, children interpreted (b) as 'the boy pushed the girl' and (d) as 'the car hit the truck'.
>
> **Conclusion:** Comprehension of complex grammatical forms like the passive is not necessarily completely mastered, even when the child is using them competently.

Maratsos (1978) found that even by the age of 6, children had difficulty understanding sentences such as 'The man was remembered by the boy'.

There are individual differences in the rate at which children acquire language skills. Wells (1981) observed the mean length of utterance of children aged 2–5, i.e. the average number of words a child used in a single utterance. For any particular mean length he found a range of about three years.

Perhaps more interestingly, there are also differences in children's approaches to language use. One distinction, between **expressive** and **referential** speech, is described in box I:

Box I: Nelson (1973)

Procedure: In a longitudinal study, the language development of children aged from one to two and a half was followed. The mother's use of language when communicating with the child was also analysed.

Results: Children could be classified into two groups. For the larger group (the **referential** group) vocabulary consisted mainly of words used for naming objects, plus a few verbs, adjectives and proper nouns. The other group (the **expressive** group) tended to do less naming. Instead, they used a lot of social expressions, e.g. 'stop it', 'I want it', as well as 'this' and 'that'. The groups were not completely distinct: individual children tended more towards referential or expressive language use. Mothers also tended to be more referential or more expressive. A mismatch between the language use of child and mother was associated with a slower start in language learning.

Conclusion: There are individual differences in the way young children use language.

But does context also affect the way in which language is used?

Activity 7: language and context

In each of these situations, which use of language would you expect to be more dominant: referential or expressive? Why?

1 Two children occupied with building bricks.
2 A child reading a book with his mother.
3 A child playing chasing games with her father.
When you have finished, see the notes on page 442.

The effect of context has been shown by Peters (1977), who found that expressive language was more commonly used in play and interpersonal situations.

These differences tell us something about language development, but also something about language itself. Linguists tend to focus on one aspect of what children have to learn, e.g. sounds *or* grammar *or* meaning, but children are given information about all these different aspects of language every time something is said to them. They must decide which of these to concentrate on. Referential and expressive language reflect different kinds of focus.

Nelson's research raises a lot of interesting questions. Do the differences she described disappear as children grow older? (Nelson found that they did.) Does birth order make a difference? (There is some evidence that firstborn children are likely to be more referential.) Is social class a factor? Are these differences related to neurological differences? As yet, the information we have is too limited to allow us to draw any firm conclusions.

- Children go through **stages** in their acquisition of language. The grammar they use becomes progressively more complex.
- Even when children are using grammatical structures appropriately, they still need time to develop a full understanding of their use.
- There are individual differences, both in the rate at which children's language development proceeds, and in the way very young children use language. One distinction is between **referential** and **expressive** language.

Psychologists have put forward many different theories to explain how children acquire language. The fundamental division is between those who take an **associationist** position and believe that language is acquired in the same way and using the same mechanisms as other cognitive skills, and the more **nativist** position of those who believe that there is some kind of innate language-specific device distinct from more general learning mechanisms. More recently, **social constructivist** ideas have become more prominent. While not dismissing earlier ideas, they suggest that the acquisition of language has its roots in the earliest interactions between infants and caregivers.

Skinner's theory

In his book *Verbal Behaviour* (1957), Skinner applied the principles of **operant conditioning**, outlined in chapter 1, to the acquisition of language. Verbal behaviour, he claimed, is just like any other kind of behaviour. It is acquired through the processes of **shaping** and **reinforcement**. Children produce sounds and imitate the sounds they hear around them. Skinner calls this kind of imitation an **echoic response**. Caregivers respond to the sounds that children make. If this response is reinforcing, the sounds will be repeated. Caregivers will shape the sounds that children make by reinforcing progressive approximations to the words and sentences of the language which children are to acquire. In this way, children will learn the phonology, vocabulary, syntax and semantics of their language community.

Activity 8: reinforcement and shaping

What examples of caregiver behaviour can you think of which would reinforce random sounds made by an infant? How could the noises a child makes be shaped to become 'mummy'?
When you have finished, see the notes on page 443.

According to Skinner, a child makes two types of verbal responses, which he called **mands** (as in *de*mands) and **tacts**. A mand is a response to a need stimulus. For example, if a child wants milk, their response to this need will be the word 'milk'. This will be reinforced by being given milk. A tact is a response to an object stimulus. A child sees a dog and responds by saying 'dog'. This will be reinforced by their caregiver saying: 'Yes, that's right' or 'Aren't you clever!' A link can be made here with the referential/expressive distinction made earlier, with mands being expressive and tacts referential.

In studies of children who have problems developing language, it has been shown that language can be developed in the ways that Skinner suggested. For example, Lovaas (1987) used the behaviour modification techniques of shaping and reinforcement with autistic children, to good effect.

Further evidence that the language environment in which children grow shapes the way in which language develops is provided by Clarke-Stewart (1973), who found a positive relationship between the amount caregivers talk to their children and the size of the children's vocabularies.

You may also have noticed that people do not talk to babies in the same way as they talk to older children or adults, but use what is known as **child directed speech** (**CDS**, sometimes also referred to as **baby talk register** or **motherese**). This way of talking to babies seems to be universal, appearing to some degree in a wide range of cultures. Not only adults use CDS; Shatz and Gelman (1973) found that even 4-year-olds use simplified CDS to an infant.

Activity 9: child directed speech

Make a list of the ways in which people modify their speech when they talk to very young babies. How might being talked to in CDS help a baby's acquisition of language?
How can the existence of CDS be used to support Skinner's theory?
When you have finished, see the notes on page 443.

There are, however, some problems with Skinner's theory. Many utterances are not mands or tacts but what Skinner calls **intraverbal responses**: one person says something and another replies. There are thousands of possible responses which could be given in any situation, and quite often what we say is not an exact repetition of what we have heard before; we use language *creatively*. Since we have not heard these exact utterances before, imitation and reinforcement cannot be the complete answer.

Skinner suggests that children learn grammatical rules through caregivers and others reinforcing correctly formed utterances. A study by Brown *et al.* (1969) in box J investigated this idea:

Box J: Brown *et al.* (1969)

Procedure: Examples of mothers' responses to their children's utterances were collected. The researchers were interested in whether mothers responded to the truth value of what their children said (i.e. whether it was factually accurate) or its linguistic correctness.

Results: Mothers tended to respond to the *meaning* of what their children say, and not to whether it is expressed accurately. A nice example of this was a child saying: 'He a girl' and the mother replying: 'That's right', i.e. reinforcing an incorrect response.
Conclusion: Skinner's belief that caregivers shape and reinforce grammatically accurate language is not supported by empirical evidence.

However, more recent research (e.g. Saxton, 1997) has shown that adults often expand on what a child has said, providing a grammatically correct version, e.g:

child: Do you know how Big Foot was borned?
adult: No, how was he born?

Farrar (1992) also found that children are more likely to repeat adult expansions than other utterances, which suggests that they attend to this feedback.

Children's speech errors in the formation of verbs in the past tense are also informative. In regular verbs in English we add -ed when talking about the past, eg 'I help' becomes 'I helped'. However, we also have irregular verbs, e.g. 'I went', 'I sang', 'I bought' and so on. These don't follow any rule and need to be learned individually. Activity 10 gives some examples of the forms of the past tense which children use as they learn irregular verbs:

▷ Activity 10: formation of irregular past tenses

Here are some examples of the stages which children go through in their production of an irregular past tense form:

1. came	1. went
2. comed	2. goed
3. cameded/comeded	3. goed/wented
4. comed	4. goed
5. came	5. went

Notice that children often start off by getting it right, and then work their way through various forms until, at stage 5, they consistently use the grammatically correct form.

How do these stages lend support to Skinner's theory?

What does this series of forms suggest is happening?

In what ways is this a challenge to Skinner's ideas?

When you have finished, see the notes on page 443.

The examples in activity 10 show how children arrive at correct grammatical forms. The acquisition of meaning seems to happen in a similar way. Young children often demonstrate **overextensions** and **underextensions** in applying labels to what they see. For instance, a child may overextend 'daddy' by using it to refer to *all* men, or use 'car' to refer to a bus, lorry, tractor or aeroplane. An example of an underextension could be the use of 'cup' only for the child's own cup, but not other cups. These errors seem to show that children are trying to discover the boundaries of categories, and to find out labelling rules, rather than imitating directly what they have heard. An early, mainly associationist, method of learning is being superseded by a more cognitive style.

Young children often demonstrate overextensions.

A final example of young children's ability to form rules is shown in box K:

Box K: Berko (1958)

Procedure: Children were shown a picture of an invented creature (a) and told: 'This is a wug'. They were then shown another picture (b) and told: 'Now there is another one. There are two of them'. They were asked to complete the sentence 'There are two ....'

This is a wug

Now there is another one.
There are two of them.
There are two _____.

Results: Three- and four-year-old children had no difficulty in completing the sentence correctly.

Conclusion: Young children can use grammatical rules with words they have never heard before.

In all these examples, Skinner's theory cannot really account for the way in which children form and apply rules. A **nativist** approach, which suggests that we have some kind of innate propensity to acquire the rules of language, fits much better, and we shall be looking at this idea in more detail in the next section.

Of course the language environment in which we grow up does influence how our use of language develops. Obviously to learn English children need to be exposed to English and not German or Tamil. But while imitation is important in learning vocabulary and accent, less of a case has been made for its role in the development of syntax and semantics.

- Skinner proposed an **associationist** model of language acquisition. Children learn through **imitating** what they hear around them. Language is learned like any other behaviour through the processes of **reinforcement** and **shaping**.

- He identified two kinds of verbal responses: **mands**, which are a response to a need stimulus, and **tacts**, which are a response to an object stimulus.

- Reinforcement and shaping can provide a partial account of how language develops. Skinner's theory can also explain the function of **CDS**.

- However, caregivers often don't reinforce their children in the way that Skinner suggests; imitative utterances are often replaced by (incorrect) **rule-based** utterances, such as the regularisation of irregular past tenses.

Chomsky's theory

The linguist Noam Chomsky was extremely critical of Skinner's theory, and his own ideas about language acquisition are in complete contrast to Skinner's ideas. Chomsky argued that language acquisition is facilitated by an innate **language acquisition device** (**LAD**), tuned to extract grammatical rules from the incomplete and often ungrammatical speech we hear around us. This device is dedicated to language acquisition, and so is unrelated to other aspects of cognition.

We are obviously not preprogrammed to understand a specific language, but are equipped with general language-learning principles and grammatical knowledge about some aspects of language which are common to all languages. These are called **linguistic universals**. One example is the distinction between statements and questions; in all languages it is possible to make statements and to ask questions.

Since a lot of information about language is already present at birth, language acquisition will take place with only very minimal input from the environment. An innate grammar is modified over time by the grammar of the language which children hear spoken. In this way, the language-learning structure becomes fine-tuned to the grammar of the particular language to which an infant is exposed.

Chomsky differentiated between what he called **deep structure** (the underlying meaning of an idea or an utterance) and **surface structure** (the specific grammatical structure used to express that idea). Let's take as an example the sentence: 'Robert likes cleaning ladies'. This has two distinct possible meanings. In other words, it represents two *deep* structures in one *surface* structure. For an opposite example, let's say we want to express the meaning (*deep* structure) of a request to shut the door. This could be expressed with a range of *surface* structures:

Please shut the door

Would you mind closing the door?

You've left the door open

or even:

There's a draught in here

You'll let the dog out!

Linguistic universals exist at the deep structural levels. The differences between all the many languages that exist relate to surface structure. The LAD represents the underlying deep structure of language rather than the differences in the surface structure.

A final term here is **transformational grammar** (**TG**), which is the process of translating underlying meaning into speech, i.e. transforming deep structure into surface structure and vice versa. Thus when we hear a spoken sentence, we do not process the surface structure, but rather transform it into its deep structure. The LAD enables us to learn the rules to transform deep structure into the various possible surface structures.

This theory can explain some aspects of language acquisition which cause problems for **associationist** theories. By the age of about four, as we have seen, children are using language pretty competently, with quite complex grammatical structures. It is certainly easier to explain the *speed* with which language is acquired if we accept that the child is preprogrammed to pick up on certain aspects of linguistic input. This also ties in with the evidence described in the section above on the process of language acquisition, which suggests that babies have an innate tendency both to attend to and produce language sounds.

Children also seem to acquire language at much the same rate, and in the same sequence, irrespective of the kind of environment to which they have been exposed. If, as Skinner suggested, language is developed through reinforcement, we would expect individuals to acquire language in different ways, since the reinforcement they have received will show huge variations. As we have seen, this is not the case. There are differences in the rate at which children acquire language, but not the wide individual differences we see in other areas of cognitive development, such as learning to manipulate numbers, or to read; ability does not seem to be a major factor in language acquisition. Dockrell and Lindsay (1998) reported that the language development of hearing children of deaf parents, who may hear no more than 10 hours of speech a week, does not lag behind that of other children.

In addition, different aspects of language, as described in the section on developmental stages of language acquisition, appear in the same order in the wide range of languages which have been studied. This suggests that language development may have *universal*, inbuilt features, which express themselves as a result of **maturation**. Further support for the importance of maturation comes from Lenneberg (1967), described in box L:

Box L: Lenneberg (1967)

Procedure: This study compared Down's syndrome children and normal children. The age at which children reached developmental milestones, e.g. the ability to sit unsupported, to walk a few steps unaided and so on, was noted. The age at which language milestones were achieved (for examples, look back to the section above on language development) was also noted.

Results: There were significant positive correlations between the achievement of the two kinds of milestones.

Conclusion: There is strong evidence that developmental milestones such as sitting unaided come about as the result of genetically determined maturation. The correlations found here between developmental and language milestones suggest that maturation is also important in language acquisition.

A final point to think about is the ability children have to segment the language they hear into meaningful units. For example, a very small child is told:

'Grandma is coming to see us tomorrow.'

Even very small children are capable of drawing out the key ideas of this sentence, i.e. 'grandma', 'coming' and 'tomorrow'. But how do they know where the breaks in the sentence come? There is no reason why the sentence should not be divided up as:

'Grand mais co mingtosee usto mo rrow.'

It would seem to make sense to propose some mechanism that predisposes children to pick up on the cues which show how sentences are segmented and thus facilitate language acquisition.

There is also some rather more concrete physiological evidence which tends to support Chomsky's ideas. The left hemisphere of the brain is associated with language. If this part of the brain is damaged, language fails to develop normally. In addition, Molfese (1977) tested electrical activity in the brain of one-day-old infants. It was found that the amount of activity rose in the left hemisphere when they were exposed to speech sounds. Since it appears so early in life, it is extremely unlikely that this could be a learned response, so again the idea that we are preprogrammed at least to respond to language seems to be supported.

While Chomsky's ideas have considerable appeal, they have also been criticised. Firstly, they seem to underestimate the role played by the **environment** in language acquisition. If you look back to the section on the associationist model, there is plenty of evidence that the environment may be providing more than the rather limited input which is all Chomsky believes is necessary for language to develop. This theory also does not very readily lend itself to testing: it lacks **falsifiability**.

A final important criticism of Chomsky's theory is that it defines language mainly in terms of the acquisition of grammatical competence. His theory does not look at the **pragmatic** aspects of language, or indeed consider language within the social context in which it takes place.

⊖ Chomsky proposed that we have an innate **language acquisition device**, tuned to extract grammatical rules from limited input.

⊖ He differentiated between **deep structure** and **surface structure**. **Transformational grammar** allows us to move from one to the other.

⊖ This theory explains the **speed** with which children become competent language users, the finding that all children acquire language at a roughly **similar rate**, and the similarity in the **order in which linguistic structures appear** in different languages. It also helps to explain how children can **segment** what they hear into meaningful chunks. There is some **physiological evidence** to support the theory. **Maturation** is seen as a major factor.

⊖ Chomsky's ideas have been criticised for undervaluing the importance of the **environment**. His theory also lacks **falsifiability**. Chomsky's theory has been criticised for looking at language in purely grammatical terms, and ignoring the **social context** within which it takes place.

Social interactionist theories

While recognising the contribution that both associationist and nativist theories have made, theorists interested in language acquisition have more recently focused on social factors. The theories we have looked at focus on the development of language and how it becomes a conversational activity. Social constructivist theories, in contrast, look at the development of conversation and how it becomes a language-based activity.

Snow (1977) suggested that we can find the beginnings of children's language in pre-linguistic 'conversations'. She is referring here to the turn-taking in interactions between caregivers and small children, to which both contribute and where the caregivers act as if the children's babbling and gestures have meaning and intention. These exchanges have been called **proto-conversations**. Trevarthen (1974) used the term **pre-speech** to describe the mouth movements of infants in these early exchanges, and suggested that they may help to lay the foundations for later verbal communication. He supported this idea with video recordings which allowed the interaction of caregivers and children to be analysed. An example is shown in figure 3:

Figure 3: a record of 10 seconds of mother–child interaction

The solid lines show when the behaviours listed at the side occur (pre-speech, smiling, etc). The shaded areas show the level of activity of mother and child, on a scale of 1–4, as the exchange progresses.

Activity 11: interpreting mother–child interaction

What can we tell about mother–child interaction from the recording in figure 3?

When you have finished, see the notes on page 443.

The meshing of the behaviour of each to the other is called **interactional synchrony**. This has also been observed in early interactions during feeding, as described in box M:

Box M: Kaye and Brazelton (1971)

Procedure: Behaviour patterns of mothers and infants during feeding were observed. In particular, the researchers were interested in the relationship between the pauses babies make while feeding, before starting a new burst of sucking, and the way mothers gently shake ('jiggle') their babies during a feed.

Results: Although mothers claim to jiggle their babies to wake them up, jiggling actually lengthens the baby's pauses. Mothers do not jiggle during long pauses, but typically start to jiggle immediately after a burst of sucking. Babies stop sucking while they are being jiggled, and start a new burst of sucking when the jiggling stops.

Conclusion: Mothers and babies mesh their behaviour with each other. Feeding shows the basic elements of turn-taking, which form the basis for later conversation.

A major theorist in this area is Bruner. In contrast to Chomsky, Bruner was more interested in the pragmatics of language than the development of grammar. He suggested that the development of language is rooted in the very early interactions of infants and caregivers. Games of 'peek-a-boo', bath routines and looking at pictures in books together all provide what Bruner called **joint-action formats**. He pointed out that routines and games develop which involve the infants and caregivers in predictable (though not identical) interactions, all of which involve the turn-taking necessary for conversation. These kinds of routines form what Bruner calls the **language acquisition support system** (**LASS**, in contrast to Chomsky's LAD):

Activity 12: LASS

Read through this exchange between a mother and one-year-old child, looking at a picture book:

Mother: Look!
Child: (touches picture)
Mother: What are those?
Child: (vocalizes a babble string and smiles)
Mother: Yes, they are rabbits.
Child: (vocalizes, smiles and looks up at mother)
Mother: (laughs) Yes, rabbit
Child: (vocalizes, smiles)
Mother: Yes (laughs)

How might this kind of exchange support the child's acquisition of language?

When you have finished, see the notes on page 443.

Bruner used the term **scaffolding** to refer to the way in which caregivers interact with infants, where adults take enough control of a situation to allow infants to make progress in a way that they would be unable to do without this support.

The role in language acquisition of interaction with others is also demonstrated in a study by Sachs *et al.* (1981), who studied the language of a boy called Jim, with deaf and dumb parents. They did not teach him sign language, believing that this would interfere with his acquiring spoken language. His main sources of language were from the television, and to a limited extent the nursery school he went to. His language skills were poor, but he acquired language very quickly with the help of a speech therapist. Jim had not been cut off from hearing language, but his exposure to language on television was relatively passive. He would have had little opportunity to learn about language as a social activity. The intervention of the speech therapist, together with the more specialised help she could provide, would give him experience of this kind of interaction, and thus support the development of language.

The nature of **autism** may also help to support a social interactionist perspective on language acquisition. Children with autism typically have problems with both language and social skills. One interpretation could be that problems with social interaction may be responsible for the abnormal language shown by autistic children.

The symptoms of autism (adapted from National Autistic Society 1978)

The social interactionist approach to language acquisition does not contradict the other models. As we have seen, there is evidence that both these theories can help us to understand how children develop language. Social interactionism can be seen as giving us additional insight into the nature of language development. It has the advantage of looking at the function of language – as communication in a social context – and how this might be related to its development.

- **Social interactionists** point out that language is basically a social phenomenon. They believe that the roots of language lie in early social exchanges.
- Early pre-verbal interactions between infants and caregivers have been called **proto-conversations**. Both children and caregivers take an active part in these exchanges. They show **synchrony** in meshing their behaviour. This turn-taking may help to lay the basis for later conversation.
- Bruner proposes a **LASS**, where **joint-action formats** help to **scaffold** the development of language.
- Social interactionism gives an additional perspective on language development, rather than being an alternative to **associationist** and **nativist** theories.

Recent developments

There have been two recent developments in the study of language acquisition which may prove useful in our understanding of how it takes place.

The first of these comes from Chomsky, who has proposed a **principles and parameters theory**. As with his earlier theory, it assumes that some features of language are universal. However, there are other features of language which vary. For example, English sentences typically follow the order of subject-verb-object, while Japanese sentences follow the pattern of subject-object-verb. Chomsky called this kind of difference **parametric variation**. Children identify the correct parameter by hearing examples from the speech around them. It may help to think of this process of **parameter setting** as being like a switch which can be put in any one of several different positions; children match the input to the relevant parameter, and set the switch accordingly.

This opens up two possibilities. Firstly, the **continuity hypothesis** proposes that all the possible parameters – i.e. the full range of possible grammatical structures – are available at birth. There is a parallel here with the way that babies make a full range of sounds, not just those relevant to their language community, as soon as they start to babble. Advances in language are then only held back because of problems like memory limitations. Alternatively, the **maturation hypothesis** proposes that the full range of innate linguistic knowledge only becomes available as the child becomes older.

However, as with Chomsky's earlier theory, these ideas are difficult to test. There is also the problem of storing huge amounts of information about all the parameters relevant to different languages.

A second development is **connectionism**, associated with Plunkett (1998), which is more in line with the associationist approach we looked at earlier. In contrast to Chomsky, connectionism proposes that there is no dedicated language-learning mechanism; the development of language is governed by the more general mechanisms which support cognitive development.

Connectionism uses computer modelling. The computer is given speech examples relating to one aspect of grammar (e.g. past tense forms), to which it must respond. Feedback is given each time on whether the response was correct or not. Computers can learn in this way not only regular forms (e.g. helped) but also irregular forms (e.g. brought). Even though it has been given no explicit rules, but only examples of speech, the computer behaves as though it were governed by rules. Although a strict parallel cannot be drawn between the way children and computers acquire language, this nonetheless questions Chomsky's belief that there must be some specific innate language mechanism which responds to the speech input heard by children.

One problem with drawing a parallel between computers and children in this context is that the computer is given feedback on every response it makes; as we have seen, this is not the case for children. A further limitation of this approach is that examples of only one particular aspect of grammar (e.g. past tense forms) are given to the computer, while children need to process information about many different aspects (e.g. word order, plurals, past tense, and so on) at the same time, which is a very much more complex task.

❺ Recent developments include Chomsky's **principles and parameters theory**. Children switch in to relevant internal grammatical structures on the basis of the speech they hear around them.

❺ The **connectionist** approach, using computer modelling, suggests that innate grammatical knowledge is not necessary for rule-governed speech to be produced.

16.4 PROBLEM-SOLVING AND DECISION-MAKING

Problem-solving

A problem can be defined as a situation where there is a gap between the present state and a desired goal; problem-solving eliminates this gap. The information-processing approach to problem-solving proposes that solving problems is carried out in various stages. Bourne *et al.* (1979) have suggested that the first step is **definition** or **representation** of the problem. This is followed by **generation** of possible solutions, followed by **evaluation** of these possibilities. Some researchers have suggested that there is an **incubation stage** between generation and evaluation of possible solutions, when there is no conscious attempt to solve the problem, but which may help to lead to a solution, while others have suggested that the incubation stage may come after an initial preparation period.

Research into problem-solving in humans looks at ways of **understanding problems**, methods of creating a mental **representation** of the problem, and the **strategies** used to solve them. Most research in this area has concentrated on the strategies people use, and it is this area which we will look at in the next section.

In humans, problems can be divided into two classes, adversary and non-adversary. We will look first at **non-adversary** problems, which only involve others to the extent that they set the problems to be solved, such as in crosswords. We will then look briefly at **adversary** problems, which involve people competing against each other, as in a game of chess.

❺ Research into the cognitive processes involved in human problem-solving has looked at how we **understand** problems, **represent** them to ourselves, and in particular the **strategies** we use to solve them.

❺ Problems can be **adversary** and **non-adversary**.

Problem-solving strategies in non-adversary problems

One problem-solving strategy is to use **algorithms**. An algorithm involves following a rule or procedure which must lead to the correct answer. For example, an algorithmic approach to a move in a game of draughts would involve systematically considering each possible move, each possible counter-move, and each possible response to that counter-move. This approach is used by computers. Success is guaranteed, so it may be a useful approach when the number of possibilities is small; otherwise, it can be extremely time-consuming.

As a less cumbersome alternative, people often use **heuristics**, where they are selective in the possibilities they consider. Heuristics are methods of solving a problem which involve taking short-cuts which often work. Unlike an algorithm, there is no guarantee of success, but it may be a more practical approach in terms of time.

The difference between algorithms and heuristics can be demonstrated by activity 13:

▶ **Activity 13: anagrams**

Solve these anagrams:
   qtiu   pilnsege   notcai
Did you consider every possible combination to solve these anagrams?
Were there any combinations of letters you didn't try, e.g. as the first two letters in a word? Were there any combinations which you thought would be more likely than others?
When you have finished, see the notes on page 443.

The heuristic devices used in problem-solving include the use of **analogies**, **working backwards** and **means—end analysis**.

Analogies

This device relies on seeing a similarity between a current problem and one which has been encountered in the past. Novick and Holyoak (1991) have suggested that there are four processes in using analogies: we need to **locate** the similar problem we have previously encountered, **compare** the two problems, **adapt** the procedures which were useful in solving the previous problem, and **develop** a schema which can be applied to the whole class of problems of which the current and previous ones are examples. Novick (1988) found that experts used analogies more often than novices, which makes sense in that experts would have broader experience on which to draw than novices.

One of the limitations with using analogies to solve problems is that a useful analogy can often be overlooked. Box N gives an example of research demonstrating this which used a standard problem which you might like to try for yourself by completing activity 14:

▶ Activity 14: Duncker's radiation problem

The life of a patient with a malignant stomach tumour can only be saved by using a particular kind of ray. The problem is that if the ray is strong enough to kill the tumour, it will also kill healthy tissue. If the ray is weaker than this, though, it will not destroy the tumour. How can the ray be used to destroy the tumour without harming healthy tissue?

If you have trouble with this, read through the study in box N.

When you have finished, see the notes on page 443.

Box N: Gick and Holyoak (1980)

Procedure: All participants were asked to solve Duncker's radiation problem. Those who could not solve the problem were asked to remember three stories. One was about a general capturing a fortress by having his army approach it from different directions, so it used an analogous idea to the solution to the radiation problem. Half the participants were told that one of the stories could be relevant to the problem they had been set, while half were not given this hint.

Results: Ninety-two per cent of participants who had their attention drawn to the relevance of one of the stories solved the problem, compared with very few of those who did not.

Conclusion: Even if there is an analogous situation in long-term memory which can help to solve a current problem, there may be only a very small probability of the analogy being identified.

However, it is also possible for previous learning to get in the way of finding a solution for a current problem. One example of this is **functional fixedness**; a classic example is described in box O:

Box O: Duncker (1945)

Procedure: Participants were asked to mount a candle on a vertical screen. Various objects were spread around, including a book of matches and a box of nails (see figure 4).

Results: Most participants had difficulty in solving this problem. They did not realise that the box holding the nails could be used to provide a mounting for the candle, having classified it as a container. Participants were more likely to use the box to solve the problem when it was empty.

Conclusion: Past experience can hinder problem-solving.

Figure 4: Duncker (1945)

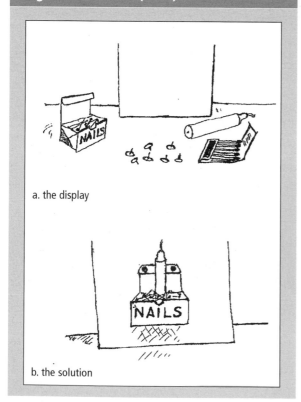

a. the display

b. the solution

We will be returning to this idea later in the chapter, in the section on problem-solving and **set**.

Working backwards

Instead of working forwards from the problem to the solution, it can sometimes be helpful if the direction is reversed: start from the desired end state and work backwards in the other direction. For example, take the problem of how a magician pulls a rabbit out of a hat. This is a difficult problem if you start from an empty hat. However, if you start from the goal state, i.e. the rabbit being pulled from the hat, it is clear that the rabbit must have been put in the hat either before or during the show. Since it would be difficult to manage this during the show, it must have been put there beforehand, so there must be a compartment where it could be hidden.

Means-end analysis

In complex problems, means–end analysis involves identifying a series of **sub-goals** between the current state of the problem and the goal state which reduces the distance between them. A **mental operator**, i.e. a move, is then chosen which allows progress to be made towards the sub-goal. For example, if the problem was to get to university, a sub-goal might be to decide which universities to apply to, or to fill in and send off the UCAS form.

Try the orcs and hobbits problem, a variant of what was previously known as the 'missionaries and cannibals' problem:

◗ Activity 15: orcs and hobbits

Three orcs and three hobbits, all on one river bank, need to cross a river so that they are all on the opposite bank. There is a boat which can hold two people, and at least one person is needed to take the boat across the river. There must never be more orcs than hobbits on either bank of the river, as the orcs would then eat the hobbits.

How many moves does it take you to get all the hobbits and orcs across the river? The smallest number possible is eleven.

When you have finished, see the notes on page 443.

This problem is clearly too complicated to solve all at once, so we might set the sub-goal of moving two hobbits and two orcs across the river. When this is achieved, we can then work on how to complete the task.

If you managed to solve the problem in 11 moves, you will have found that at one point (between moves 6 and 7; see the solution on page 443), one hobbit and one orc had to be moved back to the starting point. If we set up sub-goals, as means–ends analysis proposes, with each sub-goal bringing us closer to the final goal state, a move like this seems to be getting further away from a solution, and so might be expected to cause difficulties.

This idea was tested by Thomas (1974). He found that participants did indeed experience a lot of difficulty at this point. He also found further support for the idea of sub-goals, since typically participants would carry out several moves fairly rapidly, followed by a longish pause before another rapid series of moves.

The computational approach to problem-solving

There has been increasing interest in the possibility of modelling human thinking using computer programmes. The most influential early research in this area was carried out by Newell and Simon (1972) who developed a **General Problem Solver** (**GPS**). They devised their program by asking people to 'talk through' the problems they were solving, such as those described above, and used this information as the basis for establishing the general strategies deployed. These were then used to create the problem-solving structure of their computer program.

Newell and Simon, in developing the GPS, were aiming to develop a theoretical approach which could apply generally – therefore a *general* problem solver – rather than to just one kind of problem. Ernst and Newell (1969) found that the GPS could be applied to and solve 11 different problems, including the orcs and hobbits problem in activity 15, and the Tower of Hanoi problem in activity 16, though it sometimes seemed to do so in ways that were different from those used by people.

Newell and Simon argued that many problems can be defined in terms of a **problem space**. This consists of the **initial state** of the problem, the **goal state** and all the possible states between the two which can be created by mental operators. The process of problem-solving consists of moving through a sequence of different **knowledge states**.

As an example, let us look at a standard problem called the Tower of Hanoi:

▶ Activity 16: Tower of Hanoi

Three discs are piled in size order on the first of three pegs:

The task is to move them so that they are in the same order on the last peg. Only one disc can be moved at a time, and a larger disc can never be placed on top of a smaller one. Can you do this in the minimum of seven moves?

When you have finished, see the notes on page 444.

The rules restrict the number of possible mental operators. From the initial state, only two moves are possible, i.e. moving the smaller disc to either of the other pegs. Each of these moves changes the knowledge state, which in turn affects the possibilities available for the next move. With each move the problem is moving closer to the goal state. The mental operators used to move from initial state towards goal state are selected using heuristics, in particular **means–end analysis**. For example, in the Tower of Hanoi problem, a suitable sub-goal would be to try to get the largest disk on the last peg.

- **Algorithms** guarantee a solution to a problem but are time-consuming. As a short-cut, we may use **heuristics**.
- Heuristics include **analogies**, and **working backwards** from the solution to the problem. In complex problems, the heuristic technique of **means–end analysis** sets sub-goals between the problem and the solution.
- There is also interest in using **computers** to help us understand how people solve problems. The **General Problem Solver (GPS)** was the most influential early research taking this approach.

Set in problem-solving

In problem-solving, set is a bias or readiness to interpret information in a particular way. These preconceived ideas can prevent people from solving the problem efficiently. Set can take three forms – operational set, functional set and rule set.

Operational set refers to the notion that a problem needs to be solved using a particular operation or sequence of operations, when the person's mind is unable to shift to a different pattern:

Box P: Luchins (1942)

Procedure: Participants were given a series of problems (1–7 below). In each problem, there are three jars (A , B and C) with the different capacities shown in the table. The task is to fill and empty the different jars to end up with a specified amount of water ('goal'):

	1.	2.	3.	4.	5.	6.	7.
A	21	14	18	7	20	23	15
B	127	46	43	42	57	49	39
C	3	5	10	6	4	3	3
goal	100	22	5	23	29	20	18

Results: After working through the first six problems, participants have usually worked out that in each case the solution is to fill B, fill A from B, then fill C from B twice. The goal amount is then left in B. They apply this series of operations to the final problem, even though it is much simpler to fill B from A and C.
Conclusion: Using a particular problem-solving technique can create a set which is difficult to adapt.

Functional set refers to the assumption that the elements of a problem have a fixed function:

Box Q: Scheerer (1963)

Procedure: In the room shown in figure 5, participants were asked to put the two rings on the peg from behind the chalk line shown. They could move freely round the room while they were not actually carrying out the task, and use anything in the room. For group A, string was hanging up things with no function, i.e. an out-of-date calendar or a cloudy mirror. For group B, the string was hanging up functional items, i.e. a current calendar, a clear mirror or 'No Smoking' sign. Participants in the control group had a piece of string hanging from a nail on the wall.
Results: All group A and the control group solved the problem by using the string to tie the two sticks together. For group B, of those exposed to the current calendar, 56% failed to use the string; with the clear mirror, 69% failed. The failure rate was 53% with the 'No Smoking' sign. Group B participants reported that they hadn't thought of using the string, though none believed they were forbidden to do so.
Conclusion: Participants showed functional set, in that they did not see beyond the existing function of the string holding up the calendar, mirror and 'No Smoking' sign.

Figure 5: ring and peg task (Scheerer, 1963)

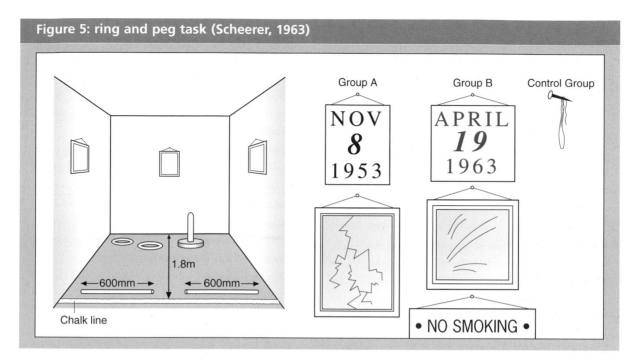

Rule set refers to the belief that there are certain rules which have to be observed when solving a problem, even when these rules have not been explicitly imposed.

▶ Activity 17: rule set

Try these problems yourself, or ask a participant to carry them out:

a Use six matches to create four equilateral congruent triangles. The length of each side of each triangle must be equal to the length of the matches.

b Draw four straight lines to connect all these dots, without taking your pencil off the paper:

•   •   •

•   •   •

•   •   •

Many people get stuck on these problems because of rule set.

When you have finished, see the notes on page 444.

Limitations of research into problem-solving

One factor which we need to bear in mind in drawing conclusions about the nature of problem-solving is the nature of the problem being investigated. You may have felt that many of the problems used by researchers are rather removed from the kinds of problems we face in real life, i.e. lack **ecological validity**. The hobbits and orcs task and the Towers of Hanoi are very clearly defined problems, with clearly specified rules. This is very rarely true of real-life problems.

Greene (1987) has suggested that everyday problems differ from puzzle problems in two main ways. Firstly, puzzle problems call on knowledge which is **domain-independent**. In other words, in contrast to real-life problems, which require **domain-specific** knowledge, solving the problem does not rely on detailed knowledge about a particular topic. Secondly, the information necessary to solve puzzle problems is present in the statement of the problem. In real-life problems, a lot of the difficulty lies in finding the relevant information which is needed to solve them. The study by Gick and Holyoak in box N gives an example of this.

Given these differences, we need to be careful in generalising about how people solve real-life problems on the basis of research using puzzle problems.

- **Set** can affect problem-solving. It can take three forms: **operational set**, **functional set** and **rule set**.
- Much of the research into problem-solving strategies has low **ecological validity**. Research findings may therefore not necessarily relate closely to the way we solve real-life problems.

Adversary problems

You will remember that in adversary problems, such as the game of chess, two (or more) people are in competition to solve a problem. The aim in adversary problems is the same as in non-adversary problems, i.e. achieving a desired goal. However, since players are in competition to reach the goal, the solution for each player needs to use a sequence of moves which do not allow the other player to achieve it or even move towards it. Each player therefore needs to adopt the **minimax strategy**, where they aim to *mini*mise the *max*imum loss the other player can inflict on them.

In a game like chess, with huge numbers of possible moves, a powerful computer would be necessary to use an algorithmic method. Human players need to take a heuristic approach, where a few possible moves are chosen and evaluated using the minimax strategy.

One area of particular interest in adversary problems is how experts go about solving problems compared with novices. Much of the research in this area has investigated the strategies used in chess; expertise is defined in terms of the domain-specific knowledge, i.e. knowledge and experience of playing chess, which a person brings to the game:

Box R: De Groot (1966)

Procedure: Five chess grandmasters (experts) and five expert chess players (novices compared to the grandmasters) were shown a particular board position. They were each asked to decide what the next move should be.

Results: The grandmasters did not consider more possible moves than the experts, but they did reach a decision more quickly, and the moves they chose were judged by independent raters to be better than those chosen by the experts.

Conclusion: Since good players study the chess games of others and can often recall details of games they themselves have played, the difference between grandmasters and experts was explained in terms of differences in the knowledge of different board positions stored in long-term memory. Given this knowledge, some possible moves could be rejected immediately.

De Groot went on to test his conclusion by asking participants to reproduce board positions from actual games, each position being presented for 2–15 seconds. The grandmasters could carry out this task with 91% accuracy, compared with only 41% for the experts. When the chess pieces were randomly arranged on the board, there was no difference in the performance of the two groups; neither group had superior knowledge on which they could draw.

Chase and Simon (1973) carried out a further study into the underlying reasons for the difference between experts and novices in chess. They asked players to reconstruct a board position on another board, while the first board could still be seen. For both experts and novices, the average number of pieces taken in at a glance was similar, but the experts' glances were significantly shorter. This led them to conclude that experts are able to recognise and encode information in chunks more quickly, and this is a factor in their superior performance.

- In **adversary problems**, people need to adopt the **minimax strategy**.
- **Experts** are better at solving problems than **novices** because they have more **domain-specific knowledge** to draw on. They are also better at **chunking** this information.

Decision-making

Decision-making can be seen as a kind of problem-solving, in that we are presented with a range of possible solutions to a problem from which we have to make a choice. Decision-making involves **values** and **probability**. For example, if you are deciding which kind of job to apply for, each possible job has value implications in terms of how interesting it is likely to be, the kind of salary it carries, the possibilities for promotion, and so on. You would also need to consider the probability of these positive outcomes occurring.

Many of the everyday decisions we make are relatively unimportant, such as deciding which video to get from the video shop. Others, however, have far-reaching consequences, such as deciding which subject to study at university. Psychologists have investigated the ways in which people make decisions and the factors which may influence this process.

One useful distinction is between **normative** and **empirical** decision-making. Studies of normative decision-making have been widely carried out in such areas as economics. They are concerned with finding out the best and most rational ways of making decisions. Empirical studies, on the other hand, look at the actual processes involved when people make decisions.

A further distinction can be made between **compensatory** and **non-compensatory models** of decision-making. Compensatory models refer to evaluating possible outcomes of decisions in terms of the extent to which the desirable aspects of a particular decision compensate for the undesirable aspects. Non-compensatory models are less precise; we do not take into account all the possible features of each possible choice when reaching a decision.

Compensatory models of decision-making

One example of a compensatory model, which also falls into the category of normative decision-making, is the **additive compensatory model**. You can try this for yourself:

Activity 18: making decisions: the additive compensatory model

Think back to the time when you needed to decide which subjects to study at A-level. Make a list of six subjects which you thought of taking, and use the following procedure to reduce the possibilities to the number of subjects you are actually taking. Make a list of the factors which you think are important in making this choice. A few suggestions are given here, but feel free to add to these or to leave out any which you don't consider important:

a How interesting the subject is likely to be.

b How much time needs to be spent on the subject outside the classroom.

c How well you get on with the teacher who will be taking the subject.

d Whether the results have been good in previous years.

e How useful the subject will be in terms of career plans.

You then need to weight each factor, using a scale from 1–10 in terms of how important you think it is, e.g:

a How interesting the subject is likely to be. (8 = pretty important)

b How much time needs to be spent on the subject outside the classroom. (3 = much less important)

You then need to rate each of your six subjects from 1–10 on each of the factors you have listed, in terms of how positively you rate it on that particular factor, and multiply this rating by the weighting to get a score, e.g:

> History – a. rating 7 (pretty interesting);
>   score = 7 x 8 = 56
>   b. rating 2 (loads of reading);
>   score = 2 x 3 = 6

Add up the scores for each subject, and pick the subjects with the highest scores.

Is this a useful way of making this kind of complex decision?

Would you use this procedure again, e.g. if choosing a car or deciding which university to go to?

What are its good points?

What are the drawbacks?

If you know someone who will soon be making the decision of which A-levels to take, test the procedure on them instead. Ask them how helpful they found this method.

There are several good things about using this model. Providing you have identified all the factors which you think are important and weighted them appropriately, the procedure is thorough and comprehensive, and will lead to the best decision. On the other hand, it takes a long time to carry out, and this may be an important reason why in practice people tend not to make decisions in this way.

Non-compensatory models of decision-making

Because they are quicker and more straightforward, we are more likely in practice to use one of the various non-compensatory models in reaching a decision. Four possible methods are shown in figure 6:

Figure 6: non-compensatory models

a. *elimination by aspects*: we pick the factor which seems to us most important, e.g. in activity 18 this could be how interesting the subject is likely to be. Possibilities which are low on this factor are eliminated. If there are still more than two possibilities, we then focus on the next most important factor to eliminate more options, and so on. We finally accept the last remaining option.

b. *maximax strategy*: we decide what is the best aspect of each option, compare these aspects, and decide on the option which has the strongest best aspect.

c. *minimax strategy*: the weakest positive feature of each option is identified. The option chosen is the one whose weakest feature is considered most important.

d. *conjunctive strategy*: a minimum acceptable value is given to each option. Criteria are matched in turn against each option, and those options which don't meet the minimum requirements are eliminated until only one option remains.

Activity 19: identifying models of decision-making

Helen is deciding what to do on Saturday evening. She has been invited to a party by friends at college, another friend has asked if she would like to go to see a film, and there is a band playing locally that she would like to hear.

Below are four ways in which Helen might have made her decision. Match each with one of the models in figure 6. Each model is used once:

1   Going to hear the band will make a change from what Helen normally does on a Saturday evening, going to the party won't cost anything, and going to the film means she doesn't have to make much of an effort, as her friend will pick her up and drop her off again. She is short of money, so decides to go to the party.

2   Helen thinks about the other people she will be with for each activity. None of her friends is interested in the band she likes, and she doesn't think that any of her close friends are going to the party. She decides to go to see the film.

3   Helen is very hard up, so she can't afford to do anything which costs much. If she goes to the party, she will have to take a bottle. She may not get a lift back so she might need to get a cab. The tickets for the band are quite expensive, and she will need money for drinks. Her friend will pay for her cinema ticket, pick her up and drop her off afterwards. She decides to go to the film.

4   Lots of her friends are going to the party, she really wants to see the film, but this may be the only opportunity she has to hear the band. She decides to go to hear the band.

When you have finished, see the notes on page 444.

We will look at just one of these non-compensatory models, the **elimination by aspects** model proposed by Tversky (1972). This strategy has the advantage of being relatively straightforward, compared with, say, the additive-compensatory model, though it may not lead to the best decision. Ideally, the most important criterion should be considered first, but what is most important may not be entirely clear – for example, cost and how much fun you are likely to have may be more or less equally important criteria when deciding what to do on a Saturday night – so the option finally chosen may depend on the order in which the criteria are considered.

Finally, people may also use a mixture of the strategies we have looked at:

Box S: Payne (1976)

Procedure: Participants were asked to choose a house or a flat from information given on cards. The strategies they used to reach a decision were noted.

Results: Most participants initially used strategies such as elimination by aspects to reduce the number of possibilities. They then made a final decision in a more thorough and systematic way.

Conclusion: In practice, a mix of strategies may be used, depending on the number of options available.

Heuristics in decision-making

When we have important decisions to make, it clearly makes sense to approach the decision-making process in a systematic way. However, sometimes we don't have all the information we need to make completely rational decisions. We also tend to try to reduce the amount of effort we need to make, and so rely on **heuristics**. The examples of non-compensatory models of decision-making, described above, also take a heuristic approach.

Two heuristics important in decision-making are the **availability heuristic** and the **representativeness heuristic**. To give you a feel for what is meant by an availability heuristic, try activity 20:

▶ Activity 20: availability heuristics

Do you think that K is more common as the first letter of a word or as the third letter of a word? If you can, ask other people the same question. Compare your answers with the discussion that follows.

Tversky and Kahneman (1973) found that most people guessed that K appears more often as the first letter of a word than as the third letter, though in fact K is three times as likely to appear in third place. They suggested that people make this error because it is very much easier to think of words beginning with K than those which have K as their third letter. In other words, those words beginning with K are more available. Decision-making may be affected by the availability of information in long-term memory.

A study by Tversky and Kahneman demonstrates how decisions may be affected by the representativeness heuristic:

Box T: Tversky and Kahneman (1973)

Procedure: Participants were given this information:

'Steve is very shy and withdrawn, invariably helpful, but with little interest in people, or in the world of reality. A meek and tidy soul, he has a need for order and structure, and a passion for detail.'

They were then asked to estimate how likely it was that Steve had a job as a musician, pilot, doctor, salesman and librarian.

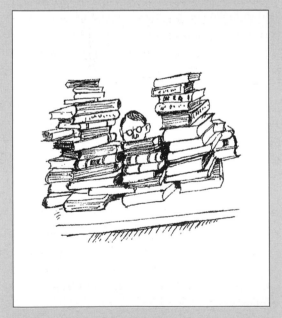

Results: Most participants guessed that he was most likely to be a librarian.

Conclusion: Decisions were affected by how well the description fitted prototypes, where a concept is defined in terms of a set of typical characteristics. Steve's characteristics fit well with stereotypes we have about what a typical librarian is like.

The representativeness heuristic relates to judgements of probability. This is a major factor in decision-making, and has therefore been the focus of a lot of research. People often make errors when judging probabilities:

Box U: Kahneman and Tversky (1972)

Procedure: Participants were told that the descriptions of people they were going to be given had been selected at random from a set of 100 descriptions. Half the participants were told that 70 of the people described were lawyers, and the other 30 engineers. The numbers and professions were reversed for the other participants. They were read a description which corresponded well to stereotypes of both lawyers and engineers, and then asked to indicate the probability of the description being either of an engineer or of a lawyer.

Results: Most participants decided that the probability of the description relating to a lawyer or an engineer was 0.5, i.e. that there was a 50/50 chance that the description related to either profession.

Conclusion: Probability judgments were influenced by the representativeness heuristic, since the description was equally applicable to both. Participants did not take into account the base-rate information, i.e. the relative numbers of lawyers and engineers they were told made up the sample.

The conclusion Kahneman and Tversky drew was supported by a further finding in this study. Participants were told a description had been picked at random, but were not given the description. In this situation, when they could not use the representativeness heuristic, they correctly estimated the probability of the description relating to an engineer or a lawyer as 0.7 or 0.3, in line with the base-rate information they had been given. In a further study (Tversky and Kahneman, 1980), people were much more likely to make appropriate use of base-rate information when they were presented with problems in which its importance was stressed.

Another example of how using the representativeness heuristic can lead to errors is shown in activity 21:

Activity 21: errors in judgement using the representativeness heuristic

Find some willing participants and ask them this question:

Linda is a former student activist, single, very intelligent, and a philosophy graduate. On a scale of 1–10, where 1 is 'extremely unlikely' and 10 is 'certain', how probable is it that she is: a. a bank cashier, b. a feminist or c. a feminist bank cashier?

This is one of the questions used in a study by Tversky and Kahneman (1983). They found that most of their participants said that it was much more probable that Linda was a feminist bank cashier than a bank cashier. Given their results, it is likely that you had similar answers. This answer clearly cannot be correct, since the category 'bank cashiers' must include 'feminist bank cashiers', as well as those with rather different views. Tversky and Kahneman called this kind of error the **conjunctive fallacy**; 'conjunctive' here means putting together different pieces of information.

So why do people make use of availability and representativeness heuristics when they so often lead to errors? One reason is that such heuristics can often be accurate. It makes perfect sense to assume that the characteristics of a sample are generally representative of the parent population from which the sample is drawn. When errors are made, it is usually because other information has been ignored, rather than because the heuristic is irrelevant.

Another reason is that heuristics give us a simple way of approaching a range of problems. People act as **cognitive misers**, in that they try to minimise mental effort. Heuristics are one way in which this can be achieved.

Other influences on decision-making

As we have seen, heuristics are widely used in decision-making and can often lead to errors. We will look briefly here at some of the other factors which can affect the decisions we make.

Sometimes we hold on to our beliefs, and let them influence the decisions we make, even when they have been shown to be ill-founded. This is called **belief perseverance**, and is very difficult to overcome. Beliefs can be challenged by deliberately considering the opposite viewpoint, but even so, ingrained beliefs can be very hard to shift.

Another factor is **entrapment**. When we have invested time or money or care in something, we can be unwilling to change direction because of the costs in terms of what we have already put into it.

Over-confidence can also play a part. We tend to remember our successes rather than our failures, and this may bias the decisions we make. For example, Lichenstein and Fischoff (1980) found that people tended to make mistakes 15% of the time, even when they were completely confident that they were correct.

Tversky and Kahneman (1986) found that people tended to avoid taking risks, even when potentially they had a lot to gain from doing so, and preferred more certain gains associated with lower risks. This is known as **loss aversion**.

Finally, **framing** refers to the way information is presented (or framed) to us. The same basic information presented in different ways can create different responses, and so lead to different decisions. For example, Levin and Gaeth (1988) found that people responded more positively to meat described as '75% lean' than the same meat described as '25% fat'.

Activity 22: factors in decision-making

Match up each of these examples with one of the factors described above. Each factor is used once:

a Penny wants to invest a legacy received from an aunt. She knows that shares as part of an ISA tend over time to be a better investment than putting money in a savings account, but that their value can go down as well as up. She decides to open a savings account.

b Mary has been married for 15 years. Her husband never helps her in the house, although she works full time; he takes no part in bringing up their children, makes no contribution to the household running costs and has had frequent affairs. She knew what he was like when she married him, but believed that he was basically a good person and that she could change him. She still thinks so.

c Some patients being offered medical treatment using a new technique were told that it had a 60% success rate, others that it had a 40% failure rate. The former were more likely to go ahead with the treatment.

d Jay prides himself on his knowledge of music and is a very successful member of his local pub quiz team. He is selected to take part in a TV quiz programme where contestants are shown each question and then decide whether or not they want to answer it. One of the questions is a musical one, and Jay is sure he knows the answer. He attempts the question and gets it wrong.

e Claire is writing a novel. She thought it would be quite quick to do, as she had the plot worked out before she started. It has gone much more slowly than she expected. She has been working on it now for over a year, and there is a long way to go before it is finished, but she is determined to see the project through.

When you have finished, see the notes on page 444.

⑤ Decision-making involves **values** and **probability**. A distinction can be made between **normative** and **empirical** decision-making.

⑤ With **compensatory models**, we systematically weigh up the desirable and undesirable aspects of the choices open to us. An example of this kind of model is the **additive compensatory model**. It is thorough but time-consuming.

⑤ **Non-compensatory models** are quicker but less systematic. They include **elimination by aspects**, the **maximax strategy**, the **minimax strategy** and the **conjunctive strategy**. We may also use a mixture of strategies.

⑤ To minimise effort in decision-making, we make use of heuristics, in particular the **availability heuristic** and the **representativeness heuristic**. The use of the representativeness heuristic can lead to inaccurate judgements of **probability** and so bias decision-making.

⑤ Other factors also influence decision-making. They include **belief perseverance**, **entrapment**, **over-confidence**, **loss aversion** and **framing**.

Notes on activities

1 The first sentence is a well-formed English sentence on all three counts. The second sentence is syntactically correct and the words are all in the English lexicon, but semantically it is unacceptable, since it has no meaning. The final sentence also conforms to the rules of English grammar – it describes where and how the plink is sitting – but 'plink', 'feltfully' and 'flong' are not in the English lexicon, and so it is semantically not an English sentence.

2 You would almost certainly be rather more formal in the way you talk to the person interviewing you than to a close friend. You would probably also emphasise rather different aspects of the job in these different circumstances. What is happening here is that you are following

unwritten pragmatic rules which affect how we communicate with others.

4 Following the rule, Jale distinguishes black and white, and Ibibio black, white, red and green (or yellow).

6 There are quite a number of possible meanings. She might, for example, mean 'The sock goes on my foot' or 'Put the sock on my foot' or 'I've got the sock on my foot' or 'The sock is on the floor near my foot' or 'The sock's got a picture of a foot on it'. You may have thought of other possibilities.

7 In the first and last examples, there would be little need to use referential language, since what the language refers to would be clear from the context. You would expect the use of expressive phrases, like 'give me that' and 'do it again'. In the second example, referential language like 'red car' and 'boy run' would make sense as a response to a book.

8 The caregiver is likely to respond by giving the child attention: smiling, touching the child and generally showing pleasure. Utterances such as the child saying something approximating to 'milk' will also be reinforced by the child being given milk. Babies make a lot of different sounds at random. By chance, some of these will sound like 'mum' or 'ma'. A mother is likely to pick up on and reinforce these sounds, since the baby saying 'mum' is very rewarding to her. For the same reason, a father is likely to pick up on and reinforce his baby saying 'dad' or 'da'.

9 CDS uses short, simple sentences. People talk more slowly than with adults or older children, and use lots of repetition and exaggerated changes in pitch. This way of talking to babies seems to serve the purpose of making it easier for babies to pick up and imitate what they hear. It has even been suggested that it can be considered an intensive form of teaching. Its existence seems to go some way, then, to supporting Skinner's belief that imitation is very important in language acquisition.

10 The initial use of correct forms suggests that children are in fact imitating what they hear, and so supports Skinner's theory. On the other hand, the form at stage 2 is not something they will have heard others say. What they seem to be doing at this point is applying the rule for forming the past tense, in this case inappropriately.

11 Both partners in this exchange are playing an active part, and seem to be responding to each other. As the mother's level of activity starts to fall at about $1\frac{1}{2}$ seconds, so the baby's level rises. Similarly, as the baby's activity level starts to drop just before 3 seconds, the mother's level starts to rise.

12 First of all, the mother is showing the child how language and features of the world correspond, in this case that the word 'rabbit' relates to the picture of a rabbit. She is also more generally

showing different things which can be done with words, e.g. naming, asking questions and so on. In addition, once the format (in this case question–answer–feedback) has been laid down, it can be used again to introduce new aspects of language. Because the format is familiar, it will make new learning easier for the child.

13 In English, 'q' must be followed by 'u', which cuts down the possibilities for the first anagram. The second and third anagrams possibly contain the very common combinations of 'ing' and 'tion' respectively, which could have provided a short-cut to a solution. It is also unlikely that you considered starting these words with 'tq', 'lg' or 'nc'. In other words, unlike an algorithmic approach, you were selective in the possibilities you considered.

14 Several weaker rays coming from different directions should be focused on the tumour.

15

443

16

Initial state

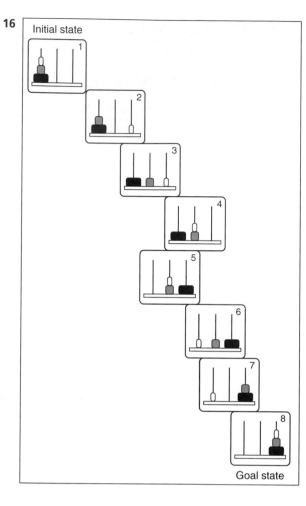

Goal state

17 **a** the matches should form a pyramid. Rule set means that people may assume that the answer has to be in two dimensions. For **b**, rule set may lead to the assumption that the lines have to stay within the square. The solution is:

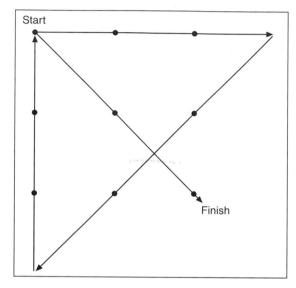

19 1c; 2a; 3d; 4b

22 **a** loss aversion **b** belief perseverance **c** framing **d** over-confidence **e** entrapment

17 Cognitive development

In this chapter we will be looking at:

17.1 Development of thinking
    Piaget's theory of children's thinking
    Vygotsky's theory of children's thinking
    The information-processing approach

17.2 Development of measured intelligence
    Genetic factors in measured intelligence
    Racial differences in intelligence
    Other factors in test performance

17.3 Development of moral understanding
    Piaget's theory of moral development
    Kohlberg's theory of moral development
    After Kohlberg: Eisenberg and Gilligan

17.1 DEVELOPMENT OF THINKING

Piaget's theory of children's thinking

Children's thinking differs in many ways from that of an adult, as shown in their beliefs, their understanding of the physical world, and their understanding of right and wrong. The Swiss psychologist, Jean Piaget (1896–1980), was interested in all these topics.

His ideas came about as a result of observations of his own three children and many others. He used a technique known as the **clinical interview**; tasks were set up for children to do and they were asked to solve problems. He observed what they did, and followed this up by questioning the children.

Piaget was a **constructivist** theorist. He saw children as constructing their own world, playing an active part in their own development. Children are **intrinsically motivated** to interact with their environment and so learn about the world they live in.

Piaget believed children's thinking goes through changes at each of four **stages** of development until they can think and reason as an adult. The stages represent *qualitatively different* ways of thinking. All children go through the stages in the same order, and each stage must be completed before they can move into the next one. Children themselves, through their actions on the environment, interacting with their biologically-determined level of maturation, bring about the cognitive changes which result in adult thinking.

A key term in Piaget's theory is **schema**, a mental representation of an action which includes the knowledge and experience we have acquired relating to that action. According to Piaget, just possessing the schema motivates us to use it. When we are born, the only schemas we have are reflexes. For example, newborn babies have a sucking schema, which they apply by sucking anything put into their mouths. Applying the sucking schema to a range of objects, without adapting it in any way, is an example of what Piaget called **assimilation:** the schema increases in terms of what it can be applied to, but is not changed or adapted in any way. Piaget referred to this steady condition, where not much change is taking place, as **equilibrium**.

However, coming across an object for which the existing schema is a poor fit creates what Piaget termed a state of **disequilibrium**, an uncomfortable state of imbalance which motivates babies to adapt their sucking schema to cope better with new objects which they put into their mouths. For example, they may need to suck a solid object like a rattle in a rather different way from a nipple. This process of adapting a schema is **accommodation**, and **equilibration** is the back-and-forth movement between equilibrium and disequilibrium.

These same principles can be applied to the way we take in and process information about our environment: assimilation is a way of exercising existing schemas, while new objects and situations create a state of disequilibrium, which motivates us to adapt schemas through accommodation.

- Piaget believed that children go through four **stages**, characterised by different ways of thinking, before they can reason like adults. His research used a technique called the **clinical interview**.
- Mental representations of actions are called **schemas**. The earliest schemas are the reflexes we are born with.
- Thinking develops through **assimilation**, **equilibration** and **accommodation.** We are **intrinsically motivated** to respond to our environment in this way. These processes result in continuing **adaptation**.

Piaget's four stages of development are called the **sensori-motor** stage, the **preoperational** stage, the **concrete operational** stage and the **formal operational** stage. There are approximate ages for each of the stages.

The sensori-motor stage (0–2 years)
During this stage, children's thinking is on a physical level: children are coming to grips with the information they receive through their **senses**, and relating these sensations to their own physical (i.e. **motor**) actions.

At the beginning of this stage, in the first few weeks after birth, children practise innate reflexes, such as sucking and grasping. Gradually these basic schemas develop as children come into contact with new objects or situations which don't fit existing schemas.

A major characteristic of this stage is what Piaget called **egocentrism**, where children's thinking focuses on themselves. When children are first born, they have no conception of the distinction between self and other. Even when this is understood, Piaget believed that their thinking is still always related to themselves. Here is an observation Piaget made which illustrates egocentrism:

> **Box A: Piaget (1963)**
>
> Piaget observed his seven-month-old daughter Jacqueline playing with a plastic duck. As she was playing, the duck slipped behind a fold in her quilt. She followed this movement with her eyes, but as soon as the duck disappeared, she did not reach out for it, and seemed to lose interest entirely. Piaget picked up the duck and showed it to her. Once he had caught her interest, he hid it very obviously under the quilt. Again, she lost interest. This same pattern was repeated several times.
>
> Piaget concluded that when the duck had disappeared, for Jacqueline it had ceased to exist. The duck existed for her only for as long as she could see it.

This observation demonstrates egocentrism, in that objects only exist in relation to the child's own perceptions. It is an example of children's lack of **object permanence**, i.e. the understanding that things continue to exist even if we can't perceive them with any of our senses. This gradually develops in the sensori-motor stage. By the age of about 8 months, children will search for a completely hidden object, but still do not seem to have developed a full understanding of the situation:

Box B: the A–B error

Procedure: A child sees a toy hidden under cloth A. She retrieves it. The toy is hidden several times under cloth A, always with the same results. The toy is then hidden under cloth B, in full view of the child.

Results: The child attempts to retrieve the toy from under cloth A.

Conclusion: The child understands the continuing existence of an object that can't

be seen. She is still egocentric, since she believes that her own actions have brought the toy back into existence. On each repetition of the toy being hidden, the reappearance of the toy has been achieved by her lifting cloth A, so this is what she does on the last repetition.

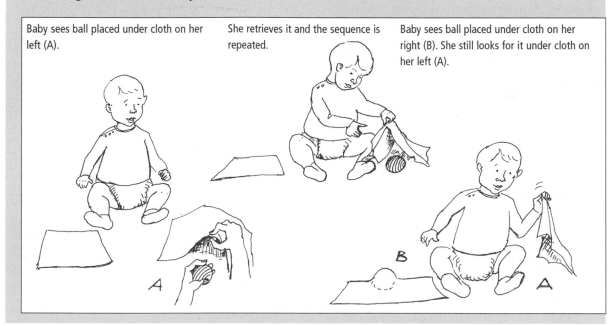

Baby sees ball placed under cloth on her left (A).

She retrieves it and the sequence is repeated.

Baby sees ball placed under cloth on her right (B). She still looks for it under cloth on her left (A).

By about 12 months babies have developed object permanence, but it is not until the age of about 18 months that they understand that something which they haven't actually seen *might* have happened.

You can test this out by hiding a small toy, in full view of a child, in a matchbox. Then hide the matchbox under a cushion. While the child isn't looking, take the toy out of the matchbox, hide it under the cushion and give the empty matchbox to the child. When the child fails to find the toy in the matchbox, he or she usually does not look for it under the cushion; according to Piaget, the idea that the toy could have fallen out of the matchbox does not occur to such children, because they have not seen it happen.

Activity 1: Piaget's interpretation of his observations

Look back at the two observations Piaget made, described in box A and box B, and the description of the matchbox task described above.

Piaget's results have been replicated many times with very similar results. However, his *interpretations* of what he observed have been questioned. Can you think of alternative ways of explaining Piaget's observations?

When you have finished, see the notes on page 481.

Later research has used methods which are simpler for children:

Box C: Hood and Willats (1986)

Procedure: Five-month-old infants were shown an object either to their left or their right. Their arms were held down so they couldn't reach out to the object. The lights were then switched off, so that the infant could no longer see the object, but their behaviour could be observed. At the same time, their arms were freed.

Results: The infants as a group reached out significantly more often in the direction in which the object had been seen, compared to the number of times they reached out in the other direction. There was, though, considerable variation between individuals.

Conclusion: Some children as young as 5 months have some degree of object permanence. This is considerably younger than Piaget suggested.

Light on, child looks at toy

Light off, child looks away

Light still off, child reaches to where toy was last seen

It has also been suggested (e.g. Diamond, 1985) that it is the demands made on the child's immature **memory** capacity that make a task like the A–B error task in box B so difficult.

There is some evidence, then, that the conclusions Piaget drew from his observations are not the only possible interpretations. It seems likely that infants are capable of rather more, rather earlier, than Piaget gave them credit for.

The other main feature of the sensori-motor stage is the development of what Piaget called the **general symbolic function**. By this he meant the understanding that one thing can symbolise or stand for another. Symbols can then be used to represent something that isn't actually present. This ability appears towards the end of the sensori-motor stage, and marks children's move into the preoperational stage.

The most important way in which the general symbolic function shows itself is in the use of **language**: for example, children can use the word 'juice' as a symbol to indicate that they would like some juice, even when the juice cannot be seen. Children of this age also start to **draw**: their art represents 'a house' or 'daddy'. They take part in **make-believe play**, where a cardboard box may be used to represent a car, and they show **deferred imitation**, the capacity to imitate something or someone not actually there at the time, e.g. 'What does the cow say?' 'Moo.'

- Thinking in the sensori-motor stage is based on relating **sensory** information and children's own **movements**.
- The sensori-motor stage is characterised by profound **egocentrism** and a lack of **object permanence**.

❺ Piaget's interpretation of his observations has been challenged. The results can be explained by children's **lack of co-ordination** and immature **memory** system.

❺ Towards the end of this stage, children develop the **general symbolic function**.

The preoperational stage (2–7 years)

The development of object permanence and symbolic thinking mark the move into the **preoperational** stage. It is called the preoperational stage because children are not yet able to carry out mental **operations** i.e. internalised (mental) actions, but think in a way which is very much tied to the concrete, physical world. The start of this stage (the **preconceptual substage**) is characterised by continuing **egocentrism** and by **animism**, i.e. believing that inanimate objects are actually alive and have human abilities and feelings.

In conversations with children, Piaget gathered a lot of data which demonstrated **animism**. Some of his examples included: 'Don't touch my garden....my garden would cry', and (holding a toy car up to the window): 'Motor see the snow'.

There are also problems with **seriation**, i.e. arranging things in order, using height or length as a criterion. An example of this kind of task is shown in figure 1. Children are given a set of five cards like those in figure 1, in random order, and asked to put them in the correct order to show what happens as an upright stick falls over.

Similarly, Piaget and Szeminska (1941) asked children to put some sticks in order by length. The children had trouble with the concept that a stick could be *longer* than a second stick but *shorter* than a third.

Children of this age have problems with **classification**, i.e. sorting tasks. They can cope quite well when they are asked to sort a mixed set of bricks into blue bricks and red bricks. They find a sorting task very difficult, though, when they are asked to use two criteria at the same time, such as size *and* colour, e.g. 'big red bricks' and 'small blue bricks'; they usually sort either by colour or by size. This shows **centration**; children focus (or **centre**) on one aspect of the situation, and are unable to take into account a second factor.

▶ Activity 2: tasks for the preconceptual substage

Try out some Piagetian tasks on 2- to 4-year-old children. For **seriation** and **classification** tasks, use the examples described above. To explore animism, you will need to ask questions such as:

What makes the sun come up in the morning?

What makes the clouds move?

Follow these up with how? and why? questions.

Figure 1: the falling stick task

Later in the preoperational stage, in the **intuitive substage**, children's thinking focuses on the most obvious features of an object, i.e. what it looks like. This is shown in conservation and class inclusion tasks.

Conservation refers to understanding that things do not change, even when their physical appearance has changed. A classic example of this is Piaget's conservation of liquid quantity study:

Box D: Piaget's conservation of liquid quantity study

Procedure: A child is shown two identical glass beakers, two-thirds filled with water. The child is asked whether they both have the same amount of water, or if one has more:

the initial display

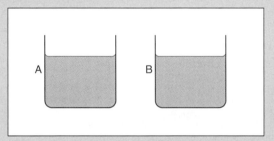

The experimenter makes minor adjustments to the water level until the child agrees that both beakers have the same amount of water. The child then sees the water from one beaker poured into a third beaker, which is taller and narrower than the other two:

the transformation

The child is then asked whether both beakers in the transformed display have the same amount of water in them, or whether one has more:

the transformed display

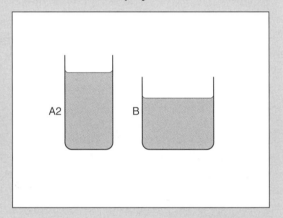

Results: Children up to the age of about 7 typically say that the taller, thinner beaker has more water. Occasionally they say that the original beaker has more in. When asked why, they give reasons such as 'Because it's taller.'

Conclusion: Children of this age are unable to conserve liquid quantlty.

Piaget believed these findings showed that children are dominated by their perceptions. Children centre on one aspect (the height of the liquid) and ignore the other aspect of width.

Children are not yet able to represent actions mentally and do not understand the principles of **compensation** (that the height of the liquid is compensated by its width), **identity** (that nothing has been added or taken away from the original display), and **reversibility** (they cannot mentally return to the initial display by pouring the liquid back into its original container).

Piaget also carried out conservation tasks on other physical properties, e.g. mass, length and number:

Box E: conservation of number

Procedure: Children are shown two rows of counters:

There are equal numbers in each row, and they are placed so that each counter in one row is directly opposite a counter in the other row. Children are asked whether both rows have the same number of counters, or whether one has more. Children usually agree that both rows are the same. The display is then transformed:

The question – whether both rows have the same number of counters or whether one row has more than the other – is repeated.
Results: Children usually say that the longer row has more counters.
Conclusion: Children of this age are unable to conserve number.

Children under seven have problems with **class inclusion**, i.e. thinking about whole classes of objects and subclasses. Imagine a child is shown a number of counters, most of them red, but with a few yellow ones. The child is then asked three questions:

Are these all counters?
Are there more red counters or more yellow counters?
Are there more red counters or more counters?

Children have no difficulty with the first two questions. For the last question, though, they tend to say that there are more red counters, in spite of having answered the first question correctly. Piaget argued that the immediate perception that there are more red counters than yellow ones prevents them from understanding the relationship between a subclass (red counters) and a class (counters).

Activity 3: tasks for the intuitive stage

If you have access to children aged 4–7, try out some conservation and class inclusion tasks. You could replicate the tasks described here.

For testing conservation, you could also try **conservation of mass**. Use two balls of plasticine, and add or remove bits until the child agrees that they have the same amount. Then roll one into a sausage shape and ask: 'Does each have the same amount of plasticine, or does one have more?' A non-conserving child is likely to say that the rolled-out shape has more plasticine.

Egocentrism is still shown in children's inability to put themselves mentally in someone else's position:

Box F: Piaget and Inhelder (1956)

Procedure: Children were shown a three-dimensional model of a Swiss mountain scene. There were three mountains of different colours. One had snow on top, one a cross and one a house. The children sat facing the model. They were asked to pick from a display of ten pictures the view they could see. Most children could pick out their own view. They were then asked to pick out the view which could be seen by a doll seated opposite them on the far side of the display.

Results: Most children under the age of 7 were unable to pick out correctly the view the doll could see. They picked out their own view or the wrong picture.

Conclusions: Children under 7 are bound by the **egocentric illusion**; they do not understand that what they see relates only to their own position. They do not understand the viewpoint of someone sitting in a different position.

According to Piaget, all these tasks show children's inability to think logically and demonstrate that children of this age are still egocentric to the extent that their perceptions dominate their judgement. However, the tasks Piaget used with preoperational children have also been criticised. Researchers have claimed that his methods mask what the child is able to do, and they criticise his interpretations of his findings.

Donaldson, in her book *Children's Minds* (1978), suggested that Piaget did not take into account the **social context** in which children carried out his tasks. He assumed that children use language in the same way as adults. Preoperational children do badly on this kind of task because they are unable to use language abstractly and divorce reasoning from the context in which it occurs; to use Donaldson's word, they are unable to **disembed**. A lot of research supports her ideas, and suggests that Piaget may have underestimated what children can do.

Let us start with the three mountains task. A similar task is described in box G:

Box G: Hughes (1975)

Procedure: Children from $3\frac{1}{2}$–5 were tested. A display of two walls, intersecting to form a cross, was set up. Children were asked to hide a boy doll from a policeman doll. A second policeman doll was then introduced, and the child was asked to hide the boy doll so that neither policeman could see him.

Results: Children managed this task successfully around 90% of the time. Even when a third policeman was added and there were six walls, the older children were successful 90% of the time, and the younger ones were 60% successful.

Conclusion: Children of this age are not as egocentric as Piaget believed. If the task is simplified, children are largely successful.

Activity 4: three mountains and a policeman

Think about the ways Piaget's three mountain task differs from the policeman task. Use these differences to try to explain why children do so much better on the policeman task.

When you have finished, see the notes on page 481.

Let us turn now to some conservation studies. One study by Rose and Blank (1974) carried out a variant of the conservation of number task. They asked the question 'Do both rows have the same counters, or does one have more?' only once, *after* the transformation had been made. Children in this variation were much more likely to conserve, i.e. to say that both rows had the same number of counters.

If you are asked a question, and then asked the same question a second time, it is usually because you got the answer wrong the first time. What children seem to be doing here is *interpreting* the second question in terms of what it would be sensible to ask in the circumstances. Between the first and second questions, one row of counters has been made longer. It may be that children believe they are meant to focus on this change, and this influences their answers to the second question in Piaget's test.

Other factors might also need to be considered:

Box H: McGarrigle and Donaldson (1974)

Procedure: The standard initial question was asked, and the child agreed that there was the same number of counters in the two rows. Then a 'Naughty Teddy' glove puppet appeared out of his box and pushed one row of counters closer together. After the teddy had been returned to his box, the second question was asked.
Results: Children were much more likely to conserve than in a standard conservation task.
Conclusion: The transformation was seen as *accidental*, and so was not considered to be an important part of the procedure which should influence the answer.

Let us look finally at a class inclusion task:

Box I: McGarrigle and Donaldson (1974)

Procedure: Six-year-old children were shown four toy cows, three black and one white. The cows were put on their sides and children were told that they were sleeping. Some children were asked the standard class inclusion question: 'Are there more black cows or more cows?' Others were asked: 'Are there more black cows or more sleeping cows?'

Sleeping cows

Results: Significantly more children answered the second question correctly.
Conclusion: Comparing a sub-class with a whole class is not something that children realise they are expected to do. The question as it stands doesn't make immediate sense to them. They therefore interpret the standard question as asking them to compare sub-class (black cows) with sub-class (white cows). The wording of the second question (including 'sleeping') emphasises what comparison is to be made, making it easier for them to show their understanding.

Piaget's idea that preoperational children are egocentric is not without merit. For example, it can help to explain why children perform poorly on seriation and classification tasks; decentration is a problem. They do seem to focus on their immediate perceptions, and have difficulty co-ordinating more than one perspective at a time. There may also be some truth in the idea that animism shows that children are egocentric. On the other hand, parents often encourage their children to be animistic ('Let's put teddy to bed now. He's very sleepy'). Nor is animism restricted to the under-7s – perhaps you swear at your computer when it doesn't do what you want it to?

Unlike adults, children can't usually give us much feedback on their mental processes, and so we must interpret what they do. However, the research examples in this section help to show that we need to think very carefully about how we interpret children's behaviour. We need to look at Piagetian tasks from children's point of view, and take into account the social context of the tasks, the extent to which tasks make human sense to children of the relevant age and to consider that children's use of language may not be identical to that of adults. In the light of this evidence, it seems that children are less egocentric in the preoperational stage than Piaget claimed.

- ❺ In the **preoperational stage**, children are still **egocentric**. They are unable to put themselves in another's position and see with their eyes.
- ❺ They are **animistic** and are unable to carry out **seriation**, **classification, class inclusion** and **conservation** tasks. They are unable to **decentre**.
- ❺ Piaget has been criticised for the **complexity** of his tasks. When the tasks are simplified, young children are much more capable than Piaget suggested.
- ❺ Piaget didn't place much importance on the **social context** of his tasks, and what makes **human sense** to the child. He also downplayed the role of **language**.
- ❺ Piaget's notion of **egocentrism** seems to have some truth. He may, however, have overestimated the degree of egocentrism of children in this stage.

The concrete operational stage (7–11 years)

When children enter the concrete operational stage, egocentrism is much reduced. Children can now carry out the tasks which were so problematic in the preoperational stage.

The most important feature of this stage is that children have developed **operations**, i.e. the ability to perform actions mentally. They are capable of performing conservation tasks because they can *mentally* move the counters back the way they were before the transformation or *mentally* pour the liquid back into the original beaker. But this stage is called the **concrete operational stage** because children need mentally to manipulate *concrete objects*; they are still not yet capable of abstract adult thought.

One problem that children of this age still have trouble with is known as a **transitivity task**. Here is an example:

> Andrew is taller than Ben. Ben is taller than Carl. Who is taller, Andrew or Carl?

If they are able to use real objects (e.g. dolls) to represent this problem, concrete operational children can solve it. As an abstract problem, they will not be able to get it right until they reach the **formal operational stage**.

The formal operational stage (11–15 years onwards)

The concrete operational thinker manipulates *things* (even if this happens mentally). The formal operational thinker can manipulate *ideas*. At this stage, children can think *abstractly*. Piaget believed that we all reach this stage somewhere between the ages of 11 and 15, and that formal operational thinking was the thinking of an intelligent adult.

Activity 5 demonstrates a further characteristic of formal operational thinking. The question was used by Dworetzky (1981):

▶ Activity 5: hypothetical thinking

Answer this question: What would happen if people had tails?
When you have finished, see the notes on page 481.

The kinds of answers you are likely to have given show a readiness to think *hypothetically*: to think about things that have never been experienced and are highly unlikely to happen. Concrete operational children are much more likely to respond to this kind of question by telling you what a silly idea it is, and in general not being prepared to consider it on its own terms.

Finally, consider the problem in activity 6:

▶ Activity 6: the beaker problem (Inhelder and Piaget, 1958)

You are given four beakers, each containing a colourless, odourless liquid. You are also given a small bottle, which also contains a colourless, odourless liquid.

The problem is to work out which liquid, or combinations of liquids from the beakers will turn yellow when a few drops of the liquid from the bottle are added. How would you go about solving this problem?

When you have finished, see the notes on page 481.

Children in the concrete operational stage tend to try various combinations haphazardly, while systematic thought is a characteristic of formal operational thinkers.

- ⊗ By the **concrete operational stage**, children have developed **operations**, i.e. mental actions. This enables them to carry out successfully the tasks they could not do in the preoperational stage. **Egocentrism** is much reduced.
- ⊗ Concrete operational children still have problems with **transitivity tasks**. They are unwilling to think hypothetically, and their approach to problem-solving is not yet systematic.
- ⊗ **Formal operational** children can think hypothetically, systematically and abstractly. Formal operational thinking is the thinking of the intelligent adult.

Educational applications of Piaget's theory

▷ Activity 7: Piaget and educational practice

Look back through the account of Piaget's theory. Make a list of the basic ideas it contains which might be useful to teachers in thinking about what goes on in their classroom. For each idea, make a note of what practical use could be made of it in a classroom situation. You could perhaps start with the principle that children learn through their own activity. The implications here would be that children need to have opportunities to be active in the classroom.

Compare your ideas with the discussion which follows.

The idea of children as **active** explorers of their environment is essential to Piaget' theory. Children who are starting their schooling are given opportunities to play with water, clay and so on, as a way of helping them to understand their physical properties by direct hands-on experience.

Children's thinking cannot be developed by **instruction**; the role of the teacher is to provide opportunities for children to find things out for themselves, related to the stage their thinking has reached.

Children's thinking is **qualitatively different** from that of an adult. Teachers need to be aware of these differences in the various stages, and adapt what they ask children to do to the stage the child is in.

Teachers need to remember that young children do not think abstractly but need to relate thinking to **concrete examples**. For example, arithmetic could be supported by the use of counters. Problems need to be related to specific examples that children can easily relate to.

Piaget sees children as **'lone scientists'**, developing as individuals, rather than learning from others in their teaching group. They move through Piaget's stages at rather different rates. Teachers cannot assume that all the children in their class reason in the same way. This puts the emphasis on individualised learning.

Children are **intrinsically motivated**. The activities provided for them should be carried out because achievement in its own right provides satisfaction for children.

Most of these ideas relate to what is now standard practice at least some of the time in the majority of primary school classrooms. A major factor in bringing this about was the Plowden Report (1967) on primary education. This report was very much influenced by what Piaget had to say, in particular the use of **activity methods** and the concept of **readiness**, i.e. matching learning to children's stage of development. It brought to public attention the idea of **child-centred learning**. It signalled a move away from rote learning and children being instructed as a class; the focus instead was on individualised learning, with intrinsically-motivated children finding out for themselves by active self-discovery the nature of their physical environment.

Educational materials and courses have been very much influenced by these ideas. One example is the Nuffield Science programme, which uses a hands-on approach to the teaching of science to younger children.

Activity 8: limitations in educational applications

Can you think of any problems which teachers might have in using these ideas?

When you have finished, see the notes on page 481.

- Piaget's ideas about children as **active, intrinsically-motivated** learners, who bring about their own development, and whose **thinking is qualitatively different** from that of an adult, can be translated into classroom practice.
- The **Plowden Report** made Piaget's ideas widely known. This report was an important influence on classroom practice in primary education.
- **Constraints** on teachers mean that it may not always be possible to put these ideas fully into practice.

Evaluating Piaget's theory

Piaget proposed a comprehensive theory to account for the differences in the thinking of children and adults, explaining the processes through which thinking develops. He has claimed that his account applies universally. This has been supported by many cross-cultural studies, including studies of conservation by Nyiti (1976) in Tanzania and Kiminyo (1977) in Kenya. Piaget used systematic methods, and his ideas are backed by a lot of research. His findings have been widely replicated.

His work has inspired a lot of other research; other theorists have built on his original ideas. It is also worth noting that many of his basic ideas – that thought changes in a systematic way through childhood, that children are active in their own development, and so on – are widely accepted. It is

generally on the more detailed points that other theorists disagree, e.g. the extent to which children are egocentric, rather than the basic concepts. Piaget's theory has also had a profound effect on educational practice.

There are, however, several possible criticisms of the theory. Firstly, there are methodological problems. The clinical interview technique in general is open to criticism, in that it did not always follow a carefully standardised procedure. It seems also that the tasks Piaget used may be too complex, leading to an underestimation of children's understanding in the sensori-motor and pre-operational stages.

Interestingly, he has also been criticised for overestimation when it comes to the formal operational stage. Many people do not reach the abstract reasoning of this stage by the age of 15. A study by Shayer and Wylam (1978) concluded that only 30% of 15- and 16-year-olds reasoned in this way. However, although Piaget believed that all adults are capable of formal reasoning, he recognised that they may have very little need to use this ability in day-to-day living, so it may not develop fully.

Another criticism has been that he largely ignored the social context within which development and testing takes place. Children are seen very much as acting alone in coming to understand their environment, with no real role for other people in shaping cognitive development. In particular, the active interpretation of test situations by children, in terms of what kinds of questions make sense to them in that context, has been overlooked. Related to this is children's use of language. Piaget saw language as reflecting thought, rather than helping to shape it, and so saw it as having little influence in test situations.

The concept of discrete stages has also been criticised. Piaget introduced the idea of **decalage**, the gradual acquisition of particular skills within a particular stage of cognitive development. For example, a child may be able to conserve number but not yet be able to conserve mass. This suggests that the boundaries between stages are not clear-cut.

In spite of these criticisms, though, Piaget's ideas represent a major step forward in our understanding of how children's thinking develops.

⊖ Piaget's theory seeks to give a **comprehensive** and **universally-applicable** explanation of children's cognitive development.

⊖ His ideas have been backed up by systematic **research**, which has been replicated many times. It has also served as a basis for the ideas of other theorists.

⊖ Piaget has had considerable influence on **educational practice**.

⊖ His methods have been criticised for being unnecessarily complicated, leading to dubious **interpretations**. He seems to have underestimated the abilities of under-7s.

⊖ His interpretations fail to give sufficient prominence to the role of **social context** and **language** in young children's reasoning.

⊖ It may be more appropriate to think of development as more continuous than the idea of discrete **stages** suggests.

Vygotsky's theory of children's thinking

Lev Vygotsky (1896–1934) was a Russian psychologist, born in the same year as Piaget. He died early, though, and his work was not readily available in translation until the 1960s, so he has been a less prominent figure in Western developmental psychology than Piaget.

The ideas of Piaget and Vygotsky provide a nice contrast. While both can be described as **constructivist**, and both are **stage theorists**, Vygotsky believed that *all* development is rooted in social interaction: Vygotsky was a *social constructivist*. He also proposed that any account of cognitive development has to take into account the **culture** within which children are growing up. Cognitive skills change and develop in the context of the culture in which they need to be used.

He talked of children acquiring **cultural tools**, ways of functioning in response to the demands of the particular culture. Examples include sign systems (like language and number), social rules and technological tools. Vygotsky claimed that cultural tools are acquired through interacting with others (through **interpersonal** processes), which children then adopt as their own: what was an interpersonal behaviour pattern becomes an **intrapersonal** (i.e. within the person) cognitive process.

Let us take as an example a child going to nursery school. The child will want to play with the toys, use the equipment and so on, but will come up against the problem of other children wanting to do the same things at the same time. These problems are solved by rules, such as taking turns, which the child comes to accept. Fitting in with these rules is the **interpersonal** stage. The child may internalise these behaviour patterns and later come to apply them to other situations. **Internalisation** means adopting behaviour we observe going on around us as our own. When internalisation has taken place, a concept has become **intrapersonal**.

One major way in which Vygotsky's theory is distinctive is the importance for him of **instruction.** He believed that the highest forms of thinking can only be achieved through appropriate instruction. Vygotsky claimed that purely abstract thinking is only found in highly technological cultures, which have a heavy emphasis on formal instruction.

A key concept here is what Vygotsky called the **zone of proximal development** ('proximal' means 'next'). By this he meant what children are able to achieve with help from an adult or another child more competent than themselves. This has been a major focus of research in recent years. A naturalistic example is given in box J:

Box J: Childs and Greenfield (1982)

This study looked at children learning to weave among the Zinacantecon people of Mexico. Weaving involves six main processes, starting with setting up the loom, and ending with finishing the garment. The first time children tackle these tasks, the instructing adult needs to intervene very frequently. However, the amount of help required drops off very quickly as children achieve 'stand-alone' competence.

For Vygotsky, language was crucial to development. Piaget believed that language only *reflected* cognitive development which had already taken place. Vygotsky's stages, on the other hand, focused on the changing relationship between language and thought.

Initially, language and thought are quite separate. Very young children can think without language, as when they are manipulating objects in play. Vygotsky described the infant's first attempts to communicate – for example, emotional cries – as having a purely social function, and suggested that in this way language occurred without thought. Gradually language and thinking merge, so that language can influence thinking, and thinking can be expressed in language.

As children develop, language serves different purposes. In the first stage, the **social stage** (0–3 years), language is used to express simple thoughts and feelings, and to control the behaviour of other people, e.g. asking for food. The **egocentric stage** (3–7 years) comes next. Language now starts to be used to direct and control children's own behaviour, but it is still **external speech**, i.e. spoken aloud. It is only in the final **inner stage** (7 onwards) that the child uses **inner speech**, when language and thought fuse together into a tool which can then be used to shape and direct thinking.

Activity 9: comparing Piaget and Vygotsky

These theories have some things in common, as well as considerable differences, some important and some fairly minor. Think of ways they can be compared to bring out both the similarities and the differences.

When you have finished, see the notes on page 481.

- Vygotsky was a **social constructivist**. He emphasised the role of **culture** in development.
- **Cultural tools** are acquired when **inter-personal** experience is **internalised** to become **intrapersonal** cognitive processes.
- The influence of other people is expressed in Vygotsky's term **zone of proximal development**. This refers to the difference between what children can do on their own, and with the help of someone more competent.
- The **stages** of Vygotsky's theory are the **social** stage, the **egocentric** stage and the **inner** stage.

These reflect the changing role of **language** and its relationship to thought as children develop. They move from **external** to **inner speech**, when thought and language become fused.

Educational applications of Vygotsky's theory

Activity 10: Vygotsky and educational practice

Look back through the account of Vygotsky's theory. Make a list of the basic ideas it contains which might be useful to teachers in thinking about what goes on in their classroom. For each idea, make a note of what practical use could be made of it in a classroom situation. Look back to activity 7, to identify the implications for education which are common to Piaget and Vygotsky.

When you have finished, see the notes on page 481.

- Vygotsky's theory has implications for education, some of which are shared with Piaget's theory.
- The importance he places on **language**, the notion of the **zone of proximal development**, and the idea of learning and development being inextricably entwined with **culture** are all relevant to education.

The information-processing approach

The information-processing approach to intelligence is somewhat different from that of Piaget and Vygotsky, focusing on the processes involved in intelligent behaviour. It sees the human mind as being like a computer. Information is put in, and is then processed in various ways, leading to a response or output. The physiology of the brain is the 'hardware' of cognition, and the processes occurring during processing are the 'software' or 'programs'. **Computer simulation** techniques are often used by researchers in this area, i.e. attempts to replicate human thinking by using computers. More generally, **task analysis** is used, breaking down the steps involved in carrying out a task. The general aims of this approach are to understand how individuals interpret, store, retrieve and evaluate information by looking at perception, memory and the use of rules and strategies.

There are two main strands to this approach. The first is **developmental**, looking at age-related changes in how information is processed. Like Piaget and Vygotsky, it is assumed that the way in which children think develops in a clear sequence, though it is not necessarily assumed that there are discrete stages in this development. It is also interested in **individual differences**, identifying and comparing the information-processing capacities and strategies of individuals, and sometimes relating these differences to performance on intelligence tests.

The developmental approach

One theorist in this area is Case (1978). One of his main propositions is **sequential development**: cognitive development follows an orderly sequence, with children becoming increasingly more proficient at processing information. Another relates to **working memory** (see chapter 2). Development is explained in terms of **M-space** (mental space), the increasing size of working memory as the child develops. This is due to brain maturation, and schemas becoming more automatic with practice, thus freeing up M-space.

However, Meadows (1995) argued that the increase in working memory capacity does not necessarily account for children's increasing ability to solve problems efficiently. She believed that this is due to increasing knowledge and experience of handling cognitive tasks.

Children certainly become more efficient at processing information as they get older. Memory recall for a string of digits, for example, increases with age (Lloyd, 1995). These differences have also been tested across a range of tasks:

Box K: Kail and Park (1992)

Procedure: Children's performance on a wide range of tasks was tested. These included reaction time, e.g. pressing a button when a light appeared, and simple addition.
Results: Older children were faster across the range of tasks they were asked to carry out than younger children.

Conclusion: Age is related to efficiency in processing information, indicated by the speed with which tasks are carried out.

The increase of speed of processing with age was also found with children in Korea, suggesting that this kind of development is universal. It is thought to be largely due to physical changes in the brain, and in particular **myelination**, in which an insulating sheet develops over nerve fibres in the nervous system. This speeds up mental activity and response time.

Children develop a basic set of rules which they can use when asked to solve problems. These rules develop with age and experience:

Box L: Siegler (1991)

Procedure: Children were shown a balance scale with pegs on which weights could be placed. They were asked to predict which way the balance would tip depending on the number and position of the weights.

Results: Children's answers seemed to depend on following one of four rules:
Rule 1: Attention was paid to the number of weights. Their position was ignored.
Rule 2: As rule 1, unless the number of weights was equal, when the position of the weights was taken into account.
Rule 3: Children tried to take both number and position of weights into account, but not systematically. They often ended up guessing.
Rule 4: Children systematically considered both distance and weights on both sides. The older the child, the more sophisticated the rule-based behaviour.
Conclusion: Children develop rules in an orderly sequence, becoming increasingly more proficient at applying them.

▶ Activity 11: rules and Piaget

Can you relate the progression of children through the rules to the sequence of cognitive development Piaget described?

When you have finished, see the notes on page 482.

While there are some parallels between Siegler's ideas and Piaget's stages, Siegler saw this development not so much as a maturational process related to age, but instead dependent on experience and practice.

A further aspect of development is **meta-cognition**. This is the awareness of and ability to reflect on one's own cognitive processes. This is one of the skills, which also include considering different strategies and planning how to solve a problem, which information-processing theorists call **executive processes**. These skills also develop as children gain in experience, in which education has a large part to play.

Individual differences

Up to now we have been looking at development in general. However, the information-processing approach also proposes that the way in which processing differs between individuals is the key to differences in intelligence. There are individual as well as developmental differences in the speed of information-processing, and there has been some interest in a possible link with intelligence, as measured on intelligence tests. Vernon and Mori (1992) found a positive correlation between the speed of conduction of neural impulses and measures of IQ.

Research has also looked at the use of strategies:

Box M: DeLoache and Brown (1987)

Procedure: The searching strategies of two-year-old children who were developing normally and those who appeared to be developmentally delayed were compared. The children were asked to search for a toy hidden in a room. Without the children's knowledge, the toy was then removed before they were asked to search for it again.

Results: For the initial search, there was no difference between the two groups. Once the toy had been removed, however, the normally-developing children searched for it in places other than where it had originally been hidden. The developmentally delayed children, however, continued to search in the same place.

Conclusion: Flexibility in the use of strategies may contribute to individual differences in cognitive ability.

Sternberg (1985) referred to a person's set of mental processes as **components**. A component is defined as 'an elementary information process that operates upon internal representations of objects or symbols'. Sternberg identified five major kinds of component:

Figure 2: Sternberg's five components

metacomponents	control processes, used in planning how a problem should be solved
performance components	processes used in carrying out a problem-solving strategy
acquisition components	processes used in acquiring knowledge
retention components	processes used in remembering
transfer components	processes used in applying knowledge from one task to a similar task

Activity 12: applying Sternberg's components

Read through this problem:

Gary bought five oranges and paid for them with a £5 note. If he received £3.75 change, how much did each orange cost?

How might the different components be involved in solving this problem?

When you have finished, see the notes on page 482.

Sternberg considered that metacomponents may be equivalent to the general intelligence measured by many psychometric tests. People who are better at these tests are faster and more accurate, but also spend more time on metacomponent processes, i.e. understanding the problem, before attempting to solve it. This means that performance is affected by the choice of strategies. Sternberg also emphasised that selecting relevant information and adapting to the changing demands of the environment are the goals of intelligent behaviour.

Sternberg pointed out that although the basic information-processing components do not change from one culture to another, the emphasis placed on different components does. For example, in some cultures physical skills may be considered more important than academic ones. We therefore need to develop the skills which help us to function in the environment we are in.

Educational applications of the information-processing approach

One obvious application of this approach to cognitive development is its use as a diagnostic tool to identify children (as in box M) whose development is not proceeding normally. This could then lead to training programmes to support their development.

In general, the approach implies that teachers should know what information is necessary, and how it should be handled, in order for children to carry out tasks successfully. They should be aware of children's limited working memory capacity. If children are making mistakes, they need to understand that this may be because rules are being misapplied, rather than simple carelessness. They need to identify which rule each child is using, so that a more useful rule can be substituted. Brown and Burton (1978) have shown how this approach can help with children's problems in arithmetic. Teachers should also encourage metacognitive knowledge by getting children to reflect on their own cognitive processes. They therefore have an instructive role, more in line with Vygotsky's ideas than those of Piaget.

Evaluation of the information-processing approach

The two main ways of studying cognitive development have been those like Piaget, concerned with the course of development, and the **psychometric approach** which we shall come to in the next section. This approach assumes that intelligence is largely innate, and is concerned with measuring individual differences in cognitive skills.

The information-processing approach can be seen as complementary to these approaches, and as providing some links between them. It seems likely that there are inborn strategies which develop with age, but experience in using strategies is also important in developing cognitive skills. This emphasis on experience suggests a role for education in supporting children's cognitive development.

The theory also has the advantage of providing a detailed account of cognitive processes. It goes beyond the Piagetian approach by identifying the individual skills necessary to carry out a task, and investigates how these develop.

However, research in this area is still in its early stages. Its findings can often be task-specific. For example, the approach cannot yet explain the differences children show when they are asked to carry out Piagetian tasks. Neither does it yet provide a credible alternative to intelligence tests.

๑ The information-processing approach describes cognition using a **computer** analogy. It is interested in the development of cognitive skills and in individual differences.

๑ **Developmental** theorists propose that development is **sequential**. It is related to an increase in **working memory**. As they get older, children become faster at processing information, and increasingly able to apply **rules**. **Metacognition** is also important to development.

⊜ There are **individual differences** in the use of **strategies**, which may be related to measured intelligence.

⊜ The theory has **educational applications** in terms of **diagnosing problems** and **supporting development**.

⊜ The theory looks in detail at individual skills in problem-solving, but is still in its early stages.

17.2 Development of measured intelligence

Piaget's theory of cognitive development is one approach to intelligence, since it looks at how the ability to reason develops in young children. However, the dominant approach in psychology has been a **psychometric** one, which takes a quantitative approach and is interested in the measurement of intelligence using standardised tests. Many of these tests give a score known as a person's **intelligence quotient** or **IQ**. While Piaget's approach looks at the general principles underlying the development of intelligence, the psychometric approach is more interested in making comparisons between people and groups of people, using the scores the tests provide.

Genetic factors in measured intelligence

There are differences between children in their performance on intelligence tests. However, the reasons underlying these differences are in question. Some theorists believe that intelligence is innate, and differences in test performance are therefore the result of genetic variation. Others believe these differences are the result of environmental factors. This issue raises a wide range of ethical and political issues, such as streaming in schools. It is therefore a key area for discussion.

At the same time, it is important to bear in mind that the question of whether nature or nurture is the more important influence is ultimately rather simplistic, since the two are interlinked. Genetic information, like a plant seed, requires the right environmental conditions to develop; but without the right 'formula' in the genes, the nutrients provided by the environment cannot be fully utilised. What is of interest here is the maximum range of measured intelligence which can be produced from the same genotype, and that different genotypes can produce within the same environment.

With this in mind, Anastasi (1958) introduced the idea of a **norm of reaction**, whereby genetic information imposes an upper and a lower limit on development. Within this range, the environment will be influential. According to Scarr-Salapatek (1971), this range is 20–25 IQ points.

There are serious problems in determining the **heritability** of intelligence, i.e. the proportion of the variation in the population that can be attributed to genetic differences. For example, selective breeding to manipulate heredity would clearly be unethical. It would also not be ethically acceptable to put some people into poor environments so that they could be compared with those in better environments. Since genes and environment cannot be systematically controlled, attempts to establish the relative contribution of each are inevitably affected by confounding variables.

Research aiming to establish the role of genetic factors in IQ rests on the principle that if differences in IQ are genetically determined, then individuals who are closer genetically should be more similar in IQ than those less close. The method used is to correlate the IQ scores obtained by different individuals. We would expect high positive correlations between the IQ scores of people who are closely related.

Three major ways in which this kind of research has been carried out are twin studies, family studies and adoption/fostering studies, and we will look at each in turn, together with longitudinal studies.

Twin studies

Researchers have compared identical or monozygotic (MZ) twins with non-identical or dizygotic (DZ) twins. MZ twins are genetically identical because they come from the same fertilised egg, and so share 100% of their genes. DZ twins have developed from two fertilised eggs and, like other brothers and sisters, share about 50% of their genes. Both MZ and DZ twins share the same intra-uterine environment before birth, though the nutrition they receive at this time and the growing space they have could well be different. While MZ twins have the same genotype, then, they may be different even at birth as a result of different intra-uterine experiences.

Studies have also compared twins reared together in the same environment with twins reared apart in different environments. Some typical results are given in box N:

Box N: IQ correlations in twin studies

name of study	MZ twins reared together	MZ twins reared apart	DZ twins reared together
Newman et al. (1937)	0.91	0.67	0.64
Shields (1962)	0.76	0.77	0.51
Burt (1966)	0.94	0.77	0.55
Bouchard and McGue (1981)	0.86	0.72	0.60

▶ Activity 13: understanding twin studies

Use the information in box N to answer these questions:

a Which are more similar in IQ, MZ or DZ twins?
b What does this suggest about the inheritance of intelligence?
c Which are more similar in IQ, MZ twins reared together or MZ twins reared apart?
d What does this suggest about the inheritance of intelligence?

When you have finished, see the notes on page 482.

The most important of the above studies is that of Bouchard and McGue (1981), who drew together the results of 111 studies of intelligence in related people. The overall conclusion they reached is that both genetic factors and environment are important, but genetics has the bigger role. But is this conclusion justified?

There are several ways in which the earlier studies can be criticised, most of which were proposed by Kamin (1974). Firstly, many of the early studies were based on small samples, e.g. Shields (1962), who studied only 37 pairs of twins. Coleman (1987) argued that the entire psychological literature on this topic is based on the study of 121 pairs of separated MZ twins.

Another problem is that many early studies used dubious techniques for assessing zygosity (i.e. whether twins were MZ or DZ). For example, Newman *et al.* (1937) simply based their assessment on how similar the twins looked, and did not include in their sample any who differed in appearance or behaviour.

Measurement of IQ was also dubious in many cases; Newman *et al.* used a test intended for a younger age group, which had the effect of artificially increasing the similarity of the IQ of participants.

Separated twins often go to similar environments, either because twins are brought up by relatives, or because the adoption agencies have a policy of trying to match the birth mother with the adoptive mother; this is known as **selective placement**. This leads to an underestimation of the effects of the environment. Kamin (1974) reported that only 13 of the 37 pairs studied by Shields were raised in unrelated families; some lived in the same street, played together and sat together at school. In the study by Newman *et al.*, twins separated by long distances (e.g. one in Alaska and one in Canada) were excluded from the study on the grounds of cost!

It is also possible that MZ twins may be treated more similarly than DZ twins – for example, they are more likely to be dressed the same or treated as if they are the same person in other ways – so environment as well as genes will be more similar.

Some separated twins sat together at school.

There is also the possibility that MZ twins may not always be identical even at birth; for example, as a result of different intra-uterine experiences, mentioned above.

Burt's study has caused a great deal of controversy, since it almost certainly included faked data. For example, the correlations obtained in different studies were identical to three decimal places. Non-existent research assistants and dubious techniques for measuring IQ have also increased suspicions that Burt manipulated the outcomes to support his genetic theories (Hearnshaw, 1979). Burt's studies were not included in the review by Bouchard and McGue for this reason.

Both the Shields and Newman *et al.* studies involved IQ testing by the researcher who knew which twins were MZ and which DZ; this could have led to experimenter bias. For example, Kamin found that the twins tested by Shields showed an IQ difference of 8.5 points (leading to a correlation of 0.84), whereas the five pairs tested by other researchers showed an average difference of 22.4 points (giving a correlation of 0.11). Kamin interpreted this difference in terms of researcher bias.

All the studies used volunteers, who may constitute a biased sample. For example, in the

Newman *et al.* study there was a large financial inducement to take part, which could have encouraged some twins to lie about their separate upbringing.

Overall, then, it seems that the heritability estimates obtained from these studies (which vary from 0.5–0.8) may not be reliable. Kamin (1974) argued further that neither the twins nor their environments were representative of the variation that exists more widely in genes or environmental conditions.

Some twin studies have not in fact been able to show differences between MZ and DZ twins; Scarr-Salapatek studied 779 twins and refused to publish non-significant results because she felt they would not be accepted. This is an example of a more general problem in psychology, i.e. the tendency to present for publication (and to accept for publication) only work in which a significant difference or correlation has been established. After all, significant findings allow conclusions to be drawn, which is not the case for non-significant results.

An interesting meta-analysis by Taylor (1980) aimed to re-analyse data from all of the published studies apart from those of Burt, after removing some of the confounding environmental factors. Taylor found only five pairs of twins who had dissimilar educational and socioeconomic environments, had not been re-united after separation, and lived with unrelated families. The correlation between their IQ scores was only 0.24. Again, though, as with many of the twin studies we have discussed, the very small sample size means that these findings must be treated with caution.

- Theorists disagree about the extent to which differences in measured intelligence are **genetic** or come about through **environmental** influences.
- One way in which this topic has been investigated is **twin studies**, comparing correlations between MZ and DZ twins.
- Some twin studies have claimed to show that intelligence has high **heritability**. Most have been criticised on methodological grounds. When **methodological problems** are allowed

for, the correlations between separated MZ twins are low.

Family studies

Studies have also examined IQ correlations between different family members, to see if more closely related individuals are also more similar in IQ. This work originates from Galton's study *Hereditary Genius* (1869), in which he investigated the family trees of 415 eminent men. He found that a large proportion of their relatives were also eminent; this was particularly true of closer relatives. From this he argued that genetic factors are important in intelligence.

However, Galton looked at a very narrow range of participants, so his sample was not representative of the general population. More importantly, it is likely that the families of the eminent men he studied would have had good educational opportunities, and would have known people who could help them to advance in their chosen professions.

More recent family studies have also been carried out. Box O shows some typical results of family studies, taken from Bouchard and McGue (1981). This excludes Burt's data, since it is likely to be unreliable:

Box O: Bouchard and McGue (1981)

IQ correlations from family studies

parent/child reared together	0.42
parent/child reared apart	0.22
siblings reared together	0.47
siblings reared apart	0.24
cousins	0.15

Activity 14: interpreting data from family studies

From the data in box O:
a Does there appear to be a genetic effect? Why?
b Does there appear to be an environmental effect? Why?
c How could you criticise this type of study?
When you have finished, see the notes on page 482.

There are other criticisms of this type of study which should also be mentioned briefly. Firstly, many of the studies which have been carried out have been flawed. For example, an analysis of 52 studies by Erlenmeyer-Kimling and Jarvik (1963) contained a great many errors in reporting and calculation.

Secondly, it has been suggested that the correlations obtained should be higher (for example for parent/child) because of the process of assortative mating. This refers to people's tendency to marry others who are genetically similar to themselves. Because of this overlap, children are likely to have more than half of their genes in common with one parent, so parent/child correlations of around 0.5 are actually rather low if intelligence is inherited.

Finally, such studies ignore the influence that family members have on one another. For example, having an extremely bright older sibling may have a detrimental effect on a younger child.

Adoption studies

Another group of studies in this section are adoption studies, in which the IQs of adopted children are compared with those of their adopted and natural parents.

Activity 15: why adoption studies?

In this kind of study, what kinds of correlation would be expected by someone who believes:
a genes are very important in intelligence?
b the environment is a crucial influence?
When you have finished, see the notes on page 482.

This approach started with Galton, who compared the progress in life of the adopted 'nephews' of Popes and other Roman Catholic priests with that of the natural sons of eminent men. When the nephews proved to be less successful, he argued that because both groups had similar environmental advantages, their lack of achievement must mean that they lacked the necessary genetic qualities. Therefore he saw intelligence as largely genetic.

There have also been some more recent and better controlled studies than Galton's. Some typical findings of adoption and fostering studies are shown in box P:

Box P: IQ correlations from adoption and fostering studies		
	parents/ natural child	parents/ adopted child
Burks (1928)	0.52	0.20
Leahy (1935)	0.60	0.18

In both these studies, data from two separate sets of families produced these correlations.

	child/ natural parent	child/ adopted parent
Skodak and Skeels (1949)	0.44	0.02
Horn et al. (1979)	0.28	0.15

IQ was not directly measured for the adopted parent in the Skodak and Skeels study, only the parent's educational level.

The obvious conclusion to be drawn from these studies is that because the correlation is always higher between the parent and the natural child, and the child and the natural parent, IQ must be largely genetically determined. At the same time, however, there have been a great many criticisms of these studies.

Firstly, not all studies have given the same results. For example, Snygg (1938) found a correlation of only 0.13 between the IQs of adopted children and their natural mothers. The correlation from the Horn et al. study in box P also shows this correlation to be rather low, bearing in mind the proportion of genes they have in common.

The principle of selective placement means that, here too, the environment provided by the natural and the adoptive parents would be similar. This would lead to an underestimation of the possible effects of the environment.

Skodak and Skeels tested their sample at several different ages. The early tests showed little difference between the correlations; it is possible that the differences observed in later tests may be due, as Kamin (1974) has suggested, to selective drop-out of the adoptive parents with lower IQs.

This study also reveals on close examination that the average IQ of the children was 117, whereas the mean of their biological mothers (few of whom had been to college) was 86. Since 50% of the adopted mothers had been to college, it could be argued that they had increased the IQ of the children compared with what would be expected on a genetic basis. This is the view of McGurk (1975), who has shown that adopted children tend to move towards the IQ level of their adopted parents – increasingly so as time goes on – and obtain higher scores than their biological parents. So the adoptive environment actually appears to raise IQ above genetic expectations.

Some of the studies, such as those by Burks and Leahy, involved separate samples of adopted and natural children, which is bound to increase the number of variables which could influence the results.

Another approach is that of Scarr and Weinberg (1977), who tested adopted children in families with a natural child of the same age. The correlations of both adopted and natural children's IQ scores with that of the mother of the family were similar, despite the fact that the adopted children were often from a disadvantaged background, and were black and living in a white adoptive family. Similarly, Schiff et al. (1978) found that adopted children from disadvantaged backgrounds, who were adopted by high-status parents, scored higher on IQ tests (average 111) than siblings who had remained with their natural parents (average 95).

The quality of the environment in the adoptive home has also been investigated. Freeman et al. (1928) rated adoptive homes on six factors, including material conditions, social activity, education of parents and their occupation. They found a reasonably strong correlation of 0.48 between these factors and the adopted child's IQ, suggesting an environmental influence. We will return to this issue of environmental quality later in this section.

Overall, then, the problems of interpretation appear to be so great that firm conclusions are difficult to reach, but it does seem that the environment may contribute more than was previously thought.

- **Family studies** compare correlations for IQ between close and more distant relatives. Generally the correlations are higher for close relatives. However, the environments in this case are also likely to be more similar.
- **Adoption studies** compare children's IQs with those of their natural and adoptive mothers. Most studies have found higher correlations with the natural mother, but other factors suggest that environment has a considerable influence.
- There are **methodological problems** with both these approaches.

Longitudinal studies

If heritability is high, IQ should remain similar throughout the life-span. This can be tested by examining the results of longitudinal studies. There have not been very many of these, but the results of one of the largest are given in box Q:

Box Q: Honzik *et al.* (1948)

Procedure: Over 250 children were studied for a 16-year period. Correlations of IQ test scores for the same individuals at different ages were calculated.

Results: The following correlations were found:

age	correlation at age 10	correlation at age 18
4	0.66	0.42
6	0.76	0.61
8	0.88	0.70
10	–	0.76
12	0.87	0.76

Conclusion: The higher correlations between different ages as the children became older seem to suggest that IQ scores become more stable with age. The correlations are in general quite high, indicating support for the genetic argument.

However, it is worth noting that with such a large sample, there can still be a lot of variation in particular individuals, which could be the result of environmental factors.

Other studies, such as that carried out by Hindley (1968), have looked at younger children, and found smaller correlations; that between IQ at 6 months and two years, for example, is 0.31. This fits in with the general pattern observed by Honzik *et al.*, although it is important to note that IQ as such cannot be measured in such young children; what is measured is the Developmental Quotient (DQ), using the **Bayley Scales of Infant Development**, which may not be measuring quite the same thing.

Some studies have shown that there are large changes over time. For example, the **Fels Longitudinal Study of Development** (McCall *et al.*, 1973) found an average change of 28 IQ points (the range being 10–74) between the ages of $2\frac{1}{2}$ and 17 years. One problem here is that it is very difficult to assess accurately the IQ of a child as young as $2\frac{1}{2}$. However, the fluctuations over the period of time when more accurate assessment is possible can be accounted for quite easily in terms of different rates of maturation.

- **Longitudinal studies** show quite high correlations between an individual's IQ measured at different ages, with the size of the correlations increasing with age, supporting the genetic argument.
- Quite large differences in IQ scores at different ages have also been found. This is hard to explain in genetic terms.

Racial differences in intelligence

Galton (1869) wrote about the genetic inferiority of African-Americans, and the large number of half-wits to be found amongst them, paving the way for research and speculation into genetically-determined racial differences. Not many years later, as part of a drive to control immigration into America in the early part of this century, IQ tests were administered to would-be immigrants. Goddard (1929) reported that more than three-quarters of the Italians, Jews and Russians tested were feeble-minded, leading to mass deportation and the passing of the 1917 Immigration Act to exclude those of 'constitutional psychopathic inferiority'. Early tests were culturally biased towards white, middle-class individuals. The tests used for immigration purposes also assumed a knowledge of American culture which immigrants would be unlikely to have. However, the issue of possible racial differences in intelligence is still with us.

In more recent times, on the basis of evidence that black Americans score on average 15 points lower than white Americans on IQ tests (e.g. Shuey, 1966), and that studies of the white population indicated that variability in IQ is 80% due to inherited differences, Jensen (1969) argued that the difference between the groups was the result of genetic differences. Eysenck (1971) also took this view, which was supported by the finding that in Britain, West Indian immigrants had been shown to have lower IQ scores than the white population, although the differences were not as large as those reported in America, varying from 5–13 points.

▷ Activity 16: race and intelligence

Jensen and Eysenck suggested that the differences in measured intelligence found between different racial groups could be accounted for in terms of genetic differences between races.

Can you think of any reasons why it might be unwise to accept this idea?
Compare your ideas with the discussion which follows.

The first thing that needs to be said is that differences observed between groups are between averages for those groups. There is in fact a lot of overlap between the groups. For example, Shuey (1966) showed that 15–25% of blacks score higher than 50% of whites. Variations within each group, then, are greater than those between groups, as figure 3 shows.

As we saw in the previous section, the 80% heritability estimate for the white population (within-group variance) is far from being an accepted figure. The argument for genetically determined racial differences is significantly weakened if IQ scores in general have not been clearly demonstrated to be largely genetically determined. Furthermore, heritability refers to the amount of variation within a population or group, not to the variation between groups; for example, IQ could be 100% genetically determined within the white population, and within the black population, but the differences between them could be 100% environmental.

Figure 3: ethnic group differences in IQ scores

This can be illustrated in the famous analogy put forward by Lewontin (1976):

▶ Activity 17: the Lewontin analogy

Two handfuls of seed are taken from the same sack, and planted in separate plots. Plot A contains more nutrients than plot B. The plants in plot A grow taller than those in plot B, but within each plot, some plants grow taller than others:

plot A

plot B

a Are the differences between the two plots due to genetic or environmental factors?

b Are the differences within the two plots due to genetic or environmental factors?

c What do your answers to (a) and (b) suggest about race differences in intelligence?

When you have finished, see the notes on page 482.

Bodmer (1972) has established that genetic differences within a race are far greater than those between races. Racial differences in fact only account for 7% of genetic differences (Rose *et al.*, 1984).

On the other hand, there is a lot of evidence for environmental differences between black people and white people. According to the US Bureau of the Census (1994), 28.2% of African-Americans live below the poverty line, compared with only 7.9% of European-Americans. Tobias (1974) has pointed out that this difference goes back for some generations; even though there have been recent improvements, the deprivation suffered by black people in terms of poverty, malnutrition, lack of educational opportunities, prejudice and discrimination could still be having effects.

A study by Tyler (1965) has shown that African-Americans in the northern states, where they have always had better conditions than in the south, were on average superior in IQ to those in the southern states – their scores were not very different from those obtained by whites. African-Americans who moved from the south to the north showed IQ gains. This adds weight to the view that environmental factors are important in IQ. Bayley (1955) found no IQ differences between young black and white children, which suggests genetic equivalence.

Scarr and Weinberg (1976) showed that for black children adopted into white families, IQ scores were 25 points higher than the mean for black children in general. At 10-year follow-up, they were found to be still higher than those who had remained in disadvantaged homes, again supporting an environmental argument.

Loehlin *et al.* (1988) found that differences between black and white children in IQ are reduced when they are matched for family income, occupation and socioeconomic status. In Britain, the Child Health and Education Study (Taylor, 1980) showed that between 1970 and 1980, the average IQ scores of Asian children fell, as did their socio-economic status. In the same study, when West Indian children were matched with white children on father's income, family size and quality of neighbourhood, the 9-point difference in IQ that had been reported fell to 2.6 points.

Racial crossing studies have been carried out, where black and white children are reared in the same environment:

Box R: Eyferth *et al.* (1961)

Procedure: The IQ of illegitimate children of American servicemen, both black and white, was tested. These children had been born and raised in Germany at a time when there was little racial prejudice.

Results: There were no IQ differences between the two groups.

Conclusion: Environmental conditions in America are responsible for IQ differences between black and white people which have been found there.

This is supported by Ogbu (1981), who has pointed out that the IQ difference between African- and European-Americans is the same as that found between deprived and privileged groups in other countries, e.g. India, Japan and New Zealand, where there are caste-like minority groups.

In America, Scarr and Weinberg (1976) found that when raised in white adoptive homes, black, mixed-race and white children had IQ scores of 96.8, 109 and 111.5 respectively. The difference between white and mixed-race children was very small. It is likely that the lower scores of the black children were the result of their being adopted later than the others, and coming from poorer backgrounds originally.

A further point to bear in mind is that black and white people do not constitute distinct biological groups; it has been estimated that 75% of Afro-Caribbeans have at least one white ancestor. Neither were the African slaves who formed the bulk of the black American population all from one race. They came from a wide range of countries in different parts of the African continent, and are generally considered to have been at least as varied genetically as modern Europeans.

Racial admixture studies have compared the IQ scores of people with different amounts of black and white ancestry. If genetics can explain differences in intelligence between races, those with more white ancestry should obtain higher scores. Witty and Jenkins (1936) found that a group of high IQ black children had no more white

ancestry than a control group with average IQs. Scarr *et al.* (1977), using better techniques for estimating the proportion of racial ancestry, i.e. blood samples rather than genealogical records, also reported no relationship between racial ancestry and IQ scores.

The measurements of IQ have been criticised for being culturally biased in ways which would penalise black people. The researchers are usually white, and their expectations may also affect test performance. Labov (1970) has argued that black children do much better when interviewed by black researchers. Although attempts have been made to devise **culture-fair IQ tests**, research using **Raven's Progressive Matrices**, one of the most popular, has shown that recent Asian immigrants perform very badly on the test, and that performance improves with length of stay in this country (Mackintosh and Mascie-Taylor,1985). This suggests that attempts to develop culture-fair tests have not been entirely successful.

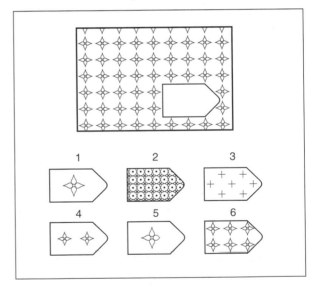

An item from Raven's Progressive Matrices

It has been pointed out that other group differences have not been treated in the same way as racial differences. For example, females have always been found to score higher on IQ tests than males; this problem was dealt with by adjusting the norms, so that they have to answer more questions correctly to obtain the same IQ score as males.

Another factor to consider in the race and intelligence debate is that in some studies mongoloid groups, such as Chinese and Japanese, show higher average IQ scores than whites – seven points higher, according to Rushton (1989) – and the mean IQ score of Asians in North America or Asia tends to be five points higher than that of Caucasians (Lynn, 1987).

◉ **Racial differences** indicate that African-Americans score lower on IQ tests than European-Americans. This has been attributed by some theorists to genetic factors.

◉ Evidence for **genetic differences** between different racial groups is weak.

◉ **Environmental differences** between the groups are large and the **testing process** itself may be biased.

◉ Many studies indicate that reducing environmental differences reduces differences in IQ scores between racial groups.

Other factors in test performance

Throughout this section, a range of factors has been mentioned which could affect measured intelligence.

Activity 18: factors affecting measured intelligence

Can you think of any other factors which might be important in a testing situation, which could help to account for why some people do not do as well on IQ tests as others?

You may find it helpful to start by thinking about educational, personal and test factors.

When you have finished, see the notes on page 482.

We will look finally in this section at two pieces of work which have brought together various factors to help us understand variations in tested IQ:

Box S: Sameroff and Seifer (1983)

Procedure: Starting in the 1970s, several hundred children were studied from birth to adolescence. The study aimed to establish the environmental factors which affect IQ scores.
Results: Ten factors associated with lower IQs were identified:

1. Mother's history of mental illness
2. An overly anxious mother
3. A mother with inflexible beliefs and attitudes about the child's development
4. Little positive mother–child interaction
5. The main family earner has a semi-skilled job
6. Poor educational standard of the mother
7. The child is from an ethnic minority
8. The child lives in a single-parent family
9. Family experience of 20+ stressful events before the child is 4
10. There are 4+ children in the family

Conclusion: There are strong correlations between measured IQ and a range of environmental and in particular family factors.

Since the study is correlational, any conclusions should be drawn with caution, but some of these factors link in with what we know from other research, such as the quality of parenting, discussed in box T. The study is helpful in indicating a broad range of specific factors.

A series of scales has been developed to identify parenting qualities:

Box T: Caldwell and Bradley (1978)

A series of checklists has been developed to assess the quality of children's home experience, called Home Observation for Measurement of the Environment (HOME). There are versions for infancy, pre-school and middle childhood; for example:

HOME – pre-school version

subscales:

1. affection, pride in the child and warmth
2. not using physical punishment
3. stimulating language use
4. stimulating academic skills

5. providing stimulating toys, games and reading material
6. providing appropriate social models
7. providing varied stimulation
8. providing a safe and clean physical environment

Correlations of around 0.5 have been found between HOME scores and later IQ scores.

A further factor which may affect intelligence test performance relates to the distinction between aptitude and attainment measures. It has always been argued that IQ tests should be measures of potential, i.e. **aptitude** tests, rather than measures of what has been learnt, i.e. **attainment** tests. The obvious flaw with this is that measurement of aptitude can only be done by sampling behaviours that have had to be learnt, so in practice the distinction between the two breaks down.

Another way of approaching this problem is to ask whether the test relies on specific or general prior experience: a test that relies on specific experience, such as a driving test, can be regarded as an attainment test, while a test that relies on more general abilities rather than specific knowledge can be regarded as an aptitude test.

One important consequence of this distinction is that tests make the assumption that everyone taking the test will have had an equal opportunity to carry out this general learning. When this is not the case, people may not be fairly assessed.

An example of this is the issue of coaching. Candidates who are not familiar with taking tests are likely to be less confident and have fewer strategies available to help them to deal with the tests – for example, knowing when to guess. They are referred to as lacking test sophistication. Studies of the effects of coaching in test-taking skills or in specific subjects have shown that it can raise scores considerably. For example, Messick and Jungeblut (1981) found that 30 hours of instruction in verbal skills resulted in average gains of 14 points on the verbal section of the SAT.

The other issue that arises here is that of cultural bias. For example, Smith (1948) has pointed out that

people from some cultures do not appreciate the need to work quickly. Others may be unfamiliar with pictorial representations of objects (Warburton, 1951). On a more subtle level, people from minority groups within Western countries may not be familiar with the language used in tests, or with the objects they are being asked questions about.

It has been shown that although Asian children who have lived in Britain for several years are not penalised by the test, recent immigrants still achieve poorer scores than white people (Mackintosh and Mascie-Taylor, 1985). This suggests that the tests used may not be culture-fair. However, it is also possible to argue that the environment the immigrants are coming to may lead to the development of higher levels of measured intelligence than the environment they are leaving. It could also be the case that the trauma of leaving their country and settling in a new one may have the temporary effect of lowering measured intelligence.

- **Educational**, **personal** and **test factors** are associated with IQ test performance.
- Specific factors have been identified which can be measured in early infancy and are associated with later IQ scores.
- Other problems with tests include confusion between **aptitude** and **attainment**, and assumptions about **equal opportunities** for learning.
- **Culture** is also an issue, since tests are culture-specific. Attempts to produce culture-fair tests have had some success but no completely culture-fair test has been developed.

17.3 DEVELOPMENT OF MORAL UNDERSTANDING

What is moral development?

As children grow, they develop an understanding of what is right and wrong. How this happens has been of major interest to psychologists. However, the study of moral development does not stop here. We may know what we ought to do (or not do), i.e. the **cognitive** aspect of morality, but we may not behave accordingly, so there is also interest in how people respond when faced with a moral dilemma (the **behavioural** dimension). In addition, there is an **affective** dimension, which refers to feelings such as guilt or shame.

The major theories in this area have tended in practice to concentrate on one of these areas at the expense of the other two. The major focus in this section is on the theories of Piaget and Kohlberg, both of whom focus on the cognitive aspect of moral development.

Piaget's theory of moral development

As you read earlier in this chapter, Piaget was interested in the development of children's thinking, so it is not surprising that he was also interested in the development of moral reasoning. His interest in moral development focused on three aspects:

1. children's ideas about **rules**
2. their **moral judgements**, and the reasoning on which these judgements were based
3. their ideas about **punishment** and justice

He investigated the first of these by playing marbles with children. He considered that looking at children's understanding of the rules of games was a way of bypassing adult influence, and so studying children's thinking directly.

Activity 19: playing marbles with Piaget

Piaget pretended not to know the rules in a game of marbles, and asked children to explain them to him. He would then ask questions such as: 'Where do rules come from?', 'Who made them?' and 'Can we change them?'
How would you answer these questions?
You could also replicate this kind of investigation with children of different ages. You don't have to use marbles; you can use any game with rules – perhaps a board game that children are familiar with.
Did the answers differ with the age of the children?

As in his theory of cognitive development, Piaget found that children reasoned differently at different ages. Below the age of about 5, he found children could not cope with this task. From 5 till about 9 or 10, they believe that rules have always existed, and are handed down by some authority – adults, older children or even God! – and so cannot be changed in any way. This does not, however, prevent them from bending the rules if it suits them! Older children understand that rules have been invented, and agree that there is no reason why they shouldn't be changed. In order to play the game at all, though, this can only happen if all the players agree. They are much more likely at this age to stick to the agreed rules.

Piaget investigated children's moral judgements by telling them pairs of stories:

Activity 20: moral reasoning

Read through these two stories:
1 A little boy called John is in his room. He goes down to the dining room for his dinner, and opens the door. He doesn't know that there is a chair behind the door, with a tray of 15 cups on it. When he opens the door, all the cups go flying, and they are all broken.

John

2 A little boy called Henry was very fond of jam. One day, when his mother wasn't looking, he climbed on a chair to reach some jam on a high shelf. It was still too high for him to reach, but while he was trying to get it, he knocked over a cup. The cup fell on the floor and was broken.

Henry

Who is naughtier, John or Henry? Why? Who should be punished more?

Try this activity with children of different ages, preferably one of 6 or 7, and an older child of 10 or 11.

It is likely that you felt that Henry was naughtier, because he was doing something which he knew he shouldn't be doing. If you tried this activity with children of different ages, though, you may have found, as Piaget did, that younger children usually think John was naughtier. The reason they give is related to the *outcome* (John broke 15 cups, whereas Henry only broke one) and not the intentions and motives of the children involved. Young children understand the idea of intentional and unintentional damage, but do not focus on this factor in their moral reasoning.

Activity 21: problems with Piaget's method

One criticism of the methods Piaget used to investigate children's thinking was that the activities he carried out with children were very complex. How could this apply to his method of investigating moral reasoning?

When you have finished, see the notes on page 482.

A study using a simpler method, focusing on just one variable, is described in box U:

Box U: Constanzo *et al.* (1973)

Procedure: Boys of 6, 8 and 10 were read variations of a story about a boy who emptied out a box of toys on the floor, either (a) so that he could sort them out or (b) just to make a mess. His mother then came into the room. She did not know what his intentions were, but in some versions of the story she approved and in some she disapproved. The children were asked whether the boy was naughty or not.

Results: When the mother disapproved, the 6-year-olds thought that the boy was naughty, regardless of his intentions, i.e. whether they had been read version (a) or (b). However, when she approved, even 6-year-olds were just as likely to judge whether the boy was naughty or not on the basis of his intentions.

Conclusion: The first finding supports Piaget's claim that young children are more influenced by the outcome of an action than by the intentions behind it. However, the second finding suggests that children make moral judgements on the basis of intentions much earlier than Piaget believed.

The first of the findings of Constanzo *et al.* gives some support to Piaget's theory, then, but is there another explanation than the one Piaget offered? Nelson (1981), using this kind of story, found that 3-year-olds assumed that if there is a negative outcome, the intentions must also have been bad. They are less good than older children at separating intentions from the outcome, and co-ordinating these two pieces of information when making moral judgements.

A further study which challenged Piaget's interpretation of his findings was carried out by Armsby (1971). This study found that even 6-year-old children are likely to judge a small amount of deliberate damage as being naughtier than a larger amount of accidental damage, but that this depends on the nature of the damage. Forty per cent of 6-year-olds (and rather less than 10% of 10-year-olds) judged the accidental damage of a TV set to be more worthy of punishment than the deliberate breakage of a cup.

Children's attitudes to punishment also change with age. Between the ages of about 5 and 10, children believe that people should pay for their misdeeds, but the nature of the punishment is not linked to the kind of bad behaviour which has been shown. Piaget called this **expiatory punishment**, i.e. a penalty is paid for the misdeed. Like rules, punishment is seen as legitimate purely because of its source. Above the age of about 10, children use the **principle of reciprocity** when considering punishment. They believe the punishment should fit the crime: for example, children who have refused to share toys with other children should not be allowed to play with the toys themselves.

In summary, Piaget (1932) claimed that children under 5 have not yet developed a moral sense. From about the age of 5, they show some understanding of rules, but see them as coming from some higher authority, and therefore not open to change. Their morality at this stage is therefore **heteronomous**, i.e. depending on the rules of others. Actions tend to be evaluated by their results, rather than by the intentions of the person carrying them out, and the purpose of punishment is to make someone pay for their crime. Piaget used the term **moral realism** to

describe this stage. Children realise that adults have the power to ensure that rules are followed, whereas children do not have the power to resist. They accept the rules of adults as absolute and not open to question.

From the age of about 9 or 10, morality becomes **autonomous,** i.e. relating to the individual. Rules can be changed, rather than being set in stone, and intentions are taken into account when judging actions. Punishment is related to the nature of the crime. Piaget used the term **moral relativism** to describe this stage. Morality is no longer tied to authority.

Links with Piaget's theory of cognitive development

You will remember that Piaget saw cognitive development as moving through a series of stages with quite distinct characteristics, which always occur in the same order. Movement through the stages is characterised by decreasing egocentrism. As children move from egocentric to operational thought – i.e. from the preoperational to the concrete operational stage – they become progressively less influenced by their own point of view and immediate perceptions, and more able to see things from someone else's point of view.

Piaget's theory of moral development has clear links with his more general theory of cognitive development. Moral reasoning, like thinking, moves through a series of stages. The shift from egocentric to operational thought is of major importance both in thinking in general and in the development of moral reasoning in particular. This shift occurs, according to Piaget, at around the age of 7, but a similar shift in moral reasoning – from moral realism to moral relativism – only takes place at around the age of 9 or 10. This suggests that the shift in thinking provides a basis for the shift in moral reasoning.

Children in the preoperational stage of thinking, who are still egocentric in their thinking, have difficulty in co-ordinating different aspects of a situation. For example, in the conservation of number task described earlier, preoperational children do not realise that when one row of counters has been spaced further apart, the increased length of the row is compensated by the larger spaces between the counters. There is a parallel here with the difficulty younger children found in co-ordinating intentions and outcome in a moral reasoning task.

The decrease in egocentrism with the shift to operational thinking also marks children's ability to see things from other people's viewpoints, as shown in the three mountains task described in box F. At the age when the shift in moral reasoning occurs, the peer group becomes more important, and the importance of adult–child relationships declines. There is therefore a shift in emphasis from obedience to negotiation. Children come to understand that rules are not absolute but the result of social agreement through negotiation with others. The intentions of others can be taken into account in making moral judgements.

Evaluating Piaget's theory

As with Piaget's general theory of cognitive development, his ideas on moral development rest on careful research. There is some evidence that morality develops from heteronomous to autonomous in the way Piaget has suggested. Linaza (1984) found the same course of development in a Spanish sample, so there is some support for Piaget's claim that this change is universal. However, this may only be true of Western cultures, since wider cross-cultural research has suggested that culture may be important in moral development.

Piaget has been criticised for setting children very complex tasks. As we have seen, later research using a simpler approach has shown that children may be able to understand moral issues at a more sophisticated level at a younger age than Piaget's theory suggests. The theory may also be seen as limited because it only looks at the cognitive aspects of developing morality, and fails to take into account behavioural and affective dimensions.

Piaget's theory could also be thought of as limited because it does not consider any development in moral reasoning beyond childhood. This point has been made by Kohlberg, whose own theory we shall now look at.

⊖ Moral development can be seen as having **cognitive**, **behavioural** and **affective** components.

⊖ Piaget believed that children's moral reasoning developed in **stages**. He investigated this by studying children's ideas about rules, moral judgement and punishment.

⊖ His belief that children move from **heteronomous** to **autonomous** morality is supported by research. However, the complex tasks he used may have led him to believe that this change takes place rather later than it actually does.

Kohlberg's theory of moral development

Kohlberg's (1963) theory built on Piaget's. Like Piaget, Kohlberg believed that morality developed in stages, and that people pass through all the stages in the same order. However, in Kohlberg's theory moral development extends beyond childhood and into middle age.

Kohlberg used stories with a moral dilemma to find out the stage of moral reasoning participants had reached. His most famous dilemma is given in activity 22:

▶ **Activity 22: the dilemma of Heinz**

Read through this story and answer the questions underneath:

Heinz' wife was close to death from a particular kind of cancer. There was only one drug that doctors thought might save her, a form of radium discovered by a chemist living in the same town as Heinz. The drug was expensive to make, but the chemist bought the radium for $200, and charged $2000 for a small dose. Heinz tried everything he knew to raise enough money, but only managed to scrape together $1000. He begged the chemist to sell it to him cheaper, or let him pay off the balance later. But the chemist said: 'I discovered the drug, and I'm going to make money from it'. Heinz broke into the man's store to steal the drug for his wife.

Should Heinz have stolen the drug? Was it morally right/wrong to steal it? Why/why not?

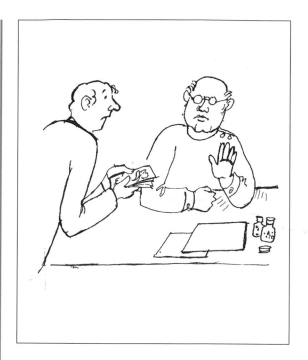

It is important that you also give reasons for your answers. Keep your answers to compare with the stages of moral reasoning Kohlberg identified, shown in figure 4.

Kohlberg defined three general levels of moral reasoning, each with two stages. The levels and stages are shown in figure 4. The ages associated with each level are very approximate:

In the first or **pre-conventional level**, reasoning focuses on the consequences of behaviour for ourselves. The moral reasoning behind our actions is related to avoiding punishment and gaining rewards. At this stage, morality is determined by the standards of adults, and the consequences if we break their rules (stage 1) or follow them (stage 2).

In later childhood, moral reasoning develops to the second or **conventional level.** We start to internalise the moral standards of others, and in particular those of adults who are important role models for us. We focus on complying with the rules and values of society. We seek to gain the approval of others (stage 3) and aim to maintain social order by showing respect for the rules of society (stage 4).

Between the ages of 16 and 20, people's moral reasoning may start to move to the third level. At this level – the **post-conventional level** – we move towards an individual conscience. In stage 5, we recognise that democratically established laws should be respected, but individual rights may sometimes be more important than these laws. In stage 6, our individual conscience determines what is or is not moral. We recognise that there are universal moral rules, and that the rules of society may need to be broken when they are in conflict with these rules.

As you can see from figure 4, the stages are defined in terms of the reasoning behind moral decisions, since it was this in which Kohlberg was

Figure 4: Kohlberg's stages of moral reasoning

level	age	stage
1. pre-conventional	6–13	1. obedience to avoid punishment 2. obedience to obtain rewards
2. conventional	13–16	3. seeking the approval of others 4. respect for authority and maintaining the social order
3. post-conventional	16–20 onwards	5. obedience to democratically accepted laws; individual rights can sometimes supersede laws 6. morality of the individual conscience in line with universal moral principles

interested, rather than whether people considered the behaviour of the characters in his dilemmas to be morally right or wrong. For this reason, his dilemmas were chosen so that a case could be made for whatever choice was made.

▶ Activity 23: matching responses to stages

Here are some possible answers to the Heinz dilemma described in activity 22. Can you match them to the stages of moral reasoning shown in figure 4?

a Heinz should not steal the drug because whatever the reason, people shouldn't take the law into their own hands.

b His family would think he was a terrible husband if he didn't steal the drug. If he let his wife die, he could never look anyone in the face again.

c He shouldn't steal the drug as he could get caught and sent to jail. He would always be worried that the police would catch him.

d If he doesn't steal the drug, he will always blame himself for his wife's death. He must do what his conscience tells him.

When you have finished, see the notes on page 482.

Evaluating Kohlberg's theory

There is some evidence to support Kohlberg's theory:

Box V: Kohlberg (1963)

Procedure: A cross-sectional study of 58 boys was carried out, testing boys aged 7, 10, 13 and 16 on a range of ten dilemmas.

Results: Each boy showed reasonable consistency in the level of moral reasoning used across the ten dilemmas. The younger boys tended to reason at stages 1 and 2, and the older ones at stages 3 and 4.

Conclusion: People use the reasoning of a particular stage of development across different moral dilemmas. They progress through the stages as they get older.

Kohlberg (1969) also found the same pattern of development in children from different cultures, i.e. Britain, USA, Taiwan, Mexico and Turkey. However, children in the less industrialised cultures tended to move through the stages more slowly. It has been suggested that his theory is culturally specific, in that the third level applies more to societies such as those in the West which value individualism, rather than those where the highest good is that of the community e.g. India and China.

In a later revision of the theory, Kohlberg (1978) concluded that most people do not move beyond level 2 moral reasoning, with only about 10% of adults moving beyond stage 4 to the third level. He also suggested (Kohlberg, 1981) that there may be a seventh stage, moving beyond moral reasoning into religious faith. A few exceptional people, such as Martin Luther King, whose lives are dedicated to humanitarian causes, may show stage 7 reasoning. Nonetheless, research such as that described in box V supports the idea of progress through the first four stages.

Martin Luther King

However, the theory has been criticised on several grounds, including the methods used:

Activity 24: evaluating Kohlberg's methodology

Look back to activity 22. Was there any other information you would have liked to have had before coming to a decision about whether Heinz was right or wrong to steal the drug? Your answer should help you to identify one of the difficulties of using dilemmas like Kohlberg's in moral development research.

Are there any other problems with his methods? You might find it useful to look back at this point to the evaluation of Piaget's theory in the previous section.

Compare your ideas with the discussion which follows.

Kohlberg's dilemmas have been criticised for being rather artificial; moral dilemmas are real problems faced by real people in a real setting. The theory rests on the assumption that we use general moral rules to identify relevant facts in the situation we are presented with. In contrast, **ethical act theory** suggests that relevant information may be more important than general moral rules.

If we go back to the Heinz dilemma, Rosen (1980) suggested different slants to the story. Suppose that Heinz' wife has been thinking of suicide for some time, and now wants to die with dignity? Suppose that the chemist is her brother, who knows her wishes and respects them, and has therefore priced the drug so that Heinz cannot afford it? What if Heinz wants to keep his wife alive so that they can both live off her trust fund, which will stop paying out when she dies? Kohlberg's dilemmas do not represent the complexity of real situations.

A related problem, which was also raised in connection with Piaget's theory, is that Kohlberg only looked at the cognitive dimension of morality. In real situations, would behaviour necessarily correspond to reasoning? What about the effect of emotions?

You may also have noted possible difficulties in matching responses to stages. How easy did you find it to match your own response to the Heinz story, or the possible responses in activity 23, to the stages outlined in figure 4? Assigning responses to stages is likely to be a question of personal interpretation, so there may well be disagreement between raters (i.e. low **inter-rater reliability**) when categorising responses.

After Kohlberg: Eisenberg and Gilligan

One criticism made of Kohlberg is that his theory concentrates on situations where there is a conflict between a rule or law, and the individual's sense of right and wrong. Eisenberg has suggested that this is rather a limited view of morality. She suggested that we also need to look at situations where there is conflict between one's own needs and the needs of others, situations which require what she called **prosocial moral reasoning**. One of the dilemmas she presented to children is given in activity 25:

Activity 25: prosocial moral reasoning

Try the following dilemma on children of different ages:

Mary was going to a friend's birthday party. On the way, she saw a girl who had fallen over and hurt her leg. The girl asked Mary to fetch her parents, so that they could take her to the doctor. But this would mean that Mary would be late for the party, and miss all the birthday food and games. What should Mary do? Why?

Did you get different answers at different ages?

Using this kind of dilemma, Eisenberg (1986) also found stages in development. Children move from focusing on their own needs, to those of others. At first answers are related to the need for approval from others and later to internalised values. She also found (Eisenberg *et al.*, 1987, 1991) that actual helping behaviour, in real situations, corresponded with the stages of moral reasoning she had identified, albeit not perfectly.

Further criticism, on the grounds of gender bias, has come from Gilligan (1977). She pointed out that much of Kohlberg's research was carried out using male participants, and that most of the dilemmas had males as the main character. This would make it easier for males to relate to the situations Kohlberg used than females.

More importantly, males are socialised differently from females. Males are encouraged to use abstract reasoning in resolving problems (the **justice perspective**), whereas women are socialised to be caring and nurturant towards others (the **care perspective**). This would mean that females would be more likely to use stage 3 and 4 reasoning, which in Kohlberg's system would mean that females are less morally developed than males. Gilligan argued instead that men and women have 'separate-but-equal' paths of development. A piece of research she carried out using female participants is described in box W:

Box W: Gilligan (1982)

Procedure: Twenty-nine females, aged 15–33, were interviewed. All of them were facing the real-life dilemma of whether or not to terminate a pregnancy. The conflict they faced was between personal choice and the traditional female role of caring for others.

Results: Participants focused less on the 'justice' dimension suggested by Kohlberg, and more on responsibility. The moral reasoning of the participants was at one of three levels: (1) self-interest, (2) self-sacrifice and (3) a balance between self-interest and sensitivity to the needs of others.

Conclusion: There is a parallel between the three levels proposed by Kohlberg and Gilligan's three levels. However, at the highest (post-conventional) level, women tend to retain their focus on personal concern for the needs both of themselves and others rather than the more abstract concerns of Kohlberg's system.

Some studies using Kohlberg's system have not found gender bias. Further research by Gilligan herself (e.g. Gilligan and Attanucci, 1988) has shown that although adult females are more likely to use a care orientation in deciding on moral issues, both males and females use both care and justice orientations to some extent.

- Using responses to moral dilemmas, Kohlberg proposed a **stage theory** of moral development which extended through adolescence into adulthood.
- His theory has been criticised on methodological grounds. The dilemmas are rather abstract, and do not look at the **affective** and **behavioural** dimensions of moral development.
- The later stages he suggested may not be universally applicable. His theory has been criticised for being **culturally specific**.
- Eisenberg suggested that Kohlberg's concept of morality was limited. She looked at **prosocial moral reasoning** in children, where there is conflict between one's own needs and the needs of others.
- Gilligan has criticised Kohlberg for **gender bias**. She stressed the importance of differences in **socialisation** between males and females.

Notes on activities

1 There have been two major suggestions to challenge Piaget's interpretations of his observations. The first is that Piaget's tasks are physically quite complex for a child to carry out. Young children are quite capable of reaching and grasping, but perhaps co-ordinating these two actions is more difficult, and this co-ordination is what is required in the task in box A (Jacqueline and the plastic duck). The other possible interpretation is that children's memory capacity may not be sufficiently developed to allow them to cope with these kinds of tasks.

4 One reason Donaldson put forward to explain the differences in performance is that the policeman task makes what she called 'human sense'. By this she meant that children are presented with the problem in a context they can relate to. All children are very likely to have had experience of hiding games, even if not from a policeman. On the other hand, experience of mountains (even in Piaget's native Switzerland) is likely to have been much more limited. In addition, the question 'What would these mountains look like from the other side?' is not perhaps the first question that would be likely to spring to the mind of a 4-year-old.

The mountains task also seems unnecessarily complicated, involving as it does right–left reversals. Many children (and quite a few adults) find this a problem, and it is not necessary in a procedure to test for egocentrism.

5 You have probably come up with all kinds of ideas: we would know if other people were pleased to see us; the fashion industry would produce tailwear; we could use them to keep flies away in summer, and so on.

6 Hopefully, you would have gone about this task *systematically*: 1 + g, 2 + g .... 1 + 2 + g, 1 + 3 + g .... 1 + 2 + 3 + g and so on, until all the possible combinations had been tested.

8 The teacher is not entirely a free agent in the classroom. Head teachers, parents and governors have expectations about what children should be able to do by particular ages. This is even more

true now that Standard Assessment Tests (SATS) have been introduced. With large class sizes in primary schools, applying Piaget's principles of individualised learning is probably not a practical option, at least not during the whole time a child spends in the classroom. At the same time, classroom practice has been very positively influenced by Piaget's ideas.

9 In considering what these theories have in common, you may have included that they both use a constructivist model, and focus on the way in which thinking changes as children develop; they both describe these changes in terms of qualitative differences; they both believe children are intrinsically motivated and are active participants in their own development; and they both believe that there is an important turning point around the age of seven.

Major areas of difference include the importance of social interaction and culture, as well as the role language plays for developing children. They also vary in the extent to which they believe thinking can be developed by tuition, and therefore in their implications for education. The nature of the differences at different periods of development also differs.

10 Vygotsky shared with Piaget the belief that children are actively involved in their own development and are intrinsically motivated, so the implications of these ideas would be similar to those discussed in the section on Piaget.

For Vygotsky, the intervention of others – both teachers and more able peers – underlies the learning process. He emphasised the zone of proximal development; if learning is to take place, the teacher's role is to present challenges to the child's current competence. Children working in groups would also be appropriate in a Vygotskyan classroom, since the more able children will assist the learning of others who are less competent.

For Vygotsky, education is cultural transmission. The knowledge and skills which are to be learned will reflect the nature and values of the culture within which learning is taking place.

11 Rule 1 relates to the idea of centration, typical of the preoperational stage, where only one aspect of the situation is considered. Rule 2 appears to be a transitional phase between the preoperational stage and the concrete operational stage of rule 3. The systematic approach in rule 4 reflects formal operational thinking.

12 The metacomponent here is how to solve the problem (i.e. £5–£3.75=x; cost/orange=x/5). The performance component is actually solving these equations. The acquisition component is learning how to solve problems like this in the first place. The retention component is holding in working memory the products of the calculations at the various stages of solving the problem (e.g. remembering £1.25 so that 5 can be divided into it), while the transfer component is being able to apply this knowledge to a new problem.

13 The MZ twins are more similar, which suggests that there is a genetic component to the development of intelligence. The MZ twins reared together are more similar, which suggests that intelligence is influenced by the environment.

14 Parents and children have more of their genes in common than cousins. There is also a higher correlation in IQ scores between parent and child than cousins, evidence of a genetic effect. However, there is also evidence of an environmental effect, because siblings reared together are more similar than those reared apart. However, one of the problems with this kind of study is that the environment is also usually more similar in closer relatives, so it is difficult to separate out the effects of genes and environment.

15 If heredity is more important than environment as a determinant of intelligence, it would be expected that adopted children's IQ should have a higher correlation with that of their natural parents than their adoptive parents, and vice versa if environment is more important.

17 The differences between plants in the same plot are due to genetic factors, but the differences between groups of plants are due to environmental factors (the nutrients).

18 Educational factors could include parental involvement in children's education and the educational opportunities children have had. Personal factors could include health and motivation, and whether they are tired and find it difficult to concentrate when they are taking it. Test factors include the cultural bias inbuilt in some tests, whether children have had practice at taking tests, and the relationship with the tester on individual tests.

21 The stories which Piaget used asked children to make judgements when two variables were manipulated, i.e. the intentions of the character in the story and the seriousness of the consequences. It has been argued that it might be easier for children, and so a better test, to look at each of these variables separately.

23 **a** shows stage 4 reasoning, **b** stage 3, **c** stage 1 and **d** stage 6.

18

Social and personality development

In this chapter we will be looking at:

18.1 Personality development
  Freud's psychodynamic theory
  Social learning approaches

18.2 Gender development
  Biological and biosocial approaches
  Cognitive-developmental theory
  Social learning theory
  Gender schema theory
  Psychodynamic theory

18.3 Adolescence
  Erikson's theory of lifespan
    development
  Adolescence in Erikson's theory
  Marcia's theory
  Is storm and stress inevitable?
  Coleman's focal theory of
    adolescence

18.1 PERSONALITY DEVELOPMENT

Personality has been defined in a number of ways by various theorists, reflecting differences in the theories they have put forward. This makes it difficult if not impossible to define personality in a way that would be universally acceptable. As a working definition, personality can be thought of as the characteristics of a person, relatively stable in different situations and across time, which make them unique as an individual. However, as we shall see, this is not without its problems.

Freud's psychodynamic theory

Chapter 1 contains an outline of Freud's psychodynamic theory; you might find it useful at this point to read through this section again. This theory attempts to explain every type of human behaviour, and has made a contribution to a range of topics. For example, later in the chapter we shall be looking at what it has to say about gender development. Freud has also put forward some interesting ideas in the area of personality, which we will be looking at here.

> ## Activity 1: key principles of Freud's theory
>
> What can you remember about the main ideas of Freud's theory, listed below?
>
> **a** psychological determinism
>
> **d** dynamic unconscious
>
> **b** unconscious conflict
>
> **e** psychosexual development
>
> **c** structure of the mind
>
> **f** defence mechanisms
>
> Check your answers with the outline given in chapter 1.

For Freud, personality is the dynamic interplay between the three mental structures of id, ego and superego. These three structures work on different principles.

The **id** works on the **pleasure principle**, seeking instant gratification and trying to avoid pain. The id can be thought of as the infantile part of the personality, since it is what we are before the processes of socialisation have started to influence us. When as adults we act on impulse, or demand that our wishes are instantly met, it is our id which is in control.

The **ego** works on the **reality principle**, tempering the demands of the id and the superego in terms of what is realistically possible. It is therefore sometimes known as the 'executive' part of the personality.

The **superego** works on the **morality principle**. During the phallic stage, pleasure centres on the genitals, and this stage is experienced differently by boys and by girls. The young boy goes through a crisis called the **Oedipus complex**. He develops unconscious sexual feelings towards his mother. He is envious of his father, and jealous of the love and attention he gets from the mother. The boy's feelings for his mother and rivalry with his father lead to fantasies of getting rid of his father, and taking his place with the mother. The hostile feelings he has for his father lead to anxiety that his father will retaliate by castrating his son, as a suitable punishment for the crime of desiring his mother. Freud believed that at this age, a boy realises that girls do not have a penis, and thinks that they have been castrated already.

To cope with this **castration anxiety**, the boy uses two ego defence mechanisms, **identification** and **introjection**. He identifies with his father and introjects (or takes in) his father's attitudes and moral values. Identification and introjection are the source of the boy's superego.

Development is slightly different for girls as they experience the **Electra complex**. The young girl becomes aware that she does not have a penis and develops **penis envy**. She blames her mother for this lack, and so transfers her love from her mother to her father. She realises that she cannot possess her father, and copes with this knowledge by identifying with the mother, introjecting the mother's attitudes and values. Freud called this process **anaclitic identification**.

Freud claimed that a girl's motive for identifying with her mother was less clear than a boy's motive in identifying with his father. Since she does not have

the powerful motive of castration anxiety which a boy has, her identification with the mother is weaker than that of a boy with his father. For this reason, Freud believed that girls have a weaker superego and therefore a less developed moral sense than boys.

Both boys and girls, then, internalise the parents' standards of right and wrong in the **superego**. The conscience represents the **punishing parent**, and the ego ideal the **rewarding parent**. The hostility that was originally directed at the same-sex parent is now also internalised, and experienced as **guilt**. The child conforms to the sociocultural rules internalised from the parents to avoid guilt.

Since the mental structures of id, ego and superego work on different principles, they are in conflict. The dynamics of personality, according to Freud, are rooted in this conflict, originating in the id and fuelled by the **libido**. The way conflict is resolved is a crucial part of personality. For example, people differ in the strength of their id drives, and in the balance in the superego between the punishing conscience and the rewarding ego ideal.

As an example of the relationship between id, ego and superego and personality, Adorno *et al.* (1950) proposed the idea of the **authoritarian personality** to explain why some people are prejudiced. His ideas are firmly rooted in psychodynamic theory, and are covered in more detail in the section on theories of prejudice in chapter 8.

People also vary in the **defence mechanisms** they use. These are strategies the ego uses to reduce anxiety by distorting our perception of reality. Freud believed **repression** to be the most important defence mechanism, and **sublimation** to be the only one that is effective long-term. People vary in the extent to which they depend on ego defence mechanisms, and in which mechanisms they tend to use.

Experience of the **psychosexual stages** also affects personality development. Freud suggested that the developmental stages which a child goes through help to form the personality of that child as an adult. Conflict experienced in a particular psychosexual stage may lead to **fixation**, which will be expressed symbolically in adult behaviour.

Let us take anal fixation as an example. A child who is fixated at the anal-retentive stage may become an anal-retentive personality; as the child tried to hold on to faeces, so the adult tries to hold on to belongings. However, a child who is fixated at the anal-expulsive stage may develop an anal-expulsive personality as an adult, becoming too generous and 'giving'. Fixations can be caused by intense pleasure associated with taboos such as smearing faeces, which may be expressed symbolically later in life by being very messy and untidy. These desires may be sublimated; for example, by the person becoming a potter who smears clay. Alternatively, reaction formation against these desires could lead to the person becoming extremely tidy and hating waste.

Freud identified two main personality types, oral and anal. However, fixation at other stages also shapes adult personality. Fixation in the phallic stage, according to Freud, was associated with exhibitionism, self-centredness and the exploitation of other people as an adult. He also associated problems in this stage with homosexuality. Fixation in latency was characterised by turning away from sexuality as an adult.

◑ Activity 2: personality and psychosexual stages

Below are descriptions of personality characteristics which may develop in an adult if the child becomes fixated at a particular psychosexual stage.

Use the characteristics to match each person with the stage or substage at which they became fixated. Check back to the section on psychosexual stages in chapter 1 if you are unsure about the characteristics of each stage:

1 Jason has a preoccupation with orderliness and punctuality. He never likes his routine to be disrupted, and you could imagine him developing obsessive–compulsive behaviour.
2 Jamila loves food and tends to be greedy. She is a smoker. She is interested in foreign languages, and is good at them, and enjoys gossiping with her friends. She has been described as a 'compulsive talker'.
3 Sally can be sarcastic and scornful at times. She bites her nails
4 Jolyon is mean and miserly. He collects matchboxes and beer mats, and likes to save the string and wrapping paper from parcels.
5 Brian avoids close relationships with women, since he finds it impossible to become emotionally involved in sexual activity. He is happier reading.
6 Mark regularly loses money gambling.
7 Khalid is excessively generous. He gives a percentage of his salary to charity each month, and buys his family and friends presents that he can ill afford.
8 Faye shows excessive displays of femininity, and would never be seen in public without full make-up and immaculately dressed. She is extremely self-centred, and has great ambitions for herself; she is prepared to tread on anybody to get to the top.

When you have finished, see the notes on page 509.

To sum up, according to Freud personality development is related to the development of and interplay between id, ego and superego, the use of defence mechanisms and the experience of the psychosexual stages. But is there any evidence to support these ideas?

One problem is that Freud's theory does not easily lend itself to rigorous testing. It is such a vast theory, covering as it does every aspect of human behaviour, that to test the theory as a whole would be impossible. However, some attempts have been made to test parts of the theory, and we will look briefly now at some of the research relating to personality development.

Fisher and Greenberg (1977) saw the oral personality as being concerned with dependence and independence, optimism and pessimism and continuing to seek oral gratification. Different clusters of characteristics would be expected to be found in those fixated in the **oral incorporative** substage and those fixated in the **oral aggressive** substage. Kline and Storey (1977) found that characteristics associated with the oral incorporative substage (dependency, optimism, fluency, sociability and relaxation) did indeed tend to cluster together, as did characteristics associated with the oral aggressive substage (independence, pessimism, verbal aggression, hostility and impatience). However, the fact that these clusters were found does not necessarily imply that they came about for the reasons Freud suggested.

Oral aggressive

Oral incorporative

Research has also investigated whether the characteristics associated with anal retentiveness (orderliness, rigidity, obstinacy and a dislike of waste) cluster together as the theory would predict. Fisher and Greenberg (1977) found support for this idea, and thus for the notion of an anal personality. Similarly, Pollak (1979) found that obstinacy, meanness and orderliness tended to cluster together. However, there is no evidence that these trait clusters come about as a result of particular experiences of toilet training. Fisher (1978) found that attitudes to cleanness predicted racial prejudice based on skin colour, suggesting that this kind of prejudice could be the result of unconsciously associating skin colour and faeces. However, this could be criticised as being highly interpretative.

Evaluation of Freud's theory: criticisms

While there is some limited empirical support for Freud's ideas about personality development, the theory itself – and so by implication those parts of it related to personality development – has been widely criticised on a number of grounds.

One major problem is the nature of the data on which the theory was based, i.e. information collected and analysed during Freud's analysis of his patients (see chapter 25 for an account of psychoanalysis). The record of clients' free association and so on in therapy hardly constitutes an objective, quantitative, reliable set of data. This information needed to be interpreted by Freud, whose interpretation might well be guided by his concern to find support for his ideas. Freud himself believed that his methods provided a 'royal road to the unconscious', allowing direct access to unconscious processes, but the charge of contamination by the interpretation of the analyst seems a hard one to refute. In addition, the case studies which he wrote up were very few in number, and were written up some time after they occurred, so it is perfectly possible that the limited data he was working on could have become distorted with the passage of time.

Another major criticism is that the theory is not scientific. Freud's theory is supposedly universal, but he generalised his results from a tiny sample of rich, middle-class, Jewish, neurotic Viennese women, living at the turn of the century, who all believed in psychoanalysis, a sample which was scarcely typical of all people.

It should be noted that this criticism does not only apply to Freud; many of the theories discussed in this book were developed on equally small and unrepresentative samples, typically first-year psychology students at American universities. However, Freud has been criticised as being a product of a particular culture, whose beliefs and assumptions have carried over into a supposedly universal theory. For example, the account of the development of girls is very much less detailed than that of boys, and Freud came to the conclusion that women are morally inferior to men – not a particularly startling viewpoint in early 20th century Vienna, perhaps, but rather less likely to find favour a century or so later.

According to Popper (1959), a scientific approach requires that ideas should be testable (and therefore falsifiable), and it is not possible to falsify Freudian theory. As an example, if you enjoy painting and playing with clay, it is because of an anal fixation and a desire to smear. If you do not enjoy these pursuits, this could be interpreted as reaction formation to your anal fixation. This kind of reasoning makes it virtually impossible to prove Freudian ideas wrong. The theory is very good at explaining events after they have occurred, but much less good at allowing testable predictions to be made.

As we saw earlier, some attempts have been made to test parts of the theory. However, only small sections of the total theory can be dealt with in this way. Some parts of it do not allow predictions to be made, and even with this kind of research, there is an element of interpretation of the findings that reduces somewhat its scientific acceptability.

Evaluation of Freud's theory: strengths
Freud's theory of personality has sometimes been described as the most controversial theory in the history of psychology. In modern times, it is hard for us to imagine the horror that the theory caused, but Freud's ideas of sexuality and its origins in childhood were quite shocking to people at the time. However, there are many positive points which can be made about it.

The theory has had a huge impact on our thinking in a range of areas. Freud's notion of the unconscious as a dynamic motivating force in our lives has an intuitive appeal, and has passed into everyday understanding with such ideas as the Freudian slip. It also challenged ideas about childhood. While not everyone would find Freud's account of psychosexual development convincing, the notion that childhood experience, particularly if it is traumatic, can continue to affect the adult is one that few would question nowadays.

Freud's work has also inspired much research and many theoretical developments. His psychodynamic traditions have been followed by many neo-Freudians, who have built on and developed his ideas. For example, we will be looking at the ideas of Erikson in the section on adolescence.

A further point which needs to be made is the application of psychoanalysis as a therapy. It is still widely used and both Freudian analysis and later variants have ardent supporters, as well as fierce critics. This is discussed in chapter 25.

Hall and Lindzey (1970) suggested that the ideas of Freud have lasted so long because they are so well-written, they have an exciting subject matter, and they challenge some of the basic, intuitive ideas we have about people.

- For Freud, the **id**, **ego** and **superego** make up the structure of personality. Personality is also affected by **defence mechanisms** and **fixation** at one of the stages of psychosexual development.
- There is limited empirical support for these ideas.
- While the theory has been heavily criticised, it has nonetheless been extremely influential and some aspects of it have intuitive appeal.

Social learning approaches
An outline of social learning theory was given in chapter 1. This theory is an extension of the behaviourist approach, but focuses specifically on

human learning. It proposes that children learn social behaviour through the processes of **observational learning**, i.e. learning through watching the behaviour of others, and **modelling**, i.e. imitating what others do. Bandura, one of the founders of social learning theory, suggested that the three sources of models are the family, the subculture and the media. His work was an attempt to make the Freudian concept of identification, mentioned earlier, more scientific by carrying out research on it in the form of imitation.

Children learn social behaviour through observational learning.

Bandura claimed that observational learning can take place without reinforcement, but whether this learning is translated into behaviour depends on the consequences of the behaviour. These ideas are demonstrated in Bandura's Bobo doll experiments, described in chapter 10 in the section on theories of aggression.

Unlike the traditional behaviourist approach, social learning theory includes a **cognitive** element. When we observe another person doing something, we interpret and evaluate their behaviour in terms of its consequences. If the consequences are seen to be positive, we are more likely to model the behaviour. We are also more likely to model behaviour which we assess as being appropriate to

us. In one of Bandura's sequence of Bobo doll studies (Bandura *et al*. 1961), he found boys were most likely to imitate a male model. We are more influenced by models who are like ourselves.

So how does social learning theory relate to personality development? For Freud, personality is an internal part of the individual which leads them to respond to a range of situations in consistent and predictable ways. In contrast, for social learning theorists like Bandura 'personality' is an external label for the sum total of a person's behaviour, and is assessed by measuring observable behaviours. Personality and behaviour are therefore essentially the same thing. Personality is a set of behaviours acquired through the observational learning process.

Mischel is another personality theorist working within the social learning theory framework:

Box A: Mischel (1968)

Procedure: A metastudy of a large number of studies into personality was carried out.
Results: Correlations between personality test scores and measures of behaviour in a variety of situations were generally low, rarely above 0.3. People did not necessarily behave consistently in different situations.
Conclusion: Behaviour is mainly determined by situational factors.

The lack of consistency in behaviour which Mischel found can be explained in terms of people being reinforced for behaving in different kinds of ways in different situations. Different models, showing different behaviour patterns, lead to different behaviours being modelled depending on the situation.

The social learning theory approach to personality is not without its critics. The main method of research is experimental, and usually laboratory-based. Development is a long and complex process, so there are limitations in trying to investigate it in this way.

It has also been criticised for focusing only on learned observable behaviours, and ignoring genetic and physiological factors in personality. This emphasis on behaviour has been challenged by research into **temperament**. Temperament can be defined as a disposition to act in particular ways, which is present early in life, and which is stable over time and across situations:

Box B: Buss and Plomin (1984)

Buss and Plomin developed the EAS system for classifying temperamental differences. The three dimensions they used were emotionality (aspects of fear and anger), activity (related to the tempo and vigour of behaviour) and sociability (seeking out the company of others).

Children vary in:

activity

emotionality

and sociability

Since consistent differences in these dimensions can be observed in very young children, Buss and Plomin argued that they have a strong genetic component. High correlations on these dimensions between monozygotic twins (who are genetically identical) are consistent with this claim.

However, even if some aspects of personality are genetically based, as temperament theorists claim, it could still be that much of the difference between individuals comes about through different learning experiences as social learning theory suggests.

A further criticism of social learning theory is that people are considered to be only the sum of what they have learned, nothing more. As Phares (1988) put it, behaviourists take the 'person' out of personality.

- ⓢ **Social learning theory** proposes that behaviour is acquired through **observational learning** and **modelling**. Personality is seen as the sum total of our behaviours, and its development is seen as a result of our learning experiences.
- ⓢ There is some evidence that people do not behave consistently across situations. This is explained by having different models in different situations.
- ⓢ This approach has been criticised in terms of its **methodology** and for ignoring **genetic factors**.

18.2 GENDER DEVELOPMENT

To start this discussion of gender development, we need first of all to define our terms. Many psychologists make a distinction between sex and gender. **Sex** refers to the biological aspects of being male or female; anatomy, physiology, hormones and so on. **Gender** refers to social and cultural aspects, including attitudes and behaviour. For example, Maccoby and Jacklin (1974) found gender differences between males and females, in that girls tend to do better than boys on tests of verbal ability, while boys tend to do better than girls on tests of visuospatial ability.

Gender identity refers to the awareness that we are male or female, **gender stability** to the understanding that gender is permanent, and **gender constancy** to recognising that gender remains the same in spite of superficial changes, e.g. in clothes, or the kinds of toys that a child prefers to play with. **Gender roles** are patterns of behaviour which a particular society sees as appropriate for males or for females.

489

One question that arises is the extent to which gender differences are due to innate, biological factors (**nature**), and how much they depend on the different experiences – personal, social and cultural – of girls and boys (**nurture**). We will be looking here at the biological and biosocial approach to gender development, cognitive-developmental theory, social learning theory (together with social cognitive theory), gender schema theory and psychodynamic theory.

Biological and biosocial approaches

Before we consider the biological approach to gender development, we need to look briefly at biological sex differences. Sex can be defined in terms of three kinds of physical differences between males and females. Firstly, it refers to whether the egg was fertilised by a sperm carrying an X or a Y **chromosome**. It can further be defined in terms of **gonads**, i.e. testes in males and ovaries in females. Finally, there are **hormonal** differences, with males producing androgens (the most important of which is testosterone), and females producing oestrogen and progesterone. While both males and females can produce all the hormones, males produce very much more of the male hormones than females, and vice versa.

Both males and females begin as an egg bearing an X chromosome. If the egg is fertilised by a sperm carrying another X chromosome, the embryo will develop as a girl, and the two gonads will become ovaries. The embryo has both male and female interior anatomy, but the male elements spontaneously disintegrate, while the female ones thicken and grow into a womb. At the same time, the exterior anatomy, which has the same beginning for both sexes, develops into female genitalia, and the result is a girl. As we shall see, even without ovaries, development follows the female route; the natural route of the human is the female one.

To become a male means interfering with that natural route. If the sperm carries a Y chromosome, the gonads develop into testes. They pump out a hormone which actively absorbs the female parts which would otherwise begin to grow, and then produce the major male hormone, testosterone.

This stops the male parts degenerating. It thickens the spermatic cord, and switches the genitalia away from the female route. The result is a male.

At puberty, under the influence of hypothalamic and pituitary hormones, the male or female gonads release hormones – testosterone in the male and oestrogen and progesterone in the female – which stimulate the development of secondary sexual characteristics such as the development of breasts and pubic hair.

A biological account of gender differences argues that innate genetic and hormonal differences between males and females are responsible for their different psychological characteristics. For example, inherent differences in musculature, testosterone levels and so on would mean that males are pre-programmed to be aggressive, while the different physiological make-up of females suits them for a nurturant role.

Usually there is little doubt about whether an individual is biologically male or female, so it is difficult to distinguish between the effects of being biologically male (**nature**), and the effects of being treated as male by others (**nurture**). Occasionally, however, the situation is not so clear-cut:

Activity 3: the Batista family

Read through these case studies:

(1) the Batista family – Imperato-McGinley (1974)

Some members of the Batista family, living in the Dominican Republic, do not follow the normal course of sexual development. Where both parents carry a mutant gene from a common ancestor, some of the children are born as girls. They have normal female genitalia and body shape, and are raised as girls.

However, at the age of about 10 their vagina heals over, and they develop testicles and a penis. They all adapt their gender identity well to their new sex, take men's jobs and marry women, and are treated as men by others.

The Batista boys are genetically male. The fertilising sperm carries a Y chromosome, and enough testosterone is produced during development to preserve the male elements of their interior anatomy. However, they do not develop male genitalia at this stage due to lack of a chemical called dihydrotestosterone. At puberty, testosterone production forces up the level of dihydrotestosterone, leading to the development of male external genitalia.

(2) Accidental penectomy – Money (1974)

One of a pair of male MZ twins accidentally had his penis removed during circumcision. It was decided to raise him as a female. His male sex organs were removed, an artificial vagina constructed, and he was given female hormones. 'She' was always treated as a girl.

According to Money, who had recommended gender reassignment, as a 4/5-year-old 'she' preferred to wear dresses, and was neater and tidier than 'her' twin, but showed some tomboyish behaviour, e.g. a liking for rough-and-tumble play. When 'she' reached her teens, a follow-up study (Diamond, 1982) found 'her' to be generally unhappy, with few friends. 'She' was confused about 'her' gender, and looked rather masculine. 'She' was later reassigned as a male.

a What evidence do these cases give for a biological view of gender development?

b On the basis of these studies, how could factors in the social environment be said to play a part in gender development?

When you have finished, see the notes on page 509.

Testicular feminising syndrome suggests that gender isn't necessarily tied to chromosomes, gonads and hormone production. In this syndrome, the egg is fertilised by a sperm carrying the Y chromosome, the gonads become testes and the female parts are absorbed. However, body cells are insensitive to testosterone, so development does not continue along the male route. At birth, the individual has normal-looking female external genitalia, but has only a very short vagina. At puberty, breasts develop, but there is no menstruation, since the person does not have a womb. Such a person is biologically male. However, they look female, are raised as females and consider themselves female.

A case of testicular feminising syndrome

A final case study also underlines the strength of nurture:

Box C: Goldwyn (1979)

Goldwyn described the case of Mr Blackwell, a hermaphrodite. Hermaphroditism is a very rare condition – Mr Blackwell was only the 303rd recorded case – in which a proportion of the person's cells are the female type (XX) and the rest are the male type (XY). It is thought that this comes about by the egg being fertilised both by a sperm carrying an X chromosome and by one carrying a Y chromosome.

Half his body was male and the other half female. He had functioning sexual characteristics of both a male and a female, with an active testicle on one side and an active ovary on the other. He had both a vagina and a penis. At 14 he developed breasts, and began to ovulate and menstruate. Further tests revealed that his brain biochemistry was female in the way that his sex hormones were regulated.

He had been brought up as a boy. He was quite certain he was a male, and his female parts were surgically removed. He went on to function as a male. His upbringing as a male seems to have been a major influence on gender development.

The surgeon who carried out the operation on Mr Blackwell also treated 25 other cases of hermaphroditism. All the people treated were in no doubt about their gender, which was always in line with the way they had been raised, either as a male or as a female. It therefore seems that biological factors alone do not account for gender development.

These findings can best be accounted for by a **biosocial approach**. This approach, while stressing the importance of biological factors, at the same time claims that it is the interaction of biological and social factors which is important. The social aspect here focuses on the idea that different characteristics of babies influence how other people treat them. One of these characteristics is the baby's sex:

Box D: Smith and Lloyd (1978)

Procedure: Mothers were asked to play with a young baby that they didn't know. A baby was dressed in pink or blue clothing and was introduced to the mother using a boy's or a girl's name. The same baby was presented to different participants as a boy or a girl. The ways in which the mothers interacted with the babies were analysed.

Results: Mothers tended to stimulate a 'boy' more than a 'girl', for example by bouncing or jiggling 'him'. The toys offered to the baby were also sex-typed, with a 'boy' being more likely to be offered a hammer, and a 'girl' given a soft toy.

Conclusion: The sex of a baby influences the ways in which parents interact with them.

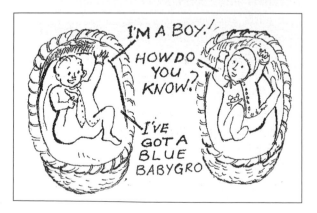

Money and Ehrhardt (1972) argued that gender identity is influenced by this kind of labelling. Being categorised as a boy or a girl on the evidence of biological differences influences how we are treated, and this further social element plays a part in developing gender identity. They argued that before the age of about 2 or 3, it is possible to change the sex of rearing without any psychological harm being done. After this sensitive period, that is no longer possible.

There is some support for this idea:

Box E: Money and Ehrhardt (1972)

Procedure: Ten individuals with testicular feminising syndrome were studied. They had all been categorised as girls at birth on the basis of their external genitalia, and raised as females.

Results: While they tended to be more tomboyish than other girls, they nonetheless showed a strong preference for the female role.

Conclusion: The interaction of biological and social factors is important in explaining gender development.

The study of accidental penectomy carried out by Money (1974), discussed in activity 3, is also relevant here. As we have seen, the considerable gender confusion experienced at puberty, and the final decision to be reassigned as a male, suggest that gender identity may not be as flexible as biosocial theories suggest.

In the light of the other evidence we have looked at in this section, the relative contribution of nature and nurture remains unclear, but most psychologists agree that both are important.

The other approaches we will be looking at are less interested in the influence of physiology, and more interested in the role of psychological factors in gender development.

- The relative importance of biological factors (**nature**) and environmental factors (**nurture**) is an issue in gender development.
- The **biological** approach explains gender development in terms of physiological differences

between males and females. The **biosocial** approach emphasises the interaction of biological and social factors, and suggests some flexibility in the development of gender identity.

❺ While biological sex differences are important, they are not the only factor in the development of gender identity.

Cognitive-developmental theory

The cognitive-developmental approach sees children as actively developing their understanding of gender. This understanding moves through stages, as a result of interaction with the physical and social environment.

Activity 4: exploring children's understanding of gender

If you have access to young children, ask them the following questions. Ideally, one of the children you interview should be 2–3 years old, and one about 5 or 6:

a Are you a boy or a girl?

b When you're ten, will you be a boy or a girl?

c When you grow up, will you be a man or a woman?

d If you have children of your own when you grow up, will you be a mummy or a daddy?

e If you wanted to, could you be a daddy/mummy?

*f If you put on a boy's/girl's clothes, would you be a boy/girl?

These kinds of questions have been used by many researchers into children's understanding of gender. In general, it has been found that children are aware of their own gender (i.e. can answer question (a) correctly) by the age of about two. However, Kohlberg (1966) found that the more sophisticated knowledge required by the other questions is not fully developed until the age of about five or six. He suggested that a child's understanding of gender has three stages:

a **gender identity** – the awareness that we are male or female

b **gender stability** – the understanding that gender is permanent

c **gender constancy** – recognising that gender remains the same in spite of superficial changes.

Gender identity has developed by around the age of two, gender stability by 4 or 5, and gender constancy by 6 or 7.

Martin and Little (1990) found evidence that understanding of gender does develop in the sequence that Kohlberg suggested, and there is some evidence that this sequence applies across cultures.

However, use of the kinds of questions in activity 4 has been criticised. How easy is it for small children to understand the questions they are being asked? For example, question (d) is grammatically complex, assumes that children understand 'have children' to mean in this context 'give birth to', and that this is something only mummies can do. Given these problems, it is possible that even if stages such as those suggested by Kohlberg do apply, children's understanding may develop more quickly than research has shown.

One way of simplifying the task for young children has been to use drawings and photographs. Emmerlich *et al.* (1977) found that children were less likely to show gender constancy when drawings were used. They typically do better with photographs (e.g. Bem, 1989), but do best when asked questions about themselves. It is possible that children understand gender constancy as applied to themselves before they learn to extend it to other people, and it is also possible that drawings and photographs confuse the issue. It is, after all, perfectly possible to change drawings permanently.

Research has also investigated young children's understanding of gender role:

Box F: Kuhn *et al.* (1978)

Procedure: Children aged $2\frac{1}{2}$–$3\frac{1}{2}$ were shown paper dolls called Michael and Lisa. They were asked whether Michael or Lisa would be likely to make statements such as: 'I like to help mummy', 'I like to fight' and 'I need some help'.

Results: Boys and girls shared some beliefs about gender roles, e.g. that girls like to help mummy, talk a lot and ask for help, and that boys like to play with cars, help daddy and say 'I can hit you'.

Boys also have beliefs about girls, which girls don't share (e.g. that girls cry and are slow). Similarly, girls have beliefs about boys, which boys don't share (e.g. that boys fight and are mean).

Boys and girls also have beliefs about positive aspects of themselves not shared by the opposite sex. For example, girls (but not boys) believe that girls look pretty and never fight. Boys (but not girls) believe that boys like to work hard and are loud.

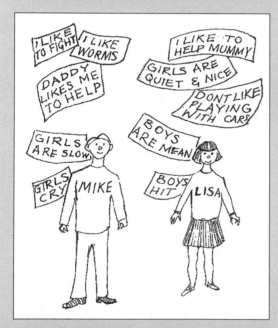

Conclusion: Gender-role stereotypes are held by very young children. There is an affective aspect to these cognitions, since the stereotypes tend to value their own sex and devalue the opposite sex.

Cognitive-developmental theory implies that there should be little gender-appropriate behaviour before gender constancy is achieved, and Kuhn's findings, as well as those of similar studies, suggest that this is not the case. Nonetheless, it is reasonable to see cognitions as contributing to gender development.

⊖ **Cognitive-developmental theory** sees gender development as passing through a series of **stages**.

⊖ Kohlberg suggested that children follow the sequence of **gender identity**; **gender stability**; **gender constancy**.

⊖ Research has offered some support to these ideas.

⊖ **Gender-role stereotypes** are present in very young children.

Social learning theory

While cognitive-developmental theory is largely concerned with children's understanding of gender, social learning theory is more concerned with gender-appropriate behaviour, and in particular with socialisation processes.

▶ ### Activity 5: social learning theory and gender development

Look back to the outline of **social learning theory** in the discussion on **personality development**. How could these principles be used to explain gender development?

When you have finished, see the notes on page 509.

The family is the most immediate source of models, but the media – e.g. children's TV and books – also provide models. For example, Leary *et al.* (1982) found that children who frequently watched TV were more likely to hold gender stereotypes, and to conform to culturally appropriate gender roles.

▶ ### Activity 6: investigating TV stereotypes

Are girls and boys portrayed differently in the media? Watch a range of TV programmes intended for children, and where children are the main actors. Before you start, prepare a checklist of behaviours. Here are some to start you off. You will probably be able to think of several you can add:

aggression (kicking, punching, shouting)
nurturing (hugging, comforting, sympathising)
leadership (planning, giving orders)

Prepare two copies of the checklist, one for boys and one for girls. As you watch the programmes, put a tick on the relevant checklist against each kind of behaviour as it occurs.

Are some behaviours shown more frequently by boys than girls, and vice versa?

Social learning theory suggests that parents and others respond very differently to girls and boys. While some studies have failed to find differences, a lot of research supports this idea, and has shown that male and female children are treated differently from birth:

Box G: Rubin *et al.* (1974)

Procedure: Parents were asked to describe their newborn infants. Male and female

infants were matched on size, weight and muscle tone, to eliminate individual differences as a possible confounding variable.

Results: Sons were more likely to be described as strong, active and well-co-ordinated. Daughters were more likely to be described as beautiful, little, delicate and weak.

Conclusion: From birth, parents have different expectations of children, based on their sex.

The findings here have parallels with those of the Smith and Lloyd study in box D, so this piece of research is also relevant to biosocial theories of gender development.

With older children, Sears *et al.* (1957) found that parents expected and even encouraged aggression in boys. A survey of children's bedrooms, carried out by Pomerlau *et al.* (1990), found that boys' rooms were more likely to contain vehicles and action-orientated toys, while girls' rooms were more likely to contain dolls and to be decorated in a floral style.

These studies can be interpreted in **operant conditioning** terms; the principles of operant conditioning are outlined in chapter 1. Children may be influenced by whether or not parents' responses reinforce gender-related behaviour. They can also be seen as supporting social learning theory, in that these behaviours could come about by modelling.

Block and Dworkin (1974) also found differences between parents, in that fathers were more likely to use sex-typed language to describe their children. They were more concerned with the cognitive development of their sons, and the development of social skills in their daughters. Langlois and Downs (1980) found that fathers were particularly hostile to gender-inappropriate behaviour in their sons.

One study, which looked in detail at parental attitudes and behaviour is described in box H:

Box H: Fagot (1978)

Procedure: A sample of 24 families was studied, each family with a child just under 2. Parents were extensively observed interacting with their children, with the child's behaviours classified under 46 headings. Parents also completed questionnaires, rating the 46 kinds of behaviour for appropriateness for boys and girls.

Results: Behaviours which occurred significantly more often in boys included play with bricks and transportation toys, and manipulating objects. Play with dolls and soft toys, dressing up, dancing and asking for help occurred significantly more often in girls. The questionnaire responses showed that parents considered playing with dolls, dressing up and dancing as more appropriate for girls, and rough-and-tumble play and aggressive behaviour as more appropriate for boys.

However, parental responses to behaviour did not always match the questionnaire responses. There was no difference in their reactions to boys and girls playing rough-and-tumble games. Girls asked for help three times as often as boys, but parents did not rate this behaviour as more appropriate for girls.

Parents considered dressing up and dancing as more appropriate for girls …

… and rough-and-tumble play and aggressive behaviour as more appropriate for boys.

Conclusion: There is some indication that parental reactions to a child's behaviour influence that behaviour, and that children's behaviour influences parental reactions. However, the relationship between parental attitudes, a child's behaviour and parental reactions is not clear-cut.

Social learning theory, then, helps us to understand children's gender development. The relationship between parental attitudes, children's behaviour and parental reactions to children's behaviour can perhaps be best understood in terms of the mutual influences of a transactional model.

However, this approach may not sufficiently take into account the child's cognitions, i.e. his or her *understanding* of gender role, and the influence this understanding can have on development. With this in mind, Bandura (1986) has adapted traditional social learning theory to put more emphasis on cognitive factors. This is called **social cognitive theory**. The child's own judgements of how they feel when engaged in gender-appropriate and gender-inappropriate play are seen to play an important part in gender development:

Box I: Bussey and Bandura (1992)

Procedure: Children aged 3 and 4 were asked to say whether they would feel 'real great' or 'real awful' when playing with a range of toys. They thought they were making these judgements anonymously.

Results: By the age of 4, boys felt 'great' about playing with trucks and robots, but 'awful' about playing with dolls and kitchen sets. The opposite was true of girls.

Conclusion: Children learn early to feel uncomfortable with gender-inappropriate behaviour. Since the reactions were given anonymously, they could be considered to be the result of the child's self-evaluation, rather than factors such as the demand characteristics of the situation.

Gender-appropriate and gender-inappropriate behaviour – see box J

Gender schema theory

Another theory which brings together social learning theory and cognitions is gender schema theory (Bem, 1981). Like social learning theory, it proposes that gender role is learned. It suggests that children develop **schemas** (or concepts) which help them to understand, organise and make sense of information. Schemas are discussed in rather more detail in chapter 2. You will remember that schemas simplify the processing of information, but can lead to distortion when new information does not fit an existing schema. Gender is the basis of a very powerful schema, which can affect the way in which children interpret gender-related information.

These ideas have been supported by research:

Box J: Martin and Halverson (1983)

Procedure: Children aged 5 and 6 were shown pictures of children carrying out activities which were either gender-consistent (boys playing with trucks) or gender-inconsistent (girls sawing wood). They were asked to recall the pictures a week later.

Results: During recall, participants tended to change the sex of the children in gender-inconsistent pictures.

Conclusion: Memory is distorted to fit in with existing gender schemas.

Since they bring together elements of social learning and cognitions, both social cognitive theory and gender schema theory have a lot to offer in terms of explaining how children's understanding of gender, and its relationship to their own gender roles, develops.

- **Social learning theory** looks at influences in the child's environment to explain gender development. Children learn by **observational learning**, **modelling** and **reinforcement**.
- Research suggests that from a very early age, parents respond differently to sons and daughters.
- The interaction of parents' attitudes, children's behaviour and parents' reactions to this behaviour may be more complex than social learning theory suggests.

497

❺ Bandura has developed **social cognitive theory**, which builds on social learning theory, putting more emphasis on cognitive factors.

❺ **Gender schema theory** also combines social factors and cognitions. A gender **schema** is developed, within which gender-related information is interpreted.

Psychodynamic theory

The major psychodynamic theory to attempt to explain gender development is that of Freud. Freud believed that 'anatomy is destiny'. For him, genital differences determine the psychological characteristics of males and females. It is not the physiological differences as such which determine gender development, though. Rather, children develop an understanding of gender when they recognise the *significance* of the differences.

The key to gender development is the Oedipus conflict, described in the earlier section on personality development. This is experienced by boys at around the age of 5–6. The equivalent process – the Electra conflict – is experienced by girls at the same age. According to Freud, the key factors in gender development are identification with the same-sex parent and introjection of their beliefs and values.

However, as in other areas of development, Freud's account of gender development has been criticised. Many theorists have questioned the validity of the Oedipus conflict, which underpins Freud's ideas on gender development. For example, a study of Trobriand islanders carried out by Malinowski (1929) found no evidence that young boys had experienced the Oedipus conflict.

▷ ## Activity 7: problems with Freud's account of gender development

The Oedipus conflict apart, can you think of aspects of Freud's theory which don't fit in with research findings in this area? You may find it helpful to look back through the discussion of other theories in this section. Can you identify any other problems? When you have finished, see the notes on page 510.

More recently, theorists working within the psychodynamic tradition (e.g. Chodorow, 1978) have given a fuller account of gender development in girls. They stress the importance of early relationships, particularly with the mother, since she is usually the main caregiver. These relationships provide a pattern for how to relate to other people. As they grow older, girls continue to follow the pattern provided by the mother, and come to understand femininity and closeness in relationships as being inextricably linked. On the other hand, boys need to establish their masculinity by breaking away from this pattern. For them, masculinity comes to be defined as a lack of closeness in relationships.

However, this approach still focuses on relationships within the family. Freud's theory was developed when the nuclear family – father, mother and children – was the norm. Variations in family make-up are now extremely common, but appropriate gender development still takes place:

Box K: Green (1978)

Procedure: Gender role in 37 children between the ages of 3 and 20 was studied. They were being brought up either by lesbians or parents who had undergone sex reassignment (transsexuals). The younger children were tested by asking them about the kinds of games they preferred, what kinds of clothes they liked to wear and what they wanted to be when they grew up. Older participants were asked about their sexual behaviour, desires and fantasies.

Results: With the possible exception of one participant, all those studied had developed heterosexual preferences and conformed to cultural gender roles. For example, the younger children expressed a preference for playing with others of the same gender. Little boys wanted to be firemen and engineers when they grew up, and girls wanted to be nurses and housewives.

> **Conclusion:** Appropriate gender development still takes place when there is no same-sex parent in the family, or when the family varies in some other way from a nuclear family.

While the family is undoubtedly an influence, at the same time it makes sense to assume that the models children use extend beyond the immediate family, as social learning theory suggests.

- ⊖ Freud links gender development to the resolution of the **Oedipus** and **Electra conflicts**. Anxiety is overcome by **identification** with the same-sex parent.
- ⊖ This has been widely criticised. The existence of the Oedipus conflict has been questioned. Gender development starts much earlier than the theory suggests. It may put too much emphasis on the influence of the family.

18.3 ADOLESCENCE

The term 'adolescence' covers from the beginning of puberty through to the ending of physical growth. It is a period during which many aspects of maturity are reached: physical, mental and emotional. At the same time, there is considerable social development and development of identity, and we shall be concentrating mainly on these areas. However, you will need to bear in mind that all these factors interact.

Many developmental theories have tended to concentrate on development through the early years of childhood. In part, this emphasis is a result of the influence of theorists such as Freud, Piaget and Bowlby, who all thought that what happens in childhood is crucial to adult characteristics. One theory which looks at development across the lifespan, and has a particular interest in adolescence, is that of Erikson.

Erikson's theory of lifespan development

Erikson's theory is descriptive, rather than based on experimental studies. He stressed that it was 'a tool to think with' (Erikson, 1950) rather than a factual analysis. Its purpose, then, is to provide a framework within which development through life can be considered, rather than to be a testable theory.

Erikson was born in Denmark, grew up in Germany and spent his professional life in the USA. There he studied college students, survivors of the second world war and American Indians. It is therefore easy to see why he concentrated on the social and cultural aspects of development.

Erikson was a neo-Freudian. He accepted Freud's ideas about stages in development, and the structure of the psyche as including the id, ego and superego. At the same time, Erikson developed and changed aspects of Freud's theory.

While psycho*sexual* development is central to Freud's theory, Erikson also emphasised the social and cultural aspects of development, so his theory is a psycho*social* developmental theory. He stressed that people are active explorers of their world, and need to understand its social realities in order to develop fully. He assumed that people are basically rational, and controlled mainly by their ego. For this reason he is called an ego psychologist.

Erikson believed that we all go through eight **stages** in our life. These stages are primarily social, in that they are to do with our relationships with others. At each stage, we face a particular conflict, which Erikson refers to as a **crisis**. Each crisis needs to be resolved before we can develop further. Each stage is related to a particular age range across the lifespan. However, he was optimistic that each crisis could be resolved at any age. Although our lives would be affected if these crises were not resolved, 'there is little that cannot be remedied later, there is much (harm) that can be prevented' (Erikson, 1950). His theory is therefore more optimistic than Freud's.

The eight stages Erikson described, and the crises which we face in each of them, are shown in figure 1:

Figure 1: Erikson's eight stages of lifespan development (1966)

1 Birth – 1 year: trust vs mistrust

social focus: the mother or other major caregiver.

If caregivers are rejecting or inconsistent, the baby does not learn to trust, and will not develop hope, i.e. trust that the world will meet their needs.

2 1–3 years: autonomy vs shame and doubt

social focus: parents

If children are not encouraged to do things for themselves, and to learn independence, they will doubt their own abilities and not develop autonomy or will.

3 3–6 years: initiative vs guilt

social focus: family

Children need to be encouraged to use their own initiative, without impinging on the rights of others. If this is not managed, the child will feel guilty and lack purpose in life.

4 6–12 years: industry vs inferiority

social focus: school and neighbourhood

Children's skills and confidence in them need to be encouraged, or they may grow up with a sense of inferiority. They need to develop a sense of competence.

5 12–18 years: identity vs role confusion

social focus: peer groups

The adolescent needs to establish a vocational and social identity, so that they see themselves as a consistent and integrated person. If this does not happen, they will not develop loyalty to people, ideas or values.

6 20–40 years: intimacy vs isolation

social focus: friends

The adult needs to form strong and intimate relationships, which show love and commitment, both in friendships and in particular with a sexual partner. Otherwise relationships remain superficial.

7 40–65 years: generativity vs stagnation

social focus: society

At this stage people need to be productive and creative, and to make a contribution to society as a whole. Otherwise they will stagnate, become too focused on themselves, and not learn to care, i.e. achieve a sense that certain things in life have meaning and importance.

8 65+: integrity vs despair

social focus: humankind

The individual will achieve wisdom, a sense of satisfaction that life has been worthwhile, and the acceptance of death. Failure to resolve this crisis leads to regret over missed opportunities and fear of death.

Adolescence in Erikson's theory

Erikson gives approximate ages for this stage of 12–18 years, but adolescence can extend from around 10 years of age into the twenties. Erikson saw adolescence as a period of psychological turmoil or **storm and stress**, which has a far-reaching effect on the self-concept. At this time physical changes bring about an altered body image, with an inevitable effect on the sense of self. Intellectual growth in adolescence allows a more complex self-concept to develop, involving what is potentially possible as well as what currently exists. At this period increasing emotional independence is developing, and decisions must be made about careers, values and sexual behaviour. All these factors are likely to lead to considerable changes at this time to the self-concept.

Erikson also believed that this period is characterised by a **psychosocial moratorium**. By this he meant a transitional time, when society allows the young person to experiment with different ideas and roles before adult commitments are made. Given space, time and encouragement, they will develop loyalty to people, ideas and values throughout life.

Many psychologists have seen Erikson's fifth stage as the central crisis of all development. At this stage, adolescents are developing their identity, and ask the question 'who am I?' The main goal at this time is to develop a lasting and secure sense of self, or **ego identity**. This has three parts: a sense of consistency in the ways they see themselves, a sense of continuity of the self over time, and a sense of mutuality, i.e. agreement between one's own perceptions of self and the perceptions of others.

First relationships at this age are not necessarily sexual – adolescents are concerned with finding themselves, as reflected by their intimates in different kinds of relationship. Erikson said that this is why 'so much of young love is conversation' (Erikson, 1968).

Difficulty in coping with this crisis means that adolescents may continue to be confused about their role in life, and unable to be faithful to people, work or a set of values. In extreme cases, particularly when they feel they cannot live up to the demands made of them, adolescents may develop a negative identity. This will lead them to behave in ways which are very unacceptable to the people who care for them. A boy with Christian parents, for example, may become an atheist.

There is some evidence that parental style is related to how well adolescents cope with this stage: (see box L on the next page).

Consistency   Continuity   Mutuality

Box L: Elder (1980)

Procedure: A possible relationship between parental style and high self-esteem, independence and confidence in adolescents was investigated.

Results: Independent, confident adolescents with high self-esteem tended to have democratic/authoritative parents. These parents respected the right of adolescents to make their own decisions, while at the same time expecting them to behave in a disciplined way. They gave reasons for the rules which they expected would be observed. In contrast, dependent adolescents, who lacked confidence and had low self-esteem, tended to have authoritarian parents, who expected unquestioning obedience and felt no need to explain their reasons.

Conclusion: Parental style is associated with the ease with which adolescents cope with the crisis of identity vs role confusion.

Because we need to make an early start in the morning

It might be a good idea to go to bed now

why?

Democratic/authoritive parents

GO TO BED NOW!

why?

BECAUSE I SAY SO!

Authoritarian parents

Activity 8: exploring Erikson's ideas about adolescence

Look back through this section to remind yourself of what Erikson had to say about this stage of development. If you fall within this age range, does your own experience, and that of your friends, support Erikson's ideas?

Alternatively, interview people of this age about these ideas. You could use an unstructured interview technique, or produce a questionnaire based on the main ideas we have looked at. As this is a rather sensitive area, you will need to assure your participants of confidentiality, and that no judgements will be made about them. You will also need to make sure that you give them enough information at the start of the interview to allow them to give informed consent to take part, and debrief them fully afterwards.

Given the nature of Erikson's theory, it is rather difficult to test empirically. One study which has attempted to do this, concentrating on adolescence, is described in box M:

Box M: Buhler (1968)

Procedure: Four hundred biographies were analysed. While Erikson's research concentrated on men, this analysis included biographies of both men and women.

Results: Buhler found that between the ages of 15 and 25, people experimented with their lives. Occupational and social choices made at this time were actually provisional, rather than for life, as Erikson implied. She also noted that at this age, for the first time, young people had a sense that 'one's own life belongs to oneself, and represents a time unit with a beginning and an end'.

Conclusion: Erikson's ideas about adolescence are basically supported. However, it is a period when identity is provisional, rather than completely formed.

Other research also supports Erikson's ideas:

Box N: Levinson *et al.* (1978)

Procedure: A sample of 40 men aged 35–45 was interviewed at length, over a period of months. They came from a variety of backgrounds, but were mostly middle class.

Results: Levinson concluded that the life cycle is ordered into four overlapping eras, each with a key task. The period between the ages of 17 to 22 he called the Early Adult Transition, with two primary tasks: –

   1 To separate from the family and

   2 To form a direction for adult life.

Conclusion: These findings broadly support Erikson's ideas about the nature of adolescence.

While there is some agreement between Levinson's findings and Erikson's ideas, Levinson has developed his own theory which focuses particularly on development in adulthood. We shall be looking at this in more detail in chapter 19.

Evaluating Erikson's theory

A major strength of the theory is that it has face validity. Many people find that they can relate what he has to say about various stages of the life cycle to their own experience.

It also develops and builds on Freud's ideas. Freud has been criticised for, among other things, seeing childhood as the main determinant of adult development, and for concentrating very heavily on sexual aspects of development. Erikson accepts many of Freud's ideas; for example, that the childhood stages he describes are important for later development. At the same time, he has built in an emphasis on the importance of social factors, and focused attention on later periods of our lives.

However, the nature of the theory has meant that it is not easy to put into a form which can be easily tested. It lends itself most readily to the use of interviews and questionnaires, which present problems of interpretation, the possibility of participants giving socially desirable answers, and so on.

However, Erikson has been a major influence on other psychologists. His emphasis on the full lifespan has encouraged others to extend the scope of developmental psychology beyond childhood, and to follow up his ideas in more detail.

- Erikson's theory builds on and extends Freud's ideas. It is a theory of **psychosocial development**. Over the lifespan, we pass through eight **stages**, in each of which there is a **crisis** to resolve.
- The fifth stage covers **adolescence**, when the crisis of **identity vs role confusion** needs to be resolved. Because of the wide-ranging changes during this period, Erikson saw it as a time of **storm and stress**. The **psychosocial moratorium** is an experimental period before adult commitments are made. During this stage, the individual develops a lasting and consistent **ego identity**.
- Research has shown that difficulties at this stage are related to **parental style**.
- Identity at this stage may be **provisional**, rather than completely formed, as Erikson suggested.
- His theory has intuitive appeal, and has been widely **influential**. At the same time, it is **difficult to test** empirically.

Marcia's theory

The most comprehensive analysis of Erikson's ideas about adolescence has been carried out by Marcia (1966). He argued that identity formation in adolescence involves both crisis and commitment. Crisis is involved in the individual reconsidering and re-evaluating existing choices and values, and this in turn leads to a commitment to a set of roles and values. He concluded that there are four identity statuses in adolescence, from least to most mature. These are described in figure 2:

Figure 2: Marcia's four identity statuses (based on Erikson's theory)

1 *Identity confusion*

This is the least mature of the four statuses. The young person's identity is diffuse, either because they have not yet experienced an identity crisis, or because they have not resolved it. They have made no commitment to their future, either in work or relationships, or to attitudes or values in life.

2 *Identity foreclosure*

There is some commitment to goals, values and beliefs, but there has been no identity crisis. Usually the young person has accepted the advice of parents or authority figures without evaluating it. Identity foreclosure can be missed out, with the individual moving directly from identity confusion to moratorium.

3 *Moratorium*

This relates to identity crisis. The young person experiments with different values, ideas, relationships and work choices. This is done with the aim of developing a stable identity.

4 *Identity achievement*

The crisis of the moratorium is resolved. A strong commitment is made to an occupation, sexual orientation and a value system, either political or religious.

Identity confusion

Identity foreclosure

Moratorium

Identity achievement

You can see that this is much more detailed than Erikson's original theory, and suggests that adolescence itself has different aspects. Unlike Erikson's theory, it is not a stage theory, since the four statuses do not necessarily follow each other in order. The theory also suggests that adolescents have to find their own way; if they follow a path set out for them by teachers or parents there may be no crisis, but perhaps no development either.

Commitment is a hallmark here: to occupation, sexual orientation, relationships and values, which all follow from experimentation. Through experimenting with different types of work, relationships and values, adolescents find the ones which suit them best. The modern practice of young people still at school taking part in work experience is a good example of giving adolescents the opportunity to try out different types of work.

Marcia's work has led to a lot of research. We will look at some examples:

Box O: Melman (1979)

Procedure: Structured interviews were used to investigate Marcia's four statuses in schoolboys or male college students aged 12–24 years.

Results: Their development was much later than Erikson implied, with only 20% of 18-year-olds achieving identity, and less than 60% of the 24-year-olds.

Conclusion: There is support for the existence of an identity crisis at adolescence, but identity development is not complete until after adolescence, and for many people, not until after the mid-twenties.

This was a restricted study, since only males were interviewed. A similar study has, however, been carried out to include females:

Box P: Archer (1982)

Procedure: The method used was similar to that used by Melman (box O). The sample included both males and females.

Results: Development was later than Erikson suggested, with only 19% of 18-year-olds having successfully resolved their identity crisis. There were also differences in identity status between four areas: occupation, sex role, religion and politics. For these four areas, more than 90% of participants had two or three different identity statuses, using Marcia's developmental structure. Stable identity was achieved most often for occupational choice, and least for political ideology.

Conclusion: Identity is achieved later in adolescence than Erikson suggested, and is achieved at different times in different areas.

This suggests that it may be an oversimplification to talk about 'identity' as a single phenomenon. From these findings, it seems that identity is complex and multifaceted: we should perhaps talk of separate identities, such as 'work identity' and 'political identity', to get a clearer picture.

▷ Activity 9: identity achievement at different periods

Erikson was writing in the 1950s and Marcia in the 1960s. Are there any ways in which life is different now, which might account for the findings in box O and box P that the identity crisis is resolved later than they suggested?

When you have finished, see the notes on page 510.

One possible influence on identity achievement has been explored in the study in box Q:

Box Q: Munro and Adams (1977)

Procedure: Identity development in college students and working peers was compared.

Results: Young people in full-time employment were more likely to have achieved religious and political identity than college students.

Conclusion: Identity formation is a social process. It may be encouraged more in the work environment than in college.

As you can see, research based on Marcia's ideas has offered many new ideas about adolescence. Development seems later than Marcia suggested, and is not homogenous, but occurs at different rates in different areas.

One important issue arising from these studies is whether going to college might actually delay development in ways that the world of work encourages. Adams and Fitch (1982) concluded from their longitudinal study that college students in fact often regress from identity achievement to moratorium.

Activity 10: social context and identity development

How might you explain research which shows that identity development is delayed, or even reversed, in young people who go to college, compared with those at work?

When you have finished, see the notes on page 510.

Both Erikson and Marcia focused on adolescence as a time when identity is achieved. However, it has been suggested that this process may continue well into adult life. Waterman and Waterman (1975) found foreclosure in many men aged 40–65, where a commitment had been made without a crisis being experienced. It must be remembered, though, that these men would have been children and adolescents between the 1930s and 1950s, so this may well be a cohort effect: for example, society's expectations at that time are likely to have been very different from today.

- Marcia based his work on that of Erikson. He proposed **four identity statuses** in adolescence: identity confusion, identity foreclosure, moratorium and identity achievement.
- Research has supported his ideas, with many studies finding identity achievement being completed later than Erikson proposed. Different areas of development may have different identity statuses at any one time.
- Identity achievement depends on the **social context** within which it develops.

Is storm and stress inevitable?

Traditionally, adolescence has been seen as a period of 'storm and stress'; Erikson's theory and Marcia's development of it both see adolescence as an emotionally intense period of considerable personal and social upheaval. But is this necessarily the case?

Box R: Rutter (1976)

Procedure: A study of 2303 14- and 15-year-olds was carried out. Data included questionnaires completed by parents and

teachers, together with interviews with some of the sample, and psychiatric assessment.

Results: Only 1 in 6 of the parents reported conflict with their sons or daughters. A rather higher proportion of the adolescents felt in conflict with their parents, but reports of serious disagreement or criticism of parents were rare. There were few cases of clinical depression in the adolescents studied. Difficulties which did emerge were usually associated with stressful situations, such as discord between parents, rather than the fact of being an adolescent.

Conclusion: Adolescence is not inevitably a period of storm and stress. It does not appear to be significantly different from other stages in life in this respect.

Coleman and Hendry (1990) have suggested that the picture many people have of adolescence as a time of emotional turmoil may be coloured by social factors. For example, films and television often portray adolescents as rebellious, and in conflict with parents and authority. In addition, many of the theorists in this area come from a clinical background. They are thus more likely to come into contact with young people who are undergoing difficulties or are in stressful situations, which may mean their perception of what life is like for the majority of adolescents is distorted.

It has also been suggested that the 'storm-and-stress' view of adolescence is culturally-based; perhaps the turmoil we associate with this stage of life is a response to the particular pressures we experience in industrialised Western societies.

The anthropologist Margaret Mead (1939) has been particularly influential in putting forward these ideas:

Box S: Mead (1939)

Procedure: Life among the people of Samoa in the South Seas was studied. In particular, the course of adolescence was described, and comparisons drawn with adolescence in Western society.

Results: In Samoa, boys and girls were familiar early on with the facts of life, death and sex. Sexuality in particular was treated in an open and casual manner, so the guilt, shame and anxiety often experienced by Western adolescents was avoided. Adolescence in Samoa was in general an uneventful time, since life as a whole was much less complex. Adolescence in Western society is a time when choices need to be made, and when the individual is under considerable pressure to succeed; this may account for the 'storm and stress' often experienced at this time.

Conclusion: Adolescent 'storm and stress' is at least in part a cultural phenomenon. While stress at this time cannot be avoided in complex industrialised societies, we can help adolescents prepare for and cope with the choices they must make at this time.

However, Mead has herself been criticised and the validity of her findings called into question. For example, Freeman (1983) pointed out that the conclusions she drew were based on interviews, and suggested that as an outsider, those she talked to may not have been completely honest with her. Moreover, all her interviews were with girls or women, so may well have provided only a partial picture. More recent cross-cultural studies have lent some support to this criticism. At the same time, Mead's work is a helpful reminder that cultural factors may have an important part to play in development. Other research also supports this idea:

Box T: Bronfenbrenner (1974)

Procedure: Child-rearing patterns and adolescent behaviour in the USA and the USSR (the former Soviet Union) were compared.

Results: Soviet adolescents were much more prosocial than American adolescents, and showed less antisocial behaviour. Soviet adolescents were encouraged to be part of adult society earlier than Americans, who were often segregated and cut off from adult activities.

Conclusion: The development of a separate youth subculture among American adolescents results from their being excluded from adult activities. Culture may be influential in how adolescence is experienced.

But segregation from the adult world will not necessarily lead to adolescents being in conflict with adult values. Musgrove (1963) argued that we need to look a little more closely at what is going on in the adolescent's life at the time. He suggested that a youth subculture with values in conflict with those of society was only likely to develop if adolescents are held in low esteem, and that this would not happen if adults treated them with respect.

We need also to look at the impact of physical changes during adolescence, in particular the start of puberty. The onset of menstruation in girls, and the enlargement of the penis and ejaculation in boys, are known as primary sexual changes. There are also secondary sexual changes; for example, the growth of pubic hair and changes in body shape such as a growth spurt and the development of breasts. These rapid physical changes have psychological implications. They affect the ways in which people respond to the adolescent, and adolescents themselves need to adjust to new and unaccustomed desires.

A further related factor which needs to be considered is the change in self-concept during adolescence. Since physical changes during adolescence are dramatic, change in body image is likely to have an important influence on the self-concept, and in particular on self-esteem.

While most girls enter puberty between the ages of 11 and 14, and boys about a year later, some children mature earlier or later than this. This has led to an interest in the psychological effects of early and late maturation.

▶ Activity 11: the psychological effects of early and late maturation

Try to put yourself in the position of a girl/boy who has reached physical maturity much earlier or later than your friends. How might you feel about this? How might it affect your self-concept? What kinds of factors might influence how you feel? Compare your answers with the discussion which follows.

All adolescents have to come to terms with the physical changes they are experiencing, and it is quite common to feel some embarrassment. There is some evidence that both early and late maturers may experience feelings of inadequacy and emotional stress. Jones and Bayley carried out a study looking at the impact of early and late maturation:

Box U: Jones and Bayley (1950)

Procedure: Psychological differences between early and late maturing boys aged 14–18 were studied.

Results: Early maturers were seen as more attractive than late maturers. They were more likely to be popular and to be given positions of responsibility. In contrast, late maturers were more childish and attention-seeking. At 17, early maturers were still more self-confident and independent, while late maturers were more aggressive.

Conclusion: Physical changes in adolescence affect the self-concept, particularly self-esteem. This may be connected with how the individual experiences adolescence.

However, this study looked only at adolescent boys. The picture seems to be very different for girls. Peskin (1973) found that girls who matured early tended to have more psychological problems and less self-confidence than those who matured later. Similarly, a study by Crawford and Unger (1995) found that early maturing girls had a less positive body image and lower self-esteem than late maturers.

▶ Activity 12: attitudes to maturation

a At maturation, muscle mass increases in boys. In girls, there is an increase in body fat.
b Changes in adolescence mean sexual maturity. How could these two facts be related to the differences between boys and girls in how physical change in adolescence is perceived? You will need to think of the opportunities and difficulties, for both boys and girls, which these changes imply. When you have finished, see the notes on page 510.

⊖ The idea of adolescence as necessarily a time of **storm and stress** has been questioned both by large-scale studies and by **cross-cultural studies**.

⊖ The extent to which young people are encouraged to take part in adult society, and **society's attitude** towards them, may be important factors in whether or not adolescence is a time of emotional upheaval.

⊖ Changes in the self-concept and **self-esteem** at this time are also important. There are both **gender** and **individual differences** here.

Coleman's focal theory of adolescence

As we have seen, there are conflicting findings about the nature of adolescence. Coleman (1974) proposed a theory which attempted to resolve some of these inconsistencies.

The important thing to remember here is that there are wide variations in adolescent experiences and expectations. For example, some young people will expect to leave home or start work at 16, while for others this change will come much later. Some will expect to find a sexual partner much earlier than others. There will be individual differences in the age at which physical maturity is reached, which as we have seen will affect the individual's experience of adolescence.

Coleman's theory took into account these kinds of variation. He suggested that individuals focus on different aspects of change at different times. For example, career choice would be the area of focus for someone about to start work, whereas it would not be so important for someone starting at university. This does not imply that the individual can only focus on one area at a time: all the problems associated with adolescence are present at all times, but at any one time, they will not be equally important. Moving through adolescence, then, involves a shift in focus on the different challenges the individual must meet.

These ideas have been explored in research:

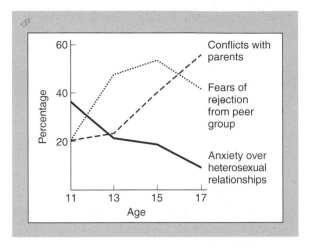

Box V: Coleman and Hendry (1990)

Procedure: A sample of 800 boys and girls was tested at the ages of 11, 13, 15 and 17. The tests included material on self-image, relationships, being alone and being in large groups.

Results: For all participants, the anxieties they expressed changed over time. Some issues tended to be prominent early (e.g. anxiety over heterosexual relationships) while others were more important later (e.g. conflict with parents). These patterns were not, however, identical for all individuals.

Conclusion: While there is some overlap, different issues come into focus at different times. The stresses associated with adolescence are spread over a period.

This research has been replicated by Kroger (1985), using samples from the USA and New Zealand, with similar results. Coleman has suggested that it is only when the individual has more than one issue at a time to cope with that problems are likely to arise. Research by Simmons and Blyth (1987) found strong support for this idea.

- **Coleman's focal theory** has suggested that the adolescent focuses on different areas of concern as adolescence progresses. The adaptation necessary at this time is therefore spread over several years.
- Adolescence is only a time of storm and stress when the individual has to face a number of issues at the same time.

Notes on activities

2 1 anal-retentive **2** oral-incorporative **3** oral-aggressive **4** anal-retentive **5** latency **6** anal-expulsive **7** anal-expulsive **8** phallic. However, some of these behaviours could be explained in terms of reaction formation. For example, in Mark's case, he could be an anal-retentive personality, and reaction formation has led to his gambling.

3 The ease with which the Batista boys adopt a male gender role suggests that biological factors are indeed important. They had been treated as girls in the early years of their lives, but this did not seem to interfere with their conceptions of themselves as male when the biological changes of puberty occurred.

In the early years, the case of the twin who had his penis removed seemed to show that nurture could outweigh nature. The behaviour of the twin who was treated as a girl corresponded to the female gender role. However, in adolescence, the gender confusion the twin experienced seemed to indicate nature reasserting itself.

5 Like other kinds of behaviour, gender-appropriate behaviour is acquired through **observational learning** and **modelling**. Adults and peers positively **reinforce** gender-appropriate behaviour by praise or approval, and **punish** behaviour which is gender-inappropriate.

7 Freud's theory claimed that children become gender-typed at around the age of 5–6. A lot of the research we have looked at, e.g. the Kuhn *et al.* study in box F, and Bussey and Bandura (box I), suggested that this may happen a lot earlier than Freud believed. This research showed that children as young as 2 or 3 have started to grasp the idea of gender, and to relate it to behaviour.

The process of identification with the same-sex parent is, according to the theory, less strong for girls than boys. There is no evidence, though, that girls have greater problems in gender development than boys.

9 The school leaving age was raised during that time to 16, so that all young people had to stay at school longer. In addition, a larger proportion than previously now choose to stay at school beyond the compulsory leaving age, or to go to a college for further training or education. The differences found in these studies may also have something to do with higher unemployment, particularly for school leavers. This could mean that young people tend to be older when they are able to start to lead more independent lives.

10 Young people at work are perhaps treated differently from those at college. For example,

they may be expected to take more responsibility for themselves, while those at college may still have many decisions taken for them. It is also possible that going to college brings people into contact with others who have very different ideas from their own. This could lead to a further re-evaluation of values and attitudes, and so a move back from identity achievement to moratorium. College might also provide a protected environment in which to explore these new ideas.

12 For boys, the increase in muscle mass is associated with social advantages, e.g. the possibility of athletic achievement and the physical presence to take a leadership role. For girls, the increase in body fat is in conflict with cultural pressures; for example, the equation between attractiveness and extreme thinness in the media's presentation of young women. Some adolescent girls may respond to this by developing the eating disorder anorexia nervosa. This is discussed in chapter 5.

Sexual maturity may also be seen in a more negative light by girls than by boys. Socially, there are often double standards as to what is seen as appropriate sexual behaviour for girls and for boys. In addition, for girls sexual maturity is associated with the inconvenience and physical discomfort of menstruation, and pregnancy may be an unwelcome possibility.

19

Adulthood

In this chapter we will be looking at:

19.1 Early and middle adulthood
   Erikson's theory of lifespan
      development
   Levinson's *Seasons of a Man's Life*
   Gould: Evolution of adult
      consciousness

19.2 Family and relationships in adulthood
   Marriage
   Divorce
   Parenthood

19.3 Late adulthood
   Erikson's theory
   Social disengagement theory
   Activity theory
   Cognitive changes

19.4 Social changes in late adulthood
   Retirement
   Bereavement and dying

As we saw in chapter 18, Erikson played a large part in expanding the interest of developmental psychologists from a focus on childhood to psychological changes across the lifespan. Before we look at his and other theories in this area, activity 1 is intended to give you some general information which you can compare with what you will be reading about in this chapter:

Activity 1: identifying changes in adulthood

How do adults change through their lifespan from young adulthood to old age? If you know an elderly person, you might find it a useful exercise to ask them how they feel they changed during various periods of their lives from their early twenties to the present day.

You could also ask what factors they believe contributed to these changes. Do they view the changes positively or negatively?

Compare your findings with the discussion which follows.

It is likely that whoever you have talked to has mentioned physical changes. They may have said that they can't move about as easily as when they were younger; for example, they are less likely to take part in energetic sports. They may also talk about cognitive change, feeling they have slowed down mentally, perhaps becoming increasingly forgetful. They may also have seen some cognitive changes as beneficial; for example, they may see themselves now as better able to make informed and sensible decisions.

They may also have mentioned personal and social changes, and may relate these directly to particular life events, e.g. marriage, parenthood, retirement and bereavement. We shall be looking in detail at the impact of this kind of experience later in the chapter. Their circle of friends and acquaintances may have shrunk, particularly after retirement. They may feel that people treated them differently when they became a parent or a widow. They may also feel that others respond differently to them as 'an old person' than when they were younger.

In personal terms, while most people feel some sense of continuity between the person they were in the past and the person they now are, they may also feel that there have been personality changes, again linked to life events. For example, they may talk about a new sense of responsibility on becoming a parent, or the need to establish themselves as an independent person after the death of their partner.

The theories and research we shall be looking at all consider some of these kinds of changes as we grow older. 'Growing old' is often seen rather negatively, in terms of physical and psychological decline. However, as we shall see, change and development during this period can also be seen in a more positive light. You may have already discovered this in the interview you carried out.

19.1 EARLY AND MIDDLE ADULTHOOD

Erikson's theory of lifespan development

Erikson's theory of development across the lifespan was described in chapter 18. Within a psycho-dynamic framework, he proposed that we pass through eight stages in the course of our lives, at each of which we have a crisis to face. You may find it useful to look back to the section on **adolescence** in that chapter, including figure 1, to remind yourself of what he had to say. Stages 6 and 7 are relevant to this section, and stage 8 to the discussion on late adulthood in the final section of this chapter.

The period from roughly 25–45 years of age is generally thought of as **young adulthood**, with some variation between theorists. Some of you may think it strange to think of 40 as 'young', but if you bear in mind that many people live well into their 80s, it is only half the lifespan. **Middle adulthood** covers the period from about 45–65 years.

Erikson viewed young adulthood as a period of settling down and making commitments, providing development had proceeded well in the earlier stages. However, as we saw in the section on adolescence in chapter 18, not everyone has formed their identity fully by the beginning of this period. The progress they have made in this area will clearly be related to their mid-adult development.

In middle adulthood, people need to be needed, and to pass on the fruits of their experience to others without thought of return. Becoming a parent may

lead to this development, while other people contribute art, music or literature: anything that is of benefit to the next generation. If the person does not develop in this way, they will become self-absorbed and stagnate. Ultimately this will lead them to regress rather than develop, and is likely to lead to an unhappy older age. If development proceeds well, the love learned earlier in life turns to a wider care for others.

Do the developmental tasks described by Erikson come to prominence during these periods? Has identity been achieved by the time the individual enters younger adulthood? Are there other factors associated with the course of development at this time?

Box A: Sangiuliano (1978)

Procedure: In-depth interviews were carried out with women in the mid-life period.

Results: Typically the women achieved a full occupational identity much later than is usual for men, and later than Erikson's theory suggests. For many, their identity merged with that of their partner, and they only established their individual identity during mid-life.

Conclusion: Women typically achieve intimacy before identity.

This study seems to suggest, then, that there are **gender differences** in the course of development. Erikson (1968) himself suggested that the sequence of stages may be different for men and women, and that women may be concerned with intimacy before identity.

This is further supported by Hodgson and Fischer (1979). In their study of undergraduates, just over 50% of the females who were rated as not yet having achieved identity were rated as having achieved intimacy. The percentage of males for whom this was true was very much smaller.

Class differences may also affect developmental patterns. Neugarten (1975) found that working-class men saw early marriage as part of the normal life pattern. The 20s were seen as a time for settling down, having a family and finding a steady job. In contrast, middle-class men and women both saw the 20s as a time for trying out different occupations and exploring what life has to offer. The 30s were seen as the appropriate time for marriage and settling down.

Since gender and social class are likely to be associated with differences in development in adulthood, both in the timing and in the ordering of stages, Erikson's stages need to be considered as flexible, rather than as describing a universal and inevitable pattern which everyone goes through. At the same time, his theory does offer a framework within which development at this time can be considered.

- ◎ Erikson's theory proposes that two stages make up adulthood, the period between adolescence and old age. Each has its own crisis. The first is **intimacy vs. isolation**, followed by **generativity vs. stagnation**.
- ◎ There may be **gender** and **class** differences in development during these stages.

Levinson's *Seasons of a Man's Life*

Like Erikson, Levinson's **life structure theory** was interested in changes during adult life. While Erikson talked about different stages throughout the lifespan, each with a different developmental task, Levinson was interested in how people experience different phases of adulthood; it is therefore a **phenomenological** account.

His initial ideas were developed on the basis of in-depth interviews:

Box B: Levinson *et al.* (1978)

Procedure: Forty men aged 35–45 were interviewed at length, for around 20 hours each, over a period of months. In addition they were given a **projective test** (the **TAT** described in chapter 8, activity 12), their wives were interviewed, and their workplace was visited where possible. They came from a variety of backgrounds, but were mostly middle class.
Results: There were different themes associated with different periods of people's lives. For example, in the period between the ages of approximately 22 and 28 people were concerned with separation, i.e. creating

psychological distance from the family, and attachments to the adult world.
Conclusion: Levinson concluded that the life cycle is ordered into overlapping eras, each with a particular focus. There are transitional periods between each era (see figure 1).

A secondary sample used biographies of people such as Gandhi and the philosopher Bertrand Russell, and fictional characters such as King Lear. The findings are explored in the book *Seasons of a Man's Life* (Levinson *et al.*, 1978).

Levinson believed that there is an underlying pattern to a person's life at any one time. Life structure develops through a series of **phases** ('seasons'), some of which are **stable** (or structure-building) which alternate with **transitional** (or structure-changing) phases. During each phase, there are biological, psychological and social adjustments to be made. Changes in role, in terms of family or work, are central to individual development. The course of development is shown in figure 1:

Figure 1: model of adult development (Levinson *et al.*, 1978)

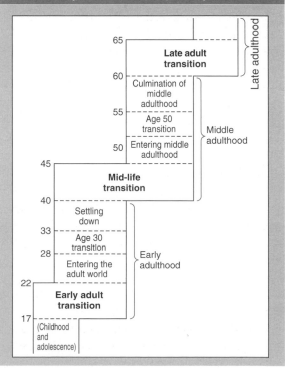

The **early adult transition** marks the move from adolescence, when separation from the family is a key theme. This separation takes many forms: moving out of the family home, becoming financially independent, depending less on the emotional support parents give, and so on.

In **early adulthood** the individual starts to explore possibilities which will lead to a stable life structure. Levinson identified four major areas which are important at this time. One of these is following a **dream**, the rather general conception of what someone wants to do with their life, and finding a place for it in the life structure. Often a **mentor** relationship is formed with an older person who guides them. The individual must make a choice of **occupation** and become established in it. At this time, **relationships** are formed, with the possibility of establishing a home and family.

The life structure is not yet fully established in the early part of this period, and some people experience a crisis at around the age of 30, as they feel that the choices made are no longer provisional and there is pressure of time on any changes which need to be made.

The end of this period is a time of consolidation, when there is a strong sense of commitment to the personal choices which have been made. The latter part of this phase has been called **BOOM** (**b**ecoming **o**ne's **o**wn **m**an).

The **mid-life transition** marks the end of one life structure and the start of another. At the same time, the process of BOOM continues. It is during this time that individuals re-examine their lives. They may compare reality with their original dreams, and modify their goals and values.

Over 80% of Levinson's sample found this period to be one of turmoil – they experienced a **mid-life crisis**, though Levinson did not himself use this term – but those who struggled with this emerged better than those who did not. On the other hand, Rutter and Rutter (1992) found the opposite; going through this period relatively calmly was associated with more satisfactory future development.

Activity 2: do we need a mid-life crisis?

Why might Levinson and Rutter and Rutter have come to such different conclusions? You will need to think about the kinds of *methodological* problems associated with carrying out an investigation of this sort, and which might be related to the different findings of these two studies.

When you have finished, see the notes on page 533.

You will remember that all of Levinson's sample were under 45, and none were actually in their 50s when he carried out follow-up interviews, so there is rather less evidence both for the remaining phases he described, and for the effect of early experience on later development.

As **middle adulthood** is entered, the individual may need to develop a new life structure. This may be brought about by **marker events**, e.g. change of occupation or children leaving home. Divorce may lead to a new relationship which will modify the life structure. However, change can also be less clear-cut, related not so much to external changes as to a change in the individual's attitude to an existing occupation or relationship. This phase is often marked by the individual becoming less self-absorbed and more concerned with future generations.

The **late adult transition** is again a period of reappraisal, as the individual is aware of the approach of old age and the readjustments it must bring. **Late adulthood** can be a time of crisis, as the individual needs to come to terms with the fact that their life is nearing its end. For some this can be a time of turmoil, for others a time to look back calmly at what has been achieved.

This theory has many strengths. If you have gone through this period of your life, it is likely that you can relate to much of what Levinson has to say. If you are still too young to have experienced any of his 'seasons' for yourself, you might like to talk to older people to find out whether they react positively to his ideas. Another of its strengths could be that it focuses specifically on adulthood, rather than necessarily seeking to fit this stage of life within a much broader theory. Finally, it is concerned with people's subjective experience of this stage of their lives, rather than viewing it objectively from the outside.

However, the theory can be criticised on several counts. Firstly, evidence to support it is limited, and methodological problems, given the nature of the topic, have already been discussed (see activity 2). The sample in the major study in box B was relatively small and exclusively male. Levinson himself later extended his studies to females:

Box C: Levinson (1986)

Procedure: Forty-five women were interviewed, following a similar pattern to the research described in box B.

Results: Men and women have different dreams. Men tend to focus on career, while for women both career and family relationships are important. There were individual differences, with some women being quite happy to sacrifice a possible career for family, and others (particularly business women) wanting to maintain both, though not necessarily at the same level.

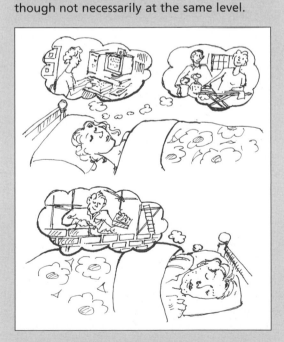

Conclusion: There are gender differences in development during adulthood.

The extent to which Levinson's theory can be applied cross-culturally is also open to question. While he claimed that his ideas could be applied universally, it seems likely that the social variation associated with class, culture and historical period influences adult development and how it is experienced. The study in box D supports this view:

Box D: Neugarten (1965)

Procedure: Over 700 people of different ages were studied over a period of seven years, using interviews and projective tests such as the TAT. The focus was on the mid-life period.

Results: There was a major shift in focus at this time, from outward events to personal reflection, and from 'time since birth' to 'time left to live'. People also internalised social norms and expectations, behaving how people 'should' be at that age, whether they were really like that or not.

Conclusion: There is a change in outlook at this time. However some lifespan changes are heavily determined by social norms.

Finally, stage theories like those of Erikson and Levinson (although Levinson refers to seasons linked to age, rather than stages) imply that there is one developmental path which everyone follows. It is also possible to focus more on individual variation. One way in which this has been done has been to look at the impact of particular life events, e.g. divorce and parenthood, and we shall be looking at this approach later in this chapter.

- Levinson sees adult development as going through a series of phases ('**seasons**'). Some of these are **stable** and some **transitional**.
- Most people can relate their own experience of adulthood to what Levinson has to say.
- The **evidence** on which his theory is based has been criticised for the small sample size and the lack of interviewees in the later phases of the lifespan.
- There may also be **class**, **gender** and **cultural** variations in development.

❺ The theory implies that there is one developmental path which everyone follows. Some theorists prefer to focus on the impact of **individual experience**.

Gould: Evolution of adult consciousness

Finally, we will look briefly at one more stage theory, the **evolution of adult consciousness** put forward by Gould (1978; 1980), which gives a slightly different and interesting slant on adult development. His theory is essentially an extension into adulthood of Freud's ideas, in that Gould viewed development in terms of the progressive resolution of **separation anxiety**, the distress shown by a child when separated from its mother. He saw development in stages related to age, in each of which we need to give up false assumptions which protect us from anxiety:

Figure 2: Gould: false assumptions to be dealt with in adulthood

1 Late teens to early twenties
'I will always belong to my parents and believe in their world.'
2 Twenties
'Doing things my parents' way will probably work out. If I can't cope, my parents will support me.'
3 Late twenties to early thirties
'Life is simple and I am in control of it. There are no contradictory forces at work within me.'
4 Mid thirties to fifty
'There is no evil in me or death in the world.'

As we move through these stages, we gradually accept our role in determining our own lives, and come more and more into contact with our 'inner core'. While the illusions represented by our assumptions protect us from anxiety, they also prevent us from becoming our own person, in touch with ourselves and reality. If we cling to our illusions, we will not be able to find meaning in our lives or in life itself.

Gould's ideas were based on medical students' ratings of recorded therapy sessions, which were then used as the basis of a questionnaire completed by 524 non-patients aged 16–50. One problem here is the methodology. The medical students, since they were students, cannot have had much experience of this kind of evaluation. This raises the issue of whether the final questionnaire was **valid**, i.e. that it was actually testing what it set out to test. In addition, there is no evidence that it was **reliable**, i.e. that it would give consistent results.

While the sample tested was reasonably large, the participants were white, middle-class adults. Given these sources of bias, how far can we extend Gould's ideas to people of a different class and culture? Note too that the oldest respondent was 50; we cannot really draw any conclusions about development after this.

❺ Gould's theory of the **evolution of adult consciousness** suggests that healthy development comes about as we give up the comfort of false assumptions to become more in touch with our 'inner core'. It has however been criticised on methodological grounds.

19.2 FAMILY AND RELATIONSHIPS IN ADULTHOOD

The theories we have looked at up to now are stage theories. Focusing on the impact of different life events can provide a rather different angle, since this looks at development within a particular social context. Some life events are **normative**, i.e. they affect most people in a particular age range (e.g. bereavement), or within a particular cohort (e.g. experiencing a particular war). Others are **non-normative**, i.e. only some people experience them (e.g. divorce). In contrast to stage theories, this approach is more interested in differences between individuals than development in general.

Early studies of the effects of life events were related to clinical studies of stress, and the consequences of the **general adaptation syndrome** (**GAS** – Selye, 1956). This suggests that if life events are stressful enough, they place a burden on our ability to adapt, leading to psychological, emotional or health problems. GAS is discussed in more detail in chapter 4.

Holmes and Rahe (1967) developed the **social readjustment rating scale** (**SRRS**) (see chapter 4), which linked life events, on a sliding scale in terms of their impact, to stress and illness. They claimed that stressful events were associated with a range of serious health problems, e.g. diabetes, heart disease, stroke and leukaemia, as well as less serious everyday problems such as headaches and stomach upsets.

While the SRRS makes a link between life events, stress and physical illness, major experiences of this kind also have psychological consequences. We will look now at the work of psychologists in three areas: marriage (or partnering); divorce; and parenthood.

❺ An alternative to stage theories is to look at the effect of **life events**. A link has been suggested between life events, stress and illness. The **SRRS** provides a way of measuring this effect.
❺ Psychologists have researched the psychological impact of a number of life events, e.g. **marriage**, **divorce** and **parenthood**.

Marriage

In modern Western societies, more than 90% of adults marry at least once. Marriage is an important transition for people, since it means making a lasting commitment to one person, accepting financial responsibilities, and perhaps, with the birth of children, family responsibilities. The nature of this transition, though, is not the same for everyone. For example, in some cultures marriages are arranged by the families of the bride and groom, who may themselves have little say in the choice of partner.

Getting married can be extremely stressful. On the SRRS, it comes seventh on the scale, just above being fired from work. Davies (1956) found that during the engagement period, people were likely to suffer from anxiety and depression, but these disorders improved once the marriage had taken place. Davies suggested that it was the decision to make the commitment, rather than marriage itself, which was stressful. At the same time, marriage may involve quite a lot of changes – adapting to another person, perhaps living in a different place, and so on

– and as Holmes and Rahe point out, it is change which brings about stress.

Over recent years, marriage rates have dropped both in the United Kingdom and in the USA. It has become much more common for people not to enter into a formal marriage, but nonetheless to form a bond with another person with whom they live in a long-term relationship, the informal equivalent of marriage. However, people who have this arrangement and then marry are more likely to divorce later than those who have not lived together informally before marriage. Bee (1994) suggested that this may be because those who choose to live together are different from people who marry without cohabiting first. Since they were prepared to go against the tradition of formalising a marriage with a partner, it may be that they are also more ready to disagree with the idea that you should stay with your marriage partner come what may.

However, it is rather misleading to talk of marriage or partnering as if it were the same kind of experience for everyone; marriages vary in the kind of relationship which exists between partners. Duberman (1973) has identified three main types of marriage:

> ### Figure 3: types of marriage (Duberman, 1973)
>
> a **traditional marriage:** the wife has responsibility for domestic arrangements (shopping, cleaning and so on) while the husband makes all other decisions.
>
> b **companionship marriage:** there is no rigid division of responsibilities along gender lines. Either partner may make decisions and assume responsibility for any area. The emphasis is on equality and companionship.
>
> c **colleague marriage:** as with companionship marriage, equality is important, but each partner takes on particular roles and responsibilities according to their interests and abilities.

Many marriages, of course, will not fit tidily into any one of these categories. In general, though, companionship and colleague marriages are becoming increasingly common. Fifty years ago, it was the social norm for marriage partners to take on the roles and responsibilities prescribed by the traditional marriage. For younger people, there is no longer the social pressure to conform to these norms.

However, the notions of equality implicit in companionship and colleague marriages may be somewhat exaggerated. For instance, Presland and Antill (1987) found that where both partners are working, there is a small increase in the amount of time men spend on housework, and a rather larger decrease in the amount of time women spend on it. Nonetheless, women are in general still considered to be responsible for running the household. Wright *et al.* (1992) found that in Sweden men were more involved in household tasks than American men, and suggested that this was linked to the Swedish government's commitment to gender equality in areas such as childcare provision. It will be interesting to see whether paid leave for both parents, proposed by the Blair government in 2000, is a step on the way to the Swedish model, and whether these kinds of initiatives will have a similar effect in the United Kingdom.

Women are in general still considered to be responsible for running the household.

Lewis and Spanier (1979) have identified several factors associated with the quality of a marriage:

Figure 4: factors influencing marital quality (Lewis and Spanier, 1979)

a Partners are similar in terms of education, religion, age and social class.

b Partners are older and better educated when they marry.

c Parents have had lasting and stable marriages.

d Parents and friends support the marriage.

e The bride is not pregnant when the couple marry.

f The husband has a secure income.

g Both partners are satisfied with the wife's work status.

h The couple share interests.

i There is a high level of interaction and communication.

j Each partner fits in with the role expectations of the other.

▶ Activity 3: what makes a good marriage?

Talk to one or two people you know who have had a long and lasting marriage. Use the list of factors given by Lewis and Spanier in figure 4 as the basis for a discussion on what factors they consider to have been important in making their marriage successful.

There is a lot of research which suggests that being married brings with it a range of benefits. Hu and Goldman (1990) found that married people tend to live longer than unmarried people, and Cramer (1994) found them to be healthier, happier and less likely to suffer from a mental disorder. A further study gives more precise information about the benefits of marriage:

Box E: Cochrane (1996)

Data for the United Kingdom show a relationship between marriage and (a) mortality and (b) mental health. Compared with married people:

a Single people are 22% more likely to die.
   Divorced people are 30% more likely to die.
   Widowed people are over 45% more likely to die.

b Single people are three times as likely to be admitted to a mental hospital in any one year.
   Widowed people are four times as likely to be admitted.
   Divorced people are five and a half times more likely to be admitted.

Divorce and bereavement, as we shall see, are both extremely stressful, but there also seem to be factors associated with marriage which may protect people from ill health, both physical and mental; for example, Kessler and Essex (1982) found higher levels of self-esteem among people who were married.

It also seems to be the case that marriage is more beneficial for men than for women. For example, Unger and Crawford (1992) found that men reported more satisfaction with their marriage than women. Bee (1994) has suggested that this may be because wives give their husbands more emotional support than they receive from them in return, and that men are less likely than women to find this kind of support outside marriage.

Interestingly, Yelsma and Athappilly (1988) compared Indian arranged marriages with love matches in both Indian and American couples. They found that people in arranged marriages reported greater satisfaction. However, it is possible that this may be the result of differences between people who accept an arranged marriage and those who marry for love.

⊖ There are different **types** of marriage, with a move away from the traditional model in which roles are prescribed by gender. More people are now living together in a more informal arrangement.

⊖ Some factors which are associated with stable and lasting marriages have been identified.
⊖ Marriage brings with it benefits for physical and mental **health**, especially for men.

Divorce

Where a marriage does not work out, the partners may choose to end it legally by divorce. This can produce considerable strains on both partners in the marriage. Divorce is the second most stressful item on the SRRS, and other items on the scale may also apply, e.g. 'change in financial status' and 'trouble with in-laws'.

One of the problems with the SRRS is that people may respond very differently to the life events listed. Divorce is a good example; for many people it is devastating, but it could also mark the end of years of unhappiness. However, there is little doubt that whatever the outcome, the process of divorce is a painful one. Bohannon (1970) has suggested that this process has several aspects, shown in figure 5. Each of these 'divorces' has to be completed before the person can re-define themselves as single:

Figure 5: stages in the divorce process (Bohannon, 1970)

emotional divorce	the marriage collapses, with conflict and anger
legal divorce	the marriage comes to a legal end
economic divorce	financial decisions must be made, e.g. about the house and/or other property
co-parental divorce	decisions must be made about the children of the marriage, i.e. custody and access
community divorce	relationships with family and friends need to be adjusted
psychic divorce	adjustment to the autonomy brought about by the end of the relationship

Looking at all these factors, Duck (1982) suggested that people who divorce go through four stages: deciding that they are dissatisfied with the relationship; telling their partner; telling their social network; adjusting to the loss. Duck's ideas about the breakdown of relationships are discussed in more detail in chapter 9.

What are the effects of divorce on the couples involved? Cochrane (1988) found that divorcees are at greater risk of mental illness, car accidents, physical illness, and death by either suicide or illness. Carter and Glick (1970) found that divorce was associated for those who did not remarry with higher death rates for pneumonia, TB, cirrhosis of the liver and suicide (in females).

Activity 4: the effects of divorce

Some people find divorce a much more traumatic experience than others. Can you suggest any factors which are likely to be associated with these differences?

Look back to the aspects of divorce outlined in figure 5 to help you get started. You could also ask people you know well, and who have been through a divorce, what kinds of factors made the experience particularly difficult for them, or helped to make it easier.

Several factors have been shown to be important: which partner suggested the divorce, arguments about the children, financial difficulties and so on. It has also been found (Chiriboga, 1982) that older people (i.e. 50+) find divorce more traumatic than younger people.

Hetherington *et al.* (1978) found that social support was an important factor in helping people cope with divorce. Without this help, they found that the effects of divorce in relation to children were to reduce warmth and control in parenting, with the consequent effects on the parent of loss of self-esteem, self-reliance and self-control.

Divorce can also be profoundly disruptive to children:

Box F: Hetherington (1979/1982)

Procedure: The effect of divorce on 48 4-year-old children, living with their mothers, was assessed over 2 years. The children were also followed up after 6 years.

Results: Initially these children showed greater anxiety, guilt, dependence, apathy, and attention-seeking and aggressive behaviour than a control group from intact families. After two years, these differences had disappeared for girls, but were still present (though to a lesser extent) in boys. At the 6 year follow-up, the pattern remained similar if the mother had not remarried. Remarriage led to an increase in problems for both boys and girls, which gradually decreased. Two years after remarriage, boys were better adjusted than girls.

Conclusion: Divorce is associated with social and behavioural problems in children. It may affect girls and boys differently.

Other research into the effects of divorce on children has shown similar findings. Hetherington *et al.* (1978) found that symptoms differ according to age, with 3–5-year-olds tending to regress to earlier behaviour, and older children showing more sadness and anger. There is some evidence that an older child able to make sense of the divorce will adjust more easily than a younger child.

There are other factors which are linked to individual differences in how well children cope with divorce. Continued supportive contact with the father is beneficial, and time spent alone with each parent helps. Continued conflict between the divorced parents prolongs distress in children. Anything that decreases the mother's stress, such as staying in the same job, a secure income and supportive friends, is also beneficial to the children.

Divorce is clearly a great life stressor. Interventions that help couples to see the divorce as a temporary failure and which offer practical

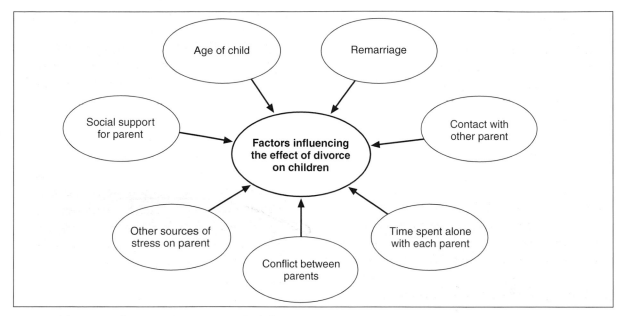

support have been found to be the most helpful, as they preserve a person's identity and self-esteem. Many people believe divorce should be treated as a bereavement, the effects of which we shall look at in the final section.

- ❺ **Divorce** is a major life event. The process itself has several aspects: **emotional**, **legal**, **economic**, **co-parental**, **community** and **psychic**. People must come to terms with all of these before redefining themselves as single.
- ❺ Some association with **ill health** has been found. A range of factors, e.g. **social support**, **age** and **finance**, affect how well divorce is coped with.
- ❺ Divorce has a profound effect on **children**. Again, several factors, e.g. **gender** and parents' **remarriage**, influence the outcome for children.

Parenthood

Becoming a parent is something many of us expect in life, but for which there is often very little preparation. It is a life event which requires us to make major adjustments. Parenthood is not specified on the SRRS, but 'pregnancy' and 'gain of a new family member' are two items which apply – along with 'change in sleeping habits'! Psychologists have been interested in exploring how new parents feel about this change in their lives.

It might be interesting to start by looking at the reasons why people become parents:

▶ Activity 5: why have a baby?

If you are a parent, think about the reasons why you decided to have a child. If not, think about why you might want to have a child, and/or put this question to people you know who are parents. How has having a child affected you/them as a person?
How has it affected your/their relationship with your/their partner?
Keep your notes to compare with the discussion in the rest of this section.

Turner and Helms (1983) have suggested several reasons why people decide to have a child. It can be a form of creativity. It can be a way of giving and receiving love and affection. One of the reasons may be to do with what society expects, i.e. conforming to social norms. It may also be a way of giving yourself a sense of purpose, and adding meaning to your life, or you may have thought it would make you happy. There are other reasons too – perhaps it was an accident, or was seen as a way of holding together a disintegrating relationship.

These different reasons may in part account for the rather conflicting data produced by research into parents' responses to the birth of a child. Some research (e.g. Bee and Mitchell, 1984) has found that the change in responsibilities, loss of income, lack of sleep and less time disrupt the marital relationship, while other research has not been so clear-cut:

Box G: Belsky (1981)

Procedure: All the existing literature on the effects of becoming a parent was reviewed to identify factors related to the impact of a new baby.

Results: The arrival of a baby was less of a crisis when:
–the parents were older
–the baby was conceived after marriage
–there was a gap between marriage and conception and
–the baby was 'easy' rather than 'difficult'
The picture was mixed if the baby had special problems. This brought parents together as often as it drove them apart.

Conclusion: Becoming a parent can be life-enhancing under good conditions, but a time of crisis under less favourable ones.

Russell (1974) found that there are class differences in terms of satisfaction with parenthood, with middle-class parents generally less satisfied than working-class parents. This may be related to middle-class mothers having unrealistic expectations of parenthood, or being more likely to be affected by having to juggle career and childcare, or perhaps resenting changes in their relationship with their partner. Bee and Mitchell (1984) found that the happiest parents were young couples who were not under any great financial pressure.

How does a new baby affect roles and relationships, and what factors seem to be important?

Box H: Cowan and Cowan (1988)

Procedure: A sample of 72 expectant parents was interviewed and given detailed questionnaires. The expectant parents were interviewed three times: during the mother's pregnancy, and when the baby was 6 and 18 months old.

Results: Parenthood produced a greater identity shift for the women, who saw themselves more as parents than the men did. Their roles became more organised along the traditional lines of men as breadwinners and women as homemakers. The women were less satisfied with this new role arrangement than the men.

There was an increase in marital disagreement amongst the new parents, though they did become better at solving their problems. Greater stress was experienced when the parents had disagreed about child-rearing before the birth. However if the parenting went well, the marital relationship benefited, and vice versa. The new parents often felt sandwiched between the needs of their own parents and the baby. There were no reported increases in stress levels generally.

Conclusion: Roles are likely to change after the birth of a baby. Cowan and Cowan said 'Babies do not appear to create severe marital distress, where it was not present before, nor do they tend to bring already distressed couples closer together.'

Duck (1994) has said that the transition to parenthood does not actually end – it is a continuous negotiation involving intimacy and power. The new division of labour relates to these issues. In a society where money is equated with power, it is clear why women could be less satisfied than men with the new arrangement.

These studies indicate that becoming a parent does not in itself create extra stress. Problems arise when the development of the parents has already been disrupted, or the relationship is already suffering. Lugo and Hershey (1979) have suggested that with careful preparation for parenthood, it can be a period of personal growth for the parents.

- Parenthood requires major adjustments, particularly in **roles** and **relationships**.
- Conflicting research findings about the response to parenthood may be related to the different reasons people have for becoming parents.
- Having a child does not in itself disrupt a parental relationship, but it also cannot repair a failing relationship.
- Parenthood can be seen as an opportunity for **personal growth**.

19.3 LATE ADULTHOOD

Most old people will tell you that they do not feel old inside – the heart has no wrinkles. However, much 'old age' psychology is about decline, which may well make people think that is all there is to being old. This is far from the truth, as the few people who have researched this area without negative attitudes have found. It is possible that beliefs about the nature of old age are the result of **negative stereotyping**:

Box 1: Goldman and Goldman (1981)

Procedure: Over 800 children aged 5–15 were interviewed about their perceptions of elderly people. The survey included children from England, Australia, Sweden and the USA.

Results: There was a tendency to talk about elderly people in negative rather than positive terms. This tendency increased with the age of the interviewee. Comments related to physical aspects of ageing, e.g. wrinkles and infirmity, and psychological aspects, such as being slow to respond or forgetful.

Conclusion: Negative stereotypes about old people are not uncommon in Western culture, and can already be formed in childhood.

Also remember that it is difficult to define 'old'; in earlier times when life expectancy was about 40 years on average, 30 would have been old. The average life expectancy is now creeping into the 80s in the Western world. People in their 70s talk about their 'old' neighbours, i.e. older than them. The period of retirement from work at 65 is the usual marker, but of course this is social, not biological. So let us try not to be ageist in our investigation into old age, and remember that much developmental work is culture-, time- and gender-specific.

Erikson's theory

Of all the lifespan theorists, only Erikson has really focused on this period. You may find it useful at this point to look back to chapter 18, figure 1 to remind yourself of what he had to say about this final stage in the lifespan, **integrity vs despair**. He believed that if people resolve all the other stages in their life, their old age can be a time of richness and acceptance, where 'wholeness can transcend the petty' (Erikson, 1950). In this way we attain **wisdom**.

On the other hand, if life's stages are not resolved, an old person can sink into despair, destroyed by unrealised goals, unfulfilled potential, and fear of death. Which pole a person comes to at the end of their life depends on what Erikson called 'triple book-keeping', the interplay between the biological, social and individual. There is some support for his ideas:

Box J: Langer and Rodin (1976)

Procedure: People on two floors of a nursing home for older adults in Connecticut participated in this study. On one floor the older people were encouraged to take control where possible; for example, choosing their own films and visits. Residents on the other floor were a control group, well cared for but with little control over their environment. Activity levels were measured for both groups.
Results: Activity levels on the floor that was given choice and responsibility were

significantly higher than controls. Unexpectedly, follow-up studies two years later found that the death rate on the choice/responsibility floor was significantly lower than controls.
Conclusion: Erikson's idea that old age can be an active and fulfilling time is supported. The retirement of the active residents did not mean a loss of purpose, control or identity, and they flourished. Where these are taken away by society from an older person, they decline and may die sooner.

There are two other major theoretical perspectives on development at this stage in the lifespan, which we will turn to now.

Social disengagement theory

In complete contrast to Erikson's ideas, Cumming (1975) has proposed **social disengagement theory**, which refers to the mutual withdrawal of society from the individual, and the individual from society. Withdrawal of society from the individual takes the form of retirement, children leaving home and moving away, the death of a partner and close friends, and so on. The individual may withdraw from society by taking less part in social activities and in general preferring to spend more time on their own:

Box K: Cumming and Henry (1961)

Procedure: A sample of 275 50–90-year-olds were studied over a period of 5 years.
Results: During this stage, society withdraws from the individual, as children leave home and become independent, and they retire from the world of work, and experience the death of their partner and friends. At the same time they are likely to take part in fewer social activities, and so start to withdraw from society.
Conclusion: This is a period of mutual disengagement.

Cumming and Henry suggested further that disengagement can be seen as a natural and positive process. The older person becomes more self-sufficient and less concerned with other people. It can be seen as a preparation for death.

There are three aspects of disengagement:

Figure 6: aspects of disengagement (Cumming, 1975)

shrinkage of life space: as we get older, we interact with progressively fewer people and occupy fewer roles.

increased individuality: older people are less governed by rules and the expectations of others.

acceptance of these changes: the healthy elderly person turns more inward. Withdrawal is a way of preparing for death.

While most people accept the first two descriptive aspects Cumming identified, the third functional aspect is more contentious. One question which arises is the extent to which disengagement is a natural and healthy process, or one that is imposed on elderly people by others. Bromley (1988) also pointed out that this view of ageing encourages a very negative view of this period of people's lives, which is seen to have no value.

That social disengagement is the general experience of everyone, and a healthy response to this stage in their lives, has also been questioned:

▷ Activity 6: thinking about disengagement

Think about elderly people who are well known to you, and talk to them about this stage in their lives. Do their later lives seem to have followed the pattern described by social disengagement theory? Are those who seem most content as disengaged as the theory suggests?

You may have found that many old people are still actively engaged socially. Although an elderly person may have lost their partner and their long-term friends, often other relationships are formed with new friends, neighbours and particularly grandchildren.

Havighurst *et al.* (1968) followed up just over half of the original Cumming and Henry sample (box K). They found that those who were active and engaged were happier than those who were not. This can also be linked with the findings of Langer and Rodin (box J), and seems to contradict the idea that disengagement is natural and healthy.

However, you may also have found that the older people you talked to are happier now with their own company than when they were younger. As with many other aspects of development, there are individual differences; some older people need roles and relationships to be content, others find satisfaction in disengagement. It is worth considering also that many people prefer to lead a life that is relatively disengaged *before* they reach this stage of the lifespan: disengagement need not necessarily be a feature only of old age.

A final point here is the possibility of a **cohort effect**: perhaps findings in this area relate to the values, attitudes and social expectations which were current at the time the studies were carried out. The age-related changes which were found may have been culturally influenced, in other words, rather than due to chronological age itself.

Activity theory

In contrast to social disengagement theory, **activity** (or **re-engagement**) **theory**, proposed by Havighurst (1964), sees older people as much the same as middle-aged people, remaining productive and active. If there is disengagement, this is because society disengages from older people. Rather than disengagement being a mutual process between society and elderly people, many elderly people are unhappy about the ways in which they are marginalised socially.

Again, you may be able to relate this idea to your findings from activity 6. However, this idea is open to similar criticisms to disengagement theory in that it does not take into account individual differences. Ageing successfully is likely to result from people finding a balance between activity and disengagement which suits them personally.

▶ Activity 7: variables in successful ageing

> Talk again to the people you interviewed in activity 6. What are the factors in their lives which lead to their being content, or make them less happy than they might be?

There are several variables which they are likely to have mentioned: health, income, family, good relationships with neighbours, perhaps living in their particular neighbourhood. For example, a family which provides good social support may be seen as a positive factor in an old person's life, while an old person whose family have moved away and are rarely in touch may see this as a negative factor. It is worth bearing in mind, then, that different responses to ageing will not only depend on individual psychological differences, but also on external factors.

Finally, it must be remembered that descriptions of this stage of the lifespan, as well as the other stages, are time-, gender- and culture-specific. This means that in another time or culture the pattern might be quite different. It is therefore important to understand that stage theories do not represent a biological map, but a social one, which could be changed.

Social disengagement theory ...

... or activity theory?

- ❺ In Erikson's theory, the focus in the final stage of the lifespan is wisdom vs. despair.
- ❺ **Social disengagement theory** sees old age as a time when there is a natural and mutual disengagement between old people and society.
- ❺ **Activity theory** considers that for healthy adjustment at this stage, old people need to remain active members of society.
- ❺ Both theories can be criticised for failing to take into account **individual differences**, and the effect of external factors. Their ideas may also be tied to a particular time and culture.

Cognitive changes

Up to now, we have focused largely on personal and social changes over the lifespan. We need also to look briefly at cognitive changes which come about as the result of growing older, and in particular changes in **intelligence test performance** and **memory**.

Early research in this area suggested that intellectual capacity declines as people get older. This research used a **cross-sectional** method, i.e. comparing the abilities of one group of older people with a different group of younger people. It is therefore possible that the differences which were found were the result of a cohort effect: these differences might relate to the different experiences of the two groups. Research using a **longitudinal** method, where the same people are tested at intervals across a period of time, has challenged these earlier findings. For example, Holahan and Sears (1995) found that many people showed little decline in their intellectual ability as they grew older. This seems to be particularly true of those who keep themselves mentally active. There are therefore substantial individual differences in age-related cognitive decline.

Maylor (1994) carried out a study of 'Masterminds', from the TV programme, and found that there was no age effect on performance in the 'specialised subject' round. On the general knowledge component, older 'masterminds' did better than younger ones. Similarly, the Older Students' Research Group (1993) found that Open University students in the 60–64 age range were the most successful academically of any age group. However, this may be because older people, who are not in full-time employment or bringing up young families, have more time available to spend on studying.

Intelligence test performance

Cattell (1963) made a distinction between **crystallised** and **fluid intelligence**. Crystallised intelligence refers to those aspects of mental functioning related to the breadth of our knowledge and experience, and the skills we have acquired. It is usually assessed by tests of general information. Fluid intelligence refers to problem-solving ability, and is tested by asking people to solve unusual problems.

Horn (1982) found that crystallised intelligence increases with age, and continues to do so until near the end of a person's life. For example, performance on vocabulary subtests of intelligence tests, which involve long-term knowledge, shows relatively little decline in old age. This supports the 'Masterminds' research mentioned above.

In contrast, Schaie and Hertzog (1983) found that fluid intelligence declines over the lifespan, beginning to do so in a person's late twenties. For instance, there is considerable age-related decline in performance on subtests which involve digit-symbol substitution, where new and arbitrary associations must be learned.

Crystallised intelligence may increase as we continue to add to and make use of our store of information and acquired skills. The decline in fluid intelligence is likely to be related to the deterioration of neurological functioning, but we may also not need to use this aspect of intelligence as much as we grow older, leading to its decline.

❺ While **fluid intelligence** declines with age, **crystallised intelligence** may increase.
❺ An increase in crystallised intelligence is associated with continued **mental activity**.

Memory

There is some evidence for a decline in memory with age. This is clearly the case if a person develops **dementia**, of which **Alzheimer's disease** is the most common form. However, it is far from being necessarily the case that memory declines with age. Diamond (1978) reported that over 90% of people over the age of 65 show very little memory deterioration. Again, this is especially true of those who keep mentally active.

Older people report that the aspects of memory which are most affected by ageing are the ability to recall proper names and more general word-finding, and to remember new information.

Difficulties in recalling names has been demonstrated in research into the **tip of the tongue (TOT)** state. You have probably come across a situation where you felt that a word that you knew well was 'on the tip of your tongue' – you knew the word was in your memory, and may even have been able to identify some of its features, e.g. the number of syllables, or initial letter, but could temporarily not retrieve it from memory:

Box L: Burke *et al.* (1988)

Procedure: Young, mid-age and older adults were asked to keep a structured diary of spontaneous TOT states over a period of 4 weeks.

Results: Proper names accounted for two-thirds of TOT states. The mean number of TOT states increased with age. Older people took longer than the other groups to resolve this state and identify the word.

Conclusion: The ability to recall proper names declines with age.

Similar results were found in a laboratory study:

Box M: Burke *et al.* (1991)

Procedure: A set of 100 questions which were found to be likely to induce a TOT state was compiled. These questions were presented one at a time to 22 young and 22 older adults, who were asked to say whether they knew the answer, did not know the answer, or had the answer on the tip of their tongue.

Results: The mean number of TOT states was greater for older than younger participants (11.9 compared with 9.9).

Conclusion: Older people have problems with word-finding.

Elderly people also have trouble remembering new information, but the ability to recall existing information is unimpaired:

Box N: Charness (1981)

Procedure: Participants took part in chess games. The quality of moves chosen for particular chess positions was assessed. Participants were also asked to evaluate end-game positions. At the end of the session, recall of the specific board positions was tested.

Results: The quality of moves and evaluation of end-game positions were related to skill but not age. Older participants were less good than younger ones at recall of board positions.

Conclusion: The moves made and the evaluation of end-game positions drew on existing knowledge of chess, acquired over many years, and so was unaffected by age. The positions of pieces on the board constituted new information, so caused problems for older participants.

Deficits in the ability to remember proper names and word-finding in general, together with a decline in the ability to remember new information, have a neurological basis. However, there are several non-cognitive mechanisms which are thought to contribute to this decline in memory.

Firstly, there may be **cohort effects**. Often, while researchers try to control for education levels between younger and older participants, the young adults tested are students, and so may be more used to taking tests and having their performance evaluated. However, there are still age differences in remembering new information when neither older nor younger participants are students (West and Crook, 1990) and when both age groups are students (Parks *et al.* 1986).

It has also been suggested that older participants lack the **motivation** to carry out what may be seen as irrelevant laboratory tasks, such as remembering lists of random numbers. However, the decline in memory for new information is still apparent in older people when more everyday tasks are used, e.g. instructions on prescription medicine bottles (Morrell *et al.*, 1990).

Expectation may also play a role. Berry *et al.* (1989) found that compared with younger adults, older adults expected to perform less well on memory tasks, and this in itself could reduce performance.

Finally, older people are likely to have less good **health** than younger people. Lachmann and Leff (1989) found that decline in performance on vocabulary tests over a 5-year period could be predicted by the number of medical problems, e.g. high blood pressure, diabetes and arthritis, reported at the time of the first test.

- In the absence of dementia, there is little memory loss with age. Problems occur with accessing **names** and **word-finding**. The ability to recall new information also declines.
- Memory loss is related to **neurological change**. **Non-cognitive factors** may also be important.

19.4 SOCIAL CHANGES IN LATE ADULTHOOD

Retirement

Since retirement is usually anticipated, some people cope with it without problems. For many, however, the world of work provides them with a routine, a sense of purpose and social contacts, so retirement can be experienced as loss; they may experience a decline in physical and psychological well-being. On the SRRS, retirement is ranked 10, reasonably near the top of the list.

For most people, adjustments have to be made. They are likely to spend more time with their partner in retirement, and there is usually a loss of income and status, leading to the development of a new role and therefore changes to the self-image. Many people also move house when they retire.

It is worth noting that the pattern of retirement has become more flexible. Traditionally, a man worked till 65 and then retired. Many people now choose when they wish to retire, and retirement may be a gradual process, with a person working part-time for a period before retirement, or continuing in part-time work after retirement.

Atchley (1982) sees retirement as a **process** and the development of a new **social role**, during which the person passes through several phases. These phases do not necessarily occur in the same order, and they are not all experienced by everyone:

Figure 7: phases in retirement (Atchley, 1982)

pre-retirement: in the remote subphase, retirement lies well in the future. In the near subphase, as retirement draws nearer, preparation and planning for retirement take place. The person may become anxious about the changes it will bring, both in their lifestyle and financially.
honeymoon: immediately after retirement, freedom from the demands of work is associated with optimism and pleasure. Activities planned before retirement are carried out.

disenchantment: initial optimism lessens, when retirement activities are found not to be satisfactory, and the person may become depressed. Activities which have been planned for retirement, e.g. travel, may no longer seem so attractive.
reorientation: a more realistic view of possibilities is developed, and new avenues are explored.
stability: people become fully adjusted to retirement and develop routines which are within their capacity.
termination: illness and/or disability limits what is possible. The person takes on a 'sick' or 'disabled' role, as opposed to 'retirement'.

Atchley's model is useful in helping us to understand the process of retirement. However, with the changes in patterns of retirement which have come about since Atchley put forward his ideas, the model may now seem rather rigid.

Most people are satisfied with their retirement. People who choose to retire usually have fewer problems than those who retire because they have reached the compulsory retirement age. Those who have the most problems are those whose health is poor, though this may often improve after retirement, e.g. if they have been involved in manual work.

Argyle (1989) linked satisfaction in retirement to several factors:

Figure 8: factors leading to satisfaction in retirement (Argyle, 1989)

a having good financial resources
b having a purpose in life
c choosing when to retire
d good health
e having a number of strong interests
f being well-educated
g being in a higher social class
h being female

Reichard *et al.* (1962) have also suggested that some personality characteristics are associated with a good adjustment to retirement, with mature and relatively passive people coping better than those who are angry and hostile.

For many people, retirement is seen very positively, and offers opportunities for fulfilment:

Box O: Young and Schuller (1991)

Procedure: People who had left full-time employment within the previous two years were interviewed. The researchers were interested in what factors were associated with satisfaction in retirement.
Results: One person in three had a very positive approach to their life in retirement. Many were engaged in voluntary work in a church or other organisation. They also tended to have a variety of interests.
Conclusion: For many people, retirement is a satisfying and productive time.

- There are **individual differences** in how well people adjust to retirement. An important factor is whether a person retires voluntarily.
- A range of factors associated with satisfaction in retirement has been identified. These include **financial resources**, **education**, **gender** and having a wide range of **interests**.

Bereavement and dying

Bereavement relates to the death of a loved one. On the SRRS 'death of a spouse' is rated as the most stressful event, while 'death of a close family member' comes quite high up the list, and 'death of a close friend' rather lower down.

Mourning and grief are a healthy response to any loss, which Freud (1917) called **grief work**. He believed that this process enables a person to internalise the lost 'object', in the same way that a child internalises their parents in order to become independent from them. According to Freud, the ability to grieve fully in later life is associated with successful identification in childhood, a good example of the importance of early development for coping with later life events.

Several theorists have discussed the processes involved in death and dying. Fulton (1970) described four stages that we go through in anticipation of a bereavement, when we know that the death of a loved one is not far away. The first of these is **depression**, when we show extreme unhappiness and grieve in anticipation. This is followed by **heightened concern** for the dying person, and a need to deal with any unfinished business which needs to be discussed with them. It can be expressed also in caring well for them. The next stage is characterised by **rehearsals for the death**, where we develop in advance ways of coping with the coming bereavement. A final stage involves **adjustment to the consequences**, when we come to terms with the changes bereavement brings, and perhaps develop additional coping strategies.

But what about the response to the bereavement itself?

Box P: Parkes and Weiss (1983)

Procedure: Clinical studies of bereaved people were carried out over several years.
Results: There are typically six stages which people need to work through:
1 Denial or avoidance.
2 Alarm, anxiety, restlessness, fear.
3 An urge to search for the lost person.
4 Anger and guilt focused on the self, the loved one, or others who press the bereaved person to accept their loss prematurely.
5 Feelings of great loss or mutilation.
6 Identification with the loved one and realisation of the loss.
Conclusion: Bereavement is a process with definite stages which people need to work through.

The researchers also noted that in the six months following bereavement, people were much more likely to suffer ill health, either physical or mental, and even death. Rees and Lutkins (1967) found that widows and widowers were ten times as likely to die

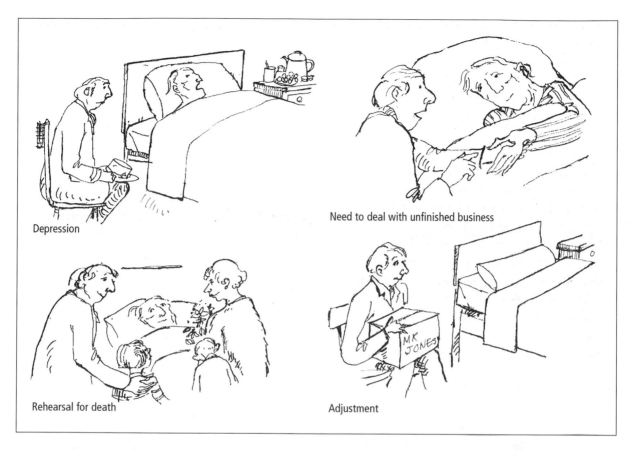

Depression

Need to deal with unfinished business

Rehearsal for death

Adjustment

themselves in the year following bereavement. Thus the time following bereavement is a critical period when people need special care.

As with other life events, there are individual differences in responses to bereavement. Barrett (1978) found gender differences: men were likely to show a more extreme response, to eat less well and to consider remarriage as a way of coping with being left on their own. They were also less likely to talk about their loss. This was a study of people aged 62+, though, so the findings may well be a cohort effect and not apply to those who are bereaved at an earlier age. Balkwell (1981) found that people were less able to cope with a sudden and unexpected bereavement, particularly with the death of a young person.

Just as with divorce, a supportive social network is helpful to people who have been bereaved. It is helpful to listen, to allow the bereaved person to express themselves, and to reassure them that their feelings are quite normal.

One of the problems of Western society is that death has become a taboo subject; it is seen as morbid to talk about it. Avoiding the subject can make bereavement more difficult to cope with. Parkes and Weiss (1983) found that the grieving process was extended where people were not encouraged to talk about their loss. At the same time, when the person is ready to move on, it is unhelpful to discourage the ending of grief by encouraging feelings of overdependence or guilt about the original relationship.

The last of Erikson's stages, integrity vs. despair, is also relevant here. The work of this stage is to come to terms with our own mortality and learn to accept death. It is during this period of our lives that we are most likely to experience the deaths of our peers, and our sense of bereavement relates not only to their loss but also anticipates our own death. Kuebler-Ross (1969) has described the stages we go through in facing our own death, which she refers to as 'the final stage of growth':

Figure 9: stages of dying (Kuebler-Ross, 1969)

denial	the person cannot accept that they are going to die. They may want another doctor's opinion, or try to find comfort in religion.
anger	this is the 'why me?' stage. The person may also be very concerned about unfinished business.
bargaining	the person attempts to bargain with God or fate; for example, 'I promise I will start going to church; just don't let me die'.
depression	it is no longer possible to avoid the fact of imminent death. There may be rapid physical deterioration at this time, and guilt feelings about letting others down.
acceptance	the person comes to terms with dying.

Kuebler-Ross points out that this is only a guide; not everyone will go through these stages, and the order can also vary. Understanding these stages can help us to understand the dying person, and also to suggest ways in which relatives can be offered support. Kuebler-Ross warns against those involved with the dying person attacking the defences put up in the earlier stages, or trying to move the person to the final stage before they are ready.

There are cultural differences in how death and bereavement are handled. In part, this is related to a culture's view of the existence or nature of an after-life. For example, people who believe in reincarnation, who see time as circular or spiral and expect the souls of the dead eventually to return to earth, are likely to have very different attitudes to mourning than those who see death as final and permanent.

Hertz (1960) proposed that for most human cultures, there are in effect two types of death, biological and social. While biological death is the end of the human organism, social death is the end of the person's social identity; there is a transitional time of days, months or even years between the two. Social death takes place in ceremonies which vary from culture to culture, but all of which have the purpose of saying farewell to one of society's members, and reasserting the continuity of society without that person.

For example, in an Irish **wake**, relatives watch the corpse for several days and nights while friends come in to say their farewells. A wake often involves feasting and drinking. Among orthodox Jews, the ceremony of **shib'ah** lasts seven days from the funeral. During this period, the bereaved stay at home and are consoled by visitors. Mourning is worn for 30 days, and recreation and amusement are forbidden for a year. The transitional period comes to an end at the end of the year, when the tombstone is dedicated. According to Helman (1994), in the Malay archipelago, the corpse is given a first temporary burial, before being reburied months or even years later at a final ceremony. Between these two burials, the deceased person is treated as though he were still alive, such as by being offered food. At the final burial, he is reborn into the society of dead ancestors, and the mourners re-enter normal society.

What these very different rituals have in common is that they all provide a standard model of behaviour which helps to relieve the sense of uncertainty and loss which a bereavement brings. Everyone knows what to do and how to act, and this helps to restore a sense of order and continuity to their lives. They also allow the bereaved person to adjust slowly to the fact of death. Skultans (1980) has suggested that the increased risk of death among those who have been recently bereaved may in part be due to the lack of these protective rituals in many sections of our culture.

As Eisenbruch (1984) has pointed out, although there are similarities in the way people grieve, it cannot be assumed that the grieving process in different cultures occurs at the same rate or even in the same sequence.

⊖ **Bereavement** is a major life event. We need to go through the grieving process in response to it.

⊖ There are **individual differences** in people's response to bereavement.

⊖ Research in this area has helped to identify ways of helping others cope with bereavement, and ways of responding which may be unhelpful.

⊖ Fulton has suggested stages we go through in preparation for an expected death. Parkes and Weiss found stages in bereavement itself. Kuebler-Ross identified stages people go through when faced with their own death. These ideas provide a framework within which responses can vary.

⊖ **Rituals** which are carried out when someone dies help to structure the experience of bereavement and make adjustment easier.

Notes on activities

2 The nature of the topic being studied limits the ways in which it can be investigated. People who are interviewed, especially on such personal matters, may be selective in what they are prepared to disclose to the person who is interviewing them. They may therefore not necessarily be giving a true picture of their experience. At the same time, what they have to say must be interpreted by the person interviewing them.

There is also the time scale to consider. If you are comparing mid-life experience and later outcomes, ideally you would need to interview people at various times during this period; a study covering 30 years or more is not really a practical proposition. If people are interviewed late in the lifespan about earlier experience, what they have to say is retrospective, and what they remember about earlier stages in their lives may have become distorted over time.

It is possible also that social changes between the time Levinson *et al.* carried out their research and the Rutter study may to some extent be responsible for the differences in their findings. Their participants may also have been drawn from rather different populations, i.e. have varied demographically.

Levinson and Rutter may also have defined 'more satisfactory future development' in rather different ways.

Determinants of animal behaviour

In this chapter we will be looking at:

20.1 Darwin's theory of evolution
  Problems with the theory of natural
    selection

20.2 Evolutionary explanations of
    co-operation and altruism in non-
    human animals

20.3 Learning theory
  Classical conditioning
  Operant conditioning
  Avoidance learning
  Evaluation of classical and operant
    conditioning theory
  Classical and operant conditioning
    theory re-interpreted
  Biological constraints on learning
  Other forms of animal learning

20.4 Social learning in non-human animals
  Foraging
  Self-recognition
  Theory of mind

20.1 DARWIN'S THEORY OF EVOLUTION

Life first appeared on earth about 4000 million years ago. Since that time, a great number of species have flourished and then their numbers have declined. Many species, like the mammoth, have become extinct, and others have gradually changed their physical forms. Darwin, in his book *On the Origin of Species* (1859), developed his theory of evolution to explain the changes in animals' numbers and physical forms.

His starting point was that the physical characteristics of an organism are important for its survival, and for its success in reproducing itself.

▷ Activity 1: the importance of physical characteristics

Think of one physical characteristic which might be important to (a) a hawk, (b) a peacock and (c) a rat, in terms of individual survival or reproductive success.

When you have finished, see the notes on page 562.

Not all offspring of members of a particular species will survive to maturity, and so be able to reproduce. For example, some will be eaten by predators, or starve if insufficient food is available. Indeed, if all offspring did survive, this would be counterproductive, since there would be too many individuals competing for limited resources, which would threaten the chances of survival of the species as a whole.

It follows that any animal which has inherited a characteristic giving it an advantage over others of the species is more likely to survive to sexual maturity. In biology, the term **fitness** refers to the ability of an organism to survive and produce offspring, which will themselves be able to survive (this is referred to as **viability**) and produce offspring (this is referred to as **fecundity**).

Fitness relates to how well an organism is adapted to its environment. Each species occupies an **ecological niche**. This term refers to a place in the total ecological environment which offers a species opportunities for survival. Only one species can occupy a niche. This is known as the **competitive exclusion principle**. A rabbit and a hedgehog occupy different ecological niches, even though they may live side by side, since the aspects of the environment which are important to their survival are different; for example, they eat different food.

Darwin suggested that species develop and change over a very long period of time in terms of how adapted they are to their environment. He developed his ideas during a five-year voyage as a naturalist on HMS Beagle. In the Galapagos islands, he observed that there were fourteen different kinds of finch. They differed in the shapes of their beaks and their feeding habits. Three examples are shown in figure 1:

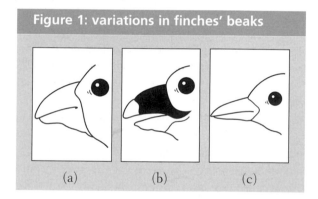

Figure 1: variations in finches' beaks

(a)   (b)   (c)

Finch (a) is a ground finch which has a short, strong beak to break open the seeds on which it feeds. The cactus finch (b) has a long, nearly straight beak for reaching into cactus flowers to get at the nectar. The warbler finch (c) has a thin, sharp beak for catching insects. Darwin believed that all these finches had ancestors in common, and that these variations in beak shape had come about in response to features of the environment. In this case, beak shape had changed over very many generations as an adaptation to the different ecological niches, in terms of food supply, offered by the different islands.

But how do these differences come about? Darwin argued that over many generations, species gradually develop in such a way that they become better adapted to their environment. This development, he believed, comes about as a result of random changes within the genotype of

individuals. From time to time a **mutation** occurs, i.e. a chance genetic variation which can be inherited by future generations. Sometimes this variation can be beneficial, in that it makes the individual more likely to survive in difficult conditions or more likely to find a mate, and thus be able to reproduce. In this case, the mutant gene will be passed on to the next generation and so survive.

It is now known that mutation is actually very rare. Variations are more likely to come about as the result of **genetic recombination**. When fertilisation occurs, the chromosomes of the new individual are formed by a combination of chromosomes from both parents. This results in new combinations which may be beneficial (or not) in a particular environment, in the same way as mutations.

Since there is inevitable competition for resources (e.g. food and mates) between members of a species, those individuals without these beneficial combinations of genes would be less likely to survive and reproduce, and would gradually die out. Many generations later, more of those members carrying the gene would be likely to survive. This is what Darwin referred to as the **survival of the fittest**; 'fit' in this context means well adapted to its environment and thus likely to pass its genes on to the next generation. **Natural selection** refers to the process by which the individual members of a species who are fittest, in this sense, are selected to pass on their genes.

A good example of natural selection is the peppered moth, before and after the Industrial Revolution. These moths were originally light in colour, but around 1850, a darker form appeared. As a result of industrial activity, surfaces in the moth's environment (e.g. tree trunks) had become blackened by soot, which meant that they provided better camouflage against predators for the darker moths than the lighter ones. By 1900, about 50 generations later, the numbers of the darker moths in industrial areas were far greater than the lighter ones, which had almost disappeared. As industrial areas were cleaned up, the darker moths became rarer, and the lighter-coloured ones more common again.

This also illustrates another point to bear in mind: individuals are only 'fit' while the environment remains unchanged. Changes in the environment are likely to mean that different variations, better adapted to the new conditions, are likely to develop.

One further point needs to be emphasised. At one time it was suggested that characteristics acquired during the lifetime of an individual could be passed on to the next generation. Lamarck (1809) believed in the **inheritance of acquired characteristics**, and gave the example of the giraffe. He proposed that because these animals have to make efforts to reach leaves on the tops of trees, their fore-legs and necks became longer. These characteristics, developed during a giraffe's lifetime, were then transmitted to their offspring. Although Darwin thought this might be possible, it is not now accepted, since the acquired change would need to lead to a change in the coding of genes, and there is no way in which this can be done.

Genes contain instructions for the development of body structure (morphology), and body structures, particularly those of the nervous system, help to determine behaviour. Behaviours can be 'hard-wired' into the system, for example as **fixed action patterns (FAPs)**. These are stereotypical behaviours which reliably occur in the presence of a specific stimulus or set of stimuli. For example, if an egg rolls out of the nest of a greylag goose, she will stand up, stretch out her neck, hook her beak over the egg and try to roll it back. The response is fixed, since even if her attempts are unsuccessful, she never tries any other method of retrieving the egg, such as by using her wings or feet. Alternatively, behaviour can be more flexible, created by the interaction of body structure and the environment, and is therefore the result of learning. It is therefore possible to talk about 'genetically determined behaviour' and a 'genetic tendency to certain types of behaviour'.

Activity 2: explaining giraffes' long necks

How could Darwin's evolutionary theory explain the development of a long neck in giraffes?
When you have finished, see the notes on page 562.

The idea that a species can be gradually changed was not in itself so startling. **Selective breeding** – i.e. breeding from individual animals showing desirable characteristics – had been a practice used to produce animals with particular characteristics long before Darwin.

Activity 3: selective breeding

What kinds of characteristics would be desirable in:
a a racehorse and
b a horse for farmwork?
You will need to think of both physical and behavioural characteristics.
When you have finished, see the notes on page 562.

Darwin proposed that these same mechanisms which are used to develop the kinds of animals we want for particular purposes could also be used to explain the whole of life on earth. He claimed that ultimately all living things are related.

He argued that it is possible to recognise relationships between different species, and suggested that this is because they have a common evolutionary history. For example, the great tit and the blue tit are now different species, but both developed from a common ancestor. Gradually over many generations, the path of development diverged to produce these two different species. In the same way, the different species of finch which Darwin observed had all evolved from one original group of finches. The evolutionary history of a species is known as its **phylogeny**.

Humans are part of this process. We are just one species among many to have evolved over time. We share common ancestors with apes – for example, we have more than 98% of our genetic makeup in common with chimpanzees – and differences between us and apes have come about by the same evolutionary processes of natural selection which have produced other species.

Darwin's theory is of central importance in comparative psychology, in that it underlies why we make comparisons between species. It suggests that animal morphology and behaviour are the result of a long process of selection, resulting in a well-adapted animal. It therefore suggests that there should be functional explanations of behaviour, i.e. explanations in terms of the function that the behaviour has for the survival of the genes which code for it. As it highlights the continuity of species, it justifies looking at the characteristics and behaviour of animal species in order to discover something about the genetics and the evolution of human behaviour.

- **Darwin's theory of evolution** proposes that species change over time. Each species occupies an **ecological niche.** Species well fitted to a niche are likely to survive, as long as the environment which provides the niche doesn't change.
- **Fitness** refers to individuals who are well adapted to their environment, and so are likely to survive (are **viable**) and pass their genes on to the next generation (are **fecund**). This is termed the **survival of the fittest**.
- Individual variation sometimes comes about as the result of **mutation**, though later theories have emphasised the importance of **genetic recombination**.
- The process by which well-adapted individuals survive to pass on their genes, while less well-adapted individuals do not, is known as **natural selection**.
- Darwin used the same principles to explain all life on earth. Ultimately all species, including humans, can be traced back to common ancestors, but gradually became differentiated.
- The theory underlies the comparison between humans and animals in comparative psychology.

Problems with the theory of natural selection

While what Darwin had to say has a lot to offer, he himself recognised that his original ideas could not always account for the facts. There appear to be two major problems.

One problem is that some animals have developed characteristics which seem to give them no advantage, and may actually put them at a disadvantage in terms of survival. An obvious example of this is the train of the peacock, which hampers the bird in avoiding predators, and makes the peacock easier to catch by providing predators with an easy way of taking hold of their prey.

Darwin himself found the answer to this problem. Fitness is to do not only with survival within a particular environment, but also with reproduction, passing one's genes on to the next generation. Mates are selected on an **assortative** basis, i.e. not randomly; some prospective mates are more attractive than others. In his book *The Descent of Man and Selection in Relation to Sex* (1871) Darwin suggested that some characteristics have developed by a process of **sexual selection**, i.e. because they are likely to increase mating success. The train of the peacock is extremely attractive to peahens, and so the males with bigger and more gorgeous trains have more reproductive success. A mating on this basis will also produce male offspring who are likely to have larger trains, and female offspring who prefer mates with larger trains.

Secondly, Darwin's theory assumed that an animal will always act to maximise the chances of its own individual survival, but this is not always the case. Social animals such as bees do not act on a selfish basis. Worker bees seem to act altruistically in spending their lives caring for the queen bee, with no individual benefit to themselves.

IT'S SUPPOSED TO BE FOR OUR BENEFIT

This problem has been solved using the concept of **inclusive fitness**, a term introduced by Hamilton (1964). Fitness is redefined not only in terms of the reproductive success of the individual but also that of its kin, with whom it has a proportion of its genes in common. It is therefore not the survival of the species or the individual which is important, but the individual's genes: fitness depends on whether or not the individual's genes can survive.

This idea has been expressed in the vivid term used by Dawkins (1976) as the title of his book *The Selfish Gene*. Metaphorically speaking, it is *as if* genes are selfish; the survival of the individual organism is of secondary importance compared with the survival of the genes themselves. Genes contribute information which helps to determine how the nervous system is structured. This will bias animals to behave in such a way as to perpetuate their own genes. In so doing, the individual (or indeed the species as a whole) may incidentally benefit. We shall be returning to the concept of inclusive fitness in the discussion of altruism in the next section.

- Darwin's early ideas raised problems when they could not easily explain animal behaviour.
- The principles of **sexual selection** and the idea of **inclusive fitness** have provided some answers.

20.2 EVOLUTIONARY EXPLANATIONS OF CO-OPERATION AND ALTRUISM IN NON-HUMAN ANIMALS

One form of co-operation is called **mutualism**, which refers to co-operation by members of the same species. As the name suggests, both individuals gain by helping the other. Davies and Houston (1981) gave the example of pairs of pied wagtails, who together protect a winter feeding territory. The benefit of improved territory defence for both of them outweighs the costs of having to share food resources.

Mutualism can also take the form of a **symbiotic relationship**, in which members of different species co-operate so that both benefit. There is usually some form of communication between them. This kind of relationship is quite common.

An interesting example of a symbiotic relationship is the cleaner wrasse, a small fish which lives among the Pacific coral reefs. Large fish let the cleaner wrasse approach them, and remove parasites from their body surface and from inside their mouths. This benefits the wrasse – it obtains food – and also benefits the larger fish because they have their parasites removed. The importance of this has been shown by the deterioration of the health of the host fish if there are no cleaners.

Cleaner wrasse removing parasites from the mouth of a fish

In another example, the honey badger has a symbiotic relationship with a bird called the honey guide. When the honey guide finds a hive of wild bees, it finds a honey badger and uses a particular display to get the badger to follow it. The badger is protected against the bees by its thick skin, and can open the hive with its strong claws, and feed on the honeycomb; it would not have found the hive without the help of the bird. The honey bird feeds on the larvae, which it would not have been able to get at without the badger.

Honey guide

This kind of relationship can also be found between animal and plant species. For example, one species of ant protects a species of young tree by eating the caterpillars which would damage the tree by eating its leaves. The tree produces a substance on which the ants feed, and which seems to serve no other function.

In these examples, co-operation, usually involving communication, is to the benefit of both species. However, it is worth bearing in mind that the animals concerned are not *aware* of this mutual benefit – they have just developed behaviours which are adaptive because both species benefit.

It is also possible for this mutually beneficial arrangement to be exploited by another species. For example, in the case of the cleaner wrasse, there is a further twist in its relationship with larger fish. Some animals have evolved in such a way as to mimic others; this mimicry gains them some kind of advantage. The sabre-toothed blenny is a good example of **aggressive mimicry**. It looks very like the cleaner wrasse. Other fish may mistake it for a cleaner wrasse and allow it to approach. It will then take a bite from the fin of the host fish before it escapes.

Another kind of co-operation is **commensalism**. In this kind of relationship, only one member of the partnership appears to benefit directly. For example, the trumpet fish will sometimes join a school of sturgeon, which provide it with camouflage. It can then take advantage of this to get closer to the small fish on which it preys. In this instance, there is no communication between the species, and while the behaviour of the trumpet fish is adaptive in evolutionary terms, the sturgeon are not affected in any way.

Some species also use **manipulation**, where one animal tricks another into co-operating:

Box A: Feare (1984)

Procedure: Sometimes female birds lay eggs in another female's nest. This has the advantage of young being reared without the costs of incubation and parental care. This process was observed in female starlings. Existing clutches of eggs were marked so they could be identified.

Results: Marked eggs were often found on the ground; females who lay an egg in another female's nest first remove one of the eggs already there to fool the host bird into accepting the new egg.

Conclusion: Females who 'helped' others by rearing their young were manipulated into showing apparently altruistic behaviour, which benefited another, without themselves receiving any benefit.

Altruism is defined as helping another in a situation where there is no obvious advantage to the helper, who may be at some personal risk in helping. The sturgeon in the example of commensalism given above seem to be demonstrating altruistic behaviour, since they do not benefit in any way from allowing the trumpet fish to join their school, though on the other hand their behaviour does not entail any risk to themselves. Mutualism and symbiotic behaviour can't really be described as altruistic, since they are based on the self-interest of both animals.

Darwin defined fitness in terms of an individual animal's ability to leave viable offspring. According to his theory, animals should show behaviours which contribute to their individual survival and ability to reproduce. There is therefore a problem in explaining truly altruistic behaviour, since help is offered in circumstances which may have adverse effects for the helper. Two explanations have been put forward to account for altruism: **kin selection** and **delayed reciprocal altruism**.

As we saw in the previous section, Hamilton (1964) suggested that what is important is not the survival of the individual animal, but of the individual's genes. His theory is known as **kin selection theory**. Even if the individual has no offspring itself, its inclusive fitness may not be zero, because its genes may be passed on by sisters, nephews or cousins. This theory explains why worker bees, who do not themselves have offspring, care for the offspring of the queen to whom they are related; they are contributing to the survival of their genes.

There are many examples of animals whose behaviour can be explained in this way:

Box B: Sherman (1981)

Procedure: The behaviour of female Belding's ground squirrels was observed to see whether there was any difference in behaviour between related and unrelated individuals. In this species, the males wander off after mating, leaving the females to rear their young alone.

Results: Close relatives (e.g. mother–daughter or sister–sister) did not fight over resources within a territory, although they were aggressive to unrelated females. They gave alarm calls at the sight of a predator when they were with a related female, but not when they were with unrelated animals.

Conclusion: This behaviour can be explained in terms of kin selection theory, since the individuals are contributing to the reproductive potential of animals with whom they have genes in common.

In some cases, such behaviour may have both direct and indirect benefits:

Box C: Woolfenden and Fitzpatrick (1984)

Procedure: The nesting behaviour of Florida scrub jays was observed.

Results: Just over half the breeding pairs had at least one 'helper', male or female, and usually related. They warned against predators and helped with feeding. The young of birds with helpers had a higher survival rate than those without. Breeding sites were in short supply, and male 'helpers' were likely to inherit the breeding site of the male bird they were helping. For helpers of both sexes, helping provided protection and increased the likelihood of survival and the possibility of future breeding.

Conclusion: For helpers of both sexes, there were direct benefits in helping (protection and inheriting a breeding site) and indirect benefits explained by kin selection theory (helping the survival of individuals with whom they have genes in common).

There are also instances of helping behaviour which cannot be explained in any of the ways described above. For example, a male olive baboon may act to allow another male to mate with a receptive female, with no apparent advantage to himself (see figure 2):

Figure 2: altruism in olive baboons

Baboon A is mating with a receptive female. Male B observes this. Male C arrives. Male B shifts his gaze rapidly and repeatedly between males A and C. Male C attacks male A, and mating is interrupted. Male B mates with the female.

How can the apparent altruism of baboon C be explained? Kin selection is not relevant because the animals concerned are unrelated; there are no immediate mutual benefits; and one animal does not use deception to manipulate another into helping. The explanation here is that baboon C is acting on the principle of **delayed reciprocal altruism**. His behaviour offers him no immediate advantage, but he acts on the expectation that B will help him in the same way (hence 'reciprocal') at some point in the future.

The obvious problem here is that there are no guarantees that this future help will be forthcoming. Baboon B could cheat by accepting baboon C's help now, but not returning this help in the future when it is needed. If delayed reciprocal altruism does in fact explain helping which is not easily explained in any other way, why does this kind of cheating not happen? We will look at a model which was developed to help us understand human behaviour, but is equally relevant to understanding animal co-operation:

▶ ## Activity 4: the prisoner's dilemma (from Axelrod and Hamilton, 1981)

Two men are arrested for a crime by the police, but the evidence against them is very weak. Each is interviewed separately and offered a deal if he informs on the other.

If they both co-operate with the police (i.e. inform), they will each get a moderate sentence. If one of them informs, but the other doesn't, the informant will be freed, while the one who hasn't co-operated will get a long sentence. If neither informs, they will each be charged with a lesser offence which carries a very short sentence.

The rewards and costs of different choices for prisoner A, expressed numerically, can be shown diagrammatically:

		prisoner B	
		co-operate	refuse to co-operate
prisoner A	co-operate	3 years	free
	refuse to co-operate	10 years	1 year

'Co-operate' means to help the police by informing on your partner; 'refuse to co-operate' means refusal to inform.

How would you respond if you were prisoner A and offered this deal?

Alternatively, you could try this out with a group of participants to see which choices are made.

When you have finished, see the notes on page 562.

Axelrod (1984) ran a computer tournament testing out different strategies for playing this game which would reward co-operation and discourage refusal to co-operate. The winning strategy was found to be **tit-for-tat**, where player A co-operates with player B on the first occasion, and on following trials just does what his opponent has done on the previous move.

This was found to be the most successful strategy for two reasons. Firstly, it retaliates when a partner refuses to co-operate, and so discourages that person from persisting in non-co-operation. Secondly, at the same time it is forgiving, by reverting to co-operation after just one act of retaliation, thus helping to restore co-operation and the benefits it can bring.

Let us look at how a tit-for-tat strategy would work in terms of animal behaviour like that of the olive baboons. If baboon B does not reciprocate the help of baboon C, then baboon C will be equally unco-operative when they next meet. If baboon B then goes on to help baboon C, baboon C will reciprocate, and both animals will enjoy the benefits of mutual co-operation.

However, there are two conditions which must be met if this strategy is to work out in practice. Firstly, it only makes sense as a strategy if the individuals can recognise each other so that cheating is identified and is therefore a costly strategy. If you can't be identified, it would be to your advantage to cheat. Secondly, the chances of the two individuals meeting again must be high. If a meeting is a one-off occasion, refusal to co-operate has the possibility of offering higher rewards than co-operation.

This explanation has been tested in practice, in relation to animal altruism:

Box D: Wilkinson (1984)

Procedure: Two groups of vampire bats were observed, all individually marked for identification. Vampire bats need to make a blood meal during the night, and if they fail to do so, beg for regurgitated blood from more successful bats. In a series of trials, one bat picked at random was kept hungry at night and then returned to the others.

Results: Of 13 regurgitations, 12 occurred between bats belonging to the same group. Starved bats which received blood reciprocated this helping behaviour significantly more often than would be expected if the exchanges had occurred randomly.

Conclusion: The findings of this study are in line with the conditions which favour the development of reciprocal altruism: helping behaviour occurred within a group of known individuals and where meetings were frequent.

- **Mutualism** describes situations where both individuals benefit from helping the other. In a **symbiotic relationship**, two species co-operate to the benefit of both. **Communication** between the species is usually required.
- This kind of relationship can be found between two species of **animals**, or between **animals and plants**. It is based on **self-interest**.
- In **commensalism**, only one species benefits and the other is unaffected.
- A third species may take advantage of a symbiotic relationship for its own advantage.
- **Manipulation** refers to situations where one animal tricks another into helping.
- **Altruism** in animals poses an apparent problem for evolutionary theory. It has been explained in several ways.
- **Kin selection theory** suggests that animals such as worker bees help those with whom they have genes in common. This helps to maximise the chances of survival not of the individual but of their genes.

- Some altruistic behaviour is best explained in terms of **delayed reciprocal altruism**. One animal helps the other in the expectation of the favour being returned in the future.
- The **prisoner's dilemma** has shown that a **tit-for-tat** strategy is most successful in bringing about the mutual co-operation necessary for delayed reciprocal altruism. This kind of co-operation only works as a strategy among individuals who know one another and who are likely to meet again.

20.3 LEARNING THEORY

As you read in chapter 1, behaviourism has been a major perspective in the history of psychology. Behaviourists have had a particular interest in learning, and in particular classical and operant conditioning. See how much you can remember about these theories:

Activity 5: behaviourism and learning theory revisited

Complete this outline of behaviourism and conditioning. The words you will need to fill in the blanks are listed below; each should be used once. If necessary, look back to chapter 1:

.... developed the behaviourist approach. He believed that.................... was an inappropriate way of carrying out psychological investigations because it was...................... If psychology was to be...................., the appropriate data should be......................., i.e. observable behaviour.

The ideas of classical conditioning were developed by.................... He showed that dogs learn by the.......................... of a...................... and a.................... When dogs learned to salivate to the sound of a bell, this behaviour was known as a........................... response. The case of......................................, who developed a.................... response to a white rat, showed that the same principles can be applied to human learning.

The principles of classical conditioning relate to.................... behaviour. However, the principles of operant conditioning, developed by ...., apply more widely. Learning takes place as the result of associating .... and its........................ A positive outcome of a behaviour is known as ...., which makes behaviour more likely to be................. Behaviour can be changed gradually by........................

stimulus	scientific	introspection
Little Albert	repeated	association
reinforcement	response	fear
consequences	Watson	subjective
Skinner	behaviour	Pavlov
reflex	shaping	objective
conditioned		

When you have finished, see the notes on page 562.

Classical conditioning

We will now take a further look at classical conditioning. To add a little detail to the bare outline in activity 5, you may find it useful to carry out activity 6:

▷ Activity 6: trying out classical conditioning

a See if you can use Pavlov's method to condition a response in someone else. You will find that blowing gently but briskly into someone's eye will make them blink. You will probably need to practise this a few times, to make sure you are the right distance away for air to reach the eye, and are not blowing so hard as to make this an unpleasant experience for your participant. Blowing down a straw or a biro tube helps to aim the puff of air. Tap with a pencil on the table for your NS/CS (the equivalent of Pavlov's bell).

b Prepare a diagram like the one in activity 4, chapter 1. Fill in the terms 'puff', 'blink' and 'tap', as well as NS, UCS, UCR, CS and CR.

When you have finished, see the notes on page 562.

A useful term here is **contingency**. This refers to a sequence of events to which an animal is exposed, when one event depends on another event. In Pavlov's experiments, salivation is contingent on the presentation of food. If the presentation of the NS (bell) is immediately followed by the UCS (food), i.e. the presentation of food is made contingent on the ringing of a bell, then conditioning will occur. Because Pavlov's procedure is known as classical conditioning, the particular sequence of events of the NS followed by the UCS is known as a **classical contingency**.

The timing of this contingency is important in the conditioning process. Ideally, the bell needs to be presented $\frac{1}{2}$ to 1 second before the presentation of food. The bell thus acts as a signal for the arrival of food. If the bell is sounded after the food is presented, conditioning is impossible, since the bell cannot act as a signal. If the gap is much longer than 1 second, the conditioning effect is weak. This principle of timing – presenting the CS at the same time or very shortly before the UCS – is known as **temporal contiguity**.

How stable is a conditioned response? Pavlov found that after a few presentations of the bell on its own, the response became weaker, as measured by the amount of saliva produced. Finally, after twenty trials or so, no saliva at all was produced by the sound of the bell. Pavlov referred to this procedure as **extinction**, and the CR is said to have been extinguished when it is no longer produced by the CS. Often, after a break in testing, even though the bell is not paired with food again, the CR of salivation can come back. This phenomenon is known as **spontaneous recovery**. This shows that the process of extinction doesn't wipe out the original learning. What seems to have happened is that the learning has been suppressed by repeated presentations of the bell on its own. This suppression is known as **inhibition**.

Another phenomenon which emerged in later research has been called **generalisation**. This refers to the possibility of a CR being given to a stimulus that is not actually the same as the CS, but very similar to it. For example, if a dog is conditioned to a particular bell, then a CR may also be given to a bell which has a slightly different pitch. However, as the difference between the original CS and the new stimulus increases, the CR will be weaker. At some point the stimuli will be so dissimilar that the CR no longer appears. This lack of a CR to a different stimulus shows **discrimination**; the animal is responding to the difference between the two stimuli. Pavlov trained dogs to salivate to a circle but not to an ellipse. He then proceeded to make the ellipse more and more circular. When the ellipse became almost completely circular, the dogs responded in what could be called a neurotic way: whining, trembling, urinating and so on. Pavlov termed this behaviour **experimental neurosis**; it comes about when the limit of the animal's ability to discriminate is reached.

It is also possible to use a CS as though it were a UCS. In this way a new NS can become a CS by being paired with an established CS. Let us assume that we have established a CR of salivation to a bell, as Pavlov did in his experiments, so that the bell reliably elicits salivation. We can now treat this bond as a new UCS (bell)–UCR (salivation) association. We can pair a new NS (e.g. a buzzer) with the UCS, in order to create a new CS–CR link between the buzzer and salivation. This is called **second-order conditioning**. You might find it helpful to draw out a diagram like that in activity 6b, inserting 'bell', 'salivation' and 'buzzer', to clarify this idea. By repeating this process, third and even fourth order conditioning is possible, though the conditioning effect becomes less marked. The term **higher-order conditioning** is used to cover second, third and fourth order conditioning.

How do Pavlov's experiments with dogs relate to learning, though? The dog salivating to the sound of the bell provides what Watson refers to as an **index of learning**: an objectively measurable change in behaviour. So the dog can be said to have *learned* to salivate to the sound of a bell. Such learning has adaptive value; salivation at the sight of food prepares the stomach for the arrival of food, and so aids the digestive process.

Watson tried to explain the relationship between stimulus and response in terms of links in the brain. He suggested that there are strong connections between a UCS and a UCR, but also other weaker links, which could form a basis for conditioning. Learning was seen as a gradual strengthening of existing weak links, and the extinction process could be thought of as weakening these links again. You need to remember that at the time Watson was working, much less was known about the brain than we know now. Even so, in the light of modern knowledge, these ideas have been found to be reasonably accurate.

- Pavlov's work on the salivary reflex in dogs led him to demonstrate what has come to be known as **classical conditioning**. A stimulus (UCS) which always produces a reflex response (UCR) can be paired with a neutral stimulus (NS). After repeated pairings, the new stimulus becomes a conditional stimulus (CS) which will produce the reflex response (CR) on its own.
- A **contingency** is the sequence of events to which an animal is exposed, when one event depends on another event. Exposure to an NS immediately followed by a UCS is a classical contingency. **Temporal contiguity** refers to the closeness in time between presentation of the NS and the UCS, necessary for effective conditioning.
- After repeated exposures to the CS alone, the CR will die out. This is known as **extinction**. After a break in testing, it is likely to return. This is **spontaneous recovery**.
- **Generalisation** refers to a CR being produced to a stimulus which is similar but not identical to the CS. **Discrimination** describes the lack of a CR to a stimulus which is sufficiently different from the CS.
- **Higher-order conditioning** is the procedure where a CS becomes a UCS in further conditioning.
- Watson suggested a **physiological explanation** of the conditioning process. Research has broadly supported his proposal that learning can be explained in terms of the strengthening of neural pathways.

Operant conditioning

We will now look in a little more detail at operant conditioning. Much of Skinner's research used an apparatus known as a Skinner box (see figure 3). This had a bar to press if rats were the subjects, or a key to peck for pigeons, and these responses by the animals were automatically recorded on a chart. Reinforcers were also presented automatically, usually in the form of food pellets to a food tray:

Figure 3: Skinner box

a for rats

b for pigeons

Skinner's explanation of what happens in operant conditioning was a move away from the stimulus–response (S–R) explanation of classical conditioning. Although the idea of a stimulus can be found in Skinner's early accounts of operant conditioning, by 1938 he no longer included it. In operant conditioning, what is important is the association between behaviour and the consequences of that behaviour. It is this sequence of events which is the contingency in operant conditioning.

Activity 7: classical and operant conditioning

Identify each of the following as examples of classical or operant conditioning. In each case, what is the association being formed?

a A hungry dog is going through the dustbins left outside a row of houses. He tips over one of the dustbins. Food scraps fall out, which the dog eats.

b When George walks into the dentist's surgery and hears the drill, his teeth tingle and he feels anxious.

c Wendy keeps a tin opener on the shelf in the porch where she feeds her cat. It rubs round her legs and purrs whenever she reaches for something on that shelf.

d A cat is outside when rain begins to fall. The cat pushes at the cat flap and lets itself into the house.

When you have finished, see the notes on page 562.

Skinner's move away from an S–R account of learning can be linked to differences in the nature of the behaviour studied in classical and operant conditioning. In classical conditioning, the response is inevitable, because it is a reflex. It is **involuntary**, since it is something over which the animal has no control, and is known as an **elicited response**, i.e. one which reliably occurs to a stimulus, such as salivation to food. In operant conditioning, there is no obvious stimulus applied immediately before a response such as lever-pressing occurs. If a rat is put into a Skinner box, it will not immediately go to the lever and start pressing – it may sniff the food tray, explore the corners of the box, and produce any number of behaviours before it presses the lever. These behaviours are **voluntary**, and freely **emitted** by the animal.

A lever can become a stimulus, in the sense that a rat who has learned to press a lever and is reinforced by food may immediately produce lever-pressing behaviour when put into the box, but it should not be seen as a stimulus during the learning period. In this kind of situation, animals emit arbitrary responses from time to time. If one of these responses is reinforced, then it is likely to be repeated. What causes confusion, and why Skinner is sometimes wrongly believed to be working within an S–R framework, may be the use of the word 'response', which suggests that behaviour must happen as the result of a prior event, i.e. a stimulus.

One of the key principles in operant conditioning is **reinforcement**. Both positive and negative reinforcement strengthen behaviour, while punishment weakens it; you may need to look back to chapter 1, figure 2 to remind yourself of what these terms mean.

Activity 8: reinforcement and punishment

In each of these examples, identify where each of these contingencies is being used:
a positive reinforcement
b negative reinforcement
c punishment
(NB: Each scenario contains several examples.)

1 John often misses the school bus because he gets up too late. His mother, who is normally pleasant and cheerful, shouts at him to get up, which he hates, and often carries on grumbling even when he has finally dragged himself downstairs. When he does get up early enough, he has time to enjoy his breakfast.

2 Peter is allowed to stay up late on Saturday and watch his favourite TV programme if he has helped his mother with the hoovering. He often helps his father wash the car after lunch on Sunday. It is Peter's job to wash up after the meal, but if his father wants help with the car, he may come in while Peter is still clearing the table and get Peter's brother to finish washing up. Peter enjoys cleaning the car, and can't stand washing up.

3 Jenny thinks her partner doesn't always pay her enough attention, as he often disappears behind the newspaper over breakfast, and likes to make straight for the sports pages when he gets in from work. He likes big band music like Glen Miller and can't stand anything classical. Jenny puts on a Glen Miller CD as background music in the morning when he talks to her, but

when he hides behind the newspaper she puts on a Beethoven CD. Sometimes she is playing this music when he gets home, but turns it off if he starts to talk to her.

When you have finished, see the notes on page 563.

I've got him well-trained! every time I run this maze he gives me a bit of cheese.

Although it initially seems to work, punishment is less effective than reinforcement in bringing about behaviour change. Estes (1970) has argued that the only effect of punishment is to suppress a particular behaviour, not to get rid of it. You may remember the term **inhibition** from the discussion of classical conditioning which expresses a similar idea:

Box E: Estes (1970)

Procedure: Two groups of rats were trained to press a lever for food. This response was then extinguished by withholding food from both groups. In addition, for the first few extinction trials, group A was given electric shocks. However, group B did not get any shocks.
Results: In the first stage of extinction, group A pressed the lever less often than group B. However, when the shocks stopped, their rate of bar-pressing increased until they were responding at the same rate as group B.
Conclusion: Punishment (the shocks) did not cause the behaviour to be unlearned. It only had the effect of temporarily suppressing it.

A distinction can be made between primary and secondary reinforcers and punishers. **Primary reinforcers** have a biological basis and are naturally reinforcing, e.g. food to a hungry animal, water to a thirsty one, or sex. In the same way, there are primary punishers: pain, extreme cold and so on. **Secondary reinforcers** have become reinforcing through learning, through the process of classical conditioning. Money is an obvious example. Most people find money highly reinforcing, but this reaction is not something we were born with: we have learned to associate money with what it can buy. In the same way, we were not born with a fear reaction to the sound of a dentist's drill, but some of us have learned to associate this sound with pain, and may find ourselves going out of our way to avoid hearing it. In this way, classical conditioning combines with operant conditioning as we learn to respond with approach or avoidance to new signals.

Skinner carried out a lot of research to find out more about the characteristics of operant conditioning, and was particularly interested in what he called **schedules of reinforcement**, i.e. the pattern of reinforcement applied to behaviour. What we have talked about so far – where every correct response is reinforced – is called **continuous reinforcement (CRF)**. But is this necessarily the best way to bring about and maintain behaviour change?

Skinner found that schedules differ in their effectiveness, depending on what you want to achieve. To establish a behaviour, continuous reinforcement is indeed the most effective method to adopt. However, once a behaviour is reliably established it is possible to *maintain* it by **partial reinforcement**, where not every appropriate response is reinforced; in fact, response rates are then better than for continuous reinforcement. Partial reinforcement can follow four different patterns:

Figure 4: patterns of partial reinforcement

fixed interval (FI) – a reinforcement is given at regular intervals, e.g. once every 20 seconds, as long as there has been at least one appropriate response since the previous reinforcement.

variable interval (VI) – as above, but instead of reinforcement being given every 20 seconds, it is given every 20 seconds on average; after 25 seconds, 15 seconds, 20 seconds, and so on.

fixed ratio (FR) – a reinforcement is given after a fixed number of responses, e.g. after every 10 responses. This pattern is kept to no matter how long it may take for those 10 responses to be given.

variable ratio (VR) – as above, but after every 10 responses on average; after 10 responses, 9 responses, 12 responses, 9 responses and so on

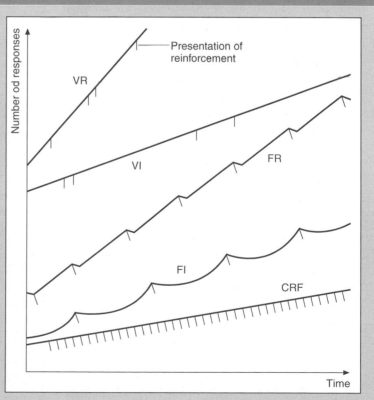

Activity 9: schedules of reinforcement

Skinner believed that human behaviour is shaped and maintained by reinforcement in the same way as the behaviour of rats and pigeons. Can you identify the schedule of reinforcement in each of these examples? Each is used once only.

1 Mike is playing the slot machines in the arcade. Every so often, the machine he is on pays out.
2 Jane works at home for the local toy factory. She gets paid for each batch of a dozen cuddly rabbits she completes.
3 Helen is revising for her A levels. She rewards herself with a 10-minute break every hour.
4 Every time William cries his mother picks him up.
5 Raj is a self-employed potter. He sends out invoices regularly at the end of the month, but some customers pay more quickly than others.

When you have finished, see the notes on page 563.

Each of these different schedules produces a typically different pattern of behaviour. They also vary in how easy it is to extinguish behaviour, when a particular schedule is operating. Behaviour on a CRF schedule is the easiest to extinguish; both FI and FR are relatively easy to extinguish. VI is more difficult, and VR is the most resistant of all. Behaviour which has been reinforced using these schedules will continue long after the reinforcement used in training has been withdrawn.

It is worth noting that generalisation, discrimination and extinction, discussed in relation to classical conditioning, also apply to operant conditioning if they are slightly rephrased to include the concept of reinforcement. A response which has been reinforced in one situation may appear in a similar situation; this will not happen if the situations are too different; and behaviour will disappear if it is not reinforced.

❺ **Operant conditioning** is the term used to refer to the work of Skinner and his followers. Skinner explained conditioning as the association between a **behaviour** and its **consequences**. There are some important differences from classical conditioning.

❺ Skinner distinguished between **positive reinforcement**, **negative reinforcement** and **punishment**. Punishment is an ineffective long-term measure, since it only suppresses behaviour.
❺ Skinner identified different **schedules of reinforcement**, which vary in how useful they are in establishing, maintaining and extinguishing a behaviour.
❺ **Generalisation**, **discrimination** and **extinction** apply to operant as well as classical conditioning.

Avoidance learning

You will remember that negative reinforcement refers to behaviour being strengthened if that behaviour means that something unpleasant in the environment is avoided. For example, a rat might learn to jump a partition in a box to escape an electric shock through the floor of the section in which it is standing. This kind of behaviour – known as **escape learning** – is straightforward to explain: it fits in well with the principles of operant conditioning. The rat jumps the partition for the negative reinforcement of the pain of the shock stopping.

Let us look at a slightly different situation. A rat experiences a light immediately followed by an electric shock through the floor of the cage. Just as in the first example, it can jump the partition to escape the shock. Very soon, the light alone is enough to make the rat jump the partition. This is called **avoidance learning**, since it allows the animal to avoid the aversive event altogether. This kind of behaviour does not fit so readily into an operant conditioning framework as simple escape learning: what is reinforcing the jumping behaviour when the light comes on?

To explain what is happening in this situation, Mowrer (1960) proposed the **two-factor theory**, the two factors being classical and operant conditioning. He suggested that the light and shock are first associated using a classical conditioning framework, the light becoming the CS for the fear response originally elicited by the shock. Jumping in response to the light is negatively reinforced because it reduces the fear.

Avoidance learning is extremely resistant to extinction:

Box F: Miller (1948)

Procedure: Rats were given shocks in a white room, which they could avoid by running through a door into a black room. When this response had been established, the door between the rooms was closed and could only be opened by turning a wheel. No further shocks were given.

Results: Rats very quickly learned to turn the wheel to escape the white room, in spite of not experiencing any shocks at this stage.

Conclusion: Avoidance behaviour means that changes in a situation are not learned. The animal doesn't test for the continuing presence of electric shocks in the white room, so the behaviour is extremely resistant to extinction.

If a rat is trained to press a bar for food, the rat's behaviour soon ceases unless the training is reinforced. The rat has learned to respond to a new situation. With avoidance learning, however, the rat doesn't stay around long enough to find out if the shocks still happen! It is not exposed to the new situation, and therefore cannot learn to respond appropriately to it.

- **Avoidance behaviour** is difficult to explain in operant conditioning terms, since negative reinforcement is not directly involved.
- This behaviour is resistant to **extinction**, since the continuing presence of something aversive is not tested.
- Mowrer explained avoidance behaviour in a **two-factor theory**, where the two factors are **classical** and **operant conditioning**.

Evaluation of classical and operant conditioning theory

In this section we will be looking at some of the ways in which the principles of classical and operant conditioning have been criticised. At the same time, this doesn't mean that they should be discarded as worthless. Their ideas help to explain a lot of behaviour, and the principles of both classical and operant conditioning have practical applications.

For example, they underlie the behavioural treatment for phobias and other anxiety disorders, described in chapter 25.

However, some theorists have not been totally convinced by an account of learning which focuses entirely on behaviour, and have suggested that we need to bring in some mental processes if we are to account for all human and animal behaviour. Tolman is the major proponent of what has come to be known as **cognitive behaviourism**. Let us start by looking at one of his experiments:

Box G: Tolman and Honzik (1930)

Procedure: Three groups of rats were run in a maze. Group 1 was always reinforced with food for reaching the goal box. Group 2 never received food in the goal box. Group 3 was not reinforced for the first 10 days of the experiment, but was reinforced in the same way as group 1 from day 11 onwards.

Results: Group 1 produced a standard learning curve. The rats showed a gradual drop in the time taken to run the maze, until they ran straight to the goal box. Times for group 2 showed little variation over the trials. Group 3 showed a similar pattern to group 2 for the first 10 days, then a sudden drop in the time taken from day 11. They caught up very rapidly with the time taken by group 3 (see figure 5).

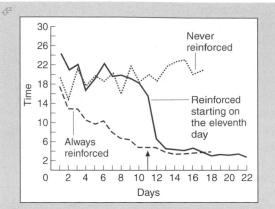

Conclusion: The very rapid learning of group 3 from day 11 onwards, compared with the gradual learning shown by group 1, suggests that group 3 had learned something about the maze during the first 10 days of the experiment. This is called **latent learning**, i.e. it was not demonstrated until it became relevant.

Activity 10 – Tolman vs. behaviourism

Why are these results, in particular the pattern of learning shown by group 3, difficult to fit into a strictly behaviourist account? (Hint: reinforcement)

When you have finished, see the notes on page 563.

Tolman suggested that in this kind of situation, the animal does not learn fixed behaviours, but instead learns *information*. In this experiment, the animal has learned something about the maze which can be used as appropriate; in this case, when the animal is reinforced for running to the goal box. The animal can use the information it has acquired to adapt its behaviour, according to the situation in which it finds itself. Tolman referred to the information about the maze which the rat acquires as a **cognitive map**.

This kind of explanation is sometimes referred to as S–S (stimulus–stimulus) psychology. What is being learned is the association between stimuli, the *expectancy* that one stimulus will be followed by another. It is basically a cognitive, information-processing account of learning: rats (as well as humans) learn facts, not responses. Another study by Tolman contrasted his ideas about learning

information and acquiring cognitive maps with traditional behaviourist accounts of learning:

Box H: Tolman *et al.* (1946)

Procedure: Two groups of hungry rats were run in a simple maze (see figure 5). They were sometimes started at A and sometimes at B. The maze provided a rich environment, with many cues giving information to the rats about where in the maze they were. Irrespective of where they started, group 1 always had to turn left to obtain food. Group 2 always had to go to a particular food box at a particular place in the maze, so they sometimes needed to turn left, and sometimes right.

Results: Group 2 learned to find food in the maze more easily than group 1.

Conclusion: When there is adequate information available, animals use it to behave flexibly, according to what is appropriate in a particular situation. The learning of fixed responses is possible, but relatively difficult.

Figure 5: The maze used by Tolman *et al.* (1946)

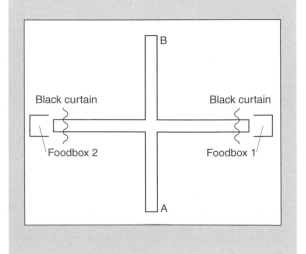

Activity 11: how is behaviour adaptive?

Try to relate the findings of Tolman *et al.*, shown in box H, to a rat in the wild. Why might the kind of learning group 2 showed be adaptive, and therefore useful for survival?

When you have finished, see the notes on page 563.

Reinforcement still has an important place in Tolman's theory. Food has reinforcing properties for a hungry rat. However, what is being reinforced is not the S–R link of classical conditioning, nor the behaviour–consequences link of operant conditioning. Reinforcement strengthens **cognitions** concerning expectancy of food in a particular place; cues in the environment become better **predictors** of food.

This is not to say, of course, that animal cognitions are necessarily the same as human cognitions. For one thing, humans can form symbolic mental representations, which affects how they process information. However, the basic principle underlying Tolman's approach is that cognitions are involved in the learning of animals as well as humans. The animal uses information which it has acquired in a flexible way, depending on the environmental conditions it meets.

Classical and operant conditioning re-interpreted

How would cognitive behaviourists describe what is happening in a classical conditioning experiment? Let us take as an example a rat which is given a mild electric shock to its feet. The rat will probably run away from the source of the shock if escape is possible. If escape is not possible, e.g. the shock is experienced from the floor of a small cage, the rat usually flinches. If the shock is now paired with an NS, say a tone, the rat will eventually respond to the tone alone. According to classical conditioning theory, the rat should again flinch, i.e. the association between NS (tone) and R (flinching) has been strengthened in the learning process. However, if at this stage escape is possible, this is what the rat will do, rather than flinching:

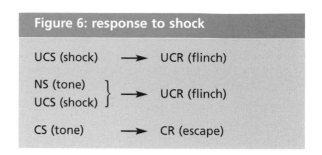

Figure 6: response to shock

UCS (shock) → UCR (flinch)

NS (tone)
UCS (shock) } → UCR (flinch)

CS (tone) → CR (escape)

Activity 12: cognitive behaviourist explanations

What is the difficulty in trying to explain the behaviour shown in figure 6 within a classical conditioning framework? How could this behaviour be explained by a cognitive behaviourist? You will need to bring in the ideas of prediction, expectancy and flexibility.

When you have finished, see the notes on page 563.

Perhaps the results of Pavlov's experiments had something to do with the very artificial situation he used. The dog had very limited options; remember, it was harnessed, so its behaviour was strictly controlled. Flexible behaviour was just not possible.

Activity 13: operant conditioning revisited

Can you restate what is happening in an operant conditioning situation, using the ideas of cognitive behaviourists? How could a cognitive account help to explain why a VR schedule is so resistant to extinction?

When you have finished, see the notes on page 563.

- The principles of **classical** and **operant conditioning** can explain a lot of learning, but doubts have been raised as to (a) whether what is learned is a **purely behavioural** response and (b) whether there are also completely **different types** of learning.
- Some theorists have suggested that we cannot totally ignore mental processes. This is known as **cognitive behaviourism**.

- Tolman suggested that what is learned is **information**, not rigid patterns of behaviour. This information can then be used flexibly in response to the demands of a particular situation; it is **adaptive**.
- Using mazes, Tolman showed **latent learning** in rats. He used his findings as evidence that their experience in the maze allowed them to form **cognitive maps**.
- Some behaviour can only be explained using the concepts of **expectancy** and **prediction**.
- Both classical and operant conditioning can be re-interpreted. In both cases, what is being strengthened is **cognitions**. In classical conditioning, this is the expectancy that the NS will be followed by the UCS. In operant conditioning, it is the expectancy that a particular behaviour will be followed by particular consequences.
- Some research into animal learning can't be explained within a strict behaviourist framework, but fits easily with **cognitive behaviourist** ideas.

Biological constraints on learning

Behaviourist ideas have also been challenged on another issue. According to behaviourists, there is no such thing as innate behaviour, beyond the few reflexes which animals possess at birth. Organisms differ only in their capacity for learning, and an animal's behavioural responses will depend solely on its history of reinforcement. But is it really the case that the behaviour of an animal reflects only its learning history, and that no behaviours have innate roots?

Within a behaviourist framework, all animals can be taught to do anything of which they are physically capable. For example, you will remember that Skinner taught pigeons to play table tennis. As long as the animal is capable of carrying out a behaviour, it should be possible to teach it to produce that behaviour using the principles of shaping and reinforcement. However, this does not seem to be the case.

Breland and Breland ran a business engaged in training animals for films, commercials and so on. In 1961, they published a paper with the title

The Misbehaviour of Organisms (a play on words of the title of Skinner's book *The Behaviour of Organisms*). In this paper they discussed some of the problems they had come across in their work. They had trained a range of animals, using the operant conditioning principles of shaping and reinforcement, but the results were not always as expected.

For one assignment, they needed to train pigs to drop coins into a piggy bank. Pigs apparently condition easily with food as a reinforcement. Initially things went well, and each pig's behaviour was successfully shaped right up until the final step. However, when it was necessary for a pig to put the second coin into the piggy bank it would pick up the coin, but would also throw it up in the air, root it with its snout, pick it up, drop it, root it again, and so on.

Activity 14: animal misbehaviour

In what ways do these behaviours not fit conditioning theory? How could they be accounted for? (Hint: the reinforcement for the pigs was food.) When you have finished, see the notes on page 564.

Further problems in the area of learning versus innate behaviour are shown in what is known as the **Garcia effect**:

Box I: Garcia and Koelling (1966)

Procedure: Before the start of the study, rats were tested on a saccharin solution to establish that they had no inbuilt dislike of the taste. Saccharin was then paired with a bell and a flashing light, both automatically triggered by the rat touching the drinking spout. Some time later (up to 12 hours in some cases) the rats were given an injection which made them nauseous and ill. Each rat experienced this procedure only once. They were then tested with: (a) saccharin solution on its own and (b) plain water, paired with the bell and the flashing light.

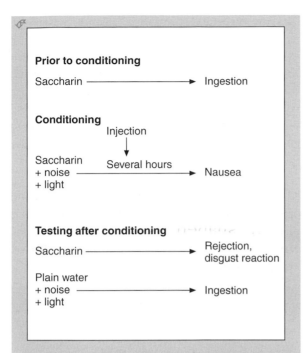

Prior to conditioning

Saccharin ⟶ Ingestion

Conditioning

Injection

Saccharin + noise + light — Several hours ⟶ Nausea

Testing after conditioning

Saccharin ⟶ Rejection, disgust reaction

Plain water + noise + light ⟶ Ingestion

Results: The rats refused the saccharin solution, and showed a disgust reaction. They drank the plain water, even though drinking it triggered off the bell and the light.
Conclusion: The rats had formed an association between the saccharin solution and nausea. They did not form this association to the bell and the light.

Activity 15: the Garcia effect

Three principles of classical conditioning are challenged in this study. What are they? How can these results be accounted for? (You will need to consider how the rats' behaviour would be adaptive in their natural setting.)

When you have finished, see the notes on page 564.

The Garcia effect describes the ability to form associations very quickly between taste and illness. The adaptive value of this kind of learning is clear. In the wild, the rat could well be exposed to food or drink that would make it ill, and it would need to learn this connection very rapidly in order to survive. When faced with a novel taste, rats typically try a very little, and will not touch the food again if there

are ill effects. This could help to explain why it is so difficult to get rid of rats with poison.

On the other hand, light or noise are not usually associated with nausea in the wild. Seligman (1970) has used the term **preparedness** to describe what is happening here: animals are born prepared to make some associations, those linked to survival, more readily than others. This idea may also be useful in explaining why people are more likely to have a phobia about snakes than, say, buttons.

- The principles of conditioning have been challenged from a biological perspective. It does not seem to be the case that all animals can be taught anything, using shaping and reinforcement. There is a tendency to revert to behaviour which is natural for the species. This is known as **instinctive drift**.
- Associations can be formed between events which are hours apart. They are very readily formed between taste and illness, where they are important to survival, but not so readily between events which are not naturally linked. This is known as the **Garcia effect**.
- Seligman used the term **preparedness** to describe how some associations are more readily formed than others. This idea can also be related to phobias.

Other forms of animal learning

So far we have looked at conditioning theory, together with modifications to it. It seems inevitable that we must include cognitive factors in an account of learning. It is also clear that there are biological constraints on learning. But although these modifications are necessary, the theorists who proposed them still accept basic conditioning principles, in particular that learning is usually a gradual strengthening of associations. But (the Garcia effect apart) is this necessarily the case?

Box J: Koehler (1925)

Procedure: Bananas were suspended from the ceiling of a chimpanzee's cage, out of reach of the chimpanzee. Several boxes of different sizes were scattered around the cage.

Results: The chimpanzee initially jumped up and down, trying in vain to reach the bananas. It then stayed relatively quiet for a time. After a while it jumped up, piled the boxes up, and climbed up to reach the bananas.

Conclusion: The chimpanzee formed a mental representation of the complete problem which allowed it to find a solution. When a sudden solution to a problem is found, this is described as **insight learning**.

Koehler's chimpanzee

Koehler carried out experiments with several chimpanzees, covering a range of problems. For example, one experiment involved using a short stick to reach a longer stick outside the cage. This longer stick could then in turn be used to retrieve a banana. He found the same kind of pattern of learning as that shown in box J. Koehler was a

Gestalt psychologist. The Gestalt school of psychology was mainly interested in perception, and suggested that we need to look at perception as a whole, rather than at separate elements which contribute to what we see. Koehler saw Gestalt principles at work in this kind of problem-solving behaviour: all the elements of the problem need to come together and form a cohesive whole in order for a solution to be found.

Koehler's ideas contrast with the idea of learning as a gradual process, proposed by both classical and operant conditioning. One possible explanation is that insight learning only applies to higher animals. However, this was demonstrated not to be the case in the study in box K:

Box K: Epstein *et al.* (1984)

Procedure: Using operant conditioning techniques, pigeons were taught to push a box to a particular section of the cage wall. They were also trained to stand on a box and peck a plastic banana hanging from the ceiling. They were then put in a situation where the banana was suspended, but the box was some distance away from it.

Results: The pigeons at first showed no behaviour appropriate to solving the task. They then suddenly started to push the box under the banana, climbed on the box and pecked the banana.

Conclusion: Pigeons are capable of insight learning.

So lower animals too show evidence of sudden insight. It seems likely, then, that the difference between the findings of classical and operant conditioning and those of Koehler are to do with the way that the problem is presented. If Gestalt theory is right, for insight learning to take place, all the elements of the problem need to be seen in relation to each other. For animals, this has been found to mean that all the necessary parts of the problem need to be in the field of vision at the same time. This was the case both for Koehler's chimpanzees and the pigeons of Epstein *et al.*

However, Koehler's studies have been criticised on several grounds. First, they can be criticised for being very open to experimenter demand characteristics. The concepts of 'sitting thinking' and 'suddenly conceiving of the solution' are not objectively observable behaviours but interpretations by the experimenter. Second, the studies were not very well controlled, particularly since the previous experience of his chimpanzees was not taken into account. However, more recent research into insight learning, where an animal's previous experience has been controlled, has had similar findings. There is thus some indication that the cognitive element of learning, and therefore learning itself, can take different forms.

- The chimpanzees in Koehler's studies showed **insight learning**, i.e. a sudden solution to a problem. This is in contrast to the gradual association suggested by conditioning theory. Koehler explained learning by using **Gestalt** principles.
- His methods have been criticised, but are useful in suggesting that there are different kinds of learning.

20.4 SOCIAL LEARNING IN NON-HUMAN ANIMALS

For animals who live in social groups, it is possible that the presence of one animal can influence the knowledge, and therefore the behaviour, acquired by another. This possibility is known as social learning. One example of social learning is the development of a fear of a particular predator. The study by Mineka and Cook (box J, chapter 22) demonstrates how a monkey could learn to fear a snake as a result of observing another monkey showing a fear response to a snake.

Social learning is also important in the development of effective interaction with others in the group. It has been suggested that for some primates, particular skills and understanding are developed over time as the individual matures and interacts with others.

In this section, we will look at some examples to illustrate the influence of social learning.

Foraging

Animals can learn food preferences from others. This ability has clear survival advantages, in that it allows an animal to learn from the experience of others; for example, it does not have to go through a trial-and-error process to identify which foods are harmful. This ability has been shown experimentally:

Box L: Galef (1988)

Procedure: A demonstrator rat was allowed to eat food with a distinctive flavour, either cocoa or cinnamon. A test rat was then put with the demonstrator for 30 minutes, but with no food present. The test rat was then allowed to choose between cocoa-flavoured and cinnamon-flavoured food.

Results: Test rats preferred food of the same flavour as that eaten by the demonstrator. This was the case even 4 hours after the demonstrator had eaten, and when 12 hours had elapsed before the test rat made its choice.

Conclusion: Interacting with a rat which has just eaten a particular food temporarily creates a preference for that food.

I think the kids are getting suspicious of us always smelling of their "Nice Greens"!

It is possible that these results could be explained by rats being **neophobic**, i.e. very unwilling to taste anything new. This was noted in the previous section, in connection with the Garcia effect. For example, the test rat could have picked up the smell of the particular foodstuff on the breath of the demonstrator, and actually be choosing between what was familiar and what was unfamiliar, rather than being influenced directly by the demonstrator rat having eaten the food. However, Galef found similar results even when the test rats were familiar with both cocoa- and cinnamon-flavoured food.

Galef and his colleagues carried out a further study to try to identify the critical features of the social interaction between demonstrator and test rat which created a food preference:

Box M: Galef *et al.* (1988)

Procedure: This study used the apparatus shown in figure 7, with a test rat being placed in the bucket part, and a demonstrator in the wire mesh basket through the side. Test rats were exposed to an anaesthetised demonstrator rat in one of three conditions: (a) with food dusted on its face; (b) with food placed directly into its stomach via a tube; and (c) with the rear end dusted with food, and the animal introduced rear end first into the basket. A fourth condition substituted the demonstrator with cotton wool dusted with food. Test rats were then offered a choice of food to establish under which of the conditions they would prefer the food associated with the demonstrator.

Results: A food preference was shown in conditions (a) and (b), and a slight preference in (c). There was no preference in the 'cotton wool' condition.

Conclusion: For a rat to develop a food preference through exposure to a demonstrator, the demonstrator does not need to be conscious, but does need to be a rat. Interaction with the front end of the rat is preferable. The test animal needs to be able to smell food at the same time as it smells the demonstrator's breath.

Figure 7: apparatus used by Galef *et al.* (1988)

Galef and Durlach (1993) suggested that these kinds of food preferences are acquired through a process of classical conditioning. However, Pearce (1997) pointed out that such food preferences last for only a few hours, whereas the effects of classical conditioning are much longer. The processes involved are therefore not as yet clearly understood.

It has also been suggested that animals can learn skills relevant to foraging by **observational learning** and **imitation**. In the days before milk was homogenised, the cream would rise to the top in bottles of milk. Blue tits would peck through the foil caps of milk bottles to get at the cream. It has been suggested (e.g. Bonner, 1980) that this skill became widespread through birds imitating others whom they observed getting at the cream in this way.

However, there is some controversy over whether this behaviour should be described as observational learning, and whether it comes about as the result of imitation. Sherry and Galef suggested that it could have come about through **social facilitation**, i.e. when the mere presence of others makes a behaviour more likely to occur, or improves performance:

Box N: Sherry and Galef (1990)

Procedure: Individual black-capped chickadees were tested in isolation to see whether they would peck at and open the foil top of a container of cream. Other chickadees were individually tested in the presence of a second chickadee in an adjacent cage.
Results: When tested in isolation, the birds were very unlikely to peck at the foil tops. However, in the presence of another bird they were very likely to do so, and finally to open it.
Conclusion: This behaviour was the result of social facilitation.

The reasons underlying social facilitation in this context are far from clear. Pearce (1997) suggested that the presence of a second bird may reduce fear or encourage behaviour relevant to foraging in the test bird. However, the results of the Sherry and Galef study suggest that this behaviour is not the result of imitation.

It has also been suggested that observational learning and imitation explain some primate behaviours. For example, Lawick-Goodall (1970) reported that young chimpanzees may learn 'termiting' from watching their parents. Termiting involves pushing a stick into a termite nest, and eating the termites which cling to it when it is pulled out. Similarly, Boesch (1991) reported on a group of chimpanzees in the Ivory Coast who used stones to break up nuts.

However, one problem with this kind of explanation is that these kinds of complex skills do not spread easily through a group of animals; for example, not all chimpanzees learn to termite, even when exposed to models showing this behaviour. If primates were willing imitators, it would be expected that these kinds of skills, very useful in foraging, would be universally acquired within a social group. Nagell et al. (1993) has suggested instead that the acquisition of such skills is the result of the combination of a number of complex processes, including trial-and-error learning.

- Animals who live in groups acquire **knowledge** through learning from others. It is also necessary for **social skills** and **understanding** to be acquired if the social group is to function efficiently.
- Rats learn temporary **food preferences** from others. The processes by which these preferences develop are not entirely clear.
- It has been suggested that some skills are developed through **observational learning** and **imitation**. Research has challenged this interpretation; such skills may be better explained by looking at the combination of a number of processes.

Self-recognition

One of the most basic social concepts to grasp is that each one of us is a self in a world consisting of ourselves and other selves. This concept, in turn, depends on an ability to recognise ourselves.

We will look in this section at the social learning which might be said to take place when an animal interacts with itself by means of a mirror. Whether animals are capable of self-recognition in a mirror depends to an extent on the species. When chimpanzees first see themselves in a mirror, they respond to the mirror image as if it were another chimpanzee, either threatening the image or making conciliatory gestures towards it. However, after a few days they learn to use it to inspect parts of their body which are not normally accessible to them, pick their teeth, and remove mucus from their eyes and noses. This suggests that they have some understanding that the image they see in the mirror is their own body.

These kinds of self-directed behaviours in front of a mirror could perhaps be explained away as coincidence; the animals just happened to be carrying out behaviours in which they engage frequently while in front of a mirror. To discount this possibility, rather more rigorous studies have been carried out, using a 'red mark' technique developed by Gallup:

Box O: Gallup (1970)

Procedure: Young chimpanzees born in the wild were tested. A full-length mirror was introduced into the cage of each chimpanzee. After ten days, the chimpanzees were anaesthetised while a red mark was put on one ear and one eyebrow. They were then put back in their cages with no mirror, to establish a baseline measurement of how often they touched the body parts which had been dyed red. The mirrors were then put back in the cages, and the number of times the chimpanzees touched their red ears and eyebrows was compared with the baseline measurement.

Results: Over the first few days, the chimpanzees developed typical self-directed behaviours towards their reflection. When their ears and eyebrows had been marked, each chimpanzee immediately began to explore the red marks when they saw themselves in the mirror. They touched their red ears and eyebrows 25 times more frequently than during the period of baseline measurement.

Conclusion: Chimpanzees can learn self-recognition.

Gallup's technique has been used to investigate whether other animals too are capable of self-recognition. This seems to be true for orang-utans (Lethmate and Ducker, 1973) and gorillas

Ape interacting with its reflection

(Patterson and Cohn, 1994). However, tests with other animals have been unsuccessful, e.g. gibbons (Gallup 1983), elephants (Povinelli, 1989) and parrots (Pepperburg *et al.*, 1995). It seems that self-recognition is limited to great apes and humans.

But why are some animals capable of recognising themselves in a mirror? It is possible that this ability is limited to animals who are able to make use of this information in some way. However, there are many research examples which show that animals who are not capable of self-recognition can nonetheless make use of mirrors. For example, Povinelli (1989) found that an elephant could use a mirror to guide its trunk to retrieve a carrot that could only be seen in the mirror. This kind of ability is perhaps the result of trial-and-error learning.

Gallup himself suggested that self-recognition indicates self-awareness. He drew on the work of Cooley (1902) and Mead (1934), both of whom were interested in the development of the self-concept in humans. Cooley used the term **looking glass self** to express the idea that our self-concept develops as the result of how others respond to us; it is essentially a social process. If the same is true of chimpanzees, it would follow that chimpanzees raised in isolation would fail to show self-recognition:

Box P: Gallup (1977)

Procedure: The same procedure was followed as for Gallup's earlier study (box O). Chimpanzees raised in isolation were tested.

Results: The chimpanzees always treated the mirror image as if it were another animal. They did not touch the red marks more often than they had touched their ears and eyebrows before they had been marked.

Conclusion: Exposure to the reactions of other members of the species is necessary for self-recognition to develop.

The results of this study lend some support to Gallup's ideas about the social basis of self-recognition. However, possible effects of being reared in isolation cannot be discounted. You will remember from chapter 3 the extensive problems experienced by the monkeys raised in isolation by Harlow and Harlow (1962).

It is clear that some species can learn to use mirrors to direct behaviour towards their own bodies. However, whether this indicates self-awareness remains open to question.

- Social learning plays a role in the development of animals which live in social groups. **The recognition of self** in a world of other selves is a basic social concept.
- In **mirror studies**, chimpanzees, orang-utans and gorillas show self-recognition. Other species do not.
- It has been suggested that this ability is confined to species which could make use of this information. However, animals incapable of self-recognition can use a mirror to solve problems.
- It is possible that great apes have **self-awareness**, but this is open to question.

Theory of mind

For animals who live in social groups, effective functioning would encourage animals to learn to understand the beliefs, intentions and desires of other animals in the group. The ability to represent the mental states of others, and so understand how they think and feel, has come to be known as **theory of mind**. It has been suggested that the ability to learn from social interactions is based on having a theory of mind. Work in this area originated with chimpanzees when Premack and Woodruff (1978) published a paper posing the question: Does the chimpanzee have a theory of mind?

Two experimental paradigms which have been used to establish whether or not animals have a theory of mind involve deception and knowledge attribution. **Deception** assumes that if animal A understands that the behaviour of animal B is influenced by what B knows about a particular situation, then animal A could manipulate the information given to animal B (e.g. use deception) in order to influence B's behaviour:

Box Q: Woodruff and Premack (1979)

Procedure: A chimpanzee saw a laboratory assistant hide food under one of two containers, and then leave the room. The chimpanzee could not reach either of the containers. One of two trainers then entered the room. If the chimpanzee pointed to the container hiding the food, the 'co-operative' trainer would bring the food to the chimp; the 'competitive' trainer would keep the food. However, if the chimpanzee directed the 'competitive' trainer towards the empty container, the chimpanzee received the food.
Results: Some of the chimpanzees were able to earn food in both sorts of trials, i.e. those involving the 'co-operative' and the 'competitive' trainer.
Conclusion: The chimpanzees deliberately deceived the 'competitive' trainer, thus supporting the idea that they possessed a theory of mind.

Activity 16: evaluating Woodruff and Premack (1979)

One problem with the findings of this study is that some of the chimpanzees tested did not apparently learn how to manipulate the behaviour of the 'competitive' trainer to earn themselves food. There is a further problem in terms of how the results should be interpreted. Many trials were necessary before the chimpanzees started to deceive the 'competitive' trainer.

Given this information, what alternative interpretation of the results of this study could be made, other than that chimpanzees possess a theory of mind? (Hint: association learning)

When you have finished, see the notes on page 564.

The Woodruff and Premack study was a laboratory study, and therefore took place in rather artificial conditions. If it is the case that animals such as chimpanzees have developed a theory of mind to

559

facilitate living with others of their kind, it is likely that this would be demonstrated in naturalistic settings. There are numerous examples of individual behaviour in a natural setting in which deliberate deception seems to be taking place:

Box R: Byrne and Whiten (1985; 1987)

a In a troop of baboons, an adolescent (referred to as Melton) attacked a younger baboon, whose screams alerted adults. Melton stood on his hind legs and looked around as baboons do when they notice a predator. The adults stopped approaching and looked round too. Melton thus avoided being punished by the adults.

b An adult female baboon gradually approached a rock behind which she started to groom a young male. The young male was hidden from the leader of the troop by the rock. The leader would not have allowed such contact if he had been aware of what was going on.

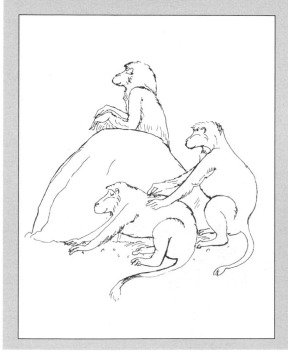

Activity 17: interpreting the behaviour of baboons

a In the examples given in box R, how could the behaviour of Melton and the female baboon be interpreted to support the idea that these animals had a theory of mind?

b Are there any other ways in which these behaviours could be interpreted?

When you have finished, see the notes on page 564.

Given the problems of interpreting animals' behaviour, these kinds of observations cannot be used either to support or to disprove the idea that some animals may have a theory of mind. A further problem, of course, is that with this kind of naturalistic observation, there is no way of knowing what the previous experience of the animals has been. It is possible that the strategies chosen in the examples given in box O had been produced by chance in an earlier, similar situation, and found to be effective; they could therefore be explained in terms of learning by association rather than theory of mind.

Pearce (1997) put forward a further criticism of this kind of evidence. He pointed out that in the case of Melton, a very complex reasoning process is being assumed by those who see his behaviour as evidence for animals having a theory of mind. It assumes he knew that (a) the adults were intending to punish him, (b) that it is possible to create false beliefs about the presence of predators by adopting a particular posture, and (c) that these false beliefs will disrupt the existing intentions of others. Pearce suggested that focusing on the complex behaviour which is involved in deception may mean that this approach is not the most useful way of trying to establish whether or not animals have a theory of mind.

The second – and potentially less complex – way of testing whether or not animals have a theory of mind is **knowledge attribution**, in other words whether animals are capable of understanding what knowledge another animal (or person) may have:

Box S: Povinelli *et al.* (1990)

Procedure: A chimpanzee was seated in view of four cups, one of which contained a piece of food. The chimpanzee was allowed to keep the piece of food by correctly identifying the cup which contained it. The chimpanzee had previously seen one of the trainers (the 'guesser') leave the room, while the other trainer (the 'knower') hid the food under one of the cups; the chimp could not see under which cup the food was hidden. When the chimpanzee came to choose a cup, the two trainers were also in the room, each pointing to a different cup. Four different chimpanzees were tested on this task.

Results: All four chimpanzees showed a preference for the cup at which the 'knower' was pointing. Several hundred trials were necessary before this preference was statistically significant for all four participants.

Conclusion: The findings are consistent with the idea that chimpanzees have a theory of mind, i.e. that they understood that the 'knower' had information not shared by the 'guesser'.

However, given the large number of trials taken by the participants before the preference became significant, it is also possible that the chimpanzees had simply learned that the person who was in the room for longer was the one who pointed to the correct cup. This possibility was tested in a final stage of the experiment in box S, shown in box T:

Box T: Povinelli *et al.* (1990)

Procedure: Once the participants were trained using the method in box S, the procedure was changed so that both the 'knower' and the 'guesser' remained in the room while the food was hidden under one of the cups by a third assistant. The 'knower' watched the food being hidden, while the 'guesser' was prevented from watching by having a bucket put over his head. The third person then left the room, and the 'knower' and 'guesser' each pointed to a different cup. A series of 30 trials was carried out.

Results: A statistically significant preference was shown by 3 of the 4 participants. However, in spite of having taken part in the previous part of the experiment, errors were made.
Conclusion: Although the performance on this task was consistent with the idea that chimpanzees have a theory of mind, the errors made mean that there is an alternative interpretation. It is possible that the animals were simply learning that the person who did not have his head covered was pointing to the cup in which the food was hidden.

Overall, research into whether or not animals possess a theory of mind has been disappointing. While the findings are consistent with the theory of mind idea, alternative interpretations are also possible. Further research needs to be carried out to clarify this issue.

- **Theory of mind** refers to the ability to represent the mental state of others. This has been investigated in primates.
- The ability to use **deception** has not been clearly demonstrated either by laboratory studies or by naturalistic observation. This approach may be too **complex** to yield clear-cut results.
- Studies investigating **knowledge attribution** are also open to different interpretations.
- While research findings are consistent with the idea that some animals may possess a theory of mind, further research is necessary for a more definite understanding of this issue.

Notes on activities

1 There are a number of possibilities here, so we will take as examples one characteristic of each. A hawk with keen eyesight is better able to locate its prey and thus survive long enough to reproduce successfully. The train of a peacock influences how attractive it is to females, and thus how likely it is to find a mate and be able to reproduce. The strength of a rat's legs will affect how easily it escapes from predators, contributing to its prospects for survival.

2 Where there is a shortage of food, only those giraffes who had longer necks would be able to reach the leaves at the top of trees, and thus have a relatively plentiful food supply. They would thus be more likely to survive and breed, and so pass genes for longer necks to the next generation.

3 There are lots of possibilities here. For example, if a racehorse is to run fast it needs to be thinner and lighter than a working horse. A horse for farmwork would need to be bred for strength and stamina. Being temperamental may not be a drawback in a racehorse, but this quality would be undesirable in a farm animal. You have probably thought of other variations which would influence breeders in their choice of animals to breed from.

4 The most rewarding response for prisoner A is to co-operate, i.e. inform on prisoner B. If A co-operates and B refuses to co-operate, A gets the best payoff, while B is left with the 'sucker's payoff', i.e. a 10-year sentence. If both A and B co-operate, the outcome is less good than if they both refuse to co-operate, but the worst outcome (the sucker's payoff, where B co-operates and A refuses to co-operate) is avoided.

5 Watson; introspection; subjective; scientific; objective; Pavlov; association; stimulus; response; conditioned; Little Albert; fear; reflex; Skinner; behaviour; consequences; reinforcement; repeated; shaping.

6 The tap starts off as an NS and becomes a CS in the course of conditioning. It is a CS when it elicits a blink on its own. The puff of air is the UCS; the blink is the UCR before and during the conditioning procedure, and a CR when it is a response to the tap on its own.

7 **a** and **d** are both examples of operant conditioning. In each case there is an

association between a piece of behaviour (knocking over a dustbin; pushing against the cat flap) and its consequences (food; escaping the rain). These consequences reinforce the behaviour and make it more likely to happen again. In contrast, **b** and **c** are both examples of classical conditioning. The relationship is between an initial NS which becomes a CS (the dentist's surgery; reaching for the shelf) which has been linked with a UCS (unpleasant experiences at the dentist's; being fed) and a UCR which becomes a CR (anxiety; pleasure).

8 For John, his mother shouting is a punishment for lying in bed, since being shouted at is something he finds unpleasant. On the other hand, getting up on time is positively reinforced by breakfast. If his mother continues to grumble when he has got up late, she is punishing getting out of bed, which could help to explain why this strategy might not be very effective.

For Peter, helping with the hoovering is positively reinforced by being allowed to watch TV. Washing the car is a positive reinforcement, since it is something which gives him pleasure, and car washing is also negatively reinforced by not having to do the washing up.

Having Glen Miller on in the background positively reinforces Jenny's partner talking to her. Reading the newspaper is punished by Jenny putting on the Beethoven CD. Talking to her is negatively reinforced by this music being turned off.

9 Mike's slot machine is on a VR schedule; the machines pay out on average after a certain number of plays. Jane is on a FR schedule – it is the number of rabbits she completes which determines her pay (reinforcement). Helen's schedule is FI – the time which has elapsed since the last reinforcement is what is crucial. William is on a CRF schedule, because his mother picks him up (which reinforces crying) each time he cries. Raj is on a VI schedule, because his customers vary in terms of the interval between their receiving the bill and sending him a cheque.

10 If the behaviourists are right, then learning can only take place if behaviour is reinforced. Group

3 were not reinforced during the first 10 days, so in theory they should only start to learn the maze from day 11. We would expect their learning to show the same pattern as group 1, i.e. a gradual drop in the time taken to reach the goal box. The rapid drop in time group 3 showed suggests that they had in fact learned something about the maze in the initial stage of the experiment, even though they were not reinforced for doing so.

11 An animal's behaviour in the wild has to be fairly flexible. A lot of animals are territorial and don't stray far, but they don't follow exactly the same route between places all the time. If there are places where they are likely to find food or can hide from predators, they need to be able to find their way there from wherever they happen to be. Flexible behaviour is therefore adaptive, in helping to ensure that animal's survival.

12 In a standard classical conditioning framework, a particular response (e.g. salivation) is made to occur to a different stimulus (e.g. bell instead of food). The response, in other words, remains the same, so this theory cannot really explain what happens in the situation shown in figure 6 where the UCR is different from the CR.

But this behaviour can easily be explained by cognitive behaviourism. The rat has learned an S–S association between tone and shock; the tone is a predictor of shock, and this information allows the rat to respond flexibly according to what is possible. In response to the CS of the tone, it will escape if possible, and otherwise flinch. In the same way, Pavlov's experiments could be explained in terms of an S–S bond between bell and food: the dog learns to expect food when it hears the bell.

13 In operant conditioning, an association is formed between behaviour and its consequences. A cognitive behavourist would say that what is being strengthened here is the expectancy that behaviour will be followed by particular consequences: the behaviour is a predictor of the consequences. This could help to explain why a variable ratio schedule of reinforcement is so resistant to extinction; because the predictability of the reinforcer is lessened, the expectation that reinforcement will still occur is strengthened.

14 The behaviour that the pigs were showing was never reinforced, and should therefore have been extinguished. At the same time, appropriate behaviour – dropping the first coin into the container – was not repeated with the second coin in spite of being reinforced.

Pigs root for food; you may have heard of pigs being used in France to root up truffles. Rooting is a fixed action pattern (FAP), i.e. a genetically preprogrammed sequence of behaviour released by the presence of food. Since food was being used as a reinforcer, the coins the pigs had to carry were associated with food; they were behaving towards the coins as if they were food. The Brelands called this tendency, for the animal to revert to behaviour typical of its species, **instinctive drift**.

15 One of the things you may have noticed was that the association was formed in spite of the nausea reaction only being produced a considerable time after the rat had drunk the saccharin solution. This is a challenge to the idea of temporal contiguity which is important in conditioning. Secondly, although the association was formed to saccharin, it was not formed to the other stimuli presented at the same time, since the rat drank the plain water even though it was paired with the bell and the light. Since all three were presented simultaneously, the disgust reaction should have been shown to all three. Finally, the rats learned the saccharin–illness association even though they only experienced one pairing. You will remember that in Pavlov's experiments, repeated exposure to the bell paired with food was necessary to strengthen the S–R bond between food and salivation.

16 Given the length of time it took the chimpanzees to develop appropriate behaviour, it is possible that this was a simple case of learning by association. The animals had learned to associate reinforcement (i.e. food) with different behaviours (i.e. pointing to the full or empty container) when different trainers were present.

17 **a** Melton could have been deliberately deceiving the adults into thinking a predator was approaching to avoid punishment. On the other hand, he might have spotted something – not noticed by the human observers – which he thought was a predator.

b It is possible that the female chimpanzee had deliberately positioned herself in relation to the rock, with the understanding that what she was doing could not be seen by the leader. However, her choice of position may just have been a coincidence.

Animal cognition

In this chapter we will be looking at:

21.1 Animal navigation
    Landmarks
    The sun
    Magnetism
    Stars
    Other possibilities
    Learning in migration

21.2 Animal communication and language
    Signalling systems in non-human
        animals
    Evolutionary development of
        signals
    Studies of natural animal
        communication systems
    Is communication in non-human
        animals 'language'?
    Attempts to teach language to
        non-human animals
    Attempts to teach language to
        non-human primates
    Naturalistic language acquisition
        in chimps

21.3 Memory in non-human animals
    Memory in navigation
    Memory in foraging

Cognition refers to mental processes such as thinking and remembering. It can be contrasted with the purely automatic response learning described in conditioning theory, discussed in chapter 20, where mental processes are not thought to be necessary in explaining behaviour. In this chapter we will be looking at the kinds of cognitive processes of which animals are capable, and the role that cognition plays in some aspects of their behaviour.

21.1 ANIMAL NAVIGATION

Animal navigation includes homing and migration. **Homing** can be defined as an animal's ability to return from a distance to its nest or burrow, or loft in the case of pigeons. **Migration** is the long-distance seasonal mass movement of members of a species. We will be concerned here with the extent to which cognitive processes are involved in these abilities, and the nature of these processes.

The distances involved in homing and migration vary enormously between different species. For example, homing pigeons have been known to cover more than 600 miles in one day. A Manx shearwater gull was tagged as travelling over 3000 miles from Boston to its home in South Wales, while the albatross covers over 4000 miles. The Arctic tern spends 2 weeks at the North Pole, slightly longer at the South Pole, and spends the rest of the year travelling between the two. At the other end of the scale, zooplankton move 1–2 metres vertically within a lake, according to the time of day.

Animals which have an established nest or burrow need to find it again because it provides protection against predators and a safe place to rear young. But what are the reasons for migration?

Activity 1: explaining migration

What reasons are there for birds and other animals to migrate?

Use your answers to think about a second question: what could trigger migration?

When you have finished, see the notes on page 593.

Successive generations of a particular species follow the same migratory pattern. They cover the same distance in the same direction, often without any opportunity to learn when and where to go. This suggests that migratory behaviour is **endogenous**: it is innate and unlearned. However, as we shall see later, there may also sometimes be a learned element.

A key issue here is what information animals use for successful homing and migration. In the next section, we will look at some of the main ideas which have been put forward, including the use of landmarks, light, magnetism, the stars and infrasound.

- Many animals have a **homing** ability. Many also **migrate** at the appropriate season.
- Migration can be for personal **survival** or for **breeding** purposes. It is triggered by environmental changes and is largely **endogenous**.
- Several **sources of information** for homing and migration have been proposed.

Landmarks

One theory, focusing particularly on the homing behaviour of pigeons, has proposed that they make use of landmarks to return to their lofts. There is some anecdotal evidence to support this idea. For example, pigeon fanciers have found that homing behaviour is helped if pigeons are allowed to explore the area round their loft.

Early in his career, Watson (whom you read about in chapter 1, in the section on behaviourism) carried out a study of colonies of sooty terns on the Tortuga islands, just off the Florida Keys. Each female tern builds a nest in the sand dunes. Watson was interested in how each tern found her nest after returning from hunting for food. In a series of experiments, he moved the nest sideways or vertically, or removed details of the surroundings. He concluded that each tern used a series of landmarks on the ground to locate its own nest, had a fixed landing place, and followed an unchanging route back to its nest.

A study of digger wasps suggests that the use of landmarks in navigation is not only true of birds:

Box A: Tinbergen and Kruyt (1938)

Procedure: A circle of 20 pine cones was arranged around the burrow of a digger wasp. While the wasp was away, the circle of pine cones was moved to a different spot.

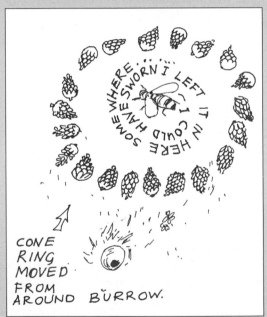

Results: On its return, the wasp tried to locate the burrow within the circle of pine cones.

Conclusion: Digger wasps make use of landmarks in locating their burrows.

In an interesting variation of this study, Van Beusekom (1948) again used a circle of pine cones, but also arranged cones in a square and an ellipse. Wasps tried to locate the burrow within the circle and the ellipse equally often, but ignored the square. The wasps were showing **generalisation** to the ellipse, and **discrimination** to the square. This suggests that their use of the information the pine cones provided was not precise, but sufficient to be useful in most situations found in the wild.

However, there are limitations to the usefulness of landmarks. Keeton (1974) found that pigeons had no problem homing from a distance of 50 miles, from where no relevant landmarks would be visible. That landmarks are not essential in homing behaviour has been tested even more rigorously:

"They could not have learned much about the route while they were deeply asleep."

Box B: Schlichte and Schmidt-Koenig (1971)

Procedure: Homing pigeons were fitted with frosted contact lenses, which allowed light to enter, but meant that landmarks could only be identified from a distance of 6 metres. They were then released 80 miles from home.

Results: Most pigeons flew in the correct direction for home. Some did not reach the loft itself, but arrived close to it.

Conclusion: Landmarks are not a major factor in pigeons' homing behaviour. If they are important, the pigeons could have been expected to fly *to* the loft, rather than *near* it.

It has been suggested that pigeons home by retracing a route they have learned while being transported to the release point, using landmarks to guide them. Walcott and Schmidt-Koenig (1973) demonstrated that this could not be the case by anaesthetising pigeons during the outward journey. They still homed, but could not have learned much about the route while they were deeply asleep. In any case, pigeons taken to the same place on more than one occasion do not choose the same route home each time.

A further possibility is that **bico-ordinate navigation** – using information about the relative position of two different landmarks (e.g. a church tower and a TV mast) – is used. However, there is no evidence that this method is actually used, so it is possible rather than likely. It would help to explain homing over unfamiliar territory, but would still not explain the ability to do this over hundreds of miles.

It seems likely that pigeons use landmarks to locate the loft in the final part of their journey home, but they must also have some other source of information to be able to cover long distances. One possibility is the position of the sun, and we shall look at this in the next section.

⊖ Animals may use **landmarks** in homing behaviour. However, pigeons are still able to home when landmark information is not available. The use of landmarks does not explain homing over long distances.

⊖ It has been shown that pigeons do not depend on **retracing** the outward route.

⊖ **Bico-ordinate navigation** is a possible explanation, but does not explain navigation across very long distances.

The sun

Kramer (1952) put forward the **map and compass hypothesis**. Animals must have an internal map which tells them in which direction home lies. For this to be useful, they would also need the equivalent of a compass, so that the map information can be converted into a bearing that relates to the environment in which they find themselves. For example, if the map component tells a pigeon that home is due west, it would then need to use the compass to tell it in which direction it should fly. One possible source of information which could act as a compass in this way is the sun.

Let us look at this in relation to the homing behaviour of pigeons. When the pigeon is released, it would observe the position of the sun. This would need to be co-ordinated with the time of day; the pigeon would get this information from its internal body clock (you can read about body clocks in chapter 12 in the section on bodily rhythms). The body clock is set by the cycle of light and dark. It therefore follows that if the pigeon's internal body clock is disrupted by manipulating its exposure to light and dark, its ability to home should be affected:

There is still a problem with this explanation of homing, because pigeons also home when it is overcast, and have even been known to do so when it is dark. However, conditioning experiments have shown that they are receptive to both **polarised** and **ultraviolet light**, to which humans are insensitive. Polarised light produces patterns which radiate from the sun, and is more noticeable in ultraviolet than in other wavelengths of light. The ability to perceive polarised light would be useful for navigation, as it would allow the sun to be located in overcast conditions, provided there is some blue sky. Von Frisch (1950) found the same sensitivity to polarised light in bees. Light, including polarised and ultra-violet light, is certainly used by animals to navigate. However, the fact that they can also navigate in the dark means that light is not the only aid to navigation.

Magnetism

Another possibility is that the magnetic properties of the earth could aid navigation. The geomagnetic field varies slightly from one location to another, and

Box C: Keeton (1969)

Procedure: In a clock-shift experiment, pigeons were kept for a while in an environment where lights were put on at midday and off at midnight. If we assume that dawn is at 6 am, this means that the pigeon's body clock was moved ahead 6 hours. They were released at 9am (when their body clock would tell them it was 3 pm).
Results: The pigeons flew at a 90-degree angle from the appropriate angle for home.
Conclusion: The sun moves through an angle of 15 degrees every hour and the pigeons' body clock was moved forward 6 hours. This corresponds to the 90-degree error in direction made by the pigeons: the pigeons inferred that the sun was in the south-west when in fact it was in the south-east. Pigeons use the position of the sun and information from their internal body clock in homing.

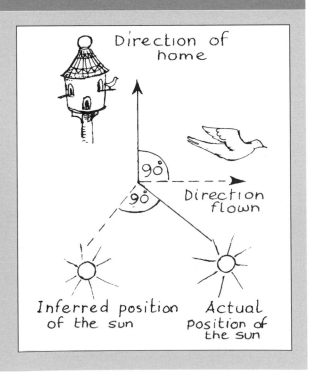

it could be that some animals are responsive to these variations. Magnetism would have the advantage of being a relatively stable form of information, largely unaffected by changes in the weather.

Walcott *et al.* (1979) found that pigeons have a structure between the brain and the skull which includes a substance called **magnetite** which is sensitive to magnetism, so potentially they have the ability to use information about the earth's magnetic field on overcast days or at night. Magnetite has also been found in the yellow fin tuna, which migrates for long distances, and in the abdomen of some bees, which also home. But can pigeons detect magnetic fields?

Box D: Bookman (1978)

Procedure: Pigeons were held at one end of a tunnel, which was surrounded by coils which could induce a magnetic field. At the other end of the tunnel were two boxes. The presence or absence of a magnetic field indicated which box contained food.
Results: Pigeons learned to use the magnetic field information to go to the box which contained food.
Conclusion: Pigeons can detect magnetism and use this information appropriately.

A curious finding of this study was that pigeons only showed this learning in pairs. There doesn't seem any very obvious explanation for this! It should also be noted that attempts to replicate this study have often been unsuccessful.

However, there is some evidence that magnetism may have a part to play in homing. Keeton (1974) fitted small magnetic coils to pigeons' heads, and found that this interfered with homing on overcast days. There was no effect on sunny days, presumably because the pigeons were then able to use the sun to navigate. Gould (1982) also found that homing was less successful when there was a magnetic storm, which distorts information normally supplied by magnetic fields.

Keeton concluded that pigeons have dual or maybe even multiple compass ability; they use the sun if possible, and if not, the earth's magnetic field.

Young pigeons use a magnetic compass, but learn to use the sun. The magnetic compass can then be used as a backup system.

Multiple compass use does not only apply to pigeons. This has been shown in **cue conflict experiments**, where different sources of information are available, which provide contradictory cues. The set of cues to which an animal responds tells us which is the preferred source of information. For example, the dunnock's preferred source of information is the earth's magnetic field, while robins prefer polarised light.

It seems likely that pigeons have a magnetic sense, but are poor at learning to apply it in conditioning experiments; in the wild, change in the magnetic field would not normally be associated with food. This can be linked to the idea of **preparedness**, discussed in relation to the **Garcia effect** (chapter 20, box I). Rats formed associations between saccharin and nausea, since in the wild nausea could well be the result of eating something unusual, but did not form an association between nausea and either light or noise, associations which would not normally occur.

Studies of turtles by Lohmann (1992) have demonstrated that the earth's magnetic field is one source of information they use to find their way out to sea after hatching, and back to the beach where they were born when it is time to breed. Lohmann also suggested that the ability to detect magnetic fields could be a basis for the 'map' component of Kramer's map and compass hypothesis. Several geomagnetic features vary consistently and predictably in such a way that they could be used in determining position.

The Earth's magnetic field may be one source of information turtles use to find their way out to sea after hatching.

⊙ Kramer has proposed a **map and compass hypothesis**. It is possible that the **sun** may act as a compass. Pigeons' sensitivity to **polarised light** would allow this information to be used on overcast days.

⊙ Pigeons and other animals are also responsive to **magnetism**. There is some evidence that magnetism is used in navigation.

Stars

Since navigation can take place at night, it has been suggested that the stars may give navigational information. Emlen (1970) carried out a study of indigo buntings, which live in North America. They fly south in the autumn and north in the spring. Before their migration, they build up deposits of fat and become restless. This restlessness is called **Zugunruhe**, a German word meaning 'migratory restlessness'. If they are kept in cages at this time, they orient themselves in the direction in which they migrate:

Box E: Emlen (1970)

Procedure: Indigo buntings were kept in cages in an aviary, cut off from their normal environment, but with the same light/dark cycle as outside. They were then divided into three groups. Group 1 stayed in the aviary. Group 2 was moved to a planetarium, and was exposed to stars rotating round the normal north/south axis. Group 3 was also moved to the planetarium, but was exposed to stars rotating round a different axis. All three groups were then tested in cages in the planetarium, with the stars motionless.

Results: The Zugunruhe orientation of group 1 was basically haphazard. Group 2 oriented themselves towards the south. Group 3 oriented themselves according to the rotation they had observed.

Conclusion: In indigo buntings, exposure to the stars is essential for successful migration. The movement of the stars is also important.

What kind of information are these birds getting from the stars? The apparent movement of the stars is due to the earth's rotation, so there is more apparent movement at the equator than at the poles. In the northern hemisphere, then, less movement indicates north. As indigo buntings migrate south, they would need to fly in the direction where there is more apparent movement.

It is perhaps worth noting that many species cross the equator when they migrate, which means they would also need to learn to respond to new constellations. In the southern hemisphere when flying south, orientation would need to change towards the stars which move least. This suggests that if the stars are used for migration, a different kind of compass would need to be used initially, with the stars being used only in the latter part of migration.

Other possibilities

Changes in air pressure produce sound. This can travel thousands of kilometres without distortion. For example, the sonic boom from Concorde has been recorded over a distance of 1000km. **Infrasound** refers to very low-frequency sound which is below the threshold at which humans can detect it, but pigeons have been shown to respond to it in conditioning experiments. When pelicans migrate, they need to find twisting columns of hot air called thermals to carry them on their way. Thermals create a storm of infrasound, which helps the birds to locate them. However, the problem with infrasound is that it is affected by interference, such as by wind or turbulence. Since this would make it an unreliable source of information, it doesn't seem likely that it would be used as the sole source of information for navigation.

Papi *et al.* (1978) suggested that **smell** may also be a source of navigational information. Pigeons may have the ability to build up complex **olfactory maps** which they can use to orient themselves towards home. There has been some fairly convincing evidence to support this idea, but it has not always been replicated. In addition, pigeons' ability to distinguish natural air (which would carry smells) from filtered air is still open to question.

It has also been suggested (Hasler, 1960) that salmon may use the sun to reach the home river mouth, but then use smell, learned as a form of **imprinting**, to find the exact tributary where they were hatched. (Imprinting is discussed in chapter 3.)

▷ Activity 2: evaluating sources of navigational information

Reread Kramer's map and compass hypothesis. From the research outlined above, what conclusions would you draw to explain:

a what animals can use as the map

b what they can use as a compass

When you have finished, see the notes on page 594.

⊖ The **stars**, **smell** and **infrasound** are possible sources of navigational information.

⊖ It is likely that more than one source of information is used. Animals differ in terms of which they are able to use, and which they prefer to use.

Learning in migration

While homing by definition includes an element of learning, migratory behaviour, as noted earlier, must be endogenous. The Atlantic salmon makes its journey to a European lake to spawn only once, so there is no possibility that this is learned behaviour.

This has been further demonstrated in finches. Two varieties of black-cap finches both spend the winter in Africa. Of these, the Finnish black-cap finch spends the summer in Finland, while the Canary Island black-cap finch spends the summer in the Canary Islands. Migration is therefore a much longer journey for the Finnish variety. If the two varieties are crossed, the hybrid offspring is an intermediate distance flier, which flies a distance halfway between that of the two parent birds. The distance flown in migration by black-cap finches is therefore entirely genetically preprogrammed.

At the same time, there is some evidence that homing and migratory behaviour can be modified by learning:

Box F: Perdeck (1958)

Procedure: Starlings were captured at their breeding grounds on the Baltic, as they were about to migrate to the north coast of France and the south coast of England for the winter. They were released in Switzerland, 500 miles away.

Results: The young birds flew in the direction which would have been appropriate at the place where they were captured. However, the adult birds altered their course to compensate for the new start point (see figure 1).

Conclusion: Adult birds can use information acquired on previous migrations to adapt their migratory behaviour.

Figure 1: adapting migratory behaviour (Perdeck, 1958)

There has also been anecdotal evidence of learned behaviour of this kind in pigeons. They have often been observed travelling on the London Underground, with Fulham Broadway and Parson's Green apparently being favoured stopping-off points, and Putney Bridge as well if it is low water. They have also been known to hitch a lift on boats in the Channel which are headed in the right direction.

Homing and migration, then, are not totally inflexible behaviours. However, this is an area where our information is far from complete.

○ There may also be a **learned** element in migratory behaviour.

21.2 ANIMAL COMMUNICATION AND LANGUAGE

In this section, we will be looking at the various ways in which non-human animals communicate. A controversial issue here is whether any examples of animal communication can be called language. One method of investigating this has been to look at naturally-occurring examples of animal comm-unication. The problem with this approach, of course, is that we cannot always know exactly what

animals are communicating to each other. For this reason, some researchers have attempted to teach animals to communicate with humans. We will be looking at some of their findings in the final part of this section in order to shed further light on the language issue.

Signalling systems in non-human animals

Communication takes place when a **message** is passed from a **signaller** to a **receiver**. There are many ways in which this can be done:

▷ ## Activity 3: methods of communication

How do we communicate? Think of as many different ways as you can in which we pass information to each other.
When you have finished, see the notes on page 594.

Like humans, animals too use a range of ways of communicating. Some of their methods have parallels with human communication – look back through what you have noted for activity 3 as you read through this next section – but they also use other kinds of senses which do not seem to exist, or are far less important, in humans.

Visual communication is quite common. For example, the display of the peacock signals courtship to a female. Many animals have ways of making themselves seem as large as possible when facing an aggressor, e.g. the pilomotor response in domestic cats, where their fur stands on end. Colour may also be used. Lack (1943) found that territorial aggression in robins was triggered by seeing the red breast of an intruder.

Olfactory communication (i.e. using smell) is also common. For example, scent plays a role in the mutual recognition of a mother goat and her kid. As another example, many animals, including cats, mark their territory using scent markers. A further kind of olfactory communication is provided by **pheromones**, chemicals which affect the hormone system of the receiver. They are widely used by animals, and are often linked to sexual communication. For example, Melrose *et al.* (1971) found that sows exposed to a particular pheromone immediately assumed the position for mating. Some moths can detect pheromones released by a potential mate at a distance of several miles.

As with humans, touch is also used. One example of **tactile communication** is used by the male of one species of spider, in which the male is eaten by the female. He strokes the female to indicate that he wishes to mate, so that she becomes receptive and won't eat him. Lawick-Goodall (1974) noted that the contact chimpanzees make while they are grooming each other can have the effect of calming animals who have been fighting.

A lot of animal communication uses **sound**:

◗ Activity 4: auditory communication

What kinds of advantages might sound offer as a communication medium? You might find it useful to compare sound with the other forms of communication described in this section, picking up on any drawbacks they might have which would not apply to sound.

When you have finished, see the notes on page 594.

⊖ Communication takes place when a **message** is passed from **signaller** to **receiver**.

⊖ Animals use various forms of communication: **visual**, **olfactory** (including **pheromones**), **tactile** and **auditory**. Auditory communication has many advantages and is widespread.

Evolutionary development of signals

Many signals given by animals are relatively **stereotyped**. It is possible that each action on the part of the signaller may trigger appropriate behaviour in the receiver, and vice versa. There is some support for this idea:

Box G: Tinbergen (1951)

Procedure: The courtship and mating display of sticklebacks was observed.
Results: The behaviour of both male and female follows a stereotypical pattern. The male does a zig-zag dance in front of the female. This induces her to deposit her

---

unfertilised eggs in his nest. When she has done this, he swims over and fertilises them. If at any point this pattern is not followed, the interaction is broken off.

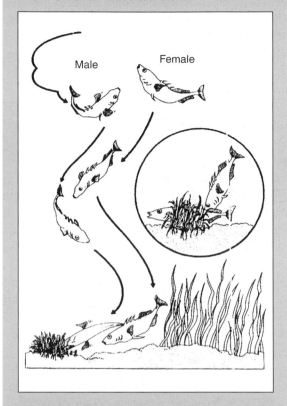

Male   Female

Conclusion: There is some evidence that both male and female act in response to the behaviour of their partner.

To understand what is happening here, we need to look briefly at some terms used in ethology:

Figure 2: ethological terms

fixed action pattern (FAP)	a sequence of innate behaviour
innate releasing mechanism (IRM)	hypothetical mechanism which opens the gate which holds back a specific drive, such as mating behaviour
sign stimulus	an aspect of an animal which causes a response in another animal

In the Tinbergen study, the zig-zag dance of the male is an FAP. This acts as a sign stimulus for the female which unlocks the gate of egg-laying behaviour (the IRM), and induces her to deposit her eggs. Similarly, the egg-laying behaviour of the female is an FAP, which acts as a sign stimulus for the male, releasing the behaviour of fertilising the eggs. In evolutionary terms, this ritual element in behaviour may contribute to individual fitness in terms of the survival of the individual and successful mating.

It is also possible that the ritualistic nature of this kind of behaviour provides an opportunity for each partner to become aware of the characteristics of the other. This could help in preventing cross-breeding between related species; a member of a different species would simply not make the correct moves, and so mating would not take place. A further reason may be that this kind of closed system is very difficult for outsiders to break into and use for their own ends.

Similar kinds of signalling rituals often take place in **conflict** situations. When red stags compete with each other for females, the two animals start the contest by roaring at each other. If the defender of a group of females can roar faster, the intruder usually retreats. This part of the contest sends the signal: 'I am in good physical shape'. If the challenger matches the defender in roaring, or outroars him, the next stage involves a parallel walk. Presumably this stage allows the two animals to assess each other's strength at close quarters, and withdraw or continue with the contest on the basis of what they have seen; many fights end at this point. The final stage involves interlocking antlers and pushing. If the contest has got as far as this final stage, there is a good chance that both animals will be injured. The earlier stages provide opportunities to bring the conflict to a close, avoiding the costs of loss of life or serious injury.

Many species also show **appeasement gestures**. These are gestures which express vulnerability and 'switch off' aggression in an attacker. For example, in one species of jackdaw the nape of the neck is a very vulnerable area, and clearly marked off from the rest of the body by its plumage. When this part of the body is offered to an attacker, aggression stops instantly. These kinds of signals serve a similar

Red stags in each of the three stages of conflict: roaring, parallel walk, interlocking antlers

Appeasement response of submissive dog

purpose as the roaring and parallel walk in stags: serious harm is usually avoided.

All the signals described so far are **honest signals**; they provide accurate information to the receiver. Sometimes, however, **deceptive signals** may be sent. An individual, in order to win a fight, may signal a willingness to fight in the hope that the prospective opponent will back off. This is a risky strategy, because the bluff may be called, and a fight may lead to injury or even death; however, if it works, it does so at very low cost. For example, lower tones in the call of male cricket frogs are associated with larger frogs. Wagner (1992) found that males may lower the tone of their call to give the impression that they are larger (and therefore stronger) than they actually are.

Dishonest signalling is also common in **predator–prey** situations. For example, hoverflies mimic wasps, signalling to predators that they are dangerous, and so avoiding attack.

- Many animals show **stereotypical** ritualised behaviour in **courtship** and **conflict** situations.
- These kinds of behaviour may have developed to contribute to evolutionary **fitness** in terms of survival and successful mating.
- In some situations, particularly in **conflict** or **predator–prey** situations, **deceptive signals** are sent. These can be successful low-cost strategies, but also carry some risk.

Studies of natural animal communication systems

We have discussed briefly the different kinds of signals that animals give and receive. We will now look a little more closely at systems used by different kinds of species, which have been of particular interest to researchers into the nature of animal communication, and the extent to which this communication can be considered to be language: bees, birds, cetaceans (i.e. whales and dolphins) and non-human primates.

Communication in bees

A swarm of bees consists of a queen, male drones and worker bees. The worker bees are sterile females. One of their tasks is to locate sources of food, and bring it back to the hive. When they find a rich source of food, they need the help of other bees. Worker bees perform a **bee dance** to communicate to other workers the distance and direction of food sources. This dance was first observed and written about by von Frisch (1950).

When she comes back to the hive, the worker gives the food she has collected to the other bees, and then performs a dance on the vertical surface of a comb. If the food source is relatively close, within 50–100m of the hive, this will be a round dance. The bee stays on the spot, and turns once to the left, once to the right, and so on for half a minute or so (see figure 3a).

When the source of food is further away, the bee performs a waggle dance. This involves running a short distance while waggling the abdomen, then turning a full circle to the left back to the starting point. This is repeated to the right, then left again, and so on. In repeating this routine, a figure-of-eight pattern is created (see figure 3b).

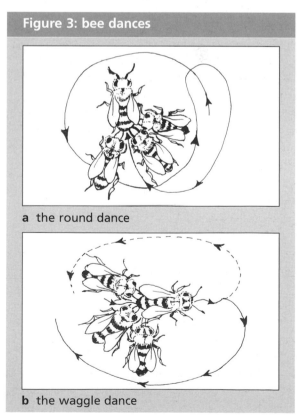

Figure 3: bee dances

a the round dance

b the waggle dance

If the food source is close by, there is no real need to communicate the direction in which other bees will need to fly in order to locate it. If it is further away, this is clearly essential information, so how do the bees use the dance to communicate how far away a food source is? On the basis of his observations of 3885 dances, Von Frisch found that the closer the source was to the hive, the more turns were included in the dance. This relationship between distance and turns is shown in figure 4:

Figure 4: the relationship between the number of turns in the waggle dance and the distance of the food source (adapted from Von Frisch, 1950)

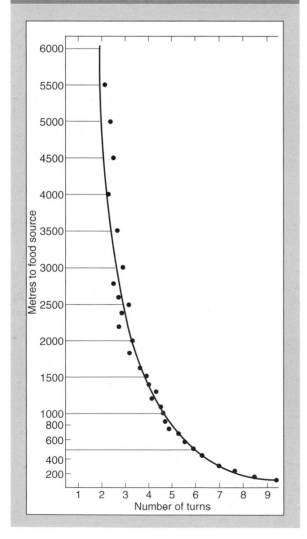

The way that direction is communicated is even more intriguing. The dance is carried out on the vertical surface of the hive, with the waggle part of the dance always at a constant angle. The size of this angle from the vertical corresponds exactly to the angle between the sun and the source of food. This is shown in figure 5:

Figure 5: the relationship between the angle of the dance and the direction of the food source

The angle between the orientation of the dance and the vertical is the same as that between the sun and the food source, as measured at the entrance to the hive.

There are still some aspects of the dance that we don't fully understand. It is thought that the liveliness of the dance indicates how rich the food source is. Bees also make small sounds during the waggle part of the dance, and bees ignore dancers who do not make these sounds, so it seems likely that sound forms part of the total message.

🖙 **Bees** communicate the distance and direction of food sources in a **dance**. The **number of turns** in the dance indicates the **distance**. The **angle** of the dance shows the **direction**.

Birdsong

Two of the main uses of birdsong are to defend territory and to attract a mate. Some birds use it for one purpose only, and some for both. It can also be used for a variety of other purposes, e.g. so that birds can identify their mates, and to warn that there is a predator about. In this section we will look at the song of chaffinches.

Bright (1984) identified 16 different kinds of song in the chaffinch which serve a range of purposes. Some of these calls are only heard at particular stages of the life-cycle. There are also regional variations, so that chaffinch songs in one area are different from those in another.

The existence of regional variations suggests that there is an element of learning in birdsong. At the same time, this does not rule out the possibility that birdsong is to a large extent innate. This possibility has been tested experimentally:

Box H: Slater (1981)

Procedure: Chaffinches were hand-reared in isolation so that they could not hear the song of any wild birds.

Results: The birdsong which developed was very different from that of normal chaffinch song. One of the chaffinches heard a wild sparrow outside the laboratory, and copied the sparrow's song.

Conclusion: Chaffinches are genetically predisposed to develop song, but the nature of that song is affected by exposure to other birds. The imitation of the sparrow suggests that chaffinches are strongly motivated to imitate.

These findings are similar to those of Thorp in the 1940s. He noted that chaffinches develop regional 'dialects', and therefore reasoned that there must be both an innate and a learned component in the chaffinch's song. He isolated a baby chaffinch, and waited until the following year, when the innate component of the song was produced. This was a very basic, abbreviated version of the normal chaffinch song. He also discovered that there was a critical period, during which a young bird needed to be exposed to an adult song if it were to produce a normal song later in life.

Some parallels can be drawn between birdsong and human language, e.g. the tendency to imitate and the transmission of dialects. It has also been found (Marler, 1991) that both birdsong and human speech are most readily acquired when young, with human infants acquiring the phonology of language from the age of about seven months.

- **Birdsong** seems to be **genetically pre-programmed**, but there is an element of **learning** in the song.
- Birdsong shows **regional variations**.

Cetaceans

Cetaceans are aquatic mammals, i.e. dolphins and whales. These animals produce a variety of sounds which can travel a long way through water. It has been suggested that whale song can be picked up by other whales several hundred miles away.

Humpback whales seem to sing only during the breeding season. They have complex songs which last up to half an hour, and are then repeated. Continuous singing lasting 22 hours has been recorded; the observation was brought to an end at this point, so it is possible that the song may have lasted longer.

Groups of whales sing the same song, with variations included over time, so that the song at the end of the season is different from that at the beginning. The elements of one year's song provide the basis for developing a new song the following year.

The song seems to have some social function. Tyack (1983) observed that a singing whale, swimming alone, would often be approached by a non-singing whale. They would swim together for a while. Then the original whale would swim away and the newcomer would take up the song.

The song may also play a part in courtship. Tyack (1981) observed on several occasions a singing male whale approaching a female with a young calf.

Sometimes the singing whale was allowed to join them, and the two adult whales would dive together for short periods, possibly to mate. At other times the female would swim away from the singer. If this kind of group swam into the path of another singing male, this new whale would try to displace the original escort. Other whales would gather round them, making a range of calls, including fragments of song.

As well as singing, whales make a range of other noises, particularly when a group of whales is engaged in a co-operative activity. An example of such an activity is bubble-net fishing, where whales create a 'net' of bubbles to trap fish, gradually drawing the net in.

Dolphins also make a range of sounds, including whistles, chirps, squeaks and rattles. Like whale sounds, the sounds which dolphins make also seem to serve a social purpose. For example, Norris and Dahl (1980) found that dolphins whistled and called to each other before moving off in a group to hunt. They also seem to whistle to each other a lot when feeding, or when they come across something unusual.

Whistling can also be a distress signal:

▶ Activity 5: signalling in dolphins

Bright (1984) described playing back to other members of the group the sounds made by a dolphin being captured. They immediately swam away quickly. Dolphins from another group showed no such response, but only curiosity.

What conclusions about dolphin communication can be drawn from:

a the response of members of the same group?
b the response of members of the different group?

When you have finished, see the notes on page 594.

Dolphins may also communicate quite complex information:

Box 1: Bastian (1965)

Procedure: Two dolphins were kept in tanks where they could hear but not see each other. One dolphin was trained to press a paddle to receive a reward. The second dolphin was then tested on the task.
Results: During the training period, the dolphins made a range of sounds. When tested, the second dolphin immediately performed the task.
Conclusion: The dolphin who had been trained had transmitted relevant information about the task to the second dolphin.

It seems clear that the sounds made by both whales and dolphins have a social purpose, and dolphins seem to communicate quite complex information. Unfortunately it has not yet been possible to identify the meanings of the range of sounds which these animals produce, or the kinds of information which are being exchanged.

- ⊖ **Whales** and **dolphins** make a range of sounds. Both seem to use these sounds for **social** purposes. Whale songs may also be part of **courtship**.
- ⊖ **Dolphins** also use sounds to communicate **complex information**.
- ⊖ It has not yet been possible to identify the meanings of the particular sounds whales and dolphins make.

Non-human primates

Like humans, chimpanzees communicate emotions by facial expressions. A relaxed animal has what is known as a **play-face**, the mouth slightly open and the teeth covered by the lips. When it is frightened it shows a **fear-grin**, with the lips pulled back exposing the teeth. A nervous chimpanzee shows a closed grin, when the jaws are closed but the teeth exposed.

Chimpanzees also communicate using **eye-contact**. They avoid eye-contact if threatened, but stare if they are threatening another animal. Like many other animals, this threat display is accompanied by a threatening posture, with the animal pulling itself up to its full height with fur erect, thus presenting a very intimidating figure.

They also make a range of noises. The threat display is accompanied by a series of hoots, ending in a screech. A milder form is the **pant-hoot**, a series of hooting noises with breathing sounds in between. This pant-hoot is also used as a social signal; groups of animals make this noise as a sign of excitement. Lawick-Goodall (1974) suggested that it is also a way of locating the rest of the group, since each animal has its own variation of the pant-hoot. Grunts are used to show contentment, e.g. during grooming, or in greeting.

One study looked at whether chimpanzees could communicate to each other about absent or hidden objects:

Box J: Menzel and Halperin (1975)

Procedure: A group of young chimps was studied. One was taken out of the cage and out of sight of the others, and shown where some food was hidden. It was taken back to the cage, and the whole group released. A similar procedure was followed when a snake was hidden.

Results: Usually the chimp led the others to the food. Sometimes, however, other members of the group would run ahead, apparently looking in possible hiding places. When a snake had been hidden, one of the other chimps would pick up a stick, and poke carefully around. This behaviour was only shown when the leader was let out with the others, and in groups which had lived together for some time.

Conclusion: Chimpanzees are capable of communicating information about something not physically present. This information is limited, since they did not communicate exactly where the food or snake was hidden.

It seems, then, that communication between chimps is limited. However, it could also be argued that in the wild this kind of communication would have very little place; for example, a chimp finding food would only need to let out a series of pant-hoots to alert the others, since they would be likely to be nearby. It seems probable, as with many of the other animals we have looked at, that communication is mainly used for social purposes among chimps.

A study of social communication in vervet monkeys has investigated further the abilities of primates:

Box K: Seyfarth and Cheney (1980)

Procedure: Vervet monkeys are vulnerable to three types of predator: eagles, leopards and snakes. These monkeys have three types of alarm call, one for each type of predator. Tape-recordings were made of these calls, which were then played back to the monkey group.

EAGLE   ALARM
(CHUCKLE)

Results: Different behaviours were shown in response to each of the calls. When they heard the 'eagle' call, the monkeys would look up into the sky and hide. They climbed trees in response to the 'leopard' call, and would search the ground carefully if they heard the 'snake' call.

Conclusion: Vervet monkey calls give precise information about predators.

Seyfarth and Cheney also observed that young monkeys would sometimes make these calls inappropriately, such as giving the 'leopard' call in response to a warthog. However, the mistakes they made were always systematic; the 'leopard' call was

only ever given if a ground-based animal was sighted and never in response to a bird. This seems to suggest that young monkeys have some understanding of categories.

If a young monkey gave an alarm call, adults would repeat it if it were appropriate, but would otherwise ignore it. This suggests that there is an element of **observational learning** in giving appropriate alarms.

- Chimpanzees communicate using **facial expression**, **eye-contact** and **posture.** They also make a range of noises which serve social purposes.
- They are able to communicate information, but only in a very limited way.
- Vervet monkeys give calls to alert others to predators. There are different calls for different kinds of predator. **Observational learning** may be involved in developing accurate use of these calls.

Is communication in non-human animals 'language'?

As we have seen, animals communicate with each other in a range of ways. But can any of these communication systems be classed as a language? This of course depends on how 'language' is defined. Many definitions include the idea that language ability is specific to humans, e.g. 'the institution whereby humans communicate and interact with each other by means of habitually used oral–auditory arbitrary symbols' (Hall, 1964). However, other theorists have looked more closely at the specific characteristics by which language may be defined.

Hockett (1960) suggested thirteen (later sixteen) design features of language, i.e. criteria which he believed must be met if a communication system is to be called a language. These include some features which relate to human spoken language, but do not apply to other forms of human language. For example, his criterion of the vocal/auditory nature of language does not apply to written language, nor to American Sign Language (ASL or Ameslan), which is generally considered to be a language in its own right. It has its own grammar, and can express anything which can be communicated by spoken English.

In a reappraisal of Hockett's criteria, Aitchison (1983) focused on four of these features:

Figure 6: Aitchison's four language criteria

semanticity: the use of symbols to refer to objects or actions.

displacement: the ability to convey information about something not physically present, or removed in time.

structure dependence: this refers to the patterned nature of language, e.g. the relevance of word order. 'The man bites the dog' conveys a different meaning from 'The dog bites the man', although the same items are used in each case.

productivity: The ability to use language creatively; to produce and understand novel utterances.

Aitchison claimed that the features in figure 6 are unique to human language, but to what extent can any of them be applied to the communication systems of other animals?

▶ **Activity 6: is animal communication language?**

Look back through the sections on bees, birds, cetaceans and primates. Do the communications of any of these animals meet any of Aitchison's criteria?

Draw out a table listing the four kinds of animals and Aitchison's four features:

	semanticity	displacement	structure dependence	productivity
bees				
birds				
cetaceans				
primates				

Note in each cell whether the criterion applies, and if it does, give an example of behaviour to illustrate it.

When you have finished, see the notes on page 594.

The main problem in studying natural animal communication to assess whether or not animals can be said to have language is that it has been impossible to translate what messages are being communicated. For this reason, psychologists have also made attempts to teach animals to communicate directly with us. This approach will not of course tell us much about how animals communicate naturally, but it can help to indicate whether some animals may have the potential for language. This question has been of particular interest to researchers aiming to test Chomsky's assertion that humans have a species-specific **language acquisition device (LAD)** which, if it exists in the way Chomsky claimed, would by definition mean that animals could not be said to have language. (Chomsky's theory of language is discussed in chapter 16.) We shall look at some of these studies in the next section.

- Hockett defined language in terms of 13 criteria, some of which can only apply to spoken human language. Aitchison identified **semanticity**, **displacement**, **structure dependence** and **productivity** as being crucial.
- Some forms of natural animal communication show some of these features, but none show them all.
- Because we cannot understand animal communication, there have been several attempts to teach language to non-human animals. These studies have the aim of showing whether animals have the potential to acquire language.

Attempts to teach language to non-human animals

There have been several projects aimed at teaching animals to communicate with us. Many of these have used primates, but we will look first at two other studies, one which attempted to train a parrot, and one involving a dolphin.

Box L: Pepperburg (1983)

Procedure: Alex, an African grey parrot, was taught the names of objects. His trainer used a colleague as a model. While the parrot could see both of them, Pepperburg would hold up an item and ask the colleague to name it. If he replied correctly, he would be praised and given the item to eat or to play with. The procedure was repeated with Alex, using the same kinds of reinforcement. The training was extended to include concepts such as colour and shape. Alex was tested on this by being shown, say, a red square, and asked either what colour or what shape it was.

Results: Alex learned in this way to identify and ask for over 50 items. He also learned to put them into categories, e.g. 'fruit'. He correctly answered questions on colour and shape significantly more often than would be expected by chance. Alex was eager to take part; Pepperburg noted that the social aspect of the model's involvement in the procedure seemed to be important in motivating him.

Conclusion: Alex showed some ability to learn language. His ability to learn concepts, such as the category of 'fruit', suggests that this was not just straightforward stimulus–response learning.

A further study investigated the understanding of grammatical language in a dolphin:

Box M: Herman *et al.* (1984)

Procedure: A dolphin called Akeakamai was trained, by means of gestures made by the trainer at the side of the pool, to understand and respond to two- and three-word sentences. (Some examples of the gestures used and the kinds of instructions given are shown in figure 7.) The expected response depended on the order of the signals she was given. For example, 'Pipe hoop fetch' meant 'Take the hoop to the pipe', while 'Hoop pipe fetch' meant 'Take the pipe to the hoop'. She was tested with a large number of sentences using items in novel combinations which she had never heard before. She was also tested on a four-word sentence.

Results: Akeakamai's level of correct responses to the instructions she was given was very much higher than could be expected by chance.

Conclusion: This dolphin showed considerable skill in language comprehension. She showed the ability to learn and apply grammatical rules in the understanding of instructions.

Figure 7: sample gestures and instruction used with Akeakamai

tail-touch   mouth   left   water

2-word: basket toss (throw the basket)

3-word: left person mouth (touch the person on your left with your mouth)

4-word: ball right frisbee fetch (take the frisbee on your right to the ball)

Activity 7: dolphin communication

Read through the study in box M and answer these questions:

1 Why do you think the order in which gestures were made was important in this study?

2 Why was Akeakamai tested on a four-word sequence?

3 Why was she tested on novel combinations of gestures?

4 How might this study be extended to test for displacement?

5 Why is this study limited as an investigation of whether dolphins have language?

Compare your answers with the discussion which follows.

You will remember the term **structure dependence** from the earlier discussion of features of language. Observations of animals in their natural habitat don't allow us to draw any firm conclusions about whether their communications have this feature. The inclusion in this study of instructions which are identical except for word order allows us to put it to the test.

This dolphin was capable of responding to this kind of rule. The response to a four-word sentence shows that she was able to extend the basic principles of the two- and three-word sequences she had been trained on.

Testing on novel combinations means that the animal cannot be forming simple stimulus–response bonds. We can therefore be reasonably confident that her comprehension fulfils the criterion of **semanticity**.

The study was in fact extended to test for **displacement**. Perhaps you thought of some of the tests that were actually used. On some trials, the instruction related to an item which was hidden from view (**spatial displacement**) and which had to be found so that the instruction could be carried out. On other trials, the instruction was given up to 30 seconds before the object was put in the pool (**temporal displacement**). Neither of these conditions caused any difficulty. In another variation, the instruction related to a missing item.

Akeakamai would spend some time searching for it and then stop, ignoring the other objects.

Akeakamai's performance is impressive. The problem is, of course, that dolphins can only demonstrate comprehension. Production is of equal importance, and dolphins are not suited to this kind of test. For this reason, most attempts to teach animals to communicate with us have used primates. It is these studies which we will consider next.

- Pepperberg's parrot Alex showed some ability to communicate with humans. He could identify, ask for and categorise items.
- Akeakamai the dolphin gave evidence of **semanticity**, **structure dependence** and **displacement** in responding to gestures. This study was limited by being able to test only **comprehension** and not **production** of language.

Attempts to teach language to non-human primates

Early studies attempted to teach spoken English to chimpanzees. Kellogg and Kellogg (1933) brought up Gua, a young chimpanzee, with their own baby. They found Gua's practical abilities developed very much faster than those of their son, but in spite of apparently recognising 95 words and phrases in spoken English, Gua only uttered three words himself. A study of a chimp called Vicki (Hayes, 1951) had similar findings. Vicki only produced the words 'papa', 'mama', 'up' and 'cup'.

The problem here is that the vocal apparatus of a chimp does not allow it to produce the wide range of sounds necessary for spoken language. This means that trying to get a chimpanzee to communicate in this way may not be a valid test of the animal's capabilities. Later studies have therefore used either sign language or artificial languages. We will look briefly at a range of these studies, and then consider what they can tell us about the communicative abilities of non-human animals.

Gardner and Gardner (1969) established the Oklahoma colony where they taught chimpanzees to use ASL, which is used by many deaf people in the USA. Their most famous chimp was called Washoe.

Washoe was initially taught by putting her arms and hands in the appropriate positions for signs in relevant situations. When she used the signs correctly in particular situations she was reinforced by praise, food and so on.

The Gardners claimed that Washoe learned 130 signs relating to objects (e.g. 'banana'), actions (e.g. 'open') and concepts such as colour and size. Washoe also spontaneously used combinations of signs to make requests, e.g. 'open food drink' when she wanted the fridge opened, and 'go sweet' when she wanted to be taken down to the raspberry bushes. You will notice here that she used language to refer to things not physically present, which suggests that her use of signs could not be described as the learning of simple stimulus–response connections. When she was no longer actively involved in the project, she was given Loulis, a young chimp, as a companion. She taught Loulis signs, though it is not clear whether or not he understood their meaning.

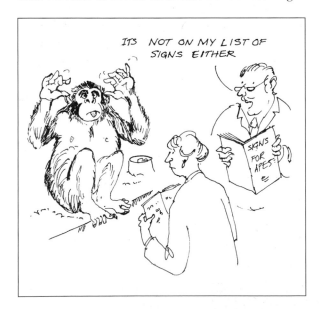

Another study using ASL was carried out on a gorilla named Koko by Patterson (1979). Patterson claimed that Koko learned to use and understand 400 signs, and could also understand the spoken equivalents of some of them, to the extent that she sometimes became muddled and signed a word wrongly, using a sign with a similar sound. A particularly nice example is when Koko wished to

remind her trainer that it was 11 o'clock, when she was used to being given a snack, and signed 'lemon o'clock'.

When she wished to communicate about something for which she had no sign, Koko spontaneously combined symbols. For example, she referred to a zebra as a 'white tiger', and a cigarette lighter as 'bottle match'. She also showed an ability to communicate about past events, on one occasion apologising to her trainer for having bitten her three days earlier.

Premack and Premack (1972) used coloured plastic symbols which could be attached to a magnetic board to communicate with their chimp Sarah. Some of the symbols they used are shown in figure 8. The colour of each symbol is shown with it in brackets:

Figure 8: symbols used by Premack and Premack

Chocolate (green)   Banana (red)   Raisin (white)

Same (orange)   Different (red)   No-not (pale blue)

Name of (pale blue)   Colour of (white)   ? (purple)

Red (light grey)   Yellow (black)   Brown (dark grey)

Sarah could follow instructions using these symbols (e.g. 'insert the banana in the pail'), but never created any new sentences of her own. However, she did learn to use over 100 symbols, including concepts such as 'colour of' and 'name of'.

Activity 8: teaching language to a chimpanzee

You could try using the Premacks' system yourself if you can find someone who will volunteer to act as a chimp for you. See if you can teach your 'chimp' simple concepts like 'name of', 'not name of' and 'colour of'. You will need to use the appropriate symbols from figure 8, together with items to match the symbols, in appropriate colours. Make sure that each concept has been grasped before you teach something else, and remember not to use any words (though plenty of positive reinforcement!).

A similar approach was developed by Rumbaugh (1977) in training his chimps. Instead of having separate symbols which could be attached to a magnetic board, he used a device rather like a typewriter keyboard with a range of symbols (**lexigrams**) which would light up when pressed, and appear on a screen:

Rumbaugh's chimp Lana learned to use around 100 symbols by this method. She also created new combinations of symbols for words she didn't know; for example, referring to a ring as a 'finger bracelet' and a cucumber as a 'banana which is green'.

Lana showed an awareness that the order in which symbols appeared on the screen could make a difference to meaning, such as by differentiating between 'Lana groom Tim' (Tim was her trainer) and 'Tim groom Lana'. This aspect of communication was stressed in training. Lana's communication was only accepted if it conformed to the grammatical rules of the language she was using (known as **Yerkish**), which were similar to those of English. A pair of chimps named Austin and Sherman were trained together in the same laboratory, and made even more progress than Lana.

We will look also at the work of Terrace (1979) and his chimp, Nim Chimpsky. You will remember the name of Noam Chomsky from earlier in this section, and the name of Terrace's chimp was a lighthearted reference to this major figure in linguistics. Chomsky was convinced that language is something which sets humans apart from other animals. Terrace originally believed that apes could be said to use language, but, partly on the basis of his work with Nim, finally came to the same conclusion as Chomsky.

Figure 9: a lexigram keyboard

Blank spaces are non-functioning keys or display photos of trainers

Nim was taught to use ASL, and like the other chimps trained in this way, appeared to use a range of signs correctly. However, the video analysis Terrace carried out, using a freeze-frame technique, showed that Nim was not spontaneously using signs to respond appropriately to a situation. Instead, the trainer was inadvertently giving cues as to which signs should be used, and Nim was merely imitating what he had been shown. Terrace argued from this that Nim had not learned that signs could be used to convey ideas.

Terrace and his team also analysed some of the video footage of the Gardners' chimp Washoe and of Koko the gorilla, trained by Patterson, and claimed that like Nim, these animals' apparent competence could also be explained by imitation. The Gardners disputed this claim, since Terrace had only looked at a very small proportion of their video footage of Washoe.

However, according to Pinker (1994), the one deaf signer who worked with Washoe, and for whom ASL was therefore the first language, claimed to be under pressure to interpret all movements of Washoe's arms and hands as signs:

'They were always complaining because my log didn't show enough signs. All the hearing people turned in lists with long lists of signs…The hearing people were logging every movement the chimp made as a sign…Sometimes [the trainers would] say, 'Oh, amazing, look at that, it's exactly like the ASL sign for give!' It wasn't.'

Pinker also queried the size of the vocabulary claimed for these animals, since the same movement made by a chimp was often interpreted by those working with them as different words, depending on the context. In addition, he gave examples of typical sentences produced by a trained chimp: 'tickle me Nim play' and 'you me banana me banana you' which are very unlike the kinds of sentences young children produce, and suggested that this is much more typical of animal communication in the wild, which the zoologist E O Wilson (1972) described as 'repetitious to the point of inanity'.

Activity 9: do non-human primates use language?

Look back through the projects described in this section.

To what extent do the communicative abilities of the chimpanzees, who were trained to communicate with their human trainers, or Koko the gorilla, meet the four criteria for language Aitchison highlighted (see figure 6)?

Compare your ideas with the discussion which follows.

All the studies we have discussed apparently fulfil the criterion of **semanticity**. It is claimed that all the animals studied learned to use over 100 symbols correctly, and in the case of Koko, many more. However, there is a certain amount of interpretation involved, given that in the case of Washoe at least, one movement was interpreted as having different meanings depending on the context. While Sarah only responded to communications initiated by her trainers, and there is some doubt about the extent to which Nim understood the correspondence between signs and objects or actions, the sophistication of Koko's use of signs and her understanding of spoken language seem to provide convincing evidence of semanticity. Additional support for this conclusion comes from Koko's ability to generalise. For example, the sign for 'straw' was also used for other items of similar appearance but for which she had no signs, e.g. a cigarette, plastic tubing and a car radio aerial.

There is no evidence of **displacement** in the communications of Sarah and Nim. However, Washoe's use of such phrases as 'go sweet', and Koko's apology for the biting incident, suggest that they may have been using language in this way.

Whether **structure dependence** was shown depended to some extent on the training methods. Sarah was trained to follow word order rules, and Lana to observe the rules of Yerkish. Both showed consistency in the order in which they used symbols. Lana demonstrated some understanding of rules in her ability to distinguish between the different meanings of 'Tim groom Lana' and 'Lana groom Tim'. However, in Washoe's training there was little emphasis on this aspect of language.

There is some evidence of **productivity** in many of the chimp communications. It is claimed that Washoe, Lana and Koko all spontaneously combined signs or symbols to create new utterances. Sarah didn't do this, but again, this may have something to do with the way her training was carried out, since it focused on her ability to respond to the questions and commands of the trainer.

One major problem with research in this area is the effect of **experimenter expectation**. There is a considerable amount of interpretation in the claims which many of the researchers make for their animals. We have already seen this in relation to interpreting a particular sign as having different meanings depending on the context in which it is made.

People involved in this research start out with an absolute belief in the existence of meaning in the gestures which their animals make, and so are very ready to interpret what they see as support for this belief. It needs also to be remembered that the nature of this research means that a close and enduring emotional tie is formed between animal and researcher, which is likely to lead to a very protective stance towards the animals' abilities. Pinker claimed that Patterson in particular was very ready to excuse any errors Koko made by claiming that the gorilla was fond of jokes, puns and naughty fibs. Many researchers have extended this defensiveness to refusing to share with other researchers their raw data, e.g. videos made of the animals' performance, and so do not allow their interpretations to be scrutinised.

⊖ Attempts to teach primates to speak have had little success because of the animals' **physical limitations**. Many projects have tried to teach animals to communicate using **ASL**, plastic **symbols** or a **lexigram keyboard**.

⊖ Some theorists, in particular Terrace, are very unwilling to accept that animals are capable of language.

⊖ It is claimed that all the animals in these projects, with the possible exception of Nim Chimpsky, showed **semanticity**. Similarly, it is

claimed that Washoe and Koko demonstrated **displacement** and both of them, together with Lana, showed **productivity**. Whether or not there was a possibility of **structure dependence** being shown seems to have depended on the training methods. The communications of some of the animals apparently showed this feature.

⊖ It is likely that the claims made about animals' language abilities have been heavily influenced by **experimenter expectation**. The nature of the relationship between animals and trainer, and the belief among trainers that animals can be said to have language, are likely to have influenced the experimenters' interpretations. Lack of access to raw data has meant that trainers' interpretations cannot be assessed by others.

Naturalistic language acquisition in chimps

We will look finally at a project using **bonobos** (pygmy chimps), carried out by Savage-Rumbaugh in the 1980s. The projects described in the last section concentrated on gradually building up a vocabulary through rote-learning, with language being used in somewhat formal testing situations. Savage-Rumbaugh's approach was different, in that she aimed to use a wide vocabulary from the start, and to use language to her animals in the context of everyday activities. In contrast to previous projects, their language experience was more like that of a human child.

Her most famous chimp, Kanzi, was trained to communicate using a lexigram keyboard, which he combined with gestures. Interestingly, he imposed his own structure on these communications, always using the order lexigram-gesture, and never the other way round, even though he was not trained to do this. This can be compared with **stage 2 grammar** in humans (discussed in chapter 16). At this stage one group of words – the **pivot class** – always occurs in a particular position in a child's two-word sentence. This has been seen as evidence for a LAD specific to humans; here we see something very similar in a bonobo.

Kanzi also learned to respond to spoken English. He was tested on this ability in a rigorously controlled way. He was given instructions by someone he couldn't see, and the assistant in the room monitoring his performance wore earphones so that she could not hear the instructions, and so perhaps unconsciously give him cues which might help him. This approach lent scientific rigour to the testing procedures, in sharp contrast to the highly interpretive nature of some of the studies described in the previous section.

Kanzi's performance under these conditions was impressive. He was tested on novel sentences, using combinations of words he had not been trained on, e.g. 'Can you put the cereal in the bowl?' and showed no difficulty in carrying out these instructions. In an even more difficult test, Kanzi was asked 'Can you get the ball that's in the colony room?'. This meant that he had to walk past another ball before reaching the colony room, but he was still successful in following these instructions.

A typical day for Kanzi was similar to that experienced by a child: he was involved with Savage-Rumbaugh or an assistant in helping to prepare meals, going for walks in the forest, playing games and so on. There was no insistence that Kanzi communicate; the conversation had a natural flow, just as it would between a parent and a small child.

Kanzi and Savage-Rumbaugh

This approach has been fruitful, and suggests that non-human animals are indeed capable of acquiring language. At the same time, there are still differences between animals and humans in terms of their language use. One important distinction made by Aitchison (1983) is that though animals may be *capable* of learning language, they are not *predisposed* to learn it. For humans, language use is central.

Terrace argued that Kanzi's use of language was *qualitatively* different from that of humans, in that he only used language to get things done, and to get what he wanted, whereas humans use language to share their perception of the world. Savage-Rumbaugh agreed that this was what most of his communication was about, but pointed out that this is also the main way in which young children use language. She also pointed out that Kanzi's communication was not totally limited in the way that Terrace suggested. For example, Kanzi also talked about his own behaviour, or where he wanted to go. Savage-Rumbaugh believed that there was a *quantitative* difference in language use between Kanzi and humans, rather than the qualitative difference that Terrace suggested.

Before we leave this topic, we need to consider the ethics of studies teaching animals to communicate with humans:

▶ Activity 10: ethics in teaching animals language

Studies of primates can be seen as very useful in helping us to assess the cognitive abilities of animals and – even more importantly – to clarify the nature of language.

Can you think of any ethical concerns these studies might raise?

When you have finished, see the notes on page 595.

- Savage-Rumbaugh developed a programme where bonobo chimpanzees acquire language as part of their daily routine.
- **Kanzi** learned to communicate using **gestures** and a **lexigram keyboard**. His ability to understand **spoken English** was impressive.
- Savage-Rumbaugh believed that Kanzi's language was only **quantitatively** different from that of humans, while Terrace believed that it was **qualitatively** different.

○ While this study shows that chimps can acquire language, they are not innately programmed to do so.

○ There are **ethical concerns** about studies which attempt to teach primates to communicate with us.

21.3 MEMORY IN NON-HUMAN ANIMALS

Memory in navigation

In the discussion of conditioning theory in chapter 20, we looked briefly at cognitive behaviourism, and in particular the idea that animals might form **cognitive maps**, mental representations of the environment which allow them to find their way around. In Tolman's study (chapter 20, box H), animals in a rich environment were better able to use cues to learn the location of food than to learn simple responses.

There are two ways in which the development of a cognitive map will give an animal an advantage: firstly, it will be able to select a novel route to a goal, and secondly, it will be able to make a detour round an obstacle. Experiments into cognitive maps have drawn on both these abilities.

A study by Morris (1981) has looked at the ability to select a **new route**:

Box N: Morris (1981)

Procedure: Rats were trained to swim in a large vat of milky liquid to a goal box containing food. The goal box was slightly submerged below the surface of the liquid. The rats quickly learned to swim directly to the food. They were then divided into three groups. Group 1 was started from the same place, but the position of the goal box was changed. For Group 2, the position of the goal box was unchanged, but they were started from a different place. For Group 3, the control group, start place and goal box were both unchanged.

Results: Group 3 continued to swim directly to the goal box, group 2 swam fairly directly to the goal box, but group 1 swam in no particular pattern until reaching the goal apparently by chance.

Conclusion: In the initial training period, rats had used environmental cues to form a cognitive map of the position of the goal box. Group 2 was able to use this information to find the goal box from a new starting point.

◐ Activity 11: explaining Morris' method

1 Why did Morris use a milky liquid in the vat, and submerge the goal box?
2 What was the purpose of including group 1 in the study?

When you have finished, see the notes on page 595.

However, Morris' study does not provide clear evidence of the use of cognitive maps. Of the six rats who took part in group 2, all but one started to swim in the wrong direction; there is no reason why the development of a cognitive map would lead to this behaviour. True, they then adjusted the direction in which they were swimming in order to approach the goal fairly directly, but this could possibly be a simple response to one of the cues provided in the environment.

Other studies have explored the ability to select a novel route in more naturalistic settings:

Box O: Gould (1986)

Procedure: Bees were trained to fly for food from their hive to point A (see diagram). They were then taken to point B in a darkened container, and released. The slope of the field at B meant that none of the features of A could be seen.

Results: The bees flew directly from B to A.
Conclusion: Before the experiment, the bees had formed a cognitive map of their surroundings which they were able to use to find the food source.

It is possible that the bees' behaviour here could be explained in much the same way as Morris' findings, without needing to assume that cognitive maps have been developed. However, a further study challenges this explanation:

Box P: Dyer (cited in Gould, 1984)

Procedure: Worker bees were trained to collect food from a boat in the middle of a lake (the lake station), and later from a boat moored at a similar distance on the opposite side of the lake from the hive (the shore station). The response of other workers to the bee dance made by the worker when returning from these journeys was observed.

Results: The workers did not respond to the dance indicating food at the lake station, but they did when the shore station was indicated.
Conclusion: Bees have a cognitive map, i.e. mental representation, of their immediate surroundings. When the information given in the dance does not correspond to the information this map provides – there are hardly likely to be flowers in the middle of a lake – bees do not act on it.

Incidentally, the lack of response to the dance indicating food at the lake station is also good evidence for a certain degree of semanticity in bees' communication.

The basic strategy used in **detour studies** is to show an animal a goal and then place it behind a barrier some distance away. If the animal selects the shortest possible route to the goal, this is some indication that it possesses a cognitive map.

Early studies by Koehler (1925) indicated that dogs could make a detour when they were shown food, choosing the shortest possible route. However, Koehler did not take into account the previous experience of the dogs he tested; it is possible that they had had experience of situations where such detours were necessary, and had developed this ability through trial and error learning.

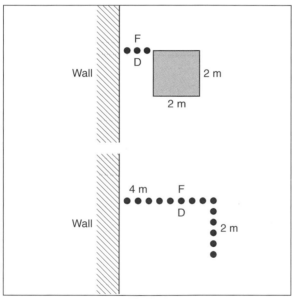

Plans of Koehler's apparatus. D=initial place of dog, F=place of food.

However, more recent and better controlled studies have had similar results:

Box Q: Chapuis and Scardigli (1993)

Procedure: A circular maze was used (see figure 10). Hamsters were trained to run from chamber A to chamber E for food (see dotted line). They were prevented from taking any other route by locked doors. After a training period, all the doors were unlocked except the one used by the rat to leave chamber A. The maze was rotated during the training phase so that it was impossible for the animals to respond to external cues.

Results: The hamsters chose the most direct alternative route (see solid line) significantly more often than would be expected by chance.

Conclusion: The hamsters had formed cognitive maps which they were able to use appropriately when the direct path, which they had learned took them to food, was blocked.

Figure 10: apparatus used by Chapuis and Scardigli (1993)

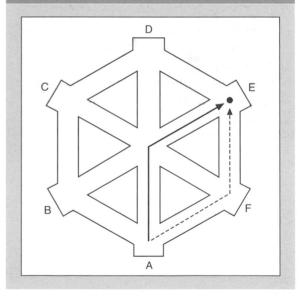

However, this does not mean that all animals have the ability to develop and use cognitive maps. Koehler also studied chickens, who rarely managed to make their way round a barrier to food. Apparently they only managed to reach the food when their attempts to crash through the barrier by chance led to them getting round it.

❺ The ability of animals to develop **cognitive maps** has been studied by testing their ability to take a **novel route** to a goal, and to take the shortest route when a **detour** is necessary.

❺ While some findings have been ambiguous, it seems likely that some animals – though not all – have this ability.

Memory in foraging

Foraging refers to the range of behaviours associated with finding food. For some species, food needs to be stored at times when it is plentiful, so that it can be retrieved when it is scarce. This involves remembering the places where it has been hidden. Some species have shown a remarkable ability to do this.

The most striking example is Clark's nutcrackers. In the autumn, these birds collect more than 30,000 seeds and bury them over a wide area in shallow holes (caches), with an average of 4 seeds per cache. They need to find these seeds again during the winter and the following spring to feed themselves and their young. Van der Wall (1982) claimed that a bird needs to revisit between 2500 and 3750 caches, which means that it needs to store information about more than 3000 locations.

It does not of course necessarily follow that the bird remembers all these locations. An alternative explanation is that other cues are used to indicate a cache. The possible use of olfactory cues has been tested experimentally:

Box R: Balda and Turek (1984)

Procedure: A Clark's nutcracker was given 26 seeds, which it hid. A diagram of the hiding places is shown in figure 11. Half the seeds were then removed from the caches, to eliminate the possibility that the bird could use olfactory cues when it came to retrieve them. The bird was allowed back a month later.

Results: The bird looked for seeds in 20 locations. The 18 caches revisited are circled on the diagram; 10 of them were sites from which the seeds had been removed.

Conclusion: With no olfactory cues, the bird had remembered the locations of most of the caches.

Figure 11: caches in the Balda and Turek (1984) study

It is also possible that nutcrackers use visual cues; for example, they may always make caches near tufts of grass. However, this possibility can also be eliminated:

Box S: Balda (1980)

Procedure: A nutcracker was allowed to store seeds in an outdoor aviary and was then removed to another cage. The sites of the caches were noted, then the seeds were removed and the floor of the cage swept, eliminating visual and olfactory cues. A week later, the places where the nutcracker probed for seeds with its beak were noted.
Results: As many as 80% of the cache sites were revisited. Very few attempts were made to retrieve seeds from non-cache sites.
Conclusion: In the absence of visual and olfactory cues, nutcrackers can retain an accurate representation of food caches.

A further study by Balda and Kamil (1992) found that nutcrackers can retain this information for at least 6 months, and possibly for as long as 9 months.

The Clark's nutcracker is not the only bird to cache and retrieve seeds in this way. In the course of a day, the black-capped chickadee will hide several hundred seeds or small insects over a wide area, in cracks in the bark of trees or in patches of moss. Hitchcock and Sherry (1990) claimed that these birds hid only one item in each place, and never used the same cache twice, but could recall the locations of the hiding places for as long as 28 days. Again, it is possible that chickadees do not remember the locations of their hiding places, but use visual or olfactory cues to locate the hidden food. However, this does not seem to be the case:

Box T: Sherry (1984)

Procedure: Captive chickadees were allowed to store sunflower seeds in holes drilled in small trees in an aviary. After the birds had hidden a sunflower seed in four or five of the 72 available caches, they were removed from the aviary for 24 hours. During this time, the cached seeds were removed and all 72 openings were sealed with Velcro.
Results: When the birds were allowed back in the aviary, they made more visits to the sites where they had stored seeds and spent more time pecking at the Velcro covers of these caches.
Conclusion: Since the Velcro covers eliminated the possibility of the chickadees using visual or olfactory cues, they remembered the sites of the seeds they had hidden earlier.

⊙ Some birds hide food, and have the ability to retrieve it much later. Studies have established that they do not rely on visual or olfactory cues, but remember the locations of their caches.

Notes on activities

1 There may be several reasons for migration. The fact that it is seasonal gives us some clues. Many animals **breed** in a particular season, and for breeding to be successful, they need to ensure that the conditions are appropriate. They need an adequate source of food, and an environment in which the young can thrive.

Migration may also be to do with personal **survival**. For example, wildebeest on the African savannah move towards rain in the dry season.

The monarch butterfly, which migrates from the north to the south of America, avoids low temperatures which would threaten survival. They cluster together into groups when the weather gets colder, which confirms the importance of warmth.

Sometimes personal survival is not an issue. For example, Atlantic salmon migrate from the Sargasso Sea in the South Atlantic to the European rivers where they were spawned. After breeding, they remain behind and die, while the new generation make their way back to sea.

Migration can be triggered by changes in the weather, the length of the day and air temperature. It may also come about in response to dwindling food supplies. Sometimes migration does not take place. However, this shouldn't be seen as a conscious 'decision' not to migrate, but rather the result of insufficient triggers in the environment, such as unseasonably warm weather.

2 There seem to be several possible sources of information for the 'compass' part of Kramer's hypothesis. It is likely that animals can draw on a range of sources: the sun, magnetism, the stars, and so on. It is possible that the main source of information used depends on the species, but it also seems unlikely that any species relies entirely on one source. The 'map' part of the hypothesis is still very unclear. Memory for visual landmarks could explain the development of a map of familiar territory, and smell may also be important. However, we still can't explain how animals acquire information about unfamiliar territory, though research into geomagnetism suggests some answers.

3 There are so many ways that it is impossible to know what you have come up with. The main point of this activity, though, was to start you thinking about the wide range of ways in which communication can take place.

One of the major ways we communicate is using language in some way – by talking or writing or even using Morse code. However, we also use non-verbal sounds, e.g. a baby's cry communicates a need to its caregiver. There are facial expressions, eye contact, posture and so on. Touch is another possibility – a kiss carries a rather different message from a punch. It is also possible to communicate without consciously intending to do so; we blush when embarrassed, and our pupils automatically dilate if we are looking at someone we find attractive.

4 Visual communication is limited because it usually requires light, and so cannot take place in the dark. The signaller and receiver need to be able to see each other, so they need to be relatively close, and with no obstacles to obscure the view. An olfactory communication will linger long after the message has been received, which may be dangerous for the signaller. Different messages require production of different chemicals, and there is little possibility with olfactory messages of using patterning as a way of distinguishing one message from another. All of these drawbacks are overcome by auditory communication.

5 The response of members of the same group suggests that a specific meaning – i.e. danger – is carried by the sounds dolphins make. The response of dolphins from another group suggests that the same sounds mean different things in different dolphin groups. This in turn implies that there may be an element of learning in dolphin communication.

6 When assessing whether animal communication shows **semanticity**, there is always the problem that animals might just be showing an automatic response to a stimulus, rather than forming a mental representation of what is being referred to. The formation of categories by vervet monkeys, shown by Seyfarth and Cheney (box K) could also be interpreted as showing semanticity. However, there is no firm evidence that bird or cetacean communication has this feature.

The bee dance clearly shows **displacement**, since it refers to a food source outside the hive. Similarly, the study by Bastian (box I) shows a dolphin understanding a communication about a task to which it has not yet been introduced. There is also displacement in the Menzel and Halperin study of chimps (box J), although the communication in this respect is rather imprecise. Again, there is no evidence that birdsong shows this feature.

None of the examples given show **structure dependence**. This is not to say, of course, that animal communication doesn't have this feature; all it means is that we do not have sufficient understanding of animal communication to come to a conclusion.

There is no evidence of **productivity** in the communication of birds or non-human primates, though again, just because we have no evidence of it doesn't mean that we can dismiss it as a possibility.

To an extent bees could be said to show productivity, since they can communicate about a virtually unlimited number of spatial locations. On the other hand, the *kind* of information they can communicate is very limited. This has been demonstrated in a further study by Von Frisch and Lindauer (1954). They placed a hive at the bottom of a radio beacon and some sugar water at the top. The bees who were shown the sugar water performed the round dance, and the other bees flew around for several hours in all directions – except up! As Von Frisch put it: 'The bees have no words for 'up' in their language. There are no flowers in the clouds.' But the bees were unable to pass on this extra, essential piece of information, so the productivity of their communication is extremely limited.

The dolphin in the Bastian study (box I) shows productivity, since it is communicating information about a novel task. However, there is no firm evidence as to whether cetaceans show this feature of language in their natural communication.

10 These studies take place over several years, during which time the procedures involved encourage animals to form an intensive social relationship with their human carers. Once the study is complete, this close relationship comes to an end, and animals are returned to what might be termed 'normal' captivity with others of their kind. Researchers involved in work of this kind are sensitive to this kind of problem, and make every effort to provide the animals with a rich and stimulating environment. At the same time, however, this environment is very different – and arguably very much less stimulating – from what they have become accustomed to during testing.

11 This was a carefully controlled study, since care was taken to avoid the possibility of the rats using cues other than those necessary to form a cognitive map, such as smell. The milky liquid prevented the rats from being able to see the goal and so use vision to swim straight to the goal. Group 1 was included to make sure that the rats weren't using other environmental cues to reach the food.

Evolutionary explanations of human behaviour

In this chapter we will be looking at:

22.1 Evolutionary theory and human behaviour

22.2 Human reproductive behaviour
   Sexual selection
   Parental investment

22.3 Explanations of mental disorders
   Depression
   Phobias

22.4 Intelligence
   Environmental factors: food and foraging
   Machiavellian intelligence hypothesis

22.1 EVOLUTIONARY THEORY AND HUMAN BEHAVIOUR

In this chapter we will be investigating the usefulness of evolutionary ideas in explaining various aspects of human behaviour. The basic principles of Darwin's theory of evolution were outlined at the start of chapter 20; you may find it useful to look back now at this material.

The basic claim made by evolutionary psychologists is that much of human behaviour can be explained in terms of its **adaptiveness**. One of the key concepts here is the idea of **natural selection**: physical characteristics which produce patterns of behaviour which are adaptive in a particular environment will be selected and passed on through the genes to the next generation, while characteristics which are not adaptive are less likely to be passed on. Evolutionary psychology is therefore concerned with innate patterns of behaviour.

Behaviours are seen as adaptive if they contribute in some way to **fitness**, i.e. the ability to survive long enough to pass on genes to the next generation, and to raise viable offspring. Even behaviour which may on the surface seem to be maladaptive – for example, mental disorders – may nonetheless have some adaptive function, or may have been adaptive in our evolutionary past.

Evolutionary psychologists have drawn on these ideas to explain a vast range of human behaviours, some of which we will discuss in this chapter.

⊗ Evolutionary ideas have been used to explain a range of human behaviours.

22.2 HUMAN REPRODUCTIVE BEHAVIOUR

Evolutionary psychologists have claimed that the mind consists of a number of specialised mechanisms or **modules**, each of which has developed through natural selection to solve specific problems faced by our ancestors, such as acquiring a mate, raising children and dealing with rivals. They have also claimed that in general these modules are universal. However, since the reproductive roles of men and women are very different, so too are their mental modules.

To understand these differences, we need to look first at **anisogamy**, i.e. differences in the gametes (sperm and ova) in sexually reproducing species. This represents a fundamental difference between males and females: males produce a large number of small, very mobile sperm, while females produce larger, relatively immobile eggs. Because eggs are large, they are produced in quite small numbers. Eggs can survive for quite a while; sperm, once they become active, are very short-lived. These differences have important consequences for sexual behaviour.

The number of offspring that a female can produce is limited by the number of eggs she can produce. She cannot increase the number of offspring she produces by mating with several males. The male, on the other hand, can increase his reproductive success by mating with several females. This means that males and females have different reproductive priorities, in terms of the strategies which are most likely to lead to reproductive success.

On this basis, it would be expected that for the male, most of his reproductive effort would be taken up in competing with other males for females, and in persuading females to mate with him, i.e. **mating effort**, while for females, reproductive effort will largely be taken up in the production and care of offspring, i.e. **parental effort.** This is true of some species, including most mammals, as shown in figure 1:

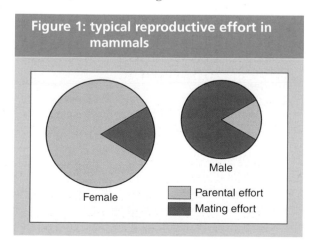

Figure 1: typical reproductive effort in mammals

Female

Male

Parental effort
Mating effort

Activity 1: differences in mating and parental effort in mammals

In terms of reproductive efficiency, why would it not make sense for a male mammal to devote more of his reproductive effort to parental effort? What would he have to lose?

Similarly, why would it not make sense for the female to devote more of her reproductive effort to mating effort? What would she have to lose?

When you have finished, see the notes on page 618.

We can already see a conflict of interest here. The male will be more interested in quantity of offspring, and is likely to leave their care to the female. On the other hand, the female will be more committed to raising a smaller number of offspring successfully. It should be possible, on the basis of these differences, to make predictions about the mating tendencies of both sexes:

Activity 2: mating tendencies in males and females

From what you have read so far, answer the following questions:

Which sex would you expect to:

a be more discriminating in their choice of partner?

b be more likely to demand elaborate courtship rituals?

c have a more easily aroused sexual response?

d be more competitive with members of their own sex?

e be larger?

When you have finished, see the notes on page 618.

These predictions are supported in a large number of species, and will be useful in the later discussion of sexual selection and parental investment.

A further important factor is the pattern of mating behaviour shown by a species. There are different patterns of mating behaviour, which can be thought of as different systems, in different species. These systems are monogamy, polygamy and polygynandry (promiscuity).

Monogamy means that one female will mate exclusively with one male. In swans, a pair bond is formed for life. In sparrows, the bond lasts for just one breeding season, and a new pair is formed the following year. However, in both swans and sparrows, mating is exclusive while the bond lasts.

In **polygamy**, one member of one sex will mate with several members of the other. It can take two forms: **polygyny**, where one male has several female mates, and **polyandry**, where one female has several male mates. Polygyny is far more common. It can be serial, as in the pied flycatcher, where males bond with several females during the breeding season, but only with one at a time; it can also be simultaneous, as in elephant seals, where a single male has a harem of females during the breeding season.

The final pattern is **polygynandry** (or **promiscuity**), where no permanent pair bonds are formed, but males and females come together very briefly in order to mate. For example, female chimpanzees will mate with most males in a group, and males will mate with as many females within the group as possible.

The likelihood of members of a particular species showing one particular pattern has been found to correlate with the weight of the testes:

Box A: Harcourt *et al.* (1981)

Procedure: Twenty kinds of primates were studied, ranging in size from the marmoset (weighing approximately 320 gm) to the gorilla (170 kg). A comparison was made between the body weight of each species, their mating patterns, and the weight of their testes.

Results: The weight of the testes increased with body weight. However, species where one male has the monopoly on mating with several females (e.g. the gorilla and orang-utan) had smaller testes relative to their body weight than species where several males mate with each oestrus (i.e. receptive) female (e.g. the chimpanzee).

Conclusion: In multi-male systems, e.g. the chimpanzee, where females mate with several males, the male's sperm has to compete with other sperm. The increased sperm production from larger testes makes the male more competitive. On the other hand, in gorillas and orang-utans each male needs to ejaculate only enough sperm to ensure fertilisation, and therefore the testes are smaller.

Short (1991) applied similar ideas to humans, and came to the conclusion that 'we are basically a polygynous primate, in which the polygyny usually takes the form of serial monogamy'. This is actually quite a common pattern of behaviour, particularly in Western societies; it is not unusual for people to have several partners in succession, either before they decide to make their lives with one particular individual, or as the result of divorce. However, you may wish to query Short's conclusion that this pattern of behaviour relates to poly*gyny* – does it relate only to men? It could be argued that the term polygynandry would be more accurate.

The different systems are also reflected in the maximum number of offspring recorded for different species:

Figure 2: maximum number of offspring for four different species (Krebs and Davies, 1987)

species	maximum number of offspring produced during a lifetime	
	male	*female*
elephant seal	100	8
red deer	24	14
human	888	69
kittiwake	26	28

In polygamous or polygynandrous species, e.g. the polygynous elephant seal, males have a much higher potential reproductive rate than females. On the other hand, in the monogamous kittiwake this potential is virtually identical for males and females

(Clutton-Brock, 1983). The data for humans come from the *Guinness World Records*: the male was Moulay Ismael the Bloodthirsty, Emperor of Morocco, and the woman a Russian, who produced her children in 27 pregnancies. The difference in potential reproductive rates which the figures of 888 and 69 represent suggests that humans may be a naturally polygynous or polygynandrous species.

It is perhaps worth noting that the maximum number of offspring for the three non-human species in figure 2 may not be entirely accurate; for example, only a tiny proportion of kittiwake broods come to the attention of human researchers. How accurate the figures are for humans is also questionable. Einon (1998) carried out a mathematical analysis, taking into account biological factors in conception and gestation, which challenges the figure of 888 as the number of offspring produced by Ismael. She calculated that if he had sexual relations 3 times a week over 40 years (he died at 55), with no interruptions for illness or exhaustion, he would be likely to have produced a lifetime total of 79 children. This figure rises to 368 if he had intercourse 14 times a week. The difference between the maximum number of offspring produced by men and by women is therefore probably not quite as striking as the *Guinness World Records* suggests, though even the more limited difference lends some support to humans being polygynous or polygynandrous.

This has led to several predictions about human sexual behaviour:

▷ Activity 3: differences in male/female sexual behaviour in humans

Males or females? Explain your choice each time in terms of reproductive success:

a .... will be more readily sexually aroused.
b .... are more likely to seek a variety of sexual partners.
c .... will be more concerned with a mate's fidelity.
d .... will be more likely to commit adultery.
e .... will be more likely to rape.

When you have finished, see the notes on page 619.

Symons (1979) provided some support for the idea that human males have an inherited tendency to be polygynous, while females are monogamous. He claimed that gay men are more likely to have a succession of short-lived relationships, while lesbians tend to form a lasting monogamous partnership. Homosexuality is not a reproductively successful strategy, but the different patterns of behaviour shown by males and females can be thought to show an underlying genetic trait.

However, in classifying mating systems we need to bear in mind a number of points. Firstly, the classification often applies to only one sex. For instance, when we say that elephant seals are polygynous we mean that this is the pattern for males. It ignores the fact that in general females are monogamous unless the male with whom they are mated is unsuccessful at defending his territory against other males. Secondly, the term 'system' implies that there are constraints on the species which mean that they inevitably follow a particular pattern. This is not the case, since other factors influence this behaviour. Thirdly, these terms should really be applied to individuals rather than species. For example, in polygamous species some individuals will have several mates, and some none at all. Finally, we should not think of each pattern as being completely distinct from the others. A female may be monogamous each year, but with a different mate, so she is in effect polyandrous. Nonetheless, this categorisation can be useful in relation to reproductive behaviour.

In the next section, we will see how the factors we have discussed influence sexual selection in humans, and the parental investment given to their offspring.

- **Anisogamy** refers to the different forms **gametes** take in the **male** and the **female** of a species. These differences have implications in terms of differences between the sexes in **mating effort** and **parental effort**.
- Patterns of mating have been classified under different **systems**: **monogamous**, **polygamous** and **polygynandrous (promiscuous)**.
- These patterns are relevant to **sexual selection** and **parental investment**.

Sexual selection

According to Darwin (1871), sexual selection refers to the selection, in evolutionary terms, of characteristics which lead to increased mating success. It depends on the advantage some individuals have over others of the same sex and species in terms of reproductive success.

Sexual selection has two components. The first is **intrasexual selection**, i.e. selection within a sex, where males compete directly with other males to fertilise females. The second is **intersexual selection**, selection between sexes, where males compete indirectly by special courtship displays or adornments which lead a female to select a particular male.

Generally females select males, and males compete for females. At the most basic level, this can be seen in the competition of sperm to fertilise eggs; the element of competition is inevitable because there are very many more sperm available than there are eggs to be fertilised. The female needs to be selective in her choice of mate because she is limited in the number of eggs and offspring she can produce, so it makes evolutionary sense for her to ensure she picks the 'fittest' mate as a sexual partner.

The female needs to be selective in her choice of male

A male can potentially fertilise huge numbers of females – for example, 5 ml of human ejaculate could theoretically fertilise twice the population of the USA. His genes are more likely to be carried on if he fertilises as many females as possible, and any adaptation which allows him to do so will be favoured by natural selection. This of course assumes that the decrease in offspring survival chances in one-parent rather than two-parent care is more than made up for by the number of extra opportunities the male gains for fertilising females. This represents the main reason why it is difficult, if not impossible, to make predictions about male sexual behaviour. If we assume a polygynous or a polygynandrous system, predictions about male behaviour will be completely different than they will if we assume a monogamous one.

The different priorities of men and of women lead to different criteria in the selection of a mate. One important aspect of attractiveness in females appears to be the ratio of the circumference of the hips to the waist:

Box B: Singh (1993)

Procedure: The measurements of the Miss America Pageant winners and Playboy centrefolds over the previous 50 years were studied.

Results: Although factors like bustline, body weight and physique varied over the years, a large hip-to-waist ratio was a consistent feature of female attractiveness.

Conclusion: A larger hip-to-waist ratio is associated with better health status, and therefore potentially better reproductive capacity. This preference in men is therefore adaptive in maximising reproductive potential.

It could perhaps be argued that the preference Singh found for a larger hip-to-waist ratio is culturally based. However, the consistency of the finding across so many years lends some support to an evolutionary interpretation.

A further study has investigated priorities in males and females:

Box C: Buss (1989)

Procedure: More than 10,000 people in 37 cultures on 6 continents and 5 islands were studied. They were asked what their priorities were in choosing a sexual partner.

Results: Men were much more likely to rate youth and good looks as extremely important, while females valued a cluster of characteristics which included good financial prospects, ambition, industriousness, older age and emotional maturity.

Conclusion: Priorities for males and females are different, and appear to be universal.

Activity 4: an evolutionary explanation of male/female preferences

In evolutionary terms, we seek to maximise opportunities of passing on our genes to the next generation, and making sure that they reach maturity and reproduce themselves. How might these ideas be linked to the widespread preferences Buss found in his study?

When you have finished, see the notes on page 619.

Activity 5: investigating male/female preferences

Run a small practical study to investigate whether Buss is right in his claim that men seek good looks in a sexual partner, while women look for a partner with sound finances.

You will need a 'Lonely Hearts' column from a newspaper. Your local paper may run one, and there is one in *The Guardian* on Saturdays. Select 20 adverts put in by males seeking female partners, and 20 in which females seek males. Count up how many adverts in each category:

 offer youth or attractiveness
 ask for youth or attractiveness
 offer good financial prospects
 ask for good financial prospects.

You will need to identify the kinds of words used to indicate these categories. For example, the word 'solvent' suggests financial resources, but this can also be indicated in more subtle ways, e.g. 'own house'.

If Buss is right, women should be more likely to offer attractiveness than men, and men should be more likely to ask for attractiveness than women. Men should be more likely to offer financial resources than women, and women should be more likely to ask for financial resources than men.

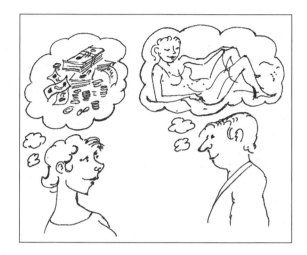

Dunbar (1995) carried out a similar content analysis which confirmed these hypotheses. However, the characteristics identified as being more important to men and to women are not necessarily those which are most valued by either. A survey by Kenrick and Simpson (1997) found that kindness, understanding and intelligence were top of the list for both sexes, supporting Buss's own finding that kindness and intelligence were consistently rated by both men and women as more important than good looks and financial prospects.

A further problem with the argument Buss puts forward is that it focuses on only one level of explanation. Historical and cultural influences may also affect our choice of a sexual partner. For example, it could be that women try to obtain resources through men because they have traditionally been cut off from economic opportunities. It could also be that a man will seek out an attractive partner because this will enhance his social status.

Eagly (1994) proposed a similar cultural explanation for human mate selection criteria. She pointed out that in the cultures studied, males are socially dominant, and suggested that if females were the dominant sex, then the preferred attributes in the opposite sex would be reversed. In other words, the choices found in this kind of research depend not on evolutionary imperatives but on social and cultural ones.

Unfortunately, there is no way of testing this suggestion directly, since there are no societies where females are socially dominant. However, the kind of reversal in gender assignment for sexual selection which Eagly suggested does occur in some animals. For example, in the seahorse the male is responsible for parental care, having a special pouch which holds infant seahorses as they mature. In this species, brightly-coloured females compete for dull-coloured males.

A final word of caution in interpreting the results of studies into sexual selection comes from Graziano *et al.* (1997). They found that if women found a man pleasant, they would find him significantly more physically attractive if he were also dominant. However, they point out that results of this kind should not necessarily be accepted at face value, since mate choice may not be entirely free, but may reflect a certain amount of social coercion. To take an extreme example, the choice of a dominant and aggressive male for a partner may be a choice to stay alive, rather than a personal preference for dominant men.

On the basis of his survey of sexual attitudes in men and women, Buss concluded that men are much more likely to be promiscuous than women. This makes evolutionary sense, because men can in principle father huge numbers of children, and promiscuity is one way in which their reproductive success can be maximised. On the other hand, a woman can only produce on average one child a year, so it is in her interests to invest time and care in making sure that her offspring survive to sexual maturity.

However, the picture is rather more complex than this. Not all men are promiscuous, and some women are, and this could also be explained in evolutionary terms. There are sound evolutionary reasons for women to be unfaithful (e.g. to gain male protection and care, or to promote sperm competition) and for men to be faithful (e.g. infidelity may lead to a man losing his sexual partner with no guarantee of gaining another). These patterns of behaviour could therefore also be seen as adaptive in evolutionary terms.

It seems, then, that the same theory can explain whatever male and female behaviours are observed, which means that the theory has no predictive value. It cannot be falsified, and therefore, according to Popper (1959), it has no value as a scientific theory, and so is of limited use in explaining human behaviour. It is also the case that other explanations – relating for example to historical, cultural and social factors – may be just as valid.

On the surface, there is also something of a problem in fitting homosexuality into an evolutionary framework, since homosexual relationships will not lead directly to a person's genes being carried forward to future generations, and so are not adaptive. However, any trait strongly selected for in part of the population – in this case being attracted to males, strongly selected for in females – will necessarily appear from time to time in other parts of the population, in this case males.

❺ Some members of a species have characteristics which increase their mating success. It is on this basis that **sexual selection** takes place. There are two components: **intrasexual selection** and **intersexual selection**.

❺ Males and females have different reproductive potential. It would be expected that **males** would prioritise youth and **physical attractiveness** in females, as a guide to their reproductive potential. For **females** a higher priority would be **financial resources** to maximise the chances of their offspring surviving to maturity.

❺ There is some **empirical support** for these predictions, but care needs to be taken in **interpreting** the findings. The theory is limited in not being **falsifiable**.

K-selected species

Parental investment

The selection of an appropriate mate is only one part of the process of maximising the chances of the individual's genes being carried forward to future generations. For many species, care of the young by one or both of the parents will be essential if the young are to stand a chance of surviving to maturity and breeding in their turn.

Trivers (1972) used the term 'parental investment' to mean: 'any investment by the parent in an individual offspring that increases the offspring's chance of surviving (and hence reproductive success) at the cost of the parent's ability to invest in other offspring' (p139). In practice, it is not very easy to operationalise terms like 'the offspring's chance of surviving' and 'cost to parents', and so there are difficulties in assessing parental investment

Several factors influence the amount of care the young of a particular species is likely to attract. In some species known as **r-selected species**, such as insects and many species of fish, little or no parental care is given. So many offspring are produced that sheer weight of numbers makes it likely that some offspring (and therefore parental genes) will survive. In these circumstances, extensive parental care is unnecessary. At the other extreme, in **K-selected species,** a lot of parental care is given to offspring by one or both parents. Human beings are a good example of a K-selected species. Species of this kind have slower development, larger bodies, fewer offspring, a higher survival rate, a higher proportion of learned behaviour and a longer lifespan than r-selected species. All of these characteristics imply a need for considerable parental investment.

r-selected species

The brain size of humans makes lengthy parental investment necessary if offspring are to survive to maturity and themselves reproduce. The size of the human brain has tripled over the last 2 million years, which has meant that the skull needed to become enlarged to accommodate it. At the same time, the size of the human pelvis is determined by our walking on two legs. The increased size of the skull made childbirth more difficult, and to compensate for this and make it possible for the baby's head to pass through the narrow birth canal, birth takes place when the infant is still relatively immature. If we were like other primates, a full term for a human pregnancy would be 21 months, by which time the head of the infant would be too large to pass through the pelvic canal. So while most animals become independent within a matter of months, humans remain dependent for very much longer.

One advantage of increased brain size is that it allows for learning, i.e. adapting behaviour to the requirements of a particular environment. This in turn means that very few behaviour patterns are wholly genetically determined and 'hard-wired' into the system, with the consequence that a period of prolonged care and education of the young – in terms of selection of relevant environmental events – is necessary for appropriate learning to take place.

In general, women tend to make a greater parental investment than men. In the past, breastfeeding made them the more likely parent to care for small children, and so to continue to provide parental investment as the period of care lengthened. Women therefore provide not only the most prenatal investment, but also the most postnatal investment. This makes evolutionary sense: since a woman has already made a considerable investment in a child by the time it is born, it makes sense for her to continue to provide for it, given her limited reproductive capability.

Mummy says she keeps a record of how much I cost 'just out of curiosity' – but I'm not so sure that I'm not going to end up with a whacking great bill!

One factor in parental investment which also leads to more parental care being offered by mothers is **paternity uncertainty**. Because fertilisation in humans is internal, females always know who their offspring are but males can never be completely sure; if they offer parental care, they may be contributing care to offspring which have none of their genes. Indeed, Fisher (1992) referred to several large-scale surveys which indicate that on average in married couples with children, about 10% of children have a genetic father different from the official 'family' father.

Statistically one of these children can't be mine –

10% CHILDREN ILLEGITIMATE

Differences between species in the parental care offered is associated with differences in mating systems, which in turn vary in terms of paternity certainty. You will remember that there are several different mating systems: monogamy, polygamy (polygyny and polyandry) and polygynandry (promiscuity). These different systems have different implications in terms of who offers parental care.

▶ Activity 6: mating strategies and parental care

For each of these systems, who would you expect to provide parental care for the offspring: the male parent, the female parent, both or neither? In terms of reproductive success, what reasons lie behind the differences in care patterns?

	care provided by	*reasons*
monogamy:		
polygyny:		
polyandry:		
polygynandry:		

When you have finished, see the notes on page 619.

Different mating systems offer a general guideline as to whether and by whom parental care is given. However, just as we saw earlier with mating behaviour, parental care is also influenced by other factors.

Since human males, as noted earlier, seem to have a tendency to be serial monogamists, it would be expected that fathers might offer parental care if they can be fairly sure that the offspring are genetically theirs. Daly and Wilson (1996) have indicated the many ways that men in different cultures have tried to increase paternity certainty; these include male sexual jealousy, domestic violence, female circumcision and infibulation, harems staffed by eunuchs and the stoning of adulteresses.

The result is that in all cultures, women typically tend to invest more time and energy than men in childrearing. Buss (1999) noted that maternal relatives other than the mother make a greater investment than paternal relatives. In addition, Daly and Wilson (1982) found that 80% of comments about the resemblance of a child to a parent pointed out ways in which the child looked like the father, while only 20% referred to the mother. This observation could be interpreted as offering reassurance of paternity. However, it is also possible that it reflects a naturally-selected tendency for human offspring to resemble their fathers; this would provide protection against infanticide by the father, and a way of extracting parental care from him.

HE'S GOT HIS FATHER'S LOOK OF WRY IRONY....

A further complication is illustrated by the Trivers–Willard hypothesis (Trivers and Willard, 1973) which looks at the effects of variance in reproductive success in species where this is greater for males than for females. In such species, some males will have great success and some little or none, whereas females will not show these extremes. Where this difference in variance holds true, males in good condition will have a greater chance of leaving viable offspring than females in good condition, since their reproductive success is likely to be greater than that of females. Therefore parents who are in good condition should show a bias towards producing sons (who will in turn have a greater likelihood of reproductive success than females) over daughters; those in poor condition should show a bias towards producing daughters. Trivers and Willard suggested that this idea could be extended to human societies, using wealth and socioeconomic status (which varies more for males than for females) as an indicator of condition. There is some evidence to support their hypothesis:

Box D: Mueller (1993)

Procedure: An analysis was carried out of the sons:daughters ratio of eminent men, using a sample of US and German elite males (drawing on information from the American and German *Who's Who*) and British industrialists (using the *Dictionary of Business Biography*).
Results: With all three samples, the ratio of sons to daughters was significantly greater than would be expected from the ratio for the populations as a whole.
Conclusion: There is some support for the Trivers–Willard hypothesis in relation to human sex ratios.

The mechanism which brings about this skewing of the ratio of sons to daughters is not clear. It is likely to be mediated through hormone production in the parents, but other mechanisms could include differential mobility or differential survival of the X and Y sperm or differential mortality of male and female embryos.

Within this framework, it would also be predicted that not all children would be cared for equally, and that male and female children would be treated differently depending on social status. It might be expected that high-status parents would invest more in sons, and low-status parents in daughters:

Box E: Gaulin and Robbins (1992)

Procedure: Breastfeeding was used as a measure of parental investment. The rates of breastfeeding in the USA, for sons and for daughters, in high-income and in low-income families, were compared. A further measure was birth spacing, i.e. the time between the birth of one child and the birth of another. A shorter period before the birth of the next child would represent a smaller investment in the existing child.

Results: In low-income families, over 50% of the daughters but less than 50% of the sons were breastfed. In high-income families, over 90% of sons compared to 60% of daughters were breastfed. In low-income families, birth spacing was on average 4.3 years after the birth of a daughter, and 3.5 years after the birth of a son. In high-income families the figures were reversed: 3.2 years for daughters and 3.9 years for sons.

Conclusion: Parental investment is linked to the sex of a child, which in turn is linked with status.

- **Parental investment** may be made by one or both of the parents, or little by either. Human infants need a lot of parental care if they are to survive to maturity; typically, most of this care is provided by mothers.
- The nature of parental care offered is influenced by the **mating system**, which in turn is linked to **paternity certainty**.
- Across cultures, men have tried to increase **paternity certainty**, thus making sure that parental investment contributes to the survival of their genes. However, most parental investment is provided by women.

- There has been some support for the idea of **differential investment** in sons and daughters being linked with **social status**.

22.3 EXPLANATIONS OF MENTAL DISORDERS

Depression

The characteristics of depression are described in chapter 24, figure 4. In that chapter, some of the biological and psychological explanations for depression are discussed. Straightforward depression is sometimes called **unipolar depression** to distinguish it from **bipolar disorder**, sometimes called **manic depression**.

Bipolar disorder is characterised by major mood swings between a state of severe depression and a state of mania, two extremes (or poles) of mood, hence the term 'bipolar'. The symptoms during the depressive phase are the same as those of unipolar depression. The symptoms in the manic phase are shown in figure 3:

Figure 3: symptoms of mania

- Increased energy, social and sexual activity
- Reckless decisions and actions
- Delusions of grandeur and persecution
- Rapid speech – more talkative
- Hallucinations
- Distractability
- Irritability
- Little sleep needed

Depression is universal; it occurs in all cultures, and is recognised as a disorder in almost all human societies. In this section we will look at evolutionary explanations for both unipolar depression and bipolar disorder. Evolutionary psychologists see depressive and manic behaviour as adaptive responses to loss and gain respectively.

In explaining how depression and mania can be adaptive, it is assumed that we have two basic needs: the need to have close emotional bonds with other people, and the need for social rank or status. Beck (1983) distinguished between **deprivation**

depression, the failure to fulfil the first of these needs, and **defeat depression**, the failure to fulfil the second.

Deprivation depression can be linked to **attachment theory**, and in particular Bowlby's ideas, discussed in chapter 3. Bowlby proposed that we have an innate predisposition to form a close bond with an attachment figure, which leads to the development of an inner model of the self as someone capable of giving affection and worthy of receiving it. Failure to form such a bond in early childhood has important implications both for future relationships and for mental health. The loss or lack of an early attachment figure will make the person vulnerable to depression.

Bowlby described a child's response to separation from the attachment figure as moving through three stages: protest, despair and detachment. The depression expressed as despair can be seen as acceptance of the loss of separation. The adaptive purpose of depression is therefore to achieve detachment.

There is some support for these ideas. For example, Parker (1984) reported that patients liable to develop depression often recall a lack of parental affection. However, people who have had serious attachment problems in childhood do not necessarily develop depression in later life.

There is no doubt that depression is sometimes associated with the loss of an attachment figure through separation or death. However, the kinds of life event which trigger depression are quite often associated with the loss of a job, or status, or financial security. These kinds of depression are hard to fit into Bowlby's theory, and relate more easily to **rank theory**, which is associated with defeat depression.

We need to affiliate with others because of the benefits that living within a social group brings: safety and access to resources such as territory, food and potential mates. However, such groups are a hierarchy, in which some individuals are more dominant and others more submissive; individuals within the group compete for rank. It has been suggested (e.g. by Stevens and Price, 2000) that depression is an adaptive response to losing rank to a competitor, in that it promotes acceptance of a subordinate position in the social hierarchy. Depression prevents the person from using resources in doomed attempts to change circumstances, and therefore also helps to maintain the stability of the social group.

Both unipolar depression and bipolar disorder can fit within this account. Price and Sloman (1987) described unipolar depression as a **yielding subroutine**, which ensures that the yielder does not try to make a comeback, assures the winner that conflict is at an end, and so allows social harmony to be restored. Mania is a component of the **winning subroutine**. It makes clear that any attempt at a comeback will be successfully resisted, and ensures that the winner has the necessary resources to resist – confidence, energy and strength – if the loser should attempt a comeback.

This model has received some empirical support:

Box F: Belsher and Costello (1988)

Procedure: Within two years of recovery from unipolar depression, about 50% of patients relapse. A review of long-term follow-up studies investigating factors associated with relapse was carried out.

Results: Factors identified included the absence of social support, a history of depressive episodes, and a tendency to evaluate life events in extreme terms. However, the most common factor was repeated criticism from a partner.

Conclusion: The rank theory of depression would predict that being on the receiving end of continual put-downs would make a person vulnerable to relapse. The importance in relapse of repeated criticism from a partner supports this idea.

Further support comes from a study linking the neurotransmitter serotonin with status. Antidepressant medication increasing the levels of available serotonin, such as Prozac, is widely used in the treatment of depression (see chapter 25):

Box G: Raleigh and McGuire (1993)

Procedure: Vervet monkeys live in hierarchical groups which include high-ranking (alpha) males and males of lower status. Levels of serotonin were measured for alpha and low status males, and for the alpha males when they had lost their status in the group hierarchy. Antidepressants were also given to a randomly chosen male once the alpha male had been removed from the group.

Results: Alpha males in each group had levels of serotonin which were twice as high as those of lower status males. When the alpha males lost their position in the hierarchy, their serotonin levels plummeted, and they showed behaviour similar to that of a depressed person, e.g. refusing food and rocking back and forth. Antidepressants prevented these behaviours. In every group tested, the male randomly chosen to be given antidepressants became the new alpha male.

Conclusion: The depression associated with low levels of serotonin may be a normal part of status competition.

It would of course be unwise to extrapolate too definitely from these findings to depression in people. However, given the large percentage of their genes which human beings have in common with other primates, it is not unreasonable to see these findings as lending some support to evolutionary ideas about depression. However, in human communities not everyone who has lost status suffers from depression, while someone of high social rank may do so. It is also the case that depressive or manic reactions are not necessarily associated with loss or gain of rank.

How can evolutionary psychology explain the greater prevalence of unipolar depression among women? Stevens and Price (2000) pointed out that this gender difference is most marked during the reproductive years of life. They argued that while depression may be advantageous to both sexes, depression during that period would be more disadvantageous to males than to females in terms of reproductive success. The pursuit of females by

males requires more determination, more energy and more initiative – all of which are reduced by unipolar depression – than the acceptance of males by females. Since evolutionary theory argues that females are necessarily more committed to a relationship than males, females may well have to yield in conflicts with a dominant partner; rank theory could well apply here.

However, there would also seem to be other reasons for gender differences in the incidence of unipolar depression during this period. The mother more than the father is likely to suffer from the demands of the child, starting with the child drawing on maternal resources for its development in the womb. Breastfeeding requires resources, and additional children will increase the demands made on the mother.

Cultural factors in terms of different expectations of the role of mothers and of fathers may also contribute to the difference in the incidence of depression in men and women. The effect of cultural factors, such as the differential distribution of power between men and women, has been supported by research:

Box H: Wilhelm and Parker (1989)

Procedure: Participants were student teachers in their early twenties who were followed for a period of five years. Given the nature of the participants, it was argued that female participants were given equal opportunities with males. The incidence of unipolar depression in males and females was compared.

Results: There was no difference between males and females in the incidence of depression.

Conclusion: The difference in the incidence of unipolar depression usually found between males and females is linked to the social inequality of the sexes.

However, the conclusion to be drawn here is not clear-cut. The similarity in the incidence of depression among males and females was due not so much to fewer females becoming depressed, as might be expected where females were given greater opportunities, but rather to an increase in depression among males. This could be because teaching is seen as a low-status occupation for males. However, it is also possible that these findings reflect a more general trend towards an increase in depression among young males, itself perhaps linked to increasing competition from women in the world of work.

A further study, relatively unaffected by the social changes which are a confounding variable in the Wilhelm and Parker study, is also interesting:

Box I: Loewenthal *et al.* (1995)

Procedure: The prevalence of unipolar depression in a sample of 339 Jews (157 men and 152 women), affiliated to orthodox synagogues in North London, was investigated.
Results: There was an equal prevalence of depression in both sexes.
Conclusion: Social and cultural factors have an important role in determining behaviour. Factors in this case include the high esteem in which women are held by this group, and the readiness of men in the sample to acknowledge depression.

A somewhat different approach has also been used to explain the adaptiveness of bipolar disorder. Goodwin and Jamison (1990) reported that bipolar illness is often associated with high intelligence and/or creativity. Many creative people are thought to have suffered from this disorder, and it has been

suggested that the manic phases have made a huge contribution to their creative energy. Examples include Vincent van Gogh, Virginia Woolf, Handel and Coleridge. Both high intelligence and creativity are attributes which are likely to increase a person's attractiveness to potential mates, an advantage which may outweigh the periods of dysfunction experienced in this disorder.

However, as with all the ideas suggested by evolutionary psychologists, it is very difficult to see how these claims about the adaptive nature of both unipolar depression and bipolar disorder could be tested in a controlled way. While research has yielded results which could be explained in evolutionary terms, it is impossible to rule out alternative interpretations. As such, these ideas remain little more than interesting speculation.

- ⊖ Evolutionary explanations have been proposed for both **unipolar depression** and **bipolar disorder**.
- ⊖ Links have been made both with **attachment** difficulties in childhood and with competition for **status** within communities.
- ⊖ Explanations in terms of **reproductive success** have been put forward for **gender differences** in the incidence of **unipolar depression**. **Cultural factors** are also important here.
- ⊖ There are adaptive advantages associated with the **creativity** often found in people with **bipolar disorder**.
- ⊖ While there is some supporting evidence for these ideas, they do not lend themselves easily to rigorous testing.

Van Gogh

Virginia Woolf

Handel

Coleridge

Many creative people are thought to have suffered from bipolar disorder

Phobias

A phobia is an anxiety disorder, an irrational fear of an object or a situation, out of all proportion to what elicits it. However, it should be noted at the outset that fear in itself is not maladaptive. Some degree of fear is important to survival and reproductive success. The dodo became extinct because, before the arrival of people, it lived in an environment with no predators, and so knew no fear.

Some phobias result in an automatic response which is relevant to the feared object or situation. For example, acrophobia (fear of heights) leads to a person physically freezing, so making them less likely to fall, while haemophobia (fear of blood) causes fainting, with its associated bradycardia and drop in blood pressure, so making the person less likely to bleed to death. However, sometimes the phobic has a choice of responses:

▶ Activity 7: a spider in the bath

Imagine that you are arachnophobic, i.e. you have an intense fear of spiders, which tend to appear in the bath. You plan to take a bath. How might you respond to the possibility of a spider in the bath?

CAN SOMEONE GET RID OF A SPIDER IN THE BATH?

When you have finished, see the notes on page 619.

It has been suggested that phobias may develop through classical conditioning (described in chapter 1). There is some evidence that phobic behaviour can develop in this way, most notably Watson and Rayner's study of Little Albert (chapter 1, box B).

However, even if phobias can be learned, it does not follow that all phobias are acquired in this way,

and there are difficulties with this explanation. One major problem is that some phobias are very much more common than others, and their frequency does not correspond with how often we are exposed to a particular stimulus or situation, or what the potential dangers are. For example, we are much more frequently exposed to cars than to snakes or spiders, and therefore have greater opportunities to acquire a phobia about them, but many more people have a phobia about spiders than about cars. This is in spite of the fact that, in the Western world, we are far more likely to be harmed by a car than by a spider. Guns, cigarettes, whisky and saturated fats are serious threats to our wellbeing, but people are much more likely to develop a phobia to open spaces than to any of these.

Seligman (1971) has explained this in terms of **biological preparedness**; we may be preprogrammed to develop fears of objects and situations which were very real sources of danger in our evolutionary past. Going back thousands of years, those of our ancestors who were sensitive to these kinds of stimuli were more likely to avoid them, and thus survive long enough to pass on their genes to the next generation, while those who were less responsive were less likely to survive, and so their genes died out.

▶ Activity 8: the adaptiveness of phobias

Some of the most common phobias are fear of:

spiders	snakes
heights	storms
deep water	the dark
being in an enclosed space	leaving home alone

Why would these fears have been adaptive in our evolutionary history?

When you have finished, see the notes on page 619.

Some modern phobias can be explained as analogues of fears which were adaptive in our evolutionary past; a phobia of going to school or to the dentist are related to fears of leaving home and of pain. Other modern fears are biologically prepared in that they contain elements of these ancient dangers. Fear of flying, for example, combines a fear of heights, enclosed spaces, falling and loud noise.

Further support for the idea of preparedness comes from the fact that it is very hard to induce a fear of something which has been selected arbitrarily, e.g. a telescope or baked beans. Little Albert was conditioned to fear a rat, a fear that is not uncommon and which would have been adaptive in our evolutionary past, since rats carry disease and may therefore present a real danger. Seligman suggested that fears can only be conditioned if we are evolutionarily prepared to form a fear response to the object or situation to which we are exposed. This may explain why it is so hard to teach young children to fear evolutionarily recent dangers, such as knives, matches and electric sockets.

Marks and Nesse (1994) went further, and suggested that phobias are innate fears which we gradually unlearn. As discussed in the section on attachment in chapter 2, children in their first year of life show a fear of strangers (or **xenophobia**) and of separation from their major care-giver. These fears make perfect evolutionary sense in terms of the possibility of infanticide which is common among primate species; similarly, Daly and Wilson (1989) reported that human infants were more likely to be abused by those to whom they are not genetically related than by kin.

Fear of the dark, of spiders and of deep water are also very common in young children. Marks and Nesse suggested that children learn *not* to be afraid of these objects and situations by **observational learning**, i.e. modelling their behaviour on the behaviour of those around them. This is the explanation Bandura provided in **social learning theory** (see chapter 1) to explain how we acquire relevant social behaviours. For example, when a young child is approached by a stranger or an animal, the child characteristically looks at its mother to monitor her responses. If the mother smiles, the child is reassured; if she shows alarm, this releases and increases the child's fear.

Adult phobias, then, are the result not of learning but of failure to unlearn inappropriate but evolutionarily relevant fear responses. There is some empirical support for this idea. The conditioning explanation would mean that the phobic object or situation, e.g. a snake, must in the past have been paired with a traumatic experience. The fear associated with this experience would then become a conditioned response to the snake. However, for many people who are phobic about snakes there is no evidence that this is the case. Maurer (1965) found that schoolchildren in Chicago were most frightened of lions, tigers and snakes. These fears fit in with an evolutionary theory of phobias, while it seems extremely unlikely that the children could have learned these fears in the way which conditioning theory suggests.

Further evidence comes from a study of monkeys:

> **Box J: Mineka and Cook (1993)**
>
> **Procedure:** Laboratory-raised macaques were shown snakes. They were then shown a film of another monkey being frightened by a snake or by a flower, and tested again to see whether they were afraid of the snake or the flower.
>
> **Results:** Before seeing the film, the monkeys showed no fear of snakes. After watching the film, they showed a fear response to a snake but not to a flower.
>
> **Conclusion:** The fear response to a snake after watching the film was not learned in response to the film, since fear was not shown to the flower. Viewing the film of the monkey being frightened by a snake triggered a preprogrammed fear response.

While this explanation of phobias seems convincing, there are nonetheless criticisms to be made of it. As with all the explanations proposed by evolutionary theorists, these ideas are not directly testable. This does not of course mean that the explanations they offer are incorrect, but rather that we have no way of knowing whether or to what extent they provide an accurate account of human behaviour, so they remain little more than speculation. In their lack of emphasis on the role that experience and culture play in shaping our behaviour, these ideas have also been criticised for being **reductionist**, i.e. limited in the kinds of factors which shape our behaviour which are seen to be important.

❺ Phobias have been explained as **learned behaviour**. However, this does not account for the **relative frequency** of different phobias.
❺ The idea of **biological preparedness** links phobias to fears which would have been adaptive in our evolutionary past. It is also possible that certain fears are **innate** and need to be unlearned through **observational learning**.
❺ There is some **empirical support** for these ideas, but there are problems with testing them. In addition, they have been criticised as **reductionist**.

22.4 INTELLIGENCE

▷ Activity 9: animal intelligence

Put this list of animals in descending order of intelligence, starting with the most intelligent.

fish	dogs	apes
humans	horses	chickens
cows	cats	sheep

When you have finished, check your results against those of Banks and Flora (1977) – given in the notes on page 619 – who gave college students a similar task.

It is likely that the order in which you put these animals, and the ratings you gave, were not widely different from the data of the Banks and Flora study. The ranking itself was not the main aim of their study; what is more interesting is that it reveals the common assumption that there is a progressive development of intelligence in the animal kingdom, with humans at the top.

Phylogeny is the history of a species showing its links to ancestral species. A **phylogenetic tree** can be used to infer relationships between an existing species and its evolutionary history. Attempting to represent the animal kingdom in an orderly sequence has a long history, going back to Aristotle. It has been referred to as the Scala Naturae or the 'Great Chain of Being'. Typically, simple creatures like sponges are at the bottom, with humans at the top, and insects, fish, amphibians, reptiles and mammals in between. (Incidentally, sometimes the Great Chain has been extended above humans to angels and to God at the very top!)

This kind of approach can be seen to link to Darwin's idea that all species have evolved from different, earlier species, and it has often been assumed that with evolution comes increasing intelligence. However, this is very much an oversimplification, and it is now clear that it is impossible to organise the relationships among various species using a simple linear scale. A better representation of the complex relationships between species is a tree-like structure like that shown in figure 4.

Another popular belief is that intelligence is related to **brain size**. The Banks and Flora data showed a strong positive correlation between rankings of intelligence and the brain size of the animals concerned.

This idea was popular with the eighteenth century psychologist Franz Gall, the founder of the pseudoscience of **phrenology**, which linked various mental functions with the bumps and depressions on people's skulls. Gall proposed that heavier brains were more intelligent than lighter ones; that on average the brains of black people are smaller than those of white people; and that women's brains are smaller than men's. These differences supposedly explained the differences in intelligence between these groups. Ironically, when Gall died, his brain was weighed and found to be somewhat lighter than that of the average female.

One problem with linking brain size to intelligence is that elephants have much heavier brains than those of humans; however, very few people believe that elephants are the more intelligent species. A more plausible suggestion is that we should look at the ratio of the size of the brain to the body. However, using this measure, humans (relative brain size of 2%) are now outclassed by the mouse lemur (relative brain size of 3%).

However, in assessing brain size we also need to take **allometry** into account. This relates to the

Figure 4: one possible version of the family tree of the animal kingdom (from Romer, 1966)

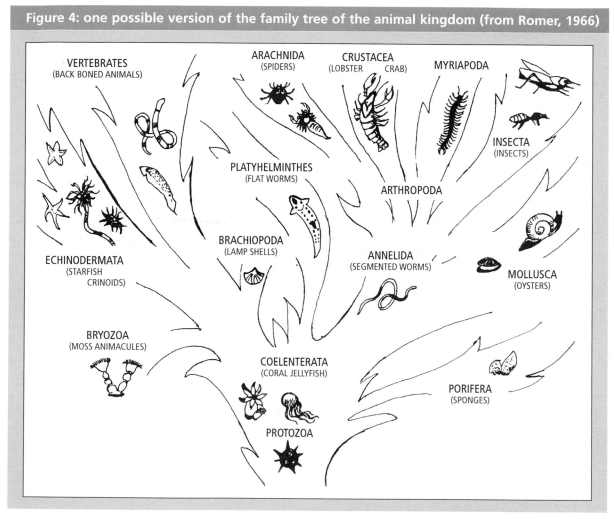

growth of one part of the body in relation to the growth of another part of the body, or of the body as a whole. Allometry looks at these changes either in one organism, or makes comparisons between different organisms. As an organism increases in size, there is no reason to suppose that all its organs (including the brain) should increase proportionately. For example, if a mouse were increased to the size of an elephant its legs would still be disproportionately thinner than those of an elephant. However, if brain weight is plotted against body size for mammals, using a logarithmic scale to create a straight line graph (see figure 5), the weight of the human brain is very much larger than expected for a mammal of our size and quite a lot larger than expected for a primate of our size.

Figure 5: brain weight and body weight (from Young, 1981)

The variance of brain size from what would be expected given body size is known as the **encephalisation quotient (EQ)**. However, a high EQ does not necessarily imply high intelligence; for example, someone with dwarfism would have a very high EQ but people with this condition are no more intelligent than other people.

While the relationship between brain size and intelligence is not a simple one, it was noted earlier that the size of the human brain increased rapidly (in evolutionary terms) some 2 million years ago. From evidence provided by fossils, Deacon (1997) pointed out that the body size of hominids has increased over the last 4 million years. However, the growth of body size during development is slower than for other mammals, while the brain continues to increase in size after birth to make it larger than would be expected. Brains take a great deal of energy to produce and to run. While the human brain makes up about 2% of body mass, it uses up about 20% of the energy we take in as food. A key issue, then, is why humans have developed such large brains. We will look now at the various ideas which have been put forward.

It is possible that the tripling in size of the human brain in the past 2 million years is the result of natural selection. Perhaps there was some change in the environment which made a larger brain an adaptive feature. However, this may not offer an entirely adequate explanation. Growth of the human brain started while brains of other closely related hominids, in the same habitat, remained the same size. This rapid increase in growth stopped about 100,000 years ago, long before the Neolithic revolution in technology and art 40,000 years ago.

Miller (1998) suggested that we need to look here at sexual selection, which could well bring about such rapid change, and in particular intersexual selection, i.e. the choices made by one sex for the features of the other. Remember that for humans, it is males who compete for females and females who choose males. Miller suggested that in our evolutionary past, humans would have assessed potential partners on a range of features, to estimate age, fertility, social status and cognitive skills. In terms of this last criterion, females may have selected males who were amusing and creative, a process facilitated by the development of language, which would allow an exchange of information to assist in choosing a suitable partner. Females would therefore select males with large brains. Miller went on to suggest that female brains would also increase in size because the increased cognitive capacity would be necessary to understand and appreciate male displays.

In support of his ideas, Miller went on to point out that males are responsible for far more art, music and literature than females, much of it produced not long after reaching maturity. Culture, in other words, is seen as a form of gender display. As such it is a form of intrasexual selection, i.e. a way in which males compete for females. Gould and Gould (1989) suggested that traditional male intrasexual competition, involving the acquisition of resources, has been transformed into a more symbolic contest in terms of ambitiousness, risk-taking and cultural expression.

Ridley (1993, p20) reported that 'most evolutionary anthropologists now believe that big brains contributed to reproductive success either by enabling men/women to outwit and outscheme other men/women or because big brains were originally used to court and seduce members of the other sex.'

However, there has been considerable criticism of ideas such as those put forward by Miller. These ideas are highly speculative and unsupported by any evidence. As an explanation of increased brain size, it seems unlikely that females would make the effort to produce and run a large brain simply for the purpose of appreciating male displays. In addition, we need to look at cultural factors which may have influenced the artistic output of men and women; for example, the opportunities open to them to develop the necessary skills, the influence of gender on the expectations of individuals, and so on.

There are currently two major theories which seek to explain the increase in brain size and therefore intelligence, and which do not focus directly on sexual selection. One looks at environmental factors, with the idea that the environment of primates poses particular problems in terms of the mental capacity necessary to gather food. The other – the Machiavellian intelligence hypothesis – relates to the highly complex skills necessary for successful group living. This idea relates to the first idea in the Ridley quotation, the ability of people to outwit and outscheme one another. We will look at each of these theories in turn. The relationships between factors in these two approaches can be seen in figure 6:

◒ It is a popular **misconception** that evolution has been **linear**, with new species becoming progressively more intelligent. A **tree-like** structure is a better representation.

◒ It is also often assumed that **intelligence** is related to **brain size**. The relationship is not a simple one. However, the human brain is very much larger than would be expected in a primate of our size, i.e. we have a high **encephalisation quotient**.

◒ Several suggestions have been made to explain the rapid **increase in brain growth** in the last two million years.

◒ There is little evidence for this change being driven by **habitat change**. Several ideas have been proposed relating to **sexual selection**. Two other theories relate to **environmental factors in foraging** and the skills necessary for successful **group living**.

Environmental factors: food and foraging

Herbivores such as cows need to spend a lot of time grazing in order to ingest sufficient food. However, this kind of foraging does not require a large brain. Most primates are unable to deal with the large

Figure 6: rival theories in accounting for increase in human brain size (from Byrne, 1995)

Machiavellian intelligence predictions

Resource distribution   Risks of predation

Large social groups

Complex societies

Enlarged neocortex

Environmental complexity predictions

High-quality diet

Complex feeding   Enlarged neocortex

amounts of cellulose involved in a herbivorous diet, and so have a more varied though largely vegetarian diet. This involves travelling around to find suitable food, locating food using a highly developed perceptual system and extracting food from its source – for example, eating fruits while avoiding the prickles and stings which are often part of the plant – all of which require more intelligence than grazing.

It has been suggested that the increased brain size of humans is related to the use of tools in extracting food from its source. For example, chimpanzees use sticks to extract termites from their nest and stones to break nuts. However, Byrne (1995) pointed out that the available evidence suggests that tools used by early man – Neanderthals and homo erectus – were only slightly more sophisticated than those used by chimps today. Moreover, as has already been noted, the rapid growth of the human brain was already over by the time of Neolithic people. It seems unlikely, therefore, that the driving force behind human brain development was simply the search for food.

Machiavellian intelligence hypothesis

A more convincing explanation has come from various related hypotheses which Byrne and Whiten (1988) have brought together as the **Machiavellian intelligence hypothesis**. The name refers to Nicolo Machiavelli, the Renaissance politician and author whose name has come to epitomise the cunning manipulation of others in political life. In this model, brain growth came about so that hominids could predict and manipulate each other's behaviour, so serving their own interests without disrupting the cohesion of the social group within which they lived.

Living in groups is a good defensive strategy; there is safety in numbers, which will also benefit the individual. A group also offers access to resources and potential mates. At the same time, the larger the group becomes, the more opportunities there are for conflict between group members. To some extent, this is kept in check in primate groups by a dominance hierarchy, with some individuals having more power within the group than others.

Another very effective mechanism is **grooming**. Primates such as chimpanzees spend far more time than is necessary for purely hygienic purposes in picking through each other's fur and removing bits of plant material, insects and scabs. It has therefore been suggested that grooming serves social ends, such as strengthening alliances between individuals, and bringing about reconciliation after a dispute.

However, the Machiavellian intelligence hypothesis goes beyond grooming to look at other ways in which behaviour can help the individual negotiate and benefit from group living. The key here is deception, one of the ways in which some primates demonstrate what is known as **theory of mind**. This is the ability to be self-aware and to appreciate that others also have self-awareness. It is discussed in more detail in the last section of chapter 20, with some research examples of this ability in primates in box Q and box S. You might find it useful to look back now over this material.

Grooming and the deception of others make quite heavy demands on cognitive skills. Primates who live in social groups must be able to recognise a number of other individuals, to remember who has given favours to whom, who has alliances with whom and is related to whom, and most demanding of all, consider how a situation would appear from someone else's perspective.

This theory would predict that there should be a strong association between time spent grooming, possession of theory of mind, and intelligence. However, there are difficulties associated with testing these ideas, perhaps the most serious of which is how an animal's intelligence might be measured. In testing human intelligence, there is considerable controversy about whether it is possible to construct a way of measuring intelligence which is culture-free, or at least culture-fair, i.e. not biased towards a particular culture. The possibility of a 'species-free' measure of intelligence is considerably more problematical.

One approach which has been suggested rests on the **triune model** of the brain, proposed by MacLean (1972), who argued that the human brain can be divided into three sections:

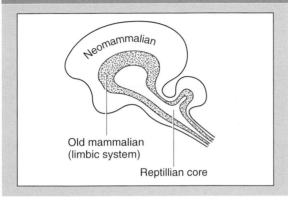

Figure 7: triune model of the brain (MacLean, 1972)

The **reptilian core** is that part inherited from our reptilian-like ancestors, responsible for basic drives and repetitive behaviour. The **old mammalian** part of the brain includes the **limbic system**. It is responsible for behaviours such as fighting, feeding and social behaviour. The **neomammalian** part (the **neocortex**) was the most recent to develop, and is responsible for higher mental functions. It is this region which is therefore responsible for the kinds of social and cognitive abilities described in the Machiavellian intelligence hypothesis. An objective way of measuring the intelligence of different species might therefore be to look at what percentage of the total brain is represented by the neocortex; it would be expected that the more intelligent the animal, the greater should be the proportion of the brain represented by the neocortex. This measure has been used to test both the environmental complexity explanation of the rapid increase in brain size, and the alternative Machiavellian intelligence hypothesis:

Box K: Dunbar (1993)

Procedure: Various species of primates were tested. The ratio of the volume of the neocortex to the rest of the brain was compared with (a) various measures of environmental complexity (to test the environmental complexity explanation of the rapid increase in brain size) and (b) the size of group within which each species lives (to test the Machiavellian intelligence hypothesis).
Results: There was no relationship between the size of the neocortex and environmental complexity. However, there was a strong correlation between the size of the neocortex and group size.
Conclusion: The percentage of the brain represented by the neocortex is unconnected with environmental complexity, and therefore does not support this explanation of rapid brain growth in humans. However, the correlation with group size lends some support to the Machiavellian intelligence hypothesis.

This research could be criticised on the grounds that the percentage of the brain represented by the neocortex is a very indirect (and therefore possibly invalid) measure of intelligence. However, research has also attempted to establish whether neocortex size correlates with direct measures of intelligent behaviour:

Box L: Byrne and Whiten (1988)

Procedure: Data were collected from studies of behaviour in primates which were instances of Machiavellian intelligence, and specifically deception. Allowances were made for the number of studies carried out on particular species in order to arrive at a tactical deception index. As a further control, examples of behaviour which could be interpreted in any other way were excluded. A possible correlation between the tactical deception index and neocortex ratio was investigated.
Results: There was a strong positive correlation between instances of tactical deception and neocortex ratio.
Conclusion: Neocortex ratio is a valid measure of intelligence in primates.

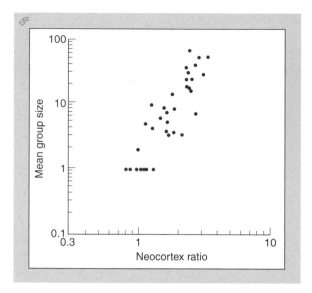

Similar studies have investigated a possible relationship between time spent grooming and group size. If grooming is a way of facilitating social interaction within a group, which brain development allows to be carried out more effectively, then it follows that more time should be spent on grooming as the size of the group increases. A study by Dunbar (1993) found a strong positive correlation between time spent grooming and group size, thus supporting this idea.

There is some empirical support, then, for the Machiavellian intelligence hypothesis as an explanation of the rapid brain growth which took place in humans some 2 million years ago. However, much of this research uses only rather indirect measures of what it aims to assess. As with all ideas in evolutionary psychology, there is no way of testing them directly even though they have some interesting and thought-provoking proposals to make.

- It has been suggested that **environmental factors** in foraging, in particular **tool use**, could account for the rapid increase in brain growth in humans. There is little support for this idea.
- The **Machiavellian intelligence hypothesis** accounts for this brain growth in terms of developing the **cognitive skills** necessary for the successful **manipulation** of other group members.
- **Grooming** seems to serve a social purpose. **Theory of mind** research also indicates that higher primates are capable of using **deception** as a way of manipulating the behaviour of others.
- Research has lent some support to these ideas, but as with other evolutionary ideas, they can be criticised for not being very amenable to testing.

Notes on activities

1 The **male** does not need to make parental effort, since his part in the reproductive process is quickly accomplished, compared with the commitment to gestation of the female. Even if a particular mating fails, or the young he has fathered fail to survive, the male has not lost much since his role is so small. In giving time to parental effort, a male would lose the opportunity of mating with other females, and thus increasing his chances of reproductive success. It may also not be sensible for him to make too much parental effort, because he cannot be sure that the offspring are his own.

A **female** could theoretically abandon her young for the male to look after and seek additional matings. However, this would be a risk, since if the male failed to look after the young, the considerable effort the female had put into producing them would be lost. The limited number of eggs a female has represent a more precious resource than a male's sperm, which is quickly and easily replaced. Because the number of eggs is limited, a female may not quickly become pregnant.

2 The answer to **a** and **b** is females, and males to **c**, **d** and **e**. A female has more to lose from a mating that fails, since each egg represents a relatively large proportion of her lifetime's production of gametes. She therefore needs to choose her partner with care, and a courtship ritual may contribute to this choice. However, males have less to lose if a mating fails, since they can easily

mate again, but they will need to compete with other males for the opportunity to do so. Size would be an advantage for males, since it would make them better able to compete.

3 Alcock (1993) predicted that all these will be characteristic of males rather than females. Ease of sexual arousal, a preference for a variety of partners, problems in remaining faithful in marriage and a tendency to force sexual activity on unwilling females all follow from the reproductive success of a polygynous male depending on mating with many partners. This will only be a successful strategy, though, if females are monogamous and make the considerable parental investment necessary to rear the young successfully. For **c**, males should be more concerned with a mate's fidelity because it is the only way they can be sure that the offspring to whom they are giving parental care are their own. However, it would also make sense for females in a monogamous species to be concerned about male fidelity, because a deserting male reduces the chances of survival of the offspring; one-parent care is not nearly as effective as two-parent care.

4 The reproductive success of men is increased if they mate with young, healthy women, as opposed to older, unhealthy women. Youth indicates that the woman is still fertile, while attractiveness provides a rough guide to age and health. In looking for a good provider, women can help to ensure that their pregnancies are successful and that their offspring survive to sexual maturity.

6 In monogamous species, both parents are likely to offer parental care. For the female, offering care makes sense because of the relatively large investment she has made in producing the offspring. For a monogamous male, offering parental care helps to ensure the survival of the offspring he has fathered, and this outweighs the extra opportunities for mating which would be possible if this care were not offered.

In polygynous species, parental care is usually provided by the female. This can again be explained from the female's point of view in terms of the relatively large investment she has

made in producing the young. On the other hand, the male must put his efforts into defending resources such as food or territory, or protecting his females from other males so that they will offer care to his offspring rather than offspring fathered by a rival male. The opposite is true of polyandrous species such as the lily trotter, where males provide care and female effort is put into defending the nest site.

In polygynandrous species, care by either parent is often very much reduced. Frequently, a male cannot be certain that he has fathered a particular offspring, and therefore any care given will not necessarily contribute to the survival of his genes. Females may offer some care, and in some polygynandrous species, such as the chimpanzee, a lot of care is given. Females cannot be certain which offspring have been fathered by males with the 'best' genes, and so cannot selectively invest parental care in offspring with the 'best' fathers.

7 It is likely that the strategies you have identified could each fall under one (or more) of four headings: avoidance (getting someone else to check the bath before entering the bathroom), freezing (staying rooted to the spot, perhaps calling for help), escape (leaving the bathroom if there is a spider in the bath and returning only when it has been removed) or attack (washing the spider down the plughole).

8 Spiders and snakes are often venomous, heights present a risk of being killed or harmed by falling, water presents the risk of drowning, and storms present the risk of being struck by lightning. In the dark, there would be less warning of the approach of predators or of detecting other hazards. Being in an enclosed space is associated with suffocation, and restricts the options available (e.g. flight) if danger threatens. Being alone means a lack of support from others if in a dangerous situation.

9 Banks and Flora did not include humans, but they did give a numerical value to the others (shown in brackets):

1. humans, 2. apes (9.2), 3. dogs (7.4), 4. cats (6.6), 5. horses (5.6), 6. cows (3.6), 7. sheep (3.4), 8. chickens (3.4), 9. fish (1.7).

Issues in the classification and diagnosis of psychological abnormality

In this chapter we will be looking at:

23.1 Classifying abnormal behaviour
      Classification systems: DSM and ICD
      Neurosis and psychosis
      The uses of classification
      Reliability
      Validity
      Ethical problems with classification
      Bias in diagnosis

23.2 Multiple personality disorder
      (dissociative identity disorder)
      The origins of DID
      The treatment of DID
      Is DID a genuine disorder?

23.3 Culture-bound syndromes (CBSs)
      CBSs in context
      Do we need the concept of CBSs?

23.1 CLASSIFYING ABNORMAL BEHAVIOUR

The medical approach to abnormal behaviour, which conceptualises mental disorders as illnesses, assumes that mental disorders can be identified and categorised systematically. This kind of categorisation can then be used to diagnose the particular disorder from which an individual is suffering, and suggest how it might be treated.

There are other theoretical orientations to mental disorders. For example, the psychoanalytic approach sees mental disorders arising from childhood experience and psychic conflict, and the behavioural approach sees mental disorders as the result of maladaptive learning. Within these theoretical orientations, classification systems like the ones we will look at in this section are seen as inappropriate. However, the medical model is the most widely accepted model of mental disorder, so it is relevant to look at the systems used by this approach.

Classification systems: DSM and ICD

The idea of classifying mental disorders goes back to the Ancient Greeks, but the first comprehensive classification system of modern times was produced by Kraepelin (1913). He suggested that there were 18 different disorders, each with its own characteristic pattern of symptoms (called a **syndrome**), its own causes (or **aetiology**), and its own typical pattern of development and outcome (or **prognosis**).

Building on Kraepelin's work, the two most well-known current systems of classification are **ICD** (International Classification of Diseases) and **DSM** (Diagnostic and Statistical Manual of Mental Disorders). The World Health Organisation was formed in 1948, and shortly afterwards published ICD. DSM was first published by the American Psychological Association in 1952. ICD is used in Britain and in most other parts of the world, whereas DSM is used in North America.

Both systems are regularly revised; DSM is currently in its fourth edition (and is therefore known as DSM-IV) and ICD is at present in its tenth edition, ICD-10. The re-writing of the systems aims to increase their reliability and validity, characteristics we will be discussing later in this section.

ICD-10 uses 11 categories of mental disorder, shown with examples of disorders in each category in figure 1:

Figure 1: categories of disorder in ICD-10

1   *organic, including symptomatic, mental disorders*: e.g. dementia in Alzheimer's disease; behavioural disorders as a result of brain damage
2   *mental and behavioural disorders due to psychoactive substance abuse*: e.g. the abuse of substances such as alcohol and hallucinogens
3   *schizophrenia, schizotypal and delusional disorders*: e.g. schizophrenia
4   *mood (affective) disorders*: depression; bipolar disorder
5   *neurotic, stress-related and somatoform disorders*: phobias; post-traumatic stress disorder; obsessive–compulsive disorder
6   *behavioural syndromes associated with physiological disturbances and physical factors*: anorexia nervosa; bulimia nervosa
7   *disorders of adult personality and behaviour*: antisocial personality disorder; schizoid personality disorder; gender and identity disorders
8   *mental retardation*
9   *disorders of psychological development*: speech disorders; autism
10 *behavioural and emotional disorders with onset usually occurring in childhood and adolescence*: disorders of attention; non-organic enuresis
11 *unspecified mental disorder*: disorders not specified in other categories

DSM-IV uses 17 categories, shown with examples of each category in figure 2:

Figure 2: categories of disorder in DSM-IV

1   *delirium, dementia, amnestic and other cognitive disorders*: e.g. dementia in Alzheimer's disease; amnestic disorders
2   *schizophrenia and other psychotic disorders*: schizophrenia
3   *substance-related disorders*: alcohol-use disorders; nicotine-use disorders
4   *mood disorders*: depressive disorders; bipolar disorder
5   *anxiety disorders*: phobias; post-traumatic stress disorder; obsessive–compulsive disorder
6   *somatoform disorders*: hypochondriasis
7   *dissociative disorders*: dissociative identity (multiple personality) disorder
8   *adjustment disorders*: adjustment disorder, with anxiety and/or depressed mood
9   *disorders first diagnosed in infancy, childhood or adolescence*: mental retardation; learning disorders
10 *personality disorders*: antisocial personality disorder; schizoid personality disorder
11 *sexual and gender identity disorders*: hyperactive sexual desire disorder; fetishism
12 *impulse control disorders not elsewhere classified*: kleptomania; pyromania
13 *factitious disorders*: Munchausen syndrome
14 *sleep disorders*: insomnia; sleepwalking
15 *eating disorders*: anorexia nervosa; bulimia nervosa
16 *mental disorders due to a general medical condition not elsewhere classified*: catatonic disorder
17 *other conditions which may be a focus of clinical attention*: medication-induced movement disorders; relational problems

Activity 1: comparing ICD-10 and DSM-IV

Look back through the categories shown in figure 1 and figure 2.

a where does a category used in one system seem to be very similar to a category in the other system?

b which two or more categories in DSM-IV contribute to one category in ICD-10, and vice versa?

When you have finished, see the notes on page 644.

DSM-IV also has a system of **multiaxial classification**, which allows a broad assessment of level of functioning. Every person assessed can be rated on five separate axes, aiming to make the psychiatrist consider as much available information as possible. This is based on the idea that disorders must be due to both physical and psychological states of the individual, as well as environmental factors:

Figure 3: the five axes in DSM

Axis I – clinical syndromes and other factors which may be a focus of clinical attention: the disorder(s) from which the person is suffering are listed, together with other problems, such as a history of abuse, and factors related to the stage of a person's life, e.g. menopause

Axis II – personality disorders: traits or behaviours generally typical of the person, over and above those related to the particular disorder(s)

Axis III – medical disorders: medical conditions, e.g. a heart condition, which might be relevant

Axis IV – psychosocial and environmental problems: stressful events in the person's life, such as a recent bereavement or poor housing conditions, which could be relevant, rated on a scale of 0 (none) to 7 (catastrophic)

Axis V – global assessment of functioning: an assessment of the person's current level of functioning, using the Global Assessment of Functioning Scale, from 0 (persistent danger) to 100 (superior functioning)

The first three axes always need to be used for making a diagnosis. For example, you may have noticed that autism is included in category 9 of ICD, but is not mentioned in DSM. Since autism is an underlying condition, it would become part of the diagnosis for a person with this disorder as the result of using axis II. Axes IV and V may be used to give a broader basis for clinical assessment.

Mental health professionals using ICD-10 also use a similar range of information to make a diagnosis. They will need to find out about the psychiatric, medical, personal and family history of the patient; their social circumstances; and their personality. They will make a cognitive assessment, e.g. of memory and IQ, test the functioning of the CNS and make a physical examination. This information can then be summarised in a grid, like the one shown in figure 4:

Figure 4: assessment grid

	biological	social	psychological
precipitating			
predisposing			
perpetuating			

This will show the factors which are the immediate or precipitating cause of the disorder, factors which have predisposed the person to develop a particular disorder, and factors which serve to maintain or perpetuate it.

Neurosis and psychosis

We need also to look briefly at the terms 'neurotic' and 'psychotic'. These terms have long been used to describe distinctions between different types of disorder:

Figure 5: the neurotic/psychotic distinction

neurotic	psychotic
only a part of the personality is affected	the whole of the personality is affected
contact with reality is maintained	contact with reality is lost
the person realises they have a problem	the person does not realise they have a problem
neurotic behaviour can be seen as exaggeration of normal behaviour	psychotic behaviour is unlike normal behaviour
neurotic behaviour is related to the person's behaviour before developing the disorder	psychotic behaviour is not like the person's behaviour before developing the disorder

In psychosis, contact with reality is lost

Making this distinction, a disorder such as schizophrenia is classified as a psychosis, while an anxiety disorder such as a phobia is classified as a neurosis.

Though 'neurotic' appears as part of category 5 in ICD-10 and 'psychotic' in category 2 in DSM-IV, they are no longer used to make broad distinctions between disorders within ICD-10 and DSM-IV. However, the terms are still in general use; for example, you will find the term 'antipsychotic drugs' used in chapter 25 on therapies. Mental health professionals still find these terms a useful way of describing different disorders in general terms, but they have fallen out of use for diagnostic purposes, for several reasons. For one thing, they are not very precise. Each term can be used to describe a range of disorders with very little in common. They were originally used because the origins of such disorders as neuroses were thought to be similar. As we will see in chapter 24 on psychopathology, this is not necessarily the case. It is much more informative to use the terms such as those used in the classification systems which refer to a specific disorder. Finally, while the table in figure 5 suggests that there are clear distinctions between neurosis and psychosis, in practice this distinction is not always clear-cut. This again means that the terms are not as useful as more precise labels.

❺ The two main classification systems are **ICD-10** and **DSM-IV**. The two systems show considerable overlap. DSM-IV uses additional information from a **multiaxial system**. ICD-10 has similar structured techniques.

❺ In practice, a distinction is often made between **neurosis** and **psychosis**, though these terms are rather too limited to be very useful.

The uses of classification

Goldstein and Anthony (1988) suggested that a good clinical classification scheme has to have three uses:

> **Figure 6: determinants of a good classification system (Goldstein and Anthony, 1988)**
>
> 1 To allow a **prognosis** to be made (i.e. to predict the future development of the disorder)
> 2 To develop **treatment plans**
> 3 To study the **aetiology** (causes) of specific disorders

One reason that classifying abnormal behaviour is useful is because classifying and diagnosing a person's illness means that mental health professionals then have a better idea of what treatments will be suitable for that person. For example, if a disorder is caused by a chemical imbalance in the brain, no amount of quality counselling will help that patient towards a cure.

Classification of the illness may also help in coming to terms with it – being able to give their problems a label, and perhaps even understand something of their cause, is often of help to patients. For example, treatment for alcohol addicts who attend Alcoholics Anonymous involves accepting the label 'alcoholic'. However, there are problems associated with labelling, which we will return to later in this chapter.

Having a classification system is also useful for researchers, as its structure can guide their research. Similarities between patients can help them to identify the cause or aetiology of a disorder. The use of labels can facilitate the communication of information between health professionals, and can also be of use in assessing improvement as the result of treatment.

There are, however, a number of serious arguments against classifying abnormal behaviour, and problems in implementing the system. There are problems in terms of the **reliability** and **validity** of the classification systems, together with **ethical problems** with their use. Another area of concern is possible **bias** in diagnosis. We will look at each of these issues in turn.

Reliability

For a classification system to be of use, it must be **reliable**; in other words, it must produce consistent results, so that the professionals using it can agree on a category for any particular patient. Reliability may be a problem in classifying mental disorders:

> **Box A: Beck (1967)**
>
> **Procedure:** Four experienced psychiatrists met and discussed the classification system they were to use during the study (DSM), to ensure they agreed on how it should be applied. They then diagnosed 153 patients during their first week in a psychiatric hospital. Each patient was interviewed separately by two different psychiatrists.
>
> **Results:** The psychiatrists agreed on a diagnosis of schizophrenia in only 54% of cases. There was even less agreement on subcategories of this disorder. Discussion about why the diagnoses were different revealed that some disagreements were due to inconsistencies in the information given by the patients and some were due to inconsistencies on the part of the psychiatrist, such as differences in judging the importance of particular symptoms. Most of the disagreements, however, were considered to be the result of inadequacies of the diagnostic system.
>
> **Conclusion:** Diagnostic systems can be difficult to use, and lead to criticisms of unreliability of classification.

A further study also illustrates concerns about the reliability of diagnosis (box B):

It seems, then, that reliable diagnosis of a mental disorder is somewhat problematical. However, you should note that laboratory tests such as blood tests are available to doctors diagnosing a purely physical illness; psychiatrists do not have these additional objective criteria. It is also worth pointing out that although many people have great faith in the reliability of doctors diagnosing medical illnesses, Falek and Moser (1975) found that agreement between doctors in cases of angina, emphysema and tonsillitis which were diagnosed without using a definitive laboratory test was no better than agreement on diagnoses of schizophrenia, and in some cases worse.

Box B: Temerline (1970)

Procedure: An interview was taped, with an actor playing the role of a person enjoying 'good mental health'. Five experimental groups (graduate students in clinical psychology; clinical psychologists; psychiatrists; law students; undergraduates) heard a famous psychiatrist say: 'I know the man being interviewed today. He is a very interesting man because he looks neurotic but is actually quite psychotic'. Since this suggestion was made by a man who was a well-known expert in his field, it was termed the **prestigious suggestion**. There was also a control 'no suggestion' group, and a group which heard the suggestion that the man was mentally healthy. The actor gave as his reason for coming to the clinic that he had just read a book about psychotherapy and wanted to talk about it.

After hearing the interview, all participants were asked to make a specific diagnosis by ticking items on a data sheet that listed various psychotic, neurotic and personality disorders, plus a 'healthy' category.

Results:

diagnosis (%)

group	psychosis	neurosis/personality disorder	healthy
psychiatrists	60	40	0
clinical psychologists	28	60	12
graduate students	11	78	12
law students	18	72	10
undergraduates	30	54	16
no suggestion	0	31	69
'healthy' suggestion	0	0	100

Conclusion: Diagnosis is not objective. The more experienced the person making the initial diagnosis, the more likely there is to be a bias towards accepting it, even when it is incorrect.

One frequently-quoted study in the area of reliability in diagnosis is that of Rosenhan (1973):

Box C: Rosenhan (1973)

Procedure: In a study titled 'On Being Sane in Insane Places', eight people with no history of mental illness were asked to turn up at different psychiatric hospitals, complaining of auditory hallucinations. They claimed to hear voices saying 'empty', 'hollow' and 'thud'. All eight people were admitted to the psychiatric hospitals, and from that point on, behaved normally. They answered staff questions by saying that they felt fine and had no symptoms.

Results: Participants noticed that staff at the hospital treated them in a very off-hand way, either answering inappropriately their questions about when they might be discharged, or ignoring them entirely. Many of their normal behaviours were reported on their notes as symptoms of their illness, such as writing a diary (required for the research) being reported as 'excessive note-taking'. Although many of the genuine patients of the psychiatric hospitals quickly recognised that the pseudo-patients did not have a mental disorder, not one of the mental health professionals detected any of the pseudo-patients.

Conclusion: If people are labelled 'abnormal', everything they say and do may be taken to be a symptom of their illness. Psychiatrists may not be able to distinguish people with mental disorders from those without mental disorders.

A follow-up study by Rosenhan involved telling a hospital about the original study, and warning staff that more pseudo-patients would seek admission over the following three months. Despite the fact that no such pseudo-patients were sent, of the 193 people who were admitted to the hospital, one member of staff 'spotted' that 43 of them were pseudo-patients. Hospital admission statistics for schizophrenia were also lower during this period. The results of his research led Rosenhan to conclude that 'it is clear that we cannot distinguish the sane from the insane in psychiatric hospitals'.

However, various researchers have commented on Rosenhan's work, and it has been suggested that the criticisms levelled at psychiatrists on the basis of his study are unfair. Perhaps the study really shows that psychiatrists can't tell the difference between someone with a mental disorder and someone pretending to have one, rather than an inability to distinguish between a person with a mental disorder and someone with no such disorder. It is also worth noting that the pseudo-patients insisted on being admitted, which in itself is a sign of serious emotional disturbance. It has been claimed that if the same study were carried out now, the pseudo-patients would not be able to gain admission, as DSM-IV would now not diagnose them as schizophrenic.

It is also argued that the reliability of diagnosing and classifying mental disorders is now greatly improved since the time when these studies were carried out. Fonagy and Higgett (1984) reported that DSM covers a broader range of disorders than previously, uses more precise language and gives more specific categories of disorders. The fact that the exact criteria ('operational criteria') for each disorder have been explicitly detailed makes the system much more objective and therefore more reliable. ICD has also been improved, including the addition of structured interviews and increased use of checklists to cover aspects such as cognitive functioning and social circumstances, which should help to make diagnosis more objective. DiNardo *et al.* (1993) reported that psychiatrists now agree at least 70% of the time on the diagnosis of a patient's main problem.

It is possible, however, that anxiety and personality disorders may never be reliably diagnosed, because there could be a large contribution from social learning to these disorders, which would result in considerable variation and overlap in behaviour patterns. Szasz (1972) also made the point that abnormal behaviour does not necessarily fit into neat categories. He suggested that any classification system may do more harm than good because it creates a case for stereotypical behaviour, forcing people with different patterns of behaviour into what is considered the 'correct' behaviour.

- ❺ Classification systems can be useful in aiding **communication** between mental health professionals, contributing to **research** into the aetiology of mental disorders, suggesting appropriate **treatment** and reassuring patients.
- ❺ There is some evidence that classification systems may have low **reliability**. However, the most recent versions of ICD and DSM are more detailed and precise than earlier versions, and are therefore more reliable.

Validity

In this context, validity means how useful the categories of a classification system are in terms of making a clear distinction between patients in one category and patients in another. Validity is related to reliability – if a classification system does not lead to reliable diagnosis, can the categories which make up the system be said to be valid? If a diagnosis is valid, it should be possible to make accurate statements about the nature of the disorder and predictions about the course it will run.

Diagnosis can have three forms of validity:

Figure 7: validity in the diagnosis of mental disorders

- ❺ **aetiological validity:** the same factors have caused the disorder in the diagnostic group. For example, if a disorder is thought to be genetic, there should be a family history of that disorder in everyone who suffers from it.
- ❺ **concurrent validity:** other symptoms, not part of the diagnosis itself, should be characteristic of those diagnosed. For example, most people with schizophrenia also have problems in personal relationships.
- ❺ **predictive validity:** there should be similarities in the course of the disorder, with patients suffering from it showing similar behaviour. In other words, a specific prognosis can be made.

However, the question of validity is not without its problems. For example, in trying to establish predictive validity, it is very difficult to operationalise or measure accurately mental states such as anxiety or depression.

As we have seen, there is also still some disagreement between the different systems used by DSM and ICD. For example, Cooper *et al.* (1972) found that a diagnosis of schizophrenia was twice as likely to be made by New York psychiatrists (using DSM) than by psychiatrists in London (using ICD), while the opposite was true of depression. This led to the ironic suggestion that the easiest way for a schizophrenic from New York, or a Londoner with depression, to be cured is to cross the Atlantic! However, as we have seen, the most recent versions of the two systems are closer than previously. The APA notes that it should not be assumed that each category of mental disorder is discrete, and boundaries may be blurred because symptoms overlap.

The main aim behind making a diagnosis or classification is to choose the appropriate therapy, so perhaps the question we should be asking about classificatory systems is whether or not the systems are useful in terms of understanding aetiologies and suggesting treatments. Heather (1976) argued that very few causes of mental disorders are known, and that there is only a 50% chance of predicting what treatment a patient will receive on the basis of the diagnosis which has been made. However, our knowledge in this area has expanded over recent years, so the picture may no longer be as bleak as Heather suggested.

The system may also work in reverse, with the response to treatment guiding diagnosis. For example, a person may be diagnosed as schizophrenic, but not respond to neuroleptic drugs which are used to treat schizophrenia. However, if they are found to respond to Lithium, which is widely used for bipolar disorder (manic depression), then the diagnosis will be changed to bipolar disorder.

Given the fact that human behaviours are so complex, it is not difficult to see why problems of validity are bound to arise in the area of categorising mental disorders. Classification may be illusory, giving the impression of the precision of a mental diagnosis, but resting heavily on interpretation and inference.

There may be difficulties in classifying disorders

Ethical problems with classification

As we have seen, diagnosis leads to **labelling** a person. While labelling can be useful from the patient's point of view, since they may find it reassuring that their problem has been identified, the idea of labelling is of great concern to many people. Public misconceptions and stereotypes of mental illness can lead to prejudiced behaviour against those labelled as mentally ill.

Poor understanding of the nature of mental illness leads to the question of how easy it would be for a person labelled as, say, 'schizophrenic' to get a job when they mention their illness at interview. You can probably imagine yourself in the position of being introduced to someone and being told that they had had a period of schizophrenia a couple of years ago. The stigma attached to that label means that you would be unlikely to think of that person in the same way as you might if they had told you they had suffered from malaria.

Gove (1990) found that the effects of labelling were not long-lasting. However, there is evidence that it can have an effect:

Box D: Langer and Abelson (1974)

Procedure: Participants, including mental health professionals, were shown a video of a young man discussing his work experience with an older man. Some of the participants were told that the young man was a job applicant, while others were told that he was a patient. They were then asked for their impressions of the man.

Results: Participants who believed the young man to be a job applicant described him as 'attractive' and 'conventional-looking', while those who thought he was a patient used descriptions such as 'defensive', 'dependent' and 'frightened of his own aggressive impulses'.

Conclusion: Our judgement of other people can be affected by labels to do with mental disorder. This is true even of mental health professionals.

Rosenhan's work in box C also showed the powerful effects of labelling: if people are labelled 'abnormal', everything they say and do may be taken to be a symptom of their illness, thus making it unlikely that staff will notice any errors in diagnosis that may have been made. If people accept the label and see themselves as 'abnormal', the label can lead to a **self-fulfilling prophecy**, in that they may start to behave in ways consistent with that label. Accepting this **sick role**, and allowing mental health professionals to adopt the **expert role**, reinforces the perceptions of those looking after patients and confirms beliefs that the diagnosis is correct.

A further ethical problem is raised by the assumption that a mental disorder has an underlying physical cause, which may lead to social and psychological factors not being given enough weight. However, the most recent versions of ICD and DSM have addressed this problem with the use of axes (DSM) and the structured investigation of additional factors which should form part of the diagnostic process (ICD). It is perhaps also worth noting that the opposite assumption – that the causes of mental disorders are psychological – can also be problematical, since it can lead to a failure to investigate possible physical causes; two examples are ME and Gulf War Syndrome.

There is thus growing awareness of these kinds of problems. Taken together with the improved accuracy of the classification systems, it is now more likely that a correct diagnosis can be made, and appropriate treatment offered.

It may help to clarify the ethical implications of classification by carrying out a cost–benefit analysis:

Activity 2: costs and benefits of classification

From what you have read so far, draw up a table and make a list of the benefits and costs of classification:

benefits	costs

When you have finished, see the notes on page 644.

- The classification systems have been criticised on the grounds that they lack **validity**; they do not make precise distinctions between disorders. In this context, validity can take three forms: **aetiological**, **concurrent** and **predictive**.
- **Ethical problems** include **labelling**, which can lead to stereotyped behaviour from patients and prejudice from others. The use of classification systems within the medical model can mean that **social** and **environmental factors** may be given insufficient weight.

Bias in diagnosis

Bias in classifying mental disorders can also be a problem. In general, diagnosticians are likely to expect – quite reasonably – that people coming to them for help are disturbed, and they may therefore be biased in how they interpret the information patients give them to fit in with their expectations. Bias can also be related more specifically to culture, ethnicity, gender and social class. The first three of these issues have been discussed in chapter 5, section 5.3, and you may find it useful now to look back at this material. We will look briefly here at bias related to social class.

People from socially disadvantaged backgrounds are more likely than those from higher socioeconomic groups to be diagnosed as schizophrenic. The opposite is true of neurotic disorders. In the USA, the Midtown Manhattan Study by Stole *et al.* (1962) found the lowest levels of disorders in the higher classes, higher in the middle classes and highest in lower classes. Cochrane and Stopes-Roe (1980) found a similar pattern in Britain.

It has been suggested that these differences reflect genetic differences, coming about through the intermarriage of people who are genetically vulnerable to particular mental disorders, but there is no evidence that this is the case.

It could perhaps be better explained in terms of exposure to more stressful life experiences, which trigger the development of disorders in people who are genetically vulnerable to them. It is certainly the case that high levels of stress correlate with the incidence of mental illness. For instance, Brown and Harris (1978) found a high incidence of depression in working-class housewives in Camberwell. Vulnerability factors included long-term adverse life circumstances, together with the impact of short-term life events and lack of paid employment.

It could also be that those in higher social classes have more ready access to 'coping resources', e.g. professional help. Umbenhauer and DeWitte (1978) found that upper-class people received more favourable clinical judgements than lower-class people, and were more likely than lower-class people to be offered psychotherapy, rather than physical

treatments, perhaps because lower-class people were considered less able to benefit from talking therapies. Other findings in this area have been similar:

Box E: Johnstone (1989)

Procedure: The diagnosis of disorders, and treatment offered, for upper-class and lower-class people was compared.
Results: Lower-class people were more likely then upper-class people to: be given a more serious diagnosis; spend longer in hospital; be given a poorer prognosis; and be offered physical treatments (e.g. drugs) rather than psychotherapy.
Conclusion: There are class differences in the diagnosis and treatment of mental disorders.

- Diagnosis may be affected by **bias** related to **culture**, **ethnicity**, **gender** and **social class**.
- People from a lower social class are more likely to be diagnosed as suffering from a **serious mental illness** and are more likely to be prescribed **physical treatments**.

23.2 MULTIPLE PERSONALITY DISORDER (DISSOCIATIVE IDENTITY DISORDER)

Dissociation is a mental process which creates a lack of connection in a person's thoughts, feelings, actions, memories and sense of identity. It can be thought of as a continuum from extremely mild to chronic. Mild dissociative experiences are those which most people experience, such as daydreaming or getting lost in a book you are reading. At the other extreme is a group of dissociative disorders, recognised by DSM-IV (1994), in which there is a disruption in 'consciousness, memory, identity or perception of the environment'.

This category includes psychogenic amnesia (an acute disturbance of memory function), psychogenic fugue (in which a person wanders off and doesn't know who or where they are, and has no memory of how they got there), depersonalisation disorder (a disturbance in the experience of self, in which the person's sense of reality and identity is temporarily distorted) and dissociative identity disorder. This was previously known as **multiple personality disorder (MPD)** when it was first included in DSM-III (1980). The name was changed to **dissociative identity disorder (DID)** in DSM-IV (1994), because the term 'personality' carries the suggestion of stability across time and situations, and refers to the totality of our psychological makeup. It is therefore inappropriate for people with DID, where personality is fragmented across two or more identities. It is the most severe of the dissociative disorders.

DID is characterised by a lack of integration of different aspects of consciousness: thoughts, memories, feelings, actions and identity. In addition to the primary personality, i.e. that by which the individual is most commonly known, there may be several different sub-identities (sometimes referred to as **alters**, from the Latin for 'other') which will be evident at different times. Cases have been reported with as few as two identities and as many as 100; according to the American Psychological Association (1994), the average number is 15 for women and 8 for men.

These identities differ from the primary personality in terms of their names, age, gender and personality characteristics. A person may switch gradually to another identity, but the changeover is often abrupt, caused by triggers which are related in some way in the patient's mind to the underlying trauma which has brought about the disorder. Stress may also lead to a changeover in identity. Some identities will be aware of the others, but before treatment the primary personality is usually unaware of the alters. However, the primary personality is usually aware of blocks of time which they can't account for, when one or more of the alters has taken over. The primary personality is often guilt-ridden, passive, depressed and dependent, while the alters may be outgoing and aggressive. Alters may interrupt each other when communicating with the therapist.

Amnesia for personal activities, both recent and long past, is common. In some cases, this may cover an extended period of childhood. Flashbacks and self-mutilation may also occur, and current relationships may be abusive. The diagnostic criteria for DID are shown in figure 8:

Figure 8: diagnostic criteria for DID (from DSM-IV, 1994)

a The presence of two or more distinct identities or personality states (each with its own relatively stable pattern of perceiving, relating to, and thinking about the environment and self).

b At least two of these identities or personality states recurrently take control of the person's behaviour.

c Inability to recall important personal information that is too extensive to be explained by ordinary forgetfulness.

d The disturbance is not due to the direct physiological effects of a substance (e.g. blackouts or chaotic behaviour during alcohol intoxication) or a general medical condition (e.g. complex partial seizures).

Note: In children, the symptoms are not attributable to imaginary playmates or other fantasy play.

The incidence of the disorder is hard to establish. Ross *et al.* (1991) have estimated that 1% of the population may be affected. Bliss and Jeppsen (1985) have suggested that up to 10% of psychiatric patients are multiples (sufferers from DID), though few clinicians would accept this estimate. One problem with establishing the incidence of DID is that, in most cases, the primary personality is completely unaware of the alters. Since the alters have a particular role to play, and fulfil a particular function in the patient's life, they are unlikely to seek treatment. Therefore, when multiples do seek treatment it is usually for some other disorder such as depression. Hacking (1995) reported that 90% of cases are women. It is also possible that it may be equally prevalent (though less diagnosed) among men.

Given the dramatic nature of the disorder, it is hardly surprising that some of the best-known cases have been popularised by being written up as novels or turned into Hollywood films. A classic example, made into the film *The Three Faces of Eve*, based on the book of the same name, is described in box F:

Joanne Woodward as Eve in the film *The Three Faces Of Eve*

Box F: Thigpen and Cleckley (1954)

A patient known as Eve White was referred for therapy because of severe headaches. She also complained of blackouts. Hypnosis was used to help her with her personal problems, which seemed to be nothing out of the ordinary.

A few days after hypnosis, the therapist received a letter from her, with a postscript in different handwriting. At her next therapy session, Eve White denied sending the letter, though she remembered starting one. She reported hearing a voice in her head. She sank her head in her hands, and when she sat up, seemed to be a completely different person. While Eve White was usually quiet, shy and anxious, she now seemed very relaxed, confident and carefree. Even her voice was very different. This 'other woman' is referred to as Eve Black.

Eve White was not aware of Eve Black, though Eve Black was aware of Eve White. Apparently Eve Black had existed from Eve White's early childhood, and her behaviour had resulted in Eve White being punished for things she was not aware that she had done. Both personalities were given a series of psychological tests, and differences emerged in IQ, memory and personality.

At a later session, a third personality – Jane – emerged. She was aware of both Eve White and Eve Black, but neither was aware of her. Therapy continued in an attempt to 'kill off' the two Eves, and to establish Jane as the dominant personality, as she seemed the best solution to the problem.

In the book *The Three Faces of Eve*, it was reported that these three personalities were eventually integrated into a stable personality called Evelyn. However, in an autobiography 'Eve' (now called Chris Sizemore) revealed that by the mid-1970s she had experienced 22 subidentities. The dissociation was so severe that the skills learned by one (such as driving or sewing) could not be shown by the others. Their handwriting, and even their EEG records, appeared to vary considerably, and their responses on psychometric tests were quite different.

Another later example, also made into a film in 1976, is Sybil:

Box G: Sybil (Schreiber, 1973)

According to Schreiber, Sybil was brought up in a small conservative town in America. Her parents were both strictly observant Seventh-Day Adventists. Sybil was a timid child, and her mother was a very controlling person, who had been hospitalised for a psychotic disorder and was probably schizophrenic. She had subjected Sybil to severe and bizarre physical and sexual abuse. Sybil herself had no memory of this abuse, but her alters did. Sybil had 16 subpersonalities, including adults, a teenager known as 'The Blonde' and a toddler called Ruthie. Clara and Mary were very religious, while Vanessa was scornful of religion. Two personalities were males, carpenters called Mike and Sid. They all had different images of how they looked, as well as different tastes in friends, food, music and so on.

Sybil was treated by a psychiatrist called Cornelia Wilbur, who collaborated with Schreiber, a science journalist, in writing *Sybil*, the book about Sybil's case. According to Schreiber, after 11 years of psychoanalytic treatment, Sybil's 16 selves eventually fused to form a seventeenth and cured self.

The case of Sybil proved a great spur to the acceptance of DID as a distinct disorder, and its inclusion in DSM-III in 1980. As Hacking (1992) pointed out, it was the first reported case to make an explicit link between severe abuse in childhood and the later development of DID. The book was a best-seller, and the notion of DID found ready acceptance in a social climate where feminism had become an active force, and where there was increasing concern about child abuse and its effects.

However, as we shall see later, the acceptance of DID in the wake of this case, and the large number of cases diagnosed since its appearance, have also been challenged. Many clinicians believe that it may be a disorder created by therapists themselves, and that if it exists at all, it is extremely rare. We shall be returning to this controversy in a later section.

Another example is the case of Billy Milligan:

◐ DID is one of a group of dissociative disorders where there is a disruption in consciousness, memory and sense of identity. **MPD** was classified as a disorder in 1980; the term was changed to **DID** in 1994.

◐ A DID patient has a **primary personality** and one or more **alters**. The primary personality is aware only of blanks in memory when one or more of the alters has taken over. The alters may be aware of the primary personality and of each other.

◐ It is difficult to establish the **incidence** of DID, but it has been claimed that it affects 1% of the population. Ninety per cent of patients are **women**.

◐ **Eve**, **Sybil** and **Billy Milligan** are three high profile cases about whom books have been written, with the first two also being made into films.

The origins of DID

Since there are different schools of thought about the nature and origins of mental disorder (see chapter 5, section 5.4), there are several theories about why DID may develop. It is generally thought to be caused by prolonged trauma in childhood, such as physical, emotional and/or sexual abuse, though there are cases where this doesn't seem to have occurred. Some psychiatrists believe that other extreme and prolonged trauma – such as the experience of natural disasters and their aftermath, or invasive medical procedures – may also cause the disorder; most people diagnosed with DID have a secondary diagnosis of **post-traumatic stress disorder (PTSD)**, described in chapter 24.

Box H: Billy Milligan (Keyes, 1981)

In Ohio, Billy Milligan was found not guilty by reason of insanity of the rape and kidnapping of three students. He reported 24 personalities. Three of these were female, including a young girl and a lesbian poet. Two of the personalities were British and Australian, both of whom were minor criminals, and another was a Yugoslav who was a weapons expert.

Billy Milligan shows the normal trend among people with DID for at least one alter to be a child, and for some of the alters to be of the opposite sex. He is unusual, however, in that 90% of cases of DID are women. This may be because males with this disorder are less likely to be diagnosed and may end up instead in prison.

In order to deal with an overwhelming trauma from which there is no physical escape, a child may 'go away' in their head. This coping strategy is typically used by children as a very effective defence against physical and emotional pain, or the anxiety associated with the expectation of that pain. Thoughts, feelings, memories and perceptions are therefore separated off psychologically, so that the trauma is in effect happening to another person, allowing the child to function as if the trauma had not occurred. Dissociation can be seen as a highly creative survival technique, since it allows some areas of healthy functioning.

While dissociation allows a temporary mental escape from fear and pain, it may result in a memory gap surrounding the traumatic experience. Because the dissociation process can produce changes in memory, people who frequently dissociate may find that their sense of personal history and identity are affected.

Psychodynamic approach

You will remember from chapter 1 that, according to Freud, one way in which we deal with painful memories is to repress them into the unconscious so that we are no longer consciously aware of them. DID is seen as an extreme case of the use of **repression** as an ego defence mechanism. Painful memories – or in this case entire identities – are repressed from consciousness (Terr, 1988). Where childhood involves extreme trauma, such as the abuse suffered by Sybil (see box G), the individual can become dependent on this style of coping. Any impulses considered to be bad would then be attributed to other identities, which from time to time surface from the unconscious and express themselves. This could explain why many of the alters are typically more exciting personalities than the very inhibited primary personality which is usually presented.

This view is supported by the fact that many DID patients report childhood abuse. However, as Bliss (1980) pointed out, not all cases do report abuse, and not everyone who has experienced severe abuse in childhood goes on to develop DID. It has also been reported (Mair, 1997) that recovery of traumatic childhood memories does not generally appear to serve a therapeutic purpose, as psychodynamic theorists would suggest.

Behavioural approach

The focus here is also on the traumatic experiences associated with DID. In most cases of DID, at least one parent is severely disturbed (as was the case with Sybil's mother) and the child learns dissociation as a way of coping with abuse. Because this technique is so effective, a child who has been repeatedly traumatised will over time automatically use dissociation whenever they feel threatened or anxious. Dissociation is experienced as rewarding because it reduces anxiety. It therefore becomes a learned response, based on its reinforcing properties.

State-dependent learning

In chapter 2, we looked at **cue-dependent forgetting**, where a person may not be able to retrieve information if they are in a different external context or internal state from that in which the information was learned. It has been repeatedly shown that information which is learned in one state (e.g. mood) is best recalled when the individual is in the same state (Eich, 1995). Sufferers from DID may acquire memories and behaviours while in a state of extreme stress, and forget this information while in a more normal state. When the stressful state recurs, these memories and behaviours return, and may seem to belong to a different person. In other words, DID patients simply have very selective memories, which means that their recall will depend on them being in exactly the same physiological state as when the memories were laid down (Putnam, 1992). This theory could explain why the primary personality is often very unemotional, while the alters are often very emotionally responsive. It is also supported by the observation that alters seem to have specific functions, and only emerge in situations where that function is called for.

Self-hypnosis

This view sees DID as a form of self-hypnosis, used by sufferers to help them forget unpleasant events

(Bliss, 1985). DID is considered to begin at around 4–6 years old, which is the age when children are most susceptible to hypnotic suggestion (Kluft, 1987). They are able to separate themselves mentally from both their bodies and their surroundings. The generally accepted finding that DID patients appear to be very easily hypnotised and highly suggestible could support such a view.

Sociocultural view

There is considerable variation in the prevalence of DID in different cultures. For example, the incidence of DID is much higher in North America than in Britain. Fahey (1988) claimed that there had been only one case in Britain in the 15 years before his article appeared. Aldridge-Morris (1989) reported it to be unknown in the former Czechoslovakia (now the Czech Republic and Slovakia), New Zealand, Australia and India.

This could indicate that the features of some cultures may promote DID. Varma *et al.* (1981) pointed out that modern Western culture has created an emphasis on role-playing, largely through the entertainment industry. Similarly, some theories (e.g. Spanos *et al.*, 1994) view hypnosis as a state of role enactment, in which imagination and suggestibility play a key part.

- DID is thought to have its origins in **abuse in childhood** or some other extreme early **trauma**, though this is not necessarily always the case. Dissociation is used as a **coping strategy** to deal with pain and fear.
- The **psychodynamic** approach sees DID as an extreme form of **repression**.
- The **behaviourist** viewpoint proposes that dissociation becomes an automatic **learned response**, reinforced by the reduction of anxiety.
- DID has also been explained in terms of **state-dependent learning**, where information acquired in a stressful situation is forgotten in a normal situation.
- It is also seen as a form of **self-hypnosis**.
- Since most cases of DID occur in North America, while it is unknown in some parts of the world, it is suggested that **culture** may have a part to play.

The treatment of DID

Spiegel (1974) reported that spontaneous recovery from DID is rare. Different therapists use different techniques, but all involve some kind of talking therapy. There are four elements in treatment which seem to be widely accepted.

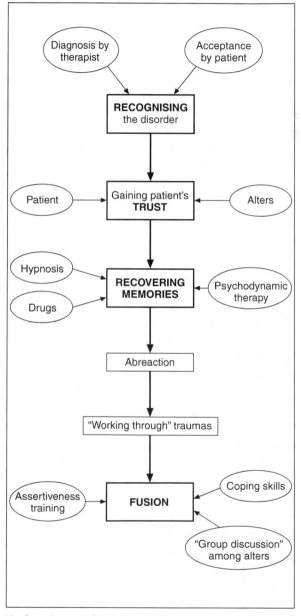

The four elements of treatment of DID

The first is **recognising the disorder**. The diagnosis must be made by the therapist, and this diagnosis communicated to the patient. This is largely an educational exercise for both patients and their families. Videotapes may be shown of subidentities, and hypnosis may be used to make subidentities aware of one another (Allen, 1993). The process can be quite difficult, since patients often react with disbelief and fear.

The therapist must then gain the **trust** of the patient. This is again a difficult process, since it applies not only to the primary personality but also to the alters.

The third process involves **recovering memories**. Using psychodynamic therapy, hypnosis or drugs, this process aims to help patients recall missing memories. This enables **abreaction** to take place, the release of anxiety through reliving intense experiences. The patient can then confront and work through the original trauma(s). This process can take months or years. During this stage, patients may become aggressive towards themselves and others (Kelly, 1993).

Finally, subidentities must be integrated into one, a process called **fusion**. Again, a range of approaches can be used, such as assertiveness training for the primary personality, or 'group discussions' between the subidentities. Coping skills need to be consolidated to reduce the risk of future dissociation.

The relatively small number of cases reported means that it is difficult to assess effectiveness, but Mair (1997) has reported that therapy may do more harm than good. Taking into account initial variations in severity, she found that there was an inverse relationship between future well-being and number of treatment sessions received; more treatment was associated with worse outcomes.

❺ Treatment for DID involves some kind of **talking therapy**. The patient needs to **recognise** that they have DID, **trust** the therapist, **recover memories** of past traumas so that they can be dealt with, and finally achieve **fusion** into one personality.

Is DID a genuine disorder?

There is considerable controversy surrounding DID, in terms of how prevalent it is and even whether it exists at all.

Some clinicians believe that DID is underdiagnosed. They argue that since it is often accompanied by other disorders – such as depression, phobias and/or substance abuse – it is often overlooked or misdiagnosed. It may also be underdiagnosed in men, since men tend to be less willing to discuss past traumas then women, and/or because men with DID are likely to end up in prison.

Conversely, a growing majority of mental health professionals believe that it is a 'fad' diagnosis and widely overused. They claim that although DID exists, it is extremely rare, and only occurs in a handful of very disturbed people. Some among this group believe that in most if not all cases it is **iatrogenic**, i.e. caused by the clinicians themselves. Frick (1995) suggested that if a therapist is on the lookout for symptoms of DID, they may make suggestions or interpretations to a patient (particularly under hypnosis) which could cause them to believe they are suffering from it, and so start to show associated symptoms.

One of the reasons why the supposed prevalence of DID has been called into question is that until recently reports of it were extremely rare. By 1970, only 100 cases of DID had been reported in professional journals. By 1990, however, 40,000 diagnoses had been made, almost all in the USA and Canada (Merskey, 1995).

It may be that there has been such a surge in cases as a result of increased awareness of DID; since it was included in DSM-III, more physicians may be prepared to accept it as a genuine disorder. The increase in cases may also be the result of more precise diagnostic criteria, so that it is less likely to be confused with disorders such as schizophrenia (Spiegel, 1974). There are also specific diagnostic tests for DID (Mann, 1995).

Advocates of DID claim that the different identities of someone with DID have different patterns of physiological functioning, for example in

EEG patterns. However, people without the disorder can also show these kinds of differences when they are in different emotional states. Moreover, Spanos *et al.* (1985) found that controls who were simulating different personalities showed EEG differences similar to those found in the different identities of DID patients.

Those who believe DID is overdiagnosed support this belief in a number of ways. Firstly, the idea of a 'fad' diagnosis could account for the sudden huge increase in the number of diagnosed cases with the rise in interest in the disorder following Schreiber's book about Sybil, and the appearance of MPD as a diagnostic category in DSM-III. They also point to the lack of coverage in the medical literature, before the appearance of that book, of disorders with symptoms like or close to those of DID.

Finally, the possible iatrogenic origin of DID cannot be discounted. The claim that the disorder may be iatrogenic is related to the fact that most diagnoses of DID are only made after long periods of therapy, usually making use of hypnosis or self-hypnosis. Since by definition hypnosis works best with those who are extremely suggestible, this treatment could lead to the sequence of events Frick described (see above). In addition, most diagnoses are made by very few therapists, who are sympathetic to the idea of multiple personalities.

An iatrogenic interpretation has been proposed for one of the earliest documented patients:

Meyer (1996) has proposed that there are four possible ways of explaining Anna O's disorder. Firstly, she may have been a true multiple, with the disorder developing independently of Breuer's influence. A second possibility is that the disorder developed spontaneously, but the symptoms were amplified by Breuer's treatment. It is also possible that she may have had some kind of dissociative disorder when Breuer started to treat her, but developed DID as the result of his treatment. Finally, she may have been faking the disorder as a way of drawing attention to herself.

Weissberg (1993) has argued that DID was induced in Anna O by Breuer. He visited her daily for most of the 18 months during which he was treating her, and she seems to have been very dependent on and emotionally involved with him. For example, for a period after the death of her father she stopped recognising anyone but Breuer, and refused to eat at all unless she was fed by Breuer. At one point she could only sleep if Breuer closed her eyes, and would not open them again until Breuer opened them for her. At the end of her treatment, Anna O announced that she was pregnant (she was not) with Breuer's baby.

Freud believed that people with hysteria, the diagnosis made for Anna O, were abnormally suggestible, and that this was likely to lead to a fragmented personality. Breuer's treatment depended heavily on hypnosis, taking Anna O back

Box I: The case of Anna O (Breuer and Freud, 1895)

Freud wrote up a case study of **Anna O**, diagnosed at the time as suffering from hysteria. She had become ill after nursing her father in his final illness, and was treated by Breuer, Freud's early mentor and collaborator. Anna had been emotionally abused by her mother, and it is possible that she had also been sexually abused.

Anna first presented with a nervous cough, though when Breuer examined her, many more symptoms emerged: headaches, disturbances of vision and hearing, and anaesthesia of her right arm and leg for which there was no apparent physical cause. She soon revealed two distinct personalities which shifted often and without warning. Her primary personality was anxious and depressed, while the alter was abusive and had hallucinations. She claimed to have two selves, a real one and an evil one, which forced her to behave badly.

to previous periods and events in her life, which may have led Anna, as a very suggestible person, to respond readily to suggestions Breuer made to her.

Spiegel (1997) spent time on research with Sybil, and has suggested that her case also may best be explained in iatrogenic terms:

Box J: Spiegel (1997)

Spiegel has put forward several reasons why we should treat the case of Sybil with caution:

a He found Sybil to be highly hypnotisable and extremely suggestible. Sybil's alters appeared only after Wilbur started to use hypnosis as a major part of the therapy she offered Sybil, although Sybil had by then been in therapy with her for five years.

b He believed that Sybil adopted personalities suggested by Wilbur as part of the therapy. He reports one conversation with her: Sybil asked him, 'Well, do you want me to be Helen?' He asked what she meant. She said, 'Well, when I'm with Dr Wilbur, she wants me to be Helen.' He asked who Helen was, and was told: 'Well, that's a name Dr Wilbur gave me for this feeling.' Spiegel concluded that with Wilbur, Sybil felt obliged to become another personality; Wilbur was helping her to identify different aspects of her life by providing names which Sybil then adopted.

c Sybil had read the literature on DID, including *The Three Faces of Eve*, which could have affected how she responded to Wilbur's suggestions.

d Sybil at one time wrote to Wilbur: '...I do not have any multiple personalities...I have been essentially lying...The dissociations are not the problem because they do not actually exist'. Wilbur dismissed this as denial, but it is possible that she forced the issue by refusing to take seriously what Sybil wrote to her.

e Sybil had a very close and continuing relationship with Wilbur which went well beyond the normal therapist–patient relationship. Even after therapy finished, Sybil moved house to be close to Wilbur when she took up a new job at the University of Kentucky, and nursed Wilbur when she became ill with Parkinson's disease. Wilbur left Sybil $25,000 dollars in her will and all *Sybil* royalties.

f Both Sybil and Wilbur benefited financially from Schreiber's book. This could have motivated Wilbur's refusal (in conversation with Spiegel) to consider any other disorder than DID (which makes for a very dramatic story) and Sybil's collusion in Wilbur's diagnosis.

It has also been suggested (e.g. Weissberg, 1993) that some people fake the disorder to avoid some social or moral responsibility. This is a possible interpretation of the case of Billy Milligan, who may have faked the disorder in order to escape the consequences of the crimes he had committed.

Spiegel (1997) claimed that cases of DID almost always occur when the person has a legal or social reason to avoid responsibility, and when health insurance is available to support the patient. The fusion which is seen as the resolution of the disorder often comes about when legal issues are resolved or there is no more insurance money.

It seems likely that DID exists, but is not nearly as widespread as its supporters suggest. However, it is impossible to prove this either way, as a result of the complexity of diagnosis and of the condition itself. Most practitioners are very careful before making such a diagnosis, and will need to see a patient over a period of time before considering DID a possibility.

◉ Some clinicians believe DID is **underdiagnosed**, while others believe it is extremely rare and **overdiagnosed**.

◉ It is also possible that some cases are **iatrogenic** in origin, with highly suggestible patients responding to suggestions made by the therapist. There is some support for this idea in the cases of **Anna O** and **Sybil**.

◉ A further suggestion is that some patients may **fake** DID to avoid social and moral responsibility.

Activity 3: true or false?

Read through these statements and decide whether each is true of DID:

a DID develops as the result of childhood abuse.

b Dissociation is an adaptive response to physical or mental pain.

c There is a similar level of diagnosis of DID throughout the world.

d People with DID are very easily hypnotised.

e Most patients are female.

f The primary personality is usually not aware of the alters.

g There was a very large increase in the number of reported cases of DID after the publication of *The Three Faces of Eve*.

When you have finished, see the notes on page 644.

23.3 CULTURE-BOUND SYNDROMES (CBSs)

DSM-IV (1994) defines culture-bound syndromes (CBSs) as:

'recurrent, locality-specific patterns of aberrant behaviour and troubling experience that may or may not be linked to a particular DSM-IV diagnostic category. Many of these patterns are indigenously considered to be 'illnesses', or at least afflictions, and most have local names.'

We have already looked briefly at some examples of CBSs in chapter 5, section 5.3, and you might find it useful to look back now to this material. However, these are only a few of the very many CBSs which have been reported.

The key aspects of CBSs are firstly that they do not have a one-to-one correspondence with a category of mental disorder in Western classifications; and secondly that when first reported, most CBSs were believed to be limited to a particular culture, or a set of related cultures, or those geographically close to one another. As we will see, however, this is not necessarily the case.

CBSs have been reported from many parts of the world. For example, koro and amok are found in Malaysia, dhat in India, and it has been suggested that anorexia nervosa and pre-menstrual syndrome are Western CBSs. We will look here at some case studies of CBSs, all of which come from China:

Box K: Qi-gong reactive psychosis (Lim and Lin, 1996)

In China, qi-gong is a development of tai chi ch'uan, a martial art and an exercise regime. The qi-gong leader is believed to project qi ('life force') into participants, thus enhancing their physical and spiritual health. Some participants, who become very involved in qi-gong, may develop psychotic symptoms. Qi-gong reactive psychosis is listed in the Chinese Classification of Mental Disorders. It is also listed in DSM-IV, which defines it as: 'an acute time-limited episode characterised by dissociative, paranoid, or other psychotic or non-psychotic symptoms'.

Lim and Lin described a 57-year-old Chinese-American man, who had started qi-gong as therapy for kidney stones. After several days, he began to hear voices, telling him how to practise qi-gong and believed he had made contact with alien beings. He suffered from both auditory and visual hallucinations.

Qi-gong is a development of the martial art of tai chi ch'uan

The symptoms of qi-gong reactive psychosis have something in common with the symptoms of **schizophrenia**, described at the start of chapter 24, and the patient was given the anti-psychotic drugs which are used to treat schizophrenics. However, it can be said to be culture-bound in that the disorder is linked to a cultural practice, and thus expresses itself within a cultural context. This is an issue we shall be returning to later in this chapter.

Another case study of a CBS is shown in box L:

> ### Box L: Suo yang (Gwee Ah Leng, in Simons and Hughes, 1985)
>
> Suo yang is the Chinese equivalent of koro, the fear that the penis is retracting into the body, with the likelihood of fatal consequences.
>
> A 34-year-old male Chinese was at a cinema when he needed to urinate. While doing so, he experienced a loss of feeling in his genitals. He thought his penis might retract and noticed it getting smaller as he looked at it. He felt cold and weak, so sat on the floor holding on to his penis for half an hour until the attack subsided.

> ### Box M: neurasthenia (Kleinman and Mechanic, in Kleinman and Lin, 1981)
>
> According to Kleinman (1981), neurasthenia is the second most common diagnosis in Chinese psychiatric hospitals. It has elements of depression and anxiety.
>
> A 41-year-old patient presented with headaches, pains in the joints, difficulty in sleeping, loss of appetite and the belief that there was something wrong with his brain which caused his scalp to sweat. The disorder was described entirely in terms of physical symptoms; most Asian cultures encourage **somatisation**, i.e. expressing emotional and psychological problems in physical terms.

While these examples relate to the DSM-IV definition, it may be misleading to talk of CBSs as a homogenous group. It is possible to divide them into several broad categories:

> ### Figure 9: categories of CBSs
>
> 1   A locally-recognised psychiatric disorder, with no apparent organic cause, which does not correspond to a Western category, e.g. **amok** (see chapter 5).
> 2   A locally-recognised psychiatric disorder, with no apparent organic cause, which resembles a Western category, but has some different features from the Western disorder which are important locally, e.g. **taijin kyufusho**. In Japan, this is an intense fear that your body or parts of your body or bodily functions are offensive to other people. It may be seen as a cultural variant of **social phobia**.
> 3   An organic disease, not yet recognised by Western medicine, with psychological symptoms, e.g. **kuru**. In New Guinea, this is a progressive psychosis and dementia found in cannibalistic tribes. It appears to

be a form of **Creuzfeldt-Jakob disease**, related to **BSE** ('mad cow disease').

4   A disorder which may or may not have an organic cause, which occurs in many cultural settings but is only classified as a disorder in one or a few, e.g. **koro** (see chapter 5). This disorder seems to occur independently as a delusion or phobia in many cultural settings.

5   Culturally accepted explanations of a disorder, which in a Western setting could be interpreted as delusions, e.g. the **evil eye**: in parts of Latin America, disease is explained in terms of the influence of an evil person.

6   Behaviours which include trance or possession states; for example, **communicating with the dead**, which could be thought in a Western context to be a sign of psychosis.

7   Syndromes which probably do not exist, e.g. **windigo**. Among the Algonkian Indians of North America, this is a syndrome of obsession with cannibalism. There is some doubt that this syndrome is real; it may rather be a way of justifying the social exclusion or execution of an individual.

Activity 4: categories of CBSs

Look back at the case studies of qi-gong reactive psychosis (box K) and neurasthenia (box M). Into which of the categories outlined in figure 9 could each be fitted?

When you have finished, see the notes on page 644.

Classing all these categories together has led to some confusion in the discussion of CBSs. Some, such as the evil eye, are better described as *explanations* of disorders, rather than disorders themselves.

In addition, many of the syndromes which have been described actually occur in many unrelated cultures, or are local variants of disorders which are found elsewhere. For example, a similar syndrome to qi-gong reactive psychosis has been described in

India, related to yogic practices. Similarly, amok was originally believed to be a Malaysian CBS. However, variants have been found in Polynesia (where it is known as cafard), Puerto Rico, Laos, Papua New Guinea and the Philippines. There is also an American term – 'going postal' – which refers to behaviour similar to that of amok. Dhat, found in India, is similar to shenkui, found in China. Koro occurs not only in Malaysia but also, as noted above, in China (suo yang), and throughout south and east Asia under various names; there was a koro epidemic in Singapore in 1967.

A further problem is that classifying a disorder as 'culture-bound' can imply that it is somehow not a real disorder, and that a patient's experience can be discounted as merely exotic.

However, the concept of CBSs is useful in that it has brought the relevance of culture to the attention of psychiatrists interested in mental disorder. In a sense, all mental disorders can be thought of as culture-bound, to the extent that they cannot be looked at in isolation from the culture within which they develop. We will look at this in a little more detail in the next section.

Activity 5: identifying CBSs

Match each of the syndromes on the left with a description on the right:

1 qi-gong reactive psychosis	a brooding, followed by an outburst of aggressive or homicidal behaviour.
2 dhat	b severe restriction of food intake, associated with a morbid fear of obesity.
3 amok	c fear that the penis will retract into the body and cause death.
4 koro	d severe anxiety over semen loss, with feelings of weakness and exhaustion.
5 neurasthenia	e psychotic symptoms developed as a result of over-involvement in a martial arts programme.
6 anorexia nervosa	f depression and anxiety, expressed in terms of physical symptoms.

When you have finished, see the notes on page 644.

◐ CBSs are defined as **patterns of abnormal behaviour** which occur **in one or a small group of related cultures.** Many CBSs have been reported from a wide range of cultures.

◐ Discussion of CBSs is complicated by them being treated as though they form a **homogenous group**. Some are **explanations** of disorders rather than disorders themselves. It has become increasingly clear that there are **variants** of many CBSs, originally linked with one particular culture, **in unrelated cultures.**

◐ The concept is useful in foregrounding the **influence of culture** on mental disorders.

CBSs in context

CBSs often seem exotic and even bizarre to those from a different culture. However, if they are considered within the cultural context within which they occur, i.e. in the context of the beliefs, values and traditions of that culture, they have their own logic.

Many of the CBSs we have looked at occur in China, and it is these which have been most researched. China has a long and well-documented medical tradition which in many ways is very different from the Western tradition. Chinese theories of medicine and the body therefore shape the experience of illness differently in China than in the West.

In Chinese Taoist philosophy, there are two complementary principles. Yang represents the male, day and heat, and is seen as active and existing through time. Yin is associated with the female, darkness and cold, and is seen as receptive and existing in space. In the healthy person, these two principles are in balance.

Figure 10: the complementary principles of yin and yang

Yin and yang as represented in the tai chi sign

Several Chinese CBSs relate to loss (or fear of loss) of yang. One of these is **shenkui**, the Chinese equivalent of dhat, the semen-loss syndrome. It is also associated with physical complaints which are thought to be the result of lost yang, for example kidney problems. According to Chinese medical theory, one of the functions of the kidneys is to turn blood into semen.

Shenkui relates logically to other disorders in the Chinese medical system which also come about through loss of yang. Hsien (1966) described two syndromes, **pa-leng** (fear of cold) and **pa-feng** (fear of wind). Since both wind and cold are yin phenomena, these disorders come about in a male as the result of fear of excessive yin, which threatens his yang.

Suo yang, the Chinese equivalent of koro or genital retraction syndrome, can also be explained in terms of the balance of yang and yin energies. The penis shrinks when cold; it therefore makes sense within this belief system for extreme cold (yin) to overpower the yang in a vulnerable man and cause his penis (the symbol of yang) to retract.

Kleinman (1986) also pointed to cultural influences in the expression of mental disorders. Many of the patients he examined who suffered from neurasthenia were survivors of the Cultural Revolution, a period in Chinese history of immense social upheaval which completely transformed Chinese society. Many people's lives rapidly changed beyond recognition, and not for the better, and their future was extremely uncertain. Kleinman suggested that this trauma could not be ignored as a factor in shaping the Chinese experience of neurasthenia.

◐ Culture-bound syndromes have an **internal logic** if considered in the broad cultural context within which they occur.

Do we need the concept of CBSs?

In comparing mental illness in different societies, there are differing viewpoints about whether we need the concept of CBSs.

The biological approach

As we saw in the first part of this chapter, the **biological approach** to mental disorder assumes that like physical illness, disorders have a biological basis. Western diagnostic categories can therefore be applied universally; CBSs represent variations of these categories due to cultural factors. For example, schizophrenia is seen as a universally-applicable category; it is only the secondary features of schizophrenia, such as the *content* of the delusions and hallucinations characteristic of the disorder, which are affected by culture.

On this basis, Kiev (1972) classified CBSs using Western diagnostic categories: for example, koro is a form of anxiety; the evil eye is a phobic state; while amok is a dissociative state. He claimed they are therefore 'not new diagnostic entities; they are in fact similar to those known in the West'.

This approach has been criticised on several grounds. Firstly, it has been claimed by some to be ethnocentric, in that it gives primacy to the Western diagnostic and labelling system. It has also been suggested that the analysis of CBSs is distorted by trying to fit them into Western categories of mental illness which may not be valid. A further criticism is that the same mental illness may play different social roles within different societies. If we are fully to understand a mental illness in another culture, we need to understand the context – social, cultural, political and economic – within which it takes place. For example, in some societies a psychotic episode is considered to be the result of social conflict, which needs to be treated by a public ritual, a view very different from Western conceptions of psychosis.

The social labelling approach

This perspective sees mental illness as a social rather than a biological fact; a disorder does not necessarily have a biological basis. Society decides which behaviour patterns are abnormal and should be labelled 'a mental disorder'. Mental illness is therefore culture-specific.

Waxler (1977) claimed that mental illness can only be defined relative to the society in which it is found; it does not have a universal existence. For example, social withdrawal, lack of energy and feelings of sadness are usually labelled 'depression' in Western societies, while in Sri Lanka the same symptoms are given little attention or treatment.

Once a person is labelled as 'mentally ill', cultural cues tell them how to fulfil that role; they learn to be ill in a way that their particular culture understands. They are then dependent on society at large for removing the label. Mental illness is therefore socially constructed and maintained, and so comparisons cannot easily be made between different cultures.

However, this approach has been criticised for neglecting the established biological basis of some disorders, such as schizophrenia, which is discussed in chapter 24, and bipolar disorder. It also ignores extreme psychoses, such as schizophrenia, which do seem to be universal, with a similar incidence in a wide range of cultures.

The combined approach

This approach brings together the biological and social labelling approaches. This perspective claims that there are disorders where Western diagnostic categories can be universally applied. Schizophrenia and bipolar disorder fit into this category, as do disorders which result from organic brain disease, such as Alzheimer's syndrome.

How the disorder manifests itself varies between cultures. For example, in a tribal society, a psychotic may believe their behaviour is controlled by witches or sorcerers, while a Western psychotic may feel controlled by extraterrestrials.

To some extent, comparisons can be made between cultures. Foster and Anderson (1978) have suggested that this comparison should be between patterns of symptoms rather than using diagnostic categories such as 'schizophrenia', as a way of overcoming the distortion inevitable when trying to fit the disorders of other cultures into these categories.

A similar comparison of patterns of symptoms can be carried out for CBSs, many of which would be classified as neuroses within the Western psychiatric model. However, this may be more difficult than for psychoses, since as we have seen, many CBSs seem to be unique clusters of symptoms which only really make sense within a particular cultural context. Not only the presentation of a disorder but also its meaning for sufferers may be difficult for Western observers to evaluate.

❺ The **biological approach** believes that CBSs can be fitted within Western diagnostic frameworks. This approach has been criticised for being **ethnocentric**. It also fails to take into account the **social role** a mental disorder plays in a particular society.

❺ The **social labelling approach** proposes that mental illness is defined in different ways in different societies, and is therefore **culture-specific**. This approach has been criticised for

ignoring the **biological basis** of some disorders, and disorders which seem to be **universal**.

❺ The **combined approach** claims that some disorders are **universal** and in these cases the use of Western diagnostic categories is appropriate. How these disorders present themselves is influenced by **cultural factors**. Comparison is possible using **patterns of symptoms** rather than diagnostic categories.

Notes on activities

1 Some of the categories are virtually the same in both systems. For example, category 2 in ICD-10 covers 'mental and behavioural disorders due to psychoactive substance use', while category 3 in DSM-IV covers 'substance-related disorders'. Since DSM has more categories than ICD, some disorders appear under a single category in ICD but are spread across different categories in DSM. For example, category 5 in ICD covers 'neurotic, stress-related and somatoform disorders'. The disorders listed appear in DSM under category 5 (anxiety disorders), category 6 (somatoform disorders), category 7 (dissociative disorders) and category 8 (adjustment disorders). However, a category in DSM can also cover disorders which appear under more than one category in ICD. Category 9 in DSM covers 'disorders first diagnosed in infancy, childhood or adolescence'. The disorders listed under this heading appear in ICD under category 8 (mental retardation), category 9 (disorders of psychological development) and category 10 (behavioural and emotional disorders with onset usually occurring in childhood and adolescence). Both systems have a category to cover any disorders not covered elsewhere in the classification system.

2 **benefits** include: reassurance of the patient; ease of communication between mental health professionals; indicates what treatment should be given; treatment may help the patient;

responsibility, and therefore blame, is removed from the patient; patients are protected from the results of their own actions (e.g. suicide).

costs include: labelling can produce stereotypes, leading to prejudice, which in turn may affect life chances; loss of rights, e.g. freedom to make choices if the patient is sectioned and treated against their will; control by others; judgements about a person are subjective, and can therefore be misguided; less powerful people are more likely to be labelled, and suffer the consequences of this; misclassification is possible; classification ignores the uniqueness of the individual.

3 **a** false – there have been cases where there is no evidence of childhood abuse. **b** true – it allows some degree of healthy functioning. **c** false – most cases are North American. **d** true – treatment often depends heavily on hypnosis. **e** true – 90%. **f** true. **g** true.

4 Both are in category 2. Qi-gong reactive psychosis resembles schizophrenia, but the link with the practice of qi-gong marks it out from this disorder. Neurasthenia has symptoms relating to anxiety and depression. However, the depressed mood which defines depression is often lacking, since the disorder is interpreted by the patient in physical rather than psychological terms, and is treated as such by the physician.

5 **1** e **2** d **3** a **4** c **5** f **6** b

Psychopathology

In this chapter we will be looking at:

24.1 The aetiology of mental disorders

24.2 Schizophrenia
    Clinical characteristics
    Biological explanations
    Psychological explanations
    The diathesis–stress explanation

24.3 Depression
    Clinical characteristics
    Biological explanations
    Psychological explanations

24.4 Anxiety disorders
    Post-traumatic stress disorder
    Phobias
    Obsessive–compulsive disorder

24.1 THE AETIOLOGY OF MENTAL DISORDERS

Psychopathology is the study of the nature and development of mental disorders. This chapter will look at a small number of the many psychological disorders described in the classificatory systems DSM-IV and ICD-10, outlined in chapter 23.

We will look at the **aetiology** (i.e. the suggested causes) of each of the mental disorders described. This is a much disputed area; just as there are different approaches to defining diseases, so different approaches suggest differences in the aetiology of mental disorders. Some theorists focus on possible **biological** factors while others stress the importance of **psychological factors**.

Within a biological framework, one focus of interest is the contribution of **genetic** factors. The possible genetic basis for disorders can be explored in three ways: family studies, adoption studies and twin studies. The rationale behind twin and family studies was discussed in chapter 5, in the section headed 'biological explanations of eating disorders'. You may find it helpful to re-read this section to remind yourself why these kinds of studies are carried out.

Adoption studies look at the occurrence of a disorder in children born to an affected parent, but adopted early in life by 'healthy' parents. The adopted child can then be compared to the biological children in their new family, or to a control group of adopted children whose natural parents are mentally healthy, to ensure that it is not the adoption process itself that causes the disorder.

Theorists with a biological perspective also seek to explain disorders in biochemical terms; for example, as an imbalance of **neurotransmitters** or **hormones**. They also suggest that disorders are the result of faulty neural structures and neuro-developmental disorders.

Other theorists stress the importance of the contribution of psychological factors. **Behaviourists** try to explain mental disorder as learned maladaptive behaviour, while for **cognitive** theorists faulty thought processes account for the disorder.

Aetiology of mental disorders

Psychodynamic explanations look at experiences in childhood and unconscious conflict. **Humanistic** explanations focus on lapsed personal development, including the effects of relationships with others. Some theorists see interactions within the **family** as being of importance.

While physiologists, behaviourists and cognitive psychologists may focus on different levels of explanation, it is also clear that biological and social/psychological factors interact. The **diathesis–stress model** suggests that some people may be predisposed to develop a particular disorder (**diathesis** refers to this vulnerability), either for genetic reasons or as the result of early experience. Whether they in fact develop the disorder will depend on the amount of **stress** in their lives.

It is important to know as much as possible about the causes of a mental disorder, so that an appropriate therapy can be offered to the patient. For example, if the disorder has a biochemical cause, then it would seem most sensible to use a drug therapy; if the disorder is related to faulty

cognitive processes, then cognitive therapy, which aims to change the way someone views the world, would seem to be a good place to start treatment. As we will see, however, a range of explanations has been offered for all the disorders described in this chapter, and in no case does any one theory provide a definitive explanation.

- Psychopathology is the study of mental disorders.
- The **aetiology** of many disorders is unclear; some theorists favour **biological** accounts, while others suggest that disorders have **psychological** causes.
- **The diathesis–stress model** suggests an interaction between the two.

24.2 SCHIZOPHRENIA

What has come to be known as schizophrenia was first described by Kraepelin, who thought that the disorder was an early form of dementia and named it **dementia praecox** ('early senility'). Bleuler first used the term **schizophrenia**, from Greek words meaning 'split' and 'mind', which is probably why it is commonly (but incorrectly) thought that people with schizophrenia have split personalities or minds. This is actually known as **multiple personality disorder**, or **dissociative identity disorder (DID)**, and is discussed in chapter 23. The split in schizophrenia is between the person and reality. It is perhaps also worth mentioning that people with schizophrenia do not have visual hallucinations, another popular misconception.

The range of symptoms shown by people who have been diagnosed as suffering from schizophrenia is extremely variable. Some theorists believe that schizophrenia is one underlying condition whose psychological and behavioural manifestations can vary from sufferer to sufferer. Others believe that schizophrenia is one underlying condition which may affect different parts of the brains of different sufferers. A third (and less widely accepted) view is that the term schizophrenia describes not just one disorder but a group of disorders, with different symptoms involved in different types of schizophrenia. However, all types of schizophrenia are severely disabling. Approximately 1% of the population are thought to suffer from schizophrenia at some point in their lives, and it affects equal numbers of males and females.

Clinical characteristics

In Britain, the diagnosis of schizophrenia depends on what Schneider (1959) called **first-rank symptoms**:

Figure 1: first-rank symptoms of schizophrenia

passivity experiences and thought disorders:
thought insertion – the belief that thoughts are being put into your head by outside forces.
thought withdrawal – the belief that thoughts are being withdrawn from your head.
thought broadcasting – the belief that your thoughts are being made known to other people in some way.

The external forces involved may be aliens or the government, and thoughts are often believed to be affected by a radio transmitter or some other kind of ray.

hallucinations:
auditory hallucinations are the most common. They often take the form of a voice in your head, commenting aloud on your behaviour or telling you what to do. When schizophrenics appear to be talking to themselves, they may actually be carrying on a conversation with the voice in their head, which to them is quite real.

primary delusions:
The main delusions are:
delusions of grandeur – the delusion that you are someone important, like the Queen, Napoleon or Jesus Christ.
delusions of persecution – the delusion that people are plotting against you, or spying on you.
delusions of control – for example, the delusion that your thoughts are able to control the movement of the clouds.

Thought insertion: the belief that thoughts are being put into your head by outside forces

If one or more of the symptoms shown in figure 1 are present, usually for more than six months, a diagnosis of schizophrenia is likely.

There are other symptoms which may also indicate schizophrenia: disturbances of thought processes, disturbances of affect, psychomotor disorders and lack of volition:

Figure 2: additional symptoms of schizophrenia

disturbances of thought processes:

thought disturbances – inability to focus thoughts and thought blocking. The individual may stop speaking in mid-sentence.

language disturbances – 'word salad', when the associations between words become too loose to make any sense; neologisms, where new words are invented.

disturbances of affect:

blunting of emotions – e.g. there is an unemotional response when the sufferer is told a close relative has died.

inappropriate emotions – e.g. the response to this kind of news could be laughing.

flattened affect – the absence of emotional expression.

psychomotor disturbances:

catatonia – unusual postures are maintained for long periods of time, in some cases weeks.

stereotypy – repetitive movements, e.g. repeated rocking.

lack of volition:

apathy, loss of motivation, social withdrawal.

Symptoms of schizophrenia fall into two categories: **positive symptoms** (ones not usually present in normal people, such as hallucinations and delusions) and **negative symptoms** (those which are usually present in normal people but are not experienced by schizophrenics, e.g. lack of motivation). Positive symptoms are also referred to as **Type I** symptoms, and negative symptoms as **Type II**.

Liddle, cited in Sterling *et al.* (1999), grouped symptoms into three clusters or 'sub-syndromes': **reality distortion** (hallucinations, delusions), **disorganisation** (language disturbance, inappropriate affective response) and **psychomotor poverty** (decreased spontaneous movement, asociality and anhedonia). These clusters are relatively independent of one another, and patients tend to show *all* the symptoms within a particular cluster.

Classification systems divide schizophrenia into a number of types. In **DSM-IV** there are five types: paranoid, disorganised, catatonic, undifferentiated and residual. The symptoms associated with each type of schizophrenia are summarised in figure 3:

Figure 3: types of schizophrenia (DSM-IV)

paranoid schizophrenia: delusions of persecution or grandeur; auditory or visual hallucinations; language and behaviour are relatively normal; often has a later onset than other types; paranoid schizophrenics tend to be argumentative and are occasionally violent.

disorganised (or **hebephrenic**) **schizophrenia**: hallucinations; thought and language disturbances; disturbances of affect; social withdrawal; usually diagnosed in adolescence or young adulthood.

catatonic schizophrenia: motor disturbances, including catatonic immobility. During this immobility, another person can move the patient's limbs into new positions in which they will be held, a phenomenon known as waxy flexibility; agitated catatonia, i.e. bouts of wild and unpredictable movement; mutism, where the patient is unresponsive; negativism i.e. resisting or doing the opposite of what has been asked.

undifferentiated schizophrenia: a sort of 'catch-all category' used for people who do show symptoms of schizophrenia, but not in such a pattern that they can be classified as disorganised, catatonic or paranoid schizophrenics.

> 🖋 **residual schizophrenia**: the category that describes people who, although they have had an episode of schizophrenia during the past six months and still exhibit some symptoms, do not show schizophrenic symptoms strongly enough to merit putting them in one of the other categories.

ICD-10 also has the category of **simple schizophrenia**, which is still used in some countries. It is used to describe the disorder where onset is early, usually during late adolescence. It is characterised by social withdrawal, loss of motivation and a loss of touch with reality. Male schizophrenics of this type often become tramps, while females may become prostitutes.

There are also other related disorders, such as **schizophreniform disorder** (where psychotic symptoms last for less than six months), **schizoaffective disorder** (where the clinician cannot decide between schizophrenia and an affective (mood) disorder, again with a relatively short duration) and **delusional disorder** (where one or more delusions are present, but without the other symptoms leading to a diagnosis of schizophrenia).

There are three phases in the development of schizophrenia. The first is the **prodromal phase**, when symptoms start to appear. The second is the **active phase**, when the major symptoms are clearly apparent. The third is the **residual phase**, when the disorder may subside, e.g. when therapy is given. Harrison (1995) claimed that approximately a third of schizophrenics regain the ability to function normally, a third are permanently in the active phase, while a third move between the active and residual phases.

- The **first-rank symptoms** of schizophrenia include passivity experiences and thought disorders; hallucinations; and primary delusions.
- **Other symptoms** include disturbances of thought process; disturbances of affect; psychomotor disturbances; and lack of volition.
- **DSM-IV** distinguishes between **five types of schizophrenia**: paranoid; disorganised; catatonic; undifferentiated; and residual. **ICD-10** uses the further category of **simple schizophrenia**. The different types have different clusters of symptoms.
- There are three **phases**: prodromal, active and residual.

Biological explanations

Genetic explanations of schizophrenia

There is a convincing amount of research that suggests that at least a predisposition to develop schizophrenia is passed on in the genes. The probability of someone developing schizophrenia is 1 in 100. However, if you have a schizophrenic parent this may rise considerably. Kety *et al.* (1968) found that children with a schizophrenic biological parent were 10 times more likely than average to develop schizophrenia. In a study carried out by Kendler *et al.* (1983), this rose to 18 times more likely.

Adoption studies

A sample adoption study, supporting the idea of a genetic cause of schizophrenia, is shown in box A:

Box A: Heston (1966)

Procedure: This study followed children born to schizophrenic mothers living in a psychiatric hospital, and either adopted by non-schizophrenic families or by the families of the mothers. There was also a control group of adopted children with non-schizophrenic birth mothers. Assessments involved interviews, psychometric tests and social ratings. Two psychiatrists and Heston separately rated each participant on a 0–100 scale of disability, and gave psychiatric diagnoses where possible.
Results: Control children were significantly less disabled than the children born to schizophrenic mothers. Sixty-six per cent of those children born to schizophrenic mothers were given a psychiatric diagnosis, compared to only 18% of the control group.
Conclusion: There is a strong genetic component to schizophrenia.

Twin studies

The results of two studies comparing the concordance rates of MZ and DZ twins are shown in box B:

Box B: concordance rates for MZ and DZ twins		
	concordance rate	
	MZ twins	DZ twins
Gottesman and Shields (1972)	42%	9%
Kendler (1983)	50%	15%

You will have noticed that despite the fact that both pieces of research found lower concordance rates between DZ twins, neither study comes close to the concordance rate of 100% for MZ twins which would be expected if the disorder were entirely genetic. Gottesman and Shields (1982) found a 58% concordance rate in monozygotic twins reared apart, which is also much lower than would be expected if the disorder were entirely genetic.

All this research suggests that although there is a strong genetic component to schizophrenia, this cannot be the complete explanation.

Prospective studies

One characteristic of the research outlined above is that it is **retrospective**, i.e. it deals with people who have already been diagnosed as schizophrenic. Some interesting research is currently being carried out using the **prospective** method which selects suitable participants and follows them over an extended period of time, assessing them at regular intervals.

In the context of assessing the genetic contribution to schizophrenia, high-risk children are identified (i.e. those with one or both parents having been diagnosed as schizophrenic), and are followed up to see if they develop the disorder themselves. A control group of similar children, where neither parent has been diagnosed as schizophrenic, is followed at the same time, so that comparisons can be made.

The main advantage of this approach is that it allows the researcher to look at the incidence of disorders which could be diagnosed at any time over many years in the individual's lifetime. It also means that the criteria by which schizophrenia has been diagnosed in the parents can be established at the outset; over the years, diagnostic criteria can change considerably, so that over time you may not be comparing like with like.

We will look briefly here at two on-going studies:

Box C: Marcus et al., (1987)

Procedure: In this study, which started in 1967, the **Israeli High Risk Study**, 50 high-risk children were matched with 50 controls. Half of each group were raised communally on a kibbutz, away from their families, and half in their families. The children were aged between 8 and 14 at the start of the study.

Results: Thirteen years later, 22 of the high-risk group and 4 of the controls had been diagnosed as schizophrenic. Sixteen were from the kibbutz system and 10 from traditional families.

Conclusion: The study provides evidence of a genetic link in schizophrenia. It is also possible that the environment within which children are raised may influence whether or not the disorder develops.

An adoption study is also being carried out, again using this method:

Box D: Tienari et al., (1987)

Procedure: In this study, which started in 1969, the **Finnish Adoption Study**, 112 adopted-away children of schizophrenic birth mothers were compared with a matched control group of 135 adopted-away children of non-schizophrenic birth mothers. The age range at the start of the study was 5–7, and all had been separated from their mothers before the age of 4.

Results: In a follow-up study reported in 1987, 7% of the index children, compared with 1.5% of the control group, had been diagnosed as schizophrenic.

Conclusion: There is a genetic component to schizophrenia.

Both these studies may well provide us with even more information as they continue to follow up participants through future years.

Neurochemical explanations of schizophrenia

It has also been suggested that schizophrenia is caused by a chemical imbalance in the brain. Years before technology enabled scientists to isolate and analyse chemicals to the extent they can today, Jung suggested that schizophrenia was caused by the presence of a chemical he named **toxin X**, which he thought would be identified in years to come. It is now thought that an excess of the neurotransmitter **dopamine** may play a part in causing schizophrenia.

There is quite convincing evidence to support this idea. The **phenothiazines** are a type of drug used to treat schizophrenia, but a side-effect of this drug is that it can produce symptoms similar to **Parkinson's disease**, e.g. trembling. Parkinson's disease appears to be caused partly by insufficient levels of dopamine in part of the brain. It was therefore concluded that phenothiazines work in the treatment of schizophrenia by interfering with dopamine activity in the brain, i.e. blocking the action of dopamine receptors.

Further evidence is provided by the fact that if non-schizophrenic people take **amphetamines** in large doses, they show symptoms similar to schizophrenia (such as hallucinations and delusions). It is known that amphetamines increase dopamine levels, so this in turn suggests that excess dopamine could cause schizophrenia. However, the findings are not clear-cut; Kammen *et al.* (1977) reported that taking amphetamines can lead to a reduction in the symptoms of schizophrenia.

PET scans (positron emission tomography) and **MRI** (magnetic resonance imaging) are modern techniques which allow us to study characteristics of living brains; these techniques are discussed in more detail in the first section of chapter 11. Early research by Iverson (1979), where post mortems were carried out on schizophrenic patients, found higher than normal concentrations of dopamine in the brain, and there have been similar findings in research using PET scans. Wong *et al.* (1986) have shown that people suffering from schizophrenia do have a greater density of dopamine receptors on cells in various parts of their brains, though these findings have not always been replicated.

It may be that the symptoms of schizophrenia are due not so much to an excess of dopamine but a more complex dysregulation of the dopamine system, with schizophrenics having an excess of dopamine in some parts of the brain, and low levels in others. For example, Davis *et al.* (1991) have suggested that an abnormally low level of dopamine activity in the prefrontal regions of the brain may lead to excessive dopamine activity in the limbic system.

If the biochemical theory regarding the cause of schizophrenia does indeed hold true, then it follows that treatment for the disorder will involve the use of drugs (**chemotherapy**) in an attempt to regulate the imbalance of chemicals. Crow *et al.* (1982) have suggested that drugs are only useful in treating positive (Type I) symptoms, and are ineffective in treating patients with negative (Type II) symptoms. This suggests that the link between dopamine and schizophrenia – the **dopamine hypothesis** – may only be relevant in explaining the disorder in some patients, and we would need to look elsewhere for the causes in other patients. It is possible that the interaction of dopamine with other neuro-chemicals may be an important factor.

There may also be **confounding variables** in this kind of research. It is possible that schizophrenics may have different life-styles from other groups of people – perhaps those in psychiatric hospitals smoke more, or suffer a poorer diet, than their equivalent control group. There could therefore be factors which produce a biochemical difference, but which do not explain the cause of the disorder.

Neuroanatomical findings

Research has shown **structural differences** between the brains of schizophrenics and controls. MRI studies, e.g. Brown *et al.* (1986), have shown that many schizophrenics have lighter brains with enlarged ventricles (cavities holding cerebrospinal fluid). However, some studies (e.g. Pearlson *et al.*,

1989) have failed to replicate this finding. It may also be that ventricular enlargement is the result rather than the cause of the disorder.

Birchwood *et al.* (1988) found that the balance of activity between the two hemispheres of the brain was disturbed in some schizophrenic patients. Some studies have identified a dysfunction in the frontal lobes of schizophrenics, while Roberts (1991) suggested that there may be abnormal functioning in the medial temporal lobe. Since this part of the brain is involved in integrating information, a dysfunction in this area could account for some of the typical symptoms of schizophrenia.

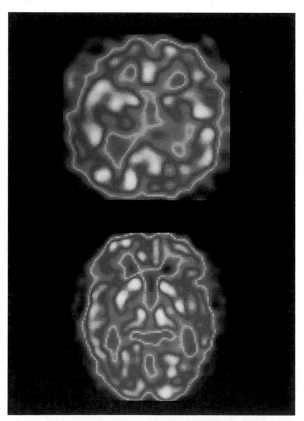

Ventricles in (top) the brain of a schizophrenic and (bottom) a normal brain

Abnormalities have also been observed in the **corpus callosum**, the bundle of nerve fibres which allow communication between the hemispheres of the brain. Some studies have found this structure to be enlarged in schizophrenics, while others have found it to be abnormally thin.

Coger and Serafetinides (1990) suggested that enlargement is associated with early onset schizophrenia and negative symptoms, while a thin corpus callosum is asociated with late onset schizophrenia and positive symptoms. There is some empirical support for this idea.

David and Cutting (1993) reported that in the brains of schizophrenics, neural connections in the hippocampus are disorganised compared to the regularly-arrayed connections in non-schizophrenics. However, this research is correlational, so some caution needs to be applied in interpreting the findings.

One possibility which has been investigated is that neurological abnormalities and schizophrenia both come about as the result of infection by a virus during foetal development:

Box E: Mednick *et al.* (1988)

Procedure: In 1957, there was a five-week influenza epidemic in Helsinki. The incidence of schizophrenia in people who had been exposed to this virus during their mothers' pregnancy was investigated.

Results: Those exposed during the second trimester of pregnancy were significantly more likely to be schizophrenic than those exposed during the first or third trimesters, or controls.

Conclusion: The second trimester is a crucial time for cortical development. Exposure to the virus at this time could therefore have led to the neurological abnormalities associated with schizophrenia.

However, Seidman (1983) has estimated that only around a quarter of schizophrenics have any form of gross brain abnormality. It is also possible that where such abnormality has been found, it may be the result of antipsychotic drugs or other as yet unidentified factors.

☉ Findings from **adoption** and **twin studies** support the idea that the cause of schizophrenia is at least in part **genetic**. There is similar evidence from ongoing **prospective studies**.

⊖ Schizophrenia has also been linked to excess **dopamine** and **structural differences** between the brains of schizophrenics and controls. It has not been possible to establish whether this link is causal.

⊖ Excess dopamine may only be linked to schizophrenia in some patients.

Psychological explanations

Some psychologists have tried to explain schizophrenia in terms of **dysfunctional families**. Bateson *et al.* (1956) suggested that some parents may predispose their children to schizophrenia by giving them conflicting messages. For example, a mother might tell her child to give her a hug while at the same time telling the child when it does so that it is too old to show affection in that way. Bateson argued that as a result of this kind of interaction, for which he used the term **double bind**, children may start to doubt their own understanding and lose their grip on reality.

R.D. Laing described case-studies of eleven families in his book *Sanity, Madness and the Family* (1964). In each family history, one member of the family is diagnosed as a schizophrenic, and Laing suggested that the cause of their schizophrenia is the way in which their family relationships work. This **family interaction model** suggests that family members communicating in pathological ways is the cause of the schizophrenia. More recently, Norton (1982) found that if parents were communicating poorly, this was a good predictor of the later onset of schizophrenia in their offspring.

However, there is a lack of evidence to support these ideas, and it seems rather harsh to blame families coping with a schizophrenic member when there is no clear-cut evidence that they are in fact responsible for it. There is also the problem of cause and effect when trying to establish a link between the ways in which families function and the development of schizophrenia. For example, Klebanoff (1959) argued that the kinds of behaviour that families show to an affected family member may well be a reasonable response to an unusual child.

In his book *The Divided Self* (1965), Laing put forward an **existential explanation** of schizophrenia. According to Laing, schizophrenia should not be seen as a disorder; what schizophrenics say and do make sense if you relate to what he referred to as their 'being-in-the world'. Their problems lie in their relationship with the world and with the self.

The schizophrenic experiences what Laing called **ontological insecurity**. The ontologically secure person meets all that life has to offer with a firm sense of his own and other people's reality and identity; this is missing in the schizophrenic. There are three forms of anxiety experienced by the ontologically insecure person. One is **implosion**, the terror associated with the possibility that the world may crash in and obliterate identity; schizophrenics experience themselves as a vacuum, which the world may come rushing in to fill. In **engulfment**, the possibility of any kind of relationship with another person threatens to overwhelm them. **Petrification** is the fear of being depersonalised by and depersonalising others. Laing believed that many of the things schizophrenics say or do make sense when seen against this background.

In *The Politics of Experience* (1967), Laing went on to propose the **psychedelic model**, that the schizophrenic is a person whose special sensitivity shows up the gross alienation which passes for normality in modern capitalist societies. What is labelled schizophrenia is a voyage into 'inner space', a 'natural healing process', which is not allowed to run its course because we are too busy treating the patient.

However, this kind of theory fell into disfavour when evidence for a genetic cause of schizophrenia began to emerge in the 1970s.

More recently, Frith (1997) has suggested that schizophrenia should be seen in information-processing terms. For example, alien control symptoms are due to faulty monitoring of intentions and plans by schizophrenics, so that they do not recognise thoughts and behaviours as being self-generated.

Interest has shifted from seeing the family as the cause of the disorder to investigating the role they might play in *maintaining it*. Brown (1972) looked at the effect of high expressed emotion (**High EE**) in the homes of schizophrenic patients returning from hospital. By this he meant homes where there were high levels of emotions such as hostility, anger and criticism. He found that schizophrenic patients returning to High EE homes were more likely to relapse than those returning to Low EE homes. This was explored further in later research:

Box F: Vaughn and Leff (1976)

Procedure: Patients returning to High EE homes were compared with those returning to Low EE homes. Data were also collected on the amount of time spent in direct contact with relatives during the period at home, as well as whether the patient was on medication.

Results: There was a 51% relapse rate in High EE homes, compared to 13% in Low EE homes. Relapse rates increased with amount of contact time, but only in High EE homes. If patients in High EE homes with high contact were also not taking medication, relapse rates rose to 92%.

Conclusion: The nature of communication within the family plays a part in whether treated patients have a relapse, though medication is also important.

The belief that High EE maintains schizophrenia is well established, and a range of other studies have supported it, across a range of cultures.

▶ Activity 1: assessing the importance of High EE

If this theory is correct, what are the implications for the treatment of schizophrenia? Can you think of any criticisms that could be made of the theory? Is it limited in any way?

When you have finished, see the notes on page 670.

Other psychological explanations have focused on the social context beyond the family. Research has shown significant correlations between **social class** and the diagnosis of schizophrenia. For example, Hollingshead and Redlich (1958) conducted a ten-year study of schizophrenia and social class in Connecticut. They found that the diagnosis of schizophrenia was twice as likely to be made in the lowest social class, especially amongst those living in densely populated, inner city areas. But does this support the **social causation hypothesis**, i.e. show that schizophrenia is caused by factors to do with social class?

The evidence here is correlational, and you will remember that correlations do not show cause and effect, so we cannot conclude that being in a lower social class causes schizophrenia. It could be that the poor education received by those in the lower social classes in Connecticut, together with the opportunities and rewards made unavailable to them, is so stressful that the individual develops schizophrenia. Alternatively, perhaps the development of schizophrenia, and the difficulties of earning a living if you suffer from the disorder, might lead to the person 'drifting' into the poorer areas of the city. This **social-drift hypothesis** suggests that the cognitive and motivational problems that the developing schizophrenic experiences can lead to their living in deprived areas, unable to obtain decent employment and unable to afford to move out of the area. There is also the confounding variable that schizophrenics in the upper classes may be less likely to come to the attention of the authorities since they are sheltered and protected by their families. Formulating conclusions from correlational studies is no easy matter.

The diathesis–stress explanation

There seems to be evidence that schizophrenia is caused by genetic, biochemical and perhaps also social and psychological factors; it is difficult to know how much weight should be given to each. The **diathesis–stress model** – suggesting that the disorder is probably the result of a combination of genetic vulnerability and environmental stress – may again have something to offer. In other words, you may inherit a *predisposition* to develop the illness, but will not go on to develop it unless stressors in your environment activate that predisposition. Amongst other things, this would help to explain why middle-class people living in a supportive family with a pleasant, enjoyable job are less likely than those who do not enjoy these advantages to be diagnosed as suffering from schizophrenia.

- ๑ It has been suggested that schizophrenia may be caused by **dysfunctional families**. Bateson's concept of **double bind** is an example of this approach.
- ๑ It is now thought that communication in families, in particular **High EE**, may be a factor in **maintaining** rather than causing schizophrenia.
- ๑ There is also a link between **social class** and the incidence of schizophrenia. The **social causation hypothesis** suggests that factors to do with class cause the disorder, while the **social drift hypothesis** suggests that people with the disorder may drift to a lower class as a result of the disorder.
- ๑ The **diathesis–stress** model suggests that we inherit a **predisposition** to develop schizophrenia, but that the disorder is developed only if this predisposition is later accompanied by **stress** from the environment.

24.3 DEPRESSION

Depression is an **affective** (or mood) **disorder**. We will be looking in this section only at **unipolar depression,** where the symptoms are those of depression alone. Depression can also play an important part in other disorders, in particular **bipolar disorder**, sometimes known as **manic depression**. This is characterised by major mood swings between a state of severe depression and mania, two extremes (or poles) of mood, hence the term bipolar disorder.

Depression is a very misunderstood disorder, frequently associated with other psychological problems. For example, we all feel sad and upset after the death of a loved family member, but clinical depression is *not* merely a feeling of sadness (although this may form a major part of the disorder), but rather a complex set of symptoms.

Depression can be relatively mild, or so intense that the sufferer is at serious risk of suicide. It can occur at any age, and it has been estimated that 5%

of adults in Britain will suffer from it at some time in their lives (SANE, 1993). The onset may be sudden or quite gradual. Nolen-Hoeksema (1988) reported that the risk of women developing unipolar depression is double that of men.

Some mental health professionals distinguish between **reactive** depression (i.e. depression in reaction to a stressful event, such as bereavement or unemployment) and **endogenous** depression (i.e. depression 'coming from within') , where there is no apparent external cause. However, these categories are not used in DSM-IV or ICD-10, the classification systems discussed in chapter 23, since it is now believed that all depression is the result of an interaction between environmental and personal factors.

Clinical characteristics

For a diagnosis of depression to be considered, a person will be experiencing some or all of the symptoms listed in figure 4:

Figure 4: symptoms of depression

- Feelings of sadness out of proportion to the person's life situation
- Poor appetite and weight loss (or increased appetite and weight gain)
- Insomnia
- Lethargy or agitation
- Loss of interest and pleasure in activities
- Loss of energy, and great fatigue
- Negative self-concept and feelings of worthlessness
- Difficulty in concentrating, and slowed thinking
- Recurrent thoughts of death or suicide

In order for clinical depression to be diagnosed, low mood will need to have persisted for at least two weeks, and a range of the symptoms described in figure 4 experienced.

Biological explanations

There is little evidence of a **genetic** link in depression. Allen (1976) found a concordance rate of 40% in MZ twins, and 11% in DZ twins. These figures suggest that genetic factors are of much less importance here than for schizophrenia (see box B).

It has also been suggested that depression is caused by imbalances in the **neurochemistry** of the body. Two theories have been put forward; one suggests that depression results from someone not having enough **noradrenaline** in their body; the second suggests that depression is the result of insufficient **serotonin**. Both of these chemicals are **neurotransmitters**, i.e. chemicals which enable a nerve impulse to pass from one nerve cell to another across a tiny gap called a **synapse**. Kety (1975) suggested that low levels of serotonin cause noradrenaline levels to become uncontrolled, so noradrenaline levels are a side effect of low levels of serotonin.

The effect of drugs on depression provides evidence supporting these ideas. For example, two groups of drugs called **tricyclics** and **monoamine oxidase inhibitors (MAOIs)** have been found to alleviate depression. Other studies have shown that these drugs increase the availability of serotonin and noradrenaline in animals' brains, providing evidence that depression may well be caused by a lack of these chemicals.

Further supporting evidence was found when **reserpine**, a drug used to treat high blood pressure, was given to schizophrenics to calm them down. One of the side effects of the drug was that it caused depression in a significant number of the schizophrenics, and its use was soon stopped. However, one of the reasons it may have caused depression in those patients is because reserpine was later found to reduce levels of serotonin and noradrenaline.

New kinds of anti-depressants have recently been developed, known as **SSRIs** (selective serotonin reuptake inhibitors), which increase serotonin levels, and **NARIs** (noradrenaline reuptake inhibitors), which increase noradrenaline levels. They are very effective in treating depression, which again suggests that depression results from low levels of these neurotransmitters.

Hormones have also been thought to be implicated in depression. Many women suffer from depression during part of the menstrual cycle (**pre-menstrual syndrome** or **PMS**), after childbirth (**post-natal depression**) and at **menopause**. At each of these times, there are rapid changes in hormone levels. Just prior to a menstrual period, oestrogen levels rise and progesterone levels fall, after childbirth there is a rapid drop in both oestrogen and progesterone, and at menopause a drop in oestrogen. It is possible that these changes in hormone levels could lead to depression.

In support of this idea, many women going through menopause and suffering symptoms of depression are helped by **hormone replacement therapy (HRT)**, which replaces lost oestrogen. On the other hand, some are not, and many women do not suffer depressive symptoms at this time, in spite of hormonal changes. A further problem in establishing the contribution of hormones is that at times like childbirth and menopause, there are often other changes taking place in a person's life. The arrival of a new baby, however much wanted, could in itself be seen as a very stressful event. The diathesis–stress model mentioned at the start of this chapter, which suggests the idea of pre-existing vulnerability, could be useful here in making sense of rather confusing findings.

- ❺ Clinical **depression** involves many symptoms including severe unhappiness, lethargy, and a loss of interest in life.
- ❺ **Twin studies** suggest that there is only a relatively weak **genetic** link with depression.
- ❺ A lack of **serotonin** or **noradrenaline** can cause depression. **Hormonal imbalance** may also play a part.

Psychological explanations

In addition to the biological ideas outlined in the last section, theorists have also suggested a range of psychological explanations for depression. We shall look now at the contributions of a **behavioural** approach, **cognitive** explanations, **psychodynamic** theory, and the effect of **major life events**.

Behavioural explanations of depression

Some behavioural theorists have related depression to **reinforcement**, drawing on the principles of **operant conditioning** outlined in chapter 1.

Lewinsohn (1974) suggested that if someone close to us dies, or we lose our job, the opportunities for receiving positive reinforcement from others are decreased. We may also be reinforced by the sympathy offered by others when we get depressed in these kinds of circumstances. When sympathy starts to wane, we are no longer offered the reinforcement of attention, resulting in even deeper depression. Lewinsohn also suggests that people who lack social skills are more likely than others to suffer from depression, since they are less likely to attract reinforcement from others.

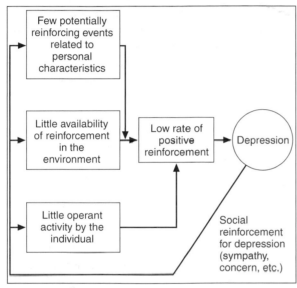

Lewinsohn's model of depression

MacPhillamy and Lewinsohn (1974) found a correlation between greater depression and fewer pleasant experiences. It seems likely that people who are depressed are less inclined to take part in activities which can bring them pleasure, and that not taking part in such activities could lead to depression. As with all correlational studies, though, cause and effect relationships are difficult to establish.

Seligman (1974) put forward his theory of **learned helplessness** within a broadly behavioural framework. His theory of depression suggested that people suffer from this disorder because they have developed a learned belief that they are not in control of their lives. He based his ideas on experiments carried out on dogs, using operant conditioning techniques:

Box G: Seligman (1974)

Procedure: Each of the experimental group of dogs was strapped into a harness and given a series of electric shocks from which it could not escape. The control group was not subjected to these shocks. Later on in the experiment, both groups of dogs were put into shuttle-boxes, i.e. boxes divided into two with a low partition over which the dogs could easily jump. They had to learn **avoidance behaviour** in this shuttle-box: if they were to avoid a prolonged electric shock, they had to jump the partition within 10 seconds of a warning signal.

Results: The control dogs learned the avoidance response very quickly, and soon jumped over the partition in response to the warning signal, thus avoiding the electric shock. However, two-thirds of the experimental dogs were unable to learn the avoidance response and just sat passively in the box, seemingly resigned to accepting the shock. Some of the dogs had to be physically pushed over the partition hundreds of times before they learnt the appropriate avoidance response.

Learned helplessness: Seligman's dogs had to be pushed over hundreds of times

Conclusion: Seligman concluded that the experimental group had learned during the initial phase that nothing they did would have any effect on the fact that they were going to receive a shock. In other words, they had learned to be helpless, and therefore were unable to 'unlearn' this helplessness and learn instead an appropriate avoidance response.

Seligman related his work on learned helplessness in dogs to depression in humans. He noticed that there were similarities between the dogs' behaviour and some of the symptoms of depression. For example, depressed people often seem to accept passively painful and stressful situations, without attempting to take action which might help them cope. Women, in particular, are more likely to suffer from depression than men, and this could be explained in terms of their relative lack of political and personal power in our society.

Some support for this idea came from a study by Roth and Kubal (1976). They found that people who had been asked to solve insoluble problems were later unable to solve as many problems where solutions were possible than a control group.

Further, Weiss *et al.* (1970) found that animals suffering from learned helplessness had lower levels of noradrenaline than controls, suggesting that the environmental stressors which create learned helplessness can also cause some of the biochemical changes associated with depression.

Cognitive explanations

Cognitive theorists explain depression in terms of the way a person thinks – their **cognitive processes**. A major theorist in the study of depression is Beck. He believed that people who are depressed make fundamental errors in logic. For example, they tend to distort what happens to them in a way which makes life seem even more hopeless. If your computer crashed when you had just typed a page of text you would probably be annoyed by the inconvenience it had caused you, but you would be unlikely to interpret the event as an example of how everything you do is doomed to failure. Beck (1991) proposed that depression is rooted in three maladaptive assumptions, which he called the **cognitive triad**: negative thoughts of self, of circumstances and of the future (see chapter 25, figure 4).

Beck suggested that depressive people draw **illogical conclusions** about events, and over-estimate their personal failings, bad luck and future difficulties, all of which lead to a **distorted reality**. He suggested that people have innate

temperamental differences, which can interact with traumatic or **negative experiences**. Depressed people, through rejection, criticism or a succession of tragedies, have negative schemas. (Schemas are discussed in more detail in chapter 2.) These negative schemas, together with the illogical conclusions mentioned previously, distort reality and lead the depressive to expect to fail at whatever they try, or to blame themselves for all misfortunes that befall them. Their negative self-evaluation schema reminds them constantly of their worthlessness. Such a conclusion may be based on one relatively trivial event; for example, failing a driving test may be taken as final proof of worthlessness and stupidity.

Beck's **depression inventory** is a way of measuring depressive symptoms. It classifies such symptoms into four groups – **moods** (feeling unhappy or unsociable); **thoughts** (seeing the future as hopeless and yourself as having failed in life); **motivation** (finding it difficult to do anything) and **physical symptoms** (such as appetite loss or insomnia). The symptoms are given a score from 0 to 3 and give the therapist a good idea of the type of depression from which the person is suffering.

Figure 5 gives you an idea of the type of item given in the depression inventory:

Figure 5: types of item in Beck's depression inventory

Unhappiness	0	I don't feel unhappy
	1	I feel unhappy
	2	I feel unhappy all the time, and can't stop
	3	I'm so unhappy I can't cope with it
Failure	0	I don't feel a failure
	1	I feel I have failed
	2	Nearly all the time I feel I've failed
	3	I feel such a failure I can't stand it

In the previous section, Seligman's concept of **learned helplessness** was linked to the behavioural account of depression. In 1979,

Seligman and his research colleagues reformulated the learned helplessness theory and incorporated the idea of **attribution**, bringing a stronger element of cognition into the theory (Seligman *et al.*, 1979). Attribution refers to what a person sees as the cause of a particular situation – for example, if you fail your driving test on the first attempt, was the failure because you hadn't had enough driving practice (an **internal attribution**: the cause was within yourself) or because the driving instructor took a dislike to you (an **external attribution**: the cause was outside your control)? Attribution theory is covered in more detail in chapter 8.

Internal and external attributions of failure

Activity 2: making attributions

Read the following situations, and try to think of (a) an internal and (b) an external attribution of a cause for each.
1 Jo achieves 98% in her German test.
2 Craig has problems assembling a flat-pack set of shelves.
3 Jonathan crashes into the back of a lorry at a roundabout.
When you have finished, see the notes on page 670.

As well as the internal/external distinction, we also use two other dimensions to make judgements: **stable/unstable** and **global/specific**. In the second example in activity 2, for instance, Craig could make either the stable attribution that he is always useless at DIY or the unstable one that this is a one-off event. He could either make the global attribution that he is always hopeless at anything practical or the specific one that he only has trouble with flat-pack assembly.

You can probably see how these ideas of attribution can be applied to depression. Depression is associated with internal, stable and global attributions of failure. It is also associated with external, unstable and specific attributions of success.

Activity 3: attributions – success and failure

a Henry does very badly on a chemistry test, and becomes depressed. How could this be explained in terms of him making internal, stable and global attributions?
b Gus does well on a physics test, but is nonetheless depressed about the result. How could this be explained in terms of him making external, unstable and specific attributions?
When you have finished, see the notes on page 670.

Research has shown that people prone to depression do tend to attribute failures or bad outcomes to internal causes; this can destroy their self-esteem and cause depression. Box H shows the results of a study carried out using Seligman's **Attributional-Style Questionnaire (ASQ)**, a questionnaire designed to discover information about people's attributions:

Box H: Metalsky *et al.* (1987)

Procedure: College students taking a course in abnormal psychology were asked to complete the ASQ, as well as a questionnaire concerning the grades they were hoping to achieve, and a checklist assessment of their current mood. Eleven days later, they were again asked to complete the mood checklist. A further five days later, when they had received their exam grade, the mood checklist was again completed.

Results: The students' results were divided into two groups according to the grades they had achieved compared to the grade they had hoped to achieve. The 'good grade' group consisted of students who had achieved a grade equal to or better than the one they had previously said they would be happy with; the 'poor grade' group consisted of those students who had achieved a grade worse than that which they had hoped for. For both the 'good grade' and 'poor grade' groups, correlations between changes in mood (as measured by the checklist) and scores from the ASQ were worked out. The results showed that for the 'good grade' group, there were no significant correlations. However, for the 'poor grade' group, depression could be predicted from the significant correlations between the two measures.

Conclusion: Students prone to attributing negative events and failures to personal inadequacies become more depressed after a negative event such as a poor exam grade.

Psychodynamic explanations

The psychodynamic view links adult depression with childhood experience and trauma. Freud, whose theory is outlined in chapter 1, argued that a loss (e.g. the death of someone we love or the loss of a job) causes us to re-experience part of our childhood and show regression. The greater the experience of loss in childhood, the greater the regression in adulthood, and thus the greater the likelihood of developing depression. Bowlby's **maternal deprivation hypothesis** (see chapter 3) also proposed that the lack of a warm and continuous relationship with one major caregiver in infancy could lead to depression in adulthood. Bowlby himself was a Freudian, and his maternal deprivation hypothesis is very much a Freudian explanation.

The evidence here is mixed. Paykel (1981) reviewed 14 animal studies investigating this idea, and found that half supported it, while half did not. It is of course unwise to extrapolate too freely from animal studies to humans, so we should be cautious in any case in drawing conclusions from this kind of research. For example, in what ways could an animal be said to be depressed? What is a warm and continuous relationship for an animal?

Unfortunately, studies of the incidence of adult depression in people who have lost a parent in childhood are also equivocal. A study by Roy (1981) found a link, whereas Lewinsohn and Hoberman (1982) did not.

Freud also made a link between unresolved hostility towards parents and depression. Since this hostility is unacceptable to the **superego**, it is turned inwards, and leads to feelings of guilt, inadequacy and despair, which may lead to suicide. As with all psychodynamic ideas, this is not easy to test, but if it is true, it is difficult to reconcile with the hostility that depressed people often show to others.

Major life events

Major life events, such as serious illness, divorce or the death of someone we love, are thought to be important triggers in reactive depression:

Box I: Brown and Harris (1978)

Procedure: Housewives living in Camberwell in London were studied. The researchers aimed to identify factors which could be associated with the development of depression.

Results: Depression was triggered by major life events, such as illness and bereavement. It was also associated with long-term problems. Several factors which made the individual more vulnerable to depression were identified: lack of paid employment, two or more children under the age of 5, lack of a

close relationship, and having lost their own mother in childhood.
Conclusion: Life events may trigger depression, but are more likely to have serious consequences in the presence of other long-term problems.

The link here between depression and the loss of their mother in childhood supports the findings of Roy, mentioned earlier in the discussion of psychodynamic explanations of depression.

You can probably relate this study to the diathesis–stress explanation of the causes of mental disorders; long-term problems make the individual more vulnerable to developing depression. This helps to explain why some people experience major life events and do not develop depression, while some develop a depressive disorder with no apparent precipitating factor.

- Lewinsohn took a behavioural view. He explained depression in terms of lack and loss of **reinforcement**.
- Seligman's **learned helplessness** theory suggested that depression is caused by a feeling of lack of control. He later reformulated his ideas to include **attribution**. Those making internal, stable and global attributions about failure and external, unstable and specific attributions about success are more likely to become depressed. The **Attribution Style Questionnaire** measures attributions.
- Cognitive theorists like Beck explain depression in terms of faulty thought processes. He suggested that depressed people draw **illogical conclusions** that distort life events. His **depression inventory** measures depressive symptoms.
- A **psychodynamic** view links depression with loss in early childhood and unresolved hostility to parents. It is difficult to test these ideas empirically.
- **Major life events** can bring about depression, but are more likely to have serious effects in those made vulnerable by long-term problems.

24.4 ANXIETY DISORDERS

Anxiety is an emotional state which can occur in many disorders, and is the main component of the disorders that will be described in this section. We all feel anxious or fearful at various times, but these feelings are not usually as strong nor as debilitating as those suffered by a person with an anxiety disorder. **Generalised anxiety disorder**, characterised by persistent and excessive worrying about a range of situations and issues, and **panic disorder**, marked by frequently recurring attacks of panic and terror, are both very common. The three anxiety disorders which we will concentrate on in this section are **post-traumatic stress disorder**, **phobias** and **obsessive–compulsive disorder**.

Post-traumatic stress disorder

Post-traumatic stress disorder (PTSD) differs somewhat from other anxiety disorders in that by definition it always follows the experience of an appalling traumatic event. Examples of relatively recent events which have triggered this disorder in some of those who directly experienced them include the Gulf War, the death of more than 90 football fans crushed to death at the Hillsborough football ground, and the Dunblane massacre when Thomas Hamilton gunned down children and their teacher at a primary school. It can also come about as the result of personal experiences such as being mugged or raped.

It is likely that most of us, undergoing this kind of traumatic experience, would react with great distress. Indeed, DSM-IV states that 'the stressor producing this syndrome would evoke significant symptoms of distress in most people'. However, for most people the stress which they experience is relatively short-lived. Although they may not forget the experience, they recover quite well, and manage to get on with their lives. It is people who fail to make this kind of recovery who are said to suffer from PTSD.

Following World War I, the term **shell shock** was used to describe the symptoms of what we now refer to as post-traumatic stress disorder, and after World War II, the disorder was called **combat**

fatigue. It was not until after the Vietnam War that PTSD was classified as a specific disorder.

A traumatic experience can lead to PTSD

Symptoms of PTSD include **flashbacks** – intrusive memories of the event which are so vivid that it is as if the experience were being relived – and frightening **dreams,** often triggered by cues associated with the event. Sufferers may have problems with **concentration**, and have a tendency to be jumpy, irritable and unable to relax. They may suffer from depression, insomnia, and a feeling of detachedness from others – sometimes known as **psychic numbing** – which makes it difficult to maintain relationships.

Green (1994) found that overall the proportion of those who develop PTSD as the result of trauma is about 25%, ranging from 12% for accidents to 80% for rapes. According to DSM-IV, it is as likely to affect children as adults, and there are no gender or cultural differences in terms of who it is likely to affect. It may occur immediately after a traumatic event. On the other hand, it is not uncommon for someone to seem to recover remarkably well from an ordeal, only to develop PTSD weeks, months or even years later.

In discussing the aetiology of the disorder, the focus is on why some people develop the disorder while others, who have experienced the same stressful event, do not. **Neurological factors**, **classical conditioning** and **psychodynamic** ideas have all been put forward as explanations of these individual differences.

Neurological explanations of PTSD

It has been suggested that there is a difference in the functioning of the **autonomic nervous system (ANS)**, described briefly in chapter 4, between those who develop PTSD and those who do not. Van der Kolk (1988) suggested that in PTSD sufferers, the system lacks resiliency, while Pitman *et al.* (1990) suggested that 'the experience of overwhelming terror can permanently alter a person's brain chemistry...because the brain structures that trigger the body's emergency response have become overly responsive.' In other words, traumatic stress impairs the brain's normal protection against excessive stimulation. Kosten *et al.* (1987) found higher than normal levels of noradrenaline in PTSD patients than in controls, again making a link with the stress response (see chapter 4). This is an area, though, where more research needs to be done to explore more thoroughly possible neurological explanations for individual differences.

Classical conditioning

Classical conditioning (see chapter 1) may be implicated in the development of PTSD. Stimuli present at the time of the trauma are linked with the response of extreme fear to the trauma itself, so the later presence of these stimuli produces a fear reaction in sufferers. An example is given by Hunt (in Bender, 1995). He interviewed veterans of the Normandy landings in the second world war, and found that those suffering from PTSD had been badly affected by media coverage of the 50th anniversary celebrations in 1994. However, a cognitive explanation, i.e. the revival of memories, would be equally valid here.

Psychodynamic explanations

The psychodynamic view of disorders looks for links between early childhood experience and the repression of traumatic memories and problems in later life. It is possible that those who have experienced trauma in childhood may be more vulnerable to trauma in later life, and thus more likely to develop PTSD. This idea has a strong parallel with the classical conditioning account.

Support for the psychodynamic view is offered by Bremner *et al.* (1993). They showed that PTSD is more common among people with a range of traumatic childhood experiences, e.g. physical or sexual abuse, parental divorce, or mental illness in a close family member, than among controls.

Diathesis–stress model

It is likely that there are three groups of factors which determine whether or not someone who undergoes a traumatic experience will develop PTSD.

The first of these is **pre-trauma factors**; past experiences may well make a person more vulnerable to the disorder. This is in line with the ideas put forward by the classical conditioning and psychodynamic accounts described above.

Secondly, there are **factors associated with the trauma itself**. There is some evidence that the likelihood of developing PTSD is in direct proportion to the amount of exposure to the traumatic event.

Finally, there are post-trauma factors. For example, vulnerability could be related to the availability of **social support systems**. In his study of veterans of the Normandy landings, Hunt (in Bender, 1995) found that the comradeship of others who had shared their experiences was an important coping mechanism.

- ➎ PTSD is an extreme and lasting response to a traumatic experience. It is characterised by symptoms such as **flashbacks**, **lack of concentration, depression**, **insomnia** and **emotional problems**.
- ➎ Individual differences in the response to PTSD have been accounted for by **neurological factors**, **classical conditioning** and in **psychodynamic** terms. The **diathesis–stress model** may also have something to contribute.

Phobias

Phobias are disorders characterised by an irrational, intense fear of an object, activity or situation, and a powerful urge to avoid that feared stimulus. The fear is disrupting to the individual's life, out of proportion to the real danger involved, and recognised as a groundless fear by the phobic person.

'Phobia' is a term commonly used wrongly to indicate fear or loathing of something, e.g. 'I have an exam phobia', but this is not the true meaning of the word. We may hate exams, and feel nervous when revising, or imagining the exam situation, or sick when entering the exam room itself, but we do not have a phobia about exams. Someone suffering from a true phobia about exams would probably be physically unable to arrive at the exam location and sit the exam due to their irrational fear.

You are likely to know something about phobias already. Try activity 4:

▶ ## Activity 4: which phobia?

Here are some common phobias. See how many you can match up with their meanings, and look up the others in a dictionary:

	fear of:	
claustrophobia		spiders
xenophobia		flying
musophobia		water
arachnophobia		heights
astraphobia		strangers
nosophobia		disease
hydrophobia		the number 13
algophobia		pain
acrophobia		enclosed spaces
agoraphobia		snakes
ophidiophobia		mice
pyrophobia		death
taphophobia		lightning
necrophobia		open spaces
aerophobia		fire
triskaidekaphobia		being buried alive

ALGOPHOBIA IS WHAT YOU SHOULD BE WORRYING ABOUT, NEVER MIND HYDROPHOBIA!

DSM-IV defines three categories of phobia: **agoraphobia**, **social phobias** and **specific phobias.** Agoraphobia literally means 'the fear of open spaces', but is better characterised as a fear of being away from home, in situations where no help is available or where escape may be difficult. It accounts for 10–50% of all phobias. Social phobias involve an intense fear of social situations and having to interact with other people. They account for around 10% of all phobias. In both these categories, most sufferers are female. Specific phobias relate to fear of a specific object (such as spiders, i.e. arachnophobia) or situation (such as being in an enclosed space, i.e. claustrophobia).

The age of onset of particular phobias, or kinds of phobia, varies. Specific phobias tend to develop during childhood, social phobias during adolescence, agoraphobia during early adulthood and nosophobias during middle age. This suggests that the causes of each type may not be the same.

Genetic explanations of phobia

There have been some attempts to establish whether there is a genetic basis for phobias. Seligman suggested that we have a **biological preparedness** to develop the more common phobias, because they were adaptive in our evolutionary past. For example, individuals who kept their distance from snakes and avoided high places where there was a danger of falling would be more likely to survive long enough to pass on their genes (and hence these characteristics) than those who did not. This theory is discussed in more detail in chapter 22. At the same time, however, further explanation of why some people develop phobias while others do not is necessary.

Family studies suggest that there is a genetic link. Solyom *et al.* (1974) found that of 47 phobic patients, 30% had mothers with phobias, compared to 19% for a control group. However, as noted before, this kind of study does not differentiate between genetic factors and the influence of the environment. It is possible that the patients learned phobic behaviour from observing their phobic mothers.

Twin studies have also supported the possibility of a genetic link. Torgerson (1983) investigated panic disorder and agoraphobia in twins, and found 31% concordance in 13 MZ twin pairs, but 0% in 16 DZ twin pairs. Interestingly, none of the twins shared the same phobia.

Psychological explanations of phobia

There have been various explanations of phobia which fall into this category. We will look here at **behavioural**, **cognitive** and **psychodynamic** explanations, together with the possible contribution of **major life events**.

Behavioural explanations

The main assumption of behavioural theories of phobias is that they are **learned** behaviours, and that this learning is based on **association**. The principles of both **classical** and **operant conditioning** can be used to explain the process. The basic principles of these theories are outlined in chapter 1.

The study of Little Albert, carried out by Watson and Rayner (1920), described in chapter 1, box B, demonstrated that a phobia could be developed using **classical conditioning** techniques. However, in terms of the usefulness of classical conditioning in explaining why people acquire phobias, the case of Little Albert only shows us that phobias *can* be acquired in this way – it doesn't mean that *all* phobias are acquired like this. Indeed, many people who have phobias of snakes, heights and plane travel say that they have not had frightening experiences with those objects or situations. So although classical conditioning may play a part in causing some phobias, there must be other processes at work that lead to other phobias developing.

It has also been suggested that **operant conditioning** may account for the learning of phobias, due to the **reinforcement** that showing fear may elicit from others. For example, if a child shows fear when confronted by a new situation such as going to school, the parent may inadvertently reinforce this fear by allowing them to stay at home, and providing extra cuddles and attention to make them feel less frightened. It is argued that eventually this can lead to the fear of the school situation developing into a phobia.

Activity 5: reinforcing agoraphobia

Agoraphobia is an irrational and intense fear of open spaces. Imagine an agoraphobic woman, unable to leave her house due to her agoraphobia. How could positive and negative reinforcement serve to keep her inside the home?

When you have finished, see the notes on page 670.

Another way that conditioning has been used to explain phobia is through **observational learning**. In **social learning theory** (see chapter 1), Bandura (1977) suggested that a lot of our behaviour is acquired through **imitation** or **modelling** others' behavioural responses; perhaps this is another way in which phobias can be caused. He has suggested that phobic reactions are learned by watching others displaying them, through a process called **vicarious conditioning**:

Box J: Bandura and Rosenthal (1966)

Procedure: Participants watched a stooge who was wired up to a complicated-looking array of electrical apparatus. Periodically a buzzer sounded, and each time this happened, the stooge quickly removed his hand from the arm of the chair and pretended to feel great pain. While the participant watched this situation, their physiological responses were recorded.
Results: Having watched the stooge suffering pain, the participants' emotional responses to the buzzer increased, as measured by their GSR (sweat response).
Conclusion: The participant had had no direct contact with pain, yet they learnt to react emotionally to a harmless stimulus (the buzzer). Vicarious learning was taking place.

You can probably imagine real-life situations in which such vicarious learning could take place. Children brought up in homes where the parents show great fear when catching sight of a spider are likely to watch the fear caused by the stimulus of the spider, and are more likely to develop similar fears.

One problem with behavioural accounts of phobias is that there is some difficulty in explaining why some phobias are more common than others. If it is a simple case of associating an object or situation with an unpleasant experience, we should be as likely to form phobias of hamsters or stinging nettles, which have nipped and stung most of us at some time, as we are of spiders or heights which often haven't hurt us at all; but this is not the case.

Seligman's concept of biological preparedness, mentioned earlier, can help to account for the relative frequency of some phobias, while still working within a behavioural framework. It could be that, as he suggested, we are pre-programmed to develop fears of objects and situations which were adaptive in our evolutionary past. Whether or not we do develop those fears could then depend on our experiences. This is not to suggest that we are born with snake or spider templates; it could be that certain configurations of stimuli, such as difference from the human form, trigger these phobias.

Support for this idea comes from the findings of a study carried out by Garcia and Koelling (1966). In this study rats were exposed to pairings of an unaccustomed food with illness, light and noise. They readily formed an association between the new taste and illness; failure to do so would be potentially fatal. However, they did not form an association between the taste and light or noise, which did not have survival implications. The findings of this study became known as the **Garcia Effect**. This is described in more detail in Chapter 20, box I.

Cognitive explanations

In the section on depression, we looked at the ideas of Beck. The kinds of ideas he put forward in that context can also be related to the development of phobias, i.e. that they are the result of irrational beliefs:

Figure 6: a possible route to developing claustrophobia
1 experience of being in a tightly-packed lift
2 thought: 'I might suffocate if I got trapped in a lift'
3 fear of lifts
4 generalisation to similar situations, e.g. tunnels, underground trains
5 claustrophobia

In this account, it is not exposure alone to a potentially fearful object or situation which leads to the development of a phobia, but rather how we think about this exposure.

Psychodynamic explanations

Within a psychodynamic framework, phobias can be explained in terms of **unconscious** (often sexual) fears. The ego defence mechanism of **repression** pushes the fear into the unconscious, where the second defence mechanism of **displacement** allows it to be expressed through fear of a substitute object. This is well illustrated in a case study carried out by Freud:

Box K: Freud (1909)
A case study was carried out of **Little Hans**, a 5-year-old boy whose phobia of horses was so strong that he was unable to leave the house. Freud interpreted this fear as an expression of the **Oedipus conflict** (see the section on **personality development**, chapter 18.) At this period of psychosexual development, the child's desire for his mother would lead to the fear that his father would castrate him. Since his fear of his father was too threatening to face, it was displaced on to horses. Freud noted that the child was particularly frightened of horses with black round their mouths and who wore blinkers. He interpreted this in terms of a resemblance to the father's beard and spectacles.

While this kind of interpretation has its appeal, it is difficult to see how these ideas could be tested. It is perhaps also worth noting that Hans's phobia had started after seeing a horse, pulling a heavily-loaded cart, collapse and die in the street. Hans's phobia only showed itself when witnessing a similar event, i.e. a horse pulling a heavily-loaded cart. A behavioural explanation of the development of Little Hans's phobia would therefore be equally possible. The fear of horses could have come about through classical conditioning, as the result of an association between the horrific event he had witnessed and horses.

Major life events

The relationship between stressful events and anxiety disorders is widely accepted and supported by research evidence. For example, Kleiner and Marshall (1987) found that 84% of agoraphobics had experienced family problems immediately before their first panic attack. At the same time, many people experience events such as a bereavement, but do not go on to develop an anxiety disorder. Again, it seems likely that we need to look to the diathesis–stress model to explain the relationship between life events and the development of phobias.

● **Phobias** are extreme, irrational fears. They include **agoraphobia**, **social phobias** and **specific phobias**.
● Seligman's concept of **biological preparedness** explains why some phobias are more common than others. It suggests that we are likely to develop fears which were adaptive in our evolutionary past.
● **Family studies** and **twin studies** suggest there may be some **genetic** link.
● Within a **behavioural** framework, the study of **Little Albert** shows that phobias can be developed through **classical conditioning**. They may also be shaped and maintained by **positive** and **negative reinforcement**, and develop through **observational learning**,
● **Cognitive** theorists suggest that phobias are acquired as the result of **irrational beliefs** about objects or situations.
● **Psychodynamic** explanations link phobias with the **displacement** of unconscious fears. Freud's case study of **Little Hans** illustrates this idea.
● **Major life events** may also trigger phobias, but are best considered within the **diathesis–stress model**.

Obsessive–compulsive disorder

Obsessions are recurring thoughts that intrude into a person's mind again and again, and are seen by the person having the thoughts as irrational and uncontrollable. Although we all sometimes have the odd irrational thought that pops into our mind unbidden, this is not to the same extent as those suffered by a disordered person, whose obsessions are so frequent that they interfere with normal life.

Compulsions are irresistible impulses to repeat a stereotyped ritual an excessive number of times. It is often a way of coping with obsessional thoughts. To use a very common example, a person obsessed with germs might cope with this obsession by compulsive handwashing.

Obsessive–compulsive disorder (OCD) is thought to affect 1–2% of the population, and often starts in early adulthood, though it can begin earlier. It often follows a stressful event, such as childbirth or family conflict, and is slightly more common among females.

Again, those of us not suffering from an obsessive–compulsive disorder may take a good luck object into an exam, or need to check that we have locked the front door before going to bed in spite of knowing really that we have already done so. However, a person with OCD might be unable to write anything in the exam if they forgot to take their lucky charm with them, or might get out of bed thirty or forty times to check that the door was locked.

A person with OCD realises that they have a problem and that their anxiety is irrational. At the same time, if they are prevented from carrying out the rituals which go with the disorder, they experience intense anxiety.

Common forms of obsession and compulsion in OCD are shown in figure 7:

Figure 7: common obsessions and compulsions in OCD

obsessions
obsessive doubts, e.g. that a task like locking the door has not been carried out
obsessive thoughts, e.g. an endlessly repeated chain of thought, often about a possible event in the future
fear of being responsible for someone's death or illness
germs, contamination and illness, where everything with which the person comes into contact is seen as a source of contamination

> **compulsions**
> *checking behaviours*, e.g. locks and electrical switches
> *washing*, e.g. washing the hands several hundred times a day
> *counting*, e.g. counting up to 6 over and over again
> *touching*, e.g. the need to touch a part of the body as part of a ritual

Obsessions often have very negative effects on personal relationships. Someone who feels compelled to count every paving stone as they walk from their house to their destination, or needs to go back over and over again to check that they have switched the iron off, is likely to be exasperating to those around them, even if they know that that the obsessive–compulsive person can't help what they are doing.

Biological explanations

Within a biological perspective, Comings and Comings (1987) found that people with OCD are more likely than those without the disorder to have a first-degree relative (parent, sibling or child) who also has the disorder. This could suggest a genetic element to the disorder, but could also be explained behaviourally; children of a sufferer could acquire compulsive behaviour through **observational learning**, as described above in the section on phobias.

Work using PET scans has shown that there are differences between the brains of obsessive–compulsive people and those not suffering from the disorder, e.g. increased metabolic activity in the left frontal lobe. This area of the cortex has a role in perseverative behaviour (see chapter 11). Whether this increase in metabolic activity directly causes obsessional thoughts is not yet clear; it could be that such thoughts arise indirectly, because of the failure of this dysfunctional area of the cortex to filter them out. Jenike (1986) reported that encephalitis, head injuries and brain tumours have all been associated with the development of OCD.

It is also possible that **serotonin** deficiency may be related to OCD, since the disorder can be successfully treated with drugs such as SSRIs, mentioned in the section on depression, which increase the availability of this neurotransmitter.

Obsessive–compulsive behaviour is also very common in patients with **Tourette's syndrome**. This is a disorder which begins during childhood, and involves tics of movement and verbal expression. The sufferer may make repetitive grunting noises, and exhibit coprolalia, i.e. shouting obscenities. The brains of Tourette's patients show a similar increase in metabolic activity to that found in OCD patients. Since Tourette's syndrome is associated with high levels of dopamine, it has been suggested by Pitman *et al.* (1987) that this may also cause OCD.

It is perhaps worth noting that many obsessions and compulsions relate to things which are important to survival; for example, hygiene, invasion of territory and the infidelity of a partner. As with phobias, there is perhaps a link here with our evolutionary past.

Behavioural explanations

Based on the principle of **reinforcement** central to **operant conditioning**, behavioural theories suggest that OCD develops as a way of reducing anxiety (the **anxiety-reduction hypothesis**). For example, the reduction of fear following hand-washing negatively reinforces the practice, which is therefore more likely to occur again. In the same way, ritualised checking may reduce fear about the imminent disaster imagined by the person if the checking had not taken place. This seems quite a reasonable way of explaining how OCD is maintained, but is rather less successful at explaining how it develops in the first place.

The development of OCD is perhaps better explained by the **superstition hypothesis**, still within the theoretical framework of **operant conditioning**. Skinner observed the development of 'superstitious' behaviours in pigeons, which he explained as coming about through a chance association between a behaviour and a reinforcer. For example, a pigeon might always move its head to the right before the behaviour which was reinforced by food, i.e. pecking at a disc; the pigeon had formed an association between the head movement and food, even though this movement was irrelevant to receiving food.

O'Leary and Wilson (1975) argued that this is how superstitious behaviour in humans is acquired, of which compulsive rituals are an extreme example. For example, among professional footballers little rituals carried out before the match are common, e.g. being last on the pitch, always putting the left sock on before the right, and so on. These kinds of behaviour have been coincidentally associated with success in the past, and failure to carry them out creates anxiety.

Cognitive explanations

Superstition could explain the development of compulsive behaviours, but does not really help to account for the other aspect of the disorder, obsessive thoughts. It has been suggested that we all have intrusive thoughts, but people with OCD are less able to tolerate them. They therefore make more effort than other people to inhibit these thoughts, which may paradoxically lead to becoming preoccupied with them. There is some evidence that this might be the case:

Box L: Wegner *et al.* (1987)

Procedure: One group of participants was asked to (a) think about a white bear, then (b) not think about it. A second group carried out (b) followed by (a). Participants' thoughts were measured by asking them to say aloud what they were thinking about, and to ring a bell whenever they thought about a white bear.
Results: All participants found it very difficult to inhibit their thoughts. Those in the second group had more thoughts about a white bear during (a) than those in the first group.
Conclusion: Attempting to inhibit a thought can lead to an increase in that thought.

However, why people with OCD should show a lowered tolerance for intrusive thoughts in the first place still needs to be explained.

The development of OCD has also been related to faulty thought processes. Carr (1974) has suggested that when a situation may have an undesirable outcome, obsessive–compulsives overestimate the probability that this outcome will occur, thinking along the lines of 'If anything can go wrong, then it will.' They therefore make exaggerated efforts to avoid sources of threat, e.g. compulsive hand-washing to avoid the possibility of becoming ill.

The idea that compulsive behaviour may be linked to a poor memory for having carried out actions has also been investigated:

Box M: Sher *et al.* (1983)

Procedure: Compulsive checkers were compared with a control group for (a) memory for having carried out actions and (b) being able to distinguish between having carried out an action and imagining having carried it out. The reasoning here was that compulsive checkers might have a poorer memory than controls in both these areas, so checking would be a way of reducing uncertainty.
Results: Compulsive checkers had a poorer memory than controls for (a). The results were less clear-cut for (b).
Conclusion: There is some support for a link between poor memory and OCD.

Psychodynamic explanations

Psychodynamic theory argues that obsessions and compulsions arise from instinctual sexual or aggressive forces which are not under control. Failure to resolve conflicts relating to anal/urethral activity leads to the person being **fixated** at the **anal stage**. The symptoms of an OCD sufferer represent a struggle between the sexual and aggressive urges of the id and the defence mechanisms of the ego. For example, when obsessive thoughts of harming someone else are experienced, the id is in control. Other symptoms may show the partially successful use of a defence mechanism. At the anal stage, the person may have an urge to soil; by reaction formation, this is converted into compulsive cleanliness. Freud's psychosexual stages and the consequences of fixation are discussed in more detail in chapter 18.

The **ego defence mechanism** of **displacement** is also relevant. Obsessive thoughts may be a way of not allowing threatening material from the unconscious to reach the conscious mind. On the other hand, obsessional thoughts about killing someone are in themselves so distressing that it is hard to imagine the kinds of thoughts for which they might be a more bearable substitute.

🟢 Obsessive–compulsive disorder (OCD) involves **recurring**, **uncontrollable thoughts**, together with **irresistible impulses** to repeat rituals.

🟢 It is possible that the cause is partly **genetic**. The neurotransmitters **serotonin** and **dopamine** may be implicated.

🟢 The **anxiety reduction hypothesis** claims that compulsive rituals are **reinforced** by a drop in anxiety. This is a better explanation of the maintenance of OCD than its cause.

🟢 The **superstition hypothesis** may help to explain the aetiology of compulsive behaviour. Obsessional thoughts may be explained by attempts to inhibit intrusive thoughts.

🟢 **Cognitive** theorists make a link with **negative thinking** and poor **memory** skills.

🟢 **Psychodynamic theory** explains OCD in terms of **anal fixation** and **ego defence mechanisms**.

Notes on activities

1 If family members contribute to maintaining schizophrenia, it makes sense for them to be included in any treatment programme. This is now widely done, and Doane *et al.* (1985) found that the recurrence of schizophrenic symptoms was less when parents reduced the hostility and criticism shown towards their schizophrenic children.

In terms of criticising the theory, if High EE in family members maintains schizophrenia, then it would be expected that schizophrenics who do not return to their families should be less likely to have a relapse. This has not been found to be the case (Goldstein and Anthony, 1988).

However, it may be High EE itself, rather than its expression within a family situation, which is responsible for relapse. This idea has the advantage of shifting blame away from family members, who are having to cope with the often far from easy situation of living with a schizophrenic.

2 Jo could make an internal attribution of her success by claiming she had worked especially hard for the test, or could make an external attribution by saying that the teacher only gave her such a good mark because her mother would have complained otherwise! Craig could see the cause of his problems with the flat pack as external if he thought that the instructions weren't clear, and some of the necessary bits were missing; or internal if he blamed himself for 'always being clumsy'. An external attribution for Jonathan might be to blame the car behind for flashing him and making him take his eyes off the road; an internal attribution might consider that he crashed into the lorry because he is a bad driver who really shouldn't be allowed on the road in the presence of other traffic.

3a An internal attribution could be that he didn't understand the material he had to revise for the test; a stable attribution could be that he is not clever enough to understand chemistry; a global attribution could be that he finds all academic subjects difficult to understand.

3b An external attribution could be that the test was very easy; an unstable attribution could be that doing well at physics just happened this once and does not mean that he will do well on future tests; a specific attribution could be that he can only cope with this one particular topic in physics.

5 The attention of others, and (at least initially) their sympathy, could be sources of **positive reinforcement**. For example, other people

would need to shop for food, and this activity could provide reinforcement through the opportunities provided for social activity when the shopper delivered the food.

Imagine the agoraphobic woman was determined to overcome her fear and leave the house to go to buy some milk. Despite her symptoms of fear (thumping heart, sweating palms, etc.) she puts on her shoes and coat and opens the front door.

As she steps on to the door step, her fear rises to an unacceptable level and she realises that she just *can't* do it. She goes back into the house, shuts the door, and takes off her shoes and coat. At this point, her fears subside and she feels an overwhelming sense of relief. These feelings are a very strong form of **negative reinforcement**. She is learning that *not* going out reduces unpleasant feelings, and she is therefore even less likely to be able to go out next time she tries.

Treating mental disorders

In this chapter we will be looking at:

25.1 Introduction

25.2 Biological (somatic) therapies
  Chemotherapy
  Electroconvulsive therapy
  Psychosurgery

25.3 Behavioural therapies
  Therapies based on classical
    conditioning
  Therapies based on operant
    conditioning

25.4 Alternatives to biological and
  behavioural therapies
  Psychodynamic therapies
  Cognitive–behavioural therapies

25.5 Issues in evaluating therapies

25.1 INTRODUCTION

This chapter will look at the various treatments or therapies available to help those who suffer from a mental disorder. Chapter 5 introduced the idea that different perspectives within psychology vary in what they see to be the causes of mental disorders, and these views determine which therapy is considered appropriate. Practitioners who adopt the medical or biological approach attribute mental illness to physical causes, and therefore advocate physical therapies. On the other hand, behaviourists who think mental illnesses are due to faulty learning will aim to condition behaviours in a different way. So the question of which therapy should be offered (or given) to any particular person is not easy to answer; the appropriateness of the different types of therapy depends very much on what the **aetiology** (or cause) of the disorder is understood to be.

Who provides therapies?
A good way to start the study of therapies is by clearing up the confusion that often relates to the mental health professionals known as clinical psychologists and psychiatrists. Their jobs do overlap in many respects, but the main difference between the two is in their training. **Clinical psychologists** have a degree in psychology, which they follow up with postgraduate training. This includes work with people with learning disabilities and those with mental disorders. **Psychiatrists**, on the other hand, are qualified physicians who have decided to continue study in the field of mental disorders after their medical degree, and have trained for an extra three years in psychiatry. **Psychoanalysts** are also sometimes confused with psychiatrists or psychologists, but are in fact practitioners who use techniques based on Freudian theory. They also undergo lengthy training, including being analysed themselves. In addition, there are a range of professionals offering other therapies. The training they have received will vary, but may include, for example, a qualification in counselling.

Your answers to the next two activities will provide a basis for the more detailed account of specific therapies which follows:

Activity 1: causes of mental disorders

Make up a table like the one below to remind yourself of the possible causes of mental disorders. See how much of the table you can fill in from memory, then use your notes and chapter 5 to help you complete the table. This exercise will help you understand the basis of the therapies described in this chapter.

	Cause of mental disorder
Biological approach	
Behavioural approach	
Psychodynamic approach	
Cognitive approach	

Activity 2: treating mental disorders

Jonathan suffers from arachnophobia, an extreme and illogical fear of spiders that makes aspects of his life very difficult. He is unable to get into bed before checking there are no spiders in between the sheets, finds it necessary to vacuum the carpets twice a day to get rid of any tiny spiders that might live there, and has been unable to go on camping holidays with his family for many years. Think carefully about Jonathan's situation, then note down some ideas of ways in which you could treat him for his phobia. Structure your notes according to the four approaches mentioned in activity 1 – how do you think each approach would suggest that Jonathan should be treated?

When you have finished, see the notes on page 697.

○ Approaches to mental disorders include the **biological** approach, the **behaviourist** approach, the **psychodynamic** approach and the **cognitive** approach.

○ The different approaches to mental disorders attribute different causes to disorders, and therefore vary in the therapies they use.

○ Professionals who carry out therapies include **clinical psychologists**, **psychiatrists** and **psychoanalysts**.

25.2 BIOLOGICAL (SOMATIC) THERAPIES

The medical/biological approach believes the aetiology of mental illness to be **organic**, or physical. For example, schizophrenia is seen to be caused by an imbalance of the neurotransmitter **dopamine**, and depression is said to be caused by low levels of **noradrenaline and serotonin**. The therapies used are therefore also physical. They are sometimes known as **somatic**, meaning to do with the body. There are three types of somatic therapy: chemotherapy, electroconvulsive therapy (ECT) and psychosurgery.

Somatic therapies differ from some of the other therapies you will learn about later, as the patient is treated by health-care experts (GPs, psychiatrists or clinical psychologists), often in a psychiatric hospital. The responsibility for the patient's cure is in the hands of the therapists.

Occasionally, therapy is given against the will of the patient, if they are considered to be a danger to themselves or others and have been 'sectioned'. Sectioning is so-called because of the use of **sections** of the 1983 **Mental Health Act** to commit people to a psychiatric institution. It means that the patient can be held in an institution against their will for up to six months. This period can then be renewed, if this is thought to be necessary for the health and safety of the patient or the protection of other people. Many people find the idea of sectioning particularly difficult to reconcile with their views on the freedom of the individual. The main concern is the possible abuse of this power to force someone into a mental hospital when they don't want to go. People who are sectioned can appeal to the **Mental Health Review Tribunal**. But if the sectioning is not repealed, powers to give treatment without the patient having to give their consent are given to the doctors. For example, sectioned patients can be given medication for three months. They can also be given ECT without their consent if permission has been given by a Mental Health Act Commissioner. Of the somatic therapies we shall be looking at, only psychosurgery needs the patient's informed consent.

Somatic therapies are also controversial because the use of various drugs can have dramatic side-effects, and because surgical intervention is irreversible.

Chemotherapy

Although it has come to be linked with drugs that treat cancer, the term chemotherapy applies equally to drugs given to treat other illnesses. In abnormal psychology, chemotherapy applies to the drugs given to try to cure patients of their mental disorders.

Davison and Neale (1986) grouped psychoactive drugs according to their effects on behaviour:

Evaluating the use of drugs

Although drug treatments can be very effective, they are not without drawbacks. For example, anti-anxiety drugs like Valium have been found to be extremely addictive, especially if used long-term. Patients develop a tolerance to them, and so need higher dosages, which makes dependency more likely. There are also withdrawal symptoms when a patient stops taking tricyclic antidepressants.

Traditional antipsychotic drugs such as chlorpromazine can also have serious side-effects, including epileptic fits and symptoms like those in Parkinson's disease, such as tremors and immobility. In addition, patients who take these drugs have a 5% chance per year of treatment of developing **tardive dyskinesia**, jerky movements of the mouth, face and tongue and sometimes also the limbs. These side-effects lead to a major problem with conventional antipsychotic drugs; since many patients find them difficult to tolerate, they stop taking them, and their mental health deteriorates.

To try to overcome these problems, a new generation of antipsychotics – known as **atypical antipsychotics** – has been developed. The first of these to be produced was clozapine, first available in

Figure 1: the four main drugs groups

1 **minor tranquillisers (anxiolytics)**, such as diazepam (e.g. Valium), which aim to reduce anxiety.

2 **antipsychotics (major tranquillisers)** such as **chlorpromazine** (e.g. Largactil), which blocks the action of dopamine in the brain, and more recently developed drugs such as **clozapine** (e.g. Clozaril), which affects both dopamine and serotonin levels.

3 **stimulants** such as amphetamines. For example, Ritalin is used for treating hyperactive children.

4 **antidepressants** which include subcategories of drugs used to treat depression. These include **tricyclics** (e.g. Tofranil), which block the re-uptake of noradrenaline and serotonin, and so prolong the effects of these neurotransmitters. **Monoamine oxidase inhibitors (MAOIs)** (e.g. Nardil) can be used for patients resistant to tricyclics. They raise the level of activity of synapses, and affect noradrenaline, serotonin and dopamine. More recent antidepressants include **SSRIs (selective serotonin re-uptake inhibitors)**, such as **Prozac**. This is now the most widely prescribed anti-depressant medication. There are also **NARIs (selective noradrenaline re-uptake inhibitors)**, **SNRIs (selective serotonin and noradrenaline re-uptake inhibitors)** and **NASSAs (noradrenaline and selective serotonin antidepressants)**. **Lithium carbonate** (e.g. Camcolit) is used to treat **bipolar disorder** (manic depression).

the UK and the USA in 1990, which has been shown to be very effective in treating the positive symptoms of schizophrenia for 30%–60% of patients. Because these new drugs are easier to tolerate, patients are more likely to continue the treatment.

However, these drugs are also not without problems. Firstly, it is not clear that they are effective in treating the negative symptoms of schizophrenia. Secondly, they also have side-effects; for example, weight gain and excessive salivation. In the case of clozapine, the most serious side-effect is an increased likelihood of the patient developing a blood disorder called agranulocytosis. This occurs in up to 1% of patients, and means that regular blood monitoring is essential.

Antipsychotics are not alone in having potentially serious side-effects. MAOIs can cause insomnia, weakness and gastro-intestinal disturbances, and occasionally mania. Tricyclics, according to Spiegel (1989), help 65% of depressed patients. They are safer and more effective (and also more expensive) than MAOIs but again, there may be serious side-effects, in particular heart problems, fatigue and insomnia. Prozac, initially hailed as a wonder drug for depression, has also been found to have a range of side-effects, including anxiety and insomnia. It has also been associated with obsessive thoughts of violence and suicide.

Lithium carbonate is extremely effective for 80% of manic depressives (Rosenhan and Seligman, 1995) and greatly reduces the risks of suicide in these patients. At the same time, side-effects include convulsions and heart problems, and some patients will not take it because they enjoy the manic part of the manic–depressive cycle, and this is affected as much as the depressive part.

Interactions of drugs with other medication also need to be considered. For example, tricyclics cannot be used if someone is taking an antihypertensive for high blood pressure, and cannot be used for at least two weeks if the patient has been treated with an MAOI. MAOIs also interact with a range of common foods, e.g. cheese, Marmite, and alcohol, occasionally with fatal results.

Activity 3: ethics of chemotherapy

Think carefully about the issues involved in prescribing drugs to treat mental disorders. Make a list of the possible problems and benefits that could arise from the use of chemotherapies. Compare your notes with the discussion which follows.

As pharmacology has progressed, many drugs have been developed to treat various mental illnesses. However, the ethical issues involved in the use of such drugs are subject to much discussion. For example, as we have seen, there are well-documented side-effects of chemotherapy, undesirable consequences of medication which can be unpleasant and even dangerous to the patient.

There is also the problem of informed consent. Do we have the right to insist that drugs are used on an unwilling patient? And to what extent can informed consent be said to have been given by someone who by definition is suffering from a mental disorder?

The debate as to whether drugs should be used to treat mental illnesses hinges on a cost–benefit analysis – do the benefits of the drug outweigh the disadvantages of its side-effects? For example, antipsychotic drugs have enabled many people to live relatively normal lives outside mental institutions, and this in itself may justify their use. Perhaps the side-effects of anti–depressants are outweighed by the benefits of the drugs when you consider the high suicide risk of a severely depressed person. On the other hand, the dangers of addiction, such as experienced by long-term users of Valium, need to be considered.

Some people who advocate the use of other therapies claim that drugs merely suppress symptoms and do not tackle the root cause of the problem; they also suggest that drugs such as the antipsychotics act as a 'pharmacological straitjacket', and are used to control patients whose behaviour we find disturbing. Drugs are also rarely the whole answer to a mental illness problem. Studies like that of Simpson and May (1982) show the importance of the relationship between physiology and psychology. They found that administering drugs is more effective if the surroundings in which they are given are supportive. Many therapists believe that a combination of drugs and psychotherapy is the most effective way of treating patients.

Electroconvulsive therapy

The procedure of electroconvulsive therapy or **ECT** (often wrongly called electric shock therapy) involves passing an electrical current of 70–130 volts through a patient's head for a fraction of a second. This induces a convulsion or **seizure**. The idea of using electricity to induce seizures was first proposed by Cerletti, an Italian doctor working in the field of epilepsy. He noticed that epilepsy and schizophrenia never occurred in the same person and thought that if he induced an epileptic fit or seizure in someone, perhaps this would cure their schizophrenia. Watching procedures in a slaughterhouse, in which animals were made unconscious by passing a current through their head, gave Cerletti the idea that he could give a seizure to a patient using this method.

ECT has had a very poor public reputation, largely as a result of serious problems with the procedure in the past. For example, physical injury was not uncommon during the convulsion, often leading to broken bones. Nowadays the procedure has been improved, and ECT is used for people whose severe depression has not been helped with drugs, though no longer for schizophrenia, where chemotherapy can be very effective.

Patients undergoing ECT are now **anaesthetised** and given a **muscle relaxant** to prevent physical injury during the seizure. The current can also just be administered to one side of the brain (**unilateral ECT**). Between 60 and 70% of depressed patients improve with ECT (Sackheim, 1988), although the effects tend to disappear within the following year.

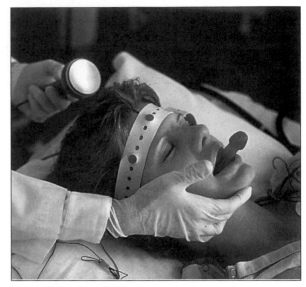

The administration of ECT

However, side-effects which still cause concern include temporary confusion and **memory loss**, though Benton (1981) found that this is reduced in unilateral ECT. Studies such as those by Sackeim (1988) suggest that memory problems are minimal if very low electrical currents are used – just enough to induce the seizure. There is also a small possibility of **brain damage** if shocks are repeatedly administered, and even death. However, the mortality rate is extremely low, making ECT one of the safest medical treatments.

Since ECT is used only for people whose severe depression means that they may be a danger to themselves, in the sense that they are at high risk of committing suicide, the possible side-effects of the treatment may be less dangerous than the risks of *not* treating that patient, and many patients do find the therapy to be extremely effective in controlling their depression. Some patients regularly attend a clinic for **maintenance ECT**, to keep their depression under control.

The issue of the placebo effect has brought into question whether it is the ECT that causes change in the patients, or whether it is the person's expectations of the effects of ECT that causes the change. A placebo is an inactive substance or procedure that can be given to a patient. It is used as a control to assess the real effectiveness of a drug or procedure such as ECT. To test for a possible placebo effect, patients go through the entire procedure of ECT (anaesthetised, given the muscle relaxant, etc.) except that the electrical current is not enough to induce a seizure.

If improvement occurs under these circumstances, it may be because doctors and psychiatrists are very powerful people in relation to the patient, so their authority may lead the patient to expect an improvement.

Studies have shown that placebo ECT is not effective in terms of treating depression, suggesting that there must be some aspect of the electrical current to the brain that does help control depression. However, Davison and Neale (1994) suggested that 'All therapies derive at least some of their power from the faith that people have in the healer'.

One ethical problem associated with the use of ECT as a therapy is that we simply don't understand how it works. Some argue that until we have this knowledge, the technique should not be used on patients. It is worth bearing in mind, though, that this is true of many medical treatments. For example, we do not know how aspirin cures headaches.

Various suggestions have been put forward to explain the effectiveness of ECT. One explanation was that it is regarded as **punishment**. However, for many years now ECT has been carried out under general anaesthetic, so the shocks are not at all unpleasant. Another possibility put forward was that the associated **memory loss** allowed the patient to restructure their view of life. Again, though, this idea is challenged by the minimal memory loss associated with unilateral ECT. However, the most likely explanation, and that now accepted by most psychiatrists, is that the shock produces **biochemical changes** in the brain, raising levels of the various neurotransmitters. These changes are stronger than those produced by drugs, so this may account for its effectiveness.

Clare (1980) suggested that ECT is abused by psychiatrists, and used too frequently, merely because it is a fairly quick and easy (and therefore relatively cheap) therapy. Organisations such as

MIND, which campaigns for mental health patients in Britain, raise the issue of **consent** – should patients who are sectioned, or detained against their will, be subjected to such harsh procedures if they do not give their permission?

Psychosurgery

Any operation carried out on the brain as a treatment for mental illness may be termed psychosurgery. Such surgery is carried out only as a last resort, generally to treat those patients with mental illnesses which have not responded favourably to other therapies. Patients must give their informed consent; a panel of medical professionals and others must agree that the patient understands what is involved in the procedure, and the risks involved.

You may have heard of **prefrontal lobotomy**, a procedure involving cutting the nerve fibres which connect the thalamus and frontal lobes of the brain. The operation was first of all known as a **leucotomy**, which suggested a clean cutting of the white fibres connecting the frontal lobes to the rest of the brain. However, once it became clear that the operation was actually destroying pre-frontal grey matter, the operation was retitled lobotomy. This technique was first used to treat schizophrenia in 1935 by Moniz, a Portuguese neurologist, who had noted its tranquillising effects in monkeys. In the following 14 years, he carried out roughly 100 such procedures, and won the Nobel prize for medicine in 1949. Moniz was later shot by a patient on whom he had carried out a lobotomy, and had to spend the rest of his life in a wheelchair.

Freeman and Watts (1942) pioneered the use of psychosurgery in the USA. They modified Moniz' original technique by inserting the scalpel into the brain through small holes drilled into the temple, or through the eye socket (**transorbital leucotomy**). Since its introduction, it has been estimated that somewhere between 40,000 and 50,000 lobotomies have been carried out in the USA alone. It has also been widely used in other countries. For example, in Great Britain around 10,000 lobotomies were carried out between 1942 and 1952, though the number has dropped sharply since that time.

Transorbital
leucotomy

Pre-frontal lobotomy/
leucotomy

Early psychosurgical procedures

These forms of psychosurgery have now been replaced by other operations which are less extreme, and so safer. **Stereotactic surgery** is now one of the more commonly performed operations. The doctor drills a small hole in the skull, and inserts a probe which is guided to specific areas of the brain and makes tiny cuts in nerve fibres, or introduces radioactive rods to destroy small amounts of tissue.

Like other somatic therapies, psychosurgery carries the risk of side-effects – epilepsy, apathy, intellectual impairment, an increase in aggression, personality change and, of course, death – though the risk is reduced with these more modern techniques.

While psychosurgery was originally used for schizophrenia, this is no longer the case now that there are drugs which are relatively effective in treating this disorder. Its use is relatively rare – only 18 operations were carried out in the UK in 1991, though the number has increased over the past few years – but it may provide relief in **obsessive–compulsive disorder** and extreme cases of **depression** when other therapies have proved ineffective.

▶ Activity 4: evaluating psychosurgery

Think carefully about the issues involved in the use of psychosurgery. What problems might be involved in its use? When would you envisage that it should be used? Note down your ideas so that you can compare them with the evaluation that follows.

Like the other somatic therapies, psychosurgery does have problems associated with its use. You perhaps thought of the fact that it is **irreversible** – once brain tissue or nerve fibres have been lesioned or destroyed, this procedure cannot be reversed. If we compare this with drug treatment, many of the side-effects of drugs can be reversed if the patient stops taking the drug.

There is also the issue of **control**. While the patient's informed consent is necessary to carry out psychosurgery, to what extent can we assume that consent *is* informed, since by definition those patients to whom it is offered are suffering from an extreme form of mental disorder? Psychosurgery is offered only when all other approaches have failed, so a patient may well be motivated to agree to anything which stands a chance of helping them if no further options are available. As with ECT, there is also the problem that we don't understand exactly how psychosurgery works. Finally, although modern procedures are safer than the original lobotomies, surgical intervention always carries a small risk.

However, psychosurgery is used only as a last resort in cases of serious mental illness, when other therapies have not worked; for example, for a suicidal patient who has not responded to other treatment. Here the possible benefits could seem to outweigh the potential costs.

678

Evaluating somatic therapies

The use of the somatic therapies remains controversial. Although the procedures have given good results in some people, they are still inconsistent and can bring about undesirable changes, e.g. to personality.

For those who advocate somatic therapies, judging when a patient is cured is not a problem – it is when their clinical symptoms stop, because the underlying chemical imbalance is restored to normal. Although this may seem obvious, you will see later in this chapter that the idea of 'cure' is not so simple, and that clinicians who adopt different approaches to therapy can disagree on when a patient is cured.

- ❧ The medical approach sees mental disorders as having **somatic** (or **organic**) causes, and therefore needing **physical** treatment.
- ❧ The three main somatic therapies are **chemotherapy**, **ECT** and **psychosurgery**.
- ❧ Chemotherapy is **drug treatment**, including antipsychotic drugs, minor tranquillisers, stimulants and antidepressants. It may have side-effects, ranging from a dry mouth to tardive dyskinesia and occasionally death.
- ❧ ECT involves passing an electrical current through the patient's brain. Its side-effects include memory loss. We are not certain how it works.
- ❧ Psychosurgery involves operating on the brain. It is irreversible, and like ECT, its effects are not fully understood.

25.3 BEHAVIOURAL THERAPIES

Behaviourists see abnormal behaviour as learned, maladaptive behaviour. It is therefore logical that behavioural treatments focus on present behaviour and the circumstances which reinforce it. Treatments focus on eliminating unwanted behaviours, and learning more appropriate ones. Methods based on both classical and operant conditioning are used.

▶ **Activity 5: conditioning**

This is a good time to check what you know about conditioning processes. What are the basic principles of classical and operant conditioning? If necessary, use the outline in chapter 1.

Behavioural treatments using **classical conditioning** focus on replacing maladaptive associations with new and more adaptive ones. We have seen from the study of Little Albert (chapter 1, box B) that classical conditioning techniques can create a mental disorder. Albert learned a phobia as a result of associating the phobic object (the rat) with the fear automatically evoked by the noise of an iron bar being struck behind his head. If a phobia can be created in this way, it should be possible to eliminate it using the same methods.

Treatments using **operant conditioning** focus on what is reinforcing (and thus maintaining) maladaptive behaviour, and eliminating that reinforcement. More adaptive behaviour is shaped and maintained through appropriate reinforcement.

Walker (1984) divided therapies using a behavioural approach into **behaviour therapy** (techniques which use the principles of classical conditioning) and **behaviour modification** (techniques which use the principles of operant conditioning).

Therapies based on classical conditioning

Classical conditioning techniques are used in behaviour therapy to eliminate unwanted behaviours and establish more adaptive ones. Behaviour therapy works on the assumption that new learning can replace existing associations. Techniques which aim to achieve this include **systematic desensitisation**, **flooding**, **implosion** and **aversion therapy**.

Systematic desensitisation

Systematic desensitisation is a technique used primarily to treat phobias, and is based on the idea that it is not possible for two opposite emotions, such as relaxation and anxiety, to exist together at the same time. This is called **reciprocal inhibition**. For example, a patient who had an irrational and all-consuming fear of snakes would first be taught relaxation techniques. Only when the patient was capable of deep relaxation would the next stage begin. The 'systematic' part of the therapy then involves very gradually bringing the patient into contact with the feared object. This contact takes place in a series of steps that form a **hierarchy** of fear.

For example, the patient, whilst in their state of deep relaxation, might first look at pictures of small snakes. When they were able to do this without feeling fearful, the next step in the hierarchy might be to look at video footage of those small snakes moving about. The next step might be to watch a film of large snakes, the next step to hold a jar containing a small snake, and the final step to hold a large boa constrictor in their arms – with various steps in between. You can see the way that the hierarchy is constructed, and have probably realised that it is not just a question of a couple of sessions looking at pictures, and then being able to sit comfortably in a pit of snakes; phobics by definition have an extreme fear of an object or situation and may be terrified even by hearing the word 'snake'.

▶ Activity 6: systematic desensitisation for an agoraphobic

Construct a hierarchy of feared situations that might be used in a systematic desensitisation programme with an agoraphobic woman. (She is so frightened of leaving her house, she has not left it for six months.) Note down your ideas so you can compare them with those below. You might like to recap on the symptoms of agoraphobia by re-reading the section on phobias in chapter 24. When you have finished, see the notes on page 697.

Phobias have been treated very successfully using systematic desensitisation:

Box A: Jones (1924)

Procedure: Little Peter was a two-year-old, living in an institution. He had an extreme fear of some animals, including rats and rabbits. This fear had become generalised, e.g. to feathers and cotton wool. In a series of 17 steps, Peter was gradually exposed to a rabbit. This was done while Peter was eating his lunch, so that the rabbit was associated with the pleasurable sensation of eating.
Results: After 40 sessions, Peter ate his lunch, while stroking the rabbit on his lap.
Conclusion: Classical conditioning techniques can be used successfully to overcome phobias.

Wolpe, who is associated with the technique of systematic desensitisation, also followed the same procedure using the patient's imagination rather than exposing them directly to the feared object. He believed that imagining progressively feared contacts would lead to lessening anxiety in real-life situations. To facilitate this, patients need also to put themselves in progressively frightening real-life situations.

This variation of the technique is also useful for rather abstract phobias, such as the fear of failure. It would be very difficult to build up a real-life hierarchy to treat this kind of phobia.

Flooding and implosion

While systematic desensitisation involves the phobic taking a series of steps which build up to the most feared object or situation, in **flooding** there is no gradual exposure and relaxation. Instead, the phobic is immediately exposed in an extreme way to the object or situation which they fear. For example, a snake phobic might be confronted with a large boa constrictor.

Implosion involves the same process, but the person has to imagine the feared object, and to help this process the therapist would describe the snake in great detail whilst the phobic is imagining it sliding up their legs and around their waist. The therapist's input is known as **stimulus augmentation**.

In both flooding and implosion, the idea is that the person's fear is kept at such a high level that it can only decrease. The concept of **forced reality testing** is also crucial here; a person is prevented from making their usual escape, and is forced to face their fear. You might find it useful to look at this point at Miller's study of **avoidance behaviour** in box F, chapter 20. In this experiment, the behaviour of the rats in running into the part of the cage where they had never experienced shocks was negatively reinforced by a reduction in fear. This could apply equally to a phobic's avoidance of the feared object or situation. Many theorists believe that the effectiveness of the techniques depends on forced reality testing. The use of a hierarchy and relaxation

techniques in systematic desensitisation may not be strictly necessary, but rather a way of making forced exposure less unpleasant.

The techniques of systematic desensitisation, flooding and implosion have had a good deal of success in treating phobias. Most studies have found flooding to be the most effective of these techniques. McGrath *et al.* (1990) claimed that systematic desensitisation is effective for phobias in 75% of cases. Wolpe (1958) used flooding with a teenage girl who had a phobia of cars. She was forced into the back of a car and driven around without stopping for four hours. By the end of the drive, during which she had become quite hysterical, her phobia had completely disappeared. There have also been impressive results using implosion. For example, Hogan and Kirchner (1967) found that 20 out of 21 people with a phobia of rats were successfully treated in this way.

▶ **Activity 7: evaluating systematic desensitisation, flooding and implosion**

What are the strengths of using these techniques to treat phobias? How might they be limited? Do you think there are any ethical issues involved in their use?

When you have finished, see the notes on page 697.

Aversion therapy

This therapy is also based on classical conditioning techniques. A patient learns to associate the stimuli linked with a pleasurable behaviour with an unpleasant reflex response, and so will come to develop an anxiety reaction to that behaviour. For example, someone trying to give up smoking might be given a specially developed chewing gum which makes cigarettes taste disgusting. Someone being treated for excessive drinking would be given a drug which, when combined with alcohol, acts as an emetic. They are then given a drink, and encouraged to augment all the associated stimuli – smelling it, swilling it around in their mouth and savouring it – and then the emetic drug makes them sick.

Operant conditioning also plays a part, since once aversion has been established, the patient will avoid the problem stimulus. This avoidance is negatively reinforced by the reduction in fear associated with it.

There are practical problems in the use of aversion therapy. Meyer and Chesser (1970) found that half their alcoholic patients abstained from alcohol for at least a year after treatment, which suggests that this treatment is better than none at all. It would provide time to use other kinds of therapy – for example, counselling – to work on the underlying problems which have led to alcohol abuse. However, if used alone its long-term usefulness is doubtful, particularly when the alcoholic returns to situations where drinking is socially reinforced, such as going to the pub with friends.

Related to this is the criticism that aversion therapy (like systematic desensitisation, flooding and implosion) only treats symptoms and not the cause of the problem. It is not interested in what led the person to become an alcoholic in the first place, so it could be argued that this kind of therapy is very limited.

Just as there are ethical controversies in the use of systematic desensitisation, flooding and implosion, there are also those who argue that inflicting pain or discomfort on people, even if they may have asked for that procedure, is not right. In particular, the use of aversion therapy for homosexual people in the days when homosexual activity was illegal was particularly controversial.

As a result of the criticisms which have been made of aversion therapy, an alternative form known as **covert sensitisation** is sometimes used. This combines aversion therapy with systematic desensitisation.

Therapies based on operant conditioning

Operant conditioning techniques use behaviour modification to increase the frequency of desired behaviours using positive reinforcement, while at the same time removing reinforcement from maladaptive behaviours.

It is necessary to plan a behavioural programme, adapted to the requirements of the particular situation (see figure 2). If you are unfamiliar with any of the terms used here, you will need to read the section on operant conditioning in chapter 20:

Figure 2: planning a behaviour modification programme

1 The specific behaviour to be changed needs to be identified. It is best to break this down into small, achievable goals, which can be easily measured.
2 The desired outcome, i.e. what is appropriate behaviour, also needs to be defined, again as specifically as possible.
3 The patient should be observed, so that a baseline measurement of the behaviour to be changed can be made at the start of the programme. This allows progress to be monitored as the programme proceeds, and may also be useful in identifying what is reinforcing (and thus maintaining) the maladaptive behaviour.
4 Inappropriate behaviour should be ignored, and thus extinguished. Appropriate behaviour should be reinforced. When the behaviour to be established is complex, reinforcement can be used to shape successive approximations to what is desired. It is important that everyone coming into contact with the patient behaves consistently.
5 Changes in behaviour should be monitored, and if necessary, the strategy modified.

Programmes using this system have been used very successfully with children, to treat thumb-sucking, self-mutilation, hyperactivity, table manners and asthmatic attacks to name but a few examples. Much of the success of these therapies with children is dependent on the fact that children are most of the time under constant supervision, so any reinforcement practices can be maintained at home and at school.

There has also been considerable success in helping children with a mental handicap. The Portage system, for example, involves parents and professionals in teaching a variety of skills to children with learning difficulties, particularly those with Down's syndrome.

Activity 8: treating self-mutilation with operant conditioning

Read the account below of a child's behaviour, and suggest how you could help him change his behaviour using operant conditioning techniques. Try to use the words **extinction**, **reinforcer** and **maladaptive behaviour** in your answer.

The boy began self-mutilation at the age of three. He pulled out his finger and toe nails, bit himself and showed projectile vomiting and head-banging. Whilst injuring himself, he often shouted 'I hate myself'.

When you have finished, see the notes on page 698.

The case you have just read about is one reported by Bull and LaVecchio (1978). The boy suffered from a genetic disorder which often leads to self-mutilation. He was treated using operant conditioning techniques such as the ones suggested in the previous activity. It was also noticed that when the boy's self-inflicted wounds were treated, he found the attention rewarding, so this treatment was subsequently carried out when the boy was anaesthetised, so that he would not form an association between injuring himself and reward. The technique of withdrawing attention led to the boy's unwanted behaviours being extinguished one by one, and taught the boy valuable social skills that

meant he could fit in more easily with his family. After 18 months, his behaviour had changed to such an extent that he was able to attend a special class in a normal school.

Autistic children have also been helped by the use of behavioural techniques. These children are socially unresponsive, have language and communication difficulties and respond to their environment in maladaptive ways. For example, they may indulge for long periods of time in repetitive behaviour, and are typically extremely distressed when their routine is altered in any way.

Box B: Clancy and McBride (1969)

Procedure: This treatment was started in hospital, so that the therapist could have maximum input, but was gradually handed over to appropriate members of the family. Practical problems such as feeding were addressed, since typically autistic children will only eat a very restricted range of foods. New foods were presented, initially camouflaged by preferred foods. At the same time, parents were helped to interact with children in games they enjoyed. The demands on the children were gradually increased. Parents were encouraged to cuddle and comfort the children. The children had to make eye contact, then make sounds and then words, in order to achieve what they wanted.

Results: Appropriate feeding was usually achieved after about a week. Bonds between parents and children also usually developed within the same time span.

Conclusion: Behavioural change can be achieved with autistic children, particularly when the family is involved.

In all cases like these, it is obviously extremely important to involve parents in the training programme, so that they can carry on with the right reinforcers at home, and children can generalise new behaviour patterns to settings outside the hospital situation.

Token economy

Ayllon and Azrin (1968) used operant conditioning techniques to impressive effect when they developed their token economy system. This involved providing tokens for desirable behaviour such as brushing teeth, making beds, or getting dressed. Tokens could later be exchanged for **reinforcers** such as a choice of television programmes, sweets or an outing. The system is ideal for giving instant, individualised reinforcement, as patients can choose the items for which they later trade in their tokens.

Many programmes similar to that suggested by Ayllon and Azrin have been brought into effect in various institutions. Studies have shown that such programmes can produce profound behaviour changes even on wards of severely institutionalised people who have been cared for in an institution for a prolonged period and become incapable of independent life outside. One such study is described in box C:

Box C: Paul and Lentz (1977)

Procedure: The token economy technique was used with a group of long-term, chronically institutionalised schizophrenic patients. Symptoms of the patients' disorders included incontinence, long periods of screaming and assaults on staff. The patients were divided into three groups, matched on variables such as age, gender, symptoms and length of institutionalisation. The three groups were:

1 The control ward, who received their normal treatment of antipsychotic drugs and little other therapy.
2 The 'social-learning' ward operated on a token economy system which covered all aspects of the patients' lives. Tokens were earned for bed-making, socially acceptable behaviour at meal times and participating in social activities. These tokens were then exchanged for meals and small luxuries. Patients also received individualised social skills training.
3 The 'milieu therapy' ward involved staff treating the patients as normal individuals and not as mentally ill people. They praised patients for good behaviour, and expected them to be active rather than passive, e.g. by participating in decisions about how the ward was to function.

Results: The patients were evaluated over the four and a half years of the research and for eighteen months by way of a follow-up study. It was seen that both the milieu therapy patients and the social learning patients showed a significant reduction in maladaptive behaviours compared to the control patients. Ten per cent of the social learning patients left the ward to live independently, as did 7% of the milieu therapy patients, but nobody from the control ward improved sufficiently to let them leave the hospital.

Conclusion: Token economy can have remarkable effects even on the behaviour of chronically institutionalised, severely mentally ill patients.

However, token economy has not been without its critics. For example, there are ethical problems involved in deprivation, though therapists would not nowadays infringe basic human rights by such tactics as only allowing privacy or meals when desired behaviours were evident. It has also been said that improvements in behaviour which are totally dependent on the provision of tokens will not last if the patient tries to transfer to life outside the hospital or institution.

However, Woods *et al.* (1984) found that changes in the hospital did often lead on to long-term changes. They noted a move from the extrinsic rewards of tokens to more intrinsic ones arising from the satisfying consequences of behaviour change. It could also be that improvements seen in patients are not due to the tokens themselves, but to factors such as changes in the practices of nursing staff, who see improvements in their patients and are thus motivated to continue behaving differently towards them.

In terms of evaluating behavioural therapies overall, critics say that behaviourists are manipulative and controlling, conditioning people against their will to perform behaviours they may not want to. In response to such criticisms, behaviourists suggest that *not* to use such techniques can be said to deprive that person of the chance of rehabilitation. The success of many of the therapies mentioned does show that people's lives can be improved drastically using behavioural techniques. Disorders as varied as nocturnal enuresis (bed wetting), habit disorders and self-injuring behaviour have all been treated successfully in this way.

Behaviourists are quite clear about what constitutes a cure. For them, once the symptoms have been removed, the patient is cured, because the symptoms are the disorder. They are therefore not interested in the causes of disorders.

Therapists using other therapeutic approaches suggest that behavioural therapies do not cure; they merely remove symptoms, for which others may be substituted (**stimulus substitution**), because the root cause of the problem has not been addressed.

- ❺ Behaviourists see abnormal behaviours as **learned**, **maladaptive** behaviours.
- ❺ Treatments are based on classical conditioning techniques (**behaviour therapies**) and operant conditioning techniques (**behaviour modification**).
- ❺ **Systematic desensitisation** involves exposing a patient to a hierarchy of feared situations, and has had much success in treating **phobias**. More direct methods, such as **flooding** and **implosion**, have also been used successfully. **Aversion therapy** involves pairing an unwanted behaviour with something which produces an unpleasant reflex response.
- ❺ **Selective positive reinforcement** has been used very successfully with children and people with learning disabilities. **Token economy** programmes use **conditioned reinforcers** in the form of **tokens** awarded for socially acceptable behaviour. These can later be exchanged for small luxuries. These programmes have been effective even with severely institutionalised patients.

25.4 ALTERNATIVES TO BIOLOGICAL AND BEHAVIOURAL THERAPIES

As well as somatic and behavioural therapies, there are several other ways in which psychological disorders may be treated, such as with counselling, based on humanistic ideas. We will be looking in the remainder of this chapter at two such approaches: therapies based on the **psychodynamic** approach and **cognitive–behavioural** therapies.

Psychodynamic therapy

Psychodynamic therapies are based on the theories of Freud (see chapter 1). The therapy associated with this theory, and which Freud himself carried out, is called **psychoanalysis**. You will remember Freud's emphasis on the importance of the unconscious and childhood experiences; these factors are seen to be of central importance in therapy. Within the psychodynamic approach, mental disorders can only be cured by uncovering the unconscious reasons underlying a disorder, and the childhood experiences which have contributed to its development. When this material has been brought into consciousness, the patient can be helped to come to terms with it. Psychodynamic therapies are therefore in stark contrast to behavioural therapies, where the causes of a mental disorder are not considered important.

Pychodynamic theories see abnormal behaviour as the result of **psychic conflict**. The ego uses **defence mechanisms** to reduce anxiety caused by conflict with the id (which gives rise to neurotic anxiety) and with the superego (which causes moral anxiety), with the result that patients are not aware of the underlying causes of their problems. The use of defence mechanisms, while providing short-term relief from anxiety, in the long term itself creates problems.

Psychoanalysis takes the form of a talking therapy. Typically, the therapy is likely to last for a period of years, during which time there are several sessions a week. The aim is to bring unconscious material into consciousness, to make people conscious of their repressed memories, wishes and experiences, and so able to deal with unconscious conflict. Unsatisfactory defences against traumatic unconscious material need to be broken down. The patient can then, with the help of the analyst, deal with the repressed material, and thus release the power it has over behaviour. This is known as **catharsis**.

Conflicts are often expressed symbolically, and it is part of the analytic process to interpret the symbols used to express unconscious fears.

▶ Activity 9: Little Hans

Read through the following account of a young boy's phobia, analysed by Freud:

Hans, who was 5 years old, had a phobia of being bitten by a horse. He was particularly afraid of white horses with black around the mouth, and wearing blinkers. He had been particularly frightened when he had seen a horse collapse and die in the street.

Given Hans' age, which stage of psychosexual development would he be in?

What might his fear of horses symbolise?

What does his fear of being bitten symbolise?

Which ego defences are being used here?

You may find it useful to look back to the material on Freud in chapter 1, and his account of personality development in chapter 18.

When you have finished, see the notes on page 698.

In psychoanalysis, a number of different techniques are used, including **free association**. The patient (or **analysand**) lies down on the couch, with the analyst sitting behind, out of sight. The analysand is encouraged to speak their thoughts and feelings, to verbalise whatever comes to mind, however silly it may seem. The aim of this procedure is to uncover unconscious material so that it can be 'worked through', and related to problems that are being experienced now. Therapists must be very careful not to direct the client's thinking; this is helped by the therapist revealing little of their own personal life. However, the analyst will ask the client to explore the significance of the associations that they make. An unexpected association of ideas, a sudden silence, the expression of strong emotions or an abrupt change of topic may be useful to the analyst in terms of identifying problem areas.

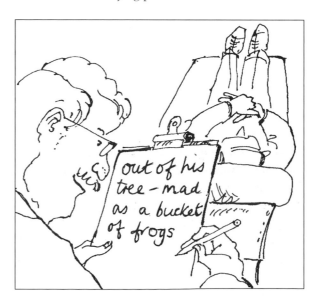

A further part of the process is transference, when the analysand projects their feelings – often repressed hostile feelings towards parents – on to the analyst. Transference indicates that repressed feelings are close to the surface of conscious awareness, and allows the analyst to identify the source of the transference (i.e. the person or situation with whom the hostile feelings are actually associated), and thus the circumstances which have given rise to these feelings. **Counter-transference** refers to the therapist's feelings about the analysand; for example, their dislike of them or attraction to them. Analysts are encouraged to use counter-transference to help them understand the analysand's transference, and the resulting defences they use.

The analyst must at this time beware of **resistance**, a phenomenon in which the analysand indulges in tactics to interrupt the session when painful memories are coming into the conscious mind. For example, clients may make a joke or look out of the window, in an attempt to distract themselves and the therapist. The ultimate form of resistance is 'forgetting' to attend therapy sessions – remember that Freud believed that this kind of behaviour was motivated rather than accidental.

Dream analysis is another technique used in classical psychoanalysis. The assumption is that ego defences are lowered in sleep, so repressed material can come into the mind, usually disguised. Such material is expressed in symbols, to protect the ego. Dreams are seen as wish-fulfillment, a way of using symbols to express unconscious desires, usually of a sexual or aggressive nature. There is more information about Freud's theory of dreams in chapter 12.

A final method involves the use of **projective tests**; for example, the **Rorschach Ink Blot** test and the **Thematic Apperception Test (TAT)**. People are asked to say what they see in the ink blot, or to tell a story based on the TAT picture (see chapter 8, activity 12). This material is deliberately ambiguous, so that people will project their own unconscious concerns and preoccupations on to it, and thus allow the analyst to start to identify possible problems.

Psychoanalysts consider someone as cured when they develop insight, i.e. an understanding of the causes of their problems, and have 'worked through'

them. The analyst judges when conflicts have been identified and dealt with, but the analysand generally recognises when the process has been completed.

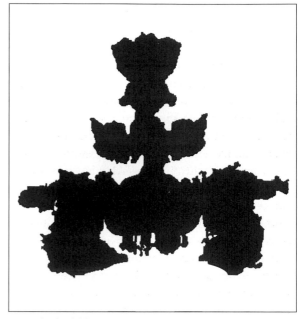

A Rorschach ink blot

Evaluating psychoanalysis

▶ Activity 10: evaluating psychoanalysis

From what you have read in this section, identify what you feel to be the strengths of psychoanalysis, as well as possible criticisms of it. Compare your notes with the discussion which follows.

There is considerable emphasis in psychoanalysis on past experience, so unlike most other therapies, it has the advantage of seeking to uncover and deal with the causes of the problems the patient is experiencing. This means that there is less likelihood of such problems as stimulus substitution, noted in the section on behavioural therapies.

At the same time, it is a painful process for the patient. By its very nature, material which has been pushed into the unconscious because it is too painful to acknowledge will be brought into consciousness, a procedure which is inevitably very distressing.

Since psychoanalysis is so time-consuming, it is also expensive, which limits who can benefit from it. It may, however, take place in a modified form. Malan (1973) used **brief focal therapy**. This cuts down on the time required by focusing more particularly on specific problems, and placing far less emphasis on the patient's past experience.

Since it is a talking therapy, which places great emphasis on communication and insight, patients need to be of a certain intellectual level. This is reflected in the **YAVIS effect**, which refers to the kinds of patient who tend to be accepted for treatment (young, attractive, verbal, intelligent and successful). Since patients must be sufficiently articulate to express their feelings, psychoanalysis has not been seen as a useful therapy for psychotic disorders, such as schizophrenia, where patients lack insight into their problems. However, some claims have been made for it even with this kind of disorder, if it is combined with antipsychotic drugs (e.g. Boker, 1992). The commitment required also means it may not be the best kind of therapy for people who are depressed.

Many psychologists are also unhappy about the degree of interpretation necessary. If we look back to the account of Little Hans (activity 9), a behaviourist could reasonably argue that the fright Hans experienced from seeing a horse drop down dead in the street would be enough to establish his phobia of horses, and that Freud's complex interpretation is unnecessary. It has also been suggested that this kind of deep analysis can lead to **false memory syndrome**, an issue which is discussed in chapter 4.

Freud's ideas have also been criticised for being very much of their time, place and culture. The theory, and hence also the therapy, is based on a small sample of neurotic middle-class Jewish women, living in the patriarchal society of Vienna at the start of the 20th century. Freud's ideas may be rather culturally limited. However, this criticism can also be made of much of psychology.

Last but not least, there is considerable dispute over whether the therapy actually works, a point most notably made by Eysenck (1952). He carried out a **metastudy**, i.e. a review of other studies:

Box D: Eysenck (1952)

Procedure: Eysenck reviewed other researchers' published work on the effectiveness of psychoanalysis (five studies) as compared to **eclectic psychotherapy** (therapy involving more than one therapeutic approach – 19 studies).

Results: Forty-four per cent of psychoanalytic patients improved following therapy and 64% of those who received eclectic therapy improved. But 66% of patients not receiving any therapy improved (this is known as **spontaneous remission**).

Conclusion: Psychoanalysis is significantly less effective than no treatment.

Eysenck's conclusion that psychoanalysis does not work seems clear-cut, but many subsequent researchers have criticised his review. For example, he defined people who dropped out of psychoanalysis as 'not cured', since they had not completed the therapy, which seems a little harsh.

Bergin (1971) looked at some of the same papers as Eysenck, but reached a different conclusion. He defined 'improvement' differently, and found that the success rate of psychoanalysis was 83% – significantly greater than Eysenck's suggestion of 44%, and also greater than the 66% for spontaneous remission. Bergin also found studies which showed that a 30% spontaneous remission rate was more realistic than Eysenck's 66%.

It is worth bearing in mind, though, that both these studies depend on subjective definitions of what constitutes a 'cure', a problem we shall be returning to at the end of this chapter.

- Freud developed the therapy of **psychoanalysis**. Its aim is to uncover unconscious conflict so that problems can be resolved through catharsis.
- Techniques include **free association**, **transference**, **dream analysis** and **projective tests**.
- One strength of psychoanalysis is that it addresses the causes of psychological disorders.

❺ Psychoanalysis may be limited in terms of the kind of patient and the kind of disorder for which it is appropriate. The degree of interpretation required has also been criticised. Some psychologists have queried whether it actually works.

Other psychodynamically-based therapies

Post-Freudians, of whom perhaps the most well known are Jung and Adler, put forward psychodynamic theories of their own, using Freud's ideas as a starting point. Their theories were also the basis for psychodynamic therapies, incorporating ideas from their own adaptations of Freud's theories.

For example, Jung disagreed with Freud's emphasis on the past, and placed considerable emphasis on spiritual development. His therapy aimed to help people explore the sort of people they were, and integrate all aspects of their personality into a harmonious and balanced whole.

Adler believed that there was rather too much emphasis on sexuality in Freud's theories. For Adler, mental disorders arose as the result of an unsuccessful drive for power, and an attempt to compensate for the resulting feelings of inferiority; he coined the term **inferiority complex**. In contrast to Freud, his emphasis was more on the present than the past, and he also gave more weight to social factors, in particular relationships with others. His therapy aimed to help the client understand their unconscious psychic processes, and develop more fulfilling relationships.

Klein focused more on the effect of a child's relationship with its mother on that child's development. She developed **play therapy** as a children's alternative to psychoanalysis. Because children cannot express their feelings verbally in the same way as adults, play therapy involves the child playing with a set of toys whilst the therapist interprets their play. An interesting and readable account of a case study successfully using play therapy is given in Virginia Axline's book *Dibs: In Search of Self* (1971).

We will also look briefly in this section at two other therapies, **psychodrama** and **transactional analysis**. These therapies lie within the psychoanalytic tradition, but in some ways are very different from traditional psychoanalysis.

Psychodrama

In contrast to psychoanalysis, psychodrama is a group therapy. It was developed by Moreno, a contemporary of Freud. Instead of talking, it uses drama to bring about the strong emotional release or catharsis which Freud believed was essential for successful therapy.

Moreno believed that many of our problems relate to the social roles we adopt – parent, child, friend and so on – which may be in conflict with each other and with our real self. In psychodrama, these conflicts are acted out in order to provide insight into the nature of the problems the individual is experiencing.

Within a group of usually 7 or 8 people, the person whose conflicts are to be the focus during a particular session is known as the **protagonist**. He provides information about the situation to be acted out to other members of the group, who will take on the roles of other people who are important in the situation. These other actors are known as **ego auxiliaries**. In **role reversal**, the protagonist may switch roles with one of the ego auxiliaries, as a way of developing insight into the problem from the point of view of others involved in the problem. In **doubling**, the group leader acts the protagonist's role with him, to provide insights into feelings and motives which the protagonist has not yet discovered. Finally, in **mirroring**, other group members act the role of the protagonist back at him, to provide additional feedback which may prove useful.

The situation is acted out with very simple props. The emphasis is not on dramatic excellence; the aim is rather to reveal the nature of the problem to the protagonist and so help him to come to terms with it and find ways of dealing with it.

In his book *Psychodrama* (1946), Moreno claims that this approach is useful for three reasons. Firstly, it helps to prevent individuals from continuing to behave maladaptively in their everyday life. Secondly, it allows the strong emotions associated with psychic conflict to be expressed. Finally, it helps to uncover the hidden causes of emotional problems.

Transactional analysis (TA)

Like psychodrama, transactional analysis is also a group therapy, developed by Berne (1964). It is also different from traditional psychoanalysis in that it focuses on the present rather than the past.

Berne believed that personality is made up of three **ego states**. The **parent** state is the part relating to the constraints of society, and is acquired from our own parents. The **child** state is unrestrained and seeks instant gratification of all its wishes. The **adult** state is the rational part of our personality, which can respond flexibly to particular situations.

▷ **Activity 11: parent, child and adult states**

Freud also saw personality as being made up of three parts. Can you relate Berne's parent, child and adult states to terms in Freud's original theory?

When you have finished, see the notes on page 698.

While Berne's three states can be related to Freud's ideas – and TA after all is rooted in psychodynamic theory – they are not identical. For Freud, the structures are to a greater or lesser extent unconscious and inaccessible to consciousness,

while Berne believed that we have full access to all three states.

Berne believed that psychological disorders come about when one of the states becomes overly dominant. He was interested in communication between people; problems can occur when people who are trying to communicate are operating in different states, which is when interactions are said to be crossed. When this happens, both people within the interaction can become angry and confused, and appropriate behaviour becomes difficult. In his book *Games People Play* (1964), Berne wrote that crossed interactions often take the form of **games**, i.e. manipulative strategies. For example, one person may deliberately taunt another. This kind of manipulation can be very destructive.

The therapy takes the form of role play, often on an individual basis to start with. A **structural analysis** is carried out of the way the individual interacts with others, to identify how ego states are used. This provides insight into behaviour, and so provides a basis for a person to make the changes necessary to have more control of their life.

After this initial work, the individual takes part in group transactions – transactional analysis proper – using role play to explore ego states and the effects these states have on others. Underlying conflicts are uncovered, and the individual is able to develop better ways of interacting with others.

Ⓢ Post-Freudians such as Jung and Adler developed therapies in line with their adaptations of Freudian theory. Klein developed **play therapy**, a psychodynamic therapy for children.

Ⓢ Other therapies derived from psychodynamic ideas include Moreno's **psychodrama** and Berne's **transactional analysis**.

Cognitive–behavioural therapies

The cognitive approach to mental disorder suggests that psychological disorders are due to faulty thinking. Therapies based on the cognitive approach therefore aim to challenge inappropriate cognitions so that more adaptive ways of thinking can be developed. Developments in cognitive therapy have led to the introduction of **cognitive–behavioural**

therapy. Behaviourists are paying more and more attention to how thoughts and expectations affect our behaviour. Such **cognitions** are seen as behaviours which cannot be easily measured, but which may nevertheless be changed in order to change observable behaviours. A lot of problems are not just learned behaviours, but are influenced by people's thought processes, too. Cognitive–behavioural therapy techniques combine procedures which help to change maladaptive beliefs with behaviour modification.

Rational–emotive therapy

This type of cognitive–behavioural therapy was founded by Ellis (1955). The rationale behind it is that psychological disorders such as depression are caused by irrational thinking and that if this thinking is changed, then the disorder will no longer exist. Distorted thinking, emotions and behaviour interact.

Ellis developed the ABC model to show how irrational thinking can lead to maladaptive behaviour. An example is shown in figure 3:

Figure 3: Ellis's ABC model

A: Activating event
Jane fails to make the final of the 200m breast stroke

B: Beliefs (about A)

Rational beliefs
Jane tells herself that she has not put in enough training, as she has been preoccupied with exam revision.

Irrational beliefs
Jane tells herself that she is not capable of swimming at that standard.

C: Consequences (of B)

Desirable emotions
Jane is disappointed with the result.

Undesirable emotions
Jane feels that she is no good at swimming.

Desirable behaviour
Jane decides to train harder when the exams are over.

Undesirable behaviour
Jane decides not to take part in any more competitive swimming.

Activity 12: using Ellis's ABC model

Alex has just received a very disappointing grade for a psychology test. Use the ABC model to describe how he might deal with this, using the irrational pathway on the right of figure 3. How might he use the rational pathway on the left? When you have finished, see the notes on page 698.

Therapists help clients to pinpoint their irrational beliefs, and then work on changing those belief systems. For example, Ellis listed eleven irrational ideas often held by his clients, such as 'I must be loved and accepted by everybody' and 'I should be competent and successful in every aspect of my life'. He pointed out that irrational thinking is often identified by words such as 'should', 'ought' and 'must'. Such beliefs control people's emotional responses and make them feel worthless and a failure.

Rational–emotive therapy or RET (often called REBT – rational–emotive behaviour therapy) is a confrontational therapy, as it involves pointing out just how damaging and illogical someone's beliefs are. Ellis's therapy involves trying to change those illogical beliefs, using logical reasoning and argument. Homework is given to enable clients to see how their beliefs relate to their everyday functioning. This may include 'behavioural experiments', where the client is instructed to take risks, carrying out behaviours which they would expect to lead to awful consequences, in order to test the reality of their beliefs.

The ultimate aim of the therapy is to enable the client to incorporate the new way of thinking into their everyday life. Ellis refers to this long-term change as **elegant**. A client will feel less of a failure, be less likely to criticise themselves, and can have a more positive sense of their own worth, and so a more rewarding life.

Ellis claimed that REBT was appropriate for such psychological problems as anxiety disorders, depression and sexual problems, though not for severe mental disturbance, where talking cures are less effective. Haaga and Davison (1989) found it to be effective for depression, aggression, anger and antisocial behaviour, though not as good as systematic desensitisation for reducing anxiety.

Activity 13: evaluating REBT

Given its effectiveness for helping with some psychological problems, what are the strengths of REBT? How might it be criticised? To help you make this assessment, you might like to compare it with other therapies you have read about.

When you have finished, see the notes on page 698.

Beck's cognitive restructuring therapy

Beck (1963) also put forward cognitive ideas, specifically for the treatment of **depression**. Like REBT, this therapy also aims to change distorted thinking, a process called **cognitive restructuring**. Beck claimed that depressive thinking is rooted in three maladaptive assumptions (see figure 4) which perpetuate automatic negative thinking:

Figure 4: Beck's triad of negative assumptions
◆ **Negative view of self** (I am a worthless person)
◆ **Negative view of circumstances** (Everything is bleak and I cannot cope with what people expect of me)
◆ **Negative view of the future** (Things can only get worse, and there is nothing I can do to change them)

For example, a person who is rejected by a friend may generalise from this information to think 'Even my friends reject me. Everybody rejects me, and always will. I am a worthless person.' Although rejection is a painful experience, people not prone to depression think in a different way from this, and may think 'My friend has rejected me. This is a shame, as I have lost a friend. But I have many other friends, and will no doubt make new ones, too.'

Beck's therapy involves first measuring the extent of the client's depression using the 21-item **Beck depression inventory** (see chapter 24, figure 5), then teaching people to change their thought

responses and then to restructure their beliefs. This is done by discussing the person's beliefs in great detail, and exploring whether or not their beliefs are actually true. For example, if a client believes 'I can't do anything right at college. I'm useless', the therapist will focus discussion on what activities the client can 'do right', and offers examples that negate the belief; it may be that although their termly assignment marks are poor, they successfully run a club or get on well with other people in their flat.

The client is also taught to identify patterns of thought that contribute to the depression, and to understand how they lead to depression by stopping them from making more realistic assumptions. Beck's therapy includes behavioural procedures such as encouraging clients to confront a potentially depressing situation and keep a detailed record of what happens. This can help to challenge negative beliefs.

Beck's work has mainly centred on depression, but his techniques have also been used successfully with phobias and anxiety (Beck *et al.*, 1985) and personality disorders (Beck *et al.*, 1990). They may even be used to treat clients with psychotic disorders. Hole *et al.* (1979) encouraged schizophrenics to reality-test their delusions, and found that for half their sample, delusions were reduced.

Stress inoculation therapy

This therapy, developed by Meichenbaum (1985), was discussed briefly in chapter 4. It proposes that people often find situations more stressful than necessary because of the way they think about them. For example, they may respond to a difficult situation with the belief that they just can't cope. If they can change the way they think, avoiding this kind of negative belief and substituting more adaptive beliefs, the stress they experience can be reduced. This therapy also has a strong behavioural element, in that it includes practising new coping skills which have been acquired. It is particularly useful in managing the anxiety associated with stress.

There are three stages involved in stress inoculation therapy. The first stage is **conceptualisation**, in which the therapist helps the person to identify and talk about their fears, and how they have tried to cope with them. The second is **skill acquisition and rehearsal**, in which general techniques for coping with stress are taught and practised, such as relaxation and making a realistic assessment of stressful situations. In the final stage, **application and follow-through**, the therapist guides the person through a series of stressful situations, to help them to develop and practise the cognitive strategies necessary for coping with stressful situations.

- **Cognitive–behavioural therapy** aims to change cognitions in order to change behaviour.
- Ellis's **rational–emotive therapy** aims to change negative and illogical thought patterns. This in turn allows the development of more positive emotions and behaviour.
- Beck's therapy is a form of cognitive behaviour therapy specifically aiming to treat **depression** through **cognitive restructuring**. It has also been applied rather more widely to other disorders.
- Meichenbaum's **stress inoculation therapy** teaches people to recognise the inappropriate cognitions they may have when they are faced with a stressful situation. They are taught coping strategies which they practise as part of the therapy.

25.5 ISSUES IN EVALUATING THERAPIES

To check that you have understood the ways the different approaches view mental disorders, and how this links in with therapies, try activity 14:

▷ Activity 14: causes and therapies

Karen is 24, and suffering from depression. She rarely gets out of bed before lunchtime, and when she does get up she lounges in front of the television in her dressing gown. Her sister sometimes telephones her and asks why she doesn't pull herself together. Karen usually bursts into tears and says how useless she feels. She says she can't even look after her dog properly any more, and everybody hates her.

Think about the possible causes of her depression according to the different approaches to therapy that you have read about. Fill in your ideas in a table like the one below. Then consider the specific types of treatment that each approach would consider suitable for Karen's depression, and complete the table.

	Cause	Treatment
Biological approach		
Behavioural approach		
Psychodynamic approach		
Cognitive approach		

Look back through the chapter to check your work.

As activity 14 demonstrates, any one of the therapies described in this chapter could be effective in helping Karen to overcome her depression. So how do we decide which one is the most appropriate?

Kazdin (1986) suggested that some therapies are more effective than others for certain disorders. As we have seen, systematic desensitisation is ideal for treating phobias, and cognitive–behavioural therapy can work very well with depression, whereas neither may be the treatment of choice for schizophrenia, where chemotherapy could be a better answer. It is therefore not very useful to try to evaluate any therapy in absolute terms, but rather to evaluate how useful it is in the treatment of a particular disorder.

Even this is not without its problems. For example, you might imagine a study which involved choosing a number of people and giving them one particular type of therapy for their mental disorder, and taking a similar group who suffered from the same disorder but not offering them the therapy. You could then compare the two groups after the same period of time by counting how many people had been cured of their mental illness, and see which therapy had been most effective.

Unfortunately, the situation is not this simple. Problems first start to arise when you consider how you could measure whether people had been cured from their disorder or not. Think back to the different approaches to mental illness; each one saw the concept of a 'cure' quite differently. For example, if the symptoms of a disorder stop, behaviourists would think the person cured whereas psychoanalysts might well think that the problem had merely become repressed more deeply.

However, some studies have tried to assess the effectiveness of different therapies for different disorders:

Box E: Smith *et al.* (1980)

Procedure: A metastudy was carried out, involving 475 studies of nearly 25,000 patients. Comparisons were made between treated groups, given a specific form of therapy, and controls, who were either given no therapy, put on a waiting list or given some other form of therapy.

Results: It was found that treatment did lead to improvement. Those who received treatment fared better than 80% of the untreated control patients. Different therapies had different effects, with behaviour therapy and cognitive–behavioural therapies being especially successful for phobias and anxiety. Neither behaviour therapy nor psychodynamic therapy was more effective than the other.

Conclusion: Therapy can be highly effective, with particular therapies being more effective for different kinds of disorders.

we have an eclectic approach — a sort of pick and mix of the best therapies....

In general, it seems fair to say that different therapies are not really comparable, but that some therapies are more effective with certain disorders than others. In practice, many therapists adopt an **eclectic approach**, i.e. selecting the best aspects of various therapies and using them together to help their clients. We have seen an example of this in the Boker (1992) study of the combined use of drugs and psychoanalysis for people with psychotic disorders.

An additional problem is the difficulty of measuring improvement in patients. For example, it is unlikely that either the patient or the therapist is going to be an objective judge about whether the patient is 'better' than when they started therapy. The patient is likely to see themselves as better, or they have wasted a lot of time in therapy which was of no use. And the therapist is unlikely to judge their own therapy as a failure.

There are also ethical problems. To measure the effectiveness of a particular therapy in an objective, scientific way, it would be necessary to allocate patients randomly to different groups, and withhold therapy from one group by way of a control. It is obviously ethically unsound to deny therapy to vulnerable, distressed people who need help. On the other hand, it would also be unethical to offer people therapy of unproven value.

Even if there is an improvement in the patient's disorder, it need not be the result of the therapy. Perhaps the increased amount of attention given to that patient, purely by virtue of having someone to talk to each week, could be responsible for their improvement. Frank (1973) argued that all therapies have aspects in common which lead to their success: therapy gives the client hope that help is at hand; they take place in 'designated places of healing', locations associated with help with problems; they have a rationale which gives clients confidence; and they include procedures which strengthen the client's faith in the therapy. While this argument does not explain why some therapies are more effective than others for particular disorders, it may nonetheless help to explain the success of therapies in general.

Another problem of measuring how effective therapies are, is in terms of whether recovery is permanent or not. If a therapist sees improvements in their client during treatment, it may be that this improvement does not carry on outside the therapy situation, or perhaps lasts only a short time after the therapy ends. The '**revolving door**' **syndrome** is a term that has been given to those who improve in the short-term, are released from hospital, then need re-admitting a short time later, again and again.

Another problem is known as the '**hello–goodbye**' effect. Patients are likely to exaggerate their problems at the start of therapy, in order to ensure that they receive treatment. They may also exaggerate how much better they feel at the end of therapy, as a way of thanking the therapist for his help. The amount of improvement as the result of therapy may therefore be distorted.

- ❺ It is difficult to evaluate the overall success of a particular therapy because therapies vary in how suitable they are for treating different disorders.
- ❺ Different approaches view the concept of a 'cure' differently. It is also difficult to measure improvement in patients or clients, and recovery may not be permanent.

Ethical issues of therapy

Another issue in evaluating therapies is the kind of ethical issues which each therapy raises. Therapy usually involves changing people's behaviour, sometimes making people behave in ways they have not chosen. It follows that there are bound to be important ethical issues in therapy, such as that of **social control**, the question of who should have the right to exert control over other people's lives.

You have already read about some of the ethical problems of using chemotherapy and ECT with mentally ill patients, but techniques such as those advocated by behaviourists have also been criticised. Token economy, for example, is often criticised as unethical, given the fact that it deprives patients of something in order to control their behaviour. For example, it is obviously not ethical to deprive patients of meals dependent on their behaviour. But it can also be argued that if therapists withhold token economy, they are depriving someone of the opportunity to improve their life. You read about the potential improvements in the lives of both staff and patients in box C. Is it more ethical to deny patients these improvements than to impose a token economy system on their ward?

Behaviour modification has been criticised for its use of pain and discomfort; for example, in aversion therapy. But other therapists have pointed out that therapies do not just involve physical pain and discomfort – what about psychologically painful therapies? Patients may uncover extremely painful memories or insights in psychoanalysis and perhaps we can't realistically expect a patient to give fully informed consent to this type of psychological distress.

However, before we condemn the use of pain we should consider whether it can be justified. Read the study in box F, and decide whether in this case the use of pain was ethically justified:

Box F: Lang and Melamed (1969)

Procedure: A nine-month-old baby, in a critical condition, was referred to Lang and Melamed, two behaviour therapists. The baby was unable to stop vomiting and regurgitation of food, despite the fact that surgery had shown no physical reason for this condition. The baby had already been hospitalised three times and was now being fed through a tube into his stomach, as doctors believed that his life was in serious danger.

The behaviour therapists delivered a series of one-second-long electric shocks to the baby's leg every time he was about to vomit following feeding.

Results: After two sessions of administering these shocks, the baby learned to avoid the shock by stopping vomiting. Within four weeks the baby had recovered fully, and follow-up examinations revealed no physical or psychological problems.

Conclusion: Sometimes the use of pain in therapy *can* be justified.

A further issue is that of **informed consent**. People should ideally be able to give informed consent before participating in any type of research. The principle applies also to therapy: patients should have some right to refuse treatment. In order for this to be effective, they need to be given enough information to enable them to judge whether they want to participate in the therapy or not. It is also possible to give patients some choice as to which therapy they would prefer, though this may be restricted by expense and availability.

As you know, people can be sectioned and treated without their consent, but the question of consent goes beyond this. For example, in behaviour therapy, the question arises of who should be allowed to control another human being, and for what purpose. It is not difficult to identify social and political reasons that might underlie a diagnosis of mental illness. The former use of aversion therapy to alter the sexual orientation of homosexuals provides an example of this kind of concern. Indeed, in the former Soviet Union, the KGB developed their own classification system, including the term 'sluggish schizophrenia', not used in other classification systems, to diagnose as mentally ill those who opposed the regime. Similar concerns were raised in the USA about the use of lobotomies, with claims from civil rights activists that they were used to control violent criminals and difficult patients in institutions, rather than to help the individual.

At the same time, the client's right to refuse treatment needs to be weighed against the rights of others. Occasionally acts of violence carried out by schizophrenics are reported in the press. For example, in 1993, Andrew Robinson, a paranoid schizophrenic, stabbed a nurse to death. In a similar incident, a man called Jonathan Zito was stabbed on the London Underground, again by a schizophrenic called Christopher Clunis. Ensuring public safety has become more of an issue with the current emphasis on care in the community.

To what extent can consent be informed, given that by definition patients are suffering from a mental disorder? Patients with schizophrenia give the clearest example of this kind of problem, since by the nature of their disorder, they often lack insight into their problem and have little contact with reality. More generally, Irwin *et al.* (1985) found that only about a quarter of patients who claimed to have understood what therapy entailed, and its possible side-effects, actually did understand when asked specific questions about their treatment.

The question of the intrinsic **inequality of power** in the relationship between patient and therapist also raises ethical issues. Ideally, both patient and therapist should be involved in deciding what the goals of therapy are to be. Therapists are increasingly turning over some control of the therapy situation to the patient. This is known as **countercontrol**, an attempt to redress the power balance. At the same time, a token economy system puts control of reinforcers into the hands of the therapist, effectively disempowering the patient.

One problem, of course, is that it is not always possible for the client to anticipate the course of therapy. Behavioural treatments, such as flooding, carry a risk of heart attacks and raised blood pressure, and clients may find aversion therapy much more stressful than they had expected. A similar point could be made about the emotional impact of psychodynamic therapy. It is therefore essential that therapists give patients as much information as possible at the outset.

But the idea that patients should merely be helped to achieve what they want to achieve is not always possible. In some situations, therapists cannot avoid making their patients aware of their own values and goals. Even such basic issues as which type of therapy is practised will affect the outcome of therapy.

One way to approach ethical problems in therapy is to carry out a **cost–benefit analysis**: do the potential positive outcomes of the therapy outweigh any problems it raises? For example, in the case of the baby treated by Lang and Melamed (1969) in box F, there can be little doubt that the baby's life was saved and the temporary discomfort he suffered was worth it. However, not all cases are as clear-cut as this, which is why therapists operate under strict rules, following the guidelines of professional bodies such as the **British Psychological Society** and the **British Association of Counselling**, while bodies such as **MIND** (the National Association for Mental Health) and **PROMPT** (Protect the Rights of Mental Patients in Therapy) oversee what psychiatrists do.

- **Ethical factors** are relevant to the evaluation of particular therapies.
- These include **social control**, the issue of **pain**, both physical and psychological, **informed consent** and the **inequality of power** in the relationship between patient and therapist.
- A **cost–benefit analysis** can be helpful in deciding whether or not a particular therapy should be used.
- Professional bodies have produced ethical guidelines. Other organisations such as **MIND** and **PROMPT** comment on ethical issues from the patients' point of view.

Notes on activities

2 If a biological approach were taken, Jonathan could be given tablets to calm his anxiety and allow him to get on with his life and go on holiday with his family. A behaviourist approach would suggest that he needs to be conditioned to learn that spiders are not dangerous or frightening, perhaps by showing him various spiders in situations that he can cope with, such as confined to a jar. A psychodynamic approach would see the fear of spiders as symbolic of some problem in Jonathan's life, probably arising from childhood experience. The treatment would be talking to Jonathan, to try and discover why he is afraid of spiders, when this fear started, and so on, and help him come to terms with the material in his unconscious which has given rise to his phobia. A cognitive–behavioural approach would see his problem as arising through faulty thinking. The treatment would challenge his beliefs about spiders, both by talking to him and by using behavioural exercises.

6 You might have suggested that having been taught the deep relaxation techniques mentioned earlier, the woman should first be asked to put her outdoor shoes on. Only when she can cope with this step should the next step in the hierarchy be initiated – perhaps standing at the front door with her hand on the door handle. Subsequent steps could include opening the front door without actually going outside; standing on the doorstep outside and closing the front door behind her; and maybe walking to the garden gate. Only when all these steps have been achieved should the woman be encouraged outside her garden and into the outside world.

7 These techniques are relatively quick, especially when compared with the years of treatment involved in such therapies as psychoanalysis, and are therefore also less expensive. There is general agreement that they are extremely effective, particularly for relatively minor phobias, such as animal phobias.

One practical limitation is that for implosion, the patient needs to be able to imagine the feared object or situation, and some patients might find this very difficult.

There are also ethical issues involved. Behaviourists are sometimes criticised for being overly controlling of people. One way in which systematic desensitisation turns over control of the situation to the patient is by helping them to construct their own hierarchy and decide the speed at which they would like to expose themselves to the feared situation or object. This choice of goals is one aspect of making therapies as ethical as possible, and can be applied also to other therapies.

8 You might have suggested that when the child started behaviour that injured himself, such as biting or head-banging (the **maladaptive behaviour**), the carers should withdraw **attention** from him – effectively ignoring his behaviour to bring about **extinction**. This is in case he sees their concern and attention as a **reinforcer**. Attention should be given to the child every time he stops the unwanted behaviour, to reinforce the desired behaviour, and withdrawn every time he starts it.

9 Freud interpreted Little Hans's phobia as evidence of the Oedipal conflict, during the **phallic stage** of development. At this stage, he would wish his father dead, so that he could take his father's place with his mother.

These emotions would be very frightening, and thus the jealousy and hatred he felt towards his father would be **repressed**. The feelings would also be **projected** on to his father, with the result that he would see him as a threatening person. Hans's fear of horses symbolised for him fear of his father. He **displaced** the fear of his father on to the 'safer' target of horses.

He was particularly frightened of horses with black round the mouth and wearing blinkers because these resembled his father's moustache and glasses. Hans's fear of a threatening father would give rise to **castration anxiety**, symbolised here by the fear of being bitten.

11 parent=superego; child=id; adult=ego.

12 Alex might think, irrationally, that the poor result means that he is not going to do well in psychology. He therefore feels he is no good at it, and considers giving up the course. More rationally, he realises that he spent very little time on revision. Although he is disappointed, he decides to spend more time on revision for the next test.

13 REBT is relatively quick to carry out; for example, compared with psychoanalysis. It is also not invasive, like somatic therapies. Given that it is not considered suitable for severe problems, the issue of informed consent is not so problematic. The goals of the therapy are clear, and it aims to empower clients, by enabling them to help themselves.

However, risk-taking homework has the potential to be very embarrassing for the client. You might also have thought that it could be difficult to define whether or not a belief is irrational, which also creates problems in terms of evaluating whether or not the therapy has been effective. Finally, it is limited in terms of the kinds of disorders for which it is suitable.

Research issues

In this chapter we will be looking at:

26.1 Planning research

26.2 Inferential statistics

26.3 Carrying out statistical tests
    Mann–Whitney U test
    Wilcoxon signed ranks test
    Spearman's coefficient r_s
    Chi square (χ^2)
    Binomial sign test

26.4 Writing research reports
    Abstract
    Introduction
    Method
    Results
    Discussion
    Conclusion
    References
    Appendices

Appendix 1: Tables for Mann–Whitney U
            test
Appendix 2: Tables for Wilcoxon signed
            ranks test
Appendix 3: Tables for Spearman's
            coefficient r_s
Appendix 4: Tables for chi square (χ^2)
Appendix 5: Tables for the binomial sign
            test
Appendix 6: Sample research report

26.1 PLANNING RESEARCH

In working through the previous chapters, you have read about a lot of varied psychological research. In planning your own research, there are several factors which you will need to bear in mind in order to make it as effective as possible.

The first consideration will be choice of topic. As you will write a report on your research, it makes sense to choose a topic in an area which you find interesting, and which links in with background theory and research, since the introduction to your report will need to show that your research hypothesis – what you expect to be the outcome of your research – is well grounded. At the same time, don't be too ambitious; it is highly unlikely that you will produce a ground-breaking study, nor are you expected to do so. For example, if you are carrying out experimental research, a comparison between an experimental and a control condition is fine; there is no need to complicate matters by making a three-way comparison. What is important is that you have produced a sound hypothesis to test, that you have planned how to test it in an appropriate way, and that in your report you communicate clearly where your idea came from, how you tested it, what your findings were and what you think they mean in terms of the hypothesis.

Once you have decided on a topic, a theory relevant to it needs to be identified, and a specific prediction that is implied by that theory (a hypothesis) needs to be made. You will then need to decide which method you are going to use to test your hypothesis. In previous chapters, you have read many examples of psychological research, using a range of methods. Some studies have used the experimental (or quasi-experimental) method, though there are many examples of other non-experimental methods, such as correlational studies, observational methods, interviews and surveys. Psychologists carrying out research choose the method which is most appropriate for what they want to investigate. Whatever the topic under investigation, there is not just one way of collecting data, so when you carry out a research project of your own, you should give some thought as to which method would be most suitable.

Before making this decision, you might find it useful to look through the account of the various methods in chapter 7 and remind yourself of the strengths and limitations of each.

Activity 1: which method?

For each of these methods of carrying out psychological research, what are its strengths? What are its limitations?

a laboratory experiments
b quasi-experiments
c field experiments
d naturalistic observation
e correlational analysis
f interviews and surveys

When you have finished, check your ideas with the material in chapter 7.

There are other issues in planning research, covered in chapter 7, which you might find useful. For example, if you are using the experimental method, you will need to consider the research design, the difference between the two conditions (the IV) and the way that you will be measuring the performance of your participants (the DV). In a correlational study, you will need to decide how to measure the variables to be correlated. You will also need to decide whether, on the basis of background theory and studies, the research hypothesis is one-tailed (directional) or two-tailed (non-directional). In practice, most research hypotheses are one-tailed. Hypotheses are discussed in chapter 7, section 7.3.

You will need to decide on the population from which your sample is to be drawn, and the sampling method to be used. Most student practicals use opportunity sampling as the most convenient method, though if your study takes the form of a naturalistic observation, you may be testing a self-selecting sample of people who happen to be where you are carrying out the observation.

Another consideration is how many participants to test. You will be analysing your data using a statistical test; all these tests require a minimum number of participants. However, these numbers are usually very low, and it is worth considering testing a few more

participants than is necessary to meet the requirements of the test to try to reduce the relative importance of random variation in the results. At the same time, the disadvantage in testing large numbers of participants, which can be extremely time-consuming, needs to be balanced against possible gains.

One major factor you will need to bear in mind is ethical issues. The final section of chapter 6 outlines ethical guidelines for carrying out psychological research with human participants, and you should reread this carefully before making any final decisions about the study you plan to carry out. In particular, you need to make sure that participants give informed consent to take part in your study, which means that the information given to them before they decide whether or not to take part should be as full as possible. You also need to make sure that they know that they can decide at any time to take no further part in the study, and can have their data destroyed.

Finally, you will need to prepare any necessary materials. These may include standardised instructions, stimulus materials, questionnaires, rating scales and so on. It is always worth running a small pilot study, testing just two or three participants, to make sure that your instructions are clear, that your materials are appropriate, and that any timings (such as the time for which participants are exposed to stimuli) are neither too long nor too short.

It is unlikely that you will be short of ideas; it is probable that several possibilities have already occurred to you as you have worked your way through the topics in this book. The main thing is to keep notes of the planning process – in which books or articles or websites you have found the relevant background material relating to theory and research, the reasoning behind the various planning decisions you have made, and so on. Once you have carried out your research, these notes will make writing the report a lot easier.

26.2 INFERENTIAL STATISTICS

The term 'inferential statistics' refers to carrying out statistical tests on data, which then allow inferences (or conclusions) about the data to be drawn. What the tests actually tell you is the probability of obtaining the results if the null hypothesis is in fact correct.

It is not possible to prove something true by observation alone. Take, for example, the assertion that 'All swans are white'. We could observe a great number of swans, and find that all of them are white. But however large a sample of white swans we observe, we cannot discount the possibility that we may at some point come across a black one. The best we can achieve, then, is a reasonable certainty that a research hypothesis which we have investigated is correct. It is for this reason that the word 'proved' is not used in relation to the research hypothesis when discussing the results of a study. Instead, the hypothesis is supported or not.

In psychological research, the 5% (0.05) level of probability is the conventionally accepted level at which a research hypothesis can be accepted. This means that we need to establish that the probability that our results could have come about by chance (and that the null hypothesis is actually correct) is 5% or less, and that we can therefore accept our results as supporting the research hypothesis with a 95% level of confidence, and reject the null hypothesis. If the results of a study reach the 5% significance level, they are said to be **significant** at this level.

The 5% level has been accepted in psychological research because it represents a reasonable compromise between making a **type 1** and a **type 2** error. If a researcher accepts that their research hypothesis is supported, whereas in fact the results have come about by chance, they are making a type 1 error. If on the other hand they wrongly infer that the research hypothesis has not been supported, they are making a type 2 error. The 5% level is stringent enough to allow a reasonable certainty in accepting the research hypothesis, while at the same time not being so stringent that genuine results are overlooked.

While statistical tests can tell us whether data reach the 5% criterion, they can also tell us whether a more stringent criterion, e.g. 1% (0.01), is reached. If so, we can then accept the research hypothesis with even greater confidence, i.e. 99%.

Standard tests are applied to psychological data to establish whether we can be sure, to the level of certainty which we have decided on, that results like those obtained could have occurred by chance alone. It is perhaps worth noting that if you are testing a one-tailed hypothesis, most of the tests cannot decide for you whether your results are in the direction predicted, or whether the difference is in the opposite direction. To establish this, you will need to look at the data before carrying out the test. For example, if you have predicted that scores in condition A will be higher than those in condition B, but the scores for condition A are in fact generally lower than those for condition B, the statistical test cannot lead you to reject the null hypothesis. It is also worth looking at your data before carrying out the test to consider how distinctively different the two sets are, and how likely it is that this has come about by chance.

26.3 CARRYING OUT STATISTICAL TESTS

There are very many statistical tests available to psychologists; which one is suitable for analysing the data of a particular study will depend on several factors to do with the research design used in the study. Here we shall concentrate on what are called **non-parametric** tests. In contrast to parametric tests, which make various assumptions about the nature of the data collected, these tests have the advantage that they can be used with any level of quantitative data, and are quick and easy to use. Their main drawback is that they are somewhat insensitive, but this is usually not too much of a problem in student practicals. We will look at five tests which relate to different kinds of simple research design.

In order to decide which test is appropriate for a particular set of data, three questions need to be answered. The first question is whether the study is looking for a difference between conditions, or whether it is looking for a relationship or association. You will remember from chapter 7, section 7.1, that experiments look for a difference, while correlational designs look for a relationship. Observational studies could look for either.

The second question concerns the level of the data.

Chapter 7, section 7.7 describes the different levels of measurement which can be used. For parametric tests, the data need to be of at least interval level, while the non-parametric tests which we shall be looking at here can be applied whatever level of measurement is used. The critical distinction for these tests is between nominal (category) data, and data which are of at least ordinal level, i.e. in the form of scores which can be put in order.

If the study is looking for a difference between conditions, the final question to be asked is whether the design of the study uses repeated or independent measures. For the purposes of choosing a statistical test, a matched pairs design is treated in the same way as a repeated measures design. See chapter 7, section 7.5, if you have forgotten what these terms mean.

We will look here at five tests. How the answers to these questions relate to choice of test is shown in figure 1.

You may wonder how the chi square test can be used to establish either a relationship or a difference. It is in fact a test of association. For example, if you were investigating whether men or women are more likely to hold open a door for someone else passing through, the test would tell you whether there is an association between gender and this kind of helping behaviour. At the same time, it could tell you whether there is a difference between men and women in this respect.

▷ Activity 2: choosing a statistical test

Read the following scenarios. For each one, decide
a   whether the researchers are looking for a difference between performance in two conditions or a relationship/association between two variables
b   what level of measurement is being used

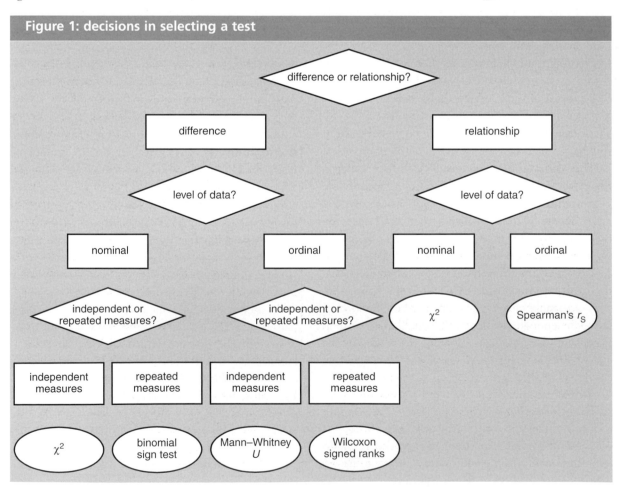

Figure 1: decisions in selecting a test

c   if they are looking for a difference, whether they have used a repeated or independent measures design.

On the basis of your answers to these questions, decide which statistical test would be appropriate to analyse the data:

1   An A-level Psychology teacher is interested in whether there is a relationship between the amount of time students spend in paid employment and how well they do at A-level. She asks students how many hours they spend each week at work, and translates their predicted A-level grades into a points score (A=10, B=8 etc).

2   Does the nature of the material to be learned affect how well it is remembered? Participants are asked to learn a list of 30 words, half of which are related to emotions (e.g. love, hate) and half of which are neutral words, matched for length and approximate frequency in the English language. They are asked to recall as many words as they can. Their scores for the two kinds of words are compared.

3   A primary school teacher is interested in the language skills of her pupils, and in particular whether there is a link between size of vocabulary and spelling ability. She gives them a vocabulary test, which requires them to match a series of words with their meanings, and compares their scores with those from a spelling test.

4   Researchers are interested in the effect on helping behaviour of watching altruistic behaviour on TV. One group of children is shown a video where friendly cartoon animals help old ladies across the road and help to carry their shopping, while another group is shown a Tom and Jerry cartoon. All the children are then exposed to situations where they could offer help. Observers decide whether each child is very helpful, quite helpful or not helpful, and compare the ratings for the two groups.

5   In a memory experiment, participants are asked to learn pairs of words. One group is asked to learn the words by repeating them over and over again, while another group is asked to create a visual image to link the words. They are then tested by being shown the first word of each pair, and asked to supply the second word. The number of words correctly remembered in each condition is compared.

6   Researchers are interested in whether information about party policy affects people's voting intentions. A sample of voters in Anytown is asked whether or not they are likely to vote for the Monster Raving Loony Party. They then attend a lecture on Monster Raving Loony Party policy, following which they are again asked whether they are likely to vote for this party. Researchers note how many people who had not originally intended to vote for the party changed their minds after attending the lecture.

7   Do children change their opinion of school subjects when they have spent some time at a particular school? Children entering Dotheboys Hall are asked to rate how interesting they find English, Maths and Science, using a scale of 1 (extremely boring) to 10 (absolutely great). They are asked to rate these subjects again when they have been at the school for a year, to assess whether there has been any change.

8   Gumrot plc have produced a new line in sweets called Dinosaur Droppings. They want to know whether there is a difference between the two possible packaging designs they have developed in terms of their appeal to girls and to boys. Sweets are displayed in both packaging designs. The number of each kind bought by girls and by boys is recorded and compared.

9   Researchers are interested in the truth of well-known sayings, in particular 'elephants never forget' and 'a memory like a sieve'. Participants are hypnotised and given a post-hypnotic suggestion either that they are an elephant or that they are a sieve. They are then asked to read and memorise a story. Recall for each group is compared, using a questionnaire on the content of the story.

10 Psychologists at Oxford Clinic for the Seriously Bewildered are interested in whether their therapy methods, which involve teaching clients A-level Psychology, can be shown to be effective. Staff are asked to rate a group of clients on the amount of bewildered behaviour they show, both before and after studying A-level Psychology.

When you have finished, see the notes on page 715.

We will now look in detail at how each of the five statistical tests in figure 1 is carried out. For each test, a formula is followed which allows you to work out what is called the calculated (or observed) value for the test you are using. This is then compared with the critical value in the relevant set of tables, included as appendices to this chapter, to indicate how likely it is that the results have come about by chance. The calculated value is first compared with the critical values at the 5% level; this is indicated on the table by $p < 0.05$, meaning that the probability of the results having come about by chance is less than 5%.

If the results are significant at this level, then the calculated value can be compared with critical values at more stringent levels. For example, $p = 0.01$ means that the probability that the results could have come about by chance is 1%, while $p = 0.005$ means that the probability that the results could have come about by chance is 0.5%. The smaller this probability, the greater the confidence with which the research hypothesis can be accepted.

It is also worth noting that, for some tests, the calculated value needs to be smaller than the critical value in the table in order to be accepted at this level, while for other tests, it needs to be larger. This is indicated in the worked examples and also at the top of each table.

Some of the tests we will be looking at – those which work on data which are of at least ordinal level – require the raw data (the actual scores which have been collected) to be ranked, i.e. put in order, in the same way that runners in a race can be put in the order in which they finish. This is done because non-parametric tests require that the ranks of the scores, rather than the scores themselves, are compared.

However, unlike the runners, in ranking for psychological tests the lowest score is ranked 1, the next lowest 2, and so on. If there is a tie of two equal scores, the next two positions are added and divided by two. Similarly, if there are three equal scores, the next three positions are added and divided by three.

Activity 3: ranking

Here is a sample set of scores which have been ranked:

scores	25	21	21	15	14	14	14	12	11
rank	9	7.5	7.5	6	4	4	4	2	1

Now rank these scores:

scores: 17   17   14   14   14   12   9   6   6

When you have finished, see the notes on page 715.

Mann–Whitney *U* test

We will relate this test to activity 9 in chapter 2. Each participant in two conditions is given a set of words written individually on cards to sort into three piles. In condition 1, they are asked to sort the words using meaningful categories, while in condition 2, they are asked to sort by the script in which the words are written. On the basis of the levels of processing theory (see chapter 2, section 2.3) the research hypothesis is that participants who have sorted by meaning (semantic processing) will remember more of the words in an unexpected recall test than those who sorted by script (structural processing).

The table of results, showing the number of words correctly recalled by each participant in each condition, is shown in figure 2. The Mann–Whitney *U* test requires that all the scores from both conditions are ranked together; these ranks are also shown in figure 2.

Figure 2: preparing data for the Mann–Whitney U test

participant	condition 1 (semantic)	rank	participant	condition 2 (structural)	rank
1	16	12	10	12	7
2	21	18	11	16	12
3	10	3.5	12	15	10
4	22	19	13	10	3.5
5	18	16.5	14	10	3.5
6	18	16.5	15	13	8
7	16	12	16	10	3.5
8	24	20	17	14	9
9	17	14.5	18	11	6
		$T_1 = 132$	19	9	1
			20	17	14.5

In this example, there are different numbers of participants in each condition; it is not necessary to have equal numbers for this test. The next step is to substitute numbers into the formula for the Mann–Whitney U test. The formula and workings are shown in figure 3.

Figure 3: calculations for the Mann–Whitney U test

For this test, the value of a statistic denoted by U is calculated using the formula:

$$U = n_1 n_2 + \frac{n_1(n_1 + 1)}{2} - T_1$$

n_1 is the number of participants in condition 1, n_2 is the number of participants in condition 2, and T_1 is the sum of the ranks in condition 1. This gives $U = 99 + 45 - 132 = 12$

We then need to work out a further value called U prime (U') using the formula

$$U' = n_1 n_2 - U, \text{ so } U' = 99 - 12 = 87$$

The smaller values of U, in this case 12, is compared with the critical values in the tables. If we are to accept the research hypothesis, the calculated value of U needs to be equal to or less than the critical value.

Activity 4: assessing the results of the Mann–Whitney U test

1 Decide whether the research hypothesis was one-tailed or two-tailed. If it was one-tailed, check that the difference is in the direction predicted by the research hypothesis.
2 Turn to the tables for this test in appendix 1, page 716, selecting the 5% level(0.05).
3 Find the value of n_1 along the top of the table, and the value of n_2 down the left-hand side. Move down from n_1 and across from n_2; where they meet is the critical value.
4 Compare the critical value with the calculated value of 12. Can the research hypothesis be accepted at $p < 0.05$? If the calculated value is equal to or less than the critical value in the table, it indicates that the probability of the results having come about by chance is less than 5%. This is expressed as $p < 0.05$. Can it also be accepted at more stringent levels?

When you have finished, see the notes on page 715.

Wilcoxon signed ranks test

To illustrate this test, we will look at a variation of the Stroop effect (see chapter 14, box K). In the

Stroop effect, people almost invariably take longer to identify the ink colour in which words are written if the words are colour words written in a conflicting colour (e.g. the word 'blue' written in red ink) than if they are words with no colour associations. As a variation on this, we will compare the time taken to identify ink colours in a set of words with a colour association, written in a conflicting colour (e.g. 'grass' written in red) and to identify the colours of a set of neutral words, matched for initial letter, length and relative frequency in the English language. The research hypothesis is that people will take longer to identify the ink colours of the colour-associated words than of the neutral words.

For this test, a statistic called T is calculated. To carry out this test, the two sets of scores are listed as shown in the table in figure 4, then the difference between each set of scores is calculated (the column headed 'd' for 'difference'). Any pairs of scores which are equal are discarded, and that participant's data are not included in the calculation. These differences are then ranked, ignoring whether they are minus or plus values (the column headed 'rank of d'). For example, differences of +1, −5 and +6 would be ranked 1, 2 and 3 respectively.

Figure 4: calculation for the Wilcoxon signed ranks test

Time in seconds to complete colour identification task

participant	condition A (colour-associated words)	condition B (neutral words)	d	ranks of d	sign of d
1	24	16	+8	9	+
2	18	18	0	omit tie	
3	32	26	+6	7.5	+
4	21	23	−2	3	−
5	28	23	+5	5.5	+
6	41	35	+6	7.5	+
7	17	15	+2	3	+
8	18	20	+2	3	+
9	20	19	+1	1	+
10	22	17	+5	5.5	+

A column 'sign of d' is added to the table as shown. All the ranks corresponding to a − sign are added and all the ranks corresponding to a + sign are added. Whichever of these sums is smaller is the observed value of T. In this case, the only value in the 'rank of d' column to have a minus sign is the rank of 3 for participant 4, so this is clearly going to be smaller than the sum of all the plus ranks. Therefore, $T = 3$.

It is worth noting that if all the differences are in the same direction – for example, if all the signs in the final column are plus – then T would be equal to 0, i.e. the sum of the minus results, in this case.

To look up the value of T in the relevant table, you will also need to know the value of n, i.e. the number of participants. In this case, $n = 9$, since we are discarding the data of participant 2, who took the same time in each condition. If the research hypothesis is to be accepted and the null hypothesis rejected, the calculated value of T needs to be equal to or less than the critical value.

Activity 5: assessing the results of the test

1 Decide whether the research hypothesis was one-tailed or two-tailed.
2 Turn to the table for this test in appendix 2, page 720, selecting the 5% level, i.e. the appropriate column headed 0.05.
3 Find the value of n, and compare the calculated value of 3 with the critical value in the table at 0.05. Can the research hypothesis be accepted, and the null hypothesis rejected, at this level? What about more stringent levels?

When you have finished, see the notes on page 715.

Spearman's coefficient r_S

In this test, a statistic usually denoted by r_S, but sometimes called rho, is calculated. We will relate this test to the data supplied in activity 18, chapter

7. The research hypothesis here is that there will be a positive correlation between students' IQ scores and A-level points scores. Ranking is again used, with each of the two sets of scores – IQ and A-level points – being ranked separately and the ranks compared. Since the research hypothesis predicts a positive correlation, it is expected that the rank for each score for each participant will be similar, i.e. that a participant with a high rank for one score will tend also to have a high rank for the other, and a participant with a low rank for one score will tend also to have a low rank for the other.

Once the two sets of ranks have been completed, the difference between the ranks for each participant is worked out (the column headed 'd') and then this difference is squared (the column headed 'd^2'). All the values in this last column are then added to give Σd^2. The sign Σ is the Greek letter sigma, and means 'sum', in this case finding the sum of the d^2 values.

Figure 5: working out Spearman's coefficient r_S

participant	IQ score	rank	A-level score	rank	d	d^2
1	125	6	20	7.5	−1.5	2.25
2	110	2	14	3	−1	1
3	127	7	24	10	−3	9
4	135	9	18	5.5	3.5	12.25
5	118	4	22	9	−5	25
6	142	10	20	7.5	2.5	6.25
7	122	5	16	4	1	1
8	112	3	10	1.5	1.5	2.25
9	128	8	18	5.5	2.5	6.25
10	108	1	10	1.5	−0.5	0.25

$\Sigma d^2 = 65.5$

Numerical values are then put into the formula:

$$r_S = 1 - \frac{6\Sigma d^2}{n(n^2 - 1)} \quad \text{where } n = \text{the number of pairs of scores}$$

$$r_S = 1 - \frac{6 \times 65.5}{10 \times 99}$$

$$r_S = 1 - \frac{393}{990} = 1 - 0.397 = +0.603$$

If the research hypothesis is to be accepted, the calculated value of r_S needs to be equal to or larger than the critical value in the table. In order to accept a research hypothesis predicting a negative correlation, the critical value is read as being a minus number, and the calculated value has to be between the critical value and -1.0.

Activity 6: using the table for Spearman's coefficient r_S

Using the table for this test in appendix 3, page 721, check to see whether the research hypothesis can be accepted at the 5% level. Do the results reach a more significant level than this? Why/why not? How would you interpret these results: do they show a very strong relationship between IQ and A-level scores? Quite a strong relationship? A weak relationship? (You may find it helpful to compare your assessment with the answers to activity 18, chapter 7).

When you have finished, see the notes on page 715.

Chi square (χ^2)

For this test, a statistic called chi square (written as χ^2 and pronounced 'ky square') is calculated. We will return to the example given earlier of a study which investigates whether men or women are more likely to hold open a door for someone else passing through. The researchers position themselves outside a department store where they can observe door-opening behaviour without making themselves too conspicuous, and keep a tally of the numbers of men and women who hold the door open for someone else, and those who are in a position to do so but do not. The numbers in each of the four categories (men who helped; men who didn't help; women who helped; women who didn't help) are entered in a table with four cells, as shown in figure 6. Each person can therefore only be counted in one cell (a requirement for the chi square test); they are either male or female, and they either hold the door open or do not. The totals of the rows and columns also form part of the table. The data and workings are shown in figure 6.

Figure 6: working out χ^2

	men	women	total
held the door open	23	8	31
did not hold the door open	11	14	25
total	34	22	56

The numbers in the four main cells in the table are the **observed values**. The table also shows totals for the rows (31 and 25), totals for the columns (34 and 22) and the overall total number of observations (56).

The first step is to work out what are called the **expected frequencies** for each of the four cells, i.e. the frequencies we would expect if the null hypothesis were true. This is done for each cell by multiplying the marginal total of the relevant row by the marginal total of the relevant column, then dividing by the overall total. For cell 1 (men who held the door open), the expected value would be:

$31 \times 34 \div 56 = 18.82$

When all four expected frequencies have been calculated, they are put in the relevant cells:

23		8	
	18.82		12.18
11		14	
	15.18		9.82

To check that your calculations are accurate, the row and column sums for both the E and the O values should be worked out; they should be the same. For example, in column 1, $23 + 11 = 34$ and $18.82 + 15.18 = 34$.
For each cell, figures need to be substituted in the formula

$$\frac{(O - E)^2}{E}$$

where O = the observed value for that cell and E = the expected value.

For the first cell (top left), the calculation is

$$\frac{(23 - 18.2)^2}{18.2} = 0.93$$

For the second cell (top right), the result of this calculation is 1.43. The results for the third (bottom left) and the fourth (bottom right) cells are 1.15 and 1.78 respectively.

The formula for chi square is $\sum \dfrac{(O - E)^2}{E}$

so to find the value of χ^2, these four numbers must be added. In this case, the value is

$$\chi^2 = 0.93 + 1.43 + 1.15 + 1.78 = 5.29.$$

To reach significance, the calculated value of χ^2 needs to be equal to or larger than the critical value in the table.

Before we can look up this statistic in the table, we need to calculate the degrees of freedom (df). This is simply the number of rows minus 1, multiplied by the number of columns minus 1. In this example, there are two rows and two columns, so df = (2 – 1) x (2 – 1) = 1. It would be perfectly possible, however, to have more rows and/or columns; for example, people could be classified as 'very helpful', 'quite helpful' or 'not helpful', as in example 4 of activity 2.

Activity 7: using the table for chi square

Use appendix 4, page 722, to find out whether the results in figure 6 are significant, and if so, at what level. You will first need to decide whether the research hypothesis is one-tailed or two-tailed.

When you have finished, see the notes on page 715.

Binomial sign test

For this test, a statistic called S is calculated. As an example, we will look at a study which compares children's performance on a standard Piagetian conservation of liquid quantity task (see chapter 7, box D) and on a similar task which makes 'human sense', in which children are told that liquid needs to be poured out of the original container into another one because the original container is chipped, and so might hurt someone. Piaget's experiments, the rationale behind them and variations carried out by later researchers are discussed in chapter 17. The children carry out the standard task and the 'human sense' task on two separate occasions, and researchers expect that children who are unable to conserve on the standard task will be successful in carrying out the 'human sense' task.

A tick or a cross is put for each participant in each condition, according to whether they conserved successfully. For those who conserved in condition B but not in condition A, i.e. responded in line with the research hypothesis, a + sign is put in the final column. A – sign is given if they succeeded on task B but not on task A, i.e. the difference is in the opposite direction from that predicted. If they conserved on both tasks, or failed to conserve on both tasks, i.e. there was no difference between the two conditions, their data are not included in the calculation.

Figure 7: working out the sign test

participant	condition A (standard task)	condition B ('human sense' task)	conserved in B but not in A
1	✗	✓	+
2	✗	✓	+
3	✗	✓	+
4	✗	✗	omit
5	✓	✗	–
6	✓	✓	omit
7	✗	✓	+
8	✗	✗	omit
9	✗	✓	+
10	✗	✓	+

The next step is to add up the number of + signs and the number of – signs in the final column. The smaller of the two numbers is the value of S. In this example, the data of participants 4, 6 and 8 would be discarded, since there was no difference in performance on the two conditions. Therefore $n = 7$; there are 6 + signs and 1 – sign, so $S = 1$.

In this example, we have looked only at the change in sign between conditions. However, this test can also be carried out when the data are in the form of scores. In this case, the final column will show a + sign when the difference between scores for the two conditions is positive, and a − sign when the difference is negative.

▶ Activity 8: assessing the results of the sign test

Use the table in appendix 5, page 733, to assess whether the results of this test are significant, and if so at what level. You will need to decide whether the research hypothesis is one-tailed or two-tailed.

When you have finished, see the notes on page 715.

26.4 WRITING RESEARCH REPORTS

Careful planning of a research project and appropriate analysis of the data are only part of research. It is also necessary to communicate clearly relevant information about the study in a report. There are conventions as to how this should be done which we will be looking at in this section. At the end of the chapter, in appendix 6 (page 724), there is a sample report written by a student, together with comments on its strengths and weaknesses. It is a study relating to the Craik and Lockhart levels of processing model of memory, which you read about in chapter 2, so you will be familiar with the material. You may find it useful to refer to the sample report as you read about how to write the various sections of a report.

Before starting to write the report, you will need to think of a suitable title. This should be concise, while at the same time giving a clear idea of the research question which you have investigated. It is a good idea to include in the title the IV and DV (or the two co-variables in the case of correlational research).

The report, with the exception of the research and null hypotheses, should be written in the past tense. It should not be longer than 2000 words, not counting any tables or appendices, so it is important to put the necessary information across succinctly. It is divided into sections, each with a different heading and serving a different function. The sections are: abstract; introduction; method; results; discussion; conclusion; references; and appendices. It helps to make the report easy to read if each section is given its appropriate heading. We will look at each section in turn in terms of what it should contain and how it should be structured.

Before we move on to the specific sections, there are a few general points to bear in mind in report writing. It is a convention that words such as 'I', 'we' and 'my' are not used. The report should be written in an impersonal style, so that instead of writing 'I read participants the instructions', you should write 'Participants were read the instructions'.

You should also aim to use a simple style throughout. Students are often tempted to use long words and write in long sentences, but this usually makes the report more difficult to read. You may find it helpful to ask someone else, who doesn't know anything about psychology, to read through your report when it is completed, and then consider rewriting any sections they find difficult to understand. You should write in sentences, and avoid lists.

Finally, make sure that there is a logical progression within each section; this can be a particular problem in the introduction and discussion sections. It pays to give particular attention to links between paragraphs, to ensure that there is a smooth transition from one idea to the next.

Abstract

The first part of a report is the abstract. This is a short summary of the report, including brief information about all the other major sections, i.e. introduction, method, results and discussion. It is therefore a good idea to write it after the other sections have been completed, even though it comes at the start of the report. In published research, the purpose of the abstract is to allow other people to have a clear and easily accessible overview of the study so that they can decide whether they would like to read about it in more detail.

The abstract should make brief reference to background theory or research, and should include the aims of the study, the research hypothesis and the expected findings. It should say how the idea was tested, who the participants were and how many were tested, and identify the test used to analyse the data. It should give the critical and calculated values from the statistical analysis, and say whether the results were significant, and if so, at what level. Finally, there should be some brief comment on any limitations of the research, and suggestions as to how the topic could be followed up in future research. It is also relevant to note any practical implications.

Introduction

The purpose of the introduction is to provide a rationale for the idea which you have chosen to test. Overall, it should not need to be longer than one and a half pages of typing. It helps to think of this section as being like a funnel, which starts from relevant but general information, and gradually becomes more specific, finishing with the research and null hypotheses.

It is likely that your study relates to a particular theory, so you will need to start with a theoretical outline. This should be quite brief, highlighting the main ideas, and mentioning the name of the theorist and the date of the theory.

From this, you will need to move on to research which supports the theory. You should be selective in what you choose to include; more is not necessarily better. Aim for between 2 and 5 studies, and use the ones which relate most closely to what you are going to be testing in your study, with the most relevant one coming last. This should lead to the aims of the study: what exactly are you trying to find out by carrying out the study?

You will then need to decide whether your research hypothesis is one-tailed or two-tailed, and justify your decision. This decision is based on the findings of the research studies you have described, but this link needs to be made explicit. You should end this section by stating the research hypothesis and the null hypothesis. It helps to set these out as separate paragraphs.

In many cases there are competing theories within the area which you have chosen to investigate. However, it is not necessary to look at more than one theory in the introduction. Alternative theories are best considered in the discussion, in the light of your findings. The exception to this is when you are testing a two-tailed hypothesis, where one theory predicts one outcome and another predicts the opposite. In this case, both theories, together with their supporting research, need to be covered in the introduction. This makes sense if you bear in mind that the aim of the introduction is to provide a clear rationale for the research hypothesis.

Method

This section of the report gives a detailed account of how the study was carried out. Think of it as being a bit like a recipe. It should be possible for someone reading this section to replicate your study exactly, so you need to include full details of how the study was carried out and samples of any materials used. The method uses four separate subheadings: design; participants; materials/apparatus; and procedure.

In the **design** section, you should state the method used – for example, that it was a laboratory experiment, or quasi-experiment, or a study using correlational analysis – and say why this design was chosen. If an experimental design is used, you should identify the experimental and control conditions. You should also say whether you used independent measures, repeated measures or matched pairs, and justify your choice. You should then identify the IV and the DV, or the two co-variables in the case of correlational analysis. If repeated measures are used, say whether counterbalancing or randomisation of conditions was used. If you are comparing two conditions, you need to state the basis on which participants were allocated to conditions.

Identify any controlled variables, i.e. factors which were kept the same in both conditions, such as the time for which participants were exposed to stimulus materials, or the conditions under which testing was carried out. Finally, you should state the significance level to be accepted, and say why this level was chosen. As noted above, the 5% level is the one conventionally used in psychological research, unless existing research is being challenged or there are safety implications in what is being tested.

In the **participants** section, you should identify the population from which your sample of participants was drawn. Say how many participants were tested overall, and how many were tested in each condition if you are carrying out an experimental or quasi-experimental design. You need to state the sampling method used, and say why your sample fits into this category. For example, you could say that an opportunity sample was tested, since people were tested on the basis of their availability and willingness to take part. It is usual to give the approximate age range of the participants, and the gender composition of the sample (though try to avoid ambiguous statements such as 'Participants were half male and half female'). There may be other information about participants which is relevant. For instance, in the example of the Stroop effect used above to show the working of the Wilcoxon signed ranks test, it would be relevant to say that no participants were colour blind.

The next subsection describes the **materials/apparatus** used. Apparatus could include a computer if you have presented stimulus materials using PowerPoint, or a stopwatch if you have timed participants' performance. You will also need to give details of any materials you have used such as tests, questionnaires or word lists. If you have prepared the materials especially for the study, you need to explain the basis on which this was done; for example, why the kinds of items used in a questionnaire were chosen, or the words in word lists selected.

You should include a sample of your materials in an appendix, and say here that you have done so. You should also include scoring systems for tests or questionnaires. You are likely to have several appendices by the time you finish the report, so number them in the order in which they are mentioned in the text, and refer to them using the relevant number. These references are usually made in brackets, e.g. (for a sample word list, see appendix 1). You are also likely to have standardised

instructions to include in this section. Even if instructions have been given verbally to participants, a written transcript needs to be included as an appendix, referred to in this subsection.

The final subsection of the method section is the **procedure**. This subsection describes exactly how the study was carried out, and you need to make sure that enough detail is given so that full replication would be possible, such as including the time allowed to carry out tasks. At the same time, you should avoid giving details such as the time of day, or a description of the room where the study was carried out, unless this is relevant to the study.

You need to note here any ethical problems (such as not giving participants full information about the study before they take part) and say how these were dealt with, or why they were not thought to be a problem. If there were no apparent ethical problems, you should say so. Don't forget to say that all participants were thanked and debriefed at the end of the study, or why debriefing was not thought to be necessary.

The method section overall should not need to be longer than a page of typing.

Results

The results section is very short. Its aim is to present the data in an easily accessible way, to give the results of a statistical analysis, to say whether the results are statistically significant, and if so, at what level. You don't need to say what the results mean in this section; this takes place in the discussion section.

You should start by presenting the data you have collected in summary form. This could take the form of a table of the means, medians or modes for different conditions (check back to chapter 7 to help you decide which measure of central tendency is appropriate). If your data are of at least ordinal level, you could also include here a measure of dispersion; for example, the ranges of the scores in different conditions.

Your summary could also take the form of a graphic representation of the data, such as a bar chart or frequency polygon (see chapter 7), and should directly reflect the hypothesis tested. Don't forget that any graphs should show *summary* data; for example, it is not acceptable to provide a bar chart showing each participant's individual score. If your study has used correlational analysis, probably the most suitable form of data presentation here is a scattergraph.

Don't forget to give any tables or graphs a title stating precisely what is shown, and to label axes on graphs, or bars on a bar chart. You should then write one or two sentences highlighting what the data seem to show.

The raw data (i.e. the individual scores of participants) should be put in a numbered appendix, and the reader should be referred to this material here. However, you do not need to include all the raw data, e.g. the detailed questionnaire responses for all participants. Remember that you should observe confidentiality about participants' data, so do not use participants' names but give each participant a number, as was done in the worked examples of tests earlier in the chapter.

The next step is to identify the statistical test used to analyse the data, and justify why this test has been chosen. For example, a Mann–Whitney test would be used if you were looking for a difference between conditions, if you used an independent measures design, and if your data were of at least ordinal level, i.e. in the form of scores which could be put in rank order.

You should state the calculated value which you have worked out using the test, e.g. the value of U for a Mann–Whitney test. Refer the reader to the calculations used to work out this statistic in an appendix. You should also give the critical value from the table. Don't forget to include the significance level of the critical value, e.g. $p < 0.05$, and whether the research hypothesis was one- or two-tailed. For a chi square you will also need to include the degrees of freedom (df).

As an example, your statement for a Mann–Whitney test should be something like: 'The critical value of U at $p < 0.05$, one-tailed, is 23', while for χ^2 it should be something like: 'The critical value of χ^2 at $p < 0.05$, one-tailed, df = 1, is 2.71'. If your results are more significant than $p < 0.05$, e.g.

if they are significant at $p < 0.025$ or $p < 0.01$, use the most significant level for this statement.

You should then compare the calculated and critical values, and say whether your research hypothesis can be accepted, and whether the null hypothesis can be rejected or must be retained. For example, this statement could be: 'Since the calculated value of U at 25 is greater than the critical value of 23 at $p < 0.05$, the research hypothesis is not supported and the null hypothesis must be retained.'

Finally, write a sentence to relate the results of the test to your study. For example: 'There was no significant difference between the number of words recalled by participants instructed to use imagery to aid recall and by those to whom no particular strategy was suggested.'

Discussion

This section of the report is usually the longest, and perhaps the most difficult to write, but also attracts the most marks in an A-level report. It is here that you explain the results of your study, and consider the implications of your findings.

The first thing to do is to make links with the theory and studies outlined in the introduction. Do your results support the background theory? How do they compare with the research findings described in the introduction?

Whether or not your results were significant, you might find it helpful at this point to consider alternatives to the theory on which your study was based. Are there other theories which could also account for the results? If your results were not significant, is there another theory which might help to make sense of them? You could also describe related research whose findings are not in line with your results, and explain these differences.

Apart from theoretical issues, you will need to consider any methodological problems. If there were any uncontrolled factors which might have influenced the results of your study, you need to identify them and suggest what kinds of improvements would need to be made to eliminate them if the study were to be carried out again.

It is also possible that a different method might be a good idea in future research. For example, if you carried out a laboratory experiment, you may have thought that it had low ecological validity, and that therefore either a field experiment or a naturalistic observation or simply more suitable materials would be a useful way of testing your idea further. If this is the case, you need to outline briefly how this could be done.

The sample of people tested could also be considered. For example, if only a very small sample was tested, they are unlikely to be representative of the parent population. Even if the sample size was adequate, the sample might nonetheless be unrepresentative in other ways.

There are quite often practical implications of research findings, which also need to be discussed in this section. For example, if a memory experiment shows a particular method of learning material to be effective, then this could have implications within education, both in terms of ways in which information might be taught and in suggesting ways in which revision for exams might be carried out more efficiently. You should also note any limitations of these kinds of implications.

Finally, you need to consider the direction which future research in the area you have been investigating might usefully take. What kinds of questions remain unanswered? How might future researchers go about answering them?

Conclusion

This should be a very short section, just two or three sentences. It should include a short restatement of the findings of the study, say what conclusions can be drawn from them, and indicate briefly any theoretical or methodological problems.

References

In the introduction and discussion sections, you will have made reference to theories and research, in each case naming the relevant psychologist(s) and giving the date of the theory or research in brackets.

In this section, you need to give full references for these names and dates, so that anyone reading your report could check your sources if they wished to do so. References need to be listed in alphabetical order.

There are standard ways of presenting references. If the reference is to a journal article, it should give the name(s) of the psychologist(s), the date of the article, its title, the name of the journal and its volume number (in italics or underlined), and the page numbers, e.g:

Allport, D.A., Antonis, B., and Reynolds, P. (1972). On the division of attention: A disproof of the single channel hypothesis. *Quarterly Journal of Experimental Psychology, 24*, 225–235.

If the reference is to a book, it should give the name(s) of the psychologist(s), the date of the book, the book title (in italics or underlined), the place of publication, and the publisher, e.g:

Gibson, J.J. (1966). *The senses considered as perceptual systems*. Boston: Houghton Mifflin.

Textbooks have a list of detailed references at the end, so usually you will be able to copy the reference from the book in which you found the theory or study. You may also have used information from a website. Some websites include references, but if not, you need to give full details of the URL.

It is a good idea at the planning stage of your research to make a note of the sources of the material you intend to use. This will make it very much easier to track down the references when you come to complete your report.

Appendices

You are likely to have several appendices which you have referred to in the method and results sections. Make sure that your appendices are numbered in the order in which they are referred to in the report, and that you use these numbers when referring to them in the main body of the report.

Notes on activities

2 **1** Spearman's r_s; **2** Wilcoxon signed ranks; **3** Spearman's rho; **4** chi square; **5** Mann–Whitney U; **6** sign test; **7** Wilcoxon signed ranks; **8** chi square; **9** Mann–Whitney U; **10** Wilcoxon signed ranks.

3

scores	17	17	14	14	14	12	9	6	6
ranks	8.5	8.5	6	6	6	4	3	1.5	1.5

4 This is a one-tailed hypothesis, because it is directional; it was predicted that people who sorted semantically would remember more words than those who sorted structurally. The critical value of U at $p = 0.05$, one-tailed, where $n_1 = 9$ and $n_2 = 11$, is 27. Since the calculated value of 12 is smaller than this, the results are significant at this level and the research hypothesis can be accepted and the null hypothesis rejected ($p < 0.05$). It is also smaller than the critical value of 18 at $p = 0.01$, and the critical value of 16 at $p = 0.005$. It is therefore significant at the most stringent level available; there is a probability of only 0.005 (or 5 in 1000) that the differences between the two conditions could have come about by chance. The research hypothesis can therefore be accepted with 99.5% confidence.

5 The research hypothesis is one-tailed, since it predicts that people will take longer to identify the colours of the colour-associated words than the neutral words. The critical value for a one-tailed test at $p = 0.05$, where $n = 9$, is 8. Since the calculated value of 3 is smaller than 8, the results are significant at this level. Since the calculated value of 3 is equal to the critical value at $p = 0.01$, the results are also significant at this level, the most stringent level available for this test for a sample of this size. There is therefore a probability of only 0.01 (or 1 in 100) that the differences between the two conditions have come about by chance. The research hypothesis can be accepted with 99% confidence.

6 There is a fairly strong correlation between the two variables being measured, though it is a far from perfect correlation. The calculated value of r_s at 0.603 is larger than the critical value of 0.564 for a one-tailed hypothesis at $p = 0.05$, where $n = 10$. The results are therefore significant at this level ($p < 0.05$). The calculated value is not larger than the critical value at $p = 0.025$, so the results fail to reach this level of significance. However, as the 5% level is the conventional level used in psychological research, the research hypothesis can be accepted and the null hypothesis rejected.

7 The research hypothesis is two-tailed, since it is just suggested that there will be a difference in the helpfulness of men and of women; there is no indication as to whether men or women are likely to be more helpful. The critical value of χ^2 for a two-tailed hypothesis at $p = 0.05$ is 3.84. Since the calculated value of 5.29 is larger than this, the results are significant at this level ($p < 0.05$). However, the critical value of 5.41 at $p = 0.02$ is larger than the calculated value, so the results are not significant at this more stringent level.

8 The research hypothesis was one-tailed, since it was predicted that children who could not conserve on a standard Piagetian task would be able to do so on a task which made 'human sense'. Where $n = 7$, the critical value of S at $p = 0.05$, one-tailed, is 0. Since this is less than the calculated value, the research hypothesis cannot be supported, and the null hypothesis must be retained.

Appendix 1: Tables for Mann–Whitney U test

Critical values of U for a one-tailed test at 0.05; two-tailed test at 0.10* (Mann–Whitney)

n_1

n_2	1	2	3	4	5	6	7	8	9	10	11	12	13	14	15	16	17	18	19	20
1	–	–	–	–	–	–	–	–	–	–	–	–	–	–	–	–	–	–	0	0
2	–	–	–	–	0	0	0	1	1	1	1	2	2	3	3	3	3	4	4	4
3	–	–	0	0	1	2	2	3	3	4	5	5	6	7	7	8	9	9	10	11
4	–	–	0	1	2	3	4	5	6	7	8	9	10	11	12	14	15	16	17	18
5	–	0	1	2	4	5	6	8	9	11	12	13	15	16	18	19	20	22	23	25
6	–	0	2	3	5	7	8	10	12	14	16	17	19	21	23	25	26	28	30	32
7	–	0	2	4	6	8	11	13	15	17	19	21	24	26	28	30	33	35	37	39
8	–	1	3	5	8	10	13	15	18	20	23	26	28	31	33	36	39	41	44	47
9	–	1	3	6	9	12	15	18	21	24	27	30	33	36	39	42	45	48	51	54
10	–	1	4	7	11	14	17	20	24	27	31	34	37	41	44	48	51	55	58	62
11	–	1	5	8	12	16	19	23	27	31	34	38	42	46	50	54	57	61	65	69
12	–	2	5	9	13	17	21	26	30	34	38	42	47	51	55	60	64	68	72	77
13	–	2	6	10	15	19	24	28	33	37	42	47	51	56	61	65	70	75	80	84
14	–	3	7	11	16	21	26	31	36	41	46	51	56	61	66	71	77	82	87	92
15	–	3	7	12	18	23	28	33	39	44	50	55	61	66	72	77	83	88	94	100
16	–	3	8	14	19	25	30	36	42	48	54	60	65	71	77	83	89	95	101	107
17	–	3	9	15	20	26	33	39	45	51	57	64	70	77	83	89	96	102	109	115
18	–	4	9	16	22	28	35	41	48	55	61	68	75	82	88	95	102	109	116	123
19	0	4	10	17	23	30	37	44	51	58	65	72	80	87	94	101	109	116	123	130
20	0	4	11	18	25	32	39	47	54	62	69	77	84	92	100	107	115	123	130	138

* Dashes in the body of the table indicate that no decision is possible at the stated level of significance.

For any n_1 and n_2 the observed value of U is significant at a given level of significance if it is *equal to* or *less than* the critical values shown.

SOURCE: Runyon R and Haber A, *Fundamentals of Behavioural Statistics* (3rd edn.), Reading, MA: McGraw-Hill, Inc (1976). With the kind permission of the author.

Critical values of U for a one-tailed test at 0.025; two-tailed test at 0.05* (Mann–Whitney)

n_1

n_2	1	2	3	4	5	6	7	8	9	10	11	12	13	14	15	16	17	18	19	20
1	–	–	–	–	–	–	–	–	–	–	–	–	–	–	–	–	–	–	–	–
2	–	–	–	–	–	–	–	0	0	0	0	1	1	1	1	1	2	2	2	2
3	–	–	–	–	0	1	1	2	2	3	3	4	4	5	5	6	6	7	7	8
4	–	–	–	0	1	2	3	4	4	5	6	7	8	9	10	11	11	12	13	14
5	–	–	0	1	2	3	5	6	7	8	9	11	12	13	14	15	17	18	19	20
6	–	–	1	2	3	5	6	8	10	11	13	14	16	17	19	21	22	24	25	27
7	–	–	1	3	5	6	8	10	12	14	16	18	20	22	24	26	28	30	32	34
8	–	0	2	4	6	8	10	13	15	17	19	22	24	26	29	31	34	36	38	41
9	–	0	2	4	7	10	12	15	17	20	23	26	28	31	34	37	39	42	45	48
10	–	0	3	5	8	11	14	17	20	23	26	29	33	36	39	42	45	48	52	55
11	–	0	3	6	9	13	16	19	23	26	30	33	37	40	44	47	51	55	58	62
12	–	1	4	7	11	14	18	22	26	29	33	37	41	45	49	53	57	61	65	69
13	–	1	4	8	12	16	20	24	28	33	37	41	45	50	54	59	63	67	72	76
14	–	1	5	9	13	17	22	26	31	36	40	45	50	55	59	64	67	74	78	83
15	–	1	5	10	14	19	24	29	34	39	44	49	54	59	64	70	75	80	85	90
16	–	1	6	11	15	21	26	31	37	42	47	53	59	64	70	75	81	86	92	98
17	–	2	6	11	17	22	28	34	39	45	51	57	63	67	75	81	87	93	99	105
18	–	2	7	12	18	24	30	36	42	48	55	61	67	74	80	86	93	99	106	112
19	–	2	7	13	19	25	32	38	45	52	58	65	72	78	85	92	99	106	113	119
20	–	2	8	14	20	27	34	41	48	55	62	69	76	83	90	98	105	112	119	127

* Dashes in the body of the table indicate that no decision is possible at the stated level of significance.

For any n_1 and n_2 the observed value of U is significant at a given level of significance if it is *equal to* or *less than* the critical values shown.

SOURCE: Runyon R and Haber A, *Fundamentals of Behavioural Statistics* (3rd edn.), Reading, MA: McGraw-Hill,Inc (1976). With the kind permission of the author

Critical values of U for a one-tailed test at 0.01; two-tailed test at 0.02* (Mann–Whitney)

n_1

n_2	1	2	3	4	5	6	7	8	9	10	11	12	13	14	15	16	17	18	19	20
1	—	—	—	—	—	—	—	—	—	—	—	—	—	—	—	—	—	—	—	—
2	—	—	—	—	—	—	—	—	—	—	—	—	0	0	0	0	0	0	1	1
3	—	—	—	—	—	—	0	0	1	1	1	2	2	2	3	3	4	4	4	5
4	—	—	—	—	0	1	1	2	3	3	4	5	5	6	7	7	8	9	9	10
5	—	—	—	0	1	2	3	4	5	6	7	8	9	10	11	12	13	14	15	16
6	—	—	—	1	2	3	4	6	7	8	9	11	12	13	15	16	18	19	20	22
7	—	—	0	1	3	4	6	7	9	11	12	14	16	17	19	21	23	24	26	28
8	—	—	0	2	4	6	7	9	11	13	15	17	20	22	24	26	28	30	32	34
9	—	—	1	3	5	7	9	11	14	16	18	21	23	26	28	31	33	36	38	40
10	—	—	1	3	6	8	11	13	16	19	22	24	27	30	33	36	38	41	44	47
11	—	—	1	4	7	9	12	15	18	22	25	28	31	34	37	41	44	47	50	53
12	—	—	2	5	8	11	14	17	21	24	28	31	35	38	42	46	49	53	56	60
13	—	0	2	5	9	12	16	20	23	27	31	35	39	43	47	51	55	59	63	67
14	—	0	2	6	10	13	17	22	26	30	34	38	43	47	51	56	60	65	69	73
15	—	0	3	7	11	15	19	24	28	33	37	42	47	51	56	61	66	70	75	80
16	—	0	3	7	12	16	21	26	31	36	41	46	51	56	61	66	71	76	82	87
17	—	0	4	8	13	18	23	28	33	38	44	49	55	60	66	71	77	82	88	93
18	—	0	4	9	14	19	24	30	36	41	47	53	59	65	70	76	82	88	94	100
19	—	1	4	9	15	20	26	32	38	44	50	56	63	69	75	82	88	94	101	107
20	—	1	5	10	16	22	28	34	40	47	53	60	67	73	80	87	93	100	107	114

* Dashes in the body of the table indicate that no decision is possible at the stated level of significance.

For any n_1 and n_2 the observed value of U is significant at a given level of significance if it is *equal to* or *less than* the critical values shown.

SOURCE: Runyon R and Haber A, *Fundamentals of Behavioural Statistics* (3rd edn.), Reading, MA: McGraw-Hill,Inc (1976). With the kind permission of the author

Critical values of U for a one-tailed test at 0.005; two-tailed test at 0.01* (Mann–Whitney)

n_1

n_2	1	2	3	4	5	6	7	8	9	10	11	12	13	14	15	16	17	18	19	20
1	–	–	–	–	–	–	–	–	–	–	–	–	–	–	–	–	–	–	–	–
2	–	–	–	–	–	–	–	–	–	–	–	–	–	–	–	–	–	–	0	0
3	–	–	–	–	–	–	–	–	0	0	0	1	1	1	2	2	2	2	3	3
4	–	–	–	–	–	0	0	1	1	2	2	3	3	4	5	5	6	6	7	8
5	–	–	–	–	0	1	1	2	3	4	5	6	7	7	8	9	10	11	12	14
6	–	–	–	0	1	2	3	4	5	6	7	9	10	11	12	13	15	16	17	18
7	–	–	–	0	1	3	4	6	7	9	10	12	13	15	16	18	19	21	22	24
8	–	–	0	1	2	4	6	7	9	11	13	15	17	18	20	22	24	26	28	30
9	–	–	0	1	3	5	7	9	11	13	16	18	20	22	24	27	29	31	33	36
10	–	–	0	2	4	6	9	11	13	16	18	21	24	26	29	31	34	37	39	42
11	–	–	0	2	5	7	10	13	16	18	21	24	27	30	33	36	39	42	45	48
12	–	–	1	3	6	9	12	15	18	21	24	27	31	34	37	41	44	47	51	54
13	–	–	1	3	7	10	13	17	20	24	27	31	34	38	42	45	49	53	57	60
14	–	–	1	4	7	11	15	18	22	26	30	34	38	42	46	50	54	58	63	67
15	–	–	2	5	8	12	16	20	24	29	33	37	42	46	51	55	60	64	69	73
16	–	–	2	5	9	13	18	22	27	31	36	41	45	50	55	60	65	70	74	79
17	–	–	2	6	10	15	19	24	29	34	39	44	49	54	60	65	70	75	81	86
18	–	–	2	6	11	16	21	26	31	37	42	47	53	58	64	70	75	81	87	92
19	–	0	3	7	12	17	22	28	33	39	45	51	57	63	69	74	81	87	93	99
20	–	0	3	8	14	18	24	30	36	42	48	54	60	67	73	79	86	92	99	105

* Dashes in the body of the table indicate that no decision is possible at the stated level of significance.

For any n_1 and n_2 the observed value of U is significant at a given level of significance if it is *equal to* or *less than* the critical values shown.

SOURCE: Runyon R and Haber A, *Fundamentals of Behavioural Statistics* (3rd edn.), Reading, MA: McGraw-Hill,Inc (1976).

Appendix 2: Tables for Wilcoxon signed ranks test

Critical values of T in the Wilcoxon signed ranks test

	Level of significance for a two-tailed test			
	0.10	0.05	0.02	0.002
	Level of significance for a one-tailed test			
	0.05	0.025	0.01	0.001
n = 5	0	–	–	–
6	2	0	–	–
7	3	2	0	–
8	5	3	1	–
9	8	5	3	–
10	10	8	5	0
11	13	10	7	1
12	17	13	9	2
13	21	17	12	4
14	25	21	15	6
15	30	25	19	8
16	35	29	23	11
17	41	34	27	14
18	47	40	32	18
19	53	46	37	21
20	60	52	43	26
21	67	58	49	30
22	75	65	55	35
23	83	73	62	40
24	91	81	69	45
25	100	89	76	51
26	110	98	84	58
27	119	107	92	64
28	130	116	101	71
29	140	126	110	79
30	151	137	120	86
31	163	147	130	94
32	175	159	140	103
33	187	170	151	112

Calculated value of *T* must EQUAL or BE LESS THAN the table (critical) value for significance at the level shown.

SOURCE: Adapted from Meddis R, *Statistical Handbook for Non-Statisticians*, London: McGraw-Hill (1975).

Appendix 3: Tables for Spearman's coefficient r_S

Critical values of Spearman's coefficient r_S

	Level of significance for a two-tailed test			
	0.10	0.05	0.02	0.01
	Level of significance for a one-tailed test			
	0.05	0.025	0.01	0.005
$n = 4$	1.000	–	–	–
5	0.900	1.000	1.000	–
6	0.829	0.886	0.943	1.000
7	0.714	0.786	0.893	0.929
8	0.643	0.738	0.833	0.881
9	0.600	0.700	0.783	0.833
10	0.564	0.648	0.745	0.794
11	0.536	0.618	0.709	0.755
12	0.503	0.587	0.678	0.727
13	0.484	0.560	0.648	0.703
14	0.464	0.538	0.626	0.679
15	0.446	0.521	0.604	0.654
16	0.429	0.503	0.582	0.635
17	0.414	0.488	0.566	0.618
18	0.401	0.472	0.550	0.600
19	0.391	0.460	0.535	0.584
20	0.380	0.447	0.522	0.570
21	0.370	0.436	0.509	0.556
22	0.361	0.425	0.497	0.544
23	0.353	0.416	0.486	0.532
24	0.344	0.407	0.476	0.521
25	0.337	0.398	0.466	0.511
26	0.331	0.390	0.457	0.501
27	0.324	0.383	0.449	0.492
28	0.318	0.375	0.440	0.483
29	0.312	0.368	0.433	0.475
30	0.306	0.362	0.425	0.467

Calculated value of r_S must EQUAL or EXCEED the table (critical) value for significance at the level shown.

SOURCE: Zhar J H, Significance testing of the Spearman Rank Correlation Coefficient, *Journal of the American Statistical Association 67*, 578–80.

Appendix 4: Tables for chi square (χ^2)

Critical values of χ^2

	Level of significance for a two-tailed test					
	0.02	0.10	0.05	0.02	0.01	0.001
	Level of significance for a one-tailed test					
df	0.10	0.05	0.025	0.01	0.005	0.0005
1	1.64	2.71	3.84	5.41	6.63	10.83
2	3.22	4.60	5.99	7.82	9.21	13.82
3	4.64	6.25	7.82	9.84	11.34	16.27
4	5.99	7.78	9.49	11.67	13.28	18.47
5	7.29	9.24	11.07	13.39	15.09	20.52
6	8.56	10.64	12.59	15.03	16.81	22.46
7	9.80	12.02	14.07	16.62	18.48	24.32
8	11.03	13.36	15.51	18.17	20.09	26.12
9	12.24	14.68	16.92	19.68	21.67	27.88
10	13.44	15.99	18.31	21.16	23.21	29.59
11	14.63	17.28	19.68	22.62	24.72	31.26
12	15.81	18.55	21.03	24.05	26.22	32.91
13	16.98	19.81	22.36	25.47	27.69	34.53
14	18.15	21.06	23.68	26.87	29.14	36.12
15	19.31	22.31	25.00	28.26	30.58	37.70
16	20.46	23.54	26.30	29.63	32.00	39.25
17	21.62	24.77	27.59	31.00	33.41	40.79
18	22.76	25.99	28.87	32.35	34.81	42.31
19	23.90	27.20	30.14	33.69	36.19	43.82
20	25.04	28.41	31.41	35.02	37.57	45.31
21	26.17	29.62	32.67	36.34	38.93	46.80
22	27.30	30.81	33.92	37.66	40.29	48.27
23	28.43	32.01	35.17	38.97	41.64	49.73
24	29.55	33.20	36.42	40.27	42.98	51.18
25	30.68	34.38	37.65	41.57	44.31	52.62
26	31.80	35.56	38.88	42.86	45.64	54.05
27	32.91	36.74	40.11	44.14	46.96	55.48
28	34.03	37.92	41.34	45.42	48.28	56.89
29	35.14	39.09	42.56	49.69	49.59	58.30
30	36.25	40.26	43.77	47.96	50.89	59.70
32	38.47	42.59	46.19	50.49	53.49	62.49
34	40.68	44.90	48.60	53.00	56.06	65.25
36	42.88	47.21	51.00	55.49	58.62	67.99
38	45.08	49.51	53.38	57.97	61.16	70.70
40	47.27	51.81	55.76	60.44	63.69	73.40
44	51.64	56.37	60.48	65.34	68.71	78.75
48	55.99	60.91	65.17	70.20	73.68	84.04
52	60.33	65.42	69.83	75.02	78.62	89.27
56	64.66	69.92	74.47	79.82	83.51	94.46
60	68.97	74.40	79.08	84.58	88.38	99.61

Calculated value of χ^2 must EQUAL or EXCEED the table (critical) value for significance at the level shown.

Abridged from Fisher R A and Yates F, *Statistical Tables for Biological, Agricultural and Medical Research* (6th edn), Longman Group Ltd (1974).

Appendix 5: Tables for the binomial sign test

Critical values of S in the binominal sign test

	Level of significance for a two-tailed test				
	0.10	0.05	0.02	0.01	0.001
	Level of significance for a one-tailed test				
	0.05	0.025	0.01	0.005	0.0005
$n =$ 5	0	–	–	–	–
6	0	0	–	–	–
7	0	0	0	–	–
8	1	0	0	0	–
9	1	1	0	0	–
10	1	1	0	0	0
11	2	1	1	0	0
12	2	2	1	1	0
13	3	2	1	1	0
14	3	2	2	1	0
15	3	3	2	2	1
16	4	3	2	2	1
17	4	4	3	2	1
18	5	4	3	3	1
19	5	4	4	3	2
20	5	5	4	3	2
25	7	7	6	5	4
30	10	9	8	7	5
35	12	11	10	9	7

Calculated value of *S* must EQUAL or BE LESS THAN the table (critical) value for significance at the level shown.

SOURCE: Clegg F, *Simple Statistics*, Cambridge University Press (1982).

Appendix 6: Sample research report

The effect of the type of processing on the amount of information recalled

Comment: A good title, linking the IV and the DV

Abstract

The Levels of Processing model of memory devised by Craik and Lockhart (1972) has three levels of processing information: structural, phonological and semantic. Semantic is the deepest level, phonological is more shallow and structural the shallowest. The model proposes that information processed at a deeper level will be remembered better than information processed at a more shallow level. This study aimed to test the idea that participants who used semantic processing would recall more words than those who used phonological processing.

An opportunity sample of twenty participants was asked to carry out a task matching pairs of words that rhymed (phonological condition) or had opposite meanings (semantic condition). The participants believed that they were being tested on the speed with which they matched up the pairs. Participants were given an unexpected recall test to see how many words they had remembered.

The Mann–Whitney U test was carried out to analyse the data. The calculated value of U was 44.5. This exceeded the critical value of 27 for a one-tailed hypothesis at $p = 0.05$, meaning the results were not significant, and the research hypothesis was not supported. This means that there was no significant difference in the number of words recalled at each level of processing.

The results may be due to theoretical flaws in the LOP model, in particular the idea that not only the level of processing but also the amount of time and effort spent on a problem may be a factor. There could also have been faults in the materials used to test participants. Some of the words were similar in meaning. This could have led to interference, or 'chunking', affecting recall.

Comment: A good, succinct summary of the background to the study, how it was carried out, what the results were, and how they might be interpreted.

The student could have made brief reference to a study supporting the LOP model in the first paragraph, and the theoretical criticism in the final paragraph could have been a little clearer.

Introduction

In 1972, Craik and Lockhart attempted to move away from models of memory such as Atkinson and Shiffrin's multi-store model (1968) by proposing the Levels of Processing (LOP) model. This concentrates on the type of processing involved in memory, rather than suggesting that there are different STM and LTM stores. It suggests that remembering information is a by-product of processing, rather than processing being a means of organising information.

There are three levels of processing. The structural level is the most shallow. It involves analysing a word by physical characteristics, such as whether it is written in capital letters or not. A deeper stage is the phonological level. Here it is the sound of the word which is examined. The deepest level of processing involves analysing the word for meaning. It is known as the semantic level. Craik and Lockhart claimed that the deeper the level of processing, the more information would be retained.

Craik and Watkins (1973) differentiated between two types of rehearsal, which relate to different levels of the LOP model. Maintenance rehearsal is the repetition of information, relating to the phonological level of the LOP. Elaborative rehearsal relates to the semantic level of processing. It may involve composing a story or devising an image to link pieces of information.

Support for the LOP model comes from Craik and Tulving (1975). In this study, participants had to perform a variety of tasks on lists of words, which corresponded to different levels of processing. They were given an unexpected recognition test. Words which had been processed at a deeper level were remembered more than those processed at a shallower level.

In the Elias and Perfetti (1973) study, participants had to perform similar tasks to those in the Craik and Tulving study on a list of words. They were presented with an unexpected recall test, a technique called incidental learning. They found words from the deeper level of processing were more likely to be remembered.

The aim of this study was to test the LOP theory by comparing recall, using an unexpected recall test, when semantic and phonological processing is carried out. A one-tailed experimental hypothesis was devised. A one-tailed hypothesis was appropriate as the LOP model and the research supporting it predicted the direction of the results. Semantic processing would induce a higher level of recall than phonological processing.

The experimental hypothesis is:

Participants who carry out a task requiring semantic processing of words will recall more words in an unexpected recall test than participants who carry out a task requiring phonological processing.

The null hypothesis is:

There will be no difference in the amount of information recalled by participants who use different types of processing.

Comment: The underlying theory here is well explained. The research studies supporting the theory are well chosen, though the description of both could have given slightly more detail about the methods followed, i.e. the nature of the tasks to be carried out. The aims are clear, and the directional hypothesis is clearly justified. The hypotheses include the IV and the DV, and are well set out.

Method

Design

The experiment used an unrelated design, with independent measures. This ruled out the possibility of demand characteristics, and eliminated order effects.

There were two experimental groups. The task for condition 1 required phonological processing (matching pairs of rhyming words). The task for condition 2 required semantic processing (matching pairs of words with opposite meanings). The independent variable was the type of processing used in carrying out each task. The dependent variable was the number of words the participants could remember.

The study was carried out in a quiet room to minimise distractions from noise. All participants were tested on their own by the same experimenter.

The minimum level of statistical significance to be accepted was $p < 0.05$, because this is the conventional level in psychological research, unless there are safety implications, or existing research is being challenged.

Comment: The information here is in general clearly and succinctly put across. However, the use of an independent measures design does not rule out the possibility of demand characteristics, though it does help to reduce this possibility. Some indication could have been given as to what kinds of order effects might occur; in particular, an independent measures design was necessary here because the recall test needed to be unexpected. This would not have been possible if a repeated measures design had been used.

Participants

Twenty participants were tested. Ten participants were alternately allocated to each of the conditions. The participants were approximately 16–19 years of age, and included males and females. An opportunity sample was drawn on the basis of availability from a population of college students.

Comment: Again, brief but to the point. The student could have indicated how many males and how many females were tested, and if there were the same numbers of each in each condition. Given that the participants were asked to process words, it might have been worth mentioning that they were all native English speakers.

Materials

Each condition required a set of cards, with one word written on each card. A sample of the cards can be found in appendix 1. The words used were selected from a dictionary on the basis that they had fewer than eight letters, and were not more than two syllables long. The words also had to be frequently found in everyday language, so participants in the semantic condition could match them by meaning.

In the phonological condition (condition 1), the words were matched by sound, by checking that the end of the word had the same phonetic groups. In the semantic condition, the second word of the pair was found by reading the dictionary definition of a chosen word and finding a word with an approximately opposite definition.

Five confederates of the experimenter were provided with one word of the pairs and asked to supply the other word, to check the validity of the pairs. A full list of all the words can be found in appendix 2.

The experiment also used a stopwatch to time how long participants took to match the words (the task they believed they were being tested on), together with standardised instructions and a standardised debrief. These can be found in appendix 3.

Comment: The student doesn't state here how many word pairs were used in each condition. This information is available in appendix 2, but it should be included here too for ease of communication. Appendix 1 contained four sample cards, one pair from each condition. This is quite sufficient, since a complete list of words was included as appendix 2.

The criteria for selecting particular words are perhaps a little wide, but this is a problem picked up in the discussion. It was a good idea to check the validity of the pairs before carrying out the study.

The standardised instructions in appendix 3 set out clearly what the task was. A detailed standardised debrief is not really necessary; debriefing participants is part of a well-planned study, but apart from explaining the deception involved and why it was necessary, the experimenter could perhaps respond to the individual participant, in terms of how much they are interested in knowing about the study.

Procedure

The procedure for one participant is described below. It was followed for all the other participants. Each participant was tested alone.

A potential participant was approached and asked if they would like to take part in a psychology study. If they agreed, they were taken to a quiet room and the oral instructions were delivered. The participant was given the shuffled word cards and timed while they sorted them into matching pairs. In condition 1 (phonological) the words were sorted into pairs of rhyming words. In condition 2 (semantic) the cards were sorted into pairs with opposite meanings.

The participant was then asked to count out loud backwards from 200 down to zero in threes, at the rate of about one number a second, to prevent rehearsal from taking place. The cards were then collected in. When the participant had reached zero they were asked to recall as many words from the cards as possible in three minutes.

Finally, the participant was thanked and debriefed. This debriefing helped to combat the ethical problem of deceiving participants to prevent demand characteristics.

Comment: The student explains clearly and succinctly how the test was carried out. However, there seems no reason why an intervening task was used between sorting and recall. This kind of task is useful when participants are aware that they are taking part in a memory experiment, and the experimenter suspects that as there is only a limited amount of information to be learned, there may be a ceiling effect, i.e. all participants are likely to get high scores. This would mean that the test would not discriminate between participants. As the recall test here was unexpected, this kind of problem is highly unlikely. However, if an intervening task were to be used, this should have been mentioned in the 'Design' section. Perhaps a little more could have been made of the ethical concerns, i.e. that the deception involved was fairly minimal and unlikely to have caused any serious problems.

Results

A summary of the data collected in the study can be seen in the table and bar chart below. The raw data can be found in appendix 4.

Table to show the mean number of words remembered in each condition

	Condition 1 (phonological)	Condition 2 (semantic)
mean number of words remembered	16	17.1

Bar chart showing the mean number of words remembered

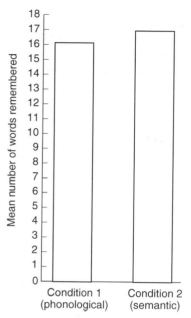

The table and bar chart show that the participants in condition 2 (semantic processing) recalled slightly more words on average than those in condition 1 (phonological processing), though the difference is very small.

A statistical test was carried out to see if this difference was significant. The experiment was a test of difference between the two conditions, and used an independent measures design. The data were determined to be of at least ordinal level, since the scores could be ranked. The Mann–Whitney U test was therefore used to analyse the data.

The calculated value of U was 44.5 (for calculations see appendix 5). The critical value of U, one-tailed at $p < 0.05$, is 27. Since the calculated value of U exceeds the critical value, the experimental hypothesis was not supported and the null hypothesis must be retained.

There was no significant difference in the number of words remembered between participants using phonological processing and those using semantic processing.

Comment: The table and bar chart are appropriate, and suitably titled and labelled. A frequency polygon showing the distribution of scores in each condition could also have been a good idea. The choice of means as a measure of central tendency was a good one, as the data were fairly precise. The range for each condition could also have been included. The use of the Mann–Whitney U test was fully justified. The results of the test were well set out.

Discussion

The difference between the two conditions was not statistically significant. The findings of this study therefore fail to support the principles of the LOP model. The results fail to replicate the findings of Craik and Tulving (1975) and Elias and Perfetti (1973), described in the introduction. It is possible that the results can be explained by limitations of the LOP model, or they may be the result of methodological flaws in carrying out the study.

Some criticisms have been made of the LOP model. Eysenck (1984) offered support to the model, as it presented memory, attention and perception as interdependent. However, he became frustrated at the lack of comment on how the information is stored and retrieved from memory. Baddeley (1978) also criticised the model for being over-simplified, and describing rather than explaining.

A specific criticism of the model is the difficulty in gauging which type of processing is being used and how much information is retained at each level. There is a circular logic in saying that more information is recalled because it has been processed deeply if the criterion for deep processing is that more information is remembered. The LOP is more of a concept than a portrayal of how memory works.

Another issue is that the model proposes that we do not automatically analyse a word in terms of meaning. It is hard to believe that a participant can look at a word and analyse it purely in terms of what it looks and sounds like, without being aware at some level of what the word means. Theories of attention suggest that automatic processing of all stimuli is unavoidable and without conscious effort. This is supported by the Stroop effect (Stroop 1935), where people take longer to identify the colour ink a word is written in if the word is a different colour word than if it is a word not connected with colour. Craik and Tulving used the term 'overspill coding' to describe the processing of a word at several levels of the model.

Sometimes it is desirable to process a word at more than one level. For example, when learning to speak a foreign language it is necessary to remember both what a word means and what it sounds like. Morris et al (1977) discovered that rhyming words (processed at a shallower level) were remembered better than words processed at a semantic level, if they were eventually to be used in a task relating to sound. This contradicts the LOP model, and suggests the eventual use of information is significant to how it is processed.

Finally, it has been suggested that the different levels of processing correspond not to how information is encoded but the amount of time and effort required to process the information. Tyler et al (1979) found that, despite both conditions using semantic processing, difficult anagrams were remembered better than anagrams which were easier to solve, because participants expended more time and energy on the harder task.

There were some methodological problems with this study. First, it has low ecological validity.

Another concern is the source material used as word cards. All the words were of varying length. Some of the pairings were obvious, using words which are frequently used together, such as 'hard' and 'soft'. The strong link between these words could lead to 'chunking', reducing the amount of information which needed to be stored. There were also similarities between some of the pairs in terms of meaning. For example, 'day' and 'night' and 'light'

and 'dark' are closely related. This could either lead to chunking or cause interference.

An An associated issue is the use of a mixture of concrete and abstract words. The semantic condition used some abstract words, whereas the phonological condition used mostly concrete words. This could have affected the results, as research (e.g. Richardson 1980) has found that imagery aids recall, and it is easier to form a mental image of a concrete word, e.g. 'cat' than an abstract word, e.g. 'justice'.

These concerns could be remedied by revising the word lists. They should contain only concrete words, with the words having the same length and frequency in the language. The pairs of words should not be extremely common, or semantically very similar.

Another issue is that participants may have found some words more personally meaningful than others, and so remember them better. Morris et al (1981) found that information which has a personal meaning is retained better than information which has no personal meaning. It is possible that participants' experiences could cause them to make semantic links between apparently unconnected words. This links to the concept of the spreading activation model of memory (Collins and Loftus 1975).

A major flaw was the relatively small and unrepresentative sample, which means that the results of the study cannot be generalised. To overcome this problem, a future study could use more participants from a wider age range.

However, the study could be modified for future research. The study focused only on retention in the short term. A modified form of the experiment could be implemented a week or two after the original study took place, to see if either form of processing produced better recall in the long term. The effect on recall of processing effort and time could also merit further investigation. Perhaps in one condition participants could be asked to pair obvious pairs of words, whilst the other group could be given more obscure words to pair, which would require more effort.

This is one theory which should be investigated further, as it has practical applications, for example in advising students on the most efficient way of revising. It suggests that strategies such as being tested are a more efficient form of revision than just reading through notes.

Comment: This discussion covered all the necessary areas: links made to the introduction, theoretical issues, methodological problems and how they might be overcome, practical applications and suggestions for future research. Good use was made of relevant theory and research, though in some cases (e.g. the Morris et al. study and the spreading activation model of Collins and Loftus) a little more detail would have been useful. It helps to think about writing for an intelligent and interested reader, but one who has no background knowledge of the theoretical area of the study.

The second and third paragraphs here raised rather general points about the LOP model, which do not help to explain the findings of this study. These kinds of points can legitimately be included in this section, but should perhaps come after the discussion of theoretical problems which might help to explain the results.

The fourth paragraph was well argued, and the argument supported by the Stroop effect. However, the concept of 'overspill coding' is not explained, so it doesn't really contribute much to the argument. Useful material in paragraphs 5 and 6, though a link with the findings of this study could have been explored. It is nice that the theoretical discussion is linked to the real world situation of language learning.

When the student comes to consider methodological problems, the point about ecological validity is sound, but needs a little more explanation in the context of this study. There were some very useful points about the shortcomings of the materials used, together with appropriate suggestions as to what improvements should be made. However, no suggestions were made about how the problem of personally meaningful words could be approached.

There were some sensible suggestions for future research, and a fairly brief mention of practical applications of this area of research, though this could perhaps have been developed in a little more detail.

References

Atkinson RC and Shiffrin RM (1968) Human memory: a proposed system and its control processes. In Spence KW and Spence JT (eds) *The Psychology of Learning and Motivation* (vol.2) London. Academic Press.

Baddeley AD (1978) The trouble with levels: a re-examination of Craik and Lockhart's framework for memory research. *Psychological Review*, 85(3), 139–152.

Collins AM and Loftus EF (1975) A spreading-activation theory of semantic processing. *Psychological Review*, 82, 407–428.

Craik F and Lockhart R (1972) Levels of processing. *Journal of Verbal Learning and Verbal Behaviour*, 11, 671–684.

Craik F and Tulving E (1975) Depth of processing and the retention of words in episodic memory. *Journal of Experimental Psychology: General*, 104, 268–294.

Craik F and Watkins M (1973) The role of rehearsal in short term memory. *Journal of Verbal Learning and Verbal Behaviour*, 12, 599–607.

Elias CF and Perfetti CA (1973) Encoding task and recognition memory: the importance of semantic coding. *Journal of Experimental Psychology*, 99(2), 151–157.

Eysenck MW (1984) Handbook of Cognitive Psychology. Hove: Lawrence Erlbaum Associates.

Morris CD, Bransford JD and Franks JJ (1977) Levels of processing versus transfer appropriate processing. *Journal of Verbal Learning and Verbal Behaviour*, 16, 519–533.

Morris PE et al. (1981) Football knowledge and the aequisition of new results. *British Journal of Psychology*, 72, 479–483.

Richardson JTE (1980) Mental Imagery and Human Memory. London: Macmillan.

Stroop JR (1935) Studies of interference in serial verbal reactions. *Journal of Experimental Psychology*, 18, 643–662.

Tyler SW, Hertel PT, McCallum MC and Ellis HC (1979) Cognitive effort and memory. *Journal of Experimental Psychology (Human Learning and Memory)*, 5(6), 607–617.

27

Issues and debates in psychology

27.1 Gender bias

27.2 Cultural bias

27.3 Ethical issues

27.4 The use of non-human animals

27.5 Free will and determinism
   Freud
   Skinner
   Rogers

27.6 Reductionism

27.7 Is psychology a science?
   Paradigms in science
   Theories and hypotheses
   The scientific method

27.8 The nature–nurture debate

In this final chapter, we will be focusing on issues which apply widely to the many topics covered elsewhere in the book. We will look at the nature of psychology, some of the problems associated with carrying out psychological research, and different views about the nature of the subject matter of this research, i.e. people.

27.1 GENDER BIAS

Psychologists make a distinction between **sex differences**, which result directly from physiological variations, and **gender differences**. For example, a difference between men and women in their capacity for nurturing is a gender difference rather than a sex difference, since it is related to the different ways in which men and women are socialised within a particular culture.

There are obvious sex differences between men and women in terms of their reproductive organs and secondary sexual characteristics. However, there are other biological differences between the sexes, which may have psychological implications. For example, the anatomical structure of the brain differs between men and women. The brains of women are less lateralised than those of men, so that damage to one side of the brain will generally have less effect on a woman than on a man. In addition, women have cerebral hemispheres which are more asymmetrical for speech, and an enlarged back part of the corpus collosum (Allen *et al.*, 1989). There is also evidence that levels of the hormone oestrogen are related to spatial ability in women (Hampson, 1990), with testosterone being similarly related to the spatial performance of men (Kimura, 1992).

While these kinds of differences and their relationship to human functioning are interesting, there is usually considerable overlap in the functioning of men and women. Maccoby and Jacklin (1974) carried out a review of research into sex differences. They found that in most areas, there were no significant differences, or that the differences were very small.

It is therefore possible to exaggerate the differences between men and women. Hare-Mustin and Maracek (1990) use the term **alpha bias** to describe theories which do this. They also describe theories which minimise or ignore any differences between men and women as showing **beta bias**. Theories with alpha bias can sometimes heighten the value placed on women; for example, research carried out by Chodorow (1978) found that women were better at relationships and more caring than men. However, research showing women in a more positive light than men is relatively rare.

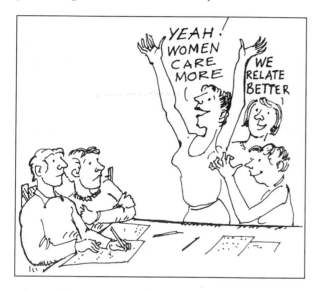

Until very recently, most psychological research was carried out by men, often using only male participants. Erikson (chapters 18 and 19), Asch (chapter 6), Sherif (chapter 10) and Kohlberg (chapter 17) are examples of male researchers who only tested other men. This has often led to **androcentrism**, where male norms and the male viewpoint are assumed to be legitimate for explaining the experiences of both sexes. It is this androcentric approach which may lead to alpha bias, in that women's perceptions, norms and behaviour are defined only in terms of the extent to which they deviate from those of men, or beta bias, when research fails to investigate what may be important gender differences.

These biases mirror a more general distinction in psychology between nomothetic and idiographic approaches. An **idiographic** approach assumes that everyone is different, and therefore focuses (like alpha bias) on individual differences. In contrast, a **nomothetic** approach starts from the general assumption that people are broadly the same, and so (like beta bias) aims to come up with universal theories.

Activity 1: alpha and beta bias

Alpha bias and beta bias are both seen as unhelpful in psychological research. Can you suggest why? How could each lead to discrimination against women?

When you have finished, see the notes on activities on page 757.

Matlin (1993) suggested that theories with beta bias mean that important experiences in women's lives may not be researched:

Activity 2: women's experiences

a Can you think of any life experiences which specifically apply to females, and which might therefore not be researched as a result of beta bias?

b Are there also experiences which are more likely to apply to females than to males, which could be ignored in the same way?

When you have finished, see the notes on activities on page 757.

It has been suggested that Freud's theory takes an androcentric approach. An outline of his theory was given in chapter 1, and there are discussions of aspects of the theory relevant to this topic in chapter 18 (gender development).

Activity 3: androcentrism in Freud's theory

Read through what Freud has to say about gender development. In what ways can these ideas be seen as androcentric? Are they examples of alpha or beta bias?

When you have finished, see the notes on activities on page 757.

Horney (1924), while a psychodynamic psychologist herself, criticised the androcentric bias in Freud's theory, and pointed to the influence of social and cultural factors on development. She suggested that his term **penis envy** should be replaced by **power envy**, reflecting women's feelings of powerlessness in a male-dominated society. Horney's arguments are forerunners of those put forward more recently within the framework of a feminist psychology.

However, Mitchell (1974) challenged the widespread feminist belief that Freud's ideas imply that women are inferior. She suggested that while his ideas have been widely interpreted in this way, and used to justify a social order where women have an inferior status, psychoanalysis is not a recommendation for a patriarchal society, but merely a description of one.

Gender bias, then, can arise either when gender differences are a particular source of focus (alpha bias), or when they are ignored altogether (beta bias). Both represent androcentrism; if women's behaviour varies from the male norm, it may be seen as inferior (alpha bias), and similarly anything outside the male world view may be ignored (beta bias). Both biases can lead to sexism, i.e. discrimination against someone on the basis of their sex.

Sexism can be shown in many ways. Malim and Birch (1998) suggested that one institutional kind of sexism is the failure to appoint women to academic posts in male-dominated universities, or if they are appointed, marginalising them into areas which are not at the forefront of academic research. Although Malim and Birch offer no evidence to support this idea, university departments have traditionally been dominated by men.

Malim and Birch go on to suggest that sexism can also be found in the formulation of research questions. For example, a study might define leadership in terms of aggression and dominance, characteristics which are stereotypically male. However, they again offer no evidence to support this claim, and it would be interesting to see if an analysis of published research confirmed these ideas.

There can also be gender bias in whether or not research is published. Research in any area of psychology which fails to find expected differences is less likely to be published than research where differences are found – the so-called 'file drawer

phenomenon' – so it is likely that research into gender which fails to find any differences between men and women might not be published.

The way in which research is carried out is also an issue. Wilkinson (1986) pointed out that traditionally much mainstream psychological research, carried out by men, has been experimental, using the techniques of manipulation and control. This approach distances the experimenter from those taking part in the study; remember that until very recently, participants were known as 'subjects'. It tends to take participants' behaviour rather than the participants themselves as the unit of study, and so ignores the personal, social and cultural contexts within which it is carried out. If gender differences are found, they may then be assumed to be the result of characteristics of the participants, rather than arising from the research context. As women have become more involved in carrying out psychological research, they have been alerted to what less distant techniques, such as interviews, with their emphasis on personal experience, might have to offer.

The use made of research findings, and the choice of words used to describe gender differences, can also be sexist.

▷ Activity 4: identifying sexism

Read through the following descriptions, and decide how each example could be seen as sexist. Can you also make links with alpha/beta bias and androcentrism?

a Based on Bowlby's maternal deprivation hypothesis (see chapter 2), a researcher sets out to investigate the possible negative effect of working mothers on children's development.

b A researcher is interested in the experience of women workers in male-dominated industries. She plans her project carefully, but fails to attract the funding necessary to carry it out.

c Witkin (1950) suggested that people could be categorised as either 'field-dependent' or 'field-independent'. One way in which this was measured was using the **embedded figures test**, in which a participant is asked to locate a figure which is embedded in a complex design, e.g:

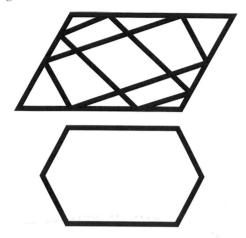

Field-dependent people are those who tend to see things as wholes, so they are influenced by external factors in the context in which they operate; in the embedded figures test, they have difficulty in separating the figure from the context. They are more likely to be women. Field-independent people, on the other hand, are less easily influenced by context. They are more likely to be men.

d Kohlberg tested only men in developing his theory of moral development (see chapter 17), which he then went on to apply to both sexes. He concluded that women reach a lower level of moral development than men.

When you have finished, see the notes on activities on page 757.

So how can gender bias in psychology be eliminated, or at least reduced? Worrell (1992) has made several suggestions:

Figure 1: reducing gender bias (Worrell, 1992)

a Alternative research methods, as outlined above, could be explored.

b Women should be studied in a natural setting.

c Researchers should collaborate with participants to explore personally-relevant variables.

d Samples of women with whom research is carried out should reflect their diversity, e.g. in age, socioeconomic status and ethnic group.

An increasing number of women are involved in psychology, and the subject 'Psychology of Women' is now an option in many degree courses. This is a recognition that in some areas women's experience may be very different from that of men, and so worthy of study in their own right. However, with such courses there needs to be an awareness of possible alpha bias, if bias against women is not to be replaced by an equally inappropriate bias against men.

⊖ There are **psychological differences** between men and women, as well as a large degree of overlap. These differences can lead to **gender bias**.

⊖ Theories which exaggerate these differences show **alpha bias**, while those which minimise them show **beta bias**. Theories biased against women by using the male viewpoint to explain the experiences of both sexes show **androcentrism**, which can be expressed in either alpha or beta bias.

⊖ Gender bias can be shown in many ways, including choice of research, failure to support research, methodology, and the choice of words when describing findings.

27.2 CULTURAL BIAS

A **culture** can be defined as the values, beliefs and patterns of behaviour which are shared by a group of people. Some theorists, e.g. Moghaddam *et al.* (1993), use a somewhat broader definition, which includes not only psychological characteristics, but also physical aspects of a culture, such as works of art and everyday structures. Triandis (1989) proposed that individuals have a **cultural identity**, which is built on norms, values and beliefs, implicitly accepted and shared by a distinguishable group of people, which are passed on from one generation to the next. Of course, there are also differences between individuals within cultures, but there will nonetheless be considerable overlap between people from the same culture.

Within any culture, there will also be **subcultures**, which also have shared value systems. For example, in Britain minority ethnic groups form subcultures. It could also be argued that there is a distinct youth subculture. However, it is likely that members of different cultures will have more in common with other members of that culture than with other cultural groups, in spite of differences between subcultures.

Cultures are shaped by a wide variety of factors, and these different influences are reflected in wide differences between various cultures, which may in turn have psychological implications. Some of these influences are **ecological**, e.g. climate and geographical features. Luria (1976) gave a striking example of how ecological factors can affect culture; he pointed out that cultures living near the Arctic circle have a wide range of words for different shades of white, but none for the different shades of red and green. A further example is the relationship between geographical features and perception, e.g. in susceptibility to visual illusions (see chapter 15). **Sociopolitical** factors also influence culture. These include political systems, migration, invasion, patterns of trade, and so on.

the bad news is that they have 36 words for different sorts of mud.

In chapter 17, the theories of cognitive development developed by Piaget and Vygotsky were discussed. Piaget grew up in Switzerland, in a Western capitalist society, where the focus was on individual choice, needs, responsibility, and personal achievement. Vygotsky, on the other hand, grew up in the former Soviet Union, under Marxism, where the emphasis was on the goals and needs of the social group, and the duty of the individual towards the group. Given Piaget's emphasis on development being driven by the actions of the individual on the environment, and Vygotsky's claim that development must be considered within the cultural context in which it takes place, the differences between their theories seem to reflect these two very different cultures.

This is an example of the distinction drawn by Hsu (1971) between **individualist** and **collectivist** cultures, discussed in the final section of chapter 9, in the context of different kinds of close personal relationships. However, there are many other ways in which cultures may differ. One example is in what are seen as priorities in life; some cultures stress the importance of work and achievement, while others are more concerned with the quality of life and relationships between people. Another example is how emotions are managed. In some cultures, it is usual to express emotions freely, while in others it is thought that emotional expression should be controlled.

You may have read about research in other cultures in many areas of psychology covered in this book. However, the vast majority of psychological research has been carried out in the Western world, and in particular in the United States, and most of the research you have read about is American or British. Since so much of the research has been carried out on such a restricted sample of people, there is a danger of cultural bias, and of assuming that what is true of one culture is universally true. For example, in Western culture, aggression may be seen as natural, so it could be assumed that this must be universally true for all cultures. A further possible source of cultural bias lies in deciding what questions are worthy of study. For example, the factors influencing initial attraction in relationships have been heavily researched, while the way that love develops in an arranged marriage has hardly been covered at all.

The restricted range of cultures within which much psychological research is carried out can lead to **ethnocentrism**, i.e. a tendency to consider the standards, norms and behaviour of one's own culture as the baselines against which those of other cultures can be evaluated, in terms of the extent to which they deviate from those of the home culture. If we take an ethnocentric approach, we have a tendency to believe that our own culture's ways of behaving are correct, and if other cultures' practices are different, they are inferior. Ethnocentrism can be contrasted with **cultural relativism**, where information about a culture is interpreted within the context of that culture.

At the same time, in many topic areas you have read about cross-cultural research. This has enabled us to test whether psychological theories are universally applicable, or related only to our own culture. More recent research into other cultures

has carried out such research as a way of looking at how different social systems link to psychological variations between cultures. However, the results of such research have sometimes been interpreted in an ethnocentric way.

Ethnocentrism and cultural relativism can be linked to the **emic/etic** distinction relating to research in other cultures. Pike (1966), drawing on the field of linguistics, noted the distinction between phon*emics* (sounds which are unique to a particular language) and phon*etics* (universal language sounds). He extended this distinction to methods used in psychological research in relation to culture.

Emics is the study of a culture from within, using its own terms, with the help of members of that culture. Participant observation can be a useful method in this approach, since it should provide a good insight into the nature of the culture. Cultural relativism underlies this approach.

Etics, on the other hand, is the study of a culture from the outside, using criteria which are assumed to be common to the culture being studied and the home culture. It rests on the assumption that there are psychological universals; Kohlberg's theory of moral development is a good example (see chapter 17). An etic approach might take the form of tests which have been developed in the home culture, and merely translated where necessary for use in other cultures. This is called the **imposed etic**, because the criteria used for the home culture are also those used in studying a different culture. The etic approach can be linked with ethnocentrism.

There has been some criticism of the etic approach, since the criteria used by the home culture may not be appropriate to other cultures. For example, in the area of helping behaviour, Western economic theories involving profit and loss, such as exchange theory and Piliavin's arousal:cost-reward model (see chapter 10), may not be relevant to cultures where individual benefit is of less importance than the well-being of the social group. Similarly, the relatively greater diagnosis of some mental disorders among immigrant populations may reflect prejudice or misunderstanding by the person making the diagnosis (see chapter 6).

A further problem is that the results of psychological investigations can be interpreted to fit political ideas. For example, cultural differences in measured intelligence were interpreted in a way which sanctioned racist policies: the interpretation of IQ scores as reflecting innate ability led to restricted immigration into the USA in the 1920s for some cultural groups.

An etic approach can lead to value judgements being made about other cultures. Any differences between the home culture and another culture can result in the other culture being seen as inferior; in other words, the etic approach can lead to ethnocentrism. Researchers may not even be aware that they are using an imposed etic. We will look at some examples of research in this area:

Activity 5: the imposed etic

Some examples of this kind of research include:
Ainsworth's Strange Situation technique (chapter 2)
Intelligence testing (chapter 17)

For each of these topic areas, consider:
1 What kinds of cultural differences have been identified?
2 If an ethnocentric view of the findings were taken, what conclusions could be drawn from this research?
3 What might be the practical implications of these conclusions?
4 What factors within the cultures being studied do you think need to be considered to understand these cross-cultural differences?
When you have finished, see the notes on activities on page 757.

The etic approach also has practical problems. In particular, it may be difficult to replicate a study exactly in another culture. Also, where similar studies are carried out, there may nonetheless be important differences; for instance, in the people tested. This is shown by replication in different cultures of the study of obedience originally carried out by Milgram (1963). Here are some examples:

Figure 2: cross-cultural replications of Milgram's study

researcher	country	sample	% showing obedience
Milgram (1963)	USA	men (gen. pop.)	65%
Kilham and Mann (1974)	Australia	women students	16%
Meeus and Raaijmakers (1986)	Holland	general population	92%

In these three studies, the differences in the percentages of those tested who were willing to harm an innocent victim are quite startling. It would be possible to interpret these differences in terms of culture, since the three studies were carried out in different cultures. However, the nature of the samples tested also varied in gender, which could mean that gender is a factor in obedience. In addition, the studies were carried out at widely different times, another possible factor. These kinds of complications are one of the factors which make an etic approach problematic.

However, Pike (1990) pointed out that the emic/etic distinction is not a rigid one, but often involves looking at the same data from two different points of view. Morever, the etic approach is not without its uses. He suggested that such an approach can give us a broad, global perspective on an issue, highlighting similarities and differences across cultures. There may also be more practical reasons for adopting it. For example, it may be much quicker than an emic approach.

Using the two approaches together may be an effective way of investigating a psychological issue cross-culturally. Berry (1990) described the typical steps, combining an emic and an etic approach, taken in comparative research between cultures:

Figure 3: steps in comparative research (Berry, 1990)

1 *emic A*: research on the relevant issue is carried out within the home culture.
2 *the imposed etic*: similar research, using the same methods and materials,

is carried out in another culture, to establish similarities and differences.

3 *emic B*: the issue under research is explored within the other culture, in its own terms.

4 *comparison between emic A and emic B*: where there is no communality between the two cultures, no comparison is possible. However, where there is some communality, comparisons can be made. What the two cultures are found to have in common as the result of following these procedures is called the *derived etic*.

However, Berry recognised that this kind of extended approach may be difficult to achieve in practice, since it is likely to be complex to plan, time-consuming to carry out and therefore also expensive.

So what leads to cultural bias? The two most important influences are to do with researchers and methodology. Researchers from cultures other than the home one may not be appointed to academic positions, or if they are, may not be promoted as readily as academics from the home culture. You will remember that a similar argument was put forward in the discussion of gender bias. Cultural bias is also likely to occur where researchers are themselves racist. The hypotheses they test in research into culture could then be based on stereotypes, which they help to perpetuate, ignoring cultural influences.

The methodology used in cross-cultural research may also cause problems. Again, the argument is similar to that advanced in the discussion of gender bias. The emphasis in most Western psychological investigations on manipulation and control of variables, with the researcher maintaining a distance from participants, may create a research context which is alien to people from other cultures.

These problems suggest what we need to be aware of, and what changes might need to be made, if cultural bias is to be reduced and hopefully eliminated. In this way, we will be able to develop a clearer picture of the role of culture in psychology.

- Much psychological research has been carried out using samples from Western populations. It is unwise to assume that information acquired through this research can be applied universally across cultures.

- Research into other cultures has been carried out as a way of linking different social systems to psychological variations between cultures. However, researchers need to be aware of the danger of **ethnocentrism**, the assumption that the home culture provides a norm against which other cultures should be judged. **Cultural relativism** looks at a culture in its own terms.

- Ethnocentrism is a particular problem when research takes an **etic** approach, i.e. studying another culture from the outside, using the criteria of the home culture. This may lead to judgements being made based on an **imposed etic**.

- Ideally, an etic approach can be combined with an **emic** approach, i.e. studying a culture in its own terms. This can lead to a **derived etic**. However, it may not always be practicable.

- Culture bias arises from factors to do with **researchers** and **methodology**. Problems in these areas suggest what changes need to be made to avoid bias.

27.3 ETHICAL ISSUES

In the last part of chapter 6, we looked in some detail at general ethical considerations which need to be taken into account when planning and carrying out research with human participants. A further ethical issue is raised by the question of **socially sensitive research**, a term used by Sieber and Stanley (1988). They defined this as psychological research which may have social implications for the people being tested, or the group to which they belong. Research into homosexuality and racial differences are examples which we shall be considering in this section.

The ethical dilemma of socially sensitive research centres round the potential uses which may be made of the findings which it produces; these can be used to enhance people's lives, or conversely to exploit or manipulate them. Ethical guidelines, such as those produced by the British Psychological Society and the American Psychological Association, are concerned with the treatment of research participants, but have little to offer in terms of the implications of any research findings for the wider group, the population from which the sample tested has been drawn.

There is some disagreement about whether some research should be carried out at all, and if it is, whether the results should necessarily be reported. For example, Scarr and Weinberg (1976) found that black and mixed-race children adopted into white families did well on IQ tests. Oden and McDonald (1978) claimed that the publication of these findings was unethical, since they were, in their view, derogatory to the black community.

The main issue here is whether researchers, in deciding whether or not to carry out and/or publish research, need to consider the use to which others may put their findings. There are many different ways in which research findings can be (mis)used; for example, by governments seeking to control people, by racists aiming to justify their ideology, or by newspapers misrepresenting research findings in order to sensationalise a topic. Can research be seen as value-free, with the researcher taking no responsibility for any use which may be made of it? Howitt (1991) argued that it is impossible to be objective and value-free, and therefore very careful consideration should always be given to applying psychological findings.

This issue of social sensitivity is not confined to psychological research. The American Psychological

Association (1982) pointed out that an atomic physicist also faces this kind of problem, since research in this area can be used positively (e.g. contributing towards finding a cure for cancer) or negatively (e.g. to create weapons of mass destruction). Similarly, in a psychological context, Skinner's development of the principles of operant conditioning could be used to train animals to help people with a disability (e.g. as guide dogs for the blind), or to deliver explosive weapons.

Activity 6: positive and negative consequences of research

Hamer *et al.* (1993) carried out research into the possibility of there being a genetic component in homosexuality – the so-called 'gay gene'. On the basis of a study of the family histories of 114 gay men, he came to the conclusion that there is a genetic component in male homosexuality.

If we accept Hamer's conclusions, what kinds of uses – both positive and negative – could be made of this information?

When you have finished, see the notes on activities on page 758.

Sieber and Stanley (1988) have suggested that there are four aspects of research which might raise socially sensitive issues:

Figure 4: potential sources of socially sensitive issues (Sieber and Stanley, 1988)

1 The formulation of the research question.
2 How the research is carried out, and how participants are treated.
3 The institutional context within which research is carried out.
4 The interpretation and application of research findings.

Sieber and Stanley's first aspect is the **formulation of the research question**. They argue that merely posing a research question can in itself be problematical. For example, questions such as Is homosexuality inherited? and Are there racial differences in intelligence? can in themselves be damaging, in that they may reinforce existing prejudices, such as homophobia or racism, by lending them some scientific credibility. On the other hand, it could be argued that to avoid research into these kinds of sensitive areas could be seen as avoiding social responsibility; such research, objectively and sensitively carried out, could help to challenge prejudice.

They then consider **how the research is carried out**, and how participants are treated. These issues are covered in some detail in ethical guidelines such as those produced by the British Psychological Society, discussed in chapter 6. One important issue here is that of confidentiality. Socially sensitive research can cover issues such as sexual habits or drug taking. There may be a serious moral quandary for a researcher who has to weigh up the confidentiality offered to participants against the wider interests of society. It would be difficult to find people to take part in socially sensitive research if participants were not offered confidentiality. On the other hand, there may be a moral duty to break confidentiality to protect wider social interests which might be threatened, such as if sexual abuse of a child were reported.

Socially sensitive research can also have implications for the researchers themselves. It was noted in chapter 6 that Milgram's famous studies of obedience attracted a lot of criticism, largely because they had told the public something about human nature which they did not want to know: that ordinary people are willing to harm innocent people if told by an authority figure to do so.

Milgram's studies also provide a nice example of Sieber and Stanley's third aspect of socially sensitive research, the **institutional context** within which research is carried out. The levels of obedience Milgram found dropped considerably when his experiment was carried out in a downtown office, compared with the high levels found when the study was carried out at Yale University. The nature of the setting within which the study took place itself exerted a coercive influence over participants.

Other kinds of settings may also be problematical; for example, if psychologists carry out psychometric testing on employees of an organisation, participants may feel obliged to take part. However, the data they provide could be used as a basis for making these employees redundant or blocking their promotion.

Sieber and Stanley's final point concerns the **interpretation and application of research** findings. We have already raised this issue in relation to Hamer's research on the 'gay gene', but you might find it useful to consider some further examples:

Activity 7: socially sensitive issues: interpretation and application of research findings

For each of the following, think of:
a ways in which the findings could be interpreted
b ways in which the findings could be used

1 Several studies have shown an average difference of 15 points between white Americans and African Americans in measured intelligence (see chapter 17).
2 Research into the effects of institutionalisation on children's social, emotional and cognitive development found that children in institutions, who did not develop a close, continuous relationship with a mother or permanent mother substitute had later problems in all these

areas (see chapter 3).

You may find it useful to read the relevant material in the appropriate chapters as a basis for thinking about these topics.

When you have finished, see the notes on activities on page 758.

It is worth bearing in mind that Sieber and Stanley were not suggesting that socially sensitive research should not be carried out. Indeed, they stated that we need to "address some of society's most pressing issues and policy questions" (p55). Although such research may legitimise prejudice, it may also be a way of challenging it, so researchers have a social responsibility to carry it out. However, researchers need to be aware of the issues such research raises, and the need for caution at all stages of the research process.

Issues surrounding socially sensitive research are linked to the influence psychologists have in society. If they have little influence, the impact of their findings, beyond the immediate sample of people tested, is likely to be minimal. However, psychological findings can have (and have had) important effects on political and social policy.

A good example can be found in the discussion of Bowlby's maternal deprivation hypothesis in chapter 3. Although Bowlby drew attention to the adverse effects on children of disrupted child care, and did a lot of good in improving aspects of child care, his ideas also helped shape and support the view that the role of women was to look after children, and influenced the implementation of public policy to bring this about. Similarly, research into the possible genetic basis of differences in measured intelligence led not only to divisive and discriminatory social policies within education, but also to compulsory sterilisation of those with low measured intelligence in some states of America. According to Gould (1981), these laws were being implemented in the state of Virginia up until 1972.

So how do psychologists influence political and social policies? Segall (1976) made some suggestions, together with the strengths and limitations of each:

Box A: Segall (1976)

There are three main ways in which psychologists can influence political and social policies:

a as *expert witnesses*; for example, by giving evidence in a court of law or making their expertise publicly available in the media. *The advantage of this kind of influence is that opposing psychological views can be presented, so avoiding biased views having undue influence. However, the information given can be accepted or rejected at will by policymakers; this is out of the psychologist's control.*

b by *policy evaluation*; for example, by taking part in research to assess the impact or potential impact of political measures, actual or proposed.
In this way, a positive social impact can be made. For example, desegregation in education in America was influenced by psychological research on the harmful effects of segregation. However, funding for relevant research, and therefore also whether it is carried out and its quality, may limit what is possible. These factors will in turn be influenced by the current social ethos, in terms of whether such research is seen as worth carrying out.

c as *social-psychological engineers*, in particular devising ways of bringing about socially desirable behaviour. For example, in his book *Beyond Freedom and Dignity* (1971), Skinner described how operant conditioning techniques could enhance people's lives.
There are very many pro-social behaviours (e.g. safe sex) which can be encouraged in this way. However, the techniques can also be used by those who have no interest in socially desirable behaviour, e.g. shop layout consultants whose only interest is in persuading us to buy more things.

If research is not carried out, then findings cannot be misused. However, neither is there any potential for benefit. We will finish this discussion with a look at one further socially sensitive area of psychological research where the findings have certainly had a positive impact on people's lives: the experience of children giving testimony in a court of law.

In cases of sexual assault against children, the child concerned may be the only person able to provide evidence for the prosecution, and there have been doubts about a child's ability to give accurate evidence. As a result of these doubts, children under the age of six were, until recently, not usually allowed to give evidence in court, and children's evidence alone could not lead to a conviction in the absence of any corroboration. Heydon, an English lawyer, identified what he saw as some of the possible problems in accepting the evidence of children in a court of law:

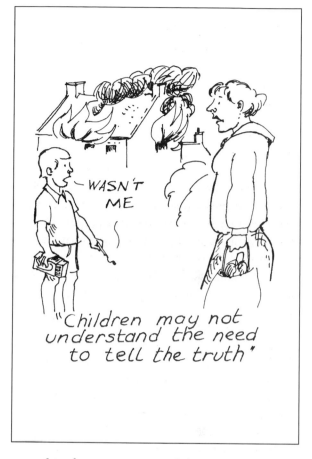

"Children may not understand the need to tell the truth"

Box B: Heydon (1984)

1 Children's powers of observation and memory may not be as developed as those of an adult.
2 They are likely to live in a make-believe world and be unable to distinguish between truth and fiction.
3 They are suggestible, so may easily be influenced in their testimony by others.
4 They may not understand the duty to speak the truth.
5 Some children may revenge themselves on adults by making false accusations.

However, Hedderman (1987) published a review of psychological research for the Home Office to establish the accuracy of these preconceptions, and found that to a large extent they were misplaced. As a result of this research, the Criminal Justice Act of 1988 established that child witnesses were to be treated in the same way as adult witnesses, and by 1990, children of any age could give evidence in a court of law if the judge believed that they were intelligent enough to do so, and able to understand the duty of speaking the truth. These changes have improved the likelihood of a successful prosecution in cases of offences against children.

For some if not most children, giving evidence in a law court may bring its own problems, and psychologists have also carried out useful research into this aspect of children's testimony:

Box C: Flin et al. (1993)

Procedure: Over a 12-month period, 89 children called to give prosecution evidence were observed.
The aim was to examine the experience of children giving testimony, and to identify problematical aspects of the procedure.

Results: Many children were asked to give evidence, including the examination-in-chief and cross-examination, for long periods of time. Half the children were rated as being 'unhappy' or 'very unhappy', and a similar percentage as 'tense' or 'very tense'. Most children were fluent and could provide some detail, though many (85%) were asked questions inappropriate to their age in terms of vocabulary or grammatical complexity.

Conclusion: There are several aspects of giving testimony in court which may disadvantage children compared with adults.

Studies like this have helped to identify the kinds of problems children may encounter when asked to give testimony. This in turn has led to research into how to make the experience as productive and stress-free as possible. For example, the Criminal Justice Act 1991 allowed video recordings of children's evidence-in-chief to be admitted as evidence. In 1992, the Home Office published the Memorandum of Good Practice on Video Recorded Interviews with Child Witnesses for Criminal Proceedings. It drew on psychological evidence (for example, the use of the cognitive interview technique described in chapter 2) to enable interviewers to get as full and as accurate an account as possible from a child witness, without there being undue influence. It also emphasised the need for closure, bringing the experience to a satisfactory conclusion to ensure that the child has not been unduly distressed, or feels that they have 'failed' if they were unable to remember something.

In this area, then, socially sensitive research has resulted in a good working relationship between psychologists and the legal profession, an increased understanding of children's ability to give testimony, and a sensitivity towards the problems this may pose for them. Though there is still research to be carried out in this area, it has become more possible for children to play an active part in the conviction of offenders.

- Research is socially sensitive when its outcome may have **social implications** for the people being tested or the group to which they belong.
- The main issue here is the extent to which possible **uses of research** findings should be considered by those planning to carry out this kind of research. However, such research can also **benefit** those to whom it applies.
- Researchers need to consider the **formulation of the research question**, **how the research is carried out**, the **institutional context** within which it takes place, and the **interpretation and application of the findings**.
- Bowlby's **maternal deprivation hypothesis** and **racial differences in measured intelligence** are examples of socially sensitive research which has disadvantaged some social groups.
- Research into **testimony given by child witnesses** is an example of the possible beneficial outcomes of this kind of research.

27.4 THE USE OF NON-HUMAN ANIMALS

Animals have been used in psychological research both in laboratory studies and in studies which observe or manipulate their behaviour in the natural environment. Both of these kinds of research raise a variety of practical and ethical issues, and are the cause of a great deal of controversy.

The practical reasons underlying the use of animals in laboratory experiments were discussed in chapter 1. In particular, these experiments rest on the assumption that since experimental animals are in many ways like humans (for example, in having a similar nervous system), it is possible to extrapolate animal findings to humans. The use of animals instead of humans allows the use of procedures which could not be used with humans, giving studies a greater degree of control, and allowing cause and effect relationships to be established. The short lifespan of animals also makes the study of genetics and changes across the lifespan more practical.

This research may lead to applications with humans. For example, Green (1994) pointed out that anti-anxiety and anti-depressant drugs could not have been developed without animal experimentation. Such studies may also benefit animals themselves. Research has made it possible to design living conditions over which the animals themselves have more control; pigs, for example, have been trained to adjust their own lighting conditions to their preferred level.

However, not everyone accepts these benefits. Barnard and Kaufman (1997) argued that the assumed similarities between animals and humans are invalid, so there is no justification on this basis for the use of animals in experiments.

The debate on the ethics of animal studies is, if anything, even more contentious than that about their practical uses. One view, put forward by Gray (1987), argued that the use of animals in research, and in particular the amount of suffering they experience, has to be weighed against the possible benefits to humans of carrying out this research. He acknowledged that there are problems in assessing suffering, and that the benefits of research may not be immediately obvious, and that there is a point where the suffering of animals becomes so extreme as not to justify any possible benefits to humans. The problem for him lay in establishing where this point is.

Another viewpoint recognises that different species have different sensibilities, and proposes that it is therefore impossible to take a general standpoint on the ethics of animal experimentation. For example, few would argue that causing the death of a meningitis bacterium is on a par with causing the death of a gorilla.

A more extreme view was taken by Singer (1991), who argued that there can be no justification in harming another sentient being, whether human or non-human. He accused Gray of speciesism, i.e. exploiting and discriminating against animals on the basis of species, in the same way that racism discriminates against people on the basis of their race.

There is some evidence that there has been a decline in the number of experimental procedures using animals:

Box D: Thomas and Blackman (1991)

Procedure: The number of animal studies carried out by psychologists in 1976/7 and 1988/9 was investigated. The number of animals used in experiments, together with the number of different species and the number of different procedures used over the two time periods, were compared.

Results: There was a significant decline in the number of animals used in 1988/9 compared to 1976/7, as well as the number of different species and the number of different procedures used. Considerably fewer studies involving drugs, deprivation of food and water, surgery and electric shocks were carried out in 1988/9 than in the time period ten years previously. However, there was an increase in the number of non-experimental studies, e.g. those involving observation of animals.

Conclusion: There has been a decline in the use of animals in experiments, but a rise in observational studies of animal behaviour.

The British Psychological Society and the Association for the Study of Animal Behaviour have produced guidelines relating to the use of animals in psychological studies. These guidelines relate both to experiments and to observational studies. They are covered by the Animals (Scientific Procedures) Act (1986), some extracts of which are shown in figure 5:

Figure 5: Guidelines for the Use of Animals in Research: summary of part of the Animals (Scientific Procedures) Act (1986)

1 *The law*: There are laws protecting the rights of animals, and anyone who fails to comply with these laws can be prosecuted.

2 *Ethical considerations*: If animals are to be subjected to stress or to any other kind of harm, the researcher needs to consider whether the benefits to be gained from research outweigh the harm involved,

and whether there might be alternative ways of testing their ideas.

3 *Species*: Researchers should have some knowledge of the animals to be used in experiments, so that if pain or suffering is involved, animals may be tested who are less likely to suffer.

4 *Number of animals*: The smallest possible number of animals should be tested.

5 *Endangered species*: These animals should not be manipulated in the wild except for the purposes of conservation.

6 *Caging and social environment*: The amount of space given to animals needs to be considered in terms of the particular species being tested. Isolation in social species should be avoided.

7 *Motivation*: If deprivation of e.g. food or water is involved, the researcher needs to consider the normal behaviour pattern of the species.

8 *Aversive stimuli and stressful procedures*: Stressful or painful procedures can only be carried out under licence from the Home Office, and when there are no viable alternative methods. Suffering should be kept to a minimum, and should be justified in terms of the scientific contribution made by the study.

In addition, a person wishing to carry out animal research needs a licence from the Home Office to do so. They will need to justify their research in terms of the scientific contribution they expect their research to make. If animals are to be subjected to stressful procedures, then these must be assessed and licensed by the Home Office.

Bateson (1986) developed a system to help researchers decide whether or not they should go ahead with planned research. This system uses three criteria: the quality of the research, the degree of animal suffering and the certainty of benefit. It can be shown diagrammatically:

Figure 6: Bateson's decision cube

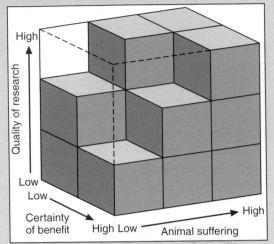

In figure 6, the solid space indicates when research should *not* go ahead, while clear space indicates when it should. Ideally, for research to be carried out, the quality of the research should be high, the degree of suffering low, and the certainty of benefit high. Conversely, research should not go ahead where the quality of the research is low, the degree of suffering high, and the certainty of benefit low.

Clearly, making these assessments about a prospective piece of research can be problematical. Judging the quality of research has an element of subjectivity, though in practice there is a high degree of agreement on this aspect of research. In addition, only high quality research will attract the funding necessary to carry it out. Assessing the degree of suffering involved can also be difficult, since different animals react differently to stressful situations. However, this becomes less of a problem as our knowledge about different animal species increases. Dawkins (1985) has suggested three factors which may be useful in making this assessment: the animal's state of physical health, signs of stress and the animal's behaviour. Evaluating possible benefits is again somewhat subjective, though the aims of the study should go beyond merely satisfying curiosity, and result in real understanding being gained.

Some of the animal research you have read about in this book was carried out before such detailed guidelines and laws were in place, and it would therefore be somewhat unfair to judge these studies by these standards. In addition, early research has provided us with enough necessary information in some areas so that there would be no need to carry out similar research today. However, you may find it useful to apply the basic principles to some actual studies:

▷ Activity 8: evaluating laboratory studies of animal behaviour

For each of the following studies, use the three criteria of Bateson's cube to decide whether the research would be justified today. In what ways does it meet (or fail to meet) these criteria?

a Skinner's studies of rats and pigeons (chapter 1, section on operant conditioning)

b Harlow and Zimmerman (chapter 3, box C)

c Brady (chapter 4, box F)

When you have finished, see the notes on activities on page 758.

Field experiments in animal behaviour raise specific issues beyond the general guidelines described above. They can be of use in broadening our understanding of animal behaviour, which can then be applied; for example, in conservation work. However, they are usually of no immediate benefit to humans, and by their very nature, they involve manipulating an animal's natural environment in some way. In a review of nearly 1000 research papers describing these kinds of experiments, Cuthill (1991) identified seven different forms this manipulation can take:

Box E: Cuthill (1991)

The main methods used in field experiments with examples

a *dummies*: using a stuffed dummy predator.

b *non-trivial handling*: repeated trapping of birds or animals for the purpose of tagging and tracking.

c *playback*: playing recordings of alarm calls.

d *food addition*: providing extra food.

e *removal*: the temporary removal of e.g. a parent animal.

f *brood manipulation*: in studies of birds, adding to or taking away eggs from a clutch.

g *phenotype manipulation*: altering an animal's physical characteristics.

▷ Activity 9: problems with field experiments

Examples of each of the kinds of studies outlined in box E are given below. For each one, identify both the short-term and the longer-term negative effects which these procedures might have:

a *dummies*: Elliot (1985) tested the response of lapwings nesting in groups to taxidermy mounts of predators – carrion crows, black-backed gulls and foxes – pulled towards them. The study took place during the breeding season. The lapwings responded to these dummy predators as if they were live. They attacked the crow, a relatively harmless predator. In response to the fox, they circled overhead and attempted to distract it from their nests, but did not attack it. Both attack and distraction responses were shown to the black-backed gull. From his observations, Elliot concluded that nesting in groups enhances the effectiveness of lapwings' responses to nest predators such as crows but not to more dangerous predators such as foxes.

b *non-trivial handling*: see Schlichte and Schmidt-Koenig, chapter 21, box B.

c *playback*: see Seyfarth and Cheney, chapter 21, box K.

d *food addition*: Elgar (1986) investigated the circumstances in which foraging in sparrows takes place in groups or individually. Individual sparrows were offered the same amount of bread, either as a lump (difficult to divide up) or as crumbs (easy to divide up). In the 'crumb' condition, the sparrow gave its usual chirrup. It failed to do so in the 'lump' condition. Elgar concluded that the benefits of communal feeding in terms of protection from predators are outweighed by the costs involved in dividing up food which is not easily shared.

e *removal*: see Perdeck, chapter 21, box F.

f *brood manipulation*: Tinbergen (1981) carried out a study of foraging behaviour in starlings with young to feed. The birds could choose between leatherjacket grubs, which were easy to find close to the nest, or more palatable caterpillars, which were less easy to find and further away. They usually foraged for caterpillars. Tinbergen added extra nestlings to the nest, thus artificially making the need for food more pressing, and in these circumstances, the parent bird foraged for leatherjacket grubs.

g *phenotype manipulation*: Andersson (1982) investigated the relationship between tail length and attractiveness to females in long-tailed widow birds. The male is about the size of a sparrow and has a tail up to 50 cm long. Male birds were studied and divided into 4 groups. Group 1 had their tails docked. The severed portions were attached with superglue to the tails of group 2 birds. The tails of group 3 were left untouched, while the tails of group 4 were docked and reattached so the length was not altered. The mating success of the different groups was measured by counting the number of nests in each male bird's territory. Group 2 birds were significantly more successful than birds in the other three groups. Andersson concluded that tail length is a significant factor in the mating success of the male long-tailed widow bird.

When you have finished, see the notes on activities on page 759.

In all these cases, there is the further possibility that the disturbance of the animal's environment involved in these kinds of manipulation may have long-term consequences. To minimise all these problems, a pilot study should be carried out to assess both the immediate and longer-term implications of what is being planned, disruption should be kept to a minimum, and follow-up studies should be carried out to assess the effects.

๑ Animal experimentation, in the laboratory and in the field, raises both **practical and ethical issues**. There has been a decline in the number of **laboratory experiments**, but a rise in **field experiments**.

๑ There are **safeguards** in the use of animals in experiments, including **guidelines** produced by professional bodies and **legal restrictions**.

๑ It has been suggested that the **criteria** for deciding whether or not an experiment should go ahead are: the **quality of the research**; the **degree of suffering** involved; and the **certainty of benefit**.

๑ **Field experiments** raise additional issues to do with **manipulation** of animals and their environment. These can be addressed by pilot studies and assessment carried out after the experiment has taken place.

27.5 FREE WILL AND DETERMINISM

An issue which has carried over from philosophy into modern psychology is the extent to which we are free to choose how to act (we have **free will**), and the extent to which our actions are determined by influences beyond our control (**determinism**). This issue arises in psychology because people are the subject of study. The mechanistic nature of much of psychological research implies that people are passive responders to stimuli, i.e. the research takes a deterministic viewpoint and fits well with a scientific approach to psychology, an issue we shall be returning to later in this chapter. However, these assumptions go against our intuitive feeling that we can make choices. For example, I have the choice to carry on typing this chapter or to go and make a cup of tea. Clearly there are some constraints on our ability to make choices, but in general we feel that we have free will.

Free will and determinism both carry important implications. If we have free will, it is assumed that we are responsible for our actions, since we could have chosen to act differently. Our legal system is based on this assumption, except in exceptional circumstances, as in the plea of 'diminished responsibility' as a defence for murder. This defence was introduced in the Homicide Act (1957), and if accepted, there is no trial, the person is automatically found guilty of manslaughter, and will be compulsorily detained in hospital.

The debate is also relevant in abnormal psychology. Mental disorders can be seen as a complete or partial breakdown of our ability to exert free will, such as in obsessive–compulsive disorder (see chapter 24), where a person is unable to control obsessive thoughts and compulsive behaviours. Control is thought to be the normal state, and loss of it, such as in schizophrenia, is an acceptable legal defence. The concept of free will makes possible the concept of blame; the concept of determinism is incompatible with it. In the field of mental disorders, then, a deterministic stance removes the idea that a person is in some way responsible for their problems.

Determinism carries the implication of predictability. If we have all the necessary information, it should be possible to identify the causes of behaviour, and the behaviour should therefore be totally predictable, and ultimately controllable. In practice, it is much easier to identify causes after an event.

The term 'determinism' can be used in different ways. James (1890) made a distinction between **hard determinism** and **soft determinism**. According to hard determinism, the immediate causes of behaviour are seen as part of a long chain of causes, so there is no sense in which we can be seen as acting freely. The soft determinism approach taken by James, in contrast, sees behaviour as free to the extent that there is no immediate coercion to act in a particular way.

In the context of this debate, the term 'free will' is also used to cover a range of different ideas:

Figure 7: the meaning of free will

1 *having a choice*: a person could have behaved differently in a given set of circumstances.
2 *not being coerced*: this is related to the idea of soft determinism put forward by James, where there is no immediate compulsion to behave in a particular way.

---

3 *voluntary*: 'involuntary' can be used to describe reflex behaviour, such as blinking when a puff of air is directed towards the eye. Other behaviour could therefore be described in contrast as 'voluntary'. Support for this distinction comes from Penfield (1947), who stimulated the motor cortex of patients about to undergo brain surgery, thus causing them to make involuntary movements. The patients reported that these movements felt different from voluntary movements.
4 *deliberate control*: Norman and Shallice (1986) defined three levels at which information can be processed: fully automatic; partially automatic; and deliberate control (see chapter 14). Deliberate control here equates to free will, while fully automatic processing equates to determinism.

Throughout this book, you have read about various 'models of the person', i.e. assumptions about the nature of human beings, which in turn determine the kinds of research questions to be asked and how this research is carried out. We will look here at the free will versus determinism debate in the context of three major figures in psychology, with very different views:

▶ Activity 10: free will and determinism: three theorists

We will look here at the ideas of Freud, Skinner and Rogers. An outline of each of their theories is given in chapter 1, with additional material in several other chapters. For each of these theorists:

a if free will and determinism are seen as two ends of a continuum, where do you think each theorist should be placed?
b what aspects of their theory led you to decide this?
c even if you think that a particular theorist should be at one extreme or the other, are there any aspects of their theory which might move

them, even if only slightly, towards the other end of the continuum?

Compare your notes with the discussion which follows.

Freud

You will remember that one of the key ideas in Freudian theory is **psychic determinism**, in that he believed all psychological processes to be strictly determined by the principles of cause and effect. This is illustrated by what he has to say about **parapraxes** (see chapter 1) and his theory of **dreams** as expressing unconscious conflict and wishes (see chapter 12). As in these examples, much of our motivation comes from material in the unconscious, where it cannot be under our control and so amenable to free will. Freud therefore believed that free will is essentially an illusion.

However, this is not the whole story. Freud accepted that there were genuine accidents; for example, being struck by lightning, which were brought about by forces outside the individual and not caused by unconscious forces. He also believed that some change, albeit limited, was possible through the use of **psychoanalysis**, the therapy associated with his theory; the goal of psychoanalysis, according to Freud, was: 'where id was, there shall ego be.' A further factor is Freud's principle of **over-determination**. Much of our behaviour has several causes, so it is possible that conscious choices can affect our decisions, even if this is not the whole story. In practice, Freud attempted to explain his patients' behaviour and neurotic symptoms in terms of their meaning to the individual, rather than in terms of causes.

Skinner

While Freud and Skinner have little in common, Skinner's theory too is very much at the deterministic end of the free will–determinism continuum, and he too saw our experience of having freedom to choose as illusory. As a radical behaviourist, his theory has no place for mental states such as thoughts and emotions. Although these internal states exist, they do not directly cause behaviour. All our behaviour, apart from the few simple reflexes we are born with, is acquired through **shaping and reinforcement**.

While some of the reinforcers and punishers which have shaped our behaviour are obvious, we are unaware of many of them. Because the causes of our behaviour are often hidden from us, we feel that we have freedom of choice; however, these apparent choices could be shown to be determined if we were able to access the complete reinforcement history of the individual. We feel our behaviour to be freely chosen to the extent that we are unaware of what has led to it.

There is clearly a conflict here with the need to see people as having freedom to choose if they are to be held morally (and indeed legally) responsible for their actions. Skinner removed the idea of morality from behaviour by defining 'good' as something which is beneficial to others and is rewarded, and 'bad' as something which is harmful to others and is punished.

In his book *Beyond Freedom and Dignity* (1971), Skinner further argued that the idea of 'autonomous man' – that people make choices about their actions – is not only false but is also harmful to the individual. This assumption means that people are constantly exposed to punishment or the threat of punishment, which are experienced as aversive. He believed that positive reinforcement was not only non-aversive, but also more effective in bringing about behaviour change. He demonstrated how this could work in his novel *Walden Two*, in which people's behaviour is shaped entirely by positive reinforcement, to their own benefit and that of the community in which they live.

Rogers

Rogers' humanistic theory is very much at the other end of the continuum from those of Freud and Skinner. There are three basic assumptions in the humanistic approach. Firstly, the psychologist takes an **experiential approach**, by focusing on people's subjective awareness of their worlds, as opposed to others' views of them. Secondly, the emphasis is on the **whole person**, taking in all the different aspects (biological, social and so on) which make us what we are. Finally, people are assumed to have the capacity for **personal agency**, i.e. they can play a part in creating the kind of person they become. This process of self-development is known as **personal growth**. This last principle suggests that the idea that we have free will is central to the theory.

The emphasis the theory places on personal growth is shown in Maslow's concept of **self-actualisation**, the idea that we are motivated to move towards becoming what we want to become, and fulfilling our potential (see chapter 13). People can be helped towards this by **client-centred therapy**. This is a talking therapy, and is non-directive in that the therapist does not suggest how the person might wish to change, but helps them to explore these possibilities for themselves by listening and mirroring back what the client tells them, and supports the client in deciding what kinds of changes they would like to make. In this therapy, people choose to see themselves and their life experiences differently. Clearly our life experiences are important, but what is crucial is our ability to choose how we will respond to them.

While Rogers believed that people were fundamentally good, and had a generally optimistic view of human nature, he was aware that we all have the capacity for more negative behaviour, such as becoming angry or treating others cruelly. However, he believed that we can choose whether or not to behave in these ways. The decisions we make depend to some extent on social conditioning, but we also have voluntary choice.

The influence of social conditioning suggests that choices are not entirely free. Negative elements brought about by social conditioning cause people to become neurotic and what Rogers calls **incongruent**, in that their true self has become distorted, and is not the self which has developed. Rogers believed that this can come about in childhood, if children are offered only **conditional positive regard**, i.e. love is offered on condition that the child behaves in certain ways which fit in with the wishes and expectations of others. To become a healthy and fully functioning person, children need to be offered **unconditional positive regard**, so that personal growth is not distorted, and the true self and the actual self are congruent.

However, even where personal growth has become distorted, there is always the possibility of change. Particularly in therapy, we can choose to focus our personal growth on changing incongruent elements of the self, to become happier and more fulfilled. There are some constraints on the choices we make, but choices are always possible.

- The **free will versus determinism** debate within psychology is concerned with the extent to which we have freedom of choice in our behaviour. This issue is particularly important in terms of **moral responsibility** and in **abnormal psychology**.
- The term '**free will**' can cover a range of **different ideas**, relevant to different areas of psychology.
- Freud and Skinner took an essentially deterministic view of human nature, while personal growth and the ability to make choices is at the heart of Rogers' humanistic theory.

27.6 REDUCTIONISM

Reductionism can be defined as the attempt to explain a complex phenomenon in terms of the units which make it up, rather than as a whole. It rests on the idea that we have the best chance of understanding something if we break it down into its simplest component parts. It stems from an idea current in biological science in the nineteenth century. This saw living organisms, including humans, as a complex of organs like the heart and liver. These organs in turn are a complex of cells. In order to understand the living organism, it was believed to be necessary to make a close study of the characteristics of these different cells.

This general approach later became a general scientific principle, and can be seen in some approaches to psychology. An early example of a reductionist approach is **structuralism**, discussed in chapter 1.

Reductionist principles have also been applied to the development of theories in the principle of **parsimony**, which states that the best explanation of a phenomenon is the simplest one which can account for all the data. Higher-level unobservable processes, such as intentions and perceptions, may be broken down into observable behaviours. The aim of this kind of reductionism is to be able to explain behaviour without having to use concepts such as 'will' or 'consciousness'. An example is Watson's belief that thinking could be defined as tiny movements of the vocal cords, where complex thought is explained in terms of very simple muscle movements.

In contrast to reductionism, **holism** takes a broader view, assuming in Gestalt terms that 'the whole is greater than the sum of its parts'. Reductionism can also be contrasted with **interactionism**, which approaches a problem from many different angles – e.g. biological, cognitive and social – and tries to explain a phenomenon in terms of how these aspects interact.

Psychological phenomena can often be explained on a number of different levels, with the lower levels taking a more reductionist approach, and the higher levels a more holistic approach. This can be related to the different perspectives in psychology described in chapter 1: psychodynamic, behaviourist, cognitive, humanistic and physiological. Let us take depression as an example:

Figure 8: levels of explanation (Rose, 1976)

sociological   systems explanations
social psychological   (holistic)
psychological (mentalistic)
physiological (systems)
physiological (units)
anatomical (biochemical)
chemical
physical   unit explanations
                                           (reductionist)

> ## ► Activity 11: explaining depression
>
> How would each of these perspectives explain depression? Which perspectives do you think take a more reductionist approach, and why?
>
>   behaviourist   cognitive
>   humanistic   physiological
>
> When you have finished, see the notes on activities on page 759.

Is reductionism necessarily a bad thing? Rose (1976) looked at both sides of this question, bringing in the idea of different levels of explanation. The levels he proposed are shown in figure 8 opposite.

As you move down through these levels, investigation becomes focused on an ever narrower area. At the top, social factors are seen as important, looking at the person in terms of their social environment.

Psychological explanations look at the individual in a broad sense, including cognitions and feelings. Physiological explanations narrow the focus on the individual to consider only their physical make-up, perhaps looking at the working of the endocrine system or neurotransmitters. This focus can then be narrowed still further; for instance, looking only at the effects of adrenaline within this system. It would then be possible to seek explanations at the level of the neuron (brain cell). The explanation becomes progressively more reductionist, looking more at the individual units which make up the system than at the system as a whole.

Different levels of explanation can all be valid. For example, a cognitive explanation of depression doesn't necessarily rule out physiological factors. Rose makes a distinction between 'explaining' and 'explaining away'. If a reductionist physiological explanation can *contribute* to a psychological explanation, then it has something to offer: it helps to 'explain' the phenomenon. It is only when such an explanation is offered *instead* of a psychological explanation – to 'explain away' a psychological phenomenon – that psychological explanations are under threat.

One problem with a reductionist approach is that in some cases it may not be very useful. For example, a piece of behaviour such as waving your hand can only be understood in terms of its meaning: are you waving or drowning? It is impossible to make sense of behaviour if it is taken out of the context in which it occurs. A purely physiological account here would provide very little understanding.

Another problem is that reductionist explanations may often have political implications. For example, concentrating on physiological explanations for depression shifts the focus away from wider social issues – poverty, unemployment and so on – which may have had a large role to play in the development of the disorder.

Reductionism can also be seen positively, in that it takes a scientific and analytical approach to its subject matter. This enables psychological phenomena to be broken down into small parts which can be readily tested in a controlled way. This has worked well with the natural sciences, and can give scientific credibility to the discipline of psychology.

Psychological phenomena are often best explained using an **interactionist** approach, i.e. looking at how different levels of explanation interact with each other:

▷ **Activity 12: the interactionist approach**

In activity 11, we saw how different perspectives can offer different levels of analysis in depression. Think about how this approach might be useful in:
a understanding schizophrenia (see chapter 24)
b understanding visual perception (see chapter 15)
c offering therapies for a mental disorder (see chapter 25)
When you have finished, see the notes on activities on page 759.

There are practical problems in taking an interactionist approach. For example, this kind of research is clearly more complex than the relatively straightforward task of looking at smaller components. Because so many factors on so many levels interact, it becomes difficult to tease out the relative contributions of any one factor and to make clear causal connections.

- A **reductionist** approach looks at complex phenomena in terms of simple units. It is contrasted with a **holistic** and an **interactionist** approach.
- Psychological phenomena can be explained at different **levels**. Reductionist explanations can be useful if they contribute towards a psychological explanation. They are less useful as a substitute for a psychological explanation.
- A reductionist approach is often not useful in understanding the **meaning** of behaviour, and is **not suitable** for some topics in psychology. Such explanations can shift the focus of study from the wider psychological and **social issues** which may contribute to a phenomenon. However, reductionism allows for a **scientific approach** to research.
- An **interactionist** approach is often useful, looking at the relationship between different levels of explanation. However, this is not without **practical problems**.

27.7 IS PSYCHOLOGY A SCIENCE?

We need to establish first of all what is meant by 'science'. If we take natural sciences like physics and chemistry as a model, there are several criteria which should be met:

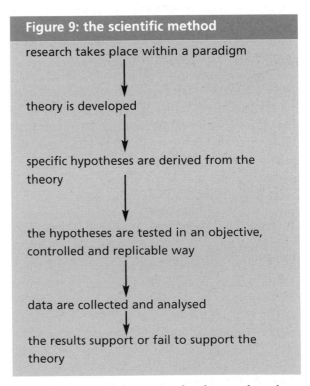

Figure 9: the scientific method

research takes place within a paradigm
↓
theory is developed
↓
specific hypotheses are derived from the theory
↓
the hypotheses are tested in an objective, controlled and replicable way
↓
data are collected and analysed
↓
the results support or fail to support the theory

We will look a little more closely at what these criteria for a science involve.

Paradigms in science

The term **paradigm** was used by Kuhn (1962) to refer to a set of assumptions, methods and terminology shared by those working within a particular scientific discipline. He suggested that there are continual revolutions in science; the contradictions inherent within a paradigm – for example, challenges to it from new evidence – build up until it must be abandoned, and a new paradigm takes its place, i.e. there is a **paradigm shift**. An example of this kind of shift occurred when Einsteinian physics replaced Newtonian physics. According to Kuhn, there are three stages in the development of science:

> ### Figure 10: stages in the development of science (Kuhn, 1962)
>
> a pre-science: there is no universally accepted paradigm
> b normal science: researchers work sharing the same paradigm
> c revolution: the paradigm no longer fits the evidence, so a paradigm shift occurs to a new perspective.
>
> Stages b and c are repeated as each existing paradigm becomes inadequate.

It could be argued from this that psychology falls at the first hurdle in terms of being a science, since there are a great many different (and contradictory) paradigms; psychology is pre-paradigmatic. For example, behaviourism has little in common with psychodynamics and both differ in important ways from the humanistic approach. On the other hand, it could be argued that psychology has gone through a great many paradigm shifts, e.g. from structuralism to behaviourism to cognitive psychology, and is therefore a well-developed science using these criteria. Perhaps these shifts have been a precursor to developing an integrated paradigm. Valentine (1982) has suggested that psychology has had unified paradigms in the past, in particular the behaviourist paradigm which dominated psychology in the 1940s and 1950s.

However, not everyone agrees that science progresses through the stages suggested by Kuhn. Feyerabend (1975) argued that science involves individuals, each following their own path, rather than conforming to paradigms, which may only serve to stifle creativity and therefore also hold back progress. This certainly seems to reflect quite closely how psychology has developed.

Theories and hypotheses

In order to qualify as scientific, theories should aim to enable scientists to do three things: understand, predict and control. One way in which they provide **understanding** is, of course, by being true. However, they should also be able to organise information in a consistent way, such that general laws can be developed. They should be parsimonious, i.e. provide the greatest degree of explanation in the simplest possible way.

For a theory to be useful, it should be possible to use it to derive **predictions**, i.e. testable hypotheses which can be used either to support or refute it. Popper (1959) proposed that a theory needs to be falsifiable. It is never possible to prove a theory correct, since we cannot observe all the data at any one time. For example, it would not be possible to prove that all swans are white. If we were to observe a sample, and note that they were all white, we could not draw this conclusion, since another sample could include a black one. However, a theory making a clear prediction can lead to a test to prove it wrong.

If theories make clear predictions, they allow us to **control** aspects of our environment and experience, hopefully in ways which improve the human condition. For example, the principles of behaviourism have been used as the basis of therapies to help people with a mental disorder (see chapter 25). Control of course raises ethical issues, such as who should have control over others, and for what reasons.

The scientific method

Within this method, the testing of hypotheses should be carried out in an objective way. The terms of what is to be tested should be operationalised (see chapter 7), and the data to be collected should be clearly defined. Research should be well controlled, so that it is possible to draw conclusions about cause and effect from the findings. This is why psychological experiments use a control group, with which the data from the experimental group(s) can be compared. Studies should also be replicable, so that it is possible for another researcher to repeat a study exactly to check the findings.

▷ **Activity 13: psychological theories and science**

Using the discussion in this section about the nature of science, to what extent can each of the following be considered scientific?
a Skinner's theory of operant conditioning
b Freud's psychodynamic approach
c humanistic psychology
When you have finished, see the notes on activities on page 760.

While some areas of psychological research adopt the criteria of a science, others do not. Since a strictly scientific approach cannot be used to investigate all the different factors which make us human, adopting it as the only way of carrying out psychological research limits the scope of what can be studied.

Problems arise in trying to fit psychology to a scientific paradigm because of the nature of what is being studied, i.e. people. Psychologists, as people themselves, come to the subject with beliefs, expectations and prejudices about the way people function. These are known as **implicit theories**, i.e. theories which have not been put to the test in any very systematic way. These beliefs may mean that it is difficult to be as objective as a scientific approach would require. For example, if you believe that watching violence on TV makes children aggressive, it may be very difficult to be unbiased in assessing the results of a study exploring this.

It is also possible that the testing situation may influence research. For example, the presence of an observer may change the behaviour of those who are being observed. People may also guess the purpose of the study. This kind of problem is referred to as

the demand characteristics of a situation. As a result of **demand characteristics**, participants may adapt their behaviour to what they think the experimenter wants or expects. This is a particular problem with children, who are usually very eager to please. A good example of a study with high demand characteristics was carried out by Berkowitz and LePage (1967), discussed in chapter 7. On the other hand, participants may act to put themselves in a good light, or behave in the way they think they 'should' behave. This factor is known as **social desirability**. See for example the discussion of the EPI in chapter 7. The physicist studying subatomic particles does not run into this kind of problem.

Some areas of psychology seem to be particularly problematical. Suppose we want to study how people behave in social situations. We can observe naturally occurring behaviour, but then the data we collect are likely to be distorted by a range of variables over which we have no control. If we put in place all the controls required by a strictly scientific approach, so that we have isolated the one variable in which we are interested, the situation may bear little resemblance to what happens in the real world. The study would then be said to lack **ecological validity**, and the conclusions we could draw about the behaviour we were studying might not be generally applicable.

▷ **Activity 14: problems of studying social processes**

a Imagine that you are planning to carry out a study to determine whether watching a violent TV programme causes children to behave aggressively. Make a list of all the variables you would need to control to make sure that any aggression shown by children after watching a violent TV programme occurred *as a result* of watching it.
b Make a list of any ways in which a carefully controlled study might differ from what happens when children watch TV in a normal, everyday situation, i.e. ways in which it might have poor ecological validity.
When you have finished, see the notes on activities on page 760.

... HE GETS AGGRESSIVE NOT WATCHING TELLY.

Since the study of psychology may pose so many problems, it has been argued that psychology can never reach the status of a science like physics or chemistry. But some of these problems can also arise in disciplines which we regard unquestioningly as scientific. For example, in physics the act of measuring may disturb what is being measured. It could also be argued that studying subatomic particles using an electron microscope is an indirect way of getting information, in the same way that observing behaviour may be an indirect way of accessing internal processes.

There is a case to be made for thinking of psychology as a science, but a different kind of science from physics or chemistry. Given the nature of the subject matter, the methods used may need to be adapted. The case study method, used by Freud and others, can be an appropriate way of collecting psychological data if used systematically. Observation of naturally occurring behaviour, though it is likely to lack the element of control achieved in scientific experimentation, also has something to offer. Introspection, as used by Wundt and by humanistic psychologists, has drawbacks, in that it is hard to derive precise measurements from it. On the other hand, it is likely to give us much richer data, and therefore a much more complete picture of what is going on.

Several psychologists have suggested that the use of the traditional scientific method in psychology should be replaced by a new paradigm. For example, De Waele and Harre (1979) have proposed that the interpretations of participants in a study should be considered the most important data. If this principle is followed instead of collecting data in terms imposed by the researcher, a wide range of ideas may emerge which may be quite different from the preconceptions of the researcher.

There is no easy answer to the question of whether or not psychology is a science. The extent to which it can (or should) be scientific will depend on the topic being studied, the aims of the study and the kinds of data you wish to collect.

- Science works by producing **theories** from which **hypotheses** can be derived and tested in a systematic and controlled way. The aim is to increase **understanding** of a phenomenon, so that **general laws** can be established. These then allow **prediction** and ultimately **control** of behaviour.
- While some areas of psychology work well using these criteria, they are less appropriate for other aspects of human functioning. Some psychologists reject the scientific approach, given the nature of what is being studied.
- The subject matter of psychology, i.e. people, can make a strictly scientific approach problematic. It may be a good idea to use a **range of methods**, which together can contribute to a fuller understanding of what it is to be human.

27.8 THE NATURE–NURTURE DEBATE

Another issue which is important in many areas of psychology is what is known as the nature–nurture debate. This links in with philosophical **rationalist** and **associationist** ideas, going back to the Ancient Greeks. For instance, Plato's philosophy takes a rationalist approach, while the philosophy of Aristotle takes an associationist approach.

In the past, theorists have taken extreme views in this debate, with some claiming that human abilities and characteristics are genetically determined and innate, i.e. we are born with them, and they will emerge as we mature. This is the **rationalist (nature)** viewpoint. Others believed that very little is present when we are born – perhaps only a few simple reflexes – and that human development is shaped entirely by environmental influences. Behaviours are learned; for example, as the result of socialisation. This represents the **associationist (nurture)** position.

▶ Activity 15: nature vs. nurture

For each of these topics, decide whether you think nature or nurture is more important:
1 The development of a clinical condition such as depression
2 Personality, e.g. whether you tend to be sociable or prefer to spend time on your own
3 The nature of intelligence: are you born with a certain level of intelligence, or can intelligent behaviour be developed?
4 Making sense of what we see
5 Children's acquisition of language
6 Levels of aggression in children
When you have finished, see the notes on activities on page 761.

The nature–nurture question is important because each position seems to have implications for the possibility of change. For example, if we assume that how intelligent we are is fixed by our genes (like eye colour), it seems to follow that we can do little to increase it. On the other hand, if it can be acquired, the implication is that all children would need to have an education tailored towards developing these abilities. The assumption is that what is genetically determined is fixed, whereas what is acquired through contact with the environment is changeable.

However, it is misleading to assume that because something is genetically inherited, it is therefore fixed. Let us take as an example the illness phenylketonuria.

···*BELIEVING IN NATURE RATHER THAN NURTURE WOULD COST LESS*···

This is an inherited condition, caused by a single recessive gene which leads to serious mental retardation, but these effects can be eliminated by adapting the person's diet. So the illness is hereditary, but its effects are not fixed.

Similarly it can't be assumed that because a characteristic is affected by the environment, it can necessarily be changed. An example here could be brain damage resulting from lack of oxygen at birth. The lack of oxygen is an environmental influence, but nothing can be done about the resulting brain damage.

▶ Activity 16: nature or nurture?

Think of nature and nurture as being the two extremes of a continuum. Where along this continuum would you place each of the main approaches in psychology: biological; cognitive; behaviourist; psychodynamic; humanistic psychology? On what factors did you base your decision?

When you have finished, see the notes on activities on page 761.

You might find it useful to look at some of the areas where the nature–nurture debate has been very much to the fore. For example, in chapter 16 three major theories of **language acquisition** were discussed:

Figure 11: the nature–nurture debate and language acquisition

Skinner: language, like any other behaviour, is learnt by the processes of shaping and reinforcement, very much a 'nurture' viewpoint. Biology has provided only the general mechanisms which allow for learning.

Chomsky: Skinner's theory cannot explain the rapid and orderly development of language. We must therefore have an innate device for organising our understanding of language (the Language Acquisition Device). Minimal input from the environment is necessary for language to be learned, so this is essentially a 'nature' viewpoint.

Bruner: Language is a social activity and has its roots in social interaction. The 'nature' part of this view is that there is an innate tendency to interact with others which makes language learning possible, and for caregivers to structure their interaction with the child to facilitate this. The 'nurture' part lies in the input of others into the interaction.

If you read the discussion of theories of language acquisition in chapter 16, you will find that there is evidence for all three theories, as well as some limitations in each case to their claims. It is clear that both nature and nurture have a part to play.

Similarly, there is a discussion in chapter 24 of the causes of schizophrenia. There is evidence from adoption and twin studies that there is quite a strong genetic component in this disorder. For example, monozygotic twins are far more likely to show concordance for schizophrenia than dizygotic twins. This suggests a 'nature' interpretation for the aetiology of this disorder. However, schizophrenia may be triggered by stressful life experiences – the diathesis–stress model of mental disorders – so this would indicate an input from 'nurture' influences. The 'nurture' side of the argument is strengthened by evidence that environmental factors, such as high expressed emotion in the families of schizophrenics, play an important part in the maintenance of the disorder.

From these two examples, it would seem to be simplistic to see the nature–nurture debate in either–or terms; both influences are important. Even trying to assess the relative contributions of nature and nurture to a particular aspect of human functioning is illogical, since it assumes that the effects of 'nature' and 'nurture' are additive, and so is just a rather more sophisticated form of asking whether heredity or environment is most important. As Hebb pointed out as long ago as 1949, this is rather like asking which contributes more to the area of a field, its length or its width.

An interactionist approach is now seen as the most appropriate way of considering the contributions of 'nature' and 'nurture'. Heredity and environment interact to produce an end result, and the nature of the interaction between existing structure and environmental input in specific topic areas should be the focus of psychological research.

- ⊝ The **nature–nurture** debate is an issue in many areas of psychology.
- ⊝ It is important because it seems to suggest how useful intervention to bring about **change** might be.
- ⊝ 'Nature' does not necessarily imply 'fixed'. 'Nurture' does not imply 'able to be changed'.
- ⊝ Nature–nurture is not an either–or issue. The two influences **interact**.

Notes on activities

1 The emphasis on difference in theories with alpha bias is likely to perpetuate stereotypes of 'what men are like' and 'what women are like', playing down the many ways in which men and women are similar. At the same time, theories with beta bias are likely to apply male standards to both men and women, giving no weight to the differing experiences of men and women, and the ways in which women's psychological functioning varies from that of men.

Both biases can lead to discrimination against women. The culture of psychology has been dominated by male standards; for example, see the similarity between 'healthy adult' and 'healthy male', and the dissimilarity of both from 'healthy female' (chapter 5, box C). As a result of alpha bias, women can suffer discrimination where they are perceived as being different from (and so inferior to) the male norm. Beta bias – for example, in Kohlberg's theory of moral development (chapter 17) – could lead to women being judged inappropriately, in this case as less moral, using male standards.

2 a Two obvious examples are pregnancy and the menopause.

b Being sexually harassed, or indeed raped, are more likely to be experienced by women.

3 Freud claimed that 'anatomy is destiny', in other words, developmental pathways are determined by sex. This could be seen as an example of alpha bias, since it focuses on differences between men and women. His ideas about gender development rely heavily on the experience of the third (phallic) psychosexual stage. Gender development is described in terms of the outcome of the Oedipus conflict, which only boys experience, and where the young boy identifies with the father and introjects the father's ideals. Freud himself recognised that his explanation of the development of girls during this stage was not without shortcomings. The account of the Electra complex attempted to fit girls' experience to the template of the Oedipus conflict, and is therefore an example of androcentrism.

4 a This approach looks at the effect of working mothers; what about working fathers? There is alpha bias here, since the research project rests on the stereotype of women necessarily being children's major caregivers, with the underlying assumption that this is the natural order of things.

b There could be several sexist reasons why this project failed to find funding. There is possibly the assumption that women's experience in this area is of no particular interest, or a failure to understand why women's experience in this setting should be any different from that of men, i.e. an androcentric viewpoint leading to beta bias.

c The choice of wording here is sexist, with 'dependent' sounding pejorative; for example, compare the use of the terms 'context-sensitive' and 'context-insensitive' to 'field-dependent' and 'field-independent'. The latter terms can therefore be said to show androcentrism, since women are compared with the male norm. The emphasis on gender differences, rather than the extent to which there is overlap between men and women in this area, is an example of alpha bias.

d Kohlberg took an androcentric approach, in that he assumed that a pattern of development derived from testing men could be automatically applied to women. There is alpha bias here, in that where women do not fit the male pattern Kohlberg developed, their development is seen as inferior. Gilligan (1977) suggested that women's moral reasoning differs from that of men since it has different priorities (see chapter 17).

5 *Strange Situation*: The patterns of attachment identified using this technique vary, with a German sample showing a high percentage of anxious–avoidant behaviour, and a Japanese sample a high percentage of anxious–ambivalent behaviour, compared with British samples. It could be concluded that these differences indicate less adequate parenting in Germany and Japan. However, this would fail to take into account the different experiences of young children in these cultures which would influence their behaviour in the Strange Situation.

Intelligence testing: American research has found that African Americans on average score 15 points lower on intelligence tests than white Americans. This could lead (and has led) to the conclusion that there must be genetic differences between these subcultures, with African Americans being inferior. In terms of practical implications, African Americans might not be offered the same educational opportunities as white Americans. However, the nature of intelligence tests and their cultural bias, together with the experience of belonging to an ethnic minority within a dominant culture, would need to be considered.

6 Hamer claimed that his research furthered our knowledge about an important aspect of human nature; he went on to point out that 'The AIDS epidemic has taught us, too bitterly, that we have more to fear from ignorance than from new knowledge about human sexuality'. These findings might also serve to reduce homophobia; if homosexuality is genetic, it is not the result of a choice made by the individual, who can therefore not be blamed for it. On the other hand, the research opens up the possibility of prenatal testing for a gay gene, leading to the possibility of termination of an 'affected' foetus, even though homosexuality is neither a disease nor an abnormality. It would also be possible for insurance companies to insist on testing to identify homosexuals, against whom it would be possible to discriminate on the basis of presumed dangerous lifestyle choices.

7 a This difference could (and has) been interpreted as demonstrating the inferiority of African Americans, with the assumption being made that these differences in scores reflect underlying genetic differences between races. Following on from this, the findings could be used to discriminate between people in terms of access to education; there is no point in offering education to those unable to benefit from it.

On the other hand, the differences could be interpreted in terms of test bias, since the tests were developed by white Americans and relate to white culture, or they could reflect the inadequacy of educational opportunities available to African Americans. In turn, this interpretation could lead to more appropriate ways of testing being devised, relating to black culture, and the identification of the causes of problems experienced by this group, leading in turn to potential remedies.

b This finding, in a study by Goldfarb (chapter 3, box E), was interpreted as lending support to Bowlby's maternal deprivation hypothesis. The later problems were ascribed to the lack of continuous care from one person, and the findings were used to persuade mothers that their role was to give their children continuous care in their early years.

A somewhat different interpretation could look rather more widely at the characteristics of the institution in explaining the poor development of children in their care, rather than focusing purely on the lack of continuous care. Such institutions were in general unstimulating places, with few playthings. Staff were discouraged from interacting with the children beyond offering basic care. From this it would follow that changes might be expected if the environment was made more stimulating, and interaction between staff and children was increased.

8 a The quality of the research here was high, since Skinner carried out a series of very carefully planned and well controlled studies. The animals would have suffered some discomfort, since they would need to be kept hungry in order for food to be a reinforcer; however, it would seem a bit extreme to characterise this as suffering. The benefits of this research have been far-reaching. The basic principles of learning established by Skinner's research have had numerous practical applications; for example, in helping children with autism (see e.g. Clancy and McBride, chapter 25, box B) and the use of a token economy system to help people with a mental disorder (see e.g. Paul and Lentz, chapter 25, box C).

b The Harlow and Zimmerman study was in general good quality research, though it is in some ways open to criticism. For example, it failed to match the surrogate mothers (their faces were very different) so that the only difference between them was whether they were covered in cloth or consisted of just a wire frame. Quite a lot of animal suffering was involved here, not only to the young animals raised in isolation, but also later on in their lives when they were unable to interact socially with others of their species. They were typically unable to mate successfully, or if they did so, made poor and neglectful mothers. They were also likely to self-mutilate. However, bearing in mind the closeness of the species relationship between monkeys and humans, some benefits did come out of this research. It suggested the importance of contact comfort for healthy psychological development, and was indirectly partly responsible, through its influence on Bowlby, for developing our understanding of the needs of young children. For example, parents are now encouraged to stay with their children when they are in hospital.

c The Brady study again was a well controlled piece of research, with clear findings. However, the suffering here was extreme, given that the 'executive' monkeys developed ulcers and died. The benefits of this research are questionable, since the fact that stress could cause ulcers was already well documented. It simply discovered that having to maintain constant vigilance could be a cause of stress-related illness.

9 a This can cause distress in animals, and it is possible that the young will be deserted.

b This kind of procedure is likely to be very stressful.

c Playback of predator calls can cause distress. There is also the danger that repetition of calls, with no predator present, may lead to habituation, so that calls relating to genuine predators are ignored.

d Animals may come to depend on the food provided, which may cause problems when the experiment comes to an end. Some studies using food addition are intended to investigate dominance or territoriality; the aggression elicited could lead to injury or even death for the birds or animals involved.

e This procedure may compromise the survival chances of the birds or animals which are removed. In this example, the young birds may not have reached a suitable spot for overwintering, and so may not have survived.

f The need to forage for extra young is likely to lead to stress for the parent bird, and additional energy demands in the search for food, compromising her survival chances and therefore also those of her chicks.

g Again, stress is likely, if only from the handling involved. In addition, the mating chances of the shorter tailed birds in this example have been compromised, and the excessive tail length of group 2 birds could make avoiding predators difficult.

11 A behaviourist approach would seek to explain it as a learned response to a stimulus situation, which has in some way been reinforced. A cognitive approach would see it as the result of the development of irrational thought patterns, while humanistic psychologists would explain it in terms of distorted personal growth. At the physiological level, it could be explained as the result of an imbalance of chemical neurotransmitters. The physiological explanation here reflects a reductionist approach; the complex phenomenon of depression is reduced to a chemical explanation. Similarly, the behaviourist explanation is also reductionist, since the explanation would focus on simple units of learning.

12 a At a physiological level, research has found that there is a genetic component to schizophrenia, and that there is a link with an excess of the neurotransmitter dopamine. However, this only gives a partial picture. A cognitive approach provides insight into symptoms such as delusions and thought disturbances. At a higher level still, there seems to be a connection between the development of schizophrenia and the experience of stressful life events, fitting in with the diathesis–stress model.

b At the physiological level, careful research has provided a lot of information about the mechanics of visual perception; for example, the processes involved in perceiving shape, colour and movement. However, study of the constancies – shape, size, and so on – have shown that cognitive processes are also important; how we interpret environmental stimuli depends on knowledge, memory and expectations. This is also demonstrated by the study of visual illusions which seem to be the result of inappropriate perceptual hypotheses. At a higher level, cultural factors also influence perception, with the physical environment within which people live influencing how they perceive, as shown by cross-cultural differences in the susceptibility to visual illusions.

c Many therapies (with the exception of psychoanalysis) are used eclectically, i.e. therapies arising from different beliefs about the aetiology of mental disorders may be used in combination. For example, in the case of depression, a physiological approach would see the causes of depression as physical, such as an imbalance of neurotransmitters, so somatic therapies such as drugs might be used. However, this would not preclude the use of other therapies, so a person might also be offered humanistic counselling (based on the aetiology being seen as a problem in personal growth) or cognitive–behavioural therapy (with the aetiology being seen as inappropriate ways of thinking). The use of different levels of analysis in combination can perhaps offer more than one level alone.

13 a Skinner's theory of operant conditioning fits well within a scientific framework. It is parsimonious in that it uses a few simple principles, such as shaping and reinforcement, to explain a huge range of human behaviour: gender development, moral development, language acquisition, and so on. The theory allows testable predictions to be developed, and the research can be carried out in the objective, controlled and replicable way essential to science. The principles of the theory have been used to control the behaviour both of animals and of humans; for example, in behavioural therapies.

b Freud considered himself to be a scientist, and to some extent his approach can be said to be scientific; for example, in its careful collection and analysis of data. However, although it is very good at explaining behaviour – Freud has something to say about virtually any topic in psychology – the theory is less good at making predictions. For example, someone who became fixated in the anal retentive substage of psychosexual development could express this symbolically as an adult by being mean and miserly. On the other hand, using the ego defence mechanism of reaction formation, they could be overly generous. The theory is therefore essentially unfalsifiable; it cannot be proved wrong. Some attempts have been made to test parts of Freud's theory in a scientific way, but its lack of predictive power makes this difficult.

c Humanistic psychology does not aim to be scientific in the way described. The scientific approach takes a deterministic viewpoint, in that it attempts to establish cause and effect relationships, and laws which can be generally applied. In contrast, humanistic psychology is interested in the individual, and what makes each person unique. It is not interested in either prediction or control; these are matters for the individual.

14 You may have suggested that you would need to control for the children's normal viewing habits, since results could be very different if the child never (or frequently) watches such programmes. Similarly, previous experience of violence from other sources would need to be considered. A child would need to watch the programme alone; otherwise any aggression could be the result of imitating other children's reactions to what they have seen. It would also be relevant to control for the child's usual play behaviour, and what is classed as 'normal' or 'aggressive' in his or her social circle.

If all these factors were controlled for, it is likely that you would end up observing a situation that is very different from a natural situation. Children often only half watch the TV when it is on. They may be eating crisps, talking to (or fighting with) their friends, going out of the room from time to time to get a drink or switching channels part way through the programme if they decide they would prefer to watch something else, and so on. This is very much less focused than a study which sits children down in front of a TV and asks them to watch what is on the screen. In a natural setting, there may also be others watching at the same time, who might comment on the programme's unreality or be critical of the violence. Again, these factors could affect how a child reacts.

Given these kinds of factors, it would be very difficult, if not impossible, to run a study in which irrelevant variables were controlled, and yet which at the same time provided evidence relating to how viewing violence might affect children's behaviour in real life.

15 For some of these topics, you may have had no problem coming to a decision; for example, it may seem self-evident that some people are born more intelligent than others because they are born to intelligent parents, or that children who grow up with parents who suffer from depression will be affected by their environment, and so be more likely to become depressed themselves. You may have been less sure about other topics. Nature–nurture is in fact an issue in all these areas.

16 *biological*: with its focus on genetic, physiological, hormonal and neurochemical factors, this is very much towards the 'nature' end.

cognitive: somewhat towards the centre; it is assumed that we have innate information-processing abilities, but how these are applied is very much determined by experience.

behaviourism: since all our behaviour apart from reflexes is assumed to be acquired by the environmental forces of shaping and reinforcement, or by the formation of stimulus–response bonds, this is very much towards the 'nurture' end.

psychodynamic: given Freud's view that 'anatomy is destiny', and his emphasis on the influence of instincts, it would be reasonable to conclude that this is towards the 'nature' end. However, how innate factors are expressed will be modified by the restrictions imposed by society via the ego and superego.

humanistic psychology: since this approach looks at the whole person, innate basic physiological needs form part of the picture. However, a more important area of focus is how the person develops through their interaction with their social world, so this approach is much more towards the nurture end.

REFERENCES

Abernathy EM (1940) The effect of changed environmental conditions upon the results of college examinations. *Journal of Psychology* **10** pp 293–301.

Abramson LY, Seligman MEP and Teasdale JD (1978) Learned helplessness in humans: critique and reformulation. *Journal of Abnormal Psychology* **87** pp 49–74.

Adams GR and Fitch SA (1982) Ego stage and identity status development: a cross-sequential analysis. *Journal of Personality and Social Psychology* **43(3)** pp 574–583.

Adorno TW, Frenkel-Brunswick E, Levinson DJ and Sanford RN (1950) *The Authoritarian Personality*. New York: Harper & Row.

Agnew HW Jr, Webb WB and Williams RL (1964) The effects of stage four sleep deprivation. *Electroencephalography and Clinical Neurophysiology* **17** pp 68–70.

Ainsworth M, Blehar MC, Waters E and Wall S (1978) *Patterns of Attachment: a Psychological Study of the Strange Situation*. Hillsdale, NJ: Lawrence Erlbaum.

Aitchison J (1983) *The Articulate Mammal*. London: Hutchinson.

Akerstedt T (1985) Shifted Sleep Hours. *Annals of Clinical Research* **17(5)** pp 273–279.

Alcock J (1993) *Animal Behaviour: An Evolutionary Approach* (5th edn). Sunderland, MA: Sinauer Associates Inc.

Aldridge-Morris R (1989) *Multiple Personality: An Exercise in Deception*. Hillsdale, NJ: Erlbaum.

Allen J (1993) Dissociative processes: theoretical underpinnings of a working model. *Bulletin of the Menninger Clinic* **57** pp 287–308.

Allen L *et al.* (1989) . Two sexually dimorphic cell groups in the human brain. *Journal of Neuroscience* **9** pp 497–506.

Allen M (1976) Twin studies of affective illness. *Archives of General Psychiatry* **33** pp 1476–1478.

Allen VL and Levine JM (1968) Social support, dissent and conformity. *Sociometry* **31** pp 138–149.

Allen VL and Levine JM (1971) Social support and conformity: the role of independent assessment of reality. *Journal of Experimental Social Psychology* **7** pp 48–58.

Allport DA (1989) Visual attention. In Posner M (ed) *Foundations of Cognitive Science*. Cambridge, MA: MIT Press.

Allport DA, Antonis B and Reynolds P (1972) On the division of attention: a disproof of the single channel hypothesis. *Quarterly Journal of Experimental Psychology* **24** pp 225–235.

Allport FH (1924) *Social Psychology*. Boston, MA: Houghton Mifflin.

Allport GW (1954) *The Nature of Prejudice*. Reading, MA: Addison-Wesley.

Allport GW and Pettigrew TF (1957) Cultural influences on the perception of movement: the trapezoidal illusion among Zulus. *Journal of Abnormal and Social Psychology* **55** pp 104–113.

Altman JS and Kien J (1989) New models for motor control. *Neural Computation* **1(2)** pp 173–183.

American Psychiatric Association (1994) *Diagnostic and Statistical Manual of Mental Disorders* (4th edn). Washington, DC: American Psychiatric Association.

American Psychological Association (1982) *Ethical Principles in the Conduct of Research with Human Participants*. Washington, DC: American Psychological Association.

Anand BK and Brobeck JR (1951) Hypothalamic control of food intake in rats and cats. *Yale Journal of Biological Medicine* **24** pp 123–140.

Anastasi A (1958) in Lerner RM (1986) *Concepts and Theories in Human Development* (2nd edn). New York: Random House.

Anderson CA (1989) Temperature and aggression: ubiquitous effects of heat on occurrence of human violence. *Psychological Bulletin* **106** pp 74–96.

Andersson B-E (1992) Effects of day care on cognitive and socioemotional competence of thirteen-year-old Swedish schoolchildren. *Child Development* **63** pp 20–36.

Andersson M (1982) Female choice selects for extreme tail length in a widowbird. *Nature* **299** pp 818–820.

Annis RC and Frost B (1973) Human visual ecology and orientation anisotropies in acuity. *Science* **182** pp 729–731.

Anthony BD (1982) Lesbian client – lesbian therapist: opportunities and challenges in working together. *Journal of Homosexuality* **7** pp 45–57.

Archer SL (1982) The lower age boundaries of identity development. *Child Development* **53** pp 1551–1556.

Argyle M (1989) *The Social Psychology of Work* (2nd edn). Harmondsworth: Penguin.

Armsby RE (1971) A re-examination of the development of moral judgement in children. *Child Development* **42** pp 1241–1248.

Aronson E (1980) *The Social Animal* (3rd edn). San Francisco, CA: WH Freeman.

Aronson E (1988) *The Social Animal* (5th edn). New York: Freeman.

Aronson E, Bridgeman DL and Geffner R (1978) The effects of a cooperative classroom structure on student behaviour and attitudes. In Bar-Tal D and Saxe L (eds) *Social Psychology of Education*. New York: Wiley.

Aronson E, Wilson TD and Akert RM (1994) *Social Psychology: The Heart and the Mind*. New York: HarperCollins College Publishers.

Asch SE (1951) Effect of group pressure upon the modification and distortion of judgements. In Guetzkow H (ed) *Groups, Leadership and Men*. Pittsburgh, PA: Carnegie Press.

Asch SE (1952) *Social Psychology*. Englewood Cliffs, NJ: Prentice Hall.

Atchley RC (1982) Retirement: leaving the world of work. *Annals of the American Academy of Political and Social Science* **464** pp 120–131.

Atkinson RC and Shiffrin RM (1968) Human memory: a proposed system and its control processes. In Spence KW and Spence JT (eds) *The Psychology of Learning and Motivation* (vol.2). London: Academic Press.

Atkinson RC and Shiffrin RM (1971) The control of short-term memory. *Scientific American* **224** pp 82–90.

Atkinson RL, Atkinson RC, Smith EE and Hilyard ER (1983) *Introduction to Psychology* (8th edn). New York: Harcourt Brace Jovanovich.

Averbach E and Coriell AS (1961) Short-term memory in vision. *Bell System Technical Journal* **40** pp 309–328.

Ax AF (1953) The physiological differentiation of fear and anger in humans. *Psychosomatic Medicine* **15** pp 422–433.

Axelrod R and Hamilton WD (1981) The evolution of cooperation. *Science* **211** pp 1390–1396.

Axline V (1971) *Dibs: In Search Of Self*. Harmondsworth: Penguin.

Ayllon T and Azrin NH (1968) *The Token Economy: A Motivational System for Therapy and Rehabilitation*. New York: Appleton-Century-Crofts.

Ayres J (1983) Strategies to maintain relationships: their identification and usage. *Communication Quarterly* **31** pp 207–225.

Baddeley AD (1966) The influence of acoustic and semantic similarity on long-term memory for word sequences. *Quarterly Journal of Experimental Psychology* **18** pp 302–309.

Baddeley AD (1978) The trouble with levels: a re-examination of Craik and Lockhart's framework for memory research. *Psychological Review* **85(3)** pp 139–152.

Baddeley AD and Hitch G (1974) Working memory. In Bower GA (ed) *Recent Advances in Learning and Motivation* (vol.8). New York: Academic Press.

Baddeley AD, Thomson N and Buchanan M (1975) Word length and the structure of short-term memory. *Journal of Verbal Learning and Verbal Behavior* **14** pp 575–589.

Bahrick HP, Bahrick PO and Wittinger RP (1975) Fifty years of memory for names and faces: a cross-sectional approach. *Journal of Experimental Psychology: General* **104** pp 54–75.

Balda RP (1980) Recovery of cached seeds by a captive *Nucifraga cariocatactes*. *Zeitschrift für Tierpsychologie* **52** pp 331–346.

Balda RP and Kamil AC (1992) Long-term spatial memory in Clark's nutcracker, *Nucifraga columbiana*. *Animal Behaviour* **44** pp 761–769.

Balda RP and Turek RJ (1984) Memory in birds. In Roitblat HL, Bever TG and Terrace HS (eds) *Animal Cognition*. Hillsdale, NJ: Erlbaum.

Balkwell C (1981) Transition to widowhood: a review of the literature. *Family Relations* **30** pp 117–128.

Bandura A (1965) Influence of model's reinforcement contingencies on the acquisition of imitative responses. *Journal of Personality and Social Psychology* **1** pp 589–595.

Bandura A (1977) *Social Learning Theory* (2nd edn). Englewood Cliffs, NJ: Prentice Hall.

Bandura A (1986) *Social Foundations of Thought and Action: A Social Cognitive Theory*. Englewood Cliffs, NJ: Prentice Hall.

Bandura A and Menlove FL (1968) Factors determining vicarious extinction of avoidance behaviour through symbolic modelling. *Journal of Personality and Social Psychology* **8** pp 99–108.

Bandura A, Ross D and Ross SA (1961) Transmission of aggression through imitation of aggressive models. *Journal of Abnormal and Social Psychology* **63** pp 575–582.

Bandura A, Ross D and Ross SA (1963) Imitation of film-mediated aggressive models. *Journal of Abnormal and Social Psychology* **66** pp 3–11.

Bandura A and Rosenthal TL (1966) Vicarious classical conditioning as a function of arousal level. *Journal of Personality and Social Psychology* **3** pp 54–62.

Banks WP and Flora J (1977) Semantic and perceptual processes in symbolic comparisons. *Journal of Experimental Psychology: Human Perception and Performance* **3** pp 278–291.

Baran SJ *et al.* (1979) Television drama as a facilitator of prosocial behaviour. *Journal of Broadcasting* **23** pp 277–285.

Bard P (1928) Diencephalic mechanism for the expression of rage with special reference to the sympathetic nervous system. *American Journal of Physiology* **84** pp 490–515.

Barnard ND and Kaufman SR (1997) Animal research is wasteful and misleading. *Scientific American* pp 64–66.

Baron RA (1977) *Human Aggression*. New York: Plenum.

Baron RA and Bell PA (1975) Aggression and heat: mediating effects of prior provocation and exposure to an aggressive model. *Journal of Personality and Social Psychology* **31** pp 825–832.

Baron RA and Byrne D (1991) *Social Psychology* (6th edn). Boston, MA: Allyn & Bacon.

Baron RA and Byrne D (1997) *Social Psychology* (8th edn). Boston, MA: Allyn & Bacon.

Baron RA and Ransberger VM (1978) Ambient temperature and the occurrence of collective violence: the 'long hot summer' revisited. *Journal of Personality and Social Psychology* **36** pp 351–360.

Barrett CJ (1978) Effectiveness of widows' groups in facilitating change. *Journal of Consulting and Clinical Psychology* **46** pp 20–31.

Bar-Tal D and Saxe L (1976) Perception of similarity and dissimilarity in attractive couples and individuals. *Journal of Personality and Social Psychology* **33** pp 772–781.

Bartlett FC (1932) *Remembering*. Cambridge: Cambridge University Press.

Bastian P (1965) Dolphin experiment, reported in Wood FG (1973) *Marine Mammals and Man: The Navy's Porpoises and Sea Lions*. Washington DC: R B Luce.

Bateson E, Jackson D, Haley J and Weakland J (1956) Toward a theory of schizophrenia. *Behavioural Science* **1** pp 251–264.

Bateson P (1986) When to experiment on animals. *New Scientist* **109(1496)** pp 30–32.

Batson CD (1990) How social an animal? The human capacity for caring. *American Psychologist* **45** pp 36–46.

Batson CD, Duncan BD, Ackerman P, Buckley T and Birch K (1981) Is empathic emotion a source of altruistic motivation? *Journal of Personality and Social Psychology* **40** pp 290–302.

Batson CD, O'Quin K, Fultz J, Vanderplas M and Isen AM (1983) Influence of self-reported distress and empathy on egoistic versus altruistic motivation for help. *Journal of Personality and Social Psychology* **45** pp 706–718.

Baumrind D (1964) Some thoughts on ethics of research: after reading Milgram's behavioural study of obedience. *American Psychologist* **19** pp 421–423.

Bayley N (1955) On the growth of intelligence. *American Psychologist* **10** pp 805–818.

Beaumont JG (1988) *Understanding Neuropsychology*. Cambridge, MA: Blackwell.

Beck AT (1963) Thinking and depression. *Archives of General Psychiatry* **9** pp 324–333.

Beck AT (1967) *Depression: Causes and Treatment*. Philadelphia, PA: University of Philadelphia Press.

Beck AT (1983) Cognitive theory of depression: new perspectives. In Clayton PJ and Barrett AE (eds) *Treatment of Depression: Old Controversies and New Approaches*. New York: Raven Press.

Beck AT (1991) Cognitive therapy: a 30-year perspective. *American Psychologist* **46(4)** pp 368–375.

Beck AT, Emery G and Greenberg RL (1985) *Anxiety Disorders and Phobias: A Cognitive Perspective*. New York: Basic Books.

Beck AT, Freeman A and Associates (1990) *Cognitive Therapy of Personality Disorders*. New York: Guildford Press.

Bee H (1994) *Lifespan Development*. New York: HarperCollins.

Bee HL and Mitchell SK (1984) *The Developing Person: A Life-Span Approach* (2nd edn). New York: Harper & Row.

Bekerian DA and Bowers JM (1983) Eyewitness testimony: were we misled? *Journal of Experimental Psychology: Learning, Memory and Cognition* **9** pp 139–145.

Bellisle F, Dalix LM and DeCastro JM (1999) Eating patterns in French subjects studied by the 'weekly food diary' method. *Appetite* **32(1)** pp 46–52.

Belsher G and Costello CG (1988) Relapse after recovery from unipolar depression: a critical review. *Psychological Bulletin* **104** pp 84–86.

Belsky J (1981) Early human experience: a family perspective. *Developmental Psychology* **17(1)** pp 3–23.

Belsky J (1988) The "effects" of infant day care reconsidered. *Early Child Research Quarterly* **3** pp 235–272.

Bem SL (1981) Gender schema theory: a cognitive account of sex typing. *Psychological Review* **88** pp 354–364.

Bem SL (1989) Genital knowledge and gender constancy in preschool children. *Child Development* **60** pp 649–662.

Bemis KM (1978). Current approaches to the etiology and treatment of anorexia nervosa. *Psychological Bulletin* **85** pp 593–617.

Bender M (1995) The war goes on. *The Psychologist* **8** pp 78–79.

Benson PL, Karabenick SA and Lerner RM (1976) Pretty pleases: the effects of physical attractiveness, race and sex on receiving help. *Journal of Experimental and Social Psychology* **12** pp 409–415.

Benton D (1981) ECT: can the system take the shock? *Community Care* **12 March** pp 15–17.

Berger R (1969) Oculomotor control: a possible function of REM sleep. *Psychology Review* **76** pp 144–164.

Bergin AE (1971) The evaluation of therapeutic outcomes. In Bergin AE and Garfield SL (eds) *Handbook of Psychotherapy and Behaviour Change: An Empirical Analysis*. New York: Wiley.

Berglas S and Jones EE (1978) Drug choice as a self-handicapping strategy in response to non-contingent success. *Journal of Personality and Social Psychology* **36** pp 405–417.

Berko J (1958) The child's learning of English morphology. *Word* **14** pp 150–177.

Berkowitz L and LePage A (1967) Weapons as aggression-eliciting stimuli. *Journal of Personality and Social Psychology* **7** pp 202–207.

Berlin B and Kay P (1969) *Basic Colour Terms: Their Universality and Evolution*. Berkeley, CA: University of California Press.

Berman J, Murphy-Berman V and Singh P (1985) Cross-cultural similarities and differences in perceptions of fairness. *Journal of Cross-cultural Psychology* **16** pp 55–67.

Berne E (1964) *Games People Play: The Psychology of Human Relationships*. New York: Grove Press.

Bernstein B (1961) Social class and linguistic development. In Halsey AH, Flaud J and Anderson CA (eds) *Education, Economy and Society*. London: Collier-Macmillan Ltd.

Berry DS (1990) The perceiver as naïve scientist or the scientist as naïve perceiver? An ecological view of social knowledge acquisition. *Contemporary Social Psychology* **14** pp 145–153.

Berry JM, West RL and Dennehey DM (1989) Reliability and validity of the memory self-efficacy questionnaire. *Development Psychology* **25** pp 701–713.

Berscheid E and Walster E (1978) *Interpersonal Attraction*. Reading, MA: Addison-Wesley.

Bickman L (1971) The effect of another bystander's ability to help on bystander intervention in an emergency. *Journal of Experimental Social Psychology* **7** pp 367–379.

Biederman I (1987) Recognition-by-components: a theory of human image understanding. *Psychological Review* **94** pp 115–147.

Bierbrauer G (1979) Why did he do it? Attribution of obedience and the phenomenon of dispositional bias. *European Journal of Social Psychology* **9** pp 67–84.

Bierhoff HW, Klein R and Kramp P (1991) Evidence for the altruistic personality from data on accident research. *Journal of Personality* **59** pp 263–280.

Birchwood M, Hallett S and Preston M (1988) *Schizophrenia: and Integrated Approach to Research and Treatment.* London: Longman.

Bjorkland A *et al.* (1983) Intercerebral grafting of neuronal suspensions. *Acta Psychologica Scandinavica* **Supplement 522** pp 1–8.

Blakemore C (1988) *The Mind Machine.* London: BBC Publications.

Blakemore C and Cooper GF (1970) Development of the brain depends on the visual environment. *Nature* **228** pp 477–478.

Bliss E (1980) Multiple personalities: a report on the cases with implications for schizophrenia and hysteria. *Archives of General Psychiatry* **37** pp 1388–1397.

Bliss E and Jeppsen E (1985) Prevalence of multiple personality among inpatients and outpatients. *American Journal of Psychiatry* **142(2)** 250.

Bliss JT (1985) How prevalent is multiple personality? Dr Bliss replies. *American Journal of Psychiatry* **142(12)** pp 15–27.

Block NJ and Dworkin G (1974) IQ: heritability and inequality. *Philosophy and Public Affairs* **3** pp 331–407.

Blount G (1986) Dangerousness of patients with Capgras syndrome. *Nebraska Medical Journal* **71** p 207.

Blumenthal JA, Burg MM, Barefoot J, Williams RB, Haney T and Zimet C (1987) Social support, Type A behavior, and coronary artery disease. *Psychosomatic Medicine* **49** pp 331–339.

Blumstein P and Schwartz P (1983) *American Couples: Money, Work, Sex.* New York: William Morrow.

Bodmer WF (1972) Race and IQ: the genetic background. In Richardson K and Spears D (eds) *Race, Culture and Intelligence.* Harmondsworth: Penguin.

Boesch C (1991) Teaching among wild primates. *Animal Behaviour* **41** pp 530–532.

Bogdonoff MD, Klein RF, Estes EH, Shaw DM and Back K (1961) The modifying effect of conforming behaviour upon lipid responses accompanying CNS arousal. *Clinical Research* **9** p 135.

Bohannon P (1970) *Divorce and After.* New York: Doubleday.

Boker W (1992) A call for partnership between schizophrenic patients, relatives and professionals. *British Journal of Psychiatry* **161 (supplement 18)** pp 10–12.

Bokert E (1970) The effects of thirst and related auditory stimulation on dream reports. Paper presented to the Association for the Physiological Study of Sleep, Washington DC.

Bolles RC (1972) Reinforcement, expectancy and learning. *Psychological Review* **79(5)** pp 394–409.

Bolles RC (1980) Some functionalist thoughts about regulation. In Toates FM and Halliday TR (eds) *Analysis of Motivational Processes.* London: Academic Press.

Bolles RC (1980) Ethological learning theory. In Gazda GM and Corsini RJ (eds) *Theories of Learning: A Comparative Approach.* Itaska, IL: Free Press.

Bonner JT (1980) *The Evolution of Culture in Animals.* Princeton, NJ: Princeton University Press.

Bonnet MH and Webb WB (1979) The return to sleep. *Biological Psychology* **8(3)** pp 225–233.

Bookman MA (1978) Sensitivity of the homing pigeon t an earth-strength magnetic field. In Schmidt-Koenig K and Keeton WT (eds) *Animal Migration, Navigation and Homing. Proceedings in Life Sciences.* Berlin: Springer Verlag.

Borbely A (1986) *Secrets of Sleep.* Harmondsworth: Penguin.

Bornstein MH (1976) Infants are trichromats. *Journal of Experimental Child Psychology* **19** pp 401–419.

Bossard JHS (1932) Residential propinquity as a factor in mate selection. *American Journal of Sociology* **38** pp 219–224.

Bouchard TJ and McGue M (1981) Familial studies of intelligence: a review. *Science* **212** pp 1055–1059.

Boulton MG (1983) *On Being a Mother: A Study of Women with Preschool Children.* London: Tavistock.

Bourne LE, Dominowski RL and Loftus EF (1979) *Cognitive Processes.* Englewood Cliffs, NJ: Prentice Hall.

Bourne PG (1971) Altered adrenal function in two combat situations in Viet Nam. In Elefteriou BE and Scott JP (eds) *The Physiology of Aggression and Defeat.* New York: Plenum Press.

Bower GH, Monteiro KP and Gilligan SG (1978) Emotional mood as a context for learning and recall. *Journal of Verbal Learning and Verbal Behavior* **17** pp 573–585.

Bower TGR (1966) The visual world of infants. *Scientific American* **215(6)** pp 80–92.

Bowers D and Heilman K (1981) A dissociation between the processing of affective and nonaffective faces. Paper presented at a meeting of the International Neurological Society, Atlanta.

Bowlby J (1944) Forty-four juvenile thieves: their characters and home life. *International Journal of Psychoanalysis* **25** pp 1–57 and 207–228.

Bowlby J (1953) *Child Care and the Growth of Love.* Harmondsworth: Penguin.

Bowlby J (1969) *Attachment and Loss: attachment.* New York: Basic Books.

Bradbury TN and Fincham FD (1990) Attributions in marriage: review and critique. *Psychological Bulletin* **107** pp 3–33.

Brady JV (1958) Ulcers in 'executive monkeys'. *Scientific American* **199** pp 95–100.

Braine M (1963) On learning the grammatical order of words. *Psychological Review* **70** pp 115–120.

Brehm JW (1956) Post-decision changes in the desirability of alternatives. *Journal of Abnormal and Social Psychology* **52** pp 384–389.

Breland K and Breland M (1961) The misbehaviour of organisms. *American Psychologist* **16** pp 681–684.

Bremner JD, Southwick SM, Johnson DR, Yehoda R and Charney DS (1993) Childhood physical abuse and combat related post-traumatic stress disorder in Vietnam veterans. *American Journal of Psychiatry* **150(2)** pp 235–239.

Breuer J and Freud S (1895) Studies in hysteria. In Strachey J (ed) (1955) *The Standard Edition of the Complete Psychological Works of Sigmund Freud, Volume 2*. London: Hogarth Press.

Brewer WF and Treyens JC (1981) Role of schemata in memory for places. *Cognitive Psychology* **13** pp 207–230.

Bright M (1984) *Animal Communication*. London: British Broadcasting Corporation.

Broadbent DE (1958) *Perception and Communication*. London: Pergamon.

Broadbent DE (1982) Task combination and selective intake of information. *Acta Psychologica* **50** pp 253–290.

Broca P (1861) Remarques sur le siège de la faculté du langage articulé suivées d'une observation d'aphémie. *Bulletin de la Société Anatomique (Paris)* **6** pp 330–357.

Bromley DB (1988) *Human Ageing: An Introduction to Gerontology* (3rd edn). Harmondsworth: Penguin.

Bronfenbrenner U (1974) The origins of alienation. *Scientific American* **231** pp 53–61.

Broverman IK, Broverman DM, Clarkson FE, Rosencrantz PS and Vogel SR (1981) Sex role stereotypes and clinical judgements of mental health. In Howell E and Boyes M (eds) *Women and Mental Health*. New York: Basic Books.

Brown GW (1972) Influence of family life on the course of schizophrenic disorders: a replication. *British Journal of Psychiatry* **121** pp 241–248.

Brown GW and Harris TO (1978) *Social Origins of Depression: A Study of Psychiatric Disorder in Women*. London: Tavistock.

Brown JS and Burton RD (1978) Diagnostic model for procedural bugs in basic mathematical skills. *Cognitive Science* **2** pp 155–192.

Brown R (1986) *Social Psychology* (2nd edn). New York: Free Press.

Brown R (1988) Intergroup relations. In Hewstone M, Stroebe W, Codol JP and Stephenson GM (eds) *Introduction to Social Psychology*. Oxford: Basil Blackwell.

Brown R and Kulik J (1977) Flashbulb memories. *Cognition* **5** pp 73–99.

Brown R, Cazden CB and Bellugi U (1969) The child's grammar from one to three. In Hill JP (ed) *Minnesota Symposium on Child Psychology* (Vol.2). Minneapolis, MN: University of Minnesota Press.

Brown R, Coller N and Corsellis JAN (1986) Post-mortem evidence of structural brain changes in schizophrenia: differences in brain weight, temporal brain area, and parahippocampal gyrus compared with affective disorder. *Archives of General Psychiatry* **43** pp 36–42.

Bruce V and Valentine T (1988) When a nod's as good as a wink: the role of dynamic information in face recognition. In Gruneberg M, Morris P and Sykes R (eds) *Practical Aspects of Memory: Current Research and Issues* (vol.1). Chichester: John Wiley.

Bruce V and Young AW (1986) Understanding face recognition. *British Journal of Psychology* **77** pp 303–327.

Bruch H (1973) *Eating Disorders*. New York: Basic Books.

Bruner JS and Minturn AL (1955) Perceptual identification and perceptual organisation. *Journal of General Psychology* **53** pp 21–28.

Bryden M and Ley R (1983) Right hemispheric involvement in the perception and expression of emotion in normal humans. In Heilman P and Satz K (eds) *The Neuropsychology of Emotion*. New York: Guildford.

Buck R and Duffy R (1980) Nonverbal communication of affect in brain-damaged patients. *Cortex* **16** pp 351–362.

Buckhout R (1974) Eyewitness testimony. *Scientific American* **231** pp 23–31.

Buhler C (1968) *The Course of Human Life: a Study of Goals in the Humanistic Perspective*. New York: Springer.

Bull M and LaVecchio F (1978) Behaviour therapy for a child with Lesch–Nyhan syndrome. *Developmental Medicine and Child Neurology* **20(3)** pp 368–375.

Burke DM, Worthley J and Martin J (1988) I'll never forget what's her name: aging and tip of the tongue experiences in everyday life. In Gruneberg M, Morris PE and Sykes RN (eds) *Practical Aspects of Memory: Current Research and Issues* (vol.2). Chichester: Wiley.

Burks BS (1928) The relative influence of nature and nurture upon mental development: a comparative study of foster parent–foster child resemblance and true parent–true child resemblance. *Yearbook of the National Society for the Study of Education (part 1)* **27** pp 219–316.

Burt CL (1966) The genetic determination of differences in intelligence: a study of monozygotic twins reared together and apart. *British Journal of Psychology* **57** pp 137–153.

Burton AM and Bruce V (1992) I recognise your face but I can't remember your name: a simple explanation? *British Journal of Psychology* **83** pp 45–60.

Burton AM, Bruce V and Hancock PJB (1999) From pixels to people: a model of familiar face recognition. *Cognitive Science* **23** pp 1–31.

Burton AM, Bruce V and Johnson RA (1990) Understanding face recognition with an interactive activation model. *British Journal of Psychology* **81** pp 361–380.

Buss AH and Plomin R (1984) *Temperament: Early Developing Personality Traits*. Hillsdale, NJ: Erlbaum.

Buss DM (1989) Sex differences in human mate preferences: evolutionary hypotheses tested in 37 cultures. *Behavioural and Brain Sciences* **12** pp 1–49.

Buss DM (1992) Mate preference mechanisms: consequences for partner choice and intrasexual competition. In Barkow JH, Cosmides L and Tooby J (eds) *The Adapted Mind: Evolutionary Psychology and the Generation of Culture*. New York: Oxford University Press.

Buss DM (1999) *Evolutionary Psychology*. Needham Heights, MA: Allyn & Bacon.

Bussey K and Bandura A (1992) Self-regulatory mechanisms governing gender development. *Child Development* **63** pp 1236–1250.

Byrne D and Clore GL (1970) A reinforcement model of evaluative responses. *Personality: An International Journal* **1** pp 103–108.

Byrne R (1995) *The Thinking Ape*. Oxford: Oxford University Press.

Byrne R and Whiten A (1985) Tactical deception of familiar individuals in baboons (*Papio ursinus*). *Animal Behaviour* **33(2)** pp 669–673.

Byrne R and Whiten A (1987) A thinking primate's guide to deception. *New Scientist* **3 Dec** pp 54–57.

Byrne R and Whiten A (1988) *Machiavellian Intelligence: Social Expertise and the Evolution of Intellect in Monkeys, Apes and Humans*. Oxford: Clarendon Press.

Caldwell BM and Bradley RM (1978) *Home Observation for Measurement of the Environment*. Little Rock, AR: University of Arkansas.

Calhoun JB (1962) Population density and social pathology. *Scientific American* **206(2)** pp 139–148.

Campbell A (1981) *Girl Delinquents*. Oxford: Basil Blackwell.

Campbell A (1984) *The Girls in the Gang*. Oxford: Basil Blackwell.

Campbell DT (1967) Stereotypes and the perception of group differences. *American Psychologist* **22** pp 817–829.

Campbell FA and Ramey CT (1991) *The Carolina Abecedarian Project*. Paper presented at the biennial meeting of the Society for Research in Child Development, Seattle, WA.

Campos JJ, Langer A and Krowitz A (1970) Cardiac responses on the cliff in pre-locomotor human infants. *Science* **170** pp 196–197.

Cannon, WB (1927) The James–Lange theory of emotions: a critical examination and an alternative. *American Journal of Psychology* **39** pp 106–124.

Cannon WB (1929) *Bodily Changes in Pain, Hunger, Fear and Rage*. New York: Appleton-Century-Crofts.

Cannon WB and Washburn AL (1912) An explanation of hunger. *American Journal of Psychology* **29** pp 441–454.

Carlson NR (1991) *Physiology of Behaviour*. Boston, MA: Allyn & Bacon.

Carmichael L, Hogan P and Walter A (1932) An experimental study of the effect of language on the reproduction of visually perceived forms. *Journal of Experimental Psychology* **15** pp 1–22.

Carr AT (1974) Compulsive neurosis: a review of the literature. *Psychological Bulletin* **81** pp 311–319.

Carroll JB and Casagrande JB (1958) The function of language classifications in behaviour. In Maccoby EE, Newcombe TM and Hartley EL (eds) *Readings in Social Psychology* (3rd edn). New York: Holt, Rinehart and Winston.

Carter H and Glick PC (1970) *Marriage and Divorce: A Social and Economic Study*. Cambridge, MA: Harvard University Press.

Carter R (1998) *Mapping the Mind*. London: Weidenfeld and Nicholson.

Cartwright RD (1978) *A Primer on Sleep and Dreaming*. Reading, MA: Addison-Wesley.

Case R (1978) Intellectual development from birth to adulthood: a neo-Piagetian interpretation. In Siegler R (ed) *Children's Thinking: What Develops?* Hillsdale, NJ: Erlbaum.

Caspi A and Herbener ES (1990) Continuity and change: assortative marriage and the consistency of personality in adulthood. *Journal of Personality and Social Psychology* **58(2)** pp 250–258.

Caton R (1977) Interim report of investigations on the electric currents of the brain. *British Medical Journal* **Supplement 5 May**.

Cattell RB (1963) Theory of fluid and crystallized intelligence: a critical experiment. *Journal of Educational Psychology* **54** pp 1–22.

Ceci SJ, Ross DF and Toglia MP (1987) Suggestibility of children's memory: psycholegal implications. *Journal of Experimental Psychology: General* **116** pp 38–49.

Chapman LJ and Chapman JP (1967) Genesis of popular but erroneous psychodiagnostic observation. *Journal of Abnormal Psychology* **72** pp 193–204.

Chapuis N and Scardigli P (1993) Shortcut ability in hamsters (*Mesocricetus auratus*): the role of environmental and kinaesthetic information. *Animal Learning and Behaviour* **21** pp 255–265.

Charness N (1981) Aging and skilled problem solving. *Journal of Experimental Psychology: General* **110** pp 21–28.

Chase WG and Simon HA (1973) Perception in chess. *Cognitive Psychology* **4** pp 55–81.

Cherry EC (1953) Some experiments on the recognition of speech with one and two ears. *Journal of the Acoustical Society of America* **25** pp 975–979.

Childs CP and Greenfield PM (1982) Informal modes of learning and teaching: the case of Zinacanteco learning. In Warren N (ed) *Advances in Cross-Cultural Psychology*. London: Academic Press.

Chiriboga DA (1982) Adaptations to marital separation in later and earlier life. *Journal of Gerontology* **37** pp 109–114.

Chodorow N (1978) *The Reproduction of Mothering*. Berkeley, CA: University of California Press.

Chorover S and Schiller P (1965) Short-term retrograde amnesia in rats. *Journal of Comparative and Physiological Psychology* **59** pp 73–78.

Cialdini RB, Schaller M, Houlihan D, Arps K, Fulz J and Beaman AL (1987) Empathy-based helping: is it selflessly or selfishly motivated? *Journal of Personality and Social Psychology* **52** pp 749–758.

Clancy H and McBride GM (1969) The autistic process and its treatment. *Journal of Child Psychology and Psychiatry* **10** pp 233–244.

Clare A (1980) *Psychiatry In Dissent*. London: Tavistock.

Clark MS (1984) Record keeping in two types of relationships. *Journal of Personality and Social Psychology* **47** pp 549–557.

Clarke AC (1952) An examination of the operation of residual propinquity as a factor in mate selection. *American Sociological Review* **27** pp 17–22.

Clarke-Stewart KA (1973) Interactions between mothers and their young children: characteristics and consequences. *Monograph of the Society for Research into Child Development* **38** (6–7, serial no. 153).

Clarke-Stewart KA and Fein GG (1983) Early childhood problems. In Mussen PH (ed) *Handbook of Child Psychology*. New York: Wiley.

Cline VB, Croft RG and Corrier S (1973) Desensitisation of children to television violence. *Journal of Personality and Social Psychology* **27** pp 360–365.

Clutton-Brock TH (1983) Selection in relation to sex. In Bendall DS (ed) *From Molecules to Men*. Cambridge: Cambridge University Press.

Coates B and Pusser HE (1975) Positive reinforcement and punishment in Sesame Street and Mister Rogers' *Neighbourhood*. *Journal of Broadcasting*. **19** pp 143–151.

Cochrane R (1977) Mental illness in immigrants to England and Wales: an analysis of mental hospital admissions, 1971. *Social Psychiatry* **12** pp 25–35.

Cochrane R (1988) Marriage, separation and divorce. In Fisher S and Reason J (eds) *Handbook of Life Stress, Cognition and Health*. J Wiley & Sons.

Cochrane R (1996) Marriage and madness. *Psychology Review* **3** pp 2–5.

Cochrane R and Stopes-Roe M (1980) Factors affecting the distribution of psychological symptoms in urban areas of England. *Acta Psychiatrica Scandinavica* **61** pp 445–460.

Coger RW and Serafetinides EA (1990) Schizophrenia, corpus callosum, and interhemispheric communication: a review. *Psychiatry Research* **34** pp 163–184.

Cohen DB (1973) Sex role orientation and dream recall. *Journal of Abnormal Psychology* **82** pp 246–252.

Cohen S (1980) Aftereffects of stress on human performance and social behaviour: a review of research and theory. *Psychological Bulletin* **87** pp 578–604.

Cohen S and Williamson GM (1991) Stress and infectious disease in humans. *Psychological Bulletin* **109** pp 5–24.

Cohen S, Tyrell DAJ and Smith AP (1991) Psychological stress and susceptibility to the common cold. *The New England Journal of Medicine* **325** pp 606–612.

Coleman JC (1974) *Relationships in Adolescence*. London: Routledge & Kegan Paul.

Coleman JC and Hendry L (1990) *The Nature of Adolescence* (2nd edn). London: Routledge.

Collins AM and Loftus EF (1975) A spreading-activation theory of semantic processing. *Psychological Review* **82** pp 407–428.

Colman AM (1987) *Facts, Fallacies and Frauds in Psychology*. London: Hutchinson/Unwin Hyman.

Colquoun WP et al (1970) Circadian rythums, mental efficiency, shift work. *Ergonomics* **13(5)** pp 558–560.

Comings DE and Comings BG (1987) Hereditary agoraphobia and obsessive–compulsive behaviour in relatives of patients with Gilles de la Tourette's syndrome. *British Journal of Psychiatry* **151** pp 195–199.

Condon WD and Sander W (1974) Neonate movement is synchronised with adult speech: interactional participation in language acquisition. *Science* **183** pp 99–101.

Condry J and Condry S (1976) Sex differences: a study in the eye of the beholder. *Child Development* **47** pp 812–819.

Conrad R (1964) Acoustic confusion in immediate memory. *British Journal of Psychology* **55** pp 75–84.

Constanzo PR, Coie JD, Grumet JF and Farnhill D (1973) Re-examination of the effects of intent and consequence on children's moral judgements. *Child Development* **44** pp 154–161.

Conway MA, Anderson SJ, Larsen SF, Donnelly CM, McDaniel MA, McClelland AGR and Rawles RE (1994) The formation of flashbulb memories. *Memory and Cognition* **22** pp 326–343.

Cook M (1978) *Perceiving Others*. London: Routledge.

Cooley CH (1902) *Human Nature and the Social Order*. New York: Charles Scribner's Sons.

Coolican H (1990) *Research Methods and Statistics in Psychology*. Sevenoaks: Hodder & Stoughton.

Cooper JE, Kendell RE, Gurland BJ, Sharpe L, Copeland JRM and Simon R (1972) *Psychiatric Diagnosis in New York and London*. Oxford: Oxford University Press.

Corteen RS and Wood B (1972) Autonomic responses to shock-associated words in an unattended channel. *Journal of Experimental Psychology* **94** pp 308–313.

Cowan CP and Cowan PA (1988) Who does what when partners become parents: implications for men, women, and marriage. *Marriage and Family Review* **12(3–4)** pp 105–131.

Cox T (1975) The nature and management of stress. *New Behaviour*, **25 Sept** pp 493–495.

Cox T, Watts CR and Barnett A (1981) The experience and effects of task-inherent demand. *Final Technical Report to the US Army Research, Development and Standardisation Group, UK.*

Coyle J *et al* (1983) Alzheimer's disease: a disorder of cortical cholinegic innervation. *Science* **219** pp 1184–1190.

Craik F and Lockhart R (1972) Levels of processing. *Journal of Verbal Learning and Verbal Behaviour* **11** pp 671–684.

Craik F and Tulving E (1975) Depth of processing and the retention of words in episodic memory. *Journal of Experimental Psychology: General* **104** pp 268–294.

Craik F and Watkins M (1973) The role of rehearsal in short term memory. *Journal of Verbal Learning and Verbal Behaviour* **12** pp 599–607.

Cramer D (1994) Personal relationships. In Tantam D and Birchwood M (eds) *Seminars in Psychology and the Social Sciences*. London: Gaskell Press.

Crawford M and Unger RK (1995) Gender issues in psychology. In Colman AM (ed) *Controversies in Psychology*. London: Longman.

Crick F and Mitchison G (1983) The function of REM sleep. *Nature* **304** pp 111–114.

Crisp AH and Kalucy RS (1974) Aspects of perceptual disorder in anorexia nervosa. *British Journal of Medical Psychology* **47** pp 349–361.

Cross HA, Halcomb CG and Matter WW (1967) Imprinting or exposure learning in rats given early auditory stimulation. *Psychonomic Sciences* **67** pp 233–234.

Crow TJ, Cross AG, Johnstone EC and Owen F (1982) Two syndromes in schizophrenia and their pathogenesis. In Henn FA and Nasrallah GA (eds) *Schizophrenia as a Brain Disease*. New York: Oxford University Press.

Crutchfield RS (1954) A new technique for measuring individual differences in conformity to group judgement. *Proceedings of the Invitational Conference on Testing Problems*, pp 69–74.

Crutchfield RS (1955) Conformity and character. *American Psychologist* **10** pp 191–198.

Crystal D, Fletcher P and Garman M (1976) *The Grammatical Analysis of Language Disability: A Procedure for Assessment and Remediation*. London: Edward Arnold.

Culebras A (1992) Update on disorders of sleep and the sleep–wake cycle. *Psychiatric Clinics of North America*. **15** pp 467–489.

Cullingford C (1984) *Children and Television*. Aldershot: Gower.

Cumming E (1975) Engagement with an old theory. *International Journal of Ageing and Human Development* **6** pp 187–191.

Cumming E and Henry WE (1961) *Growing Old: The Process of Disengagement*. New York: Basic Books.

Curtiss S (1977) *Genie: A Psycholinguistic Study of a Modern-Day 'Wild Child'*. London: Academic Press.

Cuthill I (1991) Field experiments in animal behaviour: methods and ethics. *Animal Behaviour* **42(6)** pp 1006–1014.

Cutts TF and Barrios BA (1986) Fear of weight gain among bulimic and non-disturbed females. *Behaviour Therapy* **17** pp 626–636.

Dalton K (1964) *The Premenstrual Syndrome*. Springfield, IL: Charles C Thomas.

Daly M and Wilson M (1982) Whom are newborn babies said to resemble? *Ethology and Sociobiology* **3** pp 69–78.

Daly M and Wilson M (1989) *Homicide*. New York: Aldine.

Daly M and Wilson M (1996) Violence agains stepchildren. *Current Directions in Psychological Science* **5(3)** pp 77–81.

Damasio A *et al.* (1982) Prosopagnosia: anatomic basis and behavioural mechanisms. *Neurology* **32** pp 331–341.

Damasio A and Van Hoesen G (1983) Emotional disturbances associated with focal lesions of the limbic frontal lobe. In Heilman P and Satz K (eds) The *Neuropsychology of Human Emotion*. New York: Guildford.

Damasio H (1981) Cerebral location of the aphasias. In Sarno M (ed) *Acquired Aphasia*. New York: Academic Press.

Damasio H and Damasio A (1980) The anatomical basis of conduction aphasia. *Brain* **103** pp 337–350.

Darley JM and Batson CD (1973) From Jerusalem to Jericho: a study of situational and dispositional variables in helping behaviour. *Journal of Personality and Social Psychology* **27** pp 100–108.

Darley JM and Latané B (1968) Bystander intervention in emergencies: diffusion of responsibility. *Journal of Personality and Social Psychology* **8** pp 377–383.

Dartnell H *et al* (1983) Microspectrophotometry of human photoreceptors. In Mollon J and Sharpe L (eds) *Colour Vision: Physiology and Psychophysics*. New York: Academic Press.

Darwin C (1859) *On the Origin of Species*. London: Murray.

Darwin C (1871) *The Descent of Man and Selection in Relation to Sex*. London: Murray.

David AS and Cutting J (1993) The *Neuropsychology of Schizophrenia*. Netherlands: Erlbaum.

Davidson AG (1991) Looking for love in the age of AIDS: the language of gay personals, 1978–1988. *Journal of Sex Research* **28** pp 125–137.

Davies DL (1956) Psychiatric illness in those engaged to be married. *British Journal of Preventive and Social Medicine* **10** pp 123–127.

Davies NB and Houston AI (1981) Owners and satellites: the economics of territory defence in the pied wagtail, *Motacilla alba*. *Journal of Animal Ecology* **50** pp 157–180.

Davis K (1947) Final note on a case of extreme isolation. *American Journal of Sociology* **52** pp 432–437.

Davis KL, Kahn RS, Grant K and Davidson M (1991) Dopamine in schizophrenia: a review and reconceptualisation. *American Journal of Psychiatry* **148** pp 1471–1486.

Davison G and Neale J (1986) *Abnormal Psychology* (4th edn). New York: Wiley.

Davison G and Neale J (1994) *Abnormal Psychology* (6th edn). New York: Wiley.

Dawkins MS (1985) The scientific basis for assessing suffering in animals. In Singer P *Defence of Animals*. Oxford: Blackwell.

Dawkins R (1976) *The Selfish Gene*. Oxford: Oxford University Press.

Dawson D and Campbell SS (1991) Time exposure to bright light improves sleep and alertness during simulated night shifts. *Sleep* **14** pp 511–516.

de Groot AD (1966) Perception and memory versus thought: some old ideas and recent findings. In Kleinmuntz B (ed) *Problem-Solving: Research Method and Theory*. New York: Wiley.

De Renzi E (1986) Current issues in prosopagnosia. In Ellis HD, Jeeves MA, Newcombe F and Young A (eds) *Aspects of Face Processing*. Dordrecht: Martinus Nijhoff.

De Valois RL and De Valois KK (1988) *Spatial Vision*. New York: Oxford University Press.

Deacon T (1997) *The Symbolic Species*. London: Penguin.

Delboeuf JLR (1892) Sur une nouvelle illusion d'optique. *Bulletin de L'Academie Royale de Belgique* **24** pp 545–558.

DeLoache JS and Brown AL (1987) Differences in the memory-based searching of delayed and normally developing young children. *Intelligence* **11** pp 277–289.

Dembroski TM and Costa P (1988) Assessment of coronary-prone behaviour: a current overview. *Annals of Behavioral Medicine* **10** pp 60–63.

Dement W (1960) The effect of dream deprivation. *Science* **131** pp 1705–1707.

Dement W (1972) *Some Must Watch While Some Must Sleep*. Stanford, CA: Stanford Alumni Association.

Dement W and Kleitman N (1957) The relation of eye movements during sleep to dream activity: an objective method for the study of dreaming. *Journal of Experimental Psychology* **53(5)** pp 339–346.

Dement W and Wolpert E (1958) The relation of eye movements, body motility and external stimuli to dream content. *Journal of Experimental Psychology* **55** pp 543–553.

Den Heyer K and Barrett B (1971) Selective loss of visual and verbal information in short-term memory by means of visual and verbal interpolated tasks. *Psychonomic Science* **25** pp 100–102.

Dent HR (1988) Children's eyewitness evidence: a brief review. In Gruneberg MM, Morris PE and Sykes RN (eds) *Practical Aspects of Memory: Current Research and Issues* (vol.1). Chichester: Wiley.

Deregowski J (1972) Pictorial perception and culture. *Scientific American* **227** pp 82–88.

Deutsch JA and Deutsch D (1963) Attention: some theoretical considerations. *Psychological Review* **70** pp 80–90.

Deutsch M and Collins ME (1951) *Interracial Housing: A Psychological Evaluation of a Social Experiment*. Minneapolis, MN: University of Minnesota Press.

Deutsch M and Gerard HB (1955) A study of normative and informational social influences upon individual judgement. *Journal of Abnormal and Social Psychology* **51** pp 629–636.

Devlin, Honourable Lord Patrick (chair) (1976) *Report to the Secretary of State for the Home Department of the Departmental Committee on Evidence of Identification in Criminal Cases*. London: Her Majesty's Stationery Office.

DeWaele JP and Harré R (1979) Autobiography as a psychological method. In Ginsburg GP (ed) *Emerging Strategies in Social Psychological Research*. Chichester: Wiley.

Di Giacomo JP (1980) Intergroup alliances and rejections within a protest movement: analysis of social representations. *European Journal of Social Psychology* **10** pp 329–344.

Diamond A (1985) Development of the ability to use recall to guide action, as indicated by performance on AB. *Child Development* **56** pp 868–883.

Diamond M (1978) Sexual identity and sex roles. *The Humanist* **March/April**.

Diener E, Fraser SC, Beaman AL and Kelem R (1976) Effects of deindividuation on stealing among Halloween trick or treaters. *Journal of Personality and Social Psychology* **33** pp 178–183.

DiNardo P *et al.* (1993) Reliability of DSM III–R anxiety disorder categories. *Archives of General Psychiatry* **50** pp 251–256.

Dindia K and Baxter LA (1987) Maintenance and repair strategies in marital relationships. *Journal of Social and Personal Relationships* **14** pp 143–158.

Dion K and Dion K (1988) Romantic love: individual and cultural perspectives. In Sternberg R and Barnes M (eds) *The Psychology of Love*. New Haven, CT: Yale University Press.

Dion K, Berscheid E and Walster E (1972) What is beautiful is good. *Journal of Personality and Social Psychology* **24** pp 285–290.

Doane JA, Falloon IRH, Goldstein MJ and Mintz J (1985) Parental affective style and the treatment of schizophrenia: predicting course of illness and social functioning. *Archives of General Psychiatry* **42** pp 34–42.

Dockrell J and Lindsay G (1998) The ways in which speech and language difficulties impact on children's access to the curriculum. *Child Language, Teaching and Therapy* **14(2)** pp 117–133.

Dollard J and Miller NE (1950) *Personality and Psychotherapy*. New York: McGraw-Hill.

Dollard J, Doob LW, Miller N, Mowrer O and Sears RR (1939) *Frustration and Aggression*. New Haven, CT: Yale University Press.

Donaldson M (1978) *Children's Minds*. London: Fontana.

Donnerstein E and Wilson DW (1976) The effects of noise and perceived control upon ongoing and subsequent aggressive behaviour. *Journal of Personality and Social Psychology* **34** pp 774–781.

Drabman RS and Thomas MH (1974) Does media violence increase children's toleration of real-life aggression? *Developmental Psychology* **10** pp 418–421.

Dreman SB and Greenbaum CW (1973) Altruism or reciprocity: sharing behaviour in Israeli kindergarten children. *Child Development* **44** pp 61–68.

Duberman L (1973) Step-kin relationships. *Journal of Marriage and the Family* **35** pp 283–292.

Dubrovsky VJ, Kiesler SB and Sethna BN (1991) The equalisation phenomenon: status effects in computer-mediated and face-to-face decision-making groups. *Human–Computer Interaction* **6** pp 119–146.

Duck S (1982) A topography of relationship disengagement and dissolution. In Duck SW (ed) *Personal Relationships 4: Dissolving Personal Relationships*. London: Academic Press.

Duck S (1992) *Human Relationships* (2nd edn). London: Sage.

Duck S (1994) *Dynamics of Relationships*. Thousand Oaks, CA: Sage Publications, Inc.

Duck S and Barnes MK (1992) Disagreeing about agreement: reconciling differences about similarity. *Communication Monographs* **59(2)** pp 199–208.

Dunbar R (1993) Coevolution of neocortical size, group size and language in humans. *Behavioural and Brain Sciences* **16** pp 681–735.

Dunbar R (1995) Are you lonesome tonight? *New Scientist* **145(1964)** pp 12–16.

Duncan HF, Gourlay N and Hudson W (1973) *A Study of Pictorial Perception among Bantu and White Primary School Children in South Africa*. Johannesburg: Witwatersrand University Press.

Duncan SL (1976) Differential social perception and attribution of intergroup violence: testing the lower limits of stereotyping of blacks. *Journal of Personality and Social Psychology* **34** pp 590–598.

Duncker K (1945) On problem solving. *Psychological Monographs* **58** (whole no. 270).

Dunn J and Kendrick C (1982) *Siblings: love, envy and understanding*. London: Grant McIntyre.

Dutton DC and Aron P (1974) Some evidence for heightened sexual attraction under conditions of high anxiety. *Journal of Personality and Social Psychology* **30** pp 510–517.

Dworetzky JP (1981) *Introduction to Child Development*. St Paul, M: West Publishing Co.

Dziurawiec S and Ellis HD (1986) Neonates' attention to face-like stimuli: Goren, Sarty and Wu (1975) revisited. Paper presented at the Annual Conference of the Developmental Section of the British Psychological Society, Exeter.

Eagly AH (1997) On comparing women and men. *Feminism and Psychology* **4(4)** pp 513–522.

Ebbinghaus H (1885) *Concerning Memory*. New York: Teachers' College Press (published in 1913).

Eich E (1995) Searching for mood dependent memory. *Psychological Science* **62** pp 67–75.

Einon D (1998) How many children can one man have? *Evolution and Human Behaviour* **19** pp 413–426.

Eisenberg N (1986) *The Development of Prosocial Behaviour*. New York: Wiley.

Eisenberg N and Mussen PH (1989) *The Roots of Prosocial Behaviour in Children*. New York: Cambridge University Press.

Eisenberg N, Miller P and Shell R (1991) Prosocial development in adolesence: a longitudinal study. *Developmental Psychology* **23** pp 712–718.

Eisenberg N, Shell R, Pasternak J, Lennon R, Beller R and Mathy RM (1987) Prosocial development in middle childhood: a longitudinal study. *Developmental Psychology* **23** pp 712–718.

Eisenbruch M (1984) Cross-cultural aspects of bereavement. II: Ethnic and cultural variations in the development of bereavement practices. *Culture, Medicine and Psychiatry* **8** pp 315–347.

Ekman P et al (1972) Universals and cultural differences in facial expressions of emotion. In Cole JK (ed) *Nebraska Symposium on Motivation* 1971. Lincoln, NE: University of Nebraska Press.

Ekman P, Levenson RW and Friesen WV (1983) Autonomic nervous system activity distinguishes among emotions. *Science* **221** pp 1208–1210.

Elder GH Jnr (1980) *Family Structure and Socialisation*. New York: Arno Press.

Eldridge NS and Gilbert LA (1990) Correlates of relationship satisfaction in lesbian couples. *Psychology of Women Quarterly* **14** pp 43–62.

Elgar MA (1986) House sparrows establish foraging flocks by giving chirrup calls if the resources are divisible. *Animal Behaviour* **34** pp 169–174.

Elias CF and Perfetti CA (1973) Encoding task and recognition memory: the importance of semantic coding. *Journal of Experimental Psychology* **99(2)** pp 151–157.

Ellenberg L and Sperry RW (1980) Lateralised division of attention in the commissurotomised and intact brain. *Neuropsychologia* **18** pp 411–418.

Elliott J (1977) The power and pathology of prejudice. In Zimbardo P and Ruch FL (eds) *Psychology and Life* (9th edn). Glenville, IL: Scott, Foreseman and Co.

Elliott RD (1985) The effects of predation risk and group size on the anti-predator responses of nesting lapwings *Vanellus vanellus*. *Behaviour* **92(1–2)** pp 168–187.

Ellis A (1962) *Reason and Emotion in Psychotherapy*. New York: Lyle Stuart.

Ellis GT and Sekgra F (1972) The effect of aggressive cartoons on first-grade children. *Journal of Psychology* **81** pp 37–43.

Ellis HD and Szulecka T (1996) The disguised lover: a case of Fregoli delusion. In Halligan PW and Marshall JC (eds) *Method in Madness: Case Studies in Cognitive europsychiatry*. Hove: Psychology Press.

Ellis HD, Shepherd JW and Davies GM (1979) Identification of familiar and unfamiliar faces from internal and external features: some implications for theories of face recognition. *Perception* **8** pp 431–439.

Ellis HD, Shepherd JW, Shepherd J, Flin RH and Davies GM (1989) Identification from a computer-driven retrieval system compared with a traditional mug-shot album search: a new tool for police investigations. *Ergonomics* **32** pp 167–177.

Elms AC (1972) *Social Psychology and Social Relevance*. Boston, MA: Brown.

Elms AC and Milgram S (1966) Personality characteristics associated with obedience and defiance towards authoritative command. *Journal of Experimental Research in Personality* **1** pp 282–289.

Emlen ST (1970) Celestial rotation: its importance in the development of migratory orientation. *Science* **170** pp 1198–1201.

Emmerlich W, Goldmann K, Kirsh K and Sharabany R (1977) Evidence for a transitional phase in the development of gender constancy. *Child Development* **48** pp 930–936.

Empson JAC and Clarke PRF (1970) Rapid eye movements and remembering. *Nature* **228** pp 287–288.

Epstein LC and Lasagna L (1969) Obtaining informed consent. *Archives of Internal Medicine* **123** pp 682–688.

Epstein R, Kirshnit CE, Lanza RP and Rubin LC (1984) "Insight" in the pigeon: antecedents and determinants of an intelligent performance. *Nature* **308** pp 61–62.

Erbeck J, Elfner L and Driggs D (1983) Reduction of blood pressure by indirect biofeedback. *Biofeedback and Self Regulation* **8(1)** pp 63–72.

Erikson EH (1950) *Childhood and Society*. New York: Norton.

Erikson EH (1966) Eight stages of man. *International Journal of Psychiatry* **2(3)** pp 281–300.

Erikson EH (1968) *Identity: Youth and Crisis*. London: Faber.

Erlenmeyer-Kimling L and Jarvik LF (1963) Genetics and intelligence: a review. *Science* **142** pp 1477–1479.

Ernst GW and Newell A (1969) *GPS: A Case Study in Generality and Problem Solving*. London: Academic Press.

Eron LD, Lefkowitz MM, Huesmann LR and Walder LQ (1972) Does television violence cause aggression? *American Psychologist* **27** pp 253–263.

Estes WK (1970) *Learning Theory and Mental Development*. New York: Academic Press.

Evans C (1984) *Landscapes of the Night: How and Why We Dream*. New York: Viking.

Eyferth K (1961) Leistungen verschiedener Gruppen von Besatzungskinder in Hamburg: Wechsler Intelligenztest für Kinder (HAWIK). *Archiv für Gesamte Psychologie* **113** pp 223–241.

Eysenck HJ (1952) The effects of psychotherapy: an evaluation. *Journal of Consulting Psychology* **16** pp 319–324.

Eysenck HJ (1954) *The Psychology of Politics*. London: RKP.

Eysenck HJ (1971) *Race, Intelligence and Education*. London: Temple Smith.

Eysenck MW (1982) *Attention and Arousal: Cognition and Performance*. Berlin: Springer.

Eysenck MW (1984) *Handbook of Cognitive Psychology*. Hove: Lawrence Erlbaum Associates.

Eysenck MW (1993) *Principles of Cognitive Psychology*. Hove: Erlbaum.

Fagot BI (1978) The influence of sex of child on parental reactions to toddler children. *Child Development* **49** pp 459–465.

Fahey TA (1988) The diagnosis of multiple personality disorder: a critical review. *British Journal of Psychiatry* **153** pp 597–606.

Falek A and Moser HM (1975) Classification in schizophrenia. *Archives of General Psychiatry* **32** pp 59–67.

Fantz RL (1961) The origin of form perception. *Scientific American* **204(5)** pp 66–72.

Fantz RL (1963) Pattern vision in newborn infants. *Science* **140** pp 296–297.

Farina A, Holland CH and Ring K (1966) Role of stigma and set in interpersonal interaction. *Journal of Abnormal and Social Psychology* **71** pp 421–428.

Farrar M (1992) Negative evidence and grammatical morpheme acquisition. *Development Psychology* **28(1)** pp 90–98.

Farrimond, T (1968) Retention and recall: incidental learning of visual and auditory material. *Journal of Genetic Psychology* **113** pp 155–165.

Feare C (1984) *The Starling*. Oxford: Oxford University Press.

Feingold A (1992) Good looking people are not what we think. *Psychological Bulletin* **111(2)** pp 304–341.

Feldman RE (1968) Response to compatriot and foreigner who seek assistance. *Journal of Personality and Social Psychology* **10** pp 202–214.

Femlee DH (1995) Fatal attractions: affection and disaffection in intimate relationships. *Journal of Social and Personal Relationships* **12** pp 295–311.

Festinger L, Schachter S and Back K (1950) *Social Pressures in Informal Groups: A Study of Human Factors in Housing*. Stanford, CA: Stanford University Press.

Feyerabend P (1975) *Against method: outline of an anarchistic theory of knowledge*. London: New Left Books

Fisher HE (1992) *Anatomy of love: the natural history of monogamy, adultery and divorce*. New York: Norton

Fisher RP, Geiselman RE and Amador M (1990) Field test of the cognitive interior, reported in *The Psychologist* **Sept** 1991.

Fisher RP, Geiselman RE and Raymond DS (1987a) Critical analysis of police interview techniques. *Journal of Police Science and Administration* **15** pp 177–185.

Fisher RP, Geiselman RE, Raymond DS, Turkerich LM and Warhaftig ML (1987b) Enhancing enhanced eyewitness memory: refining the cognitive interior. *Journal of Police Science and Administration* **15** pp 291–297.

Fisher S (1978) Dirt – anality and attitudes towards negros. A test of Kubie's hypothesis. *Journal of Nervous and Mental Disease* **166** pp 280–291.

Fisher S and Greenberg RP (1977) *The Scientific Credibility of Freud's Theories and Therapy*. New York: Basic Books.

Fiske ST and Taylor SE (1991) *Social Cognition* (2nd edn). New York: McGraw-Hill.

Flament C (1988) Practical activity and social cognitive representations. *Prezeglad Psychologiczny* **31(1)** 221–228.

Flin R, Bull R, Boon J and Knox A (1993) Child witnesses in Scottish criminal trials. *International Review of Victimology* **2** pp 313–339.

Flowers JH, Warner JL and Polansky ML (1979). Response and encoding factors in ignoring irrelevant information. *Memory and Cognition* **7** pp 86–94.

Flynn JP (1976) Patterning mechanisms, patterned reflexes, and attack behaviour in cats. *Nebraska Symposium on Motivation* **20** pp 125–153.

Foa UG and Foa EB (1975) *Societal structures of the mind*. Springfield, IL: Thomas.

Fodor JA and Pylyshyn ZW (1981) How direct is visual perception? Some reflections on Gibson's 'ecological approach'. *Cognition* **9** pp 139–196.

Fonagy P and Higgitt A (1984) *Personality Theory and Clinical Practice*. London: Methuen.

Foster GM and Anderson BG (1978) *Medical Anthropology*. New York: Wiley.

Foulkes D (1985) *Dreaming: A Cognitive–Psychological Analysis*. Hillsdale, NJ: Lawrence Erlbaum Associates.

Frank JD (1973) *Persuasion and Healing* (2nd edn). Baltimore, MD: John Hopkins University Press.

Franzoi SL and Herzog ME (1987) Judging physical attractiveness: what body aspects do we use? *Personality and Social Psychology Bulletin* **13(1)** pp 19–33.

Frean A (1995) Getting a kick from TV violence. *The Times* **23 Aug**, p 31.

Freedman JL and Fraser S (1966) Compliance without pressure: the foot-in-the-door technique. *Journal of Personality and Social Psychology* **4** pp 195–202.

Freedman JL, Levy AS, Buchanan RW and Price J (1972) Crowding and human aggressiveness. *Journal of Experimental Social Psychology* **8(6)** pp 528–548.

Freeman D (1983) *Margaret Mead and Samoa: The Making and Unmaking of an Anthropological Myth*. Cambridge, MA: Harvard University Press.

Freeman FN, Holzinger KJ and Mitchell BC (1928) The influence of environment on the intelligence, school achievement, and conduct of foster children. *Yearbook of the National Society for the Study of Education, Part 1* **27** pp 103–217.

Freeman J and Watts JW (1942) *Psychosurgery*. Springfield, IL: Thomas.

French J (1957) The reticular formation. *Scientific American* **196(5)** pp 54–60.

French JRP, Caplan RD and Van Harrison R (1982) *The Mechanisms of Job Stress and Strain*. New York: Wiley.

Frenkel-Brunswik E (1942) Motivation and behaviour. *Genetic Psychology Monographs* **26** pp 121–265.

Freud A and Dann S (1951) An experiment in group upbringing. *Psychoanalytic Study of the Child* **6** pp 127–168.

Freud S (1990) *The Interpretation of Dreams*. London: Hogarth Press.

Freud S (1909) *Analysis of a Phobia in a Five-Year-Old Boy*. London: Hogarth Press.

Frick W (1995) The subpersonalities controversy. *Journal of Human Psychology* **35** pp 97–101.

Friedman M and Rosenman RH (1974) *Type A Behaviour And Your Heart*. New York: Knopf.

Friedman M, Thoresen CE, Gill JJ, Ulmer D, Powell LH, Price VA, Brown B, Thompson L, Rabin D, Breall WS, Bourg E, Levy R and Dixon T (1986) Alteration of Type A behavior and its effects on cardiac recurrences in postmyocardial infarction patients: summary of The Recurrent Coronary Prevention Project. *American Heart Journal* **112** pp 653–665.

Friedrich LK and Stein AH (1973) Aggressive and prosocial television programmes and the natural behaviour of preschool children. *Monographs of the Society for Research in Child Development* **38** no. 4.

Frith CD (1997) *Schizophrenia*. Hove: Psychology Press.

Fulton R (1970) Death, grief and social recuperation. *Omega: Journal of Death and Dying* **1** pp 23–28.

Gainotti G (1972) Emotional behaviour and the hemispheric side of lesion. *Cortex* **8(1)** pp 41–55.

Galaburda A (1988) The pathogenesis of childhood dyslexia. In Plum F (ed) *Language, Communication and the Brain*. New York: Raven.

Galaburda A and Geschwind N (1982) *Neurology and neurosurgery update series* **3** pp 1–7.

Galef BG Jnr (1988) Communication of information concerning diet in social central-place foraging species: *Rattus norvegicus*. In Zentall TR and Galef BG Jnr (eds) *Social Learning Psychological and Biological Perspectives*. Hillsdale NJ: Lawrence Erlbaum Associates Inc.

Galef BG Jnr and Durlach PJ (1993) Absence of blocking, overshadowing, and latent inhibition in social enhancement of food preferences. *Animal Learning and Behaviour* **21** pp 214–220.

Galef BG Jnr, Mason JR, Preti G and Bean NJ (1988) Carbon disulfide: a semiochemical mediating socially induced diet choice in rats. *Physiology and Behaviour* **42** pp 119–124.

Gallup GG Jnr (1970) Chimpanzees: self-recognition. *Science* **167** pp 86–87.

Gallup GG Jnr (1977) Self-recognition in primates: a comparative approach to the bidirectional properties of consciousness. *American Psychologist* **32** pp 329–338.

Gallup GG Jnr (1983) Toward a comparative psychology of mind. In Mellgren RL (ed) *Animal Cognition and Behaviour*. Amsterdam: North Holland Publishing Co.

Galton F (1869) *Hereditary Genius: an Enquiry into its Laws and Consequences* (2nd edn) (reprinted 1978). London: Julian Friedmann.

Gamson WB, Fireman B and Rytina S (1982) *Encounters with Unjust Authority*. Hounwood, I: Dorsey Press.

Garcia J and Koelling RA (1966) Relation of cue to consequence in avoidance learning. *Psychonomic Science* **4** pp 123–124.

Garcia-Arraras JE and Pappenheimer (1983) Site of action of sleep-inducing muramyl peptide isolated from human urine. Microinjection studies in rabbit brains. *Journal of Neurophysiology* **49(2)** pp 528–533.

Gardner H (1975) *The shattered mind*. New York: Knopf.

Gardner RA and Gardner BT (1969) Teaching sign language to a chimpanzee. *Science* **165** pp 664–672.

Garfinkel PE and Garner DM (1982) *Anorexia Nervosa: A Multidimensional Perspective*. New York: Brunner/Mazel.

Garland H, Hardy A and Stephenson L (1975) Information search as affected by attribution type and response category. *Personality and Social Psychology Bulletin* **4** pp 612–615.

Garner DM, Garfinkel PE, Schwartz D and Thompson M (1980) Cultural expectations of thinness in women. *Psychological Reports* **47** pp 483–491.

Gaulin SJC and Robbins CJ (1992) Trivers–Willard effect in contemporary North American society. *American Journal of Physical Anthropology* **85** pp 61–69.

Geiselman RE, Fisher RP, Firstenberg I, Hutton LA, Avetissian IV and Prosk AL (1984) Enhancement of eyewitness memory: an empirical evaluation of the cognitive interview. *Journal of Police Science and Administration* **12** pp 74–80.

Geiselman RE, Fisher RP, MacKinnon DP and Holland HL (1986) Enhancement of eyewitness memory with the cognitive interview. *American Journal of Psychology* **99** pp 385–401.

Gergen KJ, Gergen MM and Barton W (1973) Deviance in the dark. *Psychology Today* **7** pp 129–130.

Geschwind N and Behan P (1984) Laterality hormones and immunity. In Geschwind N and Galaburda A (eds) *Cerebral dominance: the biological foundations*. Cambridge, MA: Harvard University Press.

Ghiselin B (1955) *The Creative Process*. New York: Mentor Books.

Gibson EJ and Walk PD (1960) The visual cliff. *Scientific American* **202** pp 64–71.

Gibson JJ (1986) *The Ecological Approach to Visual Perception*. Hillsdale, NJ: Lawrence Erlbaum.

Gick ML and Holyoak KJ (1980) Analogical problem solving. *Cognitive Psychology* **12** pp 306–355.

Gilbert GM (1951) Stereotype persistence and change among college students. *Journal of Abnormal and Social Psychology* **46** pp 245–254.

Gilligan C and Attanucci J (1989) Two moral orientations: gender differences and similarities. *Merrill-Palmer Quarterly* **34** pp 223–237.

Gilligan C (1977) In a different voice: women's conceptions of self and morality. *Harvard Educational Review* **47** pp 481–517.

Gilligan C (1982) *In A Different Voice: Psychological Theory and Women's Development*. Cambridge, MA: Harvard University Press.

Glanzer M and Cunitz AR (1966) Two storage mechanisms in free recall. *Journal of Verbal Learning and Verbal Behaviour* **5** pp 351–360.

Glass DC, Singer JE and Friedman LW (1969) Psychic cost of adaptation to an environmental stressor. *Journal of Personality and Social Psychology* **12** pp 200–210.

Goddard HH (1929) Hereditary mental aptitudes in man. *Eugenics* **2** pp 1–7.

Godden DR and Baddeley AD (1975) Context-dependent memory in two natural environments: on land and under water. *British Journal of Psychology* **66** pp 325–331.

Gold DR, Rogacz S, Bock N, Tosteson Tor-D *et al.* (1992) Rotating shift work, sleep and accidents related to sleepiness in hospital nurses. *American Journal of Public Health* **82** pp 1011–1014.

Goldfarb W (1943) The effects of early institutional care on adolescent personality. *Journal of Experimental Education* **12** pp 106–129.

Goldman RJ and Goldman JDG (1981) How children view old people and ageing: a developmental study of children in four countries. *Australian Journal of Psychology* **3** pp 405–418.

Goldstein IB (1981) Assessment of hypertension. In Prokop CK and Bradley LA (eds) *Medical Psychology*. New York: Academic Press.

Goldstein K (1948) *Language and language disturbances*. New York: Grune & Stratton.

Goldstein WN and Anthony RN (1988) The diagnosis of depression and the DSMs. *American Journal of Psychotherapy* **42(2)** pp 180–196.

Goldwyn E (1979) The fight to be male. *The Listener* **24 May** pp 709–712.

Gooch S (1980) Right brain, left brain. *New Scientist* **11/9** pp 790–792.

Goodwin DW, Powell B, Bremer D, Hoine H and Stern J (1969) Alcohol and recall: state-dependent effects in man. *Science* **163** p 1358.

Goodwin FK and Jamison KR (1990) *Manic Depressive Illness.* New York: Oxford University Press.

Goodwin R (1995) Personal relationships across cultures. *The Psychologist* **8(2)** pp 73–75.

Gottesman II and Shields J (1972) *Schizophrenia and Genetics: A Twin Study Vantage Point.* New York: Academic Press.

Gottesman II and Shields J (1982) *Schizophrenia: The Epigenetic Puzzle.* Cambridge: Cambridge University Press.

Gottman JM (1994) *What Predicts Divorce? The Relationship Between Marital Processes and Marital Outcomes.* Hillsdale, NJ: Lawrence Erlbaum Associates Inc.

Gould JL (1982) The map sense of pigeons. *Nature* **296** pp 205–211.

Gould JL (1984) Natural history of honeybee learning. In Marler P and Terrace HS (eds) *The Biology of Learning.* Berlin: Springer.

Gould JL (1986) The locale map of honeybees: do insects have a cognitive map? *Science* **232** pp 861–863.

Gould JL and Gould CG (1989) *Sexual Selection.* New York: Scientific American Library.

Gould RL (1978) *Transformations: Growth and Change in Adult Life.* New York: Simon & Schuster.

Gould RL (1980) Transformational tasks in adulthood. In Greenspan SI and Pollock GH (eds) *The Course of Life: Psychoanalytic Contributions Toward Understanding Personality Development, vol 3: Adulthood and the Ageing Process.* Washington, DC: National Institute for Mental Health.

Gould SJ (1981) *The Mismeasure of Man.* London: Penguin.

Gove W (1990) Labelling theory's explanation of mental illness: An update of recent evidence. In Nagler M (ed) *Perspectives on disability.* Palo Alto, CA: Health Markets Research.

Graf RC and Riddell LC (1972) Helping behavior as a function of interpersonal perception. *Journal of Social Psychology* **86** pp 227–231.

Grasha AF (1983) *Practical Applications of Psychology* (2nd edn). Boston, MA: Little, Brown & Co.

Gray J (1987) The ethics and politics of animal experimentation. In Beloff H and Colman AM (eds) *Psychological Survey No. 6.* Leicester: The British Psychological Society.

Gray J and Wedderburn A (1960) Grouping strategies with simultaneous stimuli. *Quarterly Journal of Experimental Psychology* **12** pp 180–184.

Graziano WG, Jensen-Campbell LA, Todd M and Finch JF (1997) Interpersonal attraction from an evolutionary perspective: Women's reactions to dominant and prosocial men. In Simpson JA and Kenrick DT (eds) *Evolutionary social psychology.* Hillsdale NJ: Lawrence Erlbaum Associates Inc.

Green BL (1994) Psychosocial research in traumatic stress: an update. *Journal of Traumatic Stress* **7** pp 341–363.

Green R (1978) Sexual identity of 37 children raised by homosexual or transexual parents. *American Journal of Psychiatry* **135** pp 692–697.

Green S (1996) Drugs and psychological disorders. *Psychology Review* **3(2)** p 25–28.

Greene J (1987) *Memory, Thinking and Language.* London: Methuen.

Greer A, Morris T and Pettingale KW (1979) Psychological response to breast cancer: effect on outcome. *Lancet* **13** pp 785–787.

Gregor AJ and McPherson D (1965) A study of susceptibility to geometric illusions among cultural outgroups of Australian aborigines. *Psychologia, Africana* **11** pp 490–499.

Gregory RL (1972) Visual illusions. In Foss BM (ed) *New Horizons in Psychology* I. Harmondsworth: Penguin.

Gregory RL (1983) Visual illusions. In Miller J (ed) *States of Mind.* London: BBC Publications.

Griffit W and Veitch R (1974) Preacquaintance attitude similarity and attraction revisited: ten days in a fallout shelter. *Sociometry* **37** pp 163–173.

Groblewski T *et al.* (1980) cited in Carlson N (1991) *The Physiology of Behaviour.* Boston, MA: Allyn & Bacon.

Gross AE, Wallston BS and Piliavin IM (1975) Beneficiary attractiveness and cost as determinants of responses to routine requests for help. *Sociometry* **38** pp 131–140.

Gross RD (1992) *Psychology: The Science of Mind and Behaviour* (2nd edn). London: Hodder & Stoughton.

Grossman K, Grossman KE, Spangler G, Suess G and Unzer L (1985) Maternal sensitivity and newborn's orientation responses. In Bretherton I and Waters E (eds) *Growing Points in Attachment Theory and Research,* Monographs of the Society for Research in Child Development **50** Serial No. 209 pp 3–35.

Grudin JT (1983) Error patterns in novice and skilled transcription typing. In Cooper WE (ed) *Cognitive Aspects of Skilled Typewriting.* New York: Springer.

Guilleminault C and Bliwise DL (1994) Behavioural perspectives on abnormalities of breathing during sleep. In Timmons BH and Ley R (eds) *Behavioural and psychological approaches to breathing disorders.* New York: Plenum Press.

Guimond S and Palmer DL (1990) Type of academic training and causal attributions for social problems. *European Journal of Social Psychology* **20(1)** pp 61–75.

Gulevich G, Dement WC and Johnson L (1966) Psychiatric and EEG observations on a case of prolonged (24 hours) wakefulness. *Archives of General Psychiatry* **15** pp 29–35.

Gunter B *et al.* (1991) Children's Views About Television. Avebury.

Gupta U and Singh P (1992) Exploratory study of love and liking and types of marriage. *Indian Journal of Applied Psychology* **19** pp 92–97.

Gur RC, Skolnick BE and Gur RE (1994) Effects of emotional discrimination tasks on cerebral blood flow: regional activation and its relation to performance. *Brain and Cognition* **25** pp 271–286.

Haaga DA and Davison GC (1989) Outcome studies of rational–emotive therapy. In Bernard ME and DiGiuseppe R (eds) *Inside Rational–Emotive Therapy.* New York: Academic Press.

Haas SM and Stafford L (1998) An initial examination of maintenance behaviours in gay and lesbian relationships. *Journal of Social and Personal Relationships* **15(6)** pp 846–855.

Hacking I (1992) Multiple personality disorder and its hosts. *History of the Human Sciences* **5(2)** p 8.

Hacking I (1995) *Rewriting The Soul: Multiple Personality and the Sciences of Memory.* Princeton, NJ: Princeton University Press.

Hall CS (1951) What people dream about. *Scientific American* **434** (May reprint).

Hall CS and Lindzey G (1970) *Theories of Personality* (2nd edn). London: John Wiley & Sons, Inc.

Hall K and Savery LK (1986) Tight Rein, More Stress. *Harvard Business Review* **Jan/Feb** *p 160.*

Hall RA (1964) *Introductory Linguistics.* Philadelphia, PA: Chilton.

Halligan PW (1995) Drawing attention to neglect: the contribution of line bisection. *The Psychologist* **8** pp 257–264.

Halmi KA, Goldberg SC and Cunningham S (1977) Perceptual distortion and body image in adolescent girls: distortion of body image in adolescence. *Psychological Medicine* **7** pp 253–257.

Hamer D, Hu S and Magnuson VL (1993) A linkage between DNA markers on the X chromosome and male sexual orientation. *Science* **261** pp 321–327.

Hamilton WD (1964) The genetical evaluation of social behaviour. *Journal of Theoretical Biology* **7** pp 1–52.

Hampson E (1990) Estrogen-related variations in human spatical and articulatory-motor skills. *Psychoneuroendocrinology* **15** pp 97–111.

Hampson PJ and Morris PE (1996) *Understanding Cognition.* Oxford: Blackwell.

Hanassab S and Tidwell R (1989) Cross-cultural perspectives on dating relationships of young Iranian women: a pilot study. *Counselling Psychology Quarterly* **2** pp 113–121.

Harari H and McDavid JW (1973) Teachers' expectations and name stereotypes. *Journal of Educational Psychology* **65** pp 222–225.

Harburg E, Erfurt JC, Hauenstein LS, Chape C, Schull WJ and Schork MA (1973) Socioecological stress, suppressed hostility, skin colour, and black–white male blood pressure: Detroit. *Psychosomatic Medicine* **35** pp 276–296.

Harcourt AH, Harvey PH, Larson SG et al (1981) Testis weight, body weight and breeding system in primates. *Nature* **293** pp 55–57.

Harding G (1993) How surgeons could navigate the brain. *New Scientist* **11/12** pp 28–31.

Hare-Mustin RT and Maracek J (1990) *Making A Difference: Psychology and the Construction of Gender.* New Haven, CT: Yale University Press.

Hargreaves DH (1967) *Social Relations in a Secondary School.* London: Routledge and Kegan Paul.

Harlow H and Harlow MK (1962) Social deprivation in monkeys. *Scientific American* **207** pp 136–144.

Harlow H and Zimmerman RR (1959) Affectional responses in the infant monkey. *Science* **130** pp 421–432.

Harrison P (1995) Schizophrenia: a misunderstood disease. *Psychology Review* **2** pp 2–6.

Harry J (1983) Gay male and lesbian relationships. In Macklin E and Rubin R (eds) *Contemporary Families and Alternative Lifestyles: Handbook on Research and Theory* pp 216–234. London: Sage.

Hartley EL (1946) *Problems in prejudice.* New York: King's Crown Press.

Hartmann EL (1973) *The Functions of Sleep.* New Haven, CT: Yale University Press.

Hasler AD (1960) Homing orientation in migrating fishes. *Ergebnisse der Biologie* **23** pp 94–115.

Hastorf AH and Cantril H (1954) They saw a game; a case study. *Journal of Abnormal and Social Psychology* **49** pp 129–134.

Hauty GT and Adams T (1966) Pilot fatigue: Intercontinental jet flight 1. Oklahoma City to Tokyo and back. *Office of Aviation Medicine Report* **65** pp 16–22.

Havighurst RJ (1964) Stages of vocational development. In Borrow H (ed) *Man in a World of Work.* Boston, MA: Houghton Mifflin.

Havighurst RJ, Neugarten BL and Tobin SS (1968) Disengagement and patterns of ageing. In Neugarten BL (ed) *Middle Age and Ageing.* Chicago, IL: University of Chicago Press.

Hay DC and Young AW (1982) The human face. In Ellis A (ed) *Normality and Pathology in Cognitive Functions.* New York: Academic Press.

Hayes C (1951) *The Ape in Our House.* New York: Harper and Rowe.

Hays RB (1985) A longitudinal study of friendship development. *Journal of Personality and Social Psychology* **48** pp 909–924.

Hazan C and Shaver P (1987) Romantic love conceptualized as an attachment process. *Journal of Personality and Social Psychology* **52** pp 511–524.

Hearnshaw LS (1979) *Cyril Burt: Psychologist*. London: Hodder & Stoughton.

Heather N (1976) *Radical Perspectives in Psychology*. London: Methuen.

Hebb DO (1949) *The Organisation of Behaviour*. New York: Wiley.

Hedderman C (1987) *Children's Evidence: The Need for Corroboration*. Research and Planning Unit, Paper 41. London: Home Office.

Heider F (1944) Social perception and phenomenal causality. *Psychological Review* **57** pp 358–378.

Heider F and Simmel M (1944) An experimental study of apparent behaviour. *American Journal of Psychology* **57** pp 243–259.

Helman CG (1994) *Culture, Health and Illness* (3rd edn). Oxford: Butterworth-Heinemann.

Helmholtz H von (1962) *Treatise on physiological optics* (vol.3). New York: Dover. (Originally published 1866.)

Helmreich R, Aronson E and Lefan J (1970) To err is humanizing sometimes: effects of self-esteem, competence and a pratfall on interpersonal attraction. *Journal of Personality and Social Psychology* **16(2)** pp 259–264.

Hendrick SS, Hendrick C and Adler NL (1988) Romantic relationships: love, satisfaction and staying together. *Journal of Personality and Social Psychology* **54** pp 980–988.

Hering E (1878) *Outlines of a Theory of the Light Sense* (translation). Cambridge, MA: Harvard University Press.

Herman J and Roffwarg H (1983) Modifying oculomotor activity in awake subjects increases the amplitude of eye movement during REM sleep. *Science* **220** pp 1074–1076.

Herman LM, Richards DG and Wolf JP (1984) Comprehension of sentences by bottle nosed dolphins. *Cognition* **16** pp 129–219.

Hermelin B and O'Connor N (1970) *Psychological experiments with autistic children*. Oxford: Pergamon.

Hershenson M, Munsinger H and Kessen W (1965) Preference for shapes of intermediate variability in the newborn human. *Science* **147** pp 630–631.

Hertz R (1960) *Death and the Right Hand*. London: Cohen and West.

Hess W (1957) *The functional organisation of the diencephalon*. New York: Grune & Stratton.

Heston LL (1966) Psychiatric disorders in foster-home-reared children of schizophrenic mothers. *British Journal of Psychiatry* **122** pp 819–825.

Hetherington AW and Ranson SW (1942) The relation of various hypothalamic lesions to adiposity in the rat. *Journal of Comparative Neurology* **76** pp 475–499.

Hetherington EM (1979) Divorce: a child's perspective. *American Psychologist* **34(10)** pp 851–858.

Heatherington EM (ed) (1999) *Coping with Divorce, Single Parenting and Remarriage: A Risk and Resiliency Perspective*. Mahwah, NJ: Lawrence Erlbaum Associates Inc.

Hetherington EM, Cox M and Cox R (1978) The aftermath of divorce. In Stevens MH and Mathews M (eds) *Mother/Child, Father/Child Relationships*. Washington DC: National Association for the Education of Young Children.

Hetherington EM, Cox M and Cox R (1979) Play and social interaction in children following divorce. *Journal of Social Issues* **35** pp 26–49.

Hetherington EM, Cox M and Cox R (1982) Effects of divorce on parents and children. In Lamb ME (ed) *Non-Traditional Families: Parenting and Child Development*. Hillsdale, NJ: Lawrence Erlbaum Associates.

Heydon J (1984) *Evidence: Cases and Materials* (2nd edn). London: Butterworth.

Hindley CB (1968) Growing up in five countries: comparison of data on weaning, elimination training, age of walking, and IQ in relation to social class from European longitudinal studies. *Developmental Medicine and Child Neurology* **10(6)** pp 715–724.

Hiroto DS and Seligman MEP (1975) Generality of learned helplessness in man. *Journal of Personality and Social Psychology* **31** pp 311–327.

Hitchcock CL and Sherry DF (1990) Long-term memory for cache sites in the black-capped chickadee. *Animal Behaviour* **40** pp 701–712.

Hobson JA and McCarley RW (1977) The brain as a dream state generator: an activation-synthesis hypothesis of the dream process. *American Journal of Psychiatry* **134** pp 1335–1348.

Hockett CF (1960) The origin of speech. *Scientific American* **203** pp 88–96.

Hodgson JW and Fisher JL (1979) Sex differences in identity and intimacy development. *Journal of Youth and Adolescence* **8** pp 37–50.

Hoffman LW (1974) Effects of maternal employment on the child – a review of the research. *Developmental Psychology* **10** pp 204–228.

Hoffman ML (1981) Is altruism part of human nature? *Journal of Personality and Social Psychology* **40** pp 121–137.

Hofling KC, Brotzman E, Dalrymple S, Graves N and Pierce CM (1966) An experimental study in the nurse–physician relationship. *Journal of Nervous and Mental Disorders* **143** pp 171–180.

Hofstede G (1980) *Culture's Consequences: International Differences in Work-Related Values*. Beverly Hills, CA: Sage.

Hogan RA and Kirchner JH (1967) A preliminary report of the extinction of learned fears via a short term implosive therapy. *Journal of Abnormal Psychology* **72** pp 106–111.

Hogg MA and Vaughan GM (1995) *Social Psychology: An Introduction*. Hemel Hempstead: Prentice Hall/ Harvester Wheatsheaf.

Hohman GW (1966) Some effects of spinal cord lesions on experienced emotional feelings. *Psychophysiology* **3** pp 143–156.

Holahan CK and Sears RR (1995) *Social Psychology: An Introduction*. Hemel Hempstead: Harvester Wheatsheaf.

Hole RW, Rush AJ and Beck AT (1979) A cognitive investigation of schizophrenic delusions. *Psychiatry* **42** pp 312–319.

Holland AJ, Hall A, Murray R, Russell GFM and Crisp HH (1984) Anorexia nervosa: a study of 34 twin pairs and one set of triplets. *British Journal of Psychiatry* **145** pp 414–419.

Hollingshead AB and Redlich FC (1958) *Social Class and Mental Illness: A Community Study*. New York: Wiley.

Holmes TH and Rahe RH (1967) The social readjustment rating scale. *Journal of Psychosomatic Research* **11** pp 213–218.

Honzik MP, Macfarlane HW and Allen L (1948) The stability of mental test performance between two and eighteen years. *Journal of Experimental Education* **17** pp 309–324.

Hood B and Willats P (1986) Reaching in the dark to an object's remembered position: evidence of object permanence in 5 month old infants. *British Journal of Developmental Psychology* **4** pp 57–65.

Horn JL (1982) The ageing of human abilities. In Wolman B (ed) *Handbook of Developmental Psychology*. Englewood Cliffs, NJ: Prentice Hall.

Horn JM, Loehlin JC and Willerman L (1979) Intellectual resemblance among adoptive and biological relatives: the Texas Adoption Project. *Behaviour Genetics* **9** pp 177–207.

Horne J (1988) *Why We Sleep: The Functions of Sleep in Humans and Other Mammals*. Oxford: Oxford University Press.

Horne J (1992) Sleep and its disorders in children. *Journal of Child Psychology. Psychiatry and Allied Disciplines* **33** pp 473–487.

Horney K (1927) Der Männlichkeitskomplex der Frau. *Archiv für Frauenkunde und Konstitutionsforschung* **13** pp 141–154.

House JS, Landis KR and Umberson D (1988) Social relationships and health. *Science* **241** pp 540–545.

Howes C (1990) Can the age of entry into child care and the quality of child care predict adjustment in kindergarten? *Developmental Psychology* **26** pp 292–303.

Howitt D (1991) *Concerning Psychology: Psychology Applied to Social Issues*. Milton Keynes: Open University Press.

Hsien R (1966) Two forms of vital deficiency syndromes among Chinese male mental patients. *Transcultural and Psychiatric Research* **3** pp 19–21.

Hsu F (1971) Psychosocial homeostasis and jen: conceptual tools for advancing psychological inquiry. *American Anthropologist* **73** pp 23–44.

Hsu LK (1990) *Eating Disorders*. New York: Guilford.

Hu Y and Goldman N (1990) Morality Differentials by marital status: An international comparison. *Demography* **27** pp 233–250.

Hubel DH and Wiesel TN (1959) Receptive fields of single neurons in the cat's striate cortex. *Journal of Physiology* **148** pp 579–591.

Hubel DH and Wiesel TN (1962) Receptive fields, binocular interaction and functional architecture in the cat's visual cortex. *Journal of Physiology* **160** pp 106–154.

Hubel DH and Wiesel TN (1977) Brain mechanisms of vision. *Scientific American* **241** pp 130–144.

Hüber-Weidman H (1976) *Sleep, Sleep Disturbances and Sleep Deprivation*. Cologne: Kiepenheuser & Witsch.

Hudson W (1960) Pictorial depth perception in sub-cultural groups in Africa. *Journal of Social Psychology* **52** pp 183–208.

Hughes M (1975) *Egocentrism in Preschool Children*. Edinburgh University: unpublished doctoral thesis.

Hull CL (1943) *Principles of Behaviour*. New York: Appleton-Century-Crofts.

Humphreys G *et al.* (1992) *Understanding Vision: An Interdisciplinary Perspective*. Oxford: Blackwell.

Humphreys L (1970) *Tearoom Trade*. Chicago, IL: Aldine.

Hurd MW and Ralph MR (1998) The significance of circadian organisation for longevity in the golden hampster. *Journal of Biological Rhythms* **13(5)** pp 430–436.

Huston M and Schwartz P (1995) The relationships of lesbians and gay men. In Wood J and Duck S (eds) *Understudied Relationships*. London: Sage.

Hutt C and McGrew WC (1967) Effects of group density upon social behaviour in humans. In *Changes in Behaviour with Population Density*. Paper presented at the Meeting of the Association for the Study of Animal Behaviour, Oxford, 17–20 July.

Hyman HH and Sheatsley PB (1954) Attitudes towards desegregation. *Scientific American* **195(6)** pp 35–39.

Ibuka N and Kawamura H (1975) Loss of circadian rhythm in sleep–wakefulness cycle in the rat by suprachiasmatic nucleus lesions. *Brain Research* **96** pp 76–81.

Imperato-McGinley J, Guerro L, Gautier T and Peterson RE (1974) Steroid 5-reductase deficiency in man: an inherited form of pseudohermaphroditism. *Science* **186** pp 1213–1216.

Inhelder B and Piaget J (1958) *The Growth of Logical Thinking*. London: Routledge and Kegan Paul.

Insko CA, Drenan S, Solomon MR, Smith R and Wade TJ (1983) Conformity as a function of the consistency of positive self-evaluation with being liked and being right. *Journal of Experimental Social Psychology* **19** pp 341–358.

Irwin M, Lovitz A, Marder SR, Mintz J, Winslade WJ, Van Putten T and Mills MJ (1985) Psychotic patients' understanding of informed consent. *American Journal of Psychiatry* **142** pp 1351–1354.

Ivancevich JM, Matteson MT and Preston C (1982) Occupational stress, Type A behaviour and physical wellbeing. *Academy of Management Journal* **25** pp 373–391.

Iverson LL (1979) The chemistry of the brain. *Scientific American* **241** pp 134–149.

Jacobs TJ and Charles E (1980) Life events and the occurrence of cancer in children. *Psychosomatic Medicine* **42** pp 11–24.

Jahoda G (1966) Geometric illusions and environment: a study in Ghana. *British Journal of Psychology* **57** pp 193–199.

Jahoda M (1958) *Current Concepts of Positive Mental Health*. New York: Basic Books.

James W (1884) What is an emotion? *Mind* **9** pp 188–205.

James W (1890) *Principles of Psychology*. New York: Holt.

Janis (1971) *Stress and Frustration*. New York: Harcourt.

Jenike MA (1986) Theories of aetiology. In Jenike MA, Baer L and Minichiello WE (eds) *Obsessive–Compulsive Disorders*. Littleton, MA: PSG Publishing.

Jenness, A (1932) The role of discussion in changing opinion regarding matter of fact. *Journal of Abnormal and Social Psychology* **27** pp 279–296.

Jensen AR (1969) How much can we boost IQ and scholastic achievement? *Harvard Educational Review* **39** pp 1–123.

Johansson G (1975) Visual motion perception. *Scientific American* **232** pp 76–88.

Johnson JH and Sarason IG (1978) Life stress, depression and anxiety: internal/external control as a moderator variable. *Journal of Psychosomatic Research* **22(3)** pp 205–208.

Johnson TJ, Feigenbaum R and Weiby M (1964) Some determinants and consequences of the teacher's perception of causation. *Journal of Experimental Psychology* **55** pp 237–246.

Johnston WA and Heinz SP (1978) Flexibility and capacity demands of attention. *Journal of Experimental Psychology: General* **107** pp 420–435.

Johnston WA and Wilson J (1980) Perceptual processing on non-targets in an attention task. *Memory and Cognition* **8** pp 372–377.

Johnstone L (1989) *Users and Abusers of Psychiatry: A Critical Look at Traditional Psychiatric Practice*. London: Routledge.

Jones EE and Davis KE (1965) From acts to dispositions: the attribution process in person perception. In Berkowitz L (ed) *Advances in Experimental and Social Psychology* (vol.2). New York: Academic Press.

Jones L and Cochrane R (1981) Stereotypes of mental illness: a test of the labelling hypothesis. *International Journal of Social Psychiatry* **27** pp 97–107.

Jones MC (1924) The elimination of children's fears. *Journal of Experimental Psychology* **7** pp 382–390.

Jones MC and Bayley N (1950) Physical maturity among boys

related to behaviour. *Journal of Educational Psychology* **41** pp 129–148.

Jones RW and Bates JE (1978) Satisfaction in male homosexual couples. *Journal of Homosexuality* **3** pp 217–224.

Jouvet M (1967) Mechanisms of the states of sleep: a neuropharmacological approach. *Research Publications of the Association for the Research in Nervous and Mental Diseases* **45** pp 86–126.

Jouvet M (1983) Hypnogenic indolamine-dependent factors and paradoxical sleep rebound. In Monnier E and Meulders A (eds) *Functions of the Nervous System, Volume 4: Psychoneurobiology*. New York: Elsevier.

Kadushin A (1970) *Adopting Older Children: Summary and Implications*. New York: Columbia University Press.

Kagan J, Kearsley RB and Zelazo P (1980) *Infancy: Its Place in Human Development* (2nd edn). Cambridge, MA: Harvard University Press.

Kahneman D (1973) *Attention and Effort*. Englewood Cliffs, NJ: Prentice Hall.

Kahneman D and Tversky A (1972) Subjective probability: a judgement of representativeness. *Psychology Review* **93** pp 136–153.

Kail R and Park Y (1992) Global developmental change in processing time. *Merrill Palmer Quarterly* **38** pp 525–541.

Kamin LJ (1974) *The Science and Politics of IQ*. Harmondsworth: Penguin.

Kammen DP van, Bunney WE, Docherty JP, Jimerson DC, Post RM, Sivis S, Ebart M and Gillin JC (1977) Amphetamine-induced catecholamine activation in schizophrenia and depression. *Advances in Biochemical Psychopharmacology* **16** pp 655–659.

Kanizsa A (1976) Subjective contours. *Scientific American* **234** pp 48–52.

Kanner AD, Coyne JC, Schaefer C and Lazarus RS (1981) Comparison of two modes of stress management: daily hassles and uplifts versus major life events. *Journal of Behavioural Medicine* **4** pp 1–39.

Kant I (1991) *Critique of Pure Reason*. (trans. Kemp N) (2nd edn). Palgrave (formerly Macmillan Press).

Karabenick SA, Lerner RM and Beecher MD (1973) Relation of political affiliation to helping behavior on election day, November 7. *Journal of Social Psychology* **91** pp 223–227.

Karlins M, Coffman TL and Walters G (1969) On the fading of social stereotypes: studies in three generations of college students. *Journal of Personality and Social Psychology* **13(1)** pp 1–16.

Katz D and Braly K (1933) Racial stereotypes of one hundred college students. *Journal of Abnormal and Social Psychology* **28** pp 280–290.

Karni A, Tanne D *et al.* (1994) Dependence on REM sleep of overnight improvement of a perceptual skill. *Science* **265(5172)** pp 679–682.

Kaye K and Brazelton TB (1971) Mother–infant interaction in the organisation of sucking. Paper delivered to Society for Research into Child Development, Minneapolis.

Kazdin AE (1986) Research designs and methodology. In Garfield SL and Bergin AE (eds) *Handbook of Psychotherpay and Behaviour Change* (3rd edn).New York: Wiley.

Keeton WT (1969) Orientation by pigeons: is the sun necessary? *Science* **165** pp 922–928.

Keeton WT (1974) The orientational and navigational basis of homing in birds. *Advances in the Study of Behaviour* **5** pp 47–52.

Kelley HH (1967) Attribution theory in social psychology. In Levine D (ed) *Nebraska Symposium on Motivation, 1967*. Lincoln, NE: University of Nebraska Press.

Kelley HH (1972) Attribution in social interaction. In Jones EE *et al.* (eds) *Attribution: Perceiving the Causes of Behaviour*. Morristown, NJ: General Learning Press.

Kelley HH (1973) The processes of causal attribution. *American Psychologist* **28** pp 107–128.

Kellogg WN and Kellogg LA (1933) *The Ape and the Child*. New York: McGraw-Hill.

Kelly GA (1955) *The Psychology of Personal Constructs*. New York: Norton.

Kelly K (1993) Multiple personality disorders: treatment coordination in a partial hospital setting. *Bulletin of the Menninger Clinic* **57** pp 390–398.

Kelman HC (1958) Compliance, identification and internalization: three processes of attitude change. *Journal of Conflict Resolution* **2** pp 51–60.

Kelman HC (1967) Human use of human subjects: the problem of deception in social psychological experiments. *Psychological Bulletin* **67** pp 1–11.

Kemp J and Thach B (1991) Sudden death in infants sleeping on polystyrene-filled cushions. *New England Journal of Medicine* **324** pp 1858–1864.

Kendler KS (1983) Overview: a current perspective on twin studies of schizophrenia. *American Journal of Psychiatry* **140** pp 1413–1425.

Kendler KS, Maclean C, Neale M, Kessler R, Heath A and Eaves L (1991) The genetic epidemiology of bulimia nervosa. *American Journal of Psychiatry* **148** pp 1627–1637.

Kennedy (1997) in *The Times* **14 April**.

Kenrick D and Simpson J (eds) (1997) *Evolutionary Social Psychology*. Hillsdale, NJ: Erlbaum.

Kerckhoff AC (1974) The social context of interpersonal attraction. In Huston TL (ed) *Foundations of Interpersonal Attraction*. New York: Academic Press.

Kerckhoff AC and Davis KE (1962) Value consensus and need complementarity in mate selection. *American Sociological Review* **27** pp 295–303.

Kertesz A (1979) *Aphasia and associated disorders*. New York: Grune & Stratton.

Kertesz A (1981) An anatomy of jargon. In Brown J (ed) *Jargonaphasia*. New York: Academic Press.

Kessler RC and Essex M (1982) Marital status and depression: the importance of coping resources. *Social Forces* **61(2)** pp 487–507.

Kety SS (1975) Biochemistry of the major psychoses. In Freedman A, Kaplan H and Sadock B (eds) *Comprehensive Textbook of Psychiatry*. Baltimore, MD: Williams & Wilkins.

Kety SS, Rosenthal D, Wender PH and Schulsinger F (1968) The types and prevalence of mental illness in the biological and adoptive families of adopted schizophrenics. In Rosenthal D and Kety SS (eds) *The Transmission of Schizophrenia*. Elmsford, NY: Pergamon.

Keyes D (1981) *The minds of Billy Milligan*. New York: Random House.

Kiesler S and Sproull L (1992) Group decision making and communication technology. *Organisation Behaviour and Human Decision Processes* **52** pp 96–123.

Kiev A (1972) *Transcultural Psychiatry*. Harmondsworth: Penguin.

Kilham W and Mann L (1974) Level of destructive obedience as a function of transmitter and executant roles in Milgram's obedience paradigm. *Journal of Personality and Social Psychology* **29** pp 696–702.

Kiminyo DM (1977) A cross-cultural study of the development of conservation of mass, weight and volume among Kamba children. In Dasen PR (ed) *Piagetian Psychology*. New York: Gardner Press.

Kimura D (1992) Sex differences in the brain. *Scientific American* **267(3)** pp 80–87.

King FA and Meyer PM (1958) Effects of amygdaloid lesions upon septal hyperemotionality in the rat. *Science* **128** pp 655–656.

Kitzinger C (1987) *The Social Construction of Lesbianism*. London: Sage.

Kitzinger C and Coyle A (1995) Lesbian and gay couples: speaking of difference. *The Psychologist* **8(2)** pp 64–69.

Klebanoff LD (1959) A comparison of parental attitudes of mothers of schizophrenics, brain injured and normal children. *American Journal of Psychiatry* **24** pp 445–454.

Kleiner L and Marshall WL (1987) Interpersonal problems and agoraphobia. *Journal of Anxiety Disorders* **1** pp 313–323.

Kleinman A (1986) *Social Origins of Stress and Disease: Depression, Neurasthenia and Pain in Modern China*. New Haven, CT: Yale University Press.

Kleinman A and Lin T-Y (eds) (1981) *Normal and Abnormal Behaviour in Chinese Culture*. Dordrecht, The Netherlands: D Reidel Publishing Company.

Kleist K (1943) Die katatonie. *Nervenarzt* **16** pp 1–10.

Kline P and Storey R (1977) A factor analytical study of the oral character. *British Journal of Social and Clinical Psychology* **16** pp 317–328.

Kluft RP (1987) The simulation and dissimulation of multiple personality disorder. *American Journal of Clinical Hypnosis* **30(2)** pp 104–118.

Klüver H and Bucy PC (1939) Preliminary analysis of functions of the temporal lobes in monkeys. *Archives of Neurology and Psychiatry (Chicago)* **42** pp 979–1000.

Kobasa SC (1979) Stressful life events, personality, and health: an enquiry into hardiness. *Journal of Personality and Social Psychology* **37** pp 1–11.

Kobasa SC, Maddi SR and Kahn S (1982) Hardiness and health: a prospective study. *Journal of Personality and Social Psychology* **42** pp 168–177.

Koehler W (1925) *The Mentality of Apes*. London: Routledge and Kegan Paul.

Kohlberg L (1963) The development of children's orientations toward a moral order: 1. Sequence in the development of moral thought. *Human Development* **6** pp 11–33.

Kohlberg L (1966) A cognitive–developmental analysis of children's sex-role concepts and attitudes. In Maccoby EE (ed) *The Development of Sex Differences*. Stanford, CA: Stanford University Press.

Kohlberg L (1969) Stage and sequence: the cognitive developmental approach to socialisation. In Goslin DA (ed) *Handbook of Socialisation Theory and Research*. Chicago: Rand McNally.

Kohlberg L (1978) Revisions in the theory and practice of moral development. *Directions for Child Development* **2** pp 83–88.

Kohlberg L (1981) *Essays on Moral Development, Vol. 1*. New York: Harper & Row.

Kosten TR, Mason JW, Giller EL, Ostroff R and Harkness I (1987) Sustained urinary norepinephrine and epinephrine elevation in post-traumatic stress disorder. *Psychoneuroendocrinology* **12** pp 13–20.

Koukkou M and Lehman D (1980) Psychophysiologie des Traumens und der Neurosentherapie: Das Zustands-Wechsel Modell, eine Synopsis. *Fortschritte der Neurologie, Psychiatrie unter ihrer Grenzgebeite* **48** pp 324–350.

Kraepelin E (1913) *Clinical Psychiatry: A Textbook for Physicians* (trans: Diffendorf A). New York: Macmillan.

Kramer G (1952) Experiments on bird orientation. *Ibis* **94** pp 265–285.

Krebs D and Adinolfi A (1975) Physical attractiveness, social relations and personality style. *Journal of Personality and Social Psychology* **31** pp 245–253.

Krebs JR and Davies NB (1987) *An Introduction to Behavioural Ecology* (2nd edn). Oxford: Blackwell.

Kroger J (1985) Separation–individuation and ego identity status in New Zealand university students. *Journal of Youth and Adolescence* **14** pp 133–147.

Kruglanski AW (1980) Lay epistemologic process and contents: another look at attribution theory. *Psychological Review* **87** pp 70–87.

Kudirka NK (1965) *Defiance of Authority under Peer Influence*. Unpublished doctoral dissertation, Yale University.

Kuebler-Ross E (1969) *On Death and Dying*. London: Tavistock/Routledge.

Kuhn D, Nash SC and Brucker JA (1978) Sex role concepts of two- and three-year-olds. *Child Development* **49** pp 445–451.

Kuhn TS (1962) *The Structure of Scientific Revolutions*. Chicago, IL: University of Chicago Press.

Kurdek LA (1993) The allocation of household labor in gay, lesbian, and heterosexual married couples. *Journal of Social Issues* **49** pp 127–139.

Kurdek LA and Schmitt JP (1986) Relationship quality of partners in heterosexual married, heterosexual cohabiting, and gay and lesbian relationships. *Journal of Personality and Social Psychology* **51** pp 711–720.

L'Armand K and Pepitone A (1975) Helping to reward another person: a cross-cultural analysis. *Journal of Personality and Social Psychology* **31** pp 189–198.

Labov W (1970) The logic of non-standard English. In Williams F (ed) *Language and Poverty*. Chicago, IL: Markham.

Lachmann ME and Leff R (1989) Perceived control and intellectual functioning in the elderly: a 5-year longitudinal study. *Developmental Psychology* **25** pp 722–728.

Lack D (1943) *The Life of the Robin*. London: Methuen.

Laing RD (1964) Is schizophrenia a disease? *International Journal of Social Psychiatry* **10** pp 184–195.

Laing RD (1965) *The Divided Self*. Harmondsworth: Penguin.

Laing RD (1967) *The Politics of Experience and the Bird of Paradise*. Harmondsworth: Penguin.

Laird JD (1974) Self-attribution of emotion: the effects of facial expression on the quality of emotional experience. *Journal of Personality and Social Psychology* **29** pp 475–486.

Lamarck JB (1809) *Philosophie Zoologique*. (trans. Elliot H) London: Macmillan.

Land EH (1964) The retinex theory. *American Scientist* **52** pp 247–264.

Land EH (1977) The retinex theory of colour vision. *Scientific American* **237(6)** pp 108–128.

Lang PJ and Melamed BG (1969) Case report: avoidance conditioning therapy of an infant with chronic ruminative vomiting. *Journal of Abnormal Psychology* **74** pp 1–8.

Langer EJ and Abelson RP (1974) A patient by any other name…: clinical group difference in labelling bias. *Journal of Consulting and Clinical Psychology* **42** pp 4–9.

Langer EJ and Rodin J (1976) The effects of choice and enhanced personal responsibility for the aged: a field experiment in an institutional setting. *Journal of Personality and Social Psychology* **34** pp 191–198.

Langer FJ, Janis IL and Wolfer JA (1975) Reduction of psychological stress in surgical patients. *Journal of Experimental Social Psychology* **11** pp 155–165.

Langlois JH and Downs CA (1980) Mothers, fathers and peers as socialisation agents of sex-typed play behaviours in young children. *Child Development* **57** pp 1237–1247.

LaPiere RT (1934) Attitude vs. actions. *Social Forces* **13** pp 230–237.

Larsen KS (1974) Conformity in the Asch experiment. *Journal of Social Psychology* **94** pp 303–304.

Lashley K (1929) *Brain mechanisms and intelligence: a quantitative study of injuries to the brain.* Chicago, IL: University of Chicago Press.

Latané B (1970) Field studies of altruistic compliance. *Representative Research in Social Psychology* **1(1)** pp 49–61.

Latané B and Darley JM (1968) Group inhibitions of bystander intervention in emergencies. *Journal of Personality and Social Psychology* **10** pp 215–221.

Latané B and Darley JM (1970) *The Unresponsive Bystander: Why Does He Not Help?* New York: Appleton-Century-Crofts.

Lawick-Goodall J van (1970) Tool-using in primates and other vertebrates. In Lehrman DS, Hinde RA and Shaw E (eds) *Advances in the study of behaviour* (vol.3). New York: Academic Press.

Lawick-Goodall J van (1974) *In the shadow of man.* London: Collins.

Lazarus RS (1982) Thoughts on the relations between emotion and cognition. *American Psychologist* **37** pp 1019–1024.

Lazarus RS and Folkman S (1984) *Stress, Coping and Adaptation.* New York: Springer.

Leach P (1979) *Who Cares: A New Deal for Mothers and Their Small Children.* Harmondsworth: Penguin.

Leahy AM (1935) Nature–nurture and intelligence. *Genetic Psychology Monographs* **17** pp 235–308.

Leary MA, Greer D and Huston AC (1982) The relation between TV viewing and gender roles. Paper presented at the Southwestern Society for Research in Human Development, Galveston, Texas.

LeBon G (1895) *Psychologie des Foules.* Paris: Alcan.

Lee L (1984) Sequences in separation: a framework for investigating endings of the personal (romantic) relationship. *Journal of Social and Personal Relationships* **1** pp 49–74.

Lee MT and Ofshe R (1981) The impact of behavioral style and status characteristics on social influence: a test of two competing theories. *Social Psychology Quarterly* **44** pp 73–82.

LeMagnen J (1967) Habits and food intake. In Code CF (ed) *Handbook of Physiology (section 6) Alimentary Canal vol 1*, pp 11–30. Washington, DC: American Physiology Society.

Lenneberg EH (1967) *Biological Foundations of Language.* New York: Wiley.

Lepper MR, Greene D and Nisbett RE (1973) Undermining children's intrinsic interest with extrinsic reward: a test of the 'overjustification' hypothesis. *Journal of Personality and Social Psychology* **28** pp 129–137.

Lethmate J and Ducker G (1973) Untersuchungen zum Selbsterkennen im Spiegel bei Orang-utans und einigen anderen Affenarten. *Zeitschrift für Tierpsychologie* **33** pp 248–269.

Levin IP and Gaeth GJ (1988) How consumers are affected by the framing of attribution information before and after consuming the product. *Journal of Consumer Research* **15** pp 374–378.

LeVine RA and Campbell DT (1972) *Ethnocentrism: theories of conflict, ethnic attitudes, and group behaviour.* New York: John Wiley & Sons.

Levinson DJ (1986) A conception of adult development. *American Psychologist* **41** pp 3–13.

Levinson DJ, Darrow DN, Klein EB, Levinson MH and McKee B (1978) *The Seasons of a Man's Life.* New York: A A Knopf.

Levy J (1983) Language, cognition and the right hemisphere. *American Psychologist* **38** pp 538–541.

Levy J, Trevarthen C and Sperry RW (1972) Perception of bilateral chimeric figures following hemispheric disconnection. *Brain* **95** pp 61–78.

Levy MB and Davis KE (1988) Love styles and attachment styles compared: their relations to each other and to various relationship characteristics. *Journal of Social and Personal Relationships* **5(4)** pp 439–471.

Lewinsohn PM (1974) A behavioural approach to depression. In Friedman R and Katz M (eds) *The Psychology of Depression: Contemporary Theory and Research.* Washington, DC: Winston/Wiley.

Lewinsohn PM and Hoberman HM (1982) Depression. In Bellack AS, Hersen M and Kazdin AE (eds) *International Handbook of Behaviour Modification and Therapy.* New York: Plenum.

Lewis RA (1972) A developmental framework for the analysis of premarital dyadic formation. *Family Process* **11** pp 17–48.

Lewis RA and Spanier GB (1979) Theorising about the quality and reliability of marriage. In Burr W *et al.* (eds) *Contemporary Theories About the Family* (vol.1). Free Press.

Lewis VJ and Blair A (1991) In Cochrane R and Carroll D (eds) *Psychology and Social Issues: A Tutorial Text.* Hove: Psychology Press.

Lewontin R (1976) Race and intelligence. In Block NJ and Dworkin G (eds) *The IQ Controversy: Critical Readings.* New York: Pantheon.

Ley RG and Bryden MP (1979) Hemispheric differences in processing emotions and faces. *Brain and Language* **7** pp 127–138.

Lichenstein S and Fischoff B (1980) Training for calibration. *Organisational Behaviour and Human Performance* **26** pp 149–171.

Likert R (1932) A technique for the measurement of attitudes. *Archives of Psychology* **22** p 140.

Lim RF and Lin K-M (1996) Cultural formulation of psychiatric diagnosis: case no. 03: psychosis following qi-gong in a Chinese immigrant. *Culture, Medicine and Psychiatry* **20** pp 369–378.

Linaza J (1984) Piaget's marbles: the study of children's games and their knowledge of rules. *Oxford Review of Education* **10** pp 271–274.

Lindsay PH and Norman DA (1972) *Human Information Processing: An Introduction to Psychology*. New York: Academic Press.

Linton M (1979) I remember it well. *Psychology Today* pp 81–86.

List J (1986) Age and schematic differences in the reliability of eyewitness testimony. *Developmental Psychology* **22** pp 50–57.

Livingstone MS and Hubel DH (1987) Psychophysical evidence for separate channels for the perception of form, colour, movement and depth. *Journal of Neuroscience* **7** pp 3416–3468.

Lloyd P (1995) *Cognitive and Language Development*. Leicester: BPS Books.

Loehlin J *et al.* (1988) Human behaviour genetics. In Rosenweig M and Porter L (eds) *Annual Review of Psychology, 39*. Palo Alto, CA: Annual Reviews.

Loewenthal K, Goldblatt V, Gorton T, Lubitsch G, Bicknell H, Fellowes D and Sowden A (1995) Gender and depression in Anglo-Jewry. *Psychological Medicine* **25** pp 1051–1063.

Loftus EF (1975) Leading questions and the eyewitness report. *Cognitive Psychology* **7** pp 560–572.

Loftus EF (1979) Reactions to blatantly contradictory information. *Memory and Cognition* **7** pp 368–374.

Loftus EF (1994) *The Myth of Repressed Memory*. New York: St Martin's Press.

Loftus EF and Burns HJ (1982) Mental shock can produce retrograde amnesia. *Memory and Cognition* **10** pp 318–323.

Loftus EF and Palmer JC (1974) Reconstruction of automobile destruction: an example of the interaction between language and memory. *Journal of Verbal Learning and Verbal Behaviour* **13** pp 585–589.

Loftus EF and Zanni G (1975) Eyewitness testimony: the influence of the wording of a question. *Bulletin of the Psychonomic Society* **5** pp 86–88.

Loftus EF, Levidow B and Duensing S (1991) Who remembers best? Individual differences in memory for events that occurred in a science museum. *Applied Cognitive Psychology* **6(2)** pp 93–107.

Loftus EF, Schooler JW, Boone SM and Kline D (1987) Time went by so slowly: overestimation of event duration by males and females. *Applied Cognitive Psychology* **1** pp 3–13.

Lohmann KJ (1992) How sea turtles navigate. *Scientific American* **266(1)** pp 82–88.

Lopez S and Hernandez P (1986) How culture is considered in evaluations of psychopathology. *Journal of Nervous and Mental Disease* **176** pp 598–606.

Lorenz K (1965) *Evolution and Modification of Behaviour*. Chicago, IL: University of Chicago Press.

Lott BE (1994) *Women's Lives: Themes and Variations in Gender Learning*. Pacific Grove, USA: Brooks Cole.

Lovaas O (1987) Behavioural treatment and normal educational and intellectual functioning in young autistic children. *Journal of Consulting and Clinical Psychology* **55** pp 3–9.

Luchins AS (1942) Mechanisation in problem solving. The effect of Einstellung. *Psychological Monographs* **54** (whole no. 248).

Lugo JO and Hershey GL (1979) *Life-Span Development* (2nd edn). London: Macmillan.

Luria AR (1976) *Cognitive Development: Its Cultural And Social Foundations* (trans. Lopez-Morillas M and Solota L). Cambridge, MA: Harvard University Press.

Lydiard RB, Brewerton TD, Rossey MD, Laraia MT, Stuart G, Beinfield MC and Ballenger JC (1993) CSF cholecystokinin octapeptide in patients with bulimia nervosa and in comparison with normal subjects. *American Journal of Psychiatry* **150** pp 1099–1101.

Lynn R (1987) Japan: land of the rising IQ: a reply to Flynn. *Bulletin of the British Psychological Society* **40** pp 464–468.

Maccoby EE (1980) *Social Development*. New York: Harcourt Brace Jovanovich.

Maccoby EE and Jacklin CN (1974) *The Psychology of Sex Differences*. Stanford, CA: Stanford University Press.

Mach (1886) *The analysis of sensations*. Reprinted 1959. New York: Dover.

Mackintosh NJ and Mascie-Taylor CGN (1985) The IQ question. In *Report of Committee of Inquiry into Education of Children from Ethnic Minority Groups*, pp 126–163. London: Her Majesty's Stationery Office.

MacLean PD (1949) Psychosomatic disease and the 'visceral brain': recent developments bearing on the Papez theory of emotion. *Psychosomatic Medicine* **11** pp 338–353.

MacLean PD (1972) Cerebral evolution and emotional processes: new findings on the striatal complex. *Annals of the New York Academy of Sciences* **193** pp 137–149.

MacPhillamy D and Lewinsohn PM (1974) Depression as a function of levels of desired and obtained pleasure. *Journal of Abnormal Psychology* **83** pp 651–657.

Main M and Cassidy J (1988) Categories of response to reunion with the parent at age 6: predictable from infant classifications and stable over a 1-month period. *Developmental Psychology* **24** pp 415–426.

Main M and Goldwyn R (1984) Predicting rejection of her infant from mother's representation of her own experience: implications for the abused–abusing inter-generational cycle. *Child Abuse and Neglect* **8** pp 203–217.

Main M and Solomon J (1990) Procedures for identifying infants as disorganised/disoriented during the Ainsworth Strange Situation. In Greenberg MT, Cicchetti D and Cummings EM (eds) *Attachment in the Preschool Years*. Chicago, IL: University of Chicago Press.

Mair K (1997) Psychological treatment for dissociative identity disorder. Paper given a the British Psychological Society conference, London. 17 Dec.

Major B (1980) Information acquisition and attribution processes. *Journal of Personality and Social Psychology* **39** pp 1010–1023.

Malan D (1973) The outcome problem in psychotherapy research. *Archives of General Psychiatry* **32** pp 995–1008.

Malim T and Birch A (1998) *Introductory Psychology*. Basingstoke: Macmillan.

Malinowski B (1929) *The Sexual Life of Savages*. New York: Harcourt, Brace & World.

Mann B (1995) The North Carolina Dissociation Index. *Journal of Personality Assessment* **64** pp 349–359.

Mann L, Newton JW and Innes JM (1982) A test between deindividuation and emergent norm theories of crowd aggression. *Journal of Personality and Social Psychology* **42** pp 260–272.

Mantell DM (1971) The potential for violence in Germany. *Journal of Social Issues* **27** pp 101–112.

Marañon G (1924) Contribution a l'etude de l'action emotive de l'adrenaline. *Revue Française Endocrinologie* **2** pp 301–325.

Maratsos MP (1978) How to get from words to sentences. In Aaronson D and Rieber R (eds) *Perspectives in Psycholinguistics*. Hillsdale, NJ: Lawrence Erlbaum Associates.

Marcia JE (1966) Development and validation of ego identity status. *Journal of Personality and Social Psychology* **3** pp 551–558.

Marcus J, Hans SL, Nagier S, Auerbach JG, Mirsky AF and Aubrey A (1987) Review of the NIMH Israeli Kibbutz-City and the Jerusalem infant development study. *Schizophrenia Bulletin* **13** pp 425–438.

Margolin D and Walker J (1981) Personal communication quoted in Carlson N (1991) *Physiology of Behaviour*. Needham Heights, MA: Allyn & Bacon.

Margolin D *et al.* (1985) Common mechanisms in dysnomia and post-sematic *Surface Dyslexia*. London: LEA.

Marks IM and Nesse RM (1994) Fear and fitness: an evolutionary analysis of anxiety disorders. *Ethology and Sociobiology* **15** pp 247–261.

Marler PR (1991) Differences in behavioural development in closely related species: birdsong. In Bateson P (ed) *The development and integration of behaviour: essays in honour of Robert Hinde*. London: Cambridge University Press.

Marr D (1982) *Vision*. San Francisco: WH Freeman.

Marsh P (1978) *The Rules of Disorder*. London: Routledge & Kegan Paul.

Marshall GD and Zimbardo PG (1979) Affective consequences of inadequately explained physiological arousal. *Journal of Personality and Social Psychology* **37** pp 970–988.

Martin C and Halverson C (1983) Gender constancy: a methodological and theoretical analysis. *Sex Roles* **9** pp 775–790.

Martin C and Little JK (1990) The relation of gender understanding to children's sex-typed preferences and gender stereotypes. *Child Development* **61** pp 1427–1439.

Masling J (1966) Role-related behaviour of the subject and psychologist and its effect upon psychological data. In Levine D (ed) *Nebraska Symposium on Motivation*. Lincoln, NE: University of Nebraska Press.

Maslow A (1954) *Motivation and Personality*. New York: Harper & Row.

Mathews KA (1984) Assessment of type A, anger, and hostility in epidemiological studies of cardiovascular disease. In Ostfeld A and Eaker E (eds) *Measuring Psychosocial Variables in Epidemiologic Studies of Cardiovascular Disease*. Bethesda, MD: National Institute for Health.

Matlin MW (1993) *The Psychology of Women* (2nd edn). Fort Worth, TX: Harcourt Brace Jovanovich.

Maurer A (1965) What children fear. *Journal of Genetic Psychology* **106** pp 265–277.

Maylor EA (1994) Ageing and the retrieval of specialised and general knowledge: performance of ageing masterminds. *British Journal of Psychology* **85** pp 105–114.

McArthur LZ (1972) The how and what of why: some determinants and consequences of causal attribution. *Journal of Personality and Social Psychology* **22** pp 171–193.

McCall RB, Appelbaum MI and Hogarty PS (1973) Developmental changes in mental performance. *Monographs of the Society for Research in Child Development* **42** (3. Serial No. 171).

McCartney K, Scarr S, Phillips D and Grajek S (1985) Day care as intervention: comparisons of varying quality programs. *Journal of Applied Developmental Psychology* **6** pp 247–260.

McClelland DC (1961) *The Achieving Society*. Princeton, NJ: Van Nostrand.

McCloskey M and Zaragoza M (1985) Misleading post-event information and memory for events: arguments and evidence against memory impairment hypotheses. *Journal of Experimental Psychology* **114** pp 1–16.

McCloskey M, Wible CG and Cohen NJ (1988) Is there a special flashbulb-memory mechanism? *Journal of Experimental Psychology: General* **117** pp 171–181.

McCormick NB and McCormick JW (1992) Computer friends and foes: content of undergraduates' electronic mail. *Computer in Human Behaviour* **8** pp 379–405.

McGarrigle J and Donaldson M (1974) Conservation accidents. *Cognition* **3** pp 341–350.

McGeoch JA and Macdonald WT (1931) Meaningful relations

and retroactive inhibition. *American Journal of Psychology* **43** pp 579–588.

McGrath T, Tsui E, Humphries S and Yule W (1990) Successful treatment of a noise phobia in a nine-year-old girl with systematic desensitisation *in vivo*. *Educational Psychology* **10(1)** pp 79–83.

McGuire WJ (1964) Inducing resistance to persuasion: some contemporary approaches. In Berkowitz L (ed) *Advances in Experimental Social Psychology* (vol.1). New York: Academic Press.

McGurk H (1975) *Growing and Changing*. London: Methuen.

McNeil JE and Warrington EK (1991) Prosopagnosia: a reclassification. *Quarterly Journal of Experimental Psychology* **A43:2** pp 267–287.

Mead GH (1934) *Mind, Self and Society*. Chicago, IL: University of Chicago Press.

Mead M (1939) *From the South Seas: Studies of Adolescence and Sex in Primitive Societies*. New York: Harrow.

Meadows S (1995) Cognitive development. In Bryant PE and Colman AM (eds) *Developmental Psychology*. London: Longman.

Meddis R (1975) *The Sleep Instinct*. London: Routledge Paul and Kegan.

Meddis R, Pearson AJD and Lanford G (1973) An extreme case of healthy insomnia. *Electroencephalography and Clinical Neurophysiology* **35** pp 213–214.

Mednick SA, Machon R, Huttunen MO and Bonett D (1988) Fetal viral infection and adult schizophrenia. *Archives of General Psychiatry* **45** pp 189–192.

Meeus WHJ and Raaijmakers QAW (1986) Administrative obedience: carrying out orders to use psychological–administrative violence. *European Journal of Social Psychology* **16** pp 311–324.

Meichenbaum D (1985) *Stress Inoculation Training*. New York: Pergamon.

Melhuish EC, Mooney A, Martin S and Lloyd E (1990a) Type of childcare at 18 months – I. Differences in interactional experience. *Journal of Child Psychology and Psychiatry* **31** pp 849–859.

Melhuish EC, Mooney A, Martin S and Lloyd E (1990b) Type of childcare at 18 months – II. Relations with cognitive and language development. *Journal of Child Psychology and Psychiatry* **31** pp 861–870.

Melman PW (1979) Cross-sectional age changes in ego identity status during adolescence. *Developmental Psychology* **15** pp 230–231.

Melrose DR, Reed HCB and Patterson RLS (1971) Androgen steroids associated with boar odour as an aid to the detection of oestrus in pig artificial insemination. *British Veterinary Journal* **127** pp 497–501.

Menges RJ (1973) Openness and honesty versus coercion and deception in psychological research. *American Psychologist* **28** pp 1030–1034.

Menzel EW and Halperin S (1975) Purposive behaviour as a basis for objective communication between chimpanzees. *Science* **189** pp 652–654.

Merskey H (1995) The manufacture of personalities: the production of multiple personality disorder. In Cohen LM *et al.* (eds) *Dissociative Identity Disorder*. Northvale, NJ: Aronson.

Messick S and Jungeblut A (1981) Time and method in coaching for the SAT. *Psychological Bulletin* **89(2)** pp 191–216.

Metalsky GI, Halberstadt LJ and Abramson LY (1987) Vulnerability and invulnerability to depressive mood reactions: towards a more powerful test of the diathesis–stress and causal medication components of the reformulated theory of depression. *Journal of Personality and Social Psychology* **52** pp 386–393.

Meyer V and Chesser ES (1970) *Behaviour Therapy in Clinical Psychiatry*. Baltimore, MD: Penguin.

Meyer RG (1996) *Case Studies in Abnormal Behaviour* (3rd edn). Needham Heights, MA: Allyn & Bacon.

Mikulincer M, Florian V and Weller A (1993) Attachment styles, coping strategies, and post-traumatic psychological distress: the impact of the Gulf War in Israel. *Journal of Personality and Social Psychology* **64** pp 817–826.

Miles LE, Raynan DM and Wilson MA (1977). Blind man living in normal society has circadian rhythm of 24.9 hours. *Science* **198** pp 421–423.

Milgram S (1963) Behavioural study of obedience. *Journal of Abnormal and Social Psychology* **67** pp 391–398.

Milgram S (1964) Issues in the study of obedience: A reply to Baumrind. *American Psychologist* **19** pp 848–852.

Milgram S (1965) Some conditions of obedience and disobedience to authority. *Human Relations* **18** pp 57–76.

Miller GA (1956) The magical number seven, plus or minus two: some limits on our capacity for processing information. *Psychological Review* **63** pp 81–97.

Miller GF (1998) How mate choice shaped human nature: a review of sexual selection and human evolution. In Crawford C and Krebs DL (eds) *Handbook of Evolutionary Psychology*. Mahwah, NJ: Lawrence Erlbaum.

Miller JG (1984) Culture and the development of everyday social explanation. *Journal of Personality and Social Psychology* **46** pp 961–978.

Miller NE (1948) Studies of fear as an acquirable drive. *Journal of Experimental Psychology* **38** pp 89–101.

Mills J and Clark MS (1982) Exchange and communal relationships. *Review of Personality and Social Psychology* **3** pp 121–144.

Milner BR (1996) Amnesia following operation on temporal lobes. In Whitty CWN and Zangwill OL (eds) *Amnesia*. London: Butterworth.

Milner P (1970) *Physiological Psychology*. New York: Holt, Rinehart & Winston.

Minard RD (1952) Race relations in the Pocohontas coalfield. *Journal of Social Issues* **8** pp 29–44.

Mineka S and Cook M (1993) Mechanisms involved in the observational conditioning of fear. *Journal of Experimental Psychology: General* **122** pp 23–38.

Minuchin S, Rosman B and Baker L (1978) *Psychosomatic Families*. Cambridge, MA: Harvard University Press.

Mischel W (1968) *Personality and Assessment*. New York: Wiley.

Mita TH, Dermer M and Knight J (1977) Reversed facial images and the mere exposure hypothesis. *Journal of Personality and Social Psychology* **35** pp 597–601.

Mitchell J (1974) *Psychoanalysis and Feminism*. New York: Vintage.

Mitchell TR and Larson JB Jr (1987) *People in Organisations: An Introduction to Organisational Behaviour* (3rd edn). New York: McGraw-Hill.

Moghaddam FM, Taylor DM and Wright SC (1993) *Social Psychology in Cross-Cultural Perspective*. New York: WH Freeman & Co.

Molfese DL (1977) Infant cerebral asymmetry. In Segalowitz SJ and Gruber FA (eds) *Language Development and Neurological Theory*. New York: Academic Press.

Money J (1974) Pre-natal hormones and post-natal socialisation in gender identity differentiation. In Cole JK and Dienstbier R (eds) *Nebraska Symposium on Motivation*. Lincoln, NE: University of Nebraska Press.

Money J and Ehrhardt A (1972) *Man and Woman. Boy and Girl*. Baltimore, MD: Johns Hopkins University Press.

Moniz E (1937) Prefrontal leucotomy in the treatment of mental disorders. *American Journal of Psychiatry* **93** pp 1379–1385.

Monnier M and Hosli L (1964) Dialysis of sleep and waking factors in blood of the rabbit. *Science* **146** pp 796–797.

Moran J and Desimone R (1985) Selective attention gates visual processing in the extrastriate cortex. *Science* **229** pp 782–784.

Moray N (1959) Attention in dichotic listening: affective cues and the influence of instructions. *Quarterly Journal of Experimental Psychology* **11** pp 56–60.

Moreland RL and Beach SR (1992) Exposure effects in the classroom: the development of affinity among students. *Journal of Experimental and Social Psychology* **28(3)** pp 255–276.

Moreno JL (1946) *Psychodrama*. New York: Beacon.

Morgan MJ (1969) Estimates of length in a modified Müller–Lyer figure. *American Journal of Psychology* **82** pp 380–384.

Morrell RW, Park DC and Poon LW (1990) Effects of labelling techniques on memory and comprehension of prescription information in young and old adults. *Journal of Gerontology* **45** pp 166–172.

Morris CD, Bransford JD and Franks JJ (1977) Levels of processing versus transfer appropriate processing. *Journal of Verbal Learning and Verbal Behaviour* **16** pp 519–533.

Morris PE *et al.* (1981) Football knowledge and the aquisition of new results. *British Journal of Psychology* **72** pp 479–483.

Morris PE, Tweedy M and Gruneberg MM (1985) Interest, knowledge and the memory of soccer scores. *British Journal of Psychology* **76** pp 417–425.

Morris RGM (1981) Spatial localization does not require the presence of local cue. *Learning and Motivation* **12** pp 239–260.

Morrow L *et al.* (1981) Arousal responses to emotional stimuli and laterality of lesion. *Neuropsychologica* **19** pp 65–72.

Moruzzi G and Magoun HW (1949) Brain stem reticular formation and activation of the EEG. *Electroencephalography and Clinical Neurophysiology* **1** pp 455–473.

Moscovici S (1961) *La Psychanalyse: Son Image et Son Public*. Paris: Presses Universitaire de France.

Moscovici S (ed) (1984) *Psychologie Sociale*. Paris: Presses Universitaire de France.

Moscovici S and Hewstone M (1983) Social representations and social explanations: from the 'naïve' to the 'amateur' scientist. In Hewstone M (ed) *Attribution Theory: Social and Functional Extensions*. Oxford: Basil Blackwell.

Moscovici S and Nemeth C (1974) Social influence II: minority influence. In Nemeth C (ed) *Social Psychology: Classic and Contemporary Integrations*. Chicago, IL: Rand McNally.

Moscovici S, Lage E and Naffrechoux M (1969) Influence of a consistent minority on the response of a majority in a colour perception task. *Sociometry* **32** pp 365–379.

Moscovitch M and Olds J (1982) Asymmetries in emotional facial expressions and their possible relation to hemispheric specialisation. *Neuropsychological* **20** pp 71–81.

Moscovitch M and Rozijn P (1989) Disorders of the nervous system and psychopathology. In Rosenhan D and Seligman M (1989) *Abnormal Psychology*. New York: Norton.

Mowrer OH (1950) *Learning Theory and Personality Dynamics*. New York: Ronald Press.

Mowrer OH (1960) *Learning Theory and Behaviour*. New York: Wiley.

Mueller U (1993) Social status and sex. *Nature* **363** p 490.

Mugny G (1984) The influence of minorities. In Tajfel H (ed) *The Social Dimension* (vol.2). Cambridge: Cambridge University Press.

Muir DE and Weinstein EA (1962) The social debt: an investigation of lower-class and middle-class norms of social obligation. *American Sociological Review* **27** pp 532–539.

Mukhametov L (1984) Sleep in marine animals. In Borbely A and Valatx JL (eds) *Sleep mechanisms*. Munich: Springer-Verlag.

Munro G and Adams GR (1977) Ego-identity formation in college students and working youth. *Developmental Psychology* **13** pp 523–524.

Murstein BI (1972) Physical attractiveness and marital choice. *Journal of Personality and Social Psychology* **22(1)** pp 8–12.

Murstein BI (1976) The stimulus–value–role theory of marital choice. In Grunebaum H and Christ J (eds) *Contemporary Marriage: Structures, Dynamics and Therapy*. Boston, MA: Little, Brown.

Musgrove F (1963) Inter-generation attitudes. *British Journal of Social and Clinical Psychology* **2** pp 209–223.

Nagell K, Olguin RS and Tomasello M (1993) Processes of social learning in the tool use of chimpanzees (*Pan troglodytes*) and human children (*Homo sapiens*). *Journal of Comparative Psychology* **107** pp 174–186.

National Association for the Education of Young Children (1991) *Accreditation criteria and procedures of the National Academy of Early Childhood Programs* (revised edn). Washington, DC: National Association for the Education of Young Children.

National Autistic Society (1987) *Building a better future for autistic people: review 1986–87*. London: National Autistic Society.

Neisser U (1963) Visual search. *Scientific American* **210** pp 94–102.

Neisser U (1976) *Cognition and Reality*. San Francisco, CA: WH Freeman.

Nelson K (1973) Structure and strategy in learning to talk. *Monographs of the Society for Research in Child Development*. **38** p 149.

Nelson K (1981) Individual differences in language development: implications for development and language. *Developmental Psychology* **17** pp 170–187.

Nemeth C and Wachtler J (1973) Consistency and modification of judgement. *Journal of Experimental Social Psychology* **9** pp 65–79.

Neugarten BL (1965) Personality and patterns of ageing. *Gawein* **13** pp 249–256.

Neugarten BL (1975) The future of the young-old. *The Gerontologist* **15** pp 4–9.

Newcomb TM (1961) *The Acquaintance Process*. New York: Holt, Rinehart & Winston.

Newell A and Simon HA (1972) *Human Problem-Solving*. Englewood Cliffs, NJ: Prentice Hall.

Newman HH, Freeman FN and Holzinger KJ (1937) *Twins: A Study of Heredity and Environment*. Chicago, IL: University of Chicago Press.

Nicholson A *et al.* (1986) Nocturnal sleep and daytime alertness of aircrew after transmeridian flights. *Aviation, Space and Environmental Medicine* **57** pp 45–52.

Nisbett RE, Caputo C, Legant P and Maracek J (1973) Behaviour as seen by the actor and as seen by the observer. *Journal of Personality and Social Psychology* **27** pp 154–164.

Nolen-Hoeksema S (1987) Sex differences in unipolar depression: evidence and theory. *Psychological Bulletin* **101** pp 259–282.

Norman DA (1968) Toward a theory of memory and attention. *Psychological Review* **75** pp 522–536.

Norman DA (1981) Categorisation of action slips. *Psychological Review* **88** pp 1–15.

Norman DA and Shallice T (1986) Attention to action: willed and automatic control of behaviour. In Davidson RJ, Schwartz GE and Shapiro D (eds) *The Design of Everyday Things*. New York: Doubleday.

Norris KS and Dahl TP (1980) Behaviour of the Hawaiian spinner dolphin, *Stenella longirostris*. *Fish Bulletin* **77(4)** pp 821–849.

Norton JP (1982) *Expressed Emotion, Affective Style, Voice Tone and Communication Deviance as Predictors of Offspring Schizophrenia Spectrum Disorders*. Unpublished doctoral dissertation, University of California at Los Angeles.

Novick LR (1988) Analogical transfer, problem similarity and expertise. *Journal of Experimental Psychology* **14** pp 510–520.

Novick LR and Holyoak KJ (1991) Mathematical problem solving by analogy. *Learning, Memory and Cognition* **17** pp 398–415.

Nyiti RM (1976) The development of conservation in the Meru children of Tanzania. *Child Development* **47** pp 1622–1629.

O'Connor R (1969) Modification of social withdrawal through symbolic modelling. *Journal of Applied Behaviour Analysis* **2** pp 15–22.

O'Leary KD and Wilson GT (1975) *Behaviour Therapy: Application and Outcome*. Englewood Cliffs, NJ: Prentice Hall.

Oden CW and MacDonald WS (1978) The RIP in social scientific reporting. *American Psychologist* **33(10)** pp 952–954.

Ogbu JU (1981) Origins of human competence: a cultural–ecological perspective. *Child Development* **52** pp 413–429.

Older Students' Research Group (1993) *A Brief History 1981–1993*. Milton Keynes: The Open University.

Olds J and Milner P (1954) Positive reinforcement produced by electrical stimulation of septal area and other regions of the rat brain. *Journal of Comparative and Physiological Psychology* **47** pp 419–427.

Oliner SP and Oliner PM (1988) *The Altruistic Personality: Rescuers of Jews in Nazi Europe*. New York: Free Press.

Orbach S (1978) *Fat is a Feminist Issue: How to Lose Weight Permanently Without Dieting*. London: Paddington Press.

Orne MT (1962) On the social psychology of the psychological experiment – with particular reference to demand characteristics and their implications. *American Psychologist* **17(1)** pp 776–783.

Orne MT and Holland CC (1968) On the ecological validity of laboratory deceptions. *International Journal of Psychiatry* **6** pp 282–293.

Orne MT, Soskis DA, Dinges DF and Orne EC (1984)

Hypnotically induced testimony. In Wells G and Loftus E (eds) *Eyewitness Testimony: Psychological Perspectives*. Cambridge: Cambridge University Press.

Ornstein R (1986) *The Psychology of Consciousness* (2nd edn revised). Harmondsworth: Penguin.

Oswald I (1966) *Sleep*. Harmondsworth: Penguin.

Page MM and Scheidt RJ (1971) The elusive weapons effect. *Journal of Personality and Social Psychology* **20** pp 304–318.

Palmer S (1975) The effects of contextual scenes on the identification of objects. *Memory and Cognition* **3** pp 519–526.

Palmer S (1992) Modern theories of gestalt perception. in Humphreys G *et al.* (eds) *Understanding Vision: An Interdisciplinary Perspective*. Oxford: Blackwell.

Papez JW (1937) A proposed mechanism of emotion. *Archives of Neurology and Psychiatry* **38** pp 725–743.

Papi F, Ioale P, Fiaschi V, Benvenuti S, and Baldaccini NE (1978). Pigeon homing: cues detected during the outward journey influence initial orientation. In Schmidt-Koenig K and Keeton W (eds) *Animal Migration, Navigation and Homing*. Berlin: Springer.

Pappenheimer JR *et al.* (1975) Extraction of sleep-promoting factor S from cerebrospinal fluid and from brains of sleep-deprived animals. *Journal of Neurophysiology* **38(6)** pp 1299–1311.

Park RJ, Lawrie JM and Freeman CP (1995) Post-viral onset of anorexia nervosa. *British Journal of Psychology* **166** pp 386–389.

Parker G (1984) The measurement of pathological parental style and its relevance to psychiatric disorder. *Social Psychology* **19** pp 75–81.

Parkes CM and Weiss RS (1983) *Recovery from Bereavement*. New York: Basic Books.

Parkin JR and Eagles JM (1993) Blood-letting in anorexia nervosa. *British Journal of Psychiatry* **162** pp 246–248.

Parks CW Jnr, Mitchell DB and Perlmutter M (1986) Cognitive and social functioning across adulthood: age or student status differences? *Psychology and Aging* **1** pp 248–254.

Parks M and Floyd K (1996) Making friends in cyberspace. *Journal of Communication* **46(1)** pp 21–32.

Parry-Jones WL and Parry-Jones B (1993) Self-mutilation in four historical cases of bulimia. *British Journal of Psychiatry* **163** pp 394–402.

Patterson FGP (1979) Conversation with a gorilla. *National Geographic* **154(4)** pp 438–465.

Patterson FGP and Cohn RH (1994) Self-recognition and self-awareness in lowland gorilla. In Taylor ST, Mitchell RW and Boccia ML (eds) *Self-Awareness in Animals and Humans*. New York: Cambridge University Press.

Paul GH and Lentz R (1977) *Psychosocial Treatment of the Chronic Mental Patient*. Harvard, MA: Harvard University Press.

Pavlov IP (1927) *Conditioned Reflexes*. London: Oxford University Press.

Paykel ES (1981) Have multivariate statistics contributed to classification? *British Journal of Psychiatry* **139** pp 357–362.

Payne J (1976) Task complexity and contingent processing in decision making: an information search and protocol analysis. *Organisational Behaviour and Human Performance* **16** pp 366–387.

Pearce JM (1997) *Animal Learning and Cognition: An Introduction* (2nd edn). Hove: Psychology Press.

Pearlson GD, Kirn WS, Kubos KL, Moberg PJ, Jayaram G, Bascom MJ, Chase GA, Goldfinger AD and Tune LE (1989) Ventricle–brain ratio computed tomographic density, and brain area in 50 schizophrenics. *Archives of General Psychiatry* **46** pp 690–697.

Penfield W (1947) Some observations on the cerebral cortex of man. *Proceedings of the Royal Society* **134** p 349.

Penfield W (1969) Consciousness, memory and man's conditioned reflexes. In Pribram K (ed) *On the Biology of Learning*. New York: Harcourt Brace Jovanovich.

Penfield W and Roberts L (1959) *Speech and brain mechanisms*. Princeton NJ: Princeton University Press.

Penry J (1971) *Looking at Faces and Remembering Them: A guide to Facial Identification*. London: Elek Books.

Peplau LA (1991) Lesbian and gay relationships. In Gonsiorek JC and Weinrich JD (eds) *Homosexuality: Research Implications for Public Policy* pp 177–196. London: Sage.

Peplau LA, Padesky C and Hamilton M (1982) Satisfaction in lesbian relationships. *Journal of Homosexuality* **8** pp 23–35.

Pepperburg IM (1983) Cognition in the African grey parrot: preliminary evidence for auditory/vocal comprehension of class concept. *Animal Learning and Behaviour* **11** pp 179–185.

Pepperburg IM, Garcia SE, Jackson EC and Marconi S (1995) Mirror use by African grey parrots (*Psittacus erithacus*). *Journal of Comparative Psychology* **109** pp 182–195.

Perdeck AC (1958) Two types of orientation immigratory starlings, *Sturnus vulgaris L* and chaffinches, *Fringilla coelebs L* as revealed by displacement experiments. *Ardea* **46** pp 1–37.

Perrin S and Spencer C (1981) Independence or conformity in the Asch experiment as a reflection of cultural and situational factors. *British Journal of Social Psychology* **20** pp 205–209.

Peskin H (1973) Influence of the developmental schedule of puberty, learning and ego functioning. *Journal of Youth and Adolescence* **2(3)** pp 273–290.

Peters AM (1977) Language learning strategies: does the whole equal the sum of the parts? *Language* **53** pp 560–573.

Peters DP (1988) Eyewitness memory and arousal in a natural setting. In Gruneberg MM, Morris PE and Sykes RN (eds) *Practical Aspects of Memory: Current Research and Issues* (vol.1) pp 89–94. Chichester: Wiley.

Peterson LR and Peterson MJ (1959) Short term retention of individual items. *Journal of Experimental Psychology* **58** pp 193–198.

Pettigrew TF (1959) Regional difference in anti-negro prejudice. *Journal of Abnormal and Social Psychology* **59** pp 28–56.

Phares EJ (1988) *Introduction to Personality* (2nd edn). Glenview, IL: Scott, Foresman & Co.

Phillips DA, Voran M, Kisker E, Howes C and Whitebook M (1994) Child care for children in poverty: opportunity or inequity? *Child Development* **65** pp 472–492.

Piaget J (1932) *The Moral Judgement of the Child*. Harmondsworth: Penguin.

Piaget J (1963) *The Origins of Intelligence in Children*. New York: Norton.

Piaget J and Inhelder B (1956) *The Child's Conception of Space*. London: Routledge and Kegan Paul.

Piaget J and Szeminska A (1941) *La Genese du Nombre Chez l'Enfant*. Neuchatel, Paris: Delachaux, Niestle.

Pike KL (1990) On the emics and etics of Pike and Harris. In Headland TN, Pike KL *et al.* (eds) *Emics and Etics: The Insider/Outsider Debate*. Newbury Park, CA: Sage Publications, Inc.

Pike KM and Rodin J (1991) Mothers, daughters, and disordered eating. *Journal of Abnormal Psychology* **100** pp 198–204.

Pike R (1966) *Language in Relation to a United Theory of the Structure of Human Behaviour*. The Hague: Mouton.

Piliavin IM, Piliavin JA and Rodin S (1975) Costs, diffusion and the stigmatised victim. *Journal of Personality and Social Psychology* **32** pp 429–438.

Piliavin IM, Rodin J and Piliavin JA (1969). Good Samaritanism: an underground phenomenon. *Journal of Personality and Social Psychology* **13** pp 289–299.

Piliavin JA, Davidio JF, Gaertner SL and Clark ID III (1981). *Emergency Intervention*. New York: Academic Press.

Pillemer DB (1984) Flashbulb memories of the assassination attempt on President Reagan. *Cognition* **16** pp 63–80.

Pinel JPJ (1993) *Biopsychology* (2nd edn). Boston, MA: Allyn & Bacon.

Pinel JPJ (1997) *Biopsychology* (3rd edn). Boston, MA: Allyn & Bacon.

Pinker S (1994) *The Language Instinct*. London: Penguin.

Piran N, Kennedy S, Garfinkel PE and Owens M (1985) Affective disturbance in eating disorders. *Journal of Nervous and Mental Disease* **173** pp 395–400.

Pitman RK, Green RC, Jenike MA and Mesulam MM (1987) Clinical comparison of Tourette's disorder and obsessive–compulsive disorder. *American Journal of Psychiatry* **144(9)** pp 1166–1171.

Pitman RK, Orr SP, Forgue DF, Altman B, Jong JB and Hertz LR (1990) Psychophysiological responses to combat imagery of Vietnam veterans with post-traumatic stress

disorders versus other anxiety disorders. *Journal of Abnormal Psychology* **99** pp 49–54.

Plowden Report (1967) *Children and their Primary Schools*. (Central Advisory Council for Education) London: HMSO.

Plunkett K (1998) Connectionism and development. In Sabourin M, Craik F et al. (eds) *Advances in psychological science (vol.2): Biological and cognitive aspects*. Hove: Psychology Press.

Plutchik R (1980) A general psychoevolutionary theory of emotion. In Plutchik R and Kellerman H (eds) *Emotion: Theory, Research and Experience* (vol.1). New York: Academic Press.

Pollak JM (1979) Obsessive–compulsive personality: A review. *Psychological Bulletin* **86(2)** pp 225–241.

Pomerlau A, Bolduc D, Malcuit G and Cossette L (1990) 'Pink or blue': environmental gender stereotypes in the first two years of life. *Sex Roles* **22** pp 359–367.

Popper K (1959) *The Logic of Scientific Discovery*. London: Hutchinson.

Posner MI and Peterson SE (1990) The attention system of the human brain. *Annual Review of Neuroscience* **13** pp 25–42.

Povinelli DJ (1989) Failure to find self-recognition in Asian elephants (*Elephas maximus*) in contrast to their use of mirror cues to discover hidden food. *Journal of Comparative Psychology* **103** pp 122–131.

Povinelli DJ, Nelson KE and Boysen ST (1990) Inferences about guessing and knowing by chimpanzees (*Pan troglodytes*). *Journal of Comparative Psychology* **104** pp 203–210.

Premack AJ and Premack D (1972) Teaching Language to an Ape. *Scientific American* **227** pp 92–99.

Premack D and Woodruff G (1978) Does the chimpanzee have a theory of mind? *Behavioural and Brain Sciences* **4** pp 515–526.

Presland P and Antill JK (1987) Household division of labour: the impact of hours worked in paid employment. *Australian Journal of Psychology* **39** pp 273–291.

Price JS and Sloman L (1987) Depression as yielding behaviour: an animal model based on Schyelderup-Ebbe's pecking order. *Ethology Sociobiology* **8** pp 855–985.

Price RA and Vandenberg SG (1979) Matching for physical attractiveness in married couples. *Personality and Social Psychology Bulletin* **5** pp 398–400.

Pringle MLK and Bossio V (1960) Early prolonged separations and emotional adjustment. *Journal of Child Psychology and Psychiatry* **1** pp 37–48.

Putnam FW (1992) Dr Putnam's response. In Chu JA The Critical Issues Task Force Report: The Role of Hypnosis and Amytal Interviews in the Recovery of Traumatic Memories. *International Society for the Study of Multiple Personality Disorder News* **June** pp 7–8.

Quaade F (1971) Spontanprognosen ved adipositas: den intestinale-shunt-operations rationale og indikation. *Nordic Medicine* **85** p 733.

Rabbie JM, Lodewijkx H and Broeze M (1985) Individual and Group Aggression under the Cover of Darkness. Paper presented to the symposium 'Psychology of Peace' at the third European Congress of the International Society for Research on Aggression (ISRA) devoted to Multidisciplinary Approaches to Conflict and Appeasement in Animals and Men, Parma, Italy, 3–7 September.

Ragland DR and Brand RJ (1988) Type A behavior and mortality from coronary heart disease. *New England Journal of Medicine* **318** pp 65–69.

Rahe RH and Arthur RJ (1977) Life change patterns surrounding illness experience. In Monat A and Lazarus RS (eds) *Stress and Coping*. New York: Columbia University Press.

Raleigh MJ and McGuire MT (1993) Environmental constraints, serotonin, aggression, and violence in vervet monkeys. In Masters R and McGuire M (eds) *The Neurotransmitter Revolution*. Carbondale, IL: Southern Illinois University Press.

Ralph M *et al.* (1990) Transplanted suprachiasmatic nucleus determines circadian period. *Science* **247** pp 975–978.

Ramachandran VS and Blakeslee S (1999) *Phantoms in the Brain*. London: Fourth Estate.

Rasmussen T and Milner B (1977) The role of early left brain injury in determining lateralisation of cerebral speech functions. *Annals of the New York Academy of Sciences* **299** pp 355–369.

Ratcliff G and Newcombe F (1982) Object recognition: some deductions from the clinical evidence. In Ellis A (ed) *Normality and Pathology in Cognitive Functions*. London: Academic Press.

Reason JT (1979) Actions not as planned: the price of automatisation. In Underwood G and Stevens R (eds) *Aspects of Consciousness: Volume 1, Psychological Issues*. London: Academic Press.

Reason JT (1992) Cognitive underspecification: its variety and consequences. In Baars BJ (ed) *Experimental Slips and Human Error: Exploring the Architecture of Volition*. New York: Plenum Press.

Reber AS (1985) *The Penguin Dictionary of Psychology*. Harmondsworth: Penguin.

Rechtschaffen A and Kales A (1968) A manual of standardised terminology, techniques, and scoring system for sleep stages of human subjects. *National Institute of Health Publication 204*. Washington, DC: US Government Printing Office.

Rechtschaffen A, Gilliland M, Bergmann B and Winter J (1983) Physiological correlates of prolonged sleep deprivation in rats. *Science* **221** pp 182–184.

Rees WD and Lutkins SG (1967) Mortality of bereavement. *British Medical Journal* **4** p 13.

Reeves AG and Plum F (1969) Hyperphagia, rage and dementia accompanying a ventro-medial hypothalamic neoplasm. *Archives of Neurology* **20** pp 616–624.

Reichard S, Livson F and Peterson PG (1962) *Aging and Personality*. New York: John Wiley.

Reinberg A (1967) Eclairement et cycle menstruel de la femme. Rapport au Colloque International du CRNS, la photoregulation de la reproduction chez les oiseaux et les mammifères, Montpelier.

Reis HT, Nezlek J and Wheeler L (1980) Physical attractiveness in social interaction. *Journal of Personality and Social Psychology* **38(4)** pp 604–617.

Richardson JTE (1980) *Mental Imagery and Human Memory*. London: Macmillan.

Ridley M (1993) *The Red Queen*. London: Viking.

Ring K, Wallston K and Corey M (1970) Role of debriefing as a factor affecting subjective reaction to a Milgram type obedience experiment: an ethical enquiry. *Representative Research in Social Psychology* **1** pp 67–88.

Rivers WHR (1901) Vision. In Haddon AC (ed) *Reports of the Cambridge Anthropological Expedition to the Torres Straits*, Volume 2, Part 1. Cambridge: Cambridge University Press.

Roberts A and Bruce V (1988) Feature saliency in judging the sex and familiarity of faces. *Perception* **17** pp 475–481.

Roberts GW (1991) Schizophrenia: a neuropathological perspective. *British Journal of Psychiatry* **158** pp 8–170.

Robertson J (1995) Recovery of brain function: people and nets. *The Psychologist* **8** p 253.

Robertson J and Robertson J (1967–73) *Young Children In Brief Separation*. A film study.

Robinson MJ (1978) Liking and disliking: sketch of an alternative view. *Personality and Social Psychology Bulletin* **4(3)** pp 473–478.

Rogers CA and Frantz C (1962) *Racial themes in Southern Rhodesia*. New Haven, CT: Yale University Press.

Rokeach M (1960) *The Open and Closed Mind*. New York: Basic Books.

Rolls BJ *et al.* (1981) Variety in a meal enhances food intake in man. *Physiology and Behaviour* **26(2)** pp 215–221.

Romer AS (1996) *The vertebrate body*. Philadelphia, PA: WB Saunders.

Rosch E (1973) Natural categories. *Cognitive Psychology* **4** pp 328–350.

Rose S (1976) *The Conscious Brain*. Harmondsworth: Penguin.

Rose S and Blank M (1974) The potency of context in children's cognition: an illustration through conservation. *Child Development* **45** pp 499–502.

Rose S, Kamin LJ and Lewontin RC (1984) *Not In Our Genes: Biology, Ideology and Human Nature*. Harmondsworth: Penguin.

Rosen BK (1980) Kohlberg and the supposed mutual support of an ethical and psychological theory. *Journal for the Theory of Social Behaviour* **10(3)** pp 195–210.

Rosen S (1970) Noise, hearing and cardiovascular function. In Welch B and Welch A (eds) *Physiological Effects of Noise*. New York: Plenum.

Rosenhan DL (1973) On being sane in insane places. *Science* **179** pp 365–369.

Rosenhan DL and Seligman MEP (1989) *Abnormal Psychology* (2nd edn). London: Norton.

Rosenhan DL and Seligman MEP (1995) *Abnormal Psychology* (3rd edn). New York: Norton.

Rosenketter LL *et al.* (1990) Television and the moral judgement of the young child. *Journal of Applied Developmental Psychology* **11** pp 123–137.

Rosenman RH, Brand RJ, Jenkins CD, Friedman M, Strauss R and Wurm M (1975) Coronary heart disease in the Western Collaborative Group Study. *Journal of the American Medical Association* **233** pp 872–877.

Ross C *et al.* (1991) The frequency of multiple personality disorder among psychiatric inpatients. *American Journal of Psychiatry* **148** pp 1717–1720.

Ross ED (1981) The aprosodias: functional-anatomic organisation of the affective components of language in the right hemisphere. *Archives of Neurology* **38** pp 561–569.

Ross L (1977) The intuitive psychologist and his shortcomings: distortions in the attribution process. In Berkowitz L (ed) *Advances in Experimental and Social Psychology* (vol 10). New York: Academic Press.

Ross L, Amabile TM and Steinmetz JL (1977) Social roles, social control, and biases in social-perception processes. *Journal of Personality and Social Psychology* **35** pp 485–494.

Ross L, Lepper M and Hubbard M (1974) Perseverance in self perception and social perception: biased attributional processes in the debriefing paradigm. *Journal of Personality and Social Psychology* **32** pp 880–892.

Roth I (1986) An introduction to object perception. In Roth I and Frisby JP (eds) *Perception and Representation*. Milton Keynes: Open University Press.

Roth S and Kubal L (1975) The effects of non-contingent reinforcement on tasks of differing importance: facilitation and learned helplessness effects. *Journal of Personality and Social Psychology* **32** pp 680–691.

Rotter JB (1966) Generalized expectancies for internal versus external control of reinforcement. *Psychological Monographs* **30(1)** pp 1–26.

Rotton J, Frey J, Barry T, Milligan M and Fitzpatrick M (1978) The air pollution experience and physical aggression. *Journal of Applied Social Psychology* **9** pp 397–412.

Roy A (1981) Role of past loss in depression. *Archives of General Psychiatry* **38** pp 301–302.

Rubin DC and Kozin M (1984) Vivid memories. *Cognition* **16** pp 81–95.

Rubin JZ, Provenzano FJ and Luria Z (1974) The eye of the beholder: parents' views on sex of newborns. *American Journal of Orthopsychiatry* **44** pp 512–519.

Rubin Z (1973) *Loving and Liking*. New York: Holt, Rinehart & Winston.

Rubin Z and McNeil EB (1983) *The Psychology of Being Human* (3rd edn). London: Harper & Row.

Rumbaugh DM (1977) *Language Learning by a Chimpanzee: The LANA Project*. New York: Academic Press.

Rusak B and Groos G (1982) Suprachiasmatic stimulation phase shifts rodent circadian rhythms. *Science* **215(4538)** pp 1407–1409.

Rusbult CE (1987) Responses to dissatisfaction in close relationships: the exit–voice–loyalty–neglect model. In Perlman D and Duck SW (eds) *Intimate Relationships: Development, Dynamics, Deterioration* pp 209–238. London: Sage.

Rusbult CE and Zembrodt IM (1983) Responses to dissatisfaction in romantic involvements: a multidimensional scaling analysis. *Journal of Experimental Social Psychology* **19(3)** pp 274–293.

Rusbult CE, Johnson DJ and Morrow G (1986) Impact of couple patterns of problem solving on distress and non-distress in dating relationships. *Journal of Personality and Social Psychology* **50** pp 744–753.

Rushton JP (1989) Genetic similarity, mate choice and fecundity in humans. *Ethology and Sociobiology* **9** pp 329–333.

Russek M (1971) Hepatic receptors and the neurophysiological mechanisms in controlling feeding behaviour. In Ehrenpreis S (ed) *Neurosciences Research* (vol.4). New York: Academic Press.

Russell CS (1974) Transition to parenthood: problems and gratifications. *Journal of Marriage and the Family* **36** pp 294–302.

Russell MJ, Switz GM and Thompson K (1980) Olfactory influences on the human menstrual cycle. *Pharmacology, Biochemistry and Behaviour* **13** pp 737–738.

Rutter M (1972) *Maternal Deprivation Reassessed*. Harmondsworth: Penguin.

Rutter M (1976) Sex differences in children's responses to family stress. In Anthony EJ and Konpernick CM (eds) *The Child in His Family*. New York: Wiley.

Rutter M and Rutter M (1992) *Developing Minds: Challenge and Continuity Across the Lifespan*. Harmondsworth: Penguin.

Rutter M and Yule W (1975) The concept of specific reading retardation. *Journal of the American Academy of Child Psychiatry* **16** pp 181–197.

Ryback RS and Lewis OF (1971) Effects of prolonged bed rest on EEG sleep patterns in young, healthy volunteers. *Electroencephalography and Clinical Neurophysiology* **31** pp 395–399.

Rydin I (1976) *Information Processes in Pre-School Children, 1: The Tale of the Seed*. Swedish Broadcasting Corporation, project no. 72–7–114.

Sachs J, Bard B and Johnson ML (1981) Language learning with restricted input: case studies of two hearing children of deaf parents. *Applied Psycholinguistics* **2** pp 33–54.

Sackheim H (1988) The efficacy of electroconvulsive therapy. *Annals of the New York Academy of Sciences* **462** pp 70–75.

Sackheim H and Gur R (1978) Lateral asymmetry in intensity of emotional expression. *Neuropsychologica* **16** pp 473–482

Sacks O (1985) *The Man who Mistook his Wife for a Hat and Other Clinical Tales*. New York: Summit Books.

Saegert S, Swap W and Zajonc RB (1973) Exposure, context and interpersonal attraction. *Journal of Personality and Social Psychology* **25** pp 234–242.

Sameroff AJ (1991) The social context of development. In Woodhead M and Light P (eds) *Becoming a Person*. London: Routledge/The Open University.

Sameroff AS and Seifer R (1983) Familial role and child competence. *Child Development* **54** pp 1254–1268.

SANE (1993) *Depression and Manic Depression: The Swings and Roundabouts of the Mind*. London: SANE Publications.

Sangiuliano I (1978) *In Her Time*. New York: Morrow.

Saxton M (1997) The Contrast Theory of negative input. *Journal of Child Language* **24(1)** pp 139–161.

Scarr S and Weinberg RA (1976) IQ test performance of black children adopted by white families. *American Psychologist* **31** pp 726–739.

Scarr S and Weinberg RA (1977) Intellectual similarities within families of both adopted and biological children. *Intelligence* **1** pp 170–191.

Scarr S, Pakstis AJ, Katz SH and Barker WB (1977) Absence of a relationship between degree of white ancestry and intellectual skills within a black population. *Human Genetics* **39** pp 69–86.

Scarr-Salapatek S (1971) Social class and IQ. *Science* **174** pp 28–36.

Schachter S (1959) *The Psychology of Affiliation*. Stanford, CA: Stanford University Press.

Schachter S (1964) The interaction of cognitive and physiological determinants of emotional state. *Advances in Experimental Social Psychology* **1** pp 49–80.

Schachter S (1971) Some extraordinary facts about obese humans and rats. *American Psychologist* **26** pp 129–144.

Schachter S and Singer JE (1962) Cognitive, social and physiological determinants of emotional state. *Psychological Review* **69** pp 379–399.

Schachter S and Wheeler L (1962) Epinephrine, chlorpromazine and amusement. *Journal of Abnormal and Social Psychology* **65** pp 121–128.

Schaffer HR (1990) *Making Decisions about Children*. Oxford: Blackwell.

Schaffer HR and Emerson PE (1964) The development of social attachments in infancy. *Monographs of the Society for Research in Child Development* **29** (whole no. 3).

Schaffer LH (1975) Multiple attention in continuous verbal tasks. In Rabbit PMA and Dormi S (eds) *Attention and Performance* (Vol.5). London: Academic Press.

Schaie KW and Hertzog C (1983) Fourteen-year cohort-sequential analysis of adult intellectual development. *Developmental Psychology* **19** pp 531–543.

Scheerer M (1963) Problem solving. *Scientific American* **208(4)** pp 118–128.

Scheff TJ (1966) *Being Mentally Ill: A Sociological Theory*. Chicago, IL: Aldine.

Schenck C *et al.* (1986) Chronic behaviour disorders of human REM sleep. *Sleep* **9** pp 293–308.

Schiff N, Duyme M, Dumaret A, Stewart J, Tomkiewicz S and Feingold J (1978) Intellectual status of working-class children adopted early into upper-middle-class families. *Science* **200** pp 1503–1504.

Schlichte HJ and Schmidt-Koenig K (1971) Zum Heimfindevermögen der Brieftaube bei erschwerter optischer Wahrnehmung. *Naturwissenschaften* **58** pp 329–330.

Schneider DJ (1988) *Introduction to Social Psychology*. New York: Harcourt Brace Jovanovich.

Schneider K (1959) *Clinical Psychopathology*. New York: Grune & Shelton.

Schreiber FR (1973) *Sybil*. Harmondsworth: Penguin.

Schwartz M *et al.* (1980) The word order problem in agrammatism. *Brain and Language* **10** pp 249–262.

Sears RR, Maccoby EE and Levin H (1957) *Patterns of Child Rearing*. New York: Harper & Row.

Secord PF and Backman CW (1964) *Social Psychology*. New York: McGraw-Hill.

Segal MW (1974) Alphabet and attraction: an obtrusive measure of the effect of propinquity in a field setting. *Journal of Personality and Social Psychology* **30** pp 654–657.

Segal A (1976) Sociocultural variation in sick role behavioural expectations. *Social Science and Medicine* **10(1)** pp 47–51.

Segall MH, Campbell DT and Herskovitz MJ (1963) Cultural differences in the perception of geometrical illusions. *Science* **139** pp 769–771.

Seidman LJ (1983) Schizophrenia and brain dsyfunction: an integration of recent neurodiagnostic findings. *Psychological Bulletin* **94** pp 195–238.

Selfridge OG (1959) Pandemonium: a paradigm for learning. In *The Mechanisation of Thought Processes*. London: HMSO.

Seligman MEP et al (1970) On the generality of the laws of learning. *Psychological Review* **77** pp 406–418.

Seligman MEP (1971) Phobias and preparedness. *Behaviour Therapy* **2** pp 307–320.

Seligman MEP (1974) Depression and learned helplessness. In Friedman RJ and Katz MM (eds) *The Psychology of Depression: Contemporary Theory and Research*. Washington, DC: Winston Wiley.

Seligman, MEP (1975) *Helplessness: On Depression, Development and Death*. San Francisco, CA: WH Freeman.

Seligman MEP, Abramson LV, Semmel A and Von Beyer C (1979) Depressive attributional style. *Journal of Abnormal Psychology* **88** pp 242–247.

Seligman MEP, Maier SF and Solomon RL (1971) Unpredictable and uncontrollable aversive events. In Brush FR (ed) *Aversive Conditioning and Learning*. New York: Academic Press.

Sellen AJ and Norman DA (1992) The psychology of slips. In Baars BJ (ed) *Experimental Slips and Human Error: Exploring the Architecture of Volition*. New York: Plenum Press.

Selye H (1956) *The Stress of Life*. New York: McGraw-Hill.

Selye H (1974) *Stress Without Distress*. New York: Harper & Row.

Sergent J (1984) Configural processing of faces in the left and the right cerebral hemispheres. *Journal of Experimental Psychology: Human Perception and Performance* **10** pp 554–572.

Serpell RS (1976) *Culture's Influence on Behaviour*. London: Methuen.

Seyfarth DM and Cheney DL (1980) The ontogeny of vervet monkey alarm calling behaviour: a preliminary report. *Zeitschrift für Tierpsychologie* **54** pp 37–56.

Shallice T (1967) Paper presented at NATO symposium on short-term memory, Cambridge, England.

Shallice T (1981) Phonological agraphia and the lexical route in writing. *Brain* **104** pp 413–429.

Shallice T and Warrington EK (1970) Independent functioning of verbal memory stores: a neuropsychological study. *Quarterly Journal of Experimental Psychology* **22** pp 261–273.

Shapiro CM, Bortz R, Mitchell D, Bartel P and Jooste P (1981) Slow-wave sleep: a recovery period after exercise. *Science* **214** pp 1253–1254.

Shapiro PN and Penrod S (1986) Meta-analysis of facial identification studies. *Psychological Bulletin* **100** pp 139–156.

Shatz M and Gelman R (1973) The development of communication skills: modification in the speech of young children as a function of the listener. *Monographs of the Society for Research in Child Development* **38** No. 152.

Shayer M and Wylam H (1978) The distribution of Piagetian stages of thinking in British middle and secondary school children: II. *British Journal of Educational Psychology* **48** pp 62–70.

Sheffield FD and Roby TB (1950) Reward value of a non-nutritive sweet taste. *Journal of Comparative and Physiological Psychology* **43** pp 471–481.

Shepherd JW (1986) An interactive computer system for retrieving faces. In Ellis H, Jeeves M, Newcombe F and Young A (eds) *Aspects of Face Processing*. Dordrecht: Nijhoff.

Shepherd JW, Deregowski JB and Ellis HD (1974) A cross-cultural study of recognition memory for faces. *International Journal of Psychology* **9** pp 205–212.

Sher JK, Frost RO and Otto R (1983) Cognitive deficits in compulsive checkers: an exploratory study. *Behaviour Research and Therapy* **21** pp 357–363.

Sheridan CL and King KG (1972) Obedience to authority with an authentic victim. *Proceedings of the 80th Annual Convention of the American Psychological Association* **7** pp 165–166.

Sherif M (1935) A study of sane factors in perception. *Archives of Psychology* **27** (whole no. 187)

Sherif M (1966) *Group Conflict and Co-operation: Their Social Psychology*. London: RKP.

Sherman PW (1981) Kinship, demography and Belding's ground squirrel nepotism. *Behaviour, Ecology and Sociobiology.* **8** pp 251–259.

Sherry DF (1984) Food storage by black-capped chickadees: memory of the location and contents of caches. *Animal Behaviour* **32** pp 451–464.

Sherry DF and Galef BG Jnr (1990) Social learning without imitation: more about milk bottle opening by birds. *Animal Behaviour* **40** pp 987–989.

Shields J (1962) *Monozygotic Twins Brought Up Apart And Brought Up Together*. Oxford: Oxford University Press.

Shiffrin RM and Schneider W (1977) Controlled and automatic human information processing: 11 – perceptual learning, automatic attending and a general theory. *Psychological Review* **84** pp 127–190.

Short RL (1991) *The Differences Between the Sexes*. Cambridge: Cambridge University Press.

Shotland RL and Straw MK (1976) Bystander response to an assault: when a man attacks a woman. *Journal of Personality and Social Psychology* **34** pp 990–999.

Shuey HM (1966) *The Testing of Negro Intelligence* (2nd edn). New York: Social Sciences Press.

Sieber JE and Stanley B (1988) Ethical and professional dimensions of socially sensitive research. *American Psychologist* **43(1)** pp 49–55.

Siegler RS (1991) *Children's Thinking*. Englewood Cliffs, NJ: Prentice Hall.

Siffre M (1972) Cited in Aschoff J (1979) Circadian rhythms: general features and endocrinological aspects. In Krieger D (ed) *Endocrine Rhythms*. New York: Raven.

Sigall H and Landy D (1973) Radiating beauty: effects of having a physically attractive partner on person perception. *Journal of Personality and Social Psychology* **28** pp 218–224.

Simmons R and Blyth DA (1987) *Moving Into Adolescence*. New York: Aldine de Gruyter.

Simons RC and Hughes CC (eds) (1985) *The Culture-Bound Syndromes: Folk Illnesses of Psychiatric and Anthropological Interest*. Dordrecht, The Netherlands: D Reidel Publishing Company.

Simpson GM and May PRA (1982) Schizophrenic disorders. In Greist JH, Jefferson JW and Spitzer RL (eds) *Treatment of Mental Disorders*. New York: Oxford University Press.

Sinclair A, Jarvella R and Levett WJM (eds) (1978) *The Child's Conception of Language*. Berlin: Springer-Verlag.

Singer P (1991) Speciesism, morality and biology: A response to Jeffrey Gray. *The Psychologist* **4(5)** pp 199–200.

Singh D (1993) Adaptive significance of female attractiveness. *Journal of Personality and Social Psychology* **65** pp 295–307.

Skinner BF (1957) *Verbal Behaviour*. New York: Appleton-Century-Croft.

Skinner BF (1971) *Beyond Freedom and Dignity*. London: Jonathan Cape.

Skodak M and Skeels HM (1949) A final follow-up study of one hundred adopted children. *Journal of Genetic Psychology* **75** pp 85–125.

Skultans V (1980) A dying ritual. *MIMS magazine* **15 June**.

Slade DD and Russell GFM (1973) Awareness of body dimensions in anorexia nervosa: cross-sectional and longitudinal studies. *Psychological Medicine* **3** pp 188–199.

Slater A, Rose D and Morison V (1984) New-born infants' perception of similarities and differences between two- and three-dimensional stimuli. *British Journal of Developmental Psychology* **2** pp 287–294.

Slater PJB (1981) Chaffinch song repertoires: observations, experiments and a discussion of their significance. *Zeitschrift für Tierpsychologie* **56** pp 1–24.

Smith C (1948) *Mental testing of Hebridean children in Gaelic and English*. London: University of London Press.

Smith C and Lloyd BB (1978) Maternal behaviour and perceived sex of infant. *Child Development* **49** pp 1263–1265.

Smith EM, Brown HO, Toman JEP and Goodman LS (1947) The lack of cerebral effects of d-tubocurarine. *Anaesthesiology* **8** pp 1–14.

Smith ML, Glass GV and Miller TI (1980) *The Benefits of Psychotherapy*. Baltimore, MD: Johns Hopkins University Press.

Smith VL and Ellsworth PC (1987) The social psychology of eyewitness accuracy: misleading questions and communicator expertise. *Journal of Applied Psychology* **72** pp 294–300.

Snow CE (1977) Mother's speech research: from input to interaction. In Snow CE and Ferguson CA (eds) *Talking to Children: Language Input and Acquisition*. New York: Cambridge University Press.

Snyder F (1966) Towards an evolutionary theory of dreaming. *American Journal of Psychiatry* **123** pp 121–136.

Snygg D (1938) The relation between the intelligence of mothers and of their children living in foster homes. *Journal of Genetic Psychology* **52** pp 401–406.

Solomon GF (1969) Emotions, stress, the CNS and immunity. *Annals of the New York Academy of Sciences* **164** pp 335–343.

Solyom L, Beck P, Solyom C and Hugel R (1974) Some aetiological factors in phobic neurosis. *Canadian Psychiatric Association Journal* **21** pp 109–113.

Spanos NP, Weekes NP and Bertraud LD (1985) Multiple personality: a social psychological perspective. *Journal of Abnormal Psychology* **94(3)** pp 362–376.

Spanos NP *et al.* (1994) Multiple identity enactments and MPD: a sociocognitive perspective. *Psychological Bulletin* **116** pp 143–165.

Spector PE (1987) Interactive effects of perceived control and job stressors on alternative and health outcomes for clerical workers. *Work and Stress* **1** pp 155–162.

Spector PE, Dwyer DJ and Jex SM (1988) Relation of job stressors to affective, health and performance outcomes: a comparison of multiple data sources. *Journal of Applied Psychology* **73** pp 11–19.

Speisman JC, Lazarus RS, Mordkoff AM and Davidson LA (1964) The experimental reduction of stress based on ego defence theory. *Journal of Abnormal and Social Psychology* **68** pp 397–398.

Spelke ES, Herst WC and Neisser U (1976) Skills of divided attention. *Cognition* **4** pp 215–230.

Sperling G (1960) The information available in brief visual presentation. *Psychological Monographs* **74** (whole no. 498).

Sperry RW (1961) Cerebral organisation and behaviour. *Science* **133** pp 1749–1757.

Sperry RW (1974) Lateral specialisation in the surgically separated hemispheres. In Schmitt FO and Worden FG (eds) *The Neurosciences: Third Study Program*. Cambridge, MA: MIT Press.

Spiegel H (1974) The Grade Five Syndrome of the Highly Hypnotisable Person. *The International Journal of Clinical and Experimental Hypnosis* **22** pp 303–319.

Spiegel H (1997) Sybil – the making of a disease: an interview with Dr Herbert Spiegel. *New York Review of Books*, April 24.

Spiegel R (1989) *Psychopharmacology* (2nd edn). New York: Wiley.

Sprafkin JN and Rubinstein EA (1979) A field correlational study of children's television viewing habits and prosocial behaviour. *Journal of Broadcasting* **23** pp 265–276.

Sprafkin JN, Liebert RM and Poulos RW (1975) Effects of a prosocial televised example on children's helping. *Journal of Experimental Child Psychology* **20(1)** pp 119–126.

Springer S and Deutsch G (1985) *Left brain, right brain*. San Francisco, CA: Freeman.

Stacey M, Dearden R, Pill R and Robinson D (1970) *Hospitals, Children and Their Families: The Report of a Pilot Study*. London: Routledge & Kegan Paul.

Standing L (1973) Learning 10,000 pictures. *Quarterly Journal of Experimental Psychology* **25** pp 207–222.

Stang DJ (1973) Effects of interaction rate on ratings of leadership and liking. *Journal of Personality and Social Psychology* **27** pp 405–408.

Stephan WG (1978) School desegregation: an evaluation of predictions made in Brown vs. the Board of Education. *Psychological Bulletin* **85** pp 217–238.

Sterling J *et al.* (1999) Schizophrenia: the causes may be out there. *Psychology Review* **November** pp 2–5.

Sternberg RJ (1985) *Beyond IQ: A Triarchic Theory of Human Intelligence*. Cambridge: Cambridge University Press.

Sternberg RJ (1986) A triangular theory of love. *Psychological Review* **93** pp 119–135.

Sternberg RJ and Barnes ML (1985) Real and ideal others in romantic relationships: is four a crowd? *Journal of Personality and Social Psychology* **49** pp 1586–1608.

Stevens A and Price J (2000) *The Voices of God: Charisma, Sex and Madness*. London: Duckworth.

Stole MJ *et al.* (1962) *Mental health in the metropolis: the Midtown Manhattan Study*. New York: McGraw-Hill.

Storms MD (1973) Videotape and the attribution process: reversing actors' and observers' points of view. *Journal of Personality and Social Psychology* **27** pp 165–175.

Stouffer SA, Suchman EA, DeVinney LC, Starr SA and Williams RM (1949) *The American Soldier: Adjustment During Army Life* (vol.1). Princeton, NJ: Princeton University Press.

Stroop JR (1935) Studies of interference in serial verbal reactions. *Journal of Experimental Psychology* **18** pp 643–662.

Sui-Wah L (1989) Anorexia nervosa and Chinese food. *British Journal of Psychiatry* **155** p 568.

Suomi SJ and Harlow HF (1972) Social rehabilitation of isolate-reared monkeys. *Developmental Psychology* **6** pp 487–496.

Sweeney K (1995) Stay calm and heal better. *The Times* **21 Dec** p 5.

Syer J and Connolly C (1988) *Sporting Body Sporting Mind: An Athlete's Guide to Mental Training*. Eaglewood Cliffs, NJ: Prentice Hall.

Symons D (1979) *The Evolution of Human Sexuality*. Oxford: Oxford University Press.

Szasz T (1972) *The Myth of Mental Illness*. London: Paladin.

Tache J, Selye H and Day S (1979) *Cancer, Stress, and Death*. New York: Plenum Press.

Tajfel H (1969) The cognitive aspect of prejudice. *Journal of Social Issues* **25** pp 79–97.

Tajfel H (1970) Experiments in intergroup discrimination. *Scientific American* **223** pp 96–102.

Tajfel H (ed) (1978) *Differentiation between Social Groups: Studies in the Social Psychology of Intergroup Relations*. London: Academic Press.

Tajfel H (1981) *Human Group and Social Categories*. Cambridge: Cambridge University Press.

Tajfel H and Turner J (1986) The social identity theory of intergroup behaviour. In Worchel S and Austin WG (eds) *Psychology of Intergroup Relations*. Chicago, IL: Nelson.

Tajfel H, Billig MG and Bundy RP (1971) Social categorization and intergroup behaviour. *European Journal of Social Psychology* **1(2)** pp 149–178.

Takahashi K (1990) Are the key assumptions of the 'strange situation' procedure universal? A view from Japanese research. *Human Development* **33** pp 23–30.

Tannen D (1990) *You just don't understand. Women and men in communication*. New York: Ballantine.

Tashakkori A and Thompson V (1991) Social change and change in intentions of Iranian youth regarding education, marriage and careers. *International Journal of Psychology* **26** pp 203–17.

Taylor HF (1980) *The IQ game: A Methodological Inquiry into the Heredity–Environment Controversy*. Brighton: Harvester.

Teitelbaum P and Stellar E (1954) Recovery from the failure to eat produced by hypothalamic lesions. *Science* **120** pp 894–895.

Temerline MK (1970) Diagnostic bias in community mental health. *Community Mental Health Journal* **6** pp 110–117.

Terr L (1988) What happens to early memories of trauma? Annual meeting of the American Psychiatry Association. *Journal of the American Academy of Child and Adolescent Psychiatry* **27(1)** pp 96–104.

Terrace HS (1979) *Nim*. New York: Knopf.

Thibaut JW and Kelley HH (1959) *The Social Psychology of Groups*. New York: Wiley.

Thigpen CH and Cleckley H (1954) *The Three Faces Of Eve*. Kingsport, TN: Kingsport Press.

Thomas JC (1974) An analysis of behaviour in the 'hobbit–orcs' problem. *Cognitive Psychology* **28** pp 167–178.

Thomas L and Blackman D (1991) Are animal experiments on the way out? *The Psychologist* **4(5)** pp 208–212.

Thompson RF (1986) The neurobiology of learning and memory. *Science* **233** pp 941–947.

Tienari P *et al.* (1987) Genetic and psychosocial factors in schizophrenia: the Finnish adoptive family study. *Schizophrenia Bulletin* **13** pp 477–484.

Tinbergen JM (1981) Foraging decisions in starlings, *sturnus vulgaris L. Ardea* **69** pp 1–67.

Tinbergen N (1951) *The Herring Gull's World*. London: Collins.

Tinbergen N and Kruyt W (1938), cited in Tinbergen N (1951) *The Study of Instinct*. Oxford: Oxford University Press.

Tipton RM and Browning S (1972) The influence of age and obesity on helping behaviour. *British Journal of Social and Clinical Psychology* **11** pp 404–406.

Tizard B (1991) Working mothers and the care of young children. In Woodhead M, Light P and Carr R (eds) *Growing Up in a Changing Society*. London: Routledge.

Tizard B and Hodges J (1978) The effect of early institutional rearing on the behaviour problems and affectional relationships of four-year-old children. *Journal of Child Psychology and Psychiatry* **16** pp 61–74.

Tizard B and Rees J (1975) The effect of early institutional rearing on the development of eight-year-old children. *Journal of Child Psychology and Psychiatry* **19** pp 99–118.

Tobias P (1974) IQ and the nature–nurture controversy. *Journal of Behavioural Science* **2** p 24.

Tolman EC and Honzik CH (1930) Introduction and removal of reward and maze learning in rats. *University of California Publications in Psychology* **4** pp 257–275.

Tolman EC, Ritchie BF and Kalish D (1946) Studies in spatial learning: II. Place learning versus response learning. *Journal of Experimental Psychology* **36** pp 221–229.

Torgerson S (1983) Genetic factors in anxiety disorders. *Archives of General Psychiatry* **40** pp 1085–1089.

Treisman AM (1960) Contextual cues in selective listening. *Quarterly Journal of Experimental Psychology* **12** pp 242–248.

Treisman AM (1964) Verbal cues, language and meaning in selective attention. *American Journal of Psychology* **77** pp 206–219.

Treisman AM and Riley JGA (1969) Is selective attention selective perception or selective response: a further test. *Journal of Experimental Psychology* **79** pp 27–34.

Trevarthen C (1974) Conversations with a one-month-old. *New Scientist* **62** pp 230–235.

Triandis HC (1989) The self and social behaviour in differing cultural contexts. *Psychological Review* **96(3)** pp 506–520.

Trivers RL (1972) Parental investment and sexual selection. In Campbell B (ed) *Sexual Selection and the Descent of Man*. Chicago, IL: Aldine.

Trivers RL and Willard DE (1973) Natural selection of parental ability to vary the sex ratio of offspring. *Science* **179** pp 90–92.

Tucker D *et al.* (1977) Affective discrimination and evocation in patients with right parietal disease. *Neurology* **27** pp 947–950.

Tulving E (1962) Subjective organisation in free recall of 'unrelated' words. *Psychological Review* **69** 344–354.

Tulving E (1972) Episodic and semantic memory. In Tulving E and Donaldson W (eds) *Organisation of Memory*. London: Academic Press.

Tulving E (1974) Cue-dependent forgetting. *American Scientist* **62** pp 74–82.

Turek FW and Losee-Olson S (1986) A benzodiazepine used in the treatment of insomnia phase-shifts: the mammalian circadian clock. *Nature* **321** pp 167–168.

Turnbull CM (1961) *The Forest People*. New York: Simon & Schuster.

Turner JS and Helms DB (1983) *Life-Span Development*. New York: Holt Rinehart & Winston.

Turner RH and Killian LM (1973) *Collective Behaviour* (2nd edn). Englewood Cliffs, NJ: Prentice Hall.

Tversky A (1972) Elimination by aspects: a theory of choice. *Psychological Review* **79** pp 281–299.

Tversky A and Kahneman D (1973) Availability: a heuristic for judging frequency and probability. *Cognitive Psychology* **5** pp 207–232.

Tversky A and Kahneman D (1980) Causal schemas in judgements under uncertainty. In Fishbein M (ed) *Progress in Social Psychology*. Hillsdale, NJ: Erlbaum Inc.

Tversky A and Kahneman D (1983) Extensional versus intuitive reasoning: the conjunction fallacy in probability judgement. *Psychological Review* **90** pp 293–315.

Tversky A and Kahneman D (1986) Judgement under uncertainty: Heuristics and biases. In Arkes HR and Hammond KR (eds) *Judgement and decision-making: An interdisciplinary reader*. New York: Cambridge University Press.

Tyack P (1981) Interactions between singing Hawaiian humpback whales and conspecifics nearby. *Behavioural Ecology* **8(2)** pp 105–116.

Tyack P (1983) Differential response of humpback whales *Megaptera novaengliae* to playback of song or social sounds. *Behavioural Ecology* **13(1)** pp 49–55.

Tyerman A and Spencer C (1983) A critical test of the Sherifs' robbers' cave experiment: intergroup competition and co-operation between groups of well-acquainted individuals. *Small Group Behaviour* **14(4)** pp 515–531.

Tyler LE (1965) *The Psychology of Human Differences* (3rd edn). New York: Appleton-Century-Crofts.

Tyler SW, Hertel PT, McCallum MC and Ellis HC (1979) Cognitive effort and memory. *Journal of Experimental Psychology (Human Learning and Memory)* **5(6)** pp 607–617.

Tyszkowa M (1991) The role of grandparents in the development of grandchildren as perceived by adolescents and young adults in Poland. In Smith PK (ed) *The Psychology of Grandparenthood: an International Perspective*. London: Routledge.

Ugurel-Semin R (1952) Moral behaviour and moral judgement of children. *Journal of Abnormal and Social Psychology* **47** pp 463–474.

Umbenhauer SL and DeWitte LL (1978) Patient race and social class: attitudes and decisions among three groups of mental health professionals. *Comprehensive Psychiatry* **19(6)** pp 509–515.

Unger R and Crawford M (1992) *Women and Gender: A Feminist Psychology*. New York: McGraw-Hill.

Uranowitz SW (1975) Helping and self-attributions: a field experiment. *Journal of Personality and Social Psychology* **31(5)** pp 852–854.

US Bureau of the Census (1994) *Statistical abstract of the United States* (114th edn). Washington, DC: US Government Printing Office.

Valentine ER (1982) *Conceptual Issues in Psychology*. London: George Allen & Unwin.

Valentine T and Ferrara A (1991) Typicality in categorisation, recognition and identification: evidence from face recognition. *British Journal of Psychology* **82** pp 87–102.

Valins S (1966) Cognitive effects of false heart-rate feedback. *Journal of Personality and Social Psychology* **4** pp 400–408.

Van Beusekom G (1948) Some experiments on the optical orientation in *Philanthus triangulum. fabr. Behaviour* **1** pp 195–225.

Van der Kolk B (1988) The trauma spectrum: the interaction of biological and social events in the genesis of the trauma response. *Journal of Traumatic Stress* **1** pp 273–290.

Van der Wall SB (1982) An experimental analysis of cache recovery in Clark's nutcracker. *Animal Behaviour* **30** pp 84–94.

Van Ijzendoorn MH and Kroonenberg PM (1988) Cross-cultural patterns of attachment: a meta-analysis of the Strange Situation. *Child Development* **59** pp 147–156.

Vanneman RD and Pettigrew TF (1972) Race and relative deprivation in the urban United States. *Race* **13** pp 461–486.

Varma V *et al.* (1981) Multiple personality in India. *American Journal of Psychotherapy* **35(1)** pp 113–120.

Vaughn CE and Leff JP (1976) The influence of family and social factors on the course of psychiatric illness. A comparison of schizophrenia and depressed neurotic patients. *British Journal of Psychiatry* **129** pp 125–137.

Veraa R and Grafstein B (1981) Cellular mechanisms for recovery from nervous system injury. *Experimental Neurology* **71** pp 6–75.

Vernon PA and Mori M (1992) Intelligence, reaction times and peripheral nerve conduction velocity. *Intelligence* **16** pp 273–288.

Visintainer M, Seligman M and Volpicelli J (1983) Helplessness, chronic stress and tumor development. *Psychosomatic Medicine* **45** pp 75–76.

Von Frisch K (1950) *Bees, Their Vision, Chemical Senses, and Language.* Ithaca, NY: Cornell University Press.

Von Frisch K and Lindauer M (1954) Himmel und Erde in Konkurrenz bei der Orientierung der Bienen. *Naturwissenschaften* **41** pp 245–253.

Von Wright JM, Anderson K and Stenman U (1975) Generalization of conditioned GSRs in dichotic listening. In Rabbit PMA and Dornic S (eds) *Attention and Performance* (Vol.1). London: Academic Press.

Wade C and Tavris C (1993) *Psychology* (3rd edn). London: HarperCollins.

Wagenaar WA and Groeneweg J (1990) The memory of concentration camp survivors. *Applied Cognitive Psychology* **4** pp 77–87.

Wagner WE Jnr (1992) Deceptive or honest signalling of fighting ability? A test of alternative hypotheses for the function of changes in call dominant frequency by male cricket frogs. *Animal Behaviour* **44** pp 449–462.

Walcott C and Schmidt-Koenig K (1973) The effect of anaesthesia during displacement on the homing performance of pigeons. *Auk* **90** pp 281–286.

Walcott C, Gould JL and Kirschvinck JL (1979) Pigeons have magnets. *Science* **205** pp 1027–1029.

Walker S (1984) *Learning Theory and Behaviour Modification.* London: Methuen.

Walster E, Aronson E, Abrahams D and Rottman L (1966) Importance of physical attractiveness in dating behaviour. *Journal of Personality and Social Psychology* **4** pp 508–516.

Walster E, Walster GW and Berscheid E (1978) *Equity Theory and Research.* Boston, MA: Allyn & Bacon.

Walton G, Bower NJA and Bower TGR (1992) Recognition of familiar faces by newborns. *Infant Behaviour and Development* **15** pp 265–269.

Warburton FW (1951) The ability of the Gurkha recruit. *British Journal of Psychology* **42** pp 123–133.

Warren CAB (1974) *Identity and Community in the Gay World.* New York: John Wiley.

Waterman CK and Waterman AS (1975) Fathers and sons: a study of ego-identity across two generations. *Journal of Youth and Adolescence* **4** pp 331–338.

Waters E (1978) The reliability and stability of individual differences in infant–mother attachment. *Child Development* **49** pp 483–494.

Watson JB (1913) Psychology as a behaviourist views it. *Psychological Review* **20** pp 158–177.

Watson JB and Rayner R (1920) Conditioned emotional response. *Journal of Experimental Psychology* **3** pp 1–14.

Waxler N (1977) Is mental illness cured in traditional societies? A theoretical analysis. *Culture, Medicine and Psychiatry* **1** pp 233–253.

Weatherley D (1961) Anti-semitism and expression of fantasy aggression. *Journal of Abnormal and Social Psychology* **62** pp 454–457.

Webb W (1975) *Sleep: the gentle tyrant.* New York: Prentice Hall.

Wegner DM, Schneider DJ, Carter SR and White TL (1987) Paradoxical effects of thought suppression. *Journal of Personality and Social Psychology* **53** pp 5–13.

Weiskrantz L (1986) *Blindsight: A Case Study and Implications.* Oxford: Oxford University Press.

Weiss JM (1972) Influence of psychological variables on stress induced pathology. In Knight J and Porter R (eds) *Physiology, Education and Psychosomatic Illness.* Amsterdam: Elsevier.

Weiss JM, Stone EA and Harell N (1970) Coping behaviour and brain norepinephrine in rats. *Journal of Comparative and Physiological Psychology* **72** pp 153–160.

Weissberg M (1993) Multiple personality disorder and iatrogenesis: the cautionary tale of Anna O. *International Journal of Clinical and Experimental Hypnosis* **41(1)** pp 15–34.

Wells G (1981) Becoming a communicator. In Wells G (ed) *Learning Through Interaction*. Cambridge: Cambridge University Press.

Werner E (1991) Grandparent–grandchild relationships amongst US ethnic groups. In Smith PK (ed) *The Psychology of Grandparenthood: an International Perspective*. London: Routledge.

Wernicke C (1874) *Der Aphasische Symtomenkomplex*. Breslau: Cohn & Weigert.

West RL and Crook TH (1990) Age differences in everyday memory: laboratory analogues of telephone number recall. *Psychology and Aging* **5** pp 520–529.

West SG, Whitney G and Schendler R (1975) Helping a motorist in distress: the effects of sex, race and neighbourhood. *Journal of Personality and Social Psychology* **31** pp 691–698.

Wetherall M (1982) Cross-cultural studies of minimal groups: implications for the social identity theory of intergroup relations. In Tajfel H (ed) *Social Identity and Intergroup Relations*. London: Cambridge University Press.

White GL, Fishbein S and Rutstein J (1981) Passionate love and the misattribution of arousal. *Journal of Personality and Social Psychology* **41** pp 56–62.

Whittaker JO and Meak RD (1967) Sound pressure in the modification and distribution of judgement: a cross-cultural study. *International Journal of Psychology* **2** pp 109–113.

Whyte WF (1948) *Human Relations in the Restaurant Industry*. New York: McGraw-Hill.

Whyte WF (1956) *Street Corner Society: The Social Structure of an Italian Slum*. Chicago, IL: Chicago University Press.

Wiesenthal DL, Endler NS, Coward TR and Edwards J (1976) Reversability of relative competence as a determinant of conformity across different perceptual tasks. *Representative Research in Social Psychology* **7** pp 35–43.

Wiggins JA, Dili F and Schwartz RD (1967) On 'status ability'. *Sociometry* **28** pp 197–209.

Wilhelm K and Parker G (1989) Is sex necessarily a risk factor to depression? *Psychological Medicine* **19** pp 401–413.

Wilkinson GS (1984) Reciprocal food sharing in the vampire bat. *Nature* **308** pp 181–184.

Wilkinson J (1988) Context effects in children's event memory. In Gruneberg MM, Morris PE and Sykes RN (eds) *Practical Aspects of Memory: Current Research and Issues* (vol.1). pp 107–111. Chichester: Wiley.

Wilkinson S (1986) *Feminist Social Psychology*. Milton Keynes: Open University Press.

Williams JE and Best DL (1990) *Measuring Sex Stereotypes: A Multination Study* (revised edn). Newbury Park, CA: Sage.

Williams RB (1984) Type A behavior and coronary heart disease: something old, something new. *Behavioral Medicine Update* **6(3)** pp 29–33.

Williams TM (1985) Implications of a natural experiment in the developed world for research on television in the developing world. Special Issue: Television in the developing world. *Journal of Cross-Cultural Psychology* **16(3)** pp 263–287.

Wilson EO (1972) Animal Communication. *Scientific American* **Sept**.

Winch RF (1958) *Mate Selections: A Study of Complementary Needs*. New York: Harper.

Winnurst JAM, Buunk BP and Marcelissen FHG (1988) Social support and stress: perspectives and processes. In Fisher S and Reason J (eds) *Handbook of Life Stress, Cognition and Health*. New York: Wiley.

Winson J (1992) The functioning of REM sleep and the meaning of dreams. In Barron JW, Eagle MN *et al.* (eds) *Interface of Psychoanalysis and Psychology*. Washington DC: American Psychological Association.

Wirtshafter D and Davis JD (1977) Set points, settling points and the control of body weight. *Physiology and Behaviour* **19** pp 75–78.

Witkin HA (1950) Individual differences in ease of perception of embedded figures. *Journal of Personality* **19** pp 1–15.

Witty PA and Jenkins MD (1936) Intra-race testing of Negro intelligence. *Journal of Psychology* **1** pp 179–192.

Wolf DG (1979) *The Lesbian Community*. Berkeley, CA: University of California Press.

Wolfgang AP (1988) Job stress in the health professionals: a study of physicians, nurses and pharmacists. *Behavioural Medicine* **14** pp 43–47.

Wolpe J (1958) *Psychotherapy By Reciprocal Inhibition*. Stanford, CA: Stanford University Press.

Wong DF, Wagner HN, Tune IE, Dannals RF, Pearlson GD and Links JM (1986) Positron emission tomography reveals elevated D2 dopamine receptors in drug-naïve schizophrenics. *Science* **234** pp 1558–1562.

Woodruff G and Premack D (1979) Intentional communication in the chimpanzee: the development of deception. *Cognition* **7** pp 333–362.

Woods PA, Higson PJ and Tannahill MM (1984) Token-economy programmes with chronic psychotic patients: the importance of direct measurement and objective evaluation for long-term maintenance. *Behaviour Research and Therapy* **22** pp 41–53.

Woolfenden GE and Fitzpatrick JW (1984) *The Florida Scrub Jay*. Princeton, NJ: Princeton University Press.

Worchel S, Andreoli VA and Folger R (1977) Intergroup cooperation and intergroup attraction: the effect of previous interaction and outcome of combined effort. *Journal of Experimental Social Psychology* **13** pp 131–140.

Worell J (1992) Feminist journals: academic empowerment or professional liability? In Williams J (ed) *Gender In Academe*. Tampa, FL: University of South Florida Press.

Wright EO, Shire K, Hwang SL, Dolan M and Baxter J (1992) The non-effects of class in the gender division of labor in the home: a comparative study of Sweden and the United States. *Gender and Society* **6** pp 252–282.

Wundt W (1896) Cited in Rosensohn WL (1963) A logical method for making a classification of emotions, using Wilhelm Wundt's theory of emotion formation. *Journal of Psychology* **55(1)** pp 175–182.

Yager J, Hatton CA and Lawrence M (1986) Anorexia nervosa in a woman totally blind since the age of two. *British Journal of Psychiatry* **149** pp 506–509.

Yarnell PP and Lynch S (1970) Retrograde memory immediately after concussion. *Lancet* **1** pp 863–865.

Yelsma P and Athappilly K (1988) Marital satisfaction and communication practices: comparisons among Indian and American couples. *Journal of Comparative Family Studies* **19** pp 37–54.

Young AW, Hay DC and Ellis AW (1985) The faces that launched a thousand slips: everyday difficulties and errors in recognising people. *British Journal of Psychology* **76** pp 495–523.

Young JZ (1981) *The Life of Vertebrates*. Oxford: Oxford University Press.

Young M and Schuller T (1991) *Life After Work: The Arrival of the Ageless Society*. London: HarperCollins.

Yovetich NA and Rusbult CE (1994) Accommodative behaviour in close relationships: exploring transformation of motivation. *Journal of Experimental Social Psychology* **30(2)** pp 138–164.

Yuille JC and Cutshall JL (1986) A case study of eyewitness memory of a crime. *Journal of Applied Psychology* **71** pp 291–301.

Zaidel E (1978) Auditory language comprehension in the right hemisphere following cerebral commissurotomy and hemispherectomy. In Caramassa A and Zuriff E (eds) *Acquisition and Language Breakdown: Parallels and Divergences*. Baltimore, MD: Johns Hopkins University Press.

Zaidel E (1983) A response to Gazzaniga. *American Psychologist* **38** pp 542–546.

Zajonc RB (1968) Attitudinal effects of mere exposure. *Journal of Personality and Social Psychology*, Monograph **Supplement 9, Part 2** pp 1–27.

Zajonc RB, Adelmann PK, Murphy ST and Niedenthal PM (1987) Convergence in the physical appearance of spouses. *Motivation and Emotion* **11(4)** pp 335–346.

Zajonc RB, Swap WC, Harrison A and Roberts P (1971) Limiting conditions of the exposure effect: satiation and relativity. *Journal of Personality and Social Psychology* **18** pp 384–391.

Zechmeister EB and Nyberg SE (1982) *Human Memory*. Monterey, CA: Brooks/Cole.

Zeigler HP and Karten HJ (1974) Central trigeminal structures and the lateral hypothalamus syndrome in the rat. *Science* **186** pp 636–637.

Zeki S (1978) Uniformity and diversity of structure and function in rhesus monkey prestriate visual cortex. *Journal of Physiology* **277** pp 273–290.

Zeki S (1992) The visual image in mind and brain. *Scientific American* **267** pp 43–50.

Zeki S (1993) *A Vision of the Brain*. Oxford: Blackwell.

Zigler EF and Gilman E (1993) Day care in America: what is needed? *Pediatrics* **91** pp 175–178.

Zimbardo PG (1969) The human choice: individuation, reason and order versus deindividuation, impulse and chaos. In Arnold WJ and Levine D (eds) *Nebraska Symposium on Motivation*. Lincoln, NE: University of Nebraska Press.

Zimbardo PG, Banks WC, Craig H and Jaffe D (1973) A Pirandellian prison: the mind is a formidable jailor. *New York Times Magazine*, **8 April**, pp 38–60.

INDEX

A-B error 447

Accommodation 446

Action slips 369–372; 380

Activity theory 525–526

Actor-observer effect (AOE) 188

Adler 689

Adolescence 499–509
  focal theory of 508–509
  psychosocial moratorium in 501, 503–505
  self-esteem in 502, 507–508
  'storm and stress' in 501, 506–508

Adoption studies
  of intelligence 465–467
  of schizophrenia 649, 650

Affiliation 209–210

Aggression 241–249
  definitions of 241–242
  gender differences in 247
  media influences on 264–268
  Social Learning Theory and 242–244
  and stress 247–249

Agnosia 296
  visual 387

Algorithms 430, 436

Alien hand 294

Allport 197, 204

Alpha bias 730–731, 757

Altruism 249–264
  delayed reciprocal 540–542
  empathy-altruism hypothesis 261–262, 271
  in non-human animals 538–542

Alzheimer's disease 302, 527, 643

American Sign Language (Ameslan/ASL) 580, 583–584, 586

Amnesia 301

Analogies 431–432

Androcentrism 731, 757

Animal communication 572–580

Animal navigation 565–572

Animism 449, 453

Anisogamy 597

Anna O 637

Anorexia nervosa 639

Antidepressants 608, 656, 674, 743

Antipsychotics 623, 674

Aphasia 287

Appeasement gestures 574

Appraisal theory 348

Apraxia 296–297

Assimilation 445

Associationism 754–755
  and language development 421–424

Attachment
  and depression 607
  and love 226
  and phobias 611

Attentuation 356–358

Attraction 211–217, 735
  competence and 216
  evolutionary explanations of 217–218
  exposure and familiarity in 211–212
  gender differences in 214
  and physical attractiveness 213–214
  proximity and 212–213, 240
  similarity and complementarity in 214–216, 239
  stage and filter theories of 218–220

Attribution theory 182–189
  and depression 659–660, 670
  and helping behaviour 257
  and relationship breakdown 224

Attributional Style Questionnaire (ASQ) 659

Authoritarian personality 198–201, 484

Autism 422, 428, 683, 758

Autokinetic effect 392

Aversion therapy 681–682, 696

Avoidance learning 548–549, 657

Bandura 242–244, 265, 488, 496, 611

Batista family 490–491

Bee dance 575–576

Behaviour modification 422, 679, 682–685, 691, 695

Behaviour therapy 679–682

Bereavement 530–533

Beta bias 731, 757

Billy Milligan 633, 638

Binomial sign test 702, 709–710, 723

Bipolar disorder 606, 628, 655, 674

Birdsong 577

Black English Vernacular (BEV) 418

Blind spot 384

Blindsight 295

Bobo doll 243, 488

Bottom-up theories
  and colour vision 387
  of pattern recognition 373–376
  of visual perception 400–402

Brain damage 273–275, 755
    and electroconvulsive therapy 676
    visual disorders 295–296
Brain size
    and intelligence 612–618
    and parental investment 603–604
Breastfeeding 604, 606, 608
Brief focal therapy 688
Broca's area 282, 283, 287, 297, 298
Bruner 427–429, 756

CAT scans 273, 279
Capgras syndrome 377
Carpentered world hypothesis 409
Castration anxiety 698
Catharsis 686, 689
Causal schemata 185–186
Cetaceans 577–578
Chemotherapy 651, 674–676, 679
Chi square 701, 708–709, 722
Child abuse 632–633
Child-directed speech (CDS) 422, 443
Chomsky 424–426, 429–430, 581, 585, 756
Circadian rhythms 304–307
Class inclusion 453
Classical conditioning 543–544, 551, 556, 563
    and phobias 610, 665, 666
    and post-traumatic stress disorder 662
    in therapies 679–682
Classification of abnormality 620–630
    ethics of 628–629
    reliability of 624–627
    validity of 627–628
Client-centred therapy 749
Cocktail party effect 356–357
Cognitive-behavioural therapies 690–693
Cognitive behaviourism 549–551, 563, 589
Cognitive interview 742
Cognitive labelling theory 345–347
Cognitive map 550–551, 589–593, 595
Cognitive restructuring 692
Colour perception
    and brain damage 295
    theories of 388
Conformity 202
Connectionism 283, 429–430
Conservation 450–451
Constancy 393–394, 397–398, 760
    colour 388–389

    in cross–cultural studies 409
    shape, in infants 407
    size, in infants 407
Corpus callosum 281, 290, 291–292, 296, 652, 730
Correspondent inference theory 183–184
Counselling 682, 685
Covariation model 184–185
Creuzfeldt-Jacob disease 641
Cross-cultural research 735–737
    into adolescence 507
    into adult development 515
    into perception 398, 408–411
    into Piaget's theory 456
    and stereotypes 194
Cue conflict experiments 569
Cue-dependent forgetting 634
Cultural bias 734–737
    in intelligence tests 468, 472, 482
Cultural relativism 735
Culture
    and adolescence 499
    and ageing 526
    and bereavement 532–533
    And depression 606, 608–609
    and dissociative identity disorder 635
    and dreams 319
    and Freudian theory 487, 688
    and gender development 494–496
    and gender roles 498
    individualist and collectivist 228–229, 262–263, 734
    and intelligence 461
    and language 414–416
    and language use 417–419
    and marriage 228–230
    and mental disorders 639–644
    and prosocial behaviour 262–264
    and relationships 217
    and sexual preference 600–602
    and sexual selection 614
    and 'storm and stress' 507
Culture-bound syndromes (CBSs) 639–644

DSM-IV 620–624, 640, 644, 645, 661, 662
Darwin 534–538, 596, 612
Decalage 456
Deception 559–560, 616–618
Decision-making 437–442
Defence mechanisms 200, 201, 484, 634, 669–670, 686
Deindividuation 244–247

Depth perception 389–392, 400
    binocular cues in 390
    in cross-cultural studies 410
    in infants 406–407
    monocular cues in 390–392
Depression 655–661
    biological explanations of 655–656
    cognitive–behavioural therapies for 691–693
    and culture 606
    and electroconvulsive therapy 676
    evolutionary explanations of 606–609
    inventory (Beck) 658, 692
    psychological explanations of 656–661
    and psychosurgery 678
    and stress 630
    symptoms of 655
Desensitisation 267
Determinism 746–749
Detour studies 591–592
Diathesis–stress model 646
    of depression 661
    of phobias 667
    of post–traumatic stress disorder 663
    of schizophrenia 654–655, 756
Dichotic listening 290, 353–362
Diffusion of responsibility 244, 250, 252
Discrimination 544, 548, 567
Disinhibition 267–268
Dissociative identity disorder (DID) 630–639, 647
    gender differences in 631
    explanations of 634–635
    treatment of 635–636
Dissolution of responsibility 253
Distinctiveness effect 379
Divided attention 351, 362–366
Divorce 519–521
Dogmatism 201
Dopamine hypothesis 651
Dreaming 318–323
    lucid 319
    nature of 318–319, 324
    and REM sleep 309
    theories of 319–323
Drive reduction theory 332–333
Dual task method 362–364
Dying 530–533

EEG 276–277, 290, 308, 321, 632
Eating disorders 332, 510

Ecological validity 353, 753
Education
    and the authoritarian personality 200
    and the reduction of prejudice 205–206
Egocentrism 446, 451, 481
Emergent norm theory 246–247
Electroconvulsive therapy (ECT) 301, 314, 674, 676–677, 679
Emics 735–737
Emotion
    and brain damage 290–291
    brain lateralisation and 340–341
    brain structures in 339–341
    disorders of expression 301–302
    nature of 338–339
    neurotransmitters in 341, 343
    theories of 341–349
Epilepsy 275, 277, 294, 676
Equal status contact 204
Equity theory 220–221
Erikson 511, 531, 731
    theory of adolescence 499–503
    theory of late adulthood 524
    theory of lifespan development 512–513
Ethics 737–742
    of animal research 743–746
    of behavioural therapies 682
    of classifying abnormality 628–629
    in evaluating therapies 694–695
    in carrying out research 700, 712
    in teaching animals language 588
    of therapies 695–697
    of token economy 684–685
Ethnocentrism 199, 349, 735
Etics 735–737
Evolution
    Darwin's theory of 534–538, 596
    and sleep 313–314
Expectancy theory 334–336
Experimenter bias 200
Extinction 543, 548, 549
Extraversion 201
Eysenck 201

F-scale 199–201
Face
    preference in infants 404–406
    recognition 290, 293, 296, 376–379, 380
    Recognition Units 378–379, 380

False memory syndrome 688
Falsifiability 218, 426, 487, 602, 752
Family studies
    of intelligence 465
    of phobias 664
Field dependence 732–733
Fixed action patterns (FAPs) 536, 564, 573–574
Flashbacks 631, 662
Flooding 681
Foot–in–the–door technique 259–260
Foraging 555–557, 746
    and brain size 616–618
    memory in 592–593
Free association 686
Free will 746–749
Freud 199, 503, 510, 634, 637, 660, 672, 685–690, 748
    on bereavement 533
    theory of dreaming 319–321
    theory of gender development 498–499, 731, 757
    theory of personality development 483–487
    on phobias 666–667
Frustration–aggression hypothesis 201–202
Fundamental attribution error (FAE) 186–188

Galvanic skin response (GSR) 291, 665
Garcia effect 552–553, 555, 569, 666
'Gay gene' 738
Gender
    and adult development 512
    and bereavement 531
    bias 730–733
    and culture 494–496, 498
    and depression 608
    development 489–499
    and dissociative identity disorder 631
    and effects of divorce 520
    and helping behaviour 257
    and intelligence test scores 470
    in obedience research 736
    and phobias 664
    and relationships 731
    and schizophrenia 647
General Adaptation Syndrome (GAS) 516
General Problem Solver 433
General symbolic function 448
Generalisation 543, 548, 567
Genetic factors in intelligence 462–466
Geon theory 373
Gestalt theory 283, 554, 750
Gulf war syndrome 629

Habituation 403, 759
Halo effect 193
Head Start 418
Hello-goodbye effect 695
Hermaphroditism 491–492
Heuristics 430, 436
    in decision–making 439–441
Hierarchy of needs 336–338
High Expressed Emotion (EE) 654, 670, 756
Holism 750–751
Homeostasis 329–332
Homing 566–567
Homosexuality 218, 231–235, 599, 602, 738
Hormones
    and circadian rhythms 304
    in depression 607–608, 656
    and dyslexia 300
    and gender development 490
    and gender differences 730
    and infradian rhythms 307
Humanistic psychology 336–338, 748–749
Hunger 326–328
    physiological factors in 326–328
    psychological factors in 331–332
Hyperphagia 326
Hypnosis 632, 636, 637
Hypothalamus 276, 282, 301, 306
    and emotion 339
    and hunger 326–328
    and thirst 328–329

ICD-10 620–623, 644, 645
Idiographic approach 731
Implicit theories 753
Implosion 681
Inclusive fitness 538, 539
Infanticide 605, 611
Inferiority complex 689
Information processing
    attention as 352, 362, 364–365, 747
    to intelligence 458–460
    in pattern recognition 373–376
    in problem solving
    and schizophrenia 651
Informed consent 674, 675, 677, 678, 695, 696, 700
Infradian rhythms 307–308
Infrasound 570–571
Ingroup favouritism 196
Inhibition 543, 546
Innate releasing mechanism (IRM) 573–574

Instinctive drift 553, 564
Intelligence
    development of measured 462–467
    evolutionary explanations of 612–618
    and gender 470
    individual differences in 460–461
    in old age
    psychometric approach to 461
    racial differences in 467–471, 739
Intelligence tests 418, 459, 470–471, 736, 738, 758
    culture-fair 470, 472, 616
    factors in performance 471–472
Interactionism 750–751
Introspection 754

Jetlag 306, 323
Jigsaw classroom technique 205
Jung 689

K–selected species 603
Kanzi 587–589
Kitty Genovese 250– 253
Knowledge attribution 560–562
Kohlberg
    theory of gender development 493–494
    theory of moral development 476–479, 731, 733, 735, 757
Korsakov's syndrome 301

Laing 653
Lateralisation of function 288–295
Language
    acquisition, theories of 421–430, 756
    and culture 414–416
    definition of 412–413, 580–581
    development 419–421
    disorders 297–300
    in Piaget's theory 456
    over-and underextensions 423
    and sexual selection 614
    and social class 417–419
    teaching animals 581–589
    and thought 413–416
Language Acquisition Device (LAD) 424–425, 581, 587, 756
Language Acquisition Support System (LASS) 427–429
Latent learning 550
Law of equipotentiality 282, 289
Law of mass action 282
Learned helplessness 657–658

Learning theory 542–553
Legislation 206
Leucotomy 677
Levels of measurement 702
Levels of processing theory 704
Levinson's life structure theory 513–515
Lexigram keyboard 585
Life events 660–661, 667
Likert scale 199
Limbic system 287, 340, 377, 617
Linguistic relativity hypothesis 414–416
Little Albert 610, 664, 679
Little Hans 666, 686, 688, 698
Little Peter 680
Lobotomy 274, 287, 677
Localisation of function 281–288
Longitudinal studies 467
Love 226–228
    in arranged marriages 229

MEG scans 280
MRI scans 273, 279, 651
Machiavellian intelligence hypothesis 616–618
Magnetism 568–570
Manic depression see Bipolar disorder
Mann-Whitney U test 702, 704–705, 716–719
Map and compass hypothesis 567–568, 594
Marriage 517–519
    arranged 229, 517, 519, 735
    and culture 228–230
    and self-esteem 519
    types of 517
    types of relationship in 210–211
Maternal deprivation hypothesis 660, 732, 740, 758
Mating effort 597
Mating systems 597–598, 619
Matching hypothesis 213–214
Means–end analysis 432
Memory
    children's 741
    loss with electroconvulsive therapy 677
    in non–human animals 589–593
    in obsessive–compulsive disorder 669
    in old age 527–528
    in problem solving 436
Mental Health Act 673
Mid-life crisis 514
Migration 565–566, 593–594
    learning in 571–572
Milgram 736, 739

Minimal groups 190–191, 203
Minimax strategy 436
Modelling 488, 509
Moral development 472–480
    Kohlberg's theory of 476–479
    Piaget's theory of 473–476
Moral realism 475
Moral reasoning 269
    prosocial 479–480
    socialisation in 480
Moral relativism 475
Motivation 325–338
    brain mechanisms in 326–329
    intrinsic 455, 481
    in old age 528
    and work 334
Multiple personality disorder *see* Dissociative
identity disorder
Mutation 535
Myelination 459

Nativism
    and language development 424–426
Natural selection 535, 596, 600, 614
Nature-nurture debate 754–756
    and gender development 490
    and intelligence 462–466
    and perception 408–411
Neurasthenia 640
Neurotransmitters 278, 673, 750
    and circadian rhythms 306
    and depression 656
    and electroconvulsive therapy 677
    and emotion 341
    and obsessive–compulsive disorder 668
    and post–traumatic stress disorder 662
    and recovery from cerebral lesions 302
    and schizophrenia 651
    and sleep 312
Nomothetic approach 731

Observational learning 488, 509, 556, 580, 665, 668
Obsessive-compulsive disorder (OCD) 667–670, 678,
    747
Ocular system maintenance theory 315
Oedipus complex 484, 498, 666, 757
Operant conditioning 544–548, 551, 563, 738, 740
    and depression 656–658
    and gender development 495

and obsessive-compulsive disorder 668–669
    and phobias 665
Operations 454
Orcs and hobbits 432–433, 443
Outgroup homogeneity effect 195

PET scans 279, 303, 387, 651, 668
Pandemonium model 374
Paradigm 751–752
Parental effort 597, 618
Parental investment 603–606
    gender differences in 604
    and human brain size 603–604
Parenthood 521–523
Parkinson's disease 275, 651
Parsimony 749, 752
Paternity uncertainty 604–605
Pattern recognition 373–379
    bottom–up theories 373–376
    top–down theories 376
Pavlov 543–544, 551, 564
Perception
    definition of 372
    of depth 389–392, 400
    of movement 392–393
Perceptual
    development 403–410
    set 398, 401
Personal growth 523, 749
Personality 185
    authoritarian 198–201
    development 483–489
    and helping behaviour 258
    and retirement 529–530
Pheromones 572
Phi phenomenon 392
Phineas Gage 273–274, 286
Phobias 623, 663–667
    behavioural therapies for 679–680
    evolutionary explanations of 610–612
Phrenology 272, 612
Phylogeny 536, 612
Piaget 734
    theory of cognitive development 445–456, 475–476
    theory of moral development 473–476
    and language 416
Pilot study 700, 746
Placebo effect 676–677
Play therapy 689

Pluralistic ignorance 252
Point light studies 404
Portage 683
Post–traumatic stress disorder (PTSD) 633, 661–663
Preferential looking technique 404
Prejudice 196–207, 739
    expression of 197–198
    and Freudian theory 486
    individual explanations of 198–202
    and IQ scores 469–470
    intergroup approach 202–203
    interpersonal approach 202
    reduction of 203–206
Premenstrual syndrome (PMS) 308, 639, 656
Preparedness 553, 569, 610, 664, 665
Principle of non–common effects 183–184
Prison simulation study 245
Prisoner's dilemma 541, 562
Problem solving 430–437
Projective tests 199, 515, 687
Prosocial behaviour 249–264
    arousal: cost–reward model 254–260
    cultural differences 262–264
    information processing approach 251–254
    media influences on 268–270
Prosopagnosia 296, 377
Protoconversations 426–427
Psychoanalysis 486, 672, 685–688, 732, 748
    in dissociative identity disorder 636
    dream analysis in 320, 687
    free association in 686
Psychodrama 689–690
Psychodynamic
    explanations of depression 660
    explanations of obsessive-compulsive disorder 669–670
    explanations of phobias 666–667
    explanations of post-traumatic stress disorder 662–663
    therapies 685–690
Psychometric
    approach to intelligence 461
    tests 632, 739
Psychosexual stages 484–485
Psychosurgery 274, 340, 677–679
Punishment 546, 563, 748

Qi–gong reactive psychosis 639, 641

REM sleep 309, 313, 316, 321
r-selected species 603
Ranking 704, 707
Rationalism 754–755
Raven's Progressive Matrices 470
Realistic conflict theory 202–203
Reductionism 612, 749–751
Reinforcement 546, 551, 552, 563, 564, 582, 670–671, 748
    schedules of 547–548
Relationships
    and attachment 210
    breakdown of 222–225, 234–235
    and culture 217, 228–231
    fatal attraction model 225
    gay and lesbian 231–235, 599
    gender differences in 731
    internet 236–238
    maintenance of 220–222, 233–234
    reinforcement–affect theory 217
    types of 210–211, 239
Relative deprivation theory 202
Reliability of classification systems 624–627
Report writing 710–714, 724–729
Response set 201
Retirement 529–530
Revolving door syndrome 695
Rogers 748–749
Rorschach ink blot test 687

Scaffolding 428
Schemas
    in attention 371–372
    and depression 658
    in perception 402
    in Piaget's theory 445–446
in problem solving 431
Schizophrenia 623, 628, 646–655, 747
    biological explanations of 649–652
    psychological explanations of 653–655
    symptoms of 647–649
Scientific method 752–753
Seasonal affective disorder (SAD) 304
Selective attention 351, 353–362
    attenuation model 356–359
    filter model of 353–356
    pertinence model 359–361

Selective placement 462, 466
Self-actualisation 336–337, 749
Self-esteem
    in adolescence 502, 507–508
    and attraction 216
    and divorce 520, 521
    and marriage 519
Self-fulfilling prophecy 195, 629
Self-handicapping 189
Self-hypnosis 634–635, 637
Self-mutilation 631, 759
Self-recognition 557–559
Self-serving bias 188–189
Sensory neglect 285
Separation anxiety 516
Set in problem solving 432, 434–435
Set point theory 327
Sexual selection 537–538, 600–603
and brain size 614–618
Shadowing 355–356, 363
Shift work 306–307, 323
Signalling systems 572–575
Significance level 701
Skinner 544–548, 738, 740, 748
    theory of language development 421–424, 756
Sleep 277, 308–318
    and age 310
    deprivation studies 315–318
    disorders 312–313
    disruption 307
    mechanisms of 312
    memory consolidation 314
    REM 309
    stages of 308–311
    theories of 313–315
Social causation hypothesis 654
Social class
    and language 417–419
    and lschizophenia 654
Social constructivist
    theory of language 426–429
Social desirability 753
Social disengagement theory 524–525
Social drift hypothesis 654
Social exchange theory 220
Social facilitation 556–557
Social identity theory (SIT) 189–191, 244
Social learning theory (SLT)
    of gender development 494–496

of personality development 487–489
    and phobias 611
Social norms 255, 262, 518, 521
Social Readjustment Rating Scale (SRRS) 517, 529
Social representations 191–192
Socialisation
    and gender 494–497, 730
    and moral reasoning 480
Socially sensitive research 738–742
Somatic therapies 673–679
Spearman's coefficient 702, 707–708
Speciesism 743
Split–brain research 275, 291–295
Spontaneous remission 688
Stereotaxic procedures 275–277, 326, 678
Stereotypes 192–196
    in animal signals 573
    and cultural bias 737
    counterstereotypes 206
    development and maintenance 194–195
    of the elderly 523
    ethnic 193–194
    gender 194, 494
    of mental disorders 644
    'storm and stress' 501, 506–508
Strange Situation 736, 757
Stress
    and aggression 247–249
    in animals used for research 744
    coping with 693
    and depression 630
    and dissociative identity disorder 631
    and divorce 520, 523
    and sleep 312, 314, 317
Stress inoculation therapy 693
Stroke 274, 287, 298
Stroop effect 365–366
Structuralism 749, 752
Sudden infant death syndrome (SIDS) 313
Suicide 655, 660, 676, 678
Suo–yang 640–641
Superordinate goals 204–205
Suprachiasmatic nuclei (SCN) 305
Sybil 632–633, 638
Systematic desensitisation 679–680

Tajfel 189–191, 196, 203
Tardive dyskinesia 674
Temperament 489, 658

Template matching hypothesis (TMH) 373
Testicular feminising syndrome 491
Thematic apperception test (TAT) 199, 687
Theory of mind 559–562, 616
Thirst 328–329
    physiological factors in 328
Tip-of-the-tongue (TOT) phenomenon 414, 527
Token economy 684–685, 695, 758
Top-down theories
    and colour vision 387
    of pattern recognition 376
    of visual perception 397–400, 402
Tough–mindedness 201
Tourette's syndrome 668
Tower of Hanoi 433
Transactional analysis (TA) 690
Transactional model 496
Transference 686–687
Trial-and-error learning 557, 558, 591
Triune model of the brain 617–618
Trivers-Willard hypothesis 605
Twin studies
    of depression 655–656
    of intelligence 462–464
    of personality 489
    of phobias 664
    of schizophrenia 650
Two–factor theory 548–549
Type 1/Type 2 errors 701

Validity 169, 170
    of classification systems 627–628
Vicarious conditioning 665
Visual
    acuity 404
    illusions 394–399, 401, 408, 734
    perception in infants 403 408
    processing 385–389
    search 375
    system, structure of 383–385

Vygotsky 734
    and language 416
    theory of cognitive development 457–458

Washoe 583–584, 586
Watson 544, 566, 750
Wernicke's area 283, 287, 297, 298, 299, 300

Wilcoxon signed ranks 702, 705–707, 720
Whale song 577–578
Working memory 369, 459

Yin/yang 642

Zone of proximal development 457, 481
Zugunruhe 570